THE PHILOSOPHY OF
C. D. BROAD

THE LIBRARY OF LIVING PHILOSOPHERS

Paul Arthur Schilpp, *Editor*

Already Published:

THE PHILOSOPHY OF JOHN DEWEY (1939)

THE PHILOSOPHY OF GEORGE SANTAYANA (1940)

THE PHILOSOPHY OF ALFRED NORTH WHITEHEAD (1941)

THE PHILOSOPHY OF G. E. MOORE (1942)

THE PHILOSOPHY OF BERTRAND RUSSELL (1944)

THE PHILOSOPHY OF ERNST CASSIRER (1949)

ALBERT EINSTEIN: PHILOSOPHER-SCIENTIST (1949)

THE PHILOSOPHY OF SARVEPALLI RADHAKRISHNAN (1952)

THE PHILOSOPHY OF KARL JASPERS (1957)

THE PHILOSOPHY OF C. D. BROAD (1959)

In Preparation:

THE PHILOSOPHY OF RUDOLF CARNAP

THE PHILOSOPHY OF MARTIN BUBER

THE PHILOSOPHY OF C. I. LEWIS

Other volumes to be announced later

THE PHILOSOPHY
OF
C. D. BROAD

Edited by

PAUL ARTHUR SCHILPP
NORTHWESTERN UNIVERSITY

NEW YORK

TUDOR PUBLISHING COMPANY

THE PHILOSOPHY OF C. D. BROAD

Copyright 1959

by The Library of Living Philosophers, Inc.

GENERAL INTRODUCTION*
TO
"THE LIBRARY OF LIVING PHILOSOPHERS"

ACCORDING to the late F. C. S. Schiller, the greatest obstacle to fruitful discussion in philosophy is "the curious etiquette which apparently taboos the asking of questions about a philosopher's meaning while he is alive." The "interminable controversies which fill the histories of philosophy," he goes on to say, "could have been ended at once by asking the living philosophers a few searching questions."

The confident optimism of this last remark undoubtedly goes too far. Living thinkers have often been asked "a few searching questions," but their answers have not stopped "interminable controversies" about their real meaning. It is none the less true that there would be far greater clarity of understanding than is now often the case, if more such searching questions had been directed to great thinkers while they were still alive.

This, at any rate, is the basic thought behind the present undertaking. The volumes of *The Library of Living Philosophers* can in no sense take the place of the major writings of great and original thinkers. Students who would know the philosophies of such men as John Dewey, George Santayana, Alfred North Whitehead, G. E. Moore, Bertrand Russell, Ernst Cassirer, Karl Jaspers, *et al.*, will still need to read the writings of these men. There is no substitute for first-hand contact with the original thought of the philosopher himself. Least of all does this *Library* pretend to be such a substitute. The *Library* in fact will spare neither effort nor expense in offering to the student the best possible guide to the published writings of a given thinker. We shall attempt to meet this aim by providing at the end of each volume in our series a complete bibliography of the published work of the philosopher in question. Nor should one overlook the fact that the essays in each volume cannot but finally lead to this same goal. The interpretative and critical discussions of the various phases of a great thinker's work and, most of all, the reply of the thinker himself, are bound to lead the reader to the works of the philosopher himself.

* This *General Introduction*, setting forth the underlying conception of this *Library*, is purposely reprinted in each volume (with only very minor changes).

At the same time, there is no denying the fact that different experts find different ideas in the writings of the same philosopher. This is as true of the appreciative interpreter and grateful disciple as it is of the critical opponent. Nor can it be denied that such differences of reading and of interpretation on the part of other experts often leave the neophyte aghast before the whole maze of widely varying and even opposing interpretations. Who is right and whose interpretation shall he accept? When the doctors disagree among themselves, what is the poor student to do? If, in desperation, he decides that all of the interpreters are probably wrong and that the only thing for him to do is to go back to the original writings of the philosopher himself and then make his own decision—uninfluenced (as if this were possible) by the interpretation of any one else—the result is not that he has actually come to the meaning of the original philosopher himself, but rather that he has set up one more interpretation, which may differ to a greater or lesser degree from the interpretations already existing. It is clear that in this direction lies chaos, just the kind of chaos which Schiller has so graphically and inimitably described.[1]

It is curious that until now no way of escaping this difficulty has been seriously considered. It has not occurred to students of philosophy that one effective way of meeting the problem at least partially is to put these varying interpretations and critiques before the philosopher while he is still alive and to ask him to act at one and the same time as both defendant and judge. If the world's great living philosophers can be induced to co-operate in an enterprise whereby their own work can, at least to some extent, be saved from becoming merely "dessicated lecture-fodder," which on the one hand "provides innocuous sustenance for ruminant professors," and, on the other hand, gives an opportunity to such ruminants and their understudies to "speculate safely, endlessly, and fruitlessly, about what a philosopher must have meant" (Schiller), they will have taken a long step toward making their intentions clearly comprehensible.

With this in mind, *The Library of Living Philosophers* expects to publish at more or less regular intervals a volume on each of the greater among the world's living philosophers. In each case it will be the purpose of the editor of *The Library* to bring together in the volume the interpretations and criticisms of a wide range of that particular thinker's scholarly contemporaries, each of whom will be given a free hand to discuss the specific phase of the thinker's work which has been assigned

---

[1] In his essay on "Must Philosophers Disagree?" in the volume by the same title (Macmillan, London, 1934), from which the above quotations were taken.

to him. All contributed essays will finally be submitted to the philosopher with whose work and thought they are concerned, for his careful perusal and reply. And, although it would be expecting too much to imagine that the philosopher's reply will be able to stop all differences of interpretation and of critique, this should at least serve the purpose of stopping certain of the grosser and more general kinds of misinterpretations. If no further gain than this were to come from the present and projected volumes of this *Library*, it would seem to be fully justified.

In carrying out this principal purpose of the *Library*, the editor announces that (in so far as humanly possible) each volume will conform to the following pattern:

First, a series of expository and critical articles written by the leading exponents and opponents of the philosopher's thought;

Second, the reply to the critics and commentators by the philosopher himself;

Third, an intellectual autobiography of the thinker whenever this can be secured; in any case an authoritative and authorized biography; and

Fourth, a bibliography of writings of the philosopher to provide a ready instrument to give access to his writings and thought.

The editor has deemed it desirable to secure the services of an Advisory Board of philosophers to aid him in the selection of the subjects of future volumes. The names of the five prominent American philosophers who have consented to serve appear below. To each of them the editor expresses his sincere gratitude.

Future volumes in this series will appear in as rapid succession as is feasible in view of the scholarly nature of this *Library*. The next three volumes in this series should be those of Rudolf Carnap, Martin Buber, and C. I. Lewis.

The entire project of *The Library of Living Philosophers* still is not on a sound financial foundation, owing to the lack of necessary funds. The *Library* would be deeply grateful, therefore, for gifts and donations. Moreover, since November 6th, 1947, any gifts of donations made to The Library of Living Philosophers, Inc., are deductible by the donors in arriving at their taxable net income in conformity with the

Internal Revenue Code of the Treasury Department of the United States of America.

P. A. S.
Editor

DEPARTMENT OF PHILOSOPHY
NORTHWESTERN UNIVERSITY
EVANSTON, ILLINOIS

ADVISORY BOARD

ACKNOWLEDGEMENTS

THE editor hereby gratefully acknowledges his obligation and sincere gratitude to all the publishers of Professor Broad's books and publications for their kind and uniform courtesy in permitting us to quote—sometimes at some length—from Professor Broad's writings.

TABLE OF CONTENTS

PREFACE

HERE, at long last, is Volume X in our LIBRARY, on *The Philosophy* of C. D. Broad. I say, at long last, because—as is also true of the next succeeding volume (on *The Philosophy of Rudolf Carnap*)—it has been a very long time in the making. In fact, most of the essays for this book were written in 1955. We apologize to one and all. But, perhaps the care with which Professor Broad has not merely written his Autobiography but also his Reply to his critics and commentators may in some way justify the delay. Of this great care the observant and critical reader will have no difficulty in convincing himself. All the undersigned can do here is to, once again, express to Professor Broad his sincere appreciation and gratitude.

Similar gratitude is due to all the contributors to this volume, who, like Professor Broad himself, have spared neither time nor effort to come to grips with this philosopher's salient and most distinguishing ideas. The editor is happy too to express his thanks to Dr. C. Lewy, who has so kindly and so painstakingly prepared Part IV of this volume, the Bibliography of Professor Broad's writings. The editor also desires to acknowledge the tireless efforts of his (part-time) secretary, Mrs. Edward C. Smith without whose aid this volume would have been delayed still more.

The order in which the contributed essays appear in Part II was determined by the order in which Professor Broad replied to his critics in Part III. There is one exception to this rule. That is the essay by Professor Robert W. Browning, which came into the editor's hands long after Professor Broad had completed and sent in his "Reply." Inasmuch as Professor Broad could not reply to it, this essay has been placed last in Part II.

Once again the editor is indebted to the Graduate Research Council of Northwestern University for its annual continuance of a small grant-in-aid to help defray some of the editorial expenses of this as well as of other volumes in our LIBRARY.

Except for some editorial labors, Vol. XI, on *The Philosophy of Ru-*

dolf Carnap, is also nearing completion and should see publication shortly after the appearance of the present volume.

May this volume too aid the reader of Professor Broad's works in clearing up difficulties in understanding and interpretation.

PAUL ARTHUR SCHILPP
Editor

KRESGE CENTENNIAL HALL
NORTHWESTERN UNIVERSITY
EVANSTON, ILLINOIS
DECEMBER 1, 1958

ABBREVIATIONS used for C. D. Broad's principal works (listed here in the alphabetical order of the abbreviations; not chronologically):

ABBREV'N	TITLE
EHP	Ethics and the History of Philosophy (1952)
EMcP, I or *II*	*Examination of McTaggart's Philosophy,* Vols. I & II (1933 & 1938)
FTET	*Five Types of Ethical Theory* (1930)
MPN	*The Mind and Its Place in Nature* (1925)
PPR	*Perception, Physics and Reality* (1914)
RPPR	*Religion, Philosophy and Psychical Research* (1953)
ST	*Scientific Thought* (1923)

C. D. Broad

AUTOBIOGRAPHY

Reply to Stace

I will begin with Professor Stace's remark that the really important conflict between science & religion is that the general spirit of science, as expressed in what he calls the "philosophy of naturalism", conflicts with any sort of religious view. We must either abandon naturalism or to abandon religion or find some way of reconciling the two.

The "philosophy of naturalism", as I understand it, holds that all consciousness (& a fortiori all personality) is completely & one-sidedly dependent on the fulfilment of certain physico-chemical, physiological, & anatomical conditions. Every particular experience depends one-sidedly on a particular occurrence in a certain brain & nervous system, & each person's dispositions, character, & personality depend one-sidedly on the particular minute structure & organisation of his brain & nervous system.

Now, on the one hand, everything to which we attach value or disvalue seems to reside in or to relate to persons, who experience sensations, thoughts, desires, emotions, etc., & have elaborately organised cognitive, conative, & emotional dispositions. On the other hand, the physico-chemical, physiological, & anatomical conditions of consciousness in general & of organised personality in particular seem to be highly specialised, narrowly localised in space & in time, extremely unstable, & altogether at the mercy of that part of the physical order which is organised at a lower level of complexity.

Any such view is plainly incompatible with what most people in the West & many in the East have understood by religion. For Christians, Jews, & Mohammedans, at any rate, the following propositions, taken quite literally, are essential. (1) The specifically moral values & disvalues, at any rate, which inhere in human persons & express themselves in their volitions, emotions, thought, & actions, are not just transitory & local by-products of conditions to which no kind of value or disvalue can significantly be ascribed & which cannot significantly be said to have any kind of preference for the one over the other. On the contrary, there is in every human being an essential factor which is existentially independent of his body & is destined to endure endlessly, though it may always need to be connected with an appropriate organism of some kind in order to constitute a full personality.

FACSIMILE REPRODUCTION OF BROAD'S HANDWRITING — FROM HIS "REPLY"

AUTOBIOGRAPHY

I WAS born at 11 P.M. on December 30th 1887, at Harlesden in Middlesex, then a pleasant enough place on the verge of unspoiled country, but now and for long since a most unattractive suburb of north-west London. The sign Virgo was rising at my birth, so, like Horace, I may describe myself as 'one of Mercury's men.' The astrologically-minded reader will note with interest that the ruler Mercury was in the fourth House and in the sign Sagittarius, and with regret that it was unaspected for good or for ill by any other planet.

The year of my birth was that of Queen Victoria's jubilee. The sun of England's overwhelming power and prosperity had already passed the meridian, though few can have suspected this at the time, and though rather more than a quarter of a century of golden afternoon remained before the nightfall of 1914.

My father, Charles Stephen Broad, was born in Bedminster, now a suburb of Bristol, in 1844. He was the youngest of the eight children of George and Eliza Broad of that city. Of these children one boy (James) died in infancy, and one girl (Ellen) died of consumption at the age of 26. George, the eldest child, died in middle life. The remaining five, Edwin, Emma, Leah, Julia, and my father, all lived to and beyond their three-score years and ten. They were all persons of marked individuality, possessed of more than average intelligence and a strong sense of humour, and they all remained in fair bodily health and full mental vigour until very near the end of their lives. The elderly Uncle Edwin and his wife (Aunt Harriet), and the three elderly aunts, Emma, Leah, and Julia, all played an important part in my early life; but one of them (Aunt Leah) stood, as I shall explain later, in a specially close relationship to me.

The Broads had been living in Somerset, in particular in the Mendip villages near Bristol, such as Winford and Dundry, for at least 150 years before my father's birth. They had inter-married in the middle XVIII-th century with a family of Huguenot refugees, named Thiery or Thierry, who had fled from France in 1650 and had settled in the Mendips. There is a quaint memorial-stone in the floor of the parish church of Hinton Blewett in Somerset, commemorating the names and virtues of the earlier members of this family. The first of my paternal

3

ancestors whom I can trace is my great-great-great-grandfather George, whom I will call George I. He died in 1773, and was presumably born about 1700. His son, George II, my great-great-grandfather, was born in 1732 and died in 1803. He married in 1757 Mary Thiery (b. 1734, d. 1802). The name Thiery frequently occurs as a middle name among his male descendants. I believe that the Thiery family is now extinct in the male line. The last holder of the name, so far as I am aware, was a Miss Thiery, who kept the village post-office in Winford early in the present century.

Many of the Broads in the XVIII-th century were stone-masons and small country builders in the Mendips. But my great-grandfather, George III (b. 1761), was a wool-stapler. He lived and died in Bedminster, and his business was carried on by his two sons, Stephen (b. 1789, d. 1884) and my grandfather George IV (b. 1796, d. 1866).

A younger brother of my great-grandfather George III, John Thiery Broad (b. 1772), became a fairly prominent and successful builder in Bristol. His house and builder's yard were in Old Market Street. His son, James Thiery Broad, inherited and developed the business. He commemorated his father by a memorial window in the church of St. Mary Redcliffe in Bristol, which is still to be seen there. My paternal grandmother was Eliza Broad (b. 1805, d. 1884), daughter of this John Thiery Broad and sister to this James Thiery Broad, and thus first cousin to her husband George IV.

John Thiery Broad was fairly well off, and his daughter Eliza had received an excellent education in the subjects then considered suitable for girls. I possess a beautifully worked sampler which she sewed at school in 1815. My grandfather employed in his business the money which my grandmother inherited from her father, and the business prospered.

Only a fool or a saint thinks business and money unimportant, and I cannot claim to belong to either of those classes. I shall therefore try to give some account of the family fortunes up to the time of my father's marriage, so far as I understand them; for they were certainly a factor which greatly influenced my life and character.

As I have said, Grandfather George and his elder brother Stephen were partners in the wool-stapling business which they had inherited from their father. There was a branch of this business at Rochdale in Lancashire, and we continued to derive a small annual rent from a warehouse there until it was sold when my father inherited it on the death of my Uncle Edwin in 1912. Stephen Broad lived for a time in Rochdale, and used to ride about to the neighbouring farms in Lancashire and Yorkshire, buying wool and fleeces. There are some amusing stories, handed down from him in my family, which illustrate life in the farms and vicarages of that rather rough countryside at that remote period. Like the stories which Manning's father used to relate about the Negro slaves on his West Indian plantations, they may be described in the Cardinal's words as 'indelicate, though free from evil *de sexu*.' One of them is perhaps worth recording here.

The incumbent of one of these Lancashire or Yorkshire parishes was one of the old-fashioned hunting parsons, more versed in field-sports than in his pastoral duties. One day, as he was about to set out for the meet, a message was brought to him that an old woman in the parish, who had long lain bedridden, was on the point of death and wished to see him. He hastily pulled a clerical cloak over his hunting dress and rushed down to the cottage, where the following conversation took place:—"They tell me, Parson, that I'm a-dying." "Have you said the Lord's Prayer?" "Yes, Sir." "Do you repent of your sins?" "Yes, Sir." "Do you believe that Christ died to save you?" "O yes, Sir." "Then you can tell the Devil to kiss your a-se!" And with that viaticum the parson was off to the meet.

At some time, I do not know precisely when, great-Uncle Stephen retired, taking his money out of the business and leaving my grandfather as the sole partner. The family tradition is that he was somewhat simple and very susceptible to flattery, and that cleverer and less honest persons than himself induced him to appear as director on the boards of several wild-cat companies and to put his capital into them. The one in which he lost most was a company for mining ochre somewhere in the west of England. My grandfather was a much shrewder man than his elder brother, and he was also an extremely generous one. He had clearly foreseen the result of these speculations, and, when Stephen had ruined himself financially, the younger brother took the elder as an honoured guest into his house, where he remained for the rest of his very long life.

Great-Uncle Stephen's lack of worldly wisdom was outweighed by his very rich and lovable personality. His nephews and nieces were devoted to him and would often relate to me stories of his doings and sayings. He had a profound contempt for the French, and in particular for the finicky way in which that degenerate race are wont to pronounce their own language. So, although he knew better, he was always careful to speak of Louis XVIII as 'Lewis Dick-Suet.' As elder brother he used to conduct the family prayers which were held daily in the dining-room before breakfast, and he would on occasion introduce special petitions for particular members of the family. Once his sister, 'Aunt Edwards,' was on a visit. She happened at the time (unknown to Stephen, but to the knowledge of the female members of the family) to be suffering from

a painful boil on her bottom. Stephen electrified the assembly by concluding his prayer with the words: "God bless my dear Sister; be a
comfort and support to her latter end!" Stephen outlived my grandfather by many years. He died in 1884, at the age of 95, shortly before
my grandmother.

My grandfather at his death in 1866 left his family very well provided for. The business was flourishing, and was carried on by his eldest
son George in partnership with the latter's younger brother Edwin.
My father, who was only in his 22nd year, had recently entered the firm.
Grandfather considered, reasonably enough, that his sons' financial
future was secure, and he left to them only comparatively small monetary legacies beside their shares in the firm. Most fortunately, as it
turned out, he provided for his widow and his daughters independently
of the business. He had invested his quite considerable savings in
ground-rents and reversions in Battersea and Camberwell, which are
inner suburbs of south London. He created for this property a somewhat complicated trust, which I shall now describe in outline.

The essential intention of the trust was to make his daughters and
their children (if any) completely independent of their husbands, if
they should marry. "Men," Grandfather used to say, "are Jack Straws!"
(It should be remembered that the Married Women's Property Act did
not become law until 1881.) The income of the trust was to go to my
grandmother for her life-time. At her death it was to be divided equally
among her daughters for their respective lives. On the death of any
daughter who was childless her share of the income was to be divided
equally among her surviving sisters. On the death of any daughter who
had children the capital represented by her share of the income was to
be divided, in such proportions as she might will, among her children.
In the end the whole of the capital was to be inherited by the descendants of the married daughters. As it turned out, the whole property
eventually devolved upon my cousins Ernest and Cyril, the two sons of
my Aunt Julia, who was the only daughter to have children.

As my grandmother was entitled to a share of the income of the business, beside the whole income of the trust, she began her widowhood in
very good financial circumstances. But in course of time a crisis arose
in the business. The subject was naturally a painful one to my father
and his brothers and sisters, so I do not know the precise details; but
the gist of the matter is as follows.

My Uncle George (in my notation 'George V'), who had become head
of the firm, seems to have been an able business-man on a rising market,
but somewhat too venturesome and liable to be caught short when the
market was falling. He had made an early and unwise marriage with

a woman belonging to a much lower level in the middle-class than that to which his family had now risen. Mary Ann, as she was called, and her relatives were indeed perfectly respectable, in the technical sense, but she was an ignorant and rather silly woman, whose grammar was by no means impeccable and whose manners hovered between plain vulgarity and affected refinement. She soon became too big for her boots, and her social ambitions led her to be extravagant herself and to be continually pressing her husband for means to support her extravagance. He was thus drawing too much money from the business, and was in no position to meet a time of difficulty in the wool-trade. When eventually such a time came, Uncle George, without consulting his brothers, took measures of doubtful legality to tide over the crisis. They were ineffectual; the firm was ruined, and he himself with his wife and five young children found it expedient to put the Atlantic between himself and his creditors and the law.

As a result of this my grandmother lost that portion of her income which was derived from the business. My Uncle Edwin and my father (still quite a young man) lost their positions and prospects as members of an old-established and respected family firm, and they also lost the legacies which their father had left them.

Uncle Edwin, who was a studious and quite a learned man (known in the family as 'Sage'), never attempted to go into business again. He lived at home during the rest of his mother's lifetime on a small private income derived from what he had managed to save and invest before the crash. My father went into business as a wine-merchant, and followed that occupation under various vicissitudes till he eventually retired in 1912 on the death of his brother Edwin, from whom he inherited a modest competence. He was never particularly successful as a business-man. I am inclined to think that his heart was not in his work. Such small success as he had was in middle life. As he grew older his business gradually faded away with the death of old customers, most of whom had been personal or family friends, and he seems to have made no particular effort to seek new ones.

The fact is that the income from my grandfather's trust was the financial sheet-anchor for all his children. Directly, or indirectly through the generosity of the sisters to their brothers, it furnished the means for a life of modest comfort for all and removed the stimulus of urgent need from any. My Uncle Edwin and my father were trustees under this trust, and my father was the active one of the two. He conducted all the correspondence, kept the accounts in his exquisite copper-plate handwriting, and for many years personally collected certain of the ground-rents. For this work he received a commission, which was a useful supplement to his income. After his death my mother continued for many years to keep the accounts and send out applications and receipts for ground-rent and to receive a commission for doing so, even after the trust had been wound up. In this way my two cousins, who had inherited the property and could easily have done the business for themselves, contributed with great delicacy and kindness toward my mother's income. When she grew too old for this work I undertook it for her, and she continued to receive the commission to the day of her death.

Uncle George and his deplorable Mary Ann did not long survive transplantation to God's own country. On their death in 1877 three of their chickens, their daughters Alice, Ellen, and Edith, came home to roost in their grandmother's house. Ellen was what is now called a 'difficult' child, and at an early age got into serious trouble (presumably in the classical way) and committed suicide. The incident was naturally not a favourite subject of conversation between my elders and myself, and I know nothing about it except the bare fact which I have stated.

Alice and Edith received an excellent education at their grandmother's expense. Alice never married. She was given a home and a small allowance by her aunts and Uncle Edwin until the death of the latter, when she inherited enough to enable her to live in modest comfort in her own flat. I saw a great deal of her when I was a child, a schoolboy, and a young man. She was my first governess, and taught me reading, writing, and the elements of English history and arithmetic. As trustee under Uncle Edwin's will I managed her affairs until her death in 1946 at the age of 83. She was a person of good intelligence and impulsive generosity. But she was somewhat too submissive and lacked enterprise and practical efficiency. My mother, who had in abundance the qualities which Alice lacked, regarded her with affection mingled with mild contempt, and felt that she should have made some effort to provide for herself instead of contentedly living on her relatives. Her intense affection for her much harder sister Edith and for the latter's children exposed her to many slights and to much occasional unhappiness, though I suppose that on the whole it was the main source of interest and pleasure in her life. Her sister's death, only a year or so before her own, was a loss from which she never recovered.

Edith married fairly early in life William Garland, a Cornishman, who became secretary to a number of highly successful gold-mining companies. He earned a handsome salary and gradually accumulated by judicious investment and speculation a considerable fortune out of his savings. On his death his wife became very much the wealthiest member of our family. She had some of the 'Mary Ann' characteristics, in a sublimated form, and none of the generosity so characteristic of her sister and her uncles and aunts. I suppose that early experience had impressed on her the desirability of 'keeping a good grip of the gear,' and in all important financial matters she was ruled by her very able and acquisitive husband.

Of George's two sons, who remained in the United States, the younger, Charles, perished unmarried in a hotel fire. Of the elder, Walter, I know nothing except that he married and had children. So presumably some at least of my remote cousins are domiciled on the safer and more prosperous side of the Atlantic.

From this long excursion into the family fortunes, with its attendant exposure of certain skeletons in the family cupboard, I return to my father and to the aunts and the uncle whom I knew as a boy and a young man.

In 1847, when my father was 3 years old, Grandfather George moved his business and his family from Bristol to London. He settled first in Bermondsey, where, as I understand, his house, his office, and his warehouse adjoined each other. From Bermondsey the family moved out to Peckham Rye, then one of the outermost south-eastern suburbs, on the edge of very beautiful hilly wooded country in Kent and Surrey, remains of which can still be seen in the gardens of the older houses in Dulwich, Forest Hill, and Sydenham. On my grandfather's death in 1866 my grandmother moved with her unmarried children and her brother-in-law Stephen to 39 The Gardens, Peckham Rye, a typical Victorian middle-class house in a newly built square surrounding a pleasant garden reserved for the use of the inhabitants. This continued to be occupied by members of the family until my Aunt Emma's death in 1909.

It was a roomy house, and it needed to be. The family included, beside my grandmother and great-Uncle Stephen, the two unmarried sons, Edwin and Charles, and the two unmarried daughters, Emma and Leah. The other surviving daughter, Julia, was married fairly early in life to her first-cousin, James Thiery Broad II, a Bristol solicitor, and moved away from London. But the family was soon supplemented by three children, the daughters of George and Mary Ann. Two of these, Alice and Edith, continued to live there after they had left school; the latter until her marriage in 1885, and the former for some time longer.

I shall now try to describe, as best I can from hearsay and inference, some of the features of life in this matriarchal *ménage* and some of the personal characteristics of its members.

My grandmother seems to have been an able and intelligent woman of a somewhat austere kind. She managed her household and her fi-

nances efficiently, and brought up her family of highly individual and
spirited children in such a way as to win their respect and to keep their
affection. Both she and my grandfather had originally been members
of the Church of England. But at some time in his early manhood my
grandfather, who had been a somewhat lukewarm churchman, became
converted by a Wesleyan Methodist preacher. His way of life was radically and permanently changed, and he carried his wife with him into
the Wesleyan Methodist community. So the children were brought up
as Wesleyans and regularly attended chapel.

Readers who have derived their ideas of Victorian Nonconformity
and the middle-class Victorian home mainly from the novels and plays
of left-wing writers of some fifty years ago, will be apt to jump to the
conclusion that life in my grand-parents' house was a drab and stuffy
existence, punctuated by religious exercises, to which resentful and
hypocritical children were driven by fanatical and gloomy parents.
They had better dismiss that romantic rubbish from their minds at
once. My grandfather was an exceptionally humane and generous man
by nature, and he did not become less so when he had found grace. It
is typical of him that, when the family cat was in the family way, he
would always insist that her normal portion of milk should be supplemented with cream in view of the increased demands upon her. He
refrained from setting up his carriage, when it would have been normal
for a man in his position to do so, in order that he might have more to
spend in charity. He was particularly kind to young Wesleyan ministers
and to students for the ministry making their first essays in preaching.
A series of these always hungry, often shy, and usually impecunious
young men would spend the week-end with my grandparents and be
regaled with solid meals and made to feel at home. They were naturally
a source of considerable interest, and often of mild amusement, to the
daughters of the house, who appraised their looks and their table-
manners with a critical eye. I derive a reflected glory from the fact that
the very distinguished Wesleyan minister whose son is now Registrary
of Cambridge University, was once in his babyhood dandled by my
Aunt Julia, when she was a young girl and *his* father was a newly
wedded young minister on a visit to my grandparents.

My grandfather had had much less education than his richer cousin,
my grandmother. But he gave an excellent education to his children.
The girls were sent to first-rate boarding-schools. All of them had
learned French, and in addition Aunt Leah had studied Italian and
Aunt Julia German. All the daughters were good musicians. There was
much singing and much playing on the piano and the harp. The latter
was a formidable gilded instrument, which had cost £80, and which

I used to admire as a child as it stood under its elaborate cover in the drawing-room. Aunt Emma was the chief vocalist and harp-player; Aunts Leah and Julia were excellent pianists. As to the boys, my grandfather would never have thought of sending them to public schools (in the English sense of that word). He would certainly have felt that such schools were only for the sons of the nobility and the landed gentry, and he would probably have thought them objectionable from the moral and religious standpoint. But there were many excellent private boarding-schools for boys, and my Uncle Edwin and my father received a very sound education in classics, history, geography, and elementary mathematics. Uncle Edwin was of a much more scholarly disposition than my father, and he kept up his Latin and Greek whilst my father had let his rust. But even my father would occasionally quote with relish long passages from Cicero's oration against Catiline, which he had learned by heart as a school exercise.

I should doubt whether my grandfather, after his conversion, would have approved of his children dancing or going to the theatre. But it is certain that under my grandmother's *régime* dancing was permitted, and the family gave an occasional ball. It was on one such occasion that my father's life-long friend, a young Dutchman who eventually married an English wife and settled in England and was known and loved by me as 'Uncle Chris,' fell into one of the numerous traps which the English language sets for foreigners. John Christian Kalshoven, then about 19 years old and a very good-looking boy and a fine dancer, was at this party on his first visit to the home of his friend Charlie Broad. My Aunt Leah, then a young woman of great attractions, said to him: "Have you met Miss X? Don't you think she is very pretty?" John Christian replied: "I cannot say. I have only seen her backside!" In later years I have often used this simple story as a warning to young Swedish friends visiting England. Uncle Chris's *faux pas* was at any rate less devastating than that of the young Swede, now a very distinguished scientific professor, who, in reply to a similar question, remarked to his hostess: "I think she looks very pregnant!"

I shall now say something of the personalities of the brothers and sisters in this Victorian middle-middle-class home, and in particular of my father and of Aunt Leah, who was a second mother to me.

All of them were well above the average in good-looks; both Aunt Emma and Aunt Leah, in their very different ways, must have been decidedly beautiful. They fell into two markedly different physical groups. Edwin, Leah, and Julia were typical Nords, with golden hair and blue eyes. Edwin and Leah were slim and tall, with very fine heads and features. Julia was plump and doll-like, with a characteristic pout of the lips. Emma and my father had dark hair and brown eyes. Emma was *petite* and elegant, my father of about middle height and slim in figure. Both my father and my Uncle Edwin lost their hair at an early age—a misfortune which I inherited—and they were markedly bald by the time I first knew them. My father, who was very much of a dandy in his younger days, had spent a good deal of time and money on practitioners who claimed to be able to restore fallen hair. It was therefore, perhaps, that he disliked the title 'Professor,' which, as he said, he associated with quacks who claim to cure baldness and with showmen who ascend from fair-grounds in balloons and come down in parachutes. Fortunately he died, *felix opportunitate mortis* in this as in so many other ways, before his son had been disgraced with that title.

All five, with the possible exception of Julia, were well above the average in intelligence and in their interest for serious subjects. Uncle Edwin, to the best of my belief, was uninfluenced by the famous 'conflict between science and religion' which raged in his late middle years. He was much the most definitely sectarian of the family, and for many years took an active part in the affairs of the chapel which he attended. In politics he was a somewhat bigoted Gladstonian Liberal. In his latter days, when Mr. Balfour introduced his notorious Education Bill which became law in 1902, and when certain Nonconformists under the leadership of Dr. Clifford played at being St. Laurences on the very tepid gridiron supplied to them, he was in his element and got great and obvious enjoyment from indulging his moral indignation to the full from the comfort of his easy-chair. His oracle was then Dr. Robertson Nichol of the *British Weekly,* and he used to read aloud, with due rhetorical emphasis, to his adoring wife (who was at heart an Anglican and a Conservative) that editor's hebdomadal philippic against the Church of England and the Tories.

My father had a deep interest in natural science and a very fair amateur knowledge of it, which he conveyed to me. He had been greatly influenced by the controversies concerning evolution and the higher criticism of the Bible. I do not know exactly where he had arrived theologically. He had certainly ceased to identify himself with any particular Christian church or sect, but I think that he retained a general theistic belief, in which the moral teachings of Christ (as distinct from theological doctrines about him) played an important part. He had a very strong antipathy to ritualistic practices and clerical pretensions in general, and to those of the Church of Rome and of High Anglicans in particular. His attitude cannot be better summarised than in the following lines from W. S. Gilbert's poem *Lost Mr. Blake* in the *Bab Ballads:—*

I have known him to indulge in profane ungentlemanly emphatics
When the Protestant churches were divided over the proper width
   of a chasuble's hem.
He sneered at albs—and, as for dalmatics—
Words cannot express the contempt he felt for them.

It may not be out of place at this point to relate how I might have become an Anglican clergyman myself, if my father had fallen for the wiles of an aristocratic tempter. Lord Henry Brudenell Bruce had been a business acquaintance of his, and had become Marquess of Ailesbury on the death of his extremely disreputable nephew, the fourth marquess, in 1894. He happened to meet my father shortly after this and said to him: "If you care to put your son into the Church, I have a number of livings in my gift and I should be pleased to appoint him to one or another of them when it falls vacant." My father duly thanked the Marquess for this extremely generous offer, but declined it, saying: "My son may well turn out to be as unfit for the Church as I should have been." "I am inclined to agree with you in principle," said the Marquess, "for the last time that my nephew chose an incumbent for one of his livings he gave it to a clergyman who was, he said, the only man he had ever met who could drink more whisky than he could."

In politics my father, like my Uncle Edwin, was a Liberal and an admirer of Gladstone, though he had no enthusiasm for Irish home-rule. They were completely at one in their dislike and distrust for Joseph Chamberlain, who had been too radical for them in his radical days, and had now, in their opinion, betrayed his leader and gone to his own place. But my father had none of his brother's self-complacent politico-religious narrow-mindedness. He regarded Uncle Edwin's Nonconformist Liberal heroics as somewhat absurd, though he was too wise to impart that opinion to his elder brother. Aunt Leah, who had lapsed into Anglicanism of a very broad type and also had an acute sense of the ridiculous, took the same line as my father.

One thing most characteristic of my father was his lifelong passion for gardening in general and for cultivating ferns in particular. His heart was much more in this than in his business, and he devoted more and more of his time to it as he grew older. He had begun to collect ferns as a very young man, and already in his father's lifetime had built a conservatory with a rockery for them. To each successive house in which he lived the ferns were taken, and in each there was a conservatory for the less hardy of them and a rockery in it or out of doors for their display. He was interested in his ferns rather for their delicate beauty and for the rarity of some of them than from a scientific botanical standpoint. He had great skill and excellent taste in building rockwork, and he liked to provide it with a pond and dripping water for ferns which needed very moist conditions. He was helped in his collection by a German friend long settled in England, a Mr. Stoltenhoff, who was a real expert. He certainly acquired and successfully cultivated many rare and exquisitely beautiful specimens. From an early age I was pressed into this hobby. I enjoyed helping to build rockwork, and especially mixing and dabbing on Portland cement, and I admired the beauty of the rock-garden as a finished product. But I never had any taste for the process of gardening itself, and I naturally often resented being taken from pursuits of my own, in which I was interested, in order to help my father plant and tend his ferns.

If resentment was felt, it was certainly never overtly shown, and there was no attempt to evade my father's requests and no question of disobeying them. He was a kind and even indulgent father, and fundamentally a just and reasonable one, and I liked and admired him, but I learned at a very early age that he would stand no nonsense. What he said went. Any attempt to argue or to disobey would arouse his wrath, and the mere expression of his anger in voice and manner was to me most formidable. Neither corporal punishment nor even the threat of it was needed to ensure my obedience when it was plain that he was in earnest, and when he was in earnest there was never the least doubt about the fact in my mind.

My father was the youngest child. He was adored by his otherwise somewhat austere mother, and by his sisters, whose feelings toward each other fell considerably short of adoration. Even his much older and somewhat puritanical brother Edwin had a very warm corner in his heart for my father, and was secretly proud of his social qualities and the popularity which they engendered.

He was extremely lively and sociable, an excellent conversationalist, and a delightful host and guest. He had both wit and humour to an exceptionally high degree. He noted and enjoyed the ridiculous incidents in life, and would describe and heighten them in turns of phrase which were often extremely happy. (His description of a man and his wife who lived nearby and were exceptionally thin and gawky as 'Bones and his Rib,' is typical.) As a young man he must have been decidedly good-looking in a way that would appeal to young women. In his early years he was in fact very much of a lady's man, without thereby forfeiting the affection of a large circle of friends of his own sex and age. Up to late middle life he was very particular to be well dressed and turned out, but he afterwards became completely indifferent to this and had to be kept up to the mark in such matters by my mother. At the back of all this lay a serious and somewhat melancholy and highly sensitive nature. He was not a demonstrative man, and he disliked displays of emotion, but he was easily and deeply moved by fine and by base actions and by the misfortunes of others, and these feelings did not end in themselves but issued in appropriate action. Friends who had suffered financial misfortunes were helped with gifts which were large in comparison with his limited means, and he was assiduous in visiting and trying to cheer by his company other friends who were slowly dying of painful and incurable illnesses.

He must have been in certain important respects a disappointed man. Though there was never any question of want or of serious anxiety, his financial position did not answer to the expectations which he must quite reasonably have entertained as a young man. Most of his friends and relatives were far better off than he, whilst he was far better qualified than most of them to enjoy and make good use of money and the social position which it gives to those who own it. He must have felt himself continually cramped by *res angusta domi,* both in displaying his social gifts and exercising hospitality and in his opportunities for helping others. All this would be rendered the more galling both by comparison with his more fortunate contemporaries and by the thought that all might so easily have been different. I hope I am right in thinking that in his later years he found in his son, and in the academic success which his son had already gained, some compensation for his own comparative failure to make good in life. I should suppose that a father identifies himself in a unique way with his only son, and feels the latter's life almost as a continuation of his own, so that the son's successes and failures are felt by the father almost as personal triumphs and defeats.

I turn now to the sisters. I will begin with one general remark. It must be a matter for surprise that two girls such as my Aunts Emma and Leah did not marry early in life. They were of more than average beauty, they had good manners and wit and many accomplishments, and they already had their own pin-money in their mother's lifetime and were certain to inherit quite decent incomes on her death. Yet Aunt Emma remained a spinster and became a typical old maid, and Aunt Leah was married only in late middle life and then only to an elderly widower who was a cousin of hers. Behind this there probably lay much which my parents and aunts did not care to impart to me, but I know something and can guess more.

Plainly there was something very queer indeed in Aunt Emma's psyche. She could be absolutely charming, and with children or young people on a day's visit she was delightful. She was extremely generous and hospitable and loved to stuff her young relatives with good food and drink and to tip them half-sovereigns when they went to her house. But, as I learned from my parents and others when I grew older, there was another and much less pleasant side to her character. From her early years she had been subject to fits of ungovernable temper. On these occasions she would first sulk, and would then either write extremely wounding and admirably phrased letters, denouncing the iniquities of this or that member of the family, or would assemble them all in the dining-room and deliver a verbal philippic before retiring in dudgeon to her room. (It was on one such occasion that she coined a phrase, long treasured in the family: "I have the determination of the Czar of all the Russias.")

I suppose that a modern psycho-analyst, who can tell us all about the suppressed complexes of a person who never existed, such as Hamlet, would find it child's play to explain poor Aunt Emma. For my own part I must be content with the following halting remarks. In the first place, it is certain that she was bitterly jealous of her younger sister Leah. Whether there was any concrete ground for this jealousy I do not know. Secondly, I know from my own experience that I have it in me to behave as Aunt Emma behaved, and to feel as she doubtless felt, when I believe myself (often quite unreasonably) to be slighted by a person whom I love. If I may judge others by myself, I would say that a *façade* of good sense and sweet reasonableness often conceals a boiling pit of half crazy suspicions and emotions:—*turris super cloacam,* to borrow and adapt a mediaeval monk's description of the female human body. Lastly, I have had the opportunity of witnessing in two of our cooks feminine tantrums which my mother recognised as resembling Aunt Emma's. Both these women in turn served us faithfully for many years. I know how devastating to family happiness such tantrums can be, and yet that their sporadic occurrence is quite compatible with predominant kindliness, efficiency, and good sense.

By the date of my birth Aunt Emma had become very eccentric indeed in her mode of life, and she became more so as time went on. She was then living alone, save for one maid-servant, in the house which had formerly contained all the family. She had for some years past ceased to use any means of public transport or to walk out of doors, though she was in perfectly good bodily health. But she still went out occasionally in a hired closed carriage. On such occasions she was wont to keep the coachman waiting for two hours or more at her door whilst she performed an elaborate toilette. Almost the last of her outings was, I believe, the immensely long and dreary drive across London from Peckham to Harlesden to be present at my christening. Soon after this she ceased to go out at all and spent the remaining 20 years of her life indoors. For many years before her death she had ceased, to the best of our knowledge, to go to bed. She then lived mainly in a large breakfast-room in the basement amidst an extraordinary litter of empty cake-boxes and biscuit-tins, sleeping at night in her arm-chair in front of an immense fire.

Notwithstanding this very peculiar mode of life, Aunt Emma would at fairly frequent intervals invite her London relatives to an evening meal, and from my early boyhood till shortly before her death while I was an undergraduate I thoroughly enjoyed these entertainments.

The meal, which was the *pièce de resistance,* was a form of 'high tea,' so elevated as to approach the sublime. It was, indeed, seldom served until about an hour and a half later than the time appointed. During this waiting period the guests would sit in the drawing-room (lighted entirely by wax-candles), getting hungrier and hungrier, whilst my aunt was engaged in culinary operations in the basement with her one maid, and my father's conversational powers would be stretched to their limit. But when the meal at last came it was supremely worth waiting for. Aunt Emma would preside over the teacups, with infinite charm and vivacity, in front of an urn, eating practically nothing herself and pressing her guests to overeat themselves. The more solid food generally consisted of boiled salmon and roast chicken; the lighter part of exquisite cakes, smothered in almond-paste, and tarts stuffed with cream, supplied by Messrs. Buzzard of Oxford Street, then one of the best pastry-cooks in London. I have vivid memories of the bread-sauce which used to accompany the chicken. It was made with cream instead of milk, and was a revelation of what bread-sauce can be but so seldom is. I have never tasted such bread-sauce elsewhere on earth (though I give very high marks to that which used to be served at my Aunt Julia's table in Bristol), and I hardly hope to be offered anything better in heaven (or Valhalla, as the case may be).

Aunt Emma, who ate extremely little herself, continued to cater regularly on much the same scale as when the whole family were living at the house. The resulting surplus of food found its way to the relatives and hangers-on of her maid and to a horde of miscellaneous undeserving poor who battened on my aunt's completely indiscriminate charity. After her death we found that she had been regularly sending money in fairly substantial amounts to a former maid, who had in fact been dead for many years, but whose relatives had continued to write begging-letters in her name.

My aunt, as one might imagine, soon quarrelled with any doctor who attended her. She had been for many years her own physician, consuming as her own patient vast quantities of magnesia in the fluid and the solid form. In her last illness she refused to see a doctor, and of course no one could force her to do so. When she died, in her chair before the fire in the breakfast-room in 1909 at the age of 78, the law required that an inquest should be held. This was a source of great distress to her surviving brothers and sisters, though nothing discreditable emerged and no blame was attached to anyone, and there was the minimum of publicity. The clearing-up of the house, which had been occupied continuously by the family for 42 years and had never been properly cleaned during the 20 or so years of Aunt Emma's sole tenancy, involved my parents and my Aunt Leah in weeks of hard and heart-breaking work. Unchanged cheques and postal orders, together with coins, amounting in all to several hundreds of pounds, were found stuffed into odd nooks and corners, so that not a single empty cake-box or biscuit-tin could be thrown away until it had been carefully inspected. It should be said, to the credit of humanity, that her maid, who must have had innumerable opportunities for robbing her, seems to have behaved with exemplary honesty.

It will be convenient to describe the youngest sister, Julia, before treating of my Aunt Leah, who was for all practical purposes one of my parents. As I have already mentioned, Julia was married early in life to her first-cousin James Thiery Broad II, and moved away to Bristol, where he was in practice as a solicitor.

Uncle Thiery was a strikingly handsome man, of very great charm, and with an affectionate and lovable but somewhat weak nature. He was highly intelligent and cultivated, was a first-rate lawyer, and had a genuine appreciation for good literature and good living. I greatly enjoyed his company from my childhood until his death in late middle age when I was an undergraduate. He would have been a better man, and would almost certainly have come to occupy a prominent and respected position in his native city, if he had married a more suitable wife than my Aunt Julia. Attractive dolls with pouting lips seldom mature well. She lacked all social ambition, and was too lazy and self-indulgent to go out with him into society or to make a home for him where he could entertain his friends and his clients in a fitting way. When he was at home her conversation with him tended to consist of utterly trivial and very repetitive small-talk (largely about money), mixed with half-jocular and half-serious nagging or ragging. Not unnaturally he began to take his pleasures away from home, and not unnaturally they tended to be detrimental to his pocket, to his reputation, and eventually to his business. There was never, so far as I am aware, any open scandal. But there were occasional financial difficulties, and, I believe, one minor financial crisis, and the family always felt that something really serious might happen. It never did. In the end poor Uncle Thiery, whose bodily health began to fail in his middle age, came to heel and crept into his quite comfortably appointed kennel. He was no villain (if no moral hero); his wife had by then (as she did not fail to remind him on occasion) a larger income than he; and *ubi thesaurus ibi cor*. I can see him in my mind's eye, sitting reading and smoking in his arm-chair after supper with his legs stretched out, whilst his wife's chatter to him and at him flowed on in a steady stream, punctuated by his distraught and monosyllabic responses to her demands that he should 'say something.' When I came to read *Middlemarch* I at once recognised the Thiery-Julia situation, presented by the hand of genius, in the characters of Lydgate and Rosamond.

Their two children, my cousins Ernest and Cyril, solved the problem of home life in their several ways. Ernest, a man of exceptional ability, intelligence, and integrity, became, like his father, a solicitor; took seriously to religion fairly early in life; and devoted himself thereafter to work among boys in the slums of Bristol, which provided him with the highest motives for spending his evenings away from home. His younger brother, Cyril, attained the same end by presumably less sanctified means. Ernest, who had undermined his health by his asceticism, died unmarried in 1931 in his sixty-first year. Cyril married in succession two sisters, and had by the first of them one son and by the second one daughter. He died in 1949 at the age of 76.

I think it may fairly be said that Aunt Julia managed, without ever committing a crime or breaking a Commandment, to warp the natures and blight the lives of three amiable and gifted men. I am sometimes inclined to wonder whether the Devil really gets as good service out of his "regular bad 'uns," like Messalina, as out of some of the less spectacular female servants whom he employs on the home-front.

So far I have painted a rather unpleasing picture of Aunt Julia. But I was really very fond of her, and greatly enjoyed the long annual summer visits which I used to make to her house from my first in 1897 until I came to live at Bristol as professor in 1920. She was in fact one of nature's aunts, though decidedly not one of nature's wives or mothers. Life at her house was much more free and easy than at home or with my Uncle Edwin and Aunt Harriet. I had no need to be on my best behaviour. I could air my views and argue and answer back to an extent which would not have been permitted elsewhere and which would certainly not have been desirable as a regular thing. Then, again, the family were better off than we were at home, so that there was a much freer use of the small luxuries of life, which I greatly enjoyed. There were many pleasant drives and outings to the houses of relatives in and around Bristol. My aunt, like most of the family, was extremely generous with money. She enjoyed good food and drink herself and liked to see her guests do so. She treated this important matter with a seriousness of which I highly approved, and she would constantly consult me as to what I liked and disliked, and would act accordingly.

Aunt Julia was certainly the least intellectual member of her family, and she was perhaps by nature the least intelligent. But I am rather inclined to think that she had good natural intelligence which she had let run to seed through laziness and self-indulgence. She was not without accomplishments. She was a good pianist and an exquisite worker in crochet. In this latter art she was really diligent, and I still own many table-cloths and other such articles bordered or inlaid with her beautiful embroidery.

She had very little hypocrisy and not much delicacy. She did not conceal or idealise her desires and feelings, and, when she was an old woman and I was a young man, she was often extremely frank and outspoken in her conversations with me. She told me that she much preferred cats to children (a sentiment which I fully share with her, but which Victorian ladies did not commonly express). She added that she would have preferred not to have children at all, and that my cousin Cyril was the result of an unfortunate accident. I found it very pleasant to be treated as an equal and a contemporary by a relative so much older than myself, and it was from her that I learned many details of the seamier side of the family's history.

Her cat for a great many years was a large tom, whom even I (who am inclined to be weak about cats) must admit to have been ugly, greedy, lecherous, and lacking in affection. She lavished good food on him and on all her neighbours' cats. She had named him *Urijah*, after a certain nonconformist minister who had enjoyed a very high reputation in Bristol and had recently died in the odour of sanctity, but (according to my aunt's circumstantial story) had had some of the characteristics for which tomcats are notorious. The cat Urijah survived his mistress for several years. He was treated with the same marked generosity by my cousin Ernest, who surely cannot have approved of his character, and died in extreme and unlovely old age.

Aunt Julia died in the early 1920's. She was the only one of the brothers and sisters who had the misfortune to survive the first world-war. She had the good luck not to survive it by long and to be too foolish to grasp and too old to feel its devastating effects in high taxation and inflation of the currency.

I come at length to the middle sister, my Aunt Leah. I am not one to indulge in indiscriminate panegyric, but malice itself would be hard put to it to say aught but good of her. She was very good-looking in her Nordic way even in late middle life, when I first knew her. She must have been really beautiful as a young woman. She had all the good qualities of her brothers and sisters without the defects of any of them. She was immensely generous, not only with her money but in her thoughts and actions; but her beneficence was consistent and judicious, as contrasted with the indiscriminate lavishness of Aunt Emma and the impulsive and largely self-indulgent generosity of Aunt Julia. She had that purity of heart which is the fruit or the root of religion at its best, without a trace of smugness or religiosity or intolerance. She was a proud woman, with great natural dignity in spite of her strong sense of fun, and with a high spirit notwithstanding all her kindliness. I would not have envied any man or woman who might venture to take a liberty with her; the offender would have been quietly but effectively put in his or her place.

Aunt Leah was as intelligent and as interested in the things of the mind as any member of her family, and she was accomplished in many ways. She was a good pianist, like her sisters, but not such a good crochet-worker as her sister Julia. She was, however, the best knitter of the family, and did much very beautiful work in wool. The accomplishment which I most appreciated was her gift for reading aloud both poetry and prose. Like my father, she was easily and deeply moved by fine and by base actions in real life and in fiction, and these emotions expressed themselves naturally in the modulations of her voice when reading aloud. In my childhood and early boyhood both she and my father read a great deal to me. I enjoyed this immensely at the time, and I am most grateful for it in retrospect. I had, and I still have, a receptive and fairly retentive verbal memory, and long before I could read for, myself I could repeat masses of poetry which had been read aloud to me. This included a considerable part of Macaulay's *Lays of Ancient Rome*. Naturally there was much in what I listened to which I could not understand in detail. But this did not diminish my enjoyment, whilst it exercised my intellect and gave room for my imagination. When I asked questions of my aunt or my father they were always treated seriously and answered to the measure of my experience and my understanding.

Aunt Leah's accomplishments extended beyond the finer arts to their humbler practical sisters. She was a first-rate cook, with a particularly light hand for pastry and cakes, and she was highly competent in all that concerns the efficient running of a household.

I think that she and my father resembled each other more closely in character than did any two other members of the family. There was

certainly a very strong bond of affection between them. I never heard
an angry word pass between them in the twenty-five years in which I
grew up in the household which they shared. Nothing would have
stirred my father's wrath more than any sign of disobedience or rude-
ness or neglect on my part toward my aunt. One of the few points in
my manners and morals on which I can honestly look back without dissatisfaction is that I had the grace to love and respect her and that I very
seldom indeed behaved ill toward her. She, on her side, devoted all
the latter part of her life to my father and me. I imagine (though I do
not care to peep and psychologise about my aunt's emotional life) that
my father was for her a kind of substitute for the husband, and I for
the children, whom she so inexplicably never had.

That no one ventured to marry my Aunt Emma is not surprising in
view of her temperament. I never heard of any suitors to her hand,
and, if there were any, they were to be congratulated, like those of
Queen Elizabeth I, on their lack of success. But no such considerations
apply to Aunt Leah, and I know, from what my parents and Aunt Julia
told me in later years, that there had been two love-affairs, each of which
ended unhappily.

The first was in my grandfather's lifetime, when she was still a very
young woman. Grandfather disapproved of the young man, who was
not in a strong position financially, and whom he did not think likely to
make good use of any financial help that might be given to him. No
doubt this affair must have been a source of grief to my aunt at the time,
but I gather that the effects on her happiness were not very serious or
lasting. The second was a very different story. Aunt Leah became
engaged, with the full approval of her family, to a man of good character and position, who was already well-to-do and later became very
wealthy. The engagement lasted for a long time, and my aunt received
many very beautiful and valuable presents from him. At length the
engagement was broken off by the two parties, under circumstances
which have always remained a mystery. The only known relevant facts
are that the man not long afterwards married a woman considerably
older than himself and considerably richer than my aunt then was or
ever would be in her own right, and that my aunt (who was, as I have
said, an extremely independent woman and the very opposite of an
avaricious one) kept all his presents. Whatever may have lain behind
these facts, it is certain that this incident was a turning-point in my
aunt's life. She kept her own counsel and consumed her own smoke, but
there was never again for her any question of a normal married life
with a man of her own age who could give her children of her own.

The reader is now as well acquainted as he need be with the *dramatis personae* in the events which followed closely upon my grandmother's death in 1884. These events may be compared to the sudden crystallisation of a super-saturated solution. My Aunts Emma and Leah had now their own incomes; one third of the income from the trust was now going to Aunt Julia in Bristol; and the question was whether the two unmarried sisters should continue to live together, and whether their two unmarried brothers, Edwin and Charles, should continue to share the home with them. I take it that Aunt Emma's intolerable temper, now freed from any control which her mother may have been able to exercise over it, soon answered that question in the negative, and was largely responsible for the spate of late marriages which very quickly followed.

Aunt Leah proceeded almost at once to marry a distant cousin, an elderly widower named Samuel Wilcox. Uncle Sam was a nice old man, whose hobby was carpentry, in which he was highly skilled. He had a fine collection of woodworking tools, some of which I have inherited and still use. He was very fond of me as a baby, and, I am told, very kind to me. I can (or think I can) just remember him. He had owned a small but fairly successful dyeing business in the west of London. (The founders of the well-known firm of dyers, Messrs. Eastman, were relatives of his.) He had retired many years before his second marriage with a decent income derived mainly from annuities. He was much older than my aunt, and it was to be expected that he would soon need a nurse rather than a wife. He did in fact enjoy quite good health until just before his death, from a sudden attack of bronchitis, terminating in pneumonia, when I was three or four years old. The marriage had neither the raptures nor the disillusionments of romance; but it had obvious conveniences for both parties, and, as both of them were kindly and considerate persons, I do not doubt that it was a happy one of its kind.

I am sure that one of my aunt's motives in marrying was to provide my father with a house and enable him to marry. He did so in 1885, and he and my mother took up their abode with Aunt Leah and Uncle Sam. From that time until aunt Leah's death in 1912 she and my parents lived together and shared expenses. I know nothing of the details of the financial arrangements, but I know that my aunt's income was larger than my father's, and I have no doubt that she was (particularly in later years) the main contributor to the common budget.

It is now time to speak of my mother, Emily Gomme. She was born in 1848 at Hammersmith, then an attractive village on the outskirts of west London. Her father, Stephen Gomme, was an architect, and her family had been settled for several generations in Hammersmith. I do not know nearly as much about them as about my paternal ancestors; but I believe that her first cousin, George Laurence Gomme, had collected much interesting information, which is presumably in possession of his descendants.

All that I can relate comes from stories which my mother used to tell me. The main points are as follows. I got the impression that her relatives were quite comfortably off. My grandfather, beside his professional income as an architect, owned a certain amount of land (at that time, of course, mainly agricultural) in or near Hammersmith. His wife was a Miss Steptoe. They had three children, two girls and a boy. The boy James went to sea and was drowned as a young man in a storm. My mother's elder sister, Aunt Maria, married and had several children. She died, not many years before my mother, an octogenarian. Three of her daughters are still (1954) living. I remember her as a somewhat formidable lady, with a very strong will of her own.

As a little girl my mother attended a school in Chelsea; she remembered being taken and fetched each day by her nurse through the fields and market-gardens which then separated Chelsea and Hammersmith. My grandmother died, when the children were quite young, of consumption. Soon afterwards my grandfather married again, and my impression is that his second wife had been a companion to his first or a governess to the children. My mother always expressed the strongest dislike of her stepmother, who, she alleged, had been most unkind to the children and had come between them and their father.

My grandfather himself died comparatively young, and he appointed under his will guardians for his children. These guardians, according to my mother, were certainly grossly careless of the interests of their wards, and perhaps positively dishonest. As a telling instance of this she would relate the following story. My grandfather owned a certain cornfield in Hammersmith. He had reason to believe that the Metropolitan Railway, which was about to build a line in that direction, would want this land, and he gave repeated instructions shortly before his death that it should not be sold until this possibility had been fully explored. He died, and the guardians, ignoring his instructions, promptly sold the field at the price of agricultural land. According to my mother, Hammersmith Broadway station now stands on that field, and the lucky buyers netted a very handsome sum when they re-sold to the railway.

However this may be, it is certain that the children in the end received little or nothing from their father's estate. My mother had been living for a number of years at the house of her uncle, William Gomme, who was a neighbour to my grandmother Broad in *The Gardens, Peckham Rye*. He had a large family of sons and daughters. Several of them were highly gifted, and one of them became a distinguished public servant and historical scholar. This was George Laurence, afterwards Sir Laurence Gomme (b. 1853, d. 1916). He combined great administrative ability with a lively and scholarly interest in English folklore, the early English village community, and the antiquities of London. He was Clerk to the London County Council during a long period, when it was growing up to its present extremely important position in the governance and education of millions of Englishmen living in Greater London. One of his sons, Arnold Wycombe Gomme, was an undergraduate contemporary with me at Trinity College, Cambridge. He became a distinguished classical and historical scholar, and held until recently the professorship of Greek at Glasgow University.

Emily Gomme was a very frequent visitor at the house of her uncle's neighbours, the Broads, and she had become almost a member of the family long before she married my father. She and Aunt Leah were already old friends and were on particularly good terms with each other, so the unusual arrangement of a joint household was easier to contemplate than it would otherwise have been. Nevertheless, on looking back I cannot but admire the complete harmony which prevailed throughout all the ensuing years between my mother and my aunt. The situation must have been fraught with occasions for jealousy and friction, and it says much for the good sense and the good temper of two such high-spirited women that they lived in perfect amity up to my aunt's death after a long illness, in which my mother devotedly nursed her.

My mother had received a good education, but she had not the intellectual gifts and interests of my father and my aunt. But she had very great practical ability in all domestic affairs, and far more energy and self-reliance than any of the Broads. She would in all probability have been much more successful in business than my father, if she had been a man, though she took the conventional view of her period that the making and investing of money were a man's affair and outside her province. She was an extremely good dress-maker, could paint and decorate and turn her hand effectively to almost any job in the house or garden, and was an excellent caterer on a limited income. She treated her servants kindly and firmly, and they appreciated this and generally stayed in her service for considerable periods. She greatly enjoyed society, and was in her element both as a hostess at home and as a guest in other houses. She had none of my father's wit or humour, though she thoroughly appreciated it and was herself quite an agreeable conversationalist on a more conventional level. She was an excellent card-player, and thoroughly enjoyed a game of cribbage or whist in her younger days and of bridge in her later years.

I think that my mother's extreme practical efficiency, enterprise, and self-reliance were not altogether good for my father and for myself. Both he and I were inclined to be passive and unenterprising, and were apt to forego things that we wanted rather than to take much trouble and run the risk of a rebuff in seeking them. The result was that the 'dirty work' of our social life tended to be handed over to my mother, who did it so well and apparently so much enjoyed doing it that we became somewhat parasitic upon her.

From what I have so far said of my mother the reader may be inclined to think of her as psychologically a pure extrovert and physically always in perfect health. That would be a mistake. Her constitution must, indeed, have been fundamentally very sound, for she lived to 90 and was remarkably vigorous in body and mind until well after her 80th birthday. But until late in life she was neither physically strong nor by any means free from nervous trouble. As a young woman she had been threatened with consumption, and in about 1895 she had a long and very serious attack of bronchitis and pleurisy. At that time her doctor discovered that there were scars of former tubercular infection in at least one of her lungs. When I was a boy she suffered at intervals from terrible headaches, accompanied by biliousness and vomiting, and she would be prostrated for a few days. These symptoms would sometimes come on suddenly and at awkward times, e.g., when she was guest at a dinner-party, and she has described to me the agony of sitting through the meal and keeping up a conversation without betraying her symptoms or disgracing herself. Later on I learned by first-hand experience to understand what she must have gone through on such occasions. All these bodily weaknesses gradually cleared up as she grew older, and between the ages of 60 and 80 she was remarkably free from illness of any kind. From about the age of 80 she began very gradually and almost imperceptibly to lose the use of her right arm. At the age of 85 she had a sudden and rather mysterious illness in the night, and the doctor did not expect her to live to the morning. She slowly recovered and seemed at the time to have regained something of her former health. Humanly speaking, she had much better have died then. She gradually sank into a state of bodily and mental weakness, which made her life a burden to herself and her attendants, and a most distressing spectacle to those who had known her in her prime. Her long groping through the valley of the shadow of death ended on Sept. 5th., 1939, two days after the entry of England into the second World War. *Sunt lachrymae rerum et mentem mortalia tangunt.*

My mother was much more sentimental and much more inclined to display tender emotion than were either my father or my aunt, who were at heart no less affectionate. I have always found such displays of affection extremely embarrassing to witness and quite impossible to respond to in kind. So, after my early years, I must often have hurt her feelings by lack of overt reciprocity. She was undoubtedly devoted to me, and she had willingly foregone many enjoyments in life for my sake. But, if I may say so, she was a little too conscious of this at times, and a little too apt to reproach me with ingratitude and lack of affection when I did not fall in with her wishes. This always had the worst possible effect on me; it made me sullen and often, I fear, ungracious. Mutual affection cannot be based on claims and counter-claims, and it does not thrive if too often dug up by the roots to see how it is growing. Neither my father nor my aunt, whose love and whose sacrifices were no less great, ever made this mistake.

The situation in this respect naturally tended to grow worse as my mother grew older. I was her only child, and as the years went by she gradually lost all objects of personal interest and affection except myself. Had I married and had children, she would no doubt have been jealous of my wife, but she would probably have spread her affection over my children. As things were, her eggs were all in one basket. All her interest and affection became concentrated on myself, though she fluctuated between treating me as a great and wise man (which I never have been or could be) and a naughty boy (which I no longer was). On the other hand, my objects of interest and affection were naturally numerous, and she was only one, and not at any given moment the most important, of them. Therefore I could not even *feel* an emotion towards her commensurate in intensity and concentration with that which she felt towards me. Still less could I *express* such emotion as I did feel in ways that would satisfy her. For one thing, as I have said, I find it most distasteful to utter the language and make the gestures of strong personal affection. For another, I knew that any attempt to do so would lead my mother to clutch at straws and overestimate the strength of the emotion which I felt and to respond with a still more embarrassing warmth. I was therefore often colder and less responsive in speech and in gesture than I was in feeling, and I thus often wounded and disappointed her. I was well aware of this and regretted it at the time, and I was still more conscious of it and regretful for it when I could reflect on the situation in absence and in a cool hour. But I never found any solution for this practical problem.

My excuse for enlarging on this delicate subject is that I think it indispensable to any honest account of my own development. My mother lived until I was in my fifty-second year, and in the course of the 21 years by which she survived my father I had more and more to do with her. The ambivalence of my feelings toward her, and the second-order reflexive emotions of self-reproach which this engendered in me, have been a very disturbing factor in my inner life.

We can now return to more objective and less painful topics. The family at *39 The Gardens* was now reduced to Aunt Emma, Uncle Edwin, and cousin Alice. But the expulsive force of Aunt Emma's personality was by no means exhausted. A year or so after my father's marriage Uncle Edwin, then in his late fifties and supposed to be a confirmed bachelor, found that he had had as much as he could bear and decided to marry. In his choice of my Aunt Harriet he fully merited his nickname of 'Sage,' for he secured some twenty years of great comfort and happiness for himself, and the means of providing after his death, far more liberally than he could have done out of his own resources, for my father and for his niece Alice.

Harriet Angelina Avery was a very old friend of the family. She had been a school-fellow of my aunts Emma and Leah. Her maiden name was Jennings, and her family had long been settled in Gloucestershire. Her father had been a missionary in India, and he and her mother had died there when the daughter, their only child, was still very young. Aunt Harriet as a young woman had been governess in several good families. In that capacity she eventually met a Mr. Thomas Avery, who was a friend of the family in which she was then employed. Mr. Avery was a wealthy and highly cultivated lawyer in Gloucester, considerably older than Harriet Jennings. He fell in love with her and married her, and they settled down in Cheltenham. They had no children, and Mr. Avery had no surviving near relatives to whom he was attached. So on his death his wife inherited absolutely his not inconsiderable estate. This included some very valuable pictures, silver, ivories, and furniture, and a fine collection of well bound books. The widow moved to Brighton, where she bought and furnished a house, and settled down there with a lady-companion at about the time of my grandmother's death. She was of much the same age as Uncle Edwin.

Uncle Edwin proposed to her and had the good luck to be accepted. They were married from the house of Uncle Sam and Aunt Leah, with my father doing the honours. After their wedding tour they returned to the house at Brighton and spent the rest of their lives there. Aunt Harriet bequeathed to my uncle her whole income and the use of all her property for his lifetime and a substantial sum of money absolutely. She left the house and its contents (except for certain pictures, silver, and ivories, which she specifically bequeathed to some of Mr. Avery's

surviving distant relatives) to my father after my uncle's death. At the
end of the second World War I presented to the Picture Gallery of
Dulwich College three pictures, all by Dutch or Flemish painters, which
I had inherited on my mother's death and which proved to be of considerable interest and value.

After their marriage Uncle Edwin and Aunt Harriet came to play an
important part in the lives of my parents and myself. They used to
spend a month or so at our home every summer, and during my boyhood and young manhood I used to spend a part of each school holiday
or university vacation with them at Brighton.

I never greatly liked Uncle Edwin, though he never gave me much
positive cause to dislike him, and though I am deeply indebted to him
for his marriage and for the financial benefit which I ultimately derived
from him. But my Aunt Harriet is another story, and I must say something further of her, as I knew her.

On the surface she was somewhat formidable, especially when I was
a child and a schoolboy. She held very definitely that children should
not be encouraged to air their opinions or throw their weight about.
She was also a valetudinarian (of the homoeopathic variety), and very
fussy about her own and other people's health, and about draughts,
noises, etc., as liable to affect it detrimentally. Then, again, her house
contained many beautiful and valuable things, which she appreciated
and did not want to have damaged or displaced, and life there followed
a very definite order and time-schedule. For all these reasons I had to be
constantly on my best behaviour when she was visiting us, and still
more so when I was visiting her. She was much the best-off of our rela-
·tives, and she and Uncle Edwin were the only ones from whom we had
expectations, so I was early impressed by my parents with the importance of 'keeping my dish upright'—to use an admirable phrase current in the Broad family. This naturally involved repressions which
were irksome to me as a child and a young schoolboy. When I became
an older boy and later an undergraduate, and had definitely rejected
Christianity and was going through a phase of rather crude and self-
conscious rationalism, it involved much control of my tongue, much
concealment of my thoughts and feelings, and a certain amount of
suggestio falsi.

That, for what little it may be worth, is all that I can say on the
negative side. On the positive side there is much to be said for Aunt
Harriet. I came to like and appreciate her more and more as I grew
older, and I can now see that I am greatly indebted to her.

To take the more material benefits first, she was extremely generous
in presents and tips, and also in gifts of books. She always kept a good

cook, and the meals were more elaborate and more delicately served than those to which I was accustomed on ordinary occasions at home. We were certainly not careless or sluttish at home, and I had to behave myself properly at table there; but it was a new, and in the end pleasant and useful experience for me, to stay in a house where everything was done with formality and in considerable style, though without any ostentation. Then, again, it was very good for me to live from time to time among beautiful and rare objects, whose owner valued them and took obvious pleasure in arranging them tastefully. It was typical of my aunt and of her standards that all her fabrics and wall-papers were designed by Morris and supplied by Liberty. The curtains and other fabrics were very beautiful, and I know from a very long experience that they never faded and never wore out.

Aunt Harriet certainly thought that as a child I was in danger of becoming a conceited prig and incurring the dislike of my elders by butting into their conversations with my own uncalled-for expressions of opinion. That risk undoubtedly existed for a clever and precocious only child, living mainly in the society of an adoring aunt and fond parents. Both the reality of the danger and the odiousness of the threatened result are now abundantly clear to me. It is often illuminating and sometimes shocking to see oneself as one sees others; and I have had frequent opportunities in later life to contemplate, in the precocious and priggish children of others, the image of what I myself may well have been when young. I am grateful to my aunt for having taken me in hand and administered, before it was too late, a salutary course of snubbing. If I was still a bit of a prig in my first years at Cambridge, I was at any rate a very much less blatant one than I might otherwise have been.

Aunt Harriet thought that I saw too little of other children when at home, and too much of my elders. In this too she may well have been right. She therefore attempted to provide me with suitable playmates from among the children of her friends, to arrange parties and outings for them and me, and so on. These well-meant efforts were not conspicuously successful. I intensely disliked other children, with their noise and their quarrels and their silly games, and much preferred to amuse myself (as I was quite capable of doing) in my own ways. Playmates chosen for one by another person start under a severe handicap, and those chosen by my aunt for me never happened to have the intrinsic charms which they would have needed in order to overcome this initial disadvantage. These attempts to make me happy in the lively company of my young contemporaries were the only serious blot on my otherwise enjoyable visits to Brighton.

As I grew older my aunt began to treat me more and more as a reasonable being who could be talked to on approximately equal terms. She was obviously very fond of me, and proud of my scholastic successes, though she was always quick to mark and to check any symptoms of uppishness on my part. I came to feel more at ease in her company, and by the time I was an undergraduate I greatly enjoyed it and gained a good deal of her confidence. She had travelled and seen something of Europe, from the point of view of a cultivated and comfortably situated English tourist of the Ruskin period, whilst my family had all been almost unbelievably stay-at-home and indifferent to this aspect of culture. I feel that I owe to her a certain widening of outlook beyond the admirable, but in some ways very prosaic and limited, vistas provided by my middle-middle-class home-life. Certainly the widening never went very far in the aesthetic direction, and I remain very much of a Philistine; but I am sure that I should have been more so had it not been for Aunt Harriet.

I am very far from regretting the training, which my relations with Aunt Harriet and Uncle Edwin gave me, in what Roman Catholic casuists call 'economy' and 'reserve,' and some Protestants in their crude way call by a harsher name. Throughout life I have found it most useful to have learned to hold my tongue, to say less than I think, and to seem to agree more than I do, when in company of authoritative persons who have made up their minds and do not mean to alter them. I recommend all young men and women to acquire this art as soon as may be, and I wish them the luck to do so as early and with as little inconvenience as I did. Truth (even if one *knew* that one possessed it) is far too valuable a commodity to be lavished on the self-opinionated, and far too inflammatory a one to be uttered without due regard to persons and occasions.

Aunt Harriet died, without any previous symptoms of illness, in her sleep at the age of 80 in or about 1910. Uncle Edwin, 'sage' in this as in so much else, managed to survive her and to inherit under the terms of her will, to the substantial benefit of my father and ultimately of myself. He died in 1912 at the age of 83. He had long suffered from chronic bronchitis, which weakened his heart, and he spent the latter years of his life in the drawing-room and an adjoining bedroom, largely in a kind of glass case which my aunt had had constructed in order to protect him from draughts. He thoroughly enjoyed this kind of life, read voraciously, and skillfully used his delicate state of health as an excuse for evading any situation that would be irksome to him.

From this by no means irrelevant digression I now return to the joint household of Uncle Sam and Aunt Leah and my parents. Shortly after my birth this was shifted from Harlesden to a house in Willesden, not far away, which Uncle Sam owned and which had become available through the termination of a tenancy. A good deal of money was spent on alterations and additions to this house, which was called *Clarence Lodge*. This is the first house and garden which I can remember.

At this house I very nearly followed the Sophoclean advice to those who have made the mistake of being born, viz., 'to return as quickly as may be to the place from which one came.' I began as a healthy infant, but had a fairly severe attack of whooping-cough at the age of about 18 months. I was recovering satisfactorily from this, and was playing about one day in the garden while my father was working there. It was a sunny day, with a treacherous north-east wind blowing. I got very hot and sweaty, and then, while my father was busy and pre-occupied, sat down in the shade in a draught and was chilled. The result was bronchitis and congestion of the lungs. I lay desperately ill for many weeks, and my eventual recovery was regarded as a kind of miracle. After that I was for many years delicate, with a poor and wayward appetite, and liable to bad colds with severe coughs. Gradually I grew out of this weakness, and I have had no serious illness since then up to the time of writing. But the long-range effects on my character and dispositions have been most unfortunate. I was for long regarded by my relatives (and soon came to regard myself) as delicate and not to be expected to have the bodily strength, endurance, enterprise, and skill of the normal boy or young man. I am well aware of having continually and half unwittingly used this as an excuse for omissions and evasions which are really due to laziness or cowardice or both. I still get a certain sardonic amusement in catching myself out at this life-long game.

My mother has told me that she disliked *Clarence Lodge* and its neighbourhood; and both were somewhat unfortunate for my Aunt Leah, who inherited the house on Uncle Sam's death.

Just at that time Willesden was in process of changing from a pleasant semi-rural district on the edge of the country into a nasty slummy suburb of London. A number of big houses, standing in extensive and beautiful grounds, happened to come into the market together through the deaths of their elderly owners, and the speculative builders seized the opportunity to cover the land with streets of workmen's cottages and shoddy small villas. I witnessed a segment of this process of defilement at near hand, and it made an impression on me which has been life-long. *Clarence Lodge* had a long garden, bordered by a lane, on the other side of which lay a pretty meadow with some fine trees and one picturesque cottage occupied by an interesting old woman who was reputed to be a 'Gypsy queen.' The trees were cut down and uprooted, the meadow was destroyed, and several roads of wretched little houses were built on the site. In the meanwhile the lane was taken over by the local authority, and my aunt, as owner of the adjoining house, had to contribute a considerable sum towards the making of the road and the incidental destruction of the amenities of her property.

I have mentioned these early experiences in Willesden, because they were certainly the seeds of that intense dislike and distrust which I have ever since felt for urbanisation and industrialisation, and of my complete scepticism about the value of the 'progress' which involves such sacrifices. For me the word 'progress' calls up a picture of farms and woods and gardens and pleasant houses destroyed, and replaced by hideous monotonous streets, crowded with dull jostling people and traversed by noisy stinking cars and motor-cycles:—

> Sad face and merry face—so ugly all!
> Why are you hurrying—where is there to go?
> Why are you shouting—who is there to call?

By 1894 the neighbourhood had become unbearable. Uncle Sam had died and Aunt Leah sold the house for what it would fetch. We moved to Sydenham on the other side of London. There for about 5 years, and then in the adjacent suburb of Forest Hill, we dwelled during the rest of my aunt's and my father's lifetimes, and my mother continued to reside there until 1924.

Shortly before we left Willesden the household was increased by the arrival of Alice Broad, the unmarried surviving daughter of fallen Uncle George. She had continued to live for a while at *39 The Gardens* after Uncle Edwin's marriage. But life with Aunt Emma was like living beside a volcano. The inevitable eruption soon took place, and the mild, pious, and somewhat lachrymose Alice was suddenly expelled with ignominy. I never knew the ostensible reason for this bit of spiteful cruelty, nor would it be of interest except to the psychiatrist to know how Aunt Emma's neurotic soul draped its unconscious urges. Aunt Leah, as usual, came to the rescue. She gave a home to Alice as one of the family, and Uncle Edwin made her a small allowance. So the household in which I grew up consisted of my parents, Aunt Leah, cousin Alice, and two maids who of course changed from time to time.

The part of London into which we moved was a very pleasant one. It consisted of good houses, all with gardens of fair size and many with extensive grounds, inhabited in the main by well-to-do professional and businessmen. The houses and gardens were well kept, and the whole neighbourhood abounded in beautiful trees, the remains no doubt of the ancient and once very extensive forest of Norwood. The district had grown up in the 1860's and onwards around the Crystal Palace, whose magnificent grounds were available to us as season-ticket holders, and which provided a fine firework-display on every Thursday evening during the summer months. There were indeed some ugly and squalid areas included in it, e.g., at Lower Sydenham, Penge, and round about Forest Hill railway station. But they were very restricted, and as it were encapsulated, like morbid growths which have failed to spread. Like all the inner suburbs of London, it slowly declined as prosperous citizens moved further afield, but in our time there was no catastrophic change such as had devastated Willesden. I suppose that the nature of the tenancies and the average real income of the inhabitants must by now have altered very much for the worse. Yet, when I paid a visit to my old haunts in the summer of 1954, expecting to be shocked and grieved, I was pleasantly surprised to find how little outward and visible change there had been, and how peaceful and beautiful the roads and the gardens still were.

My formal education had already begun before we left *Clarence Lodge*. As I have said, cousin Alice was my first teacher. I was an intelligent and biddable child, and had no particular difficulty with my lessons. I can remember learning the multiplication-tables up to 12 times 12 with the help of coloured counters as instantiations. From cousin Alice's hands I passed to a kindergarten school in Harlesden. Of my experiences there I can remember a good deal, but only two things seem to be of enough interest to record. One is that I had great difficulty with the instruction in reading the time by the clock, with its Roman numerals and the different meaning of the same figure when indicated by the hour-hand and by the minute-hand. (This still seems to me to involve rather subtle notions for a very young child.) The problem was solved by my father, who got hold of an old kitchen clock, no longer in use, and made me turn the hands to various positions under his instruction. He was not a patient man, and there were some tears, but the method fairly soon succeeded.

The other fact which I recall is probably of more importance psychologically. One of the subjects of instruction was musical drill. It was taught by a visiting master, named Currie, whilst one of the mistresses provided the piano-music. It appears that I am naturally defective in sense of time and in adjusting my bodily movements either to music or to those of other persons by sight. I could never keep step, and I never had the faintest idea whether I was in step or out of it. I was continually being called to order for this by Mr. Currie, in his rather loud voice, before the mistress and the other members of the class. I am morbidly sensitive to blame and to being unfavourably conspicuous, and I had never been addressed in that tone of voice before. I was terrified of Mr. Currie, and the prospect of these weekly lessons in musical drill was a nightmare to me. Since then I have always hated and feared any kind of drill, and have always approached the learning from others of any kind of bodily skill with an expectation of making a fool of myself and a feeling that I shall never be any good at it, which are almost sufficient to ensure failure. Poor Mr. Currie probably meant no harm, and he has no doubt for many years past been drilling some section of the angelic choir (who, it is to be hoped, have a better sense of *aevum* than I had of time) to the music of the spheres, with the happiest results. But I cannot help wishing that our paths had never crossed on earth.

Shortly after our removal to Sydenham I was sent to a preparatory school for boys in the neighbourhood. Some years later, when the school moved to Bexhill in Sussex, I went with it as a boarder. Our studies began with reading, writing, spelling, dictation, English grammar, English history, geography, French, Latin, and arithmetic. Later we were introduced to geometry and algebra, and had the choice of taking up either Greek or German. I took German. I think that the teaching in all these subjects, except perhaps the mathematical ones, was excellent. I may be unfair to my mathematical masters, because, while I was interested in the other subjects and did well in them, I was at that time very bad at mathematics and could not for the life of me see what it was all about. I remember trying to learn the first few propositions of Euclid by heart, and finding algebra completely unintelligible and boring. Euclid's *Elements* is, as I have long known, one of the world's great books. But it was not written for boys of 10 or 11, and I cannot believe that it is a suitable introduction for them to geometry. Now that I know something of the nature of algebra I do not envy the masters who have to teach it to small boys. As Lincoln said of Negro slavery in the South: "If all earthly power were given, I should not know what to do about it."

I was on the whole reasonably happy at this school. Discipline was strict, and I was rather in awe of some of the masters; but, as I have always trembled before authority, the reader must not make the mistake of inferring that we were harshly treated. We certainly were not. I was, as I have already remarked, hopeless from the start at all games. But neither the masters nor the boys were fanatical on this score. I liked some of the other boys quite a lot, and neither seriously disliked nor was seriously disliked by any of them. So it might easily have been very much worse. It was certainly very valuable for me to be taken out of the home circle under conditions which were not too unfamiliar or too alarming.

At my preparatory school I acquired the art of lying without serious compunction when in awkward situations. Hitherto I had been rigidly truthful, having been brought up to regard a lie with a kind of superstitious horror. ("Remember, *God* sees you!") This is not the place to enlarge on the ethics of truth-telling. I now think that lying is an expedient which is permissible and even commendable on occasions, but that those occasions are rarer than one likes to believe, and that it should be used as a sensible man would use a valuable but seductive and habit-forming drug.

I also acquired at this school a knowledge of the so-called 'facts of life,' which, though somewhat highly coloured and not altogether accurate in detail, embodied ancient traditional lore in homely Anglo-Saxon phraseology and sufficed as a basis for further observation and experiment.

I will complete what I have to say under this head with two remarks. The first is that I can fully support from my own memory the contention of the psycho-analysts that emotions, fantasies, and desires, which are sexual in the most literal sense, occur and play an important part in quite early infancy. I have vivid memories, going back to my third year, which are for me perfectly conclusive on this point. The second is that I am deeply indebted to the undergraduate friend who in my first year at Cambridge lent me Havelock Ellis's *Studies in the Psychology of Sex.* Young men are apt to think themselves uniquely abnormal, and either to worry or to give themselves airs about this. After reading that admirable work I realised that, however queer I might be, I was not nearly so queer as a number of persons who had escaped the lunatic asylum and the jail, had lived respected if not wholly respectable lives, and had died in the odour of comparative sanctity. Henceforth I had no trouble *in principle* with that side of my nature, though, like most of us, I have had plenty of worries and upsets on particular occasions in regard to particular individuals. I suppose that the Kinsey reports have the same salutary effects on contemporary youth as Ellis's book had on me. If so, more power to their elbow. The difference is that Havelock Ellis was very nearly a genius, whilst the compilers of those reports are American sociologists.

Two interests, which have lasted up to the present day and have given me much harmless pleasure, go back to this period and may now be briefly considered. They may be described as 'the railway interest' and 'the Nordic interest.'

When I was a boy nearly all small boys were interested both in real railways and in toy trains. German models, running either by clockwork or by steam, were absurdly cheap if extremely unrealistic, and most of us owned one or more of them. With most boys this interest died out;

with me, as with some others in each generation, it has lasted on. As an undergraduate and a young Fellow of Trinity I built a fairly long steam-railway of 2″ gauge in our garden at Forest Hill, buying the locomotive and the raw materials for the track from Messrs. Bassett-Lowke of High Holborn, and making the rolling-stock and building and laying the permanent way myself. Later, when I returned to Cambridge as a College and University Lecturer, my friends Patrick and Michael Browne, then undergraduates at Pembroke College, most kindly allowed me to build a railway in the large garden of the house *Firwood* in Trumpington Road, which they continued to own and occupy in the vacations for several years after the death of their parents. I now had more money to spend, and this line was a more ambitious construction of 2½″ gauge. Two undergraduate friends, Xan Wynne Willson and Henry Coombe-Tennant, successively helped me with the work. This line had eventually to be abandoned, when Patrick and Michael moved from Cambridge to London and gave up the house. I have never had the opportunity or the energy to build another, though I still have the locomotive and some of the rolling-stock and many rails, sleepers, chairs, and keys.

In order that a person, whose professional work is wholly intellectual and highly abstract, may keep reasonably sane, it is most important that he should have some side-occupation which involves the exercise of bodily skill, and, if possible, of constructive activity in the material world. (I never see a bat emerging from a belfry without being forcibly reminded of certain of my colleagues who have lacked such outlets.) Natural scientists have the great good fortune to be provided, in their own laboratories and as part of their professional work, with what is needed. Many other intellectual workers find in games like golf or tennis, in mountain-climbing or horse-riding or gliding, in driving and puttering about with their cars, or even in painting pictures, the means of preserving their mental balance. All these are highly worth-while activities, and I take off my hat to those who can perform them. But I, alas, am utterly incapable of any of them. So I record with thankfulness a hobby which has given me many hours of solitary happiness and also much pleasant companionship on a non-intellectual but not unintelligent level, and has helped to keep me in such measure of mental health as I have enjoyed.

I turn next to what I have called 'the Nordic interest.' So far as I can remember, this began with three novels which Aunt Leah read to me when I was a small boy, and which I read many times for myself. One was called *Ivar the Viking*. It was, I believe, by the French explorer du Chaillu. Another was a story for boys, which Aunt Harriet gave me, based on the legend of the foundation of Grimsby by a Danish Viking, Grim, and his sons. The third was Lord Lytton's *Harold,* which had been edited with a learned introduction and notes by my mother's cousin, George Laurence Gomme. I suspect that these outstanding influences cooperated with a background of highly tendentious history-lessons in the Freeman-Green-Kingsley tradition. I am aware that the picture of clean-limbed Teutonic he-men (Wykehamists before their time), respecting women, obeying Grimm's and Verner's laws, worshipping the All-Father, and laying the foundations of parliamentary democracy on the shores of the Baltic and the North Seas, has faded in the light of archaeological discovery and historical criticism. Still, that was the legend on which I was brought up, and the fact that I cannot now fully accept it with my head does not in the least diminish or reverse its influence on my heart. In point of fact, I share most of the likes and dislikes of our late dear *Führer,* though I hope and honestly believe that, 'if all earthly power were given,' I should not put them into practice with the insensate folly and the fiendish cruelty of that lunatic.

Under these influences as a small boy I imagined myself a Viking and I thought and talked and acted Viking *ad nauseam.* I had a costume, made by my mother, on the model of the very attractive young warrior standing on the stem of his ship, who featured in the advertisements of *Viking* condensed milk. My shield, sword, winged helmet, etc., were constructed with great skill by a local tinsmith. I acquired with some difficulty a human skull, which I tried and failed to convert into a practicable drinking-cup, and I used to make burnt-offerings of meat to Odin on an altar in the garden.

It is only superficially paradoxical that an almost pathologically timid and yielding and physically weak individual should thus admire and identify himself in imagination with men whose chief features were reckless courage, heroic endurance, bodily strength, and ruthless self-assertion. It is natural enough to admire in others the excess of those qualities which are in defect in oneself. Such influences of course produce their effects *in modo recipientis.* I was not made appreciably braver or more enterprising. But I did get hold of a Danish grammar and later of an Anglo-Saxon grammar, and I did take considerable pains at an early age to acquire the rudiments of those two Nordic tongues. I have reverted to my Anglo-Saxon several times in later life, though it is at the moment somewhat rusty; but I let my Danish drop altogether for many years. The traces of it were, however, a valuable help when I set myself to learn Swedish during the second World War.

In due course the Nordic interest passed from the focus of consciousness, but it remained not far in the background, ready to be revived at any moment. The activating occasion was the presence in Cambridge in, I think, 1938 of Georg Henrik von Wright, then a student of 22–23 engaged in writing his doctoral dissertation for the University of Helsingfors. Swedish culture and traditions could not have had a worthier or a personally more winning representative. When he returned to Helsingfors, I decided to learn the language and to read something of the literature and the history of Sweden. I began, before the outbreak of the second World War with a linguaphone course. I continued, during the war, with it and with some private tuition and much private reading. Then in 1944 I had a remarkable bit of luck. The British Council provided scholarships for four Swedish students, one from Uppsala, two from Lund, and one from Stockholm's Högskola, to spend the academic year 1944–5 in Cambridge. Two of them were assigned to Trinity. Both of these were singularly able, friendly, and intelligent young men. During that academic year I saw a great deal of all four Swedes, though I naturally saw most of the two who were in Trinity, and I was able in many ways to help to make their stay in Cambridge pleasanter and more profitable than it might otherwise have been during that very difficult period. This gave me excellent opportunities for practising Swedish conversation. I became greatly attached to one of the two Trinity Swedes, Ulf Hellsten. He spent a part of his vacations as guest in my rooms in College, and before his return to Sweden we made a tour together in northern England and visited the Roman wall. It was by then understood between us that I should pay a long visit to Sweden as soon as circumstances might permit.

The project materialised in 1946. I took the Easter and the Michaelmas terms of that year as sabbatical leave, and was thus able to spend some nine months on end in Sweden. I was then in my 59th year. Incredible as it may seem, this was the first time I had been out of the British Isles, and Scandinavia is still the only part of the continent of Europe on which I have set foot. Most of the time was spent in Stockholm, where Ulf had managed to get extremely comfortable rooms for me, with a landlord and landlady who soon became, and have ever since remained, very good friends of mine. Both Ulf and the other Trinity Swede, Nils Andrén, were living in Stockholm at the time, and they showed me every kindness. I also paid a visit to von Wright in Finland. I had not seen him since his Cambridge days before the War, but I had managed to keep in touch with him throughout the whole period by letter. Beside this, I made a long tour by myself in the extreme north of Sweden, extending over the Norwegian border to Narvik, and a shorter one with Ulf in Dalarna and Värmland. During this first visit I made the acquaintance of colleagues in Uppsala and in Lund. in both of which universities I gave lectures, as I also did in Stockholm's Högskola.

Everywhere I went in Sweden I was received with the greatest kindness and hospitality. I fell in love with the country and its astonishingly good-looking inhabitants, and have never since fallen out of it. Doubtless my favourable first impression was partly due to the contrast between conditions of life in Sweden and in England in the years immediately after the war. Sweden, by a mixture of luck and judicious temporary concessions to German pressure, had managed to escape by the skin of its teeth the catastrophe which had overwhelmed its neighbours and into which England had blundered. It was now engaged in gaily squandering the dollar-surplus which it had earned. I revelled in the immediate results, though I realised more fully than the average Swedish citizen that "the chastisement of their peace was upon *us,* and that by *our* stripes they were freed."

Since then I have returned each year to Sweden for a long visit. I have lost none of my old friends and have made many new ones. Cambridge attracts a steady stream of young Swedes, who come to it for purposes of study or research or simply as visitors, and I have been lucky enough to gain the friendship of many among them. I have been made a member of the Swedish Academy of Sciences, a doctor of Uppsala University, and an honorary member of Stockholm's Nation in that university. May I not add, remembering an answer in the English church-catechism:—'and an inheritor of the Kingdom of Valhalla'?

Let us now descend from these high latitudes and revert in time to my boyhood in England. I left my preparatory school in 1900 in my 13th year and entered Dulwich College, where I remained until I went up to Cambridge in 1906. The headmaster during my time at Dulwich was A. H. Gilkes, a very remarkable personality, who certainly bore some likeness to the man whom he most admired and would most have wished to resemble, viz., Socrates.

I was at first on the Modern Side, and there my studies were mainly in French, German, English literature, and English history. I should be a learned man, if I now knew all the details and subtleties of French and German grammar which I have forgotten since then. I reached the Modern Remove, the master of which was a very able, formidable and sharp-tongued man, Mr. Wade. He was an extremely good teacher, setting a very high standard and keeping us up to it. He had a cultivated and fastidious taste, and he would make very witty, if sometimes wounding, comments on our deficiencies and our pretensions. One book which we studied very thoroughly with him was Bacon's *Essays,* with elaborate notes and commentaries. In this connexion I read Macaulay's essay on

Bacon. I had been brought up on his *Lays of Ancient Rome,* and I was now led on to read his essays, and thence to his *History of England* and rather later to Gibbon's *Decline and Fall.* All of these I greatly enjoyed. They no doubt did much to enlarge my vocabulary, to give me a glimpse of how English prose can be wielded by experts, and to inspire me with the ambition to try my hand at the same game.

Like many boys, I was at that stage of my life extremely keen to be an engineer, without having any real knowledge of what the training for that profession and the practice of it would involve. My father, who knew better, was (as I now think, quite rightly) opposed to this. But there was an Engineering Side at Dulwich, one or two of my best friends were on it, and I was importunate to change over to it. At length my father, with obvious reluctance and misgivings, consented. This move, which might well have been disastrous, turned out in the end to be a necessary condition of my going to Trinity College, Cambridge, and thus of any success that I have had in later life. This happened in the following way.

There was at Dulwich, beside an Engineering Side, a Science Side. In the main they were independent of each other; the boys on these two Sides had different classrooms and a different set of masters. But there was a certain amount of interlocking in respect of physics and mathematics. Mr. F. W. Russell, who was head of the Engineering Side, had charge also of the most advanced teaching in those two subjects for the Science Side. Mr. Russell was primarily a mathematician. He had been a mathematical scholar of Trinity College, Cambridge; had taken the mathematical tripos with high honours; and had been appointed as a young man to a professorship in mathematics at Melbourne University. Soon after he had arrived in Australia and had taken up his job as professor, there occurred a very serious financial crisis in which many banks failed. The university was involved in these financial difficulties, and the upshot of the matter was that the new professor was informed that his salary could not be guaranteed in the immediately foreseeable future. He was offered and accepted a small lump-sum in compensation, returned to England, and eventually took up school-teaching.

It may be presumed that Mr. Russell was an excellent mathematician and a competent physicist, though I do not think that he ever made contributions of his own to either of these subjects. As a disciplinarian he was inclined to be petulant. As a teacher he was too difficult for many of his pupils. His habit of rapidly covering the blackboard with formulae, rubbing them out with a sponge before the boys could get them down, and then continuing the argument on the clean board, had earned him the nickname of *Sponge-Pot.* But he was a first-rate teacher for those who could follow him, and he certainly had the gift of making them see that mathematics and its applications to mechanics and to physics are fascinating and exciting.

As I have said, I was unusually backward and stupid at mathematics in my preparatory school. This defect continued at Dulwich up to and after my transfer to the Engineering Side, when I had the additional difficulty of being plunged into work, at a fairly advanced level, in subjects in which I had had hardly any previous training. But rather suddenly, under Mr. Russell's teaching, I began to see what mathematics and its applications were about. An occasion which I can still remember as most illuminating was when Mr. Russell showed us how to apply the calculus to determine the equation of the curve in which a chain hangs between two points of support. I became extremely interested in mathematics and its applications, and have remained so ever since. I have long known that I have not the gifts needed to make a first-rate or even a second-rate mathematician or mathematical physicist. But I can to some extent follow the work of others, and solve little problems for myself, and I still gain immense satisfaction from doing so.

Mr. Russell began to take an interest in me. He saw that I had the kind of intelligence which makes a good entrance-scholarship candidate, and he probably recognised that I was most unlikely to become a successful engineer. He therefore wrote to my father, strongly advising that I should be transferred to the Science Side, and that I should work with a view to trying for an entrance scholarship in natural science at Cambridge, with Trinity College as my first preference. After carefully considering the matter, and having a talk with Mr. Russell at dinner, my father agreed and the change was made. I cannot adequately express what I owe to Mr. Russell.

I now worked mainly at chemistry (inorganic, organic, and physical), physics, and mathematics. But the humaner side of our education was not neglected, and I consider that we were extremely well trained in the art of expressing our thoughts on paper in decent, lucid, and unpretentious English. I used to write a weekly English essay, at first for Mr. Hose, a master on the Classical Side with a very fine sense of style, and later, when I was in the sixth form, for the Headmaster. These essays were individually and very carefully criticised. I came to enjoy writing them, and it was plain that I had a certain gift for doing so. I am most grateful to these two men for the training and the critical encouragement which they gave me.

The upshot of all this was that I was elected to a major entrance-scholarship in natural science at Trinity College, Cambridge, at the end of 1905. I received, moreover, from Dr. H. M. Butler, then Master of Trinity, a personal letter in his characteristically kind and courteous style, congratulating me on my English Essay (which he had read) and my answers to the questions in the General Knowledge paper. The intervening period at Dulwich before going up to Cambridge in October 1906 was a very pleasant one. I could afford to relax and read what I liked. Under Mr. Russell's guidance I extended my knowledge of mathematics, and even browsed in Maxwell's *Treatise on Electricity and Magnetism,* a great but very obscurely written classic. My only other set reading was for the so-called 'Little-go' or entrance examination demanded by the University of Cambridge. For this I had to brush up my Latin, which I had not touched since leaving my preparatory school, and to acquire the rudiments of Greek to the extent of being able to translate and to answer questions upon two set dialogues of Lucian and St. Luke's gospel. This was interesting and presented no particular difficulty, and the rest of my time was free for miscellaneous reading.

Before shifting the scene from Dulwich to the banks of the Cam I will deal briefly with two topics on which I had already begun to form fairly definite views before leaving school, viz., religion and politics.

As a child I was brought up, both at home and at school, in an atmosphere in which Christianity was explicitly taken for granted as literally true. We were very definitely Protestant; but beyond that there was no strong sectarian bias. I was taught to say my prayers when I got up in the morning and when I went to bed at night. I continued to do this with fair conviction for many years, much as I brushed my teeth, and (it must be confessed) with considerably greater regularity. Hell and the Devil were not much mentioned; but they were there in the background, and I, with my natural tendency to be moved by fear rather than by hope, was much more frightened by the possibility of hell than attracted by that of heaven. I learned, however, fairly early from my father that the story of the creation in Genesis was not to be taken literally, and I learned somewhat later from him that the reliability of the Gospels on matters of detail had not survived the criticism of biblical scholars.

There the matter rested until I was about 15 or 16 years old. I was then studying natural science. At about that time the Rationalist Press Association was issuing a series of cheap reprints of writings by such men as T. H. Huxley, Tyndall, Haeckel, etc. The series included also books by sceptical scholars who were not natural scientists, e.g., Renan's *Life of Jesus* and Leslie Stephen's *An Agnostic's Apology.* I bought and read these works with avidity. At the same time I was reading with great admiration each of the successive books of social criticism and speculation, such as *Anticipations* and *Mankind in the Making,* which came from the pen of H. G. Wells. These moved me in the same general direction. My Christianity, which had probably been wearing pretty thin, collapsed and was replaced by what I should now regard as a rather smug and thin rationalism (in the popular sense of that word), based on natural science.

There was no kind of worry or regret over this; on the contrary I got a good deal of 'kick' out of feeling myself wiser than the deluded old fogies who were my elders and thought themselves my betters. I imagine that a similar phase, varying in its details from one generation to another, has been gone through by clever adolescents since the dawn of history. A sensible person, who has not forgotten his youth, will greet successive manifestations of this process with a not unsympathetic smile, which he will do well to conceal from his young friends. My father behaved with admirable good sense; and I had the decency not to do or say anything that might hurt Aunt Leah, and the prudence not to throw my weight about in presence of Uncle Edwin and Aunt Harriet. When I came to Cambridge I met many undergraduates who were passing through the same phase and deriving a good deal of satisfaction from it, and a certain number of dons who had never grown up and got past it.

When I was at school I used to have long arguments with a boy, C. H. Rutherford, who was moving in the opposite direction to me, viz., toward Roman Catholicism. Rutherford was highly intelligent, and one of the wittiest and most entertaining persons whom I have known. He went up to Cambridge a year before me, entered the Roman Church while there, became a schoolmaster at Downside, and was known to generations of boys there as *Father Anselm*. We made no impression on each other by our arguments, but he did give me a knowledge of the Roman Catholic point of view and a respect for it which I had previously had no chance to acquire. If *per impossibile* I were to become a Christian, I think I should become a Roman Catholic.

I have stated my attitude toward religion in general and Christianity in particular in my published writings, and there is no need to restate it here. The only one of the great religions which makes any appeal to me is Buddhism; and that, as I understand it, is rather a philosophy of the world, and a way of life for the *élite* founded upon it, than a religion in the ordinary sense of the word.

Turning now from religion to politics, I may summarise my development as follows. As I have said, I was brought up in the tradition of political Liberalism. During my time at Dulwich Joseph Chamberlain's campaign for imperial preference, and the reaction to it of Liberals and Unionist Free-Traders, were in full swing. In 1906, just before I left school, there was the great Liberal victory at the polls which was destined to be the beginning of the end of the Liberal party. Then followed in rapid succession the embittered controversy about Lloyd George's budget, and the closely interlocked quarrels about Irish home-rule and the powers of the House of Lords. As a background to all this was the growing fear of Germany and the race in naval armaments between the two countries, the violence of the militant advocates of women's suffrage, and continual labour unrest and strikes. Only in comparison with what was to follow from 1914 to the present day can it be described as a quiet or a reasonable period. Very few periods of European history could be so described, and there is always a danger among Englishmen of my generation of taking the utterly exceptional half-century from 1850 to 1900 as typical.

For Liberals it was, nevertheless, a period of hopeful expectation, which, although the hopes have turned out to be completely delusive, still seems to me to have been not unreasonable on the basis of our knowledge and recent experience at the time. It must be difficult for those who are now young or in the prime of life, and who feel (with good reason) that civilisation as they know it stands with a halter round its neck which some knave or fool or fanatic may at any moment draw, to realise what it was like to live in a time when that nightmare was absent, and when the development of scientific discovery and invention could be hailed as automatically beneficent. There was one writer, H. G. Wells, then one of my favourite authors, who provided, in a series of wonderfully prescient scientific romances, a foretaste of the horrors which have since become part of the texture of daily life.

So much for the public background to my personal political development. It goes without saying that I was, as a boy and for years later, an ardent and dogmatic free-trader. At the height of the Chamberlain campaign, Arthur Balfour, then Prime Minister, wrote and published a pamphlet entitled *Economic Notes on Insular Free Trade,* which was far too subtle and balanced to appeal to the protagonists on either side of the controversy. Mr. Hose set us to read it, and eventually to write an essay on it. It happened that I had studied some elementary political economy in Mr. Wade's form; the text-book was by an American economist, Walker, who was a strong free-trader. So I felt myself fully equipped to tackle Mr. Balfour and his tergiversations! I took a lot of trouble and wrote a long and elaborate essay, in which the Unionist leader was firmly put in his place and told where he 'got off.' It was no doubt a very crude and one-sided affair; but it was certainly a better essay than most boys of my age could have written, and it was my first effort to expound and criticise in writing the reasoned opinions of an author. Mr. Hose took it seriously and critically, and tactfully concealed the amusement which he must have felt at my youthful self-conceit and cocksureness.

Towards the end of my time at school I read, in translation, Plato's *Republic*. This made an immense impression on me, and that impression has been permanent. It was the first time that I had seen the presuppositions of democracy questioned. Plato's objections seemed, and still seem, to me conclusive. I have never seen any satisfactory answer to them, and experience and observation seem to me to have abundantly confirmed them and to continue to do so every day. Certainly it is no answer to call Plato rude names, such as 'Fascist' or 'Communist,' taken from contemporary political controversy; or solemnly to point out that the Platonic republic at its best would not have been very pleasant to live in, and would not have been likely to last for long without deterioration. Plato was not particularly concerned with happiness; and one of his strongest points is his recognition that even the best laid state will inevitably degenerate sooner or later, and his analysis of the causes and the stages of that inevitable decline. My scepticism about parliamentary democracy was further strengthened by the very critical attitude which Wells took towards it in his social and political writings.

By the time I left school there were at least three distinct and not easily reconcilable strands in my political views, and they have remained there ever since. One is an individualism and a distrust of the state and other collectivities, going back to my middle-class Liberal ancestry and confirmed by much that I have seen and heard in later life. Another is a profound distrust of democracy, based upon Plato and confirmed by my own observations and reflexions, and an unmitigated contempt for the imbecility and humbug of the party-system as it operates in every country which has a parliamentary government. The third is a recognition that the results of unguided and uncontrolled private enterprise in a thickly populated country under modern industrial conditions are disastrous in their waste of natural resources, their destruction of natural beauty, and their exploitation of human beings. This dates from my childish experiences of the unplanned development of Willesden, and has been confirmed, e.g., by the contrast between the industrial development of England and of Sweden. It tends to make me favour a strong central government and a considerable amount of planning, control, and if necessary coercion. But I would apply this to labour no less than to the landlord, the capitalist, and the businessman.

When I was young there was certainly too little public control, and these three other factors in production were certainly unduly favoured at the expense of the wage-drawers. Now, largely as a result of the two world-wars, the boot is almost certainly on the other foot. It is unreasonable to expect that exactly the right balance will exist at any given moment, or that, if it happened to do so, it would thereafter be maintained in changing circumstances. Speaking for myself, I have never been a supporter of *laissez faire* as such, since the very early days when I was for a moment taken in by Herbert Spencer. I have never at any time been a socialist, still less a communist. I cannot imagine myself at home in that collection of bone-heads unequally yoked with egg-heads and decorated with a broad lunatic fringe, which is the British Labour Party. As for the Communist Party, if nonsense imposed by violence attracted me, I would prefer the old vatted nonsense of the Roman Church to the thin pseudo-scientific vinegar provided by the Jesuits-without-Jesus of Moscow. To vote for a Liberal candidate in contemporary England is to throw one's vote down the drain. So, without enthusiasm, I vote for the Conservatives, mainly as a way of casting a vote against the Labour Party. Naturally one tends to become more conservative as one grows older and has more to lose. Not to be radical when one is young argues hardness of heart; to remain so when one is old suggests softness of head.

I will now take up again the thread of my life-story. I went up to Trinity in the Michaelmas Term of 1906. As a scholar I had the right to occupy rooms in college, and I lived first on Staircase L, Whewell's Court, and later on Staircase B, Great Court. I got immense pleasure and profit out of my life in Cambridge, and especially out of my association with other undergraduates. So far as my formal academic studies were concerned, I was occupied in the first two years in working for Part I of the Natural Sciences Tripos, my main subjects being physics and chemistry, and my subsidiary subjects mineralogy and botany. I had received a very good grounding at school in the first two of these, but the other two were new to me. I took the Tripos in 1908 and was placed in the first class.

The question then arose of the direction in which I should continue my studies. The most obvious course would have been to take Part II of the Natural Sciences Tripos in the subject which interested me most and which I was best at, viz., physics. But it is also quite common at Cambridge to switch to a different Tripos for Part II, and Trinity College has always taken a very wise and liberal attitude towards entrance scholars who desire to make such a change after satisfactorily completing Part I in the subject for which the entrance scholarship was awarded. A number of reasons, some positive and some negative, combined to make me decide to drop natural science and devote the next two years to working for Part II of the Moral Sciences Tripos. ('Moral Science' is

the official name in Cambridge for what is elsewhere called philosophy.)
The motives behind this decision may be briefly stated as follows.

Working for Part I of the Natural Sciences Tripos, and meeting men
who already were or were obviously destined to become first-rate scientists, convinced me that I could never become one myself. To do anything of importance in physics nowadays it is necessary either to be an
outstanding mathematician or to have the gift for seeing what experiments need doing and for designing and carrying them out. It is best if
one can combine both qualities, as Newton and Maxwell did; but the
possession of either alone to a very high degree is sufficient, as the
examples of Einstein and of Aston will show. It was plain that I did not
fulfil these conditions. I was possibly fitted to become a decent science-
teacher at a school or a minor university, or a fairly competent routine
worker in the laboratory of some business-firm, but I should certainly
never go further than that in science. On the other hand, I had already
been interested in philosophy in an amateurish way while at school, and
that interest had been greatly stimulated during my two years at Trinity. Lastly, there is at Cambridge a fairly valuable studentship, the
Arnold Gerstenberg, designed for persons who have taken natural science and have decided to switch over to moral science. The competition
for this is generally very slight, so it seemed likely that I might get it.
If I did so, I should be adequately financed by it and my Trinity scholarship for the next two years. I did not then look much further ahead.
I did not contemplate making the teaching of philosophy my profession.
I thought vaguely of trying for the Higher Civil Service and offering
philosophy as one of my subjects for the examination. That is what my
father would have liked me to do; and I think that, if I could have
passed, I should have made a reasonably good public servant and should
have found the work congenial.

At this point I will enter a little more in detail into my interest in
philosophy while at school and into the stimulus which it received when
I became an undergraduate. I cannot now remember at all clearly how
it began. But I am certain that an important factor in it was the desire
to talk big, and to impress my contemporaries and my elders by introducing into my conversation such imposing names as Kant and Schopenhauer. At this stage a German friend of my father's, a Mr. Friedlaender,
lent me his copy of Schopenhauer's *Die Welt als Wille und Vorstellung*.
It says something for the adequacy of the teaching in German at Dulwich and for my pertinacity as a boy that I read through this book. I
was immensely impressed; Schopenhauer's pessimism, and the quietism,
which he preached but did not practise, appealed to my naturally unenterprising and unhopeful temperament. Mr. Friedlaender, thinking

that a diet of undiluted Schopenhauer might not be very healthy for a boy of 16, then lent me Paulsen's *Einleitung in die Philosophie*. This I read with care and interest, and it no doubt widened my philosophic background.

From Schopenhauer I was naturally led on to Kant. I got hold of Meiklejohn's translation of the *Critique of Pure Reason*. As might be expected, I could make very little of this at the time. I think I understood what Kant had in mind in the *Aesthetic,* and could follow the arguments in parts of the *Dialectic,* but I could make neither head nor tail of the *Analytic.* (To judge from Lord Russell's account of the Kantian philosophy in his *History of Western Philosophy,* his understanding of Kant stopped short at about the same place as did mine when I was 17 years old.) An intelligent and cultivated Welshman, whom I met at a hotel in Wales while on holiday and to whom I talked enthusiastically about Kant and Schopenhauer, thought that a cooling draught of English empiricism would not be amiss. He recommended Mill's *Logic,* and I read this carefully. Lastly, Bertrand Russell's *Principles of Mathematics* came out during the latter part of my time at school. The author's namesake, my mathematical master, had bought it and glanced through it. He decided that it was more in my line than his, and he handed over his copy to me. I had tried to read it, but had not understood much of it, just before I went up to Cambridge.

To this strictly philosophical reading I must add two works of general literature which came out during my school-days and which I read with enthusiasm. These were Bernard Shaw's *Man and Superman* and Thomas Hardy's *Dynasts.* The philosophical background of both:— Shaw's talk of the 'Life Force' and Hardy's supernatural stage-machinery of the 'Immanent Will'—was derived directly or indirectly from Schopenhauer, and I therefore responded to it wholeheartedly. For the sake of completeness I must add Nietzsche's *Also sprach Zarathustra.* I bought this and tried to read it, as in duty bound. I must confess that I found Zarathustra a crashing bore, and that neither then nor since have I managed to pursue his maunderings to the bitter end.

I entered Trinity, then, as a Kantian idealist of the Schopenhauerian variety. I did so at a time when philosophy was a central topic of interest and discussion among intelligent undergraduates outside the very narrow circle of those taking the Moral Sciences Tripos. Both G. E. Moore and Bertrand Russell were indeed away from Cambridge at the time, but their influence was still extremely strong. Moore's *Principia Ethica* and Russell's *Principles of Mathematics* had recently been published, and they provided an inexhaustible theme for discussion. So too did Moore's *Refutation of Idealism* and others of his earliest published papers. Moore did not return to Cambridge until after I had left it. But Russell came back to Trinity as a lecturer during the latter part of my first residence there, and I saw a great deal of him and owe very much to him.

The philosophical atmosphere among the younger men was strongly and rather scornfully anti-idealistic. The two professors, Ward and Sorley, were indeed idealists, but they had very little influence on us. McTaggart was also an idealist, of his own very peculiar kind. No one could fail to be impressed by his extraordinary dialectical power, his wit, and his amazing quickness in discussion; but, though he had many admirers, he had hardly any disciples. For all practical purposes Moore and Russell held the philosophical field and continued to do so for many years. The two teachers from whose lectures and personal instruction I gained most were McTaggart and W. E. Johnson. As I have already given my impressions of their personalities and their achievements in my published writings, I need not say more about them here.

I was awarded the Arnold Gerstenberg Studentship in 1908, and I spent the academic years 1908–1910 in working for Part II of the Moral Sciences Tripos in the Section of Metaphysical and Moral Philosophy with the History of Modern Philosophy. The two philosophers set for special study on that occasion were Leibniz and Lotze. Lotze was rather a bore, though there is plenty of good stuff in his voluminous writings, and one cannot help liking a philosopher who refers familiarly to the Absolute as 'M.' Leibniz was exciting in himself, and was made more so by Russell's then recent *Philosophy of Leibniz* and by the fragments which had lately been discovered and published by Couturat. All went as I should have wished in the Tripos examination in May 1910, and I was placed in the first class and awarded a mark of special distinction.

In view of this it seemed not unreasonable to stay up for another year and try for a Trinity Fellowship. The subject for the Burney Prize in the University that year was *Lotze's Philosophy of Religion*. I spent part of the long vacation writing an essay on that subject. I submitted it for the prize, which was awarded to me. I also, on McTaggart's advice, submitted it in the Fellowship competition in 1910, simply as a trial exercise and not as a serious attempt. The first serious attempt would be in 1911, and, if I failed then, I should have one more chance in the following year.

In consultation with McTaggart and Russell I decided to write on a subject which would enable me to make use both of my scientific and my philosophical training. The topic which I chose in the first instance was the philosophy of mechanics. At the back of this choice lay the following facts. While I was still reading for Part I of the Natural

Sciences Tripos I had had some very stimulating personal supervision in dynamics from Whitehead, then a mathematical lecturer at Trinity. Then, in preparation for the examination for the Arnold Gerstenberg Studentship, I had studied rather carefully Mach's *Mechanics* and Poincaré's books on the philosophy of science. Moreover, Johnson, in his lectures, ostensibly on Advanced Logic, had dealt in a very original way with the notions of cause and substance in dynamics, and with those of absolute and relative space, time, and motion. These matters had also been touched upon, very briefly but most excitingly, in some of the concluding chapters of Russell's *Principles of Mathematics*.

When I got to work on my dissertation I found that the philosophy of mechanics was rather pushed into the background by more general philosophical problems. The dissertation was submitted to the Electors in the late summer of 1911, and I had the good luck to be one of the four candidates to be elected to a prize Fellowship in October of that year. The contents were published, with little alteration but some addition, as my first book, *Perception, Physics, and Reality*.

When I speak of 'good luck,' this is an accurate statement and not a gesture of graceful modesty. It is of course true to say that no one is elected to a Trinity Fellowship unless the work which he submits is of outstanding excellence in the opinion of several mutually independent experts. To that extent there is no question of luck. On the other hand, the number of Fellowships available in any year is so small compared with the number of first-rate candidates that several men fail inevitably to get elected whose qualifications are at least as good as those of their more fortunate rivals. At the latest stage of a Fellowship election no substantial injustice would, I believe, be done, and much futile discussion would be avoided, if the names of the surviving candidates were written on slips of paper, put into a hat, and drawn at random, and if the first so many whose names were drawn were automatically elected. (There would have to be some kind of preliminary weighing and discounting to allow for the fact that there are far more candidates in some subjects, e.g., natural science, than in others, e.g., classics.)

I had not counted on getting a Fellowship even at my last possible attempt, and I had almost no expectation of being elected in 1911. I had therefore accepted an offer to go to St. Andrew's as assistant to Professor Stout. Probably with a muddled intention of avoiding the ὕβρις which is said to bring νέμεσις in its train, I did not wait in Cambridge or even in London for the announcement of the results of the election, but had already left to take up my duties in Scotland. I was summoned to Cambridge by a telegram from the Senior Bursar with the good news. I missed the Fellowship Admission Dinner and the

Master's speech of welcome to the newly elected Fellows, and had to have a special admission in Chapel all to myself. I dined that night for the first time at the High Table and drank wine in the Combination Room, under McTaggart's wing, and then returned, after spending a few hours at home, to St. Andrew's. It was certainly one of the happiest events in my life—probably *the* happiest—and the one which most influenced my future career. It was not rendered any the less happy for my parents and Aunt Leah and myself by being a severe 'smack in the eye' for Uncle Edwin, who, in his 'sage' way, had opposed my first going to Cambridge and then my staying there after the end of my third year, and had never ceased to prognosticate disaster. To do him justice, when it came to the point he was as delighted as anyone, expressing his satisfaction in the *Nunc dimittis* manner which is so becoming to old age.

Under the college statutes then in force a prize fellowship at Trinity lasted for six years and involved no duties. Residence was not required, though non-residence of course entailed foregoing the free dinners in Hall and the free rooms in College which were part of the emolument. I was naturally much tempted to throw up my job at St. Andrew's and return to Trinity. Very wisely, as I think, I overcame that temptation, and decided to stay where I was and save and invest my Fellowship dividends. In that way I began that course of saving and investment which has been one of my main sources of interest and satisfaction in life. All my experience had impressed on me the importance of having private means. I was determined to make myself as soon as possible independent of the vicissitudes of employment. As my tastes are simple, and as there was never any risk of my catching my foot in the man-trap of matrimony, this was not an impossible ideal. I kept in touch with the College and enjoyed the communal life of the High Table by residing for about two months in each Long Vacation.

In St. Andrew's I came under new philosophical influences, viz., those of Professors G. F. Stout and A. E. Taylor. I have already put on record, in my contribution to *Contemporary British Philosophy*, my very great obligations to both of them, not only for what they taught me, but for their constant personal kindness to me. Looking back, I am inclined to think that Stout was one of the greatest all-round philosophers of his time. Important as are his published works, I doubt whether they do him full justice. Anyone who had as much discussion with him as I did must feel that there was a depth of wisdom, a breadth of knowledge and interest, and a critical acumen in his conversation, which is only imperfectly revealed in his writings. Stout's influence should be obvious to any attentive and instructed reader who troubles to compare my treatment of the problems of sense-perception in *Perception, Physics, and Reality* with that in *Scientific Thought.*

I was Stout's assistant until 1914, when I was appointed an independent lecturer in the University College of Dundee, then a part of the University of St. Andrew's. Before I had taken up my new post the first World War had broken out. I must now say something of this, as it affected me.

If I should be asked: "What did you do in the Great War?," my first and fundamental answer would be that which Sieyès, the framer of so many French constitutions, used to make when asked what he did under the Terror:—'*J'ai vécu.*' I will now develop this a little further.

I had not then, and I have never had since, any clear conviction that the entry of England into that war was either necessary or desirable. Certainly the results were disastrous. But that is not conclusive, since one cannot make any reasonable guess as to what the long-range consequences of alternative decisions would have been. So I had not the strong and most admirable motive which moved many of the best of my contemporaries to enlist. On the other hand, I had no 'conscientious objection' to the use of force in general or to war in particular. So I had not the motive which moved some few of the best of my contemporaries to refuse to undertake military service. But, even if I had been convinced that it was my duty to enlist, I have little doubt that my physical cowardice would have led me to try to evade it. And, even if I had been convinced that it was my duty to refuse to take part in the war, I have little doubt that my moral cowardice, in face of popular obloquy and the disapproval of friends and relatives, would have led me to conceal my conviction. I suppose that, if no other way out of the dilemma had presented itself, I should finally have enlisted under the pressure of public opinion in the circles which immediately surrounded me. In that case very likely our old friend, the Unconscious, would eventually have come to the rescue by staging some psychogenic physical disability.

Fortunately there was in St. Andrew's an alternative available, by which the appearances were saved and 'honour,' though 'rooted in dishonour,' was satisfied. Professor Irvine, at that time professor of chemistry in the university and later its Principal, was a distinguished organic chemist. His laboratory soon became engaged in important war-work. Early in 1915 I began to work there, utilising the knowledge of chemistry which I had acquired at school and at Cambridge. I became technically an employee of the Ministry of Munitions, and, as such, received exemption from military service and a badge to wear as an outward and visible sign of this. There were occasional alarms, as more and more men were needed to 'pass through the fire to Moloch' in France and in

Flanders, but I kept my place. The work was quite interesting, and, if I was not of outstanding use, I do not think that I was conspicuously inefficient.

I continued to live in St. Andrew's, travelling to Dundee three times a week to give my lectures there, and giving such help as I could in his teaching to Stout, who was now without an assistant. I worked, and in the summer vacations lived, with students of the university who were, like myself, exempted as employees of the Ministry of Munitions. This was a new, and in the main pleasant, experience for me. I liked most of them, and got on comfortably with all of them. But it emphasised for me the pleasures of privacy, and I have always had a fellow-feeling for the hymnologist who associates 'peace, perfect peace' with 'loved ones far away.'

At last, after years of nightmare and madness, the world was 'made safe for democracy,' though it was soon to become abundantly clear that democracy was not safe for the world. My father died in 1918 shortly after the armistice, and now the only surviving members of the family of his generation were my mother and Aunt Julia. I had lost in the War one and only one very intimate friend, though many of the best of my contemporaries at school and at Cambridge had given their lives. I resumed my normal life at St. Andrew's and Dundee until 1920, when I was elected to the professorship of philosophy at the University of Bristol in succession to Lloyd Morgan, who was, I believe, largely instrumental in my election. It is the city of my ancestors, and I had known it since childhood and had none but pleasant memories of my yearly visits to it. Moreover, it has tradition and character and is very beautifully situated. I was treated with the greatest kindness by my new colleagues, and I also made some very good friends outside the University. Among these I would mention Hugo Mallet and his wife Elsie (daughter of Mr. Lewis Fry), and Donald Hughes and those two very remarkable women, his sister Catherine and his wife Hope.

The University was then in a state of transition. It was greatly under-staffed, and its present magnificent buildings were in part incomplete and in part not even planned. I was maid-of-all-work in the department of philosophy. I have never had to compose or to deliver so many lectures on so many various subjects. Fortunately my health was good. I enjoyed the work, and in order to do it I had to read some subjects, e.g., psychology, which I had formerly neglected and to some extent ignorantly despised. One excellent scheme which Lloyd Morgan had initiated and carried on was a course of lectures in philosophy for the students of natural science. I of course continued this, and the lectures which I gave became the basis of my book *Scientific Thought*. I may compare myself with John the Baptist in at least one respect (though I do not share his taste for an unbalanced diet of locusts and wild honey), viz., that there came to these lectures one whose shoe-latches I was not worthy to unloose. This was Dirac, then a very young student, whose budding genius had been recognised by the department of engineering and was in process of being fostered by the department of mathematics.

In 1922 came an invitation from Trinity College, Cambridge, to deliver the second course of Tarner Lectures. (The first had been given by Whitehead in 1919.) Close on its heels there followed an invitation to go back to the College with a Fellowship and to succeed McTaggart, who was retiring, in his College Lectureship in Moral Science. I accepted both invitations with alacrity. I had been very happy at Bristol and would have been well content to stay there, and the return to Cambridge involved for the time at least a substantial sacrifice of income. But for me the attraction of life at Cambridge as a Fellow of Trinity was overwhelming.

It was at the beginning of the Bristol period that I first joined the Society for Psychical Research (April 1920), and it will be convenient to interrupt my story at this point in order to give a brief account of my interest in alleged paranormal phenomena.

I do not know when or how it began, but I can hardly remember a time when it did not exist. I can say two negative things about it. In the first place, it did not arise from any incidents or stories of incidents in my family, for I never heard tell of any. Then, again, it did not arise because so many of the early fathers of psychical research in England, e.g., Sidgwick, Myers, Gurney, Lord Rayleigh, and Gerald Balfour, had been Fellows of Trinity. It existed long before I was aware of this fact, and long before it would have had any special significance for me, if I had been. A possible contributory cause is that my father used to take, and I used to read with avidity from an early age, the *Review of Reviews*. W. T. Stead, the owner and editor of this, was a very remarkable and original man, and among his other unorthodoxies was a strong belief in Spiritualism. There were no doubt from time to time in the *Review of Reviews* accounts of alleged psychic phenomena, in which the stories would be taken seriously and regarded as manifestations of the surviving spirits of the dead.

However this interest may have arisen, it managed to coexist with and to survive the period of crude rationalism, based on natural science, which I have described. It received no encouragement from any of those whom I most admired at Cambridge. The only one of them who might have been interested in psychical research was McTaggart, who wholeheartedly accepted the doctrine of human immortality in its transmigrationist form, and who also had had mystical experiences. But in point of fact he was not interested. He was quite willing to admit that some of the alleged phenomena investigated by psychical researchers might well be genuinely supernormal, but he took no interest in the investigation of them. As regards human survival of bodily death, he thought that metaphysics could provide much stronger reasons for believing in this than could any psychical phenomena, however well established.

At St. Andrew's I found that Stout had read a good deal of the relevant literature with interest and was open-minded and encouraging. Taylor, on the other hand, took the extreme Anglo-Catholic attitude. If the phenomena were genuine, as some of them probably were in his opinion, then they were almost certainly due to evil spirits (human or non-human) and were best left alone. He was wont to refer to psychical research by the ludicrously inappropriate and emotionally-toned name of 'necromancy.' (I have often amused myself by trying to picture Sidgwick, Mrs. Sidgwick, Podmore, Piddington, and Gerald Balfour dancing widdershins round a witch's cauldron in the cellar of 31 Tavistock Square.)

At Cambridge, when I was a student, there was an undergraduate society for psychical research, which I joined. It used sometimes to meet in the rooms in King's of that once notorious Cambridge character, Oscar Browning. For me its main interest is that it enabled me to catch a glimpse of that almost legendary figure in the penultimate stages of its decay.

I joined the grown-up Society for Psychical Research in 1920. I became a member of its Council in 1930, and have remained on it ever since. I was chosen as President for the years 1935 and 1936. It is no small honour to be elected to an office which has been held by such men as Sidgwick, William James, Sir William Crookes, Sir Oliver Lodge, and Lord Raleigh, to name only some of those who are no longer alive. I have not been able to be a regular attendant at meetings of the Council, but I have from time to time been able to help in other ways as a member of some of its committees. Nor have I taken a direct part in any investigations conducted under the S.P.R.'s auspices, though I was *au courant* with the important experimental researches of Dr. Soal, Mr. Tyrrell, and Mr. Whately Carington.

In my published work I have stated my views about the relevance of psychical research to philosophy, and have tried to apply philosophical analysis and criticism to some of the notions current in psychical research. I have also expressed my astonishment at the contented ignorance and indifference of most contemporary Western philosophers in a matter which should deeply concern anyone who presumes to express reasoned opinions on the nature and status of man, on the limits and conditions of human cognition, on the inter-relations of the mental and the material aspects of the world, and so on. There are gratifying signs that, in England at any rate, this reproach is ceasing to apply to some of the younger philosophers. I regret to say that I have seen few, if any, such signs in the United States or in Sweden.

All that remains for me to say here on the topic of psychical research is this. I have had a certain number of anonymous sittings with mediums of good repute. In none of them have I received any communication which seemed to require for its explanation anything more than telepathic awareness by the medium of some of my own cognitive and emotional states. The vast majority of the statements made did not seem to require even that explanation; they were to all appearance just irrelevant twaddle. I have never witnessed any ostensibly supernormal physical phenomena under satisfactory conditions. As I know that I am quite easily taken in by the simplest of conjuring tricks, I should attach no weight whatever to any physical phenomenon that I might witness at a séance, unless the conditions had been checked beforehand and the medium and the sitters controlled throughout by an independent expert in such matters whom I knew and trusted. Even so, I should feel happier if the phenomena were recorded automatically by mechanical or electrical devices.

I should find it hard to say what hopes or fears or wishes, if any, lie at the back of my lifelong interest in psychical research. So far as I can tell, I have no desire to survive the death of my present body, and I should be considerably relieved if I could feel much surer than I do that no kind of survival is possible. The only empirical basis on which I can appraise life after death, if such there be, is what I know of life here and what mediums tell us of life hereafter. On neither basis of valuation does the prospect of survival hold any charms for me. Having had the luck, as it seems to me, to draw an eel from a sack full of adders, I do not wish to risk putting my hand into the sack again. And the prospect of an unending 'pleasant Sunday afternoon' in a nonconformist chapel on the astral plane would not attract me, even if I could find it credible. No doubt the simile of drawing a life at random, like a counter out of a bag, is in one important respect misleading. If one survives in any way, the dispositions which one has built up and the character which one has formed by the end of this life must surely be a most important factor in determining the initial equipment with which one will enter into one's next life. But this consideration does not encourage me to desire survival. For neither the dispositions which I have acquired nor the character which I have formed are such as to constitute a satisfactory innate equipment for another life.

I think that what lies behind my interest in the subject may possibly be this. I feel in my bones that the orthodox scientific account of man as an undesigned calculating-machine, and of non-human nature as a wider mechanism which turns out such machines among its other products, is fantastic nonsense, which no one in his senses could believe unless he kept it in a water-tight compartment away from all his other experiences and activities and beliefs. I should be sorry if anything so absurd and (as it seems to me) so dull and boring were to be true, and if those who take it for Gospel should happen to be right. Yet I must admit that, within the limited context in which it has arisen, viz., in the physiological and the psychological laboratory, where a man or an animal is regarded simply as an object to be investigated and experimented upon, the *prima facie* case for this view of man and of non-human nature is immensely strong. It is no accident that experimental physiologists and psychologists (who are certainly no greater fools than the rest of us) almost unanimously accept it in their professional capacity. I should therefore welcome the irrefutable establishment of alleged facts, which, if genuine, would be so palpably inconsistent with this view as to leave it without a leg to stand upon.

After this digression I resume the history of my life. I returned to Cambridge in October 1923 and took up residence in Trinity as Fellow and Lecturer in Moral Science. Just at that time, E. D. Adrian, a friend from our undergraduate days, married and vacated his rooms in College. I had the good luck to have them allotted to me. They were the rooms on Staircase E, Great Court, which Sir Isaac Newton occupied as a Fellow of Trinity. I have lived in them ever since, gradually introducing those rudimentary conditions of comfort, such as double windows, draught-excluders, closed stoves, electric water-heaters, a refrigerator, etc., which I learned to appreciate when visiting the higher civilisations of Sweden and the U.S.A. I have never understood the English indifference to needless and easily mitigable discomfort and squalor.

McTaggart had intended to continue, for a time at least, to give some of the numerous courses of lectures which he had been wont to deliver. But, while on a visit to London in the Christmas vacation 1924–25, he was stricken with a fatal illness and in a very short time died. This was not only a great personal loss to me; it also suddenly and heavily increased my load of lecturing on topics for which I had no lectures prepared. I was once more as hard pressed in the preparation of lectures as I had been at Bristol. I have stated elsewhere that McTaggart had made me his sole literary executor and one of the two general executors and trustees under his will. In the former capacity I saw through the press the manuscript of Volume II of his *Nature of Existence*.

So long as I held the post of Lecturer I gave in each year three courses, each of three lectures a week, throughout the three terms of the academic year. One of these was on the *Elements of Metaphysics* for Part I of the Tripos. Another was on the philosopher or philosophers appointed from time to time by the Faculty Board for special study in Part II Section A of the Tripos. The third was on the remaining chief European philosophers from Descartes to Hegel, both inclusive. This lecturing was the main part of my work. I had also to take for weekly essays and supervision those undergraduates of Trinity College who were reading for either Part of the Moral Sciences Tripos. As there were seldom more than 3 or 4 of these at any one time, this was not hard work. Occasionally, by permission of the College and by arrangement with the Tutors of other Colleges, I would supervise a non-Trinity undergraduate. My book *Five Types of Ethical Theory* arose out of my discussions with undergraduate pupils reading for Part I of the Tripos.

It is my custom to write out carefully and in full all my lectures well in advance of the date of delivery. So the notes of a course of lectures make a fairly adequate foundation for a book. All my books after *Perception, Physics, and Reality* have been constructed out of lectures.

Soon after my return to Cambridge an opportunity arose of selling our house at Forest Hill on favourable terms. We did so, and I bought a house at Langford in Somerset and installed my mother there. I am confident that she was happy there so long as she had health and vigour, i.e., up to the age of nearly 85. She was fortunate enough to secure the services of an excellent man and wife, Mr. and Mrs. Doughty, who remained with her for the rest of her life and devotedly nursed her in the last years of it. Doughty has since died. His wife, at the time of writing, is living in a flat in a house which I own in Clifton, and is assiduous in knitting socks and making black-currant jelly for me. She is a very fine cook, and, like many other experts in that art, she has not the temperament which makes life easy for herself or for others. But one could not have wished to have more scrupulously honest or more completely devoted servants than she and her husband, and I simply cannot imagine how I should have managed without them when my mother became unable to look after herself and her own affairs.

I used to spend a part of each vacation at home with my mother. I must confess that I found these spells of residence at home terribly trying to my nerves, and that I was very near to a breakdown at the end of each of them. I used to reproach myself with this, when I reflected that I could not stand, for a few weeks, the atmosphere of mutual tension in which my mother and the servants were living for years without respite. But self-reproach did no good, and only made the matter worse. This nervous strain was at its worst during the latter part of the middle period of my mother's residence at Langford. Toward the end it relaxed, and all other feelings were submerged in sheer pity and sorrow, mitigated only by the fact that there was no reason to believe that my mother was suffering bodily pain. When I look back on that period of my life, and write of it, I can appreciate the force of Aeneas's words to Dido:— *Infandum, regina, jubes renovare dolorem.*

In the course of editing McTaggart's posthumous work I came to the decision to devote a full-scale book to a really careful and thorough estimate of the extraordinarily elaborate and ingenious system which he had excogitated. It seemed unlikely that anyone else would undertake this; it seemed sad that his life-work should go by default; and it seemed obvious that I had the necessary qualifications. So I persuaded the Faculty Board of Moral Science to make McTaggart's philosophy the 'special subject' for Part II Section A of the Tripos in two successive years. I thus wrote and delivered the lectures which formed the basis of my book *Examination of McTaggart's Philosophy*. It has not been, and could not fairly have been expected to be, a 'best seller'; but I think it contains about the best work of which I am capable in philosophy. If some of my younger friends and colleagues of the 'common language' school were to twit me with the accusation that it consists largely of *difficiles nugae*, I should heartily agree. But I should be inclined to retort that the writings of their school consist largely of *faciles nugae*.

In 1933 Sorley retired from the Knightbridge Professorship of Moral Philosophy in Cambridge. I was not particularly anxious to exchange the position of Lecturer for that of Professor. The difference of salary was not great enough to be of much importance to me, and I preferred the duties of the former office to those of the latter. I had enjoyed supervising the very moderate number of undergraduates who had been in my charge, and I feel fairly sure that I did it well and that most of them derived some benefit from their discussions with me. As Professor one is not allowed to supervise undergraduates, and one is expected to take charge of a certain number of research students writing dissertations for the Ph.D. degree. I do not much care for this work, and I doubt whether I do it well. Research students have generally lost (if they ever possessed) the charm of youth, without having yet gained the poor consolation-prizes of wealth or eminence. Moreover, I am quite sceptical as to the value of philosophical research as an occupation for young men, and I have no idea how to organise or to direct it. However, though

I did not have any strong positive desire for the professorship, I should not have cared to see another person appointed to it unless he had been very obviously my intellectual superior. So I applied, and I was elected.

Six years of my tenure of the chair coincided with the second World War, and therefore cannot be judged by normal standards. But, after making due allowance for this, I cannot look back to my time as Knightbridge Professor with any great satisfaction. I think that my duties in preparing and delivering lectures were done well and conscientiously, and I certainly enjoyed that part of the work. With the help of such kindly and efficient younger colleagues as Dr. Ewing, Mr. (now Professor) Braithwaite, and Dr. Lewy, as successive secretaries to the Faculty Board, I got through my very simple duties as Chairman without disgrace, if without distinction. I did my best for the few research students who were put in my charge, and I do not think that any of them can have been much the worse for my ministrations. Some, who began by being bumptious and cocksure, but were not too clever to learn how difficult it is to prove or to disprove anything in philosophy, may even have derived a certain benefit from my not unsympathetic but entirely sceptical reception of all that was so obvious to them.

The one duty which I wittingly neglected was to attend the weekly meetings of the Moral Science Club. I am not quick-witted nor quick-tongued enough to take a useful part in philosophical discussion by word of mouth; and I was not prepared to spend hours every week in a thick atmosphere of cigarette-smoke, while Wittgenstein punctually went through his hoops, and the faithful as punctually "wondered with a foolish face of praise."

So far, then, I cannot seriously reproach myself. But a professor ought to be something more than an efficient and conscientious teacher and lecturer. He ought to be doing original work himself, and inspiring others to do the like. In this I conspicuously failed. What was fundamentally amiss was that such spring as there had ever been in my life had gone out of it. I no longer believed in the importance of philosophy, I took little interest in its later developments, and I knew very well that I at least had shot my bolt and had nothing further of value to contribute.

In September 1939 the second World War broke out. Almost at the same time my mother, to my unspeakable relief, died. I stored the furniture, made such provision for Doughty and Mrs. Doughty as seemed fitting in view of their inestimable services, and in due course sold the house at Langford.

The second World War was not nearly so trying to me personally as the first had been. I was now well over military age (in my 52nd year when the war broke out), and the whole atmosphere in England was much saner and cleaner than in the first World War. This was largely due to the facts that conscription was in force from the first, that there was almost universal acceptance of our entry into the war as inevitable, and that after the fall of France it was evident even to the stupidest that we were in a situation of desperate danger which threatened all alike. We are greatly indebted to the Germans for driving us out of the Continent at a quite early stage, and thus preserving us from the horrible trench-warfare, with the frightful slaughter of occasional large-scale assaults and the continual wastage of life during quiescent periods, which had characterised the war of 1914–18. We are also indebted to them for the air-attacks, which exposed civilians of all classes to something of the dangers and hardships endured by members of the fighting forces on active service, and thus softened the contrast which was such a demoralising feature of the first World War. (It is perhaps hardly decent for *me* to say this, since I was never in fact involved in any serious air-raid and never lost friends or relatives or property in one. But I am quite sure that it is true.)

My main personal problem was to decide what voluntary service I should undertake. When it became obvious that the College would soon be losing its extremely able young Junior Bursar, David Hinks, to the army, I decided with great trepidation to offer to undertake his job. The College accepted the offer, and at the same time relieved the Acting Junior Bursar of one irksome part of the normal duties of the office, that of assigning rooms and lodgings to undergraduates.

The Junior Bursar's business is to deal with all the *internal* affairs of the College, considered as a place of residence, except the catering. He is concerned, e.g., with the upkeep of the buildings and grounds, with the rents of rooms, with the furnishing of undergraduates' apartments in College, and with the provision of domestic service to all residents in College whether students or Fellows. I had had no previous experience of the kind, and had always carefully evaded responsibility and avoided administrative work. But I had taken my part on the College Council, which is the governing body of the College, had served on several of its committees, had acquired at least the rudiments of financial and business methods in managing my own affairs and acting as trustee for others, and had been interested from my early youth in the repair and maintenance of buildings. I am, indeed, rather exceptionally 'slow in the uptake' for a person of good general intelligence; but, given time, I am capable of learning most things that do not require bodily skill or courage, if I set myself and keep myself set to do so. So I gradually learned my job by doing it. I had from the outset at least one useful qualification. I can write clear unambiguous letters and reports, and, being hypersensitive myself, I can generally sense where other men's corns are situated and do not often unwittingly tread on them.

I was most fortunate in the employees of the College who held posts of great difficulty and responsibility immediately under me, viz., the Chief Clerk, the Clerk of Works, and the Matron. One could not have wished to have more efficient, diligent, faithful, and helpful heads of their respective departments than Mr. Nobbs, Mr. Bell, and Miss Lusk. They did all the dirty work, and did it supremely well under the continually increasing difficulties which the state of war imposed. I do not know what I should have done if any of them had fallen ill, been killed or injured in an air-raid, or been withdrawn by the government for other service. My colleagues on the College Council, which was my immediate employer as Junior Bursar, were always most considerate and helpful in every way, and I would wish to record particularly the constant kindness and practical encouragement which I received from the then Master, G. M. Trevelyan, and the then Vice-Master, D. A. Winstanley.

The air-raid defence organisation of the College was created and run with consummate ability by my colleague Andrew Gow, whose achievement confirmed me in a generalisation which I made long ago, viz., that a first-rate classical scholar can usually do a first-rate job at almost anything that he puts his hand to. All that I had to do in the matter was to give to Gow such help as he needed from the Junior Bursar and his staff in order to carry out his plans.

Naturally there was constant anxiety through the calling-up of men and the shortage of materials, perpetual minor irritation in dealing with government departments, and always at the back of one's mind the fear of a real crisis in the form of a devastating air-raid. But we were spared the crisis, and we muddled through the daily difficulties.

The monotony was relieved by at least two items of outstanding interest, in which the Junior Bursar had to play a prominent part. One was the installation in 1940 of G. M. Trevelyan as Master in succession to Sir J. J. Thomson, in accordance with the ancient and elaborate ritual, and the subsequent repairs and alterations to the Master's Lodge. The other was an extremely 'hush-hush' series of meetings, continuing for about a week in College in the depth of the vacation, at which high military and naval officers, American and English, discussed some of the final details of the plan for invading Normandy.

Soon after the end of the War I relinquished my temporary post, and my colleague, John Wisdom (afterwards Professor) took over for the period that intervened before Hinks was released from the army. The

College displayed its wonted generosity in inviting me to choose for myself any present or presents that I might like up to a total value of £50. It made a similar, and far better deserved, offer to Gow for his services as air-raid precautions officer. I chose a silver salver. Donald Robertson, then Regius Professor of Greek and a friend from the days when we were both undergraduates, composed a witty and highly flattering inscription for it. (As Dr. Johnson said, 'in a lapidary inscription a man is not on his oath,' and this holds for salvers as for tomb-stones.) The gifts were presented to Gow and myself, on behalf of the College, by the Master (Trevelyan) in presence of the Fellows at dessert one evening in the Combination Room. Mine now adorns my rooms in College.

So ended, very happily, a unique interlude in my life. I am extremely glad to have undertaken the Junior Bursarship and to have come through without discredit. One thing that impressed me, in the course of my duties, was the curious mixture of egotism and petty jealousy with loyalty and devoted service which exists in many men and women. I had of course caught glimpses of this, in a highly gentlemanly and sublimated form, in my colleagues, my pupils, and myself. But in the less sophisticated persons with whom I was concerned as Junior Bursar I contemplated it with the lid off. In view of what I saw I am less surprised that men are sometimes at war than that they are ever at peace.

One good thing which my tenure of the Junior Bursarship seems to have done for me is to have cured me of a distressing nervous trouble, which had begun to affect me immediately after the first World War and had lasted without intermission up to the beginning of the second. It was this. I had an irrational fear of being suddenly taken sick (in the specialised English sense of that word, as distinct from its generalised American sense) when eating a meal in a public restaurant or as guest at a private house or another College. (Most fortunately this did not apply to our ordinary dinners in Hall, or to dinner-parties in my own rooms, where I was host.) The existence of this fear made the prospect of eating out as a guest a misery to me, and, if I accepted an invitation, it tended to produce in me during the meal actual feelings of nausea, profuse sweating, and other premonitory symptoms of vomiting. In point of fact I always managed to get through these ordeals without disaster, but this nervous complaint certainly made me decline many invitations which I should have liked to accept and robbed me of much of the pleasure which I should otherwise have derived from the few which I did accept. I will not trouble the reader with futile speculations as to the aetiology of these symptoms, though it may be of interest to recall the rather similar ordeals which my mother had told me as a child that she used to undergo at dinner-parties. I consulted more than one psychiatrist; but I am probably too sophisticated in such matters to be susceptible to the kind of magic which they practise, and I derived no benefit from them. In the course of the second World War I just found that the symptoms had vanished, and up to the present they have not returned. Nor, so far as I am aware, has the unconscious staged any alternative set of unpleasant and inhibiting symptoms. For this I am profoundly grateful to it (or should it be to *them*?).

I have already described, under the head of the 'Nordic interest,' how, soon after the outbreak of peace, I took sabbatical leave and spent some 8 most enjoyable months in Sweden. After that I have nothing of interest to record (except the publication in 1952 of a collection of papers under the title *Ethics and the History of Philosophy*, and in 1953 of another such collection entitled *Religion, Philosophy, and Psychical Research*) until my retirement from the Knightbridge Professorship in October 1953 on reaching the age of 65. It would be a meiosis to say that I retired without regret, for I did so with great positive pleasure. No longer need I occupy the ambiguous position of an unbelieving Pope, or the invidious one of the veteran who lags superfluous on the stage. I had good health and a sufficient income (*pourvu que cela dure*, as Madame Mère used to say), and the right to remain a Fellow of Trinity, and, as such, to retain my rooms in College and to eat my free dinners in Hall.

I had often received invitations to go to the United States as visiting professor. While my mother was alive and in failing health this was out of the question. Then came 6 years of war, followed by my sabbatical leave in Sweden. After that I did not deem it decent to ask for further leave during the short period that remained of my tenure of the Knightbridge Professorship. But I had told my kind American friends that I would willingly consider an invitation after my retirement. They took me at my word, and I received almost simultaneously invitations to visit the University of Michigan at Ann Arbor and the University of California at Los Angeles in the academic year 1953–4. By mutual agreement it was arranged that I should spend the first semester at Ann Arbor and the second at Los Angeles. I already knew Professor Frankena, of the former university, for he had spent some time in Cambridge as a young man and had then attended some of my lectures. I happened also to have met in Cambridge fairly recently Professor Robson of U.C.L.A. and his wife, when they were on a long visit to Great Britain.

The prospect of this visit to the U.S.A. filled me with the feelings of gloomy foreboding which I always suffer at the prospect of any new experience in unfamiliar surroundings. But, as I have found in many other cases, the experience was delightful once I had made the plunge, and I look back on it now with the utmost pleasure. I could not have been treated with greater kindness and hospitality than that which I received in each of my two universities and in the many other universities and non-academic places which I visited. I made new friends, both among the young and their elders, and I met in their homes certain young friends of long standing whom I had not seen since the war. It was good fun too to be treated as a great philosopher. I do not think that this did me any harm; for my knowledge of the works of the great philosophers of the past, and my acquaintance with one or two of the very few really great ones among my elders and teachers, enables me to form a pretty shrewd estimate of my own position in the hierarchy.

This brings my life-history down to the date of writing. I might well stop there. But it is the business of philosophers to philosophise, and so I will conclude with a few general reflexions called forth by this review of my life.

The first is the enormously great part which is played by *chance,* in one quite definite and familiar sense of that word, in human affairs. I mean here by 'chance' factors which do have an important influence on a person's life, but which are either altogether outside his knowledge, or have effects which he cannot possibly foresee or rationally conjecture. (An example is the train of events which led to my becoming a Fellow of Trinity and a teacher of philosophy.) I am persuaded that men in general, and perhaps academic persons in particular, waste an immense amount of time and energy in futile private deliberation and mutual debate. The factors which they are aware of and can take account of are always a meagre selection from those which are in fact relevant and effective; the remoter consequences even of that meagre selection can seldom be predicted with any accuracy; and the consequences which the rejected alternatives would have had, if they had been chosen, can hardly ever be guessed. So why make all this fuss before coming to important and far-reaching decisions? Though I have made many mistakes, and have worried endlessly and needlessly about possible future developments, I do not think that I have often made the mistake or given myself the worry of prolonged anxious deliberation.

My second reflexion is that the fundamental defects in my character have been laziness, cowardice (physical and moral), and lack of drive and resolution by which these defects, or some of their consequences, might have been overcome.

I shall not insist here on the defect of laziness. It is genuine enough, and I have wasted a terrible amount of time in doing nothing in particular when I ought to have been reading and reflecting on the literature of my subject. Then, again, I have often, through laziness, done what I have done in a slovenly and half-hearted way. But it is obvious that I have accomplished, in spite of this, quite a fair amount of quite decent work. The really fundamental defects have been cowardice, physical and moral, and lack of drive and resolution. I imagine that the two are closely connected, and spring from a defect in what Plato calls the 'spirited' element in my nature. However that may be, the consequences have been really serious, and I must say something further on this topic.

To take the physical side first. Let the reader consider the following list of quite ordinary accomplishments which I have never managed to acquire. I cannot dance, or skate, or ski, or swim properly, or row, or play tennis or cricket or golf, or ride a horse, or sail a boat, or drive a car. Nor is this because I am such a fool as to despise these bodily skills, or because I have not *begun* to try to learn most of them. I value them all, and I should greatly like to possess them, and I have at one time or another started to acquire every one of them except skiing and sailing. Let us grant, and make the most of, the fact that I have very little natural aptitude; that I was the only child of elderly parents; and that, although I have good sight and a straight eye, I am unusually bad at adjusting my movements by sight to any swiftly moving object. Plenty of other men have had these or other initial handicaps and have overcome them.

What has been amiss in my case is perfectly obvious to me. In each instance I have been frightened, at the outset, either of getting hurt, or of being laughed at, or (worst of all) of being blamed for my lack of skill and possibly for its ill-consequences to others. I have felt with reasonable confidence that, if only I persisted through the initial stages, I should have acquired the skill in question, at any rate to a respectable degree. I have greatly wanted to acquire it, and have felt angry with myself and contemptuous of myself for not persisting. And yet in every case I have lacked the resolution to drive myself to persist, and have given up. Those who find the problem of free-will (like all other problems) a "pseudo-problem," which they can "dissolve" on their heads, will no doubt be able to tell me in what sense I *could* and in what sense I *could not* have persisted. I cannot but believe that there is a most important sense in which I *could,* and that I deserve moral blame because I could and *did not.*

I cannot, fortunately, give equally palpable instances of lack of moral courage and of its ill-effects on me. I have lived an exceptionally sheltered life, not unlike that of a monk in a monastery, only without the duties of asceticism. My daily bread has been given to me each day by the Steward, and my trespasses forgiven me no less regularly by the Chaplain. Unlike so many thousands of my contemporaries, I have never had to make a decision in face of *vox instantis tyranni* or of *civium ardor prava jubentium*. But I have never read in history or in fiction of a mean or cowardly action, done to avoid bodily suffering or to avert the anger or ridicule or disapproval of others, without recognising myself and being forced to say: "There, but for the luck of circumstances, go I." The story of St. Peter's denial seems to me to be one of the most remarkable and moving passages in the New Testament. Whatever else in that book may be doubtful or false, it surely must be true. I hope and believe that I should not, like Judas, have betrayed my Master for money, if that was Judas's motive. I am fairly confident that, in St. Peter's place, I should, like Peter, have denied him through cowardice.

I have painted a somewhat unpleasing portrait of myself. I must confess that I am not the kind of person whom I like, but I do not think that that source of prejudice has made me unfair to myself. If there should be others who have roses to strew, they can now do so without feeling the need to make embarrassing qualifications.

I will conclude with one little rose of my own. I have had, and I seem to have retained up to the time of writing, the power to make friends with the kind of young men whom I like and admire, despite great disparity in age. A certain number of such young men in England, in Sweden, and in America have plainly enjoyed my company and felt very kindly disposed towards me. Some of them seem to have gone on doing so, even when they have become middle-aged citizens and in spite of long separations in time and in space. I have derived more happiness from this than from any one other source. I hope it may indicate that the side of my nature which shows itself under favourable circumstances to certain others is less disagreeable than that which introspection perpetually presents to myself.

Written in Karlstad, Sweden: August 2nd.–August 24th, 1954

DESCRIPTIVE
AND CRITICAL ESSAYS ON THE
PHILOSOPHY OF C. D. BROAD

1

Everett J. Nelson

SOME ONTOLOGICAL PRESUPPOSITIONS IN
BROAD'S PHILOSOPHY

IN HIS Presidential Address to the Aristotelian Society in 1947 on "Some Methods of Speculative Philosophy," Professor Broad characterized philosophic activity in terms of three features: analysis, synopsis, and synthesis.[1] The first two, he says, characterize in varying degrees all work that would commonly be called philosophic, and the third "is often present in high degree but may be evanescent." Thus "Hume's work is so predominantly analytic that it might be denied to be synoptic, and Hegel's is so predominantly synoptic that it might be denied to be analytic."[2]

Philosophical analysis "consists in clearing up the meanings of all the fundamental kinds of sentences which we habitually use," e.g., causal sentences, material-thing sentences, sentences with temporal copulas, etc.[3] If we add to this the duty of stating clearly and criticizing resolutely our fundamental beliefs, we shall have what Broad called "critical philosophy" in his *Scientific Thought*.[4]

Synopsis is "the deliberate viewing together of aspects of human experience which are generally viewed apart, and the endeavor to see how they are inter-related."[5] These aspects may be different departments of fact, or regions or levels within a single department, which the common man or even the professional scientist may think of as separate rather than as mutually interrelated. Each of them may have its own coherent set of concepts and principles, but when we bring the sets belonging to different ones together we may find conflict or at least the appearance of conflict. To indicate more specifically the kinds of conflict Broad has in mind I shall mention three of his examples of synopsis.

(1) The problem of sense perception arises from viewing together

---

[1] *Proceedings of the Aristotelian Society*, Sup. XXI, 1–32. *MSP* hereafter.
[2] *MSP*, p. 3.   [3] *MSP*, pp. 3–4.
[4] P. 18. I shall use *"ST"* in referring to this book.
[5] *MSP*, p. 4.

71

the naively realistic interpretation of normal perception, the range of abnormal cases from slight variations in the appearances of the "same" object to hallucinations, and the various physical, physiological, and other psychological facts which constitute the usual argument from illusion.

(2) The mind-body problem arises from viewing together the facts, e.g., (a) that in many cases there is a high correlation between sensations and events in the receptors whereas in other cases—day-dreaming, reasoning—there seem not to be; (b) that the bodily events immediately preceding sensations are not in the receptors but in the brain; (c) that energy within the material world is conserved; and (d) that some people believe that a volition can guide an organism without work.

(3) Believers in paranormal phenomena are faced with a problem when they consider them together with normal phenomena, because the paranormal conflict with certain "restrictive principles which we . . . take for granted as the fixed framework within which all our practical life and our scientific theories are confined."[6] Examples of such restrictive principles are: (a) A can know about experiences of B only by hearing or reading sentences made by B or by hearing cries, seeing gestures or facial expressions made by B, or by inference from material records. (Post-cognitive and simultaneous telepathy would be exceptions to this principle.) And (b) an event cannot have effects until it has happened. (This would be violated by autoscopy and by precognitive telepathy.)

Conflicts like these not only call for a reexamination of the presumed facts, concepts, and principles that are involved, but also serve as a stimulus to the discovery of new concepts or principles in terms of which the conflicts may be resolved and the aspects of experience unified and reconciled.

When he wrote *Scientific Thought* Broad seemed to think of speculative philosophy as essentially synopsis and as having mainly a negative value: "Our *results* may be trivial; but the *process* will at least remind us of the extreme complexity of the world, and teach us to reject any cheap and easy philosophical theory."[7]

The unification and reconciliation to which synoptic thinking leads is the third feature of philosophic activity, namely, synthesis. In 1922 Broad did not explicitly distinguish it from synopsis as a feature of speculative philosophy because, I presume, he thought that it "can only consist of more or less happy guesses, made on a very slender basis," that speculative systems so far devised have been "moonshine," and that little more can be expected in the future, for "there is no hope of its reaching

6 *MSP*, p. 13.   7 *ST*, p. 22.

the certainty which some parts of Critical Philosophy might quite well attain."[8] But he seems to have relented since making that early judgment. In concluding his work on McTaggart's philosophy he says that he has "no doubt that it is desirable from time to time to take a synoptic view and to try to bring into a single coherent system all that is then known or rationally conjectured about the world." And he adds, "I have no doubt whatever that the attempts of such men as Aristotle, St. Thomas, Spinoza, Leibniz, and Hegel are among the greatest intellectual achievements of the human mind."[9] One needs only to read his detailed discussions and frequent reconstructions of McTaggart's views to discern a genuine sympathy with what speculative philosophers have tried to do and a lively interest in the problems they thought important. This attitude seems to be even more pronounced in the Presidential Address of 1947. In fact, if one considers what Broad has done in philosophy rather than what he has sometimes said about speculative philosophers or their productions, one finds in his earlier as well as in his later works a speculative bent, which might have been held too much in check by his exceptional analytic ability. His theory of time and existence, to mention only one of his metaphysical views, attests to his speculative interest, for this theory is certainly more than an example of analytic or critical philosophy. In this connexion it would be interesting to consider just how far this theory removes Broad from "that very numerous band of philosophers who have denied the existence of time and asserted that reality is eternal."[10] He does not deny the existence of time, yet the ultimate and underivative importance he actually gives to it seems not to be of such magnitude as to keep him from being on the best of terms with those members of that band who have been clear-headed hard-thinking philosophers.

The problem of synthesis is then to discover concepts and to construct principles in terms of them, that will apply to the synopsized regions and be such that any concepts or principles applying to one of the regions alone will be special cases of, or "at least cohere closely with," concepts or principles of the more general set. The apparent conflict or lack of connexion between the regions will then have been removed.

For examples of synthesis Broad draws from the sciences as well as from philosophy. Thus there are Galileo's analysis of kinematic and dynamical phenomena, and the work of synthesis done by Newton, Lagrange, Hamilton, and Einstein. Such intellectual activities, in that they involve "deep analysis, wide synopsis, and illuminating synthesis," are, he says, genuinely philosophical. Further and higher level possibili-

8 *ST*, p. 21.　　　9 *EMcP*, II, p. 788.　　　10 *Ibid.*, p. 787.

ties, which might result in broad synthesis, are viewing together inorganic and organic phenomena, and the animal, rational, and moral levels of mental life. As for examples from philosophy Broad mentions Spinoza's theory of bodies, Bergson's theory of the eliminative rather than productive function of the nervous system, and Aristotle's concept of matter and form. His discussions of these as well as of how synthesis takes place—how, e.g., concepts in one region may be extended to another and become pervasive modes of interpretation, thereby ordering and unifying the fields viewed synoptically—merit detailed consideration quite beyond the limits of this essay. Similarly instructive is his explanation of the importance of considering marginal, abnormal, and pathological cases. They may lead us to separate factors that are so closely associated in normal cases as to elude distinction, to discover the conditions of their association, and, as a consequence, to arrive at a view covering cases of all types.

Although I agree almost completely with what Broad has said about analysis, synopsis, and synthesis as characteristics of philosophic activity, I want to make one comment on the relation between critical philosophy and speculative philosophy, before discussing synthesis further. The confidence in the former and despair of the latter as productive of significant positive results, which Broad expressed in 1922, seem to rest on the assumption that critical philosophy is less dependent on speculative philosophy than it in fact is. Not only do we sometimes, as Broad says, "do our Critical Philosophy with half an eye on our Speculative Philosophy, and accept or reject beliefs, or *analyse concepts in a certain way*, because we feel that this will fit in better than any alternative with the view of Reality as a whole that we happen to like,"[11] but I think that in a more basic sense it is impossible to do critical philosophy or analysis without making speculative assumptions. Even the words I italicized in Broad's sentence suggest this. Take, e.g., the method of logical constructions. I agree with him that it is a valuable and important contribution to philosophy, but I think that the result of its employment is always a hypothesis or theory. Thus, that a cardinal number is a class of classes presupposes that the name "class" is denotative; or that sentence s_1, which has a number-name, means no more and no less than sentence s_2, which has no number-name, is a theory not certifiable on logical grounds. Another notable instance of critical philosophy is Russell's theory of definite descriptions; yet in view of the controversy still going on over it, few of us would venture to give it as an example of the near certainty Broad believes attainable in critical philosophy. Or con-

11 *ST*, p. 21. Italics mine.

sider the analysis of general propositions. One might here have expected decisive results, but quite the opposite has been the case. The greater the precision, flexibility, and power of our analytic tools, the greater has been the proliferation of issues, with little if any advance toward a solution of the initial problems. Nevertheless the methods of analysis and critical philosophy have been significant achievements in promoting clarity of thought, in revealing unthought-of possibilities and interrelations, and in stimulating philosophers to devise new constructions. Among their achievements or merits however is not the attainment of certainty or the avoidance of speculative commitment.

As I have pointed out, Broad believes that synopsis followed by worthwhile philosophic synthesis is possible. And everyone believes in the possibility and desirability of synthesis in the sciences. Now the question I want to raise is this: How is synthesis possible? What are the indispensable conditions of it? What do we presuppose when we believe in the real possibility of taking a synoptic view and then of being able to find concepts in terms of which we can formulate theories, laws, or principles that will apply over the areas viewed together? In asking this I am not restricting myself to new impressive syntheses of large areas: I am referring to syntheses of all definable areas of experience, from the large ones of the several recognized sciences down to the minimal ones of different data of experience. If, e.g., we understood the type of synthesis that makes possible classification, we should have gone far toward understanding the world. How is it possible to assign several things to one class and one thing to several classes, and how is it that some classifications but not others are fruitful in leading to further types of synthesis?

Since the possibility of synthesizing x and y, whether they are departments or regions or levels of fact or just data, presupposes the possibility of viewing them *together*, I want to make two remarks concerning synopsis before discussing synthesis. (1) Viewing x and y together presupposes that they, or they with the thinker, are *together*. That is to say, a necessary condition of the synopsis of x and y is that they are unified or integrated.[12] And (2) my being able to take a synoptic view of x and y presupposes something about me and about x and y and me. My viewing them together must be more than separate and distinct psychological events, "viewing x" and "viewing y." There must be a unity of consciousness, not just an atomicity of consciousnesses. Moreover there must be sufficient unity of subject and object to ground a cognitive relation. I trust that this relation will not infect every formula relating x and

12 Aspects of experience viewed together, Broad says, "co-exist and are relevant to each other and they must presumably be interrelated in some *coherent* way." *MSP*, p. 4. Italics mine.

y with a parameter representing the knower, yet we must not end up with a view having no room for him.

I return now to synthesis. Since it presupposes synopsis, a condition of it is the unity presupposed by synopsis as well as the particular type of unity or interconnexion presupposed by the kind of synthesis it happens to be. Every proposition, except a nominal definition or a sheer stipulation of a convention, asserts or denies a case of synthesis and presupposes therefore types of unity or categories that go beyond experience. With respect to the ground of any true proposition we can ask questions that cannot be answered by appeal to experience. I shall not argue for this universal proposition or for particular types of synthesis, but rather for the position that types of synthesis or categories are presupposed by empirical propositions of the kinds we find in the sciences and by the methods of inferring them. These methods are types of induction. I shall maintain that a condition of the validity of induction is that experience is grounded in a non-experiential matrix embodying types of unity which likewise are not given in experience.

Broad epitomized an attitude which worries contemporary empiricistic philosophers when he spoke of inductive reasoning as the glory of science and the scandal of philosophy.[13] We have on the one hand the prodigious achievements of modern inductive science and on the other the failure of philosophy to confute Hume's skeptical arguments, let alone to provide a positive validation of induction. The formal theory of probability has been developed to a high degree, and is successfully applied in theoretical science as well as in technology. Still the skeptical challenge to its applicability to empirical judgments and to its reliability as a guide in prediction and action has not been met. Embarrassed and puzzled by this, which they interpret as a failure of philosophy, many recent empiricists have come to question whether we might not have been wrong in thinking that there is a problem of induction. They have suggested and sometimes vociferously asserted that the credibility of the skeptical attack on induction has been due to the assumption that all reasoning is deductive, and that, as a result, induction has been condemned for not meeting standards that in fact are not appropriate to it. Therefore, they inform us, if only we would recognize induction for what it is and not confuse it with deduction, we should not have a problem of induction any more than we have a problem of deduction. I shall consider this suggestion later. I want simply to say now that, even if we grant that there is a problem of induction, I see nothing scandalous in its not having been solved. It is a philosophic problem and involves basic issues which have always concerned philosophers. Since the validity

13 *EHP*, p. 143.

of induction presupposes types of unity of the elements of the subject matter of the inference, the problem of induction inextricably involves the problem of the One and the Many. Similarly, since in induction inference proceeds from particulars to generals or to other particulars, the problem is an aspect of the problem of universals and particulars. If the problem of induction is a scandal, all philosophy is. There is no justification for singling it out for abuse, though the basis of a motive for doing so is not hard to find. It is the fact that the challenge to beliefs, which is characteristic of philosophic inquiry, becomes, through this problem, focussed on the greatest intellectual achievement and pride of the modern age.

Further, this sorry plight of inductive inference is made to seem the worse by comparison with deductive inference. Deduction has been such a fair-haired child of philosophers that the halo they have placed on it has blinded them from seeing its true nature. I shall show later that there is a "problem" of deduction corresponding to the problem of induction. I want to point out now that since deduction, no less than induction, is a kind of cognition, it is subject to the conditions of valid cognition. It involves steps and relations that do not supply their own credentials. We all believe that reasoning of any kind is more than an accidental or even a causal sequence of mental events. The steps considered as events may be causally determined; nonetheless we do not doubt that belief or assent may be "given or withheld in accordance with 'evidence.' "[14] Hence reasoning, or cognition of any kind, presupposes a special kind of relevance of one step to another; and it is in virtue of it that acceptance of a conclusion may be "justified," irrespective of the causal relations involved. There are then conditions of valid cognition, on which both deduction and induction depend. It is strange that Hume's theory of the separability of perceptions has made so little impact on the attitudes of empiricists toward deduction. It is as devastating of deduction as of induction. Its pluralism is incompatible with cognition, and makes an impostor of any idea pretending to refer beyond itself.

In opposing the doubts and denials that there is a problem of induction, I shall try to show, for one thing, that factual conditions must be satisfied if induction is to be valid. Time and again Broad has done this, and as clearly and forcefully as anyone could desire, and he has indicated the metaphysical implications of the problem. My justification for going over some of this ground again is that in doing so I shall have an opportunity to raise some points which I hope Broad will comment on,

14 *MSP,* p. 8.

and to invite certain elaborations of his views, for which everyone would be grateful.

In discussing induction he often introduced the issues by means of a game of chance example, and then went on to scientific inductions, pointing out for each type of case the laws of probability employed and the assumptions made. I shall use a gaming example too, but not for the purpose of eliciting or explaining specific laws of probability or detailed formulations of principles. My reason for employing such an example is that it is an easily understood and powerful vehicle both for stating conditions and separating issues that have counterparts in cases of induction, and for directing attention to conditions that are not satisfied by "chance" situations but must be satisfied if induction is to be possible.

With respect to playing roulette, let us contrast two cases: (1) The wheel is honest. I shall not try to define "honest," since we have a good idea what it means to say of a roulette wheel that it is honest. We could state it, for example, in terms of the mechanism and the causal factors entering into a selection; e.g., that as the wheel approaches being an honest selector the events or conditions favorable to different numbers tend, as spinning is continued, to cancel one another out. An honest wheel contains the ground of no law to which sequences of selections conform; it is not biased in favor of any number or sequence of numbers; or the probability of any selection by it is independent of its past selections.

From this condition of honesty it follows that no selection is evidence of any other, and therefore that we cannot *learn* how to win playing the wheel. Accordingly, it would not be reasonable for us to bet odds in favor of any selection over others of the same form, despite the past performance of the wheel.

(2) The wheel is not honest. This implies that it is biased in favor of some numbers, and that it embodies the ground of an evidential relation holding between certain numbers or sequences of them. Given that the wheel is biased, it is probable that there is a number x, or numbers x, y, etc., or a sequence of numbers, that will be chosen with greater frequency than at least one other possible selection of the same form. This implies that on the hypothesis of bias, the greater the relative frequency of the occurrence of a given selection, the greater the probability that a factor in the cause of its occurrences is the bias in the wheel. Such a wheel is, therefore, one with which we can learn how to win. If we are clever enough, we shall be able, by noting sequences of selections, to work out a "system" for placing bets. And if we bet and calculate our odds in conformance with this system, there will be a favorable probability of our winning. In so betting we shall be acting reasonably, provided that prior

to playing we had reason for believing that the wheel was not honest.

These cases show that no statement simply reporting past selections made by an otherwise unknown wheel implies or makes probable any statement about further selections or about bias in it. In order that betting may be justifiable, knowledge of past selections and reason for believing that there is bias are needed. No matter how striking the order of selections may have been, there is no probability that a formula expressing it will hold for further spins unless bias is probable independent of those selections. Accordingly, *that* we can learn how to win playing a wheel presupposes that it is biased. Let us call the statement that there is bias a "Principle of Bias." We may then restate our point this way: We can learn how to win if and only if a Principle of Bias is true of the wheel.

We may compare sense experience to watching the surface of a roulette wheel. Let us say that our world is a big roulette wheel. Our experience is limited to what takes place on its surface. Our senses do not tell us whether there is anything under it, which causes what happens on it. We observe various patterns of events. From them we infer laws, and by techniques and modes of construction countenanced by the scientific method, we elaborate systems, which we call sciences. Laws in them correspond to formulae in a gambler's system; and the use of the laws in prediction, or the warranted belief in their truth, presupposes the satisfaction of conditions corresponding to those grounding a Principle of Bias.

Of the types of induction, I shall limit myself to qualitative generalization, though what I shall say about it is general enough to hold in principle for the inference of laws of other types as well. Continuing to use the roulette example, we may compare generalizing to inferring, e.g., that even-numbered pockets will always be chosen after prime-numbered pockets, from the fact that they always have been. Now let us suppose that through experience of AB's we have come to believe that all A are B. What justification have we for dignifying this belief with cognitive status? It is not that we apprehended that the meaning of A includes the property B. Nor is it that our observations of AB's revealed a connexion between being an A and being a B, any more than seeing one pocket selected after another reveals the cause of that sequence. The plain fact is, as has been pointed out *ad nauseam,* that the only data we have are the conjunction of A and B in the observed instances.[15] And since our

---

[15] A generalization may, indeed, be supported by other data too, e.g., by other generalizations; hence its probability may be a function not alone of its own confirming instances. This fact however is not relevant to the basic problem we are considering.

belief goes beyond these data, they in isolation from all else are not sufficient for a cognitive justification of it.

In this situation there is only one alternative to skepticism. It is to assume that, though the existence of instances does not by itself entail either the truth or the probable truth of a lawful universal, there may be further conditions which, if known, would warrant belief in the universal, given the instances. Embracing this alternative, we inquire what these conditions are. What conditions, we ask, must be satisfied in order that some AB's may be evidence for "All A are B;" or what conditions do we presuppose are satisfied when we generalize? The answer is: The characterization of a particular by both A and B makes it probable that there is a connexion such that this conjunction of A and B is or results from a case of it. Nothing is evidence for anything else unless some instances of properties are connected with or determine others;[16] i.e., unless there are, as it were, biases in the world. Only if there is bias is an instance evidence for a generalization, or do additional instances increase the probability that they are due to a bias which grounds a stable uniformity or law.

Again our reasoning parallels reasoning in roulette. Assuming bias in the wheel, we take repetitions of sequences as evidence of further such repetitions. Assuming bias in nature, we take conjunctions of events or of properties as evidence of further such conjunctions. Just as the gambler devises a system which he believes expresses bias in the machine, so the scientist or any one of us devises a system which he believes expresses bias in nature. In formulating systems and in acting on them, the gambler, the scientist, and we alike presuppose that a Principle of Bias or a Principle of Induction is true of the subject matter—of the wheel, or of nature.

In terms of probability, we may state the argument this way: In order to pass from "All observed A's are B" to "Given these AB's, 'All A are B' is probable," we need a Principle of Induction, because the experiential report does not imply that the generalization is probable. A function of the Principle is to warrant the inference that it is probable; the Principle is therefore a condition of the soundness of the inference.

From this more or less informal argument for the view that generalization presupposes a Principle of Induction, I wish to proceed to state more precisely what I think the structure of generalization is. Let us begin with the commonly accepted proposition:

16 I do not imply that the connexion is directly between empirical properties or that A is by itself necessary or sufficient to B, or that the sufficient condition of an A's being a B resides in the nature of the particular they both characterize. Also, for my purpose it is not necessary to mention more specific conditions, e.g., finite limitation of variety, different types of connexion.

$$G/A_1B. . .A_nB = m,$$ P

in which I use Keynes's probability notation and in which G stands for "All A are B," and A_iB for an instance of G.[17] This proposition, which I shall call P, has been said to be deductively warranted. I do not believe that it is, if what is meant is that the probability of G may be deduced from a conjunction of instances. No proposition "$A_1B. . .A_nB$" entails " 'All A are B' is probable:" P is not analytic. The truth of P presupposes that the truth of an instantial proposition is evidence for the corresponding universal. It is analytic that if p is evidence for q, the truth or probability of p confers on q some probability; and it is by definition that A_iB is an instance of "All A are B;" but it is neither analytic nor by definition that A_iB is evidence for "All A are B." To imply that it is is a function of the Principle of Induction. It is, therefore, in virtue of it that instances make a generalization probable.

I suggest that the form of the argument is as follows, where PI stands for "Principle of Induction," and $\rightarrow$ is "entails:"

$$PI:\rightarrow:G/A_1B. . .A_nB = m \qquad (1)$$

By assumption: PI (2)

From (1) and (2) by the Principle
of Deductive Inference: $G/A_1B. . .A_nB = m.$ (3)

But (3) is not the terminus of the argument, for it is not an inductive conclusion. It is not an inductive conclusion because (a) the premises, $A_1B. . .A_nB$, need not exhaust the known data, (b) it refers to specific premises, and (c), due to this reference to premises, it cannot be confirmed or falsified.

The rejection of (3) as the inductive conclusion conflicts, at least verbally, with a position Broad took in his classic paper of 1918.[18] He showed that the addition of no premise to the instantial evidence for a generalization will avoid the formal fallacy of passing from "some" to "all" if the conclusion retains the form "All S are P." Then he argued that "If the validity of the process is to be saved at all it can only be saved by modifying the conclusion"[19] so that it becomes "It is highly probable on the observed data that all S's are P."[20] This change does, indeed, remove the illicit process; but as others have pointed out, it does so at the expense of replacing a conclusion that is subject to positive or negative verification, by one that is not: if the substituted conclusion is

---

[17] I shall use the notation "A_iB" and the word "instance" to stand for either a particular A that is B or a singular proposition "A_i is B," trusting to the context for unequivocalness.

[18] "On the Relation between Induction and Probability," *Mind*, N.S. XXVII, No. 108, October, 1918, pp. 389–404, and XXIX, No. 113, January 1920, pp. 11–45.

[19] *Ibid.*, p. 390.   [20] *Ibid.*, p. 391.

true, it is logically true. This probability conclusion recommended by Broad is, in fact, our proposition (3) or one closely resembling it.

We must then go on from (3) to a conclusion of the form "All *A* are *B*." This we can do by means of a Principle of Inductive Detachment having a function like that of the Principle of Detachment employed in deduction. In expressing this Principle I shall use two notions of probability; namely,

(1) A *relative* or dyadic one which is such that the expression "*p* is probable" is meaningless or else elliptical for "Given *q*, *p* is probable." This is the notion in (3).

And (2) a *non-relative* or monadic one which is such that "*p* is probable" is meaningful and complete. After stating the Principle, I shall elucidate this second meaning.

In the following statements of the Principle, the first "probable" is relative, the second, non-relative. If *p* is asserted and is our total evidence and if the probability of *q* on *p* is *m*, then the probability of *q* is *n*, where *n* is a function of *f* of *m*.[21] Applied to generalization, it is: If all observed *A* are *B* and if they constitute our evidence, and if the probability of *G* on this data is *m*, then the probability of *G* is *n*, where $n=f(m)$.

Clarification of the non-relative meaning of probability may be aided by comparing the syntax of its use with that of, for example, "reasonable." I may significantly say of a belief that it is reasonable, without giving or referring to reasons for it. Similarly, I may significantly say of a proposition that it is probable without giving or referring to evidence for it. In other words, "*p* is probable" is meaningful without being an abbreviation of an expression of the form, "On the evidence *q*, *p* is probable," just as "*x* is reasonable" is meaningful without being an abbreviation of an expression of the form, "Since *y* and *z* (called 'reasons') are the case, it is reasonable to believe *x*."

Further, just as I may be asked why I think that *x* is reasonable, with the expectation that I shall reply by giving reasons, so I may be asked why I think *p* is probable, with the expectation that I shall reply by giving evidence. But this does not entail that the meaningfulness of either "*x* is reasonable" or "*p* is probable" depends on my actually having reasons or evidence, or even on my believing that there are reasons or evidence. It is true however that "*x* is reasonable" implies that there are reasons supporting *x*. "*x* is reasonable" is inconsistent with "there are no reasons for *x*." Similarly "*p* is probable" implies that there is evidence for *p*, but it does not imply any specific evidence.

21 One might expect *n* to equal *m;* but since we lack a satisfactory analysis of either notion of probability, we can assert with confidence no more than that there is a close correspondence between their values: if *m* is high, or high compared to some other probability, then *n* is high, or high compared to that other probability.

One way to avoid confusing the non-relative with the relative meaning of "probability" would be to call the former "likelihood" and to restrict "probability" to the latter.

I have no doubt that this non-relative meaning is one we commonly employ in the practical conduct of our lives. When I advise taking an umbrella, explaining that likely it will rain, I am not asserting and am not intending to assert an *a priori* proposition which, if true, would be true by logical necessity and irrespective of the present state of the weather. If my practical wisdom is challenged, I might look again at the sky, and if it appears the same as before, I may try to make some calculations or to invoke an intuition of the value of the relation between my premises about the weather now and the proposition that it will rain. If, still convinced that I was right, I insist that it likely will rain, I am again dropping the premises and saying categorically that it likely will rain. I am allowing "likely" to continue to apply to the assertion after I have dropped a probability or evidential relation, one term of which is its premise, just as we allow "true" to continue to apply to a proposition after we have dropped an implicative relation, one term of which was its premise. Moreover the fact that I would look again at the sky when I reconsidered my judgment that it *would likely* rain shows that I did intend it to be corrigible, just as I should the assertion that it *will* rain.

As further evidence for the existence of a notion of probability not essentially involving premises, one could cite the frequency theories of probability. I should add however that the meaning I have in mind is not a frequency one. When I say that it likely will rain, I do not mean or imply that the limiting value of the terms of an infinite series is greater than one-half.

Our second meaning of probability and the Principle of Inductive Detachment which prescribes its use enable us to go on from (3) to an inductive conclusion of the form "All A are B." The following makes explicit this process and completes the outline of the argument:

Given: $A_1B. . .A_nB$ (4)

Given: (4) exhausts the relevant evidence (5)

From (3) (4) (5) by the Principle
of Inductive Detachment:[22] G is probable or likely to
degree n.[23] (6)

Further confirmation of G consists in adding new instances, $A_{n+1}B$,

[22] This step is, in fact, a two-fold operation, since in detaching the conclusion from the premises we change at the same time the meaning of "probability" from the notion in (3), which makes essential reference to premises, to the one in (6), which does not.

[23] As explained before, $n = f(m)$.

$A_{n + 2}B$, etc., to (4), thereby expanding the evidential part of (3) and increasing the value of m and of n. Or, more literally, with each new instance, the whole argument, (1) to (6), is replaced by another of the same form but constructed so that (5) is true.

The inductive conclusion is "All A are B." By virtue of (6) we may assert that it is probably true, without referring to premises, just as by virtue of a proposition's being the conclusion of a valid syllogism with true premises we may assert that it is true, without mentioning premises.

To what extent Broad would concur with the argument as I have sketched it, I do not know. My suggestion, however, that with each new instance the argument is replaced by another incorporating that instance in its premises does not seem irreconcilable with his explanation that "if I have observed n S's and they were all P it may be highly probable relative to these data that all S's are P and yet it may be false that all S is P. If I observe an $n+1$th S and it proves not to be P, I know that this does not alter the truth of the proposition that, relative to my first n observations, it is highly probable that all S is P. . . . Our original inductive conclusion does not cease to be *true,* it only ceases to be practically important."[24] Presumably Broad would say too that a conclusion based on $n + 1$ positive instances is of more practical importance than one based on n positive instances, or that the latter should in practice give way to the former. It seems then that his conception of the inductive argument is much like mine. He may say that the *argument* ends with (3), and then practice takes over. In that case I should add that the additional steps (4) to (6) are a formulation of the principles of that practice. This reference to practice suggests that (6) might be interpreted as, or as implying, "the degree of rational belief in G is n" or "the degree to which it would be rational to use G as one datum in guiding action is n."

One other aspect of Broad's treatment should be mentioned at this point; namely, his view that the addition of a premise about nature is necessary to justify induction by simple enumeration, though, as I said earlier, he denies that the addition of any premise is sufficient to save it from a formal fallacy. Whether he would introduce it into argument where I introduced the Principle of Induction—in steps (1) and (2)—I do not know, but that is trivial compared to the question whether it is needed.

In order further to clarify the nature of inductive inference I shall compare it with deduction and in this way bring out certain significant likenesses between them. (1) In any inferential situation there are (a) an evidential relation between propositions, and (b) a set of propositions,

24 *Op. cit.,* (note 18), p. 392.

at least one of which is asserted to be true or probably true. "Being true," or as I shall at times call it, "truth," is a relational property based on a relation T which is such that if a proposition p is true, then p is a referent of T and the ground of the truth of p is the corresponding relatum of T.[25]

(2) Deduction rests on a formal relation such as implication; and it employs a Principle of Inference, which has two functions: (a) To assert that, if a proposition p is true, then, if p implies q, q is true. It asserts, therefore, that implication is evidential: If p implies q, then p is evidence for q. In this role it is a Principle of Deduction. And (b) to authorize us to drop a true premise and to assert categorically what it implies. In this function it is a Principle of Deductive Detachment.

(3) Induction has a similar pattern, notwithstanding important differences. If p is inductive evidence for q, then there is an evidential relation R holding from p to q. Though pRq does not guarantee that q is true if p is true, it does imply that q has some probability if p has or if p is true. Since I shall continue to restrict myself to generalization, the only inductive evidential relation I shall consider is the relation of an instantial proposition to the corresponding universal proposition. I shall call this relation "instantiation." Accordingly, induction by generalization rests on the proposition that if p is an instance of q, then p is evidence for q; just as deduction rests on the proposition that if p implies q, then p is evidence for q. Thus instantiation in generalization corresponds to implication in deduction.

(4) The implicative relations of a proposition are essential to it. Whether propositions are related by implication can be determined by examining their structures and without knowledge of their truth-values. But, at least in the case of a contingent proposition, its truth-value is not essential to it, and cannot be determined without referring beyond it.

Now these two facts about a proposition, together with the Principle of Deductive Inference, result in the paradoxical situation of a relation guaranteeing that, if p has it to q and if p has the property truth, which is not essential to it, q will have the property truth, which likewise is not essential to it.[26] I shall call this characteristic of a relation "truth-conveyance." That implication has it is part of what the Principle of Deductive Inference asserts. This fact about implication may be known

[25] What we take T and the kind of relatum to be depends on our theory of truth.

[26] I restrict the range of q, as I did of p, to contingent propositions in order to avoid discussing such irrelevant and, I think, mistaken cases as a necessary proposition's being implied by every proposition.

a priori; nonetheless its explicit recognition is necessary to an understanding of deduction.

It should be noted too that as a consequence of its truth-conveying character and of the relation between truth and probable truth, implication conveys probable truth also. For if p implies q and if p is probably true to degree m, then q is probably true to a degee not less than m. Being truth-conveying is essential to any evidential relation.

(5) Instantiation, being evidential, is therefore truth-conveying too. It is not however identical with implication in this respect. Implication conveys to the implicate a probability not less than that of the implicans, whereas instantiation can do no more than convey to a generalization a probability less than that of the premise.

(6) In spite of the difference between these relations, their likeness reveals a close and important parallel between induction and deduction. Each rests on a formal truth-conveying relation. The proposition stating that implication is such a relation is a Principle of Deduction, and the proposition asserting that instantiation is such a relation is a Principle of Induction. Further, each kind of inference has its own Principle of Detachment.

(7) If there is a significant parallel between induction and deduction, one would expect that there would be a problem of deduction corresponding to the problem of induction. Such a problem is not commonly raised, but it can be defined: it is the problem of formulating and supporting the Principle of Inference. Since this principle has been formulated to the satisfaction of logicians and since it is accepted either as knowable *a priori* or as an axiom or postulate in a system, the "problem" of deduction appears to be a solved problem. Even if we grant this, we must not overlook the fact that the evidential character of implication rests on relations between the ground of p and the ground of q when p implies q and p is true, just as the evidential character of instantiation involves relations between the grounds of the terms involved.

In view of my position that there is a problem of induction, I want to comment on the charge frequently made today that those who think there is this problem are "deductionists." According to Professor Max Black a deductionist is one who desires, and would be satisfied by, a valid deductive argument going from self-evident first principles to the proposition that conclusions of inductive arguments are at least probable.[27] Mr. P. F. Strawson characterizes a deductionist as demanding "that induction shall be shown to be really a kind of deduction," or as demanding "that induction should be shown to be a rational process; and this turns out to be the demand that one kind of reasoning should be

[27] *Language and Philosophy,* p. 65.

shown to be another and different kind."[28] A deductionist seems then to be one who insists on judging inductive arguments by the standards of validity appropriate to deductive arguments; and who would, therefore, reject as invalid an inductive argument unless it is implemented, e.g., by adding a further premise or by changing the conclusion into a probability statement, so that it will satisfy deductive criteria.

This charge of deductionism is aimed quite generally at all who believe that there is a problem of induction and not, as one would expect, only at those who have confused induction with deduction or have tried to reduce the former to the latter. First I might make the obvious remark that even if everyone who has thought that there is a problem of induction has been a deductionist, it does not follow that there is no problem of induction. But what is much more important is that this charge diverts attention from the nature of induction instead of calling attention to those features of it that have worried philosophers not just since Hume but since they first distinguished between opinion and knowledge. Thus, induction is not a process of tracing relations between ideas but on the contrary is quite undeterred by a complete lack of such relations. It leaps indefinitely beyond the data, as if the given particulars were commissioned to speak for a universal law, or as if they themselves begat the future members of their kind. Nonetheless we must face the fact that in ordering our lives we have no alternative to trusting the inductive method. We do not demand guarantees that actions predicated on the results of the method will be successful; on the contrary, we should be grateful for some cognitive support of our belief that they will be. With respect to generalization, for example, we ask for no more than some assurance that if A's are characterized by B, there probably is a lawful universal of which they are instances. But speaking in terms of demands is misleading, for the problem is not to meet demands actually made. It is, from a logical point of view, to reveal, analyze, and state with clarity and precision the formal conditions on which the method rests; and from a philosophic point of view, to devise a theory such that if it were true, the argument would be sound. A philosopher cannot be expected to blind himself to the fact, however discomposing it may be, that the validity of the method depends on the truths of such a theory. Further, the fact that he searches for the validating conditions of induction or even that he introduces them as a premise into an inductive argument does not imply that he demands that induction be a kind of deduction or that it meet the standards of deduction. All it implies is that he wants to be able to show that induction is *sound*. We cannot

[28] *Introduction to Logical Theory*, p. 250.

blame him if it should turn out that the only criteria of *sound* argument are criteria of sound deductive argument.

Surely no set of propositions constitutes an argument except in virtue of connexions between them. A cognitive step from one to another can be warranted only by a relation such as entailment or by a constitutive principle grounded in the subject matter. The imagination may leap from one mountain top to another, but the intellect can make its way only by bridging every gap. When it cannot find at hand the necessary materials or premises, it substitutes principles, often of its own making but with confidence that they have a ground. If this demand for bridging is deductionism, then all intellection is deductionistic. Even if this is the case, we can discern the basic difference between intellection that is deductive and intellection that is inductive. It consists in different bridging materials or principles.

The Principle of Induction, which is a necessary condition of bridging the gap between particulars and universals or laws, may be formulated on two different levels: (a) A formal one, on which it states the formal conditions of induction; e.g., that variety is limited in certain ways, that certain series have limits, or that instantiation is evidential. And (b) a material one, on which it states in terms of descriptive characteristics what the world must be like in order that the formal conditions may hold; e.g., that events generate others in certain ways, that there are real connexions, or that change is grounded in development. The formal principle would be derivative from the material one and would have as its ground the facts expressed by the latter. We know from past attempts, that an exact and adequate formulation of either is complicated and difficult. Thus such statements as the Principles of the Universality of Causation and the Uniformity of Nature are unsatisfactory for several reasons, one being that they do not provide for certain probabilities required by the probability calculus. But improvements on them have been made, for instance, by Keynes and Broad; and I see no reason for believing that a satisfactory formulation is impossible. That we can criticize in detail proposed formulations for not doing all that is required of them, and that we can compare them with respect to adequacy, are presumptive evidence that we know what we are looking for. It will be more difficult to formulate the material principle than the formal one because the former not only must imply the latter but must be stated in terms of categories expressive of the unity and interconnexion presupposed by induction. The material principle will, therefore, be a metaphysical principle, and anyone trying to formulate it will have to face difficulties and problems of metaphysics. It is no wonder then that some philosophers have attempted to dispense altogether with a constitutive principle of induction.

Such a way out has been especially appealing to philosophers who have repudiated metaphysics and whose empiricism makes them suspicious of a need for and even the meaningfulness of a principle whose function seems to preclude the possibility of its being known. Modern logic teaches that an analytic principle could not fulfill the function of a Principle of Induction. On the other hand, if it were synthetic, presumably it could be known only by empirical inference, but such an inference would presuppose the Principle and hence would be a *petitio principii*. It is not surprising then that philosophers should doubt the basic assumptions of a view that requires a first principle whose function appears to them to rule out all possible grounds for belief in it. Facing this frustrating impasse, they easily convince themselves that the whole problem has been due to misjudging its nature, and in particular to construing the Principle of Induction as an assertion about the world and therefore as true or false. The problem of substantiating it would not have arisen if it had been interpreted as a rule or precept or policy of action, such as the following: If you want to discover laws of nature, use the inductive method because it is the one method by means of which it is possible to discover them. In recommending this rule they are not asserting that there are laws to be discovered, but that if there are any, the way of discovering them is using the inductive method.

My criticism of this attempt to circumvent the problem of induction, which I shall call the Precept Theory, will be two, viz.,

(1) Prescribing or following a rule of procedure is sensible only if there is reason to believe that following it will probably result in success; and any such reason will have to state or refer to factual conditions that ground and therefore validate the rule. Hence a minimal condition of the acceptibility of the maxim to generalize and keep on generalizing is some reason for believing that there are true general propositions to be discovered. The statement that there are true general propositions is true or false; hence the belief that a factual principle can be so readily avoided by substituting a rule is a sheer delusion.

(2) In presenting my next criticism, which will provide an opportunity of making explicit the need for antecedent probabilities in inductive argument, I shall again begin with the roulette example. We agree that if we knew that the wheel is honest, we should not counsel playing to win. But suppose that we have no evidence whether it is honest or not. In that case the advocate of the Precept Theory would advise: if you want to win, play and keep on playing, and lay your bets in accordance with past selections by the wheel; for if there is bias in it, sequences will

recur which will evidence its presence and be a clue to its nature. Bet, therefore, on recurrent selections.

Prima facie this seems to be reasonable advice, and indeed it may be, but *not* because of the argument given in support of it. This argument is based on the false premise that repetitions by themselves are sufficient to make it probable that they represent a bias of the wheel. A necessary condition of such a probability is, as we pointed out, earlier, that, independent of all occurrences of the sequence, it must be probable that the wheel is biased.

This argument sometimes appears in the following converted form: Given that the wheel is not biased, it is improbable that any specified sequence will be repeated oftener than any other of the same form; hence if one is repeated oftener than others, it is probable that the wheel is biased and that the given sequence represents the bias. The premise of this argument depends on the assumption that, if numbers are selected by an unbiased mechanism, any sequence is as probable as any other, and hence that the probability that each will occur as often as any other approaches *1* as the process of selection is indefinitely prolonged. This assumption follows from no experiential data. Independent of the results of previous inductive inferences employing it, we have no empirical reason for assuming that any sequence will be selected as often as any other. To argue that it will is, therefore, to argue either from ignorance or from a Principle of Indifference, which itself is a non-empirical principle of the kind the Precept Theory, if consistent, would reject.

The need for antecedent probability follows from principles of the probability calculus; e.g., from the following, in which G is a generalization and $I_1 . . . I_n$ are positive instances of G:[29]

$$G/I_1 . . . I_n.h = \frac{G/h}{I_1 . . . I_n/h}$$

The value of G/h is what we have called the antecedent probability of G: it is the probability of G on datum h but not on any of the data $I_1 . . . I_n$. Obviously, in order that the indicated fraction may have a value greater than *0*, or in order that any instance may support G, the value of G/h must be greater than *0*. This implies that there must be a supported proposition h such that G/h is probable. Accordingly, instances can make a generalization probable or increase its probability only if it has a probability independent of every one of them. And for it to have this probability there must be a proposition h capable of supplying it. Because the Precept Theory does not provide for h or for a Principle of

[29] This principle follows from the Multiplicative Axiom and the law that $I_i/G = 1$.

Induction which would imply h or underwrite a rule of induction, it makes an imposture of the maxim to generalize. It is no answer to point out that in a particular argument h may contain empirical propositions —e.g., other generalizations or theories—, for (1) the inference of them presupposed in the same way antecedent probabilities and hence $h's$ as premises, and (2) the argument in which these empirical propositions appear along with instances as data in support of G presupposes either (a) that G has an antecedent probability independent of them, or (b) that, given an instance, G is probable.[30] Alternative (b) rests on the non-empirical proposition that instantiation is evidential.

Thus we are led back again to the need for a principle in order to validate induction. And since, as Hume clearly saw, experience does not exhibit connexions or types of synthesis sufficient to ground such a principle, we are faced with the two alternatives, acceptance of a non-empirical principle or skepticism. Those of us who are not skeptics must pay the metaphysical price of our belief that we can learn from experience. That price on the formal level is, as we have repeatedly said, belief in some such principle as that series of relative frequencies approach limits or that independent variety is finite. Though such principles are not empirically verifiable or falsifiable, they are about orders of phenomena exclusively and can give us no more of an understanding of inductive inference than can the statement that a wheel is biased give us an insight into the basis of the bias. The ground of such statements about phenomena can reside only in some non-experiential matrix, just as the ground of the bias of a wheel must lie in the mechanism concealed from view. Consequently the philosophic desire for understanding can be satisfied only by a principle on the material level. It must be descriptive . of reality in terms of concepts that will not give rise all over again to the inductive problem, this time on the level grounding phenomenal orders. The skeptical consequences of the apparent unconnectedness of the data of experience cannot be removed by a theory supporting them by another plurality of unconnected elements. The categories of the theory, by being descriptive of the ground of experience, will be interpretative of experience. This becomes clearer when we remind ourselves that the problem of induction arises not with respect to uninterpreted experience, but on a level of highly organized and conceptualized experience: on the level of things, or enduring things; for example, of physical objects having qualities, standing in relations, and undergoing change. It is the level on which some series of events but not others are processes, on which uniformities and causal laws are discovered, and on which

---

[30] Simple transformations of the preceding formula will reveal antecedent probability factors other than the one we have referred to.

universal propositions are inferred. An inventory of such features found on this level would be very long indeed, and if systematized and reduced, would be a table of categories or of types of synthesis. They are not empirically observable characteristics but are modes of interpreting and synthesizing the given. It is only because experience is interpreted in terms of them that we are able to discern uniformities, generalize, or arrive at laws. It is therefore only on a categorized level that the problem of induction can arise. If we recall Broad's examples of problems resulting from synopsis, we shall see that the "facts," beliefs, and restrictive principles viewed together were all expressed in terms of such categories.

Similarly our parallel examples of generalization and roulette are on a categorized level. The AB's from which we generalize are assumed to be, or to be related to, instances of complex kinds—often natural kinds —having natures and dispositions: they are not just data. The roulette wheel is assumed to be a physical object, or system of physical objects; it has a history; it has a vast complex of properties; and it is such that it can be the ground of the kind of disposition we call a bias: it is not just the data we observe on its surface. Unless we believed it to be more than a momentary collection of unconnected data, the very thought of its having and continuing to have a bias would be nonsense. Precisely the same is true of the A's about which we generalize. Inductive inference takes place on a categorized level, and could not be valid unless it did so. Its function is to discover correlations, laws, relations of events, etc. on this level. The synthesizing categories underwrite it by being constitutive of the ground of the correlations, laws, etc. in such a way as to provide for the applicability of the probability calculus, for the ultimate antecedent probabilities indispensable to induction, and for the order of finiteness required if confirmation is to yield significantly large probabilities. These reflections reinforce my contention that the problem of induction is a metaphysical problem, not a problem of the kind appropriate to and solvable by a special science.

I am sure that all who have studied Broad's works would be most grateful for a statement of what he conceives the ground of general propositions or of laws to be, and of the relation of particulars to those generals of which they are instances. In view of his theory of time and of the relation between existence and becoming, and of his theory that processes, or the events that irreducibly constitute them, are the ultimate particulars, we should find especially interesting his conception of the types of synthesis involved in the fact that existence is continually augmented in such a way that each fresh slice continues the strands in the sum total of existence earlier than it and conforms to the formulae embodied in them. This continual augmentation, whether it is development, generation, or creation, must insure that the existentially new bears the image of the past, if prediction is to be possible.[31] The active generating of each new slice by its antecedents in their own form seems to be consistent with his theory that all it means to say that x has ceased to be present is that the sum total of existence has increased since the last phase of x. This view does not imply that any past event or process is dead or inactive, but only that it now stands in relations in which it did not when it was present. And since the *sense* of time is derivative from sheer increase of existence, the pastness of x implies no qualitative change in it. Hence if x is a process, and if the nature of a process includes "going on," then x goes on no matter how much existence has come into being since it became.

In the Preface to Volume II of his *Examination of McTaggart's Philosophy* Broad suggests that there may have been some changes in his theory of time since he wrote *Scientific Thought*. Still in the later work he emphasizes the ultimacy of becoming and implies that some past events exist at least for a short time, since events prehended in a specious present are, on his view, past. It is worth noting too that they are prehended as going on, not as embalmed in eternal quiescence. This theory of time and existence, though only one of many examples we could have chosen, is an excellent and intriguing one of how the problem of empirical knowledge inextricably involves metaphysical problems.

EVERETT J. NELSON

DEPARTMENT OF PHILOSOPHY
THE OHIO STATE UNIVERSITY

31 Also if inference of the past is to be possible.

2

Stephan Körner

BROAD ON PHILOSOPHICAL METHOD

THERE are at least two excellent reasons for examining C. D. Broad's writings on philosophical method. First, they are important as means of understanding the aims and results of his own thinking. Secondly, they are among the rare attempts which have been made at formulating clearly and systematically the methodological assumptions common to those who have made the movement known as Analytical Philosophy—in particular to its first leaders, namely Moore, Russell, and Broad himself.

Of the two parts of the present paper Part I will consist of a very brief synopsis of Broad's views as contained in (i) the article 'Critical and Speculative Philosophy' (*C.S.P.*); (ii) the introductory parts of the books *Scientific Thought (ST), The Mind and its Place in Nature (MPN)* and *An Examination of McTaggart's Philosophy (EMcP);* and (iii) the article 'Some Methods of Speculative Philosophy' (*M.S.P.*).* Although these writings cover a period of more than twenty years they are all in substantial agreement. In my summary of his views no more is intended than to recall them to the reader—perhaps also to enable him to trace some of my criticisms of them to misunderstandings.

Part II of the paper is critical. In particular, I shall argue that Broad does not distinguish between two different types of Philosophical Analysis, although their difference is of considerable methodological importance. I shall further argue that he ignores a similarly important distinction between different types of Speculative Philosophy or Metaphysics. Lastly, I shall try to show that if my objections to his account of Analytical and Speculative Philosophy are justified then his remarks on the relation between them stand in need of serious modification.

I

1. *Critical Philosophy.*

Without asserting that Critical or Analytical Philosophy and Speculative Philosophy or Metaphysics can be wholly separated from each

* For details concerning the publication of these works see the bibliography at the end of the volume.

other, Broad regards them as "two very different subjects" which "are pursued by different methods, and can expect to reach quite different degrees of certainty" (*C.S.P.*, 82). Critical Philosophy according to him has two tasks, namely (1) "to analyse and define the concepts which are used in daily life and the special sciences" (*C.S.P.*, 83) and (2) to take the fundamental propositions "which we uncritically assume in science and in daily life and to subject them to criticism" (*C.S.P.*, 84). Examples of concepts in need of philosophical analysis are 'number' and 'thing;' examples of propositions needing analysis are 'Every change has a cause,' 'nature obeys uniform laws.' Philosophical Analysis and Analysis as it occurs in the special sciences differ in their subject matter rather than in their methods and there are border-line cases between Philosophical and Scientific Analysis (see *M.S.P.*, 1).

Broad lays down "two useful general methods" in critical philosophy which he calls the *Principle of Exceptional Cases* and the *Principle of Pickwickian Senses* (*C.S.P.*, 90). According to the former it is "enormously important" to see how a commonly used concept, the meaning of which is to be clarified, applies to exceptional and abnormal cases. The principle has been familiar to philosophers at least since the time of Socrates. Broad not only formulates it clearly and uses it throughout his philosophical work; he is also the first analytical philosopher to show that the data of parapsychology constitute an important field for the application of the Principle of Exceptional Cases (see e.g. *MNP*, Preface, etc.).

An example of the application outside philosophy of the second principle, that of Pickwickian Senses, is the analysis of irrational numbers by certain classes of rational numbers; another, taken from theology, is found in Aquinas's account of the Trinity. The principle has, as Broad points out, been carried over by Russell and Whitehead into philosophy. A classical example of its use in Analytical Philosophy is Whitehead's method of extensive abstraction in defining points, moments, etc. (*C.S.P.*, 93).

2. *Speculative Philosophy.*

The aim of Speculative Philosophy according to Broad is to reach "general conclusions as to the nature of the Universe, and as to our position and prospects in it" (*ST*, 20). He distinguishes two main conceptions. of Speculative Philosophy, namely deductive and non-deductive metaphysics.

A system of deductive metaphysics is, or rather would be, one in which "important results about the structure of Reality as a whole" are reached "by deductive arguments from self-evident premises" (*C.S.P.*,

98). It is thus not its deductive order but the nature of its premises which characterises a deductive system as a deductive metaphysics. Broad has always held that the known attempts at constructing such a system have been unsuccessful, e.g. those of Spinoza, Leibniz or McTaggart. In his first methodological paper (*C.S.P.*, 98) he did admit the theoretical possibility of deductive metaphysics. Even this he now denies, his reason being that "the procedure which the example of Euclidean geometry encouraged philosophers to adopt, and the hopes which its spectacular success aroused in them, were based on serious though very natural misunderstandings." (*M.S.P.*, 30).

Non-deductive metaphysics, of which Broad gives as examples Whitehead's and Alexander's philosophical works, is the outcome—though not the deductive outcome—of "taking over the results of the various sciences, adding to them the results of the religious and ethical experiences of mankind, and of reflecting on the whole" (*ST*, 20). In order to understand the logical nature and function of non-deductive Metaphysics it is necessary to ask by what kind of proposition its results are expressed. Broad would seem to have two definite suggestions to make here.

According to one a metaphysical system might consist of empirical propositions. It could be given the form of a deductive system; and then it might be "as simple in its premises, as rigid in its reasoning, and as startling in its conclusions as Euclidean geometry. . . ." (*M.S.P.*, 30). Such a system would differ from scientific hypothetico-deductive systems at most in its degree of generality or comprehensiveness. This is certainly not deductive Metaphysics in Broad's usual sense of the term and hardly Metaphysics in the traditional sense.

According to the other suggestion all, or at least some, metaphysical propositions e.g. 'Every change has a cause,' 'All sensa are appearances,' are Postulates. They are Postulates in the sense that (a) "every one acts *as if* he believed them, and inevitably goes on acting as if he believed them. . . ." and (b) "it is certain that they do not appear self-evident on reflection; that they cannot be deduced by self-evident steps from premises which are self-evident; and that they cannot be defended by probable reasoning except on the assumption that they have a finite initial probability." (*MPN*, 217).

Broad's Postulates are neither empirical nor *a priori* propositions, i.e. propositions which are necessary *and* are recognised by us as necessary (*C.S.P.*, 87). In distinguishing between *a priori*, empirical and postulated propositions Broad rejects the Humean and logical empiricist dichotomy of propositions into those which are analytic and *a priori* and those which are synthetic and *a posteriori*. The function of his Postulates is conceived to be similar to that of Kant's synthetic *a priori* principles of which they may seem to be a pragamatist version. The logical structure of the Postulates is apparently not clear to Broad. He finds them "extremely puzzling" (*C.S.P.*, 86). He inclines however to the view that "some of the postulates may really be necessary principles which only fail to be counted as *a priori* because we cannot see their necessity" (*C.S.P.*, 88).

Although all philosophical thinking involves Analysis, Synopsis, and Synthesis, Broad finds a high degree of Synopsis and Synthesis to be specifically characteristic of Speculative Philosophy. Synopsis he describes as "the deliberate viewing together of aspects of human experience which are generally viewed apart, and the endeavour to see how they are interrelated" (*M.S.P.*, 4). As an example he instances the Synopsis of the phenomena of normal and abnormal visual perception and the corresponding physical, psychological and physiological facts. Another example is the Synopsis of normal phenomena and paranormal.

The importance of Synopsis for Philosophical Analysis had already found expression in Broad's Principle of Exceptional Cases. Synopsis, moreover, is presupposed by Synthesis which has for its purpose to supply "a set of concepts and principles which shall cover satisfactorily all the various regions of fact which are being viewed synoptically" (*M.S.P.*, 16). Synopsis and Synthesis take place at various levels at each of which the results of previous Syntheses have to be reviewed and often modified (see *M.S.P.*, 19 and *MPN*, 7).

Though it is not possible to give rules for the discovery of principles of Synthesis, speculative philosophers have in fact followed certain recognisable methods. Broad notes a practice of extending explanatory principles beyond the region or regions in which they had been found satisfactory to others in which they had not seemed obviously applicable. Aristotle's concepts of matter and form are used as an illustration of this method (*M.S.P.*, 21ff). He further emphasises again the fruitfulness of the Principles of Exceptional Cases and of Pickwickian Senses—this time not in Analytical but in Speculative Philosophy. Lastly he mentions two frequent types of Synthesis calling the one *Reduction* "which tries to show that the features which are characteristic of the higher levels [of the apparent hierarchy of fact] are analyzable without remainder into those which belong to the lower levels;" and naming *Sublimation* the other type, that "which tries to show that the features which seem to be peculiar to the higher levels are really present in a latent or a specially simplified or a degenerate form at the lower levels" (*M.S.P.*, 26).

Acceptance or rejection of a metaphysical system is the result, according to Broad, of a "total reaction" on our part, as are "our judgments on a person's character or on the expediency of a policy of action." It is thus "greatly at the mercy of subjective conditions." (*M.S.P.*, 28). This, however, does not imply that we can do nothing about it. We can "recognize and allow for sources of irrational bias" (*loc. cit.*).

3. *The relation between Critical and Speculative Philosophy.*

The legitimate dependence of Critical on Speculative Philosophy is in Broad's view very slight. The critical philosopher, as indeed every inquirer, must assume "that our minds are so far in accord with the rest of Reality that by using them carefully and critically we approach nearer to the truth" (*C.S.P.*, 96). This assumption, although it perhaps justifies the pursuit of Critical Philosophy, is of no use within it since it does not help us when choosing between alternative, perhaps incompatible, results of our analytical philosophising.

Broad expresses another more specific, and therefore, more effective speculative presupposition of Critical Philosophy which, though typical of his own method and G. E. Moore's, does not seem to me characteristic of all Critical Philosophy. We might call it the speculative principle of common-sense. Broad formulates it by saying that a philosophical theory must not be "silly," i.e. such that it "may be held at the time when one is talking or writing professionally, but which only an inmate of a lunatic asylum would think of carrying into daily life" (*MPN*, 5).

Although the *legitimate* influence of a person's Speculative on his Critical Philosophy is considered to be negligible, Speculative Philosophy may nevertheless have certain beneficial "collateral effects" on those who pursue it. Its pursuit strengthens the habit of synopsis—a habit which must be possessed by the Analytical philosopher if he is to observe the Principle of Exceptional Cases. Broad's commendation of Speculative Philosophy resembles that of an agnostic historian who praises the Society of Friends on the ground that its institutions tend to strengthen democratic habits.

Yet Speculative Philosophy may corrupt one's philosophical analyses since "we sometimes do our Critical Philosophy with half an eye on our Speculative Philosophy, and accept or reject beliefs, or analyse concepts in a certain way, because we feel that this will fit in better than any alternative with the view of Reality as a whole that we happen to like" (*ST*, 21). The explicit or implicit appeal to metaphysical principles in order to decide between alternative analyses is thus considered not only avoidable but mistaken. Indeed it seems fair to say that on Broad's view Analytical or Critical Philosophy is independent of Speculative Philosophy or Metaphysics to the extent that a change in a person's metaphysical standpoint does *not* commit him to a modification of his critical philosophy.

Speculative Philosophy is by no means regarded as similarly indepen- dent of the Critical. On the contrary: if Speculative Philosophy is to be "of the slightest use it must presuppose Critical Philosophy. It is useless to take over masses of uncriticised detail from the sciences and from the ethical and religious experiences of men. We do not know what they mean, or what degree of certainty they possess till they have been clarified and appraised by Critical Philosophy" (*ST*, 20). How great is the de- pendence of Speculative on Critical Philosophy in Broad's view may be judged from his admitting that possibly "the time for Speculative Philosophy has not yet come; for Critical Philosophy may not have ad- vanced far enough to supply it with a firm basis" (*loc. cit.*). And how small in his view is the dependence of Critical on Speculative Philosophy may be judged from the fact that he has not the slightest doubt about the assured position of Critical Philosophy, whether or not the time for Speculative has arrived; or, we may perhaps add, whether or not it is ever to arrive.

II

1. *Critical Philosophy.*

Critical Philosophy concerns itself both with concepts and proposi- tions. About the criticism of propositions Broad says little more than that it is dependent on the analysis of concepts and that it further con- sists in exposing the criticised propositions "to every objection that we can think of ourselves or find in the writings of others" (*C.S.P.*, 85). This is a general description of sound practice and does not give rise to special problems. Broad's account of the analysis of concepts on the other hand does raise difficulties which, as I shall try to show, are connected with his failure to distinguish between two very different types of Analysis. I propose to call them "analysis by the exhibition of meanings or rules" (briefly: "exhibition-analysis") and "analysis by the replacement of meanings or rules" (briefly: "replacement-analysis").

Exhibition-analysis of concepts could, very roughly speaking, be de- scribed as the exhibition of their meanings. Yet, although the points which will be raised can all be made in terms of the notoriously vague phrase "meaning of concepts," I shall nevertheless prefer to speak in terms of "rules governing the use of signs as concepts." Indeed what makes a sign a conceptual sign is its being used by a person in accord- ance with certain rules accepted by him. Some concept-governing rules cannot be clearly distinguished from other types of rule. But there are clear and uncontroversial instances: for example, the rules governing the assignment or refusal of colour-words to things; or the rules governing the use of the sign <prime-number> in a mathematical treatise.

Exhibition-analysis, then, consists in exhibiting the rules which we or other people, have accepted for the use of concepts or, more precisely, of signs as concepts. It does not, and often could not, make explicit *all* the rules governing a concept, but only those or some of those which are relevant to the philosophical purpose in hand. In the present context the most important characteristic of exhibition-analysis is the negative one that it does not involve any modification of the rules which it exhibits. In the vaguer terminology of "meanings of concepts" we should say that it does not involve any modification of the exhibited meanings. Here, as elsewhere, translation from the more to the less precise manner of speaking is easily achieved. Being easily repeatable, it will not be repeated.

It is fairly obvious that a person may be perfectly capable of conforming to a complicated set of concept-governing rules and yet not able to formulate these rules or to notice their interrelations. For example, most people conform to the rules governing colour-predicates although few among them could formulate the rules to which they conform. Indeed it is arguable, to say the least, that logicians who do not acknowledge the difference between the relation of determinable to determinate and that of class to subclass have failed to effect an exhibition-analysis of colour predicates.

We may perform an exhibition-analysis, *i.e.*, exhibit the rules which have in fact been accepted for the use of concepts, either indirectly or by the direct formulation of the rules in question. An example of the indirect method would be to indicate synonyms. Another would be to state entailments; for if a concept, say 'Q,' which is known to be governed by a rule, say 'r,' is entailed by another concept say 'P,' then the statement that 'P' entails 'Q' indicates that 'P' is governed by the rule 'r' among others. Incidentally, the last example shows that not every exhibition-analysis would be regarded as a definition in any of the usual senses of that term.

It may happen—it often does happen—that as a result of exhibition-analysis we recognise ambiguities, contradictions and other defects in the rules which we have accepted. On the other hand it may reveal to us that we suspected defects where there were none, in which case it may even remove philosophical perplexity. But in any case, although exhibition-analysis may improve our knowledge of the rules which we have accepted, it is never its business to improve or modify these rules.

Often, if perhaps not always, the practice of Analytical philosophers goes beyond exhibition-analysis. It involves *replacement-analysis, i.e.,* the replacement of one set of rules for the use of sign as a concept, by another one—a hitherto accepted set by a new set. More briefly, though less precisely, we may say that it involves the replacement of one concept by another. Not every such replacement is, of course, regarded as an analysis. To deserve this title two conditions must be fulfilled. *First,* the analysing concept and the concept analysed must stand in a specific relation to one another, a relation which justifies us in speaking of analysis at all. Nobody would consider, *e.g.,* the replacement of 'horse' by 'elephant' as an analysis. What kind of analysing- or replacement-relation is required will vary from one analytical philosopher to another. Examples are various kinds of bilateral implication, and in many cases no more than a resemblance, more or less clearly qualified, between the analysed and the analysing concepts. In this last group belong the cases of analysing vague concepts by exact, and internally inconsistent concepts by such as are internally consistent.

In this connection we may note that to demand the synonymity of analysing concept and analysed restricts all analysis to exhibition-analysis. If two signs say $<P>$ and $<Q>$ are used synonymously, then the rules governing them differ *only* in the signs which they govern. But this is to say that the two signs are used for one and the same concept. Philosophers who feel inclined to require synonymity as their analysing relation and who yet feel that this requirement is too strong to be useful for their purposes prefer, following Carnap, to call their kind of replacement-analysis, "explication" rather than "analysis."

Secondly, the analysed concept must stand in need of replacement. It must have defects from which the analysing concept is free. Some features, such as internal inconsistency or a high degree of ambiguity, are almost always considered defects of concepts, but there are others, such as incompatibility with certain scientific or metaphysical doctrines, which are defects for some analytical philosophers and not for others. Few have formulated exact criteria of satisfactoriness and defectiveness in concepts, and thus of when there is need for replacement-analysis, and when there is not. Exact formulations of the analysing relations required, and thus criteria of the success of the replacement-analysis, are equally rare.

We may turn for an example of a replacement-analysis to Broad's account of sense-perception and matter (*e.g.,* in *MPN,* chapter IV). After a careful exhibition of the rules which are normally accepted for the use of the concept 'physical object,' he replaces some of them by others. The main defect of the analysed concept is said to be that it misdescribes the perceptual situations which it is meant to characterise. As regards the analysing relation required for a satisfactory replacement-analysis we may perhaps say generally of Broad that he requires between the rules for the analysing and those for the analysed concept, the highest possible resemblance which is compatible with the removal of the latter's defects. From his discussion of the alternative theories (*loc. cit.*, 157ff) may be gleaned some further information about his criteria both for the defectiveness of concepts and for satisfactory analysing relations.

Before pointing to the more or less obvious differences between exhibition- and replacement-analysis it is worth while emphasising that they are neither of them "verbal" in any sense in which the use of the term implies an accusation of triviality. They are verbal in the sense of exhibiting or replacing rules governing the use of words or other signs, not in the sense that the satisfiability of the rules with which they are concerned depends on arbitrary choice. A person may choose to accept certain rules for the use of a sign, say <green> or <chair> or <cause>; but the capacity of these rules to be satisfied by him does not depend merely on his having accepted them; it depends also on features of the world whose existence or nonexistence is not at all in his choice. Broad illustrates this point from Cantor's replacement-analysis of the concept of continuity (*ST*, 17).

The particular difference between exhibition- and replacement-analysis with which all the other differences are connected, is of course, that between exhibiting accepted rules and replacing or modifying them. One reason why this has been overlooked lies in the fact which we have noted already, that the practice of most analytical philosophers involves both types of analysis, the exhibition of rules frequently paving the way for their modification. Another reason lies in the inclination of philosophers to consider some of the rules which govern a concept to be essential and the rest accidental; and consequently to consider only a change in the essential rules as a change in the concept. I think that Broad shows this inclination when he distinguishes between the analysis of a certain concept and the concept itself. (*C.S.P.*, 95). If, to take his example, William James and his opponents disagree about the analysis of 'consciousness' they do accept different concepts, although they will *to some extent* have the same content or be governed by the same rules. To regard the common content of these different concepts as *the* concept and to distinguish it from its analysis is not necessarily a harmful terminological choice. If, however, it obscures the difference between the two kinds of analysis then it is better avoided. There are contexts in which the difference may be important.

Of Broad's "two useful general methods" in Critical Philosophy (*C.S.P.*, 90) only the Principle of Exceptional Cases is applicable in both exhibition- and replacement-analysis. Thus if we are engaged in ex-hibiting the rules governing a concept, say '*P*,' and if *b* is a marginal or abnormal instance of '*P*,' then the question "is *b* a *P*?" might indeed force our attention to rules governing '*P*' which we might otherwise fail to notice. In a similar manner we might be helped by asking "is *b* a *Q*?" —where '*Q*' is considered as a possible analysing concept for '*P*.'

The Principle of Pickwickian Senses on the other hand is quite in-applicable in exhibition-analysis since it involves a modification of the rules which govern the analysed concepts. The purpose of its application is to improve not, or not only, our knowledge of the analysed concepts but the concepts themselves, that is to say to replace them by others.

This is perhaps the place to mention certain more specific differences between exhibition and replacement-analysis. To emphasize these dif-ferences will prepare us for the discussion of Broad's account of the re-lation between Critical and Speculative Philosophy. *First*, a problem in exhibition-analysis has always one correct answer and never more than one. A problem in replacement-analysis on the other hand may have more than one correct solution, and again it may have none.

Clearly, if we ask what the rules are which have in fact been accepted by a certain person or group of persons for the use of a sign as a concept, the correct answer must consist in indicating these rules and no others— whatever their real or alleged virtues or defects. The rules may be self-contradictory, ambiguous, too vague or otherwise unfitted to some de-sirable purpose; still they must be formulated as they actually are if our exhibition-analysis is to be correct. In the unlikely event of a sign, sup-posedly governed by certain rules, being in fact not governed by any, the correct exhibition-analysis would consist in stating this.

We have no right to assume a similar uniqueness of solution in every problem of replacement-analysis. Whether such a problem has one, more than one, or no solution, depends on the criteria of defectiveness in a concept which are accepted and on the analysing relation. It is easy to think of groups of problems with no solution. If, for instance, we regard the internal inconsistency of a concept as a defect, and if one of the usual bilateral implications happens to be our analysing relation, then no internally inconsistent concepts can be analysed. Other examples— less trivial ones—of unsolvable problems in replacement-analysis will be readily thought of. As a matter of fact, if, for the accepted criteria of defectiveness and the analysing-relation, a certain group of problems be recognised to have no solution, this state of affairs often leads to the re-laxation of the criteria. This happens all the more easily if the original requirements have not been too explicit.

It seems equally clear that a problem in replacement-analysis can—for a certain type of concept, for suitable criteria of defectiveness and for a suitable analysing relation—have more than one correct solution. If the analysing philosopher becomes aware of the multiplicity of possible solutions, and if he tends to think that every problem in Analytical Philosophy should have only one, he will be inclined to make the conditions of solution stricter. Since every problem in exhibition-analysis has one and only one solution, a philosopher who does not clearly distinguish between exhibition and replacement is quite likely to hold that every problem in philosophical analysis has one and only one solution.

I do not think that Broad anywhere discusses in a general way the question of the uniqueness of solutions or otherwise. It is my impression that for him there is ultimately only one correct analysis. He seems to hold that even if in the early stages of analysis a number of alternative analyses may appear equally correct, their number decreases with the widening of the region of thought which is subject to analysis until in the end only one possibility is left.

So far I have spoken of the possibility of equally correct solutions of a problem in replacement-analysis for one set of criteria of the defectiveness of concepts and one set of admitted analysing relations. Since these conditions change from philosopher to philosopher the number of alternative solutions also changes. It is indeed obvious that a question which has no answer for one philosophical analyst may have embarrassingly many for another.

A *second* difference between the two types of analysis will again turn out to be relevant to Broad's account of the relation between Critical and Speculative Philosophy. It is a difference in autonomy. Exhibition-analysis is autonomous in a sense in which replacement-analysis is not. The aim of the former is by every available means to find out which rules are in fact accepted for the use of the concept or concepts in question—by oneself or by somebody else. The success of our inquiry and the correctness of its result depends on empirical evidence and on no other conditions. In a replacement-analysis *the assumption which is not called in question* when we try to find out whether a certain defective concept is analysed by some other one which is not defective, is that certain criteria of defectiveness and a certain analysing relation have been accepted. Without this our replacement-analysis would be less than pointless: we could not possibly be engaged in it. The acceptance of some criteria and some analysing relation is a logical *conditio sine qua non* of any replacement-analysis; and the acceptance of particular criteria and a particular analysing relation is the logical precondition of a particular type of replacement-analysis.

A *third* difference between the two types of analysis, which is worth accentuating, lies in the kind of proposition which they respectively establish. Exhibition-analysis results in empirical propositions. Indeed the statement that a certain rule of conceptual thinking has been accepted by a group of people is just as clearly empirical as is, *e.g.*, the anthropological statement that a certain society has accepted a particular code of laws. Replacement-analysis on the other hand results in logical propositions, to the effect that *if* certain criteria of defectiveness are accepted and if a certain relation is chosen as analysing relation, then necessarily a certain concept, say '*P*' is analysed by a certain other concept, say '*Q*.' The antecedent of the hypothetical proposition is usually not explicitly formulated. The case is analogous to that of mathematical propositions formulated without reference to, and often without any clear awareness of, the postulates from which they logically follow.

To some extent replacement-analysis presupposes exhibition-analysis. Without it the deliberate modification which is involved in replacement-analysis would be indistinguishable from more or less unnoticed changes in our habits of conceptual thinking. Exhibition analysis without replacement-analysis is at least theoretically possible. And yet—as I believe —even the most austere exhibition-analyst will in fact hardly avoid modifying the rules which he merely intends to exhibit.

The work of analytical philosophers shows great differences in the degree to which the two types of analysis are represented. These differences are often reflected in their conception of Analytical Philosophy. Russell, and those who hold that *Principia Mathematica* or a similar formalism are the proper language of philosophy, are naturally driven to replacement-analysis—in particular, replacement of "vague" or "prescientific" concepts by "precise" or "scientific" ones. Russell's remarks on the method of logical constructions[1] amount to the thesis that philosophical analysis, and indeed all scientific Philosophy, is a special kind of replacement-analysis. The same is true of Carnap's remarks on explication.[2]

Analytical philosophers who are wont to expect to remove philosophical perplexities, not by improving ordinary language, but by understanding its function better, tend to concentrate on exhibition-analysis. They tend to agree with Wittgenstein's dictum that "philosophy may in no way interfere with the actual use of language; it can in the end only describe it."[3] For different reasons Moore too regards philosophical analysis, or rather the analysis practised by himself, as exhibition-analysis of a rather more restricted kind. This is clear from

---

1 See *e.g.*, *Mysticism and Logic* (London, 1918), pp. 155ff.
2 See *e.g.*, *Logical Foundations of Probability* (Chicago, 1950), pp. 3ff.
3 *Philosophical Investigations* (Oxford, 1953), p. 49e.

his requirement that "any expression which expresses the *analysandum* must be synonymous with any expression which expresses the *analysans*."[4] It is confirmed by his refusal to accept a Pickwickian sense of any expression as part of its analysis.[5]

2. *Speculative Philosophy.*

About the logical status of those propositions which express the results of the philosophical analysis of concepts, there is, as I have argued, hardly a problem. Exhibition-analysis results in empirical, replacement-analysis in logical propositions. Following Broad's classification of propositions into *a priori*, *a posteriori*, and Postulates, we should say that exhibition-analysis results in *a posteriori*, and replacement-analysis in *a priori* propositions, *i.e.*, propositions which are necessary and are recognised as such by us—either directly or by deduction from propositions which are themselves directly recognised as necessary. The position is notoriously quite different if we turn to the alleged propositions of Speculative Philosophy or Metaphysics.

As regards their logical status the following views—not mutually exclusive—may be held, and as a matter of historical fact have been held by philosophers: (1) Some or all of the alleged metaphysical propositions are more or less disguised *a priori* propositions. Many philosophical system-builders, *e.g.*, Spinoza, believed in the possibility of an *a priori* metaphysics. (2) Some or all of the alleged metaphysical propositions are more or less disguised *a posteriori* propositions. The conception of an *a posteriori* Metaphysics is implied by some statements of Brentano[6] and of Samuel Alexander.[7] (3) Some or all of the alleged metaphysical propositions, although neither *a posteriori* nor *a priori* are nevertheless indicative propositions (true-or-false). The difference between indicative and non-indicative might be explained by pointing out that of two incompatible indicative propositions only one can be true and one must be false, whereas of two incompatible non-indicative propositions, *e.g.*, two incompatible rules, neither can be true or false. The propositions which Kant regarded as theoretically, but not practically, empty would, if his account of them be accepted, belong to an indicative Metaphysics which yet is neither *a posteriori* nor (in Broad's sense) *a priori*. (4) Some or all of the alleged metaphysical propositions are not indicative propositions being either (a) non-indicative propositions or (b) not propositions at

4 Schilpp (ed.), *The Philosophy of G. E. Moore* (New York, 195★), p. 773.
5 See *e.g.*, *Philosophical Studies* (London, 1922), pp. 190ff.
6 See *e.g.*, *Über die Zukunft der Philosophie* (Leipzig, 1929), 137, also 30.
7 See *e.g.*, Introduction to *Space, Time, and Deity* (London, 1920).

all. The view that Metaphysics is not indicative or non-propositional is represented in many variants of logical positivism and pragmatism.

Broad does not consider an *a priori* Metaphysics possible. Neither does he hold that some metaphysical principles are disguised *a posteriori* propositions.[8] I know of no good reason against the elimination of these possibilities. If they are not eliminated we are left with the alternative, either (a) some or all of them are indicative propositions of some other kind or (b) they are not indicative propositions at all. Broad admits both possibilities.

He certainly holds that some alleged metaphysical propositions, *e.g.*, the principle of causality, are Postulates; and Postulates—though neither *a priori* nor *a posteriori*—are in his opinion indicative. If this were not so he could hardly assert that "everyone acts *as if* he believed them" (*MPN*, 217); and he could not without inconsistency conjecture that "some of the postulates may really be necessary principles which only fail to be counted as *a priori* because we cannot see their necessity" (*C.S.P.*, 88).

Yet Broad's methodological writings also contain frequent remarks which clearly imply that in his view some alleged metaphysical principles are not indicative propositions. Thus he compares our approval of a system of Speculative Philosophy to "our judgments on a person's character or on the expediency of a policy of action" and even asserts that in the end one "will have to recognise that certain types of philosophical theory are, as the vulgar would say, 'not his cup of tea'" (*M.S.P.*, 28). This is surely not the way to talk about indicative propositions. Again he admits that a metaphysical system might be "merely the expression of [one's] personal reaction to life" (*EMcP*, Preface). Such a metaphysical system would then be—like a musical composition—not only non-indicative but also non-propositional.

Broad does not explicitly formulate the distinction between an indicative Metaphysics consisting of Postulates and a non-indicative Metaphysics. Yet his views on the Postulates—and thus on the metaphysical principles which are Postulates—are expressed with great clarity. It is in this connection worth remembering that he does not claim to have given a satisfactory account of their logical status (*C.S.P.*, 86).

About the logical status of those alleged metaphysical principles which, being neither *a priori, a posteriori* or Postulates, are not indicative, we are left much more in the dark. Some of them are certainly not propositions, and this seems to be Broad's view of all alleged meta-

---

[8] In part I a passage (*M.S.P.*, p. 30) has been mentioned in which he calls a system of *undisguised* empirical propositions "Metaphysics." The only problem raised by this passage concerns the advisability of using the term in this sense.

physical propositions which are not Postulates. I shall nevertheless argue
that by his account of the methods of Speculative Philosophy and, even
more by his account of the methods of Critical Philosophy he is committed to the recognition of a regulative Metaphysics, that is to say to
the view that some alleged metaphysical principles are rules or regulative
propositions.

It is according to him the purpose of Synthesis, the main characteristic
of Speculative Philosophy, "to supply a set of concepts and principles
which shall cover satisfactorily all the various regions of fact which are
being viewed synoptically" (*M.S.P.*, 16). Broad explains in some detail
what he means by the term "satisfactorily covers" (*loc. cit.*). For our
purpose it is necessary to reflect for a moment on what is meant by
"supplying" concepts. To supply a concept is not to apply it. It is rather
(a) to exhibit in a more or less detailed manner the rules governing it,
(b) to show that it has certain needed characteristics, *e.g.*, that "it covers
various regions of fact," and (c) to recommend the acceptance of the
concept (*i.e.*, the rules governing it) in preference to its rejection or to
the acceptance of other concepts which lack the characteristics possessed
by it.

To recommend that a concept, say '*P*,' be accepted, *i.e.*, to recommend
the rules governing it, is *not* to analyse it. The recommendation is quite
different from the empirical statement that somebody as a matter of
fact has accepted these rules; and equally, it is different from the logical
statement that if certain criteria of defective concepts and a certain
analysing relation be accepted, then the concept '*P*' stands in such a
relation to another concept say '*Q*.' The supply of concepts involved in
Speculative Philosophy is thus neither exhibition—nor replacement-
analysis. It is recommendation of regulative propositions.

Apart from recommending the acceptance or rejection of rules governing the use of specific concepts—an example could be a certain
concept of causation—the Speculative Philosopher is also a recom-
mender of more general rules. Consider, for example, a metaphysician
who argues in favour of what Broad calls (*M.S.P.*, 26) a "reductive"
unification of that *prima facie* hierarchy of fact whose lowest level is
inorganic matter and whose highest level is man. Here, I do not think
that Broad would wish to assert that the alleged metaphysical principles
of a reductive Metaphysics are indicative propositions: they are hardly
a posteriori and they are certainly not *a priori*, nor are they Postulates
with regard to which "everyone acts *as if* he believed them" (*MPN*, 217).
Neither do I think that he would wish to hold that they are not propositions at all—intellectual nonsense. Between these alternatives lies the
possibility of their being regulative propositions. On this footing we

must regard the reductive metaphysician as recommending that a set of concepts be not accepted unless none of them is applicable exclusively to particulars belonging to a higher level of the apparent hierarchy of fact.

A stronger reason for regarding Broad—and indeed every practitioner of replacement-analysis—as committed to the recognition of a regulative Metaphysics lies in his account of philosophical analysis. Replacement-analysis, in which the Principle of Pickwickian Senses is observed, presupposes that the Analytical Philosopher accepts certain criteria of defectiveness and certain relations as analysing relations. It presupposes, in other words, the acceptance of regulative propositions to the effect that such concepts (such concept-governing rules) as have a certain characteristic, say a certain type of inexactness, should be rejected; and that they should, where possible, be replaced by concepts (concept-governing rules) free from this defect, provided that the replacing and the replaced concepts stand in a certain relation to each other.

All the rules which in exhibition-analysis are discovered as the accepted rules and which in replacement-analysis are modified, govern the use of concepts. As against this, the rules which the speculative philosopher recommends are often, if not always, not concept-governing rules, but rules regulating the choice among alternative sets of concept-governing rules. Such alternatives are available when the description of the known facts is compatible with different interpretations—*e.g.,* in terms of mechanistic or vitalistic concepts. Generally speaking, the more closely the different concepts are fitted to the perceived or perceivable, *i.e.,* the more descriptive they are, the smaller the range of choice. Conversely, the less closely fitted (the more interpretative) they are, the greater is the range of choice between them. Even the Metaphysician who, for example, by means of the apparent assertion that the universe is a causally ordered system, recommends the adoption of a certain concept of causation, is, I think, not merely recommending the rules governing the concept. In recommending them as preferable to others he is making and recommending a choice. At the very least he is recommending their acceptance in preference to their rejection.

I might note here that the difficulties which Broad finds in his own account of the Postulates may well have their root in his interpretation of them as indicative; and that those alleged metaphysical propositions which he regards as Postulates are perhaps better also interpreted as regulative. On this view the sentence, for example, that every change has a cause would be regarded as expressing the recommendation of a set of rules governing 'cause' and 'change' in preference to its rejection or in preference to other sets of rules. To argue this point in detail would, of course, transcend the scope of this paper.

Whether or not Broad's account of Postulates is acceptable, his failure to distinguish clearly between indicative, regulative and non-propositional Metaphysics has, as I have tried to show, led him to assertions about Metaphysics or Speculative Philosophy in general which, though true of one of these types, are false of the others. His failure to consider even the possibility of a regulative Metaphysics has, so I believe, in particular vitiated his account of the relation between Critical and Speculative Philosophy.

3. *The Relation between Critical and Speculative Philosophy.*

In the preceding two sections I have sought to show that Broad's account of Critical and of Speculative Philosophy has to be modified and how it must be modified; and I have tried further to show that Broad himself is, by implication, committed to accept these modifications. I have argued that within Critical Philosophy we must distinguish between (a) the criticism of propositions, (b) the exhibition-analysis of concepts expressed by *a posteriori* propositions, and (c) the replacement-analysis of concepts expressed by *a priori* propositions. Within Speculative Philosophy, after the legitimate rejection of *a priori* and *a posteriori* Metaphysics, we must distinguish three kinds: (a) indicative Metaphysics consisting of Postulates whose logical nature is, as Broad admits, problematic and which, I have suggested, might turn out not to be indicative at all, (b) regulative Metaphysics consisting of regulative propositions to the effect that a certain concept or type of concept (concept-governing rule) should be accepted in preference to others, or accepted rather than rejected, and (c) non-propositional Metaphysics consisting of sentences which do not express propositions at all.

We have now to consider how far the different branches of Critical and Speculative Philosophy are interdependent. By saying that one branch is dependent on another, I mean that a question arising within the first cannot be answered without making an assumption belonging to the second.

Firstly, that criticism of propositions which Broad describes as exposing them "to every objection that we can think of ourselves or find in the writings of others" (*C.S.P.*, 85), is not an autonomous discipline. It depends not only on a preliminary clarification of the concepts involved, *i.e.*, on an exhibition-analysis, but also on a regulative Metaphysics: for among the objections we should often find some to the effect that the concepts in question are defective, i.e., do violate certain regulative propositions. Thus, in criticising a proposition involving vitalistic concepts a mechanistic philosopher would be depending in his criticism on a regulative Metaphysics.

Pure exhibition-analysis is autonomous in the sense that it consists in formulating—and ends in formulating—concept-governing rules which are in fact accepted by the Analytic Philosopher or other people. This, as has been pointed out, does not mean that a philosopher engaged in exhibition-analysis will never go beyond it—even if his methodological pronouncements, unlike Broad's, identify exhibition-analysis with the whole of philosophy. What Broad says about the comparative independence of Critical or Speculative Philosophy is true only of exhibition-analysis. Indeed exhibition-analysis would be possible in a culture so intellectually static that the people living in it never changed the concept-governing rules which they had accepted or felt any need to change them.

Replacement-analysis depends, as we have seen, on exhibition-analysis and on regulative Metaphysics. There can be no explicit recognition of defects in the accepted concepts without explicit recognition of, at least, some of the rules governing them, i.e., without exhibition-analysis. There can furthermore be no recognition of defects without the acceptance of regulative propositions determining which concepts are to be judged defective and which not.

Broad's giving to Critical Philosophy the almost complete independence of Speculative fits least of all with the relation between replacement-analysis and regulative Metaphysics. According to him if we "do our Critical Philosophy with half an eye on our Speculative Philosophy" or if we "analyse concepts in a certain way, because we feel that this will fit in better than any alternative with the view of Reality as a whole that we happen to like" (ST, 21), we are in danger of intellectual dishonesty. It is quite otherwise. Replacement-analysis not only depends on the acceptance of regulative propositions but would not be possible without it. If we are to blame at all for doing our replacement-analysis with half an eye on our regulative Metaphysics it is because half an eye is not enough.

If the nature and extent of the dependence upon Critical Philosophy of those metaphysical propositions which according to Broad are Postulates is not very clear, this is due to the problematic character of the Postulates. If "everyone acts as if he believed them," and "inevitably goes on acting as if he believed them . . ." (MPN, 217), then no amount of Analysis, Synopsis or Synthesis can bring about a change in this situation. They would have to be regarded in Kantian fashion as the necessary or inevitable presuppositions of objective experience and of science. I feel inclined to hold that all alleged metaphysical propositions which are neither *a priori* nor *a posteriori*—and this includes Broad's Postulates—are either regulative propositions or not propositions at all. On the other hand I feel fully justified in not rushing in with a definite and general answer to a question which Broad finds "extremely puzzling." According to his own account of Postulates, however, those metaphysical propositions which are Postulates are established independently of Critical Philosophy which can at most only clarify their meanings.

The regulative metaphysical propositions which govern the selection among alternative sets of concepts do not depend on Critical Philosophy in the sense that before one accepts a regulative proposition one must have criticised it. This does not mean that the acceptance or rejection of regulative metaphysical propositions is incapable of being supported by argument—any more than the acceptance or rejection of other rules is. Neither does it mean that regulative metaphysical propositions are never subjected to criticism or to analysis of the concepts which occur in them.

Once we distinguish between the different types of Philosophical Analysis and of Metaphysics, the view that philosophical analysis is independent, or almost independent, of metaphysical assumptions becomes untenable. In practice, of course, the connection is even more intimate since, as has been mentioned earlier, regulative Metaphysics and replacement-analysis "influence" each other. Thus it often happens that, if the conditions of replacement-analysis are so strict as to admit no solution for a large number of problems, the conditions which are embodied in regulative propositions are relaxed. The possibility that certain problems in replacement-analysis admit of too many solutions may, on the other hand, lead to the conditions for correct solution being made stricter.

It must be said that some of Broad's remarks about the methods of Critical and of Speculative Philosophy seem to admit a far greater interdependence and interconnection between them than one would expect, judging by his explicit statements about their relation. To give one relevant example, the methods of Exceptional Cases and of Pickwickian Senses—the latter in the shape of the method of logical constructions—are regarded as operative both in Critical and in Speculative Philosophy (*M.S.P.*, 23ff).

To sum up: I have tried to locate the source of what seem to me to be Broad's misconceptions about the nature and function of Critical and Speculative Philosophy, in his failure to distinguish clearly between different types of each of them. I find the most important of these misconceptions in the doctrine—widely current by now in British and

American thought—that Critical Philosophy or Analysis is wholly, or almost wholly, independent of Speculative Philosophy or Metaphysics. I have not tried to praise or to defend those of his methodological theses with which I find myself in agreement: for I am as sure he has no need for my support as I am of his ability to deal with my objections.

STEPHAN KÖRNER

DEPARTMENT OF PHILOSOPHY
THE UNIVERSITY OF BRISTOL
ENGLAND

3

Robert Leet Patterson

A CRITICAL ACCOUNT OF BROAD'S ESTIMATE
OF McTAGGART

IT GOES without saying that to do justice to Professor Broad's *Examination of McTaggart's Philosophy,* a work which in comprehensiveness and thoroughness of treatment resembles a mediaeval *summa,* would involve the writing of a treatise which would at least equal, and might well surpass, in extent the *Examination* itself. It is, indeed, highly desirable that such a task should be undertaken by someone possessed of the requisite intelligence and energy. We are wont to-day to speak with a certain condescension of the "mere commentator," as though it were obvious that nobody would ever write a commentary who had the wit or originality to do anything else. And yet it is only fair to remember that much of the best work of mediaeval thinkers was done in their commentaries upon the treatises of Aristotle and upon Peter Lombard's *Sentences.* Indeed the Hindu practice of writing commentaries upon commentaries upon commentaries has, theoretically at least, much to commend it. For such procedure would involve, or at least ought to involve, the subjection of argument and response to re-examination and re-appraisal by a succession of thinkers each of whom would approach the same problems from his own individual point of view, and this worrying of a topic is the way to bring to light all the relevant considerations.

It is obvious, however, that, in an essay such as this, all that the writer can hope to do is to seize upon the most salient points in the discourse, and to discuss them as adequately as his grasp makes possible and as space permits. Yet, even so, a two-fold function devolves upon him. McTaggart was a philosopher of great logical acuteness and constructive ability, and Broad is an acute and incisive critic. Moreover in the first volume of the *Examination* there are passages marked with asterisks wherein Broad, temporarily deserting his role as critic, discusses in some detail the questions at issue from his own point of view, and these digressions constitute contributions of much value. In the second volume no passages thus marked are to be found, yet this, as Broad informs us and as we might have divined, is not because no independent thought is to be discovered there, but because it is so bound up with the critical aspect of his treatment that the twain cannot be sundered. Two eminent thinkers are thus before us, and the views of each demand our consideration.

In addition there remains the task of final evaluation, all the more requisite because Broad's criticism as a whole, apart from relatively few passages in which a possible reconstruction is outlined, is in general destructive. Yet the question, How destructive after all is it, and what of permanent value remains?, is a pressing one. McTaggart's relatively early death is one of the tragedies of contemporary philosophy, for, had he lived, he would in all likelihood, as Broad frankly admits, "have refuted some of the criticisms, have produced amazingly ingenious and unexpected answers to others, and have started to rebuild those parts of the system which really had suffered in the bombardment."[1] And, while it would be ridiculous for another to presume to speak for him, still some comments and suggestions with respect to this are plainly called for.

Turning now to the preface of the first volume we find Broad there emphasizing the importance of the study of McTaggart's philosophy upon the following grounds: (1) that it is an expression of the Absolutism which has exercised so profound an influence in every time and in every region, (2) that it is set forth with very great and unusual clarity, (3) that the discussion of the basic concepts upon which it is built retains its value whether the system as a whole stands or falls, and (4) that McTaggart's very ignorance of the details of physical science saved him from the error of trying to accommodate his philosophy to ephemeral theories enjoying only a transient popularity. With all this I am in complete agreement. I have, however, a single observation to make which has to do with the first point.

The abiding influence of absolutism, in Broad's opinion, is due to some aspect of reality which is either ineffable or at least strains the capacity of human language to express. That he should make such a judgment will astonish no one who has made a close study of his philosophy, for anyone who has done so is bound to have been impressed by his sympathetic interest in mysticism.[2] Nevertheless it is difficult to see how the clarity of McTaggart's presentation can shed any light upon the unutterable. Indeed the obvious inference would seem to be that the outlook of such a thinker as Bradley, for whom the Absolute utterly

1 *EMcP;* I, li.
2 See his *RPPR;* pp. 172–173, 190–201, 242–243.

transcends the realm of discursive knowledge and can be apprehended only in an intuitive experience which in its immediacy rivals sense-awareness, is to be preferred to that of McTaggart who, despite his mysticism, is obviously to be classed with those philosophers for whom reason is possessed of such a sacredness as to render any depreciation of it a form of blasphemy. The question as to which attitude is the right one is of the first importance, and I can only regret that Broad has not seen fit to pursue the subject farther.

In his discussion of the method adopted by McTaggart in his *Nature of Existence* and its relation to the methods employed by Kant and Hegel, Broad makes two points of fundamental importance. The first is that McTaggart reverts in the most barefaced manner to the "dogmatic" procedure of the pre-Kantian rationalists, a method which Kant believed himself to have discredited, and that this would seem to require some sort of defence. As a matter of fact McTaggart has defended his course, both in Ch. XXIX, Bk. IV of *The Nature of Existence*, where he has tried to show that no philosophical justification of the principle of induction has yet been provided, and in his *Dogmas of Religion* where he has contended that, at any rate, the principle cannot usefully be applied in metaphysical inquiry until the field, which in this case is coextensive with the universe, has been so delimited by deduction that we will have some notion of the ratio which obtains between the observed instances which furnish a basis for induction and the unobserved instances. Otherwise, to use his own illustration, our inductions are quite likely to be as wild as that of a Chinese who, upon landing in England and meeting a drunken Englishman, should forthwith infer that all Englishmen are habitually drunk. I confess that his reasoning here has always impressed me as extremely cogent.

Many philosophers would reject McTaggart's contention on the ground that no propositions are self-evident—some, indeed, write as though only one proposition were self-evident, namely, that no other propositions are so. But Broad does not reject the notion of self-evidence. What he says is of such brevity that it must be taken in conjunction with what his remarks on pages 788–789 of the second part of Volume II of his *Examination*, and with his more extended discussion of the subject in his contribution to Volume I of *Contemporary British Philosophy*. His position appears to be identical with that taken by Lord Russell in his Lowell Lectures—that the errors committed by deductive theorists and the notorious discrepancies between their conclusions suffice to discredit the whole method. It is assumed that a review of their wasted efforts will instil in the contemplating mind a feeling of futility akin to that experienced by the Gardener in *Sylvia and Bruno*.

> "He thought he saw an argument
> That proved he was the Pope:
> He looked again, and found it was
> A bar of mottled soap.
> 'A fact so dread,' he faintly said,
> 'Extinguishes all hope!' "

With respect to this conclusion three questions at once suggest themselves. In the first place, ought a method which Broad regards as theoretically possible[3] to be abandoned even if we grant that every practical application of it has thus far ended in failure? This is not the course which we adopt in the application of scientific theory. I can remember when popular opinion regarded as crack-brained everyone who believed that man would one day fly, and when the verses concerning "Darius Green and his Flying Machine" learned by every school child were taken as expressing the verdict of human wisdom. Yet aeroplanes fill the heavens to-day. Is it altogether improbable that in the realm of pure thought courageous patience may likewise be ultimately crowned with success? This leads naturally to the second question.

Is it actually the case that *nothing* has been achieved in metaphysics by the deductive method? Must the entire Hegelian dialectic be dismissed as a stupendous flash in the pan? And is the same true of all the work of Descartes and Spinoza and Leibnitz? I must say that this seems to me extremely improbable, although obviously I could make good the counter-contention only by writing a treatise on metaphysics. The chief difficulty in applying the deductive method is not the human fallibility which leads to the commission of mistakes in reasoning which can later be discovered and corrected; it is the discrepancy between the various points of departure taken by different philosophers and between the fundamental principles presupposed. In other words, it has to do with self-evidence. A proposition which, it is claimed, is self-evident may, indeed, be susceptible of further clarification, but, when this has been completed, *elle est à prendre ou à laisser.* All that one can do, as McTaggart said, is to "turn it over." And here so much depends upon depth and breadth of native insight which varies from individual to individual. For this reason I do not believe that we can expect ever to reach unanimity in philosophy any more than in politics. Yet it is illegitimate to conclude that, because all are not in agreement, everyone is completely mistaken.

The third question is in the nature of a *tu quoque.* Does the adoption of the method of pure empiricism insure against the commission of mistakes and guarantee compatibility of conclusions? Clearly it does

---

3 Muirhead (ed.), *Contemporary British Philosophy;* I, 98.

not. Is the empirical method, then, any more to be relied upon than the deductive in the work of metaphysical construction? And is not Mc-Taggart right in stressing the futility of attempting to employ induction in so vast a field? Broad's answer would surely be that constructive philosophy must proceed synoptically.[4] But precisely what does this mean? The philosopher must be guided, one gathers, by the principle of coherence. Yet plainly the synoptic method will involve more than this. It will involve, will it not, as Sorley has urged, the apprehension of certain characteristics of the whole which the process of analysis has disregarded? And such apprehension will clearly be of an intuitive nature which verges upon the mystical. Broad's emphasis upon the relevance of religious experience in this connection is suggestive. Such considerations would seem to carry us a long way toward such thinkers as Plotinus and Bergson. How much does Broad really hope for from the employment of such a method? One doubts whether his hopes are very high, since he has not seen fit to utilize it himself. Yet, here again, one would be grateful for further light.

The second point of fundamental importance to which I referred is Broad's observation that it is strange that McTaggart should have seen no need of submitting the categories upon which he builds to a rigorous criticism after the manner of Hegel. Here is an instance in which we can be quite confident as to what McTaggart would have said in reply, and, as a matter of fact, Broad has said it for him, and has answered his own criticism.[5] McTaggart's study of the Hegelian dialectic had convinced him that, as the dialectic proceeds, the negative element gradually fades out until the contrariety between thesis and antithesis disappears, and, moreover, that in every triad after the first—with two exceptions—the transition to the synthesis is made directly from the antithesis alone, and not from the thesis and antithesis conjointly.[6] Furthermore, McTaggart became convinced that the negative element ought never to have been there, that, in fact, the characteristics of existence are not triadically related. This led to important consequences. It led McTaggart to reject the distinction between the understanding and the reason, and with it the notion of degrees of truth and reality. Here, indeed, we find one of the most characteristic features of his thought, and one which distinguishes him from the majority of idealists. Whatever is true of reality is true of it absolutely and without qualification. His method is wholly positive, and the justification of it,

---

[4] EMcP, Part II, II, 788 of Contemporary British Philosophy, I, 98–100.
[5] EMcP, I, 13–14.
[6] See the Hegelian Dialectic, §§ 109–144 and the Commentary, pp. 11–12.

which has been furnished in his earlier works, is presupposed in *The Nature of Existence.*[7]

In his introductory chapter McTaggart informs us that reality— which is equated with being—and existence are both indefinable quali- ties, and that the existent is a species of the real. Broad is prepared to admit that existence may be a quality, but he is certain that reality cannot be a quality because predication of unreality would in that case, be self-contradictory. For example, when we say that Apollo is unreal we deny of something that it possesses the quality of reality; and yet the judgment must be about something and what it is about must possess that quality. McTaggart, I feel sure, would have replied that, when we affirm that Apollo is unreal, what we mean is that the description given of Apollo does not apply to anything. We judge, that is to say, that the universals attributed to Apollo in the "description" do not coinhere in any particular; that, taken together, they describe nothing, and thus constitute only a pseudo-description.[8] I do not say that this suffices, for, in thinking of Apollo, we seem to be thinking, not only of a group of characteristics plus the relation of characterisation—which is itself a characteristic—but also of a particular. There is, I think, a genuine difficulty here, but happily it is not incumbent upon me to try to solve it, since to do so would take us away both from Broad and McTaggart.

I am sceptical, however, of the distinction between reality and exist- ence, and this scepticism extends to Broad's distinction between the *subsistend* and the *existend.* I suspect that there is a confusion here with the distinction between universal and particular, and I suspect, further, that it is complicated by the Thomistic notion of existence as a kind of *act,* and by the analogous notion of subsistence as another kind of *act.* It would, then, be natural to assume that, since universals are not par- ticulars, they will behave differently from particulars, and so that the act of *subsisting* or *being* is other than the act of *existing.* This has a bearing upon Broad's criticism of McTaggart's appeal to introspection in the Cartesian fashion, as providing the certainty that something exists. It might be objected, observes Broad, that what is introspected is not existent, but merely subsistent; should my suspicion be well founded, however, the objection will fall. But, in any case, McTaggart could defend himself by pointing out that what is introspected is a par-

---

[7] See *The Nature of Existence,* I, 48, n. 1.

[8] McTaggart would have been guilty of a confusion in equating the idea of a thing with a psychical event in the mind (p. 3, n. 2): If by *idea* he meant a state of awareness, that is a psychical event; but if by idea, he meant the description of the thing, that is not a psychical event. It may have been a realization of this confusion that led McTaggart to change his view as to the reality of characteristics apart from particulars.

ticular mental state of doubt or denial, and that, as a particular, it will be an existent.[9]

The characteristics of existing particulars—i.e., the qualities which qualify them, and the relations which hold between them—McTaggart regards as themselves existent. He thus raises the question whether characteristics, taken as universals and apart from particulars, be real and non-existent. Broad objects that the degree of wisdom which characterised Socrates is itself a universal, since it might conceivably characterise somebody else, and also that this degree of wisdom is only a determinate falling under the determinable wisdom in general; from which it follows that, if Socrates be characterised by the determinate, he will also be characterised by the determinable, and hence that wisdom in general exists. The objection is, I think, well taken. Broad, however, discovers a hopeless muddle in McTaggart's suggestion that qualities and relations, being universals and not particulars, might without contradiction be at once existent as qualities and relations of existent things and non-existent in their general aspects. I believe that what McTaggart is getting at is, nevertheless, pretty clear. What he has in mind is what Broad has called "non-characterising characteristics." If there be such a universal as perfect straightness, it is quite conceivable that it should at a certain moment begin to characterise a certain particular, say a sensum as Broad suggests,[10] whereas at the preceeding moment it characterised nothing at all. McTaggart would then assert that it was real and non-existent at the preceeding moment, but that, as soon as it began to characterise the sensum, it existed in that sensum without, however, losing the reality which it before possessed.

If we start out by drawing a hard and fast distinction between the reality of universals and the existence of particulars, then, to talk of a universal as existing will be equivalent to asserting that it has become a particular, which is a contradiction in terms. I have already indicated where I think the trouble lies. Many philosophers, however, have made great play with the notion of an *instance* of a universal. What such an *instance* can be, since it would seem to be *neither* a universal nor a particular, or else *both* a universal and a particular, I cannot make out. *Non capit mea simplicitas.*

In *The Nature of Existence*, McTaggart argues that there is no justification for believing in real, non-existent characteristics. Toward the

[9] That Broad would concur is clear from his admission that it is self-evident that "nothing could appear to be a doubt or denial unless it were itself existent or contained an existent as an element." *Ibid.*, I, 22.

[10] *Ibid.*, I, 35–37.

end of his life,[11] however, he changed his mind about this and intended
to insert a footnote to this effect in *The Nature of Existence* were a
second edition issued. His earlier position is based upon his theory of
negative characteristics. Everything not only is what it is, but is not
what it is not. Since a table is not a phoenix, it will possess the characteristic not-phoenix. This will be an existent characteristic, hence
phoenix, as an element of this existent characteristic, will be itself
existent. Broad is, I believe, quite right in being sceptical about this
argument, for, as he truly says, it would be possible on McTaggart's
principles to prove that round-squareness is an existent characteristic.
The whole question of negative characteristics is, however, so closely
connected with that of derivative characteristics that we shall postpone
further consideration of it.

In his independent treatment of the question whether there be non-
characterising characteristics Broad has raised a number of fascinating
questions. What especially interests me is his discussion of *a priori* concepts, and particularly his suggestion that there are some characteristics
which posit their own superlatives. I do not think that straightness is a
valid instance, for it seems clear to me that straightness is a positive and
simple characteristic which does not admit of degrees, and that, when
we say that one line is "straighter" than another, what we mean is that
it is less curved or less jagged and so more nearly approximates to
straightness. But it does seem to me possible that *some* characteristics do
posit their own superlatives. And Broad appears to be quite right in
maintaining that the knowledge that a characteristic does posit its own
superlative is *a priori.*

An *a priori* concept is defined as one that is not empirical, and an
empirical concept is one acquired by abstraction from the data provided
by sense—experience and introspection. Broad is not certain that there
are *a priori* concepts, but, if there be such, they can be accounted for in
terms of either one of two possible theories. One of these is that of
Innate Ideas, which Broad has restated in such a way as to bring out its
latent strength, and to show how wide off the mark are most of the
criticisms which have been leveled against it. Such objections fail to
distinguish between occurrent and dispositional ideas, and between dispositions of "the first order," "second order," etc. The reflection that,
if the theory be true, there is no guarantee that any realities *in rerum
natura* correspond to our innate ideas may be disconcerting, yet it
affords no justification for rejecting the doctrine. A more fundamental

11 See McTaggart's article entitled *An Ontological Idealism* in *Contemporary
British Philosophy,* I, 252, Pt. I. cf. *Philosophical Studies* (edited by Dr. S. V. Keeling),
p. 274, Pt. I.

difficulty, however, arises when we consider that, on this view, innate ideas will be mental products, and that, accordingly, the mind must be credited with creative powers—and this seems unpleasantly like a recourse to magic.

Philosophers who feel the force of this objection may welcome the alternative theory of non-perceptical intuition, according to which the mind is capable of directly apprehending, apart from sense-experience and introspection, certain characteristics of the real. In connection with each of these theories Broad has discussed the category of causality. It is much to be regretted that, although he has in each instance referred to the closely related category of substance, he has abstained from examining it in detail, for such an examination at this point would have shed much light upon his subsequent treatment of this category. With regard to causality his suggestion that we non-perceptually intuit an intrinsic connection between such an event as the impact of a flying stone and such a subsequent event as the breaking of a window is full of interest. It is worth noting that, if the suggestion be accepted, we must presumably reject what Professor Ewing has called the "entailment" theory of causality; for, if that theory be sound, we ought to intuit a logical connection between the two events, and it is notorious that we do nothing of the sort. The consequence will be that we must conceive of causality in the terms of what Ewing calls the "activity" theory. This may be the true view. But I cannot help suspecting that Ewing is right in holding that we sometimes do intuit a relation of entailment between psychical occurrences in our own minds,[12] and that we feel compelled to posit the same relation as holding in the external world in order to account for the regularity of observed sequences, even though we do not directly discern its presence there.

McTaggart considers and rejects the contention that propositions are real, non-existent entities. It would be generally agreed, I think, that his argument is vitiated by his failure to grasp the theory which he is criticising. McTaggart supposes that his opponents maintain that a true belief must correspond both to a proposition and to a fact,[13] and he naturally objects that correspondence to a fact is sufficient. But, as Broad points out, this is not what his opponents assert. Broad agrees, however, that propositions can be dispensed with; and he develops an ingenious theory to deal with false propositions which stand like lions

12 *Idealism*, pp. 176–177.

13 A reading of the chapter entitled *Propositions* in Professor G. E. Moore's recently published book, *Some Main Problems of Philosophy*, and which consists of lectures which had already been written at the time when McTaggart was working upon *The Nature of Existence*, will reveal how easily such a misunderstanding upon his part could have arisen.

in his path. To use his own illustration, if I believe that the other side of a piece of paper is blue, I already know that it has another side, I know that the other side must be colored, and I know what the determinates are which fall under the determinable color. If, now, I believe that the other side is blue, my thought of blue stands in the relation of being "inserted" into the "noetic framework" constituted by the cognitive states aforesaid; and, if I disbelieve that it is red, my thought of red stands in a relation of being "extruded" from the same "noetic framework." If the other side be, indeed, blue, my belief is true; if it be red, my belief is false.

The "noetic framework" would appear to be constituted by the items of knowledge which I already possess with respect to the object, and which, inasmuch as they are apprehended with certainty, are, I presume, self-evident. But I admit that I am puzzled as to the relations of insertion and extrusion. My thought of blue occurs coincidentally with these various acts of cognition, but so does my thought of red. Contemporaneity of occurrence is identical, therefore, neither with insertion nor extrusion. I do not see how I can insert or extrude my thought of blue except by forming some judgment about blue; yet this suggestion I feel sure that Broad would reject, for it would clearly launch us upon an infinite regress.

We pass now to the second book in which Broad begins by considering McTaggart's treatment of characteristics. *Characteristic* is a term employed by McTaggart to designate qualities and relations, both of which terms he regards as indefinable. It is possible, McTaggart holds, for an entity to be related to itself. In this connection Broad distinguishes between indirect and direct relations; the former, he believes, can hold between a term and itself, but he considers it very doubtful whether the latter can do so. And, inasmuch as identity would be a direct relation, Broad proposes to dispense with it, and to substitute for it "co-inherence of attributes in a single term."[14] But what do we mean by a "single" term? Do we not mean that the term which is the subject of one attribute is identical with the term which is the subject of the other attribute? It is quite true that we can evade the issue by saying, as Broad suggests,[15] that neither attribute belongs to more than one term, yet is not this purely a verbal device? Is there any attribute which *may* not belong to more than one term? The issue comes out more clearly in the case of successive states. We should ordinarily say that a house which has been painted red is the same house as it was before it was painted red and when it was white; and have we any

14 *Ibid.*, I, 91.   15 *Ibid.*, p. 90.

justification for saying so unless the two colors successively characterise the same subject?

The actual connection of particulars by a relation—in other words, an existent relation—McTaggart calls a *relationship*. Qualities generate relationships, and relationships generate both qualities and relationships. The ungenerated characteristics of a particular constitute its *original* characteristics, the generated characteristics its *derivative* characteristics. The process of generation proceeds to infinity. Thus grass will have, not only the quality green, but also the quality of having the quality green, the quality of having the quality of having the quality green, and so on. All derivative qualities, except those immediately derived from original qualities, McTaggart terms *repeating* qualities, whereas original and immediately derived qualities he terms *primary*.

The question whether there be derived or relational qualities is obviously an important one. Broad's answer is in the negative; unfortunately his discussion is very condensed and concerned largely with sentence-structure. What I wish to ask is whether McTaggart's use of the phrase "true of" may not be either the effect or the cause of some mental confusion. When we say that it is true *of* grass that it has the quality green, we seem to be saying something about its nature, and to be ascribing some attribute to it. The truth of the assertion appears to depend, then, upon its possession of this attribute—namely the quality of having the quality green. Suppose, however, that we say that it is true *that* grass has the quality green. Now we seem to mean something different. We mean, I take it, that the proposition which we have just asserted corresponds to a fact, and that this fact is the standing of the proposition, grass is green, in a relation of correspondence to the fact that grass is green. Here no reduplication of quality seems to be involved. Of course, if an entity did not have the nature that it has, it could not enter into the relations that it does. If it were not, for example, extended in space, it could not stand behind or beside something else. But, does it follow that change of relations involves the generation and corruption of relational qualities? I do not see that it does, and, therefore, I think that Broad's conclusion is correct.

In like manner, if we say that it is true *of* a table that it is not a phoenix, we seem to be ascribing to the table a quality—i.e., the quality not-phoenix. But if we say that it is true *that* the table is not a phoenix, no such attribution seems to be involved. Are we not, therefore, justified in concurring in Broad's rejection of negative characteristics? I think that we are.

As to the generation of relationships by qualities and by relationships Broad's opinion is that McTaggart's view is, on the whole, sound. Without entering into the details of this discussion, I wish to direct attention upon a single point. McTaggart has said[16] that, if Smith is happy, the primary fact is the fact that he is happy, "and the fact that he is related to the quality of happiness is only derivative." In this Broad follows him. The two sentences, "A is qualified by redness," and "Redness inheres in A," express, he tells us, a single fact, and a different fact from the fact expressed by the sentence, "A is red." We must distinguish between the constituents of a fact and the form of their union. The fact that A is red is about A and redness, and not about the form of their union. There is another fact which is about A and redness and the form of their union, and this is the fact that redness inheres in A.

I find all this very difficult to follow. I should have thought, in the first place, that, whereas propositions are about facts, facts are not about anything, any more than a particular is about anything. It is true, I am aware, that we habitually use the phrase "The fact that;" but what do we mean when we say, for instance, "It is a fact that S is P?" We mean, I take it, that there is a fact corresponding to the proposition, "S is P." Broad has not given us his definition of fact, but McTaggart has given us his,[17] and he has definitely identified it with *relationship*.[18] But relationship, surely, is not about anything. And I should have thought, in the second place, that to say "A is red" is equivalent to saying, "A is qualified by redness," for it is clear that, when we say "A is red," we do not mean merely to refer to a particular and a quality and to leave their connection hanging in the air. McTaggart and Broad both believe in what Broad has called the "non-relational fact" that Smith is happy in order to escape from the infinite series of relations generated by the relation of characterisation and its two terms. Yet McTaggart himself has just shown that such an infinite is not vicious, and Broad has agreed with him! Why, then, try to escape it? And why introduce the notion of a "non-relational fact" which is quite incompatible with McTaggart's identification of fact with relationship, and is nothing other than that plurality without relations which constitutes so shocking an enigma in the philosophy of Bradley?[19]

Qualities, according to McTaggart, are either simple, compound or

---

[16] *The Nature of Existence,* I, § 69.   [17] *The Nature of Existence,* I, § 10.

[18] See Dr. S. V. Keeling's *McTaggart's Nature of Existence,* I, *Comments and Corrections* in *Mind,* XLVII, N.S., No. 188, 548, note p. 11.

[19] McTaggart appears to be motivated by a desire to escape Stout's charge that he makes the whole being of a substance consist "in its being related to something else" —i.e., to its qualities (see sec. 69). Yet McTaggart has asserted that a substance is nothing apart from its qualities, and is what it is only "in conjunction" with its qualities (see sec. 68). And what is it to be conjoined to its qualities if it is not to be related to them?

complex. Since he holds that the same is true of relations, Broad prefers to speak of simple, compound or complex characteristics. As to simple characteristics he raises no question, but he is quite unprepared to admit that there are such entities as compound characteristics. It appears to him absurd to assert that, because a particular is characterised by redness and by sweetness, it is also characterised by the characteristic "redness—and sweetness." The objection would seem to be as conclusive as it is obvious.

A complex quality has been defined by McTaggart as "one which does not consist in an aggregrate of other qualities, but which can be analyzed and defined by means of other characteristics, whether qualities or relations, or both," and, as an instance, he has given *conceit,* which is "the possession of a higher opinion of oneself than is justified by the facts."[20] Broad does not proffer an illustration of a complex relation, although, of course, he believes that there are such relations, since he accepts the notion of complex characteristics. I confess that these complex characteristics interest me, and that I should have welcomed a more extended discussion of them than has been given us by either philosopher.

From the consideration of characteristics Broad turns to that of particulars. He thinks that it is self-evident that anything that exists must possess some characteristic in addition to that of existence, and that McTaggart would have done better to say so than to try to prove it. He adds that existence, in "its primary sense," is equivalent to particularity; thus presupposing that existence and subsistence are mutually distinguishable, an assumption concerning which I have already expressed my doubts.

Inasmuch as there are incompatible qualities, it is certain, McTaggart points out, in the case of any particular, that there are some qualities which it does not possess. Broad objects that, although we can see that certain qualities are necessarily incompatible, and although such knowledge is *a priori,* yet we cannot know *a priori* that there must be incompatible qualities; hence, he maintains, an empirical premise must be introduced at this point into the chain of McTaggart's deductive arguments. How seriously are we to take this objection? The entire chain of arguments avowedly depends upon an empirical premise, namely, that something exists. Moreover McTaggart once again appeals to experience to show that the existent is differentiated into parts, although he believes that this can also be established *a priori.* It is clear then, that McTaggart does not object to appealing to experience. As he truly says, "A judgment which is directly based on a perception can be just as

20 *The Nature of Existence,* I, § 63.

certain as one which is evident *a priori.*"²¹ What he is resolved to avoid is an appeal to induction before the characteristics pertaining to everything that exists, and to existence as a whole, have been determined; but of such an appeal there is at this juncture no question. Furthermore, if the distinction between existence and subsistence be accepted, the "empirical premiss" which Broad wishes to introduce will relate to the subsistent, since it has to do with the being of incompatible universals. And universals are eternal and unchangeable realities. Yet, to talk of an "empirical premiss" with respect to them certainly seems to imply that they might have been otherwise, or not have been at all; and what sense can be made of such a suggestion? It is through experience, indeed, that we make contact with them; all *a priori* knowledge, as Russell urged²² and McTaggart agreed,²³ is empirically arrived at; yet the universality and necessity of its content are unaffected by the way in which we apprehend it.

I turn now to Broad's critique of McTaggart's treatment of substance, a topic of fundamental importance in his philosophy. McTaggart originally defined substance as something which exists and has qualities and is related without being either a quality or a relation.²⁴ In *An Ontological Idealism,* however, the definition is amended to read "that which has qualities and is related, without being itself either a quality or a relation, or having qualities or relations among its parts,"²⁵ the concluding phrase being added to exclude facts. Broad without noticing the emendation, proposes to achieve the same end by suffixing the three words, "or a fact."²⁶

McTaggart states that the original definition is also the traditional one, an assertion which Broad regards as mistaken. However this may be, I am quite certain that it does not adequately express the traditional *conception* of substance. McTaggart himself remarks that the term has often been "confined to that which, among other characteristics, is either timeless or persistent through time, or is fundamentally more one than many, or is held to be a unity of special importance," but he considers that such usage is due merely to inconsistency, and points out that his definition is applicable to groups and to events.²⁷ Now I am certain that the scholastics would have protested against either application, and that they would have been especially emphatic with respect to events. A substance, they would insist, does not exist *in alio* but *in se,*

21 *The Nature of Existence,* I, § 45.
22 *The Problems of Philosophy,* 2nd edition, p. 74.
23 *The Nature of Existence,* I, 62, n. 1.   24 *Ibid.,* § 67.
25 *Contemporary British Idealism,* I, 253.
26 *Examination,* I, 132.   27 *The Nature of Existence,* I, § 72.

or to put the point more technically, it possesses *inseity* and lacks *abaliety;* whereas an event lacks the former characteristic and possesses the latter. In all this Aristotle, I presume, would agree with them. Broad clearly does well to stress the novelty of McTaggart's conception. He is prepared, however, to accept McTaggart's definition "as a satisfactory description of a 'particular,' "[28] yet he remarks that it is strange that McTaggart should have regarded as unimportant what seems to many people so fundamental—namely, the distinction between occurrents and continuents. I agree that it is so, and I suspect that it is connected with his belief in the unreality of time.

In his independent discussion of this topic under the heading, *Processes and Things,* Broad makes the following illuminating comment. The coming-to-be and passing-away of a compound thing—a chair, for instance, to use his own example—can be analyzed in terms of the starting and stopping of certain processes in its members or elements. In the case of a simple thing, however,—if there be simple things—there would be no sense in asking whether it began to be or passed away. Such notions would be simply inapplicable to it. Hence Kant's suggestion that the soul might be a simple substance and yet might pass away by elanguescence involves the false identification of two mutually distinct concepts—that of *thing* and that of *process.* In so saying, Broad is restating in terms of post-Kantian philosophy the same point that Aristotle made in the *Eudemus*—that substance does not admit of degrees and has no contrary.

Broad is prepared to concede, however, that, although the coming-to-be and the passing-away of a simple substance are unintelligible *quoad nos,* yet we might know through revelation that there is a fact corresponding to the first unintelligible notion and that there is none corresponding to the second. This, as he points out, is to assume that they are unintelligible only in the sense in which a mathematical formula is unintelligible to a person ignorant of mathematics. But is this actually the case? Are they unintelligible because of the profundity of their meaning, or because they have no meaning at all? If the latter, they are literally inconceivable. I would urge that such is, in fact, the case. If this be so, we might deal with Broad's suggestion as Joseph deals with the suggestion[29] that, although we cannot *conceive* of a piece of paper as at once black and white all over, yet it may still *be* black and white all over. To admit that it may *be* black and white all over is, he observes, equivalent to asserting that we can so conceive of it, and thus to contradict ourselves. In like manner, if the coming-to-be or the passing-away

28 *EMcP,* I, 132.   29 See *An Introduction to Logic,* p. 13.

of a simple substance be inconceivable, to admit that either event can occur is tantamount to confessing that it is not inconceivable.

After a long discussion Broad concludes that the notion of *thing*— i.e., of substance in the traditional sense—can be dispensed with, and that of process substituted for it. He observes, however, that "many people have held that it is self-evident that any process, whether of 'change' or of 'quiescence,' must be a 'state of' or a 'process in' a thing."[30] I am, I confess, one of these people. Process, to my understanding, clearly involves a prior reality, or realities, in which it "goes on," and to seek to transform it from a relative into an absolute notion appears to me as hopeless an undertaking as to try to convince me that the moon has only one side. I cannot, of course, argue in defence of what I take to be an immediate insight; yet I would call attention to the fact that Broad himself has suggested that substance may be an *a priori* concept, and I cannot but regret that he has not seen fit to discuss the question in the present connection.

I must add that the consequences of the denial of substance seem to me sufficiently somber to produce a tremor in the breast of any thinker. For with substance goes permanence, and with permanence, change— in the strict sense of the word—and we are left with mere succession. Processes will be composed of shorter phases, which, Broad tells us, "overlap." "There is a phase," he writes, "which I sensed at the first moment, and have ceased to sense at the second; there is a phase which I sense at the second, and was not yet sensing at the first; and there is a phase which I sense at both. The nearer the two moments are together the more nearly does that which is sensed at the second coincide with that which was sensed at the first. The identity, which enables me to talk of '*this* noise' and to say that I have been 'hearing *it*' for some time resolves itself into the peculiarly intimate way in which these successive and partially overlapping noises are interrelated in respect of their qualities."[31]

Unless two successive phases be qualitatively dissimilar, I do not see how it will be possible to discriminate between them. Moreover, in view of what Broad has written with reference to the "specious present," I cannot help wondering whether this overlapping be not mere seeming, whether it be not a product of that misperception whereby we apprehend the immediate past as temporally displaced. Be that as it may, the relation between the successive phases will either be causal, in the sense that there is an intrinsic relation between them, or it will be non-causal. Since, however, the phases only partially overlap—otherwise they would

[30] *EMcP*, I, 151.   [31] *Ibid.*, I, 159.

not overlap at all but would be identical—the prior phase will exist—or will have begun to become—before the second has begun to do so. There will then be nothing for it to be causally related to, or upon which it can act. Its production of the second phase will constitute absolute creation. And, if we must have a creator, I should prefer the Deity. If, on the other hand, the relation be non-causal, similarity or dissimilarity between the successive phases will be wholly unaccounted for, and so will all the order and continuity in the existing universe. My criticism, I am aware, is in no sense original, it is that which any one would make who finds, as I do, the notion of absolute becoming absolutely unintelligible. In fact non-Buddhist philosophers made much the same points over two thousand years ago. I would add, however, that, whereas Broad thinks that McTaggart has made too much of substance, I think that he has made too little of it, and that he would have done better to have defended the traditional concept, and so to have distinguished sharply between substances and events.

We now come to the second appeal made by McTaggart to experience. The first appeal, it will be recalled, established the fact that something exists. The second appeal to experience will reveal the existence of more than one substance—to use McTaggart's terminology—or, as Broad prefers to say—rightly, I think—more than one particular. As a matter of fact, McTaggart contends, the appeal is unnecessary, since it is certain *a priori* that every particular is infinitely divisible into other particulars; yet he recognizes that this view is "novel and controversial," whereas the empirical approach will produce irresistible conviction in almost everybody. For even a solipsist must acknowledge that introspection acquaints him with successive states of his own self, and each of these states will be a particular. And, if we turn to the perceptual field, we discover that simultaneous sensations can acquaint us with a plurality of perception-data. Thus two simultaneous sensations of redness and shrillness can at once acquaint me with a color and a noise. To this Broad objects that the hyper-sceptic might urge that the same particular might be sensed as both red and noisy; and that the safer course would be to take two simultaneous sensations of the same kind, as, for instance, the sensation of a red flash and the sensation of a blue flash. It would, then, be indisputable that the two perception-data were qualitatively distinct, and that they were located in different places in the visual field. The plurality of particulars may thus be taken as established.

I propose now to turn to the consideration of the Dissimilarity of the Diverse and the infinite divisibility of particulars, which constitute the twin pillars that support the theory of Determining Correspondence

which is the most distinctive feature of McTaggart's system. In so doing
I shall ignore, so far as possible, a number of topics of great interest in
themselves, such as the theory of groups, intrinsic and extrinsic determination, and the discussion of causality, inasmuch as an adequate examination of Broad's detailed treatment of them would far exceed the
space at my disposal.

By the Dissimilarity of the Diverse McTaggart designates the principle that numerical diversity involves qualitative dissimilarity. It is thus
roughly dentical with Leibnitz' famous Identity of Indiscernibles. It is
important to note, however, McTaggart points out, that Leibnitz rejected relations; so that, for him, the nature of a particular consisted
entirely of its original qualities. But, for McTaggart, relations stand on
the same footing as qualities. Consequently the relational qualities of
a particular, together with its original qualities, constitute its primary
qualities, in contradistinction to its repeating qualities. And it is his
contention that the uniqueness of the nature of a particular depends
upon its primary qualities, whether original or relational.

The requirements, then, for exact similarity on the part of two particulars, as Broad enumerates them, will be the following: "(1) Every
original quality of either is a quality of both. (2) Every original relation
which relates either to itself relates each to itself. (3) Every original relation which relates A to any other particulars in any order relates B to
the same particulars and in the same order, and conversely with 'B'
substituted for 'A.' "[32] Broad also calls attention to the fact that Mc-
Taggart has recognized that "there must be some dissimilarity between
them which is not a mere analytic consequence of the fact that they are
two."[33] Thus it is not enough to appeal to A's identity with itself as an
individuating characteristic, for this dissimilarity depends upon a diversity which must antecedently be established.

Broad undertakes to show that the principle does not hold either in
the case of occurrents or of continuants. He turns in the first place to
sensibilia, which, he thinks, "are almost certainly of the nature of
processes."[34] It is clear, he concedes, that two sensibilia sensed by the
same mind must be differentiated either qualitatively, spatially or
temporally. Nevertheless it is quite conceivable that two sensibilia in
the form of two noises which are qualitatively exactly similar should be
sensed by two different minds. They would have no spatial relations to
each other, and it might be held either that they have no temporal relations to each other, or that they both occur simultaneously. Of course
one of the sensibilia would be sensed by one mind, and the other by the

[32] *Ibid.*, I, 172.   [33] *Loc. cit.*   [34] *Ibid.*, I, 173.

other mind, and this would suffice to differentiate them. But Broad now asks us to concede that it is at least logically possible for the two sensibilia to be unsensed by any mind; in which case they would be exactly similar yet mutually distinct.

I cannot think that this argument is a convincing one. In the first place some philosophers would contend that it is logically impossible that there should be unsensed sensibilia. On this point I am in agreement with Broad, yet the objection cannot merely be waived aside. In the second place I am not sure that noises are devoid of spatial relations, and, if they do possess such relationships they will be individuated thereby, and will also be, at least indirectly, spatially related to each other. It certainly seems as if the noise of a locomotive proceeds from the direction from which the locomotive approaches. Broad himself, be it remarked, thinks it possible that he can hear a sound "remaining stationary" or "moving."[35] And, in the third place, our two noises will either be the effects of two mutually distinct causes or of a single cause. On the latter supposition they will be, not two noises, but one noise; on the former, they will be dissimilar inasmuch as one will be the effect of one cause and the other the effect of the other cause. Of course, if the two noises be uncaused, spontaneous "emergents," this last objection will fall; but it seems to me a preposterous tax upon our powers of belief to ask us to entertain such an hypothesis.

When he turns to the consideration of continuants, Broad asks us to consider the possibility that two minds might exist through the same period of time, and that both of them might be wholly engaged in contemplating the successive steps of the same argument at the same speed, so that the successive states of each mind would be qualitatively exactly similar to those of the other. In order to entertain this bizarre suggestion, it is evident that we should have to make some further assumption. We must suppose either that the two minds came into existence simultaneously—and this would be to raise the yet unsolved question as to whether there is any sense in talking of minds coming into existence; certainly there is not should they prove to be simple substances—or else that the argument which they are both following consists of a sufficient number of steps to enable them to continue to follow it sempiternally. In the case of an *a priori* argument such as McTaggart's to show that a logical alternative is conceivable suffices to shake it; yet when the alternative proposed is so fantastic and of such doubtful self-consistency as the one before us, I question whether very much has been accomplished.

[35] *Ibid.,* I, 163.

I feel that Broad is on firmer ground when he proceeds to question the soundness of McTaggart's contention that it is the nature of a substance which individuates it. For it does appear to me that this assertion of McTaggart's is inconsistent with other statements which he has made. In accordance with his theory of compound qualities, all the primary qualities of any particular will form a compound quality. And for McTaggart, who was no nominalist, any quality will be a universal. Now there is nothing in the nature of any universal, as such, which will prevent it from characterizing an indefinite number of particulars; otherwise it would not be a universal. To assert that there is something in the nature of a quality which limits it to characterising only one particular is equivalent to asserting that the quality is as truly a particular as that which it characterises; and this would be to give the whole case away to the nominalist, which McTaggart, certainly, would never have dreamed of doing. It might, indeed, be the case that some universal did actually characterise only one particular. But this would be due to something in the nature of the universe external to the universal.

It is, of course, true that Broad and I do not believe in compound qualities. Yet this in no way hinders our pointing out that McTaggart has fallen into inconsistency. And it is possible for us to formulate a similar argument based upon what we do believe. Let the primary qualities of a certain particular, A, consist of three—X, Y, and Z. There will, then, be nothing in the nature of X which prevents it from characterising other particulars beside A; nor yet anything in the nature of Y and Z which prevent them from doing likewise. And we know that there is no incompatibility which would prevent their all characterising a single substance, since we know that they all characterise A. There is, therefore, nothing in the natures of X, Y, and Z to prevent them from constituting the primary qualities, and the only primary qualities, of some other particular or particulars. It seems clear, therefore, that it is not the nature of a particular which individuates it.

McTaggart, indeed, objects that such a view assumes that "the substance (i.e., the particular) has an individuality apart and distinct from its nature," and that this is untenable because "when we try to explain what we mean by this distinct aspect of substance—indeed, when we assert that it exists—we can only do so by asserting qualities of the substance. And these qualities are part of the nature of the substance, not something apart and distinct from that nature. It is therefore impossible to distinguish the substance from its qualities in such a way as to allow the substances to be different while their natures are the same."[36]

36 *The Nature of Existence,* I, § 95.

Is this, however, consistent with the earlier statement that "it does not follow that, because a substance is nothing apart from its qualities, it is not anything in conjunction with its qualities"?[37] If a substance be something in conjunction with its qualities—and it is that which *has* the qualities—why may it not constitute precisely the principle of individuation that is needed? For, after all, substances are particulars and qualities are universals. And to contend, as does McTaggert, that it is the nature which individuates seems to imply that the substance is nothing more than a group of qualities; and this is a view which McTaggart explicitly repudiates.[38]

I do not see, therefore, how we can do otherwise than agree with Broad in rejecting the Dissimilarity of the Diverse. It is a decision fraught, however, with important consequences. For with the Dissimilarity of Diverse will go the notions of exclusive description and sufficient description, and with these the theory of Determining Correspondence. Yet our conclusion appears inevitable. For the nature of a substance is either a universal or a group of universals, and there is no way to conjure the particular out of the universal. The attempt to do so is the sin committed by the Ontological Argument, and the Dissimilarity of the Diverse is guilty of the same offense.

Let us now proceed to examine the other pillar of McTaggart's system, namely, the infinite divisibility of particulars. About this there is not much to be said, since there are no arguments which require to be stated and evaluated. The proposition that every substance is divisible into parts—or, to use a phrase which, for McTaggart, is equivalent, that every substance has content—is, as he points out, synthetic, for "we do not mean by substance that which has content.[39] We defined it as that which has qualities and stands in relations without being itself a quality or a relation." Furthermore, the proposition is "self-evident and ultimate." "It is self-evident, because it does not need proof; and it is ultimate because it cannot be proved from any proposition more clearly self-evident. All that each of us can do is to regard it carefully, and to see whether he does accept it as self-evident."[40] This is a frank and honest challenge. But, before replying to it, one will do well to ponder the following citation from Broad.

Many philosophers who have asserted that there are simple substances took the word 'substance' in a much narrower sense than McTaggart, and did not mean to assert that there are particulars which are not themselves groups of

37 *Ibid.*, I, § 68.   38 *Ibid.*, I, § 66.
39 See Dr. S. V. Keeling's "McTaggart's *Nature of Existence,* I. Comments and Amendments, p. 549. n. 179 in *Mind,* XLVII, N.S., No. 188.
40 *Ibid.*, I, § 167.

particulars. These philosophers meant by 'substances' continuants, as distinguished from occurrents. What they meant to assert was that there are continuants which are not groups of continuants. They did not deny that their 'simple substances' had a plurality of successive total states. Nor did they deny that each total state was internally complex, and composed of a plurality of temporary occurrents. In fact Leibnitz, who is regarded as the typical believer in 'simple substances' most strongly asserted both these propositions. Now, on McTaggart's view, each total state of a continuant is a particular; each occurrent in any total state, is a particular; and *every* particular is to be called a 'substance.' So it is possible that even Leibnitz would have admitted that there can be no simple 'substances' in McTaggart's sense of the word.[41]

How true these observations are can be seen from the following statements of McTaggart.

A substance which has any parts is not simple, although its parts are so closely attached to one another that there is no known force which can separate them. Nor is it even simple if the nature of its parts is such that it can be seen *a priori* to be impossible that any of them should exist except as parts of that whole, or that the whole should exist without any one of them.[42]

McTaggart's position, then, is not so radical as it appears at first sight. For a substance which was "compound" in the above sense would clearly satisfy the metaphysical requirements of most believers in "simple" substances. What such thinkers have mostly been concerned about was to prove the immortality of the soul from its simplicity; and a soul which was "compound" only in this sense would obviously be "simple" enough to meet their need.

Let us now return to McTaggart's proposition. Broad has stated that it is not self-evident to him, and I must report that it is not self-evident to me. Of course both of us may be wrong, and McTaggart may be right. But I wish to call attention to what I take to be a confusion here, which Broad has pointed out,[43] and which reminds us of the confusion which we observed when considering the problem of individuation. Then McTaggart confused the substance with its nature; now he confuses it with its history. Yet it is plainly identical neither with the one nor the other. It is that which *has* the nature and which *has* the history. And since, for McTaggart, its history is part of its nature, the two confusions are actually only one confusion. The same confusion will reappear in his treatment of the self and its perceptions. And I think that it **may** account for the fact that he regarded the proposition before us as self-evident. It accounts also, I believe, for his talking of the filling or the

41 *Examination*, I, 344–345.   42 *The Nature of Existence*, I, § 173.
43 *Ibid.*, I, 349–350.

inside of a substance; when he does so, he is thinking of its characteristics and of the events in which it is involved. Yet, however many the qualities, the relations, or the successive states of a substance, so far as I can see there is no difficulty in assuming that the substance itself is simple.

Broad has stated it as his opinion that people who have believed in simple substances have done so because they have thought that the existence of such substances could be established by inference, not because they thought that any particulars with which they were acquainted appeared to be simple; and he has added that if anyone ever did hold this latter view, "his position would have been a very weak one."[44] Yet, if it be possible to become directly acquainted with one's own ego by introspection, as Descartes and McTaggart held, and as I believe to be the case, it is certain that one is not acquainted with it *as divided*. Indeed, throwing caution to the winds, I shall be rash enough to confess that to me it does seem self-evident that the self can neither be included in another self nor divided into two or more selves nor split into parts that are not selves.

It is, of course, clear that, if the Dissimilarity of the Diverse were established, there would be an exclusive description of every particular, inasmuch as every particular would possess a nature which it shared with no other. From this McTaggart infers that of every particular there would also be a sufficient description. By "sufficient description" he means a description which introduces no undescribed substance but is formulated wholly in terms of qualities and relations. A particular may be sufficiently described by a unique quality—simple or compound —which characterises it, or by a unique relation in which it stands. Or, again, it may be the only particular which stands in a certain relation to a particular thus describable, or it may be the only particular which stands in a certain relation to another particular which is the only particular which stands in a certain relation to a particular thus describable, and so on. But sooner or later the series must come to an end in a particular which can be sufficiently described in terms of its own characteristics, otherwise, contends McTaggart, we should be involved in a viciously infinite regress.

This conclusion Broad declines to accept for several reasons. In the first place it is possible, he maintains, to conceive of a universe all the members of which would have exclusive descriptions but none of which would possess a sufficient description. Let a universe consist of three minds, A, B and C. Let A be jealous of B on account of C, B of C on account of A, and C of A on account of B. Then each mind can be

44 *Ibid.*, I, 343–344.

described by the triadic, non-symmetrical relation in which it stands, and each can be devoid of a sufficient description.

I must admit that I feel with respect to this logically constructed universe the same kind of disquietude which Dr. Keeling acknowledged in his review of the volume before us.[45] It is obviously a universe which is incapable of actually existing. Three real, living minds would certainly possess other characteristics beside that of jealousy, and in terms of these characteristics sufficient descriptions might well be found for all of them. Broad, however, advances two further objections. Again we are asked to conceive of a universe, this time consisting of two minds, A and B. Each respects itself and despises the other. A can be exclusively described by its respect for A, and B by its respect for B. Again I confess to the same sort of disquietude which assailed me before. But, lastly, Broad suggests that an entity which possessed no sufficient description might be exclusively described as the only entity standing in a certain relation to a second entity, likewise devoid of a sufficient description, which might in turn be exclusively described as the only entity standing in a certain relation to a third entity, and so *ad infinitum*. Such an infinite series, he affirms, would not be vicious, since it need not be completed to furnish an exclusive description of the first entity, which can be exclusively described, as we have seen, by its relation to the second. Each of these entities, however, if they existed *in re*, would certainly possess other characteristics beside that of standing in a certain relation to the next term of the series, and these characteristics might well provide a sufficient description of it.

From the point which we have now reached we can envisage the difficulty which McTaggart undertook to solve by his theory of Determining Correspondence. Into the ramifications of this theory, and into those of Broad's critique thereof, I cannot attempt to enter; for a close and detailed study, such as would be involved in an attempt to do justice to both, would far exceed the limits of this chapter. I shall merely try to state the problem which confronted McTaggart, to outline the solution which he thought he had found, and to indicate the nature of Broad's criticism.

The universe, as McTaggart sees it, is composed of a number of substances, each of which constitutes a Primary whole. Each primary whole is divided into a Set of Parts, which, taken together make it up and do not do more than make it up. This set is, in turn, divisible into another set of parts which, taken together, make up the primary whole, and none of which falls within more than one part of the first set of parts. The first set, in McTaggart's terminology is *precedent* to the second, and

45 *Philosophy*, July, 1935.

the second is *sequent* to the first. Any set of parts which contains another is precedent to it; and any set of parts which is contained within another set is sequent to it. The parts of the set into which the primary whole is immediately divided are called primary parts; the parts into which these primary parts are divided are called Secondary Parts of the First Grade; those parts into which these secondary parts of the first grade are divided are called Secondary Parts of the Second Grade, and so *ad infinitum*.

Each one of this infinite number of parts into which the primary whole is thus divided will, of course, be a substance; and will, therefore, have a sufficient description. It cannot be supposed, however, that each one of this infinite number of parts will possess a unique characteristic; for such an endless conjunction of unique characteristics and characterised parts would be quite incredible. Yet we cannot hope sufficiently to describe every substance in terms of a set of its parts, for sufficient descriptions of the members of this set could be given only in terms of sufficient descriptions of the members of the set sequent to it, and these in turn could be sufficiently described only in terms of sufficient descriptions of the members of the set sequent to this set—and so we should be involved in an infinite regress which is clearly vicious.

Let us state the difficulty in terms of McTaggart's own terminology. When the occurrence of any characteristic involves the occurrence of a certain other characteristic, the first is said intrinsically to determine the second. Now X may intrinsically determine the occurrence of either Y or Z. It is then said to "presuppose" the characteristic which actually does occur. The sufficient description of a substance must either "supply" or "presuppose" the sufficient descriptions of the members of any set of parts, say, M. If it presupposes sufficient descriptions of the members of M, it will also presuppose sufficient descriptions of the members of N, the set sequent to M, and in like manner those of π, the set sequent to N. The nature of the substance in question will thus contain an infinite number of presuppositions. Why should it not do so? (The fact that no finite mind could know all these presuppositions is irrelevant.) It could not do so because there must be a Total Ultimate Presupposition which is reached by removing all those presuppositions the "fixing" of which is implied in the "fixing" of those which remain. Thus the sufficient descriptions of the members of N would imply the sufficient descriptions of the members of M, which would therefore be removed from the total ultimate presupposition. And the sufficient descriptions of the members of N would be similarly implied by the sufficient descriptions of the members of π and would in like manner be removed.

Thus the total ultimate presupposition can never be arrived at, and yet we know that there must be one.

The sufficient description of the original substance must, accordingly, "supply" sufficient descriptions of all its parts either by including or implying them. Why should it not include them? Because then it would be more than adequate. We do not need sufficient descriptions of the members of M if we have those of the members of N, since the former can be derived from the latter, nor yet of the members of N if we have those of the members of π. There must be a Minimum Adequate Description which will omit all superfluous descriptions. Yet such a minimum adequate description can never be reached, inasmuch as the sufficient descriptions of the members of any set of parts are always implied by the sufficient descriptions of the members of another set of parts, sequent to it. It follows therefore, that the sufficient description of the original substance must imply sufficient descriptions of all its parts.

How is this possible? It is possible only, McTaggart thinks, if the parts of the substance stand to each other in a relation of Determining Correspondence. I doubt whether any succinct statement of this complicated theory can make it clear to anyone who is not familiar with the chapters in which McTaggart has expounded it, but I propose to allow him to state it in his own words:

Let A have a set of parts, B and C. (The number of parts in the set may be any number, finite or infinite.) Let it be true in the first place, that each of these parts has a set of parts corresponding to each set of parts of A. In the second place, let it be true that the correspondence is of the same sort throughout, that is a one-to-one relation between the members of the sets of parts, and that it is such that a certain sufficient description of C, which includes the fact that it is in this relation to *some* part of B, will determine a sufficient description of the part of B in question. And, in the third place, let it be true that the correspondence is such that when one determinant is part of another determinant, then any part determined by the first will be a part of a part determined by the second.[46]

This will yield us, concludes McTaggart, "an infinite series of parts of A, where the sufficient description of each set of parts implies the sufficient description of the set of parts below it. And thus the infinite series is no longer vicious."[47]

Thus the parts of the substance will be, as it were, reflected into each other, and reflected back, and back again to infinity. As a matter of fact McTaggart thinks that only selves, whose perceptions are infinitely divisible into parts that are also perceptions, can fulfill the conditions of determining correspondence.

---

[46] *The Nature of Existence*, I, §197.   [47] *Ibid.*, I, §198.

Broad's criticism of this theory is of the greatest importance, for he undertakes to show by a geometrical illustration how a substance might be divided into parts within parts to infinity, thus constituting, as he terms it, a "Fundamental Hierarchy" which, nevertheless, is not a determining correspondence hierarchy, thus refuting simultaneously both McTaggart's theory of determining correspondence and also the argument which he will later advance to show that matter cannot be real. Broad asks us to conceive of a line which has a sufficient description, such as "the longest line in the only country which is ruled by a government of class-conscious proletarians."[48] Let the sufficient description be symbolized by ϕ. Let part of the line be red, and let the other part be blue. Then, by making use of the six characteristics, ϕ, red, blue, longest, half of, and co-terminous with, we find sufficient descriptions for the members of an infinite number of sets of parts. (The reader is urged to consult Broad's diagram on page 375 of vol. I of the *Examination,* together with the exposition on pages 376 and 377, to see how the thing is done.)

What are we to make of this geometrical illustration? Frankly I do not know. I am conscious of a feeling of uneasiness similar to that which I experienced with respect to the universe of three minds and the universe of two minds. Clearly no such line could exist *in rerum natura.* And what we want is something that could exist there, for there McTaggart's minds exist, although whether they be infinitely divisible, as he claims, is another question. I note that Broad confesses that he has been unable "to think of any alternative illustration of a determining correspondence hierarchy."[49]

As I glance back over the course of the argument, I am impressed by the correctness of McTaggart's estimate of the importance of his ultimate, *a priori,* synthetic judgment that every substance is divisible. On this, as he truly says, his most important conclusions rest, and the unity of his system depends. Up to this point the argument possesses great strength. It is true that I have urged that we ought to reject the Dissimilarity of the Diverse, not so much because of the arguments which Broad has brought against it as because it appears to me inconsistent with McTaggart's own view that qualities are universals and that substance is something to be taken in conjunction with its nature, a view which I believe to be sound. Yet, even if I be right in my contention, too much should not be made of this. In the case of an argument which aims at proving its conclusion *a priori,* it is sufficient to suggest a logically conceivable alternative to cause the structure to vibrate, yet more

48 *EMcP,* I, 376.   49 *Ibid.,* I, 400.

than this is required to make it fall. We have seen how difficult it is to conceive of two entities exactly similar. I should be prepared to admit that it is highly probable that there are no particulars exactly alike, that, accordingly, every particular has an exclusive description, and even that it possesses a sufficient description. If, then, McTaggart be right in his judgment that every substance is infinitely divisible, the difficulty which he seeks to exorcise by his theory of determining correspondence actually does arise. And, while Broad's geometrical illustration would doubtless disturb me, I should need something more convincing than this to lead me to abandon the theory altogether. But, if McTaggart be wrong with regard to the infinite divisibility of substance, the difficulty will not arise, and the doctrine of determining correspondence will collapse.

Passing over the remaining chapters of volume I, despite the interesting material which they contain, I now proceed to the consideration of book VI, the first division of volume II, which contains Broad's discussion of McTaggart's treatment of cogitations—a discussion which culminates in a criticism of his view of self-knowledge. For McTaggart all experiences are basically cognitive. Those which are, as Broad says, "ostensibly cognitive," he classifies as perceptions (i.e., awarenesses of particulars), awarenesses of characteristics, judgments, assumptions and imagings. Perceptions and awarenesses he subsumes under the common term awareness, and awarenesses and judgments he classifies as cognitions. Cognitions, assumptions, and imagings together constitute cogitations.[50] For perception Broad substitutes *prehension,* for assumption *supposing,* and for judgment *judging*—in the last case "to make it perfectly clear that it is the name of an experience and not a proposition."[51] He adds, however, that knowing (i.e., awareness of fact) should be ranked as a third with prehension and awareness. This is an interesting suggestion, but one wonders on what ground it is advanced. Is it that facts are complexes, analyzable into, yet not mere aggregates of, particulars and universals; and that, accordingly, knowings must be complexes analyzable into, yet not mere aggregates of, prehensions and awarenesses?

This point is, perhaps, of subordinate importance. What disquiets me, however, is the substitution of *prehension* for *perception,* a substitution which was made at the beginning of volume I, but about which something must now be said. Broad doubts "whether one could possibly prehend *any* continuant, such as a mind or a material thing, in the sense in which one can prehend an experience or a sensum. Even on the

50 *The Nature of Existence,* II, § 406.   51 *EMcP,* II, Part I, 20.

naively realistic view of visual or tactual perception one does not literally prehend a material object which one is seeing or touching. At most
one prehends a certain part of its surface as characterised in certain
ways at the present time."[52] In other words Broad would want to say
that I "prehend" part of the colored surface of an apple, but that I "see"
or "perceive" the apple. Perception thus becomes a mean between prehension and inference.

In regard to this Broad is commendably frank. In his *Scientific
Thought* he tells us that "the relation between the sensum and its properties, on the one hand, and the perceptual judgment about the physical
object, on the other, is not that of inference."[53] And in a later passage
he writes:

If there were no sensible appearances to me, I suppose that I should not
judge there to be any physical reality. But, on the other hand, there is nothing
in my sensa to force me logically to the conclusion that there must be something beyond them, having the constitutive properties of physical objects. The
belief that our sensa are appearances of something more permanent and complex than themselves seems to be primitive, and to arise inevitably with the
sensing of the sensa. It is not reached by inference, and could not logically be
justified by inference. On the other hand, there is no possibility of refuting it
logically, or of getting rid of it, or—so far as I can see—of co-ordinating the
facts without it.[54]

Precisely what is meant by the assertion that the belief in physical
objects, as distinct from sensa, is primitive is not clear to me. If Broad
means that there is an innate disposition in all men to accept such a
view, he is surely making an unwarranted assertion. Nobody does so
except a philosopher who has adopted the sensum theory. The man in
the street, who does not distinguish between sensum and physical object, or between prehension and perception, certainly does not accept
it; the sensible object and the physical object are one and the same for
him, and he thinks that he is directly aware of it. And, once the distinction between sensa and physical objects has been made, it is surely illegitimate to buttress the belief in the latter by any appeal to the primitive.

None the less, ever since Locke claimed that the belief in the existence
of physical objects "passes under the name of knowledge," many epistemological dualists have invoked something in the nature of "animal
faith" or "instinct" or a "natural propensity to believe" in order to
support the same conviction. Now I feel sure that it is because McTaggart regards such a contention as wholly specious that he defines per-

52 *Ibid.*, II, Part I, 38.   53 P. 247.   54 *Ibid.*, p. 268.

ception as he does. It is because the philosopher who accepts the sensum theory can justify the belief in physical objects, if at all, only by inference that McTaggart is opposed to any use of the term *perception* which would tend to obscure this fact. Broad, as we have seen, candidly admits that such a logical justification cannot be given. We must interpret this, I think, to mean that he does not believe that an absolute demonstration of the existence of physical objects will be forthcoming; for it is clear, both from his subsequent statements and also from his whole procedure, that he considers that, by co-ordinating the facts,[55] the hypothesis that physical objects exist can be shown to possess a high degree of probability. But, since it is necessary thus to resort to inference, there seems to be no point in retaining the distinction between prehension and perception; and I, for one, prefer the unequivocal usage of McTaggart.

My sympathies, on the other hand, are with Broad when he rejects McTaggart's view that perceptions—or prehensions—are parts of the self. It is a fact, contends McTaggart, that retrospection reveals that the self was "fuller" when it was apprehending many percepts than when it was apprehending few, and that this is best accounted for by the theory that apprehensions are parts of the self. In reply Broad suggests that the self may be more "variegated" in the former case than in the latter. This involves the hypothesis that to every relational property of the self there corresponds an original quality, and that every acquisition of a relational property causes the self to acquire the corresponding original quality. This impresses me as an extraordinary supposition. The positing of such a multiplicity of original qualities seems a desperate expedient, we should surely have to assume a pre-established harmony to account for them; moreover a quality the acquisition of which was caused by the acquisition of a relational property would seem itself to be a relational quality. But, whatever the explanation of the difference between the two states of perception may be—and I should think that it might well be found in a feeling of some sort—I should certainly hesitate to accept McTaggart's view.

It has also been contended by McTaggart that cogitations, volitions and emotions, taken together, "exhaust the self," so that it is "completely comprised in them."[56] This is impossible, he urges, on the supposition that they are only relations, for, in the first place, it is incredible that the self should be "exhausted or comprised in its relations,"[57] and, in the second place, these will not be the only relations in

55 *Essay*, bk. IV, ch. II, § 14.
56 *The Nature of Existence*, II, § 412.   57 *Loc. cit.*

which it stands. On the other hand, there is no difficulty in supposing that the parts of the self exhaust or comprise it. This whole argument, observes Broad, depends on the assumption that a continuant can be identified with its history—an assumption which is illegitimate.

McTaggart further insists that the cognitive relation makes a greater initial difference to the knower than to the known—ultimately, of course, through the ensuing activity of the knower it may affect the known to a far greater degree—and that this greater initial difference is due to the fact that the cognitive relation involves in the knower the presence of a part which constitutes a perception, which, before the cognitive relation was established, the knower did not possess and which, without it, he would not possess; whereas nothing of the kind is involved in the case of the known. But the cognitive relation, as Broad points out, is nonsymmetrical, and also causal. The relation, therefore, will directly determine a change in the knower, whereas it can only indirectly determine a change in the known; and this consideration should suffice to account for the fact in question.

It is of vital importance for McTaggart to establish, not only that perceptions are parts of the self, but also that they are divisible into parts within parts to infinity, for, only so, can they meet the demands of determining correspondence. Accordingly, he undertakes to show that one perception can be part of another perception, the perceptum which is the object of the first being part of the perceptum which is the object of the second. He appeals, in the first place, to introspection which, he thinks, enables him to discriminate perceptions of parts, which perceptions are included within a perception of the whole containing these parts. Like Broad, I am unable to emulate this achievement, although I admit that an antecedent incredulity may inhibit my power of discrimination. Next McTaggart asks us to consider an experience of a type familiar to everyone wherein a datum steadfastly contemplated gradually seems to become more complex—as when, under an increasing light, fresh details appear in the pattern of a carpet. This indicates, he believes, that the perception of the pattern is becoming more complex. Yet surely, as Broad rejoins, it is more plausible to assume that different sensibilia are successively presented, each more complex than its predecessor. It does not seem, then, that McTaggart has made out his case.

Since he holds that it is impossible ever to "prehend" a particular, we know in advance that Broad will reject McTaggart's theory that the human self can prehend itself; yet, inasmuch as the issue is of paramount importance, not only for McTaggart's system but also for philosophy in general, we must scrutinize attentively both McTaggart's doctrine and Broad's criticism thereof. To begin with it is worth observing that the self, according to the sensum theory, stands in a very different position from a physical object, for, on that theory, it is not even true that a *part* of the physical object is ever "prehended," since the sensum, which is "prehended," is not part of the object at all, but a *tertium quid*. In the case of introspection, however, there is no *tertium quid;* whatever is apprehended falls within the self. Broad does not believe that the self has parts. Neither do I. Broad even doubts "whether we have any clear idea of what we mean when we talk of a mind as 'having parts.' "[58] So do I. But let us assume for the moment that the mind, or the self, does have parts. The self will then occupy a position analogous to that of the physical object on the naively realistic view. Its genuine parts will actually be prehended.

Consider the Buddhist-Sufi parable of the blind men who examined the elephant. One grasped its trunk, another its ear, and another its leg. The first judged that it resembled a rope, the second that it resembled a mat, the third that it resembled a tree. Each grasped a part, each made a misjudgment with respect to the whole. Yet, in ordinary speech, I think that we should say that they all grasped the elephant. And, if they touched the elephant, they prehended the elephant. The parts are in the whole and the whole is in the parts; to prehend the part, therefore, is to prehend the whole. So at least it might, I believe, be plausibly argued. And so it might be urged that to prehend a part of the self is to prehend the self. Accordingly, if McTaggart be right in maintaining that whatever is observed in introspection is a part of the self, the self will prehend itself in the prehending of its part.

Let us now revert to what Broad and I hold to be the true view, that the self has no parts. What, then, is prehended? Is it not the self in its simplicity? No, answers Broad, it is an experience of the self. The self is a continuant, its experiences are occurrents.[59] The experiences of the self are parts of its history, they are not parts of the self.

Now this seems to me sound doctrine, but I do not know how it is to be reconciled with Broad's tentative conclusion that the notion of *process* can be substituted for that of *thing* or *substance*. For he has definitely stated that a continuant is a thing;[60] and things, one gathers, are substances. One would be inclined to assume that Broad has, for the nonce, taken up a different position and is arguing on the assumption that there are substances, were it not for the fact that this assumption appears difficult to reconcile with his ultimate conclusions. In any case what I prehend in introspection is, according to Broad,

58 *EMcP*, I, Part I, 137.   59 *Ibid.*, II, Part I, 142.   60 *Ibid.*, I, 142.

"a short contemporary slice of the history of myself."[61] From this it follows, I take it, that, even if, *per impossibile,* I continuously introspected from birth to death, I should never prehend myself, although I should prehend every experience which the self ever had. For, in the first place, there would be no one prehension of the entire history of the self; there would be only a succession of prehensions of successive experiences. And, in the second place, even if the entire history of the self could be grasped in one prehension, the prehension of its history would not be equivalent to a prehension of the self.

Of course Broad holds that it may be possible to "perceive" the self, and that McTaggart might consistently have defended such a view. But what is perception? Broad defines it as "a cogitative experience which includes prehension, but also includes perceptual acceptance of propositions not guaranteed by the prehensive element alone."[62] Precisely so—it is an unholy amalgam of prehensions and judgments, judgments which may quite conceivably turn out to be misjudgments. But the question now presses upon us. If the self never be prehended, how did not the notion of selfhood even arise?

Broad answers this question in what, upon his premises, would appear to be the only possible way. The concept of selfhood, he tells us, is "in part *a priori* and in part empirical." The *a priori* part is the concept of a continuant. The empirical part is provided by reflection upon the data acquired through introspection[63] at various times, and the relations subsisting between them.[64]

If this be true, it is certainly a very unfortunate state of affairs. For, to reiterate a contention which Broad has himself stated in volume I,[65] if the concept of a continuant be *a priori* in a psychological rather than in an epistemological and ontological sense, how do we know that there is any reality corresponding to it? Is the situation really so desperate? The history of the self is made up of events in which the self is involved, or of states of the self. Is not the self present in them as the whole is in the part? Can they be prehended, as it were, in abstraction from the self to which they belong?

Broad's view that the self is not prehended in the prehension of its

---

61 *Ibid.,* II, Part II, 164.   62 *Ibid.,* II, Part I, 163.

63 "One empirically conceived factor is the peculiar kind of unity which ties together various simultaneous experiences in a single specious present; another is the fact that some experiences in one specious present are ostensibly memories of certain experiences in earlier specious presents; another is the fact that certain experiences in one specious present are ostensibly fulfilments or frustrations of certain expectations in earlier specious presents; and so on." *Ibid.,* II, Part I, 168.

64 *Ibid.,* II, Part I, 168–169.   65 Pp. 52f.

occurents is obviously connected with the doubt which he evinces concerning the proposition, which McTaggart regards as self-evident that "there cannot be experience which is not experienced by a self."[66] As I have already stated, this proposition does seem self-evident to me. And it seems to me that Descartes was right in maintaining that in introspection one can discriminate between the ego which is doing the cogitating and the cogitating which the ego is doing. This is also McTaggart's view. And he undertakes to vindicate it in the following way. It is possible, he points out, to judge that one is aware of something, of anything you please—to use his own illustration, of equality. The judgment "I am aware of this awareness" is "not merely a judgment that a particular person is aware of this awareness. It also asserts that the person who is aware of the awareness is the person who is making a judgment."[67] For this asserted identity to be established it is essential that the self which makes the judgment should know the self which has this awareness either directly or by description. But it is impossible that inference should yield any description which will establish this identity. For all that can be inferred is that *some* self is the subject of this awareness, since we know that every awareness does belong to a self; inference cannot tell us *what* self is involved. If, on the other hand, the subject "which is a term in the judgment, and which is known by perception, is perceived as having the awareness,"[68] the problem is solved.

In his criticism of this argument Broad distinguishes between a "milder" and a "stronger" interpretation of McTaggart's statement, quoted above, that the judgment asserts that "the person who is aware of this awareness is the person who is making a judgment." The milder interpretation reads, "If anyone judges that he is having a certain experience, his judgment cannot be true unless this judgment and that experience both belong to the same self."[69] The stronger form reads, "If anyone judges that he is having a certain experience, he is *ipso facto* judging that this judgment and this experience belong to the same self."[70] The milder interpretation, he concedes, is true; the stronger interpretation he believes to be false. "If it were true," he writes, "every ego-centric judgment would be *identical with* or *necessarily accompanied by* a certain judgment *about itself*. The first alternative is nonsensical, and I know of no reason to accept the second. So far as my own introspection can inform me, I quite often make judgments like 'I am angry' without at the same time making a judgment like 'This judgment

---

[66] *The Nature of Existence*, II, § 400.
[67] *Ibid.*, II, § 383.
[68] *Loc. cit.*
[69] *EMcP*, II, Part I, 185.
[70] *Ibid.*, II, Part I, 186.

and this feeling of anger belong to the same self!"[71] He also points out that it is possible for a person to judge that there are plane figures of exactly similar shape and different areas without even thinking of Euclid's parallel postulate. The inference would seem to be that it is possible to judge "I am angry" without even thinking of the identity of the person judging with the person who is angry.

If this be the inference which we are expected to draw, I must say at once that it appears to me quite erroneous. If it were sound, it would surely be the case that, if someone pointed out to me the identity of the subject of the judgment and the subject of the feeling, I should be conscious of contemplating a fact of which I had before been unaware. But in reality I should be conscious of no such thing. It is one thing to formulate a judgment explicitly; it is another to make a judgment implicitly. And surely we do continually make implicit judgments. I am certainly aware that I am seated in a chair, or that I am standing upright, without making explicit judgments that I am doing so. Psychologists have told us that one reason why we feel disquietude when we stand on the brink of a cliff is that we then lack a criterion for an implicit judgment as to our erect attitude. And a motorist who could not make implicit judgments would soon lose his driver's license. The only alternative that I can see to admitting that cogitations of this kind are implicit judgments would be to assert that they are perceptions; and it is obvious that perceptions—or prehensions, as Broad would say— would suit McTaggart as well as judgments, if not better. I would urge, then, that, when I judge that I am angry, I am contemplating the identity of the subject of the judgment with the subject of the feeling, even if I do not, as most likely I shall not, explicitly formulate a judgment to that effect. If this contention be sound, the stronger interpretation is true, or, at least, nearer the truth than the milder. And the point is of importance, for the stronger interpretation involves direct awareness of the self, whereas the milder does not.

Broad styles McTaggart's theory of the self the "Proper-Name Theory," on the ground that "he uses the word 'I' as a proper name, in the logical sense, for this prehended particular."[72] In contradistinction to it Broad recognizes two other possible "analyses of ego-centric facts," which he terms respectively the "Disguised Description Theory" and the "Logical Construction Theory," the latter admitting of two forms, the "Bundle Theory" and the "Somatocentric Theory."[73] Broad writes, "In McTaggart's opinion it is impossible to prove the Proper-Name Theory directly, but it is possible to prove it indirectly by refuting the

[71] Loc. cit.   [72] Ibid., II, Part I, 174.   [73] Ibid., II, 174–176.

other two theories which are the only alternatives to it. Thus his argument *for* reflexive self-prehension consists of an argument *against* the Logical Construction Theory and the Disguised Description Theory of ego-centric facts."[74] I cannot help thinking that this passage might seriously mislead the unwary reader, who has not consulted McTaggart's text, into assuming that McTaggart undertakes to build his own theory upon the ruins of its rivals, and that, should he fail to refute any of these theories on its own premisses—as Broad thinks that he does fail in the case of the Bundle Theory—his own theory falls. In so doing he would certainly be mistaken. It is true that McTaggart does not believe that his own theory can be proved directly, but this is because the existence of the self is self-evident. All that one can do is to try, as McTaggart has tried, to bring this self-evidence into prominence by showing that no one can justifiably make any statements with respect to his self unless that self be directly apprehended. "I am certain," he writes,

that it is I who am angry, even though I am aware of no characteristic of the anger from which it could be inferred what particular self had it, and even though I am aware of no characteristic of the judgment from which it could be inferred what particular self made it. My knowledge that it is the same self, which is angry and which makes the judgment, is as immediate and direct as my knowledge that some self is angry and that some self makes the judgment. Unless, therefore, I perceive myself, and perceive myself as having anger and as making the judgment, what will be the data before me? Only the awareness of a state of anger, the awareness of a judgment, and the general principle that every state of anger and every judgment must belong to *some* self. This will not justify the conclusion that the anger and the judgment belong to the same self, and therefore I shall not be entitled to assert, 'I am angry.'[75]

If this contention be sound, the Bundle Theory cannot stand for a moment, for that theory, as "properly enunciated," denies that there is any self at all.[76]

The Bundle Theory, which derives from Hume, admits the reality of psychic experiences, and asserts that those which constitute the same bundle are inter-connected by a relation of some sort which differentiates them from similar experiences contained in other bundles. McTaggart suggests a number of different relations, shows that none of them will meet the requirements, can think of no other possibilities, and concludes that the theory breaks down. Broad complains that he has not considered the possibility that some combination of these relations might prove satisfactory, nor the further possibility that the relation might be

---

[74] *Ibid.,* II, Part I, 175.
[75] *The Nature of Existence,* II, § 387.   [76] *EMcP,* II, Part I, 176.

one that holds only between experiences and for which we have no name. Accordingly he considers that McTaggart has not refuted the theory.

The Somato-centric Theory asserts "that ego-centric facts are really about certain relations between experiences and organisms."[77] Psychic experiences which would ordinarily be said to belong to the same self are in reality connected by the same relation to the same organism. McTaggart affirmed that one can be certain that one is angry without believing that both the feeling and the judgment are caused by bodily states. Broad thinks that the theory can be refuted without appealing to a direct awareness of the self; the upholder of the view could be compelled to admit that, if it be true, his judgment that he feels anger must be connected with the same body and by the same relation as the feeling is, and then that he can be made to admit that he is surer that he is angry than he is as to what the relation is, or whether it actually holds in both instances, and thus be forced either to abandon the theory or to lapse into silence.

According to the Disguised Description Theory, when one makes the judgment "I am having such and such an experience," it "would be more properly expressed by saying 'There is one and only one particular which has the characteristic C, and this experience belongs to it.' "[78] In other words there is a self which is the unique owner of the experience, but this self is not directly apprehended. Broad believes that the theory can be refuted by calling attention to the fact that one frequently makes with complete certainty such judgments as "I am aware of desiring tea and I have a twinge of toothache," and then pointing out that it is impossible to establish by inference that the self which prehends the former experience is also the owner of the latter.[79]

It seems obvious that, were it not for his conviction that the notion of a continuant is an *a priori* concept, Broad would prefer McTaggart's view to any of the others which he has outlined. In this connection I should observe that Broad distinguishes between what he calls the "unqualified" and the "qualified" forms of McTaggart's theory, although he believes that McTaggart himself did not notice the discrepancy. According to the "unqualified" form of the theory the self apprehends itself as a self; according to the "qualified" form what is apprehended is that portion of the self which falls within the specious present, and, since McTaggart rejected the Pure Ego theory, it follows that this can be only a part of the self; hence Broad concludes that the "qualified"

77 *Ibid.*, II, Part I, 176.   78 *Ibid.*, II, Part I, 190.   79 *Ibid.*, II, Part I, 194–198.

form could be rendered compatible with the Bundle Theory as "improperly enunciated" if the latter were suitably modified.

In book VI Broad touches upon numerous topics in the discussion of which, did space permit, it would be of great interest to follow him. He reproaches McTaggart for not distinguishing between emotions and sentiments; he criticises McTaggart's theory that volitions and emotions are cogitations with volitional and emotional qualities, and reaches the conclusion that, although not established beyond cavil, it is yet highly plausible; and he makes the pregnant suggestion that desires are a special kind of emotions. But we must hasten on to consider his treatment of McTaggart's doctrine of the unreality of time.

As McTaggart presents his own theory it is developed out of a criticism of that propounded by Lord Russell in his *Principles of Mathematics*. According to Russell the relations of temporal priority and posteriority are objective, and thus independent of any conscious ego; whereas, past, present and future are subjective in the sense that they do presuppose such a consciousness, and with its removal they would vanish. Change is to be identified with "the difference, in respect of truth or falsehood, between a proposition concerning an entity and the time T, and a proposition concerning the same entity and the time T', provided that these propositions differ only by the fact that T occurs in the one where T' occurs in the other."[80]

McTaggart's objection is that this does not constitute genuine change at all. On Russell's view the statement that an entity possesses a certain characteristic at one moment, and the statement that it does not possess it at another moment, will both always be true; whereas if we are to have genuine change, the same proposition must be at one time true and at another time false. All events in the universe which occur coincidentally can be regarded, McTaggart points out, as a single composite event; and these composite events will be connected by relations of earlier and later, which relations will be unchanging, consequently these relations will not suffice to give us time, for time involves change. For relations to endure—and relations of temporal priority and posteriority must endure—there must be real time for them to persist in, and this involves past, present and future—otherwise they could no more be said to endure or to persist than can relations between numbers or letters of the alphabet. Thus the series of past, present and future events—which McTaggart terms the A series—is fundamental, and the series of earlier and later events—which McTaggart terms the B series—is derived from it.

[80] *The Principles of Mathematics*, § 442; quoted in *The Nature of Existence*, II, § 313.

Broad concedes that Russell's theory fails to account for "the transitory aspect of time," and that McTaggart is right in insisting on the fundamental character of the A series; but he dissents from McTaggart's view that time involves qualitative change. Mere duration without qualitative change would suffice. *Prima facie* there would appear to be a discrepancy between McTaggart's assertion that, if the terms of the B series did not differ in their non-temporal qualities, there would be no time,[81] and his statement to the effect that the only characteristics of an event which can change are its determinations by the terms of the A series[82]—i.e., in respect of pastness, presentness and futurity. The apparent discrepancy, however, is easily removed. Successive events in the B series will necessarily be qualitatively differentiated, for events are substances, and the nature of every substance is qualitatively distinct from that of every other substance. Every particular event, however, will always possess all the non-temporal qualities that it ever possesses, otherwise it would not remain identical with itself; but, if time be real, it cannot always be future, or present or past; these characteristics, therefore, and these only, will change.

It is clear that no event in the B series can become present in relation either to the previous or to the posterior event, for the relations of earlier and later are unchanging whereas to become present an event must cease to be future. It can become present, then, only in relation to something outside the B series. What could this something be? McTaggart suggests that it might be a moment, and has been blamed by Broad for so doing.[83] Russell, however, had already introduced moments, and McTaggart probably thought that another opponent might do likewise.[84] What he is concerned to show is that moments will not suffice to give us presentness, for, if an event can become present in a present moment, that moment cannot itself become present in relation to a prior or a posterior moment in the same series as itself, since all these moments will constitute only another B series. Any entity in relation to which an event in the B series can become present will either be a member of another time series or else it will be non-temporal. By what Broad calls the "Main Argument" McTaggart shows that a moment in another B series can become present only in relation to something outside the series, and that, if this something be a moment in a third B series, another series must be posited, and so *ad infinitum*. If the notion of event be substituted for that of moment, the argument still holds good. By what Broad calls the "Subsidiary Argument" McTaggart

<hr>

81 *The Nature of Existence,* II, § 362.   82 *Ibid.,* II, § 311.
83 *EMcP,* II, Part I, 314.   84 *The Nature of Existence,* II, § 310.

shows that a non-temporal entity could not become a term in a temporal relation without itself being temporalized.

Broad protests that McTaggart has tried to exorcise the problem of time by the use of temporal predicates and non-temporal copulas. But this is precisely the charge which McTaggart brings against Russell, and, whatever mistakes he may have committed, it is highly unlikely that he would repeat the very error which he has detected in his opponent's argument. As a matter of fact McTaggart's whole point is that temporal predicates can be used only in conjunction with temporal copulas. There would be no contradiction, he declares, in a term possessing the incompatible characteristics of pastness, presentness and futurity if it possessed them successively;[85] but the difficulty is that an event in the B series can become past, present or future only in relation to an entity which is not itself a member of another B series, and that no such entity has been discovered. Consequently, since no term can possess these incompatible characteristics simultaneously, no term can possess them at all. What follows? What follows, McTaggart urges, is the conclusion that both the B series and the A series are only appearances of a series of entities—the C series—all the members of which possess only non-temporal characteristics.

I am unable to see that Broad has refuted this contention. What he has done is to develop a rival theory of time, based on the notions of absolute becoming and of an event-particle. "Qualitative change and motion," he tells us, "presuppose qualitative or substantial persistence, and both presuppose temporal becoming."[86] The notion of absolute becoming he considers to be so "simple and fundamental" as to be incapable of analysis.[87] An event-particle is an instantaneous term which has "temporal position but no duration,"[88] and processes consist of compact series of event-particles.

The notion of event-particle clearly stands or falls with that of absolute becoming, and the notion of absolute becoming is obviously involved in—if it be not identical with—that of pure process; and this notion, as I have already stated, I find unintelligible. I shall not, therefore, discuss it directly, but shall touch upon some of the difficulties which I find in Broad's theory, difficulties which appear to me so insuperable that I think that it is quite likely that I have misunderstood him. I shall, however, state them briefly.

The basis of the notion of event-particle, Broad informs us, is the experience of "temporal boundaries."[89] By a temporal boundary he

[85] *Ibid.*, II, § 330.   [86] *EMcP*, II, Part I, 277.
[87] *Ibid.*, II, Part I, 281.   [88] *Ibid.*, II, Part I, 273.   [89] *Ibid.*, II, Part I, 275.

means the beginning or ending of a process. To use his own illustration, the hissing of a gas fire is a process and so is the striking of a clock, but if the latter start while the former is going on, one hears the boundary between the hissing-without-striking and the hissing-with-striking.[90] This boundary has temporal position but no temporal extension. It would seem, then, to be identical with an event-particle. Yet we are told that "it seems evident from direct inspection that the objects which we apprehend at any moment *are not* instantaneous event-particles, and that the notion of an event-particle is a rather elaborate and sophisticated product."[91] I am at a loss, therefore, to determine whether event-particles be, or be not, directly apprehended; this, however, is doubtless a point of subordinate importance.

What I am more concerned about is the status of an event-particle when it is not becoming; that is before it becomes and after it has become. It is evident that we cannot posit a series of co-existent event-particles, some of which are future, one of which is present, and some of which are past; for then, as Broad concedes,[92] we should have to posit a second time-dimension in which presentness could sweep along from one event-particle to another, and then a third, and so on to infinity— which is precisely McTaggart's point. What, then, is the alternative? That nothing is real except the event-particle which is present? But this will leave us with a reality which has no duration at all. I feel sure that Broad does not now hold such a view, and I am loath to attribute it to him at the time when he wrote the *Examination,* yet I do not see how to avoid doing so.

The situation is further complicated by Broad's ingenious theory of the Specious Present which is too complicated for us to examine in detail but which does involve the possession by the immediate past of the characteristic of presentedness. Each Specious Present consists of a very short period, and the succession of Specious Presents constitutes a compact series with no next terms. The contents of Specious Presents which lie close to each other will partially overlap, but a duration which is prehended as a temporal whole will not coincide with the period during which it is so prehended, nor will the two periods overlap; they will merely be adjoined. Thus the content prehended will always be actually past although it will be prehended as present—it will, so to speak, be temporally dislocated. "Thus the prehended phase is completely past at the moment when it first begins to be prehended, and it is getting more and more remotely past throughout the period during

90 *Ibid.,* II, Part I, 274.　　91 *Ibid.,* II, Part I, 282.　　92 *Ibid.,* II, Part I, 277–279.

which it continues to be prehended as a temporal whole."[93] How much of the past is real? All of it? Then we shall have coexistent event-particles, one of which is present and the rest of which are past, and, as McTaggart has pointed out,[94] the difficulty which he has raised will still confront us, even if we deny the reality of the future. Or is only so much of the past real as can be prehended within any one Specious Present? We shall not have escaped the difficulty, however, by making the past shorter. Moreover it is conceivable that the Specious Presents of various individuals may vary in temporal extension, yet the content prehended in each case must be equally real.

There is a further point which deserves notice. Broad regards it as a merit of his view that it involves only a minimum of misperception, in the sense of a slight temporal dislocation, in comparison with that of McTaggart which treats all temporal appearance as completely delusive. Yet the prior question is surely whether the notion of misperception be defensible. If not, it ought not to be employed at all. If it be, it is surely legitimate to seek to explain our difficulties in terms of it; and the theory which makes most use of it may, for that very reason be the better theory.

On the other hand, if it be possible to over-work the notion of misperception, it appears extremely likely that McTaggart has done so, for in his system it provides what might be called a blanket explanation of the principal difficulties. McTaggart has denied the reality of matter and sensa on the ground that they cannot meet the requirements of determining correspondence;[95] as we have just seen, he has pronounced time to be unreal; and he regards judgings and supposings and imagings as perceptions which are themselves misperceived. Human experience, therefore, is infected with error to a tremendous extent. But how does McTaggart conceive of misperception? With respect to this question I share the perplexity which Broad acknowledges in chapter XXXVI of vol. II. At first sight the most plausible explanation would seem to be that McTaggart believed in non-characterising characteristics—such as the qualities of shape and color and the relations of before and after—and that he thought that these appear to characterise—although they do not actually characterise—particulars. This is surely a defensible, if not a very usual, view. But we must remember that, when McTaggart

---

[93] *Ibid.,* II, Part I, 288.   [94] *The Nature of Existence,* II, § 341.

[95] Broad rejects McTaggart's contention on two counts; (1) he does not believe that particulars are all infinitely divisible, and (2) he believes that, if they were, matter and sensa might well be infinitely divisible without meeting all the demands of determining correspondence. The argument is too intricate for me to attempt in the space at my disposal to expound and criticise, but the reader will find it in Chapter XXXIII, in Part I. of vol. II.

was writing the first volume of *The Nature of Existence,* he did not believe in non-characterising characteristics; universals, he held, existed in the particulars which they characterised, and had no reality apart from such existence. It is true, however, that he held that a characteristic which does not, as such, characterise anything, will yet exist as an element in a negative characteristic; thus, on the supposition that nothing possesses color, color will nevertheless exist as an element in the negative characteristic *not-colored.* Can this rather extraordinary theory be taken as a clue to the interpretation of McTaggart's doctrine of misperception?

I am inclined to think that it can, and I would cite in confirmation of my view the following passage from p. 311 of vol. II of *The Nature of Existence.*

It seems clear that we *can* perceive substances as having negative characteristics. For we can make apparent judgments that they have not certain characteristics, and these apparent judgments must be, in reality, perceptions of them *as* not having these characteristics, which is the same thing as perceiving them as having the corresponding negative characteristics.

I believe that this passage definitely answers the question as to how McTaggart conceived of misperception. But I do not for a moment pretend that I find the answer satisfactory, or that I regard as intelligible the assertion that positive non-characterising characteristics can exist as elements in existent negative characteristics.

If the A series and the B series be both appearances, it is clear that there must be a reality of which they are appearances. And we must also conclude, according to McTaggart, that a reality which appears as a temporal series must itself constitute a series, although, of course, a non-temporal one. Such a series he refers to as a C series. There will be as many of these series as there are selves, and parts of selves, which misperceive their objects as being in time. All such selves, and all their parts, which constitute the dimension of determining correspondence are divided in another dimension into states of misperception, each such series making up a C series. In no such series do the misperceptions constitute a set of parts making up the whole without remainder; for the whole is a correct perception,[96] and it is clear that a correct perception

96 Each of the infinite number of veridical perceptions into which the self is divided in the dimension of determining correspondence will constitute the end-term of an inclusion series, all the previous terms of which will be states of misperception. The whole which they compose is, of course, also a veridical perception which contains the entire content of the self, both the correct perceptions which fall within the dimension of determining correspondence and also all the series of states of misperception which are the previous terms of the inclusion series of which it is the last term, and those which are contained within the correct perceptions which are its parts.

cannot constitute the sum of a number of misperceptions. In this sense the misperceptions are not infinitely divisible. On the contrary they are fragmentary parts, as McTaggart terms them, which is to say that they overlap, much as—to use his own illustration—the eleven inch section of a ruler overlaps the ten inch section, the ten inch the nine inch, and so on. The relation "included in" appears as that of "earlier than," and the relation "inclusive of" appears as that of "later than." Every inclusion series is bounded at one end by non-entity and at the other end terminates in the all-inclusive state of veridical perception which perceives itself to be eternal, and which perceives the included states—which appear to themselves to be in time—as also eternal.

This ingenious theory was elaborately expounded in all requisite detail by McTaggart in the second volume of *The Nature of Existence,* and has been subjected by Broad to a careful and equally detailed criticism. Into the ramifications of these discussions it is impossible for us to enter; I shall, therefore, confine my observations to a few points of fundamental importance.

In the first place Broad considers that McTaggart has not proved that the relations "included in" and "inclusive of" do appear as the relations "earlier than" and "later than." McTaggart's argument, as we have just seen—is that, since misperceptions cannot by adjunction constitute a correct perception and so make up a set of parts of such a perception, the only relation which can obtain between them is that of inclusion; and that, inasmuch as inclusion is the relation which really holds between the terms of the C series, it must be this relation, and no other, which appears as the relation of temporal priority and posteriority. But, as Broad truly says, it is difficult to think of perceptions—or prehensions, to use his own terminology—"as complex particulars, having other particulars as parts. The whole notion is so odd and unfamiliar that one hesitates to be sure about what might be possible or impossible if prehensions really were of this nature."[97] The best that can be said in reply is, I think, that, if the assumption be more plausible than any of the alternatives considered by McTaggart, and, if on the basis of it we can give a coherent account of appearances, the hypothesis ought to be accepted until one more satisfactory can be formulated. Possibly McTaggart himself would have claimed no more than this. Yet it must be conceded that the theory makes a fresh demand upon our powers of conception; for, not only are we required to admit that a correct perception can be divisible *ad infinitum* into correct perceptions, but also that each

97 *EMcP,* II, Part II, 422.

of these correct perceptions can contain within itself a series of misperceptions included one within another.

In the second place Broad acknowledges[98] that, upon his own principles, McTaggart is justified in concluding that it is the relation "inclusive of" which appears as the relation "later than," and the relation "included in" which appears as the relation "earlier than." The admission is an important one, for the consequences are of enormous significance from the point of view of our practical interests. Were it the other way around, we should *sub specie temporis* be proceeding from a heaven —i.e., the all-inclusive state—which lies behind toward nothingness; whereas, if McTaggart be right, we are *sub specie temporis* proceeding from nothingness toward a heaven which lies before us.

And, in the third place, Broad advances a very serious objection to certain statements whereby McTaggart seeks to justify the notion of misperception which plays so great a part in his system. *Sub specie temporis* every perception, asserts McTaggart, is self-evidently correct— with a single qualification. That qualification is imposed by the specious present. "And so," he writes, "at any moment, p, I perceive not only what is happening at that moment, but also what happens at the earlier moments between m and p. Thus if A existed and was X at the moment o, I may perceive it at the moment p, when perhaps it has ceased to exist or to be X. And thus A need not exist or be X at the moment at which I perceive it. What is meant is that, if at the moment p I perceive A as X, then it is self-evidently certain that X exists and is A at some moment or moments which I am then perceiving as present."[99] Since, however, time is unreal "the limitation must be restated 'A exists and is X at a point or points in the C series which appear to be present at the point in the C series at which the perception exists.' "[100]

How much error does this restatement allow for? It allows, Broad thinks, for very little. The characteristic which appears to characterise, yet does not characterise a certain term, must be real, and must actually characterise some other term close to that which it does appear to characterise.[101] Now it is clear that McTaggart needs to account for a far greater degree of error than this, since, if he is right, all spatial, temporal and sensible characteristics do not really characterise anything. What is his defence? His defence is the contention that, when we grasp the nature of the terms in the C series, the limitation upon correctness turns out to be a qualification of the correctness.[102] When we make the translation from the temporal into the eternal, we discover that the

98 *Ibid.*, II, Part II, 526.   99 *The Nature of Existence*, II, § 514.
100 *Ibid.*, II, § 515.   101 *EMcP*, II, Part I, 332–339, 447–450.
102 *The Nature of Existence*, II, § 515.

qualification "turns out to be really, 'from a standpoint involving a certain error.' "[103] The amount of error depends upon the place of the perception in the C series, and the place of the perception depends upon the *amount* of perception.[104]

An inquiry into this notion of amount would involve us in a discussion of what McTaggart terms the D series; the series, that is to say, of the "increments" formed by the overlapping of one misperception by another, which increments possess extensive magnitude in contrast to the intensive magnitude possessed by the misperceptions. This is, indeed, a "subtle teaching"—to use the Hindu phrase—and I acquiesce only too gladly in the fact that the limitations of space preclude any attempt on my part to expound it, and to examine Broad's treatment of it. Extent and clarity are notions which I find clearly intelligible when applied to perceptions, but I have not the faintest idea as to what *amount* of perception can be. McTaggart's whole doctrine of misperception Broad finds so unsatisfying that he thinks that he may have misunderstood it. This is, of course, possible, although far be it from me to say that it is probable. I know only that, if he has misunderstood it, so have I.

In the concluding chapters of *The Nature of Existence* McTaggart elaborates a theory of value which is of extreme interest and importance, and so, needless to add, is Broad's examination thereof. Here, again, I must confine my observations to a few basic issues. It is self-evident, McTaggart maintains, that only selves, or parts of selves, have value; hence no group of selves has value; all the value to be found in the group is in the selves which compose the group.[105] His contention, from a practical point of view, is of high import; for its repercussions upon the tendency to deify the state are obvious. In the concluding sentences of his essay on *The Individualism of Value* McTaggart has made them explicit, "If what I have said is true," he writes,

> it will follow that, whatever activity it is desirable for the State to have, it will only be desirable as a means, and that the activity, and the State itself, can have no value but as a means. And a religion which fastens itself on a means has not risen above fetish-worship. Compared with worship of the State, zoolatry is rational and dignified. A bull or a crocodile may not have great intrinsic value, but it has some. The State has none. It would be as reasonable to worship a sewage pipe, which also possesses considerable value as a means.

Broad declares that the proposition that groups of selves do not have value is not self-evident to him. It does not follow, if he be right—nor

---

[103] *Ibid.*, II, § 591.   [104] *Loc. cit.*

[105] McTaggart has in mind, of course, only intrinsic value. He would not think of denying that some groups of selves possess instrumental value of a high order.

does he suggest that it follows—that no intrinsic value is to be found in the individual, and that the state will be justified in treating him simply as a means. Yet if the State does possess intrinsic value—which he does not assert—the claims and counter-claims of state and individual may well turn out to be more difficult to adjudicate than if McTaggart's contention be sound.

The value of anything is determined, according to McTaggart, by two "independent variables," as Broad well calls them—(1) The intensity of certain qualities, which Broad terms "valifying characteristics,"[106] and (2) its duration. The characteristics which have been held to determine positive and negative value are (1) knowledge and error, (2) virtue and vice, (3) the possession of certain emotions, (4) pleasure and pain, (5) amount and intensity of consciousness, and (6) harmony and disharmony.[107] It is self-evident, McTaggart considers, that an experience of a relatively low degree of intensity would have value greater than that of an experience of a higher degree of intensity if it only lasted long enough after the other had ceased. Broad agrees that this is the case if the same valifying characteristics be present in both experiences, and if the degree of their intensity remain unaltered throughout each experience; if these qualifications be eliminated, the principle in his eyes is no longer self-evident. Thus he believes that McTaggart was wrong in asserting that a life in which there was a very low degree of consciousness and a very little excess of pleasure over pain, and which was incapable of virtue or love would, if only it endured for a sufficiently long time, exceed in value a life which possessed in a high degree knowledge, virtue, love, pleasure and intensity of consciousness, which was unmixedly good, and which lasted for a million years.[108] After having observed that we must assume that the first life likewise comes to an end—otherwise the comparison will be between a finite and an infinite duration—Broad points out that the second life possesses valifying characteristics not found in the first, and also that the valifying characteristics found in both vary in intensity much more in the second life than in the first, and thus provide it with an elaborate pattern as contrasted with the monotonous regularity of the other. Accordingly he thinks that even a mere fifty years of the second life might reasonably be preferred to a billion of the first.

While I am not certain as to just what Broad means by a pattern of varying intensities, I feel quite sure that he is right in his main con-

---

106 *Ibid.*, II, Part II, 663–668.

107 *The Nature of Existence*, II, § 813. McTaggart himself rejects the sixth on the ground that he can "see no good or evil under this head which does not come under one of the other five."

108 *Ibid.*, II, § 869.

tention. There are sequoias in California which are said to have been standing where now they stand when Solomon was building the temple. What reasonable man would choose a life such as that of one of these trees, even if he knew that it would be prolonged for a billion years, in preference to the relatively short span of a Plato, a Leonardo da Vinci or a Washington? It seems to me, however, that the situation is complicated by a further consideration which neither writer discusses. Does not the cessation of a value, I would ask, generate a disvalue, and is not this disvalue proportionate to the intensity and duration of the value destroyed? I should answer both questions in the affirmative. Of course I cannot argue directly for the truth of my assertion, any more than McTaggart or Broad could argue directly for the truth of the judgments which they take to be self-evident; none the less I cannot doubt it. And it is this conviction, I opine, which leads every great religion to insist that its heaven is either timeless or unending. McTaggart would say, I presume,—I do not know whether Broad would agree—that the cessation of an experience which has value would be an evil only if it caused displeasure in a contemplating mind. It seems to me that it would be an evil whether anyone knew of it or not. Otherwise should we not have to say that if a man were killed painlessly when asleep or in a state of coma, and if no one missed him after his murder, no evil had been produced thereby—except on the hypothesis that the man's spirit survived, recalled his previous life, and did not like to remember that he had been assassinated? Of course the disvalue which I think I discern would pertain, I assume, to the universe. In so far as values produced in it were destroyed, the universe would be a bad universe; in so far as they were conserved, the universe would be a good universe. From this McTaggart would certainly dissent; for his universe is only a group of selves, and no group has value. But I am not sure that the universe is only a group of selves, and I think that it does have value. I am pleased to see that Broad regards the latter contention as at least an open question.[109]

The final stage of the C series, according to McTaggart, has infinite value. The point is of vital importance for him, since it is the basis of his optimism. The infinite good of the final stage infinitely outweighs all the evil in the pre-final stages. It is for this reason that he is justified in referring to it as "heaven." The infinitude of its value is due to its unboundedness; it includes all the pre-final stages whereas it itself is included by nothing.

Broad has advanced the important objection that the argument is vitiated by a confused use of the term *unbounded*. McTaggart asks us to contemplate a series which would be like the C series in other re-

109 *EMcP*, II, Part II, 694.

spects, but which would have no first term and no last term. The value of each term would be finite, yet the value of the series would be infinite because it is unbounded. He next asks us to turn to the C series with its end-term beyond which there is nothing, and to acknowledge that the value of this term is infinite because it is unbounded. Broad's objection is that the term *unbounded* is not employed in a univocal sense in the two cases. "Plainly it is quite unjustifiable," he writes,

to argue that because 'being unbounded in at least one direction' (in the sense appropriate only to *series*) confers infinite value on any *series* of valuable terms which has this property, therefore 'being unbounded in at least one direction' (in the sense appropriate only to *single* terms) must confer infinite value on any valuable *term* which has this property.[110]

The objection is a serious one, and I regret more than I can say that we shall never know how McTaggart would have replied to it. I do not think, however, that it deprives McTaggart's view of all plausibility. Believers in the eternal have usually thought of it, as did Boethius, as an *interminabilis vitae tota atque simul perfecta possessio*, the value of which because of its very compression—so to speak—into a durationless state would exceed that of an endlessly strung out series of temporal states possessed of finite values. An infinity wholly possessed is contrasted with an infinity never realized. It is difficult, as Broad truly says, to know what we are talking about, when we speak of the eternal, because of the difficulty of conceiving of the eternal. Yet, if it be a valid conception, some such conclusion seems indicated. But McTaggart's argument does seem exposed to objection which Broad has raised.

Broad also points out that the final stage will be devoid of some of what we generally esteem the highest virtues—such as heroism and self-sacrifice. Undoubtedly it will. Is this a defect? On McTaggart's premises I do not believe that it is. Heroism and self-sacrifice are virtues which manifest themselves, it might be urged, only when character is in the process of being perfected. But in a perfect society of perfect selves the need, as well as the opportunity, to exercise them will have passed away. A hero will not cease to be a hero because he has exterminated the dragons, nor a saint cease to be a saint because he no longer feels the pull of temptation.

In two fascinating chapters Broad discusses McTaggart's doctrine of a plurality of lives, and in a third McTaggart's attitude toward theism. With respect to the former, he has written as follows:

It seems to me to be a doctrine which ought to be taken very seriously, both on philosophical grounds and as furnishing a reasonable motive to right conduct.

110 *Ibid.*, II, Part II, 751.

We have to conduct our present lives on *some* postulate or other, positive or negative, about what happens to our minds at the death of our bodies. We shall behave all the better if we act on the assumption that we may survive; that actions which tend to strengthen and enrich our characters in this life will probably have a favourable influence on the dispositions with which we begin our next lives; and that actions which tend to disintegrate our characters in this life will probably cause us to enter on our next life 'halt and maimed.' If we suppose that our future lives will be of the same general nature as our present lives, this postulate, which is in itself intelligible and not unreasonable, gains enormously in concreteness and therefore in practical effect on conduct.[111]

With all this I am in cordial agreement. Broad also remarks that the doctrine in question is "a commonplace in the Far East." It is true that the doctrine of a plurality of lives is accepted by the great majority of Hindu and by all Buddhist philosophers; yet it is, perhaps, worth while to recall that, in the case of most of these philosophers, it is associated with a metaphysic very different from that of McTaggart. McTaggart's system is a pluralistic, atheistic idealism. The nearest approach to such a position on the part of any oriental thinkers with whom I am acquainted is to be found in certain developments of the Yogacara school of Buddhism in China and Japan. The famous Advaita of Samkara is a singularism which bears a remote resemblance to that of Bradley. The Jaina, Sāmkhya, Yoga and Mīmāmsa philosophies are all absolute dualisms, and the supporters of these systems hold to the reality of matter as firmly as to that of selves.

I have stressed this point because it seems pretty clear that Broad's Compound Theory with its "psycho-genic factor" and its material brain and body involves an absolute dualism which remotely resembles the dualisms of India, and I think that it is the view to which he himself inclines. The strength of such a position seems to me quite generally under-rated, although I doubt whether in the long run it would prove satisfactory, and I, personally, would prefer a full-fledged mind to the psycho-genic factor.

For McTaggart, of course, all selves are eternal; hence it is not strictly true to say that they are immortal, since there is no time for them to be immortal in. Nevertheless they do manifest themselves throughout the whole of the apparent temporal process; hence they may be said to be immortal *sub specie temporis*. McTaggart arrives at this conclusion by showing that selves possess all the qualifications essential to primary parts of the universe. It is, he concedes, abstractly possible that they are not such parts, but mere appearances, and that the primary parts are unknown to us; but, though this is possible, there is no reason to believe it actual, or to refuse to selves the status to which they appear to be entitled.

Since Broad rejects the doctrine of determining correspondence which is the basis of the entire theory, he is chiefly concerned with the question as to whether there is any empirical evidence to be advanced in its favor. He concludes, if I understand him aright, that there is no sufficient ground for a belief in survival if one disregards the evidence offered by psychical research; and he blames McTaggart for having treated this subject altogether too superficially. I think that there is some justification for this, although it is fair to remember that much attention has been devoted to this line of inquiry and much evidence accumulated since McTaggart's death. More important is McTaggart's objection that evidence of this type is compatible with a number of different theories. Anyone who has discussed the problem with Dr. Rhine will be aware that he considers that, if one be willing to develop a sufficiently complicated theory making use of the notions of telepathy, clairvoyance and precognition, he can account for the phenomena without invoking the simpler hypothesis of survival. It does not follow, of course, that in the future some test may not be discovered and applied which will yield definite and positive results. Like McTaggart, however, I think that a metaphysical proof is both desirable and possible. And Broad has himself indicated with admirable clearness that, if the substantiality of the self can be established, we shall have what we are looking for.

Broad also blames McTaggart for not discussing the relation between the rational, human self and the psychic entities which, in his view, manifest themselves as its body. These psychic entities are undoubtedly selves which, as McTaggart tells us, are developing *sub specie temporis* much more slowly than the self which appears—to use the Leibnitzian phrase—as their "dominant monad." And some cause there must be for their attraction and subservience to this dominant monad. But I am not sure that it is fair to expect any philosopher to discover, either by empirical or *a priori* investigation, the exact nature of this cause.

As regards theism McTaggart holds that the word God should be applied only to a personal being, and that anyone who does not believe in a personal God should call himself an atheist. Broad objects that, then, we should have to say that "all Christians are atheists, since the Christian God is the Trinity."[112] It would be well to remember, in this connection, that not all Christians are Trinitarians. And I think that it would be fairer to say that the doctrine of the Trinity represents an illogical compromise between theism and tritheism. Broad agrees with

112 *EMcP*, II, Part II, 643.

McTaggart, however, in his contention that philosophy should follow the usage of religion, on the ground that the philosopher can always talk about the Absolute whereas the religious man has no adequate substitute for the word God.

Since McTaggart does not believe in time, he cannot believe in creation. The only kind of God, therefore, whom he can admit is a non-creative, non-omnipotent God. McTaggart treats this hypothesis very seriously, and arrives at the conclusion that, while it is a perfectly possible view, there is not sufficient evidence in its favor to justify its acceptance.

With regard to McTaggart's discussion of the Cosmological and Theological arguments for the existence of God, Broad objects that, in the case of the first McTaggart is not justified in treating creation as a form of causation in the sense in which he employs the term, and which involves a symmetrical relation, and, in the case of the second, he is not entitled—even on the assumption that time is unreal—to deny that between a divine self and other selves there might obtain a non-reciprocal relation of *conveyance* which, *sub specie temporis*, would appear as a relation of governance or control. I think that these criticisms are both sound and important. It is of interest, however, to observe that, in his *Dogmas of Religion,* McTaggart concedes that,

if any reality is rightly conceived as matter, then there is a considerable probability—though by no means a certainty—that any traces of order in it are due to the action of a directing person. Such a person would be greatly superior in wisdom and power to ourselves, and might be—though this would not necessarily follow—also superior in goodness. His superiority in all three over all other beings might be sufficient to entitle him to be called God.[113]

Thus McTaggart's atheism is rooted in his idealism. It is because the universe is not only composed of spirits, but is itself a spiritual unity, that the hypothesis of a divine governor can be dismissed.[114]

The Buddhists have shown us, however, how a system which is basically atheistic can include a qualified polytheism in which the "gods" are merely selves which have risen to a super-human level. McTaggart's philosophy would seem naturally congenial to such a point of view, and the speculations of Professor Ducasse in his *Philosophical Scrutiny of Religion*—speculations which, I understand, have derived some stimulus from McTaggart—appear quite compatible with his general outlook. I think that it cannot be denied, however, that McTaggart was glad to be able honestly to dismiss the theistic hypothesis, for he re-

---

[113] *Some Dogmas of Religion,* § 201.
[114] *Ibid.,* §§ 202–204; of *The Nature of Existence,* II, § 500.

garded it as unfavorable to a high evaluation of love[115] for human beings, inasmuch as most theists have insisted that the deepest devotion must be reserved for God alone.

In conclusion I must comment upon another issue which Broad has raised, although, from the nature of the case, there is not much that can be said about it. McTaggart, as is well known, ascribed "an unique and supreme goodness to love."[116] Here Broad charges him with hitting his readers "below the intellect" and of approaching "dangerously near" to "a muddled mysticism."[117] The accusation, I take it, is that of having made a false value judgment. Concerning judgments of value no direct argument is possible. I can only say that McTaggart's judgment that "when love reached or passed a certain point, it would be more good than any possible amount of knowledge, virtue, pleasure, or fullness of life could be"[118] seems as self-evident to me as it did to him. And I should wish to add, as did he, "This does not, so far as I am concerned, spring from any belief that I have reached such a point. It is a conclusion which seems to me to follow from contemplating the nature of love, on the one hand, and of the other qualities on the other hand."[119] In thus committing myself, I shall of course incur the same charge which has been levelled against McTaggart, a fate which I shall bear with equanimity.

By love, McTaggart means "an emotion which is intense and passionate." It is often found in connection with sexual desire, but also "in connection with other bonds of union—kindred, early intimacy, similarity of disposition or of opinions, gratitude, and so forth;"[120] but it can also be found, he tells us, "without any such connection in instances where it can only be said that two people belong to one another."[121] Broad, I take it, would reject the last assertion, and would discount all the bonds of connection mentioned above with the exception of the first. Love, in his opinion, "is essentially bound up, so far as our experience goes, with homosexual or heterosexual desire, or with maternity.[122] Out of these it does, indeed, develop into an "extremely complex sentiment," yet in these is it rooted. "The plain fact is that all experience of love has been love of *persons,* i.e., of wholes composed of a self and an organism which appears as a body, inter-related in a perfectly unique and extremely intimate way. McTaggart talks of loving *selves.* No one

---

115 For McTaggart, it must be remembered, love is an emotion and must, as such, be distinguished from benevolence which is volitional.

116 *The Nature of Existence,* II, § 850.

117 *EMcP,* I, Part I, 129.

118 *The Nature of Existence,* II, § 851.

119 *Loc. cit.*

120 *Ibid.,* II, § 461.

121 *Loc. cit.*

122 *EMcP,* II, Part I, 129.

in real life ever talks in this way. We no more love *selves* than we love corpses."[123]

If Broad means by this what he appears to mean, namely, that we love only the combination of a self and the physical body—or what appears to be the physical body—which it is said to animate, it seems clear to me that he is wrong. It is the self which is manifested through the body that we love, and we love it just as much when that connection has ceased to exist, and the self has either also ceased to exist or exists apart from that body. We regard the body with a strong emotion as manifesting the self that we love, but the emotion felt toward the body is other than that which is felt toward the self. It is, I think, because of his preoccupation with the physical concomitants, which undoubtedly color although they do not explain love, that Broad is led to conclude, "If love is an emotion which could exist between disembodied minds telepathically prehending each other, I should expect it to be so attenuated and impoverished as to be barely recognizable."[124]

There is an experience of which Broad is thoroughly aware which, I should have thought, might have led him to reconsider his opinion. It is an unquestioned fact that many mystics have felt a consuming love of God. Whether this love was directed upon a real object may be questioned; but the love itself cannot be questioned, nor yet the immateriality of its object if that object be real. And, since such an emotion can exist *secundum statum praesentis vitae*, there seems no reason to suppose that it might not exist with at least an equal intensity *secundum statum patriae*.

I have now briefly touched upon what I take to be the principal issues raised by Broad's *Examination*. The two most important of these are, I think, the infinite divisibility of substance and the unreality of time. In this judgment I believe that McTaggart would have agreed; for he regarded the problem of time as the most crucial of all philosophical problems, and he definitely states, that, unless the infinite divisibility of substance be granted, he does not see how any conclusions can be reached which are "nearly so desirable" as those which, he thinks, follow from it.[125] It would be interesting, indeed, to know the grounds for this last judgment. Most philosophers of McTaggart's way of thinking have laid great stress upon the simplicity of the self. Probably it would not be amiss to conjecture that what he had in mind was the fact that the infinite divisibility of substance is the chief support of the doctrine of determining correspondence, and the further fact that this doctrine is the point of departure of his proofs of the unreality of matter and sensa.

[123] *Ibid.*, II, Part I, 498.   [124] *Ibid.*, II, Part II, 786.
[125] *The Nature of Existence*, I, § 170.

If these proofs be sound, idealism becomes the only possible view. If they be unsound it can only claim, in McTaggart's opinion, to be the most probable view.

Of an importance almost equal to that of the infinite divisibility of substance is the principle of the Dissimilarity of the Diverse. Of lesser, but yet considerable, significance are the doctrines of derivative and negative characteristics. With respect to these four issues Broad, rightly I believe, rejects McTaggart's views.

On the other hand I am unable to follow Broad in his attempt to substitute the notion of process for that of substance, rightly or wrongly I do not think that he has refuted McTaggart's arguments for the unreality of time, nor am I satisfied with his critique of McTaggart's theory of the self and of self-awareness, and I cannot acquiesce in his rejection of McTaggart's value judgment with respect to the axiological primacy of love, which last seems to me to constitute an original and profound insight. And lastly—a more general consideration—for reasons which I have already indicated I do not think that Broad has made out a satisfactory case against the *a priori* method which McTaggart employs exclusively throughout the first four books of *The Nature of Existence* and to some extent in the remaining three.

It will be apparent, therefore, that I do not consider Broad's critique to be as destructive as he himself believes. I think that it has damaged, but not demolished, the system. And I believe that a competent metaphysician could rear upon the same foundations an edifice which, while it would certainly differ from its predecessor in many important respects, would nevertheless reproduce many features of the original structure.

ROBERT LEET PATTERSON

BELLE HAVEN
GREENWICH, CONNECTICUT

W. T. Stace

BROAD'S VIEWS ON RELIGION

1.

BROAD would not, I believe, maintain that his views on religion constitute a very important part of his total philosophical thinking. Practically everything he has written on the subject is contained in Section II of his book, *Religion, Philosophy, and Psychical Research* which is a collection of miscellaneous essays written at different times. The section on religion contains no more than one hundred pages. There are no doubt stray references to religious topics to be found scattered through his other writings, but they do not, I think, add anything very important to what is found here. Hence I shall confine myself to this book. Though it is small in amount, what Broad has to say is full of interest.

It might be suggested that psychical research has important bearings on religion, and that therefore Broad's writings of that subject should be considered here. I shall not follow that suggestion. Broad's interest in psychical research does not, so far as I can see, stem from an interest in religion or from a belief that it can provide any argument for religious doctrines. It is true that many people dabble in psychical research because they think it will help support their religious beliefs. But there is no evidence that Broad shares this view, and the present writer certainly does not. If certain forms of Buddhism are excepted, it may be said that the central concept of religion is that of God. And I cannot see how psychical research could ever throw any direct light on the existence or nature of that being. No doubt those who think that psychical research will support religion have especially in mind its possible bearing on the survival of the human spirit after death. But even if psychical research provided strong evidence of survival—which appears at present to be a very over-optimistic view—this would in reality do very little to support religion. For belief in God and belief in survival are logically independent of one another. A wholly atheistic and irreligious man might believe in Cartesian dualism, might hold that the mind is immaterial and therefore separable from the body, and that it is in fact separated from it at death and goes on existing indefinitely after that event. There would be nothing more religious in this view than in the scientific proposition that oxygen has a different nature from hydrogen, that although the two are combined in water they can and do exist apart. Broad thinks that "it is almost a *sine qua non* of any religious view of the world that some men at least should survive the death of the body." I do not agree with this dictum. But even if it were true that a religious view of the world implies belief in survival, the converse would not hold. Neither survival nor immortality would necessarily imply belief in God nor in any other characteristically religious doctrine. We may therefore conclude that psychical research, though it has in some people's minds a strong associational connection with religion, has no logical bearing on it. And since Broad does not assert any such logical connection, I think we shall be right to exclude his writings on psychical research from our consideration of his views on religion.

There is a very important statement regarding his general attitude to religion in the introduction to the book above named. He says there,

I have no religious beliefs and, so far as I can judge, I am completely devoid of anything which could fairly be called religious or mystical experience. I fully realize that this is a serious disability. Some people would say that for me to write on these matters is as if a colour-blind man should pose as an art critic or a tone-deaf one as an expert on music. This, however, seems to me an objection partly based on a false analogy and partly on a failure to recognize the limited nature of my undertaking. I am concerned simply with the appraisal of *arguments,* which are held by those who use them to be either demonstrable or probable. For that limited task I have the necessary training and aptitude, and I do not see why my judgment should not be as good as another's. I would add that, so far as I am aware, I have no *anti*-religious emotions or interests.[1]

It is true that strictly speaking the logical appraisal and analysis of arguments does not depend on the personal experience of the analyst. One can draw correct inferences from observations made by another person at the top of Everest or in the Matto Grosso without going to either place oneself, provided the reports received from those places are trustworthy. The requirements for the analyst are (1) that he be competent to appraise arguments, and (2) that he be impartial, i.e. that he have no bias for or against the conclusion which the argument he is appraising seeks to prove.

No one will doubt Broad's competence. But it is worth making some remarks about his impartiality. I think it worth while emphasizing how completely free from either pro- or anti-religious bias he seems (at any rate to the present writer) to be. Freedom from bias in this matter

---

[1] All references in this paper are to *RPPR*, except where otherwise stated.

should not be taken for granted. Might one not assume that a trained professional philosopher, whatever may be the degree of his competence, depth, learning, etc., will at least be in his professional work free from prejudice? Not in the matter of religion at any rate. It is usually obvious that religious philosophers are first of all religious men by temperament, early training, or what not, and that they set about searching for arguments which they think will support their already settled religious beliefs. And a strong anti-religious bias is as a rule easily recognizable in philosophers who disbelieve in religion. There is a wide-spread prejudice against religion among intellectuals in the modern world generally, in spite of a recent trend towards religion among some of them. For instance, why do the majority of psychologists contemptuously brush aside, and refuse to take seriously, the claims of parapsychological propositions to acceptance? Not merely because parapsychological studies have often been pursued by cranks or even quacks. There is a deeper reason. They are animated by a *fear* that to admit many of the abnormal phenomena alleged by the parapsychologists might open the door again to non-materialistic beliefs in something like that outmoded entity the "soul," to a belief in its survival of death, to what is sometimes called a more "spiritual" view of the world, and through these avenues to the revival of religious beliefs from which they think modern intelligent men have at last emancipated themselves after age-long struggles against the forces of superstition.[2] The fact that, as shown above, even a renewed belief in a "soul," even an immortal one, would not really provide a logical bridge to a renewed belief in religion, does not affect this psychological diagnosis of the mentality of psychologists, philosophers, and intellectuals generally. The reader may think that these remarks have very little relevance to our subject. This would be a mistake. Broad's complete impartiality as regards religion (and as regards philosophical questions generally) is an unusual mental characteristic. And it obviously lends great weight to what he may have to say.

In this section of my paper I am trying to describe certain quite general characteristics of Broad's attitude to religion before entering on a discussion of details. And there is another quite general characteristic which it is of the greatest importance that we should bear in mind,

2 According to the *New York Times* of August 27, 1955, Doctor George R. Price of the Department of Medicine at the University of Minnesota is said to have referred to psychical researchers as "cluttering up" scientific journals with their claims to have produced satisfactory evidence of extra-sensory perception, and to have suggested that this evidence may well be explained by fraud, and that the motive for the fraud might be that "good to humanity could result from a small deception designed to strengthen religious beliefs." I may perhaps be allowed to guess that Doctor Price's own motives in this are connected with an anti-religious bias and the sort of fear mentioned in the text above.

because in the end it determines his major conclusions, and also determines what I shall hold to be their general defectiveness. This characteristic is literalism. Every religious doctrine is interpreted by him in the most literal meaning of the words and sentences which are commonly used to express it. Another way of saying the same thing is that he takes the religious use of language to be factual in the same sense as the scientific use of language, or its common sense use, are. If a religious man says "God exists," he supposes that this is a proposition like "cows exist," and that it is amenable to exactly the same sort of logical or evidentiary proofs or disproofs. His entire discussion of Christian doctrines—and he confines himself mostly to Christianity, though other religions are occasionally mentioned—is carried on within what I should hold to be this rigid and narrow framework of thought. And as most religious doctrines, if understood in this way, have become practically incredible to educated people, it is a foregone conclusion that they will for the most part be condemned as either false, or as incapable of either proof or disproof, or as meaningless.[3]

The alternative to literalism is the view that all, or most, or many, instances of religious language are to be understood "symbolically." It is true that the notion of religious symbolism is most difficult to define, and gives rise to further serious problems. As a very rough statement it may be said that according to this view religious doctrines, which have traditionally been understood literally, are, all of them or some of them, myths which symbolize or embody spiritual truths. The tendency to hold this view is a matter of degree. Fundamentalism is the view that all religious doctrines are to be taken literally. "Liberal" theology usually takes some doctrines to be literal and some to be symbolic. The decision in which category this or that doctrine is to be placed is usually quite arbitrary and is determined by how much the particular theologian can "swallow" if he takes the doctrines literally. The more non-literal his interpretations are, the more "liberal" he is supposed to be. It is quite possible to carry this tendency to its logical extreme, and to hold that *all* religious language is symbolic, including such a proposition as "God exists." And it is quite possible to think that when this final step has been taken religion does not, as the literalist supposes, evaporate altogether, but that on the contrary it will then shine out in its quintessential brightness, shorn of all superstitions and false beliefs. This is the view of the present writer, and something will be said of it later. At

[3] I have noted two instances, both entirely trivial, and mentioned here only for the sake of accuracy, in which Broad departs from absolute literalism. He admits (page 220) that the relation of the first person of the Trinity to the second cannot be literally that of father to son, and (page 222) that the doctrine of the ascension of Jesus to heaven cannot be meant in its literal spatial sense.

the moment the point to be understood is that Broad's whole discussion is predicated on the quite literal interpretation of all important doctrines.

For instance, the doctrine that God is a person is understood by Broad to mean that he is a person in exactly the same sense as Tom, Dick and Harry are persons. And he analyzes at great length the everyday meaning of the word "person." He says that we apply the word to a substance if it fulfills the following conditions: "(1) It must think, feel, will, etc. (2) Its various contemporary states must have that peculiar kind of unity which we express by saying that they 'together make up a single total state of mind.' (3) Its successive total states must have that peculiar kind of unity with each other which we express by saying that they are 'so many different stages in the history of a single mind.' (4) These two kinds of unity must be recognized by itself and not only by some external observer."[4] Even Thomas Aquinas maintained that when we speak of God as loving, angry, etc., we are using these words "analogously." What in detail he meant by this I am not quite sure. But he certainly meant that we are not using them in the same literal sense as we are when we apply them to Tom, Dick, and Harry.

There are, of course, very great virtues in literalism. Its view is simple and easy to understand. It is, or at least may be, clear and unambiguous. It is a bulwark against intellectual dishonesty and against nebulous religiosity. The theologian who says that Jesus Christ was born of a virgin, ought not to be allowed when attacked to shift his ground, to repudiate the natural meaning of his words, and to take refuge in a cloudland of foggy ambiguities about "spiritual truths" which the doctrine of the virgin birth, by some arbitrary and fantastic process of interpretation, may be supposed to embody. On the whole the more literal-minded a religion is the more easily will it be confirmed or refuted by scientific and logical methods. The most literal-minded form of Christianity known to me is Mormonism. The scriptures use such expressions as "the Lord stretched forth his hand." It follows that God has hands, fingers, legs, and a body. As a matter of fact he has white hair and lives on a star named Kabob. This star has not yet been identified by astronomers but there is no reason why it should not be. It is evident that this creed ought to receive the enthusiastic applause of every positivist. For it is in principle in every detail empirically verifiable by the approved methods of science. The astronomers have only to discover and identify Kabob and after a suitable journey in a rocket ship to turn their telescopes on it to settle positively whether God is there or not. The literalists, and Broad with them, may also urge that traditionally the creeds

4 P. 160.

have always been understood literally until the modern wishy-washy spineless religiosity came along and began interpreting them allegorically in order to evade the attacks of science. But this claim probably cannot be supported. It is true that the *popular* understanding has always been literal because the vulgar cannot understand anything else. But this has not been true of the more philosophical and enlightened theologians and philosophers of religion. Even the above reference to Thomas Aquinas would suggest this. And the understanding of religious language as symbolical has in fact a long and distinguished history.

But Broad's literalism, though it has some points in its favor, has also grave disadvantages. It in fact cripples his enquiry from the outset. It is narrow and uncompromising. It catches the words of religion, but misses altogether its inner life and breath and spirit. And since nearly all contemporary religion, except fundamentalism and Roman Catholicism, at least in some degree understands its doctrines symbolically, Broad's conclusions have as a rule little relevance to contemporary religion. The result is that most of what he writes is of little more than academic or historical interest. For instance, a very large proportion of his treatment of religion is concerned with the traditional proofs of the existence of God. But these proofs cut almost no ice in religious circles now, except in the Roman Catholic communion. Present emphasis is all on the inner religious and mystical "witness of the spirit."

The professional philosopher is, of course, rightly interested in academic and historical questions. And therefore I shall devote the earlier portions of this paper to considering Broad's discussions in his own terms, that is to say, in terms of his own literalist framework of ideas. Indeed, if I did not do so, I should not be writing a paper on Broad. In later parts of this paper I shall briefly consider some of the things which ought to be said if we allow ourselves to pass outside the confines of this literalism.

2.

In his chapter on "The Present Relations of Science and Religion" Broad begins by pointing out that "there are certain peculiarities about Christianity which make it vlunerable to attacks which might be harmless to some other great religion such as Buddhism, or to religion in general." One of these peculiarities is that whereas other religions usually claim only that their founders were exceptionally good and wise men, or prophets extraordinarily favored by God, the founder of Christianity is supposed to occupy a unique position in the universe. Broad is referring to the doctrines of the Trinity and the incarnation. (We may pass by as unimportant the point that a doctrine of incarnation is found in Hinduism, for the Hindu avatars were not historical founders of the religion.) He writes:

I have not been so fortunate as to meet with any account of the details of this doctrine about Jesus which I could fully understand. But for the present a rough outline will be enough; and it may be given in the following propositions. (I) There is a single eternal and supernatural existent on which everything else that exists depends. . . . This may be called the Godhead. (II) Within the unity of the Godhead there are three and only three most intimately inter-related 'factors' or 'moments,' each of which can properly be called God. (III) . . . two of these factors . . . stand in a peculiar kind of assymmetrical dyadic relationship, which is at least imperfectly adumbrated by the analogy of fatherhood and sonship. . . . The third factor . . . is related to *both* the others by another kind of assymmetrical dyadic relation. This is denoted by the phrase 'proceeding from.' (IV) There is some uniquely intimate relation between that eternal factor in the Godhead called 'God the Son' and a certain man Jesus. . . . This relation is such that it is appropriate to say of Jesus (and of no other man) that he was divine as well as human, and to say of God the Son (and of no other factor in the Godhead) that He is eternally human as well as divine. (I must confess that I can think of no interpretation of these statements which would enable me to attach a meaning to them.)[5]

In addition to the four propositions just enumerated there are a further five propositions which, according to Broad, are also properly to be considered parts of the "rough outline" of the doctrine. But the reader has probably had enough, and I will not quote the other five. What I have quoted will perhaps suffice to give the peculiar flavor of Broad's analysis of Christian doctrines. It is scarcely fortunate for the prospect of those doctrines if taken literally. And it certainly is not intended by Broad to be so, though he does not in this passage draw any explicit conclusion.

In the same paper Broad contends that most of the arguments for the ontological propositions which are special and peculiar to Christianity (though not the argument from miracles) can be "disposed of" by logical arguments or logical analyses which are quite independent of empirical science. Science is irrelevant to such questions as

the doctrine of the existence and triune structure of the Godhead and the uniquely intimate connection between one of its differentiations and the man Jesus. The fundamental question is whether any part of this doctrine is intelligible, or whether it is nothing but meaningless verbiage masquerading in the grammatical form of intelligible sentences. Obviously that question cannot be answered by appealing to the methods or results of natural science. If any part of the doctrine be intelligible, the second question is whether it is true or false. . . . Now natural science is concerned with the interconnections between things or events in space and time. . . . Therefore the question whether

5 Pp. 221f.

nature *as a whole system* depends on a timeless and eternal existent . . . falls altogether outside the sphere of natural science.[6]

An essential part of the reason for believing the central doctrines mentioned above is, Broad says, that Jesus, who was a divine man and therefore must have known the truth, taught them or made statements from which they follow. But here there is a fundamental logical difficulty. The argument, says Broad,

> raises the question: 'On what grounds do you accept Jesus as an authority on these matters?' I suppose the answer would be: 'Because he was a being of superhuman wisdom and goodness who was in a position to know.' But this is itself the most central and fundamental of Christian doctrines, and if Christians accept *it* on the ground that Jesus asserted it, their whole position is logically circular.[7]

Is there then any independent ground for believing in the unique divine status of the man Jesus which should cause us to accept on his authority ontological propositions about the dependence of the world on a triune "timeless and non-natural existent" and his own unique relation to it? Broad mentions briefly the fact that Jesus "produced on those who knew him a strong impression of his divine nature" and the fact that "St. Paul, who never met Jesus, . . . underwent an experience which he took to be a manifestation of the risen Christ," and then turns to what he takes to be the main independent ground for believing in his divinity, namely, the miracles alleged to have been performed by Jesus, of which the most stupendous was his own resurrection.

The present writer was under the impression that reliance on miracles to prove the truths of Christianity was out of date as far as any modern-minded religious man is concerned, and that it had died somewhere in the age of Paley and Hume. However, one must make a distinction. There are, in fact, *two* arguments from miracles. One of them uses miracles, not only those of Jesus, but also those of the Old Testament, for the purpose of proving the existence of God. This is the one which is dead, and Broad does not mention it at all. The other bases itself on the miracles of Jesus only and uses them to prove the divinity of Jesus. This is the argument which Broad discusses. In the first argument, which is supposed to prove the existence of God, miracles must necessarily be defined, for that purpose, as *violations of the laws of nature*. To explain them we are asked to assume a being above nature who intervenes in its processes and interrupts its normal course and laws. It is obvious that the argument will not work at all unless the above definition of miracles is

6 P. 224.   7 P. 227.

given. But this definition is not necessary for the second argument, the one which Broad considers, and he gives, in fact, an entirely different definition.

Broad defines a miracle as a violation of certain very general restrictive principles "which we commonly assume without question."[8] He lists eight such principles. To mention two of these will be sufficient to indicate the sort of principles he has in mind. One is that "a body cannot enter or leave a closed vessel so long as the walls are intact." Another is that "a human mind cannot *directly* initiate or modify the motion of any material thing except certain parts of its own organism." It will be evident that according to this definition most of the abnormal events which are investigated by the Psychical Research Society are to be described as miracles. For instance, telekinesis is a miracle because it violates the second restrictive principle just mentioned. It is also obvious that we are not asked to regard such events as violations of natural law but rather as exemplifications of natural laws at present unknown to us or imperfectly known.

Broad thinks that "psychical research has made it far more probable than not that certain kinds of phenomena which are miraculous in the sense defined above, do occur."[9] But as regards the New Testament miracles he says:

there is no *direct* evidence for [any of them] which is comparable in weight to the evidence for some of the alleged miracles of modern mediumship. For the levitation . . . of D. D. Home we have the contemporary autographic testimony of Sir William Crooks, one of the ablest experimental scientists of the nineteenth century who was deliberately investigating the phenomena in his laboratory under controlled conditions. It would be merely impertinent to suggest that the *direct* evidence for the resurrection or the ascension, available to us here and now, is comparable to this.[10]

But even if we admit that the New Testament miracles did in fact occur "at the very utmost it would prove that Jesus was an extremely remarkable and impressive personality"[11]—as remarkable and impressive as D. D. Home one must suppose Broad means, though he does not say this. Thus the argument that miracles are good evidence of the divinity of Jesus fizzles out ignominiously.

As Broad does not discuss the argument from miracles to the existence of God I should like to supply the omission in a few sentences—the argument is not worth more than that. This is perhaps worth while because Hume's discussion, though famous, is very unsatisfactory. The argument

8 P. 232.   9 P. 234.
10 P. 229.   11 P. 227.

is worthless for the following reason. If an astonishing or abnormal event occurs which could, if we knew enough, be explained by natural laws which are not at present known to us, then obviously it could not be evidence of anything except nature and its laws. But it is impossible that we should ever have good reason for asserting that any event, however abnormal or astonishing, could *not* be explained by some law of nature not yet known to us unless we were certain that we already know all the laws of nature, unless, in fact, we were omniscient, which presumably we could never become in any finite period of time.

Practically the whole of the essay which is nominally about the relations of religion and science deals as a matter of fact with logical questions on which science has no bearing. On the question of the relations of science and religion Broad has singularly little of interest to say. In astronomy the Copernican revolution has made it difficult to believe that a person of the Godhead "came to *earth*, became *man*, and eventually *ascended* to his Father in heaven."[12] The bearing of physics on religion is trivial. The statistical conception of natural law does nothing, as some physicists (and even some philosophers who should know better) have supposed, to solve the free will problem.[13] The biological doctrine of evolution renders it improbable that man "occupies a unique status in a hierarchy of living beings."[14] These contentions of Broad are of course quite true.

I have tried elsewhere[15] to show that the really important conflict between religion and science has little to do with the clash between *particular* discoveries of science and *particular* doctrines of religion. It is rather that the general spirit of science as expressed in the philosophy of naturalism conflicts with any sort of religious view of the world whether it is embodied in the particular doctrines of Christianity, Judaism, Islam, or Hinduism. We must either abandon religion, or abandon naturalism, or find some way of combining both in our philosophy. This is the most profound spiritual problem of the modern world. It is the real question of the relations between science and religion. It had become clear by the time of Kant, who tried to solve it by his theory of the "two worlds" in one of which, the phenomenal world, naturalism is true, in the other of which, the noumenal world, religion is true. Of the relations between religion and science in this sense Broad has nothing to say.

3.

In two of his essays Broad discusses the traditional arguments for the existence of God. He devotes a great deal of subtle logical analysis to

---

12 P. 238.   13 P. 238.   14 P. 241.
15 *Religion and the Modern Mind.*

showing that the ontological argument depends on the use of phrases like "most perfect being," which are meaningless verbiage. So far as I know his treatment of this famous argument, depending as it does on an attempt to show that the argument is meaningless, not that it is fallacious, is quite original. It certainly is most acute and ingenious. But I do not possess Broad's heroic patience and I simply cannot bear to discuss the dreary logomachy of the ontological argument. Probably Broad has completely demolished the argument. But I cannot bring myself to think that it needed demolishing. Broad also, of course, discusses and refutes the cosmological argument, and here also I am going to shirk my job and not discuss what he says.

Something is still worth saying, however, of the argument from design. It is, as Kant noted, extremely appealing. And I believe it is still alive in the sense that many people, philosophers and non-philosophers alike, are still influenced by some form of it. It is the only one of the arguments for which a reasonable claim to be not wholly out of date could be made. In the nineteenth century J. S. Mill discussed it carefully and sympathetically. And even in the last few years the Belgian scientist du Nüoy has given in his book *Human Destiny* a new version of it based upon the complexity of the protein molecule.

In *Religion, Philosophy and Psychical Research* Broad says of the argument from design that it "has been so thoroughly discussed by Hume ... that there is very little left to say about it,"[16] and again that it "has been criticized very fairly and thoroughly by two of the greatest European philosophers, Hume and Kant. I have nothing to add to their criticisms. ... I shall ... set aside the argument."[17] He devotes two pages of remarks to it which I shall not reproduce. It is odd that he nowhere mentions Mill's most interesting treatment of the argument. The little Broad says in this book is largely influenced by Hume. He has, however, discussed the argument in *Mind and Its Place in Nature*. I shall discuss what he says there at the end of this section.

In spite of what he says, the classical treatments of the argument given by Hume, Mill, and Kant are entirely unsatisfactory and it therefore still stands in need of analysis. Hume, for example, contrary to common belief, *is not nearly sceptical enough!* It is, Hume says, an argument from analogy. Having made this point, the whole force of his argument is directed to showing that the analogy is a weak one. By admitting that there *is* an analogy between the observed adaptation of means to ends in nature and the adaptation of means to ends in man-made machines and artifacts, in watches, ships, houses, etc., he tacitly admits that the argu-

16 P. 170.   17 P. 190.

ment from design has *some* probative force and merely contends that it has very little. He ought to have shown that it has no probative force at all. He ought to have rejected it root and branch as a total fallacy. And since Mill is more favorable to the argument than Hume, these remarks apply to Mill *a fortiori.*

The basic error in Hume's and Mill's treatments is the tacit admission that a relation of means to end can be *observed* in nature, or at any rate the failure to dispute this basic premiss of the whole argument. The argument, being an empirical one, must start from some observed facts. Once admit that a means-end relation *can* be observed in nature, and you have to admit at least some probative force to the argument, however little. Even so, of course, the argument does not tend to prove the Christian God, but something much less, as Hume, Mill, and Broad have not failed to point out. But that is not the question now.

Suppose we begin by looking at the means-end relationship as it appears in human behavior, whether in the production of machines and artifacts or in any other way. Undoubtedly such a relation exists, but *it is always inferred, never observed.* Now if it cannot be observed in human affairs, it certainly cannot be observed in non-human nature. The point is that by its very nature a purpose, or a design, or a means-end relation is a *private* fact belonging to a stream of consciousness which can never be observed by anyone who is not the bearer of that consciousness, but can only be inferred from his behavior. I see your house on fire. I see you run out of the door. That is all I observe. That your purpose in running out of the door is to escape the fire, that the two events (1) running, and (2) escaping death by fire, have the relation of means to end is an inference of a quite complicated kind. We have an x and a y. The succession x-y is all that can be observed. A means-end relation between x and y, if one exists, is always inferred. If this is the case in human affairs, it will obviously be absurd to assert that design can be *observed* in nature. If it exists there, it must be an inference from some other observed facts. What are they?

This reasoning can be avoided by a behaviorist. He will say that purpose and the observed behavior are identical, and that therefore we do observe purpose in observing purposive behavior. But this argument is not open to anyone who uses the argument from design to prove a designing mind in nature. For his contention is plainly based upon the view that the intelligent mind which is supposed to have designed nature is distinct from nature, an invisible mind whose purposes cannot be directly seen but are to be inferred from nature.

The next question, therefore, is: from what observed facts in nature can one infer that any two things or events, x and y, bear a means-end relation to one another? It may be admitted that x and y may have to one another not only a relation of succession but a causal relation. Thus eyes are a causal condition of vision, the carrying of pollen on the legs of insects a causal condition of the pollination of flowers, protein molecules a causal condition of life. But a cause-effect relation is not the same as a means-end relation. From what observed facts in nature do we infer that the events x and y, as well as having a causal relation, have also a means-end relation.

There appear to be two considerations which have made philosophers accept this conclusion, both of them entirely fallacious. One is the extreme complexity of x. In all the alleged instances of means-end in nature x is really a vast concatenated assemblage of things or events, and this fact is always an essential part of the argument. For the argument is that all these multitudinous things or events—possibly millions of them —have to be exactly adjusted to one another, have to "cooperate" with one another, to produce y, that this could not happen "by chance," i.e. by the blind operation of mechanical laws of nature, but can only be explained by the hypothesis of a designing mind. Why? Because the chances against the required adjustment to one another of the vast number of the components of x are so enormous, millions or even billions to one, that chance will not explain it. For instance, the eye is a complicated mechanism of many parts, lens, cornea, retina, etc. and these have innumerable sub-parts down to molecules and atoms. If the lens is not perfectly adjusted to the retina, the retina to the optic nerve, the pupil to the lens, in certain definite, precise, and delicate ways, vision will not result. And of course the same argument must be carried down to the sub-parts. In Newton's example of the argument, the solar system, the complicated adjustment of the masses, distances, and velocities, of planets and satellites to one another, is necessary to produce the balanced world machine. "To compare and adjust these together *in so great a variety of bodies*[18] argues the cause [of the machine] to be not blind or fortuitous but well skilled in mechanics and geometry." In du Nüoy's version of the argument the enormous complication of the protein molecule, and enormous number of such molecules required to produce the existing life on the earth, is given as the reason which renders it necessary to adopt the hypothesis of design, since it is argued that so vastly complicated an adjustment of billions of billions of atomic parts to one another could not have come about by chance in the two or three billion years during which the universe is now supposed to have existed. The time has been too short.

This argument from complexity involves a simple fallacy. It picks out

18 *Italics* mine.

certain phenomena, such as vision, life, etc. and shows that the chances against the "cooperation" with one another of the vast assemblage of its causal conditions are millions or billions to one. This is quite true. But what is not noticed is that it is also true of every conceivable event which could happen in nature, and not merely of the selected ones. Whatever happens is almost infinitely improbable in the sense that an almost infinite number of other things might have happened instead of it, if the causal conditions had been different. Billions of causal conditions have to "cooperate" to produce any event whatever. Assume a universe which was neither created nor governed by an intelligent mind, governed only by natural laws, and having existed from all eternity, and it will still be true in such a universe that any event whatever which happened could not have happened unless a limitless complexity of causal conditions had "cooperated" to produce it, and that an almost infinite number of other events might have happened if the conditions had been different, and that, *in that sense*, the chances against whatever event did happen were beyond all calculation. Therefore, to pick out a few selected cases, such as vision or life, in which this is true, has no tendency whatever to prove design. It is not that the argument is merely a weak one, having some, but not much, probative force. It is a hundred per cent total fallacy.

Why, then, does the human mind tend to pick out these few special cases and argue from them? The answer is obvious. They are always things which we like and consider "good." We do not pick out evil things, diseases, disasters, floods, earthquakes, volcanic eruptions which may slaughter thousands of human beings, although their "cooperating" causes are just as complex, and the chances against them just as great. And this constitutes the second consideration—I will not dignify it by the name argument—which makes people transform in imagination the x-y causal relationship into a means-end relationship. There is no shadow of cogency in such a consideration. It is true that since virtuous human minds tend to produce good things, the hypothesis of a virtuous designing mind might explain the production of good things by nature. But since nature also produces evil things, since it apparently produces good and evil things at random and with no appearance of a preference for good over evil things, therefore the hypothesis of chance is a much better hypothesis than that of God, since it explains both the good and the evil things, whereas the hypothesis of God explains only the good things.

It is certain that none of the arguments for the existence of God have any value. But this, so far from being something which tells against religion is, on the contrary, something which tells vastly in favor of it. I shall explain this more fully later. For the moment I will confine myself to the following remarks. If the existence of God could be made the conclusion of a valid argument, then we should have a situation which might be symbolized by P→G. P would be the premisses, for instance, certain observed facts about the world. G would stand for God. Thus there would be a multiplicity of things, the things represented by P, and also God. In that case God would be *one thing among others*. And from this it would follow that God would be a finite existence, and this contradicts the infinity of God. But God, according to all the great religions, is Infinite.[19] This is the reason, or one reason, why there can be no valid argument for the existence of God.

Put it in another way. Ultimately the conception of God is a mystical conception, resting on mystical grounds (though the word "ground" here is not strictly accurate) and not on rational grounds. But mysticism teaches that God is wholly beyond the grasp of the logical intellect. That his existence cannot be proved by logical argument, or even made in the slightest degree probable, is merely a particular instance of this truth.

Put it in yet another way. In the proposition "God exists" what does the word "exist" means? It is often said by philosophers that "being" and "existence" are not predicates. This is true if the word is supposed to stand for some determination, quality, or characteristic which all things are supposed to have in common over and above their differentiating characteristics. "Exist" in that sense has no meaning. But as the word is used in the sentence "cows exist, but centaurs do not" it must have meaning since the sentence is true. To exist in this sense means to be one among the many things which constitute that system of things which we call by such names as nature, reality, the universe, and so on. Cows do, and centaurs do not, form a part of that system; and therefore cows exist and centaurs do not. Now in this sense God does not exist, and if he did he would be a finite part of the universe. He does not exist in the same sense as cows exist. But this is the only kind of existence which can be

---

[19] The word "infinite" as applied to God, and as it is used here does not mean the endlessness of a series, as in the sense in which it is used of space, time, and the number series. It is used here in the same sense as Spinoza uses it of Substance. The infinite in this sense may be roughly described as "that than which there is no other." The Chandogya Upanishad explains this concept of the infinity of God as follows: "Where one sees nothing else, hears nothing else, knows nothing else—this is the Infinite. Where one sees another, hears another, knows another—this is the finite." Compare this with Spinoza's statement about Substance that it is that "the conception of which does not need the conception of any other thing from which it must be formed." The infinity of a series seems to be the same, in denotation if not in connotation, as what Spinoza calls "infinite in its own kind." Hegel also makes the same distinction. The infinity of a series he calls—unjustifiably it may be—the "false" or "spurious" infinite, whereas the infinite as I use it here can be identified with what he calls the "true" infinite. To make this distinction is essential if the argument used in my text above is to be understood.

made the conclusion of any sort of inference, deductive or inductive. Therefore, no conceivable proof of God's existence could ever be valid.

Broad has discussed the argument from design in Chapter II of *Mind and Its Place in Nature*, pages 81 to 94. He begins by defining a "teleological system" as one which is such that (1) "our more or less superficial knowledge of the system suggests that it was designed. . . ." and which is also such that (2) "if we use this hypothesis as a clue to more minute investigation we continue to find that the system is constructed as if the hypothesis were true." It will be noticed that a teleological system, according to Broad's usage of the expression, is one which *appears* to us to have been designed, or is *as if* it had been designed. The problem then is: given such a system, was it *actually* designed?

An organism is by definition such a system. It gives the appearance that its parts are so made and adjusted to one another as to serve the purposes of life. It thus suggests the hypothesis of design. That is to say, it fulfils the first of Broad's two conditions specified above. The reason why this is not enough, and why the second condition is also necessary if we are to draw the inference that the system was actually designed, is that otherwise "of any system whatsoever we might suppose that it was designed to do what we actually find it doing." The hypothesis of design only becomes at all probable because it provides a clue to further investigation which tends to confirm the hypothesis. Broad only gives one example to elucidate this. If a superficial knowledge of the human body has made us suspect design (condition 1), then when we find "various small and apparently unimportant glands . . . whose secretions . . . exercise a profound influence over its growth and well-being," and when we also find "the production in the blood of antitoxins when the body is attacked by organisms likely to injure it" (condition 2) then the original suspicion that the body was designed to produce and preserve vital characteristics is in some degree confirmed.

There are of course other hypotheses, besides that of a designing mind which can be put forward to explain the characters of organisms. Such hypotheses are to be found in biological mechanism, substantial vitalism, and emergent vitalism. Broad discusses these along with the theistic hypothesis. The details of his comparison of the different hypotheses do not concern us. He draws no final conclusion and expresses no decided preference for any of them. But I think he means us to understand that there is at least a certain amount of force in the argument from design in the sense that, if anything is a teleological system, i.e. if it fulfils both conditions 1 and 2, then there is *some* degree of probability that it was actually designed, though he does not come to a decision whether this theistic hypothesis is more or less probable than the other hypotheses of mechanism and vitalism.

Since I have maintained that there is no force whatever in the argument from design, it follows that, if I am right, there must be some error in Broad's argument. My problem is to discover what is wrong with it.

Broad himself admits that, if we are to conclude that there is to be a degree of probability that a certain system was designed, it is not enough that it should fulfil condition 1, i.e. that a superficial knowledge of it should suggest design. For "of any system whatsoever we might suppose that it was designed to do what we actually find it doing." Therefore it must be the case that whatever force the argument has is due to the additional fact that the system also fulfils condition 2.

It is very difficult to see how condition 2 can make this difference. Let us suppose that the "superficial" knowledge of System S which, in accordance with condition 1, suggests design, consists of the knowledge of facts a, b, c, d, and e, which are characteristics of S. On the strength of these we suspect design, and using this as a clue we now find, in accordance with condition 2, further characteristics f, g, h, i, and j, which also seem to further the hypothesis of design. According to Broad the hypothesis of design now for the first time shows a certain degree of probability.

Now of course if a, b, c, d, and e constitute evidence which renders design in any degree probable then certainly it is intelligible that f, g, h, i, and j may constitute additional evidence which may add to the probability. But this is apparently not what Broad means. For if it were, there would be no point in dividing the evidence into two instalments, a superficial instalment a, b, c, d and e and a later instalment f, g, h, i and j. There would be no point in his two separate conditions. Obviously the evidence a . . . . . . j, taken in one instalment would have exactly the same probative force as two instalments of evidence a . . . . . . e and f . . . . . . j.

I think what Broad means is that the fact that the hypothesis of design, formed on the basis of a . . . . . . e, enables us to *predict* f . . . . . . j, confirms the hypothesis, just as Einstein's theory of relativity, suggested by certain facts, enabled astronomers to predict that certain further phenonema would be observable at an eclipse of the sun, and this tended to confirm the hypothesis of relativity.

On this there are two comments to be made. In the first place Broad has not shown any instance in which the hypothesis of design has enabled us to predict hitherto unobserved biological phenomena. The hypothesis that the human body was designed, could never have enabled us to predict the discovery of certain small and apparently unimportant glands, nor their function in influencing the growth and well-being of the body. Nor would it have enabled anyone to predict that antitoxins would be produced in the blood of a body attacked by organisms likely to injure it. Thus the analogy between the argument from design and the predictive capacity of scientific hypotheses breaks down.

In the second place, the common belief that the capacity of a hypothesis to *predict* phenomena is what especially confirms the hypothesis is a delusion. If on the strength of observed facts a . . . . . . e we erect an hypothesis H which enables us to predict observations f . . . . . . j, then the degree of probability of H is exactly the same as it would have been if we had observed a . . . . . . h, in the first place. The evidence for the hypothesis is in any case simply a . . . . . . h. Whether some of these facts were predicted or not can in no way increase or diminish the force of the evidence. What makes the hypothesis probable is that it is possible to deduce from it the facts a . . . . . . j. Whether the facts, or any of them, were deduced before or after the facts were observed makes no logical difference whatsoever.

The real truth is what Broad has himself stated that "of any system whatever we might suppose that it was designed to do what we actually find it doing." It is odd that Broad apparently does not see that if this is true of "any system whatever" it will be true of a teleological system as defined by him with its two conditions, and that by making this statement he really refutes himself. It is possible that he meant to make this statement not of "any system whatever," but only of "any system which fulfils condition 1 but not condition 2." But in that case he would have had to show how condition 2 makes any difference, and this he has not done.

That "of any system whatever we could suppose it was designed to do what it is doing" is the real refutation of the argument from design. If the fact that the parts of the eye are adjusted to one another so as to produce vision is an argument for believing that the eye was designed to produce vision, then the fact that the parts of a volcanic eruption are so related to one another as to produce the destruction of a city and the death of thousands must be an argument for believing that the eruption was designed with that end in view. The same will be true of any system whatever and whether it is what Broad calls a "teleological system" or not makes no difference.

Nor will it make any difference whether the facts about the eruption are discovered all at once or in two instalments. On a superficial examination of the disaster I find that molten lava flowed onto the city and produced death and destruction. Suppose I suspect that the eruption was designed to produce death and destruction. On more minute examination I find that the volcano saturated the atmosphere with poisonous gases and that the eruption was accompanied by an earthquake which shook down buildings and killed the occupants. In either case, whether on the strength of a superficial examination or a more detailed one, I can always suppose that whatever effects a set of causes produced was in reality designed. Therefore, unless everything that happens in the universe is evidence of design (which no one has ever maintained), nothing is. Hence the argument has no validity, and Broad's partial defense of it, like Hume's and Mill's, falls to the ground.

4.

Owing to the compression of my account of Broad's views on religion I may have given the impression that they are wholly negative and even hostile. This would be unfair to Broad. Mainly negative his views are, although there is one positive element which I have left for treatment in this final section. But hostile they never are. I have already emphasized his very genuine impartiality and complete absence of any animus or bias against religion. It is true that for the most part he decides against religious beliefs. But a judge who decides a case against a litigant is not therefore shown to have been partial, prejudiced, or animated by hostile feelings.

The positive element in Broad's treatment of the subject is to be found in what he says about mysticism. Apart from casual references there are two main passages in which he briefly discusses the subject. Although they both say much the same thing, I think it desirable to quote from both of them. The first is as follows:

Finally I come to the argument for the existence of God which is based on the occurrence of specifically mystical or religious experiences. I am prepared to admit that such experiences occur among people of different races and social traditions, and that they have occurred at all periods of history. I am prepared to admit that, although the experiences have differed considerably at different times and places . . . there are probably certain characteristics which are common to all of them and which suffice to distinguish them from all other kinds of experience. In view of this I think it more likely than not that in religious and mystical experience men come into contact with some Reality or some aspect of Reality which they do not come into contact with in any other way. But I do not think that there is any good reason to suppose that this Reality is personal.[20]

In the other passage he says:

To me the occurrence of mystical experience at all times and places, and the similarities between the statements of so many mystics all the world over, seems to be a significant fact. *Prima facie* it suggests that there is an aspect of reality

20 P. 172.

with which these persons come in contact in their mystical experiences. . . . I should say this *prima facie* appearance of objectivity ought to be accepted at its face value unless and until some reasonably satisfactory alternative explanation of the agreement can be given.[21]

He goes on to note that alternative explanations have been given by psychoanalysts and also by Marxists, but points out that both these alternatives are unsatisfactory in certain respects.

The basic agreement between mystical experiences in all cultures and ages was also noted by William James who observed that "it ought to make the critic stop and think."[22]

The very guarded and limited character of Broad's conclusions should, of course, be noted. He does not call the reality, the objective existence of which he thinks is "more likely than not," by the name God. And he thinks there is no reason to believe that it is personal.

In the first quotation he refers to mystical experiences as affording the starting point of an *argument* for the existence of God; and to regard the matter in that light, and to criticize it on that assumption, is the almost universal practice of all those philosophers who discuss the matter at all. Nevertheless, it is mistaken. It will be seen that it contradicts the view that there cannot possibly be an argument for the existence of God which ought to be considered valid by the religious man. I shall maintain that there is no such thing as an argument which *infers* the existence of God *from* the occurrence of mystical states.

One must begin by saying that the mystic himself most certainly would not regard his conviction of God, which he attains in the mystical experience, as any sort of argument or inference, however much it may appear in this light to other people. The view that for the mystic himself God is an inference from his experience, or would be seen by him to be one if he afterwards thought the matter out logically, is based on a false analogy. We use our sense-perceptions as the starting points of various inferences. And because mystical experience is often spoken of as immediate, i.e. as having within itself no sort of mediation, we suppose that it is in some way analogous to a perception. It is, we think, a nonsensuous perception, and therefore it is of such a nature that inferences might be based upon it. And we suppose that the existence of God is such an inference. But, according to my reading of mystical literature, this analogy between mystical experience and perception is utterly misleading. Since there is no state of our ordinary consciousness to which it can properly be compared, we can hardly fail to try comparisons which are misleading. There are two favorite analogies. Sometimes it is supposed that mystical experience must be a kind of *perception,* and some-

[21] P. 242. [22] *Varieties of Religious Experience,* p. 419.

times that it is an *emotion*. Thus Russell somewhere, as I remember, calls it a "noble emotion," and dismisses its claim to objectivity just because he supposes it to be "nothing but" an emotion. But that it cannot be either a perception or an emotion is made plain by one of the commonest statements made by mystics in all cultures and all religions, namely that in that experience (the word "experience" is also no doubt not a correct descriptive word for it; indeed, no word ever could be) there is no distinction between subject and object, or that that distinction is "transcended." The experience therefore is neither subjective nor objective. It is mis-described as an emotion because that word carries the implication of subjectivity. It is mis-described as a perception because in all perception there is the distinction between subject and object (this is true even of illusory perception). Hence Plotinus says it is not properly called a "vision." And that there cannot be, for the mystic, an inference from the experience to God is shown by the consideration that he cannot argue. "I have in my consciousness this inner or subjective experience and this is evidence of the objective being of God," since this argument relies on the subject-object distinction.

For the mystic, therefore, God is not objective. He is not an object. This is the reason why he cannot be said to "exist." For to exist means to be objective. But for the very same reason he cannot be called subjective or illusory. Although it is false to say "God exists," it is also false to say "God is non-existent." And if you say he must be either existent or not existent, the answer is that this either-or is a logical category which, although it is rightly applied to the sphere of finite things, does not apply to God, or to the mystical experience, which are beyond all logic. The mystics usually say that they are "above" logic or "above" reason. For this value word there is good ground. But since I cannot discuss that aspect of the matter here, I use the neutral words "outside" or "beyond."

By far the most profound statements of these matters are to be found in the Upanishads, although words carrying, less clearly, the same meanings can be found in Christian, Jewish, Islamic, or Buddhist sources (although Buddhism speaks of Nirvana in place of God). The Upanishads tell us "that experience is neither subjective nor objective"[23] and that God is is beyond both existence and non-existence.

23 This is from Swami Prabhavananda's and Frederick Manchester's translation of the Mandukya Upanishad. I have suspected the translation because of the modern and western wording. But R. E. Hume, who is one of the most scholarly translators, renders it "neither inward nor outward"; and Radhakrishnan translates it "not that which cognizes the internal (objects) and not that which cognizes the external (objects)"; and both these renderings seem to mean the same as "neither subjective nor objective." I do not read Sanskrit myself.

Since the mystical experience is beyond logic it is also beyond words, since words are logical tools. "Ineffable" is the word commonly used here. It does not mean merely that the experience is very difficult to describe because our language is too poor. It means that it is inherently and forever inexpressible in any conceivable language. And the reason is that the experience is undifferentiated, and that there are in it no distinctions whatever—no "contrasts" is Eckhart's expression, "contrast" being his word for any distinction. But all words, except proper names and exclamations, express concepts, and all concepts depend on classification and therefore on distinctions or contrasts. This is merely an application of the fact that the experience is "beyond logic" and beyond the logical intellect, which depends on distinctions. Of course it also follows that we cannot properly apply to it such words as "ineffable" or "mystical" or "divine" since these also are classificatory. You have to make the best you can of this ultimate paradox. It is clearly and especially recognized in Mahayana Buddhism where (for instance in the *Diamond Sutra*) it is insisted that there is no distinction between Nirvana and non-Nirvana. This does not mean that there is no Nirvana. It means that Nirvana is incapable of being thought, understood, or spoken of, although it can be experienced.

It will be asked: if no words can ever be framed which describe the mystical experience, why does the mystic use words which apparently aim at describing it? Why does he not obey the advice of Wittgenstein, "that whereof one cannot speak, thereof one must be silent"? Undoubtedly he is inconsistent with himself, and everything which can be written down (including of course what is written in this paper) or said about mystical experience is self-inconsistent. Let me quote a recent writer who has himself had such experience, Arthur Koestler. He writes: "Mystical experiences, as we dubiously call them, are not nebulous, vague, or maudlin—they only become so when we debase them by verbalization. However, to communicate what is incommunicable by its nature, one must somehow put it into words, *and so one moves in a vicious circle.*"[24] The circle *is* vicious, inherently and ultimately, and let us make no pretense that this can be explained away or got rid of. But then this is the logician talking again.

Koestler adds: "what distinguishes this type of experience from the emotional entrancements of music, landscapes, or love is that the former has a definitely intellectual, or rather noumenal, content. It is meaningful, though not in verbal terms. Verbal transcriptions which come nearest to it are: the unity and interlocking of everything that exists, an interdependence like that of gravitational fields or communicating ves-

[24] *The Invisible Writing*, p. 352, (my *italics*).

sels."[25] By the rather doubtful words "intellectual or noumenal content" I think what he means is that the experience has a unique quality which the mystic attempts to communicate by such words as "truth" and "reality." Since "truth" understood in its literal sense is an attribute only of propositions, which are the product of the logical intellect, the mystical experience cannot be "true" in that sense. One simply has to put up with the fact that no word will do. And one should give up trying to prove that God and religion and religious concepts are true in the indicative or scientific or literal sense. One can say that it is just as false to say that they are subjective fantasies as that they are objective facts. The ascription of truth and reality and objectivity to religious concepts serves at least the negative function of repudiating the false view that they are subjective or illusory or otherwise false.

I go back to the point that for the mystic himself his experience cannot be represented as an "argument for the existence of God." Perhaps, however, it can constitute a starting point of an argument for us, the non-mystics. But this will be true only in a very trivial sense. The argument would have two main steps. It would proceed: "(1) I, who do not have the experience, infer from the mystic's words and behavior, and from the agreement between mystical utterances in all ages and cultures, that he really does have the experience which he says he has, that he is not lying, that he is not deluded in supposing that he has the experience, and that his words are some sort of attempt to communicate the incommunicable. (2) From this experience in the mystic I infer the existence of God." The first step is no doubt inferential in the same sense as I infer from the fact that you say you are having a toothache that you really have one. This is correct, but trivial. But the second step, which is the important one, does not represent any inference at all for the reasons already given. There is an inference from the words and behavior of mystics to their experience. But there is no such thing as an inference from this experience to the existence of God, either for the mystic or for the non-mystic.

The absolute unshakeable certainly that the mystic feels about God, which is so often referred to, is also a result of the undifferentiated and non-inferential character of his experience. Because there is for him no distinction between himself and his experience on the one hand and God on the other hand, because he and his experience are simply identical with God, there is no possibility of any mistaken interpretation. It is commonly said that this utter conviction which fills the mystic's soul may convince him, but cannot be an argument for us, since the mere subjective state of a feeling of certainty is notoriously not evidence of

25 *Ibid.*

truth. I am afraid this conventional observation is a very poor comment on the question. In the first place the mystic's conviction is not a "subjective state of feeling certain." There is nothing subjective about the experience, and the sense of certainty and reality is a part of the experience, and not something which the experience produces. As usual we are applying common sense categories and criteria which have no application. If in any experience there is a possible distinction between a subjective state of mind and an objective fact, then a subjective state of a feeling of certainty cannot render certain an objective fact. But here there is no such distinction. The case seems to be as follows. The mystic is certain of God simply because he has entered into union with God, or *is* God, if that expression is preferred. As to us, we could conceivably be mistaken in our inference that the mystic has the experience which he says he has. But if we are satisfied as to that, then we ought to be as certain of God as the mystic is, since there is no further inference to be made, and therefore no possibility of mistake.

I pass finally to Broad's remark that he does not think there is any good reason to suppose that the reality with which the mystic is in contact is "personal." The doctrine that God is personal is symbolic, not literal. God is not a person in the sense in which Tom, Dick, and Harry are, as has been pointed out. The study of the utterances of mystics will show that God is consciousness, but not *a* consciousness. His consciousness is universal, not individual. Since this is not intelligible to the vulgar, the concept of personality is used. The mystical insight is that God is super-personality. According to our ordinary common sense categories either I exist as an individual or I do not exist at all. For instance, according to the common conception of immortality in the Christian religion, Tom will continue to be Tom, Dick Dick, and Harry Harry, three distinct and separate individuals, throughout all eternity. Either this must be true, we suppose, or Tom, Dick, and Harry will suffer extinction. In the same way it is supposed that God must be an individual consciousness if he exists as consciousness at all.

But all this is shown false by mystical experience. I will quote two passages, one from Tennyson who had frequent mystical experiences, the other from Koestler. Tennyson wrote: "All at once out of the intensity of the consciousness of individuality individuality itself seemed to dissolve and fade away into boundless being, and this was not a confused state, but the clearest, the surest of the surest, utterly beyond words . . . *the loss of personality (if such it were) seeming no extinction but the only true life.*"[26]

The passage from Koestler reads: "Then I was floating on my back in

26 James' *Varieties of Religious Experience*, 384. *Italics* mine.

a river of peace under bridges of silence. It came from nowhere and flowed nowhere. Then there was no river and no I. The I had ceased to exist. . . . The 'I' ceases to exist because it has, by a kind of mental osmosis, established communication with, and been dissolved in, the universal pool. It is this process of dissolution and limitless expansion which is sensed as the 'oceanic feeling,' as the draining of all tension, the absolute catharsis, the peace that passeth all understanding."[27] It is noticeable that Koestler in these words and in his whole account avoids the use of the word God. Presumably he wishes to avoid the superstitious ideas commonly associated with the word. But the "universal pool" in which personality is dissolved is exactly what in the usual mystical vocabulary is called God.

The lesson of these two passages (and plenty more could be quoted) is clear. It is false that consciousness is necessarily individual or associated with an "I." There is a universal consciousness to which even human beings can attain, and this universal consciousness in which all individual egos dissolve and cease to be distinguished from one another is the divine consciousness.

One now understands how the Hindu can assert that a soul which has reached that highest level of spiritual development in which it is freed from the wheel of reincarnation will be absorbed in God, and how this dissolution of his personality will yet not be extinction. This is certainly a higher conception of immortality than the surely absurd Christian view that Tom, Dick, and Harry will remain the same Tom, Dick and Harry for ever. If this were understood, it is possible that the enquiries and experiments of the Psychical Research Society might be fruitfully channelled in a new direction.

The conclusion is that when Broad finds no reason to think that the reality which is contacted in mystical experience is a person, this is nothing to be surprised at, because he takes the word person in its most literal sense, and God is not a person in that sense.

W. T. STACE

DEPARTMENT OF PHILOSOPHY
PRINCETON UNIVERSITY

27 *The Invisible Writing*, 352.

5

Robert G. Turnbull

EMPIRICAL AND A PRIORI ELEMENTS IN BROAD'S THEORY OF KNOWLEDGE

. . . there is both need and room for a science which shall try to analyse and define the concepts which are used in daily life and in the special sciences. There is need for it, because these concepts really are obscure, and because their obscurity really does lead to difficulties. And there is room for it, because, whilst all the special sciences *use* these concepts, none of them is *about* these concepts as such. I regard Critical Philosophy as the science which has this for its most fundamental task.[1]

PROFESSOR Broad has devoted considerable skill and effort to performing this "most fundamental task" of "Critical Philosophy" in essays and books from his earliest articles (in Moral Philosophy) to the present. My essay is largely devoted, however, to examining his performance of a philosophical task which, in an obvious sense, is more fundamental than that which he thought, in 1924, "most fundamental." This is the task of making clear and justifying the concepts *used* in analyzing and defining "the concepts used in daily life and in the special sciences" including, of course, *analysis* and *definition*. Fortunately for the present purpose, Broad has written a good deal *about* the various concepts *used* (or *to be used*) in performing the "most fundamental task" of Critical Philosophy. It is with some of his writings about some of these concepts that I shall be concerned. For the most part I shall be concerned with his doctrine of "empirical concepts," for the rest with his doctrines of "*a priori* concepts" ("Innate Ideaism" and "Non-Perceptual Intuition"), both as developed in his *Examination of McTaggart's Philosophy*.[2]

I. *Introduction*

Serious philosophical discussion has been and continues to be almost wholly "dialectical," in the sense that it proceeds from what is granted

[1] C. D. Broad, "Critical and Speculative Philosophy," in *Contemporary British Philosophy*, First series, ed. J. H. Muirhead (New York, 1924), 83.
[2] *EMcP*, Vol. I published in 1933, Vol. II (Parts 1 and 2) published in 1938 (Cambridge), hereafter referred to as *McTaggart* in the text.

(or what the writer or speaker hopes will be granted—cf. the ubiquity of 'surely,' 'it is certain,' 'clearly,' and kindred expressions in philosophical essays) to various conclusions. Certain conclusions may turn out to be at variance with each other or at variance with other propositions which seem equally to be granted (or the conclusions therefrom), in which case what has been granted is re-scrutinized (assuming that the reasoning from it is correct) and certain elements of it dropped or reformulated. Certain quite different conclusions may be thought to follow from or at least be compatible with what is granted, and argument may ensue as to there being any good reasons for preferring any of these latter conclusions to the former ones or *vice versa*. In either of these events, something *more* or *other* will be granted, and conclusions may be drawn from this or from this and what was first granted. These may turn out to be at variance with each other, and so on. Serious philosophical criticism seems to consist, largely at least, in showing or trying to show that (i) what philosopher *A* takes as granted results in variant conclusions which he has not noticed, (ii) the argument by which *A* proceeds from what is granted to his conclusions is faulty, (iii) different conclusions from those reached by *A* follow from or are, at least, compatible with what is granted, (iv) there are good reasons for preferring the conclusions mentioned in (iii) to those reached by *A*, (v) there are good reasons for claiming that what is taken as granted by *A* is by no means to be granted (having a bearing, perhaps, on (iii) and (iv) above), or (vi) several or all of criticisms (i) through (v) apply to *A*'s philosophizing.

This is, of course, highly schematic and uses several near-technical terms with calculated unclarity and ambiguity. It leaves out of account, moreover, such questions as "What is uniquely *philosophical* in either, what is granted, what is concluded, or the means of arriving at the latter from the former?" and "Are there any philosophical propositions?" I do not at any point wish to discuss these questions as such. My schematic account does, however, make possible at least three comments which are germane to the present undertaking. First, it indicates the nature of the criticisms which Broad himself has made of a large number of philosophical arguments. Apart from that of sardonic wit directed against Wittgenstein admiration at Cambridge, Russell's behaviorism, the Ph.D. degree, American professors, and what not, the image which most of us have of Broadian philosophizing is that of painstaking elimination of rival philosophical conclusions (and the arguments for them) by methods (i) through (v) above, together with both careful statement of what it seems necessary to grant (in a given connection) and the claim that Broad's own conclusions (and supporting arguments) are not open to the objections made against the rivals. Second, it suggests the pattern which must be followed if philosophical criticism is to be at all possible. Occasionally, even contemporary philosophers have written as though philosophy were revelation and their problem an evangelizing one. Of such philosophizing (if such it be) the only appropriate "criticism" seems to be counter-propaganda or *argumentum ad baculum*. Fortunately, so far as I know, there is no Broad church. Third, it suggests the pattern which I shall attempt to follow in this paper.

I might say a word in defence of limiting myself to doctrines and arguments to be found in the *McTaggart*. First, though Broad has not been a philosophical chameleon, he has, at different times held different views concerning the issues at hand and has offered different arguments at different times for the same views. It seems obviously necessary, in a relatively short essay, to limit oneself to discussion of a small number of views and arguments. (Indeed, as we shall shortly see, even *these* will lead us into areas which, if discussed with the thoroughness they deserve, would require volume-size investigation.) Second, there is reason to believe that, though Broad has occasionally written in a different vein since the late 'thirties, the arguments and doctrines of the *McTaggart* are, on the whole, mature statements of matters he "worried out" at least from the period of *Perception, Physics and Reality*. Third, the *McTaggart* treats within the compass of one work (though five years intervened between the publications of Vol. I and Vol. II) of all the issues I shall discuss in this paper. This is *prima facie* evidence that the arguments and conclusions are thought through with an eye to their bearing upon one another. Finally, the doctrines and arguments to be considered from the *McTaggart*, even if Broad is no longer prepared to defend any of them,[3] are still worthy of serious discussion and, if possible, refutation. Before turning to the material from the *McTaggart*, it will be convenient to develop a terminology and to invent various quoting devices.

With a nod in the direction of Occam, I propose to use the term '*complexum vocis*' as a portmanteau for the following items. A "TOKEN *complexum vocis*" will be, e.g., the string of marks between inverted commas in 'John is tall' or any other single string of marks or sequence of sounds which may be, or the use of which may be, on a given occasion, appropriately called 'true or false.' 'tcv' as a quoting device will indicate that a token *complexum vocis* is being referred to; so that 'tcvJohn is talltcv' e.g., may be used to refer to the set of marks placed between single inverted commas in the immediately preceding sentence. 'CLASS

---

3 I once asked Professor Carnap a question concerning his *Logische Aufbau der Welt*. He replied, "My grandfather wrote that!"

complexum vocis' will be used to refer to a class of token *complexa vocis* the members of which are related by similarity of shape or sound. Using 'ccv' as a quoting device, '^{ccv}John is tall^{ccv}' e.g., may be used to refer to the class of marks related by similarity of shape to ^{tcv}John is tall^{tcv} and the class of sounds related by similarity of sound-sequence to an "utterance" of 'John is tall.' The use of a member of a certain class *complexum vocis* on a certain occasion will be called a "PRODUCED *complexum vocis*," using 'pcv' as a quoting device. Thus, e.g., Jones' assertion on a given occasion, using a member of ^{ccv}John is tall^{ccv}, will be referred to by '^{pcv}John is tall^{pcv}.' Unless otherwise indicated in the context, I shall in what follows use the quoting device and 'produced *complexum vocis*' to refer to what is commonly called an *assertion,* though there may be, of course, produced *complexa vocis* which are not assertions. If Jones, e.g., is able to use members of ^{ccv}John is tall^{ccv} appropriately, I shall say that he has an ABILITY *complexum vocis,* and 'acv' will be used to refer to such ability *complexa vocis.* Token *complexa vocis* or produced *complexa vocis* or both are commonly said to have "meanings," whether or not they are true or false. Ignoring, for terminological simplicity, what may be some important distinctions, I shall call the "meanings" of token or produced *complexa vocis* 'MEANING *complexa vocis*' and use 'mcv' as a quoting device to refer to them. Members or the uses of members of different class *complexa vocis* may, of course, have the same meaning *complexum vocis,* as, e.g., ^{tcv}John is tall^{tcv} (or ^{pcv}John is tall^{pcv}) and ^{tcv}Johann ist lang^{tcv} (or ^{pcv}Johann ist lang^{pcv}) may both be said to have ^{mcv}John is tall^{mcv}. (Strictly, of course, meaning *complexa vocis* are only misleadingly called '*complexa vocis*'; if this is kept in mind, the advantage of keeping the terminology, as well as the quoting devices, simple outweighs the disadvantage of possible misuse.) Finally, it may be convenient, on various occasions, to refer to different members of the same class *complexum vocis* or to different produced *complexa vocis,* each of the latter being the use of a member of the same class *complexum vocis.* On such occasions I shall mark the difference by the use of numerical subscripts following the closing quotation device, as ^{tcv}John is tall$^{\text{tcv}}_1$, ^{tcv}John is tall$^{\text{tcv}}_2$, etc., ^{pcv}John is tall$^{\text{pcv}}_1$, ^{pcv}John is tall$^{\text{pcv}}_2$, etc.

Similar distinctions will be made for what shall be called '*incomplexa vocis,*' justified, at least in part, by the fact that members of the same class *incomplexum vocis* may occur in members of different class *complexa vocis,* as, e.g., members of ^{clv}John^{clv}, ^{clv}is^{clv}, and ^{clv}tall^{clv} may occur in members of ^{ccv}John is tall^{ccv}, ^{ccv}George is tired^{ccv}, ^{ccv}John is tired^{ccv}, etc. Whether all token *incomplexa vocis* may be said, in the same sense or senses, to have meaning *incomplexa vocis* is a question not decided by the terminology or quoting devices any more than is the question "What, in *any* sense, is a meaning *incomplexum vocis* or, for that matter, a meaning *complexum vocis?*"

So defined, I think it uncontroversial that there are *complexa* and *incomplexa vocis* of the various kinds distinguished and that, though the terminology and quoting devices are arbitrary, the distinctions made among them are genuine.

I propose to use the term *'complexum mentis'* as a portmanteau for the following items. A "PARTICULAR *complexum mentis*" is a particular "thought" which, if it is what the tradition calls a "judgment," may be true or false (though it may be what Broad and others call a "supposition"). I shall use 'pcm' as a quoting device to refer to particular *complexa mentis,* so that, e.g., ^{pcm}John is tall^{pcm}' may be used to refer to Jones' thought at a certain time that John is tall. 'ABILITY *complexum mentis'* will be used to refer to an ability to produce or have various particular *complexa mentis* on appropriate occasions. 'acm' will be used as a quoting device to refer to ability *complexa mentis,* so that Jones' ability, e.g., to have or produce items like ^{pcm}John is tall^{pcm} will be referred to by '^{acm}John is tall^{acm}.' As in the case of token or produced *complexa vocis,* particular *complexa mentis* may be said to have a "meaning," whether they are true or false. I should like to refer to the "meaning" of a particular *complexum mentis* as a "CONTENT *complexum mentis,"* using 'ccm' as a quoting device. Thus the "meaning" of ^{pcm}John is tall^{pcm} will be referred to by '^{ccm}John is tall^{ccm}.' The presumption is, of course, that, in at least one of the senses of 'meaning,' certain meaning *complexa vocis* may be identical with certain content *complexa mentis;* so that ^{mcv}John is tall^{mcv} may be identical with ^{ccm}John is tall^{ccm}. Again, as in the case of token and produced *complexa vocis,* it will be convenient to use numerical subscripts, when appropriate, to indicate that different produced *complexa mentis* are being referred to.

Similar distinctions may be made for *incomplexa mentis,* as ^{pim}tall^{pim}, e.g., is, in some sense, a "part" of ^{pcm}John is tall^{pcm} and ^{aim}tall^{aim} may be, in some sense, a "part" of ^{acm}John is tall^{acm}. The presumption is also, as in the case of *complexa vocis* and *mentis,* that ^{miv}tall^{miv}, e.g., is identical with ^{cim}tall^{cim}, and so on.

The following may serve as an "exemplary" summary:

1. ^{tcv}John is tall^{tcv} Token *Complexum Vocis*—a shape (or a noise).
2. ^{ccv}John is tall^{ccv} Class *Complexum Vocis*—class of similar shapes and/or noises.

3. ^{acv}John is tall^{acv} — Ability *Complexum Vocis*—an ability to use members of ^{ccv}John is tall^{ccv} correctly.

4. ^{mcv}John is tall^{mcv} — Meaning *Complexum Vocis*—The "meaning" of 'John is tall.'

5. ^{tiv}Tall^{tiv} — Token *Incomplexum Vocis*—a shape (or noise).

6. ^{civ}Tall^{civ} — Class *Incomplexum Vocis*—class of similar shapes and/or noises.

7. ^{aiv}Tall^{aiv} — Ability *Incomplexum Vocis*—an ability to use members of ^{civ}Tall^{civ} correctly.

8. ^{miv}Tall^{miv} — Meaning *Incomplexum Vocis*—The "meaning" of 'Tall.'

9. ^{pcm}John is tall^{pcm} — Particular *Complexum Mentis*—a certain thought that John is tall.

10. ^{acm}John is tall^{acm} — Ability *Complexum Mentis*—an ability to have thoughts like ^{pcm}John is tall^{pcm}.

11. ^{ccm}John is tall^{ccm} — Content *Complexum Mentis*—The "meaning" of, e.g., ^{pcm}John is tall^{pcm}.

12. ^{pim}Tall^{pim} — Particular *Incomplexum Mentis*—a certain thought, part of, e.g., ^{pcm}John is tall^{pcm}.

13. ^{aim}Tall^{aim} — Ability *Incomplexum Mentis*—an ability to have thoughts like ^{pim}Tall^{pim}.

14. ^{cim}Tall^{cim} — Content *Incomplexum Mentis*—The "meaning" of, e.g., ^{pim}Tall^{pim}.

As in the case of *complexa* and *incomplexa vocis*, I think it is readily to be granted that there are *complexa* and *incomplexa mentis* of the various kinds distinguished, especially since nothing in the terminology decides anything about the relations between (or identities of) *complexa* and *incomplexa mentis* and *complexa* and *incomplexa vocis*. Armed with this apparatus of terminology and quoting devices, let us now turn to Broad's discussion of various kinds of concepts.

II. Broad's Account of "Empirical" and "A Priori" Concepts

In Chapter III of Vol. I of *McTaggart* Broad gives an account of the "formation" of ability *incomplexa mentis* which are "empirical," "simple," and "intuitive." I shall quote the heart of that account and make it the subject of several extended comments.

It is now possible to define an "empirical concept." It is quite certain that many, if not all, simple intuitive dispositional ideas are formed in the following way, which may be illustrated by the formation of the idea of redness. I perceive from time to time things which present a characteristic kind of perceptual appearance. They "look red." I compare them with other things that look like them in this respect and look unlike them in other respects. For example, I may see objects which look round, triangular, square, etc., and all look red. Again, I compare them with yet other things which look unlike them in this respect, but look like them in other respects. For example, I compare triangular things which look red with other triangular things which look green, and with other triangular things which look blue, and so on. I perform a similar process of comparison and contrast between circular things that look red, and circular things that look green, and circular things that look blue, and so on. Eventually I am able to perform an act of abstraction, and to contemplate the characteristic of redness in separation from other qualities and in abstraction from any particular substance. Finally a disposition is formed which, whenever it is suitably stimulated, will produce an act of acquaintance with the quality of redness for its object. I have then "acquired the idea of redness." A very important adjunct to the process is to link this disposition by association with the traces left by hearing, seeing, and speaking the word *red*. When this associative link has been formed anything that excites the verbal trace will tend to excite the dispositional idea and will thus tend to evoke an occurrent intuitive idea of redness.[4]

A.

I think it is clear that Broad has identified ^{cim}red^{cim} (the content *incomplexum mentis*), in the most important sense of 'meaning,' with a certain universal, *redness*. Thus, whenever I exercise ^{aim}red^{aim}, I am, on Broad's account, having or producing "an act of acquaintance with the quality of redness for its object." Commitment to Broad's account, therefore, involves an *ontological* commitment to the doctrine of universals as well as a *psychological* commitment to the existence of "acts of acquaintance" with such universals. He writes elsewhere of certain token *incomplexa vocis* NAMING certain universals with which one having the appropriate ability *incomplexa mentis* may be "acquainted." The presumption is, then, that he would identify, e.g., ^{miv}red^{miv} and ^{cim}red^{cim}, both, of course, as the universal redness.

B.

I should think that, if I am *perceiving* a certain object, what I am doing would be commonly said to require *somehow* my having an appropriate ability *complexum mentis*. Suppose, e.g., that I am perceiving a certain red object; then the appropriate ability *complexum mentis* would include ^{aim}red^{aim}. If Peter should be the red object in question, to perceive that Peter is red (or, if you please, to perceive Peter *as* red) *might* involve only a *readiness* to produce a member of ^{ccv}Peter is red^{ccv} (not necessarily the producing of such a member), or an item like

[4] *EMcP*, I, 41.

ᵖᶜᵐPeter is redᵖᶜᵐ, or it *might* involve the *producing* of, e.g., ᵖᶜᵐPeter is redᵖᶜᵐ₁. In either case my perceiving that Peter is red would, presumably, involve having some sort of "experience" (a "red" one); and, in either case, it would involve my having ᵃᶜᵐPeter is redᵃᶜᵐ. This latter, of course, includes ᵃᶜᵐredᵃᶜᵐ. Thus, ignoring for the moment the complications of Broad's talk about "perceptual appearances" and "looking red," it would seem that, on his account, if his use of 'perceive' is taken seriously, I must have ᵃⁱᵐredᵃⁱᵐ before, by hypothesis, I am supposed to have it. Elsewhere in the *McTaggart*,[5] Broad seems clearly to agree that to be able to have what he there calls "perceptual experiences" involves appropriate ability *incomplexa mentis,* though his account of perceptual experiences does not require the having of any particular *incomplexum mentis* on the occasion of the perceptual experience. He has it in mind that a perceptual experience may involve only what Price calls "perceptual acceptance," interpreting this as some sort of "modification of experience, corresponding to the *disposition* to make a certain perceptual judgment." It goes without saying that such a modification is possible only in one who has the disposition in question; and, if the perceptual acceptance is of an object as red, then the disposition surely includes, in some way, ᵃⁱᵐredᵃⁱᵐ, as a part.

I do not intend now to press the criticism made in the above paragraph, for Broad may easily reply either that I have picked up a slight misuse of 'perceive' or that I have ignored the complications introduced by "looks red" and, perhaps, "perceptual appearance" in his account. It does, however, indicate the line of a fundamental criticism I shall be making. Broad *seems,* moreover, in Vol. II of *McTaggart* (published some five years after Vol. I), to have taken notice of this possible criticism. I say 'seems,' for the context is criticism of McTaggart's "extended use" of 'perception.' Broad proposes the substitution of 'prehension' for 'perception' where the latter is used in McTaggart's "extended sense." "McTaggart uses the name 'perception' to cover every instance of acquaintance with particulars, regardless of whether they are ostensibly material, as in visual or tactual sensation; or ostensibly mental, as in introspective reflexion; or of uncertain status, as in being aware of images."[6] A little farther on he writes

When a person has repeatedly prehended certain particulars as having a certain characteristic *C* he may "form an idea of" that characteristic. That is, he may acquire the power and the disposition to think of it whenever his attention is suitably directed, even though he is not at the time prehending any particular as having it. From ideas which have been formed in this way we

5 *EMcP*, II, 66f.   6 *EMcP*, II, 4.

can proceed to form ideas of complex characteristics which no particular that we have ever prehended has been prehended as having.

When and only when a person has formed ideas of characteristics he can make judgments and suppositions. Having formed the idea of redness from prehending certain particulars as red, he can proceed to *judge that* a certain particular, which he is now prehending, is red. This is quite different from *prehending it as* red. Again, he can proceed to judge or to suppose that a certain particular, which he is not now prehending, is or has been or will be red.[7]

Before commenting on "prehensions," I should like to cite another passage, this one from Vol. I of *McTaggart:*

Whenever I perceive a physical object, I am acquainted with a certain particular, which I will call a "sensibile." My judgments of perceptual appearance are not about the sensibilia which I sense, but they are founded upon the latter and their sensible qualities. If I choose to do so, I can attend to the sensibile and inspect it and make a judgment about its sensible qualities.[8]

Let us suppose that a certain physical object, Peter, in Broad's terms, "presents a certain perceptual appearance;" doing so, Peter "looks red." Of course, Peter looks red to me when and only when I am "acquainted with" a red sensibile. Let us call the sensibile in this case 'Sam.' The presumption is that, in this case, to say that Peter *looks red* is to imply that Sam *is red*. In another section of the *McTaggart*,[9] Broad contends that —taking the present case as an example—$^{pim}red^{pim}$ in $^{pcm}Peter$ is red^{pcm} and $^{pim}red^{pim}$ in ^{pcm}Sam is red^{pcm} have *different* content *incomplexa mentis*, the latter being a *component in* the former. If so, the content *incomplexum mentis* of $^{pim}red^{pim}$ in $^{pcm}Peter$ is red^{pcm} would seem to be a compound universal. Since Broad seems to think of simple empirical concepts as *of* simple universals (cf. the "prehensions" account above and comment 'E' below), I could not get $^{aim}red^{aim}$ (call it '$^{aim}red^{aim}_2$') where it is the ability to be aware of the *redness* which might qualify Peter *simply* by the process described on p. 41 of Vol. I of *McTaggart* (quoted above, pp. 202f.). The $^{aim}red^{aim}$ (call it '$^{aim}red^{aim}_1$') allegedly acquired by *that* process would seem to be the ability to be aware of the redness which might qualify Sam. Now it would seem that, in order to acquire $^{aim}red^{aim}_1$, I should have to compare and contrast sensibilia like Sam and *not* physical objects like Peter. How else, for $^{aim}red^{aim}_1$, would Broad's phrase, "in abstraction from any particular substance" (requiring, incidentally, sensibilia to be considered as *substances*), make sense? Thus I should not be comparing objects which "look red," etc., but sensibilia. The objects *perceived* must, as well, be sensibilia. But, if

7 *EMcP,* II, 4–5. Italics are Broad's.
8 *EMcP,* I, 35.   9 *EMcP,* II, 82.

perceiving Sam as red involves having $^{aim}red^{aim}_1$, I should then have to have $^{aim}red^{aim}_1$ *before*, on Broad's account, I have acquired it!

Broad, like a good many other philosophers, seems to have taken 'appears,' 'looks,' and kindred terms as, *in certain contexts at least*, requiring a set of "sense particulars" (sensibilia, in Broad's case) in addition to physical particulars (ignoring, as we safely may for the present purpose, "mental particulars"). If this is the case, then, if it should make sense to say of sensibilia that they might "look red" or "present a characteristic kind of perceptual appearance," and so on, we would by parity of reasoning require that there be super-sensibilia; if the same sorts of things might be said of super-sensibilia, we should require super-super-sensibilia; and so on. I submit that this possibility is absurd or would result in absurdity. If this is not the case, then Broad may not say that I have distorted his meaning in interpreting the quotation from p. 41 of Vol. I of *McTaggart* as presupposing the having of $^{aim}red^{aim}$ by pointing out that 'perceive' is in some way qualified by the use of "perceptual appearances" and "looks red."[10]

Let us now see if the "prehension" account of Vol. II of the *McTaggart* fares any better. How, according to it, do I acquire simple empirical ability *incomplexa mentis*, assuming, as Broad does, that ability *incomplexa mentis* which are *of* characteristics qualifying physical objects, are *of* composite characteristics? To acquire $^{aim}red^{aim}_1$, e.g., I should, by hypothesis, have to prehend a number of sensibilia like Sam *as red*. Prehending them *as red* must be, on Broad's account, "quite different" from judging *that* they are red, severally or collectively.

Now I should think that, if anything is true of sensibilia, it is that they are not and do not include prehensions (though prehensions may be themselves, according to Broad, prehended). Broad, indeed, finds not the "least difficulty in conceiving that there might be particulars which quite literally have sensible redness and sensible roundness even though no one is sensing them as having those qualities,"[11] i.e., that there may be unsensed sensibilia. I should therefore imagine that, in

---

[10] It may be of interest to note, in passing, that Broad's account on p. 41 of Vol. I (with its "perceptual appearances" and "looks red"), taken together with the quotation from p. 35 of Vol. I, seems to presuppose the falsity of any form of phenomenalism. On p. 51 of Vol. I, he writes, "Even if no *physical object* were really red, it seems incredible that such an object should look red to a person unless in perceiving it he was sensing a sensibile which is red." (This, incidentally, reinforces a point I have made just above in the text.) Throughout the *McTaggart*, so far as I can tell, Broad offers no good *argument* against any form of phenomenalism or in favor of his realism. He seems still in the position of *Perception, Physics and Reality* (Cambridge, 1914), which he ended by lamenting his inability to find plausible arguments against phenomenalism but still "hankering after realism."

[11] *EMcP*, II, 80.

some sense, prehensions are "mind-contributed," some sort of mental act. Further, Broad seems, throughout Vol. II, to take it as possible that I might, e.g., in prehending a sensibile *as red,* be mistaken; I might be *mis*prehending it *as red.* I should therefore think it legitimate to distinguish between particular prehensions and prehension abilities. And it would seem that I must have as many prehension abilities as I have simple empirical ability *incomplexa mentis*—probably more. Further, it would seem quite conceivable that I might have certain prehension abilities and lack others. I might, e.g., have the ability to prehend various sensibilia *as red* and lack the ability to prehend sensibilia *as green.* Broad would most likely claim that, in that case, I would be "green-blind;" for, throughout Vol II, he seems to take "sensing a sensibile" as identical with "prehending a sensibile as such-and-such." In this sense of 'sensing,' however, it does not seem either self-evident or capable of proof that, in order for a sensibile to be present in my visual field, e.g., it must be "sensed." Indeed, it seems to me that, from time to time, I am confronted with visual objects which I do not prehend, apprehend, or in any way "act" upon. But, *even if this were not the case,* the prehension of a particular *as red* would be different from the particular so prehended, as Broad himself admits.

We should then require, on his account, as many prehension abilities as there are "simple intuitive dispositional ideas" which are "empirical" for us to acquire. If so, it is hard to see how his account does anything but obfuscate the issue at hand. If prehension abilities were acquired somehow, we should need an explanation of their acquisition similar to that thought required for the concepts in question. If they are not acquired, then *Broad's doctrine becomes a doctrine of "innate ideas" at one remove.* In either case, his doctrine seems to be or to require a redundancy.

It might be objected, with certain other sections of the *McTaggart* in mind, that all that is needed is a supposedly innate "general" ability to prehend various items *as similar* to or *different* from various other items. The obvious reply is that 'similar to' and 'different from' always admit of qualification by something like 'in respect *a* and/or *b* and/or *c,* etc.' In order to acquire a battery of what Broad calls "*simple* empirical concepts," I should require a set of abilities to prehend various particulars as similar to or different from in *quite specific respects* various other particulars. And this set would contain a prehension ability for every simple empirical ability *incomplexum mentis* which I could acquire. If it is possible that qualities can all be dispensed with in favor of relations, it may be that ᵃⁱᵐredᵃⁱᵐ (like other simple empirical ability *incomplexa mentis*) is just the ability to be aware of a certain "simple" relation, in this case a certain specific color-similarity. If this thesis were generalized, we would reach the obvious redundancy reached in the last paragraph only with all ability *incomplexa mentis* being abilities to produce particular *incomplexa mentis* whose "contents" are relations. The objection therefore falls to the ground, the supposed "general" ability fragmenting into a set of "special" ones.[12]

C.

I am quite puzzled by Broad's statement: "Eventually I am able to perform an act of abstraction, and to contemplate the characteristic of redness in separation from other qualities and in abstraction from any particular substance." What is "abstracted from" what? Consider once again our friend Sam, the red sensibile. It does not seem possible that I could "abstract" Sam's redness from Sam unless Sam and its redness were two particulars, the former being, presumably, a complex somehow including the latter. In that case I might learn to "contemplate" the redness of Sam in separation from Sam and, perhaps, from the round- ness of Sam. Something like Aristotle's "present-in-predicated-of" dis- tinction would seem involved in this possibility, though both Sam and his redness are, by hypothesis, sensibilia. But, even granting this very odd possibility, the redness of Sam would be a *particular;* in contem- plating it, therefore, I would not be contemplating it "in abstraction from any particular substance." To contemplate it in the absence of itself would seem more difficult than joining Alice in contemplating the Cheshire cat's grin.[13]

Many philosophers have held or implied that universals are literally parts of certain particulars or, at least, that there is only something like

---

[12] As will come out in later comments (especially comment H), I do think that *some* "general ability" is involved in acquiring "empirical concepts." This is, how- ever, putting the matter quite crudely, the "ability" to acquire dispositions to re- spond to various environmental features with members of different class *incomplexa vocis.*

[13] The possibility remains, of course, that, e.g., only after "acquaintance" with *facts* in which redness is a component, could I acquire ᵃˡᵐredᵃˡᵐ. The problem would then be that of acquiring the ability to be "acquainted with" redness out of the context of any particular fact. The difficulties in such a view are enormous; I shall mention only two. First, on the Russell doctrine of acquaintance, it follows that whatever I am "acquainted with" I can *name,* and whatever I can *name,* I am "ac- quainted with." I think Broad assumes at least this much of that doctrine. The consequence, on the present view, would be, of course, that facts can be *named.* Second, the apprehension of facts, *per se,* would seem to presuppose the conceptual abilities in question—both logically and genetically. Any view which embodies or requires this presupposition would be, so far forth, presumed correct. Any view which denies it, or entails its denial, would, *ipso facto,* be required to explain away this apparent presupposition.

a *distinctio formalis a parte rei* between particulars and the universals characterizing them. Some have held that we can "operationally" (or "ostensively") define simple empirical *incomplexa mentis;* what I am alleged to "see" at the "ostensive step" in the "operational definition" of ᵃⁱᵐredᵃⁱᵐ (or, perhaps, ᵖⁱᵐredᵖⁱᵐ) is ᶜⁱᵐredᶜⁱᵐ. If I "see" Sam, e.g., in the "ostensive step," it may well be the case that Sam is red; but it seems sheer confusion to claim that what I "see" in the "ostensive step" is ᶜⁱᵐredᶜⁱᵐ (or, if you please, redness), unless Sam *is* or *contains as a part* ᶜⁱᵐredᶜⁱᵐ. The mistake involved here is analogous to confusing the 'is' of predication with the 'is' of identity or, perhaps better, the 'is' of 'is part of.' The obvious conclusion that it would follow from this simple "ostensivism," as from other forms of the "characteristics-are-parts-of-particulars" thesis, that, e.g., nothing but Sam could be red is hardly worth pointing out. If, on the other hand, it is held straightforwardly that a certain *timeless* universal which is not an instance of itself is literally a part of a particular, "abstracting" a universal from a particular or grasping one in the ostensive step of an operational definition would be like picking up bits of Being from the fringes of a Neo-Platonic emanation without, however, the saving grace (if such it be) of so-called "exaggerated realism" which commonly accompanies Neo-Platonism. If, furthermore, there is only a *distinctio formalis* between Sam, e.g., and redness, it would follow that I could contemplate redness only in the presence of Sam; and this would be contrary to Broad's "in abstraction from any particular substance." And I do agree with Broad that, in some sense, I can "think of redness," if I have ᵃⁱᵐredᵃⁱᵐ, without any ᵖⁱᵐredᵖⁱᵐ requiring the presence of any particular, red or otherwise (except, trivially, the occurrent idea itself).

There remains the possibility (among others, perhaps) that ᵃⁱᵐredᵃⁱᵐ, e.g., might be or require some "innate" special ability. To avoid the consequence that certain persons, e.g. babies, very young children, and "abnormal" people, literally have ᵃⁱᵐredᵃⁱᵐ, we should have to say that what is innate is the ability (a special one) to acquire the ability to think of ᶜⁱᵐredᶜⁱᵐ or to produce or have items like ᵖⁱᵐredᵖⁱᵐ—a kind of "ur-ᵃⁱᵐredᵃⁱᵐ" which is such that, only when confronted with a certain number of objects which are red and, perhaps, contrast with green, blue, etc., objects, is ᵃⁱᵐredᵃⁱᵐ itself actually acquired. What Broad calls an "act of abstraction" would then be merely the triggering off of the disposition to acquire ᵃⁱᵐredᵃⁱᵐ. Broad, however, quite expressly rejects this alternative, in the following words:

All sane human beings are born with certain very general intellectual powers, e.g., that of retentiveness, that of making comparisons and contrasts between perceived objects, that of abstracting universals from perceived instances of them, and so on. These general intellectual powers, together with the objects that we perceive in the course of our lives, suffice to account for the vast majority of our dispositional ideas. There is plainly no need to assume, for example, a special second-order disposition to account for our acquirement of the power to think of redness. The fact that we see things that look red, together with the general powers of comparison, abstraction, etc., suffice to account for the acquirement of the dispositional idea of redness.[14]

D.

I should like to make comment concerning the phrase "contemplate the characteristic of redness." This is obvious philosophers' talk; I cannot conceive so-called "plain men" talking this way, though they know perfectly well the "meaning" of 'contemplate.' The question is: "What would it be to 'contemplate redness'?" I may, e.g., contemplate the stately Norway pine just outside my cottage window, noticing carefully certain scars left in the bark by the rubbing of smaller trees next to it and by people too careless with axes, wondering at its powers of survival in the teeth of the depredations of men and nature. In similar fashion I may contemplate my typewriter, the couch over yonder, etc. I am sure that I have never in this fashion contemplated the universal redness, though I am equally sure that I have ^{aim}red^{aim}. I may also, of course, contemplate such things as my past, the fate of Hitler, or my little boy's future. These contemplations may be or involve efforts to remember "lost" details, to make generalizations, to draw (as we say) a "moral," to anticipate future events if various courses of action are pursued, etc. I may also contemplate, e.g., taking a trip, in which case 'contemplate' functions as a synonym for 'intend' or 'consider seriously.' I am sure that contemplating a universal, whatever it may be, is not, nor *could* it be, like these contemplations.

What, then, *might* I be doing if I were "contemplating the universal redness?" It seems to me that I might describe myself as contemplating redness if I were saying or thinking to myself any or all of the following things: 'If something is red, then it is colored,' 'If something is literally red, then it is not a noise or an odor or a twinge or a tickle,' '^{aim}red^{aim} is different from ^{aim}blue^{aim} or ^{aim}green^{aim} or ^{aim}yellow^{aim}, etc.,' 'Something which is red may differ from other red things in brightness and saturation,' and so on. I should imagine that contemplating a universal, say, redness, would be different from *merely* "being aware of ^{cim}red^{cim}," though the former may, on occasion, include the latter.[15] Again, how-

---

[14] *EMcP*, I, 48–49. Note the constant use of 'perceive' in connection with my remarks on Broad's doctrine of simple empirical ability *incomplexa mentis* (comment B above).

[15] See comment H below.

ever, 'being aware of $^{cim}red^{cim}$' is a phrase to which, as it were, sense must be *attached*.

I think, nevertheless, that many people who have talked about "contemplating universals" have thought that doing so was more like my contemplating the Norway pine outside my window than like what I have just mentioned. One of the rather odd consequences of their doing so is that, in discussing this alleged "contemplation," their effort has *not* been to explain or interpret or examine the implications of certain *undoubted* occurrences (like my contemplation of the Norway pine) but rather to *postulate* certain occurrences in order (as they think) to account for certain unquestioned facts (like my having $^{aim}red^{aim}$, the "aboutness" of $^{pim}red^{pim}$, and, perhaps, the fact of communication). To the man who should express doubt that there was any such activity as my contemplating the Norway pine, I should most likely reply that he was being captious, foolish, or impertinent. If he were serious and naive, however, I might well try to show him that there *are* such activities or give a name to an activity he already knows about. But to the man who expresses doubt that there are any such activities as contemplating universals (redness, e.g.), where these are supposedly like contemplating the Norway pine, a defender of such activities takes an entirely different line. He ordinarily attempts to show that, if certain things are granted, there *must be* such activities. He might reply: "You don't doubt that there are simple empirical ability *incomplexa mentis* like $^{aim}red^{aim}$, do you? Given that there are, there must be (and are) items like $^{pim}red^{pim}_1$, $^{pim}red^{pim}_2$, and so on. And, of course, the peculiar feature of items like $^{pim}red^{pim}_1$, etc, is that they are 'about' something. Now it is quite unlikely that $^{pim}red^{pim}_1$, e.g., is 'about' a red particular as such or a collection of red particulars as such; for it seems clearly to be 'about' something which characterizes all red particulars and would characterize any possible red particular. I can, furthermore, produce $^{pim}red^{pim}_1$, 'knowing the meaning of it,' without imaging or sensing or in any way being confronted with a red particular. Now, unless items like $^{pim}red^{pim}_1$ are to be only mental sound and fury signifying nothing, on the occasions of producing any $^{pim}red^{pim}$, I must be 'acquainted with' something; what more natural and reasonable than that I should be, on these occasions, 'acquainted with' redness? And, surely, if I am, on occasion, 'acquainted with' redness, it seems quite reasonable to assume that, from time to time, I can and do 'contemplate' redness."

This line of argument is specious, analogous to the several specious arguments adduced as examples by Professor Ryle to the effect that, if there are certain dispositions, there must be, as it were, "cognate" occurrents. It seems, at best, extremely risky to argue that there must be mental activities which we do not know about and do not recognize even after they have been elaborately "described." Furthermore, I think it may be readily granted that there are simple empirical ability *incomplexa mentis* and that they are, indeed, appropriately called *abilities* (or, if you please, dispositions) and that they are or involve abilities to produce particular *incomplexa mentis* on suitable occasions and that both ability *incomplexa mentis* and particular *incomplexa mentis* are properly said to be "about" something. I do not see, however, that what is thus readily granted requires, in any sense, that there must be "acts of acquaintance" with universals or "contemplatings" of them where these are construed as seriously analogous to my being acquainted with or contemplating the Norway pine. Such is the hold of the confusion of logic with psychology that the truth of logical "realism," especially in the British tradition, has been thought to necessitate the truth of psychological "realism." This fallacy, alas, has not died, but has been generously exported.

If Broad or anyone else should reply that I must be "universals blind" and that, for him at least, acquaintances with and contemplatings of universals, in the sense I find not to exist, are as assuredly "there" as my contemplating of the Norway pine, at *one* level of discussion, I should not know how to dissuade them. At that level, I should have to ape Broad in the quoting of Cromwell: "I beseech you in the bowels of Christ to believe that you may be mistaken." At *another* level, I should point out that Broad himself admits to no way of being certain that there are qualities at all.

It does not seem to me to be either self-evident or capable of proof that exact likeness of a specific kind consists in or depends on the possession of a common quality. I should think it certain that recognition of likenesses and unlikenesses precedes recognition of common qualities. And it does not seem altogether unreasonable to suggest that the notion of common qualities may be a convenient fiction to systematise and abbreviate the statement of a complicated set of interrelated facts about likenesses and unlikenesses.[16]

This opens the possibility that, when Broad thinks himself to be "contemplating" the quality redness, he is really "contemplating" the relation exact likeness of *X* (a certain specific) kind. There would be, I believe, less temptation to talk of "contemplating" relation universals than there is to talk of "contemplating" quality universals, where "contemplating" is thought of as like my contemplating the pine tree. Nor is one so easily beguiled into thinking of relations as "parts" of particulars, unless he brings a certain variety of rationalism to bear. There is the presumption, therefore, that Broad is scarcely in a position to

16 *EMcP*, I, 88.

claim that I am "universals blind" and thus to stalemate the argument.

The latest quotation is, I believe, worth a quasi-independent comment. What, *in an example,* would "exact likeness of a specific kind" be? Consider redness. Suppose that *a* and *b,* two particulars, are red. I cannot say that *a* and *b* are *exactly* alike, where this implies "in *all* respects;" for then a certain legitimate application of the principle of the Identity of Indiscernibles would require me to say that *a* and *b* are identical. If I should say that *a* and *b* are alike with respect to being red, I should ordinarily be construed as implying that their likeness "consists in or depends on the possession of a common quality." If this implication is not to be present, we shall have to use locutions like 'redlike,' 'square-like,' etc. To the relations referred to by these, what would be referred to by 'colorlike,' 'shapelike,' etc. would seem to stand as determinables to determinates. Interestingly enough, in this case, each of the most determinate relations would seem to require, for "awareness" of it, a special conceptual ability. For "more general abilities," e.g., ^{aim}color-like^{aim}, would no more account for my having ^{aim}redlike^{aim} than ^{aim}color^{aim} would account for my having ^{aim}red^{aim}. This, of course, only reinforces some arguments I made in comment B above.

E.

It is worth commenting that I, at least, do not remember doing anything like what Broad says I must have done in acquiring simple empirical ability *incomplexa mentis.* It may be, of course, that my memory is faulty or that most, if not all, of these concepts were formed in the limbo of late babyhood or early childhood. In the former case, I must plead that nobody else whom I have questioned remembers doing any of Broad's pre-conceptual actions, though all remember comparing and contrasting various objects, as it were, "post-conceptually" (and though some hold almost precisely Broad's doctrine of simple empirical *incomplexa mentis.*) In the latter case, it seems appropriate to quote a comment Broad himself once made, in a justifiably devastating review of Julian Huxley's Romanes Lecture: "Of all the sciences, that which is concerned with what goes on in the minds of babies is and must remain the most precarious."[17] Less captiously, I cannot imagine any psychological experiment or set of experiments which would afford evidence that such pre-conceptual actions are occurring or have occurred in someone else. This, in the absence of good memories in myself and my questionees, puts the psychological claims of Broad's doctrine in a rather dubious light.

[17] In *Mind,* n.s. LIII (1944), 344–367.

F.

I think the notion of *simple* as applied to concepts deserves comment. The passage quoted from p. 41 of Vol. I seems to require only that any "simple intuitive dispositional ideas" which are *empirical* are formed in the manner described. The "many, if not all" is intended to exclude "simple intuitive dispositional ideas" which are *a priori* (Broad's alternatives being "innate" and "non-perceptual"). Since he alleges to be giving a *definition*,[18] I should also imagine that Broad would claim that all concepts formed in the manner described are "simple intuitive dispositional ideas" which are empirical. This is supported by the context in which he says: "Any dispositional idea formed in the way just illustrated is an instance of an empirical concept. Any compound idea all of whose components were empirical concepts would also be an empirical concept."[19] The presumption is that all ideas "formed in the way just illustrated" would be simple empirical intuitive dispositional ideas.

The last quotation opens the way for discussing Broad's distinctions between *simple* empirical *intuitive* ideas, *descriptive* empirical ideas, and *compound* empirical ideas. "To have an occurrent intuitive idea of the characteristic x is to be experiencing an act of acquaintance which has for its object the universal of which "x" is the name."[20] "To have an occurrent descriptive idea of the characteristic x is to believe or suppose that there is one and only one characteristic answering to a certain description with whose terms I am acquainted at the time."[21] Thus $^{pim}red^{pim}_1$ may be an occurrent intuitive idea of what is "named" by $^{tiv}red^{tiv}$ or $^{civ}red^{civ}$. I doubt that Broad intends his definition of an occurrent descriptive idea to be taken literally; for, if he does, then such an "idea" is a particular *complexum mentis,* not an incomplexum at all! Thus

$$^{pcm}(\exists F)\{ \ [(Color(F)) \ . \ (Between(F, \ red, \ orange))] \ . \ [(G)$$
$$((Color(G)) \ . \ (Between(G, \ red, \ orange)))\supset (G = F)]\}^{pcm}_1$$

would, taking Broad *literally,* be an occurrent descriptive "idea." The associated content *complexum mentis* of such an "idea" could be only

---

[18] It is, more strictly, what he himself has called an "epistemological description." Cf. his "Certain Features in Moore's Ethical Doctrines" (in *The Philosophy of G. E. Moore,* ed. Paul Arthur Schilpp, New York, 1952), p. 62, where he attempts to "suggest an *epistemological description,* as distinct from a logical definition, of the term 'natural characteristic' " (*italics* Broad's). An article making the same point, entitled "Is 'Goodness' a Name of a Simple Non-Natural Quality?" appeared in *Proc. Arist. Soc.* (1933), the same year as that in which *EMcP,* Vol. I was published!

[19] *EMcP,* I, 41.

[20] *EMcP,* I, 39. Note the relevance of this quotation to comment A above.

[21] *EMcP,* I, 39.

nonsensically predicated of any particular. Part of what may have led Broad to say what he did is the consideration that any judgment (or supposition) involving such a "descriptive concept" would be compound. Even as, on the Russell theory of descriptions

^{pcm}The present king of France is bald$^{pcm}{}_1$

becomes

$^{pem}(\exists\, x)\{[(\mathrm{PKF}(x)).((y)((\mathrm{PKF}(y))\supset (y = x)))].[\mathrm{Bald}(x)]\}^{pem}{}_1,$

so

^{pcm}Jones has the color between red and orange$^{pcm}{}_1$

becomes

$^{pem}(\exists\, F)\{[((\mathrm{Color}(F)).(\mathrm{Between}(F, \mathrm{red}, \mathrm{orange}))).((G)((\mathrm{Color}(G)).$
$(\mathrm{Between}\,(G, \mathrm{red}, \mathrm{orange})))\supset (G = F))].[F(\mathrm{Jones})]\}^{pem}{}_1.$

Even if this last is a proper analysis, it by no means follows that

$^{pem}(\exists\, F)\{[(\mathrm{Color}(F)).(\mathrm{Between}\,(F, \mathrm{red}, \mathrm{orange}))].[\,(G)((\mathrm{Color}\,(G)).$
$(\mathrm{Between}\,(G, \mathrm{red}, \mathrm{orange})))\supset (G = F)]\}^{pem}{}_1$

is the proper analysis of

$^{pim}(\iota F)[(Color\,(F)).(\mathrm{Between}\,(F, \mathrm{red}, \mathrm{orange}))]^{pim}{}_1.$

Another part (though it is linked with the first) of what may have led Broad to say what he did is fear lest a so-called descriptive concept fail to have a "meaning," i.e. lest there be no universal which it is "about."

$^{pem}(\exists\, F)\{[(\mathrm{Color}(F)).(\mathrm{Between}(F, \mathrm{red}, \mathrm{orange},))].[\,(G)((\mathrm{Color}\,(G)).$
$(\mathrm{Between}\,(G, \mathrm{red}, \mathrm{orange})))\supset (G = F)]\}^{pcm}{}_1$

is, after all, true or false, the "meaning" of the various first level *incomplexa mentis* involved being assured by *their* being intuitive. But

$^{pim}(\iota F)[(\mathrm{Color}(F)).(\mathrm{Between}(F, \mathrm{red}, \mathrm{orange}))]^{pim}{}_1,$

not being true or false and, apparently, capable of only the sort of "meaning" which ^{pim}red$^{pim}{}_1$ has alone, may be entirely chimerical if, in Broad's terms, I am never "acquainted with" a universal of which it is the description. I should have thought it sufficient for his purpose, given a commitment to the theory of descriptions, to claim that a descriptive idea, though, in a sense, an *incomplexum,* is such that any judgment (or supposition) which predicates it of something is necessarily compound and necessarily contains an existential component.

To have an occurrent *compound* idea, according to Broad, consists in "thinking of" characteristics $x, y, z, \ldots$ (more than one) and "believing or making the assumption that they co-inhere in some common subject."[22] To use his example, and taking him literally, a compound idea might be:

'(Serpent) . (Fire-Breathing) . ($(\exists\, x)$ (Serpent(x)) . (Fire-Breathing(x)))'
assuming ^{pim}Serpent$^{pim}{}_1$ and ^{pim}Fire-Breathing$^{pim}{}_1$ to be "simple." This is a bit monstrous, and earlier he states that "I am thinking of the char-

[22] *EMcP*, I, 40.

acteristic C" and "I am thinking of the characteristics C_1, C_2, and C_3 as co-inherent in a common subject" may have the same "significance." This suggests, of course, that

$$\text{pcm} \, (\, \exists \, x)[(\text{Serpent}(x)) \, . \, (\text{Fire-Breathing} \, (x))]^{\text{pcm}}{}_1$$

would be, by itself, a compound idea, taking away some of the monstrosity. Again, as in the case of descriptive ideas, we have an "idea" which seems to be a *complexum mentis*. Again, I do not believe that Broad intends this literally. He seems afraid lest a compound idea be merely chimerical in that the universals referred to by the elements of one might not be "co-inherent in any particular." In this way he thinks them to differ from simple empirical ideas whose "origin guarantees their having instances."[23] I believe that Broad would have better expressed himself if he had said that a compound idea is one such that, if it were used in a judgment (or a supposition), that judgment (or supposition) would *necessarily* be compound, the components of the compound idea occurring independently in that judgment (or supposition).

Dwelling on the above at such length would scarcely be justified in itself. I have done so because a suspicion is arising on my part that a distinction needs to be drawn between simple and compound ideas and ideas of simples and compounds. It is not at all clear that a simple idea must be an idea of a simple, nor, conversely, that an idea of a compound must be a compound idea. There is reason to believe, however, that Broad, in many sections of the *McTaggart*, takes this for granted.

On p. 99 of Vol. I, he writes: "I shall try to show in the next chapter that the notion of a compound characteristic is probably a figment." His showing is as follows:

I am altogether doubtful whether there are any compound characteristics in McTaggart's sense of the word. No doubt such a sentence as "x is red and sweet" is intelligible, and no doubt it is of the same grammatical form as "x is red." But it would be most unwise to assume, on this ground alone, that the phrase "red-and-sweet" must be the name of a characteristic. And I know of no other ground for assuming it. I should have thought that "x is red and sweet" was simply a short way of saying "x is red and x is sweet," i.e. of recording the fact that two characteristics, redness and sweetness, both inhere in a common subject x. If there is anything that could properly be called a "compound characteristic," it would seem to be the relational property, if such there be, expressed by the phrase "co-inhered by redness and sweetness" and not anything expressed by the phrase "red-and-sweet."

When a set of determinable characteristics C_1, C_2, ... , are found very often to be co-inherent, it is a great convenience to have a single name "C" such that the sentence "x is C" shall be understood to mean the same as the sentence "x is C_1, x is C_2, and . . . ." But we have no right to assume that there is a characteristic of which "C" is the name and of which C_1-and-C_2-and

23 *EMcP*, I, 51.

. . . is an analysis. We feel no temptation to assume this except in cases where the language that we speak happens to have a word like "C," and it is plain that this is no valid ground for the assumption. I am therefore very much inclined to think that McTaggart's notion of Compound Characteristics is a fiction.[24]

I believe that the following suppositions are consistent with the claims of Broad which are mentioned or discussed in the preceding sections. Suppose that F and G are two simple universals. Suppose that every particular which I or anyone else has encounted which is F is also G and *vice versa*. Suppose that F is a determinate under the determinable Φ and G a determinate under the determinable Ψ. Let us make similar suppositions for a supposed H and a supposed I, the former under the determinable Φ, the latter under Ψ. Suppose, however, that our language has only one word for referring to H and F and that to them together; let it be ᶜⁱᵛrousᶜⁱᵛ. Similarly let ᶜⁱᵛdousᶜⁱᵛ be our language's word for referring to H and I together. Suppose also that our language contains only one word for the determinables Φ and Ψ; let it be ᶜⁱᵛmousᶜⁱᵛ. Now let me paraphrase Broad's account of simple intuitive dispositional ideas which are empirical.

I perceive from time to time things which present a characteristic kind of perceptual appearance. They "look rous." I compare them with other things that look like them in this respect and look unlike them in other respects. For example, I may see objects which look J, K, L, etc., and all look rous. Again, I compare them with yet other things which look unlike them in this respect, but look like them in other respects. For example, I compare J-things which look rous with other J-things which look dous, etc. I perform a similar process of comparison and contrast between K-things which look rous, K-things which look dous, etc. Eventually I am able to perform an act of abstraction, and to contemplate the characteristic of rousness in separation from other qualities and in abstraction from any particular substance. Finally a disposition is formed which, whenever it is suitably stimulated, will produce an act of acquaintance with the quality of rousness for its object.

An omniscient being would, of course, know that ᵖᶜᵐx is rous ᵖᶜᵐ is only a rather confused thought for what *for him* would be ᵖᶜᵐx if F and x is Gᵖᶜᵐ. But I—and other human beings—alas, cannot detect F-ness and G-ness as separate; various particulars just look rous to me. I think we should have to say that, on Broad's account, ᵃⁱᵐrousᵃⁱᵐ is a "simple intuitive dispositional idea" which is empirical. But, by hypothesis, it is *of* a compound; and Broad, as we have seen, does not believe that there are any such characteristics. If so, ᵃⁱᵐrousᵃⁱᵐ could not

24 *EMcP*, I, 108.

be an intuitive idea at all; for there would be no characteristic rousness to be acquainted with, though there would be F-ness and G-ness. $^{aim}rous^{aim}$ would have to be an idea expressable only in judgments (or suppositions) containing $^{pim}F^{pim}$ and $^{pim}G^{pim}$, as it were, independently. But this cannot be; for, by hypothesis, I am not able to acquire $^{aim}F^{aim}$ and $^{aim}G^{aim}$, though I have $^{aim}rous^{aim}$. In another place Broad writes: "Sometimes we can describe a certain aggregate resemblance *only* by naming or describing or pointing at certain particulars and describing it as 'the aggregate resemblance between these particulars.' In such cases, if 'C' be the name given to things in respect of this aggregate resemblance to each other, we say that 'the characteristic C is, so far as we know simple,' and we say that 'the name "C" is, so far as we know, indefinable.' "[25] On this accounting, rousness would be, so far as we know, simple.

Our difficulty now comes to this. $^{aim}rous^{aim}$ would be, on Broad's "definition," a "simple intuitive dispositional idea" which is empirical. But it would be *of* a compound. It could not, however, be a compound or descriptive idea, for it has no components except itself. Furthermore, it meets Broad's test for being *of* a simple characteristic—"so far as we know." Rousness does not *seem* analyzable, and $^{civ}rous^{civ}$ does not *seem* definable. If $^{aim}rous^{aim}$ really is *of* a compound characteristic, Broad would insist that it really is expressable only in judgments (or suppositions) in which $^{pim}F^{pim}$ and $^{pim}G^{pim}$ occur independently; but, by hypothesis, this cannot be. Thus $^{aim}rous^{aim}$ must be both simple and compound. The only serious way out of this difficulty, for Broad, would be for him to maintain that, in forming simple intuitive dispositional ideas which are empirical, we either do or must make just those comparisons and contrasts which would, on his own accounting, result in simple concepts of simple universals. The "so far as we know," in the above-quoted passage, however, indicates clearly that Broad is not prepared to maintain either of these. If he sticks to his other guns, he would therefore have to admit the possibility of a certain empirical concept's being both simple and compound.

Quite aside from Broad's admissions, the claim that we do or must make "ultimate" comparisons and contrasts seems to me most dubious. Suppose that we at least sometimes do; then is there any way of *knowing* whether we have done so or are doing so? Even if "manifest" differences between observed particulars lead us to believe truly that some similarities are of a more specific kind than others, is there any ground for believing that we have ever unearthed a similarity or likeness of a *most* specific kind? The moral of this tale, as I shall try to show before long,

[25] *EMcP*, I, 114–115.

is not to cast doubt on our having any simple concepts, but rather to cast further doubt on Broad's (or anyone else's) "abstractionist" account of concept-formation.

With this in mind and with the distinction between simple ideas and ideas of simples in mind, it seems to me that the most Broad could claim would be the following. Our simple ideas are such that "their origin guarantees their having instances" (or, rather, the universals involved having instances). There is no guarantee, however, that our simple ideas are *of* simples, though they may be, so far as we know, of simples. If compound characteristics, in "McTaggart's sense," are figments, then all our simple ideas *may* (for all we know) be of figments even though, paradoxically enough, "their origin guarantees their having instances." Further, if at least part of the function of philosophy is to arrive at analyses of characteristics, it *may* be that, on Broad's grounds, we are, in principle, cut off from reaching any "ultimate" analyses of "empirical" concepts at least. If we have a set of beliefs, each to the effect that we may contemplate characteristic such-and-such "in separation from other qualities, etc." and if these beliefs are well-founded only when the characteristics in question are simple, then every such belief may be, in fact, *false*.

G.

Let me quote from a section bearing on the application of Broad's doctrine of empirical concepts.

I see no objection myself to saying that our ideas of modality are empirical, though non-sensuous. For we have, presumably, derived them by a process of comparison, contrast, analysis, and abstraction from our acquaintance with facts which were manifestly necessary or manifestly contingent. Still, they are a very peculiar kind of empirical concept. And it must be recognized that, even if they be empirical concepts, our knowledge that a comparative relation does or does not have a superlative is *a priori* knowledge.[26]

This statement occurs in a context in which Broad is considering the idea of perfect straightness. He argues that we have two different ideas of perfect straightness, one, presumably, not involving a modal idea. The first is

a. '*x* is perfectly straight' = def. '*x* is linear and not jagged or curved.'
The second is

b. '*x* is perfectly straight' = def. '*x* is a term such that, whilst it might be straighter than something, nothing could be straighter than it.'

This latter, as it includes 'could,' gives rise to his comment quoted above

[26] *EMcP,* I, 44.

concerning modal concepts; it is with it that my comment is concerned. Elsewhere Broad states flatly that 'necessary,' 'contingent,' and 'impossible' may be predicated only of what I shall here call "compound general facts," i.e. facts which involve more than one characteristic, the expression of which involves the use (in the usual symbolism) of quantifiers and variables.

I understand what is meant by saying that the presence of a certain characteristic in anything entails or excludes the presence of a certain other characteristic in that thing, or in any other thing that stands in a certain relation to that thing. But I can attach no meaning to sentences in which a "necessity" or "impossibility" is ostensibly predicated without reference to the conveyance or exclusion of one characteristic by another. Briefly, it seems to me that "necessary" and "contingent," though mutually exclusive, are not collectively exhaustive predicates of facts. Facts must first be divided into "modal" and "non-modal"; then modal facts, and they alone, can be exhaustively and exclusively subdivided into necessary and contingent. And the sort of facts which can properly be expressed by sentences of the form "This stands in the relation R to that" are non-modal facts, if "This" and "That" function as pure proper names of particulars.[27]

Though Broad does not specifically mention "atomic" facts of other than two places or what I shall call "simple general facts" (i.e. facts involving only one characteristic, the expression of which involves a quantifier and a variable), it is clear that they belong, on his account, to the non-modal category, the variables or names or descriptions in the argument-places of the expressions of such facts being, of course, zero-level. Since Broad elsewhere defines 'conveyance' in such a way as to suggest that necessary compound general facts, as it were, lie behind necessary compound facts the expression of which does not involve the use of variables,[28] I shall assume that the entailment involved here is that mentionable in the expression of compound general facts—what Broad calls "formal Entailment." It will make no serious difference, however, in the argument to follow whether we are speaking of compound general facts or merely compound facts.

Now the quotation from p. 44 of Vol. I requires that aimcouldaim be connected with aimnecessaryaim or aimcontingentaim or both. Presumably at least part of that connection is illustrated in the following (using, as Broad does, '$\rightarrow$' as the "entailment" symbol):

$$[(x)(F(x)\rightarrow G(x))]\rightleftarrows[\text{Nothing could be } F \text{ and fail to be } G].$$

Here, of course, as the Broad account on pp. 259–260 requires, two characteristics, F-ness and G-ness, are involved. Consider *straighter*

---

27 *EMcP*, I, 259–260.

28 See *EMcP*, I, 190ff. On p. 198 he writes: "conveyance is the relation which ϕ has to ψ if and only if $\phi x \rightarrow x\psi x$."

than, a relation which he obviously thinks to obtain between particulars, the concept of which he thinks may well be simple and empirical. He informs us that one of the correct analyses of perfect straightness includes a modal characteristic, *but the only non-formal characteristic in Broadian "perfect-straightness" facts is straighter than!* 'Nothing could be straighter than *x*' mentions only *one* non-formal characteristic as does '*x* could be straighter than *y* or *z* or etc.' The obvious conclusion is that Broad's second analysis of *perfect straightness* is incorrect, or his claim that modal facts involve two characteristics is incorrect, or both are incorrect.

Leaving the worries about *perfect straightness* aside, let us consider the plausibility of the claim that modal concepts are empirical (in Broad's sense). Taking him at his word that ^{aim}necessary^{aim} and ^{aim}contingent^{aim} arise from our "acquaintance with" facts which are "manifestly necessary or manifestly contingent" and that such facts ("modal" ones) are what I have called "compound general facts," the following reflections seem in order. According to Broad's account of "implication,"[29] we might appropriately express "ontological entailment" by the following:

(i) (x) $(F(x) \rightarrow G(x))$

Suppose we "picture" the fact expressed by (i) as

(ii) $\square \rightarrow \bigcirc$.

This is, of course, misleading, but I do not think it will be dangerously so for the considerations relevant here. Now suppose that, prior to my having ^{aim}necessary^{aim}, I am "acquainted with" (ii). I shall say that (ii) "looks necessary;" it has a certain characteristic "non-sensuous" appearance.

In Broad's account of a certain particular's "looking red," it is not the particular's being red which "looks red," but the particular *alone,* as it were, which allegedly "looks red." But in the case of (ii)'s "looking necessary," it seems that (ii) *includes* the necessity! Can we remedy this by saying that something analogous to the particular alone "looks necessary?" What would it be? Certainly not what would be referred to by '$(x) F(x)$,' for this is, by Broad's account, not necessary (and probably not a fact at all). Certainly not what would be referred to by '$(x) G(x)$' for the same reasons. Neither of these is, furthermore, the fact (if such they be) which is alleged to be necessary.

Suppose we consider

(iii) (x) $(F(x) \supset G(x))$

and "picture" the fact it represents by

(iv) $\square ---\rightarrow \bigcirc$.

[29] *EMcP,* I, 190ff.

Perhaps (iv) is what might "look necessary." But (iv), as the dotted arrow indicates, *is not necessary*. It is, on Broad's own account, *contingent*. It is, as it were, a "softened version" of (ii). But the particular which "looks red" is by no stretch of the imagination appropriately called a "softened version" of that particular's being red.

Similar comments would apply to the prehension interpretation. Sam, e.g., might be prehended as red. If (ii) were (adopting an arbitrary term to express "non-sensuous" prehension) "shprehended" *as necessary*, it would be, redundantly enough, the "shprehension" of all instances of *F*'s necessarily being instances of *G as necessary*.

It might be objected that the connection between *F* and *G* is what "looks necessary" (or "contingent"); but, to keep the parallel with Broad's account of other empirical concepts, necessity (or *contingency*) would then have to be a characteristic of the connection, not of the fact. We would then have a concept of a characteristic of a characteristic of characteristics described as "empirical." Presumably ^{aim}connectedness^{aim} would also be empirical. But, first, this would make *necessity* (or *contingency*) a characteristic of characteristics and *not* of facts. Second, *necessary connectedness* and *contingent connectedness* would seem to be, as it were, determinate forms of *connectedness*, analogous to *redness$_1$*, *redness$_2$* and the determinable *redness*. One would scarcely be tempted to say that *redness$_1$* was e.g., a characteristic of *redness;* and it would seem equally unreasonable to say that *necessary connectedness* is a characteristic of *connectedness*. To say that *connectedness* "looks necessary" would be like saying that *redness* "looks red$_1$," even after allowance is made for the "non-sensuous" character of the former.

The upshot of this discussion, as I see it, is (a) that Broad's account of the modalities undercuts his own analysis of *perfect straightness* and, more important, (b) that the notion of facts having characteristics coupled with Broad's account of concepts is radically wrong. If there are synthetic necessities, they are better understood in quite a different context of explanation.

H.

Let me comment on the following:

A very important adjunct to the process is to link this disposition by association with the traces left by hearing, seeing, and speaking the word *red*. When this associative link has been formed anything that excites the verbal trace will tend to excite the dispositional idea and will thus tend to evoke an occurrent intuitive idea of redness.[30]

30 *EMcP*, I, 41, quoted above, pp. 202f.

Broad quite clearly thinks that such "verbal traces" are genetically and logically separated from and separable from dispositional ideas. Presumably, therefore, I may have the verbal traces gained by "hearing, seeing, and speaking the word *red*" and fail to have ᵃⁱᵐredᵃⁱᵐ and *vice versa*.

What might such "verbal traces" be? They are, first, by Broad's admission, acquired and not innate, though the ability (or, perhaps, abilities) to acquire them may be (trivially) said to be innate. They are, second, and again by Broad's admission (as in "excites the verbal trace"), dispositions of some sort. In the case of those traces which are to be associated with ᵃⁱᵐredᵃⁱᵐ, they are dispositions somehow involving the word *red*. Let us consider now what some of the dispositions involving the word *red* which could be called "verbal traces" might fairly be said to be.

For convenience in what follows let us use 'ᶜⁱᵛredᶜⁱᵛ' and 'ᵗⁱᵛredᵗⁱᵛ.' At a very early age English-speaking children are *trained* to respond to red objects by uttering a member of ᶜⁱᵛredᶜⁱᵛ. They are rewarded for correct responses and punished for incorrect ones. (Even before any explicit training, they are usually in an environment which includes various persons uttering, among other things, members of ᶜⁱᵛredᶜⁱᵛ to each other. Even without explicit training, but surrounded by language-users, a child may, stimulated by the reward of making his wants known and the punishment of failure to do so, learn, among other things, to respond to red objects with members of ᶜⁱᵛredᶜⁱᵛ.)

After a period of such training children normally acquire a disposition such that, when confronted with red objects, they tend to respond by uttering a member of ᶜⁱᵛredᶜⁱᵛ. If we include images of members of ᶜⁱᵛredᶜⁱᵛ among the members of ᶜⁱᵛredᶜⁱᵛ, then I think we shall be closer to the facts if we say that they acquire a disposition such that, when confronted with red objects, they tend to respond by uttering or imaging a member of ᶜⁱᵛredᶜⁱᵛ.[31]

Still at a very early age, most English-speaking persons acquire dispositions to respond to utterances of members of ᶜⁱᵛredᶜⁱᵛ, usually by pointing to red objects or going and getting certain of them. Again, in acquiring these dispositions, children are rewarded and punished for correct or incorrect responses respectively. After some training, Johnny (a convenient and exemplary youngster), e.g., acquires a disposition or

[31] See fn. 11 above. As we shall shortly see, the "general ability" involved is not merely the ability to learn verbal responses to environmental stimuli, but also to learn various verbal responses to members of various class *incomplexa vocis*. I am indebted to the writings of Prof. Wilfrid Sellars for important features of the positive account given in this section and the next.

dispositions such that, when confronted with an utterance of a member of clvredclv, he tends to point to or fetch a red object.

At the same time (and perhaps later and before) Johnny is acquiring other dispositions connected with other class *incomplexa vocis*. Let us consider for the moment only those which are, as it were, *tied* to Johnny's environment in the way (or ways), so far described, those involving members of clvredclv are "tied." These are or involve verbal responding to so-and-so objects or are or involve picking out so-and-so objects in response to utterings of members of appropriate class *incomplexa vocis*. If I might, to avoid unwarranted assumptions, call what Johnny now has "ur-concepts," I might also call the dispositions involved "observation dispositions." Interestingly enough, ur-concepts are such that their origin guarantees their "tie" with "non-conceptual reality." Further, some, at least, of Johnny's ur-concepts would involve "physical object" *incomplexa vocis,* as clvchairclv, clvtableclv, clvtreeclv, clvspoonclv, etc.

At a later date in the process of acquiring "verbal traces," Johnny would acquire dispositions to respond, in various circumstances, to utterances or imagings of members of certain class *incomplexa vocis* by uttering or imaging members of certain other class *incomplexa vocis*. Johnny may, e.g., come to respond to an utterance of or imaging of a member of clvfire-engineclv with an utterance or imaging of a member of clvredclv. Such dispositions, of course, would be linked to what I have called "observation dispositions."

Probably at an even later date, dispositions involving class *incomplexa vocis* which are commonly referred to as "syncategorematic" terms are acquired. These again are dispositions involving responses to utterances or imagings of members of other class *incomplexa vocis,* though they are not quite as simple as those mentioned in the last paragraph, nor are they all equally complex. Johnny is, at this stage, acquiring ability *complexa vocis*. In the course of such training, Johnny may properly be said to "learn how" to "use" members of clvredclv correctly. Members of clvredclv now (for Johnny) play a "role" in a pattern of verbal dispositions *and also* (some of them at least) are responses to and indicators of red objects in Johnny's environment. Johnny has acquired some dispositions to use members of class *complexa vocis,* and these are (some at least), interestingly enough, "tied" to various features of Johnny's environment by virtue of what I have called "observation dispositions."

Before turning to the "traces left by seeing the word *red,*" it may be worth mentioning that, at a relatively tender age, Johnny may be exposed to another language. He may, e.g., learn that members of clvrotclv play the same (or nearly the same) role in German that members of ^{civ}red^{civ} do in English. Having learned, as it were, the *role* involving members of ^{civ}red^{civ}, he need only allow new actors, members of ^{civ}rot^{civ}, play the same role. In this manner of looking at things, with Johnny's "language" being a system of roles, English and German would not, for philosophical purposes, be different languages, but merely different role-vehicles. (Even as the roles in chess are the same, though played with quite differently colored pieces, or, stretching a bit, Hamlet is the same role, whether played by Maurice Evans or Sir Laurence Olivier.)

The "traces left by seeing the word *red*" must, of course, come at that later stage when, as we say, Johnny is "learning to read." In the manner mentioned above of "learning German," acquiring the traces left by seeing the word *red* is, most likely, a matter of Johnny's adapting various shapes, those similar in shape to ^{tiv}red$^{tiv}_1$, to play the same role as that played by the sounds which are members of ^{civ}red^{civ}.

I think it quite evident that, as a matter of fact, nobody ever acquires anything appropriately called "the traces left by hearing, seeing, and speaking the word *red*" *haphazardly,* unless he is a hopeless idiot or a foreigner who recognizes the shapes and sounds as "language" but does not, as we say, "know their meanings."

Now let us suppose that Johnny has acquired both the "observation disposition" (or dispositions) and what I shall now call the "verbal dispositions" involving members of ^{civ}red^{civ}. He has now what Broad calls "the traces left by hearing, seeing, and speaking the word *red*." His problem now is, according to Broad, to link ^{aim}red^{aim} (which he has allegedly acquired independently of the verbal traces) with these traces. But, as we have put the matter, spelling out somewhat what acquiring verbal traces might be, the idea of "linking" the "two" by "association" seems downright silly. *In acquiring the "traces", Johnny has acquired* ^{aim}red^{aim}.

There is, however, a good reason for being disturbed at the *identification* of ^{aiv}red^{aiv} (an ability *incomplexum vocis*) and ^{aim}red^{aim}. If someone has ^{aiv}red^{aiv}, he necessarily has ^{aim}red^{aim}; but, if he has ^{aim}red^{aim}, he may or may not have ^{aiv}red^{aiv}, though he would necessarily have SOME appropriate *incomplexum vocis,* the token *incomplexa vocis* involved playing the same role as the members of ^{civ}red^{civ} play in ^{aiv}red^{aiv}, e.g. ^{aiv}rot^{aiv} or ^{aiv}rouge^{aiv}. With a somewhat hazy idea of these relationships in sight, one might well be tempted to claim that the relation between "language" and "thought" is merely "associationistic;" and, in a sense, this would be an exceedingly misleading way of making a true statement, so misleading that one might then think that the "formation of" ability *incomplexa mentis* was entirely separate from the acquiring of any appropriate ability *incomplexa vocis*. And, if one confused the philological criteria for languages' being different from one another with the philosophical or logical criteria, the temptation to do so would be even greater.

A more difficult objection to deal with has to do with the notion of *role*. There is a sense in which, if I know the game of chess, a certain knight will be a "different" object to me from what it is to the uninitiate. So also is $^{tiv}red^{tiv}_1$ a "different" object to one who has $^{aiv}red^{aiv}$ (or $^{aim}red^{aim}$, where it is connected with $^{aiv}red^{aiv}$) from what it is to the uninitiate. I do not mean to suggest (as have certain Gestalt psychologists) that what confronts one in each case is literally different. I should think it nearer to the truth to suggest that the initiate has, as it were, a "readiness" to respond to certain cues by using, in the one case, the knight, in the other, one of the members of $^{civ}red^{civ}$, in appropriate fashions. Connected with this, and again, as it were, the initiate has what might be called a "readiness consciousness" akin to the "readiness consciousness" of a runner waiting for the gun or a soldier (well-trained, that is) on patrol. (Broad himself discusses something a *bit* like this, as I noted in comment B above, in connection with Price's "perceptual acceptance," a "modification of experience corresponding to the *disposition* to make a perceptual judgment.") I should think it not dangerously misleading to describe the initiate's consciousness of the knight as a "consciousness of the role of the knight in chess" and, in the other case, a "consciousness of the role of the members of $^{civ}red^{civ}$." Now it may be that the fact of such "readiness consciousness," where it involves members of certain class *incomplexa vocis*, lends a show of plausibility to talk of "acquaintance with" universals, especially when used against rather casual arguments of so-called "linguistic" philosophers. And, of course, as I suggested in comment D above, if Jones "knows the meaning of $^{civ}red^{civ}$ (or its members)"[32] he has a batch of ability *complexa vocis* like ^{acv}If something is red, then it is colored^{acv}, ^{acv}If something is literally red, then it is not a noise or an odor or a twinge or a tickle^{acv}, etc. Furthermore, we would wish to say that $^{aiv}red^{aiv}$ was, for Jones, "tied" to his environment in the way suggested above.

If Jones has $^{aiv}red^{aiv}$, however, he not only has a "readiness consciousness" in connection with seeing, hearing, and imaging members of $^{civ}red^{civ}$, but also a "readiness consciousness" in connection with being confronted with various red objects. Of this I should be inclined to say almost precisely what Broad said concerning Price's doctrine of "perceptual acceptance" (Cf. the above paragraph and comment B).

---

32 There, under the heading of "contemplating the universal *redness.*"

Finally, if simple concepts are connected with unique roles in "language," we need not run into the "rous" conundrum (comment F above). There are, however, some complications here, in that, e.g., members of different class *incomplexa vocis* may play the *same role,* members of the same class *incomplexum vocis* may play *different roles,* and, given a distinction between simple and complex token (and class) *incomplexa vocis,* complex ones may play simple roles, and simple ones complex roles.

It is not my business, however, in an essay in a volume of this sort, to develop with the detail proper to a totally independent discussion my own theories. It was necessary at least to sketch, however, in order to render plausible my claim that Broad's account of the "relation" between "verbal traces" and "empirical concepts of the first kind" is incorrect. I find it more than a little strange that Broad, who, more than any other contemporary philosopher, has made the rest of us, "disposition conscious," should be so incredibly casual in his treatment of "verbal traces."

A Priori Concepts

At long last I wish to comment on Broad's discussions of *a priori* concepts. After finishing his account of simple, descriptive, and compound empirical concepts, Broad considers two theories which, presumably, require that we have some "simple dispositional ideas *not* formed by comparison, contrast, analysis, and abstraction from perceived instances."[33] These are discussed largely because Broad apparently considers the ideas of Cause and Substance and certain ethical ideas as especially unlikely candidates for the appelation "Empirical Concept." The two theories are those of Innate Ideas and Non-Perceptual Intuition.

According to "Innate Ideaism," in addition to the *general* ability to acquire simple empirical concepts from "perceived instances," we have a battery of *special* abilities to acquire simple concepts instances of the characteristics which they are *of* not ever being "perceived." On this theory there would be, however, *occasions* (Broad's term in *Five Types of Ethical Theory*) for the formation of the concepts in question. For acquiring [aim]fitting[aim], we should need to "contemplate certain kinds of situation with certain kinds of emotion;"[34] for acquiring [aim]cause[aim], we should need to be "presented with instances of regular sequence;"[35]

[33] *EMcP*, I, 44.   [34] *EMcP*, I, 49.   [35] *EMcP*, I, 49.

and for acquiring ^{aim}substance^{aim}, we should need to be presented "with instances of recurrent bundles of qualities."[36]

For forming the concepts in question we should need special abilities which would be triggered off by such special occasions. As Broad points out, this theory would not be open "to any of the objections which are commonly brought against" theories of Innate Ideas. The difficulty, for Broad, with it is that, if we have concepts, never having "perceived" an instancing of the characteristics which they are *of*, these might be "innate racial delusions, and the Concepts of Cause and Substance and Rightness and Duty might be instances of such racial delusions. Unless there be some kind of pre-established harmony between the human mind and the rest of nature, it would seem just as likely that our innate ideas should be delusive as that they should be veridical."[37] He is thus prepared to be sceptical of the theory he so firmly stated as true in *Five Types of Ethical Theory*,[38] and, given his own presuppositions, rightly so.

Leaving those presuppositions aside, I should like to comment briefly on his examples. I should think that, to take ^{aim}cause^{aim} first, reflection upon the roles played by such terms as members of ^{civ}break^{civ}, ^{civ}bump^{civ}, ^{civ}move^{civ}, etc. may well lead one to the conclusion that these roles are similar to each other in a way in which each is not similar to the roles played by members of ^{civ}between^{civ}, ^{civ}next to^{civ}, ^{civ}similar^{civ}, etc. (staying within the categorial frame of relations). Reflection on these (and, perhaps, other such) similarities and differences of role may well lead to the classifying of roles in various ways; in the case in hand, classifying certain roles as "causal." Interestingly enough, sentences involving members of ^{civ}cause^{civ} (or a cognate) as a main verb and members of ^{civ}breaking^{civ}, ^{civ}bumping^{civ}, etc. (or cognates), e.g.

(i) The boy's throwing the stone caused the breaking of the window,

seem to entail *either* (both), e.g.,

(ii) The boy broke the window *or* (and)

(iii) The stone broke the window.

Further, (ii) entails

(iv) There is a sentence such that its *logical* subjects involve 'boy' (or a cognate) and 'break' (or a cognate) and its *logical* predicate is 'cause' (or a cognate) and that sentence is true.

If members of ^{civ}break^{civ}, ^{civ}bump^{civ}, etc. are, in the usual acquisition of ability *incomplexa vocis,* connected with what I have called "observation dispositions," then, clearly various items in the "causal category"

---

[36] *EMcP*, I, 49.   [37] *EMcP*, I, 51.

[38] London, 1930. See, e.g., pp. 105f.

are not "innate racial delusions;" they have a "tie." If, further, in the later acquisition of a conceptual apparatus, the *role-similarity*, as it were, of members of ᶜⁱᵛbreakᶜⁱᵛ, ᶜⁱᵛbumpᶜⁱᵛ, etc. becomes enshrined in an ability *incomplexum vocis* (and, therefore, an ability *incomplexum mentis*) of its own ᵃⁱᵐcauseᵃⁱᵐ will have *indirectly* a "tie."

As I noted in the last comment on Broad's doctrine of empirical concepts, there is every reason to believe that at least concepts like ᵃⁱᵐmanᵃⁱᵐ, ᵃⁱᵐtreeᵃⁱᵐ, ᵃⁱᵐchairᵃⁱᵐ, etc. are acquired in a context involving observation dispositions. Again, the "logic" of the associated terms is characteristically different from that, e.g., of the terms associated with ᵃⁱᵐredᵃⁱᵐ, etc. Contrast, e.g., 'ᵃᶜᵛThis is redᵃᶜᵛ,' 'ᵃᶜᵛThis is a treeᵃᶜᵛ,' 'ᶜᶜᵛThis is a redᶜᶜᵛ,' and 'ᶜᶜᵛThis is treeᶜᶜᵛ.' One might, for convenience, call such concepts "is-a" concepts or, though this is misleading, "substance concepts." There are, of course, such *incomplexa mentis* as ᵃⁱᵐtickleᵃⁱᵐ, ᵃⁱᵐtwingeᵃⁱᵐ, ᵃⁱᵐflashᵃⁱᵐ, etc., each having a *somewhat* similar status. The former "is-a" concepts, however, play a role in "action-term" sentences which is not commonly, if at all, played by the latter. That role, incidentally, has been admirably described by Broad himself in the *McTaggart* under the heading "The 'Nature' of a Continuant."[39] Now I should like to suggest that the role-similarity of such "is-a" *incomplexa vocis* could easily, as it were, be given a name, i.e. a token or class *incomplexa vocis*, ᵗⁱᵛsubstanceᵗⁱᵛ or ᶜⁱᵛsubstanceᶜⁱᵛ, this, in turn, being a vehicle for ᵃⁱᵐsubstanceᵃⁱᵐ. To "think of" ᶜⁱᵐsubstanceᶜⁱᵐ would then be, as it were, to "think of" the role-similarity which obtains between members of the one variety of "is-a" concepts. In this way, given the connection of "is-a" concepts with observation dispositions, ᵃⁱᵐsubstanceᵃⁱᵐ would, at one remove, have "empirical status."

Ethical concepts present a somewhat different problem. Putting the matter as simply as possible,[40] they have, as it were, a different sort of "tie" with one's environment, an "action-provoking" one. Our exemplary friend Johnny hears various members of ᶜⁱᵛoughtᶜⁱᵛ, e.g., very early in connection with the doing of various actions and becomes conditioned to respond to some such utterances by doing the appropriate action and to respond to "seeing" various actions by uttering members of ᶜⁱᵛoughtᶜⁱᵛ. Later, members of ᶜⁱᵛoughtᶜⁱᵛ come to play roles in a system of responses to members of various other class *incomplexa vocis* (some, of course, being "empirical"), still, however, preserving their "tie" with action. Johnny learns certain moral truths. Further, he learns to perform certain actions *because* he ought, i.e. "oughtness" enters the

39 *EMcP*, I, 264ff.
40 See Wilfrid Sellars, "Obligation and Motivation," in *Readings in Ethical Theory*, ed. Wilfrid Sellars and John Hospers (New York, 1952), pp. 511–518.

230   ROBERT G. TURNBULL

causal order as an intentional object in a thought "triggering off" what might be called one of Johnny's "moral dispositions." ^{aim}Ought^{aim}, as well as ^{cim}ought^{cim}, in these terms, is, however, still "simple" and not "naturalistic," i.e. the *incomplexa vocis* associated with it play a role not assimilable to that played by any term which is directly or indirectly connected with observation dispositions, nor, I might add, to that played by terms in the so-called "imperative mood." In a sense, the acquiring of ^{aim}ought^{aim} requires a "special ability," i.e. the ability to acquire what might be called "verbal-action" dispositions (and, indeed, whatever abilities are involved in "connecting" "ought-roles" and "is-roles," as in connecting ^{aim}ought^{aim} and ^{aim}promise^{aim}). It is worth noting that Broad himself, in 1951, published an article advocating (or *nearly* advocating) a theory which has interesting similarities to that so hastily sketched above.[41]

My point in sketching possible accounts of ^{aim}cause^{aim}, ^{aim}substance^{aim}, and ^{aim}ought^{aim} is that these accounts are compatible with the general one sketched in my last comment on Broad's doctrine of empirical concepts. Though they have certain superficial similarities to "Innate Ideaism," they are not open to the peculiar charge that the concepts involved might be "racial delusions." This odd charge is largely a result of Broad's "abstractionism."

Finally we come to Broad's doctrine of "non-perceptual intuition," a doctrine which, given the foregoing, can be discussed rather briefly.

On such a view as this we have only to postulate in the human mind a general power of non-perceptual intuition. Categories, ethical relations, etc., will be relations or types of structure actually present in reality, but incapable of manifesting themselves sensuously or introspectively, as colours, shapes, and spatio-temporal relations can do, and as psychological qualities and relations can do. When our perceptual experience takes certain specific forms this power of non-perceptual intuition is stimulated, and we intuit these objective types of relation and structure in the perceived objects.[42]

The main difficulty here is precisely the difficulty I found in Broad's account of simple empirical concepts, viz. the "abstracting" of universals from "instances," in this case, "non-perceived" ones. We might, to coin arbitrary terms, talk here of "shperception" and "shprehension"

41 "Hägerström's Account of Sense of Duty and Certain Allied Experiences," *Philosophy*, XXVI (1951), pp. 99–113. Incidentally, in a symposium for the Aristotelian Society ("Are There Synthetic *A Priori* Truths?," with A. J. D. Porteous, Reginald Jackson, *Arist. Soc. Suppl.* Vol. XV, 1936) Broad, in suggesting the desirability of a philosopher's having broad acquaintance with other than Indo-European languages, *seemed* to be aware of the possibility of a language's differing from another in being or containing different *roles*. pp. 102ff.
42 *EMcP*, I, 52.

and then invoke most of the arguments I have urged against Broad's doctrine of empirical concepts, urging again that the doctrine of non-perceptual intuition becomes a doctrine of innate ideas at one remove.[43]

III. *Conclusion*

In an attempt to comment on a few short passages from the *Mc-Taggart*, I have been forced at several points to "show my hand" in a context which does not allow for the proper development and defense of the views involved. However vulnerable those views may be as developed in this paper, I hope it is clear that they have a *prima facie* plausibility when considered against the background of my criticisms of Professor Broad's doctrines as stated in the *McTaggart*. My fundamental criticisms of those doctrines are made possible, I believe, because of Broad's dogged persistence in seeing his problem almost entirely in terms of the "thinking in presence—thinking in absence" distinction. I hope to have shown that seeing the problem in this way obscures—or tends to obscure—some more fundamental aspects of the problem. My admiration for the rigor and clarity of Professor Broad's discussions of most philosophical issues to which he has given his attention leads me to believe that his discussion of the "concepts" issue where it cuts deeper than the "thinking in presence—thinking in absence" distinction requires may be equally admirable.

ROBERT G. TURNBULL

DEPARTMENT OF PHILOSOPHY
STATE UNIVERSITY OF IOWA

[43] For another sort of attack on "non-perceptual intuition," perhaps more damaging in that it assumes a frame more like Broad's, see Gustav Bergmann, "A Note on 'Non-Perceptual Intuitions,'" *Philosophy and Phenomenological Research*, 10 (Dec., 1949), 263–4.

6

Brand Blanshard

BROAD'S CONCEPTION OF REASON

BROAD conceives of reason as having three functions: "(i) The intuiting of necessary and universal connexions between characteristics. . . . (ii) The drawing of inferences, demonstrative or problematical, from premises. . . . (iii) The formation of *a priori* concepts." "The three cognitive functions which I assign to reason," he writes, "may be called respectively 'Intuitive Induction,' 'Ratiocination,' and 'Formation of *A Priori* Concepts.' "[1]

Does this description of reason accord with the traditional views? Few philosophers who have used the term have defined it with Broad's clarity, and this has furthered their tendency to use it for widely different things. Its meaning varies all the way from the sort of faculty that is at work in logic and mathematics to the sort of faculty that enables one to conceive wisely the ends of life and to order one's conduct accordingly. So long as the term is left in this vague state, "reason" can be appealed to in support of almost anything. Broad points out that applications of it have been made, by Kant for example, that are plausible "only so long as the concept of a rational being is left unanalysed in an atmosphere misty with the incense of adoration."[2] But, though philosophers have often used the term in a very wide and loose sense, it is safe to say that those who have belonged to the rationalist tradition have generally included Broad's three factors in its meaning; this would be plainly true of Descartes and Spinoza, Leibniz and Kant, Hegel and McTaggart. On the other hand, it is equally clear that this way of conceiving reason is not that of most empiricist thinkers, who would deny the existence of some, or perhaps all, of these factors. Hume denied the existence of *a priori* concepts. Spencer held, though not consistently, that there was no such thing as intuitive induction. Mill maintained that there was no such thing as ratiocination if that included, as it does for Broad, the grasp of necessary connections.

1 *Five Types of Ethical Theory*, 105f.   2 *Ibid.*, 127.

233

Broad seems eager to go with the empiricists as far as he can. The way we come by our empirical concepts and beliefs is fairly straightforward and familiar; whereas, if we do have *a priori* concepts and insights, they are relatively mysterious; it is not at all clear how we could have come by them; and such desperate sallies as Socrates' theory of recollection and Kant's transcendental deduction are witnesses to this fact. Nevertheless, Broad is convinced that in none of the three functions of reason can an *a priori* element be dispensed with. With this view I agree, and it would give me much pleasure to do something in its defense. But, there is no one who stands in less need of such defense than Broad; and besides, the purpose of these essays is not so much to vindicate as to question, and so to evoke from their eminent subject some further words of wisdom. I shall therefore offer a few critical comments on certain points of detail in Broad's exposition of the three functions of reason. It may be well to begin with the simplest, namely *a priori* concepts.

I

Broad believes in *a priori* concepts, and finds them in widely diverse types of knowledge—not only in logic and mathematics, to which many philosophers would confine them, but also in metaphysics and ethics. The geometer's concepts of straight lines and circles have an *a priori* element in them; but the same may be said equally of the metaphysical concepts of substance and cause and of the ethical concept of fittingness. Broad's discussion of these ideas, particularly the minute dissection contained in various chapters of his massive masterpiece on McTaggart, seems to me most illuminating. But I have queries at several points.

Take the concept of exact straightness. Is this empirical or *a priori?* Broad answers that we may think of straightness in two ways; that if we think of it in the first way, the concept will be entirely empirical; whereas, if we think of it in the second, we cannot avoid an *a priori* element. Let us look at the first or empirical notion. "Empirical" here need not mean that we have experienced physical things bounded by perfectly straight lines, nor even that we have experienced sense data that had perfectly straight edges. Broad thinks it highly probable that we have in fact sensed such data, but he holds that, even if we have not, we might still come to conceive of straightness in empirical fashion. We have sensed a great many lines, and therefore are prepared to conceive the purely empirical concept of linearity. The lines we have sensed have had various degrees of jaggedness and curvature, and the resulting concepts of these characters are also plainly empirical. Now our concept of straightness may be, and often is, a compound one consisting of the positive concept of linearity and the two negative concepts of non-jagged and non-curved. All three of these concepts are empirical. Hence the concept of straightness that we reach when we put them together is equally empirical.

I do not find this very convincing. We start with a genus "line" conceived to have three species, curved, jagged, and straight. Curved and jagged are allowed to be positive concepts or kinds, whereas straight is not; at the point where it is supposed to appear in the classification we are confronted by a hole. A straight line has no character that distinguishes it from a curved line or a jagged one; it is just a line from which both these characters are absent. It is as if a division were proposed of triangle into equilateral, isosceles, and a third class described only as neither of the others. Now I cannot think that straightness has so vacuous a character, nor do I think that, if it had, we should be able to talk about it with the degree of clearness that we do. The trouble is not that the notion of a genus with some species only negatively defined is meaningless; we can meaningfully hold that within the genus color there are colors we have never experienced. But I do not think that our thought of straightness has anything like the negative character of "color that is neither blue nor red nor green nor any other that we can imagine." If a man agrees that a thing is colored, but denies that it is blue or red or green, we assume that it is in virtue of his knowing or believing that it has some definite color that excludes these. If he is unable to imagine any color that might exclude them, we should hold him to have been talking idly. Now when a man denies that a line is curved or jagged, is his mind in this way a blank as to the form of line that excludes these others? I can not think so. If jaggedness and curvature are positive qualities, so is straightness. The suggestion that straightness is an empirical concept compounded of a positive generic quality and two specific negatives seems to me to do less than justice to the degree of definiteness of our thought.

But Broad is not wholly committed to this view. Even if one were to convince him that the idea of straightness were positive and perfectly definite, he would probably still say that an empirical account of it could be given. For he is inclined to hold that we have in fact had sensory experiences of the perfectly straight. This does not mean, of course, that we have seen edges of physical yardsticks in which no microscope, however powerful, could reveal any curve or jaggedness. It means that among our *sense data* there have been edges that did seem to us to be quite straight, and that it is far more difficult and dangerous to deny that our sense data are what they seem to be than to deny that the structure which they suggest to us as belonging to physical things is what it seems to be. Broad concedes that mistakes are possible about one's own sense data. But he sees no reason to believe that we have *never* experienced the perfectly straight. He thinks, therefore, that the empirical account of the idea is in all probability sound. But we have also attributed to him the view that in such ideas an *a priori* element is inescapable. This calls for explanation.

Here we come to Broad's second way of conceiving straightness. It is just as valid a way as the first; it arises out of the fact that a straight line is a member in a series. We can see that some series *must* have limits, while others *cannot* have limits. A poker may get warm, and then hot, and then white hot; is there any maximum temperature beyond which it would be meaningless to speak of increasing hotness? If it reached the temperature of the interior of the sun, would it then have reached the impassable limit? Our imagination may, of course, have given out before then, but that is no ground for setting a limit to what might be, and it seems clear that no such limit can be fixed. Now consider another series. We have seen some lines that were very jagged, such as the edge of a cross-cut saw; we have seen others that were much less jagged, like the edge of a cabinet-maker's saw; and we have seen some that were so nearly straight that we have had to look closely to see any irregularities at all. Does this series, like the series of hots, have no upper limit? On the contrary, we can see that it does have a limit beyond which the suggestion of growing less jagged would be meaningless; when the line has reached zero jaggedness, it is straight, and the still straighter would be nonsense. Broad admits that the series from which we start here is an empirical series. He further admits, as we have seen, that the idea of perfect straightness may be an empirical idea also. Where, then, does the *a priori* element come in? It comes in at the point where we perceive that one empirical series *must* have a limit, whether we have experienced that limit or not, while we can see with equal clearness that other series *cannot* have limits, no matter how far we go. This perception of a "must" and a "cannot" about an empirical series is not itself an empirical insight, for such necessities are not given in sense. We do grasp them nevertheless. And it would appear that the only possible account of them is that they are *a priori*.[3]

This seems to me a judicious way of dealing with the geometrical *a priori*. If it is accepted together with the stricture offered on the first account, it does, to be sure, imply that our thought of geometrical figures is more complicated than it seems. When we think of the lines that bound a triangle, we are not thinking of three empirical lines that are non-jagged and non-curved; we are thinking of the limits of three series,

3 *EMcP*, I, 42–45.

which we see from the nature of the case to be necessary limits. Does this involve more wheels within wheels than one can introspectively verify? Yes, I think it does. We are not normally aware, when we think of such lines, of thinking of series at all. But we can see on reflection that, if our geometrical reasonings are to hold, it is something of this kind that we must mean.

We have been discussing an *a priori* concept in geometry. But Broad is inclined, as we saw, to accept such concepts in metaphysics also, and it is time we considered an example or two of these. An important place among them seems to be held by the concept of substance, which Broad discusses at length in his examination of McTaggart. McTaggart used the term so widely as to include under it both Gibraltar and a sneeze, and Broad points out that this was because he never took seriously enough the distinction between events and things, "occurrents" and "continuants." If these are to be lumped together in McTaggart's manner, Broad thinks it better to give the class the name of "particulars." What, then, is a particular? It is something that exists, has qualities, and is related, but is not itself a quality, a relation, or a fact. McTaggart sought to prove that there must be such particulars by an argument Broad puts as follows:

A quality has existence only by qualifying, either positively or negatively, some existent. A relation has existence only by relating terms which are existents. . . . Now it is impossible that the existence of anything should be derived in this way, from the existence of something else whose existence in turn is derived in this way from that of something else, and so on without end. . . . Now there are existents. Therefore there must be particulars.

"This argument," Broad adds, "seems to me conclusive."[4]

A particular, then, is an existent that is neither a quality nor a relation, though it possesses both. What sort of entity is this? Qualities we know, and relations we know; but what sort of thing can that be which is neither the one nor the other nor any compound of them? It is evident that we are confronted here with the well-worn problem about substance that produced such contradictory answers from Aristotle and Locke on the one hand and from Hume and Bradley on the other. Broad is impatient with these controversies.

The objections are, I think, all variations on Locke's theme of a substance being 'a something, I know not what.' It is said, quite truly, that no idea corresponds to the phrase 'particular not characterized by any characteristics.' It is concluded that no idea corresponds to the word 'particular' itself. This plainly does not follow, and it is not in fact true. When I say of something that it is a particular I mean that it has the formal characteristics of having quali-

4 *EMcP*, I, 133.

ties, of standing in relation, of being an existent, and of not being a quality or a relation or a fact. All this is perfectly intelligible.[5]

I must confess that I did not find this account intelligible when I read it on the appearance of McTaggart's book; and, though I am somewhat shaken to find that Broad, with an eye that misses nothing in the way of fallacy or confusion in his author, is ready to give this notion of substance so clean a bill of health, I still find it unintelligible. He seems to think that difficulties which for a long line of empirically minded philosophers have appeared plain and fundamental are no more than elementary confusions. What are these difficulties? They may be put as follows: We say of a lump of sugar, to use Bradley's instance, that it is white. What is this "it" which is white? Is it some one of the other qualities? Obviously not; it would be absurd to say, for example, that sweetness is white. Is it then the other qualities taken together? No again; for it is equally absurd to say that the group composed of sweetness plus hardness etc., is white. We seem to be asserting the qualities neither of each other nor of the group, but of something that lies beyond them, something not to be identified with any qualities or relations whatever, which is capable of owning them without *being* any or all of them. Now when we ask what this is, we are confronted by a dilemma. If we answer in terms of characteristics, we have failed, it is alleged, to catch the *it* that owns these characteristics. On the other hand, to answer the question, What?, by specifying no characteristic at all seems equivalent to saying nothing.

This dilemma, we may remark in passing, is one of the sore points in the current debate between "essentialists" and "existentialists." The existentialist insists that "being" is prior to "essence," in the sense that existence is not only wholly different from essence, but both logically presupposed by it and practically more important. The essentialist asks what this "existence" means. The existentialist may answer first that it is what distinguishes practical decision and action from mere theorizing. The essentialist answers that theorizing is itself a kind of practice, as truly existent as any other. The existentialist explains that what he has in mind is the distinction between mere essences or abstractions on the one hand and actual existents on the other. The essentialist then points out that abstraction may mean no more than considering a character in isolation from others, that the sweetness and whiteness of the sugar need not lose anything when so considered, and that it is therefore incumbent on the existentialist to say what it is that distinguishes an existent sweetness from an abstracted sweetness. At this point the existentialist's tactics vary. Sometimes he says that what he means by an existent sweetness is

[5] *Ibid.,* I, 135.

one that occupies a position in space and time. But this plays into his critic's hands, since he is defining existence in terms of spatial and temporal relations, which are characteristics, and this is what he is supposed to avoid. Sometimes he says that what gives existence is concreteness; what exists is events or things, and these are inexhaustible syntheses of qualities and relations. This equally surrenders his case, and for the same reason. If he is more guarded, he will probably complain that the demand on him is question-begging, that to ask what distinguishes an existent from an essence or set of essences is to set up the answer beforehand in terms of essence, whereas the very point he is insisting on is that no answer is possible in those terms.

How would Broad deal with this question? Fortunately he has considered it explictily in his *McTaggart*. Professor Stout had raised the question in the following form:

> What is the subject itself as distinguished from the attributes? It would seem that its whole being must consist in being that to which its attributes belong. But how can the whole being of anything consist in its being related to something else? There must be an answer to the question: What is it that is so related?[6]

To this Broad replies:

> If the question means: 'Under what *category* does that which has qualities and stands in relation fall?,' the answer is that it falls under the category of Particularity. If the question means: 'What *kind of thing* is that which has these qualities and stands in these relations?,' the answer consists in mentioning certain of its fundamental properties, which either logically entail the rest or are, in the actual world, trustworthy signs of the presence of the rest.[7]

Neither of these answers seems to me to meet Stout's difficulty. The first answer, that the subject falls under the category of particularity, leaves the question still open how particularity is to be understood, which is itself the question before us. The second answer deals effectively with one possible meaning of "What kind of thing?," but a meaning that is pretty clearly not that of Stout. It is true, as Broad points out, that when we ask "What is that?," the normal and satisfying answer is something like "That is a horse" or "That is a bit of gold." What we are asking about in such a case is a particular or individual as a whole, an existent with all its attributes on its head, not that special component within it which is supposed to be distinct from its attributes. But the reply that would be appropriate to the simple, common-sense question is quite inadequate to the subtle question Stout was asking. He was not asking whether a certain lump before him was a lump of gold or silver; he was

6 *Studies in Philosophy and Psychology*, 255f.
7 *EMcP*, I, 137–38.

assuming this question to be already answered, and answered in Broad's way, by a grasp of characteristics, and he was going on to the further question, what is the *it,* supposed to be distinct from all the thing's characteristics, in which they inhere? That seems a legitimate enough question, and I cannot think that either of the suggested interpretations does it justice. "If the question be interpreted in either of these two ways," Broad writes, "there seems to be no difficulty in answering it. If it be interpreted in neither way, I must confess that I do not know what it means, and I do not believe that it could be answered in terms of any theory." I suspect that it is because Broad has himself interpreted it in a third way and tried to give an answer where no satisfactory answer is possible that his account is so puzzling. He holds that to reduce a particular to qualities and relations is absurd. He holds that there is something in it distinct from its qualities and relations, which has them, or owns them. But, when we ask for an account of this "it," what we get is an account not of the "it" that is distinct from its characteristics, but of the whole composed of the "it" *plus* its characteristics. We are still left in the dark about the "it" itself.

Broad is the clearest-headed of philosophers, and to find oneself differing from him on so elusive an issue is not calculated to breed confidence in one's own insights. But, since a good deal hangs on the outcome, I am tempted to try a little further to show that the question he dismisses is a real one. One must agree with him, I think, on the following: (1) There is a very large difference between things that are merely thought of and things that actually exist, dollars merely contemplated and dollars in one's pocket. (2) For common sense, qualities and relations are, as he says, thought of as having existence only when taken to qualify some existent which is distinct from them. Hence, if appeals to ordinary usage could settle philosophic questions, one could stop here. But Broad has never been the victim of this passing fashion. (3) The argument most often used to show that common sense is wrong here, is an invalid one, as Broad points out. "It is said, quite truly, that no idea corresponds to the phrase 'particular not characterized by any characteristics.' It is concluded that no idea corresponds to the word 'particular' itself. This plainly does not follow. . . ." Agreed. To take a case in principle the same, it would be meaningless to talk of a picture with no lines, shades, or colors. But one cannot conclude that it would therefore be meaningless to talk of a picture that did have lines, shades, and colors, or that one's meaning was exhausted by the sum of these. Where then do we differ from Broad?

We differ in holding that, if you are to make a valid distinction, there must be content or character on both sides. Broad insists that a particular has two sides, on one of which you can place its characteristics and on the other side—what? Sometimes it seems as if he is conceiving this too as a set of characteristics. "When I say of something that it is a particular I mean that it has the formal characteristics of having qualities, of standing in relations, of being an existent, and of not being a quality or a relation or a part." But he does not say that the particular *is* these characteristics; that view he rejects in the most emphatic way; what he says is that it *has* them.[8] Between "it" on the one side and the characteristics on the other (including the having of them, which is itself a characteristic) there is supposed to be a fundamental distinction. And my complaint is that on one side of the divide is everything on which a distinction could be based, and on the other side nothing at all. The "it" that is supposed to stand over against its characteristics as that which has them turns out, after all, to be Locke's "something I know not what."

It is perhaps graceless to carp at another's moves in this fashion without laying one's own cards on the table. There is no space here to defend an alternative position, but I may say that a particular does seem to me to be a pattern of characteristics and nothing more. To the question what makes this pattern in any given case particular, the answer, I suggest, does not lie in an unthinkable "it," but in the set of relations that at once connect this group with others and distinguish it from them, most obviously the relations of space and time. If it is said that these terms mean *this* space and *this* time, and that one is thus returning to particulars at one remove, I answer that spatial and temporal relations seem to me to be universals, and that I see no reason in principle why there should not be a plurality of spaces and times.[9] If there are, they in turn could only be distinguished from each other in terms of their interrelations. On this view, could one ever arrive at the fully unique and particular? Yes, but at one point only, namely when one arrived at the whole of things. The universe is unique because two universes would be self-contradictory.

Broad is inclined to take the notion of substance, as McTaggart called it, or particularly, as he himself would call it, as an *a priori* concept of reason. If what we have said about it is correct, it is not really this, in spite of its universal and unquestioning use by common sense. It is a concept that dissolves into something unintelligible. If one asks why, then, common sense has adopted it so firmly, the explanation is to be found not in logic or the theory of knowledge, but in psychology. Promising suggestions toward this end have indeed been given by James, Ward, and Stout.

---

8 Cf. *MPN*, 30.   9 Nor does Broad. Cf. *EMcP*, I, 177.

So far, we have been discussing the use by reason of *a priori* concepts in geometry and metaphysics. But Broad holds that such concepts play an important part in ethics also. "Ethics involves both *a priori* concepts and *a priori* judgments; and these, by definition, are the work of Reason. We may therefore admit that Reason is essential in ethical cognition."[10] What *a priori* concepts do moralists use? Broad includes among them the concepts that are most distinctively ethical: "If such terms as *right, ought, good,* etc., be *sui generis* [as he holds that they probably are] I think it almost certain that the concepts of them are *a priori* and not empirical."[11] Let us confine ourselves to one of these concepts, that of rightness. According to Broad the rightness of an act is a function of two factors, its fittingness and its utility, and in the recognition of each of these an *a priori* element is involved. To see that an act has utility is to see that it has certain consequences; this, to be sure, is a merely empirical insight; but to see that these consequences, in virtue of certain of their empirical features, are intrinsically good is a quite different kind of insight; it is necessary and *a priori*. And just as "x is good" involves the *a priori*, so also does "x is fitting." "I think that there are also self-evident propositions of the form: 'Such and such a type of intention or emotion would necessarily be fitting (or unfitting) to such and such a kind of situation. In any possible world it would be fitting to feel gratitude toward one's benefactors and unfitting to feel pleasure at the undeserved suffering of another."[12] Fittingness is an *a priori* relation grasped by reason.

Now while I regard Broad as one of the soundest of moralists on the place of reason in ethics, I have doubts about this concept of fittingness. There are two points to be considered: (1) whether fittingness is an *a priori* concept, and (2) whether it is a characteristic on which rightness directly depends.

(1) An *a priori* insight apprehends its terms as connected necessarily and therefore without exceptions. (In discussing the grasp of such connections, it is hardly worthwhile to insist on the difference between *a priori* concepts and intuitions.) Is our grasp of the fittingness of a kind of action thus necessary and universal? In most cases when one turns from an empirical statement like "these leaves are green" to an *a priori* one like "these two leaves and these two are four," one feels that the transition is abrupt and sharp; one is crossing a clearly marked boundary between one kind of knowledge and another; and the kinds are so plainly different that as a rule there is no difficulty in seeing when the transition is made; the leap from ordinary judgments about things felt

or heard into logic, arithmetic, or geometry is unmistakable. Does one find anything like this in turning from empirical judgments to this about fittingness? It seems clear, on the contrary, that many judgments of fittingness have no necessity in them, and if any of them are really necessary, they are separated from the others by such fine shades as to raise doubt all along the line. It is true that at times one can arrive at a difference of kind through traversing differences of degree, as no one has made clearer than Broad. The fact remains that if the judgment of fittingness is necessary and universal, one would expect a sharper difference between it and others, and a more general agreement about it, than one finds in fact.

Consider what one does find. The Christian thinks it fitting to turn the other cheek. The old Adam in man finds it fitting that he should, if he can, give a scoundrel the drubbing he deserves. Many Easterners of all levels of intelligence hold the eating of animals to be highly unfitting; most Westerners would dismiss such an attitude as over-squeamish. American Protestants consider that the attempt by the church to raise money by bingo games is grossly unfitting, while Catholic churches resort to such games without compunction. Victorians thought it unfitting that women should ride astride, or take their dips in the sea unstockinged; their successors would find a like unfittingness in their doing anything else. Sidgwick, who was a very good moralist and a very good man, thought it most unfitting that a clergyman who had doubts about some of the 39 articles should consent to signing them; Rashdall, who was also a good moralist and a good man, took the opposite view. Is it fitting to attend bullfights? Is it fitting to suffer fools gladly? To perform a "mercy-killing?" To tell a "white lie?" To swear an oath in either the legal or the vulgar sense?

It may be that when any such issue arises, there is some act that would be seen by a clear enough head to be *the* fitting one, and seem to be so with self-evident necessity. But I doubt it. When the doctors so disagree, when civilized peoples so disagree, when a civilized majority can so rapidly and lightly reverse itself, I find it hard to believe that we have here anything very similar to the *a priori* concepts of logic and mathematics. Not that I should infer from these variations, as subjectivists do, that there is no objectively right act to be found; I follow Moore, Ross and Broad, as I understand them, in holding that there is such an act, which it is our duty to find and do if we can. What I doubt is whether we can find the compelling element in fittingness. It is notorious that what is taken as fitting in the way of dress, manners, and speech varies in fickle fashion with custom or habit, and it is extremely hard to draw any clear line between the fitting in manners and in morals. Broad remarks somewhere, I think, that there is no *a priori* unfittingness in wearing brown boots with a dinner jacket; but there are plenty of people who would regard this as more grossly unfitting than eating meat, or marrying a deceased wife's sister. In these latter they would see nothing unfitting at all, while others would regard them as serious breaches of a propriety that is clearly moral. So long as the argument on any of these matters is conducted simply on a basis of fittingness, I doubt if it could ever produce agreement.

(2) But whether fittingness is an *a priori* relation or not, it might still be an ultimate right-making character. Broad thinks it is. He considers that there are two independent factors on which the rightness of an act depends, its fittingness to the situation and the goodness of its consequences. Sometimes the one and sometimes the other of these is plainly the dominant consideration; often both are involved and even compete against the greater utility of an alternative action. Here Broad would agree, I take it, with Prichard, Carritt, and Ross, and the case they make for this view is both familiar and extremely persuasive.

If I do not accept it, it is because I have not yet been convinced that in determining the rightness of an act, its fittingness can be counted as an element independent of the goodness involved in it. I cannot think that when one weighs the goodness of an act's consequences against its fittingness, one is weighing two completely different things against each other; it is because the fittingness is itself good, or belongs to an intrinsically good scheme of things that it counts; what are weighed against each other are the two goodnesses, not goodness on the one hand and something quite other than goodness on the other. In short, fittingness is not itself an ultimate source of obligation. Only goodness is. If fittingness is to be taken into account, as it no doubt should be, it is not for itself, but because it is the bearer or sign of goodness.

How is this to be shown? One way is to consider the logic of comparison. Diverse things can be compared only in respect of something they have in common. One thing can be sweeter than another only if they both have taste, one thing larger than another only if they both have size, one thing better than another only if they both have value; whereas it would be meaningless to compare a value with a size, or a size with a taste. Now if, in considering what we ought to do, we can weigh the fittingness of an act against the goodness involved in it, there must be some common property with respect to which they can be compared. If fittingness, or the order to which a given form of fittingness belongs, can be called intrinsically good, there is in principle no difficulty, for one good is then being weighed against another. But how is fittingness as such to be weighed against goodness? Where is the common property in respect of which the comparison can be made? It may be answered that such a property is to be found in obligatoriness itself; to produce a certain amount of goodness has one degree of obligatoriness, to produce a certain fittingness has another degree of obligatoriness; and since these are degrees under the same determinable, they are comparable with each other. I am not satisfied. For sometimes we weigh fittingness against goodness without any resort to obligatoriness, as when we consider which of two communities would be the better, a less happy community in which people behaved fittingly or a happier one in which they behaved less fittingly. Here it seems clear that we are throwing fittingness and happiness into the same scale and weighing these as goods against each other. Nor is the case really different when we try to decide what to do. We then weigh fittingness against goodness with a view to finding which gives us the stronger ground for obligation, but the property "being a ground of obligation" is hardly itself the ground whose greater amount on one side or the other gives us the reason for our decision. Suppose we compare two prospective goods with each other, and decide in favor of one of them; if we are asked why we took B to be more obligatory than A, we answer that it is because B is a greater good. It is suggested that when we now compare this good with a certain fittingness, C, and decide for the latter, this sort of answer is no longer valid; indeed no answer is possible at all; fittingness is not obligatory because it is good, but simply because it is fittingness; and between it and goodness there is no ground of comparison but obligatoriness itself. This leads to the odd consequence that it may be our duty to produce a state of things with no goodness whatever, or to produce a state of things that is less good than some alternative state. These are paradoxes that I cannot accept.

Again, when two fitnesses conflict with each other, we usually settle the issue in terms not of fitness but of good. Consider the miscellaneous lot of fitnesses that we listed a moment ago. In all these cases there are sharp differences of opinion as to what it is most fitting to do. I am inclined to think that none of them would in the end be settled on that basis. One must walk warily here, for Broad does not hold, of course, that fittingness is the sole ground of rightness, and to argue that in some or even all such cases we allow fittingness to be over-ridden by goodness would be nothing to the purpose; Broad could admit it with perfect consistency. My point is a different one. It is that even when we ostensibly settle such issues on the ground of greater fittingness, this greater fittingness resolves itself on scrutiny into the greater good of the situation involved in it. When the old Adam in a man breathes in his ear that the right treatment for a scoundrel is to give him a drubbing, the first justification is always that this is the natural or fitting thing to do; there is no reference to goodness in "an eye for an eye and a tooth for a tooth;" the rule expresses what is taken as the obvious fitness of things. But it is notorious that, as reflection sets in, the rule gets modified. Do we describe this modification rightly by saying that as our knowledge of the ill consequences grows, we see that the evil of the drubbing outweighs its moral fittingness? I do not think so. It is rather that as we come to see the evil involved, the moral fittingness itself declines, and that when we see that little good or none would be produced by the drubbing, we regard it as morally unfitting.

Nor is the case essentially different, in the other instances, though in some of them it is perhaps more complicated. Should we use animals for food? The utilitarian may approach this issue confidently, arguing that the good involved in such use to human kind outweighs enormously the animal pain and loss of life. His opponent would argue, rightly I think, that this is less than the whole story. Our practice in regard to animals is bound up in intimate fashion with a great range of ideas about them and attitudes toward them, ideas regarding their level of sensation and feeling, attitudes of sensitiveness or indifference, sadism or sympathy. The deontologist is surely right in saying that whether or not one should butcher sheep is not a matter merely of the pleasures and pains involved. The entire order of one's thoughts and attitudes toward sub-human minds is involved. Indeed we must go farther. Like Mr. Joseph, I do not think that such an order of ideas and attitudes can itself be appraised in isolation; we are bound to consider the plan of life generally to which this order belongs. It may be said that resort to such large and vague considerations is still consistent with the appeal to fittingness, since one order of life as a whole is being pronounced more fitting than another. One may say so if one wishes; but I suspect that at this level the distinction between fittingness and goodness has disappeared.

To sum up on fittingness: we have seen that Broad regards reason in ethics as dealing with *a priori* concepts and that among these concepts fittingness plays a very important part. Regarding it we have, first, suggested some doubts as to whether it is to be properly described as *a priori;* and secondly, we have argued that whether *a priori* or not, its place in ethics is hardly as independent and basic as Broad suggests. If it is objected that this latter consideration has taken us somewhat outside of Broad's conception of reason, we should answer that here is a case where the good has priority over the fitting.

II

We noted at the outset that for Broad reason has three functions, the forming of a *priori* concepts, the intuiting of necessary connections, and the drawing of inferences. It is time we turned to the second of these functions. The main points of interest in Broad's treatment of it seem to be as follows:

(1) The necessities we grasp through intuition include both formal and non-formal types.

(2) In the grasp of both types, the process by which they are apprehended is commonly, though not always, one of "intuitive induction."

(3) The grasp may be either analytic or synthetic.

(4) Among non-formal synthetic necessities are some that belong to causality.

(5) The conventionalist view that necessary statements express merely relations among our ideas is false; in some cases they reveal the actual structure of things.

I should like to comment briefly on each of these theses.

(1) It is a popular doctrine of the day that the only necessary propositions are those that state formal relations, such as those of logic and mathematics. Broad denies this. We have just found him contending that the fittingness of an act to a situation may be as truly a necessary insight as one in logic itself. Again, we can see that the same surface cannot be at once red and blue. These are not insights into formal connections. They are necessary nonetheless. Necessity is therefore not confined to the merely formal.

It is not always clear what is meant when a statement is called formal. Sometimes the term is applied to any statement within the field of logic and mathematics. The assertion that all equilateral triangles are equiangular would then be formal. But it is not formal in the sense that it is without reference to any special kind of subject-matter; for it applies exclusively to figures in space, and among these exclusively to one kind of figure. Sometimes the term is restricted further to apply only to those statements that apply equally to any subject-matter; thus the three traditional laws of thought are held to be equally valid in discourse about numbers, apples, and emotions. In that new and ascetic discipline known as syntactics, the term is often taken to mean the sort of statement that has no content or meaning at all. This seems to me a waste of the word. A statement with no meaning states nothing, and if so, why call it a statement? When it is said that necessary statements are confined to formal ones, what is most sensibly meant is the second of the above ideas, that they are confined to those statements that make no reference to one kind of subject-matter rather than to any other. The equation of the necessary with formal in this sense, and of statements that contain any references to empirical kinds with the non-necessary, is often assumed unquestioningly. Broad is too well acquainted with the range of actual thinking to make any such assumption. He sees that if we cannot intelligibly call the same surface blue and red whereas we can intelligibly call it blue and square, our insight is more than formal; we see that a given color excludes another color from the same surface in a way that it does not exclude a shape. One may differ from Broad about the necessity of this or that statement and I have already expressed doubt whether statements of fittingness are really necessary; but as against those who would confine necessity within the bounds of logic, he seems to me altogether right. To put the matter slightly otherwise, those who believe that necessary statements are purely formal must take this statement itself as either formal and necessary or not. It is pretty clear that they do not mean the former. And if they mean the latter, namely that it is an empirical statement which may therefore have exceptions, the exceptions swarm to light on even a casual inspection. It is Broad whose thought on these matters is in the best sense empirical as opposed to the curious dogmatism of many who lay claim to the name.

(2) Many of our necessary insights are achieved, according to Broad, through intuitive induction. This process is intuitive in the sense that its insights are immediate; there is no reasoning from grounds or premises. It is inductive in the sense that it proceeds through instances. Contemplating a particular triangle on the blackboard, we see that if it is equilateral it must also be equiangular, and that this must hold of triangles generally. Contemplating a particular surface, we see that it cannot be at once red and blue, that this holds of surfaces generally. This process is of course very different from that of inductive generalization, such as the passing from a few cases of inverse variation of pressure and volume to Boyle's law. In this latter process, no necessity is seen to link the characteristics, and if they are held to go together universally, it is only because we assume that nature behaves according to laws, an unproved and perhaps unprovable assumption. In intuitive induction, on the other hand, we see that certain of the characters before us are linked indissolubly. Broad believes, as we have seen, that this process is at work in many insights of ethics, for example in our grasp of the fittingness of a certain attitude or the goodness of a certain experience. Cases of this kind raise the question, What is the empirical stuff in which the necessary connection is here presented? One can hardly say that it is sense data, as in the cases of the triangle and the colors; we do not apprehend the unfittingness of Nero's matricide through anything given in

sense. Broad's interesting suggestion is that the empirical vehicle in moral cases is emotion; "it seems to me arguable that *wrongness* would never have been recognized by Reason without the stimulus and suggestion of the emotion of disapproval. . . ."[13]

This notion of intuitive induction is apparently as old as Aristotle, but its recognition under this name and its clear distinction from cognate processes by Cambridge writers—for it is stressed by W. E. Johnson and F. R. Tennant as well as Broad—has been a useful bit of work. But its precise status in Broad's thought is not clear to me. For one thing, I am not clear how much of our *a priori* knowledge is supposed to be covered by it. Many of the theorems and axioms of geometry are held to be known in this way, as opposed to those propositions that are known only by demonstration; but are *all* immediate *a priori* insights achieved in this way? I am not sure what Broad would say. Again, what is the relation between intuitive induction and the process he describes in the *McTaggart* as non-perceptual intuition?[14] In both processes we lay hold of non-sensible and necessary relations through the aid of the empirically given, but in the pages on non-perceptual intuition intuitive induction is not referred to. Whether Broad would identify the two I do not know. Once more, I wish we might have had from Broad some discussion of the practical dangers and difficulties connected with intuitive induction. He recognizes how easy it is to think one sees something intuitively as necessary and to find oneself later mistaken. Euclid's axiom of parallels seems to a great many people self-evident, and to a great many not. Some statements about causality seem to many self-evident and Broad himself admits four of them to this status, while many philosophers would deny any such statements to be self-evident. A discussion by so acute a student of thought as Broad of the pitfalls to be avoided in this region would be most helpful.

(3) In his Aristotelian Society paper of 1936, "Are there Synthetic A Priori Truths?," Broad dealt with the newly published view of Professor Ayer in *Language, Truth and Logic* that all *a priori* statements were analytic. He professed great difficulty in understanding what Ayer meant, and came up with the astonishing conclusion that on the latter's theory, all *a priori* statements must be synthetic, and that the analytic was a sub-class of the synthetic. The argument was powerful, though rather naughty. Of course Ayer never meant to say anything remotely like this, but his unguarded language left his defences wide open. He had said than an analytic proposition records our determination to use words in a certain way, and that its office is to call attention to linguistic

---

13 *FTET*, 179.   14 I, 51–53.

usages. But clearly statements about our own intentions or about other people's usages are empirical; and since for Ayer all empirical statements were synthetic, these too must be synthetic. And then the preposterous conclusion did follow that all analytic *a priori* statements are really synthetic and empirical. What Broad was doing here was taking the new linguistic theory of the *a priori* at its face value and reducing it to palpable absurdity. And his argument apparently took effect, for the positivists soon dropped the view that such statements reported linguistic fact and took the very different line that they expressed resolutions about usage, a position that is hardly more persuasive. But this was not the only shock that Broad's paper gave to the positivists. He maintained that if the examples commonly given of analytic assertions were typical, such assertions never occurred. "All equilateral triangles are equilateral." No one talks that way or thinks that way. What we have is a sentence without an assertion, a "quasi-propositional sentence," not anything true or false. His position here was the same as Joseph's. "To utter a tautology," Joseph used to insist, "is not to judge, for in all judgment we advance to the apprehension of a new element in the being of a subject already partially apprehended."[15]

Now if this is true, it follows that all actual thinking is synthetic. Would Broad accept this conclusion? He clearly would if by synthetic one means non-analytic and by analytic such silly sentences as the above. But he prefers to give "analytic" a wider meaning. "It seems clear to me that a term may in fact be complex and in fact have a certain analysis, and that people may yet use it in the main correctly without recognizing that it is complex or knowing the right analysis of it. In that case the proposition which asserts that it has such and such an analysis will be analytic, but will not be tautologous."[16] Suppose, for example, that the word "good" actually means *abc,* but that a man does not realize that *c* is present as a component element. In that case the statement that good means (among other things) *c* would be an analytic statement, but it would be neither arbitrary nor verbal nor tautologous; it would be a statement of a formerly unrealized fact about a meaning.

In the light of this wider sense of "analytic," would Broad be content to say that *a priori* statements were analytic? Plainly not. He would hold, I take it, that in the statment "all equiangular triangles are equilateral," there is no reasonable ground for saying that equilateral is an *analysis* of equiangular, or contained in it. Granting that the classes of equiangular and equilateral triangles have the same extension, it does not follow that the intensions of equilateral and equiangular are either the same or

15 *Introduction to Logic,* 2nd ed., 208–209.
16 *FTET,* 173–174.

overlapping. They are two sharply distinct concepts between which as applied to triangles, one sees a connection of reciprocal necessity. Of course such necessity is not always reciprocal. To see that whatever is colored must be extended is not to see that whatever is extended is colored, for the man born blind experiences extension without color. But one-way necessity is nonetheless necessity. And what sort of relation is this? It is clearly not implication, if this means material implication, for in that relation there is no must; "what is colored is extended" would mean only that color in fact never appeared without extension, whereas part of what we mean is that it *cannot* so appear. The relation is one of entailment. And I think Broad would say that on no sensible interpretation of "analytic" could the term be applied to entailment. Whether the term is taken in the Kantian sense, in which the predicate concept is contained in the subject concept, or in Prof. Ayer's sense in which "a proposition is analytic when its validity depends solely on the definitions of the symbols it contains," or in the sense of being guaranteed only by the law of contradiction, Broad would maintain, I think, that there are necessary propositions which are non-analytic. Why do so many present-day analysts rule these out? If their ground is empirical, their confidence is misplaced, since to an empirical generalization an exception may admittedly turn up. Broad thinks that the more probable ground is a belief which can only be described as itself synthetic and necessary. "I strongly suspect that some people accept the theory that there are no synthetic *a priori* propositions because the epistemological principle that *no* synthetic proposition *could possibly* be self-evident (which is certainly a synthetic proposition) *does in fact* seem to them self-evident."[17] In all this I agree entirely.

(4) Broad differs more sharply still from currently fashionable views when he deals with causation. Some philosophers of the day keep a firm rein on their admiration for all their predecessors except Hume, and consider that on the subject of causality and indeed on much else he said practically the last word. Broad disagrees. "I would venture to suggest that we might make better progress in dealing with causation if we were occasionally to stop 'thinking of the Old 'Un,' and to cease pretending *not* to know certain things which we probably all do know, merely because, on his absurd theory of knowledge, it is difficult to see how we *could* know them."[18] He thinks that there are at least four propositions about causality that we can see with self-evidence to be necessary: 1. every change has a cause; 2. the cause of any change contains a change as an essential factor; 3. if a change issues from a moment t, then all

changes which are factors in its causes are changes which enter into *t;* and 4. a given change in a given process issuing from a moment cannot have more than one total cause.[19] It will be noted that these are all extremely general propositions about causality as such. Would Broad hold also that there is necessity in particular causal laws? There are passages in which he seems to deny this unequivocally. "When I say that a certain change which issues out of *t* is caused by certain changes which enter into *t,* all I mean is that, if such changes as these had not entered into *t,* then such a change as this would not have issued out of *t.*"[20] This is just the sort of statement that is made by holders of the regularity view. Again, regarding propositions about mind-body inter- action, he says, "It is certain that propositions of the latter kind can never express anything but contingent brute facts of regular co-exist- ence and sequence."[21] Could Hume ask for more? And yet there is no doubt that Broad would reject any attempt to identify causality with regular sequence. Where does he stand?

He thinks that causality involves something between implication and entailment. On the regular-sequence view, the link between cause and effect is essentially one of material implication; $p \supset q$ means in this con- text that whenever p occurs, q occurs, and that whenever q is absent, p is absent. Broad is clear that we mean more than this when we say that one event causes another. Some kind of *must* is involved. But what kind? Is it logical entailment? Occasionally he speaks as if it were. "Suppose I decide at a certain moment to make a certain movement. Either this movement follows or it does not. If it does, a certain change issues from that moment, with regard to which, it seems to me, I *know* that *this* change would not have issued from that moment unless *that* decision had entered into that moment." [22] It is hard to see how one could *know* this unless the proposition that this movement occurred entailed the proposition that the decision had occurred. Yet Broad shrinks back from the entailment view just as he does from the regular-sequence view. It seems plain to him that particular causal laws lack the sort of necessity possessed by logical or mathematical statements. He puts the matter so well that I am tempted to quote him at length:

Suppose we compare the two propositions 'Anything that had shape would have extension' and 'Anything that had inertial mass would have gravitational mass.' The former corresponds, and can be seen to correspond, to a fact which is necessary. The necessity of this fact is itself necessary, and so on without end. The second, if true at all, corresponds to a fact of which one can only say

19 *Ibid.,* 232–243.   20 *Ibid.,* I, 238.
21 *Ibid.,* III, 606–607.   22 *Ibid.,* I, 243.

that it *is* necessary, but its necessity is contingent. To put it in another way. If the law is true, then 'there *could not be* (in the actual world) things which had inertial mass and lacked gravitational mass.' Yet, even if the law be true, 'there *might have been* (instead of the actual world) a world in which there were things which had inertial mass and lacked gravitational mass.' But on the other hand, 'there *could not have been* a world in which there were things that had shape and lacked extension.' It may be noticed that in English we have the three sentences: 'Nothing has ϕ and lacks ψ,' 'Nothing can have ϕ and lack ψ,' and 'Nothing could have had ϕ and lack ψ.' The first expresses a Universal of Fact, the second a Universal of Law, and the third an Absolute Necessity.[23]

It is in the second of these classes that causal laws belong; they express necessities, but contingent necessities. Broad candidly adds, "The notion of a necessity which is contingent looks like, and probably is, sheer nonsense." But at least when he was writing the *McTaggart* he could see his way to nothing better.

It does not seem to me that contingent necessity is "sheer nonsense." Indeed it is a notion which seems to answer, at least in many cases, to the facts of scientific explanation and which is used by the logical empiricists as the key idea in such explanation. According to them, the standard way of explaining an empirical fact or law is to subsume it under a wider law. One sees a bridge mirrored in the surface of a river, and asks why the image occurs. The explanation is given by bringing the fact under a law of reflection familiar to physicists. But why does the law itself hold? We must proceed as before; we bring the law under a more general law, this time presumably under the Clerk-Maxwell theory of electro-magnetic waves, which brings under a single principle a large variety of optical facts, not only reflection but also refraction, diffraction, dispersion, and interference.[24] Now for the logical empiricists the occurrence of the image in the river would be a case of contingent necessity. In explaining it, one brings it under laws of wider and wider generality; and one can see that if these laws are taken to be true and the subsumption correct, the explanation of the particular fact follows logically. But the only necessity involved is that of the if-then process. In the concluding proposition about what causes the image there is no more necessity than in the generalization from which we start, and in that generalization there is no necessity at all. Outside the formal sciences of logic and mathematics, where explanation is necessary because analytic, no explanation explains in the sense of rendering the *explicandum* intelligible to reason. In the end, the connection between any empirical fact or event and any other is a mere *de facto* togetherness.

[23] *Ibid.*, I, 242–243.
[24] I take the example from H. Feigl in *Readings in the Philosophy of Analysis*, p. 512.

Now when Broad assigns to causal laws a contingent necessity, he appears to be saying, as positivism does, that though they have no necessity in themselves, they still follow with necessity from something else in the constitution of the world. But this something else is itself not necessary because in another world it might be otherwise. Hence in particular causal laws there is something surd and opaque to reason.

There is no way of proving this view mistaken. We cannot, with our present fragmentary knowledge, show that the world is rational through and through, i.e., that to the question Why? about facts and events there is bound to be an answer in terms of necessity. The true issue is whether, in view of the knowledge that we have, it is more reasonable to assume the presence of necessity in causal law, even though yet undiscovered, or, assuming its absence, to give up the search for it. Of course if one starts as the positivists do with a general denial that we can see in causation, taken in general or in particular, any trace of necessity, the negative presumption is plausible enough. But I think Broad would regard that as dogmatism. He admits that we have necessary insights into the general nature of causation; he admits, though more hesitantly, that we have such insights into some particular cases. And my argument would be that if he goes that far, he ought to go farther. He ought to admit the presumption to be reasonable that in every causal law there is at least a latent necessity.

Consider what he concedes to the rationalist. He concedes that whenever we say "This change is caused by that," the particular case comes to us framed in a matrix of necessities. We can see that the change we are accounting for must have a cause, that this cause must itself be a change, that all the factors in this change must enter into the moment from which the effect emerges, and that there must be one total cause and one only. He concedes that when we have willed a movement we can sometimes look back and say we *know* that the movement would not have occurred without the volition. He concedes that when we have made an inference we can sometimes see that the necessary linkage between premises and conclusion was itself a condition of the conclusion's coming to be.[25] He would say, I think with McTaggart, that if a hundred instances of characteristic A had been observed and all had been found to be instances also of B, we should never suppose the connection merely accidental. To be sure, he holds that if we can see no *a priori* connection between the characteristics, this conclusion is unwarranted; "we are not justified in attaching, on inductive grounds, any assignable final probability to any alleged causal law, no matter how numerous and how

25 *Arist. Soc. Proc.,* Sup. X (1931), 154.

uniformly favourable the empirical evidence may be."[26] Is the common-sense conclusion, then, just "a blind impulse?" He does not say this; "it is just conceivable that we have some kind of rational insight in some such cases . . . though we do not reach our conclusion by any known process of reasoning. . . ."[27]

Though Broad admits this as a possibility, he does not take it very seriously. He likes to stay in clear daylight; he has a deep distrust of hunches, vaticinations, and pontifical obscurities, and his readers have profited greatly from this distrust. But here he seems to me over-sceptical. I think the philosopher may quite justifiably accept as a postulate that wherever there is causation there is a necessity which links the terms through their special natures, whether at the time we can see it or not. Broad doubts whether in fact we ever see anything of the sort; and the doubt is justified if necessity means logical entailment between such ideally precise terms as we have in "equiangular triangles are equi-lateral." But I see no good reason for confining necessity to such cases. The sharp line that is now so commonly drawn between necessary and contingent propositions does not correspond to the facts; there is a wide territory between the extremes in which necessity is present in varying degrees of clearness. Consider such cases as the following. A man is facing an operation without an anaesthetic, and the prospect arouses fear. Is it really as unintelligible to us why fear should arise here as it is why water should be formed when hydrogen and oxygen unite? A man is told that his casually purchased ticket has just won the Irish sweepstakes, and he is delighted. Is his delight as intrinsically unconnected with the character of the news as it is with the state of the weather? Someone tells us that Reno is farther west than San Diego, and we say "How odd than an inland state should project farther west than a point on the Pacific coast!" Is there any sense in saying that, given the thought in mind a moment before, the occurrence of the thought that followed is as much a mystery as it would have been if we had remarked instead about the Dalai Lama? Hume and Wittgenstein would presumably have said yes, since they held that no existent is necessarily linked with any other. Common sense would certainly reject this, and though it would not distinguish itself if it tried to single out the terms in any of these cases and the necessary thread connecting them, it is surely right in insist-ing that the nexus is not one of togetherness merely, however often repeated. If we find that all animals that chew their cud are cloven-footed, we stand before the fact baffled; we must accept it, but we see no sort of necessity in it. If we meet with the kind of occurrence just

26 *EMcP*, I, 226.   27 *Ibid.*, I, 227.

mentioned, we do not feel at all baffled; we see not only that Y followed X; we see more or less clearly *why* it followed, i.e., why X should have produced it rather than anything else.

It may be said that these are all special cases, involving mental causation, and that such insight as we have in them approaches or attains the vanishing point when we turn to physical or even psycho-physical causation. This must be admitted. Though we have no doubt that when one billiard ball strikes another, the second will roll away, or that when we next touch a live coal, it will feel hot, we have no notion why. Broad goes so far as to say "it is certain that propositions of the latter kind can never express anything but contingent brute facts of regular co-existence and sequence."[28] I draw back at that "never." The only good ground for saying that we can never discover a reason for fire's giving us a burning sensation is there is no such reason to discover, that what nature presents us at this point is mere brute conjunction. And how could one possibly know that? Granting that we cannot at present give a confident answer, I think the presumption is on the other side; "is there any man of science," Bosanquet once asked, "who, in his daily work and apart from philosophical controversy, will accept a bare given conjunction as conceivably ultimate truth?"[29] There is not. I cannot think this mere prejudice. Indeed we can see on reflection that unless the conviction held in common by the plain man and the man of science is true, then every inductive argument used by science is invalid. If we grant that C necessitates E, we can validly infer that if C occurs, E will follow, or that if E is absent, C too must be absent. But if C and E merely happen together, with no further relation connecting them, then neither the togetherness of C and E in a case before us, nor any run of such cases, however long and unbroken, will give us the least ground for inferring that E will follow C in the future. If a perfectly constructed die were thrown a hundred times and in each case showed a six, could we infer that on the next throw it would probably show another six? Clearly not. If the conjunctions in nature were really contingent, there would be no more ground for expecting that they would continue as in the past than for expecting a leap into novelty. On any theory like Hume's the conformity of nature to law will be, as Montague used to insist, simply "an outrageous run of luck." An inference to the future can be justified, as Broad points out, only if the run of cases can be taken as establishing a presumption that more than chance is involved, that a link of necessity is present. May it be so taken? Only, Broad replies, if we can start by assuming that necessary connections do sometimes occur in nature, and are therefore

28 *EMcP*, III, 606–607.
29 *The Distinction between Mind and Its Objects*, 60.

among the alternatives that the empirical facts might support. Now do we know that they do occur? Only, he goes on, in the case of such clear *a priori* necessities as link equiangularity with equilaterality; we never meet them in the sphere in which induction moves. Hence there is no antecedent probability of their existence in this sphere, and hence again, the inductive case for their existence remains without force.

To my mind, the case is less hopeless than this. There are two reasons. (a) It is not true that in the region where induction operates we are always moving among bare conjunctions. There are many instances of the type just cited in which we can see that the antecedent is such as to tend by its own nature, and not by chance merely, to produce the consequent. Granting that the connection is less satisfactory than in the angles case, it is clearly more than mere togetherness. We do have evidence, therefore, that there are sequences in nature in which intrinsic connections are at work, and hence that the antecedent probability of their presence in other cases is more than zero. It may be said that, at best, all this would show is their existence in the mental field, and that we have no evidence for their existence outside this field. I do not think this is strictly correct. Nor has Broad himself invariably thought so. There is a significant passage in *The Mind and Its Place in Nature* that suggests a different view of our knowledge of the mind-body connection than the sceptical passage we have cited.

Is the connexion between cause and effect as mysterious and as little evident in the case of the voluntary production of bodily movement as in all other cases? If so, we must hold that the first time a baby wills to move its hands it is just as much surprised to find its hand moving as it would be to find its leg moving or its nurse bursting into flames. I do not profess to know anything about the infant mind; but it seems to me that this is a wildly paradoxical consequence, for which there is no evidence or likelihood. . . . It is perfectly plain that, in the case of volition and voluntary movement, there *is* a connexion between the cause and the effect which is not present in other cases of causation, and which does make it plausible to hold that in this one case the nature of the effect can be foreseen by merely reflecting on the nature of the cause. The peculiarity of a volition as a cause factor is that it involves as an essential part of it the idea of the effect. . . . It is simply silly in view of this fact to say that there is no closer connexion between the desire to move my arm and the movement of my arm than there is between this desire and the movement of my leg or my liver. . . . It is therefore by no means unreasonable to suggest that, in the one case of our own voluntary movements, we can see without waiting for the result that such and such a volition is the necessary condition of such and such a bodily movement.[30]

Broad says, as we have seen, that if inductive argument is to be validated, what we need is some antecedent probability for the hypothesis

[30] Pp. 102–103.

that necessary connections exist in nature. Is he not here offering us the very evidence that he holds we need?

(b) As soon as the postulate of a necessary connection is installed by such antecedent probability among the alternatives that induction might establish, we see that the confirmation it receives from experience is overwhelming. Wherever we turn (except perhaps in atomic physics, which Broad thinks is probably no exception after all) we find that nature behaves as if the effect were appointed by the character of the cause. To the assumption "same cause, same effect," there is not one undisputed exception in history. The likelihood that such stability would hold on the hypothesis that the connections were those of chance is of course beyond any precise calculation, as is the likelihood on the other side that they are cases of necessity. But on the basis Broad himself has provided us, namely that there is *some* antecedent probability for necessity, the hypothesis that this is at work becomes at once enormously preferable. And as we have seen, it is the only hypothesis that makes inductive inference anything but a leap in the dark. It may be replied that we cannot accept a theory as true because it would confer on such inference the validity we want for it. Agreed; but the case is stronger than that. The point is that we have made millions of inductive inferences which have been verified by the event, that this confirms the presumption that such inferences are valid, and that this validity implies that cause and effect are connected necessarily. The postulate of such a connection therefore is the most reasonable postulate with which a philosopher can confront the facts.

(5) We have become familiar in recent years with the suggestion that *a priori* statements express conventions only. They are alleged to be rules announcing how we propose to use certain words, and since rules of this kind are obviously matters of choice, we can change the rules at will. There are even alternative logics, no one of which can be said on merely *a priori* grounds to be more applicable to the real world than any other. Where does Broad stand as regards such suggestions?

So far as I know, he has not said a great deal about them. But in the *McTaggart* he has made some remarks that bear on them significantly. Assuming that we probably do have *a priori* concepts, he asks how we have acquired them. Two accounts seem possible. According to the theory of innate ideas we have, for example, "a disposition to form the idea of Cause when presented with instances of regular sequence; a disposition to form the idea of Substance when presented with recurrent bundles of qualities," and so on.[31] Is there any objection to this view? Broad points out that, if carefully stated, it can easily escape the com-

31 *EMcP*, I, 49.

mon objections about assigning abstract ideas to idiots and infants. But there is one consideration that may give us pause about it:

> if the theory of Innate Ideas be true, we have no guarantee that our innate ideas may not be as fictitious as our idea of dragonhood or phoenixhood. On this theory the notions of Cause, Substance, etc., are *read into* perceived objects by human minds. . . . There might be innate racial delusions, and the concepts of Cause and Substance and Rightness and Duty might be instances of such racial delusions. Unless there be some kind of pre-established harmony between the human mind and the rest of nature, it would seem just as likely that our innate ideas should be delusive as that they should be veridical.[32]

The alternative to this theory, with its implications of scepticism, is one of "non-perceptual intuition." On this view, "categories, ethical relations, etc., will be relations or types of structure actually present in reality, but incapable of manifesting themselves sensuously or introspectively, as colours, shapes, and spatio-temporal relations can do," and through our power of non-perceptual intuition we apprehend their presence directly. Broad is apparently inclined to this view.

To me also it seems more responsible than the current conventionalist theories. These give the impression at times of being advocated by minds in blinkers, which are able to see sharply enough the propositions they are analyzing, but have little sense of the implications of their analysis for the rest of our knowledge. If logic is really a set of conventions whose clearness and distinctness are no guarantee of their objective validity, then we have no ground for thinking that any belief we ever hold is true or any inference valid. It may be replied that one cannot change one's analysis of meanings merely because it is awkward for one's theory of knowledge; if it commits us to scepticism, that does not prove it wrong; scepticism may after all be right. There are more answers than one. (a) Such scepticism is gratuitous. Nature apparently behaves in accordance with the three "laws of thought," for example, and until something like an exception can be alleged, the hypothesis of discordance seems idle. And (b) not only has no exception occurred; it seems safe to say that none can occur; such an occurrence is really unthinkable. To say that the law of contradiction is invalid is, I suppose, to accept as true the proposition that a proposition and its contradictory may both be true. Does one accept this of the proposition itself? If one does, one cannot assert it is as true rather than false. If one does not, one is accepting as valid the law one is attempting to deny. (c) When the conventionalist is arguing the case for conventionalism, he seems to have no question of the objective validity of the rules in accordance with which he is arguing. It is because he thinks his case a valid one that he believes others

32 *Ibid.*, 51.

ought to accept it. But one can hardly be permitted to dodge back and forth in this way, and to call the same things, as it suits one's purpose, conventions and objective structures. If such laws are conventions, then the laws in accordance with which one is arguing are themselves conventions, and the argument has no claim to objective validity. If they are taken as objectively valid, then the argument to prove they are not assumes that they are.

The theory of non-perceptual intuition implies the falsity of the view so widely accepted nowadays that a priori knowledge never supplies us with information about the nature of things. Many who have accepted this view have no doubt thought of 'information' in terms of such highly specific items as 'this is red' or 'that is hot'; and no doubt it is futile to look to a priori knowledge for information of this kind. But knowledge is nonetheless knowledge because it is highly general. Broad thinks it self-evident, for example, that "any existent must have some positive original quality beside existence or stand in some positive original relation."[33] Such an insight tells us nothing about one thing rather than another. But it does not cease to be information because it tells us something about everything that has ever existed or will exist. The doctrine that we have no a priori knowledge of the real world is really an unsubstantiated dogma.

III

I have now completed what I have to say about two of the three components of reason as Broad conceives it, namely, a priori concepts and the intuition of necessary connections. I turn to a much briefer comment on the third function, which is described as "ratiocination" or "the drawing of inferences, demonstrative or problematical, from premises."

The one question I shall raise about it is whether there is any process of this kind in ordinary perception. Broad has expressed himself repeatedly and emphatically to the effect that there is not.

It would be false psychologically to say that we infer from the nature of the objective constituent and from any other knowledge that we may have that it is part of a larger spatio-temporal whole of a certain specific kind. It is perfectly evident that we do nothing of the sort. Of course we can talk of 'unconscious inferences' if we like; but at most this means that we in fact reach without inference the kind of conclusion which could be defended by inference if it were challenged. A little later he says of the perceptual level: To believe so and so at this level really means to act as it would be reasonable to act if one believed so and so, and to be surprised if the action turns out to be a failure.

[33] EMcP, I, 131.

And again:

It would be false psychologically to say that this belief exists at the purely perceptual level in the form of an explicit judgment; we must rather say that the percipient adjusts himself automatically in ways that would be reasonable *if* he held this belief, and that the belief is represented at this stage by the bodily feelings which accompany these adjustments and by the feelings of satisfaction or frustration which arise according to the results of acting as if one held the belief.[34]

A similar view has been expressed by Professor Price.

Arguments over whether a certain level of mental development should be assimilated to one above or one below are likely to be futile; there are always analogies supporting each side. I can only say that the weight of analogy here seems to me to favor the old view of Mill and Spencer that what goes on in perception is better understood by finding in it the beginnings of inference than by calling it an "acting as if." Suppose we see a weight marked "100 lb.," walk over to it, brace ourselves, give a mighty heave, and, since it is really made of cardboard, nearly fall over backwards. Have we judged or inferred? On certain points we can only agree with Broad: there has been no preliminary doubt whether this is a weight or not; there is no explicit distinction between data and conclusion; there is no appreciable interval of time between their appearances. We must agree further that the inference, if inference there be, is not a necessary one; things with the looks and markings we saw do not have to be weights. Nevertheless it seems clear to me that a rudimentary inference has occurred.

Certainly more than an "acting as if" has occurred. A mode of behavior can be neither true nor mistaken, and we have plainly made a mistake; is not the natural way of describing what happened to say that we took something, though mistakenly, to be a 100-pound weight? Nor am I comfortable when I read, "the belief is represented at this stage by the bodily feelings," since it is not easier to see how feelings can be mistaken than how actions can. It may be said that neither the data nor the conclusion in this case has the explicitness of full-fledged inference. Admitted. But the important point is that the judgment, the data on which it is based, and the passage between them were all there. That the judgment was there is shown by the recognition that we were mistaken, for only judgment can be mistaken. That the data were there is evident. That some sort of passage occurred seems to be admitted by Broad's own language in various places. "In ostensible sense-perception, whether veridical or delusive, I sense a certain sensum . . . and I automatically and uncritically base on this experience a belief that there is a certain

34 *MPN*, 151, 153, 154.

physical thing or event, outside me in space . . ."[35] When a man has an auditory perception, he hears a sound and "he founds upon this a perceptual acceptance of a proposition of the form: 'There is a noise of this character going on now outside my body . . .' "[36] Now to accept a *proposition* which one *bases* or *founds upon* certain data seems to me what inference means. The fact that the data, the passage and the conclusion are not explicitly singled out is less important than the fact that they are all there, and that the process gives us, what only an intellectual process does, namely truth or falsehood. I do not think that the process which occurs can possibly be understood unless we recognize that it is in principle the same kind of thing, in condensed and implicit form, as we find it in full-blown inference.

I can hardly close this article without admitting that I never differ from Broad with any confidence. He combines acuteness, precision, and clarity in a way that, so far as I know, is without parallel. He might have cut a larger figure if he had written obscurely enough to evoke a crop of doctoral dissertations on what he could possibly have meant. Not that he has avoided, like some of his contemporaries, the profounder issues of speculation. No one who knows his great *McTaggart* could say that. He has proved that, to be a rigorous analyst, one need not forfeit one's interest in the traditional themes of "God, freedom, and immortality;" indeed he has written on just these themes with refreshing force and illumination. But he never lets down the bars. The argument is always close, the expression always precise, while yet the prose flows along with astonishing swiftness, purity, and ease. These things seem to have held of his writing from the beginning. Some philosophers appear to be born, not made.

BRAND BLANSHARD

DEPARTMENT OF PHILOSOPHY
YALE UNIVERSITY

35 *Proc. Arist. Soc.*, Sup. XVI, 183.   36 *EMcP*, II, 67.

7

L. J. Russell

SUBSTANCE AND CAUSE IN BROAD'S PHILOSOPHY

I.

T*HINGS and processes.* I shall deal only with the independent discussions of Substance and Cause in Broad's *Examination of Mc-
Taggart's Philosophy.* Broad's examination of the concept of substance
arises out of his criticism of McTaggart's definition, which involves that
any particular event, such as a flash of light, or a noise, would be a substance. Broad holds that this would go against the common opinion
"that there are at least two fundamentally distinct kinds of particulars"
(I, 139), viz. occurrents or "events" or "states" and continuants or
"things," and, while not suggesting that an opinion is right because it is
the common opinion, he does think that anyone who diverges from the
common opinion ought to show good reasons for doing so. It is the lack
of any consideration of this common opinion which is in his view the
main defect of McTaggart's treatment of substance (142).

Broad's own discussion is concentrated on the contrast between processes and things, and the basic example of a process he uses throughout
is that of a noise going on during a period of time, with or without
changes in loudness, pitch or timbre. It should be noted that he describes
the noise itself, without reference to any "things" causing the noise or to
any sentient being hearing the noise, as an existent particular, as a substantive of which characteristics can be predicated; and he distinguishes
between any short temporal section of it, during which it is not changing in quality, and the determinate quality of which, during this period,
it is a manifestation. The quality itself is a universal, the manifestation
of the quality is an occurrent particular. For Broad this distinction is
an ultimate one, in the sense that, even if it should turn out on examination that the manifestation of the quality consists of this manifestation
and nothing more—e.g. that as so manifested the quality is not a quality
of a "substance"—this would not tempt him to identify it with the
determinate quality itself (133–4).

He begins by considering linguistic usages. In our language we have names for processes and names for things, and there are many forms of expression which are appropriate when we are characterising processes which would be quite inappropriate for characterising things. Processes can be said to start, go on, stop; and these expressions are not used of things. We say of things that they started to exist, went on existing, stopped existing; and Broad thinks that these expressions are significant only in regard to compound things, which are produced by the bringing together of simple things. He says that he can give no meaning to such phrases as "coming to be" and "passing away" as applied to simple things; but adds (145–6) that an individual might nevertheless have good reason to believe (e.g. on divine authority) that certain simple things, such as souls, did come to be, by creation.

I am perplexed as to what kind of "meaning" Broad is seeking after here. He finds no difficulty in speaking of a process as starting and (as we shall see) holds that he can see no reason why all processes should not come to an end without needing a cause for so ending. To say that a process starts at t seems to me to say no more than that it was non-existent immediately prior to t and existent at and immediately after t. Reference to some cause seems not to be involved as giving any part of the meaning of the phrase; if such reference were involved it would be difficult to give meaning to the statement that a process comes to an end without a cause. And I can see no objection to saying of a simple thing that it was non-existent immediately prior to t and existent at and immediately after t. What I think important in Broad's view is that he finds nothing in the concept of a process incompatible with the thought of a process as beginning or ending, whereas the concept of a simple thing or substance does seem to put a very high degree of pressure on him to think of the thing as continuing to exist without beginning or end— though as we have seen he does not go so far as to assert that a simple thing if it exists must necessarily exist without beginning or end. Broad would certainly not be willing to regard this difference as merely a matter of definition of terms. If the concept of a simple thing is to be accepted at all, it would on his view have to be accepted as an *a priori* concept, and its possibility explained on the lines developed on pp. 47ff. Meanwhile it should be noted that at this stage in his discussion he is not accepting the concept of a simple thing as ultimate, but merely asking what would have to be said about simple things if they were accepted as ultimate; and that he is asserting that there is a fundamental difference between the concept of a process and the concept of a simple thing in regard to the possibility of their beginning and ending.

A further important difference between the language we use about processes and the language we use about compound things is this. Processes go on *for* longer or shorter periods of time, things persist or endure *through* time. Again the parts of a process are its successive temporal parts, whereas the successive temporal phases, in relation to a thing, are parts not of the thing itself but of its history (146–7).

I think the important point here is that the distinctions made foreshadow the conclusion Broad comes to later, that a process can be completely described by describing it as the manifestation of varied characteristics during its successive temporal phases, whereas, if we are to follow the clue of ordinary language, a thing cannot be completely so described.

A further distinction mentioned by Broad suggests the same conclusion, viz. that while we can say that we hear the same noise at two different times, and see the same chair at two different times, the word "same" has not an identical meaning in the two cases. The two noises may have been successive, though not adjoining, parts in a single process. But the earlier noise is no longer present when I hear the later noise, nor was the later one present when I heard the earlier one. And we cannot say this of the chair. The chair I now see is the very same chair as the one I saw before.

If we ask, what does a thing have that processes don't have, one very important contribution to an answer is found in dispositional properties. Such a property states what would happen if the thing were in a different state, or were in different circumstances. Thus a substantive can have a dispositional property only if it is the kind of thing that can be in various states, and can stand in different relations to other things at various times while remaining the same substantive (149).

Thus we speak of something as poisonous or as fusible. Such adjectives, Broad says, are properly conjoined with thing-names and not with process-names (148). "Red," as applied to a pillar box, is dispositional in the sense that the pillar box would look red to any normal observer who viewed it in daylight. "Red" as applied to something seen by me on a given occasion is non-dispositional, since it means something which could not possibly be expressed by a conditional sentence. I take it that this means that a visual sensum is something whose nature is exhaustively described when its actual characteristics in its existing relationships have been stated; and that Broad holds that the same is true of processes in general.

II.

Can either Things or Processes be dispensed with? Having noted the differences between the language we use of processes and the language we use about things, Broad goes on to the important question whether, if we are to say adequately all we want to say, it is necessary for us to use both thing-names and process-names, or whether one of them could be dispensed with, and if so, which (151).

He begins by asking, must every process be a state of, or a process in, some thing? and his first point is, that even if we admit that some processes seem to involve reference to things, not all do so. When a movement is taking place, we can always ask what is moving, and sometimes the answer refers to a thing, e.g. a golf ball. And this question is different from the question what is causing the movement to take place. On the other hand, when a noise is going on, we can ask what is making (or causing) the noise, but can we ask what is the subject of the noise, in any sense similar to that in which the golf ball is the subject of the motion?

Broad stresses the fact that our language has no verb "to noise" (153). There are of course a large variety of verbs to express the action of making the variety of noises which occur: shriek, wail, howl, buzz, hoot, etc., and these verbs all have a thing as their subject. But he contends that in each case the subject of the verb is the thing which makes the noise, and that it cannot be regarded as the subject of which the noise is a quality. If one agrees with this, but insists that the noise, considered as an existing process, must nevertheless be thought of as dependent on the vibrations of air, or some other material thing, his reply is exactly the same. The noise is not a quality of the vibrations. If one accepts this, and concludes that it must follow that noises are not processes objectively existing at all, but that when we say there is a noise going on all we mean is that we hear a noise going on, Broad would reply by an analysis of the situation in which we are hearing a noise, into the act of hearing and the noise heard. Even if the noise heard is regarded as mental, still it is not the mind, or any part of the mind, of which the noise is a quality, so that it is still necessary to accept the conclusion that a noise is a process which is not a state of, or a process in, anything.

It should be noted that Broad's admission that in some instances of a movement there is a thing which moves, is only provisional, and he discusses it at a later point in his argument, giving reasons for concluding that even these cases may be capable of interpretation in terms of processes alone. But even if this conclusion were accepted, there would still be justification for the distinction he makes, in the argument under consideration, between a movement and a noise. A movement is a change of place, and for this to be apprehended something other than the change of place itself must be apprehended, as the subject moving. When a coloured patch moves in my visual field, what moves is not a thing, but still the coloured patch is the subject of movement. But when a noise is going on, the case is different. Nothing other than the noise itself needs to be apprehended. There are not two things, the noise itself and that which "noises." This is reinforced by the argument (155) that when a subject ceases to move I can still apprehend it at rest, whereas when a noise ceases, I can't apprehend any quiescent subject. Everything I was apprehending ceases to exist when the noise ceases.

All this, he holds, throws great doubt on the suggestion that every process is a process in a thing or a state of a thing. If there were a process in a thing which was not a state of the thing itself, it would still need to be a state of some part of the thing (154). He concludes this part of his argument with the statement "we must . . . be prepared to admit the possibility of what I will call 'Absolute Processes.' " (156)

The question arises, is a noise, described as Broad describes it, a complete process? It is non-mental, it is an occurrence, it has particularity, it is a substantive which can have various changing qualities. It has been carefully separated from anything which can be said to make or produce it, and from any of the vibrations of particles with which it is correlated by physicists. If his arguments are sound, Broad has shown that it cannot be described as a quality of anything. But are the characteristics he has given it sufficient to enable it to qualify as a complete or an absolute process?

To call something an absolute process seems to imply that it could exist by itself, even though it may need something else to cause it to begin to exist or to change. And Broad does assert in a later part of his discussion that while a cause is needed for any change in a process, no cause may be needed for the persistence of a process which has once begun, provided it continues without any change in quality. "The mere unchanging continuance of a process does not, as such, raise the question, 'Why?' " (232). Can anything of this sort be said of a noise? A hoot can persist after the owl has stopped hooting, but not when the air has stopped vibrating; and even though you insist that the hoot is not a quality of the vibrating air, this does not give it the status of an existent independent of the air.

Broad's example of a noise raises difficulty in other ways. He agrees with McTaggart (168) that whenever there is a hearing of a squeaky noise, there is a squeaky noise. But he holds (174) that "there is no ground for saying that a noise heard by me and a noise heard by you are themselves either spatially coincident or spatially separated. If anyone thinks otherwise he is probably confusing the sensibilia with certain physical events of which they are believed to be manifestations." He also thinks that while it is *logically* possible for unsensed sensibilia to exist, yet there are good reasons for doubting whether there are *in fact* any—as is shown by his discussion, already referred to, of red (a) as a quality of a pillar box and (b) as the visual sensibile which I see when I look at a pillar box. ". . . it is almost certain that the pillar box is red in the dispositional sense, . . . it is highly doubtful whether it is red in the non-dispositional sense, . . . it is quite certain that the sensible is red in the non-dispositional sense, and . . . nonsensical to say that the sensibile is red in the dispositional sense."(149)

What all this comes to is that, if a noise *is* a process, it is a very peculiar process. For (if there are no unsensed sensibilia) it exists only so long as it is being sensed by some one individual, and it seems as if *this* noise is sensed only by *this* individual. Its existence then seems to be bound up with the behaviour of this sensing individual. If I shut my eyes, the red I was sensing ceases to exist. If I go far enough away from the source of a noise, the noise I was hearing ceases to exist. None of this seems to support a conclusion in favour of noises (or any other processes described entirely in terms of sensibilia) as being absolute processes. If noises are existents at all, they seem to exist (on Broad's theory) only as constituents of a total situation which contains an individual actually sensing them. It is only in this sense that it can be said that whenever there is a hearing of a squeaky noise, there is a squeaky noise, if Broad's general account of sensibilia is to be accepted.

It does not seem to me, then, that Broad's arguments go far enough to establish the possibility that there are "Absolute Processes."

III.

Can things be dispensed with in favour of Processes? This however is only one stage of his complete analysis. He has shown that it is doubtful whether all processes are states of things. He next asks "whether processes could be dispensed with in favour of things and certain facts about things" (156), answering in the negative. He deals with this rather summarily, and I do not need to discuss his treatment. More important for my purposes is his question whether Things can be dispensed with in favour of Processes.

In answer to this question he considers the assertion that there cannot be a movement without something that moves. Even in the case of the motion of a wave or of a shadow (transmission of state, as he calls it) there are strong grounds for saying that an accurate description of the situation involves reference to the periodic movements of some stuff (which he calls translation of stuff). Even if what appears as the translation of macroscopic bodies in space were resolved by the atomic physicist into transmission of states in space, these states would still be states of periodic translation of microscopic particles of some other "stuff."

But, he suggests, this other "stuff" could itself be dispensed with if we were willing to accept as fundamental the notion of a Substantival Absolute Space, on Newtonian lines, and the notion of the pervasion of particular regions of this space by different determinate qualities at different times. For then "there would be no 'things' as distinct from regions of Absolute Space; and the latter would not of course 'move' in any sense of that ambiguous word. Ultimately, nothing would be said to 'move' except qualities; and a quality would 'move' in the sense that it pervaded now one and now another region of Absolute Space." (158).

He concludes "It might be suggested then that one must admit *either* translation of stuff *or* Substantival Absolute Space, but that, if you are prepared to accept the latter, you can dispense with the former."

This begins as an *argumentum ad hominem,* directed against Professor Prichard, but I think the final suggestion is independent of this reference.

Broad goes on next to justify in detail the kind of language in which we speak of a process as the same process through a period of time, while changing in certain characteristics, or remaining unchanged in certain characteristics. I can speak of *this* noise, and say that I have been hearing *it* for some time, while it has been getting louder, or again has not changed in loudness, but has altered in pitch. He gives an analysis of statements of this kind in terms of equivalent statements which do not contain any word or phrase "standing for an identical Thing or Subject which *persists through* a period of time." (162). All he has then to do to get rid of Things as ultimate is to resolve the residual "periodic translation of microscopic particles" which might be claimed to underlie the apparent movement of macroscopic bodies, into transmissions of microscopic absolute processes; and this, we have seen, he holds can be done in terms of the pervasion by determinate qualities of different regions of absolute substantival space at different times.

He has however one final matter to clear up. Processes he asserted have no dispositional properties, in the sense in which Things are said to have them; and unless this distinction can be shown not to be ultimate, we shall not be able to dispense with the notion of Things. He promises to discuss this in a later section. When we turn to this later discussion (Ch. XIV) we find no explicit reference back to the earlier discussion, so that we are left to decide for ourselves how the later discussion bears on the problem whether things can be dispensed with in favour of processes.

What he actually does (265 f.) is to discuss "certain things which we all tacitly presuppose in science and common life when we use the conceptions of Cause and Substance," and to show that they cannot all be accepted while being taken literally. We believe that a thing might have been in different circumstances from those in which it in fact was, and that it would then have behaved differently. The dispositional qualities a thing is said to have are qualities which it would show if its circumstances were different. But, he holds, we also believe that the circumstances in which a thing is at any moment are completely determined by the natures and the previous states of the substances in the universe, including the thing itself. And these two beliefs are inconsistent.

We shall see that in his discussion of causality Broad concludes that we have no rational ground for accepting complete determinism. In the present discussion of the common-sense scientific view however he indicates how consistency can be secured without rejecting complete determinism, provided the statement about dispositional properties is given a different interpretation (276). When I say that this metal would dissolve in *aqua regia*, I do not need to presuppose that it could now have been in *aqua regia* instead of where it is, and assert that it would then dissolve. What my statement can mean is that metals of this kind have been found to dissolve in *aqua regia*, that this is one of their constant properties which they will continue to have in future, and that what holds of other metals of this kind holds of this one. The evidence for my statement about this metal consists in experiences of it in the past in other circumstances, in which it has behaved in ways characteristic of its kind.

It follows from this interpretation that statements about dispositional properties can be given meaning without assuming that their substantives could have been in circumstances other than they ever were or are now in, and that hence so far, the possession of dispositional properties is no bar to the replacement of statements about things by statements about processes which make no reference to things. And we may note, to strengthen his case, that we do, (in spite of his denial on p. 148) apply certain dispositional words to processes. Noises are liable to cause fatigue; a smell may cause nausea; a soft light may be soothing, and so on; and consideration of such properties may lead us on occasion to take steps to prevent a process from occurring, or to ensure that it will occur. A process could not now be in a different state from that it is now in. But in saying that a noise with particular characteristics is liable to cause fatigue, all we should have to be able to assert would be that noises of this kind—i.e. noises with identical or very similar characteristics—have been observed in the past to cause fatigue in percipients, and that this is one of the properties which noises with identical or similar characteristics will be found to have in future under similar circumstances. Taken literally, a dispositional quality would not be able to be attributed to a process. A process would only have the qualities it was actually observed to have, and it would have them only in a non-dispositional sense. A process occurring at a different time with identical characteristics would not be the same process. Nevertheless it would still be significant, and for both theoretical and practical purposes important, to attribute dispositional properties to it.

The result then of Broad's discussion of dispositional characteristics in Ch. XIV seems to me to show—so far as it goes—that these are no bar to his suggestion that things can be dispensed with in favour of processes.

But this does not seem to me to be the end of the matter. He notes (166) that even if we did "dispense with" the notion of Things, this would "not mean that the notion of Things is invalid: but only that it is less ultimate than the notion of Processes." This raises a question which Broad does not himself discuss: viz. can the ultimate characteristics we attribute to Things be satisfactorily dealt with, if we accept the view that a complete and satisfactory account can be given of everything that exists without using words which refer to Things?

For Things, as Broad describes them, partly in his own confessions, and partly in his account of "what we all tacitly presuppose in science and common life when we use the concepts of Cause and Substance," have not only dispositional properties. There is a further important respect in which what we attribute to Things differs from what Broad has said about Processes. While compound things can, through natural occurrences (I must avoid the word "processes" here) come into existence and cease to exist, Broad confesses (as we have seen) that he cannot conceive of simple things as doing either, and he thinks that common sense and science would agree with this. Processes can start and stop. Two processes may be identical in characteristics; they cannot be the same process. Simple things, on the other hand, are continuants, and for them to come into being or cease to exist is unintelligible.

Suppose then we take processes as ultimate, what account are we to give of this characteristic of things? It seems clear that the only kind of continuant we could justify would be one which could theoretically come into being or cease to exist, though we might have no empirical grounds for asserting of any particular continuant that it had either come into being or ceased to exist at a particular moment of time. Its usefulness as a tool for investigation of processes might depend on our refusal to accept absence of specific evidence for its presence during a particular period of time as a positive ground for concluding that it had ceased to exist. But this would not justify our going so far as to say that its ceasing to exist was unintelligible.

Let us look at this. If one accepted the view that all existents were absolute processes in Broad's sense, what need would there be for introducing the concept of a continuant?

Take Broad's favourite example of a noise. Although noises as heard by us pervade space, yet each noise has a source; it proceeds from a particular part of space, which may be more or less voluminous. We relate the noise to some occurrence or set of occurrences, taking place within this volume, and producing it. If we interpret these occurrences in terms of processes, we shall have to admit the existence of unsensed processes if we are to maintain the beliefs about causation which Broad thinks are self-evident. For example, he holds it certain that if a change in some quality of a noise issues from a moment t, a change in some process must have entered into that moment. I hear a descending note which I identify as a whistle of a bird sitting on a tree. The change of the note in pitch demands a cause, and I find it in the changes in movement in the bird's throat. But I may see neither these changes nor the bird itself. If I interpret the bird and the movements in its throat as a set of processes (visual, tactual, olfactory, etc.) I must regard these as going on even though neither I myself nor anyone else is aware of them. When the noise ceases, I may think of the particular throat movements as ceasing, but at the same time I think of the throat as a part of the bird, and I do not think of the bird as ceasing. If I look in its direction I shall still see it. Again, even though I may interpret what I see in terms of processes, I think of these processes as related to the same bird. When I see the bird move to the ground and hear it start its song again, I link the visual process with the change of source of the sound, but I do not regard the visual process as the cause of the change of source. I relate both the auditory and the visual process to something different from either, in the bird itself. And my explorations of the processes I am actually aware of, and my expectations about what processes I shall experience under what conditions, are enormously facilitated by these causal references to something which continues to exist and to remain the same, in spite of not being perceived continuously, and even—as explorations relate more and more to what Broad has called microscopic processes—in spite of never being perceived at all, on account of their unperceivability. Perhaps then the concept of a Thing enables us to manipulate without embarrassment the notion of a process which continues to exist when it is not perceived, and which can be referred to by a variety of percipients as the same process for all of them, in spite of the general account of processes as something which, as perceived by me, cannot be the identical process perceived by you (cf. 174) and of which it is doubtful whether you can say that it exists when it is not being perceived (cf. 149).

If the account I have given corresponds to the exigencies of our situation when we are trying to understand Processes, then it looks as if, on the supposition that we start with a view which reduces what exists to Absolute Processes, we shall then find it desirable to introduce the notion of Things in order not to contradict ourselves too flatly in our theoretical account of what a process actually consists in. But this seems to involve that we cannot consistently derive the notion of a continuant or Thing from the notion of a Process; in short, if we begin by dispensing with Things, we must, to be consistent, do without them altogether. And yet it does not seem as if we can do so without too great a sacrifice.

IV.

Causation. In his discussion of causal statements Broad refers only to processes. After explaining what he means by the phrases "a change enters into t," "a change issues from t," he states four propositions which seem to him "*prima facie* self-evident," and two which do not seem to him to be so (232 f.).

The four self-evident ones are (i) Every *change* has a cause; (ii) The cause of any *change* contains a *change* as an essential factor; (iii) If a change issues from a moment *t*, then all changes which are factors in its cause are changes which enter into *t;* (iv) A given change in a given process issuing from a given moment cannot have more than one total cause.

The ones which do not seem self-evident are (v) Every change must have an effect; (vi) If a change has an effect, the latter must contain a change as an essential factor.

All these statements are general. Broad holds that the first four are known to us to be true even though we cannot give an analysis of any of them. If indeed an analysis of any of them is offered in terms of a statement or a set of statements which are *not* self-evident, this he argues is an indication that the analysis is not correct (235). And he confesses that he is unable to give a satisfactory analysis of the statement that A causes B, where A and B are particular changes. He does however make some explanatory comments which may help us to see more clearly what he means by the phrases "a cause," "the cause," "total cause," which occur in the first four statements.

He distinguishes "every change is caused" from "every change is completely determined by causes," on the ground that the latter entails the former, but the former does not entail the latter: and this is important for an understanding of his basic propositions. "When I say that a certain change which issues out of t is caused by certain changes which enter into t, all I mean is that, if such changes as these had not entered into t, then such a change as this would not have have issued out of t. To put it in an equivalent way, any moment *from* which a change of *this* kind issued would be a moment *into* which changes of *those* kinds had entered" (238).

To use Broad's own symbols, let B be an event issuing from t with a certain characteristic ψ_1, and A be an event entering into t with a certain characteristic ϕ_1. Then to say that the ψ_1 changes were caused by the ϕ_1 changes is to say only that if the ϕ_1 changes had not entered into t the ψ_1 changes would not have issued from t. We can abbreviate this conveniently into the statement, "If not ϕ_1 then not ψ_1," the symbol ψ being associated with a process issuing from t, ϕ with one entering into t.

The "equivalent" statement must be noted. It seems to be provided as showing the significance of the difficult phrases "had not entered into t," "would not have issued out of t," and is a generalisation, where the original statement is a statement about a particular case. We can abbreviate it into "Whenever ψ then ϕ." And Broad distinguishes this statement from the statement of complete causal determination, which requires in addition the proposition "Any moment *into* which changes of *those* kinds (ϕ) entered, would be a moment *from* which a change of this kind (ψ) issued," which we can abbreviate "Whenever ϕ then ψ." "Whenever ψ then ϕ" is self-evident, "Whenever ϕ then ψ" is not. If we distinguish in the usual way between necessary and sufficient conditions, we can say that the causal statements Broad regards as self-evident refer only to necessary conditions of a ϕ kind for the issuing of a ψ kind of event, and do not entitle us to speak of sufficient conditions.

This is confirmed by his discussion of the indeterminist position. He agrees that an indeterminist who accepted only propositions of the kind "Whenever ψ then ϕ" could argue that at a particular moment t, his deliberations could issue either in a decision having the characteristic ψ_1, or in one having the characteristic ψ_2 or ψ_3 etc., or in no decision at all. If ψ_1 issues, then ϕ_1 must have entered into t, if ψ_2, ϕ_2 must have entered, and so on. Thus, if all the alternatives ψ_1, ψ_2 etc. are to be open to him, then all the corresponding ϕ_1, ϕ_2 etc. must have entered into t. If the ϕ's are of such a sort that the entering of ϕ_1 into t is incompatible with the entering of any of the other ϕ's, then it will follow that the only alternatives open to him are the decision ψ_1, or no decision at all (239–241).

A cause of a change, then, in Broad's sense, is not a preceding change in the presence of which the change will occur, but merely one in the absence of which the change will not occur.

We must now ask, whether this is all that is involved when Broad speaks of *the* cause of a change, as he does in propositions (ii) and (iii), and in what sense he speaks of a "total cause" in proposition (iv). I shall take the latter question first. Proposition (iv) is expressed negatively. It does not assert that a given change must have one total cause. It only says it cannot have more than one. In his explanation of the proposition (234) he does however speak as if every change did have one total cause. If the proposition is not to be trivial, he says, the total cause of a given change issuing from t must be something less than the sum total of the innumerable changes in the innumerable processes entering into t. It must be a selection from this sum total. Hence, he goes on, "our proposition then . . . denies that *more than one* selection from the changes which enter into t can be the total cause of any change which issues from t." If we insist on the strict meaning of the phrase "*the* total cause" it would seem clear that there could be only one total cause, and that if our denial is to be significant Broad should have written "*a* total cause." The fact that he has written "*the* total cause" seems to indicate that he did not seriously consider the possibility that a change might not have one total cause; and later on in the same paragraph he makes his view clear: "Taking any particular change, the question which we ask, and to which we know that there must be an answer, is, 'What is *the* cause of it?,' not, 'What is *a* cause of it?' And the fact that the question is put in this way implies that we hold that every particular change has one and *only one* total cause" (234).

We have seen previously that he insisted that when he says that it is self-evident that every change has a cause he means only that for every ψ_1 issuing from t there is a ϕ_1 entering into t of such a sort that we can say "Whenever a ψ kind issues a ϕ kind enters." ϕ_1 is a necessary but may not be a sufficient condition for the issuing of ψ_1. If we keep to this, the total cause of any given ψ_1 would be the sum total of the conditions necessary for ψ_1 to issue, where these conditions may not be sufficient for the issuing of ψ_1. Similarly for the total cause of an event with a multiplicity of characteristics. We can perhaps go even further than this. For in his discussion of the indeterminist position he agreed that when all the conditions necessary for ψ_1 are present, then, in the absence of all the conditions necessary for ψ_2 or ψ_3 . . . , if any change of ψ kind occurs, ψ_1 will issue. But, he added, it is still possible that no ψ kind of change will issue at all. He speaks (241) as if we could in this case say ϕ_1 is a sufficient condition for ψ_1; but this is not quite correct. ϕ_1 is a sufficient condition, not for ψ_1, but for the alternative ψ_1 or nothing. And if by a sufficient condition is meant a set of ϕ changes whose entrance into t makes it necessary that the corresponding ψ changes issue from t, then on Broad's view we can have no assurance that any condition is sufficient. When a process has issued from t, we know that there must have been necessary conditions entering into t; but anything we say about sufficient conditions must rest on empirical generalisations. We might (as he says in his discussion of general laws) have empirical grounds for believing a proposition of the kind "whenever ϕ then ψ," and we should then say that the ϕ process was a sufficient condition for the ψ process. But we should always have to admit that in any particular case it was possible that the ϕ process should not be followed by any ψ process.

In his discussion of the proposition that every change must have an effect (which he does not regard as self-evident) Broad takes a rather different line, which seems to me not to give us what we want to know. He argues (237) that "it does not seem self-evidently impossible that there should be a certain moment at which all processes stop and no process begins." What we want to know is not whether a universal stoppage is logically possible, but whether he would say the same about any one particular process. A fire is burning in the grate; the total conditions necessary for its continued burning are present, and no conditions which will prevent it from continuing to burn are present. Even so, if we take what Broad has already said, there is no kind of necessity that it will continue to burn. Our expectation that it will do so is purely empirical. The present has necessary connections with the past; it has no necessary connections with the future.

It seems to me that in this whole discussion Broad is committed to using the phrase "total cause" in a way which is different from its ordinary meaning. As ordinarily used, it would be true to say that if the total cause of a particular event enters into t and if no causes enter into t of such a sort as to prevent the particular event from issuing, then the event will issue from t. The necessary conditions (ϕ) in Broad's sense would not be enough to constitute a total cause in the ordinary sense. For they give us only "If ψ then ϕ;" to make the cause total we shall have to be able to add "If ϕ then ψ." To say this is not of course to condemn Broad's use of the phrase. It is merely to show how he is using it in this discussion.

Elsewhere he uses it in its more usual sense. In his Inaugural Lecture on "Determinism, Indeterminism and Libertarianism" (reprinted in

Ethics and the History of Philosophy) he notes that if an event is completely determined in respect of some characteristic, then there is a set of true nomic, occurrent, dispositional and background propositions which together entail the propositions that this characteristic will occur in a precisely determinate form.[1] The determinate factors of an event completely determined in all respects he speaks of as the total cause of the event; and it seems as if he prefers not to speak of a "total cause" in the case of an event not completely determined.[2] "If Y is the total cause of Z, and X is the total cause of Y, I call both Y and X 'causal ancestors' of Z. Similarly, if W were the total cause of X, I should call Y, X and W 'causal ancestors' of Z. And so on. If at any stage in such a series there is a term, e.g. W, which contains a cause factor that is not completely determined, the series will stop here, just as the series of human ancestors stops with Adam."

This seems a different use of the term "total cause" from that already discussed. With the usage in the *Examination,* W might still have a total cause, viz. the set of conditions necessary (even though not sufficient) for W to occur; so that the series of causal ancestors would not stop with W. It would stop only with a causal ancestor which entered into the time series without any necessary conditions in that series. With the usage in the Inaugural Lecture an event has a total cause if and only if it is completely determined.

There is an interesting argument in the *Examination* which bears on this matter (235–6). Broad is considering one "very common analysis of the statement that a certain particular event B was caused by a certain particular event A," to the effect that (a) B issued from t with a characteristic ψ, (b) A entered into t with ϕ, and (c) whenever ϕ enters into a particular moment (past, present or future) ψ issues from it. And he argues that this analysis is inconsistent with the self-evident principle that B cannot have more than one total cause. For an event A' with characteristic ϕ' might have entered t as well as ϕ and it might be true that whenever ϕ' enters into a particular moment, ψ issues from it. If so we should have to say that B was caused by A' besides being caused by A. Broad does not give a particular example; but we might take the case of a person being shot through the heart by two bullets simultaneously, either of which would cause death by itself. Now it seems clear that the proposed analysis could quite easily take care of a situation of this sort, by including in ϕ all the actual factors of ϕ' etc., which entered into the actual moment t, of which it could be said that whenever ϕ' enters into a particular moment ψ issues from it. Thus in our example, the

[1] *EHP,* 208.   [2] *Ibid.,* 211.

two bullets would be said to be the total cause of death, and the analysis would hold. Whenever two bullets enter a man's heart in this precise way, death occurs. But the analysis would not suit Broad's account of a cause given in the *Examination,* if by total cause is meant only the sum total of conditions in the absence of which death would not occur. For either bullet might be absent, so long as the other bullet was present. And there would be no way of avoiding the admission that each bullet separately was the total cause of death. I think that this may have weighed with Broad in causing him to reject the analysis.

In his discussion of the analysis of Causal Statements (241f.) Broad describes as the "orthodox" analysis of singular causal statements such as "A caused B" an analysis very similar to the one he has rejected. In the new analysis the particular propositions are the same: A with ϕ entered, B with ψ issued. But there are two general propositions instead of one, and they are expressed more explicitly in general form. "(i) From *any* moment into which there entered changes having the characteristics ϕ, ϕ' . . . , there would issue a change having the characteristic ψ. (ii) From *no* moment into which any such changes as are mentioned in (i) *failed* to enter would a change having the characteristic ψ issue." The first of these is the proposition Broad has objected to, the second is the proposition he has stressed in his own account.

Broad's difficulties with this analysis turn (a) on the meaning of the words "would" and "would not" and (b) on what reason we have to believe statements such as (i) and (ii). There are two questions which might fall under (b). The first is the question what reason we have for believing that, in the case of any observed ψ, there is *some* ϕ, and in the case of any observed ϕ there is *some* ψ related in the ways given in propositions (i) and (ii). The second is the question what reason we have for believing that a particular ϕ and a particular ψ are related in these ways. The first question Broad has already dealt with, accepting (ii) as self-evident, and rejecting the view that (i) is self-evident but admitting that we might have good empirical reasons for believing it in particular cases. The second question is the traditional problem of generalisation.

Broad goes on to say that he feels "the gravest doubts" whether the orthodox analysis of singular causal propositions is right. He gives two reasons. Firstly, he thinks that it is "quite certain that, in many cases when I judge that 'this caused that,' I am not thinking at all about general laws and possible parallel cases." Secondly, the propositions that every change issuing from a moment has a cause and that this cause contains as essential factors changes which enter into the moment, seems self-evident, while the propositions giving the orthodox analysis of "A causes B" do not seem self-evident.

I find myself in some perplexity about both these reasons. For they do not affect only the orthodox analysis. They affect Broad's own accounts of cause. We have seen that he gave (238) one half of the orthodox analysis, viz. proposition (ii), as the general part of what he meant by the singular causal statement that a certain change is caused by certain other changes. Thus we might have expected him to say that what was wrong with the orthodox analysis was its inclusion of a general proposition which was not an essential part of this meaning. The fact that he does not take this line may suggest that he intends his doubts to apply to his own discussions.

I cannot accept his view of singular causal propositions. He says (244) that he thinks that there are occasions when I know that a particular change B would not have issued from a particular moment t unless the particular change A had entered into it. He agrees that it may well be a pre-condition of this knowledge that I should already have had experiences of B-like changes issuing from moments into which A-like changes entered. But the statement about this B is not a generalisation from these previous experiences. His view however involves more than this, viz. that my statement that this B had this A as its cause does not have as part of its *meaning* any reference to general cases.

Now it seems to me that I could not really be said to *know* that this B had this A as its cause unless I were ready to admit that the ϕ and the ψ characteristics are connected by a general law. Innumerable changes beside ϕ enter into t. How am I to select ϕ as the set with this intimate relation to ψ unless I know more about it than I can know from this particular instance? My only clue to what more I must know about ϕ will have to be determined by the meaning I attach to the notion of cause. Thus I cannot see how any meaning of "cause" could be restricted to its use in singular instances. The notion of cause seems to me to be essentially a notion involving a general law.

I shall not deal with the important questions arising out of the claim in the *Examination* that the four causal statements about changes are self-evident, partly because I have discussed them elsewhere, and partly because Broad has raised wider questions about *a priori* knowledge and about self-evidence in relation to causal propositions in later papers, which it would be desirable to take into consideration. I wished to confine myself to the discussions in the *Examination*, because of their great intrinsic interest and importance, and because I know of nothing comparable in the history of the subject. They seem to me to stand as a classic example of analysis, and it is relatively unimportant whether Broad himself would still accept their conclusions. What would be of interest would be his present reflections on his offspring, now that it has come of age.

L. J. RUSSELL

THE UNIVERSITY OF BIRMINGHAM
ENGLAND

8

Norwood Russell Hanson

BROAD AND THE LAWS OF DYNAMICS

THE laws of dynamics exercise philosophers. For statements of these laws are obviously empirical. Yet often they seem to resist the idea of disconfirmation. Evidence against the laws is sometimes impossible to conceive.

Newton stressed the empirical basis of dynamics. It is fitting that Professor Broad, who inherited Sir Isaac's rooms at Trinity College, inherited also his interest in the evidence supporting the laws. Thus Broad regards statements of the laws as substantive, descriptive, empirical propositions. Myriad confirmations[1] and a central place in the system of dynamical concepts; these are the only reasons why a macrophysical world in which the laws do not obtain is difficult to imagine.

Others are impressed by the resistance of dynamical laws to falsification. Poincaré is typical of those who view them as conventions, or definitions, or procedural rules, or boundary conditions.[2] Here the empirical aspects of the laws must be explained, or explained away.

Thus, seen through classical dichotomies, classical mechanics is challenging. It springs from empirical propositions against which disconfirmation is not always conceivable,—for this would result not in conceptions which negate those in dynamical law statements, but in no coherent conceptions at all. Apparently we must explain away either the conventional aspects of dynamical laws, or their contingent features, They are not to be allowed to float betwixt and between.

Kant refused to explain away either. He was a better observer of physics than some of his critics. For him, being 'betwixt and between' was a virtue of Newton's dynamics.

So much for the celebrated question 'What is the logical status of the laws of dynamics?' To this Broad, Poincaré and Kant have given important, but single-valued answers.

1 In the physics of molar bodies moving at moderate speeds through 'middle sized' spaces.

2 Cf. e.g., *The Foundations of Science* (Science Press, Pa., U.S.A.), pp. 28, 97, 99, 102, 106, 125, 318, 328.

281

The question itself, however, is misleading. It is like asking 'What is *the* use of rope?' The replies to this are no fewer than the uses for rope. There are as many uses for the sentences which express the statements of the laws of dynamics as there are types of context in which they can be employed. In trying to provide *the* answer to the above query, Broad, Poincaré and Kant have shown how versatile physicists are with the sentences and formulae of dynamics. There is no such thing as *the* law of inertia, *the* law of force, *the* law of gravitation.

Let us set the Broad position into this broader context. I - III will play the history of physics against the history of philosophy, contrasting the actual scientific uses of the laws with philosophical commentaries on the status of dynamical law statements. This ought to raise certain philosophical questions in IV about the relation of the uses of law sentences and the logic of law statements, about the ways in which the latter can be *a priori,* and about one other matter.

Since he is himself a most dynamic body, Professor Broad may no longer be in the position he marked out so clearly forty years ago.[3] This article then, may draw him out to correct misinterpretations of his early views, and to divulge more about his current position. What follows is a philosophical litmus paper. It is hoped that it will not be so base as to incline Professor Broad to acidity in his reply.

I

Dynamical law statements often help to explain physical events. An event is explained when it is traced to other events which require less explanation.

Suppose that on striding into my study I slide abruptly across the floor. It has just been polished. There is no more to say, no need for further explanation. This means not that there is no further explanation, but only that it is too obvious. The effect on perambulation of highly polished floors is no secret. That my floor has been polished is all the explanation needed for this undignified entrance. The general reason why shoe leather slips on polish is not of immediate relevance in explaining why I slipped. Trace an event to incidents which are commonplace and we are rarely interested in tracing it further.

When, however, events are explained by linking them to the laws of motion, this cannot be because the *explicans* is commonplace, like polished floors. Aristotle was able to detect the commonplace. Yet he would have denied at least part of the First Law of Motion, viz.,

3 In *PPR* and *ST.*

Corpus omne perseverare in statu suo quiescendi vel
movendi uniformiter in directum, nisi quotenus a
viribus impressis cogitur statum illum mutare.[4]

This is not obviously true; indeed, the Philosopher treats it as obviously false.[5]

Some Newtonians, however, felt that this law statement explained events not because it expresses an obvious commonplace, but because it needs no explanation. Similarly, that the area within a circle is the maximum for any closed curve of that perimeter needs no explanation. This is what circles are. A statement of the first law of motion sets out how bodies do move; there is nothing further to explain.[6] Dynamical explanations derive from statements like the first law. Why expect that it could itself be explained dynamically?[7]

So the first law describes a kind of event, inertial motion, whose explanation is not obvious, but which in principle requires no explanation at all. What is to be said of this as a comment on the status of statements of the law of inertia?

Certainly some events need less explaining than others. That the Earth moves needs less explaining than that it moves in an ellipsoidal orbit, rotates on its axis, and is carried with the sun through our galaxy. These latter require all the explaining the former does, and more besides.

If that to which I refer when accounting for events needs more explaining than that to which you refer, then your explanation is better than mine. Thus, since Galileo's cosmology required less explanation than did that of his Ptolemaic adversary, Galileo's was better.[8] Because Aristotle's account of the natural motion of bodies required more ad hoc explanation than that rendered in the law of inertia, Newton's was the better explanation.[9]

The best explanation, then, must show how an event which needs

---

[4] Newton, Philosophiae Naturalis Principia Mathematica, Axioms.

[5] Aristotle, De Caelo (tr. Ross), Oxford University Press, 276a (22ff.), 277a (14ff.), 294b (32ff.). Physica, 256a (5–21), esp. 11, 29 & 30, 256b, 258b, (10ff.), 260a (1.12ff.), esp. 265a (13, & lines 28–35), 266b (25–35) & 267a.

[6] Cf. Galileo, "It does not seem expedient to investigate what may be the cause of acceleration." Discorsi, 3rd Day, Opere VII, p. 202, & Newton ". . . I have not been able to discover the cause of those properties of gravity from phenomena . . . it is enough that gravity does really exist, and act according to laws which we have explained. . . ." Principia, Conclusion.

[7] Principia, Cf. Cote's Preface to the Second Edition (1713).

[8] Cf. Dialogues Concerning the Two Chief World Systems (Univ. of Cal., 1953), The First Day, esp. 45, 52, Second Day, esp. 114, 115ff., 188ff., 248, 253, 257ff., The Third Day, esp. 320ff., etc.

[9] On the lunar motion alone Newton's account is superior. Aristotle and Ptolemy could make the same observations as did Newton.

no explanation, e.g. inertial motion, is connected with observed events. But by this it appears that the goal of physics is to explain the contingent in terms of the *a priori*, to account for events needing explanation in terms of those which need none at all. This idea is not absent from the history of mechanics. Latter-day Newtonians treated dynamical law statements as if they needed no explanation whatever.[10] For various reasons they seemed prescriptive, immutable, *a priori*. Indeed, this is what they were designed to be,—the ultimate shackle in chains of physical explanation.[11] Many physicists have used dynamical laws thus.

Apparently the first law of motion needs no explanation because it could not be false. Yet it tells us what happens in nature, what would happen if certain conditions were realized. Thus the empirical grounds for asserting the first law are events like slipping on a polished floor, or observing how a round rock moves across ice with only slightly diminishing velocity until it slows to a halt. When the law seems not to hold, the reason can always be found,—ground glass on the ice perhaps, or the discovery that the rock is a lodestone, etc.

So the law encapsulates and extrapolates much information about events. Yet it seems also to be beyond disconfirmation. It could not but be true. It needs no explanation. It is self-explanatory, like the statement that the area enclosed by a circle is the maximum for a closed curve of that perimeter. Apparent disconfirmations only reveal that some condition of inertial motion is not fulfilled. Some other law of nature,—e.g. of friction, or of magnetic attraction,—is intruding.

"But surely, after having been kicked across the smoothest ice, a rock could stop abruptly. It could return to where it was kicked, or even describe circles.[12] This could happen without ground glass, magnets, or anything else. Is this not possible?"

Here some will reply "Yes," others "No." The latter might continue: "once in motion a rock cannot suddenly stop unless something stops it. It cannot return to the kicker's toe unless something brings it back,—a magnet, or a jet of air, or invisible threads. It cannot turn circles unless guided by e.g. imperceptible grooves in the ice. It would not be a rock, not even a physical body, unless when free of impressed forces it was

---

[10] Atwood and Whewell and Lagrange may be cited; the Royal Society of the late 18th and early 19th centuries was full of physicists of this temperament.

[11] Cf. esp. Helmholtz. "To understand a phenomenon means nothing else than to reduce it to the Newtonian Laws. Then the necessity of explanation has been satisfied. . . . The task of physical science is to reduce all phenomena of nature to forces of attraction and repulsion the intensity of which is dependent only upon the mutual distance of material bodies. Only if this problem is solved are we sure that nature is conceivable. . . ." *Über die Erhaltung der Kraft* (Berlin, 1847).

[12] Compare Galileo, *op. cit.*, 28–32.

'in statu suo quiescendi vel movendi uniformiter in directum.' Anything else is unthinkable."

When others would regard anomalous events as falsifying the law, such a person says "that shows the presence of some hidden mechanism.[13] Either that or what we took for a rock is not a rock at all." The law of inertia is less vulnerable to experience for him than for others. He may even regard anything which apparently disconfirms the law as itself guaranteeing that despite appearances the moving body was not free of impressed forces; or really did move in a straight line; or is no ordinary physical body. We all reason this way sometimes. Physicists observing rocks on ice certainly do so. In the ordinary mechanics of middle-sized bodies a statement of the first law is practically invulnerable. It could not be false. Whatever proves a body's motion not to be rectilinear also proves that it is acted on by forces.

Thus a form of words 'If A then B,' at first used so that what it expresses could be false, comes to express what could not be false.[14]

Alcohol boils at 78.3°C. Many people, even alcoholics, do not know this. But most of them know what to look for when asked 'Is that fluid alcoholic?,' 'Is there alcohol in the beaker?,' 'Is the liquid in the beaker boiling?' and 'What does the thermometer indicate?' They know how to answer 'What did the thermometer indicate when the alcohol boiled?'

It always reads 78.3°C.;[15] we learn this empirically. So invariant is this that it is virtually part of what we mean by 'alcohol,' at least in science. A fluid that does not boil at 78.3°C. is not alcohol. That it should be is inconceivable. So too the suggestion of a rock moving in a circle *proprio motu* over ice makes the physicist's imagination boggle.

In general, to say that something is A (e.g., alcohol), is to remark a characteristic cluster of properties a_1—a_n (e.g., a clear, bright, liquid with a unique odour and viscosity). To say that something is B (e.g., boiling), is also to remark a cluster of features b_1—b_n (e.g., an agitated fluid whose surface is broken with bubbles and steam). Put A in circumstances C (where c_1—c_n involves being in a hot beaker containing a thermometer registering 78.3°C.). The result of a few trials of this might be summarized 'if A is put in C it becomes B.' If presently we find a_1—a_n in circumstances c_1—c_n, but b_1—b_n *absent*, we might quickly say 'So it is not really true that any A placed in C becomes B.'

[13] This reasoning led to the discovery of Neptune by J. C. Adams and U. J. Leverrier, (1846); the greatest triumph of Newton's mechanics. The companion stars of Sirius and Procyon were also discovered before they were seen.

[14] Cf., Pap, A., *The a Priori in Physical Theory* (New York, 1946), pp. 1–55; Lenzen, V. F., *Physical Theory* (New York, 1931), pp. 10–15, & parts I & II.

[15] When the fluid is free of impurities and the experiment free of abnormalities. These conditions will be assumed.

If however, we never happen upon a_1-a_n in c_1-c_n where b_1-b_n are absent, then the property 'becoming B in C' may get 'built into' the meaning of 'A.' We are not bound to do this. But we may do this and often we do do this. When we do, the form of words 'A in C is B' becomes a formula permitting us to infer directly, and without possibility of error, from something's being an A in C to the presence of B.

At first 'A in C is B' simply summarized a few trials of A in C. The occasional absence of B could have been countenanced,—just as we can now countenance a piano with red keys, or a Cambridge winter without rain. B's absence would only have led us to deny that *every* case of A in C is also B. But when 'b_1-b_n' is put into the meaning of 'A is in C,' the absence of B when A is in C is inconceivable. Whatever colour its keys, a piano must be a percussive stringed instrument. A Cambridge winter must include Saint Valentine's day, whatever the humidity. And whatever else alcohol may do it must boil at 78.3°C.

Undeniably, the laws of physics, the laws of dynamics in particular, are used sometimes so that disconfirmatory evidence is a conceptual possibility, and sometimes so that it is not. This is not the historical point that physical laws begin life as empirical generalizations, but (through repeated confirmations, and good service in theory and calculation) they graduate to being 'functionally *a priori*.' Lenzen and Pap mark this well. Broad concedes the point, but, insists that the 'cash value' of dynamical law statements always rests in their original relation to observation. Poincaré demurs: the laws of physics must, of course, keep in touch with experience. But the possible orderings of experience are limitless.[16] We enforce upon the subject matter of physics the one we choose. Our choice is determined by whether or not the ordering systematises what we know, and predicts new phenomena as well.

These authors seem to regard the shift in a law's logical character,—or meaning, or use,—as being of primarily historical interest. They all agree that at any one stage in the development of physics a law is treated in just *one way,* as empirical or as 'functionally *a priori*.' In 1687 the law of inertia was essentially an empirical extrapolation, while in 1894 it functioned in an *a priori* way.

---

[16] Compare James, ". . . all the magnificent achievements of mathematical and physical science . . . proceed from our indomitable desire to cast the world into a more rational shape in our minds than the shape into which it is thrown there by the crude order of our experience." *Essays in Pragmatism* (Hafner, 1948), 38.

and Sigwart: "That there is more order in the world than appears at first sight is not discovered *till the order is looked for*. . . ." *Logik*, bd. 2, 5.382.

and Weyl: "we do not find but enforce the general principles of natural knowledge. . . ." *Philosophy of Mathematics and Natural Science* (Princeton, 1949), 148, lines 26–28.

This is inadequate. It derives from the belief that a law-sentence can at a given time have but one type of use. But the sentence on page 283 can express as many things named 'The Law of Inertia' as there are logically different uses to which that sentence can be put. Now, just as in 1894 and in 1687, dynamical law sentences are used sometimes to express contingent propositions, sometimes rules (recommendations, prescriptions, regulations, conventions), sometimes *a priori* propositions where a falsifying instance is unthinkable, i.e., psychologically inconceivable, and sometimes formally analytic statements whose denials are self-contradictory. Most philosophers, and this may include Broad, have not appreciated the variety of uses to which law sentences can be put at any one time,—indeed even in one experimental report. Consequently, they have thought that what physicists call 'The Law of Inertia' is a discrete, isolable proposition. It is in fact a family of statements, definitions and rules, all expressible via different uses of the Latin sentence on page 283. They have tried to make plausible single-valued answers to a question which differs little from 'what is *the* use of rope?' Once having decided this, they must deprecate other obvious and (for their theses) awkward uses of dynamical law sentences.

II

After this cursory discussion of the contingent and *a priori* aspects of the law of inertia we may consider in detail the mighty second law:

Mutationem motus proportionalem esse vi motrici impressae, et fieri secundum lineam rectam qua via illa imprimitur.[17]

With many physicists Broad stresses the experiential root of the second law, as with the first. This rests in the sensations accompanying muscular exertion when we pull, push and lift.[18] This effort we call *force,* our experience of which is direct and not further definable.

The direction of a moved body's acceleration is that in which we work our muscles. So, like acceleration, force is representable in vector notation.

Different amounts of force are required to produce a given acceleration in, e.g. a cannon ball and a tennis ball. A given amount of force will produce different accelerations in these bodies. However, the direction of acceleration is constant for all bodies, cannon balls and tennis balls alike. Therefore, to each body must be assigned a certain scalar

17 *Principia,* Axioms.
18 Cf. e.g., Broad, *ST,* 162. Compare Mach, *Science of Mechanics* (Open Court, 1942), pp. 244–246. & Joos, *Theoretical Physics* (Blackie, 1951), p. 82, line 4.

property. Let us call it *the inertial mass m*. The simplest equation embracing all of this is:

$$F = ma = m \frac{dv}{dt} = m \frac{d^2r}{dt^2} \quad [19]$$

Forces derive from many sources, of which muscle power is one variety.[20] Physics in general is concerned with the nature of these. Mechanics simply takes forces as given, whatever their nature. It is concerned only with computing their effects, not their genesis.[21]

$F = m \dfrac{d^2r}{dt^2}$ allows essential computations to be made. But within mechanics questions about what 'F' represents are irrelevant.[22]

Nonetheless, '$F = m \dfrac{d^2r}{dt^2}$' has many distinct uses within mechanics.

Consider these accounts:

I. 'F is *defined* as $m \dfrac{d^2r}{dt^2}$. In dynamics that is what 'F' means. It would be self-contradictory to treat 'F' as if it were not strictly replaceable by '$m \dfrac{d^2r}{dt^2}$.''

II. 'It is psychologically inconceivable that F should be other than $m \dfrac{d^2r}{dt^2}$. A world in which this did not obtain might be possible. But it is not a world of which any consistent idea can be formed. On this equation rests all macrophysical knowledge. Were the world not truly described thus, the system, so useful in dealing with machines, tides, navigation and the heavens, would crash into unthinkable chaos.'

III. 'Perhaps, despite all appearances, $F = m \dfrac{d^2r}{dt^2}$ is false,—unable adequately to describe physical events. Perhaps another set of conceptions could be substituted. Nonetheless this would be unsettling. $F = m \dfrac{d^2r}{dt^2}$ facilitates the collection and organization of a mountain of facts and theory. It patterns our ideas of physical events coherently and logically. So a statement of the second law cannot be falsifiable in any ordinary way, as are the statements which follow from initial conditions in accordance with this law.'

[19] m is assumed constant. A more cautious formulation would be $F = \dfrac{d}{dt} (mv) = \dfrac{du}{dt}$, which leaves open the question of the constancy of mass. (Cf. Kaufmann, W., *Göttinger Nachrichten*, Nov. 8, 1901.)

[20] *Principia*, p. xvii, lines 26–27.

[21] *Ibid.*, p. 5 (last para.), & p. 192 Scholium.

[22] As Broad suggests, *PPR*, 349, lines 8–10.

IV. '$F = m \dfrac{d^2r}{dt^2}$ summarizes a large body of experiences, observations, and experiments of mechanical phenomena. It is as liable to upset as any other factual statement. Disconfirmatory evidence may turn up tomorrow. Then we should simply write off $F = m \dfrac{d^2r}{dt^2}$ as false.'

V. '$F = m \dfrac{d^2r}{dt^2}$ is not a statement at all, hence not true, false, analytic, or synthetic. It asserts nothing. It is either

a) a rule, or schema,—by the use of which one can infer from initial conditions, or

b) a technique for measuring force, or acceleration, or mass, or

c) a principle of instrument construction. To use such an instrument is to accept $F = m \dfrac{d^2r}{dt^2}$. No result of an experiment in which this instrument is used could falsify the law. Or

d) it is a convention, one of many ways of construing the phenomena of statics, dynamics, ballistics and astronomy.

e) '$F = m\dfrac{d^2r}{dt^2}$' demarcates the notation we accept to deal with macrophysical mechanics.'

Our concern here (a–e) is not with the truth or falsity of statements of the second law. We are interested only in the utility of $F = m \dfrac{d^2r}{dt^2}$ as a tool for controlling and thinking about dynamical phenomena.

The actual uses of '$F = m\dfrac{d^2r}{dt^2}$ will support each of these accounts.[23] This means not just that among physicists there have been spokesmen for each of these interpretations. A particular physicist, on a single day in the laboratory, may use the sentence '$F = m\dfrac{d^2r}{dt^2}$ ' in all the ways above, I–V, without the slightest inconsistency. Examples of this follow.

Every physics student knows of Atwood's machine. Two unequal masses, m_1 and m_2, are fixed to the ends of a (practically) massless thread, running over a (practically) massless, frictionless pulley.

---

[23] These accounts (I–V) are neither exclusive nor exhaustive. In particular, V overlaps with I–IV. A definition or an empirical generalization can function as a rule of inference. So V is not necessarily an alternative to I, II, III or IV, as some philosophers have supposed. Furthermore, IV may be construed in either of two ways,—where $F = m\dfrac{d^2r}{dt^2}$ is regarded as an historical statement of how the physical world has behaved up until the present moment (a possible but rather bizarre position), or where it is taken as a general descriptive statement which nonetheless involves expectations as to the future. Finally, 'psychologically inconceivable' is probably not the best expression for denoting what II intends. It suggests an inflexible reactionary grumbling 'unthinkable' or 'inconceivable' at anything new or unfamiliar. Something much more serious is meant, as the sequel may disclose.

Assign the following arbitrary values to m_1 and m_2:

$m_1 = 48$ gm.

$m_2 = 50$ gm.

Then,[24]

$$a = 980 \frac{50-48}{50+48} = 980 \frac{2}{98} = 20 \text{ cm/sec}^2$$

This is predicted by the second law of motion.

A well-known physics book follows a similar account with the query:

Suppose we perform the above experiment and find experimentally a value for *a* which agrees with the predicted value . . . *Does it mean that we have proved Newton's second Law?*

The author continues,

. . . this question is absurd, since Newton's second law is a definition and hence incapable of proof . . . the Atwood machine is essentially a device for measuring the acceleration of gravity *g* by the determination of *a* rather than a setup for the verification of Newton's second law.[25]

This exemplifies account I. Physicists do use the second law-sentence to express a definition when they need to. They have done so for three centuries. When so used, any statement potentially contradictory to what the second law-sentence expresses may be dismissed as absurd.[26]

---

[24] By the second law, the unbalanced force on m_1 is $f - m_1g = m_1a$. The unbalanced force on m_2 comprises its weight m_2g, plus the upward pull (F) of the string. This can be expressed as $m_2g - F = m_2a$

Thus

$F = m_2g - m_2a$
$\quad = m_2 (g-a)$

Substituting this in

$F - m_1g = m_1a$:

$m_2 (g-a) - m_1g = m_1a$

or $\quad m_2g - m_2a - m_1g = m_1a$

This is the same as $\quad a(m_2 - m_1) = g(m_2 - m_1)$

And from this it follows that

$$a = g \frac{m_2 - m_1}{m_2 + m_1}$$

[25] Kolin, A., *Physics* (McGraw-Hill, 1950), pp. 46–47. Compare Humphreys and Beringer, *Atomic Physics* (Harper, 1950), ". . . Newton's laws are not physical laws . . . but are definitions of the basic concepts in dynamics . . . Newton's second law provides us with a working definition of force. . . ." (pp. 38–39.)

And Clerk Maxwell, *Matter and Motion* (London, 1920), ". . . 'impressed' force . . . is completely defined and described in Newton's three laws of motion. . . ." (III, 40, p. 27.)

And Poincaré, *Science and Hypothesis* (London, 1905) ". . . This law of motion . . . ceases to be regarded as an experimental law, it is now only a definition," (p. 100).

[26] Compare Newton, *Principia*: ". . . (this) will make the system of the two bodies . . . to go forwards *in infinitum* with a motion continually accelerated; which is absurd and contrary to the first law . . ." (p. 25), (the first law is, of course, but a special case of the second, i.e., where $\Sigma F = 0$). Similar arguments can be found throughout the *Principia*.

George Atwood himself found it useful so to use the second law-sentence.[27] However, were the second law nothing but "a definition and hence incapable of proof," Atwood wasted his time in writing the *Treatise*. For his famous machine was invented solely to demonstrate the empirical truth of statements of the second law.

In the 18th century a statement of the second law was regarded universally as a 'substantive statement;' a contingent, universal, descriptive proposition. Atwood remarks:

> . . . the laws of motion . . . ought not only to be strictly consistent among themselves, but with matter of fact . . . since any single instance which could be produced of a disagreement or inconsistency, would invalidate the whole theory of motion. . . ."[28]

The object of Atwood's neglected *Treatise* was to show that attacks by Bernoulli, Leibniz and Poleni on the validity of the second law rested on the evidence of improperly constructed apparatus.[29] He aimed to verify the law statement as a substantive statement of fact.[30]

With an accurate scale mounted behind m_2, a well-made pendulum, a silk thread of negligible mass and a light pulley (mounted in four friction wheels), Atwood showed that when $m_1 = 48$ gm., and $m_2 = 50$ gm., then the acceleration of m_2 is indeed 20 cm/sec^2.[31] The results were carefully recorded and generalized. They squared with the predictions of the second law. For Atwood this fully confirmed the law.

The point is, if Atwood thought his experiment to *verify* the law, then it must have been possible, in his view, that the machine *could*

[27] Atwood, G., A TREATISE ON THE RECTILINEAR MOTION AND ROTATION OF BODIES, WITH A DESCRIPTION OF ORIGINAL EXPERIMENTS RELATIVE TO THE SUBJECT. Cambridge 1784. Cf. p. 4, ". . . the laws of motion have been esteemed not only physically but mathematically true. . . ."

[28] *Op. cit.,* p. 30.

[29] *Op. cit.,* p. 33. "Many experiments have been produced . . . to disprove the Newtonian measure . . . it immediately belongs to the present subject to determine whether the conclusions which have been drawn from these experiments arise from any inconsistency between the Newtonian measures of force and matter of fact . . . ," p. 30.

[30] In this he only obeyed Newton's dicta:
". . . the qualities of bodies are only known to us by experiments, we are to hold for universal all such as universally agree with experiments. . . ." (III Appendix, Rule Three).
". . . we are to look upon propositions inferred by general induction from phenomena as accurately or very nearly true . . ." (Rule Four).
". . . particular propositions are inferred from the phenomena, and afterwards rendered general by induction," (p. 547).
". . . analysis consists in making experiments and observations and in drawing general conclusions from them by induction . . ." (*Optiks,* 1721, p. 380).

[31] Cf. *Treatise,* pp. 298ff., and the careful drawings of the apparatus.

have turned up evidence against the law-statement. If nothing can falsify a proposition, nothing can verify it either. It was logically possible that m_2 should have accelerated at 5 cm/sec², or 50 cm/sec².

This exemplifies account IV. There the second law-sentence was used to express a contingent universal statement, against which disconfirmatory evidence might weigh at any time. Doubtless this commended itself to Professor Broad when he wrote:

> . . . It is certain that the Second Law, as originally stated, was not intended for a definition of force but for a substantial statement about it. Unquestionably the sensational basis of the scientific concept of force is the feelings of strain that we experience when we drag a heavy body along, or throw a stone, or bend a bow.[32]

It is certain also, that Newton often puts the law-sentence to this use.[33]

So we have two distinct uses to which physicists have put '$F = m\dfrac{d^2r}{dt^2}$.'

They have used the sentence which expresses the law-statement in different ways; as the result of definitions (account I), and as an empirical generalization (account IV). Other uses must be considered as well, although the foregoing constitutes our salient contrast.

Account II tendered a use of the second law-sentence which, while it expressed what obtains in nature, still seemed inhospitable to any idea of evidence against the second law. Indisputably physicists do use laws thus, now as in the 18th century. Thus Atwood says:

> [The] Laws of Motion are assumed as Physical Axioms; . . . although the mind does not assent to them on intuition, yet as they are of the most obvious and intelligible kind . . . appear the most proper to be received as principles from which the theory of motion in general may be regularly deduced. . . .[34]

He continues:

> These three physical propositions, having been assumed as principles of motion, reduce the science of mechanics to mathematical certainty, arising not only from the strict coherence of innumerable properties of motion deduced

---

[32] *ST*, 162, and compare 163 (bottom), and 164 (lines 16–18).

[33] ". . . (in) the laws of Nature . . . there appears . . . not the least shadow of necessity. . . . These therefore we must . . . learn . . . from observations and experiments. . . . All sound and true philosophy is founded on the appearances of things. . . ," (*Principia*, Cote's Preface).

". . . such principles . . . are confirmed by abundance of experiments. . . ." (p. 21, Scholium)

Compare further references in the *Principia*, pp. 24 (lines 28–29), 294, 325–326, 398 "*. . . the laws observed during the motion of bodies acted on by constant forces admit of easy illustrations from matter of fact.*" (My italics); also pp. 308, 329, para. III.

[34] *Op. cit.*, 2.

from them a priori, but from their agreement with matter of fact. . . .[35]

And then

. . . there is no kind of motion but what may be referred to (these) three easy and obvious propositions, the truth of which it is impossible to doubt. . . .[36]

Compare William Whewell writing in 1834:

. . . the laws of motion . . . are so closely interwoven with our conceptions of the external world, that we have great difficulty in conceiving them not to exist, or to exist other than they are . . . If we in our thoughts attempt to divest matter of its powers of resisting and moving, it ceases to be matter, according to our conceptions, and we can no longer reason upon it with any distinctness. And yet . . . the properties of matter . . . do not obtain by any absolute necessity. . . there is no contradiction in supposing that a body's motion should naturally diminish. . . .[37]

Physicists often use dynamical law-sentences as described in account II. They regard them as empirically true, and yet such that evidence against them is unthinkable.

Philosophers may say that these physicists are confused. This might be hasty. Certain physical systems, e.g. classical mechanics, *are* empirically true of certain subject matters, e.g. the dynamics of 'middle-sized', low speed particles. But then the fundamental propositions on which the system rests must in some sense be empirically true as well. However, these are often treated as axioms; they *define* the subject matter to which the system can apply. Then, nothing describable within the system could refute the laws. Disconfirmatory evidence counts against the system as a whole, not against any of its fundamental parts; it only shows that the system does not hold where it might have held. No part of classical mechanics enumerates contexts in which it will apply. So no part of

---

35 *Op. cit.*, 4. Atwood was trying to say something about physics which is true and important, however unreceptive may be our own logical predilections. Contemporary physics abounds with comparable statements. They are the backbones of systems which explain, describe and predict ranges of physical phenomena. Yet any idea of disconfirming them seems impossible within the system. Thus "The laws of mechanics are the same for all reference frames," and "Nothing travels faster than light" are used within Relativity physics as descriptive of the universe, and yet in a way prescriptive of the universe of discourse. Similarly, an electron whose 'state' could be *exactly* specified (abrogating the Uncertainty Relations) is a conceptual impossibility within wave mechanics. We must not forget, moreover, that the reason we feel sure there are neutrinos is that, if there were not, the Principle of the Conservation of Energy would not hold. This is unthinkable. Cf. Fermi, E., *Elementary Particles* (Oxford Univ. Press, 1951), 2.

36 Atwood, *op. cit.*, 279.

37 Whewell, W., *Astronomy and General Physics* (London, 1834), 211f.

the system is proved false when it is discovered not to apply in some context.[38]

So dynamical law-statements are empirically true, because the system in which they are set is empirically true. But counter evidence does not disconfirm them. Only in terms of these statements can evidence relevant to the hypotheses of the system be appreciated as confirmatory or disconfirmatory.

Account IV minimizes this systematic setting of the second law of motion. Sometimes it is right and proper to do this. But often the physicist is concerned with the *system* of dynamics, within which nothing disconfirms the law statements because they 'select' those types of phenomena to which the system applies.

Suppose no alternative systems of concepts were available with which to describe and explain a type of phenomenon. The scientist would then have but one way of thinking about the subject matter. Aberrations in the perihelion of Mercury made 19th century physicists uncomfortable. But to have scrapped celestial mechanics then would have been to refuse to think about the planets at all.[39] In this sense classical dynamics[40] is empirically true of macrophysical phenomena. What system could offer a 'more accurate' account of a collision between billiard balls? Yet dynamics is true in such a way that the idea of evidence which would falsify its laws often cannot be formed.

Account II would on some occasions be supported by most physicists, in theory and in practice.[41]

38 Compare Wittgenstein: ". . . that it can be described by Newtonian mechanics asserts nothing about the world; but *this* asserts something, namely, that it can be described in that particular way in which as a matter of fact it is described . . ." *Tractatus*, 6.342.

39 ". . . the relegation of a question to being a 'false' problem is only possible and can only become fruitful on this condition; it must create the freedom necessary for the establishment of the required abstract interconnections . . . ," Heisenberg, *Philosophic Problems of Nuclear Science*, (Faber 1952), 47.

40 Or its equivalent in the wave mechanics of large quantum numbers, or in the relativity mechanics of small space-time regions.

41 The synthetic *a priori* view of dynamical law statements, first articulated by Kant (*Kritik der Reinen Vernunft*, 1781), and later by Natorp (*Logische Grundlagen der Exakten Wissenschaften*) and Cassirer (*Determinismus und Indeterminismus in der Modernen Physik*, Göteborg, 1937) is not to be dismissed as a quaint philosopher's invention. It was an important, if misguided, attempt to do justice to actual uses of dynamical law formulae in physics. Physicists still try to do justice here; thus Professor Peierls writes "People sometimes argue whether Newton's second law is a definition of force or of mass, or whether it is a statement of an objective fact. *It is really a mixture of all these things;* . . ." *The Laws of Nature* (Allen & Unwin, 1955), 21. Compare Broad "This mixture of convention and observation is a very common feature in scientific laws . . . ," *ST*, 160. These remarks are important. But law statements are not *mixtures* of the synthetic and the *a priori*, of definition and fact, of convention and observation. The second law formula can be used in physics in many

This leaves accounts V and III to be discussed.

V is familiar enough. When invoked as an 'inference pattern' the second law is not likely to be called into question by any of the conclusions which it warrants. Would $(p \cdot (p \supset q)) \supset q$ be upset by any conclusion drawn in accordance with it? In Atwood's machine, if initial conditions are given as $m_1 = 48$ gm., and $m_2 = 50$ gm., and we wish to infer *by way of the* second law to the acceleration of m_2, then (if we are not just testing the law, but actually using it) the inference pattern itself will not come under suspicion. It is accepted as a way of reasoning from initial conditions to conclusions.[42]

Similarly, the second law can be a "statement of how force is to be measured for scientific purposes." Broad accepted this view in 1913.[43] Ten years later[44] he dismissed it for the reason that the measurement of the rate of change of momentum is not the only way to measure force. This strengthens the thesis that Broad's account is single-valued. Does it follow from the fact that there may be alternative ways of measuring force that measuring the rate of change of momentum is not *a* way of measuring force? Surely the second law-sentence has been used thus. Newton infers from his pendulum experiment that, since different masses have identical constant accelerations towards the earth's centre, *a constant force* is acting whose magnitude is proportional to the masses

---

different ways. This does not make the second law statement a *mixture,* whatever that metaphor may mean.

Nor does the discovery of limitations in the application of classical mechanics damage Kant as extensively as some believe. In contemporary physics propositions are employed in precisely this way,—as descriptively true of phenomena, and yet against which evidence cannot (within the system) be conceived. A few examples are: dp $(v_1 - v_2) = qT \, dT/T$, or $dp/dT = qT/cv_1 - v_2)T$ (the Clausius-Clapeyron differential equation of the vapour pressure curve,—dependent on the Second Law of thermo-

dynamics); H $\left(\dfrac{\partial S}{\partial q_k}, q_k \right) = E$ (the Hamilton-Jacobi equation in celestial mechanics;

$f(i) = Ne - u \, (i) \, /kT / \Sigma e - u \, (i) \, /kT \Delta \tau_i$
(the Maxwell-Boltzman Law of Energy Distribution);

$$\nabla^2 \psi + \frac{8\pi^2 m}{h^2} (E - U)\psi = 0$$

(the Schrödinger Equation of Wave Mechanics);

$$U(r) = -\frac{e_2^2}{8\pi^3 \hbar} \int \frac{e^{(i/\hbar)p.r} d^3p}{\mu^2 c^2 + p^2} = -\frac{e_2^2}{2\pi^r} e - uc/\hbar) \, r$$

(the Yukawa potential with its characteristic range equal to the Compton wave length for the Pion).

42 The *Principia* abounds with this use: Cf., e.g. p. 14 (Cor. I, 9), p. 17 (Cor. III, 2), p. 20 (Cor. V, 5), p. 21 (Cor. VI, 2, and Schol. L. 3), p. 25 (31–32), p. 42 (Prop. II, 1 and 6), p. 44 (1, 6, 14), p. 136 (9), p. 162 (1. 6), p. 164 (6), p. 166 (19), p. 169 (2, 11) . . . etc., and see especially p. 244 (Schol. 8), p. 327 (Section vii, 11), p. 368 (1), p. 410 (13), p. 414 and p. 442 (11).

43 *PPR,* 322, lines 20–25.   44 *ST,* 165.

of the bodies concerned.[45] This use of law-sentences predominates in the work of engineers, which inclines some philosophers to regard the second law as *nothing but* a principle of instrument design, or of notation, or of inference.[46] The fundamental formulae of dynamics have such uses, but not to the exclusion of others equally important. The same might be said of Broad's emphatic 'single-valued' conclusions:

> The second law, is, therefore, neither a definition nor a statement as to how force is to be measured; but is a substantial proposition, asserting a connexion between two independently measurable sets of facts in nature . . .[47]

The second law-sentence can sometimes be used to express a definition, sometimes a statement of how force is to be measured, sometimes a substantial proposition (often with disconfirmatory evidence easily conceivable, but sometimes not). What physicists call "the Second Law" really consists in everything that can be expressed via different uses of '$F = m\dfrac{d^2r}{dt^2}$'.

III

Account III has not yet been discussed. To bring out this use the Law of Gravitation will serve better than the second law. But before continuing, an apposite quotation from Broad's first book may prepare the way. He writes

> The true proof of the law (of inertia) is to be found in the explanation that it offers of projectiles' paths and of planetary motion . . . The nature of the evidence for the Second Law . . . is in fact precisely the same . . . viz. that all mechanical processes can be analyzed in this particular way. . . .[48]

This suggests that Broad's answer to our leading question may be more than single-valued, and it catches the spirit of the next few pages.

[45] *Principia,* § VI, 303–326.

[46] Wittgenstein seems at times to suggest this:

"Newtonian Mechanics . . . brings the description of the universe to a unified form . . ." *Tractatus,* 6.341.

"Mechanics determines a form of description by saying: All propositions in the description of the world must be obtained in a given way from a number of given propositions—the mechanical axioms. . . ."

The position is adopted explicitly by Watson: ". . . what we have called the laws of nature are the laws of our methods of representing it . . ." *On Understanding Physics* (Cambridge Univ. Press, 1938), 52.

and by Toulmin: "Laws of Nature do not function as premises *from which* deductions to observational matters are made, but as rules of inference *in accordance with* which empirical conclusions may be drawn from empirical premises," *The Philosophy of Science* (Hutchinsons, 1953).

[47] *ST,* 165.   [48] *PPR,* 336f.

Consider how Newton discovered the law of gravitation. With other 17th century physicists he accepted Kepler's laws as empirical facts. These were as follows:

1. Each planet moves in an ellipse with the sun in one focus.
2. The radius vector from sun to planet sweeps out equal areas in equal times.[49]

These two laws were given in 1609, although the Second was discovered first.

3. The squares of the periods of the planets are proportional to the cubes of the mean distances.

This law was given in 1619.

Imagine planet P moving elliptically. The sun S is at a focus of the ellipse.

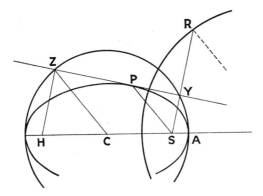

By 2, P is attracted to S. If P's velocity at time t is denoted by v, and if the length of SY (the perpendicular on the tangent at P) is denoted by p, we have

$$pv = h$$

Produce SY to R, SR being numerically equal to v. If HZ is the perpendicular on the tangent at P from H (the other focus), SR is parallel and proportional to HZ. Obviously these lines are parallel. For the ratio of the lengths we have

$$\frac{SR}{HZ} = \frac{SR \cdot SY}{HZ \cdot SY} = \frac{h}{b^2}$$

[49] This is a geometrical interpretation of the principle of conservation of angular momentum. Kepler's Second Law follows directly from Newton's as follows: A central force is one whose representative vector always points to a fixed point, O. Its magnitude may be any point function, $F = f(x, y, z)r$. The law of areas furnishes two additional first integrals of Newton's second law, thus: form the vector product of r with each side of the equation representing the law. Since F is in the direction of r, and since the vector product of two parallel vectors is zero, it follows that $O = m[r(d^2r)/dt^2]$ or $[r(d^2r)/dt^2] = O$, from which the integral may be given $[[r \cdot dr/dt] = 2c]$. The geometrical significance of $[r \cdot dr/dt]$ is as follows: $[r \, d \, r]$ = twice the area swept out by a radius vector in time dt. Dividing the area for dt by dt we get the area swept over by the radius vector in unit time, i.e., the areal velocity. Thus $[r \cdot dr/dt] = 2c$ states that the areal velocity is constant for motion under a central force, which is Kepler's Second Law.

(this follows from the property of the ellipse, SY . HZ $=$ b²). If C is the centre of the ellipse, CZ is parallel to SP. We need polar coordinates, r denoting SP, and $\odot$ the angle ASP measured from the perihelion A. Turn SR through a (positive) right angle. Then the path R is a hodograph of the motion of P. The velocity of R represents the acceleration of P, and will be perpendicular to SP. This is verified as follows: the velocity of R is parallel to that of Z, and the locus of Z (and Y also) is the auxiliary circle of the ellipse. The velocity of Z is perpendicular to CZ. Therefore the velocity of R is perpendicular to CZ, and thus perpendicular to SP.

The acceleration of P is in the direction PS. Its magnitude is measured by the speed of R which h/b² times the speed of Z (that is, the speed of R is (h/b²)a$\dot{\odot}$). Since r² $\dot{\odot}$ $=$ h, the speed of R is μ/r^2, where $\mu =$ h² a/b². Thus *the acceleration of P is in the direction PS and of magnitude* μ/r^2. This is the main result we seek.

Furthermore, the area swept out in unit time by the radius vector is ½ h. Therefore the periodic time σ for the elliptic orbit is 2 Δ/h, where Δ is the area enclosed by the ellipse. Thus

$$\sigma = 2\pi \, a \, b/h$$

Now, as we said, $\mu =$ h² a/b². Substituting for h in these two equations we get

$$\mu = 4\pi^2 a^3/\sigma^2$$

By 3, a^3/σ^2 has the same value for all the planets, i.e. the coefficient μ is the same for them all. The acceleration at distance r (from S) is the same for all the planets. Therefore the force on each planet is proportional to its mass.

This reasoning parallels Newton's own. Clearly, from here it is a short step to the law of gravitation. The attraction on a planet of mass m is proportional to m/r². If there is a universal law of gravitation, it is expected that the masses of any two particles will appear symmetrically in the formula for the attraction. Thus the general law

$$\gamma(Mm)/r^2$$

[in the example above μ is γ M, where M is the mass of the sun.[50]]

It is in terms of this move from Kepler's laws to $F = \gamma(Mm)/r^2$, that account III may be discussed. For as Newton here uses the sentence expressing the law, the statement of the law is clearly empirical. He sets out a property of any pair of particles (punctiform-masses). Alternative states of affairs are possible.[51] What the law-sentence expresses need

[50] Kepler's laws would be fulfilled precisely when M tends to infinity, γ tends to zero, and γM tends to a finite limit.

[51] Consider Kant's first published work, *Thoughts on the True Estimation of Living Forces* (1746–49), in which he writes:

"this law [of gravitation] is arbitrary . . . God could have chosen another, for instance the inverse threefold relation . . ."

(Paragraph 10)

And compare Whewell:

". . . no reason at all satisfactory, can be given why such a law [of gravitation] should of necessity be what it is; but . . . very strong reasons can be pointed out why, for the beauty and advantage of the system, the present one is better than others. . . ."

Op. cit., 216.

be neither necessary nor unfalsifiable. Indeed, before 1671 Newton set aside the law because he calculated a lunar deflection of 0.044 inches. The observed value was 0.0534.[52] The discrepancy arose from Newton's treatment of a degree of the earth's circumference as 60 miles in length. In 1671 Picard corrected this to 69 miles. This brought about close agreement.

Yet the law did remarkable work. It could not be just one more falsifiable, empirical, general statement, like "all cobblestones in Trinity Great Court contain flint," or "All flint strikes fire with steel." For the law of gravitation unifies the laws of Kepler and Galileo into a powerful unified pattern of explanation.

Here the law does not simply 'cap' a cluster of prior observations. It does not summarize them. Rather it is discovered to be that from which the observations may be generated. It requires not an actuary who can squeeze a general functional relationship out of columns of data, but a Sherlock Holmes who, from a set of apparently disconnected events (a bark, a footprint, a *faux pas*, a stain) can conclude 'The gamekeeper did it.' It requires a Newton who, from the laws of Galileo and Kepler, observations of the lunar motion, the tides, and the behaviour of falling bodies, could infer to $F = \gamma(Mm)/r^2$,—from which follows all these things, and others as well, but nothing incompatible with any of them.

The conceptual situation is not unlike this:

"If you accept these axioms all of mathematics follows"

It is objected,

'But why should I—they seem neither clear nor obvious.'

Answer,

'Because if you do accept them all of mathematics follows. What could be a better reason?'

Similarly:

'If you accept the law of gravitation, the laws of Kepler and Galileo are synthesized, and explained, and a universal mechanics follows.'

'But why should I; the empirical truth of the law is not directly obvious, nor can what it asserts be easily grasped.'

52 The moon's distance is 60 times the earth's radius. If the law is true, the moon is deflected from its inertial motion $1/60^2$ of the distance a body falls in a second at the earth's surface. This distance is 193 inches. $1/60^2$ of this is 0.0535 inches, very close to the recently observed 0.0534 inches.

'Because *if* you accept the law of gravitation the laws of Kepler and Galileo are synthesized, and a universal mechanics follows. What could be a better reason?'

This kind of reasoning gave birth to modern theoretical physics, work within which might be described as observation-statements in search of a premise. For compare

'If you accept the concept of an electron as having properties α, β, γ, (e.g. a motion formally analogous to a wave group, collision behaviour like a classical punctiform mass, no exactly simultaneous position and velocity), then a comprehensive explanation of A, B, C (e.g. electron diffraction, cathode ray deflection, limited experimental precision) will follow.'

'But why should I accept this concept of an electron? Indeed, it is simply inconceivable. The entity described can be no more than an ingenious mathematical combination of physical parameters.'

'Because if you do accept it a comprehensive and systematic explanation of A, B, C will follow. What could be a better reason?'[53]

This procedure of working backwards from observations to formulae in terms of which the observation-statements and their explanations fall into a pattern is fundamental in modern physics. Yet, like accounts II and III, it is least appreciated by philosophers, so attentive are they to the indispensable, but sometimes overestimated, empirical correlations discovered by men like Boyle, Cavendish, Ampère, Coulomb, Faraday, Tyndall, Kelvin and Boys. They tend to regard physics as a kind of mathematical photography and its laws as a formal picture of particular regularities. But the physicist often seeks not a general description of what he observes, but a general pattern, in terms of which what he observes will organize, and can be explained. Thus do observations come to cohere intelligibly. We ought not to expect the same kind of coherence and intelligibility in the fundamental formulae which so order observations. This would be like expecting a mechanical explanation of the laws which make mechanical explanation possible, or like expecting that, since 'glue' explains why stamps adhere to envelopes, the name of some similar substance will explain why the glue adheres to the stamps. The great unifications of Newton, Clerk Maxwell, Einstein, Bohr and Schrödinger, were preeminently discoveries of terse

---

[53] Compare Russell's remark: "The reason for accepting an axiom . . . is . . . that many propositions which are nearly indubitable can be deduced from it, and that no equally plausible way is known by which these propositions could be true if the axiom were false, and nothing which is probably false can be deduced from it." *Principia Mathematica* (C.U.P.), 2nd ed., I, 59, VII.

formulae from which descriptions and explanations of diverse phenomena could be generated. They were not discoveries of undetected regularities. It is precisely this which now drives theorists to search for the root of all our inverse square laws (dynamical, optical, electrical), for a formalism in quantum physics which will not be so abundant with infinities (which must be 're-normalized' by procedures which are, mathematically, quite *ad hoc*), and which drives Heisenberg to dream of "a single formula from which will follow the properties of matter in general."

This is behind accounts II and III.

The law of gravitation provides a kind of conceptual Gestalt, a pattern for mechanical thinking. Hence it is not falsifiable in the way that the statements patterned by the law are falsifiable. It made the laws of Kepler cohere for Newton in a way in which they did not cohere for Kepler himself. That the equation could do this puts it into a special class of uses of law-sentences, one which has affinities with Account II. Nonetheless here $F = \gamma(Mm)/r^2$ is clearly empirical. But its use is different from that of any gross generalization about all observable members of a certain class, and different again from a rule of inference, a definition, or a principle of measurement. And if its use is non-trivially different, its meaning is different, and if its meaning is different its logic is different.

From this use it is a short step to treating the law according to account II. Here it is an empirical assertion about the relations between particles in the universe, but it is psychologically inconceivable that evidence against it should turn up. One might risk saying that here the law of gravitation is regarded as *a priori* because it is synthetic, i.e. it synthesizes a diversity of observation statements.

Thence to account V, where the law provides a pattern of inference, a way of reasoning from initial conditions (e.g. the present position and disposition of Venus), to predictions (e.g. the position and disposition of Venus at sunrise). Since Newton, this has been a central use of the gravitational law-sentence.

With the mounting success of classical mechanics in the 19th century the law of gravitation often came to be construed according to account I,—a definition.[54]

Nothing could contrast with this more than the uses of the gravitational law-sentence, in the last three centuries, as a straightforward empirical hypothesis,—in the manner of account IV.

[54] Cf., e.g. Hertz, *Die Principien der Mechanik in Neuem Zusammenhange Dargestellt* (Leipzig, 1894).

We saw how Newton once abandoned his gravitational theory as an hypothesis which did not square with the facts. The 18th century found scientists, e.g. Clairault and Buffon, disputing whether or not the law was the necessary and inevitable law of any gravitational force.[55] Newton had found that the line of the moon's apsides sweeps through the heavens with a velocity twice as great as his law of gravitation seems at first to give.[56] This was the only failure of the theory. It was discovered later that apparently insignificant formal residues (dismissed in the course of the lengthy calculation) were cumulatively important. Until then however, the law-statement seemed to be at fault. Clairault tried to help; he introduced a small additional force varying inversely as the square of the fourth power. Buffon countered that the force could not vary according to any law other than the inverse square. So many facts support the law that this single discrepancy must be explained away. Clairault objected that the facts do not prove the law to obtain exactly. He notes that in cohesion, capillary attraction, and various other cases forces vary according to laws other than inverse square. Into this controversy came experimentalists, all eager to exploit the method indicated by Newton of how γ might be determined if only M and m were known. When M is of astronomical dimensions the problem is unmanageable. But in 1740 Bouguer proved that the mass of mountains was measurable. In 1774–76 Maskelyne actually measured the mass of Mount Schiehallion. In doing so he observed the deflection of a plumb line on opposite sides of the mountain.[57]

Then came Cavendish in 1798. Using a delicate torsion balance, he discovered that there exists an observable attraction between a heavy and a light metal ball.[58] As he says,

These experiments were sufficient to show, that the attraction of the weights on the balls is very sensible, and are also sufficiently regular to determine the quantity of this attraction. . . .[59]

Cavendish considers the objection "that it is uncertain whether, in these small distances, the force of gravity follows exactly the same law as in greater distances." He concludes that "There is no reason, however, to think that any irregularity of this kind takes place. . . ."[60]

---

[55] Whewell, W., *Astronomy and General Physics*, 226ff.

[56] The apsidal line ought, according to the *Principia*, move round once in 18 years. It is observed to do so twice in that period of time.

[57] *Philos. Trans. of the Royal Society* (1775).

[58] *Philos. Trans. Royal Society*, (1798), 469–526.

[59] *Op. cit.*, 484.   [60] *Op. cit.*, 522.

Naturally one possible result of this experiment was that *no* deflection should have been observed in the test spheres. That a deflection was observed, confirming the general statement that there exists an attraction between all physical bodies, rests on the possibility that the results of Cavendish's experiment might have turned out to be wholly disconfirmatory. Had this been so $F = \gamma(Mm)/r^2$, in this test would simply have been false.

More finely designed was the delicate experiment of C. V. Boys in 1895.[61] [Note the recent date; the law of gravitation is regarded as an empirical hypothesis late in the history of dynamics,—certainly after the axiomatic treatment of Hertz. This counters the view of Pap and Lenzen, who regard the move *empirical hypothesis→functionally apriori principle* as the standard evolutionary pattern in physics.] The ideas of Michell and Cavendish were adopted in a modified form. Boys' apparatus had an accuracy of 1 in 10,000.[62] With it Boys discovered the force of attraction between a large, freely swinging lead ball M, and a tiny, freely swinging gold ball m. This was 6.6576 x 10⁻⁸ dynes. Incidentally this shows the density of the Earth to be 5.5270 times that of water.

Thus for over two centuries '$F = \gamma(Mm)/r^2$' had a use as an empirical statement, potentially falsifiable. From Newton to Boys (1895) the fact of gravitational attraction was something to be established within experimental mechanics. Yet from Newton to Hertz (1894) the gravitational law formula had important uses as providing a principle of inference within axiomatic mechanics. The law was often set out in texts in definitional form. It was assumed as a principle of instrument construction. Finally it was invoked in those ways alluded to earlier,—sometimes as an empirical truth whose contradictory was consistent but psychologically inconceivable, and sometimes as an empirical truth unifying other bodies of information, but whose contradictory was both consistent and conceivable. These last reflect the success of the *system* of classical mechanics in forming our physical ideas. The scope of that system, and all its component laws, has decreased in this century. But now as before, law-sentences and formulae can be used in a variety of ways in the conduct of experiments and in their reports. This can appear

61 'On the Newtonian Constant of Gravitation,' *Phil. Trans. Royal Society,* (1895), 1–72. Boys' work climaxed a series of experiments aimed at the determination of the attractive force between any two point masses, beginning with Michell and later Cavendish, *Op. cit.,* through Reich (*Comptes Rendus* 1837), Baily (*Phil. Mag.* 1842), Cornu and Baille (*Comptes Rendus* vols. 76 & 86). All of these physicists treat $F = \gamma (Mm)/r^2$ as a straightforward empirical proposition.
62 *Ibid.,* 70.

contradictory only when the laws of a system are thought to be single-valued in their use.

IV

The fact is then, that physicists are more versatile with the sentences which express the laws of dynamics than philosophers have appreciated. Single-valued accounts of the nature of dynamical laws, e.g. those of Broad, Poincaré and Kant,—are supported somewhat by the practices of physics. Consequently each fails to be supported completely and exclusively. 'The Second Law of Motion', 'The Law of Gravitation'; philosophers have construed these as the names of discrete propositions. In physics they are umbrella-titles. They cover everything that '$F = m \dfrac{d^2r}{dt^2}$, or '$F = \gamma \dfrac{Mm}{r^2}$' can be used to express,—definitions, *a priori* statements, heuristic principles, empirical hypotheses, rules of inference . . . One experimental report may employ a formula to express each of these in turn. This raises questions.

It may be argued that this only shows that 'Laws of Dynamics' has a different force for philosophers than for physicists. More strongly, Broad may urge: 'the foregoing is tainted with 'psychologism.' Why should every use by physicists of '$F = \gamma \dfrac{Mm}{r^2}$' be relevant to the philosophical question 'What is the logical status of the Law of Gravitation?' Is it certain that every use of '$F = \gamma \dfrac{Mm}{r^2}$' in physics is a correct use? A physicist's uses of dynamical law-sentences are not germane to the question of what the laws of dynamics are. Nor is what he thinks about the laws,—any more than his behaviour when drunk, doped, or distracted. Nor are the vagaries involved in discovering a law pertinent to an assessment of the logic of that law.'

This rests on a realism that is difficult to accept. What concept have we of the laws of dynamics other than that gained by studying the uses to which dynamical law sentences are put in physics? Short of becoming Newtons ourselves how else could we grasp the meaning of dynamical laws? Philosophers can but record, compare and analyze the positions of these laws in the system of concepts that is classical mechanics, i.e. the uses of dynamical law-sentences by physicists (who are remarkably seldom drunk, doped, or distracted). There is no workable concept of what are the laws of dynamics other than what these law-sentences can be used to express within mechanics.

Philosophy of physics is unique in this respect. Most specialized disciplines become pure philosophy when pursued to their fundamentals. Physics becomes pure 'natural philosophy.' When pursued to its fundamentals it is a conceptual analysis, criticism of criteria and revision of methods and ideas. The most eminent inquirers here have not been academic philosophers, but men like Newton, Clerk Maxwell, Einstein, Bohr, Schrödinger and Heisenberg. They discovered what the laws of mechanics *are* and what their status is within physics. The philosopher of science, unless he is also one of these eminent physicists, can only try to understand and elucidate what these laws do in the solving of physical problems. This is just to trace the way in which mechanical laws are in fact used in solving the research problems of physicists. To go further, to make recommendations about the *real* nature of dynamical law statements or about how law-sentences ought to be used, is just the job that the theoretical physicist is trained for. If the philosopher of physics wishes to venture into this territory the standards by which he must expect to be judged will change accordingly.

'But surely, not all the uses of dynamical law-sentences are equally relevant to understanding the nature of the laws of dynamics?'

I am not impressed by this remark as much as Professor Broad may persuade me I ought to be. Agreed, nothing could be more relevant to understanding the nature of dynamical law statements than some proof that they are *a priori* or that they are contingent. But is not this only a way of remarking certain typical uses to which the sentences expressing these statements can be put? To use a law-sentence so that it expresses a statement whose contradictory is regarded as self-contradictory, is for that statement (in that context) to be analytic. Evidence offered in support of the statement's negation would be dismissed without further consideration. And for the law statement to be characterized as 'contingent' is only for a certain typical use of its law-sentence to be specified with respect to which evidence against the statement expressed is regarded as possible. Here one stops using the sentence to express anything true the moment such counter evidence is established.

Is this psychologism too? Does it not matter to one's understanding of the logic of statements how people use the sentences which express them? Can we say: 'it is irrelevant how anyone uses law-sentences, or what anyone thinks about dynamical laws. The question is whether or not a dynamical law-statement is *itself* necessary or contingent.' What are the Laws of Dynamics themselves other than what dynamicists express by the use of dynamical law-sentences? What is the concept intended in the question? Is there a philosophical alternative to the physical concept of the law of force or of gravitation? If so, by what criteria is it to be judged? Can the logic of a proposition be grasped in any way other than by learning how the sentence expressing that proposition is used on particular occasions by particular individuals? The point of characterizing the logical status of the laws of dynamics lies only in delineating how, e.g. '$F = m \dfrac{d^2r}{dt^2}$' and '$F = \gamma \dfrac{Mm}{r^2}$' are used by physicists in doing physics. But these uses are not limited to those describable by 'necessary,' or 'contingent.' All the uses of dynamical law-sentences are perhaps equally relevant to understanding the nature of the laws of dynamics. There is no reason for regarding accounts I and IV as specially to be preferred, although without doubt these constitute the major dichotomy.

A further possible objection: 'the foregoing sections confuse the process of discovering a law of dynamics with the role the law plays within mechanical theory. What does it matter whether Newton discovered the law of gravitation by mathematical reflexion on Kepler's Laws, or by experiments of the Cavendish-Boys type, or even by contemplating his navel? The essential consideration is the uses to which the gravitational law-sentence is put. Just because two laws are discovered in different ways, it does not follow that they will serve different types of purpose within physical theory.'

Certainly we do not regard it as a logical feature of Kekule's conception of the benzine ring that it came to him whilst he gazed at the flames in his fireplace. Yet it is an important fact of the history of physics that when a law is discovered in a merely empirical way,—as Boyle's followers 'found' the celebrated gas law in his neat columns of data,—the law is construed as a merely contingent regularity for a considerable period thereafter. At present Boyle's law is set in a far flung system of kinetical and thermodynamical concepts. Ostensibly falsifying evidence would be scrutinized otherwise now than in the 17th century. For then all that was involved was two sets of empirically determined, mathematically correlated magnitudes. No theoretical or conceptual crises would have resulted had phenomena turned up in 1680 which cut against Boyle's regularity. The law of gravitation, however, was not discovered in any such merely 'empirical' manner. From the outset it rested on conceptual factors absent in Boyle's regularity. For the way Newton arrived at his law was as systematically beautiful as Boyle's techniques were experimentally ingenious. So far as use goes, an experimentally discovered law is regarded as being more open to upset than is one of the

Newtonian sort, though as we saw earlier, for Newton the gravitational law was not absolutely invulnerable. This obtains until, like Boyle's law, it becomes central in one of the concept-systems we call a 'physical theory.'

Once embedded in a theory, of course, a law which was originally grossly contingent joins a family of other assertions all expressed by the same law-sentence. Some members of this family can only be described as *a priori*. Further observations may be made about this.

A law-sentence can express an *a priori* proposition when its user maintains the latter in the face of all experience. He may do this because he regards the idea of potentially falsifying evidence as (1) impossible on logical grounds, i.e. self-contradictory, or (2) impossible on physical grounds, e.g. inconsistent with a conservation principle, or (3) consistent, but psychologically inconceivable. (3) could be dismissed as logically irrelevant. But one might risk the heresy of saying that this is at least debatable. If not one physicist today has even a workable conception of x (e.g. a high speed electron at a geometrical point), this will certainly affect the use, and hence the meaning and the logic, of terms and formulae with microphysics. The logical point is that some laws *are* maintained in the face of all experience. (1), (2) and (3) are reasons why this is done; all three have been invoked as the reason for our inability to characterize an elementary particle as a moving point-mass. A man might hold to a law against all counter experience because, e.g. a Pope or a Commissar, instructs him to do so. We may deplore his reasons. The logical issue however, remains unaffected. In fact he uses the law-sentence concerned in an *a priori* manner.

Dynamical law-sentences are used in many unspectacular contexts as expressing what is non-contingent. Just as a collar stud used to replace a lost pawn *is* a chess token, so a proposition which has a contradictory which is (1) logically impossible, or (2) physically impossible, or (3) psychologically impossible *is a priori*. Here when a genuine disconfirmatory instance does appear, rather than qualify the law, it is made inapplicable to the recalcitrant instance. In strict logic these two procedures may be equivalent. In physics they would always be felt to be distinct in important ways.

Besides, in most cases wherein a dynamical law must be qualified it is due to the effect of some other law. Thus the laws of gravitation and friction qualify the First Law of Motion. Inertial motion never occurs in a pure form since unbalanced forces always act on moving bodies.

Suppose that '$F = m \dfrac{d^2r}{dt^2}$' is used in such a way that its employer will maintain it in the face of all possible experience. Does it follow from this that the law is not an empirical hypothesis? No. Account II gave a use of the second law-sentence in which the law expressed was an empirical hypothesis. Its contradictory was therefore not self-contradictory. Nonetheless here the statement of the second law would have been maintained whatever happened, since any alternative would have been psychologically inconceivable,—conceptually untenable.

In account I empirical disconfirmation of what is expressed by '$F = m \dfrac{dt^2}{d^2r}$' was logically impossible. In account II empirical confirmation of what is expressed by way of the second law-sentence is logically possible, but psychologically, or practically impossible. Of course practices in physics can be changed, as Professor Broad will be quick to observe. Whole systems of concepts can be thrown over, or limited in scope. What is and is not possible psychologically can be changed accordingly. Given the supremacy of Newtonian mechanics absolutely unquestioned, then empirical disconfirmation of the second law statement is impossible. But this supremacy has never been completely unquestioned, not in Newton's day, nor even in the confident years of the early 19th century. So account II is concerned only with limited areas of physical practice, not with matters of principle.

Suppose however that '$F = m \dfrac{d^2r}{dt^2}$' were used so that what it expressed was *in principle* not subject to empirical disconfirmation. (It is physical principles that are being considered.) Does it follow that (in that use) the contradictory of the Law expressed is self-contradictory? 'The second law statement (as a matter of principle) is not subject to empirical disconfirmation,—is this not only a necessary but also a sufficient condition for the proposition 'The second law statement is analytic'? Or are there uses of dynamical law-sentences in which what is expressed, though it is not subject to empirical disconfirmation, even in principle, is still not for that reason analytic (in the sense that its contradictories are self-contradictory)? Is there a sense of *a priori* which is different from 'analytic' and also from 'functionally *a priori*'?

Today we have a certain perspective on the Second Law of Motion. Perhaps we have too much perspective to be able to feel the force statements of that law must have had for those 18th and 19th century physicists who regarded it as a supreme empirical truth, yet in principle incapable of being disconfirmed. Let us consider some statements which at this moment control our physical thinking in an exactly comparable way, e.g.

1. "It is impossible to devise an engine which will deliver more work at one place than is put into it at another."[63]

2. "A perpetual motion machine of the second type (thermodynamical) is impossible."[64]

3. "Nothing travels faster than light."[65]

These are for us like what the second law statement must have been for early 19th century physicists. To deny what they assert would not be self-contradictory. But to say that therefore their denials are only psychologically inconceivable would strike any practicising physicist as frivolous. Consider this further.

"Today is Monday and yesterday was Friday."
"Two dozen makes 25."

These are absurd, false *a priori*. They could not possibly be true no matter what happens. There are plenty of *a priori* statements which are not purely formal, i.e. which do not arise strictly from certain uses of 'and,' 'not,' 'another,' 'either-or,' 'all' . . . etc. For example: 'Your first cousin once removed cannot be your parent's cousin's child,' and 'The Stars and Stripes has more stars than stripes.' The necessity of these cannot be grasped simply from knowing the use of logical operators. We must appreciate also the uses to which 'cousin,' 'parents,' 'stars and stripes' are actually put.

[63] This is the law of the impossibility of perpetual motion of the first type (mechanical); which is itself a special restricted version of the general law of conservation of energy, $T_2+U_2=T_1+U_1=constant$ [where kinetic energy $\frac{1}{2}mv^2$ is denoted by T and potential energy is denoted by U]. This energy principle in turn represents only a first integral of Newton's Second Law since only v (i.e. ds/dt) appears.

Compare ". . . if the devisers of new machines, who made such futile attempts to construct a *perpetuum mobile* would acquaint themselves with this principle, they would . . . understand that the thing is utterly impossible by mechanical means." Huygens, *Horologium Oscillatorium*.

[64] This is but another formulation of the second law of thermodynamics. The highest attainable efficiency for an ideal heat engine (a Carnot engine) requires an expenditure of work as follows: $W = \eta Q_1 = \eta Q^3/(1 - \eta)$ A super-Carnot engine with an efficiency higher than η would, when coupled with a Carnot engine, give us the practical equivalent of a *perpetuum mobile* of the second kind. But both experience and thermodynamic theory (supported now by the quantum theory of heat) show that such an engine is impossible.

[65] I.e. $U = C\left[\dfrac{(1 - v/c)(1 - w/c)}{1+vw/c^2}\right]$,—it is impossible to combine several Lorentz transformations into one involving a relative velocity greater than c (the velocity of light). For it is obvious that in the equation above, which is the typical result of such a combination, U cannot be equal to or greater than c so long as v and w are smaller than c. Cf. P. G. Bergmann, *Theory of Relativity* (New York 1946), 43.

"In his doctoral thesis he successfully designs a perpetual motion machine."

"This entity travels faster than light."

To grasp the absurdity here we must appreciate how differently we would proceed to determine the truth or falsity of "This machine is more efficient than that," "This is the most efficient machine ever built" and "This machine is perfectly efficient." We must understand the differences between "This man runs faster than that one," "This train travels faster than that van," "This bullet travels faster than that aeroplane," "Light travels faster than this bullet" and "This entity travels faster than light."

This is not like the differences between "This is a Stars and Stripes" and "This is a Jolly Roger." The truth-value of these last statements is determined by procedures of the same type. The procedure for determining whether or not something travels faster than light is different in principle from those involved in determining whether one man runs faster than another, or whether trains travel faster than vans, or aeroplanes, or bullets. No physicist would dream of trying to settle experimentally someone's claim to have constructed a *perpetuum mobile*.

"No machine is perfectly efficient."

"It is inconceivable that any machine should be perfectly efficient."

" 'This machine is a *perpetuum mobile*' could not but have been false."

Compare these with

"What he said $\begin{cases} \text{must have been false} \\ \text{could not but have been false} \\ \text{could not have been true} \end{cases}$ since he said

'Today is Monday and yesterday was Friday.' "

There is a difference between the simple logical moves which show that someone's statement could not but have been false when what he said was 'Today is Monday and yesterday was Friday,' and the complex non-logical moves which show that someone's statement could not but have been false when what he said was

'He has designed a *perpetuum mobile*.'

'He has discovered a particle which moves faster than light.'

Yet all of these decisions turn on matters of principle.

When statements like the last two are used by physicists so that as a matter of principle there is no procedure which could show them to be true, then we will hear it said of them that they could not but have been false,—no matter what had happened. The physicist himself would be the first to remark that these statements are not false like any gross contingent statement which might have been true but is false. Nor are they false like a false mathematical or logical statement, or like a statement which simply fails to obey prior definitions. But neither will the physicist agree that these statements are false as are 'I am not now reading these words,' 'The earth is flat,' and 'Cambridge is not the finest University in the world.' These may express what is psychologically inconceivable. But perpetual motion machines and velocities greater than c are not just psychologically inconceivable. The physicist will say that they are *impossible in principle*.

A last matter for Professor Broad's consideration: To say that when '$F = m\dfrac{d^2r}{dt^2}$' is used in the several different ways set out earlier, different propositions are being expressed, is true enough. But this minimizes the important fact that everything expressed by the use of '$F = m\dfrac{d^2r}{dt^2}$', hangs together in a most intimate way. In some sense you and I do say the same thing when we put it that '$F = m\dfrac{d^2r}{dt^2}$' even though we may express quite different propositions. Mine may be one against which empirical evidence is possible. For you the idea of such evidence may be self-contradictory. But in a particular dynamical problem (e.g. the determination of the noon position of Venus on Dec. 2nd 1957), our paper calculations will be identical, our predictions indistinguishable and our explanations very similar. Would it not be wrong to suggest therefore that we were doing entirely different sorts of things? Saying that we express different propositions when we use the second law-sentence in our different ways does seem to do this. But that we do express different propositions is undeniable. Dare one speculate that the same thing may be said with different propositions,—indeed different types of propositions?

With this I turn to Professor Broad's Reply for elucidation of his own views on Dynamics as these thoughts and questions bear on them.

Norwood Russell Hanson

The University of Cambridge
England and
Indiana University

9

Georg Henrik von Wright

BROAD ON INDUCTION AND PROBABILITY

IF I had to name the most important contributions to inductive logic from the period between the two great wars, I should without hesitation mention the following ones: Keynes' *A Treatise on Probability* (1921), Nicod's *Le Problème Logique de l'Induction* (1923), the chapters on induction and causality in the second and third volumes of Johnson's *Logic* (1922, 24), and Broad's papers, "Induction and Probability" (I–II, 1918, 20), "The Principles of Problematic Induction" (1927), and "The Principles of Demonstrative Induction" (I–II, 1930). To these might be added F. P. Ramsey's posthumous essay "Truth and Probability" and R. A. Fisher's criticism, in various publications, of the Bayes-Laplacean doctrine of so-called inverse probability. I believe that few informed people would disagree with the choice.

It has struck me that all the authors mentioned are Cambridgemen. (Nicod studied and worked at Cambridge during the first great war, and his published work is in the spirit of British philosophy.) There thus exists something which can be called a Cambridge tradition in modern inductive logic.

If Broad's writings on induction have remained less known than some of his other contributions to philosophy and less influential than the works of some of the other authors mentioned above, *one* reason for this is that Broad never has published a book on the subject. It is very much to be hoped that, for the benefit of future students, Broad's chief papers on induction and probability will be collected in a single volume,— possibly with some contributions of his to other branches of logical theory.

The following is a list of Broad's writings in inductive logic:

(1) "Induction and Probability." I and II, *Mind 27* and *29,* 1918 and 1920. 15 + 35 pp.

(2) Critical notice on J. M. Keynes, *A Treatise on Probability, Mind 31,* 1922. 14 pp.

(3) Critical notice on W. E. Johnson, *Logic,* Part II, *Mind 31,* 1922. 15 pp.

(4) "Mr. Johnson on the Logical Foundations of Science," I and II, *Mind 33,* 1924. 20 + 15 pp.

(5) *The Philosophy of Francis Bacon.* Cambridge 1926. Reprinted in *EHP.*

(6) "The Principles of Problematic Induction." *Proceedings of the Aristotelian Society, 28,* 1927–28. 46 pp.

(7) "The Principles of Demonstrative Induction," I and II. *Mind 39,* 1930. 18 + 14 pp.

(8) "Mechanical and Teleological Causation." Symposium. *Proceedings of the Aristotelian Society,* Suppl. Vol. *14,* 1935. 30 pp.

(9) Critical notice on R. von Mises, *Wahrscheinlichkeit, Statistik und Wahrheit, Mind 46,* 1937. 14 pp.

(10) "Hr. Von Wright on the Logic of Induction," I, II, and III. *Mind 53,* 1944. 24 + 23 + 22 pp.

(11) Critical notice on W. Kneale, *Probability and Induction. Mind 59,* 1950. 22 pp.

In the following I shall refer to these works using the numbers within brackets. [ ]. I shall use [1^I] and [1^{II}] to refer to part one and part two respectively of [1]; and similarly [7^I] and [7^{II}].

As an inductive logician, Broad has acknowledged[1] his indebtedness both to Keynes and to Johnson. A few words about the relation of his work to theirs may be called for.

Both parts of [1] were published before the appearance of Keynes' *Treatise.* There are two important points, on which Broad can be said to have anticipated Keynes' work. One is the mathematical treatment of the probability-relation between a generalization and its confirming instances. By virtue of it, Broad ought to be regarded as the founder of that branch of modern inductive logic, which may appropriately be termed Confirmation-Theory.[2] The second point is the idea of Limited Independent Variety.[3] This idea, in inductive logic, ultimately goes back to Bacon. With Broad in [1] it takes the form of a theory of natural kinds, with Keynes that of a theory of generic properties or of "legal

---

1 [7^I], 302.

2 I use "Confirmation-Theory" here to mean a theory of the way in which the probability of an inductive generalization is affected by the confirmation of individual instances which fall under it. In recent years the term has acquired an inflated use and come to mean the study of the probability-relation, as such, within a so-called range-model.

3 Cf. Broad's statement on the relation of his views on induction to those of Keynes' in [2], 81.

atoms" in nature. The two theories are, as far as I can see, rather far removed from each other. In [6] Broad gives some interesting further developments of the *Keynesian* form of the idea of limited variety. (See below under I and II.)

The relation of Broad's work in inductive logic to Johnson's is of a more complex kind. As far as technical terminology and fundamental distinctions are concerned Broad obviously owes much to Johnson. His paper [7] very closely follows Johnson's lines, and it seems a fair characterization to say that its primary aim is to improve upon Johnson's not too clearly formulated theory of demonstrative induction. It accomplishes, however, much more than this. The first part of [7] opens up a new and fruitful approach to the old subject of formalizing the "canons" or "methods" of induction by elimination. The second part is less original; I cannot suppress a feeling that the subject would have profited more, had Broad attempted to give an independent treatment of the theory of inductively correlated variations, rather than a perfected statement of the Johnsonian "figures" which, as Broad himself shows, rest on the use of untenable postulates. (See below under III.)

The rest of the present essay is divided into four sections. In the first three sections I examine, in order, Broad's three main publications in the field of inductive logic. Those are the three papers mentioned in the opening paragraph above and subsequently listed under numbers [1], [6], and [7]. Having examined them, I draw in the concluding section attention to some points in the remaining eight relevant publications which seem to me particularly interesting. All through my essay I have tried to concentrate on questions which I consider important from the point of view of the subject as a whole.

I

In [1] Broad proposes[4]

to prove three points, which, if they can be established, are of great importance to the logic of inductive inference. They are (1) that *unless* inductive conclusions be expressed in terms of probability all inductive inference involves a formal fallacy; (2) that the degree of belief which we actually attach to the conclusions of well-established inductions cannot be justified by any known principle of probability, unless some further premise about the physical world be assumed; and (3) that it is extremely difficult to state this premise so that it shall be at once plausible and non-tautologous.

I shall here deal with these three points in order.

1. It is not quite clear to me what Broad means by the "formal

4 [1¹], 389.

fallacy" which an inductive argument is alleged to commit, unless its conclusion be stated "in terms of probability." But, as far as I can see, the "formal fallacy" is nothing but the fact that (ampliative) induction is an *inconclusive* type of argument. It would seem to follow from this, that an inductive argument which does *not* commit a fallacy must be *conclusive*.

What then is the correct way of formulating an inductive argument? Many logicians have thought that by introducing an additional premiss —often referred to under the name of the Principle of the Uniformity of Nature or Law of Causation—the formal fallacy of ordinary inductive reasoning can be avoided. This, however, is disputed[5] by Broad. The argument which he gives[6] I find neither clear nor convincing. I should have thought that, unless the form or content of the additional premiss is restricted in advance, it is perfectly possible to state inductions in the form of demonstrations without mentioning "probability" in the conclusion. This, I believe, is implicitly admitted by Broad too in [7].

Broad seems to think that the formulation of inductive conclusions in terms of probability "accords with what we actually believe when we reflect."[7] Now, what I think we all admit upon reflection is that, in so-called ampliative or problematic inductions, the conclusions do not follow logically from their premisses, *i.e.* that the falsehood of the conclusion is consistent with the truth of the premisses. But to clothe this admission in a probabilistic terminology—as is often done by philosophers—is not an altogether good idea. It leads to conflict with a view on *certainty* which seems to me quite sound to entertain. That I shall die is *certain* ("as certain as anything") although my immortality is logically compatible with the mortal nature of any number of men in the past. There are numerous inductions, the conclusions of which are in this same sense "certain." To say that they are, after all, "probable" only, is but another way of saying that they are not *logically* "certain." But this is a bad way of putting it. It tends to obscure an important distinction, *viz.* the distinction between those inductive conclusions which are *certain*, though not logically certain, and those which are not certain in *any* sense of the word and which for *that* reason may be called *probable* only.

It seems to me therefore that the formulation of inductive conclusions in terms of probability is not only not necessary from the point of view of logic, but actually conflicts with a perfectly respectable use of "certainty" in connexion with induction. I believe that this criticism is of some relevance to a discussion of the so-called justification of induction. It does not, however, affect the rest of Broad's argumentation in [1] about the relation of induction to probability.

5 [1¹], 390.   6 [1¹], 390f.   7 [1¹], 391.

2. Let us, for present purposes, by the *factual premiss* of an inductive argument understand a proposition of the form "All observed S's have been P." Let the conclusion, stated in terms of probability, be either of the form *i*. "It is probable to degree p that all S's whatever will be P" or of the form *ii*. "It is probable to degree p that the next S to be observed will be P."

I believe that the problem behind the second point which Broad wishes to establish in [1] can be formulated as follows:

If an inductive argument is to be formally in order, *i.e.* conclusive, it is *necessary* that to its factual premiss be added some further premiss or premisses which are formal principles of probability. These principles are a sort of logical laws; they hold true "in all possible worlds."[8] The question now is, whether the addition of such formal principles to the factual premiss also is *sufficient* to make the argument conclusive. Broad shows that the answer is negative. In order to make inductive arguments conclusive still further premisses are needed. These premisses are not logical laws but material assumptions concerning the constitution of nature. In showing all this Broad is, I think, perfectly successful.

Broad distinguishes between induction "by simple enumeration" and induction "by the hypothetical method,"[9] and proceeds to consider each case separately. The distinction, though in itself important, appears to me in this connexion somewhat confusing. The essential difference between the two cases which Broad examines is that they represent two different types of approach to the problem of how to assign a probability to an inductive conclusion. The first approach is the classical doctrine of so-called Inverse Probability, founded by Bayes and Laplace. The second is a new approach, of which Broad and Keynes are the pioneers.

A. Induction by Simple Enumeration. Let the factual premiss of the inductive argument be that m counters have been drawn, without replacement, from a bag and all of them found to be white. What is the probability that the next counter which will be drawn is white? And what is the probability that all the n counters, which originally were in the bag, are white?

According to the Laplacean doctrine, the answer to the first question is given by the formula $\dfrac{m+1}{m+2}$ and the answer to the second question by the formula $\dfrac{m+1}{n+1}$.

Broad states the formal and material assumptions which he thinks are

8 [1¹], 392.   9 [1¹], 389.

needed for a correct derivation of the two formulae. Among the assumptions there are two crucial ones about *equi-probability*.

The first assumption of equi-probability is to the effect that all the possible proportions of white counters in the bag are initially equally probable. Of this assumption Broad in [1] takes the view that it is true on logical grounds alone. Or more precisely: he views it as a legitimate application of a "Principle of Indifference" which he takes to be logically necessary.[10] He does not note the difficulty caused by the fact that several different so-called *constitutions* of the bag may answer to one and the same *proportion* of white counters in it. In [6] Broad is aware of this difficulty. (See below p. 328, bottom.)

The second assumption of equi-probability is to the effect that each individual counter in the bag has the same probability of being drawn.[11] This assumption is "material," *i.e.* its truth does not follow from laws of logic and necessary principles of probability alone. But is it really needed for a correct derivation of Laplace's formulae? As far as I can see it is *not* (unconditionally) needed. It is needed only if we wish to make the transition from the proposition that the *proportion* of white counters in the bag is p to the proposition that the *probability* of drawing a white counter from the bag is p. It is needed, in other words, to make the definition of a degree of probability as a ratio among favourable and unfavourable alternatives of equal probability applicable to the case under discussion. But the problem can be treated independently of this way of defining degrees of probability, within a so-called uninterpreted calculus. Then Broad's two assumptions about equi-probability may be replaced by the *one* assumption that any given value of the probability of drawing a white counter is initially as probable as any other value. This assumption, in my opinion at least, is "material."

Broad now goes on to consider[12] "how far the attempt to establish laws of nature by simple enumeration is parallel to the artificial example just dealth with" of the counters in the bag. Two cases are distinguished:[13] laws about the qualities of classes of substances ("All crows are black") and laws about the connexion of events ("All rises of temperature are followed by expansion").

One main difference between the artificial and the "natural" cases has to do with the second assumption of equi-probability mentioned above. All counters in the bag *may* have the same probability of being drawn, but all individual crows certainly have not the same probability of being observed. This is so for two reasons. First, because "we clearly

10 [1¹], 394, *b* (iii).   11 [1¹], 394, *c* (i).
12 [1¹], 395.   13 [1¹], 395.

cannot have observed any of the crows that begin to exist after the moment when we make the last observation which we take into account when we make our induction."[14] And secondly, because our observations are confined to a restricted region in space, and "the blackness of the observed crows may not be an attribute of all crows but may be true only of crows in a certain area."[15] The same difference between the artificial and the "natural" cases is there for laws about events. Broad also points out other differences, but I shall not mention them here.

The second assumption of equi-probability, it was just said, is needed only if we wish to associate with the formulae $\dfrac{m+1}{m+2}$ and $\dfrac{m+1}{n+1}$ the "classical" definition of probability as a ratio among equi-possible unit-alternatives. In the case of crows and blackness this would amount to saying that the proposition that there is a probability to degree p that a random crow is black *means* that any one crow is as likely as any other to be observed and a proportion p of them all are black. Broad has conclusively shown that, on *this* definition of probability, use of the Laplacean formulae cannot be extended from the artificial to the "natural" cases of inductions about substances and events. This, I think, is enough to refute, if not all, at least the great majority of the attempts to apply the Laplacean formulae to cases in nature.

The Laplacean formulae are also discussed by Broad in [6]. We shall therefore have occasion to return to the subject later.

B. *The Hypothetical Method.* Under this heading Broad considers, how the probability of an arbitrary proposition h is affected by the confirmation of some logical consequences, c_1, c_2, etc. of it. An important special case is, when h is a law (hypothesis, generalization) and c_1, c_2, etc. particular instances of the law.

Let the factual premiss of a certain inductive argument be that a certain hypothesis h has been confirmed n times in succession. How can this factual premiss, $c_1 \& \ldots \& c_n$, be used to probabilify the conclusion h?

About this Broad proves[16] something which may be called the Fundamental Theorem of Confirmation. It states, loosely speaking, that the probability of h increases each time the number n of successive confirmations increases, provided that a) the probability of h prior to any confirmation is $>$o, and b) the probability of the new confirmation relative to the previous confirmations is <1.

Substantially the same theorem was proved by Keynes in his *Treatise on Probability*.[17] But whereas Broad's proof is brief and elegant,

14 [1¹], 395.   15 [1¹], 396.
16 [1¹], 400–402.   17 *Op. cit.*, ch. xx.

Keynes' is unnecessarily complicated for the purpose. From the formula deduced by Broad, but not from the formula given by Keynes, it can be immediately seen that the increasing probability of the hypothesis approaches 1 as a limit, if and only if the probability of n successive confirmations approaches the initial probability of the hypothesis. Keynes states the condition in an equivalent but much less perspicuous form. This takes him into a very obscure discussion of the question whether the condition could be fulfilled in nature. The problem of convergence towards 1 is not discussed by Broad.

The more the probability of a new confirmation relative to the previous confirmations falls short of 1, the more does this new confirmation contribute to increase in the probability of h. "This," Broad observes,[18] "is the precise amount of truth that there is in the common view that an hypothesis is greatly strengthened by leading to some surprising consequence which is found to be true."

The Fundamental Theorem of Confirmation, one might say, makes the probabilification of inductive conclusions through factual premisses depend upon two additional premisses about extreme probabilities. The first additional premiss concerns the initial probability of the conclusion. The second is about a certain probability-relation among the factual premisses.

Of both the additional premisses it holds good that no assurance of their truth can be obtained from necessary principles of probability theory or pure logic. Their truth-ground, if any, must be some feature of the actual physical world. Which it might be in the case of the second premiss, Broad does not consider. But in the second part of [1] he deals very elaborately with the possible truth-grounds of the assumption that laws for the explanation of observed phenomena possess, prior to confirmation, a finite probability.

Of the relation, finally, between Induction by Simple Enumeration and the Hypothetical Method Broad says[19] that the former is a special case of the latter. Now this may be true under some definition of the two methods. But it does not hold for Broad's conception of them in [1]. It is an essential feature of what Broad here calls the Hypothetical Method that the conclusion h should *entail* the factual premiss $c_1 \& \ldots \& c_n$. Only on this condition can the Fundamental Theorem be proved. But in that which Broad here calls Induction by Simple Enumeration there is no corresponding relation of entailment between conclusion and factual premiss. This makes a difference between the methods which, I

18 [1¹], 402.   19 [1¹], 400.

think, is of some relevance to the discussion of their material presuppositions which follows in the second part of [1].

3. In several places[20] Broad makes apologetic remarks about the unsatisfactory nature of the discussion in the second part of [1] and about the doubtful character of the suggested ideas. It must, I believe, be admitted that there is much in this paper which is obscure, but also that it contains a wealth of interesting material. Much of the material is more relevant to the metaphysics of nature than to the logic of induction. In order to see clearly what is relevant in it to inductive logic, I think it is useful to distinguish the following three questions:

i. Which are the assumptions about nature which Broad thinks are necessary in order to make inductive conclusions, formulated in terms of probability, follow logically from factual premises and formal principles of probability theory?

ii. Do these assumptions really serve their purpose of making inductive arguments formally valid?

iii. Are these assumptions true?

Broad does not keep these questions sharply apart, which makes the discussion of them somewhat difficult. But I think we may eventually assess the value of his arguments to all of them. I shall discuss the three questions in order.

i. We found above that use both of Induction by Simple Enumeration and of the Hypothetical Method require certain "material" assumptions about probabilities, and we tried to state which these assumptions were. In the case of enumerative induction an assumption of equi-probability of alternatives is required. In the case of hypothetical induction we need two assumptions about not-extreme probabilities. Actually, the discussion in the second part of [1] touches only upon *one* of these three assumptions, *viz.* the assumption that laws have a finite initial probability. Thus the discussion, even if it were in itself quite satisfactory, would necessarily fall short of achieving *everything* that is needed to make inductive conclusions follow logically with probability from their premises.

Of the assumption about nature which is to assure a finite probability to laws, Broad says,[21] that it must be an assumption which favours laws, *i.e.* propositions of the type "All *S*'s are *P*" or "No *S*'s are *P*" at the expense of statistical generalizations, *i.e.* propositions of the type "*p*% of the *S*'s are *P*." This, I think, is false. For, from the point of view of the Fundamental Theorem of Confirmation, laws and statistical generalizations do not count as alternative hypotheses. This follows from what was just said about the relation between enumerative and hypothetical induction (in Broad's sense). Thus in discussing the problem of finite initial probabilities, we need not look round for a principle which *favours* laws as against statistical correlations. But we certainly must look for some principle *about* laws.

Here the idea of Limited Independent Variety suggests itself to the inquirer. If we had some assurance that, loosely speaking, the number of alternative laws for the explanation of a given phenomenon were necessarily finite, then there *might* also be assurance that the initial probability of any given one of these alternatives is not vanishingly small. This possibility Broad may be said to explore in [6]. In [1] he takes another route. It starts from considerations about the meaning of the idea to which philosophers have referred by some such name as Uniformity of Nature.

How is the "axiom" about Uniformity of Nature—Broad calls it *Unax* —to be formulated? Broad first suggests[22] the following formulation:

> if any individual a has the property ϕ and the property ψ (*e.g.*, is a swan and is white) then there is some property χ other than whiteness (*e.g.*, that of being European) which is possessed by a, and such that everything that is both ϕ and χ (*e.g.*, is a European swan) is also ψ (*e.g.*, is white).

This seems to come very near the core of certain familiar views of universal determination in nature. Yet, as Broad points out,[23] this formulation cannot be final. It is deficient in at least two respects:

Firstly, it is too general. It puts no restrictions upon the nature of the properties ϕ, ψ, and χ. It is plausible enough to think that the whiteness of a swan is due to the presence of some property (or conjunction of properties) such that any swan with this property is white. But how many people would hold that the "swanness" of a white object is due to the presence of some property (other than the defining criteria of being a swan) such that any white object with this property is a swan?

Secondly, *Unax* in the above formulation entitles us to conclude from the conjunctive occurrence of two properties ϕ and ψ in a single individual a to the existence of some general law connecting these two properties. And this seems too bold a conclusion. In most cases, we would wish to witness quite a number of conjunctive occurrences of ϕ and ψ before we would feel justified in suspecting the existence even of *some* law connecting them. "Yet," Broad says,[24] "it is very difficult to see what principle about *nature* there could be which makes *number of observed conjunctions* relevant at just this point."

22 [1II], 13.   23 [1II], 15f.   24 [1II], 16.

Broad thinks[25] that both these difficulties can be overcome, if *Unax* is modified in the following way: We demand that ϕ should be a property defining a Natural Kind.[26] The modified principle then says that, if the individual of the kind defined by ϕ possesses a further property ψ, then there is some property χ such that all members of the kind, which have χ, also have ψ. (χ may be the same as ϕ.) The uniformity principle, thus modified, Broad calls *Unax*.

ii. We now move on to the question, whether *Unax* can help to make inductive conclusions, formulated in terms of probability, follow logically from factual premises and necessary principles of probability theory. As already explained (p. 321), the only help which *Unax might* give, is to assure a finite initial probability to laws of nature.

The way in which, according to Broad,[27] the theory of natural kinds may be relevant to considerations of inductive probability can be briefly described as follows:

A natural kind is a region in nature containing a "blob."[28] The question then is whether "this habit of heaping instances round a comparatively few possible states is typical of nature as a whole."[29] Now suppose, for the sake of argument, "that nature as a whole really distributes its instances uniformly among possible sorts."[30] Then we shall have to go on to assume "that the position of the human race is in some way wildly abnormal so that the parts of nature which have fallen under its observation have been utterly non-typical of the whole."[31]

The last assumption would mean, either that human beings happen to live in a spatio-temporal region which is very unlike the rest of the universe, or that some limitations in our perceptive powers or interests have prevented us from noting all but instances of a few possible sorts.[32] After examination,[33] the second alternative is rejected. We are left with the first alternative.

Now if the heaping of individuals about kinds be a peculiarity of a small section of the universe, whilst elsewhere the distribution is nearly uniform, it is highly unlikely that human observers will have happened to fall just into this part of the universe. The larger we suppose the universe to be compared with the part of it which has this peculiarity the less likely it is ante-

---

25 [1II], 16.
26 As far as I can see Broad nowhere defines the notion of a Natural Kind. He would probably (cf. [1II], p. 16) accept Mill's definition.
27 The question is discussed in sections 10–13 and 20 of the second part of [1].
28 [1II], 26.   29 [1II], 27.
30 *Ibid.*   31 *Ibid.*
32 *Ibid.*   33 [1II], 27f.

cedently that—human experience should have fallen totally inside this peculiar region.[34]

The objection may be advanced[35] that the human race arose from definite causes in a definite part of the universe and that therefore the talk of its being "shot at random" into the world is nonsense. Broad tries to show[36] that this objection is invalid. The talk of causes of the origin of the human race presupposes that the part of nature which has fallen under human experience is not peculiar in its nomic structure, but that causation operates outside this part in the same way as it operates inside it. The objection thus begs the question. I am not quite convinced by Broad's argument, but shall not subject it here to closer examination. Broad's conclusion anyway is that

it is highly improbable that the general characteristic of confinement to kinds, which we have noticed, extends but slightly beyond the limits of human experience. We thus seem justified in disregarding the possibility that this characteristic of the experienced world does not extend beyond it, as an argument against induction.[37]

How, if at all, is Broad's probability-argument about induction and natural kinds relevant to the question of initial probabilities of laws of nature and thus to the question of a correct formulation of inductive arguments in terms of probability? There is no answer to this question in Broad's paper, and the question itself is not quite clearly presented.[38] In one place he says,[39] quite rightly I think, that his argument may be used to probabilify the *general* view that there are kinds and nomic connexions in nature, rather than used to probabilify any *special* generalizations about such and such kinds or such and such causal relationships. Thus he comes himself near to admitting that his argument cannot, in combination with the Fundamental Theorem of Confirmation, be used to raise the probability of any single inductive conclusion appreciably above the zero-level.[40] I think that this admission is necessary and that *Unax* and the theory of natural kinds cannot—unless strengthened very much beyond the content Broad gives to these ideas—be used for securing finite initial probabilities to (some) laws of nature and thus for satisfying *one* of the conditions for increase in the probability of inductions through confirming instances.

iii. The answer to the second of our three questions above is thus, I

34 [1ᴵᴵ], 29.   35 [1ᴵᴵ], 29f.
36 [1ᴵᴵ], 30.   37 [1ᴵᴵ], 43.
38 Cf. the conclusions in section 20 of the second part of [1].
39 [1ᴵᴵ], 31.
40 Yet this appears to be implicitly contradicted by the remarks on p. 44 in [1ᴵᴵ].

believe, negative. The general principles about the constitution of the physical world which Broad discusses in [1] do not serve the purpose of making inductive conclusions, formulated in terms of probability, follow logically from factual premises and necessary principles of probability theory.

It follows from this that the question of the *truth* of the general principles is not directly relevant to the discussion in [1] of the nature and justification of inductive inferences. By this I mean that, even if we could prove these principles to be true, we should not, from what we are being told in [1], know how to use them to probabilify inductions. This I shall take as an excuse for not discussing here the problem of truth in question. But I do not wish to say that the theory of natural kinds in [1] could not be further elaborated so as to become relevant to the problem of a "rational reconstruction" of inductive arguments in probabilistic terms. And, quite apart from this, the theory itself is of great interest.

I shall conclude my examination of [1] by briefly drawing attention to two points in Broad's theory of kinds, substances, and causation, which, though scarcely directly relevant to the problem of probabilifying inductive conclusions, yet seem to me very important. I regret that I cannot possibly do justice to the wealth of ideas contained in Broad's own discussion of the topics.

a. The assumption of the existence of kinds of substance involves an assumption of the existence of substances. In speaking of the species *swan* we assume that there are individual substances, *i.e.* persistent physical things, which may be identified as swans. But what is our evidence that there are such things? A persistent thing may, somehow, be regarded as a complex of its "states."[41] Such states are what we observe of the thing. Now saying of two observed states, separated in time, that they are states *of the same thing* involves rather complicated assumptions about the existence of unobserved intermediate states, related to one another and to the two observed states in a certain way. Our evidence for these assumptions consists of observations on series of states of other substances *of the same kind*. Thus the three notions of natural kinds, of individual substances, and of plausible inductions are seen to be interdependent. Kinds presuppose substances; the evidence for substances is inductive; the warrant of the plausibility of inductions are kinds.

I am not sure that I quite understand Broad's argument about the relation of the assumption of kinds to the assumption of substances and particularly not about the relation of substances to their states. But the

41 [1^{II}], 20f.

circularity as regards the basis of induction, which Broad points out, seems to me to be unavoidable. It does not follow that the circularity is necessarily of a vicious kind, nor does Broad say that it is. As far as I can see, he does not investigate the possible consequences of the circularity in question to the problem of justifying induction.

"The world as it presents itself to superficial observation," Broad says,[42]

fulfils to a highly surprising extent the condition of consisting of permanent substances of a few marked kinds.—But it does not fulfil it altogether. The position is that it fulfils it so well as to raise the expectation that a modification of the definition of permanence and of kinds, which shall be in the spirit of the original definitions, can be found, and that with this definition the universe will *strictly* consist of permanent substances belonging to a few ideal kinds.[43]

The required modification is accomplished, when we make use of causal notions to account for α) why the properties of the states, a series of which constitutes a thing, do not always remain constant throughout the series but sometimes come into being, vary, and pass away, and β) why contemporary states of different series, which constitute substances of the same kind, are not exactly alike but deviate more or less from what may be called the "norm" or "ideal" of the kind.[44]

Thus by an extension, in terms of causality, of the notions of substance and kind we may restore the ideas of permanence of substance and ideality of kinds. "The permanence of first-order properties and their exact similarity among all instances, which first suggested kinds and permanent things, breaks down; but it is replaced by *permanence of laws*."[45]

There is also another way, in which causation becomes involved in the notion of a kind, *viz.* when a kind is defined (partly) in terms of causal properties of substances. This happens, for example, when it is regarded as part of the definition of silver that it is the kind of substance which gives a white insoluble compound with chlorine.[46]

Thus the notions of substance, kind, and causation can truly be said to form "parts of a highly complex and closely interwoven whole and any one of them breaks down hopelessly without the rest."[47]

That there is a connexion between the three notions mentioned can hardly be denied. The connexion, moreover, is probably of such a character that inductions about properties of kinds of substance (such as "all crows are black") depend for their formal validity (either in Broad's

42 [1ɪɪ], 39.
43 A kind will be called "ideal," if its instances are *exactly* similar. See [1ɪɪ], p. 38.
44 [1ɪɪ], 37 f.   45 [1ɪɪ], 40. Italics mine.
46 [1ɪɪ], 34.   47 [1ɪɪ], 44.

sense in [1] or in some related sense), not only on some general principle about natural kinds (such as *Unax*), but also on some or several general principles about causation between events. What precisely this dependence is, cannot, I think, be seen from Broad's paper. But what he has to say about the matter is sufficiently interesting to be a challenge to others to try to make these intricate connexions in the conceptual groundplan of nature more perspicuous.

II

1. In [6] Broad takes the same view as in [1] as regards the correct formulation of problematic inductions, *viz.* that their conclusions should be stated in terms of probability.[48] This opinion was criticized above (p. 316 bottom).

If from a premiss of the form "All observed S's have been P" we draw a conclusion (as to the probability of a proposition) of the form "All S's whatever are P," we have what Broad calls[49] a Nomic Generalization. If from a premiss of the same form we draw a conclusion of the form "The next S to be observed will be P" we have a Nomic Eduction. If from a premiss of the form "A certain proportion of the observed S's have been P" we draw a conclusion of the form "A certain proportion of the total number of S's are P" we have a Statistical Generalization. And if from a premiss of the same form we draw a conclusion of the form "The next S to be observed will be P" we have a Statistical Eduction.

The term "eduction" Broad has from W. E. Johnson. The distinction between eduction and generalization is certainly useful. But I am not quite happy with Broad's (and Johnson's) way of making it. Since the matter is of more than terminological interest, I shall dwell upon it for a moment.

Suppose the conclusion of an inductive argument were of the form "The *n* next S's will be P." How shall this case be classified? It would seem that, if *n* equals 1, we have a case of eduction, and if *n* equals the total number of unobserved S's we have a generalization. Further, if *n* is greater than 1 but less than the total number of unobserved S's, we have a third case which is *neither* eduction *nor* generalization, and if *n* equals 1 and the total number of unobserved S's is also 1, we have a fourth case which is *both* eduction *and* generalization.

Broad does not make a sharp distinction between an inductive conclusion which applies to an (at least "potentially") infinite multitude of unobserved cases and one which applies to a numerically restricted

---

48 [6], 1f.   49 [6], 2.

multitude. Instead of "infinite multitude" we may (here) also say "open class" and instead of "numerically restricted multitude" we may also say "closed class." This distinction is far from unproblematic. There are some indications that Broad has wished to avoid the problems relating to the notions of generality and infinity with which this distinction is intimately connected. Yet I think that this distinction is necessary for the purpose of classifying inductive conclusions. And I would myself reserve the name "generalization" for inductive conclusions about open classes, and use the term "eduction" for inductions about closed classes.

Now, as far as I can see, the theory of inductive probability which Broad develops in [6] and which is a variant of the doctrine of inverse probability applies only to inductive conclusions about *closed* classes. This theory is thus a theory of what I would call the probability of eductions, as opposed to (genuine) generalizations.

The theory of generators, on the other hand, which Broad also develops in [6] and which may be characterized as a further elaboration of some suggestions made by Keynes, is a theory about the logic of nomic connexions in nature. And it is at least highly plausible to think that generalizations about such connexions are propositions about *open* classes. This makes it difficult to see how the theory of generators could be relevant to Broad's theory in [6] of the probability of inductions, although the purpose of the former may be said to be to warrant certain assumptions about nature which turn out to be necessary in the latter. As we shall see later, Broad does not succeed in linking the two theories with one another. I would myself doubt whether such a link can be found. I should venture to maintain that the theory of generators is relevant neither to Broad's nor to any other version of the doctrine of inverse probability (Bayes's Theorem, Laplace's Rule of Succession, *etc.*) but to quite another type of theory of inductive probability. This other type of theory deals with the probability of generalizations relative to confirming evidence (instances) entailed by the generalization. This theory, though founded by Broad in [1], is not treated by him in [6]. Thus [6] consists in fact of two parts which are not relevant to one another.

2. As in [1], Broad first considers the drawing of counters from a bag *without* replacement. He produces a very handsome derivation, which makes no use of integration, of the formula $\dfrac{m+1}{m+2}$ for Nomic Eduction and $\dfrac{m+1}{n+1}$ for Nomic Generalization. These are called Laplace's First and Second Rules of Succession. The proof requires the two assumptions of equi-probability mentioned in [1] and discussed above on p. 318.

The assumption that all proportions of, say, red counters in a bag are initially equally probable, which Broad accepted in [1], is now rejected on the ground that several different so-called *constitutions* of the bag may answer to one and the same *proportion* of red counters in it.[50] Broad speaks of it as the false[51] assumption of equi-probability. As an alternative to it he considers the following assumption which he thinks is true:[52] Any individual counter is as likely to have any specific colour as any other. (The number of distinguishable colours is assumed to be ν.) Under this assumption the Laplacean formulae cannot be derived. Instead we get for Nomic Eduction the, somewhat disappointing, result that the probability that the *next* counter will have a certain colour is not at all affected by the fact that all drawn counters have had this colour.[53] For Nomic Generalization, however, we get a formula showing that the probability that *all* counters will have a certain colour increases with the number of already drawn counters which have been found to have this colour.[54]

In calling the one assumption of equi-probability false and the other true Broad evidently thinks that the first can be shown to be an invalid and the second a valid application of a Principle of Indifference. In [1], moreover, he regarded this principle itself as an *a priori* truth of probability-theory.[55] In [6], he does not mention it among the formal principles of probability and logic, necessary for his proofs.[56] I regret that Broad has nowhere discussed in detail this most important and controversial idea in the philosophy of probability.[57]

I do not believe myself that there is any way of *proving* or *disproving* either assumption of equi-probability. The distinction between constitutions and proportions gives no conclusive evidence against the Laplacean assumption. The distinction only shows that there is no *obvious* way of "splitting up" the situation into unit-alternatives of equal "weight" even in the seemingly simple case of proportions of counters in a bag.

It is noteworthy that Broad does not consider, as an alternative to the rejected assumption of equi-probability, the assumption that all constitutions of the bag are initially equally probable. If I am not mistaken, the assumption of equi-probability of constitutions would lead to the same, disappointing, result in the case of Nomic Eduction as does Broad's assumption about equi-probability of colouring, *viz.* that no

---

50 [6], 7. See also above p. 318.   51 [6], 7 and *passim*.
52 [6], 7 and *passim*.   53 [6], 8.
54 [6], 9.   55 See above p. 318.   56 [6], 3.
57 In [2] Broad discusses, in some detail, Keynes' and in [11] Kneale's version of the Principle of Indifference.

amount of favourable evidence in the past can affect the probability that the next ball is, say, red. This "eductive inefficiency" of the assumption of equi-probable constitutions, incidentally, has been used by Carnap[58] as an argument *for* (a modified form of) the original Laplacean assumption of equi-probable proportions.

Broad goes on to consider some probability-problems in connexion with the throwing of a counter with two faces. These problems are equivalent to problems of drawing counters from a bag *with* replacement. I shall here skip the mathematical part of the discussion and proceed to the important notion of *loading*. We say that the counter is loaded to a degree *s* in favour of red, if, and only if, the antecedent probability of its turning up red would be *s* for anyone who knew in detail how it was constructed.[59]

3. The notion of loading is not peculiar to problems on throwing counters. It is present also in problems on drawing with or without replacement. In stating the above First Premise of Equi-probability we assume that the counters have an equal load in favour of being drawn.[60]

Now Broad makes an extremely interesting suggestion about the evaluation of a load or, as I should prefer to call it, antecedent probability. If I understand him rightly, he wants to say that *any* such evaluation has, in the last resort, to rely on some assumption of *equi-probability*. We could not, for example, evaluate the probability of a counter falling with the red side upwards unless we knew the antecedent probabilities of its striking the table at each of the possible angles. And these antecedent probabilities, Broad goes on to say,[61] could not be evaluated without some assumption about equi-probability. This assumption could be, *e.g.*, that it is equally probable that the counter will strike the table at any given angle as at any other.

"The notion of loading," Broad says,[62] speaking of throwing a counter, "is the notion of a constant cause-factor which operates throughout the whole series of throws and co-operates with other and variable cause-factors to determine the result of each throw." I am not sure in what sense the term "cause-factor" should be understood here. The load, I should have thought, is a certain antecedent probability. Is this probability *itself* a cause-factor? Or does the cause consist in some features of the physical world (other than probabilities), which may be held "responsible" for the load? (Such features could be, *e.g.*, properties of the counter and conditions under which it is being thrown.)

58 *Logical Foundations of Probability,* § 110 A.
59 [6], 12.
60 [6], 14f. I hope this is a correct rendering of Broad's idea.
61 [6], 17.   62 [6], 13f.

The question is of some importance, since Broad now goes on to maintaining that "every inductive argument, whether it be a nomic generalization, an education, or a statistical generalization, equally presupposes the notion of causal determination."[63]

If, for the sake of argument, we assume that every inductive conclusion in terms of probability is dependent upon the notion of load, *i.e.* upon antecedent probabilities, *and* that every load has ultimately to be evaluated in terms of equi-probabilities, then the following question arises: Does Broad's statement about the dependence of induction upon causation amount to anything *more* than the said dependence of induction upon antecedent probability *and* of antecedent probability upon equi-probability? If the answer is in the negative, then I think that Broad's formulation above somewhat overstates the nature of the dependence in question. I hope Broad could illuminate this point in his reply.

I shall not here restate or examine the Fundamental Causal Premise upon which, according to Broad, any inductive argument (in terms of probability?) rests.[64] This premiss is, as Broad observes,[65] not the same as the Law of Universal Causation.

4. After his discussion of the causal presuppositions of the theory of inductive probability, Broad returns to the Rule of Succession. The probability, which the Laplacean rules confer upon eductions and generalizations could presumably be increased, if we could replace the Laplacean assumption of equi-probability of degrees of loading by some other assumption which favours a high degree of loading (in favour of a certain result in the experiment). This other assumption Broad calls an Assumption of Loading. "It is required," Broad says,[66] "not to validate inductive arguments as such, but to validate the claims of *some* of them to produce *high* probabilities."

As far as I can see, it is one of the objectives of the Theory of Generators to justify such Assumptions of Loading.[67] Exactly *how* the theory is supposed to do it, I have not however been able to figure out. (*Vide infra.*)

5. When from the "artificial" cases considered in sections 2–4 we pass to "natural" cases such as inductions about the properties of substances or the causal concatenation of events, a number of differences should be noted which affect the conditions of applicability of the formulae of inverse probability. Broad's comments in [6] on this topic are similar

---

63 [6], 15.   64 [6], 15.   65 [6], 16.

66 [6], 18.   67 Cf. [6], 22, 36–38, and 45.

to his comments on it in [1].[68] The following three points are emphasized:

i. The number of members of a natural class (such as the class of all swans) is *unknown*. Broad says[69] that "it is almost certainly very great as compared with the number that have been observed up to any given moment." As a consequence of this the value $\dfrac{m+1}{n+1}$ will be vanishingly small, and the Laplacean formulae will anyway be useless for assessing the probability of nomic and statistical generalizations.—I would myself have gone a step further and said that the number of members of a natural class is "potentially infinite" and that we therefore have no right to assume even that it is *some* finite number n. The Laplacean formulae for nomic and statistical generalizations have no *application* to natural classes.

ii. The same object (*e.g.* a swan) may be observed several times without our noticing the identity. Thus we may be led to thinking that the number m is greater than it really is. This will lead us to over-value inductive probabilities.

iii. Our observations are from a limited region in space and time. This means that the assumption breaks down, according to which every individual in the class has an equal chance of being observed by us. On the function and necessity of this premiss of equi-probability we made some comments above on p. 318f.

The upshot of all this is, according to Broad,[70] that if the application of inductive arguments to nature is to lead to reasonable probable conclusions, then

a) "we must have some reason to believe that something analogous to 'loading' exists in nature, and that certain kinds of 'loading' are antecedently more probable than others," and

b) we must somehow get over the objection which follows from *iii* above as regards equi-probability.

I must confess that I do not see how Broad's demand under *a)* is linked with his observations on the difference between the artificial and the natural cases. Nor can I see how the Theory of Generators and Limited Independent Variety, which Broad now proceeds to develop, satisfies either demand. We now pass on to an examination of this theory.

6. The germ to the Theory of Generators is found in the second half of the part on induction and analogy in Keynes' *Treatise*.[71] Its

---

68 See above p. 318.   69 [6], 19.
70 [6], 22.   71 Cf. [6], 23.

development by Broad, however, is an essentially original and important contribution of his to logic. It is worth a much more detailed presentation and discussion than can be given to it in this essay. The subject is rather technical. I hope someone would take it up for further development and I believe that this should happen within the framework of a Logic of Conditions. This framework was developed and used by Broad himself in [7] for his theory of so-called demonstrative induction which we shall examine in the next section of the present paper.

The Theory of Generators is based upon certain assumptions which may—with some simplification—be stated as follows:[72]

Let us assume that we are given two mutually exclusive sets of characteristics (properties). We call them a set of generating and a set of generated characteristics respectively. The first contains n and the second N (logically and causally independent) members. The number n is finite and smaller than N. Every single member of the second set is "generated" by some member or conjunction of members from the first set. This means that whenever the member or conjunction of members from the set of generating properties is present, then the member in question from the set of generated properties will be present too. One and the same member from the set of generated properties may be generated by more than one member or conjunction of members from the set of generating properties. If this actually is the case, we say that the member in question of the set of generated properties has a Plurality of Generators.

We shall call the assumptions underlying the Theory of Generators by the name of the Principle of Limited Variety.[73] We may distinguish two forms of the Principle: a stronger form which excludes and a weaker form which admits Plurality of Generators.

Broad does not state explicitly, whether it is essential to the Principle of Limited Variety that the number N too should be *finite*. But in at least one place his argument presupposes that N is finite.[74] The assumption of a finite N seems to me to lessen considerably the *prima facie* plausibility of the Principle of Limited Variety as a proposition of the Metaphysics of Nature.

The sense in which the Principle of Limited Variety may be said to *limit* variety in nature is worth some special comments:

Consider any true Nomic Generalization which holds between two mutually exclusive sets of generated characteristics.[75] An example could

72 [6], 25f.   73 [6], 42.
74 See [6], 30f., and below p. 335.
75 Cf. Broad's definition of a *generalization* in [6], 25.

be the proposition that anything which has C_1 and C_2 and C_3 also has C_4 and C_5. C_1, C_2, and C_3 are called subject-factors, C_4 and C_5 predicate-factors. Now assume that C_1 and C_2 and C_3 are, in the above sense, generated by G. Then, by laws of logic, C_4 and C_5 are also generated by G. Thus the truth of the Nomic Generalization in question may be attributed to the generating capacity or, as Broad calls it,[76] *fertility* of the generator G. Since, on our assumption, the number of generating characteristics and conjunctions of characteristics is *finite* (it is 2^n-1), it follows that *all* Nomic Generalizations which hold true for sets of generated characteristics may be thus attributed to the generating capacity of a limited, finite number of generators.

Unless we assume that N too is finite, there is nothing to exclude a generator from having *infinite fertility*, *i.e.* from having the capacity of generating an infinite number of generated characteristics. (Indeed, if N *is* infinite, there must be at least one generator of infinite fertility.) Thus the Principle of Limited Variety, without the assumption of a finite N, does not entail that there is a finite number of irreducible nomic connexions (between generating and generated characteristics) in nature.

We now come to the question, how the Theory of Generators is relevant to the antecedent probability of Nomic Generalizations (for generated characteristics). Broad conducts two different arguments to show that this antecedent probability will be greater than 0. The second argument leads to a somewhat stronger conclusion than the first.[77]

According to the first argument,[78] the antecedent probability of an arbitrary generalization can be expressed as a product of two probabilities. The one is the probability, given the Principle of Limited Variety, that the (combination of) subject-factors of the generalization are generated by (the conjunction of) exactly r members of the set of generating characteristics and the (combination of) predicate-factors by (the conjunction of) exactly s members of the set mentioned. The other is the probability that the s generating factors required by the predicate are wholly contained among the r generating factors required by the subject. Broad thinks that the product-probability will be greater than 0.[79] This commits him to holding that both factors of the product are greater than 0. The second factor he identifies with the ratio of the number of ways of choosing s things out of r things to the number of ways of choosing s things out of n things. One gets the impression that

76 [6], 25.   77 Cf. [6], 31.
78 [6], 27.   79 [6], 31.

he regards this identification as something unproblematic,—which it hardly is. The ratio in question is, on our assumptions, certainly greater than 0. The first factor Broad does not attempt to evaluate numerically. He explicitly says[80] that he does not see how to do it, and mentions some difficulties which seem to me to be very much to the point. And, for all I can see, he has not even proved that the factor must be greater than 0. For *this* reason already Broad's first argument seems to me to be inconclusive.

The second argument requires some interesting Lemmas. Of the relative values of n and N Broad proves[81] that if $n \geqq N$, then there *may be no* true generalization (for generated characteristics), and if $n < N$ then there *must be some* true generalization. Now it is part of the assumptions that $n < N$. If, moreover, some of the possible Nomic Generalizations (for generated characteristics) is true, then, by laws of logic, some *such* generalization must be true, the subject of which is the conjunction of all but one of the generated characteristics and the predicate of which is the one remaining generated characteristic. There are in all N Nomic Generalizations of this description. From this Broad concludes that the antecedent probability of any of them will be at least $1/N$. If N is finite this fraction is greater than 0.

It is to be noted that the second argument presupposes that N is *finite*. (The first argument is independent of this assumption.) It further presupposes that the antecedent probability of a generalization can be linked with a ratio of true generalizations. (In this respect the first and the second argument resemble each other.) The nature and justification of the link is not made clear.

The upshot of the matter seems to me to be that Broad has *not* been completely successful in showing how the Theory of Generators assures a finite antecedent probability to Nomic Generalizations. Assume, however, for the sake of argument, that he had succeeded in showing this. What further implications would follow for the theory of the probability of inductions?

As far as I can see *nothing* would follow which is relevant to the theory developed by Broad in the first half of [6], *i.e.* to the probability-theory of what he in [1] calls Induction by Simple Enumeration. But *something* important would follow for the probability-theory of what Broad in [1] calls the Hypothetical Method. It would follow that *one* of the two conditions which are necessary, if the probability of a Nomic Generalization is to be increased through confirmation, is fulfilled. But it would not follow that the second condition is fulfilled.

80 [6], 30.   81 [6], 27–30.

The reasoning has so far been conducted on the assumption of the strong form of the Principle of Limited Variety which excludes Plurality of Generators. Later Broad indicates[82] how the reasoning may be modified so as to apply also under the weaker assumption admitting Plurality of Generators. Then the question of evaluating probabilities on the basis of combinatorial calculations becomes still more tricky and dubious.

We shall not here discuss at length the plausibility of the assumption that properties which occur in nature can be divided into exclusive sets of generating and generated characteristics. Broad shows,[83] very elegantly I think, how we may *dispense* with this division altogether and yet retain everything that is essential to the Principle of Limited Variety. Instead of postulating the existence of a distinct set of generating properties, we assume that the one set of (generated and generating) properties falls into a finite number of what Broad calls[84] *coherent sets.* A set of characteristics is said to be coherent, if no member of the set can occur without all the remaining members occurring. This simplifies the Theory of Generators. But it does not help us to clear up the problem concerning its relevance to the probability of inductions.

It is clear that—whether or not we wish to dispense with the assumption of a distinct set of generators—we could not profitably discuss the plausibility of the Principle of Limited Variety unless we first made clear, to what sort of "characteristics" or "properties" this principle is intended to apply. It may well be the case that for some kinds of characteristic the principle has a certain *prima facie* plausibility, whereas for other kinds it has none.

Broad thinks[85] that the characteristics ought to be *determinables.* It would be absurd, he says,[86] to suppose that the members of the set of generating properties are determinates. The reason he gives is that any determinable may have an infinity of determinates falling under it. And if the generating properties are determinables, the properties which they (or their conjunctions) generate must be determinables too. This, in Broad's view, follows from the nature of determinables and determinates.

The restriction of the characteristics, to which the Theory of Generators may apply, to determinables diminishes its importance to inductive logic. The theory could then, if at all, only serve to probabilify generalizations of the type which Broad in [7] calls Laws of Conjunction of De-

82 [6], 34–36.   83 [6], 38–41.
84 [6], 39.   85 [6], 41f.
86 [6], 41.

terminables. Of them Broad says[87] that "only the most backward sciences are content with such generalizations."

Neither in [6] nor in [7] does Broad define the notions of determinable and determinate. I think he intends to use them in the same sense as W. E. Johnson. But the precise meaning of the terms with Johnson is not clear to me. (Indeed, I find Johnson's use of them ambiguous and confused.) I have therefore not been able to form an opinion of the seriousness to inductive logic of the alleged restriction of generator-properties to determinables. I hope Broad could illuminate the point in his reply. Of the notions of determinable and determinate we shall have to make a few more remarks in connexion with the discussion of [7].

7. The Principle of Limited Variety was thought by Broad to be an ontological precondition, "if inductive arguments are ever to be able to establish reasonably high probabilities." Leaving aside the problem of necessity and sufficiency of this condition, we raise the question: Can we know, whether it is in fact fulfilled? Broad calls this the *epistemic* question.[88]

Broad regards it as excluded that we could know the Principle of Limited Variety with *certainty*. But he thinks that an argument can be conducted in favour of the principle's *probability*.

I shall not reproduce here the formal part of the argument. Its material content consists of two probability-assumptions.

The first rests upon an analogy:

We do know that we can actually construct out of simple parts of the same nature complicated structures which behave in very different ways, *e.g.*, watches, motor-cars, gramophones, *etc*. The differences in observable behaviour are here known to be due simply to differences in arrangement of materials having the same properties; and these materials, and the structures formed of them, are parts of the material world. Relative to this fact it does seem to me that there is a finite probability that the variety of *material* nature at any rate, should arise in the same way.[89]

Broad observes,[90] that there is no similar ground for believing in a Principle of Limited Variety as far as *mental* phenomena are concerned.

The material basis of the second probability-assumption involved in Broad's argument is the observed fact "that there is a great deal of recurrence and repetition in nature."[91] "Now, if the Principle of Limited Variety were true, there would be recurrence and repetition in nature; whilst if it were not, there is very little reason to expect that there would be."[92]

87 [6], 41f.   88 [6], 42.   89 [6], 43.
90 [6], 45.   91 [6], 43.   92 [6], 43f.

I do not find Broad's probability-argument either from the analogy with machines or from the observation of regularity in nature very convincing. A conclusive test of the argument's validity would, however, require that the argument itself is first given a much more rigorous formulation than is the case in Broad's paper.

Someone may think that the question of the truth or probability of the Principle of Limited Variety is anyway greatly diminished by the fact that the principle can do, if anything at all, even less than Broad thought in [6] to strengthen inductive arguments. Its role as an ontological precondition of induction is doubtful, to say the least.

But quite apart from its relevance, if any, to induction, the idea of limited variety in nature seems to me highly interesting. If I may conclude by expressing a personal opinion on the matter without giving sufficient reasons for it, I should say that the interest does not lie in the question of the *truth* of the idea so much as in the problem of its *formulation*. As we have seen, it is not obvious which assumptions should be regarded as essential to the Principle of Limited Variety (p. 333) nor is it obvious which aspect of reality constitutes its field of application (p. 336). To consider various alternatives to the solution of these problems is to deepen our insight into the conceptual network of thinking about nature and is *therefore* already a major task of a Natural Philosophy or Metaphysics of Nature. It is my belief that the nearer we come to accomplishing this task, the less will the problem of truth worry our minds. The craving turns out to be for clarity—not for truth or probability.

* * * * *

There are some errata in the mathematical formulae occurring in [6] which may confuse readers and therefore are worth listing:

P. 17 formula (8): for ρ_{m+1} read ρ_{n+1}.
P. 18 formula (9): the same mistake as in formula (8).
P. 25, line 22: for 2^N . . . 1 read $2^N - 1$.
P. 28, line 1: for $n \leq N$ read $n \geq N$.
P. 28, line 2: for $n > N$ read $n < N$.

III

1. In the widest sense, a *demonstrative induction* may be defined as follows: "P and i_1 and . . . i_n, therefore G." G is a generalization, of which i_1, etc. are instances. P is the so-called supplementary premiss. The argument is conclusive, *i.e.* the generalization follows logically from the conjunction of some of its instances and the supplementary premiss.

Following W. E. Johnson, Broad[93] gives a more restricted definition. He requires that P be a hypothetical proposition. The consequent of this hypothetical proposition is G. The antecedent is either an instance i of G or an existential (particular) proposition, entailed by G. The minor premiss is i.

An example of a demonstrative induction in Broad's sense would be: "If hydrogen can be liquefied, then every gas can be liquefied. Hydrogen can be liquefied. Therefore every gas can be liquefied."

The idea of a theory of demonstrative induction can be said to be implicit in Bacon's treatment of induction. It was, as far as I know, first formulated explicitly by Archbishop Whately,[94] whom Mill followed in his often quoted *dictum* that "every induction may be thrown into the form of a syllogism by supplying a major premiss."

It is noteworthy, however, that when Broad later in [7] gives a formal re-statement of Mill's methods he does not state them in a way which answers to his own pattern of demonstrative induction. I do not myself see any plausible way of stating them thus. But I believe that they can be stated so as to answer to the more general pattern mentioned above. How this is to be done, I shall not discuss here. Therefore I think that the Johnson-Broad definition of demonstrative induction stands in need of modification, if it is to fit, as it is obviously intended to do, some of the most important types of conclusive reasoning in connexion with induction.

2. In the traditional theory of the so-called methods of induction the notions of cause and effect hold a prominent place. As Broad observes,[95] the word "cause" is used very ambiguously both in ordinary life and in science. Sometimes the cause is being thought of as a necessary, sometimes as a sufficient, and sometimes as a necessary-and-sufficient condition of the effect.[96] The various kinds of condition are characteristically different in their logical properties. It may be shown that these properties are the only aspect of the notions of cause and effect which is relevant to the logical mechanism of *induction by elimination*. Elimination-theory, *i.e.* the main bulk of inductive logic in the tradition of Bacon and Mill, may therefore most conveniently be approached by way of the Logic of Conditions. To have inaugurated this approach seems to me

93 [7¹], 302ff.   94 *Elements of Logic*, bk. iv, ch. i, § 1.   95 [7¹], 304.
96 Sometimes the relation of "cause" to "condition" is even more complex. Thus, e.g., in the classical theory of inverse probability, which is also traditionally said to be a theory for estimating the probability of causes, "cause" (usually) means a member of a disjunction which is a necessary condition of a certain phenomenon. For such causes Broad (in [10], 16) has introduced the term *substitutable requirements*. See also below p. 343.

to be Broad's greatest over-all contribution to inductive logic. His ideas place an old subject on a new basis and open interesting prospects for further investigation.

3. In [7], before proceeding to develop a logic of conditions, Broad observes that there are two different types of causal laws. The first he calls Laws of Conjunction of Determinables. For example: cloven-footed animals chew the cud. The second he calls Laws of Correlated Variation of Determinates. An example would be the law for gases, stating that $P = RT/V$. A science in an early stage mainly has to be content with laws of the first type. The more "advanced" a science is, the more prominent are within it laws of the second type.

I believe that Broad is here aiming at a distinction which is very fundamental to the logical study of induction. But I am not quite satisfied that the distinction should be formulated as Broad does it here. My difficulty has to do, among other things, with some unclarities in the notions of determinable and determinate. (See above p. 337.)

These notions are obviously *sometimes* relative notions. "Bird" is a determinable relative to "raven" and a determinate relative to "animal." But it would be rash to maintain that there are no absolute determinates. And if there are, there are presumably also laws for their nomic connexions.

It seems to me, therefore, that we must accept as a third type of causal law Laws of Conjunction of Determinates. The fundamental dichotomy in the division of laws should—whatever be its precise nature—rather be formulated in terms of the contrast between *conjunctions* and *correlated variations* of characteristics than in terms of the opposites *determinable* and *determinate*. I shall in the following speak of conjunction-laws and variation-laws.

There are logical relations between the two types of law. Any variation-law, as far as I can see, entails a conjunction-law. (This seems at least to hold for Broad's conception of the two types.) For example: the formula $P=RT/V$ of correlated variations entails that pressure depends uniquely on temperature and volume. The entailed proposition may be called a conjunction-law. I understand that the first premiss in each of the four Johnsonian "figures of induction," which Broad explains in the second part of [7], is a conjunction-law in this sense.

I agree that this type of premiss is necessary for the correct formulation of the figures. And it is probably right to think—as seems to be implied by Broad's description of the situation in the opening paragraph of the second part of [7]—that methodical search of variation-laws *presupposes* methods for the establishment of conjunction-laws. These methods evidently must be methods of elimination. (The reader is asked to consider, *how* we may convince ourselves that, say, the pressure of a gas depends on its temperature and volume and on no other factors.) To give a precise account of them within the framework of a Logic of Conditions is therefore a primary task of any satisfactory logical theory of induction.

4. Broad in [7] is, as far as I know, the first to have given systematic attention to the logic of the various notions of condition. Besides in [7] he has also treated the subject in [8] and, with considerable additions to his original theory, in [10]. It is not necessary here to enter deeply into the technicalities of the subject. I shall confine myself to a few observations of a general nature:

i. Broad defines[97] "*C* is a sufficient condition of *E*" as meaning "Everything that has *C* has *E*," and "*C* is a necessary condition of *E*" as meaning "Everything that has *E* has *C*."

It is worth observing that the two notions are interdefinable. If *C* is a s.c. of *E*, then $\sim C$ (the absence of *C*) is a n.c. of $\sim E$ (the absence of *E*). That oxygen is necessary for life is equivalent to saying that absence of oxygen is sufficient to extinguish life.

This relation between the two types of condition, which follows from Broad's definitions of them, appears to be quite in order. Broad, though recognizing[98] "negative factors," does not mention it.

Another relation, however, which can also be deduced from the definitions, appears debatable. It is this: If *C* is a s.c. of *E*, then *E* is a n.c. of *C*. If rainfall is sufficient to wet the ground, then the ground becoming wet is necessary for rainfall. This sounds odd. The oddity, obviously, comes from the fact that the above definitions contain no reference to what may be called a *direction of determination*. In the realm of natural events and continuants, the conditioning factor is somehow *prior to* the conditioned factor. It is at least highly plausible to assume that this "priority" has to do with the notion of temporal succession. (This certainly holds for what Broad calls[99] the popular-scientific notions of cause and effect.) In Broad's (and my) Logic of Conditions, however, the asymmetry between conditioned and conditioning factors has vanished.

Broad maintains[100] that, from the point of view of "the logical manipulation" of the causal notions it is not necessary to pay attention to the idea of temporal succession. He *may* be right as far as the canons of induction by elimination are concerned. (I have certainly been inclined to think so myself in the past.) But I am sure that a fully satisfactory Logic of Conditions cannot be based on definitions of the various notions of condition in terms of universal material implication only.

97 [7¹], 306.   98 [7¹], 311.
99 [7¹], 310.   100 [7¹], 310.

A logical theory which accounts for the notion of a "direction of determination" is needed. And I believe that such a theory, once it has been
created, can serve to give a much fuller account also of the logic of
inductive methods than can the Logic of Conditions in its present
form.

It should be added in fairness to Broad's theory that it avoids some
of the oddities, which result from the definitions, by means of a device
to separate determining factors or C-factors as Broad calls them from
determined factors or E-factors.[101] This device, however, is purely
notational. It does not help us to overcome any real difficulties in the
theory.

ii. Postulates. The Logic of Conditions, as developed by Broad in [7],
uses two "postulates." The first Broad calls the "Postulate of Conjunctive Independence." It states, roughly speaking, that the (simple) C-
factors should be capable of independent presence or absence. Independence is here understood in the strong sense of both logical *and*
causal independence. The second postulate is called the "Postulate of
Smallest Sufficient Conditions." It says that any E-factor has, in every
instance of its occurrence, a Smallest Sufficient Condition. This means
that "whenever the characteristic E occurs, there is some set of characteristics (not necessarily the same in each case) such that the presence of
this set in any substance carries with it the presence of E, whilst the
presence of any selection from this set is consistent with the absence of
E."[102]

The second postulate is a greatly improved form of what most authors
on induction and scientific method vaguely refer to under the name of
Law of Universal Causation. It is clearly "extra-logical." It seems to
me to be in the interest of the logical purity of the theory to develop
the Logic of Conditions independently of this postulate. With its aid,
but not without it, one can prove, for example, that any factor which
is common to all the s.c.'s of a given E is a n.c. of E.[103] It is of some
importance to notice that, contrary to what there may be a tendency to
believe, the truth of this theorem does *not* follow from the definitions
of the notions of condition and principles of pure logic alone. It would
therefore give a clearer picture of the case, if the existential assumption
on which this theorem depends were stated as part of the theorem
itself and not as a postulate of the entire theory.

iii. Complexity of Conditions. The most serious insufficiency of
Broad's Logic of Conditions in [7] is that it neglects disjunctive necessary
conditions. In [10] Broad corrects his theory on this point. In [10] other

---

101 [7¹], 305.   102 [7¹], 307.   103 [7¹], 308, Proposition (6).

important additions are also found. Among them is the introduction of the notions of *contributory condition* and *substitutable requirement*. If C_1 and C_2 are disjunctively necessary for E, they are called substitutable requirements of E. If they are conjunctively sufficient, Broad calls them contributory conditions. (In [8] he had coined the not very happy name "relatively necessary conditions.") A contributory condition which is a common ingredient in all the sufficient conditions of a phenomenon he calls an *indispensible contributory condition*. It is important not to confuse indispensible contributory conditions with necessary conditions.[104]

iv. Plurality of Conditions. Cause and effect are said[105] to stand in the relation of total cause to total effect when, roughly speaking, the effect is a conjunction of all the factors, of which the cause is a s.c. It follows that one and the same total effect may have several total causes, but that one and the same cause can have only one total effect. If, however, we allow disjunctive effect-factors (as I think we should do), then there is a sense in which we may speak of a plurality of effects too. For then we may have that C is *sometimes* followed by E_1 and *sometimes* by E_2. But even in this case the effect would be unique in the sense that C would *always* be followed by at least one of the two factors, E_1 and E_2. (Disjunctive effects are worth a closer scrutiny.)

Broad's statement[106] that, even under the Postulate of Smallest Sufficient Conditions, an effect may have *no* n.c. is of course false, if we admit conditions of a disjunctive form. It is of some interest to note that the postulate in question actually is equivalent to saying that every E has a *necessary-and-sufficient* condition, *viz.* the disjunction of *all* its s.c.'s.

5. Broad's formal statement of Mill's methods does not seem to me quite happy. Broad's reasoning, unlike Mill's, is entirely correct. But Broad, like Mill, fails to notice that there is an essential asymmetry between the two methods of Agreement and Difference, when used for the search of conditions of given phenomena. The Method of Agreement is (primarily) fitted for the task of finding the necessary conditions of a given phenomenon. In Mill's terminology: finding the effect of a given cause. Or as Broad put it:[107] finding *of what* a given phenomenon is a sufficient condition. The Method of Difference again is fitted for the converse task of finding the sufficient conditions of a given factor. In Mill's terminology: the cause of a given effect. In Broad's: finding *of what* something is a necessary condition.

104 [10], 17.
106 [7^I], 312.
105 [7^I], 311f.
107 [7^I], 313.

Broad's description of the reasoning employed and the suppressed premises needed, when the two methods are used for their primary task, is confined to the special case, when there are only two "instantial" premises and no admission of Complexity of Conditions.

Broad also formalizes a use of the Method of Agreement for finding sufficient conditions and a use of the Method of Difference for finding necessary conditions of a given phenomenon. For this purpose he has to rely on *universalized* instantial premises, *i.e.* premises of the form "*all ABC* is *abc*," etc. (The same form is used also in Broad's account of what I called the primary task of the two methods, but here the universalization is inessential—and therefore in my opinion misleading.) This universalization of the premises he nowhere explains.[108] It makes it possible for him to "read off" relations of sufficient conditionship directly from the instantial premises themselves. (For example: that *ABC* is a s.c. of *abc*.) From the relations, thus established, in combination with suitable "suppressed premises" the desired conclusions follow. The reasoning is quite correct. But I doubt whether the resulting figures can be called formalizations of Mill's canons. As far as I can see, there is no universalization of the instantial premises even tacitly presupposed in Mill's description of his methods.

Mill's description of his Joint Method is notoriously confused, and Broad has no difficulty in subjecting it to a devastating criticism.[109] Then he goes on to suggest an interesting improvement of the method. Broad's improvement makes clear the proper purpose of the Joint Method, which is to *combine* the use of a canon for eliminating possible necessary conditions with the use of a canon for eliminating possible sufficient conditions so as to obtain a method for ascertaining the necessary-and-sufficient conditions of a given phenomenon. Broad seems to think[110] that this combined method, though "important and legitimate," is not "absolutely conclusive" and, if I understand him rightly, in this respect different from the methods of Agreement and of Difference when correctly formalized. This view of the matter, however, is mistaken. The mistake is suggested by a peculiarity in Broad's description which, I think, ought to be corrected. The proper conclusion of the first part of the method, as described by Broad on p. 316 in [7¹], is that *a* is the only possible (simple) necessary condition of *A*. The proper conclusion of the second part again is that non-*a* is the only possible (simple) necessary condition of non-*A* or, which means the same, that *a* is the only possible (simple) sufficient condition of *A*. Taken in com-

---

108 I think the reader of Broad's paper will have to consult Johnson's *Logic*, pt. II, ch. X, especially § 4 and § 5 for an explanation.
109 [7¹], 315f.   110 [7¹], 317.

bination, the conclusions of both parts amount to saying that a is the only possible (simple) necessary-and-sufficient condition of A. This is just *as* certain a conclusion as any corresponding result obtained by means of the methods of Agreement and Difference. Broad's reservation to the conclusion of each part: "strong presumption, though never a rigid proof," is therefore out of place.

6. The second part of [7] treats of Laws of Correlated Variation of Determinates. Considered as an original contribution to the subject, this part is not nearly as important as the first part of [7]. It is essentially a formalization of W. E. Johnson's[111] "figures of demonstrative induction." The basic ideas are Johnson's. But technically Broad's treatment constitutes a great improvement. Not only is it much clearer but it also puts right some errors in Johnson's account. On one point Broad makes a rather severe criticism of Johnson's views (*vide infra*).

The rather formidable looking symbolism which Broad employs in this paper need not deter any reader. As a notation it is perfectly perspicuous, and the ideas expressed by its means are very simple. (There are, incidentally, some minor misprints in the formulae: capital C being printed for small c in a number of places.) Indeed, there may be some justification for saying that these ideas are almost trivial. Without wishing in the least to exaggerate neither the intrinsic logical interest nor the practical scientific importance of a correct formalization of the ideas behind Mill's methods, it seems to me undeniable that they far outweigh the interest and importance of anything that has hitherto been accomplished in the study of Laws of Correlated Variation. This study is, as a branch of inductive logic, still almost undeveloped.

Broad first states the postulates, which are needed for the purpose of constructing the figures in the form of rigid demonstrations.

The first postulate needed specifically for establishing correlation laws Broad calls the "Postulate of the Uniqueness of the Determinate Total Effect." Let C and E stand for determinables and c and e for arbitrary determinate values under them. Let C and E be related as total cause to total effect. (See above p. 343.) Then the postulate says that, if the value c of C is *once* accompanied by the value e of E, then c of C will always be accompanied by e of E. This postulate may be said to serve the purpose of universalizing instantial premisses.

The second postulate Broad calls the "Postulate of Variational Independence." Let C and E again be related as total cause to total effect. Let C be a conjunction of some m and E a conjunction of some n determinables. The postulate now says that any given distribution of determinate values over the m determinables in C is a (logical and

111 *Logic,* pt. II, ch. X, §§ 8–20.

causal) possibility, and so is also any given distribution of determinate values over the n determinables in E. I hope this is a correct rendering of the thought behind Broad's formulation[112] which I do not find myself quite clear.

From this postulate, in combination with the first postulate, Broad deduces[113] a number of consequences relating to the (finite, denumerable, or non-denumerable) number of determinates under the cause- and effect-determinables. (If disjunctive determinables are allowed, Broad's conclusions would seem to require some modification.) Of most interest seems to me his discussion of the question, whether there can be an infinite number of determinates under the total cause and yet only a finite number of determinates under the total effect. The postulates are compatible with this possibility. Broad discusses[114] an example from science which looks like an actualization of it. But he also shows that, on closer examination, the case is, in the aspect under discussion, different from what it looks like. I wish someone could produce a genuine example and I should feel pretty certain that such examples exist.

The third and last postulate which is needed Broad calls the "Postulate of Variational Relevance" (or Irrelevance, depending upon the way it is formulated). Let C and E be related as total cause to total effect. Let C be a conjunction of m determinables. Consider a distribution of determinates over the m determinables. Then consider another distribution which we get from the first by replacing the value of the determinable C_i by a different value, the values of all the other $m-1$ determinables in C remaining unchanged. The postulate now says that, if to these two distributions correspond two different determinate values of E, then to any two different values of C_i there will, the values of all the other $m-1$ determinables, remaining unchanged, correspond two different values of E.

On this third postulate Broad makes the important comment that it certainly cannot be universally valid. Any law which takes the form of a *periodic* function will not satisfy it. For, it is characteristic of such laws that, when the values of the cause-factors differ by a multiple of the "period," the value of the effect-factor repeats itself. And, as Broad points out, not only is there no *a priori* objection to such laws, but some important natural phenomena are in fact governed by laws of this kind.

Of the first postulate I should like to point out the following: Let us consider what it would be for the postulate to be false. It would mean

---

112 [7^{II}], 427.   113 [7^{II}], 427–431.   114 [7^{II}], 429f.

that, *although* C is a sufficient condition of E, it may happen that to one and the same determinate value c of C there would on some occasions answer a value e_1 of E, on other occasions a value e_2, etc. This possibility is certainly not ruled out by the mere fact that C is a (smallest) sufficient condition of E. For this only means that to *any* occurrence of C in *any* of its determinate values c there answers an occurrence of E in *some* of *its* determinate values e. And, granted that there is this regularity, why should there then also be the further regularity to the effect that the e which answers to a given c must always be *one and the same* value e? I doubt whether any good reasons could be given for the truth of the postulate. Unfortunately I have not been able to produce any good example of a case, where the relation of C to E is that of cause to effect and yet the relation of c's to e's is not a many-to-one or a one-to-one correspondence.

Having stated the postulates, Broad restates and explains Johnson's "Figures of Induction." The statement of the figures is elegant and perspicuous and supercedes Johnson's own statement of them completely. I shall not dwell upon the topic here, since I find it of minor interest only. It should be noted that Broad's formalizations of these "figures" actually answers—unlike his formal statement of Mill's methods—to the general pattern of demonstrative induction which, following Johnson, Broad sketches at the beginning of the first part of [7] and which I ventured to criticize for being too narrow. (See above p. 339, top.)

IV

Broad's critical notices and papers in Mind [2], [3], [4], [9], [10], [11] may be said to constitute a running commentary on the developments in inductive logic from the appearance of Keynes' *Treatise* in 1921 to Kneale's *Probability and Induction* in 1949. Broad has a rare talent for synoptic presentation. This makes some of his reviews excellent summaries of the reviewed works. When he makes criticisms, it is usually not in order to express a divergent opinion from the author's on some controversial issue, but in order either to point out some factual error or to suggest a clearer formulation of what he understands to be the author's intended meaning. His criticism of errors seems to me nearly always conclusive and his criticism of formulations is such as to oblige both the authors and the readers of the reviewed books to gratitude.

1. In his review [2] of Keynes' *Treatise* Broad touches upon a question which he calls "extremely puzzling" and of which he says that he knows of no writers except himself and Keynes, who have even raised it. The self-reference is to Broad's first published book *Perception, Physics, and Reality.* The question could be put thus: Why do we prefer probabilities relative to many data? Keynes does not answer it. Broad, however, has the following suggestion to make:[115]

> I think that our preference must be bound up in some way with the notion that to every event there is a finite set of conditions relative to which the event is certain to happen or certain not to happen. So long as the evidence is scanty a high probability with respect to it does not make it reasonable to act as if we knew that the event would happen, because it is reasonable to suppose that we have only got hold of a very small section of the total conditions and that the missing ones may be such as to be strongly relevant in an unfavourable direction. If the probability remains high relative to a nearly exhaustive set of data we feel that there is less danger that the missing data may act in the opposite direction. In fact, what we assume is that a high probability with respect to a wide set of data is a sign of certainty with respect to the *complete* set of relevant data.

This is a most interesting suggestion. It seems to me that it contains something which is possibly not right, but also something which is essentially right and points towards a solution of the puzzle.

What I doubt is the suggested connexion between preference for many data and belief in determinism. For obviously we prefer probabilities relative to many data, not only in the case of very high or very low probabilities, but also in the case of intermediate probabilities. This preference, moreover, seems to be quite independent of whether the intermediate probabilities show a tendency or not to approach extreme values (0 or 1) when the number of data is increased.

I would suggest myself that the preference in question is bound up, not with belief in determinism, but with the idea that there exists something which could be called "complete sets of data which are relevant to the probability of a given event." (This notion is not unproblematic, but we cannot discuss its problems here. *If* determinism, in the sense of the above quotation from Broad [2], is true, there exist, for every event, such complete sets of relevant data. Some such set, moreover, is then included in every set of conditions relative to which the event in question is certain to happen.)

If this suggestion is accepted, then our preference for probabilities based on many data can be grounded on the following second-order probability-argument: The more data we actually consider when we determine the probability of an event, the more probable does it become that the set of considered data will include a complete set of relevant data. This argument, unless I am mistaken, is essentially the "point"

115 [2], 78.

of Broad's suggestion, although he limits it (unnecessarily, I believe) to sets of determining conditions only.

The nature and validity of this argument demands further clarification. It cannot be given here. I believe that the argument easily can be "formalized" within the calculus. There is no strong reason for thinking that the second-order probability in question has a different "meaning" from the first-order probability. But there is reason to think that we cannot, in normal cases, estimate its numerical value.

The question, why we prefer probabilities relative to many data, seems to me to be one of the fundamental questions in the philosophy of probability. To have been the first to state the question clearly and to suggest an answer to it, is a noteworthy merit of Broad's.[115a]

2. From Broad's very full review [9] of von Mises' *Wahrscheinlichkeit, Statistik und Wahrheit* I shall select one point for discussion. It concerns the notion of a so-called "collectivity," *i.e.* a potentially infinite sequence in which the relative frequency of a certain randomly distributed characteristic is assumed to approach a limiting value. This notion seems plausible enough when regarded as an extrapolation from experiential sequences such as throws with a die or other outcomes in games of chance. But, as Broad observes[116] "the case of vital statistics would seem to be somewhat different." Consider, for example, the probability that a certain Mr. Smith, who is now 40, will survive his next birthday. There is an important lack of symmetry between his case and that of a die. It has to do with the fact that, to quote Broad, "each man can die but once." We can carry out experiments with *one and the same die* to see how often, in average, it shows, say, a "six" and then extrapolate a limiting-frequency from the observations. But we cannot experiment with *one and the same man* of 40 to see how often, in average, he survives his next birthday. The experiment would require that we could make a man live through his 40th year any number of times. And this would be possible only if human bodies, like watches, could be "wound up" after each lifespan.

Unless I am completely mistaken, the discovered asymmetry has far-reaching consequences for probability-theory. If the notion of a collectivity is to apply to the case from vital statistics at all, the collectivity must be identifiable with some class of 40 years old men, of which Mr. Smith is a member. Depending upon the choice of this class, the probability may be different. *This* need not be a cause of worries, since it is plausible to think that all probability is *relative* to some evidence.

115a For a discussion of Broad's question see J. Hosiasson, "Why do we prefer probabilities relative to many data?," *Mind 40* (1931).

116 [9], 480.

The difficulty is one of being able to identify the collectivity in question with any class at all, of which Mr. Smith is a member. For it is plausible to think that the death-rate in every potentially infinite class of human beings will be subject to *alterations* following changes in the climatic, economic, hygienic, *etc.* conditions, under which the members of the class happen to live, and there is usually no ground for thinking that the rate in question will approximate even to *some* limit. And as a consequence of this instability in the conditions determining the frequencies in such classes, the notion of a frequency-limit and therewith also von Mises' notion of a collectivity threatens to become *inapplicable* to them. This, I believe, is the force of Broad's observation.

Cases in which statistical observation is relevant to the determination of probabilities seem on the whole to be more like the above case from vital statistics than cases from games of chance. (In games of chance, probabilities can as a rule be hypothetically determined on the basis of *a priori* considerations, pertaining to the nature of the chance-machine itself.) It is interesting to note that von Mises' theory, which is sometimes called the *statistical* theory of probability, seems to be particularly ill-suited to deal with probabilities in statistics! The doubt which Broad raises about the applicability of the notion of a collectivity to vital statistics seems to me therefore to be extremely important. And it has *not* received the attention which it deserves.

3. A main theme of [8] and [11] is the character of laws of nature. Roughly speaking: are laws "mere" generalizations from observed uniformities or are they principles of necessitation? Speaking in particular of causation: is the regularity view or the entailment view of the causal relation right? In [8] (p. 102) Broad writes:

> My conclusion is as follows. Either (*a*) I do rationally cognize some principle which, in conjunction with suitable empirical premises, would justify me in believing certain laws of functional *entailment,* although I cannot elicit or formulate any such principle; or (*b*) no empirical evidence, however regular, varied, and extensive, gives me the slightest ground for believing a law even of functional *regularity.* I should tend, *prima facie,* to reject (*b*), as contrary to common-sense and to my own unquestioning convictions when not philosophizing about induction. But, when I realize that rejecting (*b*) entails accepting (*a*), I become more and more doubtful as to what I ought to hold.

This seems to me to be a good way of expressing the traditional dilemma in the philosophy of induction since the days of Hume. Few have seen the dilemma with such extraordinary clarity as Broad. He has, as far as I know, never been very hopeful about a way out of it. It is perhaps a fair characterization to say that he has objected with his sentiment to the idea that induction has no justification, and equally objected with his intelligence to the consolation-grounds offered by the anti-Humeans.

I believe that there is a way out of the dilemma, but I doubt whether Broad would accept it as being even a possibility. This way starts, not with the question whether there *exists* any ground for belief in induction, but with the question what we *call* a "grounded" as opposed to a "groundless" inductive belief and what we *mean* by "rationally to believe" a generalization. I would suggest that, ultimately, what we call grounds of rational belief in induction are what Broad in the above quotation calls "empirical premisses," *without* the additional support of some "principles" (about determinism, limited variety, equiprobability, or the rest). I think, in other words, that the argumentation in the above quotation is wrong. Rejecting (*b*) doth *not* entail accepting (*a*). The dilemma, as Broad sees it, simply does not exist. I shall not here do anything to vindicate my own position and beliefs in the matter. My aim with these remarks has merely been to provoke, if possible, some comments of Broad's on the problem of "the ground of induction." If I succeed, I know that readers of this volume will be grateful.

4. In his lecture [5] on *The Philosophy of Francis Bacon* Broad has given an appreciation of the greatest of all workers in the field of inductive logic. Besides an excellent synopsis of the plan of the Great Instauration and summary of the main content of those parts of the gigantic work which were completed, the paper contains an original and valuable attempt to clarify the meaning of "limited independent variety" as a basic principle in the inductive philosophy of Bacon.

The supreme task of science, according to Bacon, is to find the forms of simple natures. Since the form is a necessary-and-sufficient condition of the nature, it follows that any simple nature can have only one distinct form. The number of forms and simple natures must thus be the same. Since the forms are assumed to be few in number, the number of simple natures must be few too. Broad goes on to conclude[117] that Bacon by "simple natures" evidently means *generic* physical properties; *i.e.* determinables such as colour, temperature, density, *etc.* and *not* determinates falling under them. This seems to me logical, and would tend to make the postulated limited variety useless for the purpose of guaranteeing the certainty of most inductions.

Broad next distinguishes four different senses of possible Limited Variety in the material world. The first is that nature is composed of *kinds* of substance. This requires limited variety in the sense that each

117 [5], 131. Quoted from *EHP*.

kind should be uniquely distinguished from all the rest by a comparatively small number of characteristics. (It is *this* form of limitation in nature and its relevance to induction which Broad himself had considered in [1].) If to the requirement just mentioned is added that the *number of kinds* itself should be comparatively small, we get a second form of the limited variety postulate. A third form is that the various specific modifications in a single generic property, such as colour, can be reduced to modifications in a single numerical determinable, such as frequency of lightwaves. A fourth form is that the various generic properties or simple natures reduce to specific differences of some few supreme genera. For example: colour and temperature may both be reduced to specific forms of movement.

Broad thinks[118] that, though Bacon did not distinguish these various cases of limited variety from each other, he meant to assert them all. It seems to me that the fourth case comes nearest to Bacon's actual conception of the constitution of the material world. I doubt whether he can be said to have contemplated limited variety in the first of the above senses.

Broad's paper on Bacon concludes with the often quoted question, whether we may venture to hope that, when Bacon's next centenary is celebrated, Inductive Reasoning, which has long been the glory of Science, will have ceased to be the scandal of Philosophy. I think this hope is not unfounded, in view both of recent progress in the logical study of induction and of recent investigation into the nature of the alleged "scandal." Progress in both branches have largely come from one and the same geographical quarter, Cambridge—the birth-place of modern logic and modern philosophical analysis.

GEORG HENRIK VON WRIGHT

UNIVERSITY OF HELSINGFORS
FINLAND

118 [5], 132.

10

C. W. K. Mundle

BROAD'S VIEWS ABOUT TIME

WE are indebted to Professor Broad for many penetrating discussions covering a wide range of problems concerning or involving temporal concepts. It is beyond the scope of this paper to survey in detail the conclusions that Broad has reached about such matters as the measurement of time and the interpretation of Relativity theory, Kant's antinomies, or theories about memory and precognition. It is the fundamental notions about time which Broad employs in dealing with such specific problems that I wish to identify and discuss. No more can be attempted here, since we find in Broad's writings three different ways of thinking about time: the first in his article on Time in the Hastings' *Encyclopaedia of Religion and Ethics,* published in 1921 *(ERE);* the second in *Scientific Thought,* 1923 *(ST);* the third in Volume II, Part 1, of his *Examination of McTaggart's Philosophy,* 1938 *(EMcP).* Since Broad has apparently abandoned both of his earlier accounts, it might appear fairer to him to discuss here only what he says in *EMcP.* However, although I shall spend less time on his earlier views, I do not think that I should ignore them. For Broad's third account of time is, in some ways, less complete than its predecessors, and it is difficult to interpret without reference to the latter. Moreover, I think that, on this subject, we can learn most from Broad by trying to understand how and why he has changed his mind. The fact that he has changed his mind is not, of course, being adduced as a criticism. If it were, Broad has met it in advance in the Preface of *EMcP,* where he says: "I am not much interested in the question whether my present views . . . are or are not consistent with those which I published in 1923," adding "it is not considered disgraceful to learn as well as to live" (p. lxxiii). However, one who has been asked to discuss Broad's views about time can scarcely refrain from asking in what respects Broad's views have changed, and why; and Broad does not help one to answer these questions, since, in presenting both his second and his third accounts, there is no explicit mention, never mind criticism, of his preceding account. My programme then is to discuss what is fundamental in each of Broad's ways of thinking about time. What I shall, perhaps arbitrarily, treat as fundamental are his accounts of the analysis of a certain class of temporal statements and the metaphysical theories which he links with each of these.

The First Account. Broad discusses the analysis of temporal statements in section 3 of his article in *ERE* under the heading "Relation of Time to Logic." He takes his problem as being to remove the appearance that a certain class of propositions, exemplified by "Queen Anne is dead" and "*e* is present," are "at the mercy of time" in respect of their truth-value, being true at some times, false at others. The class in question is described as "propositions which assert the occurrence of particular events," and it is contrasted with two other classes: (i) "eternal truths" which "deal with timeless relations of timeless objects," and (ii) "hypotheticals asserting temporal relations between classes of events" (i.e. law-propositions which purport to be true at any time, and are sometimes called "omni-temporal"). The restriction of his attention to "propositions which assert the occurrence of particular events" is not, I think, appropriate to Broad's purpose, which I take to be the analysis of the function of tensed verbs or the temporal predicates ". . . is past (present or future)"—or, more generally, the function of any grammatical devices which perform the function that these do in English. Tensed verbs are not employed only in statements which assert the occurrence of events; they are employed also in statements which predicate a quality of a continuant (e.g. "John is (now) thin"), and these, too, are "at the mercy of time." An adequate account of the function of tensed verbs must be applicable to their use in contexts which Broad ignores; including their quite common use in law-statements (e.g. "if you heat metal, it *will* expand"), and their occasional use in analytic statements (e.g. "No dodo *could have* suckled its young"). Having entered this caveat, let us return to Broad, who simplifies the problem by concentrating, in all three accounts, on the use of tensed verbs in statements which assert the occurrence of an event, usually a fall of rain.

Broad adopts in *ERE* the nowadays orthodox solution, according to which the function of a tensed verb or temporal adjective is performed in the analysans by a timeless copula and a temporal relation—earlier, simultaneous or later. He says, for example, of "It is raining" that, although the "verbal expression . . . is incomplete and stands for no definite proposition; . . . as actually asserted, the words would be taken to express my judgment of the proposition 'It is raining at the time at which I say "it is raining." ' " Similarly, "*e* is now past" is rendered: "*e* is at (or occupies) a moment earlier than my assertion that *e* is now past." Broad points out that whereas, in conversation, the context makes the time-reference of such statements unambiguous, the written word may fail to do this, and that the remedy is to make the time-reference explicit, by saying "*e* is at t," where t is "some definite moment fixed by some system of dating from a well-known and presumably unique event." This account differs, *prima facie,* from the current token-reflexive type of analysis by introducing a reference to moments, which events are said to 'occupy'; but this is not significant, for Broad goes on in section 5 to argue that moments and momentary events can be treated as logical functions of events of finite duration. The qualms which Broad was later to feel about the timeless copula did not apparently trouble him then, for he sums up: "The laws of logic are essentially concerned with the timeless copula, and they presuppose that statements containing tenses are reduced in the way suggested above."

In the next section ("Past, Present and Future"), Broad proceeds to the metaphysical plane. He considers the statement that only the present exists, and pronounces it "mere rhetoric rooted in confusions." Admittedly, the whole history of the world is not a complex of co-existing parts as a table is; but this, he claims, "does not mean that it is not a whole, or that one part of it exists any less than any other part. To say that *x* no longer exists, or does not yet exist, simply means that it occupies a moment before or after my statement about it." Broad proceeds to speak of past events *continuing* to exist: "An event must continue to *be,* if it is to continue to stand in relations; the battle of Hastings continues to precede the battle of Waterloo, and therefore both these events must eternally be at their own respective moments." That Broad is assuming that future as well as past events must "eternally be" is made clear by his claim to solve the problem of reconciling God's foreknowledge with men's free-will: "The facts that at a certain moment t_1 God can have a state of mind whose *immediate object* is the volition of a man at some later moment t_2, and that no amount of knowledge of events before t_2 would enable Him to infer the volition at t_2, are perfectly compatible" (*my italics*). Broad attributes the view that only the present exists to two errors:

(i) the confusion of two different senses of "co-existence." "In one sense the parts of any related whole co-exist; in another only those events that occupy the same moment of time co-exist." The fact that the whole course of history does not co-exist in the latter sense does not, Broad tells us, prevent it from co-existing in the former sense, as "a related whole all of whose parts have being";

(ii) "the belief that past, present, and future are essential characteristics of objects in time in the same way as before and after are, instead of being analysable into the temporal relations of states of mind and their objects."

Regarding the first of these alleged errors, one might comment that the first of the two senses which are said to be confused seems to be a new use of the verb "to co-exist." At any rate it is a very uncommon one, for it is not mentioned in the *O.E.D.* Moreover, although, in its new use, the verb is apparently intended to correspond to the existential quantifier in being timeless, Broad does not seem to be accepting the implications of its supposed timelessness. For, in the ensuing paragraph, Broad takes it that he has shown that "the whole course of events is in a certain sense a *totum simul*," and the use of "simul" seems to imply that we could say that all events co-exist in the familiar sense of this verb, that they all exist at the same time, that they all exist *now*. Again, Broad's speaking of past events as "continuing to be" implies that one is entitled to say, for example, of the Battle of Hastings, that it *now* exists. A tendency to fail to distinguish between using a verb timelessly and using it in the present tense is something that we shall find recurring in Broad's accounts of time.

Regarding the second alleged mistake of those who say that only the present exists, Broad speaks here of the temporal adjectives as being analysable in terms of temporal relations between "states of mind and their objects," though states of mind had not been mentioned in his foregoing analysis. What Broad says here is very reminiscent of the view expressed earlier by Russell:[1]

past, present and future arise from time-relations of subject and object, while earlier and later arise from time-relations of object and object. In a world in which there was no experience, there would be no past, present or future, but there might well be earlier and later.

Broad seems, like Russell, to have been thinking spatially of time, conceiving 'objects' (events) as constituting a linear series along which 'subjects' travel, and assuming that 'past' 'present' and 'future' refer to *external* relations between subjects and objects. The model implicit in such thinking seems to be that which Broad describes in his later accounts as the policeman's bull's-eye theory. That Broad was thinking on these lines in his first account is confirmed by what he says in the section on 'Time and Space.' The alleged difference between time and space—that nothing in space corresponds to the distinctions between past, present and future—is said to "rest largely on confusions." As an analogy to the distinction between past and future, Broad suggests that

[1] "On the Experience of Time," *Monist*, 1915, 212.

between being in front of and behind one's body. He claims that the reason why this analogy is incomplete (namely that our practical and cognitive attitudes towards past and future are different) is "extraneous to the nature of time."

The Second Account. There are some striking differences between Broad's first account of time and the account he develops in *ST.* He now emphasises the differences between space and time, and concludes that we must "treat past, present, and future on their own account, without expecting any help from spatial analogies" (p. 59); he adopts a metaphysical theory which "accepts the reality of the present and the past, but holds that the future is simply nothing at all" (p. 66); and he offers us a new type of analysis of statements containing tensed verbs, according to which one finds in their logical form "an extreme difference between judgements which profess to be about future events and those which are about past or present events" (p. 77). There is a surprising gap in the arguments Broad uses in developing his second account—he nowhere discusses, or even mentions, the type of analysis of temporal statements which he adopted in *ERE.* The explanation seems to be that Broad assumed that the latter type of analysis is logically dependent on the type of metaphysical theory that he had associated with it in his first account, and that such a theory involves thinking spatially of time in one or other of two ways which he now describes and rejects:

(i) The policeman's bull's-eye analogy, i.e. thinking of

the history of the world as existing eternally in a certain order of events. Along this, and in a fixed direction, we imagine the characteristic of presentness as moving, somewhat like the spot of light from a policeman's bull's-eye traversing the fronts of the houses in a street. What is illuminated is the present, what has been illuminated is the past, and what has not yet been illuminated is the future (p. 59).

Broad's criticisms of this model in *ST* are similar to, but less clearly formulated than those given in *EMcP,* so, to avoid repetition, I shall summarise what he says in *EMcP* (pp. 277–80). The objection is that this model commits one to an infinite regress of time-dimensions, for the following reasons: (a) "If anything moves, it must move with some determinate velocity. It will always be sensible to ask 'How fast does it move?'" Since the series along which presentness is supposed to move is temporal, the question becomes "how great a lapse of time 1 does presentness traverse in a unit of time 2?"; (b) the acquisition and the loss of the characteristic of presentness by an event would have to be treated as an event of the second order; so that every first-order event would have a history (in time 2) of indefinite length, at a certain stage in which there is an outstanding second order event "the acquisition and the immediately subsequent loss of presentness."

(ii) The second alternative which Broad considers and rejects is the attempt "to resolve the difference between past, present, and future into differences in the cognitive relations of our minds to different events in a series which has intrinsic order but no intrinsic sense" (p. 60). The suggestion here seems at first to be that what "moves along the series" is not presentness but consciousness, in which case this model would be open to the same objection as the first. But Broad treats it differently. He interprets it as implying that we should "define an event as past for O if O cannot perceive it but can either remember it or remember something contemporary with it." Broad disposes of this suggestion without difficulty. One wonders, however, whether anyone can have seriously defended such a view. For no one but a solipsist would assume that there have been no events earlier than any that he can remember: and if the relation *earlier* has to appear in the definiens, why bring in memory at all, instead of saying that 'past' means 'earlier than this?'

This is all that Broad does by way of eliminating alternatives to the account of time for which he is preparing the reader. His own view is presented as the solution to two connected paradoxes concerning the predicates 'past,' 'present' and 'future': "(i) Every event has all these characteristics, and yet they are inconsistent with each other. And (ii) *events* change in course of time with respect to these characteristics" (p. 62); the connection between (i) and (ii) being that if we take the obvious step to avoid (i), we are committed to asserting (ii). Broad admits that there is something very odd in talking of events as 'changing' ("to talk of events changing seems almost unintelligible"), but he nevertheless persists in so doing, and his own theory is presented as providing the only available account of what can be meant by such talk. Broad employs some queer (and surely superfluous) arguments to show that the sense in which an event is said to change, cannot be the same as that in which a thing like a signal lamp is said to change, e.g. in colour. His solution is to distinguish "two quite different senses in which an entity can be said to change its relational properties." When Tom becomes taller than his father, "we simply have a difference of relation between different corresponding sections of two existing long events." (Notice the equation of Tom and his father with 'long events!') Whereas, when Tom ceases to be the youngest of the family, "the difference is that a certain entity has changed its relational properties because a second entity, which did not formerly exist (and therefore could stand in *no* relation whatever to T), has begun to exist." Broad claims that it is obvious that "the change that happens to an event when it ceases to be present" is like 'the change of Tom' when he ceases to be the youngest of the family.

Broad goes on to tell us that 'we must recognise that the word "change" is used in three distinct senses': '(i) Change in the attributes of things,' '(ii) Change in events with respect to pastness' (i.e. from being present to being more and more remotely past), and '(iii) Change from future to present.' The third kind of change is christened 'Becoming,' the verb 'to become' being used intransitively as a synonym for 'to come into existence.' Becoming is treated as the most fundamental kind of change, on the ground that the analysis of each of the other species of change involves reference to the coming into existence of events. The new metaphysical theory is formulated as follows:

> Nothing has happened to the present by becoming past except that fresh slices of existence have been added to the total history of the world. The past is thus as real as the present. On the other hand, the essence of a present event is, not that it precedes future events, but that there is quite literally *nothing* to which it has the relation of precedence. The sum total of existence is always increasing, and it is this which gives the time-series a sense as well as an order (pp. 66–7).

Whereas Broad treated it as a merit of his first account that it explained divine foreknowledge, he treats it as a merit of the new theory that it explains the common view that there can be no certain knowledge about the future (pp. 78–9). Indeed, Broad draws from this theory the paradoxical conclusion that judgements which are ostensibly about future events are neither true nor false at the time at which they are made. The reasoning which led Broad to this conclusion is disclosed in his statement: "Today, when I make the judgment [that tomorrow it will be wet], there is no such fact as the wetness of tomorrow and there is no such fact as the fineness of tomorrow. For these facts can neither of them begin to be until tomorrow begins to be" (p. 73). This shows that Broad was using 'fact' in such a way that a fact, like an event, comes into existence at a particular time, has a date of birth. Even so, the paradoxical conclusion would not follow unless Broad had also assumed that the verb in the sentence 'there is no such fact as the wetness of tomorrow' is not timeless but is in the present tense.

Finally, Broad offers us his new analyses of statements containing tensed verbs (p. 76). 'It has rained' is rendered:

"There is an event which is characterised by raininess, and the sum total of existence when the judgement is made includes all and more than all which it *includes* when this event *becomes*" (1) (*my italics*). 'It will rain' is rendered:

"The sum total of existence *will increase* beyond what it is when the judgement is made, and some part of what *will become will be characterised* by raininess" (2) (*my italics*).

When we consider these analyses on their own merits, the difference in form appears to be the product of some arbitrary juggling with tenses. Presumably the italicised verbs in (1) are not intended to be in the present tense, for such a statement would then imply that the rainy event in question is becoming at the time of speaking; but if, in (1), 'includes' and 'becomes' are to be interpreted as timeless, why not use timeless verbs in (2), in place of the italicised verbs in the future tense? If grammatical or stylistic considerations are held to require the use of the future tense in (2) (as indeed they do), they equally require that the verbs italicised in (1) should be in the past tense. The main comment to be made on this passage is that it reveals clearly that Broad was treating the verb, in the phrase 'There is an event . . . ,' as being in the present tense. For he prefaces his analysis of 'It will rain' by saying: 'It cannot mean anything that begins with the statement: "There *is* an event," for the only events that there are [i.e. that *now* exist] are the events that have become up to the time when the assertion is made.' The issue raised here, concerning the interpretation of the existential quantifier, will be discussed later.

Let us now consider critically the metaphysical theory which is supposed to solve the two alleged paradoxes concerning 'past,' 'present' and 'future.' It seems odd that Broad should here follow McTaggart in treating the first of these as if it presented a genuine problem. In both his earlier and his later accounts Broad briefly dismissed this view of McTaggart's, by saying that there is no contradiction to be avoided. If Broad was, at this period, persuaded by McTaggart's arguments to regard 'every event is past, present and future' as involving a contradiction, he should have seen that the alleged contradiction would not be removed by his new theory; for although the latter implies that futurity is not a characteristic of any event, the alleged contradiction would still arise concerning pastness and presentness—as McTaggart later pointed out.[2] Regarding the second paradox, it would appear that the only solution that is required is to stop speaking of events as 'changing,' to follow Professor J. J. C. Smart[3] in insisting that '*things* change, *events* happen.' I shall not, however, argue that Broad's theory is adequately disposed of simply by pointing out that it is not required to solve the alleged paradoxes. There are other considerations which may incline us to think of time as Broad does in his second account.

2 *The Nature of Existence*, II, § 341.
3 "The River of Time," *Mind,* Oct. 1949, 485.

The main objection to Broad's theory is, I think, that he has not fulfilled his professed intention to "treat past, present, and future on their own account, without expecting any help from spatial analogies." He seems rather to have merely altered his spatial model—instead of thinking of presentness (or consciousness) creeping along the linear order of events, he is now apparently thinking of the Universe growing longer in the time-dimension as a line grows longer when one draws one's pen across a blank page. That Broad is still thinking spatially of time seems obvious from the language in which he formulates his theory, e.g. in talking of 'slices of existence' being 'tacked on to' the history of the world. The implications of this way of thinking are reflected by the way in which Broad uses the terms 'event' and 'object' or 'thing.' I drew attention earlier to the passage where Broad speaks of Tom and his father as 'two existing long events.' This surprising equation was not a slip. Let us consider how it comes about.

Broad introduces his discussion of time by defining 'an event' as "anything that endures at all, no matter how long it lasts or whether it be qualitatively alike . . . at adjacent stages of its history" (p. 54). He illustrates this definition by telling us that, in his usage, the history of the cliffs of Dover is just as much an event as a flash of lightning or a motor accident, since "the only relevant difference between the flash and the cliffs (sic) is that the former lasts for a short time and the latter for a long time." The foundations for Broad's theory could scarcely have been less soundly laid! It is not in order to complain that the history of the cliffs of Dover is not the sort of thing that can be said to 'happen,' for Broad admits that his definition is contrary to common usage. The trouble is that his examples do not fit his definition. According to the definition, the predicates whose applicability defines 'events' are *enduring* and *having a history,* yet these predicates do not seem to be both applicable to any of his examples. Obviously, the history of the cliffs cannot be said to have a history, nor to endure. According to the definition, what would qualify as an event would be the cliffs themselves. The flash of lightning *might* be said to have a history (lasting a fraction of a second), but not to endure; and neither of the defining predicates seem applicable to an accident. Obviously, Broad did not, in giving this definition, say what he meant to say. In what follows, Broad usually uses the term 'event' to refer to what would normally be called processes; he takes it as being of the essence of an event that it can be divided into shorter events (phases), and that it can stand in such relations as temporal overlapping with other events. The definition of 'event' that was appropriate to his purpose is the one implicit in what he says about processes in Volume I of *EMcP*, (pp. 142–4), i.e. anything which can be said to start, to go on (happening) throughout a finite period, and then to stop. Some of Broad's examples would still not qualify as events, e.g. the signal lamp's changing from red to green, of which we can scarcely ask 'for how long did it go on?' Broad seems guilty of the error to which Smart has drawn attention[4]—making the category of 'event' too catholic, and including in it what Ryle calls achievement-words, (e.g. 'overtaking') as well as task-words (e.g. 'pursuing') and process-words (e.g. 'running'). Broad's definition of 'event' shows a failure to recognise that most of the temporal predicates which are applicable to processes are not applicable to things, and *vice versa*. Of course, some temporal predicates are applicable to both, e.g. '—lasts a long (short) time,' and it is Broad's employment of this predicate in his definition ('no matter how long it lasts') that makes the definition appear plausible.

The inappropriate definition of 'event' doubtless played its part in leading Broad to identify things like Tom with long events, but Broad did not just slip uncritically into this way of speaking. There is a later passage (pp. 405–10) in which he argues that we *must* conceive a material object as a four-dimensional entity:

> The notion of an object with nothing but spatial dimensions is an abstraction. You can divide up the object into thinner and thinner slices normal to its time-dimension, and these slices will approximate, as you make them thinner, to purely spatial figures. In the limit each will be a purely spatial figure, in general of three dimensions. But these *are* not the object, nor are they literally even *parts* of it. The object is the whole four-dimensional strand of history. . . . A person who refuses to identify an object with its whole history must either identify it with a *momentary section* of that history or with a *uniform slice* of it. If he does the former, the object is a mere abstraction, incapable of existence. If he does the latter, his restriction to the uniform part of the whole strand of history is clearly arbitrary (pp. 409–10).

Now if one has accustomed oneself to thinking spatially of time, the dilemma that Broad presents here may seem unanswerable; for if one is persuaded to think of material objects as four-dimensional, then obviously their parts must be four-dimensional, must be phases of their history, *events* in Broad's peculiar sense of this word. And this implies that its travelling from Perth to Dundee last night is a part of my motor car, and that its resting overnight in my garage is an adjacent part thereof. Admittedly we can (or can learn to) think of objects in this way. The physicists sometimes do so (and Broad is preparing the reader for an exposition of Relativity theory). But to argue that we *must* so think of objects is to ignore the fact that we do not usually do so, that what we normally think of as the parts of a motor car are its engine, wheels, etc.,

4 *Op. cit.*, 489.

and this seems to imply that we conceive material objects as three-dimensional entities. Professor Smart has recently argued[5] that what we should say is that, in ordinary language, the logic of material object-words is neither purely three-dimensional nor purely four-dimensional; not the former since the concepts of change and staying the same are applicable, e.g. a cricket ball has a history and may change in shape, etc.; not the latter for the following reason: "Suppose our four-dimensional geometry is interpreted as a geometry of space-time. (As in the Minkowski representation.) Then time now does enter in, but not the terminology of change or staying the same. Let 'cricket ball$_4$' be the expression which in our four-dimensional representation refers to the cricket ball through its entire history. Then it makes no sense to talk of the cricket ball$_4$ changing or staying the same. For the cricket ball$_4$ to change we should need a second time dimension, a fifth dimension, for its changing (or not changing) to be in." Now does this argument dispose of Broad's second account of time? This might be challenged. When Smart speaks of 'the cricket ball through its entire history,' he is presumably using 'history' to include episodes which are now future, as well as those which are now past (i.e. the sense in which Broad used 'history,' when, in his first account, he spoke of the whole course of history as co-existing). Obviously cricket ball$_4$, so conceived, could not change without there being a further time-dimension. But when, in *ST*, Broad says: "The object is the whole four-dimensional strand of its history," he is using 'history' in its normal sense to include only episodes which have *hitherto* taken place; so he might answer Smart by saying that his account *does* permit cricket ball$_4$ to change, namely by growing longer in the time-dimension, so that future 'slices' of it may differ in quality from their predecessors. The most plausible defence of Broad's theory would be, not that it solves the alleged paradoxes concerning the temporal adjectives, but that it enables us to reconcile the physicists' conception of Space-Time with the fact, stressed by Broad in his accounts of the specious present, that things are sensibly presented as moving and otherwise changing, *without* committing us to the policeman's bull's-eye model with its vicious consequences. But although, as stated, Smart's criticism applies only to Broad's first account, it can be pressed further. At first sight the spatial analogy implicit in the second account (a line growing longer) is an improvement on its predecessor (something moving along the line). The former does not, like the latter, suggest that we, the observers, are not 'in' time. But this difference does not free the new model from what Broad treats as decisive objections to the old one. Broad's first objection to the latter may be adapted as follows: If anything grows, it

5 "Spatialising Time," *Mind*, April, 1955.

must grow at some determinate rate. It will always be sensible to ask how fast it grows, and this question will have to be interpreted to mean 'what is the "thickness" (the time 1 duration) of the "slice of existence" which is added in a unit of time 2 ?' This objection might, I think, be countered by answering it on the following lines: 'When one speaks of the Universe as *increasing* or *growing*, one is speaking metaphorically. In this context these verbs do not, of course, have the same implications as when one speaks, e.g., of a tree growing; in particular, one must remember that the sort of growth to which the Universe is subject is not a change *in* time, but a change *of* time, and when this is understood it is obvious that the question "how fast does the Universe grow?" is meaningless.' However, if such an answer were judged permissible in the case of Broad's second model, his first model could be defended in just the same way: 'When one speaks of presentness *moving*, this verb is being used metaphorically. This kind of movement is a change *of* time, not a change *in* time, so questions about the *rate* of such movement do not arise.'

The Third Account. One of the difficulties in interpreting what Broad says in *EMcP* is to know whether he has recognised the point that I have been making in the last paragraph, namely that in respect of committing one to a regress of time-dimensions, his first account and his second account stand or fall together. When, in *EMcP,* Broad criticises a spatial model, it is always the policeman's bull's-eye theory that he considers. If he had realised that his second theory was open to the same objections, one would have expected him to acknowledge this. It is not easy to judge, from what Broad says in *EMcP,* to what extent he wishes to deviate from his second account. The fact that he still treats Becoming (now 'Absolute Becoming') as the key concept, might well lead a hasty reader to think that Broad is simply giving us a new exposition of his preceding theory. Let us consider what Broad says in Chapter XXXV, which, as he tells us in the Preface, contains what he would "now say (very hesitatingly) about time." This is presented as an 'Account of the Phenomenology of Time.' Broad distinguishes between 'the Extensive Aspect' and 'the Transitory Aspect of Temporal Facts.' By the former he refers to the respects in which temporal relations are analogous to spatial relations. "Every experience has some duration. It is, in this respect, like a finite straight line and not like a geometrical point." Consequently, the temporal relations which hold between any two experiences of the same person cannot be reduced to the familiar trio (earlier, simultaneous and later), but correspond to the various (thirteen) spatial relations (partial and complete overlapping, adjacence, etc.) which may hold between two sticks lying in the same straight line. By 'the Transitory Aspect' Broad refers to the sort of facts that are described by saying that an experience "keeps on becoming less and less remotely future . . . becomes present . . . retreats continually into the more and more remote past." Broad argues, first, that even in respect of the Extensive Aspect spatial analogies break down, for the following reasons:

(i) "In the temporal series there are two intrinsically opposite directions, earlier-to-later and later-to-earlier. In the linear spatial series there is no *intrinsic* direction. If direction is to be introduced, this must be done *extrinsically*," e.g. by reference to something which moves along the line, or to the right hand of an observer, or a compass needle. (Up to this point, Broad's argument is a restatement of points made in *ST*.)

(ii) "Spatial extension and the occurrence of spatial relations *presuppose* temporal duration. . . . Shape and size are commonly ascribed to particulars which persist through periods of time and have histories . . ."; and Broad goes on to make some points which were not recognised in his second account: "Temporal relations *directly* relate *events or processes*; they do not directly relate the continuants of which events and processes constitute the histories. Again, it is the events or processes which are temporally extended, i.e. which are longer or shorter in the temporal sense. The continuants, of which these events or processes constitute the histories, *endure through* periods of time." Broad seems here to be acknowledging the error which led, in *ST*, to the equation of Tom with a long event; acknowledging that temporal predicates like 'endures' are not applicable to event- or process-expressions, and that temporal predicates like 'divisible into (temporally) shorter slices' are not applicable to thing-expressions.

Concerning the Transitory Aspect of temporal facts, there are, Broad says, two points to be considered: "(i) the characteristics of pastness, presentness, and futurity; and (ii) the fact that every event is continually changing in respect of these characteristics." In discussing (i), Broad asserts that "neither presentness, in the strict sense, nor any absolutely determinate degree of pastness or futurity, can characterise a temporally extended term. Such a term cannot be *present* as a whole." Broad here assumes, without argument, that 'present' is applicable, 'in the strict sense,' only to a durationless instant or an instantaneous 'event-particle.' (Broad did not adopt this thesis in his second account, where he was prepared to speak of an event being present *throughout* a finite process of sensing. Cf. *ST*, p. 350) . Broad attributes our ability to form the conception of an event-particle to the fact that "we often prehend events as having boundaries," and he illustrates this by reference to sounds. (This account of the empirical basis of the concept of an instant or momentary event avoids the obscurity of Whitehead's theory of extensive abstraction which Broad invoked for this purpose in *ST*.)

Broad proceeds to discuss point (ii) under the heading 'Absolute Becoming.' What he does in this section is, first, to criticise "the attempt to represent temporal becoming by means of motion," i.e. the policeman's bull's-eye theory. I have summarised earlier the arguments he employs here. He then presents a cryptic argument purporting to show that the concept of Absolute Becoming is indispensable. He points out that, although sentences like 'this event became present' are of the same grammatical form as 'this water became hot' and 'this noise became louder,' the former cannot 'record facts of the same kind as the latter.' The reasons given are that 'any subject of which we can significantly say that it "became hot" must be a more or less persistent substance'; and that 'any subject of which we can significantly say that it "became louder" must be a more or less prolonged noise process. . . . But a literally instantaneous event-particle can significantly be said to "become present"; and, indeed, in the strict sense of "present" *only* instantaneous event-particles can be said to "become present." To "become present" is, in fact, just to "become," in an absolute sense' (p. 280). Now I find this passage extremely puzzling. What Broad set out to discuss was our old friend, the paradox about events changing. In his second account, it was in order to give a meaning to this use of 'change' that the concept of *becoming* was introduced, and it did so by virtue of meaning 'coming into existence.' Does 'becoming' still have this meaning? I shall argue that, if it does, the other things Broad says seem to commit him to a new and peculiar metaphysical theory; that if it does not, it is difficult to see what it can mean.

First let us suppose that 'becoming' still means 'coming into existence.' Now according to his second account, whatever has come into existence remains forever in existence. Broad does not, in *EMcP*, explicitly repudiate this feature of his second account, but there is some evidence that he has abandoned it. Certainly he nowhere speaks in *EMcP* of past events as still existing or continuing to exist, but this is inconclusive. He does not speak now of present events as existing, and the change may be due to his realising the grammatical inappropriateness of predicating 'existence,' in any tense, of events or processes. But for Broad such grammatical considerations do not settle metaphysical questions. (He argued in Volume I of *EMcP* that 'Things can be dispensed with in favour of Processes.') Possibly Broad is still thinking of past events as being real in a sense in which future events are not, and his failure to say so might be due to the fact that, in chapter XXXV of *EMcP*, he is attempting to give only a phenomenological description. However, I doubt if this can be the correct interpretation, for (i) in a paper[6] published in 1937, we find Broad arguing that in respect of their existence, past and future events are on a par; and (ii) Broad does occasionally speak in *EMcP* of events becoming *and passing away*. (Cf. pp. 308 and 315.) I think that we must assume that if '(absolute) becoming' ≡ 'becoming present' ≡ 'coming into existence,' 'passing away' ≡ 'becoming past' ≡ 'ceasing to exist.' How then are we to interpret the doctrine that events, i.e., strictly event-particles, become and pass away? This might appear intelligible provided that there was supposed to be some interval between the moment when an event-particle came into existence and the moment when it ceased to exist; if, for example, one said that an event-particle exists (persists) throughout the duration of the so-called specious present. Broad, however, debars himself from saying this, by his account of the doctrine of the Specious Present (pp. 281–8). He describes this as 'a verbal trick' for evading the difficulties in holding both of the following propositions: that "if anything which a person prehends at any moment must be present, it must be instantaneous," and that "prehended objects *are* prehended as persisting unchanged or as changing." Being unwilling to reject either of these propositions, Broad presents his own account of the specious present in the following language: "what a person prehends at any moment is of finite duration," but, whereas the whole of this 'object' is said to be *presented* at that moment, Broad insists that only an instantaneous cross-section of this total object can be *present* at that moment (p. 283). In other words, Broad adopts the view that the content of the specious present (what a person is now 'prehending') is—apart from its later boundary—to be described as *past*. In view of this Broad would appear to be committed to a metaphysical theory according to which each event-particle is created and annihilated at successive instants (if it makes sense to talk of *successive* members of a series which is supposed to be compact); and according to which the answer to the question 'what exists at present?' ('what is now real?') would have to be 'a set of simultaneous instantaneous event-particles' (though, during the time that it takes you to utter this phrase, an infinite number of such sets would have been born and died!). I do not exclude the possibility that Broad was willing to embrace such conclusions. Perhaps, when he wrote that 'qualitative change (i.e. changes in Things or Processes) involves absolute becoming' (p. 281), he was thinking of event-particles as the rock-bottom entities, the stuff of which Processes, and

---

6 'The Philosophical Implications of Precognition.' *PAS. Supp. Vol.* XVI, p. 180. Broad argues here that if one objects to the notion of precognition on the ground that it implies that a person stood in some relation to something which 'only began to exist at some later moment,' this objection would apply equally to memory, since a remembered event 'no longer exists' when it is being remembered.

hence Things, are composed. Yet the conclusions to which Broad seems committed, on the hypothesis that 'becoming' is being used in its earlier sense, are so paradoxical that it would appear more reasonable to regard them as disposing of the hypothesis in question.

If we reject this hypothesis, how *are* we to interpret Broad's use of 'becoming' in *EMcP?* Broad might reply that I have wantonly ignored his statement: 'To "become present" is just to become in an absolute sense, i.e., to "come to pass" in the Biblical phraseology, *or, most simply "to happen"* ' (*my italics*). This shows, it might be said, that he is using 'becoming' with no metaphysical implications, but simply as a synonym for 'happening.' If, however, this was Broad's intention, what he says in this passage is, to say the least, misleading, since: (i) his argument is presented in terms of 'what we can significantly say,' and event-particles do not figure among the things of which we can say that they are (were or will be) happening; (ii) Broad says (p. 281) that it seems to him certain that 'absolute becoming is involved in mere continuance without qualitative change,' i.e. without any change in the qualities (or positions) of Things or Processes. This statement would make sense if 'becoming' were being used in its earlier sense. Broad would then be repeating what he said in *ST*: "if every fresh slice of existence were qualitatively indistinguishable from all its predecessors, there would still be this continual becoming" (p. 91). But if 'becoming' is a synonym for 'happening,' this statement does not seem to make sense—we should not say that anything was *happening*, if there were 'mere continuance.'

I may have profoundly misunderstood what Broad says about Absolute Becoming in *EMcP,* but I cannot help suspecting that this concept is a sort of hangover from Broad's second account, for which there is really no room in his third account. Broad has now stopped predicating 'existence,' in any tense, of events and processes. What then is the point in his continuing to say that changes in Things (like becoming hotter) and in Processes (like becoming louder) involve Absolute Becoming, and in his speaking of the latter as if it were a third kind of change ('becoming present'), whose subject must be a third type of entity, an event-particle? Surely the so-called 'Transitory Aspect of Temporal Facts' just *is* the fact that *things* change and that we observe them changing. If Broad still wishes to maintain[7] that some processes, notably noises, are not states of things, on the ground that, although things *make* noises, they are not *subjects* of noises in the sense in which a golf ball is the subject of a process of moving, this is not the place to debate this issue. Let us simply ask—what is one leaving out of one's account of the transi-

---

[7] As he did in Vol. 1 of *EMcP*. Cf. 151–6.

tory aspect of experience, if one confines oneself to talking about changes
in things and/or processes?

Finally we must consider what Broad says, in *EMcP*, regarding the
time-reference of statements. His main thesis is that tensed verbs cannot be eliminated in any adequate analysis of temporal statements. He
emphasises that when we express a temporal statement in the form '*e*
is present (past or future),' the verb is in the present tense (p. 272). The
source of the infinite regress, which McTaggart used as an argument
against the reality of time, is attributed to his mistaken assumption that
any temporal statement can and should be expressed in a sentence containing a temporal adjective and a *non*-temporal copula (p. 314). But
Broad sides with McTaggart in thinking that 'A-characteristics' (pastness, etc.) cannot be defined in terms of 'B-characteristics' (i.e. temporal
relations like *earlier*). Broad supports this claim by examining and rejecting the type of analysis which he had himself adopted in his first
account, and which he here attributes to Russell (pp. 303–8). For our
purpose, it will be sufficient to mention Broad's preliminary formulation
of this type of analysis: 'any utterance U of the type-sentence (to use
Ramsey's phrase) "It is raining now" means "An occurrence of rain in
the neighbourhood of the speaker who utters U is simultaneous with this
utterance." ' Broad comments, as if it were an acknowledged corollary of
such an analysis: "Unless there were people who uttered type-sentences
of these kinds, nothing would be past, present or future; though events
would still be simultaneous or successive." Does the token-reflexive
analysis have this paradoxical implication? It seems to me that Broad
has here expressed in a very misleading way something that does follow
from this type of analysis, namely, that if there were no utterances of
sentences of the relevant types, nothing would be earlier than, simultaneous with, or later than such an utterance! This is a tautology which
should cause no one discomfort. (Broad's statement does cause discomfort (to me at any rate) because, when he says "nothing would be past,
present or future," one is disposed to assume that 'past' 'present' and
'future' are being used in their normal sense, so that 'past' is to be interpreted as meaning earlier than the time when Broad penned this sentence, or earlier than the time when one reads it. Broad's hypothetical
statement is thus paradoxical, because the apodosis is (or seems to be)
an instance of the type of sentence whose non-existence is postulated in
the protasis.) More could be said about this paradox, but this is not the
place, for Broad does not base upon it his case against the token-reflexive analysis. He objects to the alleged self-reference of an utterance, saying: "I am very doubtful whether this is possible at all; and I am fairly
certain that, when I make such an utterance, I am not making a judge-

ment about the utterance which I am making." Broad certainly seems to be wrong in suggesting that such self-reference is impossible. (Cf. my intoning 'This is middle C.') However, he admits forthwith that this objection can be avoided by taking as the analysans: "an occurrence of rain is simultaneous with *this,* where *this* is some particular, other than the utterance itself, which he [the speaker] prehends simultaneously with making the utterance."

Broad now advances two objections which he treats as decisive. The first concerns the copula in the analysans ('is' in 'is simultaneous with'). If this were the temporal copula 'is now,' the analysis would have failed in its purpose, so presumably it is intended to be a timeless copula. Against this interpretation Broad protests that no one but a philosopher talking philosophy ever does talk in this way. His first two counter-examples are, however, unfortunately chosen. Consider the first: 'we do not say "The Battle of Hastings precedes (or *is* followed by) the Battle of Waterloo." We say "The Battle of Hastings preced*ed* (or *was* followed by) the Battle of Waterloo." ' But according to the view being criticised, the latter sentence should be rendered, not by the former, but (roughly) by 'The Battle of Hastings precedes the Battle of Waterloo *and both precede this.*' Broad's thesis is not, however, affected by this slip, for he would still object to the allegedly timeless verbs in the revised analysans. He does protest against rendering 'it will rain' by 'an occurrence of rain *is* later than this,' commenting: 'what we say is "An occurrence of rain . . . *will* follow (or *will* happen later than) *this*." ' Broad concludes that "the obvious artificiality and awkwardness of the sentences which express temporal facts, according to this analysis of them, are a sign that we are trying and failing to force temporal facts into the mould of non-temporal facts about abstract objects such as numbers;" and he now makes it clear that he is assuming that the Russellian analysis commits one to the metaphysical theory with which he associated it in his first account: 'The theory seems to presuppose that all events, past, present and future, in some sense "co-exist," and stand to each other timelessly or sempiternally in determinate relations of temporal precedence.'

Broad's second objection to the Russellian analysis is that it leaves altogether out of account the transitory aspect of time. 'On the theory which we are discussing, there is no question of events "becoming" or "passing away." ' Broad does not make it clear whether he wishes to attribute this defect to the Russellian analysis as such, or to the metaphysical theory which he takes it to involve. In the former case, the objection is surely unwarranted. One can scarcely complain about rendering 'it will rain' by 'an occurrence of rain is later than this,' on the ground that the analysans leaves out the transitory aspect of time. If one included in the analysans a statement that all or any events are transitory, one would plainly be saying more than one says by saying 'it will rain;' and there is nothing to prevent anyone who accepts the Russellian analysis from going on to say that, of course, all events (including the one referred in the analysans by 'this') are transitory. Presumably Broad's basic objection to the Russellian analysis is that it requires one to think of the whole course of history as co-existing, and hence requires one to conceive change on the analogy of the policeman's bull's-eye.

This brings us to a fundamental issue whose discussion I have deferred—the interpretation of the logicians' timeless copulas, particularly the existential quantifier. I find it difficult to avoid the conclusion that Broad's accounts of time are largely the outcome of treating the allegedly timeless verbs, in which the logicians' symbols are interpreted, as if these were *really*, or *also*, in the present tense. (I am not suggesting that this is the whole story, for, of course, the propensity to spatialise time did not originate when logicians started conjoining 'event' with 'exists;' still, I think it is an important part of the story.) I have drawn attention to passages in his earlier accounts where Broad seems to be doing this. In *ERE,* he combined speaking of all events as co-existing timelessly, with saying things which imply that future and past events *now* exist. In *ST,* Broad was no longer willing to speak of future events in ways which imply that they now exist, but was still willing to speak thus of past events. In *EMcP,* Broad is no longer willing to speak thus of past events. I suspect that he now protests so strongly against the logicians' allegedly timeless use of verbs, because it was his interpretation of this which had led him to his earlier conclusions about the existence of past and future events. If I am right, the critic may urge that they led Broad to such conclusions only because he interpreted ' $\exists$ x' ('There is an event such that . . .') to mean 'An event *now* exists (albeit timelessly) such that . . .;' and that we can reinstate the orthodox analysis of temporal statements by saying that it has no metaphysical implications, provided that we remember that the timeless verbs *are timeless*, are no more in the present tense than in any other tense. However, I do not think we can rest content with this answer, with its suggestion that Broad's views about time are based upon a howler. If Broad's interpretation of ' $\exists$ x' is a mistake, the fact that Broad has made it shows how insidious is the temptation. Certainly Broad is not alone in making it, and indeed logicians often speak as if their calculi commit them to spatialising time. To take a recent example, Professor Quine[8] writes: "The four-dimensional view of space-time is part and parcel of the use of modern formal logic and in

8 "Mr. Strawson on Logical Theory," *Mind* (Oct., 1953), 442.

particular the use of quantification theory, in application to temporal affairs." Quine may not wish to be interpreted as making a metaphysical statement, but the reader could scarcely be blamed for not realising this, when he finds Quine speaking of 'the denizens of space-time' as being 'thing-events, four-dimensional beings.'

If Broad is charged with misinterpreting ' ∃ x,' he is, I think, entitled to press the question 'what on earth can be meant by this supposedly timeless use of "There is (exists)," when what one is talking about are entities that are 'in' time, e.g. events, whose individuality depends upon their dates?' The answer that I should give is, briefly, as follows: that ' ∃ x' should be interpreted as timeless only when the universe of discourse comprises abstract entities like numbers or triangles; that when the universe of discourse comprises events or processes, ' ∃ x' should be interpreted as 'There has occurred or is occurring or will occur an event (process) having the property(ies) . . . ;' and that when the universe of discourse comprises things (continuants), ' ∃ x' be interpreted as 'There has existed or now exists or will exist a thing having the property(ies). . . .' In other words, I am recommending (i) that we treat ' ∃ x,' in certain common contexts, as involving a disjunction of past, present and future tenses, and (ii) that we avoid begging the question whether events (or processes) and things are entities of the same type. Regarding (i), the disjunctive interpretation of ' ∃ x' was mentioned recently by Mr. P. F. Strawson,[9] and rejected for, I think, insufficient reason. Strawson considers the disjunctive interpretation satisfactory for the interpretation of law-statements; but he considers it inadequate in the case of statements which are about persons or incidents, and whose time-reference is normally expressed by means of a tensed verb, his objection being, that the time-reference of such a statement would then be left ambiguous. But surely the ambiguity is to be resolved by a subordinate clause. To illustrate, 'There will be an earthquake in Ireland' would be rendered: 'There has occurred or is occurring or will occur an event having the properties of being an earthquake, being in Ireland, and being later than this.' I can see no inconsistency in treating the participles in such subordinate clauses ('*having* the properties of *being*') as timeless, while denying this of ' ∃ x;' for the function of the former is to express what W. E. Johnson called 'the characterising tie' and not to assert the existence or occurrence of anything. Admittedly my proposed rendering of existential propositions is extremely clumsy, but the point is to show that we do not need to introduce a timeless use of 'exists,' in order to render temporal statements in such a way that their truth-value is not

[9] *Introduction to Logical Theory*, 151.

'at the mercy of time;' and it is, I take it, to secure this, that it has been thought necessary to treat ' ∃ x' as timeless.

The second point in my recommendation is this: that whatever views he may wish to defend *qua* metaphysician, the logician should not assume, *qua* logician, that all statements that are about entities in space and time must be so formulated that only one type of entity can constitute the value of the argument (*either* events *or* things *or* strange hybrids called 'thing-events'). One of the points which is high-lighted by Broad's discussions of time is that most of the predicates that are applicable to things (continuants) are not applicable to events, e.g. 'enduring,' and 'existing,' and also dispositional properties like 'combustible;' and that most of the predicates applicable to events are not applicable to continuants, e.g. 'simultaneous with—' or 'happening.' Logical calculi should not be thought to require us, though of course they permit us, to perform such intellectual acrobatics as are involved in resolving 'my watch is anti-magnetic' into a statement about event-particles or processes or 'thing-events.' In brief, I submit that if ' ∃ x' is interpreted with discrimination, according to context, there is no need to accept the view, implicit in what Broad says in *EMcP* and made explicit by Strawson, that the device of quantification cannot be adapted, so far as time-reference is concerned, to ordinary language, as well as to the language of physics.

By way of a post-script, I want to add a few words concerning Broad's views about the specious present. The two different accounts of this concept which Broad offers us, in *ST* (pp. 348 *et seq.*) and in *EMcP* (pp. 281 *et seq.*), are among his most important contributions to a philosophy of time. I have here ignored the earlier account and said very little about the later, mainly because I have discussed both in a recent paper.[10] I should like, however, to correct a mistake I made in the latter. I criticised Mr. J. D. Mabbott for attributing Broad's interest in the specious present doctrine to a desire to 'discover the unit of temporal experience,' for assuming that Broad was thinking of a person's experiences as consisting of a row of sense-data laid out, so to speak, end to end, and was concerned about the 'length' of an individual sense-datum. I attributed Broad's interest in the specious present doctrine to the fact that it enables one to claim to be directly acquainted with instances of temporal relations, in terms of which other temporal concepts could be defined. My interpretation was unwarranted, for, neither in *ST* nor in *EMcP* did Broad define 'past' and 'future' in terms of temporal relations, as I was then assuming he would wish to do. The interpretation I attributed to Mabbott was correct, or nearly so, for Broad's second account of time.

10 "How Specious is the 'Specious Present'?", *Mind*, (Jan. 1954).

For, in *ST*, the main use to which Broad puts his account of the specious present is in formulating his (peculiar) definition of 'a sensible field' (p. 353), and he goes on to define the maximum duration of a sensum by reference to his concept of a sensible field (p. 354), and he speaks of successive sensible fields as being 'adjacent,' i.e. as 'joining together at the ends' (pp. 354, 361, etc.). What Broad says about the 'joining up' of successive sensible fields and sensa involves some arbitrary assumptions, which are not made explicit. To elucidate these would require some tedious geometrising, on which it seems unnecessary to embark, since Broad seems to have recognised the inadequacy of this way of thinking, if one judges by his statement in *EMcP*: "Writers on this subject sometimes make statements which would imply that the contents of two successive Specious Presents are adjoined. . . . This is quite impossible" (p. 284).

I am painfully aware of the incompleteness of this paper. So many topics discussed by Broad have been neglected, so many important questions have been left unasked. Since much of my commentary has been critical, I should like to end by saying that I think that no other philosopher has written so stimulatingly about time, or has brought out so clearly the implications of a variety of different ways of thinking about time. If, in the end, we cannot rest content with any of the accounts that Broad has offered us, we may still agree with his dictum that Time provides 'the hardest knot in the whole of philosophy' (*ST* p. 84).

C. W. K. MUNDLE

DEPARTMENT OF PHILOSOPHY
THE UNIVERSITY COLLEGE OF NORTH WALES
BANGOR, WALES

11

C. J. Ducasse

BROAD ON THE RELEVANCE OF PSYCHICAL
RESEARCH TO PHILOSOPHY

PROFESSOR BROAD published in 1949 an article, entitled "The Relevance of Psychical Research to Philosophy," which has several great merits.[1] One is, that it furnishes the most analytical and hence the philosophically most fertile definition yet proposed of the term "paranormal" as applied to the various queer kinds of occurrences called Telepathy, Clairvoyance, Precognition, Psychokinesis, Levitation, Apparitions, and so on. Another merit is that, unlike much that is written to maintain or impugn the reality or the importance of such phenomena, Broad's article is based on extensive acquaintance with and unprejudiced appraisal of the available evidence that phenomena of these kinds sometimes occur. And still another merit is the compelling character of the arguments the article presents for the contention that those phenomena, in so far as real, render imperative a thoroughgoing scrutiny of the limits of validity of certain basic principles, which scientists and philosophers generally assume today to have not merely very wide but wholly unlimited validity.

Sharing as I do Broad's conception of what constitutes paranormality; also his conviction that some paranormal events occur; and also his estimate of the philosophical importance of the fact that they do occur, the criticisms and suggestions I shall offer in what follows will necessarily concern a few special points rather than any of Broad's fundamental contentions in this field. What I propose to do is first to summarize the argument of Broad's cited article, and to offer some brief comments on the epistemic status of the principles, conflict with which by an event makes it "paranormal." Then I shall consider, as a particularly telling illustration of the relevance of paranormal phenomena to philosophy, the acute philosophical problem concerning time and causality which arises out of the occurrence of so-called Precognition, and which is dis-

---

[1] *Philosophy*, XXIV, 1949, 291–309. The article was recently reprinted with others of Broad's papers in the book, *RPPR*, pp. 7–26. Page references for that article in what follows will be to the book, *RPPR*.

cussed by Broad in that article and more fully in others of his writings. After this, I shall submit to Broad's judgment a solution of that problem, which seems to me to avoid the difficulties in other proposed solutions of it, to which he calls attention. And finally, I shall examine and comment upon Broad's statements as to what certain paranormal phenomena suggest to him concerning one of the problems over which philosophers have most puzzled—that of the relation between the individual's mind and his body.

I. Paranormal Events and Philosophy.

In the article mentioned above, Broad points out that the business of philosophy, as exemplified by what the great philosophers have undertaken, involves at least two closely connected activities—*Synopsis* and *Synthesis:*

> Synopsis is the deliberate viewing together of aspects of human experience which, for one reason or another, are generally kept apart by the plain man and even by the professional scientist or scholar. The object of synopsis is to find out how these various aspects are inter-related. Synthesis is the attempt to supply a coherent set of concepts and principles which shall cover satisfactorily all the regions of fact which have been viewed synoptically.

Any given set of synthetic concepts and principles will therefore be philosophically important in proportion to its capacity to integrate all of the various kinds of human experience.

Now, there are certain synthesizing principles—Broad proposes to call them *Basic Limiting Principles*—which have this capacity, and therefore that philosophic importance, in a high degree; for they "cover very satisfactorily an enormous range of well-established facts of the most various kinds." Moreover, because their proved range of validity is so vast, "we are quite naturally inclined to think that they must be all-embracing;" and we therefore "unhesitatingly take them for granted as the framework within which all our practical activities and our scientific theories are confined."

But, Broad then goes on, "just in proportion to the philosophic importance of the basic limiting principles is the philosophic importance of any well-established exception to them;" and there are numerous reports of events which appear to constitute such exceptions. These alleged events are what psychical research investigates: "Psychical research is concerned with alleged events which seem *prima facie* to conflict with one or more" of the basic limiting principles. Any event which seems *prima facie* to do this, Broad calls an *Ostensibly Paranormal Event;*

and a *Paranormal Event* would then be an event which really does so conflict.

The fact, however, is that a substantial amount of very good evidence —some experimental, some spontaneous, and some of an intermediate character—has been obtained during the last hundred years, that events truly paranormal in the above sense sometimes actually occur. Hence

the speculative philosopher who is honest and competent will want to widen his synopsis so as to include these facts; and he will want to revise his fundamental concepts and basic limiting principles in such a way as to include the old and the new facts in a single coherent system. (*RPPR* pp. 7–9)

Such, in outline, is Broad's argument for the philosophic importance of psychical research. That this importance is great cannot, I believe, fail to impress itself on any philosopher who takes the trouble to familiarize himself in some detail with the existing evidence that events paranormal in the sense defined do sometimes occur and who, with those events in mind, considers the basic limiting principles which Broad formulates.

II. The "Basic Limiting Principles," and some Comments upon them.

The Basic Limiting Principles listed by Broad fall into four groups. The *first* group relates to *Causality* and contains three principles.

Principle I. 1. "It is self-evidently impossible that an event should begin to have any effects before it has happened." (p. 9)

That an effect is not anterior in time to its cause is an intrinsic part of what we mean by the words, "cause" and "effect;" that is, Principle *I*.1 is analytic, hence quite certain, and hence not susceptible to revision. Therefore the paradox involved in any seeming violation of it will necessarily have to be resolved by showing, as I shall try to do farther on, that the basic limiting principle violated is not really Principle *I*.1, but some other, which, unlike *I*.1, is not analytic, and therefore is susceptible of revision.

Principle I. 2. "It is impossible that an event which ends at a certain date should contribute to cause an event which begins at a later date unless the period between the two dates is occupied in one or other of the following ways: (i) The earlier event initiates a process of change, which continues throughout the period and at the end of it contributes to initiate the later event. Or (ii) the earlier event initiates some kind of structural modification which persists throughout the period," and which "begins to co-operate at the end of the period with some change which is then taking place" so as, together, to cause the later event. (p. 9)

The essential import of this detailed statement of Principle *I*.2 may be put by saying that *no event can cause another event at a temporal distance from it,* except through an intervening causal chain of events. (The *enduring* of a structural modification is, of course, an event.)

Principle I. 3. "It is impossible that an event, happening at a certain date and place, should produce an effect at a remote place unless a finite period elapses between the two events, and unless that period is occupied by a causal chain of events occurring successively at a series of points forming a continuous path between the two places."

Summarily again, this means that *no event can cause another event at a spatial distance from it,* except through an intervening causal chain of events.

With regard to Principles *I.*2 and *I.*3, the question arises as to what exactly it means to speak of two events as occurring "at a distance" from each other in time or/and in space. That is, exactly how are the spatial and temporal boundaries of an event to be defined. Consider for example the physical event caused by the striking of a bell. How long does it last and how far does it extend from its temporal and spatial beginning? At least in the case of events of this general type, it would seem that an event is essentially a field; and therefore that one can speak of a boundary of an event—and therefore of time and space distance intervening between it and a boundary of another event—only, pragmatically, as the locus in time and space where the given event is capable under given circumstances of causing an effect of such specific kind and magnitude as one happens to be interested in. If so, the time and space boundaries of events can be defined only in terms of causation, and the principles (*I.*2 and *I.*3) that there can be "no action at an empty distance," temporal or spatial, are then analytic.

The *second* category of basic limiting principles concerns *limitations of the action of mind on matter.* Only one principle is formulated by Broad under this heading:

Principle II. "It is impossible for an event in a person's mind to produce *directly* any change in the material world except changes in his own brain." (p. 9)

The status of Principle *II* is only that of a generalization from ordinary experience, formulated in language employing the terms "mind" and "brain" in their ordinary unanalyzed senses. It may be, of course, that the tissue of a living brain is in fact the only kind of physical material capable of being affected directly by events in the mind to which that brain "belongs;" but if interaction between mind and matter is possible at all—and Broad has conclusively shown that the principle of Conservation of Energy does not stand in the way of it—[2]

2 *MPN,* 103ff.

then there is no *a priori* reason why interaction could not, under conditions different from the normal ones, occur between a mind and material objects other than its brain. Principle *II,* therefore, is only an empirical generalization of very wide but not necessarily universal validity.

The *third* category of basic limiting principles has to do with the *dependence of mind on brain.* Here again, only one limiting principle is listed:

Principle III. "A necessary, even if not a sufficient, immediate condition of any mental event is an event in the brain of a living body."

This principle, however, is rather elaborately specified by Broad, substantially as follows: For each different mental event, a different brain-event; and for qualitatively dissimilar, and similar, mental events, brain-events respectively dissimilar, and similar; the mental events of one same person, conditioned by brain-events in the same brain; the mental events of two different persons, conditioned by brain events in two different brains, except that in cases of multiple personality a single brain is involved, and that in sleep or delirium some of the mental events—although conditioned by a single brain—are so loosely interconnected or connected with the waking mental events "that they scarcely belong to any recognizable person."

This principle, of course, is not analytic and is not even known to be true, although it is widely accepted today by psychologists and biologists. Its epistemic status is that of a hypothesis, somewhat hastily supposed to be alone capable of accounting for facts, such as those mentioned by Broad on pp. 534–5 of his *The Mind and its Place in Nature,* which appear to stand in the way of the Instrumental Theory of the Body-Mind relation—facts, for example, such as that a brain injury may transform a cheerful and benevolent person into a morose and malevolent one, etc.

The *fourth* group of basic limiting principles relates to *limitations on ways of acquiring knowledge,* and comprises four limiting principles:

Principle IV. 1: "It is impossible for a person to perceive a physical event or a material thing except by means of sensations which that event or thing produces in his mind."

"Sensations" means here the sort of mental states caused directly by stimulation of the sense organs together with the sensory nerves. This principle, again, is only a widely valid generalization from ordinary experience.

Principle IV. 2 is, in substance, that it is impossible for one person to know what experiences another person is having or has had, except by hearing or reading, and understanding sentences, or copies or translations of sentences, uttered or written by the other person; or by hearing cries or seeing facial expressions of, or movements made by, the other person, and interpreting them; or by seeing, and making inferences from, material objects made or used by the other person in the past, or copies thereof. This principle too is an empirical generalization.

Principle IV. 3: "It is impossible for a person to forecast, except by chance, that an event of such and such a kind will happen at such and such a place and time except" either "by inference from data supplied to him by his present sensations, introspections, or memories, together with his knowledge of certain rules of sequence which have hitherto prevailed in nature;" or by inference from such data or/and rules communicated to him by trustworthy other persons; or by accepting from them inferences they have so made; or by non-inferential expectations, based on past regularities of experience, and now aroused by some present experience. Forecasting of an action or experience, of oneself or of another person, on the basis of knowledge of a preceding intention to act so as to cause it, constitutes a special case of one or another of the preceding alternatives.

Principle IV. 4: "It is impossible for a person to know or have reason to believe that an event of such and such a kind happened at such and such a place and time in the past except" on the basis of "present memory, or [of] testimony based on present memory or on records of past perceptions and memories;" or of explicit or implicit inference, by oneself or an informant, from present sensory, introspective, or mnemic data together with knowledge of certain laws of nature.

It should be noted that the impossibility which Principle *IV* 3 asserts is ultimately based on the assumption that, otherwise, Principle *I*.1 (to wit, that an event cannot cause anything, or in particular a perception of it, before the event has itself occurred) would be violated. Similarly, the impossibility asserted by Principle *IV*.4 rests on the assumption that otherwise a violation of Principle *I*.2 would be involved; (that is, of the principle that an event cannot cause anything at an empty temporal distance). That these are the bases on which tacitly rests the belief in the impossibility of so-called Precognition and Postcognition is shown by Broad, with full regard to all the necessary distinctions, in another acute paper, "The Philosophical Implications of Foreknowledge."[3]

Broad does not contend that the above nine principles are the only basic limiting principles there are, nor that they are all logically independent of one another; but only that they are "important restrictive principles of very wide range, which are commonly accepted today by educated plain men and by scientists in Europe and America." (pp. 9–12) As stated earlier, their relevance to psychical research lies in the fact that

[3] *Aristotelian Society Proceedings*, Suppl. 16, 1937, 177ff.

"paranormal" events, which are what psychical research is concerned with, are events that conflict with one or another of those limiting principles.

III.   "Precognition," Cognition, and Premonition.

From Broad's general argument, now outlined, in support of the contention that paranormal events have important bearings on some of the problems of philosophy, let us now turn to the striking illustration of this fact which the well-established sporadic occurrence of so-called Precognition furnishes. Broad discusses it in detail in the other paper already referred to, "The Philosophical Implications of Foreknowledge," which was presented by him at the 1937 meeting of the Aristotelian Society, and was then commented upon by Professor H. H. Price, whose comments were in turn commented upon by Broad. Occasion will arise in later sections to cite various of those comments.[4]

We need first to be quite clear as to what the term Precognition is intended to designate. Instances of "precognition" are ones where the content of a dream or vision, or of a "hunch," or (experimentally) of a guess, eventually turns out to correspond to a later event; and where the correspondence is not plausibly explicable as chance coincidence, nor as due to inference, nor as due to habits of expectation built up in the past by non-causal regularities; nor as due to subsequent action by the experient, motivated by the experience and contributing directly or indirectly to cause the later event.

Although the term Precognition, or Foreknowledge, is now customarily used to refer to all such instances, it is a rather unfelicitous one for the purpose, since the great majority of them are not really instances of cognition or knowledge at all, in the ordinary sense of these two terms. "Cognition" or "Knowledge" ordinarily designates not merely presence to the mind of an *idea* (as distinguished from a conation or an affective state;) nor merely of an idea which happens to be *veridical* in the sense of corresponding to a fact; nor even merely of an idea veridical in this sense which in addition is *believed;* but rather, to presence of a veridical idea that is believed *and belief of which at the time is based on some more or less reliable sign, i.e., evidence, that the idea is veridical.* Most of the instances of so-called Precognition or Foreknowledge, however, are *not* marked off at the time, or in retrospect anterior to verification, by any such sign. As Broad points out, "much of the evidence adduced for supernormal precognition is really evidence for the occur-

4 *Loc. cit.,* 177–245. This paper will be referred to in what follows by the initials, P.I.F., of its title.

rence of images which were *not* prospectively referred by the experient at the time when he had them, but were shown by subsequent events to have been *in fact* pro-presentative."[5] Indeed, the events which eventually show this may be posterior to the experient's death, or may for some other reason never become known by him, but only by some other person.[6]

If the dream, vision, or guess which eventually turns out to have been veridical was accompanied by a feeling of conviction, then it constitutes a veridical *premonition* or "hunch;" but even then it does not constitute cognition or knowledge unless the experient somehow *knows*—as would seem possible only by induction from past experience —that that feeling of conviction is a *reliable* sign of the veridicality of the experience; for probably the majority of the premonitions or hunches people have turn out to have been delusive.[7]

The fact emphasized in these remarks—that very few, if any, of the precognitions or even premonitions shown by later events to have been veridical are really *cognitions*, i.e., are really knowledge in the ordinary sense—is important to keep firmly in mind; for otherwise some quite gratuitous puzzles arise as to "free will" and as to the possibility of interfering with what the future has been precognized to be going to be. These puzzles are gratuitous because rooted in failure to realize that to know what the future has been "precognized" to be going to be, is not in the least to *know* precognitively what the future is going to be.

IV.   Three objections to the possibility of precognition.

In Broad's last cited article, he examines three philosophical objections commonly felt to rule out the possibility of precognition.

The first is an epistemological one. I shall not discuss it, for Broad argues that if it were valid it would then rule out equally the possibility of memory; which is veridical non-inferential cognition too, but of events in the past instead of the future; and Broad's careful and detailed argument for this seems to me to rest on a sound analysis of memory and of sense perception.

Another objection, which Broad also attacks, is the "fatalistic" one. For brevity, I shall put it as follows: No future event can be precognized unless it was predetermined. But some future events depend on voluntary decisions. Therefore these future events cannot be precognized

---

5 *P.I.F.*, 188.   6 *P.I.F.*, 194.

7 In the *Jl. of the A.S.P.R.* for July, 1955, F. C. Dommeyer describes an interesting example of a recurrent dream containing no internal indication of its precognitive character, but which came to be recognized as precognitive because, over many years, it never failed to be quickly followed by receipt of otherwise unexpected money.

unless the voluntary decisions on which they depend were themselves predetermined. But to suppose a decision to be both predetermined and voluntary is a contradiction. Therefore no future event that was dependent on a voluntary decision can have been predetermined. Hence precognition of such events is impossible.

Broad attacks this objection on the ground that what the possibility of precognition requires is not that future events be *predetermined,* but only that they be *predeterminate*—saying that to speak of the future as already predeterminate means only that, although the truth or falsity of present judgments as to what the future will be becomes *known* only in the future, the judgments themselves do not become true or false in the future but are so already now.

I believe that future events are indeed predeterminate in this sense, although—because truth and falsity are not events and therefore have no dates—it is really no more correct to say that a judgment is true or false *now,* than to say that it will become true or false at some future date.[8] But, granting anyway the predeterminateness of future events, it seems to me that the proponent of the "fatalistic" objection could, with some plausibility, reply that, if it is a contradiction to suppose a decision to be both voluntary and predetermined, then it is equally so to suppose it to be both voluntary and predeterminate.

For reasons to be stated farther on, however, I do not myself think a contradiction is involved in supposing a decision to be both voluntary and predetermined. Like Broad, I regard the "fatalistic" objection as invalid, but on grounds different from those on which he condemns it.

One of the reasons why I regard it as invalid is that the alleged impossibility of precognizing a future event that depends on a subsequent voluntary decision rests on the tacit assumption that precognition is cognition in the ordinary sense, i.e., in the sense of belief based on evidence sufficient to certify the truth of what is believed. But, as pointed out in Sec. *III* above, precognition is in fact very seldom cognition in this sense. Hence, the impossibility of voluntary interference with a "precognized" future event lies in the fact that, at the time of would-be interference, one has no way of telling whether one's voluntary act will be preventive of, or on the contrary instrumental to, the future event; for, at that time, one does not *know* what the future event will be, but only that one has had a vision, dream, or hunch that it will be such and such.

Consider, for example, the often mentioned case of "Lady Z," who had dreamt that, on a drive, she saw her coachman sway on his seat and

8 Cf. the writer's paper, "Truth, Verifiability, and Propositions about the Future," in *Philosophy of Science,* 8, No. 3, July, 1941.

fall to the ground, smashing his hat; and who, when actually on a drive the next day, seeing the coachman indeed swaying and about to fall, remembered her dream and called to a policeman who then caught the coachman as he fell, so that the latter did not actually hit the ground or smash his hat. In this case, obviously, the correct conclusion is not that the future is only in part the effect of causes, nor that precognition is only of probabilities; but, quite simply, that the dream— which was not *knowledge* at all—was veridical only in part—only in that part of it which the later event verified; and non-veridical beyond that point. Also, that the remembering of the dream, and Lady Z's action thereby caused, were what then determined the non-occurrence of the erroneous last part of the dream.

Another reason why the "fatalistic" objection to the possibility of precognition is invalid is that, contrary to what the objection assumes and to what Broad, mistakenly I think, concedes, the assumption that a decision cannot be both voluntary and completely determined is unsound—resting as it does on the gratuitous identification of predeterminedness with predictability from exhaustive knowledge of past and present events.

For note that, if the context (antecedent and present) of a decision is *unprecedented* in that the elements of that context have *never before* in the history of the world been all so combined and in the same magnitudes, then it follows that experience of the past and present, no matter how extensive, would not enable one to predict exactly what the decision will be. But that the decision will then be unpredictable does not mean that it will have been uncaused, i.e., not determined; for whereas predictability depends on knowledge of causal laws, which is obtainable only by induction from past experience, causation itself does not so depend. Causation is the triadic relation between: (i) a given concrete state of affairs S; (ii) the occurrence of a concrete only change C in S at a time T; and (iii) the occurrence at the immediately sequent time T1 of another concrete change, E, in S—the *concrete* changes C and E, *qua so related in the concrete S* being respectively termed "cause" and "effect."

Causation, in short, is the very relation which the canon of the so-called "method" of Single Difference *describes,* and not a relation other than it but inferrible from it. What is inferrible—from comparison of several experiments, and by noting the respects in which the three elements of each resemble the corresponding elements of the others— is some causal *law;* which, however, is causal not in virtue of its being a regularity of sequence (since there are non-causal regularities of sequence), but in virtue of the fact that each of the concrete sequences generalized in the law is itself in its own individual right a causal sequence in the sense stated above.

Once causation in the concrete has thus been distinguished from such abstract regularities of causation as may be inductively discovered, it becomes evident that no contradiction at all is involved in saying, on the one hand, that an event, for example a voluntary decision, is—to the extent that its antecedent and present context is unprecedented in the history of the universe—indeed unpredictable even with exhaustive knowledge of past and present events; and in saying, on the other hand, that as in the case of any other event, that decision is determined by a cause, which is the immediately antecedent only change in the state of affairs in which that decision is the immediately sequent change. Man's freedom does not consist, as the "fatalistic" objection tacitly assumes, in his decisions being uncaused, for they too are effects of causes; but in the fact that some of them do cause what he intended. In so far as they do so, man is free; but his freedom is limited, since there are many things which his decisions are impotent to cause to occur. The confusion which infects the question of determinism arises from the taking of "determinism" and especially of "predeterminism" to mean, tacitly but quite gratuitously, that *all* future events are effects of antecedent events that will cause them *no matter what voluntary acts men could perform*. But this is true only of some future events—for example, eclipses of the moon. In the case of some other future events, on the contrary, some of the links in the chain of causes and effects which determine the occurrence of those future events *consist of human volitions*—which have their causes, but are in turn causative; and causative sometimes indeed of what they intended; but often, instead, of something unintended and unforeseen.[9]

The remaining and most important of the three objections to the possibility of precognition, which Broad considers, is the "causal" objection. In substance, it is that precognition is impossible because any case of it would be one where an event F, which at a time T is future and therefore as yet non-existent, nevertheless causes at time T another event, E—specifically, a veridical ostensible perception of F, in the form of, let us say, a dream. But that a *posterior* event should cause an *anterior* one is impossible according to Basic Limiting Principle *I*.1, which, being analytic, is perfectly certain.

Broad states that he has no theory of his own to suggest, as to the *modus operandi* of precognition; and that in his opinion the only

---

[9] The above remarks on determinism, causation, and freedom are of course much too brief to have dealt adequately with these difficult questions. A fuller treatment of them may be found in Part *II* of the writer's book, *Nature, Mind, and Death*.

theory of it worthy of consideration at all is that set forth by J. W. Dunne in the book *An Experiment With Time;* but that, because of extravagances in it which he has pointed out in another article,[10] it cannot be accepted as it stands. Broad then states that he will venture "a perfectly fantastic suggestion" (P.I.F. p. 199,) which, he emphasizes, "may be simply nonsensical" (p. 203); namely, that time may be two-dimensional—its second "before-after" dimension standing to the familiar one in a manner analogous to that in which the South-North space dimension of the earth's surface stands to the West-East dimension: "Then an event which is 'after' a certain other event, in the only temporal dimension which we ordinarily recognize, might be either 'after' or 'before' or 'simultaneous with' this other event in the second temporal dimension. . . ." (p. 200.)

Broad hazards this suggestion, very hesitantly, as the only one which would "make sense of a purely prehensive analysis of veridical foreseeing and of memory" (p. 203)—this, however, not recommending it much to him since he regards any such analysis of them as incorrect. So the chief interest which the idea of a second dimension of time has for him is that it might be a way of getting around the "causal" objection to the possibility of precognition.

Is the theory, however, intelligible, at all, or—as Price asks in his comments on Broad's paper—is the theory "nonsensical as Dr. Broad himself half suspects?" (p. 224.) The great difficulty, which Price, and Broad with him, find in it concerns the "*becoming* aspect of Time;*" that is, the fact that, "to use the language which Professor Broad has himself used elsewhere, the past is what *has become,* the present is what *is becoming,* the future is what has *not yet become.*" Price then mentions a "very curious theory," which some people apparently want to hold, but which—for reasons I shall cite later—he doubts is tenable; the theory, namely, that

all events in the universe, whether psychical or physical, are related by relations of *earlier and later* (in a single dimension of course), but only psychical events are subject to *becoming.* Thus a given physical event E_2 would be *later than* a certain other physical event E_1, and *earlier than* a third physical event E_3: but it could not be called *past, present,* or *future,* nor could we say of it that it has become, is becoming, or is yet to become. What *is* future, present, or past is not the physical event, but the *cognition* of it and perhaps the emotions directed on it. (p. 227)

Broad endorses Price's criticisms of this theory, and adds for himself that he is inclined to think that "the notion of earlier and later is inextricably interwoven with the notions of becoming and of pastness,

[10] "Mr. Dunne's Theory of Time," *Philosophy,* X, No. 38, April 1935, 168–85.

presentness, and futurity; so that the suggestion that there might be a series of terms to which the latter notions did not apply, but which were nevertheless ordered by the relation of earlier and later, is really unintelligible." Hence, in order to avoid this objection the theory would have to be restated somewhat as follows: What we commonly call a 'series of physical events inter-related by the relation of earlier and later' is not really a series of *events* and is not really ordered by the relation of *earlier and later*. In itself it is a series of non-temporal terms ordered by a non-temporal relation, for which we have no name. The terms are called 'events' and their relation is called 'earlier and later' only in respect of the relation of the whole series to genuinely temporal series of cognitions and emotions in the minds of persons who observe it and are emotionally affected by it.

Broad adds that although "this restatement makes the theory more coherent, it obviously does not remove any of Professor Price's objections to it. Rather does it reinforce those objections." (p. 243)

I have cited here the theory to which Price refers and which Broad restates in somewhat different form, but to which both of them find insuperable objections, because the theory I would now propose as avoiding the "causal" objection to the possibility of precognition resembles closely in some respects that "very curious theory." But I believe that the objections to the latter which Price and Broad formulate, and which I shall consider in due time, do not apply to the theory I shall now outline.

V. A Theory of the Relation of Causality to Precognition.

The theory about to be outlined, which for brevity of reference may be labelled theory Theta, does not profess to give an account of the *modus operandi* of precognition, but only to show that precognition does not, as it *prima facie* seems to do, require causation of a present event by an as yet future one. That is, the paradox in precognition arises from violation not of Basic Limiting Principle *I*.1, but of one of the others.

Also, theory Theta concerns precognition only (a) of events which are *physical* but which (or physical signs of which) are eventually perceived by the precognizer or by someone else; or (b) of psychological events which are perceivings of *physical* events (or of physical signs of them), by the precognizer or by someone else. That is, theory Theta does not consider and does not purport to resolve the causal paradox in cases, if any, where the event precognized is a psychological event *that*

*is not a percept of a physical event or of a physical sign of a physical
event.* So far as I know, however, there are no such cases.

The fact from which theory Theta starts is that no definition of the
adjectives "past," "present," or "future," *simpliciter,* i.e., applied categorically, can be given in purely physical terms; and hence that physical
events, *in themselves,* i.e., apart from the psychological events which are
percepts of them, are not categorically either past, present, or future.

To physical events considered independently of percepts of them, the
predicates "past," "present," or "future" are therefore applicable not
categorically but only conditionally. That is, one can say of a physical
event E so considered, that it is future to (or temporally after or beyond)
a certain other one D *from a certain third C;* but not simply that it is
future. Similarly, one can say of D that it is past relatively to (or temporally before or *cis*) E *from C;* but not simply that it is *past.* And, concerning any one of them, say E, one can say that it is simultaneous with
(or co-present with) a certain other one, S, *relatively to a certain third,* Q;
but not simply that it is *present* or *now.*

This state of affairs entails that the serial time order of physical events
in themselves *has no intrinsic direction.* For the physical event E, although future to D *from C,* is on the contrary past to D *from a fourth
event F* so selected that E is temporally between D and F. This follows
from the fact that the relation "temporally between," which determines
the serial order of physical events, does not determine one rather than
the other of the two theoretically possible directions within that order.
In terms of entropy, all that could be said would be that, in one of the
two directions, entropy never decreases; whereas in the other direction
it never increases, and this does not, *in itself,* i.e., independently of our
perceptions of physical events, specify as "real" one rather than the
other direction in the series of physical events.

The three terms, "past," "present," "future," as predicated categorically instead of, as above, conditionally, are essentially psychological
terms. Their meaning lies in the fact that psychological events, as
experienced, have in different degrees a certain characteristic which is
distinct from intensity, from clearness, and from interestingness. Nor
is it, as suggested by J. D. Mabbott,[11] the characteristic which Hume
has in mind when he speaks of "force of vivacity," since by this Hume
means what differentiates the believing of something from the mere
imagining of it.[12] I shall, more or less arbitrarily, call "liveness" the
characteristic to which I refer. It cannot be described but can easily be
identified introspectively in the concrete.

[11] "Our Direct Experience of Time," *Mind,* April 1951, 162.
[12] *Treatise of Human Nature,* Part *III,* § V, 86 (Selby-Bigge Edition).

Consider, for example, one's auditory experience as he hears or imagines the sound of some word—say, the word "inductively." The characteristic here denominated "liveness" then is that which, as that *whole* word is heard, is possessed in its maximal degree by the syllable "ly;" in somewhat lower degree by the syllable "tive;" in still lower degree by the syllable "duc;" and so on. And possession of this characteristic in its maximal degree by a psychological event—here, by the sound "ly"—is the meaning and the whole of the meaning of the statement that the event concerned is "strictly present" in the psychological sense of this term.

On the other hand, being "speciously present" through "strictly past" is the name of the status, in the serial order of psychological events, of e.g., the other syllables of the word "inductively" when the syllable "ly" is strictly present. That they are then speciously present means that, although "strictly past," they have then not yet lapsed from consciousness in the sense of needing to be recalled if one wishes to attend to them. Each of them is termed "earlier" or "less recent" in proportion to the degree of inferiority in liveness it has when the syllable "ly" has the maximal degree of liveness. To experience a psychological event as "earlier" than another means nothing more and nothing less than that. Psychological events which, at the moment, can be attended to only if recalled are termed not then speciously present, but simply "past." And "future," *simpliciter,* is the name of the status, in the serial order of psychological events, of whatever psychological events are neither past nor speciously present nor strictly present. Broad rightly rejects William James' conception of the specious present as including a bit of the future. The fact that the specious present is thus not a "saddleback" automatically disposes of the theory of precognition suggested by Saltmarsh, according to which precognition would be made possible by a subliminal specious present, *analogous to,* but longer at the forward end than, the supraliminal specious present.[13] Psychological events that have been experienced can of course be *considered,* reflectively, in any order one pleases; but psychological events can be *actually experienced* only in the order of their respective degrees of liveness, and thus of recency, at the time of the one strictly present. This entails that *the time-series of psychological events has intrinsic direction.*

To what was said above concerning the "strictly present," it should be added that, even within the sound "ly," we could if we would distinguish the "l" sound from the "y" sound—which latter would then

13 Saltmarsh, H. F., "Report on cases of apparent Precognition." *Procs. S.P.R.,* 1934, 42, 72–93.

alone be "strictly present." But when one analyzes a given psychological
event into its shorter component events, he quickly reaches components
which, psychologically, are temporally atomic because no temporal parts
can be distinguished within them. Moreover—and this is the essential
point—application of the term "strictly present" to a psychological
event is governed not by the differences of liveness we could discriminate if we specially tried, but by those which we actually do, and do
not, discriminate. In introspective experience, *esse est percipi*.

At this point, I shall pause in the outlining of theory Theta in order
to compare its account of the specious present with that offered by Broad.

The characteristic which, in what precedes, I have denominated "liveness" is I believe the same as that which Broad had (unknown to me until
recently) earlier termed "presentedness."[14] I nevertheless retain "liveness" in my account because this term seems to me less likely to generate
confusion, such, for example, as appears to underlie W. Kneale's statement in his review of Broad's book,[15] that "to say that *a* has a lower
degree of presentedness than *b* is surely not the same as to say that *a*
is presented earlier than *b*." What I believe Broad would hold (and I
then with him) is that to say that *a* is *prehended* (not, as Kneale has it,
presented) "earlier than" *b means* that *a* has a lower degree of presentedness (i.e., of what I call instead "liveness") than *b* has. That characteristic, under either name, is, as Broad rightly asserts, "the experiential
basis of our notion of *presentness* in the strict sense." (p. 288.) Also,
Broad's diagrammatic representation of the specious present as a wedge
(vs. a saddleback) is I think quite appropriate.

On the other hand, the notion of "instantaneous event-particles,"
which Broad introduces into his discussion, seems to me not only as
he says "a rather elaborate and sophisticated product" (p. 282), but,
psychologically, pure myth. That notion is useful in mathematical
physics, but importation of it into psychology is illegitimate and gratuitously trouble-making because no psychological events are instantaneous
in the mathematico-physical sense; but only in the psychological sense
already stated, that no parts actually are, or in some cases can be,
empirically discriminated within them. An event is either a change, or
a state's remaining unchanged, and an atomic psychological event is
atomic in the empirical sense just stated, which is the only one not psychologically incongruous. Psychological time is thus "granular," not
infinitely divisible as the time of mathematical physics is postulated to
be. I would therefore insist that, in Broad's statement that presentedness
"is the experiential basis of our notion of *presentness* in the strict

14 *EMcP*, II, 282.   15 *Mind* (Oct. 1939), 509.

sense," the relevant "strict sense" is the psychological strict sense, not the mathematico-physical one.

Again, it seems to me wrong to speak, as Broad does, of a "series of successive Specious Presents" (p. 285). What are many and successive are the *events,* which pop into *the* specious present at the perpendicular end of the wedge which represents it. And the arrow, pointing right, which Broad uses to represent "lapse of time," should point left instead and represent the order of decreasing "presentedness" or "liveness" within the specious present; for it is in terms of *this* that "lapse of time" gets defined. Again, Broad's assumption that "all Specious Presents

```
. . . . p , p , p :   Past events, some accessible to memory
. . . . e , e , e :   Events strictly past, but speciously present
            E :   The event strictly present
? , ? , ? . . . . :   Events as yet future
```

of the same mind are of the same duration" (284) is I think illegitimate because, in one mind, there are not several specious presents but only one, through which, as it were, crawls an endless variously mottled snake. It is its mottled markings, i.e., the events, which are many and successive. Moreover, *psychologically,* "duration" is a term applicable *within* the specious present, that is, to events there, but not *to* the specious present itself, which is not an event at all. What varies is not the "duration" of the specious present—to which this term is not applicable—but the number of events it contains. When a given event E is (psychologically) strictly present, the number of events speciously present may be, say, five; and when another given event F is strictly present, the number of speciously present ones might be, say, only three —or as the case may be, seven, etc.—according, apparently, to the degree of intrinsic interestingness of the events concerned, or to their relevance to what happens to be our governing interest at the time. What seems to me all-important to remember in connection with statements about the specious present is that they must not be worded in temporal terms, as if we already somehow knew, independently, what such terms mean; the fact being, on the contrary, that "presentedness" or "liveness" and its degrees are the experiential basis not only, as Broad says, of our notion of presentness, but of our notion of "earlier" and "later," and thus *of our notion of time.*

I return now to the exposition of theory Theta. The account of it, so far as already given, makes evident that, in any attempt to show that precognition does not involve violation of Basic Limiting Principle *I*. 1, we have to take account of two different time-series. In one of them— that of physical events in themselves—no event is categorically past, present, or future; and, because the series of those events has no intrinsic direction, no event in it is categorically earlier, or categorically later, than a given other, but only earlier than it *from a certain third,* and later than it *from a certain fourth.* In the other time-series, on the contrary—that of psychological events—the serial order does have an intrinsic direction; and always, in that series, some one psychological event, simple or complex, is categorically present, and all others categorically past or categorically future. That is, in that series, "earlier" and "later" are dyadic relations, not triadic as in the other series.

The physical series, however, gets related to the psychological one by the fact that some psychological events are percepts of physical events. Then the physical event perceived, in virtue of its being object of a percept categorically present, is spoken of also categorically as present; but, let it be noted, it is categorically present, i.e., present *simpliciter,* only in the *elliptical* sense of being object of a percept itself on the contrary present categorically in the *literal* sense described above, which applies only to psychological events.

Now, we ordinarily assume naively that a physical event can be perceived only if it is present; (or more exactly, on reflection, if it is past by the amount of time—negligible in most cases for practical purposes—occupied by the causal process extending from the physical event concerned to the sense organs and from them to the brain cortex). But what on the contrary is made evident by the preceding remarks is that *present perception* of a physical event (which event *in itself* is neither present nor past nor future) *automatically confers categorical presence on that event* in the elliptical sense stated, which is the only sense in which a physical event ever is categorically present at all.

From this, however, it evidently follows that no causal paradox is really involved in so-called precogniton; for what really occurs there is only that one individual physical event, although occurring of course only once, nevertheless is *present several times* because perceived at several psychological times—once, perhaps, at night in a dream; and again, perhaps the next day, in ordinary waking perception. That it can be present several times without itself occurring several times is an automatic consequence of the cardinal fact that, *in itself,* it is neither present nor past nor future but acquires presentness by being perceived and as often as it is perceived.

This account of precognition, however, still leaves to be answered the question as to what then differentiates a veridical precognitive dream-percept from an ordinary veridical waking percept. The answer, so far as it goes, is that, in the case of the dream percept, the qualitatively relevant sense organ—say, the eye—is not functioning; but on the contrary is functioning in the case of the ordinary waking percept. That a percept, i.e., an ostensible perceiving, *can* be caused somehow otherwise than through the functioning of the sense organs at the time is proved, of course, by the frequent occurrence of hallucinatory percepts, whether oneiric or waking ones. But that a hallucinatory percept should happen to be veridical—except as a pure matter of chance— *still is something paranormal*. It is paranormal, however, *not* as violating Basic Limiting Principle *I*.1, which is analytic and therefore certain; but as violating the weaker, ultimately empirical Basic Limiting Principle *IV*.1, to wit, that physical events can be veridically perceived only by means of sensations (if, by "sensations" as distinguished from hallucinations, we mean vivid images caused at the time through the functioning of the sense organs).

VI.   *Do Broad's and Price's objections apply to the theory outlined?*

Let us now ask whether any of the objections formulated by Broad or Price to the theories of precognition they examine apply to the theory outlined in the preceding section.

(a) First, it should be noted that the two time-series—the physical and the psychological—of which that theory takes account are not, like the two series in Broad's two-dimensional-time conjecture, "perpendicular" to each other. Theory Theta is therefore untouched by Price's objection that two-dimensional time would commit us to a "Double Now"—one for each dimension—so that an event which is "now" in one of them might be "past" or "not yet" in the other (P.I.F. p. 225). In theory Theta, "now" has no purely physical meaning, and is predicable at all of a physical event only in the elliptical sense that that event is object of a percept that is "now" in the literal sense.

(b) Let us consider next the notion of *becoming*, in connection with which both Broad and Price find that difficulties arise for the two-dimensional-time theory and for the other theory they examine. Both speak of *events* as becoming—Price objecting, for instance, that the "very curious theory" to which he refers—mentioned in Sec. *IV* above— would not enable one to say of a physical event "that it has become, is becoming, or is yet to become" (p. 227); and Broad, that according to it physical events, as such, "do not become and pass away."

"Becoming," however, is predicable of events, if at all, only in the rather unusual sense in which "becoming" means occurring, happening, befalling. "Becoming" is normally transitive and predicable only of continuants. Water, for example, becomes hot, or frozen, etc., but the event, "water's becoming hot," does not itself become, in the same sense of the word; but only in the different sense for which "occurs" or "happens" are the normal terms. As J. J. C. Smart says:[16] "Events happen, things become, and things do not just become, they become something or other." Broad, Smart goes on, "agrees that events do no *change* but he says that they *become,* and by this he means that they *come into existence,*" but "this use of 'become' is no more applicable to events than is the ordinary transitive use. . . . We can say when the inauguration of a new republic occurred and we can say that the new republic came into existence then, but we cannot say that the inauguration came into existence." (p. 486) Similarly, the birth of a baby occurs, but it is the baby, not the birth, which comes into existence. " 'Become'," Smart insists, "is a transitive verb; if we start using it intransitively we can expect nothing but trouble." (p. 486)

The notion of becoming is relevant to events in that some of them are, not becoming, but *becomings,* i.e., changes in or about something otherwise continuant. Also, in that some other events are *non-becomings:* for example, the question "What occurred then?" admits equally of the answer "The door opened," or "The door remained closed." The latter too describes an event, but one which—to use Dr. Charles Mercier's term—is an "unchange" in the state of a substance or continuant.

In the light of these remarks, it seems to me that Broad's and Price's objection to the theories mentioned, namely that they do not admit of our saying that an event becomes and passes away, or "has become, is becoming, or is yet to become" is at best most unfortunately worded. But I am not sure that to point this out is automatically to dispose of the difficulty they felt in those theories; for perhaps the difficulty could be restated in terms of "occurring" instead of in terms of "becoming." If so, it would be, I suppose, that to say of an event that it is "past," "present," or "future," is to say of it, respectively, that it *has occurred, is occurring,* or *has not yet occurred;* and that, unless this can be said of that about which one speaks, it is not an *event* at all.

This, it seems to me, has to be admitted, but only because the use there of the tensed forms of "to occur" virtually makes that statement a tautology. What is needed is an account, in psychological terms, of the difference between the three statuses of events which are describable, indifferently because synonymously, as "being past" or as "having occurred;" as "being present" or as "occurring;" and as "being future" or as "not having yet occurred." A psychological account of that difference

16 "The River of Time," *Mind,* (Oct. 1949), 481–94.

is what theory Theta offers. And that theory, it will be remembered, distinguishes—as Broad and Price omit to do—between the dyadic and the triadic sense of "earlier" and "later." In the dyadic, categorical sense, these terms are predicable, *literatim,* only of psychological events: these alone are categorically past, present, or future; or earlier and later. Physical events, on the other hand, are, *in themselves,* "earlier" or "later" only in the triadic, conditional sense (earlier or later than . . . from . . .); and are "earlier" or "later" in the dyadic, categorical sense—and categorically past, present, or future—*not in themselves* but only in virtue of the fact that some of them are perceived; and hence only in the *elliptical* sense which "being object of a past, present, or future percept" constitutes.

Broad might perhaps wish to say that unless something A is earlier or later than something else B in the *dyadic, categorical* sense of "earlier" and "later," A and B are not literally events at all. This would entail that physical events would be "events" only in an elliptical sense corresponding to that in which alone they are categorically past, present, or future. But insistence on thus tying literal eventhood to being in the categorical, dyadic "earlier-later" relation would, it seems to me, be highly arbitrary.

(c) Certain other objections to the "very curious theory," which are formulated by Price and which Broad apparently means to include in his general endorsement of Price's criticisms, rest on assumptions which seem to me unwarranted. Price writes, for instance, that, on that theory, "psycho-physical and physico-psychical causation would become an extraordinary puzzle. In the physical world causation will be reducible to *order* (of a quasi-geometrical sort) . . . the effect merely has to be *further on in time than* its cause (in accordance with some law or other)," whereas "physico-psychical causation will involve over and above this the notion of *production;* for in this sort of causation the effect has to be *brought into being* by its cause." (p. 227)

But mere sequence—even if regular and even among physical events— is not the same thing as consequence. An event which is further on in time is not a consequence of an earlier one unless the regularity of their sequence is a *causal* regularity—which, for example, is not the case with, in babies, the regular sequence of, first, growth of hair and later, growth of teeth. As pointed out earlier in a different connection, a causal regularity is ultimately differentiated from a non-causal one by the fact that in each instance of the causal one the event termed "cause" is the single change occuring in a certain state of affairs, immediately before and adjacent to occurrence in it of another change, then termed "effect." So one cannot say, even of physical events, that, on the "very curious theory"—or on the theory Theta—the effect *merely* has to be regularly further on in time than its cause.

Hence there is no such difference between physico-physical causation on the one hand, and on the other, physico-psychical or psycho-physical causation, as Price claims; namely, that in the latter two, but not in the former, the notion of *production—of bringing the effect into being—*is involved. For these expressions are mere synonyms of "causation" and of "causing"—the definition of which presupposes nothing at all as to the nature, physical or psychological, of the events that happen to figure as its terms in one or another instance.

Price goes on to say that "psycho-physical causation would be even more puzzling [than physico-psychical causation]. For here the cause would *come into being,* but the effect would not; the effect would just be." (P.I.F. p. 227)

But, for one thing, Smart's criticism quoted above, of Broad's speaking of events as "coming into existence," applies equally to the synonym "coming into being." That is, the cause would, simply, *occur* at some particular time in the time series of psychological events. And the effect would not—any more than the cause—"just be," but would occur too— at some particular time in the time-series of physical events.

In psycho-physical causation, the true difference between the cause-event and the effect-event would be that, whereas the cause-event (being a psychological event) would be present categorically and literally at a certain psychological time; the physical event, on the contrary, which would be the (immediate) effect, would not *in itself*—i.e., independently of its status as effect of a psychological event—be categorically or literally past, present, or future. That physical event would be categorically future to, i.e., (immediately) later than, its psychological cause, only in the *elliptical* sense of being effect of a psychological event present in the *literal* sense.

That is, just as, in the case of perception of a physical event, presence, or rather more or less nearly immediate pastness, in the *elliptical* sense, is conferred on the physical event by its status as object of, i.e., as more or less nearly immediate cause of, a *literally* present percept; so, in the case of volition (or other psychological causation) of a physical event, presence, or rather more or less nearly immediate futureness, in the *elliptical* sense, is conferred on the physical event by its status as object of, i.e., as more or less nearly immediate effect of, a *literally* present volition.[17]

---

[17] The conception of the nature of Objective Reference, on which the statements in the above paragraph are based, cannot be explicated here, but may be found in Ch. 15 of the writer's *Nature, Mind, and Death.*

In connection with psycho-physical causation, it is interesting to notice incidentally what would be the kind of paradoxical event analogous to that which, in the case of physico-psychical causation, precognition constitutes. That analogue would consist in present causation of a physical state of affairs by a movement, volition of which is not motivated by any present need nor by present foreseeing of the future need which the presently caused physical state of affairs will eventually serve. Something like this would seem to be what some biologists mean by "telefinalism." A plausible apparent example would be nest-building by birds. Another, less familiar, is that honey bees protect from bacterial decay the honey they will eventually need for food "by injecting a droplet of poison from the sting within each honey-cell from time to time. This is why honey will not sour within the hive."[18] It can hardly be supposed that the bee (i) *knows,* in the sense in which bacteriologists do, that the honey, left to itself, would ferment; (ii) *desires* that it shall not ferment; (iii) *believes* that sting-poison inhibits fermentation; and (iv) that (i), (ii) and (iii) together *motivate* the bee to inject the poison. But this is what it would mean, to suppose that the bee's action is consciously purposive in the sense in which pasteurization of milk by dairymen is so.

(d) As will be remembered, Broad adds to his endorsement of Price's criticisms the remark that

the notion of earlier and later is inextricably interwoven with the notions of becoming and of pastness, presentness, and futurity; so that the suggestion that there might be a series of terms to which the latter notions did not apply, but which were nevertheless ordered by the relation of earlier and later, is really unintelligible.

Hence, in order to avoid this unintelligibility, we should have to say that "what we commonly call 'a series of physical events interrelated by the relation of earlier and later' is not really a series of *events* and is not really ordered by the relation of *earlier and later.* In itself it is a series of non-temporal terms ordered by a non-temporal relation, for which we have no name." (P.I.F. p. 243)

The objection formulated by the first of these two statements, however, does not apply to theory Theta, because that theory makes, but Broad ignores, the distinction between the dyadic, categorical sense of "earlier" and "later," and their triadic, conditional sense. When this distinction is made, the unintelligibility which would indeed result from divorcing "categorically earlier, or later" from "categorically past, present, or future" vanishes. The proposal, in theory Theta, is only to divorce "*conditionally* earlier, or later" from "*categorically* past, present, or future;" and *these two* are not inextricably interwoven at all.

[18] *Animals looking into the future,* by W. A. Kepner (Macmillan, 1925), 23.

Finally, concerning the remedy which Broad proposes in the second of the two statements quoted above, for the unintelligibility he has in view, it need be said only that theory Theta is in no need of such remedy, since it holds that "what we commonly call a 'series of physical *events* inter-related by the relation of *earlier and later*'" really *is* a series of physical events; and holds that they are ordered by the relation "temporally between," which generates *two* possible earlier-later directions within the series it orders, but does not label one "real" and the other "fictitious" as on the contrary does the dyadic, categorical relation of earlier and later which, in its *literal* sense, obtains only among psychological events; and obtains of physical events only in the elliptical sense derivative from perception of them.

In bringing to a close the discussion of precognition which has occupied the preceding four sections of the present essay, it is perhaps well to recall that precognition is only one of the several kinds of paradoxical phenomena to the study of which psychical research is dedicated; and yet that, as we have seen, crucial questions—concerning causality, time, perception, events, substances, and other basic philosophical concepts—are involved in any attempt to render intelligible the fact that some well-attested cases of precognition occur which cannot plausibly be accounted for either as chance coincidences, or as due to inference or to habits of expectation.

The importance of those questions, I submit, would by itself be amply sufficient to vindicate Broad's contention, to which the title of the present paper refers, that some of the phenomena psychical research investigates are relevant to philosophy, and that philosophers who ignore them do so at the possible peril of their conceptions of man and of the universe. But additional support for this contention will become manifest if we now turn to Basic Limiting Principle *III*, and to the bearing which paranormal facts with which it clashes have on one of the most important problems with which philosophers have occupied themselves, namely, that of the mind-body relation.

VII. The Mind-Body Relation and the Individual's Destiny.

Basic Limiting Principle *III*, as will be remembered, concerns the dependence of mind on brain, and asserts that "a necessary, even if not a sufficient, immediate condition of any mental event is an event in the brain of a living body."

Evidently, this principle would rule out altogether the possibility that the individual's mind survives the death of his body; and, that survival is impossible is indeed today the opinion, or anyway the professional opinion, of the majority of biologists and psychologists. As pointed out earlier, however, Basic Limiting Principle *III*—being based on the fact that *normal* experience whether of scientific or of common kinds presents us with no minds not connected with living nervous systems, and also on such facts as that certain brain injuries alter or destroy certain mental capacities—is only an empirical generalization. Hence it is open to revision and would have to be revised if evidence of some other sort should exist that a person's mind survives after death. Broad therefore considers the various arguments that have been offered as proving survival.[19]

These are, first, the contention of some persons that the truth of survival is self-evident to them, or has been divinely revealed to them personally; second, the argument based on what is alleged to be authority; and third, arguments purporting to establish survival by deductive reasoning from *a priori* premises. Broad comments briefly on these three kinds of arguments and—warrantedly, I think—dismisses each as having patently failed to prove or to establish a probability that survival is a fact. He then gives the whole of Ch. XI to consideration of the ethical arguments for immortality, as presented "with admirable persuasiveness, brevity, and clearness" by Professor A. E. Taylor. Critical examination of them, however, leaves Broad—and, I think, again quite justifiedly—with "no confidence that Professor Taylor has produced any ground whatever for believing in human immortality." (*MPN*, 512)

This leaves to be considered only the empirical arguments for survival. They are the ones based on certain *paranormal* occurrences, and especially on the "Cross-Correspondences" between the scripts of several automatic writers isolated from one another.

These scripts, it may be mentioned here for the benefit of readers not familiar with them, "correspond" not only in the sense of having a common topic, but also in that whereas each script by itself is unintelligible or at best pointless, they have on the contrary when considered together a clear and pointed meaning, as would be the case with the fragments of a mosaic. Moreover, the purported discarnate authors of the scripts state in them that the dividing of a single theme into individually pointless fragments, each communicated independently by a different automatist, is a device by which those authors aim to prove that, although now discarnate, their minds are still active, purposive, and planning; i.e., are still living.

Broad states that he does not propose to discuss in detail these and the other relevant paranormal facts, but presupposes that many of those elicited by the careful work of the Society for Psychical Research are

19 In § IV of *MPN*.

genuine "in the sense that they have been correctly reported and that they are not simply due to fraud or self-deception." He assumes this, he states, "on the basis of a fairly careful study of the literature; of a knowledge of the kind of persons who have controlled the policy of the Society and taken part in its investigations; and of some investigations of my own"—these grounds, he adds, being exactly of the same kinds and of the same weight as those he has for accepting "the existence of certain rare physical phenomena which are difficult to reproduce to order, and of certain rare diseases which competent doctors have described." (MPN, 514)

Taking then as reasonably well-established the paranormal occurrences referred to, and survival as one among other hypotheses that would account for them, Broad, in Ch. XII, considers first the question of the antecedent probability of the survival hypothesis. As to this, he concludes that *normal* experience, whether of scientific or of common kinds, furnishes no evidence of survival; but that this does not constitute the least evidence against survival, since it would do so only under the assumption that, if survival were a fact, there would be *normal* manifestations of it; and this assumption is illegitimate since the only normal manifestations of a mind to others are those given by its living body; and this body is destroyed by death.

VIII. The Instrumental Theory of the Mind-Body Relation.

The question then is as to what conception of the mind-body relation will best account not only for the *normal* facts commonly alleged to prove that brain events are necessary conditions of mental events and hence that minds cannot survive bodily death; but also for the *paranormal* facts alleged to prove that some minds do survive after death.

The first conception to suggest itself as perhaps capable of accounting for both of those sets of facts is termed by Broad the Instrumental Theory of the mind-body relation. As he describes it, it seems identical in essentials with Cartesian Interactionism, since it regards the mind as a substance existentially independent of the body but connected with it for a time, during which the two interact. This conception, Broad says, "is consistent with a good many of the facts which are commonly held to prove the existential dependence of mind on body," and yet it would allow survival. Nevertheless, he thinks that it cannot be maintained in that simple form.

One example he gives of a difficulty in the way of it is that of a man who as a result of some brain injury loses for a time his power to remember certain events. "It can hardly be maintained," Broad writes, "that, in any literal sense, he still remembers the events; and that all that has been damaged is his power of manifesting this knowledge to others by speech or writing" as on the contrary is the fact in the quite different case of aphasia or agraphia. If it be maintained that his mind still has the power to remember those events, but is prevented from exercising it by the brain injury; or, in the case of a benevolent man made malevolent by a brain injury, that he is still benevolent but now expresses this trait by acts of hostility; then what is left of the mind when it is considered apart from the brain "is so abstract and indefinite that it does not deserve to be called a mind." (MPN, 535)

IX. Broad's Compound Theory of the Mind-Body Relation.

The above conclusion is what causes Broad to offer, as preferable to the Instrumental Theory, what he calls the Compound Theory of the mind-body relation. It supposes that what we know as a mind is a compound of two factors, one of which Broad calls the Bodily Factor, and the other the Psychic Factor—or, in the later statement of the theory in his *Examination of McTaggart's Philosophy* (604), the Psychogenic Factor. Neither of the two factors separately has the characteristic properties of a mind—"just as salt is a compound of two substances neither of which by itself has the characteristic properties of salt." (MPN, 535). Thus, mentality would be an "emergent characteristic," arising out of the combination of the bodily and of the psychic factor.

The psychic factor, Broad goes on to point out, might be universal and unique; that is, there might be "only one psychic factor for all minds;" or on the contrary the fact might be "that there is a different psychic factor for each different mind;" or again, and perhaps more plausibly, that there is a different psychic factor for each *human* mind, but perhaps only one psychic factor for a whole species of such animals as earwigs. (MPN, 537–8)

Broad states that "there is very little that can at present be said with certainty" about the nature of the psychic factor. (MPN, 651). It would have no claim to be called a "consciousness," for it would not, as that term suggests, be relating and unifying sense data. But if the supposition that it persists after death is to explain the paranormal facts which suggest that it so persists, "it must be capable of carrying traces of experiences which happened to the mind of which it was formerly a constituent." Broad thinks that "there is at present no reason to believe and strong reason to doubt that it has the higher factors of mentality" such as Referential Cognition; but it may have some of the lower, such as Sentience, (MPN, 651) though Broad does not "see anything in the facts to require or to suggest this hypothesis." It might be material, but if so it is "an unusual kind of matter. . . . not destroyed by the breaking up of the body with which it was connected; it does not manifest itself to sense perception; and it does not produce ordinary physical and chemical effects." If it is material, and if the so-called "ectoplasm" which is alleged to be involved in the alleged phenomena of materialization and telekinesis exists, "it would then be possible to suggest that . . . ectoplasm . . . is identical with the Psychic Factor, which is required to explain some of the mental phenomena of Psychical Research." (MPN, 652)

On the positive side, then, what Broad supposes about the psychogenic factor he postulates for each person is (a) that it is "associated with the person's brain from birth to death," (b) that the experiences he has during life "modify his psycho-genic factor in characteristic ways," (c) that the psycho-genic factor "may persist, with these modifications, for some time after the person has died and his brain has disintegrated," and (d) that "while in this separated state, it may occasionally enter into temporary association with the brain of some living person," termed a medium, "whose psycho-genic factor has been temporarily dissociated or loosened from his brain" (EMcP, 605)—this giving rise to a "mind-kin" temporarily animating that other person and having "some of the memories and characteristic traits of the dead man and some of those of the living medium." (EMcP, 605)

X. Merits and Defects of the Compound Theory.

The merits Broad claims—justly, I think—for the Compound Theory outlined are several. First, it is free from the difficulties he found in the Instrumental Theory, and yet would account for "all the correlation between mind and body which could ever be discovered." Moreover, it accords with what we know about minds, for "on the one hand, it seems a mistake to ascribe perception, reasoning, anger, love, etc., to a mere body. On the other hand . . . it is almost equally difficult to ascribe them to what is left when the bodily factor is ignored." (MPN, 536) The Compound Theory "is compatible with all the facts which everyone admits; it has nothing against it except a superstitious objection to dualism; and it leaves open the possibility" that the debatable but fairly well attested paranormal phenomena which it would explain are genuine. "At the same time it does not compel anyone to accept them." (MPN, 550). Its great merit is that "it leaves open possibilities, and allows us to investigate alleged facts without an invincible a priori prejudice against their possibility. And yet it allows us to be as critical as we like about each of these alleged facts, and about the evidence which is offered for each of them." (MPN, 551). Also, it "has certain advantages for those who favor the theory of metempsychosis as Dr. McTaggart does," which Broad thinks ought to be taken more seriously than it has been by Western philosophers and theologians (EMcP, 639), for "instead of a single *mind* which *animates* a successive series of organisms we should have a single *psychic factor* which *combines with* such a series of organisms to form a successive series of minds." (MPN, 551)

But the Compound Theory as formulated by Broad is clearly open to certain criticisms. One is that on the basis of what Broad postulates for the "Psychic Factor," this factor really has no title at all to be termed "psychic." This may be what, in his later *EMcP* (p. 604) led Broad to call that factor "psycho-genic," instead of, as in the earlier book, "psychic." But if, as the Compound Theory supposes, a mind emerges out of the combination of *two* factors, then the Bodily Factor has exactly the same claim to be described as "psycho-genic" as does the other factor of the combination. The latter, then, is a mere "X," described solely in terms of capacity to explain the facts which it is postulated in order to explain. Since no account is given of its intrinsic nature, no basis is provided for predictions from it of facts not yet observed but of kinds susceptible to observation, which, if eventually observed to be as predicted, would support the supposition that the factor postulated really exists; but in the contrary case would disconfirm that supposition. Thus, since the nature of the postulated factor is neither described, nor observable, nor is inferrible like that of dispositions from observations of bodily or mental behavior, Broad's account leaves that factor a mere *deus ex machina*.

Again, the sense in which it "combines" with a brain is left wholly mysterious. The analogy of chemical combinations sheds no light on this point; for the terms in which the nature of chemical combination is describable are obviously inapplicable to the case of on the one hand a material brain, and on the other a factor which, even if itself also material, as Broad allows to be possible, consists of matter quite unlike any we know.

Lastly—although what is about to be mentioned is not a defect of, specifically, the Compound Theory—Broad's statements at various places in *MPN*, as to what a mind is, or as to what constitutes materiality or mentality, do not seem to me to provide sharp enough conceptions of the meaning of those terms. Instead, those statements have rather the character of incidental descriptions. And, in so far as especially the notions of a "mind" and of "mentality" are left indefinite, the contention of the Compound Theory that a "mind," or that "mentality," emerges out of the combination of a brain and a (mysterious) psychogenic factor remains correspondingly itself rather obscure.

XI. A Modified Version of the Compound Theory.

Certain modifications can, I believe, be made in Broad's Compound Theory, which, while preserving the merits he justly claims for it, will eliminate the defects pointed out in the preceding section, and will at the same time virtually effect a reconciliation between it and the Instrumental Theory.

The first suggestion I would offer is that the factor which, when combined with the bodily factor, generates a mind, may be conceived as genuinely psychic without conceiving it as being itself a mind. The basis of this possibility lies in the distinction between the innate dispositions of a mind, called aptitudes, and the dispositions which, on the basis of those aptitudes, it acquires between birth and death as a result of its experiences, passive and active. Those innate aptitudes are true cases of what Broad calls "supreme dispositions" of a substance (EMcP, 267); that is, dispositions that are not themselves acquired but are dispositions to acquire on relevant occasions certain other dispositions, of various degrees of determinateness. The aptitudes or "supreme dispositions" of a mind do not by themselves constitute a mind, but they are the "germ" from which a mind gradually develops as a result of direct interaction between this psychic germ and the bodily germ consisting of the brain of the neonate whose body as a whole is the physical vehicle of that psychic germ, and through which body that psychic germ indirectly interacts with that body's physical environment.

The conception being outlined regards that psychic germ as a (psychic) substance in the same sense of "substance" as that in which (physical) substances are so, for example the relatively blank neonate brain from which the highly organized adult brain develops, or that adult brain itself, or indeed a piece of wood, iron, paper, or any other of the things commonly called substances. In all these cases equally, I assume that the *nature* of a substance at a given time—as distinguished from the *history* of that substance up to that time—is exhaustively analyzable as a set, or rather a system, in part hierarchical, of dispositions, some of them innate and others acquired. The *history* of a substance, on the other hand, is the series of *exercisings* of its dispositions, and will therefore include the acquisitions, by that substance, of dispositions which it had the disposition to acquire and which the occurrence of events of the appropriate kinds occasioned it to acquire. That is, the history of a substance is the series of its states and changes.[20]

Further, a disposition is here taken to be essentially a causal connection, i.e., a causal law, and, in virtue of its causal character, inherently triadic. That is, to say of a substance S that it has a disposition D is to say that, in circumstances of kind C, occurrence of an event of kind E causes S to respond in manner R. According as both E and R are physical events, or both psychic events, or one psychic and the other physical, the disposition in which they respectively figure as cause-event and as effect-event is termed a *physico-physical,* or a *psycho-psychical,* or a *physico-psychical,* or a *psycho-physical,* disposition. On this basis, a substance, of which some at least of the supreme dispositions are physico-physical, and which has no psycho-psychical dispositions, is termed a *physical substance;* whereas one, among whose supreme dispositions some at least are psycho-psychical, and which has no physico-physical dispositions, is called a *psychical substance.* (For brevity from this point on, the four kinds of dispositions will be referred to respectively as phy-phy, psy-psy, phy-psy, and psy-phy, dispositions.)

When, at death, an animal body ceases to be "animated" by the mind it had until then, the brain of that body is automatically deprived of its normal opportunity to exercise its phy-psy and its psy-phy dispositions, since a psychic substance, with which the brain can directly interact, is an intrinsic part of the state of affairs on which depends the normal possibility of exercise of dispositions of those two kinds by a brain. From that moment, the brain can exercise only such phy-phy dispositions as it retains. But if some of the phy-psy and psy-phy dispositions of a brain are not immediately destroyed at death, but only deprived of possibility of exercise, then, if it were possible, as Haitian Voodoo beliefs apparently assume it to be for a time after death, that a dead body's brain should become temporarily connected again with some mind, that brain would temporarily be able again to exercise such of its former phy-psy and psy-phy dispositions as death had not de-

---

20 The above account of the nature of substances does not have in view the notion of substance as substratum—the "something-I-know-not-what" of Locke—but is offered as an analysis of the meaning the term "substance" has when predicated in such common assertions as that bread, or wheat, or a tree, or gold, etc., is a substance. The mere sketch of this analysis in the text, which I hope is as much as my argument calls for, obviously ignores a number of important questions relating to that conception of substance; in particular, the question of the distinction between the nature and the existence of a substance. An examination of those questions, and a statement of the answers to them I would give, may be found in Ch. 10 of *Nature, Mind, and Death* (Open Court, La Salle, Ill., 1951); and, on pp. 222f of the same book, a statement of what I conceive the criterion of materiality or physicality to be; and on pp. 292–4, the criterion of mentality or psychicality.

stroyed; and the body to which it belongs would for the time be what I take Voodoo lore to mean by a "zombie."

Considering death, on the other hand, from the side of the mind, and assuming that it survives the death of the body it had been animating, the death of its body automatically deprives that mind of its normal opportunity to exercise its phy-psy and psy-phy dispositions, since existence of a living brain with which that mind can directly interact is an intrinsic part of the state of affairs on which depends the normal possibility of exercise of such dispositions by that mind. After death, it could then exercise only psy-psy dispositions; and its *post mortem* life could therefore be only of one or another wholly subjective sort unless it should then exercise certain paranormal capacities it had but which until then had remained latent—capacity, for instance, to affect and be affected by other minds telepathically; or, exceptionally, capacity to be affected clairvoyantly by some physical objects or to affect physical objects psychokinetically; or, as a special case, capacity to affect and to be affected by events in the brain of a medium. In this special case, the medium would manifest exercise, by that surviving mind, of some of the phy-psy and psy-phy dispositions it had acquired and exercised during its incarnate life; but probably with distortions due to the fact that the medium's brain, which that mind is then using, is different in various respects from the brain which had been that mind's own.

Among the dispositions of that mind, which it would thus be temporarily able to exercise by using the medium's brain, would be some of those which its memories, and indeed all its acquired knowledge, constitute. For it is here of cardinal importance to realize that possession of a particular memory, or more broadly of any piece of knowledge, essentially consists in having acquired, and retaining, a particular *disposition*. Thus, for example, "to know who was Plato's teacher" is to be such that, if the question: "Who was Plato's teacher?" is heard, or presents itself in some other way to one's mind, then this event, under "ordinary" circumstances, causes in one's mind occurrence of the believed idea that Socrates was Plato's teacher. Evidently, possession of a *memory,* for example, a memory of the particular occasion on which one originally learned that the teacher of Plato was Socrates, analyzes in a precisely parallel manner as *itself an acquired disposition*—specifically, a disposition to respond, under "ordinary" circumstances, to the question: "On what occasion did one learn that Socrates was Plato's teacher?" by a description or a mental image of that occasion.

In this connection, it is necessary to repeat and emphasize that a disposition, being a causal connection, is an inherently triadic affair. Its terms are not only a kind E of cause-event and a kind R of response as effect-event, but in addition a certain kind C of circumstances, without which occurrence of a case of E does not normally cause occurrence of a case of R. It is essential to keep this in mind because, in the case of at least the acquired phy-psy and psy-phy dispositions of a mind, a certain state of the brain, as well as a certain state of the mind, may well be a necessary, or a normally necessary, part of the circumstances under which occurrence of a certain question or other sort of mental associate of a memory-idea causes the arising of that idea, i.e., the *recalling* of the event concerned.

This possibility is what robs Broad's objections, cited earlier, to the Instrumental Theory of the mind-body relation, of the force they otherwise would have. After an accident involving concussion of the brain, it often happens that the person concerned is unable *to recall* the accident, and also the events he had experienced during some hours preceding the accident. This means that, for instance, the question: "What occurred at three o'clock on that day?" then no longer causes recall by him of the fact (say) that his brother had come to see him at the time mentioned; whereas in the normal circumstances C, that question would have caused such recall; that is, it would cause it now, were it not for the abnormal circumstance consisting of the brain state instituted by the concussion. Yet, that he does retain a latent memory of his brother's visit V is shown by the fact that, when he is put in the abnormal state H called hypnosis, that same question Q can then cause him to recall his brother's visit. The point may be summarily put as follows:

Question Q, under normal circumstances C, causes recall of V.

Question Q, under abnormal circumstances K, does not cause recall of V. But question Q, under abnormal circumstances *K plus H,* does cause recall of V. Hence memory of V was not destroyed, but only made inaccessible by the normal means Q under the abnormal circumstances K.

Analogous considerations would account for the other fact, which Broad mentions as an objection to the Instrumental Theory, that a brain injury may change a man's character from cheerful and benevolent to morose and hostile. For to say that a man's character is cheerful and benevolent means that he habitually responds, in the manner describable in those terms, to certain common situations. It does not mean that he has *no* disposition to moroseness and hostility, but only that, *in the kind of circumstances consisting of his normal brain state,* not that disposition, but the disposition to cheerfulness and benevolence, which he also has, is the one which occurrence of those common situations causes to be exercised. It is a fact of everyday observation that hunger and abnormal physical fatigue cause a normally patient person to respond with irritation to situations he would under normal circumstances have met with patience. Hence it is very plausible that common situations, which under normal circumstances call into exercise a man's cheerful and benevolent disposition, should, after the drastic change made in those circumstances by destruction of a part of his brain, call instead into exercise the morose and hostile disposition which is also a part of his total make-up.

To the account now outlined of the proposed revision of the Compound Theory, two hypotheses may be added. They are relevant to the supposition that metempsychosis occurs—a supposition which, like Broad and McTaggart, I regard as worthy of more attention than it has received in the West. The two hypotheses to be added to the proposed version of the Compound Theory correspond to and have the same effect as the two which, in the original version, would harmonize the theory with the possibility that metempsychosis is a fact.

The first of the two proposed hypotheses is that, just as brain tissue normally degenerates irreversibly before long after death, and thereby loses not merely the possibility—which connection with a mind constitutes—of *exercising* its phy-psy and psy-phy dispositions, but also *loses those dispositions themselves;* so does a surviving mind undergo, although possibly at a much slower rate, a progressive loss of *its* acquired dispositions, leaving only its supreme dispositions, i.e., its aptitudes, which, as already noted, do not by themselves constitute a mind, but only the germ of one. This hypothesis would account for the patent fact that, if a person has had a life anterior to his present one, he anyway does not bring to the present one the dispositions he had acquired in the preceding life—for example, the dispositions which his memories and all his other knowledge constituted. They get lost, whether suddenly or, as here hypothesized, gradually, during the interval between death and rebirth. And, if gradually, then the paranormal possibility of manifestation, through a medium, of some of that discarnate mind's acquired phy-psy and psy-phy dispositions exists only for a finite time after death—be it days, months, or years, few or many—a length of time, moreover, which may be very different for different persons.

Now, however, if metempsychosis not only should be a fact, but in addition were to be such as to make evolution of the human "spirit" possible, then it would be necessary to assume that the psychic factor as conceived in the proposed revision of the Compound Theory—i.e., the aptitudes or supreme dispositions of the individual's mind—not only persists after death, but also undergoes some enhancement, diminution, or alteration, as ultimate effect of certain activities or experiences of life; for example, perhaps, that long maintained earnest effort during life to acquire the capacity to play a musical instrument, or the capacity to solve mathematical problems, etc., not only results, proximately, in acquisition of such capacity, but also, ultimately, in enhancement of one's aptitude to acquire the kind of capacity one thus strives for; which enhanced aptitude only, but not the musical or mathematical or other skill one had acquired, is brought to the new birth.

XII. *Advantages of the Modified Compound Theory.*

In summary conclusion, I now submit that the effect of the suggested modifications of Broad's Compound Theory would be as follows.

The theory as modified is not open to the criticisms of the original theory set forth in Sec. IX; for the "psychic" factor is now psychic in fact, instead of, as in the original theory, only in name. Moreover, the particular nature which the psychic factor has in particular persons is now capable of being ascertained to some extent by means of psychological aptitude tests.

Again, the sense in which the psychic factor "combines" with the bodily factor to generate a mind is no longer mysterious; for, in the revised form of the theory, "combination" of the two means direct causal interaction between the bodily "germ" and the psychic "germ" constituted respectively by the neonate's brain, and by the psychic substance whose nature consists of his psychological aptitudes.

Further, the manner in which a mind emerges—not all at once but gradually—out of interaction between the two factors and exercise of the internal, i.e., the psy-psy, dispositions of the psychic factor, is to some extent observable.

On the other hand, the virtues of the original form of the theory are virtues also of the modified form. The latter too is "compatible with all the facts which everyone admits" and, like the original form, "has nothing against it except a superstitious objection to dualism." (*MPN*, 550). Like the original version, the revised one too leaves open possibilities which a monistic theory would arbitrarily exclude; and yet it allows us to be as critical of particular alleged facts as we care to be. Again, that not only a mind's aptitudes but also some of its acquired dispositions persist for some time after death is as conceivable as is persistence of the mysterious "psychic" factor of the original theory; and, the supposition that temporary connection between the persisting acquired phy-psy and psy-phy dispositions of a mind, and the brain of a medium, is no less plausible, and is more intelligible an explanation of mediumistic communications, than is the supposition that, on these occasions, what connects with the medium's brain is a factor of wholly unknown nature.

Moreover, if as the modified form of the theory permits us to suppose, a surviving mind's activities are wholly subjective ones, or objective also only in the social sense telepathy would make possible, then the fact noted by Broad, that the communications from purported surviving spirits are commonly vague as to the nature of their *surroundings*, is as well accounted for as well as by the original form of the theory. On the other hand, the modified theory would in addition account for the fact that the *occupations* of the purported surviving spirits are usually reported by them as concerned with *other spirits;* specifically, as consisting in the "helping," "comforting," "enlightening," etc., of them.

Finally, the fact emphasized in the statement of the modified theory, that memories are essentially dispositions; that dispositions are essentially causal connections; that causal connection is an essentially triadic relation (the third term of it being the circumstances under which alone an event of kind E normally causes an event of kind R); and that physical and more specifically *cerebral* conditions are a part of the circumstances on which depends the possibility of exercise of phy-psy and of psy-phy dispositions—all this adequately accounts for the observations Broad cites, that certain brain injuries affect memory or can alter character.

C. J. DUCASSE

DEPARTMENT OF PHILOSOPHY
BROWN UNIVERSITY

12

A. G. N. Flew

BROAD AND SUPERNORMAL PRECOGNITION

PROFESSOR BROAD'S 'The Philosophical Implications of Fore-knowledge' (*P.A.S.* Suppl. Vol. XVI) was published in 1937, nearly twenty years ago, and it is not among the papers selected for reprinting in *Religion, Philosophy and Psychical Research*. So probably he now wishes to withdraw from or to advance beyond some positions which he then adopted. This is the more likely because psychical research (para-psychology) has made in recent years considerable progress, in which the emphasis has shifted from investigation of spontaneous and mediumistic material to more manageable, statistically assessable, but duller, quanti-tative experiments.

I.

The topic is not foreknowledge unqualified, not even supernormal foreknowledge simply, but "non-inferential veridical precognition." The first term is too wide: it would cover such perfectly ordinary cases as that of the lobby correspondent not surprised to hear the Postmaster-General announce Government support for the commercialisation of television, because he had been successful in his job of getting advance information about this forthcoming political move. The second expres-sion, with its qualification "supernormal" is still too wide; for it would cover such cases as this. Suppose some wonder human calculator able to do the calculations which the electronic computers did on the early returns in the 1952 U.S.A. presidential election, and like them coming up with the prediction of an Eisenhower landslide; then this would cer-tainly have been a case of supernormal foreknowledge inasmuch as it "required supernormal powers of calculation and inference" (p. 179). "We must begin by noticing that veridical precognition would not raise any special *a priori* difficulties if it consisted in inferring propositions about the future from general laws and from singular facts about the present or the past" (p. 179).

The sort of thing which Broad means by "non-inferential veridical

411

precognition" is quite radically different. Suppose someone has a hunch which turns out to have been right, or a night dream or waking vision which is found to correspond with some actual later happening. Suppose that it seems to be out of the question: *either* to account for this correspondence as the product of successful inference, whether conscious or unconscious, from information acquired through the usual channels; *or* to refuse to account for it on the ground that it is a coincidence, that some hunches are bound to come off, that some dreams and visions are bound to prove veridical, (and that presumably this is just one of those cases which is bound to happen "by the law of averages"). Then Broad would be inclined to describe this as a case of "non-inferential veridical precognition." We say "would be inclined to describe" rather than "would describe." Because parapsychological investigation is an excessively tricky business which, as all experience goes to show, calls for extremes of caution. Because among the various possible hypotheses which he discusses are one or two which he would probably agree disqualified any case in which they held to be a genuine as opposed to a merely ostensible case (e.g. (ii)–(v) on p. 195). And because the main purpose of his whole paper is to discuss "the *a priori* objection which many people feel against the very notion of veridical supernormal precognition" (p. 179); which, we shall take it, amounts to an objection to any such form of words on the grounds that, like "squares whose diagonals are commensurate with their sides" (p. 179), it does not constitute a logically proper possible description. We say "through the usual channels" since this is not intended to be more than an interim definition. Later we might perhaps want to avoid thus allowing as precognitive: *either* the possible case in which the subject—the person having the hunch, dream, vision, or what not—had exploited information acquired through the usual channels not directly but indirectly, getting it in the first instance telepathically from someone else who had himself to rely on the usual channels (cf. (iv) and (v) on p. 195); *or* the possible case in which the subject had exploited information not acquired through the usual channels but clairvoyantly from physical materials already available but not normally accessible to him at the time of having his hunch, dream, or vision. In future we shall, except in verbatim quotations, usually write "Pψy" instead of "non-inferential veridical precognition" or "supernormal precognition" or any other variants: using a shorter expression for the sake of brevity; and choosing this particular shorthand for various reasons some of which we mention later.[1]

[1] For a full statement see my *A New Approach to Psychical Research* (Watts, 1953), Ch. IX.

In 1937 the evidence available to suggest that $P\psi y$ might be something more than a fanciful speculation consisted almost entirely in spontaneous and mediumistic material. But this anecdotal evidence has since been reinforced by that of some quantitative experiments. The general idea of these is this. Suppose you take a pack of twenty-five cards consisting of five different suits of five identical cards. Arrange conditions to make cheating, whether conscious or unconscious, by the use of knowledge acquired through the usual channels impossible. Randomize the order of cards in the pack. Then set a subject to guess the values of the cards in each position in the pack. Granted always that your precautions to prevent cheating have been adequate, subjects might be expected to get a guessing average of one right in every five. So if any subject achieves scores significantly better, or significantly worse, than this mean chance expectation: it is a reason for saying that some new factor is involved. We shall call any such statistically significant correlations between series of guess values and series of target values "ψ-correlations." When it is impossible for *anyone* to know by any normal means the value of the target card when the guess is made we shall speak of "clairvoyance conditions." When someone is acting as what is called "an Agent" by turning up and looking at each target card in turn while the subject is making his guess we shall speak of "telepathy conditions." One might at first be inclined to define "pre-cognitive ψ-correlations" as "statistically significant correlations between the values of a series of guesses and the values of a series of targets: where each member of the target series became available only after its opposite number in the guess series had been made; and where it was impossible for the subject to have known on the basis of any information acquired through the usual channels what the targets were going to be." But if once you allow the possibility of simultaneous ψ-correlations established under telepathy and clairvoyance conditions you may want to amend this definition in such a way as to disqualify any correlation achieved in circumstances where the subject could have got, either telepathically from other people or clairvoyantly from things, relevant information available to those other people or in those things, but not through the usual channels to him at the time when he made his guess. Otherwise your definition will admit as certainly precognitive cases which could equally well be described in terms of simultaneous telepathy or clairvoyance. Once this amendment has been made the distinction between telepathic and clairvoyant conditions may be extended to apply also to precognitive cases: though it is impracticable to use card values as the targets in the search for precognitive ψ-correlations under clairvoyance conditions.

The merits of such quantitative experiments as a method of investigation are four: two which apply with peculiar force in this particular field; and two which are just the general truisms of modern science. First, a competent experimenter can decisively exclude the possibility of normal knowledge and inference: whereas in handling spontaneous and mediumistic materials, experience has richly confirmed what common sense had always suspected, that this is exceedingly difficult to do. Second, by repeating identical procedures he can get results to which he can apply statistical techniques of assessment: he can calculate whether, and if so to what degree, the excess, or the deficiency, of hits is statistically significant; and this may be taken as offering a quantitative measure of how reasonable or unreasonable it would be to dismiss any striking correspondences between guess series and target series as coincidental. Third, if he does succeed in producing any ψ-correlations he can hope that others will be able both to repeat his experiments and thereby to confirm his results. Fourth, by varying his procedures he can "put Nature to the question" (Bacon) and hope thus to learn more.

The development of the quantitative form of experiment has also made it possible to give rather more precise meanings to the various terms we have been introducing: though they are naturally still not always used in accordance with such ostensive or operational definitions as we have been giving. The discovery of precognitive ψ-correlations in quantitative experiments would be evidence for saying that non-inferential veridical precognition (Pψy) in spontaneous and mediumistic cases was a genuine phenomenon; always assuming that "the *a priori* objection which many people feel against the very notion" can be met. Indeed, if the latter occurred, the former would presumably be its experimental, statistically assessable form.

Broad was not there concerned "to state or appraise the evidence which has been produced for the occurrence of supernormal foreknowledge" (p. 178); and neither are we here. But he did mention H. F. Saltmarsh's examination of the then available British evidence, 'Report on Cases of Apparent Precognition' (*Proc. S.P.R.,* Vol. XLII); with which it is now possible to compare the relevant sections of Dr. D. J. West's extremely sceptical 'The Investigation of Spontaneous Cases' (*Proc. S.P.R.,* Vol. XLVIII). Soal's own report on the experimental work hailed by Broad as 'The Experimental Establishment of Telepathic Precognition' (*Philosophy,* 1944), is 'Experiments on Precognitive Telepathy' (*Proc. S.P.R.,* Vol. XLVII). Soal and Bateman have recently produced a general survey of the experimental work, *Modern Experiments in Telepathy* (Faber, London, 1954: Yale U.P., New Haven, 1954) while D. J. West's *Psychical Research Today* (Duckworth, 1954) reviews the entire field.

Anyone interested in the empirical material might refer in the first instance to these sources.

Broad began by assuming "that the quantity and quality of the evidence are such as would make the hypothesis that veridical supernormal precognition occurs worth serious consideration *unless* there be some logical or metaphysical impossibility in it" and noticing that "a great many people feel that the hypothesis of veridical supernormal precognition is in this position" (p. 179: author's italics here and elsewhere unless the contrary is stated). "It is . . . important to discover why this *a priori* objection is felt, and whether it is valid or not. This is a question for professional philosophers . . . which I shall make the central topic of my paper" (p. 179). Now there are today many philosophers who would object radically to this project: not, or not only, on the ground that parapsychology is an academically disreputable business which no philosopher of standing ought to take seriously, much less to support; but instead, or additionally, on the ground that logic and metaphysics are by themselves constitutionally incapable of providing guarantees against the occurrence of anything. Hence *a priori* objections of this sort *must* be as misguided as the efforts of "the professor of philosophy at Pisa, labouring before the Grand Duke with logical arguments, as if with magical incantations, to charm the new planets out of the sky" (Galileo, quoted E. A. Burtt *Metaphysical Foundations of Modern Physical Science,* pp. 66–7). Broad himself has dealt with the former objection more than once, very faithfully. To the latter it may be replied. First, that a general conviction that no arguments of a certain sort can be sound is not always a sufficient reason for refusing to examine particular cases, especially where these are widely or eminently supported: for instance, well-grounded assurance that the existence of God cannot be proved in the way in which it is apparently *de fide* for Roman Catholics to believe that it can,[2] does not provide a sufficient justification for refusing to countenance the examination of the *Quinque Viae* of Aquinas, or similar recent attempts. Second, granted that logic and metaphysics cannot provide guarantees that anything will not happen, still philosophical analysis can sometimes reveal that some ostensibly possible descriptive expression does not in fact make sense: and hence if this expression has been applied to any actual occurrences or logical possibilities, these must have been thereby misdescribed. Third, the *a priori* arguments deployed against the possibility of $P\psi y$ may be, and in fact have been, usefully provocative and philosophically illuminating

---

2 "Si quis dixerit, Deum unum et verum, Creatorem et Dominum nostrum, per ea quae facta sunt, naturali rationis humanae lumine certo cognosci non posse: anathema sit" (*Concilium Vaticanum: Canones de revelatione,* 1: Denzinger 1806).

in other directions. You do not have to think that the logical truism "An effect cannot precede its cause" guarantees us against the occurrence of Pψy, nor for that matter do you even have to assume that "the quantity and quality of the evidence" make "the hypothesis that veridical supernormal cognition occurs worth serious consideration;" to see philosophical value in being forced to appreciate how very far from arbitrary is the matter of definition which makes this a logical truism.[3]

II.

"I think that the *a priori* objection which many people feel to the very notion of veridical supernormal precognition can be dissected into at least three parts. . . . I propose to call them the 'Epistemological,' the 'Causal,' and the 'Fatalistic'. . . ." (p. 179). We shall try as far as possible to follow Broad in this division.

The Epistemological Objection. This "may be put as follows. To say that a person P had a non-inferential veridical cognition of an object O at a moment t is to say that the object O stood at the moment t in a certain relation to the person P, viz., in the relation of being cognized by P. Now an object cannot stand in any relations to anything unless and until it exists. . . . So the phrase 'non-inferential veridical precognition by P of O at t' involves a plain contradiction. It implies that O stood in a certain relation to P at a time when O did not exist, and therefore could not stand in any relation to anything" (p. 180). Clearly there is something terribly wrong with this objection: "if it were valid at all, it would be just as fatal to memory of events in the past as to veridical non-inferential cognition of events in the future. . . . Since memory is certainly non-inferential postcognition, and since we are not prepared to reject the possibility of veridical memory, there must be something wrong somewhere. . . ." (p. 180) Broad's way of showing what this is is first to "try to analyse the experience of ostensibly remembering an event" (p. 182) in order to find "the solution for memory; it will then be easy to apply it to non-inferential precognition" (p. 180).

"Such an experience contains two utterly different but intimately connected factors. In the first place, the person concerned is imaging a certain image, visual or auditory or otherwise. This image is a *contemporary* existent; and, if the person who is imaging it attends to the question of its date, he has no hesitation in saying that it is present and not past. The second factor is that the experient uncritically and automatically takes for granted that there was a certain event in his

---

[3] See the discussion 'Can an effect precede its Cause?' in *P.A.S.* Suppl. Vol. XXVIII (1954).

own *past* life, of which this image is the present representative; and he automatically bases on certain qualities of his present image certain beliefs about the character and the recency of this assumed past event. These two factors may be called respectively 'imaging' and 'retrospectively referring' " (p. 182). "What is meant by saying that the retrospective beliefs are 'based upon' awareness of a present image and its qualities is roughly as follows. These beliefs would not have occurred when and where they did if the experient had not then and there been aware of an image; and the propositions believed by him would have been different in detail if the image had been different in certain respects" (p. 183).

On the basis of this analysis Broad would dispose of the objection to the possibility of veridical memory by arguing that this "rests entirely on the tacit assumption that to remember an event is to have a present prehension of an event which is past" (p. 184): which is mistaken because though *"something* is prehended, viz., an image . . . this is contemporary, and . . . not the remembered event." While though something is judged or believed on the basis of this prehended image, this something is a *proposition* and "this proposition, like all propositions, has no date. . . . There is no difficulty in the fact that it can be the object of a present act of believing" (p. 185). Ostensible foreseeing (ostensible non-inferential precognition) can then be analysed analogously, and the reply transposed to meet the parallel objection to its possibility. "When a person has an ostensible foreseeing the experience involves two factors. He images a certain image, which is, of course, contemporary with his act of imaging. And he automatically, uncritically, and non-inferentially bases upon his prehension of this image a belief that there *will be* an event of a certain kind, of which this image is the present representative. . . . *Something* is prehended, but it is the present image and not the foreseen future event. Something is judged or believed, viz., a timeless proposition. . . ." (pp.186–7). Finally Broad notices the possibility "that there could be 'pre-presentative' images on which the person who has them bases *no* prospective belief at the time, just as there are retro-presentative images on which the person who has them bases no retrospective belief at the time" (p. 188). Which is apparently realized since "Much of the evidence adduced for supernormal cognition is really evidence for the occurrence of images, which were *not* prospectively referred by the experient at the time when he had them, but were shown by subsequent events to have been *in fact* pre-presentative" (p. 188).

Comment. (i) Broad has stated the Epistemological Objection in such a way that it would apply not merely to Pψy, nor even (as he points out) just to memory as well as to Pψy; but to all knowledge, about not only the future but also the past. "To say that a person P had a non-inferential veridical cognition of an object O at a moment t is to say that the object O stood at the moment t in a certain relation to the person P, viz., in the relation of being cognized by P. Now an object cannot stand in any relations to anything unless and until it exists. . . ." (p. 180). Yet in deploying his reply he claims that the "objection to the possibility of veridical memory (and therefore, presumably, *mutatis mutandis* the parallel objection to Pψy—A.F.) rests entirely on the tacit assumption that to remember an event is to have a present prehension of an event that is past. This would entail that the event, which *no* longer exists, nevertheless stands to the act of remembering, which is *now* occurring, in the direct two-term relation of prehended object to act of prehending" (p. 184). Whereas the objection was to the idea of anything being in any sort of relation to anything else unless and until it exists: the reply only claims to show that veridical memory does not involve the peculiarly direct relation of *"prehension or acquaintance"* between entities which could not be so related; while admitting that here "there *is* a relation, though a very indirect one, between this past event and the present experience of ostensibly remembering" (p. 185). What Broad is in fact dealing with is: *not* The Epistemological Objection, which he formulates as a case of a general metaphysical difficulty about any knowledge of the past or future; *but* a particular difficulty about Pψy misconceived as a sort of perception of the future. If you insist on thinking of Pψy on the model of perception, then the question is bound to arise: "How could there be such a thing, for if I can perceive something it must be present to be perceived?" This is a particular difficulty and one which has certainly been felt. Thus J. W. Dunne in his *An Experiment with Time*— one of the books to which Broad referred to illustrate what he would mean by "supernormal precognition"—claims that in Pψy "we habitually observe events before they occur" (Faber, London: Third Edition, 1934, p. 7). Then by valid inference from this misdescription he concludes that the future must really be present, and on this absurdity erects his logical extravaganza, 'the Serial Theory of Time.' The more recent introduction of the term "Extra-Sensory Perception (E.S.P.)"—a complete misnomer even when applied to non-precognitive ψ-correlations—has done nothing to discourage the idea that Pψy is logically impossible: ". . . precognition—foreseeing arbitrary events in the future that could not by any stretch of the imagination be inferred from the present—that is something which is almost impossible for our minds to grasp. How can anyone see things that do not yet exist?" (D. J. West, *Psychical Research Today,*

p. 104.) "The fact is that most people who have tried to theorize about non-inferential precognition have made needless difficulties for themselves by making two mistakes. In the first place, they have tried to assimilate it to sense-perception, when they ought to have assimilated it to memory. And secondly, they have tacitly assumed an extremely naïve prehensive analysis . . . (which) is simply nonsensical when applied to ostensible remembering or ostensible foreseeing" (Broad, p. 187). And once this is recognised then indeed the possible particular objection that $P\psi y$ could not occur because it must involve the presence of the future, which is absurd, "vanishes in smoke" (p. 187): though the general Epistemological Objection, for what it is worth, remains.[4]

(ii) Broad is here insisting that mental imagery is an essential element in "the experience of ostensibly remembering an event" (p. 182). Whereas "I may image a certain image, and it may be uniquely related to a certain one event in my past life in such a way that it is *in fact* the present representative of that past event; and yet I may not base upon it a belief that there was such an event . . . the second factor cannot occur without the first. One must be imaging an image in order to have something as a basis for retrospective reference" (p. 182). Of course as "retrospective reference" is defined in terms of being "based upon awareness of a present image and its qualities" (p. 183), then this must be true; but necessarily. I do not think that Broad was definitely and deliberately enunciating this as merely a self-made truism. And in any case no *ad hoc* manoeuvres with the meanings of the neologisms of analysis can be allowed to conceal: *either* that "He is remembering the test explosion at Eniwetok" does not entail "He has a mental image of the test explosion at Eniwetok;" *or* that there are in fact some people in whose experiences of ostensibly remembering events mental imagery plays no part. We might support the first proposition by pointing out that appeals for more careful introspection play little part in everyday attempts to rebut memory claims; and the second by citing passages from Sir Francis Galton and Sir Frederick Bartlett. But here it is more appropriate to call in evidence the Broad of 1925. In Chapter V of *The Mind and its Place in Nature* he offers a full-dress account of memory, at pains to deny several of the things taken almost for granted in 1937. Thus after giving an outline account of perception he goes on, "Now, in spite of some appearances to the contrary I believe that the opposite is true of perceptual memory. I believe that what is primarily known by memory is propositions. . . . Certain groups of such propositions are recognized to have a common subject; and the object is 'remem-

---

4 Cf. Plato, *Republic*, 477ff., and H. L. A. Hart's 'Knowledge by Acquaintance' in *P.A.S.* Suppl. XXIII (1949).

bered' only in so far as it is known as the common subject of such a group of remembered propositions" (p. 248). And later, "The essential factor in the memory-situation is that peculiar feeling which seems to justify the judgement that a certain characteristic fits or fails to fit a certain past object. The characteristic need not be, and generally is not, presented to our attention by means of imitative images" (p. 248). A sting in the tail: "I think that the function of imitative images in perceptual memory has been greatly exaggerated. It is perhaps relevant to add that I am a strong visualizer, and that memory with me does in fact generally involve imitative imagery; so, if I am wrong on this point, my mistake is certainly not due to identifying a personal defect with a law of nature, as the Behaviourists do when they deny the existence of images" (p. 249).

I do not know why he backslid between 1925 and 1937. But it is perhaps worth remarking that Broad was in the twenties anticipating in this particular case that general onslaught on the importance of mental imagery in the analysis of certain concepts which Wittgenstein was to deploy in the thirties and forties; though the move to instate a "peculiar feeling" as "the essential factor" would not have appealed to Wittgenstein.

Whatever the reason which led Broad to change his mind and to insist that mental imagery is an essential element "in the experience of ostensibly remembering an event," this insistence was carried over into his discussion of $P\psi$. Since "In talking of memory" he said "that a person may be aware of an image, which is *in fact* retro-presentative, without at the time basing any retrospective belief on it. . . ." (p. 187); he concludes that it is likely that there would be 'pre-presentative' images on which the person who has them bases *no* prospective belief at the time. . . ." (p. 188). Similarly since he has refused to allow that retrospectively referring can occur without imaging, he takes no account of the possibility that prospective reference might likewise occur without imaging. Now we have recognized the former possibility we can also recognize the latter; if it makes sense to speak of precognitive hunches privately illustrated with mental pictures, then surely it must also make sense to speak of precognitive hunches not thus illustrated. And in fact even before the days of quantitative ψ-experiments cases of ostensible $P\psi$ in which the subject made no explicit reference to any mental imagery seem to have occurred: while successful subjects in quantitative tests have sometimes denied that their guesses have even been accompanied by, much less based on, pre-presented mental pictures of the target cards.

III.

The Causal Objection. Broad states this as follows. "At the time when a certain person had an image which was pre-presentative of a certain event, that event cannot have had any causal descendants. And, in many cases, its causal ancestors lay wholly outside the experient's body and mind. How then could we possibly account for the occurrence in this person at this particular moment of an image which is pre-presentative of this particular future event? The pre-presented event had no causal representative, either ancestor or descendant, in the experient at the time when his pre-presentative image of it occurred" (p. 190). The genealogical metaphor, developed in a preliminary review of differences between the problems for causal explanation presented by memory and by Pψy, explains itself: "Any *past* experience of mine may have causal *descendants* in all the later stages of my history. But an experience which has not yet happened can have no causal descendants until it has happened. It may, of course, have causal *ancestors* in the earlier stages of my history" (p. 190).

The upshot is that "it would seem to be legitimate to infer that all possible theories about veridical ostensible foreseeing must be variations on the following four themes:—(i) that the concordance between an ostensible foreseeing . . . and a certain subsequent event, however detailed it may be and however numerous may be the instances of it, is merely a chance coincidence. (ii) That the precognitive experience is only ostensibly non-inferential, but really depends on inference either in the subject himself or in some other mind. . . . (iii) That the ostensible foreseeing . . . is a cause-factor in a causal ancestor if the event which subsequently fulfils it. (iv) That there is a certain causal ancestor which has a series of successive causal descendants; that the ostensible foreseeing . . . is an effect-factor in one of the earlier of these, and that the event which subsequently verifies it is an effect-factor in one of the later of them" (p. 198). To these four, after suggesting that something might be done with the idea of an additional two spatial dimensions,[5] he adds "a perfectly fantastic suggestion" (p. 199): "the hypothesis of a two-dimensional time" (p. 204).

Comment. (i) The Causal Objection is supposed to be an "*a priori* objection . . . to the very notion of veridical supernormal precognition" (p. 179), an attempt to show that there is "some logical or metaphysical impossibility in it" (p. 179). Yet as stated here it seems to have no force at all, and is certainly not an objection of this kind. To complain that if Pψy were a genuine phenomenon ". . . could we possibly

5 This is the suggestion developed in 'Mr. Dunne's Theory of Time' in *RPPR*.

account for the occurrence in this particular person at this particular moment of an image which is pre-presentative of this particular future event?" (p. 190) does not by itself constitute a reason for saying that Pψy does not as a matter of fact occur; much less an argument to the conclusion that the very notion is logically vicious. From the premiss that it would be impossible to give a causal account of Pψy, the conclusions that Pψy is either impossible or even antecedently improbable cannot be derived: without calling in some suitable additional premiss about the ways of the actual world we live in. While to derive from the same premisse the conclusion that the very notion of Pψy is logically vicious we should need a necessarily true premiss about the impossibility of uncaused correlations of the appropriate sort. Broad gives us no reason to think that he is expecting us to take as given any such additional premisses.

(ii) Not in fact having formulated any *a priori* causal objection to the notion of Pψy, what Broad actually does in the part of this paper in which he is officially supposed to be meeting such an objection is to form a schema of all the possible types of causal account which might be attempted; including his own "perfectly fantastic suggestion" (p. 199). Although he declared at the beginning "I am not going to put forward or to criticize any theory about the *modus operandi* of veridical supernormal precognition, supposing it to be possible and supposing that there is satisfactory evidence that it occurs" (p. 178). However there is considerable reason to doubt whether anything falling under any of the original four types of theory should be counted as *explanations* of the *modus operandi* of Pψy: but rather as alternative ways of *explaining away* any appearance of it. This is clearly so with members of Broad's first two categories. To say that "the concordance . . . is merely a chance coincidence" (Option (i)) is certainly to deny the reality of Pψy: "Let us consider what a person means when he says that the available evidence suffices to show that there is veridical foreseeing. . . . He means that there is an amount of accordance between such subsequent events and ostensible foreseeings which is too great to be ascribed to 'chance coincidence'" (pp. 196–7). Again anything which comes under Option (ii) ("only ostensibly non-inferential") is explicitly excluded from the class of Pψy even by the rough and ready definitions we have given. With the second two categories, because our definitions do not explicitly disqualify their members, the situation is not quite so clear. Nevertheless, though our definitions in this respect resemble those formulated by parapsychological experimenters, it is quite certain that in practice they would refuse to allow that any experiments could constitute proof of Pψy if these failed to rule out: *both* the possibility of the subject influencing the determination of targets; *and* the possibility that the correlation between guesses and targets could be accounted for in terms of a common causal ancestry. Thus Professor J. B. Rhine and his colleagues at Duke took the suggestion that their subject, Hubert Pearce, might be influencing supernormally (by "psychic shuffle") the order of the cards which he was ostensibly precognizing as a *counter-hypothesis* to the "precognition hypothesis (Ch. XV 'The Problem of Time' in *New Frontiers of the Mind* and Ch. V 'The Problem of Time' in *The Reach of the Mind*). This counter-hypothesis falls ·under Broad's Option (iii): ("the ostensible foreseeing . . . is a cause-factor in a causal ancestor of the event which subsequently fulfils it"). While one reason why experimenters try to generate random series as targets is to exclude the possibility that correspondences between guess and target series might be attributed to a general or a particular human propensity to make guesses in accordance with some sort of pattern or system. Where this can be done the correspondence is explained away as due: not to genuine precognition; but to the fact that the experimenter, whether deliberately or unwittingly, permitted the use of targets which corresponded to a greater or lesser extent, with the guessing habits of his subject. This case could, rather awkwardly, fall under Broad's Option (iv): (the common causal ancestor).

We have illustrated our points with reference to the experimental work rather than to spontaneous and mediumistic material such as Broad had in mind when he wrote; yet they do apply to both. The development of the experimental work has certainly made it far easier to appreciate the validity of these points. But it would, I think, be a mistake to suggest that it was only as a result of developments here that parapsychologists came to use "precognition" and associated terms in such a way that cases falling under Broad's Options (iii) and (iv) would be disqualified. However this sort of discussion of what so-and-so really meant about this or that, when he was never himself forced squarely to face and pronounce on precisely this issue, is as tricky as it is unrewarding; and it would require a detailed examination of old parapsychological texts to settle the question.

(iii) In the light of the previous subsection it is now possible to formulate a causal objection which is forceful and of the appropriate type. For it appears that "Pψy" and associated terms are so defined as: *both* to require that precognitive ψ-correlations should not be "mere coincidences;" *and* to disqualify all cases which are causally explicable. To say in this context that a concurrence is not a mere coincidence is to say that there is some causal connection between the things in question, that there is some explanation of their concurrence. But apparently

Broad's Options (ii)—(iv) together exhaust all the possibilities of causal connection, and hence of explanation. Therefore "the very notion of veridical supernormal precognition" apparently involves a contradiction: for it would seem to involve that one and the same correspondence was *both* causally explicable *and* causally inexplicable. We shall now try to meet this reformulated causal objection.

(iv) Broad himself suggests how one of the two jaws of the apparent contradiction may be prised open: though he of course did not present his suggestion as this; but rather as a way of explaining Pψy. Considering the four options defined (see quotation above) he concludes: "the fundamental difficulty of the subject is this. It is alleged that ostensible foreseeings have been verified by subsequent events too often and too accurately to allow us to accept the first alternative. On the other hand, many of the best cases are such that it is impossible to bring them under any of the remaining three alternatives unless we postulate additional dimensions of space or agents and causal laws which are quite unfamiliar and for which we have no independent evidence. If I were faced with a choice between these evils, I should consider that the least of them is to postulate additional dimensions of space, provided that this will account for the facts" (pp. 198–9). He then makes some remarks about J. W. Dunne's Serialism[6] before going "in off the deep end" with the "perfectly fantastic suggestion" that there might be two time dimensions, and it might thus be possible for an event which preceded another in one time dimension to follow it in the other.

Now it might be argued that, even if sense can be given to talk of postulating further spatial or temporal dimensions, still no such manoeuvres could do anything to meet the causal objection as we have re-formulated it. For these would here presumably be ways of showing that the apparently precognized events are not really being *pre*cognized. What is being 'cognized' is something somehow going on *now*, albeit in another spatial dimension.[7] Or something which in some sense has already happened, though in the other dimension of time. So any ostensible cases of Pψy which could be explained along such lines would be thereby by definition disqualified as true cases: for the 'verification' would not really be later than the hunch or guess. But this slick move will not, I think, quite do. It seems completely adequate, if you look only at the more or less explicit definitions usually provided for "Pψy" and associated terms. Yet it is pretty clear from the actual usage of those

---

[6] Treated at length in 'Mr. Dunne's Theory of Time' in *RPPR*.

[7] This Broad is elsewhere at pains to underline: "It is extremely important to notice that, on this theory of 'precognition,' no event is ever 'precognized' in the strict and literal sense" (*RPPR*, p. 80).

who introduced and employ these, and particularly from their reactions to suggestions that all cases of ostensible Pψy might be explained in terms of new dimensions of space or time, that to say that here is a case of Pψy is not to rule out by definition *all* causal explanation, but, permits causal explanation as long as this involves 'postulating new dimensions' or other equally revolutionary innovations. The slick answer is not sufficient to dispose of Broad's suggestions. But it serves to bring out an unexciting point, perhaps unrecognized: that any explanation of Pψy, if there really is such a phenomenon, *must* be revolutionary; that this necessity has been made logical not contingent.

The question therefore remains: whether or not there could be a significant theory in the suitably revolutionary directions indicated by Broad. About this we fortunately need say nothing, for the heavy onus of proof surely lies on anyone who wants to deny the possibility. Yet Broad's instinct was surely right when he looked rather to spatial than to temporal innovation for a key. For while on his remodelling of Dunne's theory what is 'cognized' is not the later event but an earlier otherwise identical event occurring somewhere else, "in other dimensions of space;" his "perfectly fantastic suggestion" about a second time dimension could commit him to saying of two events, x and y, that x could be "before y in one of the temporal dimensions, whilst y is before x in the other of them" (p. 203). Whatever difficulties there may be in giving physical as opposed to purely mathematical meaning to such talk of further spatial dimensions (and Broad is fully aware of the seriousness of these difficulties[8]) it seems to involve no obvious contradiction. Whereas it surely is, as again Broad clearly was inclined to think,[9] a contradiction to say that the *same* event occurred *both* before *and* after another event.

(v) It is also possible to ease back the other jaw of the apparent contradiction.

(a) There is surely room for the suggestion that to say of some remarkable concurrence of phenomena that it is "not a coincidence" does not commit you to saying that they are *causally* connected but only to saying that they are *somehow* connected. I do not pretend to know whether the concept of coincidence is or is not at present determinate in this respect. (Though surely mathematicians may already speak of striking correspondences as not coincidental when the possible con-

---

8 ". . . as I have tried to show, it is not very easy to put a concrete interpretation on the various elements in the formal theory" (*RPPR*, p. 85).

9 "the suggestion that time may have more than one dimension may be simply nonsensical" (p. 203).

nections they have in mind are not causal but logical?) Yet whether it is or not, or even supposing that it is determinate and carries the former and strong rather than only the latter weak implication: still any adjustment necessary to ensure that it involved only the latter would be in itself very small. More drastic is the supplementary move required to give this small adjustment any point in an empirical context: we should have to admit the possibility of empirical but non-causal connections. This would involve allowing that there might be laws of the form, 'In such and such conditions subjects of such and such a sort always (or to such and such a degree above bogey) guess right:' *where the possibility of causal explanation (of the correlation as opposed to the occurrences correlated) is ruled out.* Now this may be a very disquieting thought to all of us set in our complacent intellectual ruts. Nevertheless it involves no sort of logical impropriety: since we have and can have no synthetic *a priori* guarantee that all phenomena can be subsumed under the sorts of laws we prefer and have been accustomed to discover; or even that they can all be subsumed under any laws at all. The connection expressed in such a law would be non-causal inasmuch as: *ex hypothesi,* the guess series must share no common causal ancestry with the target series; the subsequent target series (logically) cannot contain causal ancestors of members of the preceding guess series; and, *ex hypothesi* again, members of the guess series must not be involved in the causal ancestry of members of the target series. It might be suggested that the first and third conditions could not in principle be satisfied; for the same reason as that for which it is often contended that "Every event has a cause" is in principle unfalsifiable. But whatever may be said about the possibility or impossibility of absolutely knock-down verification or falsification here, it is surely possible to describe a situation in which there could remain no reasonable doubt but that they had been satisfied. It would be proper to say that such a law expressed a connection because this law would be a reliable basis for prediction: if the specified sort of guesser was operating under the specified conditions the values of his guesses would constitute reliable signs of the values of the appropriate target cards. Of course you would have to recognise that the law contained tacit qualification to the effect that it did not apply where steps were taken to interfere with the occurrence or values of the target series: for if it proved impossible, or even unexpectedly difficult, to prevent the fulfilment after the prediction had been made this would constitute very strong reason for saying that the predictions were among the causal ancestors of their fulfilments; and hence that the third condition was not satisfied after all.[10] Also it is difficult to see how, if at all, such a law could be elevated from its 'merely empirical' status and explained by a theory: though such feats of guessing might be made to appear less disquietingly isolated from the rest of the course of nature if it turned out that they were associated with other psychological capacities (cf. J. B. Rhine *The Reach of the Mind,* Ch. IV). But neither of these points constitute any reason for ruling out the notion of such a non-causal connection *a priori:* for plenty of respectable laws are limited in scope; and we have no synthetic *a priori* guarantee that all laws are in fact in turn explicable by other laws or theories.

Two pieces of comment, not essential to the main argument. *First;* the present suggestion has some similarity to Jung's ideas about "synchronicity phenomena." For such a law as we have indicated might paradoxically but pointedly be called a law about the regular occurrence of a certain sort of coincidence. While "synchronicity phenomenon" is in fact only a pretentious neologism for "coincidence," with a built-in suggestion that these are commoner than you would think (cf. 'Coincidence and Synchronicity' in *S.P.R. Journal* Vol. XXXVII pp. 198–201). This similarity might easily be overlooked: because of Jung's terminological peculiarities; because he associates the idea with so many of his own characteristic inventions; and because he exploits it for his own, it seems, wilfully anti-scientific and anti-rational ends. *Second;* if once we have decided that these logical possibilities have in fact to be taken seriously, it is surely important to raise without prejudice the question whether the occurrence of each particular item in the guess series and of each particular item in the target series, as opposed to the correlations between these two series of occurrences, is either in fact or even in principle completely explicable in terms of antecedent circumstances. It is too often assumed by those convinced of the reality of Pψy that it is neither. Thus Dr. D. J. West, Research Officer of the S.P.R. insists: "In a successful ESP test, there is a correlation between cards and calls which shows that one of the associations available to the subject, and effective in determining his choices, is the target order" (*S.P.R. Journal,* Vol. XXXVI, p. 695). But, as we shall urge in (b) below, a correlation could not *show,* but at most *suggest,* anything of the sort: while in any properly conducted ESP experiment the possibility of the target order being available to the subject, by any normal means, is *necessarily* excluded; though of course we are concentrating, as West was not, on Pψy as opposed to ESP in general. Our question may well be at present useless heuristically; if there is

10 Compare the legend of Oedipus the King, the relevance of which is considered in IV (iv.)(b) below.

no practicable experimental approach to its solution. But speculatively it is interesting. If West is right: then it should be possible to find some way of distinguishing $P\psi y$ guess series from those which are not so correlated with a target series, other than by checking the guess against the target values; and perhaps to find some not arbitrary way to give sense to a distinction between 'ψ' and 'chance' hits within a $P\psi y$ guess series.[11] If West is wrong: then $P\psi y$ correlations would confront us with situations reminiscent of the old occasionalist picture of mind-body relations or its secular version, the picture of psycho-physical parallelism: since the values of the items in the guess series and the values of the items in the target series would both be explicable satisfactorily but separately in orthodox causal terms; while the correlation between the two series was not susceptible of further explanation in these terms, even though it might be subsumed under some law of the type we have been suggesting.

(b) No conjunction, however elaborate, of propositions stating correlations, even one-one correlations, ever *entails* a causal conclusion. Thus there is no formal contradiction in the occasionalist suggestion that physical and mental processes might be in perfect one-one correlation eternally; and yet not be causally connected. Thus any phenomenalist analysis of the notion of causation on Humean lines must be formally inadequate: because it is committed to an exclusively extensional analysis of an essentially intensional notion; because it is committed to the hopeless project of trying to breed subjunctive conditionals (which all causal propositions entail) out of material implications (in terms of which all possible evidence for causal verdicts can be expressed).[12] This philosopher's point about the entailments carried by assertions about statistical significance might one day become important for science, and is certainly relevant to our present consideration of an *a priori* objection to the notion of $P\psi y$. It is relevant to us because it implies that were $P\psi y$ to be defined only in terms of statistical significance without any built-in commitment to the conclusion that this significant correlation is "too great to be ascribed to 'chance coincidence' " (p. 197): no contradiction could arise between this positive part of the definition and that negative part in which various types of causal connection are implicitly and explicitly excluded. (We should state, what the references to Hume will have suggested, that we are not

---

[11] The intended implications that neither of these things is at present possible may surprise: but cf. for the former and uncontroversial, *A New Approach to Psychical Research*, Ch. VIII and p. 114; and for the latter and disputed, *ibid.*, pp. 117–119 and *S.P.R. Journal*, XXXVII, 285–6 and 354–5.

[12] For further explanation of and argument for these conclusions see my 'Can an Effect precede its Cause?'

here concerned with the very important distinction between 'merely statistical' and 'more substantial' evidence for causal connection: for our present purposes both the evidence of overall deviations and the evidence of variations in the 'effect' concurrent with variations in the experimental conditions are equally assertions about statistical significance (cf. *A New Approach to Psychical Research*, p. 93). It might become important for science if it should in fact be found that in some sphere—parapsychology for instance—statistical significance happens to be a less reliable pointer to the subsistence of causal connections and/or the possibility of finding laws than it has so far elsewhere turned out to be. (To accept defeat or disappointment would at present be at best disgracefully premature: but of course our prime concern here is not with the tactics of research but with the *a priori*).

It is often and, I think, rightly insisted that far higher thresholds of statistical significance should be demanded in parapsychology than elsewhere, that we are entitled to require far higher minimum 'odds against chance' before feeling called upon to take notice of experimental results: because of the enormous antecedent improbability of the alleged phenomena; because, that is, we have an enormous mass of evidence to indicate that the world is not that sort of place at all. The analysis of the negative side of the implicit definition of supernormal precognition which was deployed in reformulating the Causal Objection suggests what is at least another way of looking at, and possibly a substantially different point about, this need to be cautious before moving from statistical significance to "not a mere coincidence" in this particular case. We can take it that supernormal precognition is defined to involve correlations which are not merely statistically significant but also more than coincidental: Broad is emphatic that this should be so, that veridical foreseeing "does not mean simply that in many cases a later event, which a person had no rational ground for expecting, *happens* to accord to a very high degree with an earlier experience in this person of veridical foreseeing. He means that there is an amount of accordance . . . too great to be ascribed to 'chance coincidence'" (p. 197). Since, to satisfy the definition again, every causal connection other than one with some hypothetical revolutionary new range of entities in another sphere must have been ruled out, by this move we here become committed: *either* to the postulation of a new world for which there is no other evidence; *or* to the postulation of a new type of non-causal law, of which we have at present no specimens. The moral is: not that the reformulated causal objection has revealed a contradiction in the notion of supernormal precognition; but that the peculiarities of the notion which this has helped to bring out

justify an appropriately peculiar caution about moving from statements about statistical significance to the verdict of supernormal precognition.

IV.

The Fatalist Objection. This arises because it is thought that the precognition of any event the occurrence of which was apparently dependent on some voluntary human decision must imply: *either* that
"the event which subsequently fulfilled the precognition did *not* really
depend on the voluntary decision on which it seemed to depend" (p.
205); *or* that "if it did, then that voluntary decision must have been
already completely predetermined at the time when the precognition
took place" (p. 205). And "many people find it highly repugnant,
both intellectually and emotionally, to admit either of these alternatives about voluntary decisions and the events which apparently depend on them" (p. 205).

Comment. (i) Again we recall that this too is supposed to be an "*a
priori* objection . . . to the very notion of veridical supernormal precognition" (p. 179), an attempt to show that there is "some logical or
metaphysical impossibility in it" (p. 179). Yet again as stated it does not
appear to be this sort of objection at all: it is only *a priori* in the sense
in which all prejudices are *a priori,* in virtue of being formed and
maintained regardless of any contrary evidence; and certainly has not
the slightest tendency to show that there is any "logical or metaphysical
impossibility" about the very notion. It looks as if you might as well
say that the person, for instance, who rejects Roman Catholic dogmas
about Hell, on the ground that this idea of Omnipotence creating in-
subordinate men for eternal torment is the most unspeakable horror
ever imagined by the mind of man, or anyone else who rejects some
view for no better reason than that he would not like it to be true,
is raising an *a priori* objection, offering a reason for saying this uncon-
genial view involves a "logical or metaphysical impossibility." But it
can be presented as unequivocally the right sort of objection by making
explicit the objectors' assumptions that we *know: both* that our decisions do sometimes affect issues; *and* that we are often free to decide
between alternatives (which supposedly implies that these decisions
must be in principle unpredictable).

(ii) Broad counters by arguing that precognition does not after all
carry implications incompatible with either conviction. There is far
more in his arguments with which we might take issue, but we shall con-

centrate as before on aspects of most continuing interest.[13] We do not wish to deny either assumption of the Fatalist Objection: we do certainly know some propositions of the form 'If he had decided differently, things would have turned out differently;' and we do certainly know that we are sometimes free to decide between alternatives. But it is crucial to the Fatalist Objection that this latter proposition should entail that such decisions are not completely determined, are not even in principle predictable: for unless this proposition does carry this entailment there is no contradiction in *both* asserting it *and* asserting the possibility of Pψy; even allowing that this assertion does commit you to denying *either* the causal efficacy *or* the in principle unpredictability of voluntary decisions. And that it carries this entailment we do deny. But we shall not here deploy any arguments to support this denial: because that would trespass on territory allotted to other contributors to this book; and because others and we ourselves have already elsewhere defended this now orthodox view less sketchily than is here possible. Instead we shall try to argue against Broad's reply to the Fatalist Objection: first, that precognition must involve that events precognised are predetermined, i.e., in principle predictable; and, second, that this does not involve as a necessary consequence that everyone was helpless to prevent events precognised.

(iii) Broad defines "already completely predetermined" as meaning "there is a set of facts about the dispositions, the mutual relations, and the internal states at or before the moment t of the various substances then existing, which together with the laws of matter and of mind, *logically entails* that an event exactly like e will happen after an interval t'-t. . . ." (p. 204): i.e. that an event e is completely predetermined if it can be unequivocally predicted on the basis of a knowledge of laws plus a knowledge of antecedent circumstances. Furthermore he holds it to be self-evident that "The occurrence of e at t' could not be *inferred with certainty* at an earlier moment t from facts about what has existed or happened at or before t unless it were already completely determined at t" (p. 207). But he mistakes this proposition to be entirely irrelevant because "no one supposes that veridical ostensible foreseeing consists in inferring from facts about the past and present *with complete certainty* that certain events will happen in the future" (p. 207). That Pψy should *consist in* such inference is indeed ruled out, by definition: but to recall this is entirely insufficient to prove the point. For if—as Broad certainly would—you intend to take Pψy to involve

13 Thus we shall say nothing about Broad's notion of the predeterminate: to do so is not essential to us; and we could add nothing to the contribution made by D. F. Pears in 'Time, Truth, and Inference' (*P.A.S.* 1950–1, reprinted in *Essays in Conceptual Analysis,* Macmillan, London, 1955).

that there must subsist laws connecting precognitive occurrences with precognized events: then from a sufficient knowledge of these laws and the circumstances surrounding the precognitive occurrence it must be possible to deduce that the event precognized will in fact occur; and hence it follows that precognized events must be predetermined. Though precognition cannot, by definition, *consist in* inference from the present to the future: knowledge of its laws must *make possible* such inference. Even supposing the precognitive hunches themselves were in principle unpredictable (see III (v)(a) above) still the events precognized must be predetermined: so long as Pψy is taken to imply the subsistence of a connection, as opposed to a mere correlation, between the guess series and the target series.

"I can infer from events in the less remote past that Julius Caesar decided in the more remote past to cross the Rubicon. No one imagines for a moment that this fact shows that Caesar's decision to cross the Rubicon was completely pre-determined at any previous date." So far so good. "Suppose now that an augur at Rome had foreseen those later events from which *we* infer that Caesar had decided at an earlier date to cross the Rubicon. Obviously, he could have drawn precisely the same conclusion about Caesar's *then future* decision as we draw about his *now past* decision" (Italics the author's; as always unless otherwise stated). Fair enough. But then Broad asks: "if the possibility of our making this inference from these data does not require Caesar's decision to be completely predetermined, why should the possibility of the augur's making the same inference from the same data require this?" To which surely the answer is short, simple, and sufficient. What makes the crucial difference precisely is the *dates: we* should be inferring from knowledge of what as a matter of fact occurred later plus knowledge of social laws, *after the event;* whereas the augur would have been inferring from similar knowledge of social laws plus knowledge of the laws of precognition, *before the event.*

(iv) The second point we wish to argue is: *not* that freedom to decide between alternatives does not entail that the decisions must be in principle unpredictable, which proposition is to be left unargued here; *but* that the predictability of some event does not entail that that event could not have been prevented by human agency, a related but entirely distinct proposition. Now I think that the reasons which have misled many philosophers—and here as so often this term should be recognised to cover not merely professionals but also laymen in their more philosophical moments—into this mistaken conclusion have been of two sorts. First, they have confused logical necessity with physical compulsion. Second, they have thought that if anyone's future behaviour is to be known in advance, whether normally or paranormally, then he must be as helpless to refrain from this particular behaviour as was Oedipus to frustrate the fulfilment of the prophecies of his incest and patricide.

(a) Using a knowledge of general laws and particular circumstances for prediction we conclude from these as premises that such and such *must* happen. It is tempting to take it that our knowledge of general laws and particular circumstances has thereby been shown to imply that something is *compelled* or *necessitated* to happen. But this is a complete mistake. The *must*, the *necessity* belongs not to the conclusion but to the inference: which moves from the premisses stating general laws (about what does as a matter of fact happen) and premisses stating circumstances (about what has happened and is happening); to the conclusion stating what will as a matter of fact, not what is logically necessitated to, happen (granting the truth of the premisses). No happening could be logically necessitated. While to show that someone was constrained to act in such and such a way: it is neither necessary nor sufficient to show that his behaviour could have been predicted; but it is essential to show that pressures had been deployed on him. "But when . . . we change *will* into *must,* we introduce an idea of necessity which most assuredly does not lie in the observed facts and has no warranty that I can discover elsewhere . . . what is this Necessity, save an empty shadow of my own mind's throwing?" (T. H. Huxley, 'On the Physical Basis of Life' in *Lay Sermons, etc.,* 1870).

(b) Mr. M. A. E. Dummett has recently provided us with an example of the second mistake by arguing that "It is of course true that if anyone *knew* whether or not something was going to happen, he would do nothing now designed to make it happen, for this would be either redundant or fruitless; in this sense you cannot change the future either: what will happen will happen" ('Can an Effect precede its Cause?', *P.A.S.* Suppl. Vol. XXVIII, p. 41). Now if *"knew"* is to be interpreted normally then this is clearly false: the Headmaster may know what he is going to do to Smith without this making his exertions either redundant or fruitless; and if in fact he idly does nothing then he did not really know he was going to beat Smith. I may in this everyday sense know something which is going to happen, and know that I shall be instrumental in bringing it about, and hence that my efforts will be neither redundant nor fruitless. But the context suggests that perhaps *"knew"* is to be interpreted as having "precognition. . . . I do not mean crystal gazing but a faculty exactly analogous to memory" (*ibid.,* p. 43). Yet if so this faculty would have to be, to preserve the perfection of the analogy with memory, fallible. So if I were able to "remember forwards in this way"[14] this would certainly not put me in any better position in principle than I now am when I make a proper memory claim; and would certainly not have the slightest tendency to show that any efforts of mine must be fruitless or redundant. Yet what I suspect that Dummett was really after was some third interpretation, a sort of Prichardian knowledge, knowledge claims which could only be relevantly and appropriately disputed by assailing the integrity of those who made them: because their very occurrence must somehow entail the occurrence which it is claimed will happen. Whichever interpretation we take it seems that one source of Dummett's error must be a failure fully to appreciate that one event, even when it is the event of making a sincere claim to know or to remember (or to precognize), cannot *entail* another, that events cannot be logically necessitated to occur (see (a) above). While another source, which would tend to reinforce the first, is presumably a failure to make a distinction between, on the one hand, honest knowledge or memory claims and, on the other hand, genuine knowledge and memory: while "He remembers (knows) that p happened" does "He claims that he remembers (knows) that p happened and he is not lying" does not entail "p happened" (cf. *ibid.,* p. 61; *Philosophy,* 1951, pp. 56–8; *S.P.R. Journal,* Vol. XXXVII, pp. 353–4; and Broad, pp. 181–2). If you fail to appreciate this point it becomes so much the easier to think that the occurrence of memory (or precognitive) claims logically necessitates the occurrence of the events remembered (or precognized).

But now even if we do suppose a precognitive faculty which is in fact always to be right (and hence to be in at least one important respect unlike memory); and if human nature is also supposed to remain otherwise unaltered: *then the world would have to be supposed so changed that all our efforts to avoid anything 'precognized' to be going to happen to us would have to be made as a matter of fact ineffective.* This third supposition has to be made because without it, human nature being what it is, people would sometimes try to prevent and, the world being as it now is, they would often succeed in preventing, the occurrences which they had 'precognised' as going to happen. What gives the story of Oedipus its cobra fascination is precisely that in his case over the prophecies of patricide and incest not merely both the first two but also the third supposition is realised: the prophecies (the 'precognitions') are both appalling and right; he is human enough to try to prevent their fulfilment; *yet things so work out that his efforts are made not merely ineffective as precautions but actually important steps in the causal process which leads to the fulfilment of the prophe-*

[14] Cf. Carroll, *Through the Looking Glass,* Ch. V.

cies. It is quite wrong to think that evidence of the predictability of human behaviour in general, or evidence of the reality of precognition in particular (whether or not it is, unlike memory, always on target); must by itself tend to show that we are all as helpless—or indeed worse than helpless—as Oedipus. For predictions, whether normal or paranormal, do not as such have to be about the occurrence of things we should for any reason, whether good or merely cantankerous, wish to avoid; nor do they have to be available to us (and thus able to provoke us into avoiding action). While just to show that prediction, whether normal or paranormal, is possible is not by itself sufficient to show that the people whose behaviour is thus predicted could not (especially had the prophecies been made known to them!) have prevented the fulfilment of the predictions by acting in ways different from those in which as a matter of fact they are acting and are going to act, other ways in which they were not constrained from acting. To show that we are as a matter of fact as helpless—or worse than helpless —as Oedipus it would be necessary to show that when we try to avoid some threatened horror we as a matter of fact fail—and that our efforts to avoid turn out to have been links in the causal chains leading to the occurrence of the horrors we had thereby attempted to prevent. So far as I know there is no parapsychological evidence which suggests that anyone is ever in the Oedipus situation about a 'precognition;' although there *is* some evidence of people having what appear to be precognitions of what it seems would have happened had the precognitive experience itself not led to the taking of evasive action which, unlike that taken by Oedipus, was effective.

This second perplexity about avoidability arises from the same fundamental source as the notorious general methodological difficulty about prediction in the human sciences. Predictions about human affairs, *if they are made known to the people involved,* may become unconsidered and disruptive factors in the very affairs with which they are concerned: thus knowledge of Marx's predictions has surely been a considerable factor making both for the verification and for the falsification of those very predictions; while the publication of the predictions of British psephologists in 1955 looks to have been at least one factor making for the falsification of their arrogantly overconfident forecasts. The source is the dual nature of man and the complexity of the interrelations of our two aspects. "It must never be forgotten that we ourselves are both actors and spectators in the drama of existence" (Niels Bohr).

ANTONY FLEW

UNIVERSITY COLLEGE
KEELE, STAFFORDSHIRE
ENGLAND

13

William C. Kneale

BROAD ON MENTAL EVENTS AND EPIPHENOMENALISM

1

IN HIS chapter on The Unity of the Mind near the end of *The Mind and Its place in Nature* Broad asks the question

Can we take the notion of "mental event" as fundamental and define the notion of "mental substance" in terms of mental events and certain relations between them: Or must we conceive a "mental event" as consisting in the fact that a certain Centre has at a certain time such and such a determinate quality, or such and such a determinate relation to other things?[1]

His cautious answer is that he can find no *a priori* objection to taking the notion of mental events as fundamental.[2] In the second volume of his *Examination of McTaggart's Philosophy* he defends the Bundle Theory against the criticisms of McTaggart and leaves us again with the conclusion that none of the arguments commonly advanced against that theory are sound. Although he does not commit himself in either place to acceptance of the theory, he declares that it has great advantages over the Pure Ego Theory for those who are concerned with the facts of abnormal and supernormal psychology; and in both works he goes on to say that he is inclined to favour epiphenomenalism, i.e., an account of the relation between mind and body according to which there can be no mental continuant other than something constructed from mental events.

Such a theory of mental events is very widely held in modern times. We may even say that it is the orthodoxy of modern physiologists and medical men. But its philosophical implications have never been worked out by anyone else with the care they receive from Broad, and that is why I have chosen this part of his work as the subject of my essay. For the convenience of the reader I shall begin by summarizing the relevant sections of his doctrine, allowing myself some of that liberty

[1] *MPN*, 587.   [2] *MPN*, 603.

of re-arrangement which he uses in his *EMcP*. Then I shall consider some objections that may be urged against his terminology. When *MPN* was published thirty years ago, Broad said in his preface that he would watch with a fatherly eye the philosophic gambols of his younger friends as they danced to the highly syncopated piping of Herr Wittgenstein's flute. Since he wrote those words the frolic has become a sombre cult in which it is a mark of devotion to show impatience at the language of all older philosophy. Against criticisms from this side I shall argue that the plain philosopher has his rights no less than the plain man, and I shall try to show that what Broad wrote thirty years ago is still worth serious discussion. This is not to say, however, that it is all true, and I shall in fact go on to raise some objections to the epiphenomenalism which he offers as his last word on the subject.

2.

Although Broad does not commit himself without reservations to the view that mental events are prior to mental continuants in the nature of things, there can be no doubt that he regards them as prior for us. By this I mean to say that while he thinks it necessary to leave open many questions about the status of minds and material things and even sometimes professes to be uncertain about their existence, he never has any doubts about the occurrence of mental events. That is why he considers behaviourism a silly theory and dismisses it without the old-fashioned courtesy that he is prepared to extend to most of the speculations of his predecessors. In one discussion he writes

I often know without the least doubt that I am having the experience called "seeing a chair" when I am altogether uncertain whether my body is acting in any characteristic way.[3]

And in another place he says

It is evident to me on direct inspection that the behaviourist form of Materialism is false. For it seems quite clear to me that statements which contain psychological terms cannot be translated without loss or gain of meaning into statements which contain no such terms but are wholly about bodies, physical processes in them, and physical transactions between them. I defy anyone to translate his own statement "I am now hearing a squeaky noise" into a set of statements of the latter kind.[4]

In these examples, and presumably in any others he might cite against behaviourism, the mental events of which he speaks belong, as he would say, to some mind, but he remarks several times that there is no good reason for assuming that all mental events belong to minds:

3 *MPN,* 614.   4 *EMcP,* II, 604.

It is very far from certain that all mental events must occur as members of those sets of interrelated mental events which we call "Empirical Selves." We might then strongly believe that a certain movement of an external body is the outward expression of a certain mental event which does not belong to our mind; and yet we might be very doubtful whether this external body is animated by a mind at all. E.g. I might feel tolerably certain that, when an insect is injured and writhes about, there is a feeling of pain which is no part of my mind and is intimately connected with these writhing movements of the insect's body. And yet I might be very doubtful whether the insect's body is animated by anything that could reasonably be called a "mind." This feeling might be quite isolated. Or, if it be in fact a member of a group of interrelated simultaneous and successive mental events, this group might be so poor in content and so loose in structure as not to deserve the name of "mind."[5]

Those mental events which belong to minds may be called experiences, but it would be unfortunate to use "experience" as a synonym for "mental event" precisely because this usage would obscure the possibility noticed above:

All experiences are mental events; but I think it would be in accordance with usage to say that, if there be unowned mental events, they should not be called "experiences." So I will define an "experience" as a mental event which is owned by some mind.[6]

The mental events which are human experiences may be of various kinds. In *The Mind and its Place in Nature* Broad writes:

If "mentality" means the peculiar characteristic of human minds, we must admit that it is complex. Its factors may be divided first into Affective Attitudes and Other Factors. The relation between them is that it is logically possible for the Other Factors to occur without any of the Affective Attitudes, while it is not logically possible for any of the Affective Attitudes to occur without at least one of the Other Factors. Secondly, we can arrange the Other Factors in a hierarchical order, such that the earlier could occur without the later but the later could not occur without all the earlier ones. The order is Sentience, Acquaintance, Intuitive Referential Cognition, and Discursive Referential Cognition.[7]

Sentience is just feeling somehow, e.g. cross or tired, whereas acquaintance is a relation to an object such as a sensum or an image. Broad says in one place that it is the converse of *manifestation*.[8] If, as some philosophers have argued, crossness and tiredness are qualities manifested by objects, e.g. by organisms, sentience may be omitted from the list of mental factors on the ground that there is nothing more fundamental than acquaintance. In his *Examination of McTaggart's Philosophy* he uses the word "prehension" as a substitute for "acquaintance" and allows

5 *MPN*, 319–320.   6 *MPN*, 375–376. Cf. *EMcP.*, II, 151.
7 *MPN*, 637.   8 *MPN*, 634.

himself to say that a particular is prehended as so-and-so.[9] Referential cognition is judgement or supposal about things or events with which we are not at the moment acquainted and perhaps never can be. Perception of a material object is an example of intuitive referential cognition, and thought of such an object when it is not perceived is an example of discursive referential cognition. When Broad says that each later item in his list presupposes all the earlier items, I do not think that he means that every instance of discursive referential cognition necessarily involves intuitive referential cognition within itself, but rather that there could not be a mind which had discursive referential cognition without ever having intuitive referential cognition. On the other hand he undoubtedly holds that perception involves sensation (i.e. the prehension of sensa), and he says explicitly in one place that *all* mental processes seem to involve sensations or prehensions of images.[10] In any case a mental event of a higher kind is not to be supposed complex in the sense that it is constituted by some interconnexion of mental events of a lower kind. For according to Broad none of the items in his hierarchy is reducible to an item or items below it in the hierarchy or indeed to anything at all.[11]

Of minds as distinct from mental events Broad writes

I do not know how to define a "mind," but I think it is evident that a thing could not be called a "mind" unless it had a peculiar kind of content and a peculiar kind of structure. Its content must be the kind of events which we call "mental" and observe when we choose to introspect. And these mental events must be interconnected in a very peculiar way. It is possible that mental events can exist only as factors in those peculiar complex wholes which we call "minds," but I do not see any very good reason to believe this. It is also possible, and much more likely, that nothing but mental events can be interconnected in the peculiar way which is characteristic of the structure of a mind.[12]

The unity of a mind through time involves mnemic connexions between mental events occurring at different dates, but even this kind of unity cannot be *explained*, as Locke thought, by reference to memory. For *ostensible* memory is not enough to guarantee identity, and it is a mere triviality to say that any experience of which a man has genuine memory must have happened to him.[13] Minds (or selves, as he often calls them in his *EMcP*) have also a transverse unity, i.e. a single mind may own several experiences simultaneously. Admittedly the ownership of men-

9 *EMcP*, II, 4.   10 *EMcP*, II, 598.
11 *MPN*, 638.   12 *MPN*, 390.
13 "Locke's Doctrine of Substantial Identity and Diversity," in *Theoria,* xvii (1951), 24.

tal events by a mind cannot be *defined*,[14] but we should not suppose that there is therefore no alternative to the Pure Ego Theory. There may be a characteristically mental form of structure, i.e. a pattern of relationship which cannot hold between terms that are not constituents of minds;[15] and if anyone challenges us to name the basic relation which holds between all the events constituting a single mind, it may perhaps be sufficient to say that they are sympsychic.[16]

The notion of a mind as something which endures for a time and passes from one experience to another is a specification of the abstract *a priori* concept of a continuant, and the specification is by empirical differentiae:

One empirically conceived factor is the peculiar kind of unity which ties together various simultaneous experiences in a single specious present; another is the fact that some experiences in one specious present are ostensibly memories of certain experiences in earlier specious presents; another is the fact that certain experiences in one specious present are ostensibly fulfilments or frustrations of certain expectations in earlier specious presents; and so on. When people say that the character of selfhood is simple and that the concept of it is empirical, I suspect that what they mean is often no more than that the empirical factors in it are quite unique and peculiar and cannot be defined in terms of the empirical factors in the notion of material thinghood. This seems to me to be plainly true.[17]

Since a mind or empirical self is something with a history, it cannot, according to Broad, be prehended by a momentary act of introspection any more than a material thing can be prehended by a glance. Introspective knowledge of ourselves and our states should be compared rather with *perceptual* knowledge of material things and their states. This is a point to which he often recurs, and from it he draws the conclusion that we have no good reason to assume that introspection can give exhaustive and infallible information about the self which does the introspection.[18] No doubt a person who practises introspection cannot be totally deceived like a man who suffers from a sensory hallucination; for his belief that he himself exists must be correct. But he may be mistaken in the accounts he gives himself of his experiences, and there may be many important facts about himself which he is quite unable to discover by this method.[19]

When he turns to consider the status of mental events in nature and their relation to the physical, Broad inclines to epiphenomenalism, but

14 *MPN*, 376.   15 *MPN*, 582.
16 *EMcP*, II, 178.   17 *EMcP*, II, 168.
18 *MPN*, 277–278, 327; *EMcP*, II, 169, 199, 259, 498.
19 *MPN*, 284–286.

he is careful to explain that his reasons are only empirical. We can conceive several alternative theories each of which is free from internal contradiction and consistent with all the facts of observation; but epiphenomenalism is the most economical, since it makes no provision for the occurrence of mental events out of association with an organism. If we had any reason to believe in the existence of minds apart from bodies, it would be necessary to reject epiphenomenalism, but it can be reconciled with all the well-attested results of psychical research by the single additional assumption of a psychogenic factor which may itself be material. Admittedly this theory does not commend itself to unscientific common sense, but the objections we feel against the view that mental events never cause bodily events can be overcome, and in the light of all the information we now have epiphenomenalism seems to be the most reasonable hypothesis about the relation of mind and body.[20] Sometimes he calls it Emergent Materialism to mark its place in his scheme of possible theories.[21]

When first announcing his preference Broad says cautiously that he considers "some form of epiphenomenalism" to be the most reasonable view.[22] His reason for using this form of words is that he has already distinguished two varieties:

Epiphenomenalism may be taken to assert one of two things. (a) That certain events which have physiological characteristics have *also* mental characteristics, and that no events which lack physiological characteristics have mental characteristics. That many events which have physiological characteristics are not known to have mental characteristics. And that an event which has mental characteristics never causes another event in virtue of its mental characteristics, but only in virtue of its physiological characteristics. Or (b) that no event has both mental and physiological characteristics; but that the complete cause of any event which has mental characteristics is an event or set of events which has physiological characteristics. And that no event which has mental characteristics is a cause-factor in the causation of any other event whatever, whether mental or physiological.[23]

Some readers may be inclined to dismiss the first of these suggestions as senseless, but Broad asserts in two places that there is no absurdity in the supposition that one and the same thing or event may have both mental and material characteristics.[24] The most he is prepared to allow is that we never prehend any particular as having both characteristics at once and have no clear idea of what we are suggesting or asserting when we say that there might be such a particular. Perhaps he thinks nevertheless that this reflection is enough to discredit the first of the

20 *MPN*, 114–121, 476, 533–535; *EMcP*, II, 604–605.
21 *MPN*, 647.   22 *MPN*, 476.
23 *MPN*, 472.   24 *MPN*, 628; *EMcP*, II, 139–141.

two forms of epiphenomenalism which he has distinguished; for in his latest discussion of the theory he says roundly

Epiphenomenalism asserts connexions between events which are heterogeneous in kind, *viz.*, between events which are described wholly in spatio-temporal and kinematic terms and events which are described wholly in psychological terms.[25]

But his immediate purpose in making this remark is to draw attention to a proposition which he explained very clearly in his earlier work, namely, that the doctrine of the one-sided production of mental events by physical is not merely a scientific hypothesis of the ordinary sort but also a metaphysical suggestion involving a distinction between two kinds of causation neither of which is covered by the definition of a cause as an invariable antecedent.[26]

3.

The main burden of the criticism now commonly brought against philosophizing like this is that it involves a mistaken conception of philosophical method. According to the critics, Broad and those who think with him have failed to realize that the philosopher's proper task is the removal of perplexities arising from misuse of language. Instead of considering whether we have a customary use for this or that queer phrase such as "the self," they proceed to inquire about the nature of what it is supposed to denote, and argue as though they were engaged in some branch of natural science. In particular, they talk as though their work were like that of astronomers, who map the heavens with meticulous care and invent new names for newly distinguished objects but often have to admit that they cannot settle some of the most interesting questions because of the limitations of their means of observation. If the critics are right, philosophical problems can always be solved, or rather dissolved, with certainty by attention to the normal use of words, and the procedure of Broad and his friends is just muddling. For an array of technical terms bamboozles the reader into thinking that he cannot make progress unless he accepts the terminology of his betters, and so makes him fail to notice small but fateful departures from ordinary usage, such as the employment of the word "self" as though it were not merely a reflexive pronoun but the name of a special kind of entity.

It is not my business to discuss Broad's conception of philosophical

25 *EMcP*, II, 606.   26 *MPN*, 116.

method, and I shall therefore content myself with two general remarks about this line of criticism.

First, it is by no means obvious that the striking changes which have been made in the style of philosophical discussion during the past thirty years are all for the good. When Broad published *MPN* (and I began the study of philosophy), it was quite common for philosophers to confess that they were puzzled. There were, of course, some such as Prichard and Moore who showed a passionate attachment to their views, but even these could be heard speaking of questions on which they found it very difficult to make up their minds. On the other hand, if we hear a modern philosopher expressing perplexity, we may be almost certain that he is giving a dramatic performance and will presently wind up by showing us the way to his own intellectual serenity. How indeed could anyone admit that he was really puzzled by a philosophical problem while still proclaiming confidently that *all* philosophical problems arise from misuse of language? Such behaviour would be as odd as a public complaint of pain by a preacher of Christian Science. For my own part, I think there must be a serious mistake in any account of philosophy which makes men ashamed to admit perplexity. No doubt philosophical problems are of a kind to be solved by clear thinking; but this is not to say that the raising of them is a sign of muddled thinking, or that their solutions must all be covered by one formula such as that about delivering men from misuse of language.

Secondly, the dangers of technical terminology have been greatly overestimated. Some readers may be intimidated by phrases like "Emergent Materialism," but to most laymen the unfamiliar words printed with initial capitals are a sign of need for extra vigilance. Nor is there much to be feared from a novel philosophical use of an ordinary word like "self." If readers accept the use in spite of its oddity, they do so presumably because it seems to serve a useful purpose. In my view there is now more danger from the use of slogan phrases such as "Statements of necessary truth tell us nothing about the world," "The meaning of a word is its use," "People are what we meet." For in each of these cases a form of words which is acceptable only as the expression of a triviality seems to acquire importance from its repetition until the hearer or reader is inclined to accept it also as the epigrammatic formulation of a thesis which is by no means trivial. Thus an assertion that statements of necessary truth tell us nothing about the world is obviously correct, but not very interesting, if it is supposed to mean that such statements give us no information of contingent facts. On the other hand it is false if it is taken to mean that statements of necessary truth are made true by human whim. Let us by all means agree that philosophical patter should be suspect, but let us train our intellectual noses to sniff at modern talk of "the behaviour of psychological concepts" as much as at older talk of "the nature of the Empirical Self."

There is not much to be gained, however, from philosophical discussion at the level of "You're another!," and so I pass on now to consider some detailed criticisms that critics of the school to which I refer have brought or might bring against Broad's use of the phrase "mental events."

It has been suggested that there is something philosophically improper in talking of mental events as Broad does because the word "event" does not occur like that in ordinary speech; and a similar objection has been brought against his use of the word "experience" to cover all sorts of feeling, thinking, and wishing. Apparently the critics hold that the word "event" should be used only in such contexts as "The two events of the year 1953 were the coronation of the Queen and the climbing of Everest" and the word "experience" only in such contexts as "What a wonderful experience it must be to survey the world from the summit of Everest." So far as I know, these criticisms have never been put in print, and the reader may perhaps suspect that I have invented them in order to bring ridicule on the cult of ordinary language, but I remember well hearing them both during oral discussions in the ancient universities of England, and I propose to take them seriously because it is important to understand what can and what cannot be proved by an appeal to common usage.

The most frequent uses of the words "event" and "experience" at the present time may perhaps be those of which I have just given examples, but they are certainly not the only uses of the words in the speech of educated men. "Event" meant originally the same as "outcome," and "experience" the same as "trying for oneself," but both have acquired many special senses. Thus "event" has often been used for an item in the programme of a sports meeting, and "experience" for a feeling which some people say they have from time to time in connexion with religious thoughts. As might be expected, we can easily find confirmation here for the well-known principle of philology that the meaning of a particular utterance depends not only on its phonetic quality but also on its context, that is to say, on its relation to the circumstances and behaviour of the speaker and in particular on its relation to his other utterances. If philosophers who advise us to study ordinary language intend only to draw attention to this principle and caution us against theorizing about meaning as though it were something that belonged to words apart from all imaginable contexts, then what they say is salutary. For we have a constant temptation to assume that every language must be like an artificial code in which each recognizable sign has one and the same meaning on all occasions. And we are sometimes inclined also to forget that any utterance is correct in one important sense, though not necessarily true or elegant, if it serves its purpose in the context in which it occurs. But it is foolishness to talk as though the speech of plain men discussing football pools had an authority lacking in the works of all learned persons. A natural language is something that grows in use, and learned persons have at least as much right as anyone else to contribute to its growth. Customs of theirs which have little connexion with the common interests of all men can never become universal, but they may for all that be well-established. Thus when Broad uses the word "event" as he does, he merely reverts to an early general sense underlying all the special usages of modern times, and I do not believe that any reader competent to follow a philosophical discussion of any kind ever had any real difficulty in understanding him on that account. His use of "experience" is rather more sophisticated, but here again he has plenty of authority on his side, and I feel reasonably certain that philosophers who object to it are not really unable to understand what he says, but rather unwilling for one reason or another to concede some thesis stated by means of the word.

I do not wish to maintain, however, that all Broad states or suggests by means of this technical terminology is correct. It seems to me, for example, that it is unwise to talk of referential cognition as a variety of mental event. Originally "cognition" meant the same as "knowledge," but it was used for a time by psychologists to provide a contrast with affection and conation in a division of modes of consciousness, and it was then held to cover believing and supposing as well as knowing. Broad seems to use it in the same way as the psychologists of an older generation, and I think it may therefore be assumed that he regards knowledge as a kind of experience. If so, he is guilty of two mistakes. In the first place he is including a capacity among experiences, where it has no place; and in the second place he is ignoring the difference between description and evaluation. In normal usage the word "know" does not refer to something that lasts for a few moments, but rather to an ability that is manifested in various ways at intervals during a period. For this reason it is rather queer to talk of knowledge as an act or event, though not perhaps so queer as some recent critics have supposed, since in many languages a noun which we translate by "knowledge" is derived from a verb which has the sense of the English "realize" or "recognize." Thus in Greek we have γνῶσις from γιγνώσκω, in Latin cognitio from cognosco, and in German Erkenntnis from erkennen. But even these verbs and the English word "realize" cannot be said to describe a kind of experience.

It is true that a man who realizes something must have an experience in the moment of realization, but this need not differ in kind from the experience of a man who suddenly feels convinced of something that is not the case. When I say of someone that he realized something in a certain moment, I do indeed ascribe to him an experience, but I call it realization in order to express my own judgement of its value. If later I become doubtful of the sufficiency of his reason for believing what he did, I must withdraw the word "realize" and substitute a neutral description such as "thought," though I have learnt nothing new about his past state of mind.

Here we have good ground for objecting to some of the things that Broad says about experiences and mental events, but not for rejecting his basic terminology. In order to make these points against him I have found it convenient to use the same terminology, and I am not alone in this. Thus the late Professor Wittgenstein, from whom the criticisms are derived, wrote frequently of *Erlebnisse* and *geistige Vorgänge* while insisting that understanding was not one of them.[27] Professor Ryle, on the other hand, maintains that there is a radical mistake in using the word "mental" as Broad does. He says indeed "I am not denying that there are mental processes,"[28] but his examples are doing long division and making a joke, and it appears presently that he wants to use the adjective "mental" as though it were equivalent to "intelligent" and applicable to kinds of behaviour. He has to admit, of course, that plain men talk of mental imagery and that it is common in scientific contexts to speak of sensations as mental; but he says that neither usage has any evidential value against his view because both are due to contagion from the false Cartesian dogma of the ghost in the machine.[29] If the facts were as he says, the philosophical howler which he attributes to Descartes would be even more extraordinary than he thinks it is. For how could even the most perverse metaphysician come to speak of minds as Descartes does, if before his time men had used the word "mind" and the partially equivalent words in other languages only to talk of "abilities, liabilities and inclinations to do and to undergo certain sorts of things, and of the doing and undergoing of these things in the ordinary world?"[30]

According to philologists the English word "mind" and the Latin *mens* from which we get our word "mental" are connected in origin with words for remembering (μιμνῄσκω, *memini*), awaiting (μένω, *maneo*), admonishing (Μέντωρ, *moneo*, *mahnen*), and purposing or intending

27 E.g., *Philosophische Untersuchungen*, I, 305ff.
28 *The Concept of Mind*, 32.
29 *Ibid.*, 34–35, 200–201.   30 *Ibid.*, 199.

("mean," *meinen*). But we need not rely on conjectural etymologies to prove our case. For most of the notions just mentioned can still be expressed by use of the English word "mind." Here for example are some of the phrases in which it can occur: "I cannot recall it to mind," "That puts me in mind of a story," "I dismissed it from my mind," "He gave his mind to the problem," "His mind was wandering," "There was something on his mind," "He made up his mind," "I had a great mind to do it," "He was in two minds," "I gave him a piece of my mind," "He told me what was in his mind," "The thought passed through my mind," "His mind was filled with gloomy forebodings," "You have set my mind at rest," "He saw it with his mind's eye," "My mind to me a kingdom is," "The poor fellow is out of his mind," "Use your mind, boy, think!." If we take account of the verb, we may add: "Mind you, he is no fool," "Mind the step!," "Mind the baby," "Do you mind if I open the window?." Clearly there is no simple definition that can be substituted for the word "mind" in all these contexts. And the reason is not that a word which originally meant the same as *res cogitans* has come to be used in a variety of idiomatic phrases. On the contrary, the phrases I have cited are among the basic usages of the word, and talk of mind as a substance is an innovation of philosophers. But a list of the basic usages is not a collection of items related one to another only by different partial resemblances, i.e. in such a way that while A resembles B and B resembles C there is nothing in common to A and C except their being like B in some respect. For there is one idea involved in all the usages, namely, that of thinking as a private event, and this, of course, is the reason why philosophers with their passion for simplification have talked of minds as thinking substances. I do not wish to suggest, however, that thinking is a simple notion which we should take as one of our indefinables. On the contrary, it is obviously complex in various ways. But it is important to connect the notion with our use of the word "mind" because we can show in this way that talk of minds is not equivalent to talk about behaviour and tendencies to behaviour of various sorts. It is true that men may think through action, and in particular through speech (as we admit when we use the phrase "thinking aloud"); but this is possible only because they can perceive their own actions. In short, all talk of minds presupposes the occurrence of experiences.

4.

The merit of Broad's use of the phrase "mental event" is that it directs attention to the occurrences which we should consider when we engage in the philosophy of mind and does so without prejudging any issue except that of behaviourism. But it may perhaps lend undeserved plausibility to the epiphenomenalist theory which Broad finally accepts. At the beginning of *The Mind and its Place in Nature* he defends common-sense interactionism against many of the objections that have been urged against it in the name of science, but at the end of this book and again in his *EMcP* he says that epiphenomenalism is a more reasonable hypothesis in the light of the information collected by scientists. This change of front is surprising, since it is not preceded by any new assessment of the empirical evidence, and I can only suppose that something in the philosophical analyses which come between the two pronouncements has made him think the evidence more favourable to epiphenomenalism than he was once prepared to allow. But the only result of his analyses that seems relevant is his conclusion that minds (or, as he sometimes says, selves) may be constructions from mental events. It has often been argued that the development of empirical science points the way to epiphenomenalism because it involves an assumption of the conservation of physical energy without any corresponding assumption of conservation in the psychical realm. When it is contended that mental unity can be explained satisfactorily by talk of relations between mental events, this argument seems much stronger, and it may well come to be thought that interactionism is bound up with a discredited metaphysical theory of mental substances. For those who call themselves interactionists commonly say that minds and bodies act upon each other; but minds that are only constructs from mental events cannot act upon bodies or suffer the action of bodies on them any more than tunes can interact with fiddles or plays with theatres. The mere fact that natural scientists who venture an opinion on the status of minds often take epiphenomenalism for granted is no good argument in favour of the doctrine, and I do not think that it is likely to impress Broad, who is too well-versed in the history of thought to be much influenced by intellectual fashions. His acceptance of epiphenomenalism as a plausible theory calls therefore for some explanation such as that I have suggested. Whatever the cause, the result is unfortunate; for epiphenomenalism is a thoroughly unsatisfactory doctrine which commits its holders to theses even stranger than those they hope to avoid. In what follows I shall draw attention to some of these implications, dealing first with those that concern the notion of substance and then with those that concern the notion of causation.

One consequence of epiphenomenalism is the proposition that mental events happen to nothing in that sense in which events have been commonly supposed to happen to substances. For it is agreed by all upholders of the theory that there are no mental substances (as distinct from continuants which may be described as logical constructions from mental events); and it is impossible that mental events should happen to any substances which epiphenomenalists are disposed to admit. The latter point, however, is not conceded by all epiphenomenalists. Some of them, including at times Broad himself, suggest that mental events may perhaps be said to happen to bodies, and even that they may perhaps be numerically identical with neural events, as the morning star is numerically identical with the evening star though recognized in a different way. I have already commented on this suggestion and drawn attention to the fact that Broad seems to abandon it in his latest references to epiphenomenalism. It is sufficient, therefore, to add here that if a body were said to have experiences we could indeed by an effort give some sense to the phrase, but not the sense required by the suggestion. For we should understand that the person owning the body had experiences, not that the experiences happened to the body in the same sense as that in which physical events might be said to happen to the body.

On various occasions Broad has written sympathetically of the theory of independent events first propounded by Hume, and he may therefore find nothing disturbing in the consequence I have just tried to draw from epiphenomenalism. But I think he should be disturbed by it; for it is incompatible with what he says about prehension (or acquaintance) and about introspection. If mental events do not happen to substances (except maybe in a secondary or derivative sense of the phrase), no mental event can be the prehension of anything, because prehension is supposed to be a simple and unanalysable relation between a prehending subject and an object such as a sensum or an image. Clearly a mental event which does not happen to a subject in any sense whatever cannot be a prehension, nor can a mental event qualify for the title merely by happening to a subject in the sense of being sympsychic with some other mental events though it might have occurred without being so related to any other events. The difficulty for Broad's theory of introspection is different, but connected with that we have just noticed. Because he is not a momentary event but an entity which endures for some time, he wishes to maintain that his introspective knowledge of his own mind must be something like his perception of a material thing. But it is essential to the epiphenomenalist theory that minds are not objects of the same type as material things, and it seems to follow from this that introspection cannot be like perception except in a very superficial way. Just as talk of prehension is plausible only so long as we assume that mental events happen to mental substances, so the suggestion of a detailed analogy between introspection and perception is plausible only so long as we think of minds as entities of the same general type as material things. It is not indeed essential that we should think of minds as substances; for we might perhaps defend the analogy by arguing with Hume and Russell that both minds and material things are logical constructions from neutral elements. But in either case we should be committed to a philosophical theory very different from epiphenomenalism.

The considerations I have just put forward are only *argumenta ad hominem*, which Broad could easily evade by abandoning what he has said about prehension and introspection; and I must admit that I cannot produce any conclusive general argument against the theory of independent events. Sometimes, indeed, I find myself inclined to think it may be true. But the theory is undoubtedly queer, and Broad himself shrinks from full acceptance of it even when he is not concerned at the moment with prehension or introspection. For although he sometimes talks as though he thought it possible for mental events to happen without happening to any substance, he declares that the notion of a mental continuant (i.e. something to which mental events happen) is empirical only in being the application of an *a priori* concept to empirical material. If mental events could happen without happening to any substance, a mental continuant would be merely a logical construction from such mental events as were found to be contingently related in a certain way. Why then should it be said that there is something *a priori* in the notion?

In the philosophy of Hume the doctrine of independent events is associated with the view that causes are no more than invariable antecedents. Broad has pointed out, however, that it is impossible to reconcile epiphenomenalism with the Humean analysis of causation since there is undoubtedly causation between mental and physical events in the only sense in which according to Hume there is causation anywhere. I am not disturbed by his rejection of Hume's view, but I do not find that he has succeeded in explaining satisfactorily that usage of the word "cause" in which he thinks it reasonable to say that mental events are caused by physical events but never themselves cause other physical events.

Apparently epiphenomenalism involves a distinction between two kinds of causation, which may conveniently be called horizontal and vertical since they are represented by horizontal and vertical lines in the diagram commonly used for exposition of the theory:

Mental   β
                  ↑
Physical   A → B → C

Horizontal causation is necessitation of one physical event by another physical event earlier in time, whereas vertical causation is necessitation of a mental event by a simultaneous physical event. Broad allows also for the possibility of what might be called diagonal causation, i.e. direct necessitation of a mental event by a preceding physical event, but I do not think we need consider this complication, since in those cases where the dependence of mental on physical is generally agreed it seems natural to think of the two as simultaneous. We assume, for example, that after-sensations occur *so long as* our sense organs and our central nervous system continue to be in an excited state after the cessation of stimuli.

Now β may be a wish for the occurrence of a bodily movement C, but according to the epiphenomenalist doctrine it cannot be a cause of C. What is the force of this denial? Having assumed that β cannot occur without a certain physical event B in a brain and that B necessitates C, we must allow that the occurrence of β is a sufficient condition for the occurrence of C. Why then should we not say that β is a cause of C? Obviously it cannot be a cause of C by purely horizontal causation, since it is a mental event and horizontal causation is a relation that holds only between physical events; but this is a triviality about the technical terminology we have introduced, and we must assume that epiphenomenalists mean something more important. Broad offers two suggestions; first, that according to epiphenomenalism the sequence ABC would have been unaltered if there had been no β, and second that B is an indispensable link in the chain of causes leading to C, whereas β is not. These formulations are presumably intended to be equivalent, and it seems to me that they are both open to the objection that if B and β are inseparable we cannot possibly get any direct empirical evidence to show what B would produce by itself. Even the epiphenomenalist admits that β is a sure sign of C; when he nevertheless asserts that it is not a cause, his reason must be that he thinks he has some insight into the way in which one event produces another and can therefore say that B is the only active partner in the pair Bβ.

Once we have posed the problem of body and mind in the fashion suggested by the epiphenomenalist's diagram we find it reasonable to look forward to a time when we shall know enough about the fine structure of the nervous system to show that A must be followed by B and B by C according to purely physical laws. But even such an advance of knowledge would not entitle us to say that β was not a cause of C; for one sort of explanation is not necessarily incompatible with another, and in his talk of vertical causation the epiphenomenalist has already allowed for a kind of connexion not covered by physical theory. When he decides to say that mental events are never causes, he seems to be acting in an arbitrary and even paradoxical manner. For the word "cause" was undoubtedly first used to assign responsibility to conscious beings, and some philosophers of science have even maintained that there is no place for it in advanced physical theory.

These difficulties about substance and causation are small, however, in comparison with the great paradox of epiphenomenalism, that is, the suggestion that we are necessarily mistaken in all our ordinary thought about human action. It is true that in ordinary life we do not talk of interaction between mind and body or use phrases like "mental event" and "physical event;" but we constantly speak of thoughts, desires, intentions, and actions in a way which is declared incorrect by the epiphenomenalists. Thus a man who is describing his movements in detail may say "The sight of a postman opening a letter box reminded me that my wife had asked me to get some stamps, and I paused for a moment to think out the easiest way of carrying out her commission. Then I turned left because I had decided that it would be best to go to the General Post Office, but I found the crowds and traffic in the main street so disagreeable that I changed my mind and decided to get the stamps at a smaller office on the way home." Here mental events are cited in a naive untheoretical fashion as causes of other events, both mental and physical, and this, I suppose, is why Broad has described interactionism as the view of common sense. At any rate he is under no misapprehension about the fact that epiphenomenalism runs counter to common sense; but to my great surprise he writes as though he did not regard this as a very serious objection to the theory. In his inaugural lecture on *Determinism, Indeterminism, and Liberatarianism* he cocks a similar snook at common sense when he says "it is . . . highly probable that the notion of categorical obligability is a delusive notion, which neither has nor can have any application" though most people, including himself, think it is expressed by a common use of "ought" and "ought not."[31] It would have been less surprising, because more in accordance with the current practice of philosophers, if in each case he had tried to reconcile his view with common sense and argued that it was opposed only to some other philosophical view. But he makes no attempt to prove that epiphenomenalism can be squared with common sense, and here at least I think he is right. What shocks me is the cheerfulness with which he rejects opinions in his philosophical moments while admitting that he continues to share them with all his fellow men during the rest of his life.

I must admit, however, that I find it very difficult to argue against

31 *EHP*, 206 and 217.

Broad's position in a way that satisfies me. Many attempts have been made to show that epiphenomenalism is in some way self-refuting, but none that I have seen appears to me conclusive. And I do not like to fall back on the device of trying to embarrass my opponent by asking him in a solemn tone such questions as, "Do you really mean to say that no one ever changed his direction because he had just remembered a commission from his wife?" Sometimes conversions may be secured by this technique, but I doubt whether I should have any success with Broad, who has been exposed to a great deal of such propaganda from persons more forceful than myself, and in any case I do not think this method of controversy leads to an increase of understanding. Perhaps the best I can do is to conclude by drawing attention to two features of the situation which seem to me very curious indeed.

In the first place the proposition which Broad asks us to reject, namely, that mental events are sometimes causes of physical events, is one which belongs to the hard core of common sense. Many beliefs that were at one time accounted parts of common sense have since been abandoned, and others which at one time seemed surprising have become part of the common sense of our age. But the belief that our thoughts affect the movements of our bodies is one which always forms part of common sense; and although Broad asks us to give it up, I am sure that he does not think we *can* give it up for long. I am confident, for example, that when he sits down to reply to this criticism he will do so with no doubt at all about the possibility of determining by his thought what shall appear upon the paper. For it is evident that we cannot apply the epiphenomenalist theory to ourselves in the moment in which we debate what we shall do. I do not suggest that this by itself proves the falsity of epiphenomenalism, but rather that it establishes a special status for the belief which epiphenomenalists reject. If anyone asks for a justification of it, we should not reject his demand as senseless, but we may properly reply that belief in the efficacy of thought is presupposed in all debates about the efficacy of thought.

Secondly, the considerations that lead Broad to favour epiphenomenalism are of a very peculiar sort. Although he makes it clear that epiphenomenalism involves a metaphysical doctrine about causation, he does not maintain that it can be established by *a priori* argument. And although he says that he is moved by empirical considerations, he does not suggest that belief in the causal efficacy of mental events could ever be refuted by the production of counter-examples. He presents the issue as though it were one of choice between explanatory theories, and tells us that epiphenomenalism gets his vote because it is simpler and more elegant than any of its rivals; but the nearest he comes to indicating

an empirical test is when he says that epiphenomenalism would be untenable if we had good reason to believe in the occurrence of mental
events out of association with bodies. Now I think we can at least understand the suggestion that there might be mental events out of association
with bodies, and so I suppose we must allow that Broad's epiphenomenalism is like a scientific theory in excluding some conceivable states
of affairs, but I do not think it is adequately specified by an account of
the imaginable situations which it excludes. For, as I have already tried
to explain, it is not at all clear to me that mental events must be supposed to be without effects merely because they are inseparably associated with bodily events. When Broad declares for epiphenomenalism,
he seems to be making a choice on purely aesthetic grounds without
either *a priori* or empirical arguments to back his preference. Whether
or not the epiphenomenalism which he adopts in this way can properly
be described as a theory, I shall not attempt to decide, but I find it very
strange indeed that it should be set up in rivalry to common sense.

WILLIAM C. KNEALE

EXETER COLLEGE
OXFORD UNIVERSITY

14

H. H. Price

THE NATURE AND STATUS OF SENSE-DATA IN
BROAD'S EPISTEMOLOGY

I.

TO THE best of my knowledge, the term "sense-datum" occurs only once in Professor Broad's major writings, and then only in a non-technical sense (*PPR*, 68). His own term is 'sensum,' and his special version of the sense-datum epistemology is called, by himself, "the Sensum Theory." In examining any philosopher's views, it is best to use his own terminology so far as one can. I propose then to discuss the nature and status of *sensa* in Professor Broad's epistemology.

We must notice, however, that although Prof. Broad has worked out the Sensum Theory so fully, he has always insisted that there are alternatives to it. In *Scientific Thought* he mentions only one alternative, the theory of a Multiple Relation of Appearing. In *MPN*, ch. 4, he mentions another as well, the Multiple Inherence Theory. In that chapter both these non-sensum theories are stated in considerable detail, and they are then compared with the Sensum Theory. We shall probably be justified in thinking that Prof. Broad himself prefers the Sensum Theory to the other two, if only because he has thought it worth while to devote some three hundred pages of his most important book to the detailed exposition of it. (*ST*, 227–548). But though it is convenient and usual to speak of 'Professor Broad's Sensum Theory,' we should remember that he has never absolutely committed himself to it.

A more important point is that he has always doubted whether the Sensum Theory applies equally well to all the different varieties of sense-experience. This is because the Sensum Theory is based upon an *act-object* analysis of sensation. Having a sensation of red, it says, consists in being aware of a particular which is red, and smelling a smell consists in being aware of an odorous particular. Now Prof. Broad holds that the various types of experiences which are traditionally called 'sensations' can be arranged in a series or scale, from visual sensation at the top end to organic sensation at the bottom. The scale runs as follows: (1) sight, (2) touch, (3) hearing, (4) smell, (5) temperature-sense, (6) taste,

(7) organic sensation. At the top end of the scale, the act-object analysis is the obvious one. When I experience a visual field, it is natural to say that I am being aware of, or intuitively apprehending, a number of coloured and shaped particulars (visual sensa) which are spatially related to one another. But when one turns to the bottom of the scale, the act-object analysis is not nearly so plausible. Having a toothache *could* be described as being aware of an organic sensum with a 'toothachy' quality. But it is much more natural to think of the term 'toothache' as an internal accusative, specifying the way one feels; I have a toothachy feeling, or feel toothachily. This is still more obvious when one considers 'all-overish' organic sensations like feeling tired. One *could*—just—say 'I am aware of a mass of organic sensa which is pervaded throughout by a "fatiguy" quality.' But the ordinary expression 'feeling tired' seems to fit the experience much better. Here the word 'tired' is an internal accusative which describes the *way* one feels. If we now turn to the middle range of the scale, we find that the act-object analysis is the more natural one for touch and hearing, while the internal accusative analysis is the more natural one for taste. Smell (and I think Prof. Broad would add, the sensation of temperature) is just on the borderline. If I smell onions it is about equally plausible to say either (a) that I am aware of an 'onionish' olfactory sensum or (b) that I just have a smell-experience with an 'onionish' quality.

This notion of a scale of sense-experiences already occurs in Prof. Broad's first work, *PPR* (pp. 64 *et seq.*). He returns to it in *Scientific Thought,* and again in his British Academy Lecture, *Berkeley's Argument about Material Substance.*[1] I propose to consider what he says about it in *Scientific Thought* (pp. 254 *et seq.*). He maintains there that *if* we are compelled to apply the one analysis or the other throughout the whole series, the act-object analysis is to be preferred. Each of the seven different types of experiences traditionally called 'sensations' would then be analysed into an act of sensing, having a sensum of one kind or another for its object. We *can* just bring ourselves to say that someone who has toothache is intuitively apprehending a toothachy particular; whereas we *cannot* bring ourselves to say that someone who sees a tomato is experiencing in a red, round and bulgy manner—that the expressions 'red,' 'round,' 'bulgy,' 'in the middle of the visual field' are no more than internal accusatives describing the way he is seeing. But why should we suppose that one and the same analysis must apply to all the experiences traditionally called sensations? Prof. Broad sees no good reason why we should. Let us say, then, that the act-object analysis does apply to sight, touch and hearing, but does not apply to

[1] *Proceedings of the British Academy,* 1942.

organic sensation. By this account of the matter, there are visual sensa, tactual sensa and auditory sensa. But there are no organic sensa. The traditional phrase 'organic sensation' may suggest that there are; but really there are only bodily feelings of various sorts, and these are not analysable in the act-object manner at all. It follows that the sensum theory is *not* a theory of all the types of experience traditionally called 'sensations,' but only of sight, touch and hearing.

There are however two 'loose ends' in this solution of the problem. First, it is not clear whether the act-object analysis applies to smell and to the sense of temperature. Perhaps we may assume that Prof. Broad does not wish to apply it to taste, (though like most philosophers he has very little to say about this sense). We may infer this from the fact that 'taste-sensa' are not mentioned in his elaborate account of the Perceptual Object (*ST*, chs. 9 and 10).[2] I shall have more to say about the Perceptual Object later. For the moment, it is enough to remind the reader that the perceptual object is a very complex group of sensa, roughly equivalent to what common sense calls 'a thing.' Within this complex group of sensa there are a number of sub-groups—a visual sub-group, a tactual sub-group, and often other sub-groups as well, for example an auditory one. Now 'heat sensa' are explicitly mentioned in Prof. Broad's account of the perceptual object (*ST*, 309f). It seems, then, that the act-object analysis does apply to temperature sensation. But oddly enough, nothing is said about smells at all. It seems fairly plain, however, that smell-sensa have as good a right to be included in the perceptual object as auditory sensa or heat sensa. They have somewhat similar spatial properties. Like auditory sensa and heat sensa, they are spread out around the region where the object is said to be located. Their intensity is greater at places which are near to this region and smaller at more distant places. Moreover, in special cases the smell sensa may be spatially dissociated from the visual and tactual constituents of the object in somewhat the same way as echoes and mirror-images. The smell of a fox may remain in a place for some minutes or even hours after the fox has gone away. I can still smell a smell of cabbages in the kitchen long after the cabbages have been removed to the dining-room.

So much for the first loose end. If I have tied it up correctly, Prof. Broad's sensum theory, with its act-object analysis of sensation, does apply to the sense of temperature, as well as to sight, touch and hearing; and in consistency it ought to be applied to smell too. The frontier line, so to speak, which divides the sensum domain from the feeling domain would be drawn between smell and taste (not a very easy place to draw it,

2 The term 'Perceptual Object' is first introduced on p. 330.

because it is not in practice at all easy to distinguish tastes from smells).

I turn to the second loose end which is left over in Prof. Broad's solution of the problem about the scale of sense-experiences. Here again I must refer the reader to Prof. Broad's discussion of the Perceptual Object in *ST*, chs. 9 and 10. It will be remembered that kinaesthetic experience plays a very important part in these chapters. Public space (as opposed to the private space of a single sense-field) is identified with the 'movement continuum' which we conceive of by correlating kinaesthetic experiences with visual ones. Now in his account of the movement continuum Prof. Broad always speaks of kinaesthetic *sensations* and never of kinaesthetic *sensa*. He evidently regards kinaesthetic sensations as a specially important sort of 'bodily feelings' and does not wish to analyse them in the act-object manner. I am not myself complaining of the term 'kinaesthetic sensation.' It is perfectly intelligible even to the speaker of ordinary language, provided he knows a little Greek. But unfortunately Prof. Broad has previously drawn a sharp distinction between 'true sensations' on the one hand and 'bodily feelings' on the other. (*ST*, 257) 'True sensations,' in that passage, are experiences to which the act-object analysis applies; they consist in the sensing of one or another sort of sensum. If he wishes to stick to this terminology, he should not have spoken later about kinaesthetic sensations, but only about kinaesthetic *feelings*. I think, however, that it would be better to abandon the notion of 'true sensations.' Instead, Prof. Broad could distinguish between sensations of the act-object type and sensations of the 'feeling' or internal accusative type. This would allow us to speak of organic sensations in general, and of kinaesthetic sensations in particular, as we are all accustomed to do.

II.

So much for Prof. Broad's own solution of the difficult problem of the scale or series of sense-experiences, from sight at the one end to bodily feeling at the other. I shall now venture to offer some criticisms and to suggest that the problem is even more complicated than he thinks it is. Prof. Broad has always insisted that visual experience is the stronghold, so to speak, of the act-object analysis. He says it is all but impossible *not* to distinguish two distinct factors in every visual experience, an act of sensing on the one hand, and a visual sensum which is its object, on the other. But, fortunately or unfortunately, there are several different sorts of visual experience. We can agree that an act-object analysis does seem the most plausible one for focal vision. But what about non-focal vision?

As we pass from the focal part of the normal visual field, with its clearly differentiated and sharply-individualised colour expanses, and move towards the margin, the act-object analysis seems less and less compelling. It is not utterly absurd to suggest that marginal and near-marginal vision is rather a kind of 'feeling' than a kind of intuitive apprehension. Now it is at least logically possible that there might be a percipient whose visual fields contained no focal part at all. Perhaps people with very defective eyesight do actually experience visual fields of this kind, in which clear outlines and sharply-individualised colour expanses are entirely lacking. Such a percipient, I believe, would not find the act-object analysis so compelling for *his* visual experience. Vision for him might be more like what hearing or smelling are for us.

Another kind of visual experience which is perfectly normal, though not very common, is the experience one has when one lies on one's back and gazes upwards at a cloudless blue sky. Here again the visual field is not divided up into sharply-individualised 'colour patches.' There is just one single visible expanse, bright blue in the middle and fading away gradually into colourlessness towards the margins. This visual experience, again, does not *demand* an act-object analysis. On the contrary, it is not wholly unlike bodily feeling.

We should also consider certain abnormal visual experiences. There is a very interesting kind of visual experience which one has when one is just on the point of fainting for some time, without actually losing consciousness. The visual field which is characteristic of this fascinating psycho-physical state is almost impossible to describe. One can only say that it is 'confused' and highly unstable. There are no clearly-delimited shapes which 'stay put,' as the shapes in the centre of the normal visual field do. There are constant changes of visual depth. The walls of the room appear to move in and out. Doors and windows appear to lean over first to one side and then to another. This rather phantasmagoric kind of visual experience does not seem to fit the act-object analysis particularly well. The same could be said, I think, of the visual experience one has when one is just coming out of a fainting-fit or other period of unconsciousness. Again, when one is completely dazzled for a few seconds by some very intense illumination, does *this* visual experience fit the act-object analysis either? Is it natural to describe it in the sensum terminology?

We should also consider the distinction which some psychologists have drawn between surface colours and film colours. (For this purpose, I am going to regard black, white and grey as colours.) Philosophers are accustomed to assume that in all vision we are aware of coloured *surfaces*. But this does not seem to be true. There are film colours as well as colours spread out over surfaces. Let us consider what we see when we look into a cloud, or a mist, or a haze of smoke. Here we are not aware of a surface at all. What we see does have the property of 'visual depth,' but it is an unusual sort of depth. A surface is *at* a depth —'over there'—but it does not have a depth *within* it. Its colour is only skin-deep, so to speak. A film-colour does have a depth within it. Here the colour is not just skin-deep, but has a kind of visible thickness. It extends 'out and away' in the depth-dimension, whereas a surface colour does not. Professor D. Katz tries to indicate this peculiarity of film colours by saying that they have a 'spongy' character. Sometimes a film colour is not *at* a depth at all though it has a depth within it (for example, when we are wholly immersed in a cloud or mist). Sometimes it is at a depth—as when we look into the smoke of a bonfire from ten yards' distance—and yet not quite in the way that a surface-colour is. Even though it is 'over there,' it does not have a sharply-delimited beginning or end in the depth-dimension.

But these are not the only examples of film-colours. Prof. Katz has pointed out that almost any coloured surface can be turned into a film colour by viewing it through a paper tube. Or we may look through a small hole in a screen of some kind. We do not often look into a room through the key hole. There may easily be moral objections to such a phenomenological experiment. But if we can bring ourselves to try, we may be somewhat surprised to find that the view has a distinctly film-colourish character. One may notice the same thing if one attends to the view which can be seen through a hole in a wall, or a crack in a fence, or a small gap in a thick hedge. Moreover, it could be argued, I think, that in any fairly wide prospect, such as the view seen from the top of a hill, the more distant parts of the landscape have a distinctly film-colourish character, though the nearer parts consist of coloured surfaces. I suspect that philosophers live too much indoors, or in confined spaces such as city streets and college quadrangles. Here surface-colours do predominate, at any rate in the central part of the visual field. Moreover, we ought to consider the kind of vision we have in twilight and semi-darkness, an experience which does not occur at all frequently if we live most of our lives in well-lit rooms or streets. In twilight and semi-darkness, nearly everything we see has something of the 'internal depth' or 'sponginess' which is characteristic of film-colours.

Now I think it must be admitted that film-colours are ignored in Prof. Broad's account of the phenomenology and epistemology of visual experience. (They are also ignored by the sense-datum philosophers, or by the other sense-datum philosophers if we may count Prof. Broad as a sense-datum philosopher.) The question is whether this omission has any relevance to our present problem concerning the act-object analysis of sensation. I find this question very puzzling. But I would venture to suggest that for film-colour vision the act-object analysis does not have quite the 'feel of inevitability' which it has for surface-colour vision; and that when the *entire* visual field consists of one more or less uniform film-colour (as when we are wholly immersed in a translucent cloud or mist) the internal accusative analysis feels quite as plausible as the act-object analysis, if not more so.

Let us now turn to the opposite end of Prof. Broad's scale of sense-experiences—organic sensation. Here Prof. Broad finds the act-object analysis forced and unnatural, though not absolutely impossible. As we have seen, he concludes that organic sensation is best described as 'bodily feeling' and that the internal accusative analysis is here the most appropriate one. I venture to suggest that this is an over-simplification. Organic sensation is no more homogeneous than visual sensation; and as the act-object analysis fits some sorts of visual sensation better than others, the internal accusative analysis fits some sorts of organic sensation better than others. It is very plausible for 'all-overish' organic sensations like feeling tired or feeling feverish. It does seem very strange to say that one is sensing a complex organic sensum which is pervaded throughout by a 'fatiguy' quality. But when we consider sharply localised organic sensations, such as a toothache or an itch in one's left big toe, the act-object terminology does not seem so strange. It would not be at all odd to say that one senses an achy or an itchy sensum located in this or that part of one's total organic sense-field. A stomach-ache, though it does not have sharp boundaries, could be fairly described as a voluminous achy sensum with a kind of shape. Nor do I see any oddity in speaking of kinaesthetic sensa. Finally, it must be remembered that tactual sensation always has an organic component or aspect; and Prof. Broad has no hesitation in applying the act-object analysis to tactual sensation.

If I am right so far, the distinction Prof. Broad wishes to draw between 'act-object' experiences and 'internal accusative' experiences (feelings) does not divide the whole scale or series of sense-experiences into two clear-cut parts—sight, touch, hearing, thermal sensation and smell on the one side, taste and organic sensation on the other. On the contrary, it looks as if the distinction might have to be drawn *within* each member of the series. At any rate there is a case for drawing it within sight at the one end, and within organic sensation at the other. And if so, the scope of the Sensum Theory—the range of experiences to which it is applicable—will be a good deal more limited than Prof. Broad admits it to be. To be sure, its scope will be enlarged a little by the inclusion of some organic sensa; not all organic sensations will be written off as 'feelings,' as they formerly were. But this gain is much more than counter-balanced by the *exclusion* of several sorts of visual experience; and presumably several sorts of touch, hearing, thermal sensation and smell will have to be excluded from the Sensum Theory's scope on similar grounds. To make matters worse, the line between 'act-object' experiences and 'internal accusative' experiences *within* any one sense-modality does not seem to be a hard and fast one. Just how far from the focus must a part of the visual field be, before the act-object analysis ceases to be applicable? If one is somewhere near fainting but not quite on the brink, does one apply the sensing-and-sensum terminology to one's visual experience or the internal accusative terminology? If an ache is localised, but only vaguely, shall we call it a sensum, or shall we just say we feel achily?

III.

Can anything be done to clear up these difficulties? Perhaps we might get some light on them if we put the word 'object' in the plural for a moment and spoke of an 'act-object*s* analysis.' The language of sensing and sensa is appropriate when the sense-field divides itself up into a number of sharply differentiated and, so to speak, well-individuated items. This condition is most completely fulfilled in the focal portion of an indoor and well illuminated visual field, where we have a number of clear-cut visible surfaces, distinguished from each other by well marked colour contrasts, and each located at a determinate visual depth. As we pass from the focal part of the visual field towards the margin, this clear-cut individuation of visible surfaces begins to fail, and we fairly soon reach a point where there is, as we say, 'confusion' or 'indistinctness' (in the visual, not the conceptual sense of those words). This part of the visual field does *not* divide itself up into a plurality of well-individuated items—'patches' or 'expanses'—and we approach nearer to a condition of Bergsonian interpenetration. Moreover, in the marginal and near-marginal part of the visual field we are all colour-blind. The one property which 'stands out' in this part of the visual field is *movement,* and no doubt there are good biological reasons for this. But as a psychologist has remarked, it is 'movement without anything that moves,' very unlike the visible movements one is aware of in the focal part of the field, where there is a clearly delimited *something,* a coloured and shaped particular, which does the moving or to which the movement happens.[3]

It is still possible to say that in marginal and near-marginal vision we are 'intuitively apprehending' something. But now if we use the word 'object' we must put it in the singular. There is just one residual sensum, whereas in the focal part of the field there are usually many sensa. Or perhaps (if only our linguistic rules would permit it) we really need to speak here *neither* in the singular *nor* in the plural. This part of the visual field is so to speak just 'an etcetera,' and we cannot properly describe it either as one or as many; or still more outrageously, we are tempted to say it is both. I cannot but think that none of the languages we are accustomed to use, neither ordinary nor technical, is really adequate for the description of marginal and near-marginal vision; and if we try to use them we find ourselves uttering paradoxes rather like those of the mystics.

Let us now reconsider some of the other examples mentioned earlier (pp. 461–3 above). There is, for instance, the experience one has when a clear blue sky fills the whole field of vision. Here again the important point is the absence of sharply-individualised and clear-cut visual items. What will not apply here is an act-objects analysis. What will not fit is the term 'sensa,' in the plural. But one could still say that there is a visual sensum, in the singular, or that the object (in the singular) of our awareness is just the whole visual field. The near-fainting kind of vision mentioned on p. 461 is in some ways similar. It is true that there is certainly plurality here. We are experiencing a 'many,' not just a 'one.' But it is not the sort of 'many' which we have in the focal part of the normal visual field. For now there is such instability and confusion that the visual field just will not divide itself up neatly into a number of clearly-individuated units. Here again we can speak of 'the object' of our awareness or intuitive apprehension, but not of 'the objects' of it, or only with extreme discomfort. What we sense is either one variegated and highly unstable sensum, or it is just the visual field as a whole. Or perhaps we might be tempted to say that here again, as in marginal and near-marginal vision, neither the language of plurality nor the language of unity quite fits.

Let us now consider film-colours. The relevant point here is not so much what I called their internal depth (Prof. Katz's 'sponginess') but rather the fact that this internal depth has neither a clear-cut beginning

---

[3] I once walked along the sidewalk beside a main road full of fast moving traffic. Gazing resolutely straight ahead, I tried my hardest to find words to describe my marginal vision of a passing motor car. The best phrase I could think of was 'a dark flash.'

nor a clear-cut end. One cannot say that the 'visual thickness' of a film-colour extends just from *this* depth to *that*. Thus in the depth-dimension a film-colour does not have the precise localisation which a surface colour has. Moreover, it very often lacks precise localisation in the lateral and vertical dimensions as well.[4] This is why film-colour vision does not fit an act-objects analysis so easily as surface-colour vision does. There is a lack of clear-cut individualisation. In the extreme case, where we are wholly immersed in a cloud or a mist, the whole visual field is filled by a more or less uniform film-colour, and does not break up into a plurality of spatially-related items at all. Here the act-objects analysis is entirely unsuitable. The sensum language, which (if I am right) is essentially a language of *sensa* in the plural, can no longer be applied.

We can now see why Prof. Broad puts hearing, temperature, sensation and smell in the intermediate part of his scale or series of sense-experiences, and why he thinks that the act-object analysis becomes as it were less compelling here, though still applicable. It is because there is a certain degree of 'interpenetration' here. In each of these three types of sense-experience there is localisation, but the localisation does not have anything like the clear-cut character which it has in the focal part of the normal visual field or in the 'epicritic' (as opposed to the 'protopathic') type of touch. Indeed, in his discussion of hearing in *ST*, 308, Prof. Broad seems to me to exaggerate this 'interpenetration.' He says that every sound is present everywhere in the auditory field, though it is 'more' present in some parts than in others. I think this is only true when we are hearing several very loud sounds at the same time. I am now hearing the gentle sound of my clock ticking and the chirping of some birds outside the window. I do not think it is true that both these sounds are present *everywhere* in my auditory field; even if we add that one is 'more' present in one part of it and the other in another. It seems to me sufficient to say that one is on (or from) the right and the other on the left. However this may be, the localisation of sounds is always somewhat vague. Sounds may have a voluminous character, but they do not have shapes. (It may perhaps be different for creatures with moveable ears, capable of convergence; perhaps for a dog or a donkey sounds do have shapes, though even so the shapes are probably 'fuzzy-edged' at the best.) In smell, and in the experience of radiant heat, localisation is usually still vaguer than it is in hearing. Should these

---

[4] There are occasional exceptions: e.g. looking into a tank full of water. Here the water has a film-colourish character—a faintly-green tinge with a certain 'visual thickness.' But in the left-to-right and up-and-down dimensions the film-colour is sharply bounded by the borders of the tank. So too when one looks into a smoke-filled room through an open doorway. The film-colour is sharply bounded by the internal edges of the doorway.

considerations make us hesitate at all about applying the act-object analysis to these three types of sense-experience? I think not. Whether localisation is good, bad or indifferent we can still say that we are *being aware of* something, or intuitively apprehending something. What we should hesitate about is not the act-object analysis but the act-object*s* analysis. Does the something we are aware of divide itself up into a plurality of co-existent parts or items, and are they sufficiently differentiated to justify us in saying that we are sensing several sensa (in the plural)? The answer is 'Yes' in some cases and 'No' in others.

We can now suggest a solution for the difficulties raised on pp. 463f. Perhaps the doubts which we have about applying the act-object analysis to certain sorts of sense-experience arise from a mistaken assumption. We assume, wrongly, that wherever the act-*object* analysis is applicable, the act-*objects* analysis must be applicable. There certainly are experiences, within each of the sense-modalities, to which the act-objects analysis will not apply; from this we conclude, wrongly, that the act-object analysis will not apply to them either. Or perhaps we may put it this way:—in some cases, but by no means in all, the act-object analysis takes the special form of an act-objects analysis. If a certain experience is analysable in the act-objects manner, this of course entails that it is analysable in the act-object manner. But the converse entailment does not hold. It may still be true that one is aware of something (is 'intuitively apprehending' something) even though one is not aware of it in a discriminating way, and even though one cannot be aware of it in a discriminating way, because the 'object' of one's awareness contains no clear-cut distinctions within it and does not break up into a plurality of well-differentiated items.

I conclude, then, that the act-object analysis does apply to all the different types of experience traditionally called sensations, from visual sensation at the one end to organic sensation at the other. But in some sorts of sense experience (and they are to be found within each of the sense-modalities) the act-object*s* analysis does not apply. Here, though we can still distinguish between the sensing and the sensed, we cannot distinguish between sensing and *sensa* in the plural. Either we must just say that there is one sensum, or else we must say that there is no sensum at all, but only a sense-field.

As we saw earlier, Prof. Broad thinks that there are cases when the act-object analysis *can* be applied, but only in a forced and artificial manner; having a headache would be an example. I suggest that in saying this he is partly right and partly wrong. He is partly wrong, because he has not distinguished between 'act-object' and 'act-objects.' He is partly right, because the applicability of the act-object*s* analysis really is a matter of degree; it depends upon the *degree* of internal differentiation which a particular sense-field has. In my attempt to describe how a sense-field breaks itself up into a plurality of different sensa, I have had to use terms like 'clear cut,' 'sharply contrasted,' 'well-individuated.' All these characteristics are matters of degree. As I have tried to show, they are sometimes present in some degree even in organic sensation, but seldom or never in the degree which they normally have in the central part of a well-lit indoor visual field. A toothache, or a twinge of pain in the right ankle, is seldom as 'clear cut' as the visible surface of a white teacup placed on a brown table;[5] it is seldom as 'well individuated' as the visible surfaces of walls, windows, chimneys, human passers-by, pavements etc. are in a city street or a college quadrangle, either in daylight or in artificial light. But if we compare these two pains with what we experience in twilight vision, or with the more distant parts of a rural landscape seen on a hazy day, the results are rather different. It could well be said that the toothache or the twinge in the right ankle is *as* clear-cut, *as* well individuated as the visible appearance of an owl seen in twilight, or of a wood on the horizon on a rather misty autumn afternoon.

IV.

I have been arguing that the act-object analysis does apply to all the different forms of sense-experience, while the act-object*s* analysis only applies to some of them, in a greater or lesser degree, but not to all. Would it follow from this that the 'feeling somehow' analysis, with its internal accusatives, is just a mistake? It certainly looked plausible in some cases, and they are not confined to organic sensation and gustatory sensation, as Prof. Broad seems to think, but are to be found in all the different sense-modalities. Is this plausibility wholly spurious, a result of the mistaken assumption that where we can distinguish act and object we must also be able to distinguish act and object*s*? Our conclusion would certainly be a much more neat and tidy one if we could just reject the internal accusative analysis altogether. But obviously we cannot. There must be some good ground for using expressions like 'I feel tired,' 'I have a headache.'

I wish to suggest, however, that the ground for it is metaphysical rather than epistemological. I do not mean that the ordinary man who

---

[5] It is remarkable how often articles of furniture (especially chairs and tables) and pieces of crockery are used as examples in philosophical discussions of perception; and Prof. Broad's own favourite example is a penny. Such artificial objects as these are *designed* to have clear cut visible and tangible boundaries, so that they can be easily found and moved about.

speaks in this way is influenced by a metaphysical theory. But I think he does have something which might be called an unconscious metaphysical attitude. This metaphysical attitude is not absolutely stable or constant, as we shall see. But it governs the greater part of his everyday thought and behaviour. It consists in a tendency to identify himself with his body, or at any rate to regard his body as part of himself. The important part of the expression 'I feel tired' is the personal pronoun. From the purely epistemological point of view, the fact is just that he is aware of an undifferentiated organic sense-field pervaded throughout by a certain sensible quality; and this is an act-object situation (though not of course an act-objects one). But he takes this organic sense-field to be a state of his body, and he takes his body to be himself or at any rate part of himself. Thus he regards organic sensation as a kind of *self-consciousness;* and he says 'I feel tired' rather as he says 'I feel surprised' or 'I feel doubtful about such and such.' Nevertheless, this self-body identification is not absolutely invariable even in the experience of the most ordinary and un-Cartesian man. There are occasions when he regards his body as not-I. He has begun to do so when he calls it 'my body' (instead of just 'me'). 'My body feels itchy all over,' 'all my limbs feel like lead.' Here the word 'feels' has changed its meaning. It is no longer a self-consciousness word (cf. 'I feel surprised') but has become a sensible-appearing word (cf. 'the room feels warm,' 'this surface feels sticky'). 'My body feels itchy all over' is not so very different from 'this piece of wood feels smooth all over.' And if someone says 'my head aches,' 'my left forefinger smarts just here,' these again are sensible-quality verbs like 'glitter' or 'sparkle.' Indeed, it could be argued that 'my head aches' is just a straightforward piece of sensum terminology, *plus* the reference of the sensum to a material object, which that terminology of course allows. In these cases, then, the ordinary identification of self and body is suspended; and organic sensation is regarded as a way of getting information about a specially important and interesting material substance, but not as a form of self-consciousness. Consequently, the internal accusative language of '*I* feel so and so' no longer applies.

Thus when the internal accusative language does apply, this is not because the act-object distinction is absent, but because the object of awareness is identified with the 'I,' or at any rate regarded as part of it. The grounds for applying or refusing to apply the internal accusative analysis are not epistemological at all. The decisive point is something quite different—what one might loosely call the fluctuating boundary of the self. Sometimes the self is identified with the body; sometimes the two are distinguished, and the body is no longer 'me' but just a piece

of living matter with which I am very closely connected for weal or woe.
But what I have called the fluctuating boundary of the self may fluctu-
ate in the opposite direction too. *Any* sense-field, even a visual one, may
be regarded, on occasion, as part of oneself. It may be relevant here to
refer to the Neutral Monist theory, which holds that mind and matter
'overlap,' and that sensa or sense-data or sensible appearances are constituents of both. Strange as this theory is and untenable as it may be, it
is not just an arbitrary invention of certain eccentric philosophers. If
we take it not as a piece of metaphysics, but as a phenomenological description, there really are experiences which it fits. One can become
so completely 'absorbed' in the visual field that the ordinary antithesis
between 'me' on the one hand and the visible scene on the other is temporarily abolished. Sometimes this 'absorption' needs a deliberate effort
to initiate it, sometimes it just happens of itself. One loses the 'spectator
attitude' (still more, of course, the practical attitude). The view is experienced as a constituent of oneself, something that one lives through,
a part of one's own biography. That is one way of describing the experience.[6] Another is to say that the self is completely emptied of its contents, and there is nothing left but the visual field itself.

This Neutral Monist experience perhaps happens most easily when
the sense-field does not contain a plurality of clear-cut and sharply individuated items. A predominance of film colours over surface colours,
an absence of abrupt colour-contrasts, a vagueness in respect of visual
depth, are all favourable conditions. The discriminating type of sensory awareness (where 'act-object' takes the special form of 'act-object*s*')
tends to bring back the distinction between self and other-than-self. Perhaps the reason is this. When we are aware of a well-individuated sensum, we have a very strong tendency to take it as a constituent of a material thing or a physical event. Some philosophers, Prof. Broad among
them, distinguish between sensing and perceiving. Using this terminology, we may say that the discriminating kind of sensory awareness
is very closely connected with perceiving, i.e. with the 'referring' of
sensa to environmental things and events; and perceiving, in its turn, is
closely connected with the practical attitude, with action and incipient
action and readiness for action. Once we are in this perceptual-practical
attitude, which is of course our biologically-normal one, the distinction
between self and not-self is too obtrusive and insistent to be got rid of.
A house or an apple or a river, presenting itself in or through a well-
individuated sensum, is so very obviously something other than me and
independent of me. It is, so to speak, something with a life and a career

[6] I suppose this is what Wordsworth has in mind when he speaks somewhere of
people 'for whom high mountains are a *feeling*.'

of its own, quite distinct from mine, and something to which I must adapt myself in one way or another if I am to get what I want. (This animistic language does correspond to something in our naive perceptual attitude.) With the undiscriminating kind of sensory awarenesss— awareness of the act-object but not of the act-objects type—perception of physical things and events is much vaguer, and may even lapse altogether, if the experient is fortunate enough to be a somewhat 'dreamy' and unpractical person.

Nevertheless, this Neutral Monist experience *can* occur when the sense-field is 'clear and distinct' (in the sensory, not the conceptual meaning of these words) with clear-cut distinctions and sharp boundaries between one part of it and another. We may absorb ourselves in a visible landscape (or, I suppose, in the sound of a symphony) in an *aesthetic* way; and this is certainly compatible with clarity and distinctness. But it is still necessary, I think, that the pattern of the whole should predominate over the individuality of the parts. Some kind of Hegelian terminology seems to be needed here. The clear-cut divisions have to be taken not as separate and so to speak autonomous items, as they ordinarily are, but as 'moments' within a patterned whole. To be still more Hegelian, discrimination, though it is still there, is 'transcended' or 'taken up into a higher unity.' Such phrases, considered in a cool hour, may seem utterly nonsensical. But I am venturing to suggest that there are some sense-experiences which provide us with an ostensive definition of them.

So much for the difficult problems which arise from reflection on Prof. Broad's scale or series of sense-experiences. If I am right, we do *not* have to conclude that there are any sense-experiences to which the act-object analysis is inapplicable, though certainly there are some, in each part of the scale and not only in taste and organic sensation, to which the act-objects analysis is inapplicable. Even when the act-objects analysis will not fit, we may still distinguish between the sensing and the sensed, the awareness and what one is aware of. But in so far as the notion of a sensum is bound up with the act-objects distinction, we do have to say that there are sense-experiences in which we are not aware of *sensa*, but rather of a sense-field as a whole. I have also tried to show that when the internal accusative ('feeling somehow') language is appropriate, its appropriateness does not depend upon epistemological considerations at all. Whether it fits or fails to fit depends upon the point at which the distinction between self and not-self is drawn; and the boundary between self and not-self is not fixed once for all, but fluctuates. Even the somatic sense-field can be part of the not-self; and in some rather unusual cases, even the visual field can be part of the self.

V.

So far I have been discussing what may be called internal questions, *within* the general conceptual framework of Prof. Broad's philosophy. I have spoken freely of 'sensations' and 'sense-experiences' and have only been asking what kind of analysis applies to them. I have assumed, as Prof. Broad does, that all perceiving does contain sensation or sense-experience as an essential element, whatever else it may contain besides; that when something is seen, or touched, or heard, it is at any rate certain that a visual sensation or a tactual sensation or an auditory sensation is occurring.

But there are many philosophers nowadays who reject these assumptions. They hold, accordingly, that the questions I have so far been discussing are of no importance or interest, except perhaps to future historians of early 20th century philosophy. They would agree that there are organic sensations. But they hold that there are no other sorts of sensations at all, and that the adjective 'organic' should therefore be dropped, because it suggests that there *are* other sorts of sensations. The word 'sensation' (it is said) should be reserved for such experiences as aches, itches, twinges of pain, feelings of fatigue, etc.; and it is pointed out that this is the way the word is generally used in ordinary everyday English. There may of course be *ocular* sensations, as when one has a feeling of eye-strain, or one's eyes ache or smart. But though these may sometimes accompany seeing, they are not visual sensations in the traditional sense of that expression. And if there *are* no visual sensations or visual sense-experiences, and no tactual or auditory or olfactory sensations either, there is not much point in asking how these nonexistent occurrences are to be analysed.

Consider these alleged visual sensations, for example. Analyse them as you please, in the act-object way or any other. Say if you please that visual sensation consists in being aware of or intuitively apprehending visual sensa. You still cannot show us that there are in fact any such entities as visual sensa or that you are in fact aware of them. Or rather (for it is not just a question of fact) you cannot show us that the terminology, the conceptual apparatus, of the sensum theory does anything at all to clarify such concepts as 'seeing something,' 'hearing something,' 'touching something.' On the contrary, its effects are obfuscating rather than clarifying. The sensum theory distracts our attention from the crucial fact that what is seen or heard or touched is a physical object or a physical event, and even makes it seem impossible that such objects and events should ever be perceived at all, just as the traditional theory of Representative Ideas did. Indeed, the sensum theory is admittedly just a tidying up and reformulation of that ancient and vicious doctrine.[7]

Of course, if these critics are right, it is not only Prof. Broad's sensum theory which is refuted, or shown to be non-sensical, but all the different varieties of the sense-datum theory; and not only these, but all theories which analyse perception (other than proprioceptive) in terms of sensations, whether or not the sensations themselves are analysed in an act-object manner. If the critics are right, Berkeley is refuted no less than Prof. Broad; and Lord Russell and Professor G. E. Moore no less than Berkeley. But here we are concerned only with Prof. Broad's sensum theory. It is, I am afraid, true that Prof. Broad's sensum theory has come to seem incredible to many present-day philosophers. They do not trouble to consider its details, because it appears to them mistaken in principle. Can anything be done to disarm their objections?

There is an impression that the sensum theory is trying to deprive us of something. We thought we saw trees, books, mountains, lightning flashes. The sensum theory is supposed to say that we do not really see these things at all. We thought we saw material objects and physical happenings. Instead, we are only allowed to see a kind of coloured façades, and private and evanescent ones at that. Moreover, the sensum theory is often supposed to hold that these façades are 'flat,' i.e. two-dimensional. Similarly, we thought we heard physical and public sounds; but the sensum theory is supposed to say that we are quite mistaken in thinking so, and that all we 'really' hear are just private and evanescent entities called auditory sensa.

But this is a misunderstanding of what the sensum theory is maintaining. Almost all the philosophers who have used any variety of the sense-datum terminology, and certainly Prof. Broad, distinguish in one way or another between sensing and perceiving. There is a familiar and easily recognisable experience which we call seeing a tomato. The sensum theory does not say that this *just* consists in being aware of a bright red colour-expanse with a roundish shape. It says there is another element in the experience as well, and an equally essential one, namely the believing or the taking for granted that this colour-expanse is related in a specially intimate way to a physical tomato. This belief or quasi-belief *about* the sensum is the perceptual part of the experience of seeing, as opposed to the purely sensory part. Moreover, Prof. Broad is careful to point out that words like 'see' 'hear' 'touch' are commonly used in a *perceptual* sense, and he tells us explicitly that he himself will always use them in their perceptual sense, and does in fact abide by that decision (*ST*, 248). If anyone says 'I do not see sense-data, I

---

[7] *ST*, p. 238 'The doctrine of "representative ideas" is the traditional and highly muddled form of it.'

see material objects' Prof. Broad will heartily agree with him. He has never maintained that we do see sense-data (or rather sensa). He has only maintained that we *sense* them, or as he sometimes says, intuitively apprehend them. Nor has he denied that we see material objects. What he has done is to propose an analysis of what this seeing of them consists in. It consists, he thinks, in holding a certain sort of belief, or quasi-belief,[8] about some visual sensum which we sense, the belief that this sensum is related in a specially intimate way to such and such a material object (or sometimes, to a physical event, such as a lightning flash).

Moreover, the objection that sensa are 'mere façades' amounts to saying that the sensum theory regards all visual perception as hallucinatory or at least illusory. On the contrary, Prof. Broad has taken a great deal of trouble to explain how illusory and hallucinatory perceptual situations differ from normal ones; and he certainly does not deny that normal perceptual situations very frequently occur. Finally, the allegation that the Sensum Theorist's visual sensa are 'flat,' i.e. two-dimensional, is just a rather surprising mistake. In most of the varieties of the sense-datum theory a good deal is said about visual depth. In most of them, and certainly in Prof. Broad's sensum theory, depth (i.e. three-dimensionality) is held to be an *intrinsic* property of visual fields, and not merely, as Berkeley thought, a mnemically-superadded one. Indeed, Prof. Broad might almost be accused of discussing visual depth *ad nauseam*.

Does the sensum theory really deprive us of anything at all? Suppose you see a cat from a particular point of view at a particular moment. How much do you claim to see of it? In answering this question, take care to limit yourself to what you actually see here and now. Obviously you do not see the far side of the creature, but only its near side and perhaps a little of its top side. From this distance you do not see its whiskers, and still less the individual hairs of its coat. You do however claim to discern certain visible properties of it: a variegated tabbyish colouring and a certain humpish shape, more easily drawn on paper than described, the whole located at a certain visible distance from you. Now these are just the visible properties which the sensum theory attributes to a certain visual sensum in your present visual field. To be sure, it does substitute the technical phrase 'at a certain depth' for the common sense phrase 'at a certain visible distance from you;' and when you talk of 'what I see of a certain object from here now,' *it* prefers to talk of 'a certain visual sensum in your present visual field.' But the specific visual properties which you mention in answering the question 'what do you see of this object?' are just the ones which *it* mentions in

8 The term 'quasi-belief' does not occur in *ST*. It is first introduced in *MPN*, p. 215.

answering the question 'what characteristics does this particular visual sensum have?' Then what have you been deprived of? Have you really been deprived of anything which can be visually discerned from one particular point of view in one specious present?

Perhaps someone may think he *has* been deprived of the cat itself, though not of the visible properties which he claims to discern in it here and now. The visible properties may be the same, but surely the entities they are attributed to are very different? A visual sensum is not a cat, nor even a part of a cat. He may also think he has been deprived of the right to what he sees of this object in *other* specious presents or from other points of view. But neither of these complaints is justified. The sensum theory admits most handsomely that there may well be or have been other visual sensa (your own or other people's), related to this present one in a specially important way which Prof. Broad has analysed in great detail in *ST*, chs. 9 and 10. Sensa thus related to each other are co-constituents of the same 'perceptual object,' as Prof. Broad calls it. A perceptual object also contains tactual sensa among its constituents, and sometimes auditory, thermal and (I think) olfactory ones as well. It is public to an indefinite number of observers; it continues through a period of time, in some cases a long one. The cat the plain man speaks of is in Prof. Broad's language a perceptual object; and we have not been deprived of it at all, though possibly we might fail to recognise this familiar and agreeable animal in the very complex verbal dress in which Prof. Broad clothes it. I shall have more to say about the doctrine of the Perceptual Object later. Here I only wish to point out that it is an essential part of Prof. Broad's sensum theory. We shall hardly do justice to the sensum theory if we only consider what its author has said in the first dozen pages of his exposition of it.

VI.

Let us now consider the relation between the terminology of sensa and the everyday language of the ordinary percipient. Some modern common-sensical philosophers profess not to be able to understand the terminology of sensa at all. They speak as if it had been introduced abruptly 'out of the blue,' like some strange kind of mathematical calculus, and had no relationship whatever with our ordinary ways of describing what we see or touch or hear. If these philosophers were right, it would be rather surprising that so many people of quite moderate intelligence have in fact managed to learn to use the sensum terminology. We may notice too that any second-year medical student easily learns to use the closely connected terminology of visual sensations, auditory sensations, etc., un-commonsensical as it may be. It is true that Prof. Broad, writing in 1923, does not explicitly consider the Sensum Theory from this linguistic point of view. Nevertheless, he does in effect give us all the instructions we need for making the passage from everyday perceptual language to the language of sensa. If there is a gulf between the two, he has provided us with a bridge across it. His bridgehead on the common sense side is the notion of *appearing*. Appearing has various determinates under it: looking so and so, sounding thus and thus, and feeling so and so for the various types of experience which common sense, in its heavy-handed way, lumps together under the title of 'touch.' It frequently happens that some object we perceive appears to have some quality which it does not really have. The field on the hillside looks purplish-grey from here, but it is really green. A distant waterfall looks stationary, but it is really in rapid movement. At sunset, the sun sometimes looks egg-shaped. A very loud explosion sounds faint at ten miles' distance.

Philosophers have thought that there is something puzzling here. How can an object appear to have a quality (or a relational property) which it does not really have? How can there be a half-way house between having a characteristic and not having it? We must notice, of course, that appearing ϕ is not the same as being believed to be ϕ. I do not for a moment believe that the distant waterfall is stationary. But it does *look* stationary to me from here, two miles away. Prof. Broad emphasises this point himself. It is therefore unfortunate that he sometimes uses the word 'seem' instead of 'appear' ('look,' 'sound,' etc.). 'That seems ϕ to me' can very well express my *belief*—though not perhaps my full conviction—that it is ϕ.

Prof. Broad's own example is the round penny which looks elliptical. It is not a very happy example, especially as he uses it so frequently. In actual fact pennies do not very often look elliptical. This is partly because they are small objects, and can only be seen at all from relatively short distances. The result is that, in adult vision at any rate, they are usually seen stereoscopically. The nearer edge of the penny usually has a smaller visual depth than its farther edge. Moreover, a penny is a very familiar sort of object, and with familiar objects, especially when seen from short distances, the phenomenon of Shape Constancy is particularly marked. The apparent shape is closer to the real shape than it would be if the laws of perspective alone applied. A better example would be a large circular pond seen obliquely from four hundred yards away. This really does look elliptical.

Whatever we may think of Prof. Broad's illustration, there certainly is a problem about appearing. Let us see how he proposes to solve it.

'The solution which the sensum theory offers is to "change the subject." *Something*, it admits, is elliptical, and something is round; but they are not the same something. What is round is the penny, what is elliptical is the sensum' (*ST*, 244*fin*–245). This gives us the terminological instructions we need. Whenever the ordinary percipient says that an object O appears ϕ (looks, feels, sounds ϕ as the case may be) we are to say instead that he is sensing a sensum which actually *is* ϕ. And we are to say this whether or not O does in fact have the characteristic ϕ which it appears to have. From here the waterfall looks stationary, though it is in fact in movement. Very well, then. We are to say that I am sensing a visual sensum which *is* stationary, though the material object it belongs to is not. A similar terminological treatment will apply to hallucination as well. Here our bridgehead on the common sense side is an 'existential appearing' statement (as opposed to the 'attributive appearing' statement so far considered). On a dark evening while I am walking along Turl Street in Oxford, there appears to me to be a tabby cat in a dark angle of the wall, though in fact there is no cat there. The equivalent statement in the sensum terminology would be 'I sense a tabby coloured sensum of a familiar sort of shape (more easily drawn than described) but there is no material object to which it belongs.'

We now see how we are supposed to make the transition from ordinary everyday perceptual language to the language of sensa. The most important step is the one Prof. Broad calls 'changing the subject.' *Ce n'est que le premier pas qui coute.* As we shall see, there are cases where the cost of this step is quite considerable. But first we must notice that 'changing the subject' is not the whole of it. We also have to retain the predicate. To speak more accurately, we have to retain the adjective or adjectival phrase which followed the 'appearing' verb, for instance the word 'stationary' in the example of the waterfall. But for brevity's sake I shall henceforth speak of 'changing the subject and keeping the predicate' and shall mean by 'the predicate' the sensible quality or sensible relational property which some object appears to the percipient to have. The important point is that in the terminology of sensa this quality or relational property is to be attributed to a sensum; and we are to say that this sensum does actually have it. This is the sense in which we have to 'keep the predicate' when we 'change the subject.'

It is rather unfortunate, perhaps, that Prof. Broad presents his sensum terminology to us as a solution of the problem of illusion. In the examples considered in this passage, a material object appears to have some characteristic which it does *not* really have. It looks elliptical; in actual fact it is not elliptical, but round. But of course a thing can perfectly well appear what it actually is. The envelope is rectangular;

and from here it does look to me rectangular. What is the equivalent for this in the sensum terminology? Shall we say 'I sense a visual sensum which is rectangular, and it belongs to a material object which is also rectangular?' If we do say this, we must notice that the term 'rectangular' does not have the same meaning in both clauses, and consequently the word 'also' is inappropriate. As applied to the sensum, the word 'rectangular' means an ostensibly definable visible quality. As applied to the envelope it has what Prof. Broad calls a Pickwickian sense. To find out what this sense is, we must read the whole of his very elaborate analysis of the perceptual object. To put it very roughly, he holds that when we call the envelope rectangular we are referring to a region of discontinuity in 'the movement continuum.' We are saying that this region of discontinuity has a rectangular surface (in a sense of 'rectangular' which is defined in terms of the movement continuum); and we are saying that this region is occupied, in a very complex and highly Pickwickian sense of the word 'occupy,' by a very complex group of sensa, of which this present sensibly-rectangular visual sensum is a member. The movement-continuum itself is roughly what other philosophers have called 'public space;' and it, in its turn, is analysed in a rather complex manner in terms of kinaesthetic sensations and the visual experiences which are correlated with them.

Thus if someone asks what is the sensum theory's equivalent for 'O both looks ϕ and actually is ϕ,' Prof. Broad does have an answer, though it is an exceedingly complicated one, and to find out what it is we must read chapters 9 and 10 of *Scientific Thought* as well as chapter 8. This, then, is not a genuine objection to his proposal for 'changing the subject and keeping the predicate.'

But there is another objection which is more difficult to answer, and so far as I know, Prof. Broad has not discussed it anywhere. We have already seen what difficulties arise from Prof. Broad's scale of sense-experiences. Unfortunately there is a kind of scale of appearings too. Let us consider the visual type of appearing. Our ordinary expression for this is 'looking ϕ.' So long as ϕ is some visible quality or visible relational property (e.g. 'just to the left of so and so') no great difficulty arises about keeping the predicate, though if it is a spatial predicate we shall have to allow for the complications mentioned just now. The wood looks purplish-grey from here; the sensum *is* purplish-grey. The distant pond looks elliptical; the sensum *is* elliptical. But doubts may begin to creep in when we consider a distant cumulus cloud which looks bulgy ('visually solid'). Very distant objects, far beyond the range of physiologically-stereoscopic vision, do often look bulgy when there are strong contrasts of light and shade, though in other conditions they

may look flat. The trouble is that this bulginess is a mnemic phenomenon, due to tactual and kinaesthetic associations. Though Berkeley was
no doubt mistaken in thinking that *all* 'visible solidity' is a mnemic
phenomenon, his tactuo-kinaesthetic theory of visible solidity really
does apply to this sensum of the distant cumulus cloud. Still, perhaps
there is no very serious trouble for the Sensum Theory here. Bulginess
is after all a perfectly good visible quality, in the sense that there is such
a character as *non*-mnemic bulginess which is frequently exemplified
in our visual fields. So perhaps we need not mind saying that a visual
sensum actually *is* bulgy even when it owes its bulginess to mnemic
factors.

But we can think of other examples where Prof. Broad's plan of
changing the subject and keeping the predicate does not seem to work
so easily. Ice and snow often *look* cold. Walls *look* hard, and water
looks wet. (This, of course, is a mnemic phenomenon again.) But when
I see the ice and it looks cold, can we say that my visual sensum *is*
actually cold? Perhaps we just can, if we distinguish between coldness
as a causal property belonging to physical objects, and coldness as a
sensible quality, the quality you sense when you actually lay your
hand on the ice. Perhaps we *can* just say that the visual sensum of the
ice is cold in the sensible quality sense of the word 'cold,' though to
say that a sensum is cold in the causal property sense of the word 'cold'
would, I think, be sheer nonsense. (Similarly with the wall which looks
hard. We should have to distinguish between hardness the causal property, the capacity which walls have to resist changes of shape and penetration by other objects, and hardness the sensible quality, which you
sense when you feel the wall with your hand or run into it in the dark.)

Some philosophers have denied that ice does look cold, or that walls
can look hard, on the ground that coldness and hardness are not visible
properties. I think this is sheer a priorism. Questions of phenomenological fact are not to be settled by *a priori* arguments. It is not enough
to say that when I see the ice I *believe* that it is cold or believe that it
would feel cold if I were to touch it. It just *looks* cold, as it looks
gleamy and semi-transparent. Moreover, a piece of theatre backcloth
skilfully painted to resemble an iceberg may still *look* cold, though we
do not believe it to be cold. A photograph of a wall can look hard,
though we are fully aware that what we are seeing is only a portion of
a quite soft piece of paper.

We may now pass further along our scale of lookings. What are we
to say about 'he looks ill,' 'he looks angry' or 'he looks English?' We
can certainly change the subject here, and talk about a visual sensum
we are sensing. But we cannot keep the predicate. No visual sensum

can *be* ill or angry or English; or rather, it makes no sense to say it can. And here again we cannot get out of our difficulty by changing 'looks' into 'is believed to be.' He *looks* English, but I do not at all believe he is. I have the best of reasons for believing that he is a Dutchman.

Let us now consider a rather different and perhaps more disputable example. It could, I think, be said that what we see usually looks material or corporeal. The remark is no doubt an odd one. But it does have a point, because there are occasions when things do *not* look material or corporeal. Instead, they look, as we say, 'dream-like' or 'insubstantial.' The more distant parts of a very extensive prospect do sometimes look dream-like or insubstantial, especially in a rather hazy atmosphere, and so does a distant landscape glimpsed suddenly through a hole in a cloud. On the other hand, the nearer parts of the prospect, especially if brightly illuminated, do not look at all dream-like or insubstantial. And that is the point of saying that they *do* look material or corporeal, though we should not usually mention the fact, because that is the way we expect the majority of visible objects to look. Now here again we can of course 'change the subject,' as Prof. Broad recommends. But can we keep the predicate? Can we assert that a visual sensum *is* material or corporeal?

Finally, since all my examples so far have been visual, I will mention some non-visual ones. We could say of someone that he 'sounds excited,' or of a piece of music that it 'sounds mediaeval.' But we obviously cannot say of an auditory sensum or series of auditory sensa that it *is* excited or *is* mediaeval. Again, it may well be that to a dog a human being can smell angry or smell frightened. But we can hardly say of an olfactory sensum that it *is* angry or frightened.

VII.

What is the sensum theorist to do about this scale or slippery slope of appearings where we can always 'change the subject,' but seem to pass gradually from examples where we can 'keep the predicate' quite comfortably to cases where we can only keep it with doubt and difficulty, and from these again to others where we obviously cannot keep it at all? Obviously he must deny the continuity of the series. He must make a clean cut somewhere. He is obliged to say that everywhere along the scale you must 'change the subject.' If you do not, you are not using the sensum terminology at all. But he must say that you can only 'keep the predicate' up to a certain point in the series and no farther. Beyond that point you will have to transform it into something more complex.

He looks angry (to me, now, from here): that is, I sense a visual sensum of his face, and this sensum has a certain visual *Gestalt*-quality which commonly characterises sensa of angry faces. In addition, we might have to begin by transforming the common sense statement which we are being asked to translate. For 'he looks angry' we might first substitute 'he looks *as if he were* angry' or he 'looks *like* an angry man;' and we might then say 'I sense a visual sensum which is like a visual sensum of an angry face.'

I am not at all sure that such an expedient does full justice to the phenomenological facts. I suspect it of being over-sophisticated and over-intellectualised. It seems to me that the concept or idea of anger 'blends' with the colour and visible shape of the face in a more intimate way than this explanation allows. Is there anything propositional about looking angry, as the phrase 'as if he were angry' suggests? 'He looks angry' is a description of a fairly primitive type of percept, and we have good reason to think that infants and even domestic animals can experience a percept of this sort.

But setting these doubts aside, where exactly is the clean cut to be made in our series of appearings? I think that the latest point at which the sensum theorist can make it is just after 'ice looks cold' (with its parallel examples 'looking hard,' 'looking wet,' etc.). We can perhaps keep the predicate so long as it falls under some sense-modality or other. We can—just—say that the visual sensum of the ice *is* cold or hard or wet, because these adjectives, suitably interpreted, are the names of sensible qualities. To be sure, these qualities are tangible, not visible. But it is perhaps not quite incredible that a visual sensum might acquire tangible qualities, in addition to its visible ones, given suitable mnemic conditions. And if the sensum theorist digs his toes in and says '*A priori* it might not have been expected that visual sensa could also have tangible qualities, but as a matter of fact they sometimes do,' I cannot see how he is to be refuted. Moreover, looking cold does not seem to differ in principle from looking bulgy (which can also be the result of tactual associations) and I do not think a sensum theorist can possibly deny that the visual sensum of the distant cumulus cloud actually *is* bulgy.

On the other hand, in the examples which come after 'looking cold' in our series—'looking ill,' 'looking angry,' 'looking English,' 'looking corporeal' (as opposed to 'dream-like') 'sounding mediaeval'—the adjective which follows the word 'look' is *not* the name of a sensible property. These characteristics, unlike coldness or bulginess, do not fall under any sense-modality at all. Here it is impossible to keep the predicate when we change the subject. 'A looks ϕ' can no longer be equivalent to 'there is a sensum which actually *is* ϕ.' Instead, we shall have to say something like this: 'there is a sensum which actually has a characteristic ψ, and sensa which have this characteristic commonly belong to ϕ-ish entities.'

So much for the bridge which Professor Broad constructs to take us across from everyday perceptual language to the technical language of the sensum theory. We are to start from the common sense language of appearing, and then we are to change the subject while keeping the predicate. There are difficulties about carrying out these instructions when we consider the many different types of appearing which are recognised by common sense. We can always change the subject, as the Sensum Theory requires, but we cannot always keep the predicate. Still, if I am right, these difficulties are not insuperable. It may be possible to make a 'clean cut' in the series of appearings in the way I have suggested.

VIII.

Nevertheless, even where we *can* 'keep the predicate,' some will still feel that the sensum language does not give us the full equivalent of the common sense perceptual language from which we started. They will feel that something important has been left out. I have already referred to the objection that the Sensum Theory 'deprives us of something.' It may be worth while, in conclusion, to say a little more about this. On p. 534 of *Scientific Thought* Prof. Broad mentions, and dismisses, a criticism which might be made of Lord Russell's theory in *Our Knowledge of the External World* and *Mysticism and Logic*, chapters 7 and 8: it might be said that this theory 'makes sensa too substantial and self-subsistent, whilst it makes physical objects too ghostly.' Perhaps some will think that this objection applies to Prof. Broad's own theory too. Moreover, they would have some ground for thinking so, if the objection were interpreted, as it could be, in a phenomenological rather than an ontological sense. In his discussion of 'the quasi-belief about the sensum' (*MPN*, 215f) Prof. Broad does seem to be saying that while sensa present themselves to the mind in a full-blooded manner, material objects present themselves to the mind in what may well be called a ghostly manner. Let us recall his distinction between sensing and perceiving— the sensing of sensa on the one hand, and the perceiving of material objects on the other. Sensing is the intuitive apprehension of actually presented particulars. But perceiving, in this passage, seems to fade away into a mere behaving-as-if, accompanied by certain feelings and occasionally by images. It seems that we are not *conscious* of material objects in any way at all. This account of perceiving, as opposed to sensing, seems to me altogether too somnambulistic. It is true that something like what Prof. Broad describes does happen sometimes; for example, when we walk home along a familiar street, successfully avoiding lamp posts, puddles, and passing motor cars, and arrive at our destination hardly knowing how we got there, without any clear recollection of anything perceived on the way. But how very different this quasi-perceiving is from the perceiving which occurs when we are wide-awake and alert and attentive to minute details in our physical environment, for example, when one is carefully searching for a rare flower in a wood full of undergrowth. It must however be noticed that the doctrine I am criticising only occurs in *The Mind and its Place in Nature*. There is nothing at all like it in *Scientific Thought*. In that work, indeed, Prof. Broad appears to go too far in the opposite direction. 'We are not as a rule interested in sensa, as such, but only in what we think they can tell us about physical objects, which alone can hurt or harm us.' It is like what happens when we are reading print in a familiar language. We attend to the meaning, and hardly at all to the printed words. (*ST*, 247.) So far, so good. According to this passage, we do attend to material objects, and do not just behave in a somnambulistic manner as if they were there. But then Prof. Broad adds the shocking remark 'Sensa themselves "cut no ice." ' On the contrary, they sometimes cut a great deal. In the English Lake District or the Scottish Highlands roads are built, hotels put up, and buses run, all for the sake of the *visual sensa* which can be sensed from certain places. Much ice is cut by the visual sensa obtainable in picture-galleries, and concert halls are erected, at vast expense, in order to provide people with complex series of auditory sensa.

But the objection about 'making sensa too substantial and physical objects too ghostly' is more naturally interpreted in an ontological manner, as an objection to someone's account of what a physical object is, or to his account of what it is that we perceive (as opposed to his account of the experience of perceiving). And if it is so interpreted, Prof. Broad has an answer to it. His answer is the doctrine of the Perceptual Object which I have mentioned several times already.

As we have seen, the perceptual object is a very complex group of sensa. Sensa themselves are private, but the perceptual object is public, in the sense that many different people's sensa are constituents of it. It is 'neutral' as between the different sense-modalities. There are tactual as well as visual sensa among its constituents, and sometimes auditory sensa and thermal sensa as well. It is located in public space (the space of the 'movement-continuum'). Or rather, each of the sub-groups of sensa into which it may be divided—the visual sub-group, the tactual sub-group, etc.—is located in this public space in its own appropriate and highly complex manner. Moreover, in some sense of the word 'contain' the perceptual object contains possible sensa as well as actual ones—those which *would* be sensed if there were to be appropriately placed observers, as well as those which *are* sensed. So far Prof. Broad's perceptual object looks something like the phenomenalists' object, though he has analysed its structure far more carefully than the phenomenalists themselves have. But on pp. 389–392 of *ST* a purely phenomenalistic account of the perceptual object is explicitly rejected. In addition to the sensa which are its constituents, the perceptual object contains other constituents which fill up the gaps between one actually-sensed sensum and another. These 'gap-filling' constituents are actual physical particulars and not merely unfulfilled possibilities.

The criticism we are discussing, the charge that Prof. Broad's theory 'makes sensa too substantial and physical objects too ghostly' really amounts to saying that Prof. Broad has misdescribed what we perceive (as opposed to what we sense). But the truth is, I think, that he has not yet described it at all in the part of his book which such critics probably have in mind. His description of what we perceive, as opposed to what we sense, is not given in *ST,* ch. 8, the chapter on 'The Theory of Sensa,' but in ch. 9 ('The Positions and Shapes of Sensa and of Physical Objects') and in ch. 10 ('The Dates and Durations of Sensa and of Physical Objects and Events'). If we consider these later chapters, we shall find a very elaborate account of what we perceive, that is, of the perceptual objects of which we take our sensa to be constituents; and I do not think that this answer to the question 'what do we perceive?' is after all so unacceptable to the plain ordinary percipient, if only he were able to understand the complicated and highly technical language in which it is stated.

The ordinary man's perceptual belief might perhaps be formulated thus:—'There is more of the same sort as *this,*' where 'this' is what he is immediately aware of here and now. Reading ch. 8, we might think Prof. Broad wishes to substitute 'There is something of quite a different sort from *this,* to which *this* is related by a relation of "being an appearance of." ' Here the physical world does seem to have retreated behind a veil of all-too-substantial sensa, and to have been degraded to a mysterious and rather ghostly status. But when we consider the doctrine of the Perceptual Object, we find that Prof. Broad does after all accept the formula 'there is more of the same sort as this.' For the 'this,' in Prof. Broad's terminology, is the sensum which one is sensing at the moment; and it now turns out that the object in whose existence we believe consists largely of other sensa. It also turns out that many of our perceptual beliefs are true; and when our perceptual belief is true, there really *is* 'more of the same sort as this.' To be sure, Prof. Broad's perceptual object contains constituents which are not sensa, as well as constituents which are. But I do not think the plain man would be worried by this. He is quite ready to believe the physicists when they tell him that stones and trees contain invisible and intangible constituents. I would suggest then that when we consider Professor Broad's theory as a whole ('perceptual objects' and all) his account of what we perceive turns out to be much much less shocking to common sense than his critics suppose. His perceptual objects are not so ghostly after all, even if we still feel that his sensa are too substantial.

H. H. PRICE

NEW COLLEGE
OXFORD UNIVERSITY

15

Konrad Marc-Wogau

ON C. D. BROAD'S THEORY OF SENSA

Broad has dealt with the theory of sensa and related subjects in a number of papers, most circumstantially in the books *Perception, Physics and Reality* 1914, *Scientific Thought* 1923 (= *ST*), *The Mind and its Place in Nature* 1925 (= *MPN*), *Examination of McTaggart's Philosophy* Vol. II, 1938, and the articles "Prof. Marc-Wogau's Theorie der Sinnesdaten" (= *Mind* 1947) and "Some Elementary Reflexions on Sense-Perception" (= *Philosophy* 1952). The following considerations are restricted mainly to the theory of sensa as it is expounded in the two works *ST* and *MPN*, and do not take into account some important modifications which Broad's views have undergone in later writings.

In the exposition and discussion of Broad's theory I shall make use of the two terms "perceptual situation" and "objective constituent" in the sense in which Broad introduces them in *MPN*. In this work he declares: "I will call such situations as are naturally indicated by phrases like 'I am seeing a chair' or 'I am hearing a bell' by the name of 'Perceptual Situations'" (*MPN*, 141), and he maintains that every perceptual situation of this kind, where I perceive something, contains in addition to myself something to which I find myself standing in an asymmetrical two term relation (*MPN*, 150). In a perceptual situation I find myself in direct cognitive contact with something, and this "something" is the objective constituent of the perceptual situation. I shall also speak about sensa as such objecitve constituents or as parts of objective constituents. This is in full agreement with Broad's terminology.[1]

In talking of the objective constituent of a perceptual situation in the sense mentioned certain of the fundamental presuppositions of the

[1] In the summary *MPN*, 219 "objective constituent" is said to be "a sensefield with a certain outstanding sensum." From the explanation of the term "sensum" it is, however, evident that also a sensum, and not only a larger whole, of which sensum is an outstanding part, can be said to be an objective constituent. "I give the name of sensa to the objective constituents of perceptual situations. . . ." (*MPN*, 181f.)

theory of sense-data have implicitly been assumed: that in a perceptual situation we find ourselves in a *cognitive* relation to a sense-datum, that this relation has the character of *direct* awareness or acquaintance, that it is a two term relation, and that what we directly perceive is a particular existent. These presuppositions are, however, by no means self-evident, and have often been questioned and criticized in the course of the discussion of the last decades. One thing is evident: unless we accept them, we have to reject the theory of sense-data. It is not my intention here to discuss these presuppositions more closely or to enter into the arguments against them. In the following I shall discuss only one main thesis in the theory of sense-data together with Broad's arguments in its favour.

The term "theory of sense-data" (or Broad's term "sensum-theory") can be conceived as an inclusive name for a number of different theories which have, however, one fundamental thesis in common. It can be characterized by the following two propositions:

I. In every perceptual situation we directly perceive an objective constituent or a sense-datum (sensum).

II. The objective constituent (or the sense-datum) is never identical with the physical object which we profess to perceive, or even with part of it.

It is my intention to deal particularly with proposition (II) and with the arguments for it. Different types of the theory of sense-data conceive the relation between propositions (I) and (II) in different ways. The terms "the directly perceived" ("sense-datum") and "physical object" can be given such a content that proposition (II) follows with logical necessity from proposition (I). On the other hand it can also be assumed that proposition (II) does not follow from proposition (I) on account of the meaning which is connected with the terms "sense-data" and "physical object," but that a sense-datum factually is never identical with the physical object or part of it.

My first objection against Broad's exposition of the theory of sensa concerns a certain lack of clarity found there in this respect. I shall illustrate this by comparing some passages in *MPN,* where the question whether "the objective constituent of the perceptual situation" can be "quite literally a spatio-temporal part of the perceived object" is discussed in detail. In numerous instances the idea seems to be that the theory of sensa cannot admit the objective constituent to be part of a physical object in *all* perceptual situations. On the other hand the theory does not entail that this could not be the case in *some* perceptual situations.

The theory of sensa "insists that the objective constituents of perceptual situations are *seldom, if ever,* spatio-temporal parts of the physical objects which it (i.e. common-sense) claims to be perceiving" (*MPN*, 184).

The theory of sensa "cannot admit that, when we say that we are seeing a certain physical object, the objective constituent of our visual situation is *in general* a spatio-temporal part of the physical object which we say that we are seeing. On this theory, then, the objective constituents of *most, if not all,* perceptual situations cannot be spatio-temporal parts of physical objects" (*MPN*, 181).

"It is just as *possible, logically,* for the Sensum-theory to make this . . . claim as for the other two theories. It might assert that from one specially favourable position, the objective constituent is literally a part of the physical object" (*MPN*, 193).

According to these pronouncements proposition (II) is not to be taken as a logical consequence of proposition (I). For the validity of the former Broad also adduces certain arguments intended to show "that we can never be sure" (*MPN*, 201) or that "we may not believe" (*MPN*, 219) that the objective constituent in a perceptual situation is part of the physical object. Other utterances, however, produce a different impression.

"I give the name 'sensa' to the objective constituent of perceptual situations, on the supposition that they are *not* literally parts of the physical object which we are said to be perceiving" (*MPN*, 181f.).

Other theories of perception admit that the objective constituents in perceptual situations are parts of physical objects. But "this cannot be admitted on the Sensum Theory; the relation must be less direct and more complicated than common-sense believes" (*MPN*, 182).

"It is no doubt true that sensa cannot be parts, in literal and straightforward sense, of physical objects" (*MPN*, 189).

Here the reservations "in general" or "most, if not all," italicized by me above, are missing and proposition (II) is considered as a doubtlessly true proposition, the meaning of which seems to follow from the way in which the concept *sensum* has been understood.

According to my opinion this vaccillating attitude towards proposition (II) has to be seen against the background of the different ways in which Broad introduces the concept *sensum*.

In the chapter "Theory of Sensa" in *ST* the term "sensum" is first explained by the following description:

"Whenever I truly judge that *x* appears to me to have the sensible quality *q*, what happens is that I am directly aware of a certain object *y*, which (a) really does have the quality *q*, and (b) stands in some peculiarly intimate relation, yet to be determined, to *x*" (*ST*, 239).

Thus sensa are described here as what is directly perceived in a perceptual situation, or as objects of "direct awareness." The quotation must, obviously, not be taken as a definition in strict sense. It describes situations, in which sensa are perceived, but it does not indicate a necessary condition of the presence of a sensum. Broad is of the opinion that it is "logically possible and indeed quite plausible that there might be unsensed sensa" (*ST*, 516). Thus the property of being object of "direct awareness" is not necessarily inherent in sensa, since also unsensed sensa can exist. But the quotation maintains in any case that sensa, *provided they are perceived*, are objects of direct awareness. Evidently, from the description given it does not follow, that *y*, i.e. a sensum, could not be identical with *x*, i.e. the perceived physical object, or with a part of *x*. This is also pointed out by Broad.

"At the present stage, for all that we know, *y*, might sometimes be identical with *x*, or might be literally part of *x*" (*ST*, 239).

Some pages further on another explanation of the concept *sensum* is encountered. There one reads:

"Under certain conditions I have states of mind called sensations. These sensations have objects, which are always concrete particular existents like coloured or hot patches, noises, smells, etc. Such objects are called sensa" (*ST*, 243).

Here sensa are introduced as objects of experiences of a special kind— sensations; and these objects are exemplified. Still some pages further on Broad distinguishes between different meanings of the vague common expression "to see something:" "In one sense we see a penny; in a somewhat stricter sense we see only one side of the penny; in another sense we see only a brown elliptical sensum" (*ST*, 248). Broad maintains that the two first meanings refer to acts of perceiving, the last again, to acts of sensing. If sensum is characterized as object of sensation or act of sensing, and if physical objects are understood as objects of acts of perceiving, then it follows from what has been said, that sensa cannot be identical with physical objects or parts of such. A physical object or a part thereof is obviously an object of perceiving, and not of sensing. The designation of sensum as object of sensation or act of sensing, and of the physical object as object of the act of perceiving leads here to the result, that proposition (II) must be said to follow from proposition (I) with logical necessity. To the earlier characterization of sensum as object of direct awareness has here been added the characterization of the physical object as the object of the act of perceiving, which has not the character of direct awareness. One can, however, ask what evidence there is for this last assertion, that physical objects are not objects of direct awareness. To me the simplest explanation seems to be, that physical objects, i.e. objects like coins, bells, etc., are supposed to be "bits of matter," whereas the objects of sensation or "direct awareness" are supposed to be of an entirely different nature, as appears from Broad's exemplification.

It is obvious that Broad introduces sensa in different ways, partly by their description as objects of direct awareness, partly by the description as objects of sensation, and partly by exemplification. But it is not at all self-evident that these ways of introducing sensa mark out exactly the same objects. It is not self-evident that the class of what is directly perceived in perceptual situations coincides with the class of what can be objects of sensation, or with the class of such objects as coloured patches, hot patches, sounds, smells, and the like. Broad seems to assume that the classes mentioned coincide. He claims to find by "inspection" that what is directly perceived in perceptual situations has just the character of coloured patches, and the like, i.e. of such objects which are assumed to be objects of sensations. And he is of the opinion that "direct inspection" is "the only relevant evidence in such a matter" (ST, 34f.; MPN, 246).

I interpret Broad's idea in the following way. The description of sensa as what is directly perceived in a perceptual situation is the fundamental description. Now inspection shows, that what we directly perceive in a perceptual situation are just coloured patches, hot patches, and the like, thus just what can be characterized as objects of sensing. The exemplification of sensa is based upon the testimony of inspection, whereas their description as objects of direct awareness has to be best understood as a proposal of how the term "sensum" should be applied. What is called "the testimony of inspection" corresponds, I assume, to what the psychologists believe themselves to find when giving a so-called purely phenomenological description of the experience. Now, the assertion that what is experienced in a perceptual situation has the character of coloured patches, sounds, etc., is, like every phenomenological description, an empirical assertion. It is evident that this empirical assertion can be wrong. It is wrong, according to my opinion, for a multitude of perceptual situations. To this point I shall return later on.

The interpretation given here of Broad's introduction of sensa leads naturally to the following interpretation of his assertion that a sensum can never be identical with a physical object or part thereof. Broad is of the opinion that it is certainly *logically possible* from the point of view of the theory of sensa (i.e. that it is not excluded by the characterization of sensa as the directly perceived) that a sensum be identical with, or part of a physical object, but that the inspection of what is directly perceived witnesses against this ever being the case.

Irrespective of the way in which the concept *sensum* is introduced it is obvious that the answer to the question whether a sensum can be identical with or part of a physical object must depend on the way in which the physical object is characterized. According to Broad "physical object" in this connection is to be understood in the way in which common-sense makes use of this expression (or perhaps better still, in the way in which common-sense takes such expressions as "body" or "material object," as the term "physical object" can hardly be said to form part of the vocabulary of common-sense). Broad also attempts to indicate what characterizes physical objects in this sense.

If the physical object, e.g. a penny, is interpreted as in Broad's *philosophical theory* about the physical object, it follows, of course, immediately that no sensum can be identical with a physical object or part of it. The penny as understood by common-sense, Broad calls "perceptual object" (*ST*, 330), and in his theory he conceives this object as a group of constituents of different kinds. A penny is not one single homogeneous object but "a number of correlated constituent objects of different types," viz. visual, tactual, and others. But these constituents are themselves groups of sensa, visual, tactual, and others. A visual sensum is thus only a member of a group of visual sensa, which together with other groups of sensa (e.g. tactual sensa) form the object of perception, the penny. Consequently a particular visual sensum cannot reasonably be said to be identical with, or part of, an object of perception.

Starting from this theory about the nature of the physical object, the thesis of the sensum-theory that sensa cannot be identical with, or parts of, physical objects must present itself as an immediate consequence. But for Broad the theory about the nature of the physical object is not a point of departure; it has rather to be considered as an interpretation, which Broad is inclined to accept, since in his opinion it is impossible for certain reasons to assume that what is directly perceived in a perceptual situation can be a physical object or part of it. In the examination of proposition (II) of the theory of sensa we can thus completely ignore Broad's own final interpretation of the nature of the physical object. He also thinks that the meaning of the term "physical object" ought to be determined according to what common-sense, and not what a philosophical theory puts into this term, when the thesis is put forward that sensa cannot be identical with a physical object or part thereof.

In order to characterize what common-sense means by "physical object," when common-sense speaks e.g. about a penny as a physical object, Broad enumerates a number of features which an object must possess in order to be called a physical object. In *MPN*, 146f. he enumerates the following five characteristics:

(1) to continue its existence during a time which is longer than that of our specious present,
(2) to have a three-dimensional extension in space,
(3) to be independent of perception,
(4) to be public, i.e. perceptible by several persons at the same time, or by the same person at different times, and
(5) to possess, in addition to the properties of which we become aware in a perceptual situation, a multitude of other properties, even such as we perhaps never perceive.

We shall first assume that Broad with these characteristics wished to state some conditions which must be fulfilled if an object shall be called a physical object according to the linguistic usage of common-sense. We can then examine whether these five characteristics really indicate necessary conditions for the use by common-sense of the term "physical object," and we can, furthermore, ask the question whether or not they or some of them are occasionally ascribed to sensa, i.e. to what is directly perceived in a perceptual situation.

To me it appears obvious that characteristic (2) indicates such a necessary condition for the use of the term "physical object" by common-sense. To speak about something, which is not extended in three dimensions, as a body or a material object, is incompatible with ordinary linguistic usage. Something without any extension at all is not a body, and neither is a surface a body. But the characteristic (2) is not confined exclusively to physical objects. A visual sensum also is extended in three dimensions according to Broad (ST, 410). It is thus not feasible to adduce characteristic (2) as an argument for the impossibility of the identity of a sensum with a physical object or part of it. It might be that Broad puts more into this characteristic than just the extension in three dimensions which, according to him, can pertain also to visual sensa. About the physical object he says in MPN, 196 that "it is supposed to be literally extended in Space, having a bounding surface of a certain geometrical size and shape. . . ." He might mean that a visual sensum, a coloured patch, though extended in three dimensions, in contrast to the physical object is not closed in three dimensions. Broad says, e.g., that by a bell (which is a physical object) common-sense means something which has a closed surface with an inner side as well as an outer side, and which is not "merely a patch with indefinite boundaries" (MPN, 149). He seems to be of the opinion, that although three dimensions pertain to both sensa and physical objects, only physical objects are limited in three dimensions, while visual sensa are merely patches with indefinite boundaries. If this is the case he appears to me to have given a description of the directly perceived which is incorrect from the phenomenological point of view, a description which obviously contradicts the results of experimental psychology. What we perceive in a natural attitude is not a patch with indefinite boundaries, but just a three-dimensional whole. It is true that on perceiving, e.g., a sphere I do not perceive its entire surface in the same way in which I perceive the side of the sphere which faces towards me. I am not able to determine merely by an analysis of my perception the colour of the off-side of the sphere, just as little as I can pronounce about the interior of the sphere. But in order to give a description of the directly perceived I shall naturally use the expression "sphere," thus a word which designates something extended and closed in three dimensions, and not "surface of a hemisphere" or something similar.[2] When a natural attitude is taken towards the seeing of things the sensible field is perceived as structurally composed of figure and background. Then the figure which appears against the background—as already pointed out by E. Rubin in his paper *Synsoplevede Figurer,* published in 1915[3]—is experienced as a thing, i.e. as a uniform whole, which is definitely limited in three dimensions. It follows from the distribution of the perceived into figure and background, that we can be said to experience in the example chosen here not only the sphere as a closed whole, but a sphere against a background, which extends behind the sphere. The description of the perception of two trees against a blue sky, as given by Broad in *ST,* contradicts fundamentally these observations of the Gestalt-psychology. There we read:

If e.g. we are in fact looking at two trees, standing up against a cloudless sky, our field of view will consist of two characteristically shaped green patches separated and surrounded by a blue extension. In the visual field there is nothing to correspond to the notion of empty space, for the whole field is occupied by some colour or other *(ST, 33).*

Rubin tells that the subjects in his experiments often had the direct impression of the background continuing behind the figure, and that abstract knowledge or assumption did not play any part in it. Neither is the figure which has the character of a thing experienced as lying upon or in contact with the more diffuse background, but as being at a certain distance from this background. There is plenty of room for empty space in our organized sensible field.[4]

[2] Broad denies this as late as in *Mind* 1947 (p. 109)!

[3] German edition 1921, *Visuell wahrgenommene Figuren.*

[4] The description applies to perception under what I have called here "natural attitude," and what is called by German psychologists "Einstellung auf die Dinge." Under a different, more artificial attitude ("Einstellung auf reine Optik") an experience *can,* of course, be realized, where the directly perceived can be described as has been done by Broad in the quotation given. This fact I believe to be the reason why descriptions of the directly experienced of the type given by Broad are not more easily recognized as unrealistic.

The phenomenological analysis shows also that the directly seen figure is experienced as something three-dimensionally closed. Thus the characteristic (2) does not indicate a property which pertains exclusively to physical objects and never to sensa as the directly perceived.

With regard to characteristics (3) and (4) it is easily seen that they indicate something which is as a rule satisfied, when common-sense talks about physical objects. Commonly we talk about bodies which are independent of perception in the sense that they exist whether they are perceived or not; and we talk about the same physical object which is seen at the same time by several persons or by the same person at different times. There may be some doubt whether these characteristics constitute a *necessary* condition for the application of the expression "physical object;" but it is not necessary here to enter into this question. It is, however, important that according to Broad independence of perception and publicity can also be thought to pertain to sensa. He declares it logically possible that there may exist sensa which are never perceived by anybody, and that sensa perceived on one occasion by one person are perceived also by another person (*Philosophy* 1952, p. 15). The characteristics (3) and (4) can thus not be adduced as arguments for the assertion that sensa cannot be identical with physical objects or parts of such.

With characteristic (1) the case is different. If we assume with Broad that sensa never have a duration which exceeds the specious present, and if an object must have a longer duration in order to be called a "physical object," it then follows from the above that a sensum cannot be a physical object or a spatial part of it. But does (1) really indicate a condition which must be fulfilled by an object in order to be called a physical object by common-sense? I do not think so. It is quite natural for common speech to call a physical object with long duration, e.g. this penny struck in 1900, and which I now hold in my hand, and a short section of the history of this object, e.g. the penny during the short while when it lay upon the floor recently, as one and the same penny, or as one and the same physical object. And there is no limit to the shortness of such a section in the history of the penny. The brief section also is called a penny or a physical object. But objects which have an infinitely short history are also called physical objects. A drop of water which has just formed and which after an instant falls upon a hot stone and evaporates, should we not call this a material object? And has the physicist the feeling of not closely following common speech when he talks about particles of matter with infinitely short duration? Neither do I think that it contradicts linguistic feeling, when the world is described as a spatial whole of physical objects—houses, persons, trees, etc.—in certain relations, even if it is assumed that the world has been created an instant ago and will be annihilated after an instant. Yet if this is correct it does not follow from the short duration of sensa that they cannot be identical with, or parts of physical objects.[5] There remains now characteristic (5) to the effect that the physical object also possesses a multitude of other properties apart from those which are directly perceived in the perceptual situation. If this characteristic indicates a necessary condition for the use of the term "physical object" by common-sense, and if it is at the same time assumed that sensa never have properties other than those with which they are perceived, then it would result from the above that a sensum can never be identical with, or part of a physical object. I am, however, unable to convince myself that the characteristic indicates a necessary condition for the use of the term "physical object" by common-sense. I have the impression that the following can be derived from the linguistic usage of common-sense: (a) If a person professes to see in the hand of another person a brown round penny, and if this other person has the feeling of something hard and cold, common linguistic usage considers it natural to say that the two perceive the same physical object, "the brown, round copper-penny." But is it against common linguistic usage to speak about a body or a material object, when a brown, round three-dimensionally closed something is perceived without any thought about other properties? (b) We are in the habit of distinguishing between two perceptual situations which from the phenomenological point of view can be exactly identical, e.g. when I see a landscape and when I have a hallucination as of a landscape. We differentiate between them by saying that real trees and meadows, thus physical objects, have been perceived in the first perceptual situation, but not in the other. And we must go beyond these two perceptual situations in order to distinguish between them. We inquire if other persons also have perceived the same landscape, and we also ask whether the perceived objects have likewise other properties which trees and meadows are expected to possess. The characteristics (4) and (5) indicate criteria by means of which we distinguish

[5] It is worthy of notice that Broad in another context ascribes to common-sense an opinion about physical objects into which the presupposition of a duration or "history" of the physical object does not enter. He says that "in ordinary life" we distinguish between the object and its history. "We say e.g. that there is a certain object, such as a penny, and that it may either rest or move. . . . These events, we say 'happen to' the object and its history is just all the events that happen to it. You might, we think, have an object without history, but you could not have a history without an object" (ST, 406). This seems to imply, that according to the usual way of thinking an instantaneous thing would not be an absurdity. And it is just against an idea of this kind that Broad turns when he maintains: "no merely momentary object could really exist" (ibid.).

perceptions of real objects from hallucinations, or criteria for the question whether or not the perceived object possesses the reality which is demanded of a physical object. In other words, it is impossible to decide by analysis of the objective constituent in a perceptual situation whether the perceived is a physical object or not. In order to do this it is necessary to go beyond the perceptual situation. But if it is established that the perceptual situation was no hallucination, then the property of being a physical object is predicated of the perceived, and nothing in the linguistic usage of common-sense indicates that the subject, of which the property is predicated, could not be the objective constituent of the perceptual situation, i.e. the object of direct awareness in the perception.

The circumstance that Broad is of a different opinion depends, I believe, on the fact that he has understood characteristic (5) (and also the other characteristics!) in a way different from that adopted above. I have assumed that the five characteristics indicate conditions which must be fulfilled by an object, if it is to be called a physical object according to the linguistic usage of common-sense. Beyond this Broad seems to see in these characteristics also an expression of what common-sense holds of the meaning of the term "physical object." He says about them that they "would generally be admitted to be part of, or to be entailed by the *definition* or the *commonly accepted description* of a 'physical object'" (*Mind*, 1947, 104). Broad thus assumes that common-sense has a theory about the nature of the physical object, and that this theory determines its way of the use of the term "physical object." According to this theory the physical object is a particular existent with all the properties which it can be discovered to have in different perceptions, and perhaps also with other properties; in the different perceptions it reveals only some of its properties. If this is what common-sense understands by "physical object," then it follows obviously that an objective constituent in a perceptual situation, which does not have all these properties, but only a part of them, could not be said to be a physical object. This whole train of thought appears to me to rest upon an erroneous presupposition. It is possible to establish a certain regularity in the linguistic usage of common-sense, indicating when common-sense speaks about a physical object and when not, and when it speaks about *one* physical object, and when about two. I consider it, however, extremely doubtful that common-sense should have a theory about the meaning of the term "physical object."

A remark may be inserted here about the rôle played by the conception "common-sense" in Broad's philosophy, and which may, perhaps, throw some light on what has been said here about the use of the term "physical object" by common-sense. Broad often speaks about the opinions of "common-sense" or "educated common-sense" (also of "practically everybody" or "ordinary people"). He ascribes to common-sense definite opinions, often even on very intricate philosophical questions. He speaks, e.g. about "the common-sense notion that the temporal relations between the sensa in the same sense-history are dyadic" (ST, 369), and says that "common-sense believes that the pervasion of anything by a colour is a two term relation between this thing and this colour" (MPN, 175). Common-sense is also said to react in different ways to philosophical theories, to become more or less shocked by them.

Now it is not quite clear which rôle the assumed opinions of common-sense are supposed to play in Broad. Sometimes the impression is created that he would like to give preference to the theory which is closer to common-sense, when choosing between different philosophical theories. He says: "in philosophy it is equally silly to be a slave to common speech as to neglect it" (MPN, 148), where "common speech" is to be taken just as an expression for the opinion of common-sense. Broad says, that it seems plausible to analyse the meaning of "I see a chair" as a two term relation, obviously just with regard to "common speech" (MPN, 148). Broad speaks on the other hand condescendingly of "poor dear Common-sense" (MPN, 180), whose opinions are such that they cannot cover all facts, and adds: "in face of the facts we can only advise common-sense to follow the example of Judas Iscariot, and 'go out and hang itself' " (MPN, 186).

The question that Broad has in mind when talking about the opinions of Common-sense is of great importance, since according to him the critical philosophy has to analyse the concepts of common-sense. In order to obtain clarity in this matter, we shall ask the question: how is this analysis to be understood? Logical analysis can be understood in at least the two following different ways. Firstly, in the meaning of G. E. Moore when he says that "both analysandum and analysans must be concepts, and if the analysis is a correct one, must in some sense be the same concept."[6] This implies that the term for analysans can be used in all the cases and only in the cases where the term for analysandum is used,—like "brother" and "male sibling" in Moore's known example. On the other hand, however, the analysis can also be understood in Carnap's meaning of explicatio, according to which the explicatum (or the analysans "is to be similar to the explicandum (analysandum) in such a way that, in most cases in which the explicandum has so far been used,

---

[6] Schilpp (ed.), The Philosophy of G. E. Moore, (Library of Living Philosophers), 666.

the *explicatum* can be used; however, close similarity is not required, and considerable differences are permitted."[7] For instance: the transition from the word "fish" as it is used in common speech, where it includes also whales, to the term "fish" of natural science, which does not include the whales. Analysis in this sense implies, in distinction from the analysis in Moore's meaning, a certain change in the denotation of the terms.

One sense in which it might well be said that a philosophical analysis shocks common-sense, is this, that the *analysans* has another denotation than the term for the common-sense-concept, which forms the *analysandum*. The use by natural science of the word "fish" comes into conflict with the linguistic usage of common-sense, and can in this respect shock common-sense. However, when Broad says that common-sense can be shocked by philosophical theories he aims at something different, if I have understood him correctly. The offence which he assumes is based upon the presupposition that common-sense has itself certain theories about the facts, which some of its terms aim at, theories which now come into conflict with philosophical theories. Common-sense can then be shocked by a philosophical theory in the same sense in which one philosophical theory can be shocked by another: common-sense makes certain assumptions which are rejected by the philosophical theory, and does not accept other assumptions made by the philosophical theory. This presupposition, viz. that common-sense has definite opinions about certain of the fundamental concepts which are analysed by philosophy, appears to me very doubtful.

That common-sense should have opinions about these fundamental concepts seems to mean that common-sense is ready to give a definite answer to the question what a certain term signifies. Broad speaks about "the common-sense belief that the objective constituents of perceptual situations are literally spatio-temporal parts of persistent physical objects" (*MPN*, 153), and he explains how this is to be understood: "if you asked the ordinary man to make this reference (i.e. reference beyond the objective constituent) explicit, he would say that the objective constituent is literally part of a certain physical object of larger size and longer duration" (*MPN*, 154). It is obvious that common-sense uses such terms as "perception," "body" or "material object," and such in a sensible way and understands them without difficulty; but it is highly improbable that it should have an idea of how they ought to be analysed. One might ask oneself, if the reaction of common-sense to the question into the meaning of such terms as are usually

[7] R. Carnap, *Logical Foundations of Probability*, 7.

analysed by philosophers would not be just the one which is described
by the often quoted words of St. Augustine about time: "*Si nemo ex
me quaerat, scio; si quaerenti explicare velim, nescio.*"

If this is correct then it is meaningless to ask whether the assumption
that sensa are identical with, or parts of physical objects contradicts
what common-sense thinks about the nature of physical objects. A
question which can be asked within reason is whether or not this
assumption contradicts the common-sense use of the term "physical
object." The above argumentation was intended to show that this is
not the case.

It appears from what has been said that neither the way in which
sensa are characterized, nor the way in which common-sense uses the
term "physical object" entail that sensa cannot be physical objects or
parts of such. Now, Broad also feels compelled, like many other adherents of the theory of sense-data, to adduce special arguments in
favour of this fundamental thesis of the theory. In the remainder of
this essay I shall discuss some of these arguments which Broad seems
to have considered as particularly weighty at least in his earlier writings.

1. *The Argument from Delusive Perceptual Situations.*

This argument is meant to demonstrate that perceptual situations in
which a real thing is perceived, e.g. when I say "I see a brown penny,"
have not the physical object (the penny) as constituent. Broad starts
from a delusive perceptual situation, the "I see a pink rat" of the drunk-
ard, and reasons in the following way:

    a. It is obvious that a pink rat is not a constituent in the perceptual
       situation of the drunkard. A pink rat is no constituent in anything.
    b. "There is no relevant internal difference between the veridical
       and the delusive perceptual situations."
    c. Consequently: it is reasonable to assume that a physical object is
       constituent in neither case (i.e. not even in a perceptual situation
       where a real thing is perceived) (*MPN*, 156).

From an internal likeness between the two kinds of perceptual situations the conclusion is drawn here that they are like each other also in
the respect that a physical object is not constituent in them. The conclusion appears, however, hardly reasonable. This becomes evident
from the following, formally entirely analogous argumentation, which
leads to a conclusion which Broad is not prepared to accept:

    a_1 It is obvious that what Broad calls the epistemological object
       (*MPN*, 141), in a delusive perceptual situation has no counterpart
       in what he calls an ontological object (*MPN*, 141). (This is an

analytical proposition which follows from the definition of "delusive perceptual situation.")

$b_1 = b$.

c_1 Consequently: in no case, i.e. not even in veridical perceptual situations, does the epistemological object have an ontological object as its counterpart. (This is a contradictory proposition.)

In discussing my criticism of the argument in question Broad maintains in a later paper that the argument would be made conclusive by the premiss that the objective constituent "cannot have characteristics beside those which it is visually prehended as having." But he admits that this premiss "begs the question" (*Mind,* 1947, 106). Thus Broad seems to have abandoned the argument.

2. *The Argument from Continuity.*

The starting point in this argument is the relativity of perceptions. The objective constituents of different perceptual situations which we refer to the same physical object, often exhibit incompatible properties. Broad's example is the perception of a penny. If I look straight down upon the penny I am aware of a round sensum, if I look at the penny from an increasingly slanting direction then the sensa I am aware of have an increasingly elongate, elliptical shape. And furthermore: on touching the penny and viewing it at the same time at a slant my tactual sensum is round, but my visual sensum elliptical. The only conclusion which can, strictly speaking, be drawn from these facts is that not all objective constituents of these perceptual situations can be parts of the same physical object; it is, however, compatible with facts that the objective constituent in one or in several of these perceptual situations is part of the penny. Thus also Broad maintains in an already quoted passage that the theory of sensa finds it logically possible to assert that in a specially favourable perceptual situation the objective constituent is part of the physical object. He is, however, of the opinion that certain facts are against this possibility. An argument which is often adduced in this connection is the *Argument from Continuity.*

The reasoning is as follows. Let me look straight down upon a penny, and then gradually change my position with regard to it. I then see first something round, which might be the penny itself or at least a part of it, but thereupon I gradually become aware without any sudden discontinuity of something elliptical, a sensum, which cannot be identical with the round penny or part of it. Now, it must appear extremely remarkable (a) that a hardly noticeable change in my position should result in such a radical change that from a direct awareness of the physical object I turn to being aware of something which cannot be a

physical object, and (b) that two sensa which are "practically indistinguishable" with regard to their internal characteristics should be
so different in another respect that one of them is part of a physical
object, while the other cannot be it.[8]

As a rule the argumentation has been carried out in this way on the
supposition that the described alteration in the form of the directly
seen should completely follow the change in shape of the picture upon
the retina. When Broad in papers dating from the 20's describes the
change of the directly seen he makes this presupposition. When discussing the example of the penny he maintains: "What we sense visually
is not round, except when we are in that very special set of positions
from which we are said to be looking straight down on the penny. And
even if we confine ourselves to this series of positions the sizes of the
various round patches which we sense are not the same for different
positions in the series" (*ST*, 275; cf. 246). Later Broad has admitted that
he, like many other adherents of the theory of sense-data has not taken
into account what psychology calls the phenomena of the constancy of
size, shape, and colour, when describing the object of direct awareness.

Older theories started from the erroneous presupposition that a successive change of the conditions of perception must result in a successive
change in size, shape and colour of the object of direct awareness. It
was assumed that the visual size of a perceived object changes in proportion to the decrease in size of the picture upon the retina, when
the observer increases his distance from the object; that the visual
shape of a perceived object changes uninterruptedly while the position
of the observer with regard to the object undergoes a continuous
change; and that a gradual change in the illumination should result
in an equally gradual change of the colour in the object of direct awareness. That we consider a penny as round, even if we become aware of
the penny from rather different directions, was, naturally enough, explained as a re-interpretation of the visual impression: it was believed
that the directly perceived shape of the penny would be changed in
accordance with the laws of perspective at the same time as the position
of the penny is altered in relation to the eye; yet the association with
tactual sensa or with our knowledge about the constancy of the shape
of the penny leads us—associatively or by some kind of conclusion—to
graft this constancy of shape upon the given impression. The philosophical theories of perception have had great difficulty in abandoning
this mode of thought, and have only step by step been forced to give
way to an entirely different idea which was maintained by more recent
psychology. The description, indicated above, of the immediately given

[8] The variant (a) is found e.g. in Price, *Perception*, 32; Broad gives the variant (b).

has shown itself to be erroneous. The changes in the impressions are not continuous and do not faithfully follow the changes in the physiological and physical conditions of perception. We are directly aware of the penny as something round not only in the special situation when we look straight down upon it, but also under a quite considerable alteration of its angle to the eye. Its size is perceived to be about the same whether we view it from a distance of, let us say, thirty centimetres or a metre, etc. The establishment of these so-called phenomena of constancy forces us to describe the object of our direct awareness in an entirely different way. It is not necessary here to enter into these now well known and generally recognized facts. One point only requires particular insistence.

Let us consider the phenomenon of the constancy of size. It is an established fact that *in normal attitude* we are not aware of any change in the size of an ordinary object, even when the distance to the object is considerably altered. A person at the farthest end of the room does not appear smaller than a person in my immediate proximity, although the size of the picture upon the retina is essentially different in the two cases. But the phenomenon of constancy has a certain limit. If the distance is considerably increased, if e.g. we look from the Eiffel tower at a person in the street below, this person appears like an ant. It would, however, be a mistake to believe that the size I am aware of remains constant within a certain circle around me and then decreases gradually outside this circle in proportion to the decrease in size of the picture upon my retina. It is not possible to draw a distinct limit between what is inside and what is outside this circle. The limit is vague, i.e. if I compare the size of a person I am aware of in my proximity and the size of a person at the distance of five metres, then I take them definitely as equal; if, on the other hand, I compare the size of a person I am aware of in my proximity and that of a person at the distance of 200 metres, I take them definitely as different; but there exists a wide belt within which a comparison of size does not give any clear information. To continue: the phenomenon of constancy asserts itself also for distances outside the assumed circle. When we ascend from the second to the third floor of the Eiffel tower the size of the persons in the street which we are aware of does not diminish gradually in proportion with the changes of the picture upon the retina. No, in spite of considerable changes of the distance the perceived impression of size can remain constant also outside the inner circle for the phenomenon of the constancy of size. These facts together with analogous facts concerning shape have to be kept in mind when taking up an attitude towards the *Argument from Continuity*. On account of them it is altogether im-

possible to talk about a *continuous* change in the impression of size
or shape when the perceptual conditions are altered.

Now, Broad is of the opinion that the *Argument from Continuity*
does not lose weight even when the phenomenon of constancy is taken
into account. The consideration of the phenomenon of constancy only
"shifts the point of application of the Argument from Continuity,"
since it is still necessary to distinguish between sensa which cannot be
parts of the physical object (e.g. on account of their size and shape which
differs from those of the physical object) and sensa which might possibly
be parts of the physical object. And it is still necessary to say that "the
two classes melt insensibly into each other" (*Mind,* 1947, 113). It
appears to me as if Broad in this way of reasoning did not consider that
the term "insensible transition" between the classes of sensa now has a
meaning which differs from that in the original argumentation. In the
original argumentation it meant that there exists a "dividing line"
between two hardly distinguishable sensa such that the sensum on one
side of this line is identical with the physical object, whereas the sensum
on the other side is such that it cannot be identical with a physical
object (cf. *Mind,* 1947, 110). But now the "insensible transition" between the two classes signifies something entirely different, viz. that
the boundary between them is vague. About certain sensa we can say
with certainty that they belong to the one class, about others that they
belong to the other; but the border area contains sensa about which it
cannot be said with certainty whether they belong to the one or the
other class. The transition can be compared with the transition from
forest to grove, obtained by the successive cutting down of one tree
after the other. The vagueness of the terms "forest" and "grove" has
the effect that we never can say that the accumulation of trees will no
longer be a forest but a grove, when the next tree is cut down. Without
the passing of a distinct limit the forest is "insensibly" transformed into
a grove. Nobody will pretend that on account of the fact that the
transition is of this insensible character certain accumulations of trees
should not justifiably be called forest and not groves. In the same way:
from the fact that, starting from the perception of a round sensum, we
arrive by a successive change of position "insensibly" at the awareness
of an elliptical sensum which cannot be part of the physical penny, it
does not follow that it would be "unreasonable" to assume the original
sensum to be part of the penny.

3. *The Argument from the finite Velocity of Light.*

The fact that the velocity of light is finite is adduced by Broad as an
argument against the opinion of naïve realism that the objective con-

stituent in a visual perception is or can be identical with the physical object or part thereof. The argument is expounded in *ST*. *One* point in this connection is that when two persons have sensa of a physical object, these sensa, however like they may be, cannot reasonably be called one and the same sensum, if the persons are placed at different distances from the object; the reason lies in the fact that there exists between the sensa of the two persons a certain difference in time, since the light from the object does not reach them simultaneously; and further: neither of these sensa can be said to be identical with a part of the object, since there exists a certain interval between the time when the object sends out the light which causes the act of sensing, and the sensa which are sensed in this act. This, albeit, very inconsiderable difference in time—an interval which lies below the threshold of what can be registered by our senses—shows that here there can be no question of one and the same sensum of which both persons are directly aware, and that the object of direct awareness cannot be the physical object itself or part of it.

This way of reasoning considered as argument for the object of direct awareness not being part of the physical object, seems to be of interest only in those cases where it is a question of exceedingly small differences in time. If the differences in time are great, then the distance to the physical object is so great that the sensum is clearly distinguished from the physical object not only with regard to time, but also with regard to size and other qualities, and thus already on this account cannot be identical with the physical object or part of it. If we should attempt to identify, e.g. the visible moon, this luminous disc of the size of a plate in the sky, with the astronomical moon or part of the latter, the argument could obviously be adduced against it; but such an identification is absurd already on account of the circumstance that the sensum of the moon is tremendously smaller than the astronomical moon, and of the circumstance that the moon as object of direct awareness is localized in another place than the astronomical moon. Broad seems to want to describe our perception of a celestial body as if we experienced an impression of light as pervading the region where the celestial body is actually found (*MPN*, 166f.). The correctness of this description must, however, be questioned. The distance to the spot of light or the luminous surface is not experienced in this way. The luminous disc is perceived at a distance where no celestial bodies are found. I should like to describe my experience of the distance to the visible moon with the words of the servant-girl in Popelius' *Reading for Children*, when she answers to the question about the distance to the moon: "Sometimes longer and sometimes shorter. When it is lowest near the edge of the wood, it can be reached with a roasting-spit of just the right length."

In the case of perception of objects in our proximity, where the subjective estimation of the distance is more or less correct and where the size we are aware of corresponds to the real size of the object, a number of arguments are eliminated which would exclude the possibility that the sensum we are aware of should be identical with the physical object or part of it. Yet the reason which is adduced in our argument, the difference in time between the sensum and the physical object, still exists, even if the difference in time is very small in this case. It is therefore of interest to test the argument just on such perceptual situations.

An important premiss which is presupposed by the argument, and which Broad rightly points out (*Mind,* 1947, 121), is that what is sensed is "strictly simultaneous with" the act of sensing. If this presupposition is not adhered to, then what is sensed by two persons can be said to be the same sensum, even if the acts of sensing are not simultaneous, the persons being at different distances from the source of light. It can then also be said that the sensa sensed by the persons, and the physical object are identical, in spite of the fact that the physical object and the persons' acts of sensing are separated in time. This is the criticism of the argument which appears to me most obvious.[9]

Now, one of Broad's utterances about the acts of sensing seems to allow us to question the strict simultaneity of the sensed and the act of sensing. With regard to the two acts "sensing" and "remembering" he points out in *ST,* 348: "The two kinds of act are markedly different when a long gap in time separates the act of remembering from the object remembered. As the time-lapse between act and object decreases, the distinction between sensing and remembering grows fainter, and no absolutely sharp line can be drawn where one ends and the other begins." Farther on in the book Broad gives a stricter account of the term "act of sensing" by inserting into its definition a claim of strict simultaneity (*ST,* 358); but the passage just quoted in which the vagueness of the term is underlined seems to stand in closer contact with normal linguistic usage. "Strict simultaneity" of the act and the object of direct awareness need not be an indispensable condition for calling the act an "act of sensing."

In the discussion of Broad's sensum-theory it may be of interest to stress another premiss for the argument. When discussing this argument, Broad assumes a premiss which is—as far as I can see—invalidated by

9 For the discussion of the premisses of the argument see my book *Theorie der Sinnesdaten* (1945), p. 63ff.

the linguistic usage proposed by him for the term "sensum" in another connection.

The argument starts from the following assumption. We cannot talk about *one* sensum which is directly sensed by two persons if the objective constituent in the perception of one of them differs in time from the objective constituent in the perception of the other; and we can not say that a sensum is identical with a physical object or part thereof, if any difference in time exists between them.— This assumption appears highly reasonable if sensa are taken as something momentary, without extension in time. In this case it appears natural to distinguish just on account of the difference in time between the sensum at the time t_1 and the sensum at the time t_2 as two sensa, and furthermore between the sensum at the time t_2 and the physical object at the time t_1 as two different things. (Cf. *ST*, 346.) The case can assume a different aspect if the sensa are supposed to persist for a certain time. It has to be remembered that an adherent of the theory of sensa has to propose rules for the use of the expressions "*one* sensum" (as distinguished from "two sensa"), "the same sensum" (as distinguished from "different sensa"), and "the same" or "two different objects" (as applied to a sensum and a physical object). From the linguistic usage proposed by Broad with regard to "sensa" it seems to follow that a difference in time, of an order of size like the one considered here, does not exclude that two sensa which differ in time may be called *one* sensum, and that a physical object and a sensum which differs in time from it may be called *one and the same* thing.

Let us now consider some of Broad's theses which are of importance for the train of thought in question. Concerning the duration of sensa Broad proposes the linguistic usage that *one* sensum shall not have longer duration than a specious present. Unless I have entirely misunderstood Broad's theory of the specious present the following seems to be a fundamental assumption: if we have to do with an act of sensing of shorter duration than a specious present, then we sense in it one and the same sensible field as long as the act persists (*ST*, 351). This means that if the act of sensing lasts from t_1—t_3, then the same sensible field is sensed at the time t_1, at the time t_3, and at any moment between t_1 and t_3, e.g. t_2. Let us now suppose that I perceive during a time t_1—t_9, which is longer than a specious present, an object which does not change during this time. Then also what I am *directly* aware of or sense remains unaltered. The act or process of sensing which takes place in such a situation can, according to Broad, be split into successive "bits" which are shorter than a specious present, e.g. t_1—t_3, t_4—t_6, t_7—t_9. In every one of these bits a sensible field is sensed, the perduration of which does

not exceed a specious present. In the totality of the longer act a succession of sensible fields is sensed. Instead of "sensible fields" we can
here talk about sensa, since "sensum," according to Broad, can be defined as a part of a sensible field, and since in the example chosen sensum
has the same duration as the sensible field $(ST, 354)$.— Now, the following case is possible according to Broad:

A certain place in a sensible field may be occupied by a sense-quality (e.g. a
colour of a certain definite shade, brightness, and saturation) throughout
the whole duration of the sensible field. We should then say that a sensum
of this colour has persisted and rested in one sensible place throughout the
whole duration of the field. Of such a sensum we can only say that it cannot
last longer than the sensible field of which it is a part (and therefore not
longer than the duration of a Specious Present), though, of course, it may be
continued by qualitatively indistinguishable sensa, occupying similar sensible
places in successive sensible fields $(ST, 355)$.

To me a difficulty seems to lie in this train of thought of Broad for
the reason that the longer act of sensing can be divided into shorter
parts in many different ways. A time, different from t_1, e.g. t_2, can be
chosen as starting point of the division. We should then obtain the acts
t_2—t_4, t_5—t_7, etc., and sensible fields or sensa which in regard to time
partly overlap the sensible fields or sensa which had been accepted in
the aforementioned division. According to the first division at t_3 we
experience the sensum which is sensed during the entire act lasting from
t_1—t_3, but according to the second division at t_3 we experience the
sensum which is sensed during the entire act lasting from t_2—t_4. These
sensa will partly overlap in time. As now the division of the long process
of sensing can be carried out in an unlimited number of ways, the consequence arises that at t_3 a countless number of overlapping sensa are
sensed.— This seems to be a consequence of certain fundamental assumptions made by Broad about the act of sensing, sensum, and specious
present. Nevertheless Broad uses the word "sensum" so as to be able to
say that *one* sensum is sensed at t_3 or in the act of sensing t_1—t_3. If this
linguistic usage with regard to the expression "*one* sensum" is followed,
it appears also possible to speak about *one* sensum in the case of overlapping but otherwise indistinguishable sensa, which in the example
of the argument are sensed by different observers. There seems also to
be nothing to prevent one from saying that the physical object and the
sensum, which is qualitatively indistinguishable from the former, are
one and the same object, in spite of the difference in time between
them.

The difficulty which has now been dealt with must, of course, not be
taken as an objection to the *Argument from the Finite Velocity of Light*.

It only shows that by adopting the argument one has also adopted a premiss which entails important consequences for the elaboration of the theory of sensa, consequences which Broad—as far as I can see—has not observed.

In this article I have examined some of the arguments for a thesis adopted by the adherents of the theory of sensa, viz. that sensa can never be identical with, or parts of a perceived physical object. I am convinced that the arguments in favour of the thesis are not conclusive. By saying so I do, however, not wish to maintain that the thesis itself must be wrong.

KONRAD MARC-WOGAU

UNIVERSITY OF UPPSALA
SWEDEN

16

John W. Yolton

BROAD'S VIEWS ON THE NATURE AND
EXISTENCE OF EXTERNAL OBJECTS

BROAD'S sensum theory, like the sense-datum theories of Russell and Price, takes as its point of departure a belief in external, physical objects. Broad does not seek to prove this belief but only to indicate the grounds for increasing its probability, assuming it has an initial finite probability. In order to achieve this end, at least two tasks present themselves: to characterize the nature of the external objects and to explain how we come to know them. If we do know these external objects, it must be through our senses, since sensation appears to be the first source of our knowledge of our environment. Broad's method of procedure is to ask what the conditions must be for anything to be a physical object and then to examine his sense experiences to see whether they can in fact yield such knowledge. His general solution has been to deny a direct acquaintance with externality by insisting upon a realm of sensa which serves as an intermediary between observer and the external world. The sensum theory is, in other words, a distant relative of Locke's representative theory. But Broad, like Russell, has been concerned to circumvent the scepticism of Locke's theory by a search for a means of bridging the gap, epistemically and semantically, between sensa and physical objects. Russell has appealed to the postulate of isomorphism as a means of making sense-data yield some knowledge of the external, physical world. Broad takes this same postulate as one of the principles of meaning permitting the derivation of physical object statements from sensum statements; but he adds two other principles to strengthen his analysis, the criterion of physicality and the principle of extensive abstraction. An account of Broad's views on the nature of external objects must examine the nature and implications of the criterion of physicality from which his analysis starts, analyze the formulations he offers for the structure of the physical world, and endeavor to decide whether he has succeeded in working from sensa to a knowledge and linguistic formulation of this external physical world.

1—The Concept of Externality

Broad has variously formulated the concept of external physical objects. The composite picture yields ten different prerequisites for physicality. In "Phenomenalism,"[1] a physical object is said to require four conditions. (I) "It must be neutral as between various observers;" (II) "we must be able to talk of its remaining constant while many of the sense-data connected with it change, and *vice versa;*" (III) "we must be able to state causal laws in terms of such objects;" and (IV) "there must be a sense in which they persist when I cease to be aware of the sense-data connected with them." In "The External World,"[2] these conditions were shortened to (I) publicity and (II) the ability of yielding diverse appearances, with the added requirement that (V) the appearances of shape, size, and position must resemble that which appears. In *Scientific Thought,* these two lists are merged into one with another new condition added. The properties are referred to 'a bit of matter.' A bit of matter must (I and II) be independent of minds but "capable of being observed by many minds," that is, it must be independent and public (p. 229); (VI) be neutral between the various senses such that we observe the same piece of matter by our different sense organs (p. 231); (IV) persist and interact with other bits of matter whether observed or not (p. 232); and (VII) have a permanent shape, size, and position in space in addition to being capable of moving from one position to another (p. 232). Condition (III) of "Phenomenalism" does not reappear explicitly either here or later. In *The Mind and its Place in Nature,* the list is reformulated and again increased. There the prerequisites are ascribed to physical objects. Any physical object is said to (VIII) be a strand of history which endures and has a unity and continuity; (VII and IX) be literally (as opposed to Pickwickianly) extended in space with a size, shape, and spatial relations with other such objects; (IV) persist and interact with other objects when not perceived; (I) be perceptible by many different observers and at different times; and (X) have other qualities besides shape, size, and spatial order, some of which may never be perceived (pp. 145–47; cf. a similar list on pp. 195–96). This last condition is meant to include more than primary qualities, although the additional, qualitative nature need not, and (he finds reasons for saying) usually is not the familiar secondary qualities of color, sound, etc., but something similar, e.g., mass or electric charge (p. 207).

Prominent in this concept of externality is the distinction between appearance and that which appears, the distinction which in Broad's own theory is designated as that between sensa and scientific objects.

---

[1] *Proc. Arist. Soc.,* XV (1914–15), 233.   [2] *Mind,* XXX (1921), 387.

This distinction is both a primitive and a derivative belief in Broad's account. "The belief that our sensa are appearances of something more permanent and complex than themselves seems to be primitive, and to arise inevitably in us with the sensing of the sensa." (*ST*, 268)[3] Neither psychologically nor logically can we work from appearances directly to that which appears. "On the other hand, there is no possibility of either refuting it [the belief] logically, or of getting rid of it, or . . . of co-ordinating the facts without it." (*Ibid.*) But this primitive belief refers only to what Broad terms the "constitutive" properties of the physical world, i.e., "that there are things which are relatively permanent, which combine many qualities, and which persist and interact at times when they are not appearing to our senses." (*ST*, 267) This primitive belief is covered by conditions (II), (IV), and (VIII). The further specification of the external physical world, that is, all the other conditions but especially (VII) and (IX), is derivative and arises only late in the development of the individual or of the race. Neither physical space nor time nor matter is given; all three are constructed from the common experiences of man.

The common-sense notions of a single Space, a single Time, and persistent bits of Matter which exist, move, and change within them are by no means primitive. They must be the results of a long and complex process of reflection and synthesis, carried out by countless generations of men on the crude deliveries of their senses . . . (*ST*, 228; cf. p. 95)

His criteria of physicality, which he offers as "the irreducible minimum of characteristics that a thing would have to possess in order to count as a physical object" (*MPN*, 146), cover both the primitive and the derivative components of the belief in an external world.

Although Broad has recognized and dealt with various ontological alternatives as expressions of this elaborate criterion, has, for example, allowed that the distinction (which he thinks is imperative) between sensations, sense-data, and physical objects may be interpreted in a phenomenalist way by making physical objects functions of sense-data or sensations ("Phenomenalism," 228), he has himself consistently favored at least the retention of sense-data and physical objects. He treats phenomenalism (in *PPR*) as derivative from naive realism, just as his own form of realism is taken as an inevitable alternative to naive realism in the face of the various arguments from illusion. But if we were to replace this psychological order of acceptance of these three ontologies by a logical ordering, renaming them slightly in the process, I think we could see more clearly how Broad's particular realist on-

---

3 Broad's major works will be referred to in abbreviation, in line with the policy being followed throughout this volume.

tology emerges from his point of departure, that is, from his criterion of physicality. I would define, and place first in logical order, *phenomenalism* as the doctrine which says matter is just a collection of sense qualities which exist only when perceived. Next would come *phenomenalist-realism,* or naive realism, as the modification of phenomenalism which asserts that sense qualities can and do exist unperceived and that matter is never more than can be disclosed through perception. Last would appear Broad's own position of *dualist-realism* which makes matter not only mind-independent but conceives of it as never known directly in perception. With this classification in mind, we can see that acceptance of the primitive aspect of the complex belief in external objects does not, by itself, lead us to a dualist-realist rather than a phenomenalist-realist ontology. This part of the belief only requires us to conceive the world as independent of mind but revealed in perception. It is the derivative part of this belief which packs into the criteria of physicality the dualist-realist hypothesis. The distinction between literal and Pickwickian inherence (condition IX) brings this ontology into focus, since it is one way of saying that appearances differ *in kind* from that which appears, at least in its spatial properties. The further development of Broad's ontology includes a widening of the area of type-distinction between phenomenal qualities and the non-phenomenal world. There are good grounds for rejecting phenomenalist-realism in favor of a dualist-realism, as Broad labors to show; but it should be recognized that the acceptance of a dualist ontology is not, in this theory, solely the result of arguments presented in the face of phenomenalist-realism, since the dualist ontology is implicit in the derivative aspect of the fundamental belief Broad says arises inevitably in all of us. If this is the nature of our belief about the external world, it is strange that the familiar plain man should have for so long been interpreted as holding to the phenomenalist-realist ontology. If Broad has correctly formulated this ontology in his criterion, it has never been phenomenalist-realist, but always dualist-realist. Even in the earliest formulations of "Phenomenalism" and "The External World," with the clear distinction between appearance and that which appears, the dualistic nature of the belief should have been clear.

The fact that the criteria in "Phenomenalism"—the closest Broad comes to restricting the concept of externality to the phenomenalist-realist ontology—do not exactly fit my formulation of phenomenalist-realism (since he goes beyond the sensible qualities to include a referent of these qualities, i.e., physical objects) illustrates what I mean in saying his criteria are already dualist in nature. Broad purports to be expressing the conditions for physicality which would be acceptable for everyone, a kind of neutral ontology. But this proffered neutrality really masks the ontological bias of Broad (and of other sense-datum philosophers). On the level of ordinary experience, our ideas of physical objects are built up entirely on the basis of phenomenal qualities.[4] We learn to distinguish veridical from non-veridical experiences quickly, still within the phenomenal confines of everyday experience. What we mean by a table in ordinary experience is precisely this particular collection of sensible qualities situated in this particular place in my study; that brown, oval-shaped object, made of oak, etc. From this particular specification of this table, Broad goes on to generalize a concept of tableness or physicality. A physical object then becomes what his various formulations of physicality claim, that is, a permanent, public, independent object with shape and size. It is only after he is armed with this conceptual abstraction from ordinary experience that Broad offers his arguments against a phenomenalist-realism. Appeal to the particularizations of physicality employed in ordinary experience are no longer made. The abstracted criterion replaces the phenomenological description of practical life. Relevant to the criteria, the experiences of ordinary life can no longer confirm a belief in phenomenalist-realism: this is precisely the structure of Broad's argument for dualist-realism. I do not wish to say that Broad has misformulated the ontology of ordinary experience, since that claim is not necessary for my argument that his criteria of physicality already contain the ontology with which he concludes his many arguments against phenomenalist-realism. I think it is misleading to suppose that there is an ontology of ordinary experience. What we as philosophers do is to impose various ontological frameworks upon our everyday world. Neither Broad, nor any of the other sense-datum philosophers, nor their critics, have seemed to me to recognize the status and genesis of their respective ontologies. It would be purely diversionary for me here to attempt to show that we can impose a different ontology upon experience and hence arrive at a different conclusion from Broad about the nature of external objects and our knowledge of them. All that I wish to emphasize is the way in which his final analysis of physicality depends upon his initial postulates. If we abide by Broad's formulation of the minimum conditions for physicality, the situation is not that the plain man reluctantly relinquishes his belief in phenomenalist-realism, but rather that he comes to realize the correct nature of his basic belief. In short, with Broad's complex criteria of physicality, it is impossible to accept anything other than a dualist ontology.

However, the problem of exegesis is rendered difficult by certain pas-

4 Martin Lean expresses this point well, *Sense-Perception and Matter*, 18-25.

sages in the early *Physics, Perception and Reality;* for, in the context of
a discussion of the nature of causation and its relation to objects, Broad
is led to offer a clearly phenomenalist definition of 'thing.' The question
which he there raises is "what is meant by 'one thing.'" This breaks
down into two sub-questions: (1) "What distinguishes it [one thing] at
a given moment from other things at that moment?," and (2) "What
makes us call a certain succession of states the states of one thing that
persists through time?" (p. 92) The answer to the first is "Homogeneity
at a given moment of sense qualities within a definite boundary in
space. . . ." (*Ibid.*) The fundamental notion in the concept of 'one
thing' is that of "certain sensible qualities having extension and shape."
(p. 94) The answer to the second sub-question is simply that the changes
of a state must appear continuous. Both questions, in other words, are
given a phenomenalist analysis very similar in nature to the analysis in
terms of families of sense-data which Price developed some years later.
What makes the situation within the context of Broad's theory even
more puzzling is that he says this analysis of the individuation of a
'thing' is in accord with what common sense means by 'one physical
thing.' Even the conditions (I) to (IV) of the early "Phenomenalism"
article would seem to go beyond this phenomenalist reduction. However, he points out that inference is required to unify the sensible appearances defining a physical object in this way.

For . . . it is partly a matter of inference, and partly a matter of definition, to
identify a seen with a felt boundary, either as to position or to shape. And
then the identification is not a 'finding identical' of the objects of two different sense-perceptions, but a correlation of them with a third unperceived
common shape through their correlation with each other. (*PPR, 95*)

The common unperceived space referred to here is not the constructed
physical space of his developed theory, but the sensory or phenomenal
space of perception; his point is that only after reflection upon tactual
and visual sensible space orders do we come to identify them as one and
the same order. Taken strictly, they are two different orders of space,
but practically we learn to treat them as one. (pp. 16–29) Broad goes on
in this context to deny the necessity of the idea of substance in the concept of one physical object, after the fashion of Russell's elimination
of the substantival implications of 'this' in the *Inquiry into Meaning
and Truth.*

What is true in the substance theory then has no special reference to the unity
of a thing with a number of qualities but refers to the relations of instances
to their universals, a relation which would equally hold in a case of particular which was an instance of only a single universal. (*PPR, 97*)

To the usual arguments for substance from the reality of change ('X has changed' means 'there is an X over and above its manifestations and it is the latter which has changed'), Broad replies with Hume that complete identity of successive states is not required for the concept of 'one thing.' "All that is necessary is that the successive objects of observations should be continuous with each other." (p. 103) Such continuity can be accounted for on a purely phenomenalist basis. Broad thus draws the conclusion:

For we now see that what constitutes one thing in the physical world is nothing of a deep or recondite character, and that its nature is just its qualities from moment to moment in the relations in which they constitute a thing. (p. 104)

This clear formulation of the phenomenalist-realist position on the nature of 'thing' is immediately sublimated in the subsequent discussion in *Physics, Perception, and Reality*. In the very next chapter on phenomenalism, he introduces the familiar distinction between perceptions and the objects of perceptions. Phenomenalism is said to hold "not merely that the objects of all our perceptions exist only when they are perceived, but also that there are no permanent real things with laws of their own that cause these perceptions and in some measure resemble their objects." (p. 164) Broad points out that the phenomenalist is forced to include in his ontology his own past perceptions as well as perceptions of other people, else his account of the world will be unduly restrictive and non-predictive. But once phenomenalism has been modified in this way, has, that is, been expanded beyond solipsism, the question is then "whether the processes by which the phenomenalist . . . arrives at his belief in all these other perceptions would not equally justify the plain man's assumption of a real world more or less like what he perceives." (*PPR*, 168; cf. 178) Broad's answer to this question is in favor of the realist, as opposed to the phenomenalist, assumption, in favor of a realism which goes beyond phenomenalist-realism to a dualist-realism. The clear formulation of 'thing' in a phenomenalist-realist language in chapter two of *PPR* served certain purposes in his discussion of causation; but what seems most strange is that he never shows any awareness that the language he there used in talking about the external world is inconsistent with the language used in subsequent discussions of the subject. It is even inconsistent with his own formulation of the criteria of physicality (I) to (IV) offered before the Aristotelian Society during the same academic year as the publication of *PPR*. In his discussion of the ontology of phenomenalism he seems not to have discerned that his account of 'thing' in that book was an alternative phenomenalist formulation to the description of phenomenalism offered in his direct discussion of that ontology, although it is true that the formulation in chapter two is implicitly phenomenalist-realist rather than pure phenomenalist. The force of his own dualist ontology has obscured this lapse into phenomenalist-realism; it is a lapse which may perhaps be taken as a kind of presagement of more fundamental difficulties within his system, the difficulties of an adequate linguistic formulation of his dualism.

There can be no doubt, however, that despite this peculiar discussion in *PPR*, Broad's own preferences, even in that work, are for the dualist-realist ontology. He does not claim that this ontology can be proved correct, but only that it is the best explanatory postulate for our phenomenal experiences. "The notion of persistent physical objects is logically merely a hypothesis to explain such correlations between perceptual situations" as we commonly find in our experiences. (*MPN*, 152; cf. *PPR*, 180–85; *ST*, 278) This postulate is elsewhere described as a category or "innate principle of interpretation."

From the very nature of the case the notion of "Physical Object" cannot have been derived by abstraction from observed instances of it, as the notion of "red" no doubt has been. For the objective constituents of perceptual situations *are* not instances of this concept; and it is only in virtue of these postulates that we can hold that they are "parts of" or "manifestations of" instances of this concept. The concept is not "got out of" experience until it has been "put into" experience. (*MPN*, 217)

I think it important to note Broad's recognition of the categorial nature of his physical ontology, for this is just the point that needs to be emphasized against those critics of the sense-datum theory who argue that physical object words can only be derived from our phenomenal experiences.[5] The meanings for physical object words in Broad's dualist ontology are extra-ordinary and do transcend phenomenal experiences. No violation of meaning-genesis has been made so long as we properly recognize the source of these transcendent meanings, which lies in part in the criteria or category of physicality laid down by Broad at the beginning of his analysis. I am not at all sure that even Broad recognized the necessity, within his particular ontology, of deriving physical object meanings from his criteria and not from phenomenal experiences; but this is a problem for the third section of this paper. What is important to note at this point is Broad's insistence that the category of physicality as formulated by him in his complex criteria presupposes a structural isomorphism between phenomenal and physical realms: "what is real

---

[5] E.g., Lean, *op. cit.*, 25, 28, 35.

but imperceptible resembles that which we perceive." (*PPR*, 222) More specifically: "There is a certain physical object and a certain part of it which can be called '*the* part of *the* physical object' which has this sensum as an appearance." (*MPN*, 183) Unlike Russell, who appeals to the same structural postulate, Broad does not seek the isomorphous features in all sense experiences but only in tactual experiences, which hold a privileged position in his analysis of our knowledge of externality.

Our conclusion, then, is that it is most probable that there is a real counterpart corresponding point for point to what is perceived in most (perhaps in all) tactual perceptions that we have of figure, though doubtless more differentiated than the tactual objects themselves; and that events in this reality are the causes of our visual perceptions . . . (*PPR*, 265)

The concept of externality embedded in the criteria can thus only be elaborated by appeal to the doctrine of structural similarities between phenomenal and physical realms.

2—*Material Particles and Geometrical Points*

There are two separate tasks involved in any account of the physical world: an indication of the general conditions or prerequisites for physicality and the qualitative description of physical objects. The criterion, which has turned out to be an elaborate categorial imposition upon the data of ordinary experience, accomplishes for Broad the first task while the doctrine of structure renders possible the second. Although there are no reasons against assuming an isomorphism between secondary as well as primary phenomenal qualities, Broad argues that there is no need to postulate a correlation in the physical realm with anything other than primary qualities, e.g., shape, size, or position. The secondary phenomenal qualities can be explained by a primary physical world. Tactual sensations bring us into contact with the external object, although it is rather difficult to state just what is known in such experiences. In *Physics, Perception, and Reality,* the importance of tactual sensations was stated in a tentative manner: if we ever do come into contact with the physical world, the coincidence of visual and tactual sensations may be considered one example. (p. 236) In his *Examination of McTaggart's Philosophy,* the experience is given a phenomenological description. "In tactual perception we seem to ourselves to be prehending the surfaces of independent material things, close to our own bodies, and to be exploring the latter and interacting with them."[6] In *Scientific*

6 II, pt. I, 62; cf. "Some Elementary Reflections on Sense-Perception," in *Philosophy,* Jan. 1952, 6.

Thought the suggestion is advanced more positively. "When we actively feel a body we are trying to penetrate a certain region of the movement-continuum from various directions, and are failing to do so. And our failure is marked by characteristic tactual sensations." (p. 341) What Broad wants to be able to say is that physical or scientific objects are within the region thus marked out in the movement-continuum in a *literal* way: "the felt boundaries are the boundaries of a volume which is *in* the movement-continuum in the same literal sense in which a tactual sensum is in its tactual field. . . ." (*ST*, 341)

But what precisely do we learn from the tactuo-resistant experiences? Whatever is *in* the general area marked out in the movement-continuum of these experiences cannot be said to have "the peculiar sensuous reality that we experience" (*PPR*, 248), since the physical world of Broad's dualist ontology is a world without observers. Thus, it would seem that we can ascribe primary qualities to this world only in the sense that "it will agree in having distinctions where we perceive spatial [or tactual] distinctions and where other people agree with us in perceiving them." (*PPR*, 249) The objective is not so much to give a *qualitative* description of the physical world (since the term 'quality' may itself apply to the non-phenomenal world in only a very indirect fashion) as it is to offer a *geometrical* formulation sufficient for the uses of science. Thus, besides locating the physical object in the movement-continuum, tactual sensations are said to reveal the correct geometrical shape of that object. (*PPR*, 262; *MPN*, 171–73) But Broad requires tactuo-resistant sensations to play another important role in delimiting and characterizing the physical world of external objects. In general, for all sensa the world of matter serves as part cause of the phenomenal world. In finding our movements impeded by certain sensory defined areas in the movement-continuum, are we experiencing more than geometrical properties of the physical world? Condition (III) of Broad's criteria stipulated that we must be able to state causal laws in terms of physical objects. What is even more important, we must be able to state causal laws connecting physical and sensory worlds. In his discussion of causation in *Physics, Perception, and Reality,* Broad made it clear that he wished to define 'cause' in a non-activist sense, i.e., as uniformity. Thus to say that a certain tactuo-resistant sensation is caused in part by a certain feature of physical objects means that the sensa stand in certain uniform relations with the physical object. In *Scientific Thought,* this uniformity is spoken of as a 'fixing,' according to general rules, of the filling of one region by another. A general formulation for causation (or generation, as he refers to it here) takes the following form:

If any determinate c of the determinable C inheres in a region r of the Space-Time S, then a certain correlated determinate γ of a certain correlated determinable Γ inheres in a certain correlated region ρ of a certain correlated Space-Time Σ. (ST, 541)

In the case of physical causation, the region S and Σ are in the same space-time realm. There are other simplifying conditions for causation within the physical realm which need not concern us here, since the important question is what is involved in the causal relation between physical objects and sensa. Broad recognizes that the relation in this case becomes more complex because of the differences between the space-time realms of the two causal factors. But he insists that the causation of sensa does not differ in kind from that of physical objects. (ST, 542) Thus, presumably what he wants to say about physical-phenomenal causation is, like the other physical-phenomenal relations, that for changes in the one there can be assumed correlated changes in the other. Causation is a primary quality since it applies to the physical realm, but it cannot be said, I think, that resistance sensations yield any insight into this primary quality since they disclose no more of the causal (i.e., uniformity) connections between phenomenal and physical than do sensa such as color, for secondary as well as primary phenomenal qualities stand in a causal relation with the physical world. It is only because of the assumption of structural similarity, and certain other special assumptions regarding tactuo-resistant sensations, that these sensa play any more determinate role than others. The causal relation in the phenomenal realm can be said to be similar to the same relation in the physical realm because the postulate of isomorphism stipulates a correspondence and because a uniformity principle can be stated to cover relations in both realms. But the causal principle does not thereby add any qualitative information concerning the physical world which was not already present in the structural postulate. In general, the belief that the physical world has the primary qualities in the same way that we experience them is replaced by the belief "that there is a one to one correspondence between perceived geometrical distinctions in the object of tactual perception and certain permanent ones in the reality events in which cause the perception." (PPR, 263)

The opposition between sensuous and geometrical plays a central role in Broad's attempt to elaborate his account of the physical world. He wants to maintain both that all we know of the physical world depends upon sensa, and that nonetheless the sensuous aspect of sensa must be eliminated in using them as descriptive-indicators of the scientific, physical world. Like Russell, Broad has consistently maintained that the significant features of the physical world are constructed from the

sensuous world of ordinary experience. His most detailed treatment of
the constructionist thesis occurs in his various accounts of physical
space. The question concerning space in the physical sense is whether
we can think of the physical world as being a spatio-temporal whole
analogous with the sensory whole of our various sense-histories. (*ST*,
454) The justification, as always for any feature in scientific formulations, is whether such a manner of thinking summarizes all of the data
of our sensory world. Space-time is not an entity but a system of relations. "When we talk of the properties of physical Space-Time we are
simply enumerating certain very general structural characteristics of
that spatio-temporal whole which is the physical world." (*ST*, 457)
More generally, for any space, whether physical or sensible, "We assume
a class of entities which we call points and we assume certain kinds of
relations between them and other relations which only relate certain
selections of them."[7] A straight line, for example, is a selection of certain
points in the space to which it belongs. Space-time in the physical world
is a system of relations between the various components of whatever it
is that inhabits that world. But the only account of the spatial or
temporal relations of the physical world which Broad offers is geometrical. (*ST*, 457ff) The requirement of abstracting the sensuous elements of experience before we arrive at a description of the nature of
external physical objects is once again interpreted as a task for geometrical formulation. The analogy between the sensuous world of
ordinary experience and the observerless world of physics lies in their
corresponding geo-chronometries. But a geo-chronometry of the physical world, however useful to physics, is insufficient by itself to tell us
what it is that has these spatio-temporal relations. Although there is a
tendency in some passages for Broad to equate the physical world with
the geometrical tools used in dealing with it, there can be no doubt that
he meant to separate the two. In the early article on space already referred to, he very consciously distinguished between space and the
matter which encloses it. To make such a separation "we must suppose
that pieces of matter are related in a certain peculiar way to points of
space." (*Mind*, XXIV, 466) We are thus confronted with two sets of
spatial relations relevant to the physical world of matter: material and
geometrical relations, the latter being unextended. We have, in other
words, a sharp distinction between material particles and geometrical
points. Spatial relations between material particles, or points in matter,
cannot be stated without reference to the relations between the corresponding geometrical points and their relations to material particles.

---

[7] "What do we Mean by the Question: Is our Space Euclidean?," *Mind*, XXIV,
(1915), 465.

The statement "the material point A is twelve miles to the SW of the material point B at the moment t" means, "the material point A is at the geometrical point a at t and the material point B is at the geometrical point B at t and the geometrical point a is eternally twelve miles SW of the geometrical point B." (*Ibid.,* 466–67)

Geometrical points are timeless while material points are subject to time. Like the general concept of externality, space is a feature not given in experience but added to it by way of interpretation. (*Ibid.,* 470) Perceived shapes, sizes, and spaces are found in experience but physical space is not. Any physical space is "conceptual in the sense that" it is "constructed in order to deal with certain sets of experienced objects according to a certain definite plan." (*Ibid.,* 472–73) In the example just quoted, reference to geometrical points renders the material location precise. None of the perceptual data which is summarized by this precise spatial interpretation can be said to be *in* the physical space thus constructed. "This is because physical space and physical bodies are only constructed to deal with certain important data of sight and touch and not with all perceptual data even of waking life." (*Ibid.,* 474)

If we pursue this constructionist thesis closely, it would seem to lead us to the conclusion that all that is required in the concept of external physical objects is a precise geometrical formulation enabling physicists to manipulate and predict the features in the phenomenal world. The world of physical objects would be replaced by the world of geometry. Geometrical points would surplant material particles. Broad has raised the question about the reality of space, saying that this question has two possible meanings. It could mean, "Are the points of physical space of the same logical type as particular sense-data?," or it could mean "Can all observable movements be stated as functions of physical bodies with the qualities that have been ascribed to them and of Space with the qualities that have been ascribed to it in the particular system of physics and geometry under discussion?" (*Ibid.,* 476) The first alternative is indeterminate, although Broad finds no reasons for an affirmative answer. The second alternative is the one Broad favors. Physical space is real in the sense of being a function of observable objects, but the space which is physical and the space which is geometrical tend to merge into one. For the geometrical points which are required to deal with physical position are themselves real in the same way that physical space is real: "in the sense that they are determinate functions of real series of actually existing particulars." (*ST,* 51) But Broad wishes to make the physical world something more than just a geometrical function of phenomenal events. In *Physics, Perception, and Reality* he remarks that all of the laws of motion are stated about what we perceive but are meant to apply to the imperceptible in the sense that "they are laws about that aspect of it [appearance] and its changes to which we believe there to correspond a real counterpart." (pp. 345f) Mathematical analysis is held distinct from that which it analyzes.

Are we justified in supposing that the causes of the perception of a piece of wood and of a piece of iron of the same size and shape are differently aggregated collections of the same kind of small but finite real bodies differing only by their number and arrangement, and such that when, for purposes of the second law of motion, we make the mathematical analysis into particles, we can assume the same laws connecting configurations with acceleration, and explain the observed differences in terms of the differences of number and configuration? (*PPR*, 351f)

Particles in the sense of geometrical points must be carefully distinguished from *material* particles or the material qualities which are formulated by the language of mathematics. Strongly as the constructionist thesis is expressed in Broad, I think it correct to say that it never becomes so dominant as to lead him to deny an ontological realm of material particles which are the real counterparts of our phenomenal experiences. He considers the physical world to have various levels, where the levels are "stages where certain disintegrating agents, which have previously been effective, cease to be so." (*ST*, 401) The first level in the physical hierarchy is, however, not at all clear. "The sort of scientific object which is specially connected with a perceptual object, like a chair, may be called a *first order* object." (*Ibid.*, 400f) We are told that the first order scientific object is "supposed . . . to consist of a great many molecules arranged in a pattern in space" and these are called the *second order* objects. Does Broad mean to say that interposed between the molecules and the perceptual chair there is another imperceptible scientific object? His classification would seem to claim just this, but I do not see what kind of object he has in mind. Be that as it may, we move down in the physical scale by subdividing the molecule into atoms, "characteristically arranged in space and moving in characteristic ways in time." These *third order* objects are themselves arrangements "of positive and negative electrons, with characteristic types of motion," which constitute the *fourth order* objects in the physical world. The classification here is of an open nature, since Broad leaves the way clear to further disintegrating forces.

Matter and the geometry of matter, then, Broad means to separate. There is a realm of real objects classifiable in the manner just indicated, possessed of such qualities as position, motion, spatial arrangement, shape, etc. These primary qualities are referred to as material qualities. (*PPR*, 346; *MPN*, 592) In *The Mind and its Place in Nature* he develops a precise terminology for referring to the material qualities possessed by the various order objects of the external physical world. Space and time are positional qualities, while color and temperature are non-positional qualities. "Every particular existent is characterized by some determinate form of the determinable quality of Temporal Position." (*MPN*, 592) In addition, every instance of a non-positional quality "must *also* be characterized by some determinate form of the determinable quality of Spatial Position." These are the material qualities, distinguished from immaterial qualities which do not need to be characterized by spatial position. Under the impetus for mathematical precision in his formulation, Broad wants to say that every particular existent of a material sort must be both instantaneous and punctiform; that is, each existent is characterized by just one determinate form of the qualities of temporal position and spatial position. The result of this restriction yields point-instants which are the material counterpart of the geometrical points used in the mathematical formulation of physics. Besides the single determinate form of space and time, each point-instant must have a determinate form of one or more non-positional qualities. (*MPN*, 593–94, 207; cf. *PPR*, 265) This is condition (X) of his criteria for physicality. Moreover, there are some qualities which can characterize only groups of point-instants, not the particular point-instant itself, which are dependent upon the particular relations between the individual members of such groups, such as duration, shape, and size. These Broad calls Extensional qualities. They are so defined that they are the results of groupings of instantaneous, punctiform point-instants. In fact, Broad continues in this same context to build up a detailed definition of a material substance. (pp. 596f; cf. *ST*, 215–17) Material particles, which themselves define material substances, are functions of material point-instants sharing the same determinate quality of spatial position, whose determinate qualities of temporal position "form a continuous series, so that the whole composed of these point-instants has a certain determinate duration," and each of which shares in the other necessary material qualities. With appropriate alterations in the conditions of the groups of point-instants, Broad extends this process of construction to the derivation of finite bodies with all the necessary features of a physical object as laid down by his criteria of physicality. We could map the composite picture of physicality by means of the following diagram.

Diagrammatic Map of Broad's Physical World

Levels of Reality				*Qualities*
First Order – ⟨?⟩		imperceptible particles and groups of particles derived from puncti-form, instantaneous point-instants	shape size position mass time motion or change electric charge	Formulated in mathematical, geometrical terms derived from phe-nomenal experi-ences by extensive abstraction.
Second Order–molecules				
Third Order–atoms				
Fourth Order–electrons				

The above diagram is as complete as Broad's dualist ontology permits, but he seems to have thought he could include our own physical bodies in the map of externality. In fact, he treats our own bodies in many ways as the paradigm of physical objects. He points out the special peculiarities about the relation we have to our bodies. The sense-object by means of which I am related to this object remains constant through-out my movements and adjustments with other sense-objects. In order to have contact sensa of this object we do not need to move around since it is always within the contact area. (*ST*, 439) "My trunk is the *only* physical object which appears throughout the *whole* of my visual sense-history as a positionally uniform sense-object; and it is the only physical object which I can touch whenever I like . . ." (*Ibid.*, 440). Moreover, tactual sensations of this object are accompanied by certain somatic sensations, such as the awareness that it is *my* body that is being touched.

My own body is thus known to me by tactual exploration as a closed surface which resists my efforts to penetrate it, like any other physical object. But it is marked out from the other closed surfaces that I feel by the qualitative pe-culiarity of the tactual sensa, and by the fact that I do not have to walk up to it and cannot walk away from it. (*Ibid.*, 441)

Furthermore, the kinaesthetic sensations which accompany these sensa are taken by Broad as sense-perceptions of the inside of this particular body. We can never have inside sensa for other bodies. It is this peculiarity which suggests to Broad an empirical origin for our general concept of physical objects, although this is clearly not meant to sup-plant the *a priori* nature of the category of physicality. But assuming that we can take communication as involving more than a private soliloquy, we learn that other people have bodies of the same sort as we do, having insides as well as outsides, connected to our general sense field in the same peculiar fashion.

I thus come to recognize that there are plenty of other bodies besides my own, having internal processes; although I cannot *perceive* these processes in any body except my own. So the fact that I cannot perceive such processes elsewhere ceases to be any reason for supposing that they do not *exist* elsewhere. (*ST*, 443)

Since we can learn that somatically felt changes are correlated in this instance with optically experienced changes, we come to formulate the belief that what is optically filled in any instance is physically filled as well. But although this may be an accurate account of part of the psychology behind the belief in other bodies, there is a peculiarity about this account of human physical bodies which seems to escape Broad. Where, for example, would we place this object on our map? Presumably if it is to be a genuine physical object, the description contained on our map must be applicable. But Broad does not say that somatic sensa place us in contact with electrons or molecules nor that what we know in these special experiences are imperceptible but finite real particles. When we take somatic sensations as experiences of the insides of our bodies we are not using the term "inside" in the sense that we would, were we to say that inside every physical object lies its imperceptible structure. Experience of pains, of hunger, etc., may be taken as different from experiences of tactual or visual sensations; but, if we are to use the vocabulary of "inside" and "outside" in this connection, it is comparable to speaking of the inside and outside of my desk. Inside my desk are hollow spaces filled with paper clips, notes, pencils, etc. Had I peculiar visual powers I could perhaps have experiences at the same time of the outside surface and of the inside of this desk. But whether we are inside or outside in this example, we are still in the phenomenal world. We have not left the world of sensa and penetrated to the physical world which stands as the postulated correlate to our sensa. We might be able to picture Broad's dualist ontology by saying that our tactual sensa bring us as close to physical objects as we can ever get sensuously and that this experience is almost like touching my desk or my body on the outside. But the situation is not the same with physical objects as it is with the phenomenal objects of our sensuous experience, since I can never penetrate beyond the tactual sensa and obtain a sensuous experience of the physical object which lies just on the other side. In fact, the concept of lying on the other side of my tactual sensa is misleading, since we are here dealing with two different kinds of space and hence of positional qualities. The inside of my physical body to which Broad refers is still a sensuously felt inside and hence part of the phenomenal world. In short, the attempt to place our own physical bodies on the map of physicality results in their being pushed off the map and being placed on the map of phenomenality. The phenomenal object called our body does have a peculiar and special role to play in our experiences, but on the particular dualist ontology advanced by Broad it cannot be taken as a physical object: we are no closer to the physical aspect of our bodies than we are to any other physical object. Broad has apparently forgotten, in these passages, the commitments required by his own ontology and by his other clear acceptances of the sharp separation between sensuous and physical. Like the phenomenalist-realist account of 'thing' in *Perception, Physics, and Reality*, this attempt to single out the body as the paradigm of all physical objects has a strangely phenomenalist character totally inconsistent with his ontology.

Just as his account of the relation between material particle and geometrical point indicates a concern to keep the material and the geometrical provinces separate, so the material realm of physical objects must be kept strictly distinct from the phenomenal realm of sensa. The physical body we call our own cannot be placed in the physical realm so long as we mean by that body what Broad has clearly intended to mean, i.e., the body we know through tactual and kinaesthetic sensations. Physical and phenomenal have been inconsistently blurred. It is the sharp separation of these two realms which is entailed by Broad's criteria of physicality laid down in advance of any further analysis. But the two examples we have remarked of his apparent transgression against the dualistic requirements of his criteria—that of the early definition of 'thing' and the equating of the phenomenal body with a physical body—are not the only tendencies in Broad's analysis leading towards the undermining of his dualism. The constructionist thesis which we have been examining in this section involves a similar two-fold separation to that between physical and phenomenal. The construction of physical objects from punctiform, instantaneous particulars described in *The Mind and its Place in Nature* is not meant to enable us to pass from the imperceptible world of physical objects to the phenomenal world of sensa. It is a construction indigenous to the world of matter alone, although in order for the construction of finite material but imperceptible bodies to be useful and meaningful for the world of ordinary experience, it must be possible to work from the formulation to the phenomenal world. For example, while dealing with the meaning of causation, Broad says that it must be thought of as a relation between durationless states. He observes that it is no objection to say that these states cannot be perceived, for neither can the causal laws.

Both causal laws and the momentary states into which perceptually continuous change of quality is analyzed are discovered by reflecting upon and rea-

soning about what we do perceive. It then becomes quite irrelevant to the validity of causal laws whether the states in terms of which they are formulated
really exist, so long as it is always possible to retrace one's steps from these
durationless states to what we actually do perceive . . . (*PPR*, 117f)

Broad thought he had a method whereby this retracing could be
achieved. But the problem here is one of working back from the formulation used in dealing with the external world to the world as we know
it in sensuous experience. The constructionist thesis has, in other words,
two forms within Broad's ontology. It assumes the form of a derivation
of meaningful concepts to apply to the external world from the phenomenal world of ordinary experience. This derivation, which I shall
refer to as the *linguistic construction,* is achieved by his use of Whitehead's method of extensive abstraction: it involves the defense of
mathematical and geometrical concepts as formulations of the nature
of the physical world. But the constructionist thesis also takes the form
of a derivation of physical objects from instantaneous, punctiform
abstractions. This *ontological construction* occurs wholly within the
physical realm. The two constructions are of course closely related,
since the material qualities used in the second construction are themselves defined in terms of the first construction, that is, in terms of the
mathematical and geometrical language of physics. In fact, the problem
for the dualistic ontology Broad is trying to defend is actually how to
keep the two constructions sufficiently separated to prevent the loss of all
meaning to his ontological concepts. It is debatable whether Broad has
been able to achieve this required separation; for the point-instants
used in the second construction to derive the world of physical objects
seem dangerously near to collapsing into the geometrical points of the
first construction. If we decide that this danger is not only imminent in
his system but actually eminent, then I think we can say that the constructionist element in Broad's physical ontology has triumphed over
the realist factors and renders invalid the concept of a realm of matter
distinct from our mathematical formulation.

3—*Linguistic Formulation and Phenomenalist Transcendence*

Language should not be taken as a particular revealer of the structure
of reality, but a theory of reality is meaningful and understandable only
if it can be formulated in a language. While there are difficulties connected with formulating a language for phenomenalist and phenomenalist-realist ontologies, there are very special problems in a dualist-
realist theory which arise from the phenomenalist transcendence required by such an ontology. Similar linguistic problems arise with
metaphysical or theological formulations: how can our words mean

more than is revealed in phenomenal experiences? Any theory of ostensive definition is clearly phenomenalist in its restrictions, since it is impossible to indicate that which is not directly experienced. Physical object words initially and ordinarily refer to phenomenal qualities, but the requirements of Broad's physical ontology necessitate a non-phenomenalist language for physical object words. The linguistic construction for physical objects referred to in the last section represents Broad's attempt to offer such a non-phenomenalist formulation. The requirement here is for a non-sensuous conception and linguistic expression, a requirement which is achieved by looking through the sensuous content of our phenomenal experiences to their geometrical structure. The observerless world is interpreted as being geometrically similar to the phenomenal world, and the linguistic problem becomes that of deriving geometrical from sensuous terms. The danger, remarked in the last section, of the second construction within Broad's system—the construction of physical objects from point-instants—coalescing into the geometrical formulation for physical objects, reappears on the linguistic level as the problem of determining whether the geometrical formulation is an adequate linguistic description of the non-phenomenal world.

The problems here and their proffered solutions can best be dealt with by first schematizing the various linguistic components employed by Broad for this task.

Linguistic Map for Broad's Dualist Ontology

I *Phenomenal Objects*	II *Transcendent Meaning Principles*	III *Physical Objects*
1. Quality words learned by direct acquaintance, e.g., red, extension, round.	1. Criterion of Physicality	1. Geometrical words learned from mathematics and geometry.
2. Statements comprised of quality words referring to groups of sense qualities.	2. Postulate of Isomorphism	2. Quality words borrowed from phenomenal statements, e.g., extension, shape, size.
	3. Principle of Extensive Abstraction.	3. Statements translating quality words into geometrical words.

The statements translating quality words into geometrical words (III, 3) rest for their meaning upon the three meaning principles (II, 1, 2, 3). The criterion of physicality (II, 1) functions as a directive stipulating that our physical object words must have meanings which go beyond the phenomenal realm; such words are to have an extra-ordinary meaning. The force of the postulate of isomorphism (II, 2) consists in saying that besides the dualism of II, 1, we must replace our quality words and statements (I, 1, 2) by non-sensuous terms. That is, what the postulate calls for, with its emphasis on structural or geometrical relations, is precisely a non-sensuous language. But in order for the move from ordinary phenomenal statements to the abstractive statements of II, 2 to be made, we need some principle showing that a transition can be made from sensuous to geometrical. Thus we have II, 3, the principle of extensive abstraction. It is this principle which plays the final decisive role in Broad's attempt to construct a meaningful language for his physical world, since it enables him to relate the formulation of physical laws to the perceptible events of our phenomenal experience, while at the same time permitting him to say the language refers to the imperceptible world of electrons, atoms, and molecules. He borrowed the principle of extensive abstraction from Whitehead, who used it, oddly enough, to avoid the kind of dualism which Broad's ontology requires.[8] As Broad interprets Whitehead's principle, it consists in defining the geometrical terms—points, lines, and areas—as "series of converging volumes." (ST, 45) The geometrical terms thus defined are not the limits of converging series but are to be identified with the series themselves, although unlike the series which are perceptible, the points or lines are not. The only reality for such concepts is, as we have seen, as functions of the converging series. Broad endeavors to give as concrete a picture of the process of derivation as he can by showing how far the geo-chronometry of an "idealized sense history" can be said to be analogous to the geo-chronometry of the physical world. What is involved is a careful but persistent elimination of the sensuous properties together with a steady narrowing of the spatial and temporal features of the sense history. (ST, 459f) We begin by extending, conceptually, the temporal and spatial field of a particular sense history so that there are no limitations imposed by sensation or memory, e.g., the sense-history stretches indefinitely into the past, and the spatial field includes what could be grasped could we see all around ourselves at once. We then reduce this extended sense-history until we arrive at smaller and smaller slabs or slices, both temporally and spatially. Thus, the history can be conceived as composed of a great number of instantaneous, punctiform slabs. Quality words are thus transformed into geometrical words and we have the translation required by III, 3.

The distinction between the two components of his constructionist

8 Cf. The Concept of Nature, p. 30. "What I am essentially protesting against is the bifurcation of nature into two systems of reality, which, in so far as they are real, are real in different senses. One reality would be the entities such as electrons which are the study of speculative physics. This would be the reality which is there for knowledge; although on this theory it is never known. For what is known is the other sort of reality, which is the byplay of the mind."

thesis—the linguistic and the ontological construction—is never made by Broad as clear or as decisive as I have argued his position requires. Thus, the derivation of the linguistic construction from phenomenal experiences frequently appears as an ontological construction for the physical world; but the fate of his realist ontology depends upon the ability to keep these two constructions distinct. Even though the linguistic construction can be legitimately derived, in the way Broad intends, from phenomenal experience, the validity of this formulation for his ontology requires that it be an adequate expression for the ontological construction while remaining distinct from it. But its adequacy as a meaning-principle for physical object words seems clearly to rest upon the postulate of isomorphism, since it is this postulate which specifies that the external physical world is an analogue of the geometrical features of the phenomenal world. On the directive of the principle II, 2, Broad has reduced the physical world to point-instants. This principle demands a geometrizing of the physical world; II, 3 provides the meaning for such geometrizing while showing how the isomorphous relations of structural features between phenomenal and physical realms can be exemplified. Were it not for II, 2, there would be no justification at all for saying III, 3 applies to or is the linguistic expression of the physical world; we would have merely another formulation for the phenomenal world. In other words, it is the postulate of isomorphism which enables Broad to escape an unknowable substance doctrine, but he escapes this doctrine only by feeding into his meaning-principles the features required by his conclusions. Just as the dualist ontology he advocates as a necessary modification of the ordinary view of the physical world was found to be an imposition upon ordinary experience, so the specific form this dualism takes is the result of the imposition of the postulate of isomorphism upon II, 1. The logical status of both the category of physicality and the postulate of isomorphism is the same: they are explanatory devices capable of rendering intelligible our phenomenal experiences. Like Russell, Broad has been motivated throughout his analysis of perception and reality by a concern to defend the views of science and of common sense. The latter requires some modification over what Broad assumes it to be initially, but the realm of science and the phenomenal realm are allowed to meet only on the grounds of geometrical similarity. The features of ordinary experience can then be allowed to yield information about the external world, and some part of the ordinary non-philosophical belief is thereby preserved. The phenomenal world is related both ontologically and semantically to the physical world by the abstractive process of rendering the sensuous qualities into geometrical concepts.

When Broad is presenting the abstractive process required by the principle of extensive abstraction, he does not always indicate that he understands that the language thus abstracted from phenomenal experience cannot be taken as a physical language for his dualist ontology without explicit appeal to the postulate of isomorphism. But the postulate is the implicit assumption behind the second part of *Scientific Thought*, which tells us very little directly about the physical object words such as shape, size, extension or motion. He assumes throughout that the appearances tell us about their physical correlates. In effect, the bulk of his analysis there is concerned with the quality words that refer to sensa; he leaves us, presumably, to make the necessary abstractions to physical reality. But there are many terminological slips in this and other of his discussions which could lead us to conclude that he has forgotten the requirements of his own ontology. He speaks of physical objects moving away from us and talks frequently of watching physical objects. (*ST*, 413) All that we can watch are sensa on his theory: the conclusion to physical objects is an inference based on his postulate of isomorphism and upon the experienced sensa. The same ambiguity attaches to some of the criteria in the category of physicality. For example, condition (I) asserts that physical objects must be public, perceptible to more than one observer, while condition (VI) says that physical objects must be neutral between the different senses. But the intrasensorial or interpersonal publicity allowed by Broad's dualism is at best only derivative from sensa and dependent upon the assumption of a similarity between appearance and that which appears. Interpersonal publicity is in effect phenomenal publicity, although Broad does not concern himself with justifying the belief in a common phenomenal world. If our phenomenal experiences are interpersonally similar, and if there is a world of objects behind the phenomenal world standing in a causal relation to this phenomenal world, then we can say physical objects have a causal publicity, e.g., that for similar phenomenal experiences there are similar or the same physical objects. In *The Mind and its Place in Nature* Broad violates the proper dualist mode of speech even more openly by arguing that the question of whether any given perceptual situation, besides having an epistemological object, has an ontological or physical object as well, cannot be settled by linguistic considerations alone: "the question can be settled only, if at all, by a careful enquiry into the nature and connexions of *things*." (p. 143) But it is one of the sceptical consequences of his own ontology that we can never enquire into the nature and connection of things in the physical sense: our enquiry is restricted to sensa. What these various terminological slips reveal is not, I think, a fundamental impossibility in the position Broad wishes to defend (as some of the sense-datum critics have claimed) but a failure to maintain the sharp distinction required by the phenomenalist and dualist modes of speech. The failure does, indeed, gloss over some important problems of verbalizing the dualist ontology and of assessing carefully the full significance of the postulate of iso-morphism. It is also related to the other lapses into phenomenalist lan-guage remarked in the previous sections of this paper, but I read both these lapses and the terminological slips as oversights in an otherwise consistent system.

Are we to conclude, then, that Broad has been successful in keeping the linguistic and ontological constructions separated, that is, has avoided constructionism in favor of realism? A decisive answer cannot be given to this question. On the one hand, he has succeeded in offering a linguistic formulation which satisfies the phenomenalist transcend-ence required for his dualist ontology by providing a basis for physical meanings in a set of meaning-principles. He has not tried to pass directly from the quality words and statements of phenomenal experiences to the extra-ordinary physical object words of the external world. Such a direct passage can no more be made on his system linguistically than it can epistemologically. On the other hand, the linguistic construction thus emanating from the three transcendent meaning-principles pre-sents us with a considerable conceptual problem. The physical world which is expressed by the linguistic construction is a world without observers and hence must be radically different from the world of ap-pearances. But the task of conceiving what this non-sensuous world is like is hardly resolved by reference to geometrical formulations, since the components of such formulations are commonly taken to be points, lines, surfaces, and areas. When we abstract from any familiar phenome-nal object and state its geometrical dimensions and relations, we do not ordinarily think we are dealing with other reals of an ontologically different sort from the phenomenal objects. As Broad admits, geo-metrical points are real only in the sense that they are functions of actually existing particulars. We cannot interpret the physical world of Broad's theory as having a reality like geometrical points, since this would reduce the ontology to a mere formulation. That Broad means the physical world to be a function of the phenomenal world in the sense that its geometrical features are the analogue of the phenomenal qualities is beyond doubt. But he just as clearly intends the physical world to be more than a formulation of certain abstract features of the phenomenal world. How then are we to conceive of it? We saw in the previous section that Broad relies upon physics at this juncture in his analysis: he presents a picture of the physical world in terms of the material particles—electrons, atoms, molecules—referred to in physics. But he was not content with saying the material particles, like the phenomenal objects of ordinary experience, have a similar geometrical structure. He found it necessary to make the material particles themselves constructs of point-instants, without making clear how a point-instant differs from a geometrical point. Is a point-instant another ontological ingredient in the physical real along with the other levels discriminated on the map of the physical world? Presumably not, or he would have so specified them. Besides, it is clear, I think, that point-instants stand to the electrons, atoms, and molecules of the physical world in much the same relation as do the points and lines abstracted from the phenomenal world by the principle of extensive abstraction: just as the phenomenal world can be reached by tracing backwards along the abstractive process from the points to the qualities, so the physical objects of the external world are obtained by a constructive process from point-instants. If we take the point-instants in the ontological construction as distinct from the geometrical points of the linguistic formulation, then it would seem that we have in effect two different formulations, the one applying to the phenomenal world, the other to the physical world. If on the other hand, we interpret point-instants as identical with geometrical points, then we have one formulation for two different realms. But on neither alternative do we have a clear understanding of what is being formulated: we do not know how we are to conceive the components of the physical world apart from the formulation. Every attempt to conceive or to say what the physical world is like ends in a retreat to the abstract geometrical formulations of points or point-instants. We have a formulation without knowing what it is that is being formulated. In short, I do not think the linguistic formulation which Broad offers for his ontology instructs us how to separate the formulation from that which is formulated, the appearances from that which appears. A world of geometrical properties only (which his postulate of isomorphism seems to require) is indistinguishable from the geometrical formulations which apply to the phenomenal world.

Thus, I would conclude by suggesting that the difficulties of Broad's analysis of the nature of external physical objects are difficulties of conception and not of formulation. We can follow him into his requirements of isomorphous similarities between phenomenal and physical and into his use of the principle of extensive abstraction. But our conception falters when asked to fill in the contents of the physical world while separating these contents from the formulation which expresses them. Broad has a notable predecessor in his suggestion that the contents are geometrical shapes and figures, for Plato advanced the same suggestion in the *Timaeus*. Plato's spokesman in that dialogue admitted that the ontology advanced there was at best a fanciful or conjectural account. Broad has the sanction of modern science behind his account but I think he has not made the ontology of geometrical solids any more understandable than did Plato. It is especially incumbent upon him to enable us to distinguish our talk about the physical world from that physical world itself. The alternatives are a constructionism which denies the significance of this distinction or a sceptical substance doctrine in modern guise.

JOHN W. YOLTON

DEPARTMENT OF PHILOSOPHY
KENYON COLLEGE

17

William K. Frankena

BROAD'S ANALYSIS OF ETHICAL TERMS

AS BEFITS a Knightbridge Professor of Moral Philosophy, C. D. Broad has written a great deal on ethical topics over a long period of time. He has not, however, published any systematic work of any length on ethics. Most of his writings on ethics are either brief or incidental to a treatment of other topics, and many of them are discussions of the views of others rather than statements of his own. His only long work on ethics is largely historical, interpretative, and critical, and offers very little in the way of a constructive system of moral philosophy.

But, though Broad has not written one of this century's important original books on ethics, he has exerted a considerable influence on its moral theory. Possibly no one has done more recently for the emendation of the human understanding in matters meta-ethical than he has. Few if any worthwhile contributions to ethical theory have appeared in English since 1930 which have not been significantly affected by Broad's writings. His younger contemporaries have depended heavily on his expositions and critical discussions of other peoples' views, and have found his classifications and analyses of possible theories, his definitions, distinctions, terminology, and machinery useful or stimulating. To many of them he has seemed to throw a clear light over "the main problems of ethics" which they have regarded as preferable to any answers to those problems which he might have given under the cover of greater darkness. I am myself one of these younger contemporaries whom Broad has helped in his own way, and if I now go on to ask a few questions or to complain a little about what he has written, I hope I may be forgiven.

In this paper I shall ignore Broad's views on normative and psychological questions, and concern myself only with his opinions on meta-ethical ones, that is, with his analysis of ethical concepts, characteristics, terms, judgments, or sentences. This is appropriate, for Broad's own interest in ethics, when not historical, has been a theoretical and not a practical one. My purpose, however, is not to evaluate Broad's meta-ethical views, but only to try to determine what they are. It may come

537

as a surprise to many that there should be any problem about this, since Broad is always so incomparably clear. This is because people have associated him with the position advanced in *FTET*, and have not followed carefully his subsequent writings. When one does study all of his works in sequence, however, one finds that there is a real difficulty in determining what Broad's analysis of ethical terms is, or even whether there is any such thing at all. Before 1934 his position is clear enough, although it is only tentatively espoused, but after that his writings are singularly non-committal. One senses that his position has changed, but one is hard put to it to say just how. At any rate, I have found the problem of deciphering Broad's views after 1934 most intriguing, and propose here to write out my attempts at solving it, in the hope that they may be of interest to others and move Broad to tell us what his views really are.

I shall begin with an account of Broad's meta-ethical position prior to 1934, and then go on to give a chronological review of his later writings.

I

It is, as we shall see, hardly fair today to tax Broad with simply assuming that ethical judgments are cognitive in the sense of being true or false. It is just, however, to say that before 1934 he always did assume that they are. In an article on ethics in 1914 he says, "Any proposition, whether about goodness or anything else, is either true or false."[1] This statement is not made as part of a discussion of the nature of moral judgments, but, even so, it shows how implicitly he then believed that such judgments are cognitive. When he returns to ethics in 1928, and in the years immediately following, he again takes it for granted that ethical terms stand for characteristics, and is only concerned with the nature of these characteristics, our cognition of them, and their relations to one another and to non-ethical characteristics. In *FTET*, for instance, he defines ethical characteristics as "whatever characteristics are denoted by the words 'good,' 'bad,' 'right,' 'wrong,' 'ought,' and 'duty,' and by any other words which are plainly mere synonyms for some word in this list," and then he adds that "the first and most fundamental problem of pure ethics is whether these characteristics are unique and peculiar," without ever asking whether ethical terms do denote characteristics at all.[2] That he did not ask this question then is, of course, not surprising, for it had not yet come to the fore as it has

[1] "The Doctrine of Consequences in Ethics," *Int. Journal of Ethics,* 24, 1913–14. p. 298.
[2] P. 257.

since—in fact, Broad was himself one of the first to call attention to it in 1934.

In accordance with this assumption Broad usually distinguishes, during the years before 1934, only two kinds of meta-ethical theories: naturalistic and non-naturalistic ones. The former he generally defines as theories which hold that ethical characteristics can be analyzed without remainder into non-ethical ones, the latter as theories which deny this.[3] As a result he has to call naturalistic certain views which Moore had regarded as metaphysical and not as naturalistic, namely, views which define ethical characteristics by reference to metaphysical or theological ones. Thus he regards Spinoza and Paley as naturalists— Paley as a theological naturalist! Sometimes, however, he suggests a rather different definition. He defines a "natural" characteristic as "any characteristic which either (a) we become aware of by sensing sensa which manifest it or by introspecting experiences which manifest it; or (b) is definable wholly in terms of such characteristics and the notions of cause and substance," and a "non-natural" characteristic as one of which neither (a) nor (b) is true.[4] On this account a naturalistic theory would not have to say that ethical characteristics can be analyzed into non-ethical ones; it could claim that goodness, etc., are unanalyzable natural properties. Non-naturalistic theories, on the other hand, would not need to insist that ethical properties cannot be analyzed into non-ethical ones; since there seems to be no reason for thinking that ethical properties would be the only non-natural ones, a non-naturalist might argue that ethical properties can be analyzed into non-natural non-ethical ones, which is what Moore's metaphysical moralists held.

In one place in *Five Types* Broad speaks of three "analyses" of "x is good:" the phenomenalist analysis, the causal analysis, and the *a priori* concept analysis.[5] It is clear that he would regard the first as a form of naturalism, and the last as a form of non-naturalism, but what of the second? "The causal analysis would be that goodness is the property which *causes* a thing to be generally approved by men." Such an "analysis" does not exhibit goodness to us, and, strictly speaking, it does not analyze it either. It only describes it in Russell's sense; it defines goodness by giving a definite description. For all it says, then, goodness itself, if ever known by acquaintance, may turn out to be natural or it may turn out to be non-natural. Broad does not evaluate this theory here or elsewhere in his writings, and he goes on in *FTET* to subscribe to

---

[3] Cf. *FTET*, 257.
[4] "Is 'Goodness' a Name of a Simple Non-Natural Quality?," *Proc. Arist. Soc.*, XXXIV, 1933–34, 264.
[5] Pp. 109–110.

the *a priori* concept analysis. I mention it because it shows that even before 1934 he took seriously at least one type of theory which, like the emotive theory, cannot be labelled naturalistic or non-naturalistic, although it is still a theory which regards ethical judgments as true or false, and ethical terms as in some sense standing for characteristics, though not naming them.

In the 1914 article Broad takes no stand on the issue between naturalism and non-naturalism, being concerned with the views of Moore and Russell about the relation of the rightness of an action to the value of its consequences. In the 1928 article he is concerned with the "analysis of some ethical concepts," but the only strictly ethical concept he takes up is rightness. With regard to it he says,

> I very much doubt whether "rightness" can be defined. I am almost certain that it cannot be defined in non-ethical terms. And I see no reason to think that it can be defined in terms of other ethical concepts, such as "good." At any rate, I do not know, and cannot think of, any satisfactory definition. . . . Rightness is a species of fittingness or appropriateness . . . but [this] is not a definition of it. For, so far as I can see, rightness is a quite unique kind of appropriateness, just as red is a quite unique kind of color.[6]

Here, then, Broad is almost certainly a non-naturalist, at least about rightness. In *Mind and Its Place in Nature* (1929), again, while considering the logical status of ethical arguments with factual conclusions, he says,

> I assume . . . that there are certain purely ethical characteristics, i.e. characteristics which cannot be identified with or defined in terms of non-ethical or "natural" characteristics. I should consider that the characteristics of being "intrinsically good" or "right" or "a duty" are examples of purely ethical characteristics.[7]

The non-naturalistic view thus adumbrated is more fully presented, though still rather briefly and with characteristic tentativeness in *FTET* (1930), partly in passing and partly in a concluding *confessio fidei*.[8] (1) "I . . . think it very likely, though not absolutely certain, that Ethical Naturalism is false, and that ethical characteristics are *sui generis*." (2) Our concepts of ethical characteristics are *a priori* and not empirical. Sometimes this is asserted categorically; sometimes hypothetically, as being almost certainly true if ethical concepts are *sui generis*. Always it is added that if ethical concepts are *a priori*, then they are the work of reason, although it is admitted that reason cannot form these concepts unless experience provides it with suitable occasions in the way of feelings of approval and disapproval. (3) There are syn-

---

[6] "Analysis of Some Ethical Concepts," *Journal of Phil. Studies*, 3, 1928, p. 295.
[7] P. 487.   [8] Cf. pp. 178–179, 268–270, 281–283.

thetic necessary propositions connecting ethical with certain non-ethical characteristics, and they can be seen to be necessary by reason through intuitive induction. This again is sometimes asserted categorically, and sometimes hypothetically, as being true if ethical naturalism is false. (2) and (3) together make Broad a rationalist and an intuitionist, of what he calls the milder sort, both about ethical concepts and about universal ethical judgments. (4) "I am almost certain that 'right' and 'ought' cannot be defined in terms of 'good.' But I am not sure that 'x is good' could not be defined as meaning that x is such that it would be a fitting object of desire to any mind which had an adequate idea of its non-ethical characteristics."

The grounds on which Broad maintained this non-naturalistic theory are only scantily indicated. There is no mention of the naturalistic fallacy. The open question argument used by Sidgwick and Moore is carefully weighed and found wanting.[9] No examination is made of possible naturalistic theories other than that of Hume, except by way of a restatement and discussion of Sidgwick's critique of four such theories.[10] In discussing Hume, however, Broad gives an interesting argument which can be generalized against all naturalistic theories. Perhaps because he assumes that all ethical theories are cognitive, he interprets Hume, I think incorrectly, as maintaining a certain kind of naturalistic theory which he calls "phenomenalistic." According to Hume, he says, "goodness is the characteristic of *being* generally approved by men."[11] Commenting on this position, Broad remarks that Hume's arguments against the rationalists neither refute his opponents nor prove his own case.

. . . it remains possible that he is right and they are wrong. I cannot profess to decide the question here; but I will end by pointing out one consequence of Hume's view. This is that every dispute on questions of right and wrong is capable of being settled completely by the simple method of collecting statistics . . . by experiment, observation, collection of statistics, and empirical generalization. This seems to me simply incredible. I should accept the view that there is a point in any ethical dispute . . . beyond which further argument becomes futile. . . . But . . . the logical consequences of Hume's theory is not [this. It] is that all such disputes *could* be settled, and that the way to settle them is to collect statistics of how people in fact do feel. And to me this kind of answer seems utterly irrelevant to this kind of question. If I am right in this, Hume's theory must be false.[12]

We may take this as objecting to all psychological theories of the sort which Broad later calls "public" or "transsubjective" on two scores:

9 Pp. 173–174.   10 Pp. 166–170.
11 P. 109.   12 Pp. 114–115.

(a) that not all ethical disputes can be settled by argument, (b) that none of them can be settled by "experiment, observation, collection of statistics, and empirical generalization." But the same two objections would seem to rule out all other forms of naturalism, as well as what Broad calls the causal analysis, leaving only non-naturalism as a possibility for him, since he has not yet envisaged the emotive theory or any other kind of non-cognitive theory.

Some points in the sort of view presented in *FTET* are worked out by Broad in *EMcP*, Volume I (1933).[13] He expounds two epistemological theories to which a non-naturalist may resort in order to explain the formation of *a priori* concepts: the theory of innate ideas and that of non-perceptual intuition. He also gives an elaborate and interesting treatment of other topics relating to intuitionism, namely, the nature of analysis, the kinds of definition, and the meaning of simplicity or indefinability. All of these discussions are valuable to anyone trying to understand the intuitionist position. Broad prefaces them, however, with a remark in which one senses a growing uncertainty about non-naturalism in ethics. He says,

. . . although it is quite clear that no naturalistic analysis of ethical characteristics with which I am acquainted is satisfactory, it is certainly not clear to me that none could be satisfactory. Still, we may say that the view that our concepts of ethical characteristics are a priori is quite plausible enough to be worth consideration.[14]

II

Before 1934, then, Broad was a cognitivist in his conception of the nature and function of ethical judgments, and, with some uncertainty, an intuitionist or non-naturalist. After that, however, he no longer takes it for granted that ethical terms stand for characteristics or properties. He still talks, a good deal of the time, as if they do, but he always mentions at crucial places the possibility that they do not. Apparently he was led to take this possibility seriously through reading an unpublished work by A. E. Duncan-Jones in which an emotive theory of ethical terms was expounded, but it was, of course, kept before his mind's eye by Ayer, Russell, Stevenson, and the others who propounded non-cognitive theories after 1933.[15] However, Broad not only is aware throughout this period of the possibility of what he calls "the Inter-

13 Cf. pp. 38–53, 111–127.   14 P. 47.

15 The emotive theory may also have been called to Broad's attention by R. B. Braithwaite, "Verbal Ambiguity and Philosophical Analysis," *Proc. Arist. Soc.,* 28, 1927–28, and by W. H. F. Barnes, "A Suggestion about Value," *Analysis,* 1, 1933.

jectional Analysis" of ethical utterances; he might be aware of this and yet be a convinced intuitionist, as Ross and Ewing are. He may also be giving up the non-naturalism of his earlier works. At any rate, he never again commits himself, even tentatively, to any form of non-naturalism, though he nowhere explicitly rejects it in all its forms; and he shows occasional signs of being inclined to some other kind of position, though he nowhere accepts any such position in so many words.

Thus we come face to face with the problem of this paper: what position about the analysis of ethical expressions, if any, is Broad inclined to subscribe to after 1934, and on what grounds? To answer this question it seems best to make a chronological review of his ethical writings from 1934 on, in an effort to follow act by act the play of Broad's mind.

The first essay which bears on our problem is entitled, "Is 'Goodness' a Name of a Simple Non-Natural Quality?"[16] Here Broad states Moore's theory of value and reviews it "in the light of our present knowledge and beliefs." His article is very clear and helps a great deal in seeing just what Moore's position implies, and what questions are involved in evaluating it. But when we ask what it reveals about Broad's own state of mind, it turns out to be very difficult to interpret. It can be regarded as being wholly noncommittal on Broad's part, for he does not say that he denies or even doubts any of the six propositions he ascribes to Moore, but it can also be interpreted as questioning or implicitly rejecting every one of these propositions.

Three parts of the essay are important for our purposes. Discussing the question whether "good" stands for a characteristic at all, Broad introduces Duncan-Jones' emotive theory, which is very similar to that proposed a little later by Ayer. Following Duncan-Jones he points out that it has a ready explanation for the fact that all attempts to define ethical words in purely non-ethical terms seem to leave out something essential, namely, that this is because "the interjectional, rhetorical, or imperative force which the original sentence derived from the ethical word in it, has vanished."[17] Then, on his own, he argues "that this theory may be further supported by reflecting on how we learn ethical words as children," concluding that Duncan-Jones' view is "quite plausible enough to deserve very serious consideration" and must be refuted before one can take up the question whether "good" stands for a simple non-natural quality.[18] Moore, he goes on to claim, does not refute it. But Broad does not refute it either; he only supposes "for the sake of the argument" that it is not true, and, even so, in the rest of the dis-

---

[16] *Proc. Arist. Soc.*, XXXIV, 1934, 249–268.
[17] P. 252.   [18] P. 253.

cussion he mentions the possibility that "good" does not stand for a property at every point at which it is relevant.

Continuing with the question whether the property denoted by "good" is analyzable, Broad does not say either that it is or that it is not. He insists that it cannot be proved to be unanalyzable, and shows at some length that the attempt to prove that no analysis can be satisfactory "involves some very fundamental and difficult logical points."[19] He seems to feel, though he does not assert, that these difficulties cannot be overcome, but he does not draw the conclusion that goodness is not a simple quality. He agrees that naturalistic analyses seem either to leave something out or to be too complex, but adds, "I am not much impressed with the importance of a widespread feeling that a proposed analysis is unduly complex." As for the feeling that such analyses are inadequate—he reminds us again that Duncan-Jones' theory will account for it. And, of course, he adds that, even if "good" does not name a natural property, it may still be analyzable "partly in ethical and partly in non-ethical terms."

The last question is whether or not "good" stands for a non-natural characteristic. Broad first finds Moore's account of the distinction between natural and non-natural properties unsatisfactory, and offers the alternative epistemological definition of the distinction which was quoted above. Next he contends that, if goodness is simple, then it is "almost certainly" non-natural. I find this contention doubtful, but so far all is clear. Now, however, Broad says, ". . . I do not think that it has been proved or could be proved that 'good' is the name of a simple quality. Indeed, I am now going on to argue that there are considerable epistemological difficulties in holding that 'good' is the name of a simple quality."[20] He then argues that, since it is almost certain that goodness is non-natural if it is simple, then one who regards it as simple almost certainly must hold (1) that we can have intuitive ideas of non-natural properties, and (2) that there are *a priori* notions and our notion of goodness is one of them; adding that, if one believes also that goodness has necessary connections with certain natural properties, then he must hold (3) that we can make synthetic *a priori* judgments.

I find this puzzling. In the last sentence quoted, Broad implies that one who holds goodness to be simple is involved in serious epistemological difficulties, namely (1), (2), and (3), and this seems to be intended as throwing doubt on Moore's position. But, on the other hand, Broad does not himself take (1), (2), or (3) to represent serious epistemological difficulties. About (1) he writes, "although [the principle that we cannot have intuitive ideas of non-natural properties] does seem to me highly

19 Pp. 254–259.   20 P. 267.

plausible, I am not prepared to accept it as self-evident. I am therefore not prepared to conclude that no characteristic of which I can have an intuitive idea could be non-natural."[21] In connection with (3) he says similarly, "I do not find this principle [that there can be no synthetic a priori judgments] in the least self-evident myself. . . ."[22] As for (2), he does not say so here, but in other passages, some written earlier and some later, he makes it quite clear that he also does not find the view that there are no a priori concepts self-evident, and even shows signs of believing that there are such concepts.[23]

The point is that the "epistemological difficulties" which Broad finds in Moore's position will lead one to reject this position only if one is inclined to be an empiricist, and Broad does not seem much inclined to be one. He does seem to find empiricism "plausible," but this can hardly mean that he is ready to accept it. But then, although his article does bring out the epistemological consequences of the view that goodness is simple, and so may confirm the opponents of this view in their denial of it, it does not tell us what Broad thinks. So far as I can see, he says nothing which is incompatible even with Moore's form of non-naturalism. But, even if he means to reject this, he may still be subscribing to a non-naturalism which defines "good" in terms of "fitting," although, of course, almost everything that he says about Moore's theory will also apply to any other non-naturalistic position. But what he says is also compatible with an emotive theory, and even naturalism does not seem to be definitely excluded by it.

III

Broad's inaugural lecture, *Determinism, Indeterminism, and Libertarianism,* also published in 1934, may give us some light on his state of mind. Broad argues here that our ordinary moral judgments involve the notion of categorical obligation or obligability, and that categorical obligability almost certainly entails more than indeterminism and very probably entails libertarianism. But libertarianism is "self-evidently impossible." "It is therefore highly probable," he concludes, "that the notion of categorical obligability is a delusive notion, which neither has nor can have any application."[24] We need not evaluate the argument, for it is only this conclusion that concerns us. While it is somewhat hypothetical, it seems to commit Broad to saying that the non-naturalistic kind of ethics to which he had subscribed is very probably

21 P. 267.   22 P. 268.
23 Cf. *EMcP*, I, 47, and a quotation given below from "Some Reflections on Moral Sense Theories."
24 *EHP*, p. 217.

mistaken, centering as it does on the ordinary notion of moral obligation. In fact, stopping where it does, it suggests a kind of ethical scepticism, according to which morality involves the notion of a relational characteristic of obligability which cannot be reduced to non-ethical terms but which is delusive in the sense of not applying to anything.[25] This seems to be what one of Broad's colleagues felt when he said after the lecture, "If that is what you really believe about your subject, I should think that, if you *had* any duties, the first of them would be to resign the Chair." Broad's reply is amusing, but it hardly helps to end our quest for his analysis of ethical terms: "I can see what he meant, but I have seldom allowed conscientiousness to degenerate into fanaticism and I have continued to draw my salary ever since."[26] I still wish *I* could see what *he* meant.[27]

With the interpretation of the 1934 article on Moore in mind, one reads with interest Broad's contribution to a symposium on the question "Are there Synthetic A Priori Truths?" (1936).[28] For if he here finds it unlikely that there are, then one has some reason for concluding that he there meant to be throwing doubt on intuitionism in general. And, indeed, Broad does say here that "the theory that all ostensibly a priori propositions are analytic . . . has enough plausibility to be worth serious consideration."[29] His main point, however, is that the principle that all truths are either analytic or empirical must itself be either *a priori* or empirical. If it is *a priori,* then it is a synthetic *a priori* truth, for it can hardly be regarded as analytic. To be consistent, therefore, one must hold that it is an empirical generalization about statements. But then it is only probably true and to determine its truth

---

[25] Of course, Broad may be thinking that fittingness is different from moral obligation and not delusive.

[26] *Op. cit.,* pp. x–xi.

[27] In his class lectures at about this time Broad recurs to the causal analysis or descriptive theory of the meaning of ethical judgments, according to which "x is good" means "There is one and only one characteristic or set of characteristics whose presence in any object which I contemplate is necessary to make me contemplate it with approval, and x has that characteristic or set of characteristics." He says he regards this as "the most satisfactory account of what I mean when I make a first-hand judgment of the form 'This is good' or 'This is bad'. . . ." This seems to mean that he has given up intuitionism, without accepting naturalism or the emotive theory. The descriptive theory, he points out, leaves open the question whether there is a characteristic answering to the description or not, and whether, if there is, it is natural or non-natural. It is true that he applies it only to "good" and "bad," and not to "right" and "ought," but presumably the same reasons that lead him to apply it to the former would also hold of the latter. Then these unpublished lectures may be taken to confirm the hypothesis that Broad moved away from non-naturalism after 1934, though perhaps not in the direction of naturalism.

[28] *Proc. Arist. Soc. Supp.,* XV, 1936.   [29] *Op. cit.,* p. 110.

. . . what is wanted is a detailed examination of (and not vague 'gas' about) logic, arithmetic, algebra, geometry, and ethics, in order to see whether representative propositions in each of these ostensibly a priori subjects can all be shown to be synthetic empirical propositions about certain kinds of linguistic usage.[30]

Since the paper stops at this point, we are left wondering. Does Broad believe that all ostensibly *a priori* propositions can be shown to be analytic in the sense of being empirical propositions about certain kinds of linguistic usage or does he not? Most readers probably assume that he does not. But he does not say so, and he does say that this theory is plausible enough to warrant serious consideration! In short, his discussion here does nothing to unveil the mystery we are probing.

In 1938, in his *EMcP* II, Part II, Broad makes two statements relevant to our problem:

I think it must be admitted that, when this confusion [mistaking a necessary and reciprocal synthetic connection between goodness, on the one hand, and some set of non-ethical characteristics, on the other, for an *analysis* of the former in terms of the latter] is avoided, no proposed definition of "intrinsically good" or "intrinsically bad" in wholly non-ethical terms seems to be at all plausible.[31]

This seems to rule out the possibility that Broad is moving toward some form of naturalism. He then says, about Osborne's view that "x is intrinsically good" means "x is an object which it is fitting for a human being to desire as an end,"[32]

It seems to me that, *if* there is a pair of characteristics of which "intrinsically good" and "intrinsically evil" are names, it is quite plausible to suppose that they can be analysed in this way. Any reader who is interested to know what I have to say on the whole subject may consult my paper, "Is 'Goodness' a Name of a Simple Non-Natural Quality?"[33]

This tells us that the 1934 paper contains Broad's views on the analysis of "good" but helps little to tell us what those views are. It does say, however, that *if* "good" stands for a property, and the italicized "if" indicates that Broad has a real doubt about this, then it stands for the non-natural property of being fitting to desire. From the two statements taken together then, it seems reasonable to infer that Broad would choose between the emotive theory and Osborne's form of non-naturalism, rejecting naturalism and Moore's kind of non-naturalism.

But which position does he prefer, that of Duncan-Jones or that of Osborne? In "Ought We to Fight for our Country in the Next War?"

---

[30] *Ibid.*, p. 116.   [31] P. 659.
[32] See H. Osborne, *Foundations of the Philosophy of Value*, (1933), 94.
[33] *Loc. cit.*

written "some years before the outbreak of the second World War,"
Broad gives an excellent and typically intuitionist or non-naturalist
account of ethical arguments and reasoning, but perhaps we should not
read anything into this fact. He then writes about the question stated
in his title,

> . . . I have no idea what is the right answer to this question, and, if I had,
> I should not be able to prove it to people who accepted different ethical princi-
> ples and premisses from those which I accept. I am not sure indeed that it is
> the kind of question to which there is an answer, even laid up in Heaven, as
> Plato might say.[34]

The first part of this passage could have been written by an intuitionist;
it is, in fact, reminiscent of Broad's comment on Hume. The second
part, however, could not, for an intuitionist would have to think that
there was an answer at least in heaven. Indeed, as Broad implies in his
remark on Hume, a naturalist would have to think there was an answer
too, though probably not in heaven. This passage, therefore, seems to
indicate that Broad is disposed to choose the side of Duncan-Jones.
    This interpretation, however, appears to be cancelled out by the
paper on "Conscience and Conscientious Action" (1940).[35] It is true that
Broad is careful to speak, not of "moral cognitions," but of "ostensible
moral cognitions," thus avoiding a cognitivist commitment, and that
he goes on to work out definitions of "having a conscience" and "being
conscientious" which can be accepted by an emotivist. In less guarded
moments, nevertheless, he talks like an intuitionist, and, what is more
to the point, he refers to emotivists as "ethical sceptics" in such a way
as to imply that he is not one of them.

IV

Broad's next piece is a review, in 1940, of Ross's *Foundations of
Ethics*.[36] He says that he is not impressed by Sir David's argument to
show that "good," in at least one of its senses, is the name of a non-
natural quality, and that he believes the following account of the facts
to be equally plausible. Admiration is an emotion which it is appropriate to feel in the presence of any of a large number of natural
characteristics like courage and intelligence. " 'To be good' . . . simply
means 'to have one or other of the natural characteristics which make
an object fit to be admired.' " Each of these natural characteristics
counts as a fitting-making characteristic, and there is no need to have
both a non-natural quality of goodness, grounded on these natural
characteristics, and a non-natural relation of fittingness grounded on

---

[34] *EHP,* p. 240.   [35] *Ibid.,* pp. 244–262.   [36] *Mind,* 49, 1940. See p. 237.

this non-natural quality, as Ross has. Even if we discount the fact that Broad merely claims that this account and that of Ross are equally plausible, which may be going too far, we learn here only that Broad rejects the Moore-Ross view that "good" in one of its senses stands for a simple non-natural quality. The sentence quoted suggests a form of non-naturalism similar to that of Osborne and Ewing, but it does not necessarily commit Broad to such a position. Everything depends on what he would say about the term "fit," and this he does not indicate.

In 1942 Broad published a revised version of part of his 1934 paper on Moore, introducing some important changes but still leaving us in the dark about the drift of his own thinking.[37] Then he argued that maybe "good" does not stand for a characteristic at all, but if it does stand for a *simple* one, then it almost certainly stands for one which is non-natural, and there are "epistemological difficulties." Here he repeats that "it is by no means certain that ['good'] is the name of a characteristic at all," and he argues as before that, if it names a simple characteristic, then it almost certainly names one which is non-natural. But he adds that if "good" names a complex characteristic there is also good reason to think that it names a non-natural one. For, he says,

I know of no proposed definition of goodness in purely natural terms which is in the least plausible. But . . . it would not be unplausible to suggest that "x is intrinsically good" means that x is something which it would be *right* or *fitting* to desire as an end.[38]

In other words, if "good" stands for a characteristic at all, that characteristic is probably non-natural.[39] Broad does not, however, say that then Moore is involved in epistemological difficulties, as he did earlier. He first comments that "anyone who saw reason to doubt the existence of non-natural characteristics . . . might fairly use this conclusion as an argument to show that 'good' is *not* a name of a characteristic at all."[40] Does he say this because he doubts the existence of non-natural properties? In the next sentence he writes, "It will be worth while to develop this line of argument a little further." Then he points out as before that Moore's position involves admitting *a priori* concepts and synthetic *a priori* truths, and again says that the empiricist denial of these epistemological doctrines is highly plausible but not self-evident. Is he denying Moore's view then? If so, on what ground? And which

[37] "Certain Features in Moore's Ethical Doctrines," *The Philosophy of G. E. Moore,* ed. by Paul A. Schilpp. See pp. 57–67.

[38] Pp. 64–65.

[39] For a brief discussion of his argument see my "Some Arguments for Non-Naturalism about Intrinsic Value," *Philosophical Studies,* I, 1950, 56–57.

[40] P. 65

view is he inclined to espouse instead, an emotive theory or Osborne's kind of non-naturalism? If the latter, why does not what he says about Moore's theory hold against his own? All that seems clear is that he is still rejecting naturalism.

Next in the sequence of Broad's ethical writings appear two pieces on evolutionary ethics—a discussion in 1942 of C. H. Waddington's views on the relation between science and ethics, and a review in 1944 of Julian Huxley's *Evolutionary Ethics*. Nothing of interest here occurs in the latter.[41] In the former, however, Broad ends by stating as follows a view which he claims is what Waddington really had in mind.[42]

(i) There is a certain group of interconnected emotions which may be called "ethical." Examples of these are moral approval and disapproval, feeling of guilt, feeling of obligation, and so on. An ethical belief is a belief which is toned with one or more of these emotions. Such emotions act as motives for or against doing actions towards which they are felt, and so we have specifically *moral* motivation. (ii) The study of young children shows that in the main ethical emotions become attached to actions which hinder or promote the adjustment of the child's social relations with his family in general and his parents in particular. He acquires a moral motive against doing the former and for doing the latter. (iii) A certain kind of ethical emotion becomes attached to a certain kind of action through the child doing such actions impulsively or instinctively and then finding that the reactions of his parents are satisfactory or unsatisfactory to him. (iv) From this we infer that the "function" of ethical emotions is to enable individuals to live in social relations with each other; just as the "function" of the lungs is to aerate the blood, and that of the heart to distribute it throughout the body. (v) In particular cases a type of action which is detrimental to social harmony may have become associated with an approving ethical emotion, or one which would conduce to social harmony may have become associated with a disapproving ethical emotion. In such cases we say that ethical judgments about such actions are "false." This just *means* that these particular ethical judgments fail to perform that "function" which is characteristic of ethical judgments as a whole in human life. To call an ethical judgment "false" would be like calling a certain state or process in the heart or lungs "unhealthy" or "abnormal." (vi) A study of the genesis of ethical emotions and beliefs in the infant and of the part which they play in making family-life possible *suggests* to us the function of such beliefs and emotions in the life of the race. But in order to determine the latter more precisely it is necessary to consider the main trend of change in social relations throughout human history. We then recognize that the "function" of ethical beliefs and emotions is to keep human social relations changing in this direction and to prevent them from deviating from it or reverting within it. To call a particular ethical belief "false," then, means that it fails to perform this, which is the characteristic function of ethical belief as such.

[41] This review in *Mind* is reprinted in *Readings in Philosophical Analysis*, ed. by H. Feigl and W. S. Sellars.

[42] "The Relations between Science and Ethics," *Proc. Arist. Soc.*, XLII, 1942, 100G–100H.

This passage is interesting because the view here expounded is similar to the view which Broad himself seems to accept in the essay to be taken up next. Here, however, he only throws it out "as a suggestion for critics of Dr. Waddington to consider." He does not criticize it himself, but it looks as if he would, for he says,

I do not propose to criticize it myself here and now. But I would conclude by asking [Waddington's critics] to look with a very attentive eye at the notion of "function," which plays so large a part in my statement of the theory. I wonder whether this has not teleological and perhaps even ethical overtones which carry us beyond the methods and presuppositions of ordinary natural science.

The last sentence appears to imply that Broad is of the opinion that "ethical overtones" lie "beyond the methods and presuppositions of ordinary natural science." Indeed, earlier in the paper he asserts categorically that an ethical belief cannot be supported or refuted by the methods of natural science, that is, by sense-perception and introspection aided by experiment and generalized by problematic induction. In other words, Broad is still against naturalism.

V

We come thus to the most important of Broad's writings on ethics after 1934, namely, "Some Reflections on Moral Sense Theories" (1944–45),[43] which I find exciting because in it Broad seems to be propounding and defending a kind of naturalism after all. He considers here only "deontic sentences" like "That act is right," and begins by distinguishing three "analyses" of such sentences: (1) interjectional or emotive theories, (2) subjective theories (autobiographical, transsubjective, etc.), (3) objective theories (some naturalistic, others non-naturalistic). Of all these theories, he says, only three are worth serious consideration: the interjectional theory, the moral sense form of the transsubjective dispositional theory, and objective theories of a non-naturalistic kind.

About the interjectional theory he says very little, namely, that it "can be swallowed only after one has undergone a long and elaborate process of 'conditioning' which was not available in the eighteenth century."[44] This only explains why Richard Price would not have taken the theory seriously; it does not necessarily imply that Broad himself has not undergone the conditioning required to swallow it.

The only objective or non-naturalistic theory which Broad takes up

43 *Proc. Arist. Soc.*, 45. This article was occasioned by a reading of Richard Price and is reprinted in *Readings in Ethical Theory*, ed. by W. S. Sellars and J. Hospers. My page references are to this volume.
44 P. 365.

here is the naively realistic form of the moral sense theory. By this he means the view which thinks of deontic cognition as a naive realist thinks of the perception of yellow. This view Broad definitely rejects, after discussing it at some length, and he seems at the same time to be rejecting Moore's theory, for he remarks that Moore in *Principia Ethica* was probably tacitly assuming something like a naively realistic interpretation of both ethical and perceptual judgments.[45] But does he mean to be rejecting all other forms of non-naturalism too? He does not say, for he is concerned only with moral sense theories, and does not seem to regard the Osborne-Ewing form of non-naturalism as naively realistic. He does remark once more that,

. . . if ethical terms . . . are simple and non-naturalistic or are complex and contain a non-naturalistic constituent, then the concepts of them must be wholly or partly *a priori* . . . and such judgments as "any act of promise-keeping tends as such to be right" must be synthetic and *a priori*. Now it is a well-known and plausible epistemological theory that there are no *a priori* concepts and no synthetic *a priori* judgments.

But then he adds,

If I am right, anyone who feels no doubt about this epistemological theory can safely reject the analysis of moral judgments which makes them contain non-naturalistic constituents. On the other hand, anyone who feels bound to accept that analysis of moral judgments will have to reject this epistemological theory.[46]

He does not tell us whether he accepts this epistemological theory or that analysis of moral judgments.

Later on in the essay, however, he finally makes clear what he thinks of epistemological objections to non-naturalism. About the argument that there are no *a priori* concepts he writes,

For my part I attach very little weight to this argument. I can see nothing self-evident in what I will call for short "Hume's Epistemological Principle," and I am not aware that any conclusive empirical evidence has been adduced for it. It seems to me to be simply a useful goad to disturb our dogmatic slumbers, and a useful guide to follow until it begins to tempt us to ignore some facts and to distort others. I am inclined to think that the concepts of Cause and of Substance are *a priori* or contain *a priori* elements . . .[47]

As for the contention that there are no synthetic *a priori* propositions— he observes that "Such an argument would have different effects on different persons," indicates that he is neither unmoved nor overwhelmed by it, and concludes that "it is rather futile to rely on a gen-

[45] P. 370.   [46] Pp. 363–364.   [47] P. 378.

eral argument of this kind."[48] We must infer, then, that he does not really mean to argue against Moore on epistemological grounds, as he seems to in the 1934 paper.

By the transsubjective dispositional form of the moral sense theory, Broad means the view that "x is right" means "Any normal person would feel a peculiarly moral pro-emotion towards x, if he were to contemplate it in a normal state." It is then a naturalistic theory similar to that which Broad ascribes to Hume. But Broad does not therefore attack it, as one might expect. Instead, he shows how it may be defended against attack. He states the three main difficulties of the theory, including some that Sidgwick and he had in mind in criticizing such theories as Hume's, and then proceeds to show, not that the theory cannot answer them, but that it *can*. The three questions are,

(i) Can it deal with the fact that judgments like "That act is right" seem always to be grounded upon the supposed presence in the act of some non-ethical right-inclining characteristic, such as being the fulfilment of a promise? (ii) If so, can it deal with the further fact that the connexion between a right-inclining characteristic and the rightness which it tends to convey seems to be necessary and synthetic? And (iii) can it deal with the fact that it seems not only intelligible but also true to say that moral pro-emotion is felt towards an act in respect of the characteristic of *rightness* and moral anti-emotion in respect of the characteristic of *wrongness?*[49]

We need not run through Broad's answers to these questions in detail. The important point is that he concludes that the naturalistic theory under discussion can deal plausibly with these facts and then stops. He does not actually say that he accepts the theory, but he seems inclined to. Two passages are of especial interest. In the first Broad is explaining part of the answer to the second question, and what he writes sounds very like the view which he ascribes to Waddington in one of our earlier quotations.

The defensive part of the argument might take the following line. Civilised men throughout human history have been assiduously conditioned in infancy and youth by parents, nurses, schoolmasters, etc., to feel moral pro-emotions towards acts of certain kinds and to feel moral anti-emotions towards acts of certain other kinds. Moreover, if we consider what kinds of acts are the objects of moral pro-emotions and what kinds are the objects of moral anti-emotions we notice the following facts about them. The former are acts whose performance by most people on most occasions when they are relevant is essential to the stability and efficient working of any society. The latter are acts which, if done on many occasions and by many people, would be utterly destructive to any society. On the other hand, the former are acts which an individual is often strongly tempted to omit, and the latter are acts which he is often

48 P. 379.   49 P. 376.

strongly tempted to commit. This is either because we have strong natural impulses moving us to omit the former and to commit the latter, or because the attractive consequences of the former and the repellent consequences of the latter are often remote, collateral, and secondary. It follows that any group of men in which, from no matter what cause, a strong pro-emotion had become associated with acts of the first kind and a strong anti-emotion with acts of the second kind would be likely to win in the struggle for existence with other groups in which no such emotions existed or in which they were differently directed. Therefore it is likely that most of the members of all societies which now exist would be descendants of persons in whom strong moral pro-emotions had become attached to acts of the first kind and strong anti-emotions to acts of the second kind. And most existing societies will be historically and culturally continuous with societies in which such emotions had become attached to such acts. These causes, it might be argued, conspire to produce so strong an association between such emotions and such acts in most members of every existing society that the connexion between the emotion and the act seems to each individual to be necessary.[50]

About this answer Broad says,

No doubt this line of argument will produce different effects on different persons. For my part I am inclined to attach a good deal of weight to it.[51]

In the other passage, which comes at the very end of the essay, Broad is concluding his answer to the third question.

What is happening when a person is said to be feeling a *first-hand* moral emotion towards an act in respect of his belief that it is right or that it is wrong? I can give only a very tentative answer to this question, based on my own imperfect introspection of a kind of situation with which I am not very familiar.
   It *seems* to me that in such cases I do not first recognise a quality or relation of rightness or wrongness in the act, and *then* begin to feel a moral pro-emotion or anti-emotion towards it in respect of this knowledge or belief. What I seem to do is to consider the act and its probable consequences under various familiar headings. "Would it do more harm than good? Would it be deceitful? Should I be showing ingratitude to a benefactor if I were to do it? Should I be shifting onto another person's shoulders a burden or a responsibility which I do not care to bear myself?" In respect of each of these aspects of the act and its consequences I have a tendency to feel towards the act a certain kind of moral emotion of a certain degree of intensity. These emotional dispositions were largely built up in me by my parents, schoolmasters, friends and colleagues; and I know that in the main they correspond with those of other persons of my own nation and class. It seems to me that I call the act "right" or "wrong" in accordance with my final moral-emotional reaction to it, after viewing it under all these various aspects, and after trying to allow for any permanent or temporary emotional peculiarities in myself which may make my emotional reaction eccentric or unbalanced. By the time that this has happened the features which I had distinguished and had viewed and reacted to separately have fallen into the background and are again fused. They are the real mediating

---

[50] Pp. 379–380.   [51] *Loc. cit.*

characteristics of my moral pro-emotion or anti-emotion; but I now use the omnibus words "right" or "wrong" to cover them all, and say that I feel that emotion towards the act in respect of my belief that it is right or that it is wrong.[52]

What makes this passage especially interesting is the fact that, although he does so tentatively, Broad seems to be giving as his own an account of what happens in a first-hand deontic judgment which cannot be accepted by an intuitionist, but only by one who holds what he calls an "Emotional Reaction" theory. Thus he seems at last to have parted company with the non-naturalists altogether.

In doing so, if this is what he is doing, Broad appears to think of himself as adopting an emotional reaction theory of a naturalistic kind, namely, a transsubjective dispositional form of the moral sense theory, as he so winsomely calls it. It should be remarked, however, that what he says is also compatible with an emotional reaction theory of a non-cognitivist kind. In fact, the passages quoted seem to me to fit in with some kind of interjectional analysis better than with any naturalistic one.

It is possible, then, that Broad has not clearly distinguished and chosen between the above two kinds of emotional reaction theory, even if he has given up non-naturalism. I may, however, be misinterpreting him in suggesting that he has done the latter, for he does not openly declare himself and is characteristically non-committal throughout most of the essay.

VI

In any case, the end of our quest for Broad's analysis of ethical terms is not yet, though we have not far to go. There is the well-known paper, "Some of the Main Problems of Ethics" (1946).[53] In it Broad writes as if he were subscribing to "the Objective Analysis" of ethical judgments, as he himself points out, but he reminds us that ethical terms may not stand for characteristics at all, and he stops on occasion to explain what account emotional reaction theories will give of the matter in hand, for example, of the notion of right-making characteristics. He does, in one place, point to a certain difficulty for "any form of the Emotional Attitude analysis," but it is a difficulty to which he himself has supplied an answer in the paper on moral sense theories.[54]

[52] Pp. 387–388.
[53] Reprinted from *Philosophy*, 21, in *Readings in Philosophical Analysis*, ed. by H. Feigl and W. S. Sellars, pp. 547–563.
[54] See *op. cit.*, p. 561.

Of more interest for our purposes is a paper on "Hägerstrom's Account of Sense of Duty and Certain Allied Experiences" (1951).[55] Hägerstrom is one of the pioneer proponents in this century of an interjectional or emotive analysis of ethical utterances, and Broad has recently translated a volume of his essays into English. In the present paper Broad gives a somewhat sympathetic exposition of Hägerstrom's theory, calling it a form of "ethical subjectivism" or "ethical positivism," and claiming that "none of its Anglo-Saxon adherents has made so thorough and ingenious an attempt . . . to show how the various aspects of the admitted facts can be fitted into the theory." Near the end, presenting Hägerstrom's views about rightness and the sense of duty, Broad says, "Hägerstrom first considers in detail and rejects, on what seem to me to be adequate grounds, various attempts to identify [i.e. define] 'rightness.' "[56] Now, I take Hägerstrom to be rejecting all naturalistic definitions of 'right' in favor of a non-cognitive theory. Is Broad here doing likewise, rejecting even the kind of moral sense theory to which he seemed earlier to subscribe? If so, is he favoring an interjectional analysis or a non-naturalistic one? Or is not that kind of moral sense theory included among the "various attempts to identify 'rightness' " which he is denying? Or is he not distinguishing between it and the emotive theory? It seems to me quite possible that he is not, since they are both emotional reaction theories. This possibility is borne out by the fact that the positive account of moral emotions and judgments which Broad ascribes to Hägerstrom is strikingly similar to that which he himself suggests at the end of the moral sense paper. In fact, both accounts seem to be compatible with either an emotive or an intersubjective moral sense theory. Even if we assume that he has given up non-naturalism then, we cannot be sure which of these two other kinds of theory Broad is inclined to hold.

Our last exhibit, a review of S. E. Toulmin's *Examination of the Place of Reason in Ethics,* is no less puzzling.[57] Toward the end Broad restates Toulmin's estimate of the strong and weak points in the subjectivist, imperativist, and objectivist accounts of moral indicatives, and of the places of each of them in a correct and adequate account of moral phenomena. Since he says, "I find myself in general agreement with much in Toulmin's position as thus summarized," I shall quote his summary.

---

[55] *Philosophy,* 26, 99–113.

[56] P. 110. One of these "adequate grounds" seems to be the open question argument which he found inadequate in *FTET.*

[57] *Mind,* 61, 1952.

(1) Moral phenomena in general, and the experiences which we express by moral indicatives in particular, are unique and peculiar. The only satisfactory way to investigate them is to do so *directly*. If we try to force them into moulds derived from reflecting on non-moral phenomena and the verbal expressions for these, we shall inevitably distort them. (2) The experiences which are expressed by moral indicatives resemble in certain respects judgments asserting an emotional reaction of the speaker towards an object, and in certain respects the experiences which are naturally expressed by uttering interjections or sentences in the imperative. But in each case there are unlikenesses which are as important as the likenesses. (3) Each of the three theories has arisen through concentrating on the resemblance to one of these non-moral parallels and ignoring the unlikenesses to it and the resemblances to the other non-moral parallels. (4) The two theories which admit that moral indicatives express *judgments, viz.,* the objectivist and the subjectivist theories, agree in making a certain tacit assumption. They both assume that two judgments about the same thing can logically conflict only if they refer to one and the same *property,* which one person assigns to the object and the other denies of it. Seeing that moral judgments can logically conflict, the objectivist concludes that the words "good," "right," etc., must be names for properties of a peculiar kind. Seeing that there are no such properties, the subjectivist concludes that moral judgments cannot logically conflict and therefore can only assert or deny that the speaker is reacting emotionally in a certain way to the object. (5) Mr. Toulmin rejects this common assumption. He holds that moral judgments *can* logically conflict, but that they do *not* assert or deny a property of an object. In order that they may logically conflict "all that is needed is a good reason for choosing one thing rather than the other. Given that, the incompatibility of 'This is good' and 'This is not good' is preserved. And that, in practice, is all that we ever demand" (p. 43). (6) Mr. Toulmin thinks that the imperativist makes the same tacit assumption as the objectivist and the subjectivist. But the imperativist's reaction is to deny both their alternatives and so to conclude that moral indicatives do not express judgments of any kind. (7) This line of thought is made plausible by concentrating upon singular sentences describing a concrete perceptible fact, like 'The cat is on the mat,' and taking them as the type of all sentences which can possibly express judgments. Here and here only it is sensible to talk of a *correspondence* between the elements and the structure of the sentence, on the one hand, and those of a certain fact to which the sentence refers, on the other, and to say that truth or falsity consists in the concordance or discordance between sentence and fact. Since moral indicatives plainly do not answer to this pattern, it is assumed that they cannot be true or false, i.e., that they cannot express judgments. But, then, it must be noted that the vast majority of sentences which admittedly express judgments obviously do not fit into this pattern.[58]

One cannot help wondering how much of this Broad accepts. Does he, for example, agree "that moral judgments . . . do *not* assert or deny a property of an object?" If so, then he is here rejecting both naturalism and non-naturalism, in favor of a view which he would have to call "in-

[58] P. 100.

terjectional," though Toulmin would object to this label.[59] But, perhaps, this is not part of what Broad agrees with Toulmin about. In the next paragraph he goes on to say that he does not clearly understand Toulmin's positive account of what is expressed by moral indicatives.

One aspect of this is stated in Chapter VI under the heading "Gerundive Concepts." These concepts fall under the general formula *"worthy* to be treated in a certain way." . . . Mr. Toulmin states definitely that gerundive concepts cannot be identified with or defined wholly in terms of *de facto* subjective attitudes. . . . There is nothing particularly new or startling in this aspect of the theory. It has been very fully developed, e.g., by Sir W. D. Ross and by Dr. Ewing. "Worthiness to be treated in a certain way" is in fact our old friend "fittingness" and, as such, I have no quarrel with it.

The last part of this passage seems to imply that Broad has not given up non-naturalism after all, at least not the Osborne-Ewing form of it. But, if this is so, it is difficult to see how he can be agreeing with very much in Toulmin's position.

Yet, in a sense, it is dramatically fitting that the last episode in our story should be this review of Toulmin. For this review may itself reflect something of the state of mind in which Broad has been since 1934—unable to decide finally between the three received types of ethical theory, seeing truth and error in each of them, and not discerning any tenable fourth alternative. This would explain why he finds so much to agree with in Toulmin's book, and at the same time why Toulmin's view does not seem clear or satisfactory to him. It would also explain why his ethical writings after 1934 have the character we have found them to have.

VII

We must now see what our story adds up to. Is there an "analysis of ethical terms" to which Broad is subscribing, at least tentatively, after 1934 or at the present time? It may be that there is not—that he is a sceptic in meta-ethics, if not in normative ethics. There is no such analysis which he explicitly accepts even in the cautious way in which he accepted non-naturalism in 1930. On the other hand, there is none which he clearly rejects with any kind of finality, so that he may be a non-naturalist, or an emotivist, or a naturalist. It may also be, of course, that Broad has been and still is undecided, sometimes favoring one analysis, sometimes another. We have seen that for every one of the main types of meta-ethical theory, there are some places where Broad seems to lean toward it as at least plausible and others where he seems to oppose it. But, though it is possible that Broad is a non-naturalist

[59] Broad should also object to it if he accepts (2).

still, or that he is uncertain, or that he is a sceptic, it is in my opinion reasonable on the basis of the above evidence to adopt the following hypothesis: that

(1) Broad has been doubtful of non-naturalism since the early thirties and has now essentially given it up, though on what grounds is not clear,

(2) he is still reluctant to accept any form of naturalism according to which ethical disputes can be settled by "experiment, observation, collection of statistics, and empirical generalization,"

(3) he has been moving, uncertainly but definitely, toward an emotional reaction theory of some sort, but

(4) he is undecided as between an interjectional form of the emotional reaction theory, like those of Duncan-Jones, Ayer, and Hägerstrom, but involving a unique moral emotion, and a transsubjective dispositional form of the emotional reaction theory, also involving a unique moral emotion. That is, he is undecided between the theory that a moral judgment simply *expresses* a unique moral emotion of the speaker, and the theory that it *asserts* that any normal person will feel this peculiarly moral emotion toward the object in question if he contemplates it in a normal state. In the paper on moral sense theories Broad appears to prefer the latter, but the rest of the time he prefers the emotive theory to any form of naturalism. It may be, however, that he is not always concerned to keep the two theories apart in his mind, for as we have seen, the passage at the end of the moral sense paper where he comes closest to accepting an emotional reaction analysis is compatible with both of them.

In fact, there may not be much difference in effect between the two theories just described. On either of them one can adopt Broad's favorite notion of right-making characteristics, and one can account for the apparent necessity of the connection between them and "rightness" along lines which Broad himself indicates. Again, on both of them, ethical disputes are "settled" in the same way, namely, by an empirical investigation into the presence or absence of these right-making properties. On neither view would the dispute directly involve any further enquiry of a statistical sort into what people approve. This is clear in the case of the emotive theory, but it may come as a surprise that it can be true of any emotional reaction theory of a naturalistic kind. Even Broad seems usually to think that for any theory of the latter sort an ethical enquiry is really a statistical one. Yet, when he explains how the transsubjective dispositional form of the moral sense theory can account for the apparent necessity of judgments like "Promises ought to be kept," he also shows that it does not necessarily make such judgments statistical. According to this theory such a judgment says, "Any act of promise-keeping would tend to call forth a moral pro-emotion in any *normal* human being who might contemplate it when in a *normal* state." Now the latter statement, Broad points out, may be contingent or it may be analytic, depending on the definition of "normal," and he himself seems to prefer to regard it as analytic, like "Any sample of *pure* water boils at 100°C. under normal atmospheric pressure," even though it is "founded on a whole mass of interconnected empirical generalizations."[60] If it is contingent, then it is statistical and Broad's objection to Hume applies, but if it is analytic this is not true.

It may be argued that the dispositional view has the advantage of allowing ethical judgments to be true or false and ethical disputes to be capable of being settled as scientific questions are settled. This will be true if the accepted definition of "normal person" includes "approving of the kind of action in question when in a normal state." But then, if one is really doubtful of the validity of the ethical judgment under discussion, he will simply shift his disagreement to the definition of "normal," and, if he does, how will the new dispute be resolved? Broad says that the definition of "normal," like that of "pure water," is founded on a mass of empirical generalizations, among which will be generalizations about what is approved. Then a statistical study is involved at least at second remove, but, in any case, it cannot be claimed that the definition follows logically from the conclusions of such a study.

If this is so, however, an emotivist may contend that he can do as well as a naturalist, if he is given the same empirical generalizations about what we approve. For then he can claim that "agreement in attitude" will follow upon "agreement in belief," that ethical disputes can therefore be "settled," and that, if ethical judgments cannot be true or false, they can be justified or unjustified, reasonable or unreasonable. On both views, the statistical generalization that people tend to approve certain sorts of action or qualities of character will be of central importance, but on neither will it be a working part of any ethical dispute— it will not constitute a direct reason for any ethical statement but will only be presupposed by the whole process of giving reasons for such statements.

To conclude—I may be entirely mistaken in my hypothesis about Broad's later views. If so, I should be only too happy to be told the truth about them, and so, I believe, would many of his other readers. If not, it would be equally gratifying to know which form of the emotional reaction theory he prefers, if he has any preference, and to have a fuller statement of it. In either case, it would be good to hear the grounds on which he takes the position he takes and rejects those he

---

[60] Sellars and Hospers, *Readings in Ethical Theory*, p. 382.

rejects. For example, if he holds the transsubjective dispositional form of the moral sense theory, on what ground does he do so? Is that analysis of rightness a rendition of what we ordinarily mean or is it like the definition of pure water as what, among other things, boils at 100°C. in an atmospheric pressure of 76 centimeters of mercury? If the latter, how would he defend his analysis against others?

WILLIAM K. FRANKENA

DEPARTMENT OF PHILOSOPHY
UNIVERSITY OF MICHIGAN

18

R. M. Hare

BROAD'S APPROACH TO MORAL PHILOSOPHY

WHEN, as a student beginning moral philosophy, I first read *Five Types of Ethical Theory* (then as now one of the most-used text-books in the subject), I remember being scandalized, as were many of my contemporaries, by its concluding passage:

We can no more learn to act rightly by appealing to the ethical theory of right action than we can play golf well by appealing to the mathematical theory of the flight of the golf-ball. The interest of ethics is thus almost wholly theoretical, as is the interest of the mathematical theory of golf or of billiards. And yet it may have a certain slight practical application. It may lead us to look out for certain systematic faults which we should not otherwise have suspected; and, once we are on the look out for them, we may learn to correct them. But in the main the old saying is true: *Non in dialectica complacuit Deo salvum facere populum suum.* Not that this is any objection to dialectic. For salvation is not everything; and to try to understand in outline what one solves *ambulando* and in detail is quite good fun for those people who like that sort of thing.[1]

We had just returned from a war during which we had been personally confronted with a number of moral questions which did not admit of an easy answer. Many of us hoped that philosophy might be of assistance to us in answering these questions. Indeed, that was what made us study this subject, rather than others more obviously relevant to practical problems. We were no doubt wrong to object to Broad just because his idea of fun differed from our own. But could it be that when people found the money to pay the stipends of philosophical professors, their main object was to enable these professors to amuse themselves?

The dislike of a priggish undergraduate for his prescribed reading may seem a matter of no importance; yet I have mentioned it because it is one of the purposes of this paper to show how unjust, in many respects, this criticism was. It was founded upon ignorance—ignorance of both the historical and the logical reasons which had led Broad to write in this way. It is worth while to examine these reasons; for moral philoso-

[1] *FTET,* 285.

phers have often found themselves subjected to criticism of this sort, especially in the present century. The criticism takes many forms, but the cause of the dissatisfaction is usually the same. I shall endeavour to show that the tendency in modern ethics which has provoked this dissatisfaction owes its origin to the work of the intuitionist school, of which Broad is an able representative. This fact should be obvious to anyone who has understood what has been happening in ethics during the past fifty years; but it is worth while to draw attention to it, since it is commonly thought that more recent writers are to blame for the tendency.

A proper treatment of the problem requires a survey of the development of philosophers' views on the point at issue during the first half of this century, together with an attempt to set the question in its true light. Since both these tasks will take me some distance away from Broad's own writings, I wish to explain that my object in this paper is not directly to discuss (let alone to criticise) what little he has written about the scope of moral philosophy. It might indeed be said that on this, as on other questions, Broad has been very chary of expounding his own views; his fame rests on his admirably clear discussion and criticism of the views of others. But since his writings give evidence of a consistent attitude to this question; and since the attitude is a widely-held one and the question itself of fundamental importance, this seems too good an opportunity to miss of raising the question, and thus compelling Broad, in his reply, to say, more fully than he has done, what he thinks about it.

*   *   *   *   *

In a volume devoted to Broad's philosophy, a historical survey of recent developments might appropriately have started with Sidgwick; but for reasons of space I shall not go so far back. I shall start with Moore. I do not know whether, when Moore wrote "The direct object of ethics is knowledge and not practice," he was consciously controverting Aristotle's equally famous remark on the same subject;[2] but it may fairly be said that the publication of *Principia Ethica* in 1903 marks a great break with tradition, and the beginning of a new way of thinking about this question—as about so many others. This is not to say that the distinction which Moore made between ethical theory and moral judgment had not been made before in ethics; it was made, in different words, by Socrates.[3] But it owes to Moore its prominence in recent

---

[2] G. E. Moore, *Principia Ethica*, p. 20; Aristotle, *Eth. Nic.* p. 1103 b 27: "Our enquiry has as its object, not the knowledge of what goodness is, but that we may become good men." It may be that Aristotle's enquiry was not in fact so different from Moore's as these quotations would seem to imply.

[3] See, for example, Plato, *Euthyphro*, 6 d.

ethics. The distinction is that between two questions, both of which might be expressed by the words 'What is good?' This question might, says Moore, be taken as meaning 'What (sorts of) things are good?'; but it might be taken as meaning 'How is "good" to be defined?'[4] And though Moore included under the name 'ethics' attempts to answer both these questions, he regarded the latter question as prior and treated it in the first half of his book; and it was his attempt to answer it (an attempt whose results were startlingly negative) which has provided the stimulus to nearly every important development in ethics from that day to this.

It has recently been suggested by Dr. Raphael[5] that, while recent moral philosophers have, with a one-sidedness which he condemns, concentrated on the question which Moore treated first in his book, the second half of the book was what counted most "outside the circle of professional philosophers." Lord Keynes and the Bloomsbury group are instanced in support of this contention. But what inspired Keynes and his friends were not just Moore's opinions about what things were good, treated simply as opinions—as such they were not perhaps strikingly distinctive. It is quite clear from Keynes' *Memoirs* that the reason why Moore was treated as a prophet was not merely that he propounded certain value-judgments (though these value-judgments *did* inspire them), but also that he had important new things to say about the nature of value-judgments and the way they are made. And Moore's doctrine about method was the direct outcome of his refutation of naturalism.[6]

As Keynes' biographer puts it,

The doctrine of indefinability has the consequence that decisions about what is good depend on direct intuition in each particular case. The interpretation given in Oxford to this consequence was widely different from that in Cambridge. In Oxford—no doubt owing partly to the special attention paid to Aristotle's *Ethics*—great reliance was placed on what may be called traditional morality, embodying the intuitions of wise men through the ages. In Cambridge the doctrine of intuition was interpreted—anyhow by those disciples who were to be for many years the intimate intellectual companions of Keynes—as giving fairly complete licence to judge all things anew.[7]

[4] Moore, *op. cit.*, 3–5.

[5] In an unpublished paper, "Recent Oxford Contributions to Ethics," read to the Oxford colloquium on Contemporary British Philosophy, 1955.

[6] I shall use the term 'naturalism' to cover any theory which is refutable by the argument which Moore used, or a recognisable reformulation of that argument: that is, roughly, any theory which treats an evaluative expression as equivalent to a descriptive expression. I have given my own reformulation of Moore's argument in *Language of Morals*, ch. 5.

[7] R. F. Harrod, *Life of J. M. Keynes*, 77.

"How did we know (says Keynes himself) what states of mind were good? This was a matter of direct inspection, or direct unanalysable intuition about which it was useless and impossible to argue."[8] Yet Keynes and his friends *did* argue; and their arguments were of a sort which is in one respect strikingly similar to those employed in the most recent philosophical discussions in Oxford about ethical questions. Moore's disciples used the methods of linguistic analysis (of which Moore has a good claim to be called the modern inventor) in order to clarify evaluative questions. This was the only form argument *could* take, since once the issues were clarified, there was no further place for argument. "We spent our time (says Keynes) trying to discover *precisely what* questions we were asking, confident in the faith that, if only we could ask precise questions, everyone would know the answer."[9] And of these arguments he says, "It was a method of discovery by the instrument of impeccable grammar and an unambiguous dictionary. 'What *exactly* do you mean?' was the phrase most frequently on our lips."[10] Thus, in deciding a question of value, argument (traditionally the province of moral philosophers) was confined to the elucidation of terms. Once these were understood there was nothing left to argue about; the individual had to make his own judgments of value, and, provided that the verbal elucidation had been done properly, individuals would not (so it was thought) disagree. It was only this pious hope which distinguished this kind of intuitionism from the most extreme form of subjectivism—and this should remind us that these two doctrines, superficially so different, are not in fact very dissimilar.

Keynes also says that, preoccupied with this intoxicating business of evaluating personal experiences under the powerful illumination provided by the analysis of meaning, they paid scant attention to what Moore had to say about morals, in the narrow sense in which it means "our attitude towards the outside world." "There was one chapter in the *Principia*," he says, "of which we took not the slightest notice," namely

8 Keynes, *Two Memoirs,* 84.

9 *Op. cit.,* 89. Moore's remarks on p. 6 of *Principia Ethica* might seem to conflict with Keynes' description of his method; he there says that his business is not with "proper usage, as defined by custom." The truth is that neither Moore nor analysts of the generation which succeeded him are tied, as lexicographers are, to the *actual* current usage of words (though these may guide them). Their only concern is that, however words are being used, it should be explained how they are being used. But this is not to be taken as a licence to evade the discussion and elucidation of problematical concepts by the subterfuge of substituting for them concepts which do not raise the same problems; see my *Language of Morals,* 91ff. The transition from 'words' to 'concepts' is here crucial.

10 *Op. cit.,* 88.

the chapter called "Ethics in relation to conduct."[11] This disrespect towards morals led the outside world—even including D. H. Lawrence, whose actual evaluations were not so far removed as were conventional people's from those of Moore's disciples—to regard the group with suspicion, in the same way, and for the same reasons, as it has suspected the disciples of some later philosophers who have insisted on the distinction which Moore made current. What, according to Keynes, repelled Lawrence was "this thin rationalism . . . joined to libertinism and comprehensive irreverence."[12]

*   *   *   *   *

The implications of the new division of moral philosophy made by Moore became very apparent nine years later, when Prichard (the first of the Oxford School of intuitionists referred to by Mr. Harrod) published his famous article "Does Moral Philosophy rest on a mistake?" The article concludes with the following statement:

If we do doubt whether there is really an obligation to originate A in a situation B, the remedy lies not in any process of general thinking, but in getting face to face with a particular instance of the situation B, and then directly appreciating the obligation to originate A in that situation.[13]

By 'general thinking' Prichard seems to have meant the sort of thinking which had occupied the greater part of many books on moral philosophy up to his day. These books consisted of a number of different sorts of discussion, not always clearly distinguished by their authors;[14] Moore had pointed the way to a proper classification of these different elements in moral philosophy—a classification which, when insisted on, seemed to make certain of the elements irrelevant to certain others. A typical work of moral philosophy of the old type contains three main kinds of observation. First, there are statements of fact about how things stand in the world—in particular, statements about what sorts of actions will have what sorts of results. Secondly, we have statements about the

[11] *Op. cit.*, 82; Moore, *Principia Ethica*, ch. 5.
[12] *Op. cit.*, 75f, 78, 98, 103.   [13] *Moral Obligation*, 17.
[14] Kant's question is perhaps here pertinent: "whether it would not be better for the whole of this learned industry if those accustomed to purvey, in accordance with the public taste, a mixture of the empirical and the rational in various proportions unknown to themselves—the self-styled "creative thinkers" as opposed to the "hairsplitters" who attend to the pure rational part—were to be warned against carrying on at once two jobs very different in their technique, each perhaps requiring a special talent and the combination of both in one person producing mere bunglers!" (*Groundwork*, iv; Paton's translation, 56). Kant objected not so much to the same person doing both jobs (he did himself) but to doing them "at once." The force of Kant's warning is not weakened by the discovery that there are, not two, but at least three jobs.

nature of the concepts used in moral thinking, or, as a modern would put it, about the meaning or function or use of moral words. Thirdly, the books generally conclude with some statements of moral principle which are held by the author to have been established by what has gone before.

Now Hume, in a well known passage, which Prichard echoes in this same article, had shown the impropriety of the direct passage from the first of these three kinds of statement to the third.[15] But many moral philosophers (including perhaps Hume himself) seem to have supposed that the second kind of statement could help us out of this difficulty; that discoveries about the nature of goodness, obligation, etc., could somehow provide a bridge over the gulf between factual statement and moral principle. Moore's exposure of the "naturalistic fallacy," extended by Prichard to cover "ought" as well as "good," seemed to have put this approach to the subject out of court once for all. The way to settle moral problems, when all the necessary fact-finding had been done, was by intuition. The study of the moral concepts, or the attempt to analyse moral terms, did indeed need undertaking; but its results were purely negative, and its sole use was to proclaim that they were negative, in order to prevent the unwary from falling into naturalistic errors. And since both Moore and Prichard had proclaimed this in clear tones, it is not surprising that, when Broad came on the scene, there seemed to be not much scope for the traditional sort of moral philosophy—the sort which claimed to be able to reach conclusions of moral principle.

* * * * *

This explains very clearly the feature of Broad's book which, as an undergraduate, I found unattractive. It too consists of three elements, but they are not the same three as I mentioned above. To mention first the element which occupies least space, there are some moral observations, many of them very wise, and all expressed with admirable clarity and pungency. These are to be found scattered throughout *Five Types*. They are not, however, represented as the results of any peculiarly philosophical enquiry; in so far as Broad judges moral issues, his tendency is to judge them as a man, not as philosophy professor. This is much to his credit, and makes the judgments themselves more valuable than they might otherwise have been.[16] But the separation between ethical theory and moral judgment is in *FTET* almost complete.

---

[15] Hume, *Treatise III*, 1, i, last para.; Prichard, *op. cit.*, 4.

[16] For an example of a judgment by Broad on a specific moral issue, see the devastating comparison between the personal morals of Sidgwick and Green in *FTET*, pp. 12 and 144. Some later papers contain very penetrating applications of ethical theory to moral problems, and perhaps indicate a change of attitude since *Five Types*. See especially the last two papers in *Ethics and the History of Philosophy*.

The second element in *FTET* consists of analytical studies of the various moral concepts, together with an accurate and painstaking classification of the different theories which might be held about the meaning of moral judgments and their epistemological status. The third element consists of historical studies of particular philosophers, whose views are dissected and displayed in terms of the aforementioned classification. It is perhaps not unfair to say that only by including this valuable historical matter was Broad able to fill a book about moral philosophy—so attenuated had the subject become through the work of his predecessors.

The history of moral philosophy in the years when Broad's own thought was developing not merely explains, but in large measure justifies, his approach to the subject. For, although there were ambiguities in Moore's presentation of his argument against naturalism, and although few people nowadays would accept an intuitionism of the type advocated by Prichard, yet the facts about the nature of moral discourse that led these writers to the views which I have described are indeed facts; and they do indeed render impossible of fulfilment the traditional programme of moral philosophers, that of using logical considerations, arising out of the meanings of the moral words, to get them from an "is" to an "ought." And Broad, by refusing to engage in these traditional endeavours and devoting himself instead to enquiries of a historical and analytical kind, was showing himself an honest man. He has never joined the ranks of those who, not liking the effects of the distinction made by Moore, seek to blur it—a thing which it is easy enough to do if, deliberately or by reason of an ocular defect, the subject is put sufficiently out of focus. I must therefore admit that my juvenile irritation at Broad's remarks was entirely unjustified. Yet there remains with me a certain dissatisfaction, not with Broad, but with the state of the subject. Since dissatisfaction of this sort has been voiced recently in more than one quarter, it may not be inapposite to discuss its cause; by this means I may perhaps draw Broad himself into the debate.

*   *   *   *   *

It is still frequently said of present-day moral philosophy that it has become 'impoverished' by concentrating on the analysis of concepts. I take this word from a broadcast talk by Mr. J. W .N. Watkins. As I have indicated, those who make this kind of attack upon recent writers do not often go back far enough in their search for whipping-boys. The distinction between the analysis of moral concepts and the actual propounding of moral judgments is implicit in the work of Moore, and its consequences are plain for all to see in the work of the intuitionist school. Yet sometimes writers, who do not like the way moral philosophy is done at the present time, attribute this distinction, and the ethical method which it suggests, to a more recent school of ethical writers, of whom Professor Ayer is the most controversial representative. To see how this accusation has come to be so misdirected is not irrelevant to the study of Broad's philosophy, since it is evident from his writings that, unlike some intuitionists who were not in the thick of the controversy at Cambridge, he took the new developments of the twenties and thirties seriously enough to understand them; and, although he did not accept the new ideas, they had a considerable impact on his thought.[17] The predicament in which these new developments had placed the moral philosopher provides an additional explanation of Broad's attitude to the subject.

I am not well enough versed in the recent history of ethics to be able to identify with assurance the first clear statement in modern times of what came to be known as the Emotive theory. If we ignore such earlier hints as that to be found in Berkeley's *Principles*,[18] and consider only the theory as recently maintained, we can trace it back, in a clearly-formulated shape, at least as far as Ogden and Richards' *Meaning of Meaning* (1923).[19] By 1925 Ramsey was able to write "Most of us would agree that the objectivity of good was a thing we had settled and dismissed with the existence of God. Theology and Absolute Ethics are two famous subjects which we have realized to have no real objects."[20] It is surprising, therefore, that Ayer's own *Language, Truth and Logic,* which appeared more than ten years later, created such a stir, and is still the principal butt of those who wish to attack the theory. The explanation is that the chapter in that book devoted to ethics is a masterpiece of philosophical writing, whose clarity, sharpness and earnestness could rouse even the most dogmatic from their slumbers; and that it was written in Oxford, where philosophers had been sleeping longer and more deeply, and therefore more resented being woken up.

Ayer, however, stepped so easily into the leadership of the new school in England, that it is to the common criticisms of his views, and his replies to them, that we must look if we are to understand the present state of the subject. The most important thing, historically, to notice

[17] See especially Broad's discussion in *Proc. Arist. Soc.,* XXXIV (1933–34) 249ff. of the views of Duncan-Jones.

[18] *Principles of Human Knowledge,* Intro. § 20.

[19] See especially p. 125. The theory or something very like it was developed much earlier by certain Scandinavian philosophers, the most important of whom, Hägerström, has recently been translated by Broad. See also H. Ofstad's article in *Philosophy and Phenomenological Research,* XII (1951), 42ff.

[20] F. P. Ramsey, *Foundations of Mathematics,* 288, referred to by Ayer, *Philosophical Essays,* 231.

about Ayer is his enormous debt to Moore. The general debt of the emotivists to Moore, and the close relation of their views to his, has been recognized by Professor Stevenson, and half-acknowledged by Moore himself.[21] But very striking confirmations of this debt are to be found in the pages of *Language, Truth and Logic*. If Moore had not written *Principia Ethica*, any philosopher of an empiricist turn of mind who espoused, like Ayer, a verificationist theory of meaning would have been drawn irresistibly to some form of ethical naturalism, whether of a psychological kind which maintains that moral judgments are statements that the speaker, or that people in general, have certain feelings, or of some kind such as the utilitarian, which holds that they are statements about non-psychological empirical fact. But Ayer had understood Moore well enough not to take either of these ways out; and the brilliantly clear statement of the impossibility of naturalism which *Language, Truth and Logic* contains is nothing but a refinement of Moore's argument.[22] Even when he turns to criticise Moore, Ayer reveals his debt to him by the seriousness with which he takes Moore's arguments; but the clearest and neatest indication of the relation between the two philosophers is in the following two passages, the first from *Principia Ethica* and the second from *Language, Truth and Logic*:

In fact, if it is not the case that 'good' denotes something simple and indefinable, only two alternatives are possible: either it is a complex, a given whole, about the correct analysis of which there may be disagreement; or else it means nothing at all, and there is no such subject as ethics.[23]
Having upheld our theory against the only criticism which appeared to threaten it (Moore's), we may now use it to define the nature of all ethical enquiries. We find that ethical philosophy consists simply in saying that ethical concepts are pseudo-concepts and therefore unanalysable.[24]

Moore thought that he had disposed of one of the possibilities which he lists—that what "good" denotes is a complex (naturalism); and with this conclusion Ayer agrees. Yet in the years since *Principia Ethica* Moore's own suggestion, that it was a simple indefinable non-natural quality (intuitionism) had ceased to satisfy anybody; and Moore himself has since confessed (in 1942) that "in *Principia* I did not give any tenable explanation of what I meant by saying that 'good' was not a natural property."[25] These two possibilities excluded, only the third seemed to Ayer to be open; and he seized it with relish.

21 *The Philosophy of G. E. Moore*, ed. Schilpp, 546f. Cf. C. L. Stevenson, *Ethics and Language*, 272f.
22 Ayer, *Language, Truth and Logic*, 2nd ed., 104f.
23 Moore, *op. cit.*, 15.
24 Ayer, *op. cit.*, 112. Ayer's later writings show more moderate views.
25 *The Philosophy of G. E. Moore* (Schilpp), 582.

The continuity of ethics in the present century is therefore much greater than has sometimes been thought by those who looked at developments from too close quarters. The two results of Moore's work which are important for our purpose may be summed up as follows: he established that it was impossible, by studying the nature, function or analysis of moral concepts, to build a logical bridge between factual premisses and moral conclusions; and he showed that our moral judgments are the result of something which we have to do for ourselves, and which cannot be done for us or forced on us by appeal to any definition or empirical observation. Whether we call this something an intuition, as did the earlier writers, or a feeling of approval, as did the later, is a question of small relative importance, resting on a verbal distinction which nobody has ever succeeded in making clear. Intuitionists and emotivists are on the same side in this at any rate, that they make it difficult to see much direct connection between ethical theory and moral judgment. Broad lies precisely on the dividing line between these two schools—superficially so different but actually so closely related; and that is why I am doing my utmost to elicit from him, in his reply, a statement of his present views about this question.

*   *   *   *

In order to indicate some of the possible moves, it is useful to consider how Ayer has fared in answering his critics. The first criticism which was made was that his views on ethics were morally damnable, in that they were an encouragement to all who read them to stop caring about morality and live as they pleased. The accusation of libertinism was not new, as we have seen. To this Ayer's reply has always been:

> I am not saying that morals are trivial or unimportant, or that people ought not to bother with them. For this would itself be a judgment of value, which I have not made and do not wish to make. And even if I did wish to make it, it would have no logical connection with my theory. For the theory is entirely on the level of analysis; it is an attempt to show what people are doing when they make moral judgments; it is not a set of suggestions as to what moral judgments they are to make. All moral theories, intuitionist, naturalistic, objectivist, emotive, and the rest, are neutral as regards actual conduct. To speak technically, they belong to the field of meta-ethics, not ethics proper.[26]

Ayer here rebuts the charge that his theory entails depraved moral views, by saying that it entails no one moral view rather than another. Ayer is quite right to claim here that this is true, not only of his own theory but of intuitionism too; in this respect, as we have seen, there is no difference between the two theories.

[26] Ayer, *Philosophical Essays*, 245.

In using this defence, however, against the accusation that he is a corrupting moral influence, Ayer lays himself open to another attack. If ethical theories are neutral as regards actual conduct—if judgments of value can have no logical connection with such a theory—then what **is** the point of ethics? This is, as I have said, a question which is frequently asked, not only about Ayer's work, but about that of other ethical writers of the present time; I have more than once been asked it myself, in a somewhat hostile spirit. It is a question which anyone must face who holds that ethics is concerned with the analysis of moral concepts.

It might be replied to this accusation that ethics, like any branch of learning, should be pursued for its own sake. The ethical philosopher is in the same position as the pure mathematician, or the Hebrew scholar; his discoveries may turn out to have a practical use, but this ought not to be his concern. Ethics is a branch of logic, and has many points of intimate contact with other branches of that subject. It is at least *as* important to study the logic of words like 'ought' as it is to study that of words like 'all;' and since in fact the different branches of logic illuminate one another, the logician has very good reason to study *any* sort of word that interests him. Moreover, unless philosophy is going to be given up altogether, logic must surely be allowed to survive; and if logic, then the branch of logic called ethics.

This reply, however, is not much more likely to satisfy some of the attackers than is Broad's own reply that ethics is "fun." For not only do many people take to ethics just because they think that they will learn something which will help them in making moral decisions; they take to philosophy itself because ethics is part of philosophy, and cannot be understood without studying the whole subject. In the eyes of these people (who include many, though not all, of the great philosophers) ethics cannot be justified merely because it is part and parcel of philosophy, since the justification of philosophy itself is that its study is of value to ethics. Some people may be happy to go on sorting out philosophical perplexities without worrying about whether they are doing any service to their fellow men. But it may be doubted whether the subject would ever have got started if it had not been thought to have more relevance to men's needs than that. To this it might be retorted that chemistry would never have got started if people had not hoped to enrich themselves by turning base metals into gold; and that it is no slur on philosophy to say that the first incentive to its pursuit was a false hope of finding an alchemy that would extract evaluative conclusions from factual premises. But chemistry has at least *become* useful; whereas it is often said that ethics has now lost whatever use it formerly had.

Be this as it may, the defence of ethics which we have been considering is not the only possible one. It may be said that ethics *clarifies* moral issues by bringing out the exact use of the words used in discussing them, and thus guarding against verbal confusions. This claim also excites a good deal of antipathy. For most people think that they know well enough how to use the moral words, until the philosopher gets at them; the philosopher, it is said, increases rather than diminishes the confusion. This kind of thing was said of Socrates when he pressed his paralysing demand for an analysis of moral concepts, and it is said today.[27] It is also said that in fact ethical philosophers have not, by analysis, succeeded in clearing up any perplexities about moral questions that really perplex people.

To this it might be replied that to feel quite clear about the use of the moral words may be a sign of the most radical confusion about them. Meno, in the dialogue bearing his name to which I have just referred, felt quite clear that he knew what virtue was; but his attempts to say *what* it was show how little he understood what sort of concept he was trying to define. Certainty about the use of moral words is often a sign of dogmatism; and the extreme kind of dogmatism is naturalism, the view that our own moral views are true in virtue of the very meanings of words. The analytical study of concepts like "good" has at least this negative effect, that it may show people that they really have to make up their own minds about questions of value, and cannot have these questions answered for them by definition. And this is no small gain.

*   *   *   *   *

But few people really think that their moral problems can be solved, in the last resort, by anyone but themselves. They do not need a philosopher to tell them this. What they want the philosopher to do is to give them some assistance in solving those problems. And when it is seen that this assistance cannot take the form of showing that certain answers to the problems are true by definition, they will ask what form the assistance *is* going to take.

To this question I can only suggest the answer that has satisfied me, and ask Professor Broad whether he agrees with it. I took to moral philosophy because I was perplexed about moral problems; and I am quite satisfied that the study of the logical function of the moral words has considerably reduced my perplexity. I now know a great deal better (though I am far from knowing with clear certainty) what I am doing when I am asking a moral question; and this makes it a great deal easier to answer the question. Moral issues, as anyone can observe who watches how they present themselves in real life, come to us as a confused mixture

27 See, for example, *Meno,* 79e ff.

of questions of fact and questions of value, together with a large element of questions concerning the meanings of words. In the more difficult cases we cannot begin to answer these questions till we have established to which of these classes they belong. Everyday moral discussions are full of confusions between questions of fact, requiring empirical investigation, questions of definition, requiring an agreement on how to use words, and questions of value, requiring evaluative decisions. It is often not impossible to answer these various sorts of questions, once we have sorted them out; and ethics is a training in doing this.

This, however, is not the only contribution of ethics to the solution of moral problems. It has also a more positive role. For it may be that once we know what we mean by calling a question a *moral* question, we shall stop wanting to answer it in certain ways. By this I most emphatically do not mean that, as some writers have seemed to maintain, moral conclusions of substance can be derived by means of some quasi-logic from·factual premises in virtue of a definition of the word "moral."[28] This would be nothing but a highly sophisticated form of naturalism. What I intend may be illustrated by an example. I think that it can be maintained, by means of logical considerations alone resting on the meaning of the expression "morally wrong," that what is not morally wrong for me to do in this situation is not morally wrong for anyone to do in a similar situation. The word "similar" is here to be taken to mean that whatever qualitative predicates can be truthfully applied to one situation, can be truthfully applied to the other; and "qualitative" is to be taken as excluding overt or implicit use of singular terms and also of evaluative terms in the predicate. This statement is not sufficiently precise, but it will do for my present purpose.[29] Now the statement that I have just made is not a statement of substance; it is logically compatible with absolutely any single act being either wrong, or not wrong. No synthetic judgment follows from the statement; if true, it is analytically so in virtue of the meaning of the words "morally wrong." But if I am asking whether a certain act which I am contemplating is morally wrong or not, this analytic statement may be of considerable import to me. For if I realise that the judgment, that it is not morally wrong for *me* to do this act to a certain man, entails the judgment that it would not be wrong for someone else to do a similar act to me, were the situation similar, then I may feel disinclined to say that it is not morally wrong; I

28 For a criticism of a theory of this sort, see my review of Professor Toulmin's *Reason in Ethics* in *Philosophical Quarterly*, I (1951), 372ff.

29 I have tried to state this thesis more clearly, and to defend it, in *Proceedings of the Aristotelian Society*, LV, (1954–55), 297ff; and I have given an example of the practical effect of the thesis in *The Listener*, LIV (1955), 651f.

may feel inclined, rather, to say that it *is* morally wrong. And so I may eliminate from the alternatives offered to my choice a possibility that was previously open.

I say "I may feel inclined." Whether I *do* feel inclined will depend on two conditions. The first is that I have sufficient imagination to visualise myself in the position of the other man. The second is that I am averse to suffering that experience which I imagine myself suffering, were I in the other man's place. So we have, in all, three conditions which determine my inclination to say that a certain act would be wrong. The first is, that I should understand the word "wrong" sufficiently to know that its use is governed by the principle which I enunciated in the preceding paragraph. The second is, that I should have sufficient imagination. The third is, that I should have certain likes and dislikes of certain experiences. It is to be noticed that none of these conditions presuppose any previous moral opinions of substance on my part; so that the argument which I have used does not rely upon any suppressed moral premises. It is also to be remarked that, though I have stated these distinctions in terms which have a psychological ring, an exact statement of them would reveal my contentions to be analytic.

Broad, in discussing Kant, deals with this question in greater detail than I have had the space to do.[30] I do not know whether the above statement of the case carries the argument a step further than he does. I have some hope that a restatement of Kant's doctrine on these lines might go some way to meeting Broad's objections to it, and make unnecessary the introduction of moral intuitions to deal with the difficulties which Broad finds. Kant would certainly have objected to my restatement, because it makes a moral decision depend on inclination; yet I do not myself find this objectionable; for I am not *defining* "wrong" in terms of inclinations, but only saying what would in fact incline me to say that a certain act was wrong.

I do not, however, wish to defend this thesis here; I am not unaware of certain possible objections to it, objections to which, however, there are possible answers. I have introduced the thesis only as an illustration of the sort of bearing which an ethical theory, in the restricted sense of a theory concerning the analysis of moral terms, may have on moral decisions. In this example, ethics bears on morals in two ways. The first is by making the sort of suggestion which I have made in the two preceding paragraphs—a suggestion that the conditions which determine a person, given that he knows the facts of the case, to come to a certain moral decision can be divided into three classes, viz., understanding the

[30] Broad, *FTET*, pp. 123–131.

meaning of words, imagination, and likes and dislikes. The second is by establishing, by the methods of logical analysis, that the words 'morally wrong' have such a meaning that the statement which I said was analytic is in fact analytic. Whether or not the piece of ethical theory which I have just put forward is tenable, the question 'Is it tenable?' has clearly a bearing on moral problems.

It is obvious that the discussion of the two ethical issues which I have just mentioned will bring a great deal of philosophy with it. The first one will involve us in a great variety of questions concerning the philosophy of mind: 'Does it make sense to speak of imagining oneself in another's position?,' 'What is an inclination?,' and so on. The second will lead us into the middle of a tangle of related logical questions—questions which are the lineal descendants of some of the most important problems of metaphysics—questions concerning the principle of individuation, the difference between things and qualities, and the identity of indiscernibles. Thus ethics is studied because it has a bearing on morals, and metaphysics and the philosophy of mind because they have a bearing on ethics—though in neither case are these the only reasons. Broad may therefore have been over-modest when he made so small a claim for the practical utility of ethical studies. At any rate, I should like to ask him whether he is now prepared to go a little further.

I reach, therefore, the following conclusions concerning Broad's approach to moral philosophy:

(i) Broad's inclination to understate the bearing of ethical studies on moral questions is the historical result of the work of Moore, as extended by Prichard, and carried still further by the emotivists.

(ii) This tendency is implicit in intuitionism, and is not to be laid at the door of post-intuitionist writers.

(iii) Intuitionists and post-intuitionists are right in holding that no definition or analysis of moral terms can enable us logically to derive a moral conclusion from factual premises.

(iv) Both they and their opponents however, are wrong if they suppose that ethical studies, as understood by intuitionists and post-intuitionists, can have no, or negligible, importance for moral questions.

R. M. HARE

BALLIOL COLLEGE
OXFORD UNIVERSITY

19

Ingemar Hedenius

BROAD'S TREATMENT OF DETERMINISM
AND FREE WILL

1. Professor Broad has treated determinism and free will most completely and instructively in his inaugural lecture "Determinism, Indeterminism and Libertarianism." Broad gave this lecture in 1934 when he was made Knightbridge Professor of Moral Philosophy in Cambridge. The lecture was published for the second time in 1952 in Broad's book "Ethics and the History of Philosophy." In the following pages, I shall discuss some of the views to be found in this lecture. I am not taking up what Broad has said about the problem of free will in "Five Types of Ethical Theory" (1930), because his inaugural lecture appears to represent a more developed stage in Broad's treatment of these problems.

2. It is appropriate to speak about positive and negative actions; i.e. actions which have been done or are being done, and actions which have not been done or are not being done. Thus, the non-execution of an action is referred to as the execution of an action, i.e. of a negative action. This may be bad English, but I allow myself this terminology all the same. The expression "to do an action" is therefore an abbreviation here of the expression "to do or not to do an action." By "actions" I shall mean both positive and negative actions.

3. Broad's starting point is the statement that "obligability entails substitutability." He calls an action "obligable" if and only if it is an action of which "ought to be done" or "ought not to be done" can be predicated. He calls an action "substitutable" if and only if the one who carried it out was not compelled to do so, but could in fact have done something else instead. The point of the lecture is to determine the nature of all such substitutability which according to Broad's supposition is necessary for the obligability of an action. Broad further assumes that a certain extremely complicated sort of substitutability is both a necessary and sufficient condition for obligability. The lecture ends with an analysis of this concept of substitutability. The final result is that this concept of "substitutability" has no application. Thus, according

to Broad, there are no actions of which we can say with truth "ought or ought not to have been done."

I do not believe that the fundamental premise of Broad's argument is correct. One can express oneself in approximately the following way: "It was lucky for X that X broke his leg so that X could not go to Y, since going to Y was just what X ought not to have done. From a moral point of view, X's duty was to avoid going to Y." This statement seems significant to me and is an example of correct linguistic usage. But it entails the following statement: "X was forced to do an action which he ought have done" or, in other words, "X could not have done anything else than what was X's duty."

If statements of this kind are at times completely sensible, the premise for the whole of Broad's argument is incorrect. The statement that "ought" entails "can" does not appear to be true in general. A person may have done something which he ought to have done without this action being substitutable.

4. It would be interesting to examine whether the relationship assumed by Broad between obligability and substitutability is applicable to any special class of obligable actions. One could presume that this would be the case for obligable actions which were *not* executed. A change in the previous quotation gives the following sentence: "It was bad luck for X that X broke his leg so that X could not go to Y; for going to Y was just what X ought to have done. From a moral point of view X's duty was to go to Y." If Broad's statement applies to this case, the clauses "going to Y was just what X ought to have done" and "it was X's duty" are just as preposterous as the clause "A is black" would be in a statement where amongst other things it is maintained that "A does not have any extention." For my part, however, I cannot see that this is the case.

I find no fault with sentences which state that X was forced to do his duty. But sentences which maintain that X was forced to do an action which it was X's duty to avoid doing *can* sound slightly strange. It also seems natural to say that if X was forced, he did not act contrary to his duty. But I cannot honestly see that it would be *nonsense* to state that X was forced to do what he should have avoided doing.

The difference between both cases depends perhaps on the difference in emotive meaning between statements saying that someone did what he ought, and statements saying that someone did what he ought not to have done. I believe that Professor Broad is sympathetic to such theories as G. E. Moore's or W. D. Ross's, concerning the analysis of the ethical "ought." Even philosophers of this trend ought however to agree that statements on "ought" and "ought not" *also* have a certain emotive meaning. In the first of the two cases, the emotive meaning appears to be a positive emotive attitude towards a certain action, in the latter case a negative attitude. But everyone knows that the positive attitudes are usually (though not always) much weaker and less interested than the negative ones in such cases. X did what X should have done—all right, anything else would have surprised me. I accept such a piece of information more or less as impersonally and as calmly as I accept the good news that my salary has been paid this month as usual. The statement "X did what he should" has little more emotive meaning than this. This emotional effect will hardly be impaired if we learn that X himself cannot take the credit for doing his duty, but was forced to do what X should do. So called social control has little to do with personal commendation, but rather with personal censure.

The emotive meaning of "X did not do what X should have done" has a far greater intensity and a more personal note. The emotive meaning here is often not only an expression of regret about an action, but also tends to point towards disapproval of the person who performed the action. If so we must suppose that X himself was the cause of his own action, and this is impossible for us if we get to know that X was forced. Instead, we must then disapprove of the circumstances or persons who forced X. To express such feelings, we often have more effective means than the phrase "X ought not to have done A," which appears therefore, at least on occasions, to lack what we wish to express *emotionally*. But from an *informative* point of view, "X should not have done A" may be the adequate expression.

These are speculations. But I think that something *similar* to what I have said is the case. It feels, of course, slightly awkward, in the case, to say "he acted contrary to his duty, but was forced to do so." For that reason alone, it does not however need to be nonsense. It is perhaps just a little unnecessary. And anything apart from the fact that it is unnecessary need not be implied in the objection that if X was forced, X did not act contrary to his duty. We can compare the following dialogue. "He stole because he was hungry"—"Oh, then in that case, he was not a proper thief." The objection need not state that it is nonsense to say that he who steals from hunger is a thief. The objection may only state that it is unnecessary and against the grain to use such strong terms to express the fact that the hungry man "appropriated someone else's property with the intention of keeping it."

I do not know whether there are any obligable actions which *qua* obligable must be substitutable. The obligability of actions which were, as a fact, done is far from always of such a nature. I believe we can very often say *with meaning* about X, that he did what he ought or ought not to have done, and still add that X was forced and therefore could not have acted otherwise. But I will not deny that it sometimes sounds slightly odd to express oneself in that way.

5. It is possible that "ought" entails "can" in the case of conceivable actions which have not been done, but are possible in the future.

But of course, even here, one has to remember the emotive meaning which "ought" has, when predicated of some particular action which is considered possible in the future. "You ought to do such and such a thing now" has a very great similarity to a command. But one does not order a person to do what we know he cannot avoid doing, or what we know he cannot do. If one says that a person ought to do a certain thing, which he either cannot avoid doing or else cannot do, one may not be talking nonsense in the same way as in the sentence "X is white, but has no extension." One may perhaps only be saying something which lacks practical purpose and therefore seems somewhat stupid.

The circumstances are perhaps also different, depending on whom one is talking to. If one is talking *to* the person who ought or ought not to do something, it is *very* awkward to say: "You ought to do so"—or "I ought to do so"—when I know that he—or I—cannot avoid doing so or cannot do so. But it is *less* awkward to say, not *to*, but *about* a person: "X ought to do this now—and luckily, he cannot avoid doing so," or "unfortunately, he cannot do so." The difference in awkwardness between these cases possibly lies in the fact that the emotive meaning is only similar to a command in the first case, but not at all in the second.

Broad's statement that "obligability" entails "substitutability" is least improbable if it is adapted to *some* conceivable actions which have not yet been done, but will possibly be done in the future. Curiously enough, Broad does not seem to have had such actions in mind at all. He deals wholly in his lecture with already accomplished actions, or conceivable actions in the past which were not done.

6. In the above, "ought" has been taken in a certain ethical sense, and I have had in mind the sense which is most common and most central in moral arguments about right and wrong. Broad also discusses another sense of "ought" which he calls "the comparative ought." He distinguishes between two different kinds of comparative ought, one non-ethical and one ethical. Let us see whether any of these comparative "oughts" entails "can." I will start with the non-ethical comparative "ought."

An example of the non-ethical use of the comparative "ought" is found in the statement "A car ought to be able to get from London to Cambridge in less than three hours." This statement suggests what cars on an average are capable of (possibly what a very good car of fifty years ago was supposed to be capable of), and therefore Broad calls the "ought" which occurs in such statements "comparative."

Broad says that this non-ethical "ought" can also be predicated of human beings, and I suggest the following example for this: "A mathematician ought to be able to solve second degree equations." Such an "ought" does not entail "can." The statement is considering what a mathematician ought *to be able* to do and in no way implies that every mathematician really is able to do what he ought to be able to do. We have a great liking for the use of statements containing this comparative "ought," when we come across a mathematician who is unable to do what he, in the comparative sense, ought to be able to do. The most common and most typical way of using the non-ethical comparative "ought" is therefore a usage which does not entail "can." A mathematician, who cannot solve a second degree equation, even if he tries his utmost to do so, is an example of a mathematician who is not capable of what he ought to be capable.

But perhaps this comparative use of "ought" is still ethical? I shall not discuss the question of terminology. *This* "ought" quite certainly does not entail any "can." But all the same, it is *possible* that it will occur in statements which according to normal linguistic usage are considered as purely ethical.

7. Broad has also considered another kind of comparative "ought" which has a stronger ethical tone. He supposes that this "ought" entails a kind of "can," that is to say, the kind of substitutability which he calls secondary. An example of this "ought" can be said to occur in the statement "A man ought not to cheat at cards."

If I have not misunderstood Broad, he presumes that the following implication provides part of the meaning of this ethical comparative "ought."

X ought not to have cheated at cards ⊃ X cheated at cards, and the average decent man does not do this, and anyone who does falls in this respect below the average, and a man who does this either has a very low ideal of human nature or else a very weak and unstable desire to approximate to the ideal which he has.

I take the liberty of calling this implication "Broad's implication." I think Broad is right in presuming that his implication is often present when we say that someone ought not to have cheated at cards. But I think it is misleading to make a definite distinction between this "ought" and the "ought" which is most common and most central in ethical discourses. At any rate, this ethical comparative "ought" resembles the ethical categorical "ought" much more than the comparative "ought" which occurred in the example about the mathematician.

The first part of Broad's implication is an ethical statement. The second part is possibly a purely descriptive statement.[1] Most certainly, the second part cannot be a logical analysis of the first part. But the implication can be of another kind. Some people may perhaps assume that the second part, according to some synthetic law *a priori*, states a necessary condition for the truth of the first part, and that this is the meaning of "⊃." Such an interpretation, for reasons which I shall not go into here, seems improbable to me. I am more inclined to accept the explanation that "⊃" expresses the fact that the first part very often *suggests* the second part. But "⊃" does not express that the second part is part of the first part's meaning or that the first part *logically* entails the second.

There are many parallels to such a mode of suggesting. When someone makes the statement "The earth is round," it can imply the statement: "On the average, educated people believe the earth is round, and those who do not believe it have either not been to a good school or else have forgotten what they learnt at such a school." When such an implication is present, it is appropriate to say that the first statement "suggests" the second. But to say that the first statement logically entails the second, or, even worse, that the second is part of the logical analysis of the first, would be a grave error. It is a very loose and in no way "logical" form of implication which is present here.

In the cases where Broad's implication is relevant, it is also true that we *suggest* that X's action was what Broad calls "secondarily substitutable." This is more or less self-evident, because the second part actually states that X would not have wished to cheat, if X had adopted higher ideals earlier in his life, if he had a stronger and more persistent desire to live up to his ideals. To indicate complete secondary substitutability, we need only add, that X would not have cheated on the occasion in question, if he had wished with a certain degree of intensity to avoid doing so. But the fact that the statement "X ought not to have cheated at cards" *suggests* that X's action was secondarily substitutable, in no way means that the statement also *entails* this, and I do not think that the statement does this.

I do not know whether we ever use an ethical "ought" so that it entails "can." I can find no reason to believe this and I am quite sure that we often use an ethical "ought" which does not entail "can" at all.

8. Broad's implication seems to be a variant of another implication, which it closely resembles, namely, the following: "X should not have done A ⊃ through doing A, X deviated from the valid norm N, and the reason for this was that X either lacked the will to conform to N or else

---

[1] Broad may believe this. Cf. his essay on Bishop Butler in *FTET*, pp. 56–60.

was too weak-willed to do so." I take the liberty of calling this "my implication." The main difference between my implication and Broad's is that Broad's contains additional clauses concerning the nature of N, namely that N is a part of any kind of high ideal of human nature, that N is conformed to by the average decent man, and that those who do not conform to N fall below the average. These additional clauses can however scarcely influence the logical relationship between "ought" and "can" in these types of statements.

I should think that both Broad's implication and mine are relevant to a very great number of ethical statements to the effect that people ought to have acted otherwise than they did. It also seems as if the more abstract implication, which I obtained through leaving out the comparative element in Broad's implication, is relevant to an even greater number of statements to the effect that people ought to have acted in another way. Indeed, this implication may have occurred so often that it has probably given rise to the error that "ought" entails "can." Some philosophers may have thought that this implication has meant "entailment," and the fact that it only means "suggesting" has been overlooked. The great frequency of my implication may also have played a part in the origin of this error.

9. The premise for Broad's argument concerning determinism and free will is therefore probably incorrect. It is rather improbable that "obligability" entails "substitutability." But if we speak of "moral responsibility" instead of "obligability," all of Broad's arguments have relevance and a great philosophical value. In what follows, I shall assume that the question does not refer to what "ought" entails, but to what "moral responsibility" entails. The fact that we must have been *able* to do or avoid the actions for which we are morally responsible, is obvious to me, and in this sense, "moral responsibility" (or "imputability") entails "substitutability." Broad's lecture casts much light upon this question.

The two implications which we considered in the previous section may be typical of those cases where we wish to suggest that X was morally responsible for an action which X did, but which X ought not to have done. If we say that X did, but ought not to have done A, we do not necessarily suggest that X is morally responsible for having done A. But *if* we wish to suggest that X is morally responsible for A, we suggest something like Broad's implication, or perhaps even more commonly, my implication. Of course, it is also possible that we are suggesting something *more* than appears in these two implications. Broad's lecture has interesting things to say about exactly this.

The fact that we ought to do something, and the fact that we are morally responsible for it being done, are two different things. It is possible that our concept of "moral responsibility" (or "imputability") entails such a strange form of substitutability that the predicate "morally responsible" (or "imputable") can have no application. Even if this is the case, it does not follow that the terms "ought" and "ought not" lack application.

10. My next point must be a few words about the term "moral responsibility." My starting point is the assumption that X is morally responsible for having done A, if, and only if the fact that X has done A is sufficient to make X a fitting object for moral disapproval or approval.

"Action" is here, as before, "positive or negative action."

"Moral disapproval" can take many different forms. For instance, hatred, scorn, loathing or wish to punish, but also milder forms of the same group. Common to these negative feelings is the attitude that X, through his bad action alone, deserves to suffer, to meet opposition or at least to be blamed. The positive equivalent to this is moral approval. This can take several different forms, whose common feature is the attitude that the one who is responsible for a good action is *eo ipso* deserving of reward, success or at least praise.

Another characteristic of moral approval and disapproval is that these reactions are subordinated to a principle, which the person who approves or disapproves is prepared to apply also to other similar cases. Dislike or liking which cannot be supported by a general principle, cannot be moral approval or disapproval. The person who gives *moral* approval or disapproval to other people's actions must have at least *some* similarity to a judge, who judges according to a law.

The meaning of the expression that someone is a "fitting" object for moral approval or disapproval, has a certain complication. I think it necessary to distinguish between two different meanings of this expression.

The first meaning is that it is *true* that X has done an action, which according to a certain moral principle ought to evoke moral approval or disapproval in those looking on. Thus X can be a suitable object for moral disapproval because he has done A, although in fact no one disapproves of him for this. This is the case if X has done A; but no one believes X has done A. X can also, as a matter of fact, be the object of disapproval for having done A, without X however being a fitting object. Those who disapprove of X may believe that X has done A, although this is not the case.

This definition of the expression "X is a fitting object for moral approval or disapproval" can be called the "sociological" definition of the expression. With this definition, X's moral responsibility becomes a product not only of X's behaviour, but also of the social milieu in which X's actions has taken place. In milieu M, X is perhaps morally responsible for having done A, but in N, X may not be morally responsible for having done A. I wish to call this concept of responsibility the "sociological" concept of moral responsibility.

One cannot sensibly ask what form of free will the sociological concept of moral responsibility entails *in general*. It is necessary to keep to a concept of responsibility which is found in a certain social milieu. In the present case, this does not offer any difficulty. I am of course thinking of the concept of responsibility which is to be found in the social milieu common to Professor Broad, to me, and to most of the readers of this book. The point is to find certain assumptions which in this milieu are entailed in the assumption that X was morally responsible for A.

The second meaning of the expression that "X is a fitting object for moral approval or disapproval" is not satisfied with the fact that X has done something to which a general principle which in fact occurs in a certain milieu is applicable. An additional clause is necessary: the general principle must be morally right. But if a moral principle is right, it must be so in all social milieus, provided that the principle has been fully formulated. A moral principle can be right, even if it is not adopted by any social milieu. If a moral principle is wrong, it is wrong in all milieus. In this sense, X's moral responsibility (or lack of moral responsibility) is something *absolute,* if we add the above-mentioned clause.

This definition of the expression, that X is a "fitting" object for moral approval or disapproval, can be called the "ethical" definition of the expression. With this definition, the statement "X was morally responsible for doing A" becomes a moral judgment. The statement entails that it is morally right to make X the object of moral reaction. The opposite: that it is morally wrong to react morally to X because X has done A, is entailed in the ethical statement, that X is not morally responsible for having done A.

11. An analogical distinction applies to the predicates "ought" and "ought not." "X ought to do A" can be a sociological statement. Then its meaning is that there is a norm which demands that X does A. But the statement also can be ethical and mean that X must do A according to a norm which is ethically right. In his lecture, Broad has not been interested in this distinction, and he has not said, whether he is discussing the sociological or the ethical "ought."

However, Broad expresses himself in a very resolute way about the "ought" he is considering. Thus, for instance in the following quotation:

People constantly make judgements of obligation . . . and such judgements have constantly been made throughout the whole course of human history. Every single one of these judgements has been false unless there have been cases in which actions which *were* done could have been left undone and actions which *were not* done could have been done.[2]

If Broad with "judgements of obligation" had had in mind judgements using the sociological "ought," his statements would be contrary to well-known historical facts. In the social milieu which Sophocles describes in his tragedies, it is true that Oedipus ought not to have married his mother, and also both well-known and true that Oedipus could not help doing so. It would be unreasonable to think that Broad overlooked such facts. I therefore believe that he has not had a sociological definition of "ought" in mind, but has been considering the ethical definition of "ought."

In my criticism of Broad's argument concerning free will, I shall substitute the concept "moral responsibility" (or "imputability") for his concept "obligability." It may then appear that I should take the concept "moral responsibility" in its ethical sense and not in its sociological sense, in order to stay as close as possible to Broad's own line of argument. All the same, I am choosing to take the conception in its sociological sense.

The fact that I am in this way departing even further from Broad has no great significance, however. I am choosing the concept of moral responsibility which is found in the social milieu common to Broad, to me, and to the readers of this book. Whichever of us wishes, can therefore alter my argument very easily so that it acquires an ethical bearing.

12. In the following, I am therefore discussing "moral responsibility" (or "imputability") where Broad talks about "obligability." The first question then is, whether Broad is correct in his opinion that "obligability" entails "secondary substitutability." The fact that an action A was secondarily substitutable for X means that A would not have been done if X had willed with a certain degree of force and persistence to avoid A, and that, if X had willed differently in the past, X's conative-emotional dispositions and X's knowledge of X's own nature would have been such, at the time when X did A, that X would have willed to avoid A with enough force and persistence to prevent X from doing A.[3]

In my opinion, it is true that "X is morally responsible for having

2 *EHP*, 197.   3 P. 203.

done *A*" entails "*A* was secondarily substitutable for *X*." To comment further on this very admirable section of Broad's essay would only ruin it, and I urge the reader to study it himself and gain wisdom from it.

13. Secondary substitutability belongs to a type of freedom which Broad calls "conditional substitutability." Such freedom is distinguished by the fact that "could" in "*X* could have done *A*" means "would, if certain conditions had been fulfilled which were not." Some sort of conditional substitutability is necessary for the existence of moral responsibility. But according to Broad, such substitutability is not sufficient. He thinks that a *categorical* freedom is also demanded.

Broad may also be right in this. But I am not sure that categorical freedom, which is as necessary as conditional freedom for the presence of moral responsibility, is of the nature which Broad assumes.

According to Broad, categorical freedom has two constituents, which he calls the negative and the positive condition. The negative condition for an action to be categorically free is that a desire which caused the action was not completely causally determined in respect of strength and persistence. Broad's explanation of what such a lack of causal determination means, is very interesting and admirably clear. It is probable that moral responsibility for an action entails the fulfillment of this negative condition.

The positive condition according to Broad is that *X*'s desire to do *A* (i.e. the action, for which *X* is morally responsible) was determined by *X*'s putting forth a certain amount of effort to reinforce *X*'s desire for *A*. Moral responsibility according to Broad requires that this effort factor was completely determined "*by the agent or self,* considered as a substance or continuant, and not by a total cause which contains as factors *events in* and *dispositions of* the agent."[4]

This condition can, according to Broad, never be fulfilled, since a substance or continuant can never be a cause-factor. Only events can be cause-factors. The conclusion is that no action ever can be imputable and no man morally responsible for any action.

But I do not feel convinced that our idea of moral responsibility would demand *this* positive condition. Without a doubt, moral responsibility requires that the agent's personality or self be the cause of the action for which he is responsible. But I cannot see that this idea involves the adoption of any abnormal or fantastic form of causality. In what follows, I shall try to give a more benevolent interpretation of our conception of the ego as the cause of certain actions.

14. It is not primarily the actions or even desires or volitions which we judge morally, but rather the personality which lies behind them,

4 P. 214f.

and which we consider decides the direction of the will-impulses and thus the actions. It is only secondarily, as manifestations of a good or bad character, that actions or desires are judged morally good or bad.

It is easy to produce evidence of this. We excuse an unpremeditated action, occurring through an unlikely impulse of will, if it is bad, and we do not consider it of any great merit if it is good, as long as we clearly understand that the action depended upon a chance or a coincidence which seems to us inexplicable. And even when unpremeditated actions are morally imputable, it is usually because we consider them to have been caused by carelessness or other weakness in the agent. An impulsive good deed, occasioned by the inspiration of a moment, can of course also arouse our moral admiration, but only if we believe that the impulsive person's way of behaving expresses real generosity. The repetition of a piece of villainy is held to be something extra reprehensible, because it gives even stronger evidence of a bad character than the first crime. We disapprove most of all of inherent wickedness which gives rise to evil actions all the time, and our disapproval is almost as great, whether the occasions of really doing harm are actually many or few. An imprisoned villain is almost as great a villain as one who is free. And one can also approve or disapprove morally of a person now for what he did before. It is therefore not only his execution of the admirable or reprehensible action, which one judges morally, for if that were the case, one's reaction would only be applicable to an action in the past. In fact, we have to answer for our actions long after we have done them. One judges the character which expressed itself in the action and which one presumes is still there. On the other hand, a repentant sinner, who has done a number of really evil deeds and not yet done anything good which might more or less be able to compensate for what he has done before, can often reckon on greater indulgence than a person who continues with common petty wicked deeds the whole time.

We also take the motives into account. The noble robber who steals from the rich to help the poor is not a real villain, although his whole existence is just one series of criminal actions. If one means well, but happens to act badly, one goes free of censure and perhaps even gets praise. If one means to act badly, but happens to act well, one gets no praise and may even be blamed. The fact that we give such importance to the motives is because these are considered to be surer measures of the genuine standard of character than the external actions. It is the character we wish to judge. This is also evident from the fact that we consider actions which were done after the agent had had a chance to consider the various possibilities and then made his choice, to be particularly indicative of a person's moral standard and, therefore imputable. When one has only seen one possibility, the responsibility is not as great, even if, in reality, there had been several possibilities, as long as there was no question of careless thoughtlessness. We know that the different possible actions which may be considered are not in themselves more or less tempting. What is most tempting depends on what needs and interests, in short, tendencies, I already have. Different people, confronted with the same alternatives, make a different choice, because they themselves are different. It is the character which makes the decision when one chooses. Therefore, one is considered morally responsible to a very great extent, when one has had the chance of considering things.

When we get the opportunity of acting according to our own choice, our true nature is revealed, since it is this which in such cases decides our behaviour. We are then also manifesting in a typical way the categorical freedom which is necessary for moral responsibility.

15. This concept of freedom of will involves problems, and certain reflections seem even to suggest that it is absurd.

Can the personality alone decide the behaviour, uninfluenced by either compulsion or circumstances, for instance particularly strong mental strain and exceptional temptations, or chance impulses and whims? How can the personality alone bring about something? It seems quite easy to show that this idea is preposterous.

Some event must always occur to provoke an action, the tendency to which is an integral part of the personality. We call these particular events, which must occur, stimuli. It is often external situations or objects which make an impression on me through my sense-organs and which in this purely external way, give me the necessary stimuli. I see by my watch that my usual mealtime has come round, and by this stimulus, my need for nourishment is actualized into a will impulse to go and eat. Or I read an advertisement in a book seller's catalogue and that gives my already existing tendency to obtain philosophical literature, a stimulus to order the advertised work. In the other case, a purely inward happening is the stimulus, for instance the result of a conclusion ("She is probably at the office now, so if I go there, I shall meet her") or an idea, arisen through association ("I have a plan") and that works as a stimulus. All these examples represent cases when we say that I act freely and on my own responsibility.

The fundamental needs are necessary for something to happen: if my need for nourishment happens to have been suspended for instance because I had a late lunch, the fact that it is five o'clock does not stimulate me to eat; if my interest in buying books has palled, the advertisement does not stimulate me, etc. But stimuli are just as necessary. It follows from this that the personality is never the only cause of behaviour. All willed deeds, whether we consider that they involve moral responsibility or not, actually depend just as much on external circumstances, which are external or chance in relation to the personality, as on the personality itself. Opportunities make the thief just as much as a bad character.

The stimuli which we consider to be compulsion or "sheer" coincidence, or look upon as particularly strong mental strain or exceptional temptation, do not, from a purely causal point of view, assume a separate position in relation to more "normal" stimuli, they do not influence our choice more strongly. From a purely causal point of view, things are exactly the same in both cases. The cause of an action is always divided. One part is a stimulus and the other part a certain personality, and both parts are equally necessary for an effect and one does not exert greater influence on the effect than the other. All talk of compulsion is in any case misleading, when causal connections are considered.

16. According to these reflections, there should not be any real difference between force, chance, and free manifestation of the personality. Such a conclusion would however make impossible a way of looking at things which plays a great part in many sciences.

An example will illustrate this. Supposing a terrible hurricane rages over a forest. Trees are struck down like matchsticks, but not all of them, for some remain more or less undamaged. What was it that caused a number of trees to fall? The fact that they were weak, less solid or were attacked by insects etc., we say. But the others held firm because they were thicker, stronger or healthy inside etc. In such a case we put the cause for the trees falling on to the trees themselves, not on to the hurricane—although it is obvious that the hurricane was certainly a very important cause.

However unmotivated such a way of looking at things may seem at first sight, a sensible idea lies behind it, which will be discussed later. But first we shall vary the thought-experiment somewhat. Supposing the forest-area which was ravaged by the hurricane, was only a small part of a larger forest. When we find that many trees have been struck down in this large forest, but only within this limited area, we say: it was the hurricane, which happened to pass by just here, which destroyed these trees. Now we may seem to be arguing in complete contradiction to before. We are no longer saying that the cause for the trees falling was their own nature. We are now blaming the hurricane altogether—although it is obvious that the fallen trees' own nature, their weakness etc. was certainly a very important cause. We are considering exactly the same trees and exactly the same hurricane as before, and we are giving the cause of exactly the same event.

The logic ruling this way of speaking, seems to be the following. When a certain stimulus causes an action by one or more individuals, and we have to explain the action in question, we always start with a certain class of individuals and say that one or more individuals in this class has behaved in a certain way which has had such and such a cause. If now the stimulus (in this case the hurricane) which causes a certain action (here the striking-down of the trees) upon one or more individuals in the class I am considering, is common to all or most of the individuals in the understood class, then we do not consider the stimulus in question to be the cause, but the nature of the one or more individuals of the class, who have behaved in the way in question. This is the situation in the first case when we start with the trees in the stormravaged area. The reason why we, in this case, will not consider the hurricane as the cause, is that the hurricane struck all the trees in the limited forest area I am *then* thinking of. It is the factor in the matter which is not common to all, which we consider to be the cause; in this case, the weakness etc. in the trees which were struck down. If again the stimulus which brings about the action, is not common to all the individuals in the class I am concerned with, then the stimulus is considered the cause. This is the situation in the second case when we are concerned with the more extensive forest-area. Only a certain number of trees in this large forest was struck by the hurricane, and in this case, we therefore say that this was the cause of the destruction.

The fact that it is always the exception, the factor not common to all, which we call cause, is also evident from the fact that when neither stimulus nor nature are common to all individuals of the understood class, we call both stimulus and nature causes. If we notice that this is so in the second case (when we had the more extensive forest in mind) it is natural for us to describe the cause of the destruction in this way; that there has been a bad storm and unfortunately certain trees were so weak that they were struck down. Behind this more exact way of expression lies the thought that the felled trees at least partly had themselves to blame. But in the first case when the hurricane could be left out on account of its being self-evident, it was completely the fault of the weak trees. The fact that it makes good sense to use the term "cause" in this relative way is evident from the fact that it is not unusual in a number of sciences, biology and psychology among others.

17. This quite reasonable way of thinking also lies behind our way of ascribing moral responsibility and free will to ourselves and to others. We always start with a large group of people, people of our own

society or in general, people in the countries with the same customs as we have. We take a certain type of personality as the normal, within this group of people: with fairly strong sexual, nourishment and rest-needs, a fairly strong ability to put up with discomfort, not too great a consideration for his own economy or self-assertion, a type of personality which is fairly aggressive but not tyrannical and not on the other hand too benevolent, in short, an average sort of character. When we get to know of actions by certain individuals in this group of people, which are sufficiently pronounced as good or bad to be able to arouse approval or disapproval on our part, we must then be of the opinion that the individual has acted freely in the sense that his action was caused by his personality, in order that our reaction to him can have any moral accent. This means that the action which we judge morally, is considered to have been caused by a stimulus, which everyone, or nearly everyone in the understood group of people is exposed to, but the direction of which is decided by the personal endowments of the agent, which make him depart from the above sketched average character.

An example, which can be varied, will make this clear. Let us suppose A knocks B to the ground. This action does not entail moral responsibility for A, if A had good reason to believe that only by knocking B down could A save himself from being killed by B. In this case, A's action has been caused by a stimulus, which is so unusual that it is given as a cause. At the same time, A's personality has also contributed to the action, but it has not shown any unusual qualities, only the normal instinct of self-preservation. A has not done anything else than what anyone else would at least have wished to do in the same situation. We say in this case that A acted as he did, because he was compelled, indeed, that it was not of his own free will that he knocked B to the ground.

Exactly the same behaviour by A becomes an act of free-will on the other hand, if A knocks B to the ground without believing his life is threatened by B, and only with the intention of afterwards taking B's wallet. The stimulus in this case is the knowledge that B is in such a situation that if anyone knocks B to the ground, he can afterwards take B's wallet. Practically everyone within the understood group of people has been exposed to such a stimulus many times in his life. It is indeed only an insight into the very easily-understood cause-connection between certain possible events concerning a person with a wallet. We all have plenty of insight into such obvious connections, although we do not actualize them into conscious thoughts. These stimuli make no impression on us. A, on the other hand, was interested in the cause-connection in question, he actualized his self-evident knowledge into conscious thought and acted thereupon. For that reason, he is considered to be a scoundrel. And the cause of his behaviour was not the stimulus which brought about the action, but rather his own bad character. He acted of his own free will, showed himself as he really was, and therefore can be considered to be morally responsible.

This case also shows that the compulsion which we consider occurs in the first case (when A knocked B to the ground in self-defence) does not mean that A was compelled to use force, because this was necessary for a certain end (to save his own life). Compulsion in this sense also occurs in the second case, when B is robbed. In order to obtain the wallet, A must strike B to the ground, and he may have considered this as a very unpleasant but unfortunately necessary means to his end. The fact that compulsion in this sense occurs, has nothing to do with the question as to whether A acted of his own free will, either in the first or second case.

Lastly, suppose that B is A's adversary and has, in all kinds of ways, caused A harm and damage in A's private life, and that B sneers at A in a despicable way because of his inferiority in social, economic and human respects. If A cannot stand this and knocks B to the ground, the responsibility is shared between him and the circumstances—not perhaps necessarily between him and B, since B may not have meant to be so offensive, but was in a good mood and wanted "a bit of a joke." A has acted under the strain of exceptional circumstances; that is to say, he has been exposed to an unusual stimulus and the stimulus is therefore considered to be part of the cause. At the same time, A himself is partly to blame for the occurrence, since he showed less self-control than most people. And that was *also* a cause of the incident.

18. But one may perhaps wish to object that these examples do not have anything to do with freedom of will, but only illustrate three different cases: the occurrence of a blameless action, an extremely reprehensible action and a not completely blameless action. The only commentary which would be relevant to the examples would, in such a case, be that we consider self-defence to be blameless, external force to obtain another person's possessions to be very reprehensible, and force under provocation to be not completely blameless.

Such an objection would, however, rest on an oversight. The interesting thing is just this, that when we are trying to clarify for ourselves what distinguishes the three situations from each other from a moral point of view, we are letting the concept of freedom decide the moral differences; *provided* that we consider that one and the same action has been done in all three cases. Of course, we *can* also make a completely different assumption and say that three different actions have occurred; an act of self-defence, an attempted robbery, and an unpremeditated attack. In this case, we only have to apply our moral principles, adapted to the three kinds of actions and in this case we can without further discussion assume that all three actions occurred of free will. But we can also start with the assumption that one and the same action has occurred in all three cases: that one person deliberately struck another to the ground. If we wish to start with *this* assumption which is no less correct than the other,[5] and clarify how one and the same action can be blameless in one case, extremely reprehensible in another, and not completely blameless in a third, we must judge by reference to the concept of freedom. In such a case, it will be obvious to us that the first case was an act of compulsion (*A* could not have acted otherwise), the second case was one of complete freedom (*A* chose freely) and the third case one of partial compulsion (*A* yielded to too great a temptation). Of course, legal judgement cannot consider the question thus, but the normal sense of justice can and often must argue so, since it does not normally have so many and such well-defined paragraphs as criminal law, and thus lacks the opportunity of making sharp distinctions between different kinds of actions.

INGEMAR HEDENIUS

THE UNIVERSITY
UPPSALA, SWEDEN

[5] To ask oneself, whether one and the same action can be said to have occurred in three different cases or three completely different actions is indifferent from a logical point of view. Both sides can have their say, and the phraseology one chooses depends upon whether one tends to consider the similarities rather than the dissimilarities.

20

Helmut Kuhn

EXISTENCE IN C. D. BROAD'S PHILOSOPHY

1.

THE following remarks, offered by an admiring but somewhat puzzled reader of Professor Broad's writings, are designed to raise a question which, to my knowledge, has never been dealt with by this distinguished author, at any rate not explicitly or not in the particular terms in which I am going to couch it. I wish to inquire into the place that could be accorded to existence in Professor Broad's scheme of thought. Without laying claim to the title of an "existentialist" I propose to use the term "existence" in the now widely accepted sense which has accrued to it from Kierkegaard's vocabulary as revived by the contemporary existentialist school of thought. That is to say, almost throughout I shall be putting aside that wider and, from the point of view of both common usage and philosophical tradition, more natural meaning which opposes the existence or "thatness" of a thing to its essence or "whatness." This wider metaphysical concept of existence, closely connected as it is with the problem of reality, has been discussed by Professor Broad in his attempt to evaluate the metaphysical lesson taught by science. In *PPR An Enquiry into the Information that Physical Science can Supply about the Real* (1914) he tried to discover "how much natural science can actually tell us about the nature of reality." He returned to the same question in *ST* (1923) with a heightened sense of the complexity of "the problem of the external world and our supposed knowledge of it," (p. 5) but without radically modifying his earlier views. And finally he subjected McTaggart's disquisitions on existence, reality, and their mutual relationship to a searching analysis.[1] The conceptual net woven by the author in these admirable books is so fine that no shade of opinion, no variety of doctrine, no shift of perspective is allowed to go unnoticed, uncatalogued, unevaluated. But it catches very few metaphysical fish. Yet the outline of a metaphysical theory, or, to put it more conservatively, of a metaphysical attitude is discernible. Professor Broad presents himself as a realist both in critically pointing out the weakness of

[1] Cf. his *EMcP*, I, (1933), Book I, chaps. II–IV.

the phenomenalist position and in positing existents as causal factors producing sensory awareness; as an agnostic in refusing to commit himself to any particular theory concerning the nature of these existents; as a physicalist in giving preference to the findings of physics in tentatively forming and analysing hypotheses as to what that unknown reality might conceivably be like. The fitness of the last of these three titles can be questioned in view of the philosopher's lively interest in psychical research which confirms him in his leaning toward a selective or rather eliminative and, at the same time, pragmatic view of sense perception. Each person, he writes, in a passage of Whiteheadian flavor, "is at each moment potentially capable of remembering all that ever happened to him and of perceiving everything that is happening anywhere in the universe. The function of the brain and nervous system is to protect us from being overwhelmed and confused by this mass of largely useless and irrelevant knowledge by shutting out most of what we should otherwise perceive or remember at any moment, and leaving only that very small and special selection which is likely to be practically useful."[2] But even while examining paranormal experiences such as clairvoyance, telepathy or psycho-kinesis he is concerned with relating them to normal experiences as viewed in the light of modern physics. This approach precludes from his field of vision one trait of existence to which McTaggart has called attention and which has played an important rôle in the discussions about existence: the relevance to practical life of existence as over against essence or reality. In distinguishing the real from the existent (the reversal of the proposition "everything that exists is real" does not hold) McTaggart affirmed that we can "have an interest in the real, even though it should not be existent. But it is only that interest which we have in knowledge for its own sake. All our other interests—in happiness, for example, in virtue or in love—deal exclusively with the existent, the study of which would thus in any case have a special importance for us."[3] As this "special importance" is ignored by Professor Broad, his probings into the real as discovered by physical or psychical research sheds little if any light on the life of the individual and his human interests: the author's ethical reflections, developed as on an altogether different plane, seem neither hindered nor helped by his findings about existence in general. Thus, in raising our problem of "existence" in the narrower, anthropological sense of the term we may be justified in confining our attention almost exclusively to Professor Broad's writings on ethical and religious problems. Indirectly only and by its guiding principles rather than by its

2 *RPPR, Selected Essays,* (1953), 23.
3 *The Nature of Existence,* I, Cambridge, Univ. Press, 8.

specific results will his philosophy of science be seen to have a bearing on the question at hand.

2.

What, precisely, is this question? By existence in the narrower "existentialist" acceptance of the term we do not simply mean "man" or "human nature," nor do we, by raising the question of existence in connection with Professor Broad's philosophy, ask what sort of philosophical anthropology is expressed by, or involved in, his philosophical writings. Existence, whatever restrictions we place upon the application of this concept, must have something to do with "being." Adopting the Kierkegaardian and post-Kierkegaardian usage, we may define it as that particular mode of being which is exhibited by the human person. The question of existence will then involve the problem of the existence of the human person, but it will give this problem a poignancy which, on the whole, is foreign to philosophical anthropology or to the phenomenology of personality. In modern existentialist parlance the term "existence" raises the wider problem of Being under the form of the narrower problem of the particular type of being that characterizes man. It is designed to initiate a query which ostensibly concerns man and human nature, but whose cutting edge is sharpened by an ontological interest. The study of man is to teach us something which transcends man.

The theory called "personalism" tries to base philosophy on a grand dichotomy. "Persons" are distinguished from "things" as forming an altogether separate realm of entities. Structural characteristics and laws discovered in the realm of things, the exponents of this theory urge, need not apply to persons and *vice versa*. The peril to be warded off— the Cartesian error typified by the definition of mind as *res cogitans*— consists in the violation of a frontier. Concepts derived from "things" must not be allowed to invade the realm of persons, under pain of distorting the phenomena of human life and of dehumanizing man. This personalist argument does not yet quite attain the level of existentialist criticism of philosophy but it may be considered a propaedeutic toward it. One further step must be taken. In distinguishing two classes, persons and things, we assume an underlying concept of being which undergoes the personalist bifurcation. Being, it is affirmed, is instanced either by 'things' or by 'persons.' Things and persons, however different in other respects, are both 'entities.' Now this seemingly harmless and inevitable assumption may get the personalist involved in the very mistake which his dichotomy is designed to obviate. In the overarching Being, in that apparently innocuous, colorless "entity" there may yet lie hidden the obtrusive 'thingness' of things which threatens to cloud our vision of persons and personal life. Is it correct to say that persons 'are' in the same sense in which trees or houses or stars can be said to be? To be means for that which has being to be such and such, to be circumscribed by 'whatness' or 'quiddity.' This, at any rate, is what we aim at if, in our quest of knowledge, we ask: What is this or that? However highly specialized or formalized our questions are, they ultimately conform to this basic pattern. They demand answers which reveal essences, that is to say, comprehensible abiding structures of something real. But the assumption that we, as persons, 'are' in that same sense may be misleading. Perhaps we become guilty of falsifying our answers by asking the wrong questions—questions which prejudge a decisive point of ontology, thus blocking the one road that could bring us nearer to the goal of human self-knowledge.

Of course, we all have self-knowledge, i.e. knowledge of personal existence, irrespective of the philosophy we hold. And this immediate self-knowledge—a knowledge of acquaintance—is invoked, tacitly or explicitly, wherever philosophers talk about the self, the human mind, and the like. Too often, though, they fail to realize to what extent their refined concepts actually depend upon that naive, pre-conceptual self-awareness. Now this reflexive awareness, source of all we can possibly know about the self as an instance—for everyone the unique instance—of personal existence, does not, we may contend, show us the self as entity, fixed and bound by its essential structure, nor even as a flux, a becoming, a tendency toward ever fresh formation. We know of ourselves rather as an origination of which we ourselves are the originators. And our self-awareness does not involve a vantage-point beyond that originating process. It is part and parcel of that process. The process is inherently awareness of itself—self-knowledge and self-projection at a time. Self-origination, not self-creation—passivity inextricably interwoven with spontaneity. There is the swelling and subsiding wave of inner life, and there is also the riding of the wave, and riding, in this metaphor, signifies steering, determining, choosing. This self-process, whether viewed as a suffering or as a doing, is projective, i.e. open toward an indeterminate future. Even its remembered past is present under the form of futurity. By this temporal structure it rebels against subjection to the domain of essential structures, to a concept of Being which is dominated by the ideal pastness of the Aristotelian τό τί ἦν εἶναι or of the German *Wesen* with its affinity to the past tense '*gewesen*.' Here then, in the generally hidden substratum of ontological concepts, 'thingness' may come to invade, or rather to infiltrate, subjectivity: an 'essentialist' concept of Being forces upon the recalcitrant data of self-experience a pattern borrowed from object-experience.

The self reveals itself to primary, i.e. introspective experience as a process of origination. Either of two mutually exclusive inferences will follow: (1) The self, it may be inferred, has no nature or essence at all. It is not fixed and bound by its own 'whatness.' Rather than being 'such and such' it produces itself as 'such and such a one.' It 'is' not but it produces its own Being under the original form of existence. No theory, of course, can entirely dispense with essences or natures, not even, if it deals with things human, with something like human nature. This is true also of the theory of the self as absolute self-origination. But in fidelity to its own principle it will have to maintain that essences, including the essence of human nature, derive from the ontological origination which takes place in the ego, nay which *is* what, constrained by language, we awkwardly call the nature of the ego. Thus we arrive at the famous principle of existentialism: existence is prior to essence.

There is perhaps a suspicion in our minds that this very idea of an existentialist metaphysics—a variant, evidently, of metaphysical idealism—is fanciful and impossible of execution. J. P. Sartre can take credit for disproving this suspicion. In *L'Être et le Néant* he makes the valiant and not entirely unsuccessful attempt to develop the idea of the priority of existence into an elaborate system. But, on closer examination, we may find that the devil is here driven out by Beelzebub. In the interest of a more adequate understanding of subjectivity (the ego or the human person) a radical revision of metaphysical principles is undertaken. But the result is another distortion of selfhood, complementary to the one under attack and no less fatal for the integrity of the observable phenomena. The "reification" of the self is replaced with its deification. The price paid for systematic consistency is the suppression of the component of passivity in the originating process of selfhood. Existentialism of the German brand is characterized by its anti-Cartesian pathos: Cartesian dualism is charged with responsibility for assimilating the ego as *res cogitans* to the *res extensa*. Sartre, in grafting the principle of existentialist critique on a thought animated by the Cartesian tradition inadvertently makes it clear that the justly dreaded assimilation may take on the form of assimilation by opposition. His *pour-soi*, the character of subjectivity of selfhood, is conceived as the antithesis to *l'en soi* which roughly corresponds to Descartes' *res extensa:* So the self as non-thing or nothing (*néant*) becomes the creator of things. The very radicalism of the opposition betrays its dependence upon the principle which it negates.

(2) The data of experience may justify a more conservative conclu-

sion. We may envisage the possibility of a metaphysical framework which allows a place to existence, its self-determination and futurity within a world of contingent facts, without surrendering the idea of structural constituent principles of mundane reality. Within this framework it should be possible to restore the missing link between the narrow "existentialist" concept of existence and its comprehensive metaphysical significance. E. Gilson, by invoking the Thomist idea of the act of existence as supervening upon the actualization of essences or quiddities, has conferred a degree of plausibility upon this idea by developing it as a principle of the interpretation of the history of occidental philosophy. But so far we are unable to point to a contemporary work where, in a metaphysical context, a constructive rather than a destructive rôle is assigned to existence.[4] Yet the bare outline of the idea may be useful as a tool of criticism, especially if we round off our observations on the Self as process of origination with a supplementary remark.

The Self is experienced not only as self-origination but as the awareness thereof. As originator of its own life, the Self is aware of its origination. Hence, in acting out itself it is burdened as well as animated by the care for itself. In existing it is concerned about its own existence. And this concern (Plato called it ἐπιμέλεια) is absolute—for an obvious reason. All other goods which we may care about and strive after are merely elements in the life of the Self as a whole. Even those among them which seem intrinsically good are ultimately good only as contributing to the goodness of the whole. Their goodness is relative to the absolute goodness of the life to be lived. The heightening of self-awareness is, therefore, for the individual an awakenening to the fullness of his self-concern, and out of this process a new shade of meaning grows upon "existence." We now understand why existence can be used in a neutral as well as in an emphatic or elative sense, the first being related to the latter as potency to actuality. We may exist as though we did not exist.

3.

We restate our question: Is there room for existence in the metaphysical frame of reference as denoted or suggested in Professor Broad's philosophy? And in asking this question we think of existence as defined in terms of our phenomological sketch of the existence of the human person. An examination of Professor Broad's writings leads me to answer in the negative. The question as such, I believe, can hardly be regarded as unfair or irrelevant. For Professor Broad, like every philosopher, is

---

[4] I hardly dare to mention in this connection my own fumbling and sketchy attempts, especially in *Begegnung mit dem Sein*, Tübingen, 1954.

to no small extent concerned with the human person and its ontological status. At the same time, I am far from imagining that my criticism, even if it should be considered cogent, has the effect of invalidating Professor Broad's metaphysical principles. The reader may decide that the criterion is based on a misconception of human nature and thus dismiss it as unjustified. In anticipating this adverse criticism of my criticism I still feel that I may not have wasted my time in engaging in this critical skirmish. Since the principles held by Professor Broad are shared by a large group, perhaps a majority, of contemporary philosophers, the issue transcends the particular occasion, and our discussion may serve to throw into prominence a central problem of modern philosophical thought.

In a theological context Professor Broad defines "person" as a substance characterized by four attributes: first, its ability to think, feel, will, etc. Second, its unity as a present state of mind; third, its historical unity; and fourth its being aware of these two types of unity.[5] This, in a way, is a model definition. The genus "substance" is so high up in the scale of principles that no personalist could take exception to this generic placement. The four attributes taken together add up to something like a specific difference. The specifying force of two and three is perhaps a little weakened for those who remember that the two types of unity correspond to, or are derived from, the same dual unity—the "vertical" unity of state and the "horizontal" unity of duration—which Professor Broad discovers in the physical object. The two types of unity are fundamentally the two dimensions, spatial and temporal, which determine the thingness of things. Descartes' *res* is still with us. Person is a *res cogitans*, and the *cogitatio*, the effective principle of differentiation, is expressed by the fourth attribute: the person "must not only be in fact a mind, but must also know that it is a mind."—The personal self is self-consciousness—*res se ipsam cogitans*. The dynamic character of selfhood, the fact that the unity is not simply there but that it has to be perpetually affirmed and established, that it is a self-unifying unity—this seems to go unnoticed. But there is still the first attribute: the substance under examination "must think, feel, will, etc." There, certainly, under the title of feeling and especially of will, the structural feature which we are looking for must be comprised. Just how important is 'will,' that step-child of Cartesian psychology, for Professor Broad's conception of the human person?

The definition of person to which we refer is taken from an essay dealing with "The Validity of Belief in a Personal God" and it serves the purpose of furnishing a basis for a theological discussion. So in

5 *RPPR,* 160.

fairness to the author we must look for further evidence before we can reach even a tentative conclusion. The book on *MPN*, especially chapter VI, on "Introspection," may be the appropriate place. Professor Broad, here as elsewhere, proceeds by a dialectical method. In approaching a problem he starts from points of view, opinions, theories. These he enumerates, and examines one after another until, after painstaking comparison and scrutiny, he feels entitled to give a slight preference to one of the competing solutions which is then presented as probably the right one or, at any rate, the one which seems to be most closely approaching an adequate statement of the hitherto available evidence. This method impresses the reader with a high sense of intellectual conscientiousness, of noble detachment and unflinching impartiality. But occasionally a slight sense of frustration may trouble his peace of mind. The method, to be sure, is dignified by an ancient tradition. As it is employed by Plato we seem to witness an august tribunal sitting in judgement over passionately disputing claimants. Practiced by Professor Broad the method makes us feel rather like clients in an optician's shop. One pair of spectacles after another is put to the test of our eyes: which makes us see most clearly? An excellent and wholesome procedure. But so busy are we with comparing and testing the lenses that little time is left for an inspection of the things to be looked at. Did we really see more than just an alphabet printed in letters of varying size?

"We are alleged by certain people to have an introspective knowledge of ourselves and of some of our mental states" (*loc. cit.,* 276). In the paragraphs which follow this opening statement of the section on "The Objects of Introspection" the author spends most of his time in discussing the hypothesis of a Pure Ego. We resist the temptation of tracing the sinuous path of this analysis which is taken up again and brought to a conclusion at the end of the book in Chapter XIII "The Unity of Mind." Instead we stop on page 283 where the question is raised, "whether, and in what sense, we can have introspective knowledge of the Empirical or the Total Self." In weighing this question it will be natural for the reader to find his curiosity raised to a high pitch of expectancy. He is about to be ushered into the inward life of the mind and to recapture perhaps that vertiginous excitement of which one of the earliest explorers of this *penetrale amplum et infinitum* has left us an unforgettable account, and he may feel that he has to arm himself against being overwhelmed by the humbling experience of intellectual impotence to which the great pioneer confessed: *animus ad habendum se ipsum angustus est.*[6] However, crossing the threshold this imaginary reader may be strangely disappointed. The furnishings of that enormous

---

[6] Augustinus, *Confessions,* X, 8.

room, so he shall discover, are designed by Professor Broad in an exceedingly severe style. The things our eyes meet with are the two already familiar types of unity, and the observations suggested by the definition of 'person' are corroborated. This time the author favors us with the unequivocal enunciation of his principle: "The Empirical Self is, for the present purpose (i.e. for answering the question as to whether, and in what sense, we can have introspective knowledge of the Empirical or Total Self) precisely analogous to a physical thing." Follows the explanation: "each is a long strand of history whose successive slices have a certain continuity with each other and are themselves composed of various overlapping events united in a characteristic way" (283). Descartes, in defining subjectivity opposed to the physical *res* its replica, the mental *res cogitans*. Hume duplicated the mechanics of physical atoms by his mechanics of impressions and ideas. Professor Broad follows suit. In assailing the confusion of language caused by Cartesian Physicalism, Professor Gilbert Ryle writes:

The working of minds had to be described by the mere negatives of the specific descriptions given to bodies; they are not in space, they are not motions, they are not modifications of matter, they are not accessible to public observation. Minds are not bits of clockwork, they are just bits of not-clockwork.[7]

So the fascination with the physical object as the ideal model of all objectivity obstructs the philosopher's vision and inveigles him into a misreading of experience. The Self which he imagines to be composed of 'slices' is little more than a myth engendered by the idolatry of physics. And yet, Professor Broad is the contemporary of a philosophical movement aimed at liberating the mind from the Cartesian stranglehold. Bergson's *Les données immédiates de la conscience* appeared in 1889, William James's *Principles of Psychology* in 1890. The German *Geistes-*

---

[7] *The Concept of Mind,* London 1949, p. 20. This withering attack on the Cartesian tradition begins on almost apocalyptic tones. But the Book with the Seven Seals with which it then presents us turns out to be an English Dictionary. Language unaffected as it is by the more radical conclusions drawn by philosophers may be of great help in uncovering philosophical errors. But it is unable to provide answers to philosophical questions. In examining the question of the relevance of psychical research to philosophy, Prof. Broad writes: "Suppose that philosophy consists in accepting without question, and then attempting to analyse, the beliefs which are common to contemporary plain men in Europe and North America, i.e., roughly the beliefs which such persons acquired uncritically in their nurseries and have since found no occasion to doubt. Then, perhaps, the only relevance of psychical research to philosophy would be to show that philosophy is an even more trivial academic exercise than plain men had been inclined to expect." (*RPPR,* 8). Is the first of these two sentences a teasing reference to 'Analysis'? Be that as it may, Prof. B.'s more recent publications show a marked influence on him of the analytic school of thought. "I think that failure to recognize that ambiguity (in the word 'conscience') often leads to misunderstandings and disputes which are mainly verbal" (*EHP,* 245) —passages like that have become numerous in his writings.

wissenschaft and Phenomology, profiting from the work of these pioneers and joining hands with French, Italian, Belgian, Dutch and Scandinavian scholars, have labored to rouse modern thought from its dogmatic physicalist slumber. Why has so clear-sighted a thinker as Professor
Broad ignored the evidence presented by a cloud of witnesses? An answer
may be submitted in his own words: "As so often happens in philosophy,
clever people accept a false general principle on *a priori* grounds and
then devote endless labour and ingenuity to explaining away plain
facts which obviously conflict with it."[8]

Are we to reach the conclusion that there is no place for 'person' and
'mind' in the thought of the author of *MPN?* This certainly would be a
gross exaggeration. The mind, viewed with the peculiar foreshortening
which the Cartesian principle entails, is still mind. It is, in the first
place, a knowing mind. But knowledge too suffers truncation. It is reduced to the kind of knowledge to which D. H. Lawrence scornfully refers in writing: "Keep knowledge for the world of matter, force, and
function. It has got nothing to do with being"[9]—the knowledge which
concentrates on the non-historical aspect of reality, the re-iterative pattern of events, and which, within this limited field of vision, renders possible both prediction of future events and control over them. In short,
the mind under analysis is the mind as conceived within the Positivist
tradition of nineteenth century thought—the mind of the *homo faber*
who, through knowledge, rises to mastery first over nature and, ultimately, over himself and society. The claim advanced in the name of
Man is of breath-taking boldness. But the garish light of the hopes which
once attended this claim has become dimmed to doubt and resignation.
Professor Broad chimes in with the chorus of those who lament the 'cul-
tural lag.' The greatest immediate threat to the further progress of the
human mind, is, he thinks, "the *unequal development* of these three
branches of knowledge; i.e., the relatively high degree of our control
over inorganic nature, combined with our still very rudimentary knowledge of biology and genetics, and with the complete absence of a scientific psychology and sociology."[10] While a growing disharmony between
the human organisms and their new environment imperils man's emotional equipoise, science provides him with ever fresh means of destroy-
ing life on a vast scale. Can we still hope that knowledge and control of
life and mind will catch up with physics? So far, "physics and death
have a long start over psychology and life."[11] This was written two decades before Hiroshima. We do not know whether Professor Broad still

[8] *EHP,* 229f.
[9] *Studies in Classic American Literature,* (New York: 1923), 102.
[10] *MPN,* 664f.   [11] *Ibid.,* 606.

hopes to avert disaster "by deliberately altering the emotional constitution of mankind, and deliberately constructing more reasonable forms of social organization."[12] But by putting together the inadequacy of his concept of mind on the one hand and the enormity of the expectations with which he burdens it on the other, we can realize that it is the greatness of the mind rather than its insignificance which makes it hard to find room for it in nature. In fact, how can mind, viewed as the manipulator of nature, be placed within nature? Yet there is a nemesis of this imputed greatness. Nature reclaims mind for its property so imperiously as to swallow up personal existence along with its core of spontaneous action. This happens in the essays devoted to moral problems.

The mind attaining knowledge and control over the mind—there is a sunk and a raised part to this Positivist tenet. It debases the mind by putting it on a level with matter controlled by technology; and again it deifies the mind by raising it to the rank of the lord and master of history. It robs man of the high hopes of a creature second only to the angels, and again offers up to the goddess humanity the incense of the religion of progress. Professor Broad, less hopeful than the representatives of Classic Positivism of the nineteenth century and therefore more keenly aware of the latent contradictions of the Positivist mode of thought, muses in a quizzical mood over the "paradoxical position of man, half animal and half angel, completely at home in none of the mansions of his Father's house, too refined to be comfortable in the stables and too coarse to be at ease in the drawing room."[13] For Professor Broad, writing as he does in the twentieth century, the vision of the drawing room of the future, imperfectly foreshadowed by psychological and sociological laboratories, has become singularly dim. So, in applying himself to moral problems, he finds little to say about man's angelic nature; nor, in fact, does he make common cause with the detractors of our race. Nothing is farther from the mind of this gentlemanly philosopher than cynicism. But man as an agent, as an existing being, gets all but blotted out. He is engulfed by nature which, in its turn, is enslaved by physical necessity.

4.

Coërced by his pre-occupation with physical reality as the model of everything real, the philosopher, so we have seen, is debarred from obtaining an adequate view of the self in its peculiar nature—that nature which we roughly circumscribe by the term 'origination.' The existence of the self is further characterized by its concern about itself. In existing, the person is concerned about his own existence. This is an absolute con-

<hr />

[12] *Ibid.*, 665.   [13] *FTET* (New York and London 1930), 284.

cern, and from it there derives the absolute validity of moral obligations
and moral claims on the person. Moral laws may have their ultimate
source in a divine command. But even so the command can become
effective only by appealing to a human response—to man's willing-
ness either to obey or to rebel; and his response in its turn springs from
man's natural concern about himself. So the two concepts, existence and
absolute or categorical obligation, are inseparable from each other. By
negating the first, we obliterate the second, and *vice versa*. In his essay
on "Determinism, Indeterminism, and Libertarianism,"[14] Professor
Broad endeavors to make it appear probable "that the notion of categorical obligability is a delusive notion, which neither has nor can have
any application."[15] The argument runs about as follows. Moral obligability entails substitutability. Unless we might have done otherwise
than we actually did any judgment applying to that action and expressing obligability is void of meaning. Obligability, however, is predicated upon libertarianism, which is indeterminism plus the assumption
that "the self or agent, taken as a substance or continuant," by completely determining the direction and the intensity of the effort, operates as "the non-occurrent total cause."[16] Now while indeterminism has
at least a *prima facie* possibility, libertarianism is impossible. For "in so
far as an event *is* determined, an essential factor in its total cause must
be other *events;*"[17] and the putting forth of an effort is quite clearly
an event, with other events for its causal ancestry. So along with libertarianism the idea of categorical obligability collapses. We wonder
whether, after this supreme act of critical demolition, an ethics can still
be thought possible. A tentative answer is perhaps suggested in Professor Broad's paper on "Conscience and Conscientious Action,"[18] where
he safeguards the meaning of the 'ought to' by buttressing it with a
radically subjective interpretation of conscience.

The pleasure with which we follow the author in preparing to ad-
minister a mortal blow to one of the first principles of ethics is but
slightly marred by the same kind of foreknowledge which haunts the expert reader of detective stories. Given Professor Broad's premises the
outcome is clear from the start. He knows of only one kind of causation,
the one instanced by physical knowledge and embracing two components: the preceding events (efficient cause) and the "nomic premisses," a somewhat reduced version of what is traditionally called the
"formal cause." The illustrations used for clarifying the Principle of
Causality are billiard balls and a flash of light, and the language is
strained to the utmost by enforced abstraction. For we move in a uni-

14 *EHP*, 195–217.   15 P. 217.   16 *Ibid.*
17 P. 215.   18 *Op. cit.*, 244–262.

verse of discourse in which the words denoting human actions and attitudes have no birthright—they are all of them tainted with the connotation that the agent might act, or might have acted, otherwise. They do not naturally fit into a world ruled by physical determination, and even the device persistently employed by Professor Broad—the limitation of analysis to past actions—is not sufficient to bring about a satisfactory assimilation. Any attempt to view action as action in process would bring down upon the writer a host of troublesome problems. So it is as carefully avoided as an analysis of deliberation, the intellectual strategy, as it were, of action in progress, and one of the great topics of traditional Aristotelian and post-Aristotelian ethics. But above all no consideration is given to the question as to whether there might not be types of determination other than physical determination, supplementing it rather than suspending it, not in need of any supposed gap in the closed ranks of physical causes but operating on an altogether different level of reality. The billiard balls, in Professor Broad's illustration, move in strict conformity to the laws of physics. But their motion is likewise determined by the intention of the players. And the two statements, one relating to the efficient, the other to the final cause, far from contradicting each other, are interdependent. The players can determine the cause of the balls only because it is already determined—within the limits of physical causality. We can, generally speaking, act on reality because we can rely on its responding to our action in conformity to physical laws. It seems rather odd to try to discover in what is the basis for action a disproof of its possibility, action being, by its very nature, doing one thing rather than another, deciding upon one course of action from among several possible courses. All this sounds much like common-sense, and there is in it nothing like the boldness with which Professor Broad faces up to angry or alarmed recriminations from the man in the street who happens to dabble in philosophy. But occasionally common-sense and ordinary language are better guides to metaphysical truth than physics.

But does physics, the science of whose methods and methodological problems Professor Broad is an accomplished conoisseur, really support a causal monism which, as we have seen, is destructive of the possibility of action? There is a paradox implied in physicalism. Modern physics, Newtonian and post-Newtonian, is mathematical physics, i.e. a measuring science. It focuses on that aspect of real events which, as amenable to metrical determination, reveals them as a-historical, as timelessly temporal, and, therefore, as producible and reproducible, as subject to experimental tests and technological control. We shall not say, with D. H. Lawrence, that physical knowledge "has got nothing to do with Being." But we do affirm that, by its method, it is unable to grasp concrete or historical Being. Its limitation is its strength. By performing the act of mathematical abstraction as exemplified by the notion of infinite rectilinear motion, it wins mastery over nature—or rather over that stratum of nature which lends itself most readily to that abstractive analysis, i.e. inanimate matter. Physics reveals nature as pliable to human purposes, and it offers tools for subjecting it to human ends and choices. Thus it was able to engender those enthusiastic expectations as to the future perfection of Man and Society which are still alive, though not very alive, in Professor Broad's early literary work. The very science, hailed for long as the liberator of man, now serves, through a generalization of its methodical principles, to strip man of the privilege of his human liberty. But it is not our business to meet Professor Broad on his own chosen ground, the theory of physical knowledge. Suffice it to say, in conclusion, that his philosophy, metaphysically speaking extreme naturalism, ontologically speaking, extreme essentialism, is by its very principles hard put to it to come to terms with existence.

Knowledge cannot only be put to use by an act of application which follows cognition. By itself it is part of the life of the knower who, as a human being, applies himself to the business of living his life. This inherent practicality is particularly marked in ethics, and it is understandable that Professor Broad, at the end of his book on *Five Types of Ethical Theory*, expresses misgivings as to the relationship between his theoretical findings and moral reality. In the course of his analysis things have become so complicated that he may seem to have made "the fact of right action inexplicable. Quite simple people, there is no reason to doubt, often act rightly in quite complicated situations. How could they possibly do so if the problem is so involved as we have made it out to be?"[19] He solves the puzzle by comparing the moral agent to a player, playing a ball rightly at tennis or cricket, his own analysis to the mechanical and hyrdodynamical theory of the action of the racket or bat and the flight of the ball. This analogy will become truly fitting if, for the second anologon, modern science, we substitute mediaeval Aristotelian physics, an admirably complicated theory, which, however, clinging as it did to the idea of a bodily contact between mover and moved as a prerequisite of accidental motion, was in no position to account for the momentum of a flying body such as a ball. Yet even at that time and in spite of physics balls continued to fly. So in our own time people continue to act and to act differently from the way they might act and, more often than not, differently from the way they ought to act, and all that on a vast scale and in spite of Professor Broad's analytical demolition of the principle of action. There is comfort in this for the friend of on-

19 *Loc. cit.*, 284.

going life, but it is disturbing to the friend of theory. Professor Broad's mind is not unruffled by this disturbance. His quaint remark about salvation being not everything and about trying to understand in outline what one solves *ambulando* in detail being quite good fun for certain people does not have a very cheerful ring. The thinker, defeated by existence, retreats into the melancholy fastness of esoteric resignation. He finds that there are no good reasons for crediting man with a capacity for free choice, nor for crediting God with a capacity to exist. Yet he cannot possibly wish to have that sort of knowledge bruited about. Though he takes a gloomy view of the prospects of Christianity he does not contemplate its anticipated doom with any degree of pleasure. He finds a profound truth in Christ's parable about the house that has been swept and garnished, but in the place of the evil spirit that was cast out seven worse demons move in. Human nature—"ordinary human nature," Professor Broad writes—abhors a vacuum, and with alarm he views two new religions which have entered into the clean-swept place and possessed it, Communism and Fascism. A deepening gloom settles down over the philosopher's intellectual landscape. Applied science, once a Prometheus Phosphorus, has become transmogrified into blind Samson preparing to uproot the pillars of the house and bury pure science with it in the ruins. And the light that was to guide man towards the terrestrial Jerusalem designed for him by the science of society and the science of mind must be put under a bushel. The pioneer turns traditionalist and quotes with approval Belloc's ironical nursery rhyme: "Always keep hold of Nurse, for fear of finding Something Worse."[20]

Under the Neon light of Physicalism all things take on a uniform color, and it is difficult to tell persons from objects, the existence of man from the 'being there' of things. Existence also in the broad ontological sense of the term can no longer hold its own against an unitarian conception of structural Being. Professor Broad, it is true, makes a special point of distinguishing between 'existential' and 'characterizing' propositions.[21] The negative assertions *Cats do not bark* and *Dragons do not exist* seem both to be about some sort of animals. But this, he affirms, is an illusion created by similarity of grammatical structure. The second proposition does not characterize dragons and, in fact, it is not at all about dragons—it is about the dragon-characteristics. What propositions of this type assert is "that these characteristics do apply to something or that they do not apply to anything, as the case may be. 'Cats exist' is equivalent to 'The defining characteristics of the word "cat" apply to something.' Again 'Dragons do not exist' is equivalent to 'The defining characteristics of the word "dragon" do not apply to anything.' Suppose,

20 *RPPR*, 243.   21 *Op. cit.*, 182.

e.g., that a 'dragon' is defined as a reptile which flies and breathes fire. Then the statement affirms that nothing combines the three properties of being a reptile, of flying, and of breathing fire. Such statements are neither tautologies nor contradictions."[22] Precisely, but it may be doubted whether they are really relevant to the problem of existence. In fact, there is something that combines the three properties, and we know exactly what we are talking about when we refer to dragons. In that sense dragons are. But they are imaginary entities rather than existents. Again there *are* numbers and there *are* generic conceptions, and without them science would be impossible. But neither numbers nor *genera exist,* and it is this distinction upon which the problem of existence hinges.

Professor Broad deals with existential propositions in connection with an attempt to refute the Ontological Argument. It was Anselm's error to try to find, on the basis of a strictly logical argument, the answer to a metaphysical question. His modern critic, while rejecting Anselm's conclusion, shares his fundamental mistake. Limiting himself to a merely formal analysis and writing with the bold strokes which express the self-assurance of the scientist up-to-date in his field rather than with the gracefully hesitant pen of the sceptical philosopher which he generally adopts ("the right analysis as is now well known . . ."), he does not succeed in coming to grips with the problem of existence. He lacks the metaphysical frame of reference within which alone the problem can be envisaged. Again this framework, in order to allow for a place to 'existence,' must be wide enough to include what the existentialists are aiming at when they talk of 'existence,' a concept of subjectivity untrammeled by physicalist prejudices. Man is not responsible for the existence of things real. But it is perhaps correct to say that as philosophers we arrive at a just appraisal of existence only through an understanding of that particular kind of existence which is ours.

HELMUT KUHN

UNIVERSITY OF MUNICH
GERMANY

[22] *Op. cit.,* 183.

21

Robert W. Browning

BROAD'S THEORY OF EMOTION

P*REFATORY.* In the following paper we aim, first, to present and to ask certain questions about Broad's basic analysis of emotion, and, second, to present and to ask several queries about some useful distinctions which he proffers for the discussion of emotions.

Observation of Broad's methodology, of course, may engross some persons more than the substantival issues. On the former we shall lightly touch. The material questions here to be raised are of considerable intrinsic interest. A few of them may be weighty in their indirect bearings. Although space will not permit the development of these themes in more than the most prefatory manner, justification of the topic may appeal (a) to the currency of interest in aspects of the subject, (b) to the possibility of precipitating a statement of a change of views on the part of Broad, and (c) to the relative neglect of certain large topics, descriptive and genetic, about the contents of subjectivity.

(a) No remark is necessary as to the timeliness of the subject of emotion; and leading emotivists in metaethics would be among the first to acknowledge, I believe, that pro-emotion and anti-emotion had better not be left as surds. One needs a general theory of emotion and an emotivist is under obligation to distinguish moral pro-emotion and moral anti-emotion from ordinary first-personally interested pro-emotion and anti-emotion. Physiological evidence as to whether the thalamus or the hypo-thalamus are always involved in emotional excitation does not help. Whether emotivists will find much help in Broad, whose psychology is less in the current vein than, say, Stevenson's, is another matter; but stimulus may well come from quarters which are not in fashion. Whether refutation of emotivism might derive from further theory of emotion is still another question, and on it I shall not take space to offer a very complicated trivial guess, but I may opine that the odium which has been attached by not a few morally concerned thinkers to emotivism does not properly attach to generic emotivism (assuming this sort of moral concern) but to generic emotivism plus certain widespread assumptions about emotions. Put another way, would one still call it emotivism if one held that all "moral" decisions and all "moral" ostensible judgments are the registration of certain emotions, but that certain emotions are intrinsically appropriate toward certain objects? This uncommon line of thought is not alien, I believe, to certain developments found in Broad's writings. Whether or not such an eclectic or unusual line be the line of advance, and whether or not it be called a species of emotivism, I happen to have a presumption that progress may come from better discrimination of what is already possessed implicitly in moral emotions as undergone; and Broad is a quite uncommonly good introspector.

(b) The Broad of *Five Types of Ethical Theory*, the Broad who hailed so favorably the work of the Provost of Oriel, the Broad of sundry discussions of objective fittingness, was pretty plainly a cognitivist in ethics. Within a little more than the last decade, there has been a Broad offering "Some Reflections on Moral-Sense Theories in Ethics,"[1] in which one species of emotional moral-sense theory—although not endorsed—is defended against three major criticisms and is shown to be in accord with our author's introspection of first-hand and second-hand moral emotions. A delicate task is indicated for any attempt to determine in what senses this theory is non-cognitivist (as the terms "dispositional" and "emotional" suggest) and in what ways it is cognitivist (as qualifying it as "transsubjective" and as calling it a "moral sense" theory may connote). Is it a non-interjectional emotive theory? One wonders if perchance Broad is producing something of which he once said he knew of no instance in the previous history of philosophy, namely, a theory at once non-naturalistic and non-rationalistic, a theory for which moral concepts and moral judgments are both empirical although something in morals is "irreducible" to the non-moral.[2] More recently, Broad has, with the maximum caution and the "minimum of comment and criticism," drawn attention to Hägerström's "ethical subjectivism" or "ethical positivism" and commended it for its ingeniousness with respect to "various aspects of the admitted facts."[3] And he has engaged in the great labor of love of translating from the Swedish the collection of essays of Axel Hägerström, entitled *Inquiries into the Nature of Law and Morals*.[4] I should be pleased if I or some other essayist in the present volume elicited an autobiographical statement from Broad on his exact position with respect to psychological naturalism

[1] *Proc. Arist. Soc.*, N.S., XLV (London: Harrison and Sons, Ltd., 1944–45). References in the sequel will be to the reprinting most convenient for Americans, in Wilfrid Sellars and John Hospers, *Readings in Ethical Theory*, 363–388 (New York: Appleton-Century-Crofts, Inc., 1952). Hereafter this reference will be abbreviated as S&H.

[2] *FTET*, 267.

[3] "Hägerström's Account of Sense of Duty and Certain Allied Topics," *Philosophy*, XXVI: 99–113 (April 1951).

[4] Stockholm: Almqvist & Wiksell, 1953.

and to emotivism in ethics; but I hasten to add that I am not among those critics who apparently are so heavily laden with a forensic tradition in philosophy that they value a clean confident categorical assertion of a thesis well above a careful qualified analysis of the issues.

What we shall do here is only to make some explorations in the anteroom to Broad's psychology. I should very much wish sometime to encompass at least his psychology of morals; I have found, however, that I cannot go properly into this subject until I have worked more intensively with his theory of emotion, which is a theory in which emotions are ostensibly cognitions and which is a theory of desires and aversions (and hence at least part of an account of motivation and decision). Although Broad has published no general treatise on moral psychology, he has published several very important papers on the subject and his more than incidental comments in the area are rather extensive. Particular subtlety is not required to notice the canny way in which he takes in the psychological theses and assumptions of selected historical moralists. And he was wont to precede his own classroom lectures on ethics with a course of lectures on moral psychology, portions of which in modified form have found their way into print. One treatise would be required to expound his views and another to make thorough criticism. Let it be added that the present time is at once one in which ethical advance is likely to come in conjunction with penetration in moral psychology, and one in which originality is likely to generate potent myopic ethical whimseys unless these be inhibited by a well-rounded secondary sense of moral phenomena or a lively first hand sense of moral situations. If Butler, as Broad says, has "the solid common-sense" of an English bishop of the eighteenth century, Broad himself has the solid common-sense and analytic habits of an intellectual descendant of Henry Sidgwick. He commands the respect of quite varied groups, ranging from the heirs of philosophical idealism to the latest pseudopodia of analysis. In the last few decades naturalism has ceased to move on the momentum of pricking pretensions and has largely got over the habit of gross antecedent oversimplification. Most naturalists, too, want to face the phenomena in their full richness.[5] In implementing

---

5 Professor Wilfrid Sellars does seem a bit too confident that "animal learning theory [possibly future rather than present] provides the key to all psychological phenomena," but he explicitly recognizes "It is only by absorbing the insights of rationalism that a pragmatic empiricism can do justice to the facts." "Language, Rules and Behavior," in Sidney Hook (ed.), *John Dewey: Philosopher of Science and Freedom* (New York: Dial Press, 1950), pp. 298, 301. He calls upon his fellows not to "leave the field of cognitive and moral psychology to the rationalists," for we are no longer living in the "good old days before the failure of nerve, when the climate of opinion was favorable to empiricism" and when consequently "the empiricist got away with murder." 300.

this intent, a reading of Broad would be complementary to reading novels and reading the book of life. If one could run through all Broad's *obiter dicta* and then could show the organization of issues to which these judgments pertain, one would have a pretty good map of moral phenomena. The projects referred to, however, would lead us around in the main building; here we can explore the foyer.

(c) It will be plain that, as it seems to me, there are large and mostly unformulated problems with respect to consciousness and its contents. Answers to them would be highly speculative at present; most of the questions may properly belong to psychology, descriptive and genetic, but psychologists have understandably found it happier to work with more creditable methods toward more assured results elsewhere. Despite the actual diversity in movements and contents—and the much greater diversity one tends to assume on indirect physiological evidence—I am impressed by the normal "unity" of consciousness and the continual fusion and elimination which this presumably requires. Besides an infinitude of questions of detail, there are gross questions of how distinguishable strands and modalities in the field of awareness are related, if they are related in regular ways. How are what are called "emotions" related to what are taken as "knowings"? How are they related to desires? Can any activity, conative, affective or cognitive (to use the old but still useful set of labels) be viewed as more fundamental than others, assigned any primacy in the causal order? Do these "activities" constitute three inseparable aspects of all experience, or how separable are they? What is determinative of their respective dominances in phases of experience? Are there characteristic linkages and distinctive interweavings? Is pattern brought into them by looking at them as functional, as tending toward survival of the individual and the species and even toward production of richness of experience?[6]

In the attempt to avoid disastrous length, references to the genesis of certain of Broad's views and comparisons with predecessors or contemporaries will be omitted. One may entertain the biographical supposition that our author came to his theory of emotion primarily under two motivations: he hoped to resolve some tangles concerning the relation of cognition and emotion in moral experience; second, he set himself to come to terms with McTaggart's theory of emotion. Comparable in influence with the latter would stand G. F. Stout. It would be of

6 The interminable list could go on. In describing and analyzing what is found on reflexively looking at experience, is a distinction of form and content useful? Is a distinction of object and tone exhaustive? Is a distinction of relations and qualities best? What signification in description of consciousness should be assigned to what is figuratively called "focus" and "fringe," "lowering of the threshold," "raising to explicitness," etc.? More importantly, what if anything do these phenomena show about the structure of the self?

more than incidental interest to note similarities of Broad's views to characteristic idealistic theses, although surely Broad's major habitudes of mind place him with the epistemological realists.

In the present essay we must likewise wholly eschew the problems of the psychology of decision and therewith, of course, questions of the intensity and organization of motives and more especially of whether there is any distinctively moral motive and of how (if it exists) it is related to beliefs on the one hand and to non-moral motives on the other. Broad has had quite a bit to say upon these topics, largely under the schema of hierarchies of dispositions, but we must not attempt to encompass these themes here.

Our task in the main is exposition, supplemented with critical comment. We do not pretend to do ethics here nor definitively to draw outcomes of Broad's psychological approaches for moral theory; however, we shall not restrain ourselves entirely from making references to the area (nor from offering opinions therein), for patently Broad has had in mind various problems of the analysis and genesis of ostensibly normative statements in considering emotions—at first allowing them an ancillary status and lately sketching for a class of them a possible essential and focal rôle.

I am aware that the following assumptions of mine will be repeatedly evident in the sequel—doubtless along with other assumptions of which I am unaware and of a multitude of others I do not deem worthy of mention. Neither philosophy nor the sciences contain a proven theory of the relation of somatic events to conscious events. The nature of what is native in the functioning human being is not known, nor its ranges of influence, particularly with respect to predispositions toward certain patterns of thinking and modalities of feeling; correlatively, the limits of conditioning are most vague, and therewith any grounded notions of the novelties which are possible and of the conceivable novelties which are actually impossible for the given fabric. However, native dispositions do to some extent answer to features of the environment— thanks to evolutionary selection. The psycho-physical organism is sensitive in many ways that are not manifest in consciousness. Degrees of activity and quiescence, of vividness and dullness, of sharp focus and fuzziness are characteristic of conscious content. Acts of attention appear to be able sometimes to bring to the center of the stage what has been peripheral, whether the latter be substantival or adjectival, or whether it adverbially qualifies the process. Consciousness appears to exercise some administrative rôle; its evidently highly dependent powers seem to vary greatly. Continuing the figure of speech, the intelligence in intelligent beings either is or remains close to the central government of the organism; however, there remains much sensitivity in the less focal and less vocal departments. Speculatively one may wonder if there are not feeling tones unknown to the seat of government but having their base, so to speak, out in the provinces. Experiences, or at least experiences which we centrally notice, are not wholly devoid of intentionality. Phylogenetically and ontogenetically, one may view the intellectual activities as emerging from a sensitive matrix or from overlapping sensitive matrices, and as being selected, due to functional causes, into a position of dominance. Customary views, taking high degree of consciousness with relatively sharp definition of intentional objects as marks of intellectuality, have tended—augmented, no doubt, by the discipline found necessary for public science—sharply to separate intelligence from emotion. This is evidently useful for much of practice, but it is misleading as to origins. Furthermore, it can be dangerous for practice when it leads to the abstracted counters being treated as the realities and to sources of further data being dismissed because they fall far below the extant standards of precision for respectable concepts.

In the present essay, I probably express many very poorly founded opinions, including opinions on issues which are matters of fact. I shall thus die many deaths of electrocution on the electrified fences which colleagues have set up between philosophy and science, and—much worse to me—my departed spirit will have sounded (owing to brevity) as if it supposed issues of fact were settled by what "felt plausible" or "seemed probable" to it.[7] I am quite sensitive to the latter point, but I

[7] Broad has been assigned penance for this misbehavior. In no way confined to reactions to his psychology is the acknowledged distress of those who do feel that the sort of "issues" which Broad brings up are not really issues or at least ought to be talked about in quite some other way. Professor John Wisdom has expressed his "horror" quite vividly: "Even among the purest analysts there lingers still the use of the words 'plausible,' 'unplausible'—shocking survivals of the scientific theory, i.e., the theory that philosophy is science, only grander and stricter. Professor C. D. Broad has never been properly cured of this idea. To the horror of his friends he would suddenly lapse into representing rival philosophical theories as rival hypotheses about what must be the case among the entirely unobservable or obscurely observable in order to account for what is undoubtedly the case amongst the immediately observable. The business of philosophers becomes at once that of finding which is the most probable of these hypotheses in view of the varied and conflicting evidences we have which bear upon them." Wisdom regretfully notes a little later that "this way of putting things" unfortunately "fits our feeling that philosophy is somehow about what world we are in and not merely the make up of the meanings of words." (In: Paul A. Schilpp (ed.), *The Philosophy of G. E. Moore*, 426–428.) Using some of his later terminology, Wisdom would, I suppose, say that there is systemic "categorical confusion" manifest in Broad's practice. The contextualist Professor Arthur E. Murphy would, I take it, suggest that there is confusion of contexts in typical sorts of questions Broad asks and in the way he answers them. (Cf., "Two Versions of Critical Philosophy," *Proceedings of the Aristotelian Society*, N.S., XXXVIII: 143–160.)

Granting that the generally lucid Broad has not always been as clear as one might

will only observe that some philosophical and methodological purists speak as if there were no intermediate loci between the following attitudes: "I leave that question totally to the future of science," and "Science has established this formulation with such-and-such a probability." Although one appreciates the piety of the first and the precision of the second, still between these two there is a lot of room, and it may not be wholly unprofitable to move around in it. No one can jump instantly from the first status to the second. Like other citizens, philosophers are not devoid of temporary squatter's rights on the misty flats of cognition. It is appropriate, with looseness and vagueness, to speak of some things before they can be spoken of with accuracy. At any rate, the large questions—and they are questions as well as gropings, freighted with the human concern of orientation which has been the moving life of metaphysics—cannot be put with neat precision nor answered with more than guesses.[8]

---

wish in distinguishing modes of speech from hypotheses, and granting that on occasions he may impress one as a rationalist speaking of antecedent probabilities and marshalling informed arm-chair arguments with respect to certain hypotheses, I am glad to hail a philosopher who feels the incoherencies in our common assumptions and does not dissolve them by showing that one can purchase potatoes and talk with one's groceryman without having the difficulties arise. Having an unusual command of English, he avoids, on the other hand, cultivating an elaborate linguistic discipline, the schema of which runs the danger of proscribing certain sorts of meaningful answer.

[8] Speculative philosophy, said Broad, "can only consist of more or less happy guesses, made on a very slender basis." Its fascination and its relation to man's practical interests has resulted in much "moonshine," bringing all of philosophy into "undeserved disrepute." However, speculative philosophy, even at the present time, "is of value to scientists, in its methods, if not in its results," as a reminder of the extreme complexity of the world. ST, 21f. Cf. J. H. Muirhead (ed.), Contemporary British Philosophy (London: George Allen & Unwin, 1924), 96ff.

I would not try to invoke the authority of either Broad or Whitehead in defense of any unnecessary unclarity. Both were advocates of clarity. The latter was concerned to recognize the unclarities which are inevitable, to note that the full meaning of the supposedly exact involves a context the apprehension of which is not exact; hence he cautioned against misplacing concreteness upon abstractions.

I certainly do think that Broad mixes psychology and critical philosophy and speculative philosophy (for instance, in MPN), and I do not object at all to his doing so. It exemplifies a healthy absence of professional hypersensitivity about whether one has a distinctive task in an age of specialization, and it illustrates, I believe, that too much emphasis could be placed on Broad's own formulations of the separation of philosophy and the sciences. In the formulations which were published in the 1920's Broad gave the label "critical philosophy" to labor upon two fundamental tasks of philosophy, neither of which he regarded as "purely verbal;" but neither did he regard them as utilizing the particular results of the special sciences or as competing with them. The first branch comprised the analysis of the "concepts that we daily use in common life and science," determining "their precise meanings and their mutual relations." The special sciences clarify their concepts only "so far as this is needful for their own special purposes." ST, 16. The disinterested and more thorough inter-departmental clarification of such notions as substance, cause, space, time, etc., as well as truth, implication, probability, class, good, bad, right, wrong,

What we do then in considerable measure may amount to an amateur's ramblings in old analytic or structural psychology. This admission does not constitute total self-condemnation; it seems to me that some sensible questions can be raised from such a point of view even if correct answers do not significantly yield an increase in manipulative power. There is a topography to be described, although even a correct account does not make one monarch of all one surveys.

This is the agenda. To Broad's distinction of the data of sensation from other content, we cannot attend, nor, of course, to his circumspect but not unusual view of sensory data (including pain and localized sensory pleasures, which are rightly distinguished from pleasantness and unpleasantness). His demarcation of emotions, or rather, their analysis, will be our starting point, followed—after an intrusion of our own—by consideration of the cognitive factors in emotions and then by a brief report on their tonal aspects. Broad carefully avoids confusing questions of present structure with questions of genesis; this is admirable; however, I strongly feel that his general treatment would be better if it were more functional throughout instead of at a few spots where his analysis is suspended to allow some acute observations on

---

etc., was allocated to critical philosophy. The second branch of it gave careful formulation to, and resolute criticism of, "a number of uncriticised beliefs, which we constantly assume in ordinary life and in the sciences," such as "that nature obeys uniform laws, that we live in a world of objects whose existence and behaviour are independent of our knowledge of them, and so on." The examination was to be effected by exposing the beliefs "to every objection that one can think of oneself or find in the writings of others." *ST*, 17f. The second branch was also not supposed to conflict with the sciences, but I do not see how this could be guaranteed in advance, short of a compartmentalization of levels. For, "all conclusions from experiments rest on some of these very assumptions which it is the business of Philosophy to state clearly and to criticise." *ST*, 19. What does "rest on" mean, and what if the assumptions cannot stand under the criticism?

Nor do I see why the second branch was not continuous with speculative philosophy, unless it was because Broad was much more sure of common sense realism (unspecified in details) and of the general assumptions used in science than he was of common beliefs concerning "the religious and ethical experiences of mankind," which latter, along with the former and along with the results of the sciences, received consideration by speculative philosophy in its attempt to frame "some general conclusions as to the nature of the Universe, and as to our position and prospects in it." *ST*, 20. (He has, on occasion, appealed to common sense in characterizing some theories as "silly," e.g., metaphysical behaviorism, certain forms of idealism, and Hobbes' theory of sympathy. *MPN*, 5f. *FTET*, 65.) Perhaps speculative philosophy was highly general and very hypothetical science, devised in areas of the widest perennial human concern.

In a more recent writing, the central distinction Broad makes is between analysis, on the one hand, and synopsis and synthesis, on the other. Some of what was formerly in critical philosophy is now incorporated in the successor to speculative philosophy. "Some Methods of Speculative Philosophy," *Proceedings of the Aristotelian Society*, Suppl. 21 (1947): 1–32.

natural or social selection. Of course I see no reason why introspective psychology (conceived widely or narrowly) should not be done, and Broad is uncommonly good at introspecting and inspecting. I shall draw lengthy attention to his interesting application to emotional tones of principles found useful in dealing with color experience. Here he provides a number of relevant points for the inquirer who is disposed to look for similarities across supposedly isolated contents of consciousness (the dissimilarities being no less significant for theory). The result does diminish a little the mystery of the protean qualitative flow which is continually being produced in what is called the stream of consciousness. Then, next, we shall turn to certain distinctions which Broad justly recommends for dealing with emotions: properly placed *vs.* misplaced emotions; appropriate *vs.* inappropriate emotions; motivated *vs.* unmotivated emotions; and first-hand *vs.* second-hand emotions. In the first three, the discussions of error or pathology in emotions is of major interest. It is particularly unfortunate that in some cases our author does not exhibit the methodology or render explicit the criteria upon which instances of the types of error are pronounced. Tacitly his few remarks upon appropriateness seem to me much more subtle than all the simplified talk of pro-emotion and anti-emotion which is current and to which Broad himself later resorts. The last two distinctions are especially used in locating and describing what he finds on introspecting the processes of a deliberated moral situation. By exceeding the strictures of the text, one could construe this famous description as disclosing an inclination to endorse an emotive theory in the form of a trans-subjective dispositional moral sense theory; whether such a theory would be a noncognitive theory is the topic on which we close.

1. *Demarcation of Emotion.*

In his *Examination of McTaggart's Philosophy*, Broad wrote:

Prima facie there are two and only two fundamentally different kinds of experiences, viz., those which do and those which do not have "epistemological objects." The former are all cogitations, of one kind or another. The latter are feelings. In language the distinction is expressed in the following way. We say *what* we are cogitating, and we say *how* we are feeling.[9]

Here the genus of "experiences" has "two fundamentally different" species, namely, cogitations and feelings. Cogitations presumably are "ostensible prehensions, or ostensible judgings, or ostensible supposings, or ostensible imaginings, or some combination of these."[10]

[9] *EMcT*, II, 133.   [10] *Ibid.*, 132.

What appears to be the same view is given in a recent article, where emotions are explicitly treated:

> Emotions . . . are cognitions with a certain kind of psychical quality. . . . Experiences may be divided into those which *do not* and those which *do* have an "epistemological object." The former may be called *Pure Feelings.* The natural question to ask with regard to a feeling is: "*How* are you feeling?" And the natural answer is to utter some adjective (or, more properly, adverb) such as "Hot," or "Tired," or "Cross." To feel tired is to be feeling *in a certain way;* it is not to be *aware of a certain object,* real or fictitious. On the other hand, there are many experiences about which it is natural to ask: "What is the *object* of your experience?" or "What is it *about?*" If a person says that he is seeing or hearing or thinking, it is natural to ask: "*What* are you seeing?" or "*What* are you hearing?" or "*What* are you thinking about?" And the answer that one expects is the utterance of some substantive or phrase equivalent to a substantive, e.g., "A red flash," "A squeaky noise," "The square-root of minus 1." I shall say that experiences of the latter kind "have an epistemological object" or are "epistemologically intentional." All such experiences may be called *Cognitions.*[11]

The word "cogitation" has been changed to "cognition," but this, I believe, is of no material significance. Antecedently some readers, including myself, would have a broader connotation for "cogitation," than for "cognition," but this prejudice is destroyed by Broad's illustrations of the latter and by his immediately requesting us to notice that "an experience may be epistemologically intentional, even if it be a *delusive quasi-perception* or a thought of something which does not and perhaps could not exist." The stringency of the first quotation in saying that there are "two and only two fundamentally different kinds of experiences" is somewhat cancelled by the qualifying phrase, "*prima facie.*" But whether the second quotation is giving a schema in which there will be three different basic kinds of experiences (against two for the first) is an open question, although it is plain that the introduction of a subdivision of cogitations in the first could provide a three-fold distinction with the honor of a distinctive niche for emotions.

In passing, let it be noted that the classification seems to be made from what—anyway in a wide sense—is an introspective standpoint.[12]

---

[11] "Emotion and Sentiment," *Journal of Aesthetics and Art Criticism,* XIII, 203. (December, 1954). Hereafter references to the text of this article will be abbreviated: *JAAC.*

[12] I foresee no significant harm in my persisting in using "introspection" as the omnibus term which Broad has shown it to be. The narrow application which he specifies is certainly unusual. He rightly observes that "the treatment of introspection by philosophers has been much less careful than their treatment of perception." *MPN,* 275. He notes three "extremely different kinds of cognition" which often get classified as introspection: (1) attention directed to "the objective constituents of visual, tactual, and auditory perceptual situations" to discern their own properties;

The very extended connotation and denotation of "cognitions" is consonant with this psychological orientation; within it one is relieved of responsibility for distinguishing and confining oneself to veridical cognitions. In the context of his discussion of emotion there is no dwelling upon manifestations of emotion as in classic chapters of Darwin or on the physiological correlates as in the work of Cannon. Whether the cortex is involved in animal emotion, whether the stimulation of the thalamus or of the hypothalamus is crucial, are sorts of questions which simply do not arise. Nor whether emotions are releases of previously repressed tendencies of a hypothetical *id*. The causes of emotions are scarcely more than touched upon; likewise with their relationships to instinct. Even whether they are perceptions of one's own visceral reactions or are *ex post facto* recognition of various kinesthetic innervations does not receive treatment, unless chiefly in indirect reference to Spinoza rather than to Lange or James. However, it may be immediately replied that with so many writers ready to investigate correlates of emotions, causes of emotions, functions of emotions, disfunctions of emotions, it is exceedingly important to have someone clarify what

---

(2) attention directed to bodily feelings; and (3) noting of our own "heterogeneous mental events such as perceptual memory situations" where there is reference to an epistemological object external to the situation. The first kind and most of the second Broad proposes to baptize as "inspection." Nor is the third psychological introspection, because of its external reference, but he will call it "epistemological introspection" and allow that it contains psychological introspection. 288–291, 315. Introspection is intuitive knowledge (not inferential and not discursive, although it will issue in judgments) of the mind itself or of its states. Inspection does exist; and Broad is sure that introspection does also, for otherwise how could I "distinguish between the *existence* of noises and toothaches and the *sensing or feeling* of them"? 311. It is a "curious superstition" that introspection "must give exhaustive and infallible knowledge of its objects." 285. That we are having an emotion must be known by introspection, but I have not noticed Broad categorically saying that we inspect the emotional tone. If the case were parallel with that of sense experience, there would be no question. But the case does not seem to be parallel, in Broad's view, for he often seems to be treating the emotional tone—found in answer to the question "how are you feeling?"—as an adverbial property qualifying the process, and not as the "what" or part of the "what," which is the object.

I do not intend to collide with Broad over introspection. Professor Wolfgang Köhler, however, has raised one qualm which is never easy to lay. It is not, of course, that introspection may be in error; Broad perfectly agrees. And Broad seems clear in his distinction of *perceiving with* a portion of the sense-field and *inspecting* the selected portion of the sense-field itself as an object of attention "with a view to learning accurately *its own* apparent characteristics." MPN, 297. The uneasiness is simply the generalized fear that elements may be postulated and then produced by a discipline antecedently committed to finding or making them. In that case, as surely used to happen, "introspecting" which did not find the proper elements was not taken as carrying any disconfirmatory weight but only as giving evidence that the subject had not yet learned the art. Cf. *Gestalt Psychology* (New York: Liverright, 1947), Chap. III.

emotions are, so that *their* correlates may be found, their causes located, their functions assessed—and not the correlates, causes and functions of some other things substituted unwittingly for them. Broad's approach is introspective, but it may serve in clarifying what emotions are before the experiential material of reference is lost by behavioristic denotations or psycho-analytic systemic connotations. Some qualifications which we would like to append to this immediate reply may be inferred from our general treatment.

We add here the opinion that any plausible emotive theory of ethics will be rooted in more than a behavioral view of emotion. A behavioristic definition of emotion will not be serviceable—or will be serviceable only because it is surreptitiously more. Of course the great ambiguity of behaviorism has remained concerning how language is to be taken. If linguistic phenomena are construed as noises or motor marks, an emotive theory of human morals will be practically on a par with an emotive theory of the morals of salamanders. If, on the other hand, language is to be taken for what it means and for how it is used in experience, then to divest one's self of one's own acquaintance with its use and of one's own observation of one's own intentions of meaning and expression would be—if it were possible of enactment—a colossally foolish renunciation. But it is far from completely possible; and the protagonist of such a view, whether he be actual or now more often a straw man, is an instance of self-deception or of public hypocrisy.

Common language, I suppose, is not devoid of wisdom; it makes many distinctions which can usefully be employed, and it doubtless manifests the results of some lengthy selective processes with respect to demarcations and with respect to supposed connections. However, I think it safe also to suppose that many usages of common natural language are rather rough; it will not be the mark of good philosophical prospecting to attempt to pump more wisdom out than has been deposited. Specifically, I do not believe that the ordinary usages of "emotion," "desire," etc. are very precise. Thus such a question as "How is desire really related to emotion"? will mean: "Taking the major denotations of 'desires' and 'emotions', how are these related, if indeed there is some characteristic way or ways?" From what is thus discovered one may provide or suggest criteria for stipulating more precise usages.

There are before us both material theories and questions of definition. There are material queries, such as the following. What kinds of phenomena occur in a roughly demarcated area? Which kinds seem to occur separately? Which kinds seem to occur only in complexes? What are the causes of these phenomena? What effects do these phenomena have? Then there are questions of definition—questions of fact for report of usage and questions of policy concerning stipulation. How has Broad used such terms as "emotion," "cognition," "feeling"? Throwing the policy decisions of stipulation into the present tense, one may ask: How shall we label separated sorts of things? How shall we label discriminated aspects of things? Shall we do some of our labelling on the basis of causes (in addition to present manifest intrinsic properties)? Possibly emotional moods and emotions often do get so labelled. Shall we do any labelling on the basis of effects (in addition to inspected or introspected intrinsic natures)? Possibly desires are a species of emotion, given a separate name primarily because of different effects. Presuming hereafter (to an admittedly somewhat reckless extent) upon the more or less definite discriminations in common sense, we may obviate asking every token or sentential question twice, once as a question of linguistic policy and once as a question of fact using someone's antecedent definitions. Indeed, much more than such repetition would be required were we to hold ourselves to formulating the locutions (descriptive, metaphorical, directive, etc.) which presumably would succeed in denoting or elliptically conveying to others the discriminations of feelings, cognitions, emotions, etc. which one acknowledges in one's own experience.

Avoiding such heavy chores, let us proceed, with the main focus of our attention on Broad's theory. At the outset, three terminological notes had better be offered. Broad does not identify "feeling" with hedonic tone—as occurs (misleadingly, I think) in more than a little current usage. Secondly, Broad, we reiterate, expressly employs "cognition" very comprehensively, so that it includes partly delusive and even wholly delusive cognitions and includes imaging, supposing, etc. Thus the phrase "veridical cognition" is not redundant; and mere entertaining of conceptual objects is classed as cognition. Thirdly, we offer on our own the observation that ordinary fluent experience seldom pays much attention to emotions unless these have appreciable or considerable intensity; moreover, if the theorist decides to analyze "emotion" he is likely to fix upon dramatic illustrations for his models, as the phenomena are there more vivid. A sliding of usage away from what may be a great lot of its proper referents, because these are feeble, gentle and hardly noticeable, is a consequence.

Impressionistically speaking, not only is Broad's demarcation of emotion an introspective one but the intimated theory of emotion is dominantly a cognitive one. An emotion is an ostensible cognition with an accompanying tone. Much of our author's discussion would fit an assumption that cognition is primary—prior temporally and causally. In some manner, in independence of emotional tone, an ostensible cognition is made, and then a qualitative response arises to it. Secondly, in most of the illustrations given by our author, the "object" of an emotion is typically the occupant of the conscious foreground; it is not a "situation" and not an object which importantly includes a complex of scarcely discriminated background factors. To each of these views, hypothetical or actual, it is possible to oppose a theory—most lamentably vague, I admit—which would construe cognition in some wider sense, like sensitively taking account of a situation, and which would hold that the relatively sharp cognitions emerge out of the primary matrix of vaguer feeling.

To the second charge, if it be one—and I do find myself inclined to intend it as one—the defender of Broad could at least observe that when an author makes illustrations he naturally chooses clear-cut ones for the purpose of making them at all, and that Broad does refer to very vague and indeterminate objects. To the first impressionistic observation, there is explicitly in the text a possible exception which is fatal to something. Broad indicates that possibly there are objectless moods and that the "feeling" of the mood is the same in quality as the "emotional tone" of some emotions.[13] He further pretty plainly accepts that pure moods, if they exist, sometimes generate, or latch on to, an object. When they have got an epistemological object, veridical or non-veridical, they are "emotions"—they meet the requirements of the definition. In such a case, obviously the interpreter cannot assert the primacy of the cognition—rather the reverse. However, on the question as to whether it is the case that there are objectless moods, Broad gives no definitive answer (and I must admit that I sympathize with his reticence). Either, says he, there are objectless moods or there are emotions with extremely indefinite objects (which bears upon the second point above). This possibly crucial illustration, then, is left in an indeterminate status.

The illustration, of course, may be viewed in quite different ways. It may be taken as clearly refuting the interpreter who ascribes to Broad the "primacy" of cognition in emotion. Secondly, it could be used,—if the interpreter could make out that Broad is elsewhere clearly holding the alleged primacy of cognition,—to claim that Broad is himself furnishing a refutation of himself. Thirdly, interpretations aside, it may be seen as *prima facie* indicating that, on a common definition of emotion, there are quite different species of emotion to be marked off by their respective modes of causal origination and by the dominance of one or other of their "components" in the process. The third is the most interesting (and potentially the most fertile) of the three, although—and partly because—the quest for monism in the area does lure me.

---

13 *JAAC,* 205.

Broad, has spoken, with the qualification of *"prima facie,"* of "two fundamentally different kinds of experiences." It appears that emotions are experiences which represent a union of these two, that emotions have a cognitive component (veridical or non-veridical) and a feeling component. This would suggest that there might be cognitions alone and feelings alone, and that sometimes the two have some kind of association, juncture or fusion, making them a third and compound sort of thing, an "emotion." Now surely we are using the results of analysis in too wooden a way if we intimate that there is an independent succession of cognitions and an independent succession of feelings and on occasion an association of members of the two. We are not denying that occasionally such an accidental or arbitrary connection is made; the case of a mood latching on to a proximate object may illustrate it. However, when we are concerned with such an illustration it is chiefly because we feel it is pathological. The kinds of emotions with which we should normally be concerned in aesthetics and morals would be emotions in which plainly the emotion is felt to be grounded in the nature of the object (and possibly in which the nature of the object is not adequately disclosed save in emotion). Talk of wholly independent ingredients of experience getting asscociated will not do. There is at least some intimate fusion, and apparently some kind of inner dependence, perhaps with a "primacy" of one or other factor. Chemical combination does not appear to be a very happy metaphor.

However, in making an exegesis of Broad one would hesitate to go to the opposite extreme and to interpret him as saying that all experience is a continuing organic whole and that what have here been called "components" are only aspects which are noted by distinctions of reason. It would be possible but it would not be most plausible to view him as holding that all experiences are emotions but that sometimes one aspect and sometimes another is predominant, with the result that the given occasion is labelled a "cognition" or a "feeling" or an "emotion" in accord with the felt emphases in the experience itself. He clearly entertains the possibility of feelings occurring alone, and he may entertain the idea of pure cognitions. It is also not beyond the bounds of possibility to conjecture that, instead of two components or aspects, there are three (or more). Too much space would be taken if we here followed a textual inquiry into Broad's intimated presumptions on these themes.

The problem, to be sure, is not just Broad's. If we do not follow the habitudes of the last generation in wholly eschewing introspection, we also are confronted by manifold questions. How are cognition and tone related? Are they in organic unity?—even in such organic unity as to permit no ascription of primacy or priority? Is there one or other order of precedence? Are both orders of precedence empirically found? How relatively distinct or independent does one or other source seem to be? What, if anything, do answers to the foregoing indicate about the phenomenal unity of the self?—about any trans-phenomenal unity of the self? These questions are too much to treat of here, and I do not have the answers reserved for elsewhere. At most I have a few inclinations of directions of exploration and belief. I intend here only to intimate certain tensions toward opposed accounts. After this little excursion we shall return to Broad's classification of emotions, in terms on the one side, of their ostensible cognitive components, and, on the other, of their tonalities.

2. *Primacy of Feeling Marked by Differentiation* vs. *Pluralism of Elements of Experience.*

On the one hand, I find myself disposed to see all conscious sensing, perceiving, emoting, desiring, waiting, hoping, etc., as generically having the same existential status, and as all being embedded in the stream of feeling. (When relatively definite in form and when reflexively noticed, this has been called the "stream of consciousness;" I do not especially object to this label, but I think it is encumbered with a heavy weight of associations and I believe its use has some tendency to obscure the vaguer forms of feeling.)

On the other hand, the discontinuities in what we may generically label "feeling" seem very marked. From either of two approaches this is the case. If one thinks of the career of the immediate content of consciousness, he notes in this longtitudinal view the frequent interruptions of relatively smooth courses in process by the insertion of new contents not called for by their predecessors and needing assimilation. If one attempts after the manner of structural psychology to observe, classify and relate these contents, they do not seem to exhibit continuity. If one entertains the idea of trying to set up all content of feeling upon one spectral cone he forthwith sees the immense difficulties. Are not impressions and ideas more distinct than Hume thought them to be? Are not each of the senses, as Helmholtz, asserted, radically separate from each other, and qualitatively quite discontinuous with the other senses, even though in some cases certain relations are set up between the interpreted data of different senses, visual, tactual, proprioceptive and auditory? Sounds cannot be translated into colors, and there seems to be no gradual transition mediating between them. How is one even to relate spatial perception to color expanse (for the first is introspected in Köhler's sense of introspection)? Taste itself seems to have four parameters; and so on.

However, one may counter, at least these distinctions have been got by differentiation of feeling. Nor are they *given* as distinctly as we have intimated or as they are now distinguished in the interpretations which are accepted in common sense. Outside information (although Whitehead and a few others would say that ultimately it is equally inside data) may have intruded on the qualitative data; for instance, knowledge of the different end-organs involved, knowledge of the historical appearance of these organs, knowledge of different transmitting organs and different excited nerves, glands, etc., have affected the interpretation of the data and may have become funded intimately with it.

Whether the matrix is conceived as a unity undergoing differentiation into more explicit structure or is conceived as quasi-independent organizations bringing some structures together or producing them, it does seem to be an empirical fact that mood, tonal quality, is somewhat regulative of what structures are brought above the threshold of consciousness. This seems to be the case in what is later deemed sound observation as well as in what is later adjudged to be projection.

When there is a tensional mood there will be discriminations made that would not otherwise be made. Further, when there is a tensional mood about certain matters, there will be not only discriminations made but inhibitions operating.

Mood *seems* very much to regulate the spotlight of attention; in this way it seems to regulate what epistemological structures emerge into consciousness. For instance, taken in its gross aspect the body is able to be receiving data from a number of senses for conscious attention; in fact, attention marks an amazing selectivity when one comes to consider the infinitudes of what might be attended to.

The word "seems" has been deliberately employed in order to recognize that mood may not be in the "executive" order; it may register bodily sets and organizations which are in that order. Those who have a notion of productive causation (like the author and, like, I think, Broad) will have seriously to consider epiphenomenalism; those who believe that they have no more than a correlation view of causation have no first-level obligation to consider it but only to note correlations. Here, we cannot take up the issue of epiphenomenalism, but will pass over it with only the observations that phenomenally consciousness seems to itself to be doing something, that it is biologically a nonfunctional sport if it is not, and that still if epiphenomenalism is true the phenomena are just as wonderfully complex as they happen to be and that what many of us will need to do, on giving up certain notions of mind, is to revise our inherited notions of the capacities of "matter," if that term may still be used.

On the other hand, at least a serious qualification is to be made to any sweeping assertion of the determination of cognitive data and cognitions by mood or general feeling. When there is enough of a disposition to be receptive to a stimulus in a certain channel—i.e., not to block it out from attention—the stimulus may give rise to a cognition which is quite alien to the placid mood in which it started to arise. A man having a picnic with his girl friend on a meadow may not be so amatory as to preclude auditory sensations from a cow's brother charging across the greensward. Thereupon, let us say, he tosses the fair damsel over the fence and clambers over forthwith. His original mood, pleasantly toned, incorporating taste of delectable food and anticipation of osculation with the fair maiden did not positively welcome the hoofbeats, snortings and lowered horns of said animal—but fortunately his mood did not prevent the perception of these phenomena. His subsequent feeling of fear is apprehended as grounded in his perception of the bellicose bull and the dangerous situation oriented about the animal. The fear is not grounded in this sense in the previous happy mood, although that constituted a background condition in the causal ancestry of the fear since it did not inhibit the auditory data. Now along with development of the fear tone, there is a career of unfolding perceptions; i.e., the fear-emotion develops, with both the cognitive aspect and the tonal aspect being marked by change. If the latter does not change in quality it surely changes in intensity; and probably, in the illustration, maximum intensity is not reached until several seconds after the picnic party is safely over the fence. This, I believe, is a truth in the James-Lange theory, and it lends support (if one restricts "emotion" to what we would call the very vivid emotions as we should prefer not to do) to their asserting that the emotion is the feelings of various bodily changes, activated in the extreme situation. Some functionalists would add the suggestion that this maximum of feeling of fear after the crisis of the incident (or maximum of feeling of rage when inadequately vented) is the process of the body discharging energies quickly marshalled for the emergency but unused in it; to get back to equilibrium in a less disturbed situation, some energies have to be consumed in the process of demobilization. When mobilization is constantly maintained, ulcers and sundry other neurotic disorders will ensue, for the bodily organization is not built for remaining continually on a war footing.

Is the pronounced dangerousness of the situation a discursively known relational property, and is it first discerned inferentially on the basis of several perceptions? Or is it more directly cognized, non-inferentially perceived? Or, assuming that sometimes the dangerousness is an intellectually cognized relational property, is this a derived status—has it come about as a highly differentiated form of something previously had qualitatively? The illustration given would perhaps suggest the first. However, other imagined situations will be presumptive of the last. E.g., take animal experience: when the stag sniffs the tainted gale, or the household dog watches the movers come and carry all the furniture out of the old dwelling. It is as reasonable as any alternative to suppose that the animal feels a quality of apprehensiveness or apprehensively feels what he feels, and does not set out his diagnosis in any verbal patterns.

It may be very rash, but I am inclined to believe not only that an interpreted feeling—interpreted as indicating a relational complex—can be so quickly recognized that it seems non-inferential but that in the alchemy of the creative processes of sensation and feeling a discerned relation can "become" a quality, that is, a felt quality may arise in its place as economical surrogate for it—and possibly may arise even as an enriching piece of aesthesis.

Put another way, one might suggest that there is a difference between dangerousness and apprehensiveness; the former involves a clearer idea of the dangers; the latter can be very indefinite. Now I further suggest that a *quality* of dangerousness can arise from what has been cognition of actual dangers, whereas I suspect that apprehensiveness is something in which mood or tone has preceded. If dangerousness comes out of it, it is because differentiation has proceeded to greater definiteness.

Pontificating for a moment, one reason life isn't richer for more persons than it is—despite all their success and gadgets—is that they cannot drop into enjoyment but remain in the practical mood of manipulation with anxiously toned relational ideas in the foreground because of the utility of these. The relational properties can be funded into the richness of a complex whole; a cultivation of the arts of appreciation would tend to effectuate this consequence more widely, but the operation is considerably inhibited in our culture.

Thus I am selecting for emphasis *two introspective patterns,* or at least two patterns for which introspection readily affords some plausible evidence. Different phenomena suggest different patterns of conceiving. Some phenomena suggest a unity not made out of ingredients and not separable into parts, an organic whole embodying tonal aspects and (referential and representative) cognitive aspects. Such a whole must be acknowledged to be developing, growing, protean, ever undergoing the becomings of novelty, as Bergson and James less inadequately than others have conveyed. Notable are experiences in which one feels that he is trying to articulate what he already has in inchoate form, in which one is attempting to make explicit what he possessed in implicit form. And one knows enough what he has implicitly that he can more or less tell whether a candidate rendering will do; at least he frequently perceives candidate articulations which are inadequate. This is a phenomenon on which we should like to fasten. The pattern suggested may be labelled that of *"differentiation" of feeling.* There is no necessity to contend here, we must hasten to concede, that the whole life of thought is just a development of itself, with nothing needed outside or from the outside. This flat phenomenal scheme seems to us most unreasonable; there seem to be somatic conditions of consciousness, and sensations do break in upon developing trains of thought. And, in inquiry, one positively seeks such breaking in of new data. But, at the least, some thinking, some clarification of epistemological objects, some coming to an explicit realization of what one feels or has, is characteristic of some experiences. They suggest one pattern.

Not entirely incompatible with the foregoing but significantly different and more hospitable to the concessions is some scheme which allows for less unity, more semi-independence of the aspects. If these aspects can vary independently, they seem more like *factors or even separate ingredients.* The factors do not vary proportionately. Nor inversely; there is no law that an increase in one means a decrease in the other, parallel to Whitehead's suggestion that a refinement of attention to presentational immediacy involves a loss of sense of causal efficacy. Again, it might be argued that there is sometimes a temporal gap between the appearance of one factor and its correlated other supposed aspect. Definitely there are distinctive phenomenal differences—feelings of one of the so-called aspects being "founded on" the other. An emotion, as Broad holds, seems to be toward its "object" and seems to have the qualities which it does have largely in respect to the supposed properties of that "object."

Thus we have one pattern which suggests the primacy of a unity, with phenomena of moving differentiation therein. And we have, secondly, the intimations of organizations which, though linked, are possessed of semi-independence. Cases of dependence of feeling-tone upon ostensible cognition have just received allusion. Cases of the reverse order, of the apparent priority of mood, have previously been noted. And general reference, of course, can here be made to psycho-physical organizations which under proper stimulations produce perceptual or conceptual knowledge and organizations which produce mood and tone. The apparent relative independence can rather easily, although still only superficially, be given an explanation in somatic terms. It is appropriate to add, however, that the contemporary history of medicine, physiology and psychology is one of increasing recognition of interdependence (after earlier assumptions of greater separateness) and of the influence of the whole on the parts.

If the former view is carried far, one tends to look at all perceptions as abstractions from concrete emotions. Even primary qualities are an abstraction from relational structure found in the concrete. One will not say that emotions are simply the stirring of the viscera, while vision and touch give the external world, quite disctinct from all emotion although occasionally stimulating it; if a transcendent world is known it is through discriminations emerging in content, which generically is feeling or emotion. However, one would have to acknowledge that many times when the primary properties are abstracted they seem to be the most prominent part of the emotion; the emotion may be relatively mild otherwise. Of course, it may *ad hoc* be plausibly suggested that in part men learn to attend to certain features and this diminishes the vividness and felt intensity of others. Further, from an evolutionary point of view, one will remark upon the selection and development of certain senses for relatively focal rôles in the life of the organism (smell is more important to a dog than to a man) as well as upon the selective processes carried out by such senses in daily commerce with the environment. (Super-imposed upon these selectivities are—in the case of man— the short-cuts and the biases, advantageous and disadvantageous, which are culturally induced.) Thus, although the sketch of a view is at first primarily concerned to describe what is now the case phenomenally in man's experience, one is easily led to introduce some major theses of a causal sort and with an interesting and sweeping phylogenetic bearing.

It is not exceedingly rash to interpret Broad as holding a view of experience in which there are two continuing complexes. There is the sensory continuum, containing all the objective constituents; longitudinally it is made up of "sense-histories" of data from each organ. When one of the histories is, so to speak, cut transversely, the resulting section is a "sense field." Differentiated areas or parts of sense fields are "sensa." Secondly, there is the subjective continuum of feelings, largely a function of past experience and of anticipated experience in ostensibly present cognition. Perhaps this continuum includes vague bodily feelings, but it does not include pains and other localized somatic data for these sensations.

One may still argue over some questions. Are these two originally two, and is their apparent interpenetration or fusion an actual subsequent interpenetration? Are the two an arbitrary division of what is originally one? Are the two a non-arbitrary learned distinction, based on utility, of what originally was one? Is the listing with equal status a distortion of Broad's intent; should what we may call the "noun plus adjective" status of the former be accorded a substantial or other primacy over the "adverbial" status of the latter?

The classification may reflect, not two antecedently separate sources getting accredited as such but a non-arbitrary sorting, immemorial in the psychical development of each sane individual, effected on some functional basis. Then, may not the former, which seems to us now to be primary and is dignified as affording data from the external and internal environments, be seen as having originally the same status as all the rest in the continuum of feeling, although justified learning has produced the abstraction and the quasi-autonomy?

Desires are classified by Broad as emotions. The critic cannot both hold that this classification is mistaken and that those emotions which are desires (or some of them) refute a view of the priority of cognition. However, *if* one goes with Broad in accepting this classification, then one may rightly argue that in the cases of some desires (therefore, of some emotions, at least) there is a "priority of tension" over cognition. Surely in the cases of emergence of desires for water, food, elimination, etc., a tension has preceded the learning of the object; and fairly often even in our well-learned habitual desires still the consciousness of tension momentarily precedes the awareness of the epistemological, being, indeed, the stimulus for the latter. (On other occasions, e.g., vision or mention of food, the object is the stimulus.) To be sure, this argument has a gap in that it does not prove that the consciousness of tension is the tonality in the desire which emerges; but I should think that this is a reasonable assumption in the form that it is continuous therewith and is the "same" except as it undergoes modification with increased definiteness of the object (or, of course, with intensification of organic stimuli).

Interestingly, some of the clearest cases in which cognition apparently precedes feeling, in desires, are instances of what we might call "second-hand" and habitual desires. Presumably the dispositional trait toward desiring lies latent but is excited into manifestation by the confrontation with a perceptual or conceptual object. The apparent cases are not confined to learned desires. The infant on being confronted visually with the yellow ball may desire possession, and proceed to kinesthetic, tactual, and gustatory appropriation and exploration. (Likewise with direct aversions.)

Broad in his later phases may be repudiating the primacy of the ostensibly cognitive, largely at the price of denying cognitive status to some matters which formerly he had accorded such a status. He is certainly entertaining—and may be holding—the view that in a fresh "morally" problematic situation one gets a toti-resultant emotion to the situation and upon its favorable or unfavorable character pronounces "right" or "wrong" upon some projected course. Component ostensibly factual cognitions have preceded the decisive emotion, but the decisive emotion is not founded on any moral cognition but rather is misleadingly expressed as if it possessed such.[14] Possibly, Broad is also in agreement with Hägerström in taking the conative impulse to be primary in experiences of intending a course of action, in feeling first-personal duties and in ascribing obligations to others. The differences in strengths of such an impulse may make the difference between weak consideration of a line of action and intense moral conviction about it. Such experiences are still epistemologically objective, but the apparent judgment which may emerge from them is a case of *quasi*-judging.

Even the earlier Broad cannot affirm the priority or the primacy of cognition in all emotions, since it cannot be affirmed about moods which have become emotions by producing or latching on to an object. But he might affirm a primacy of cognition in *normal* emotions in one or other of two ways. He might assert the temporal priority (although pretty highly telescoped in practice) of cognition as stimulus with tonality following as response. He might maintain the priority of the content of the cognition, as having a noun status, over the tonality, as having an adverbial status. Even if he affirms such priorities may one not still rashly want to counter the first or suggest a modification of the second by asking: "Aren't perhaps some of the properties of the object registered in, if not indeed discerned by, the tonal aspects of the emotion rather than entirely being found first by neutral processes of cognition which have subsequently stimulated the tonal reaction? Might not the emotive intuitionist be right that value is 'known' by feeling, and 'known' with appropriate nuances which are not caught by the single axis of pro-ness and anti-ness?"

I shall not intrude upon the genetic questions. It is plausible that such unity as consciousness possesses as an existing function (as well as in its momentary content) is due to its organic base, and that both maturative processes and learning processes normally produce such unity—and occasionally do not produce it, in cases of multiple personality. I do not know whether the natural history of consciousness starts with presences of pain sequences and pleasure sequences, and then somehow achieves—possibly with the help of the variations brought by motor behavior—differentiation of objects. I do not know whether consciousness starts with a fitful flash here and a momentary trickle there,

14 *S&H*, 387f.

or not. Anyway, in our experience it never gets over its sporadic character; all of us sleep and some of us have been under general anaesthesia. However, we will remark upon some characteristics of processes of conscious awareness when one is having experiences, and therein we will use some preferred terminology and classification.

The total "field of consciousness" is in one sense a unity and one object, but in another more important sense it is not a unity and it may have several objects at a time. Often there is a "dominant experience" going on, but it is accompanied by both its own periphery and by miscellaneous other items. Often two or more preëminent experiences are running concurrently, each with its own periphery, each competing or almost competing with the other, and each co-present with other items to be deemed miscellaneous with respect to them.

When a new possible "experience" is first emerging, I think it not infrequently exhibits the pattern of "differentiation." Indeed, if it is genuinely novel, I suppose that it always does so.

However, when the experience is "of" a familiar thing and proceeds with a learned pattern, the perceptual recognition of the exciting cause, functioning as a sign, is prior to the main development of the experience; but, even then, presumably the perception arises out of dimmer and less differentiated feeling. These familiar experiences may be labelled "second hand" in a somewhat different sense than Broad will employ the term. The organism goes from recognition of the situation to its habitual network of responses, albeit with some internal economies and with previous cognitions and adjustments being funded therein.

In conceptual emotions, as Broad will use the term,—at least in the more contemplative ones—the cogitation apparently precedes the main development of the emotion, even if the conception is explored further during the process. One may have some doubts whether this holds true of processes of aesthetic creation.

I do attach considerable importance to these observations about patterns of subjective unfoldment, not as mere psychological points about temporal order but because I think explicit intentionality arises within certain feelings, and arises in such a way as to be felt to have been implicit there. The order is not uniformly (1) explicit cognition and (2) emotional tone. It is sometimes the reverse, except that I am not treating the latter as a mere tone; it is my point that it is sometimes implicitly intentional and thus also implicitly ostensibly cognitive. This reversed order is not always pathological, as it is in those cases where a dominant mood latches on to some object which happens to move into ken. I thus presume that there are feelings which are not just to be viewed as occurrences, as effects and causes, but which may be described as implicitly (and sometimes explicitly) "feelings that . . ." It is to be added that far from assuming them to be rare I suppose them to be common and even to pervade the background of most of our conscious and semi-conscious existence.

Perhaps an undue amount of space has been given to the simple illustrative description of two familiar processes; however, the intent is to signalize two ways in which dominantly immediate or qualitative experiences contain cognitive factors. Since in one case there is probably widespread acceptance of the phenomenon, I have not stressed the lapsing of perceptions which once were highly conscious into unattended habit, owing to much repetition of the schema; and it is not difficult to suppose that the feeling aspects might sometimes diminish less in vividness than the recognition of the initial signs. On the other hand, I have emphasized—since there is little acceptance of the idea—that there may be implicit cognition in what are dominantly feelings but the content of which has not been definitely noticed in consciousness. "Implicit cognitions," I hold, obtain in experiences which are dominantly feelings; and these may belong to either of two kinds, (a) a pre-discursive implicit content, or (b) a post-discursive implicit content. Obviously these observations do not pertain to "tone" when it is defined as pure tone, devoid of any intentionality whatever, incipient or overt.

3. Classification of Emotions by their Cognitive Components.

If, as is premised, concrete emotions contain both a cogitation or ostensibly cognitive aspect and an affective aspect, one has two fundamental grounds for classifying emotions: on some basis relating to the modes of ostensible cognition in them or the kinds of cognitions; and on some basis relating to their affective aspect.

Broad holds there are three kinds of cognition: intuitive; perceptual; and conceptual. (i) "Intuitive cognition is direct prehension of particular existents. . . . So far as we know, a human being is capable of prehending particulars of three and only three kinds, viz., sensibilia . . . , his own mental images, and his own experiences." (ii) Perceptual cognition involves not only prehension of particulars but also "non-inferential beliefs or quasi-beliefs," which "go beyond the information" supplied by the prehension of particulars. Again Broad enumerates three important sub-species: sense-perception, reminiscence, and self-perception.

The intuitive bases of these are respectively the sensing of sensibilia, the imaging of mental images, and reflexive acquaintance with one's own experiences. In each case the presence of intuitive cognition, and the absence of explicit inference or even of a noticeable process of associative transition, is likely to make it seem that the cognition is *wholly* intuitive.[15]

(iii) Conceptual cognition includes "all those processes which operate with general ideas or abstract concepts," and thus take in the ranges of thinking not previously noted. One can conceive, entertain, imagine, believe, and the contents may not be directly present or even existent. ("Cognition," it may again be editorially noted, is used by Broad in an unconventionally wide sense.)

With these distinctions, Broad proceeds to classify emotions "by their character as cognitions." He doubts whether *purely intuitive cognitions* "have any marked emotional tone"—such cognitions anyway being "very rare in grown persons"—but manages an illustration with the "primitive fear" which Watson said is manifested by infants on hearing a loud clap.[16] A wide range of emotional tones may accompany *perceptions*. Presumably all of these—and perhaps additional ones—can also qualify *conceptual cognitions,* on the assumption that experienced sorts of stimuli can be thought of and perhaps others besides.

With respect to this classification of emotion on the basis of their cognitions, a few comments are in order.

First, let us consider intuitive cognition. There is a terminological question whether the prehending of sense data, or of images, or even of particulars of one's own experiencing, should be called "cognitive." Should the first species of Broad's first class of emotions be wiped out, with one definitional fiat, or perhaps with one large counter-assertion concerning the texture of the facts? Or, is some more modest criticism apparently in order? Or, verbal matters aside, has our author already embraced the substance of any material criticism?

There are those who would deny that animals or infants have any "objects," apparently on the grounds that all objects lie in cognition and there is no knowledge without linguistic formulation and without, in principle, public confirmability. This seems to us lamentable on several counts, although of course to the basic stipulation of such a strict meaning for knowledge we could only offer counter-definitions and strong appeals to usage and convenience. To some data apparently there is only private access, and I do not see any good reason why these should not confirm formulated statements concerning them or to which they are relevant. Ordinarily we do treat as knowledge a lot of unformulated noticings and recognitions and knowledges of how to do. Although language very greatly facilitates the making of discriminations, it is reasonable to suppose that some discriminations are prior

15 *JAAC,* 204.   16 *Ibid.,* 205.

to linguistic tagging, and it is perfectly sensible to call such discriminated things or features in conscious experience by the label "objects." Even if one accepted the narrow definition of knowledge, one might well acknowledge that there are objects of many or all emotions although one would refuse to call them "cognitions." Behaviorally we do interpret animal activity and inferred animal emotion as directed at certain objects. We are quite with Broad in eschewing those tendencies which move toward permitting only extrospective knowledge; it is right of him to affirm inspective and introspective knowledge, and not to be persuaded by definitions which presumably would slant inquiry and suggest theoretical approaches along with preëmpting a favorable piece of vocabulary. And materially it is plausible that small children, who plainly do not yet speak language and probably have registered little of auditory language, do have perceptual emotions and probably have intuitive emotions; but we are troubled as to discriminating between a reaction and an intuitive emotion of a direct sort. (Whether there is any other kind—whether there are mediated intuitive emotions —will be touched on in a moment.)

There is a more reasonable terminological issue here; and there is a consequence of how wide will be the denotation of "emotion" and of what will be investigated as emotion. Elsewhere we wonder if Broad— contrary to many writers but with our applause—has a very wide notion of emotions, not restricted to the vivid and dramatic cases. Here it would seem his view is exceedingly wide; perhaps all having of sensibilia, all having of images, all prehended experiencing, is also a having of emotions, for these "cognitive" experiences are toned.

However, it seems to us that one is near the boundary line (and probably over it) of what ought sensibly to be called a cognition when one has, for instance, the "startle" phenomenon. Should all instinctive reactions in which there is any consciousness of the reaction be called an "emotion"? There are writers who would insist that all emotions are instinctive (as against those who would affirm that human emotional responses are very largely learned—not only in virtue of man's extending of the scope of objects but also in virtue of the conditioning of the qualitative responses themselves). I do not know whether any of these psychologists would make a simple conversion of the proposition that all emotional responses are instinctive responses. In any case Broad would not, for not all instinctive responses are conscious or epistemologically objective. Pretty plainly some reflexes and tropisms are beyond the pale; but perhaps Broad has already been too latitudinarian in treating immediate havings of sense data and images as cognitive.

It is appropriate to distinguish between immediate experience and attending to immediate experience with the result that there are "objects" found in immediate experience. Definitions may be made such that the latter, as having objects, is cognitive, while the former, as not having carved any objects in immediacy, is not. Following this scheme would greatly reduce the scope of the class of intuitive cognitions and therewith of emotions even if every case of a cognition is also a case of an emotion. For in normal experience we do not have our sensibilia as objects.

Broad himself has cautioned against taking the results of an analysis of factors inferentially presumed to be requisite to experience for an analysis of what is in experience as consciously undergone. And his account of emotion is one in terms of experience as consciously undergone. Sense-data, let it be observed, may be inferred as requisite in ordinary practical activity and perceptual experience, but normally one is conscious of the perceptual objects and not of data presumed to be operative in the process. Repeatedly Broad shows an awareness of this issue; this is no guarantee that he, like the rest of us, may not have occasional lapses.

He is circumspect when he observes that "*purely* intuitive cognitions are very rare in grown persons. Intuitive cognitions occur mainly as constituents of perceptual or conceptual cognitions."[17] This statement, plainly enough, cuts down on any antecedently supposed extraordinary width of emotions which are *purely* intuitive on their cognitive side. It is to be noted that it does not necessarily cut them severely down as entering impurely into emotions which are partly perceptual or partly conceptual. This raises another question.

There is an issue of whether emotional tones are evoked, or tend to be evoked, by *unnoticed* things and qualities, and whether the embodiment of such emotional tones should be said to be emotions—for what are their objects? Empirical evidence does point, for example, to the conclusion that there is both an affect on the nervous system from physical sounds beyond the range of auditory reception and an affect on ensuing emotional tonalities; there are similar effects from largely unnoticed traffic noises; and businessmen are advised by the manufacturers of certain vibration-deadening construction materials to protect their secretaries and themselves from these unheard sounds and these scarcely noticed sounds. If there is a tendency, let us say, of a shrill voice to produce emotional shading of a certain sort independently of what is being said by the voice, and independently of its being noticed as shrill, should the concrete experience resulting both from what is said and the tone of the saying it be regarded as a mixed emotion—"mixed" not only in quality but in being partly an intuitive emotion and partly a perceptual

17 *Ibid.*, 205.

one? Or should the effect of the shrillness be considered only when it is noticed, as when one might say, "The old lady is really a pleasant person; it's a pity she has an irritating voice."

I would suggest that Broad should not count as emotions, on his own terms, cases in which the qualitative response is conscious but the "object" or stimulus or differential cause is unconscious, for he has declared emotions by definition to be epistemologically objective (although, of course, not necessarily veridical in their discriminated objects). Broad is violating this principle if, as I suspect, he allows intuitive cognitions to occur in a wholesale but impure way in perceptual and conceptual emotions, as is suggested by his statement, "Intuitive cognitions occur mainly as constituents of perceptual or conceptual cognitions." However, I will not only draw attention to the conditional clause but I will moderate the whole judgment by observing that in my own view consciousness is a matter of degree (in probably more than one dimension), spoken of more or less aptly in terms of focus and fringe, level of explicitness (as against implicitness), extent of differentiation (as against undifferentiation), articulateness (as against inchoateness of feeling), degree of attention, degree of vividness or intensity, etc.

Armed with the distinction between having immediate experience and making differentiated features within it into objects, we should be hesitant to attribute the latter activity to infants; but we should suppose that young infants have not yet made a differentiation between subjective experience and an external world and that in this sense their sensibilia are objects although they have not been made into objects by any effort of turning attention away from perceptual interpretation and toward immediate quality. We are inclined to believe that adults do, with discipline, have some pretty pure intuitive experiences. If there are very few introspectionists trained by Tichnerians today, still there are analytic philosophers trying to descry just what is given—such as can serve to ground basic sentences. Artists of various sorts frequently contemplate aspects of their respective media in a mode of attending to pure sensibilia, and appreciators of works of art sometimes contemplate both selected aspects (qualities and relations) and whole *Gestalten* in this manner; especially do devotees of abstract art do this. I think that sensibilia may be made objects of inspection when the main intent is other than this act of inspection or the qualities thereby had, for instance when a musician is comparing the quality of tone produced by two or more instruments or a scientist is attending to the quality of a datum because of its evidential rôle. (John Dewey speaks sometimes as if this is the only time a scientist has a sense datum, namely, when it is instituted for its evidential rôle.)

Thus I would not withdraw from Broad's usage, and I would materially suppose there to be intuitive cognitions and therewith emotions the cognitive aspect of which is intuitive. On the whole, as Broad observes, emotions belonging to this class are relatively mild, but the generalization could easily be exaggerated. The aesthete may not take kindly to being told that his emotions are anything other than intense. If we count in the class a babe's emotion when crying at several cooking pans having nosily cascaded on the floor nearby, his response is hardly mild. Of course, trained introspectors (or inspectors, as Broad would say) are normally possessed of quite mild emotions when discriminating sense data or images; and naturally nearly all emotions are relatively mild when compared with terror or intense anger.

We have cautioned against supposing that because sense data or sensory events at least are inferred to be involved in perception that therefore there are emotions of which these are in whole or in part the cognitive components. But if it is true that there is quite a bit of peripheral noticing of sensory qualities along with ordinary perception, or even some running attention thereto (as when an auditor at a concert is mainly "perceiving" the movement of the concerto but is also attending to the tonal qualities), then there are a lot of emotions the cognitive aspects of which are partly intuitive. Similar remarks could, one supposes, be made with respect to the intuition of images in dominantly conceptual emotions.

I do not know whether Broad would hold that all pure intuitive emotions are direct, or whether he would allow that even intuitive emotions may be "motived." One presumes that a young infant's emotions are direct and that those of animals are direct; but I can well conceive an appreciator of an abstract painting, or of a tone made on a musical instrument, speaking of a quality of the quality to which he is attending and citing this quality of the quality as more particularly evoking or mediating his emotion. In a simple case let us say that he feels gaiety on contemplating a yellow and states that the brightness and warmth of the yellow mediate his gaiety.

We turn now to the problem of the boundaries between perceptual and conceptual emotions. I have a little difficulty on being clear about the differentia or differentiae of conceptual emotions. Primarily, however, I guess I should not assert a difficulty with understanding the differentiae but with applying them in such a way as to sort out emotions cleanly with respect to them. One possible line of distinction which might be offered is that between particulars and universals; universals would have to be conceptually cognized, and emotions in which these cognitions afforded the epistemological object would be conceptual emotions. I do not believe, however, that this is Broad's distinction, and therefore we are freed from any need to discriminate different meanings of, or species of, universals. His criterion might be negatively put by saying a conceptual emotion is one which contains a cognition which is not an act of "perceiving or remembering but is only expecting or believing to exist or feigning to exist;" and conceptual cognition is positively said to "include all those processes which operate with general ideas or abstract concepts." The objective idealists, perhaps better than anyone else, maintained that the work of conception informs the activity of perception. This need not confuse matters for making distinctions of reason, but it does leave an enterprise of sorting in an indeterminate state. Broad rightly draws the same consequence, whether his basis is exactly the same or not.

A great deal of cognition, which seems *prima facie* to be purely perceptual, turns out on closer inspection to be partly conceptual. It seems likely that all one's cognitions of other persons' minds and of their experiences consists of conceptual cognition based on one's perception of their bodies, their gestures, their speech, and so on.[18]

We are already acquainted with saying there are some emotions which are partly intuitive and partly perceptual. From the citation one gathers that a given cognition can be partly perceptual and partly conceptual, and the ambiguity over the application of the criterion is whether a cognition will make the emotion in which it is embodied a "perceptual emotion" by being partly perceptual and whether it will make the same emotion a "conceptual emotion" by being partly conceptual, or whether there is some further stipulation to avoid the overlapping nomenclature. One way in which the ambiguity can be removed is simply by adding such qualifiers as "purely," "partly," "mainly," etc.

The material consequence of these considerations is that there is a blurring or mixing both of intuitive emotions with perceptual emotions and of perceptual emotions with conceptual emotions. Indeed, an emotion which would be dominantly perceptual would also be conceptual as having conceptual interpretive elements and would also (on occasion) be intuitive as having intuitive elements tending to excite particular emotional tones. Likewise a dominantly conceptual emotion which nevertheless had perceptual elements would be perceptive and perhaps also intuitive. A considerable group of ordinary emotions would have all three elements. However, at the extremes there would be pure cases: there would be emotions the epistemological object of which is entirely conceptual, including objects believed to exist; and there would be—

18 *Ibid.,* 204.

largely confined to infants, on Broad's view—emotions purely intuitive on their cognitive side.

4. On the Classification of Emotions by their Emotional Tones.

Notice has been taken of one way in which Broad has classified emotions, namely, by the kinds of cognitions which are contained in them. Along this course naturally an indefinite number of more specific classifications could be made on the various bases of division of the epistemological objects of emotion. This will not be pursued here.

Similar attention could be directed to the fact that emotions can be classified—in accord with whatever principles of division might there seem pertinent—on the basis of emotional color or tone. No doubt if men attended carefully to the task, they could make a large number of discriminations between actual emotions, even on the basis of tonality; in fact, some men do do this, but their mode of reference to discriminated tones is not by attaching abstract nouns. Fears, angers, desires (viewed as emotions) and many other actual emotions are probably given these rough headings on the basis of tonality; but finer shadings within these are usually indicated in other ways than by naming. Contrary attitudes are taken by different persons toward what would neutrally be called the "same object;" the labels for their attitudes would normally be on the basis of the differences in tone and disposition. What is hoped by one man is an object of apprehension to another and hence is not referred to by what is common but by what is different, namely, the attitude or non-cognitive aspect of the emotion. However, it is not to be denied that further distinction of an attitude or its occurrent or predisposed tone is frequently given by more delineation of the object and its relation to the patient. I should want to say that an emotion is toward a whole situation, but this is not to fail to recognize that some features of the situation are much more in the focus than others, more relevant and differential than others. We often communicate by assuming the hearer will recognize the tonality from a description of the object to which reaction is being made. (Of course the correlation which this elision banks upon cannot be used directly in communicating concerning "inappropriate" or "abnormal" tone of response; it may still be employed indirectly, as when one might say, "He heard the judge pronounce sentence as if listening to a joke on TV.")

In any extended effort at public naming of shadings of emotional tone, one is confronted by the difficulties which grow out of privacy of occurrence of the referents, the evanescence of the finer nuances, and the fact that normally the feeling tone is not in the center of attention but usually leaves that focal position to the epistemological object. The critic may object that in non-artistic gross practical life, we do not have many difficulties over color, and that the experiencing of color (as of other sense data) is as private in occurrence as emotional tone. In one important but presently irrelevant sense, many (including Broad, I think) would hold that color data are "objective" in a sense in which emotional tones are not; but, accepting the statement of the critic, I should still like to observe that the other differences hold as important matters of degree. Usually, if one wishes, one can go on gazing at the illuminated physical source of a color datum, and, if one is interested in doing so, no great effort or technique is required in inspecting the properties of the datum. In emotional tone, on the other hand, the datum shifts under scrutiny; there is a sort of long recognized Heisenberg principle of indeterminacy concerning the changing of the datum under observation; this alteration of datum has been banked upon by Buddhists, Stoics and Spinoza as an instrument of moral control. In addition, I might add, we do have difficulties in communicating about color, and there we happily can often have recourse to samples; if we were as concerned about certain shadings of color as we are sometimes concerned about certain shadings of tone in personal relations (as indicative of attitudes), and if we could not resort to sending a color patch, we should likely have kindred difficulties in communication. Elliptical modes of denotation are resorted to; ultimately connotation is not available, although from context and metaphorical use something resembling it is employed. Broad's analogy of color is one such metaphorical context.

Broad's own references to emotion are made through ostensive references to fear, anger, pity, etc., rather than by basic connotative definition. I think he might well say that ultimately "definition" could not be analytic anyway; some of the adverbial qualities are presumably simple, probably *qua* qualities all of them are, and the so-called mixed and blended ones likewise could not be ultimately defined without some sort of indexical act, an act which in this case cannot be effected by the forefinger but which rather has to be elliptically induced by symbolic means which are ever unable to say what they ultimately mean. Similarly, Broad refers to emotional moods ostensibly—crossness, apprehensiveness, etc.

As an item of theory, it is worth noting that in *Mind and Its Place in Nature* Broad did consider the question "whether it is necessary to assume a plurality of different determinable relations of reference to an object as well as a plurality of different determinable mental qualities."[19] He observed that the "pure ego theory" could not avoid the plurality of relations of reference; other theories theoretically could, and the simpli-

[19] *MPN*, 572f.

fication was attractive, but I think he rejected the suggestion for them also—he certainly did in the form proffered in Russell's *Analysis of Mind*.[20] It is plain enough that he has dismissed this ingenious idea along with pan-objectivism.

Broad would have us note several facts about the naming of emotions and sentiments. (*a*) A lot of ways of feeling and suffering are not named; for instance, in any case of sensing, I suppose, it makes sense to ask *how* as well as *what*, but we have almost no vocabulary for the former since our attention is normally on the latter. (*b*) Of the large number of names given to emotions and sentiments, some are given with respect to their emotional quality and some with respect to their objects and some (we should interpolate) with respect to both. " 'Envy,' e.g., is the name of a certain kind of emotion called forth by witnessing another person getting what one wants for oneself. 'Jealousy' seems to be the name of an emotion of much the same quality, where what one wants for oneself and what the other person gets is the affection of some third person."[21] If there is some shade of difference in the emotional quality, Broad continues, it is nevertheless clear that the different names are given with respect to the different objects. Thus the "same" emotional quality may have different names in different concrete emotions. Verbs asserting emotions, like nouns naming them, may vary primarily with some other relation to the object rather than total response. There is at least considerable generic commonness between desiring, hoping and "being glad that . . . ;" but differences in tense, and more particularly relationship to whether or not an outcome is known, is determinative of different proper usages. Apparently the same generic range of tones may be referred to with different words, and lots of different tones within a range will be devoid of any differential label. Broad has suggested that the controversy between psychoanalysts and their opponents as to whether sexual emotion exists in very young children may be over a verbal issue. (*c*) A name may not only be used to cover a great range of emotions but in cases of "mixed" emotions and sentiments may be used ambiguously. Suppose the sentiment or blended emotion to have one peculiar characteristic constituent and several other ingredients "collectively as essential." The label is likely sometimes to be used to name the peculiar ingredient and sometimes to name the concrete whole (and sometimes, one might add, to name different collections of factors temporarily regarded as the essential ones). This rendering is complicated by still another possibility which Broad points out: "It may be that what distinguishes" some particular emotional quality "from all

20 *Ibid.*, 580ff.   21 *JAAC*, 213.

others is some pattern-quality due to the particular proportion in which emotional factors, each of which occurs elsewhere, are here blended," and that "there may be no single factor in this blended emotion which does not also occur in some other blended emotion."[22]

Of general theoretical importance is some hint of Broad's genetic account of a lot of qualities of emotion. It may be got in an analogy which he sets up with visual qualities, and which is substantiated by several noteworthy empirical observations.

5. *The Analogy of Color.*

A consideration of analogies between visual color data and emotional tones is of intrinsic interest. In lieu of any actual classification of emotional qualities, it may indirectly refer to some of the principles thereof. In addition, it is in connection with his use of the analogy that Broad makes a few brief remarks indicative of his ideas of a genetic account of emotional qualities. A few adumbrations of his theory of primary and mixed emotional tones, moreover, will afford opportunity to touch upon our author's definition of sentiments.

Certain further theoretical respects in which we feel the analogy to be noteworthy, positively and negatively, will be mentioned in ending the section. It may be remarked in advance that the development of the analogy comes off better than I would have initially anticipated. The reader of Broad feels that his author must have carried out an extended comparison of emotional qualities and color qualities.

It feels to me as if feeling has a texture which is not adequately conveyed by metaphors of monotonous tone or of uniform color and yet which is not constituted by the epistemic intentionality of the experience. But I may be mistaken in this. What I am fussily noticing may receive an adequate account in some metaphoric explanation by Broad: reference is especially made to the shading, blending, mixing, and linking of emotions, to the Gestalt-effect found in phases of experience, and to the formation of sentiments.

Broad tersely records similarities between visual and emotional qualities on the basis of the fact of variegation and of the phenomenon of blending, and he asserts that emotional tones have analogies with shades, primary colors, complementary colors and pattern qualities.

First, there is the fact of *variegation.* "At any moment one's total visual field consists of adjoined visual sensa, some of one color and some of another. In this sense we can say that it can be 'more or less variegated' in respect of color. Similarly at any moment one's total experience will

[22] *Ibid.,* 214.

consist of many distinguishable cognitions and feelings." Moreover, as a variegated "visual sense-field" may be predominantly of one color, so may one's total state of mind be "emotionally variegated and yet predominantly of one emotional tone."[23]

Next, we had better get before ourselves an extended citation from Broad; it is foundational to the analogies with primary colors, shades, complementary qualities, and blended colors. It also expresses some views on questions of genesis, and contains a number of empirical observations.

> I think we may fairly assume that there is a certain fairly small number of primary species of emotional tone, just as there is a limited number of primary colors, and that the vast majority of human beings are born with dispositions corresponding to each of them. Let us call these 'primary emotional dispositions.' I should suppose that the emotional tones of fear and of anger, e.g., are certainly primary, and that the corresponding emotional dispositions are innate in the individual and common to the race. Probably some innate emotional dispositions do not come into action until certain stages of development, e.g., puberty, have been reached.
>
> Now these primary emotional dispositions are either very specialised or very generalised in respect of the stimuli which originally excite them. The disposition to feel fear, e.g., seems to be excited at first only by sudden loud noises and by the experience of falling. So the original stimulus is here very specialised. The disposition to feel anger, on the other hand, is aroused from the first by the thwarting of *any* impulse. So here the original stimulus is highly generalised. In course of experience these primary emotional dispositions become generalised or specialised, as the case may be. . . .
>
> I do not think that a given kind of emotional tone remains completely unaltered in quality as the objects of the emotion become extended and more subtle. No doubt there *is* a qualitative likeness, e.g., between fearing a sudden noise, fearing an interview with one's headmaster, and fearing God. . . . But there is a difference in the emotional qualities of these various experiences of fear. This might be compared to differences of *shade* between various instances of the same color. . . .[24]

Here are, in addition to opinions on genesis, brief statements of the

[23] Quoted approximately from Broad's lectures on Moral Psychology. I am deeply indebted to Professor William Frankena for loan of his careful notes, taken in the mid-thirties. As Broad has not seen fit to publish the original notes—a decision which, I feel, is much to be regretted,—I quote most hesitatingly and sparingly.

[24] *JAAC*, XXX, 210f. I shall happily abstain from going into the ontology of dispositions, whether the ontology would yield neural physiology or a substantial spiritual self or something else. I do think that somewhere we need realistic correlates or grounds for "laws," and that mere statements of correlations are less than fully satisfying in science as well as in metaphysics. But one always has a healthy uneasiness at the thought of Occam, which may here recall the remark of Bentham: "Now disposition is a kind of fictitious entity, feigned for the convenience of discourse, in order to express what there is supposed to be permanent in a man's frame of mind. . . ." *Principles of Morals and Legislation* (Oxford, 1879), 131.

analogies with *primary colors* and with *shades*. (There is absence of analogy, I think it safe to observe, on the matter of the variation in specialization or generalization of stimulus and on the alterability of these through experience; probably the very high degree of specialization of the sense organ of vision destroys the similarity here.) With a little development the analogies of complementary colors and of blending are evident.

In the "mixing" of emotions, there is sometimes the phenomenon called *blending* by Broad and others. More carefully than some of his predecessors Broad explained in his lectures how he uses this term.

There is no sense in talking of qualities being "mixed" or "compounded" as substances can be. Purple in itself is just as simple a quality as red or blue. It is called a mixture of red and blue in respect of two relational properties which it has. One of these is non-causal and the other is causal. The first is the fact that any shade of purple resembles pure blue to some degree and resembles pure red to some degree and does not resemble any other primary color. . . . The second is that if a stimulus x acting alone would produce a sensation of a pure red sensum, and a stimulus y acting alone would produce a sensation of pure blue sensum, then the stimulus xy acting together on the same part of the retina will produce a sensation of a purple sensum. I propose to call mixture in this sense "blending."[25]

Perhaps an aspect which is here implicit should be rendered explicit, namely, the continuity of the series of possible shades of color or of blended emotional quality. "The particular shade of blended emotion which is felt on any particular occasion will presumably depend on the relative degree of excitement of the various emotional dispositions. . . ."[26] This causal relational property does justify one in saying that, although

[25] It will be noticed that Broad here clearly has two relational properties in mind, and that presumably his definition of blending requires their logical product, which we shall call "blending$_3$." He does not mean "blending$_0$," an actual mixture. We shall find it useful to separate his two relational properties and at least to treat of one in separation from the other. Using them for differential connotation, we then get qualities which may be arbitrarily labelled cases of "blending$_1$," and of "blending$_2$."

Correlative with his two different relational properties entering into his definition of blends and with the cluster of ideas normally about each, are two different implicit notions of "primary tones." In neither case, strictly, would the pure primary tones have to exist, although it is fairly plain that Broad assumes that infantile experience does have them without being able to name them. In the first meaning a primary tone would be what *would* be produced in a mind (under normal conditions) excited by an unmixed stimulus to an innate primary emotional disposition. Here, when blends are made, they are at least blends in the sense of results of mixtures of stimuli. In another meaning, a primary tone might simply be an extrapolation by an experiment in imagination or conception to some extremity of an abstracted factor of what one is acquainted with.

[26] *JAAC*, 211.

Broad denies mixing in the sense of mixing substances, he does properly mean a mixing of stimuli, after the manner familiar in what James called "brass instrument psychology." Some interpreted empirical consequences of the account of blending are at once drawn by Broad.

(i) It may be that certain primary emotional dispositions, e.g., those of anger and of fear, are *directly* linked from the first. Others become linked only indirectly in the course of experience.

(ii) Probably a *grown* person hardly ever has an experience with a *pure* primary emotional tone. The notions of the pure primary emotions, like the notions of the pure primary colors, are ideal limits.[27]

A special independent status has been assigned by us to a third consequence, to point up the analogy on *complementarity*. Perhaps some primary emotional qualities will not blend; they "would have to each other the kind of opposition which there is between complementary colors, such as red and green or blue and yellow."[28]

Lastly, there are *pattern qualities:* ". . . there are certain emotional adjectives, such as 'sad' and 'cheerful,' which apply to a total phase of experience as a whole rather than to any part of it." They "*depend on* the qualities and relations of the constituent parts of the whole," but "they are not *reducible* to these."[29] In his Lectures, Broad compared these to adjectives "like 'bright' and 'dull' as applied to the visual field."

He further noted that normally introspection might first catch either the pattern quality or certain constituent qualities, but not both simultaneously and equally. Trained introspection, however, should be able

---

[27] *Ibid.,* 211. One will not quarrel with the notion that a grown person "hardly ever" has pure emotional tones. But, with a good spectrum, he may see relatively pure visual colors, purity being defined with the aid of the physicist in terms of uniformity of wave-length of the electro-magnetic vibrations exciting the sensation. I cannot think of any occasions in which one's total visual field would afford such purity, but a thin slice of the variegated field may offer it to a very high approximation. The arbitrariness of primary colors could be argued. But primacy is not arbitrary where there is a real genetic primacy. Serious complications arise if Broad's assertion that "pure primary emotions" are only "ideal limits" means to do more than to deny pure *occurrent* emotions after infancy; for he has previously assigned, it seems to me, an existent and causally productive role to pure emotional *dispositions.*

[28] *Ibid.,* 211. On complementarity, our author must have in mind some phenomenon or phenomena of color wheels, and not spectral colors. Perhaps the noncausal relational property is not exemplified. For, in the causal sense, all colors blend when projected upon a seen surface. (Ultra violet and infra red do not blend, for they do not appreciably affect the eye—except by damage in the first case.)

Spectrally, any colors which together give the sensation of white light are "complementary." Any portion of the spectrum, plus the remaining portion, is thus complementary.

[29] *Ibid.,* 212.

to bring out both, as a good musician—to shift the analogizing to the auditory sphere—can hear both the constitutent notes and the pattern qualities of a chord or of a melodic phrase. In addition, then, sadness or blitheness of the composition may come to him as an "objective" property.

Since we have been mentioning blended qualities and since the excitation of a sentiment yields a blended emotional tone this is a good place to introduce (as Broad does) the topic of *sentiments*. It might equally well be discussed (I will remark) in relation to the cognitive aspect of emotional dispositions, for, as we shall immediately see, the unity of a sentiment on Broad's conception of it is the unity of being bonded to the complex epistemological object. His usage of the term is somewhat peculiar; but, in view of the variety of usage generally, he is certainly entitled to make the convenient stipulation which he offers.

His usage is not peculiar in normally referring to sentiments as dispositional. Impressionistically I think he uses "emotions" prevailingly in the occurrent sense. Definitions are not such as to preclude speaking of provoking, eliciting, awakening, evoking or expressing a sentiment, nor such as to preclude usage of "emotional dispositions," etc. Sentiments are not the whole range of emotional dispositions, and emotions are not all occurrent sentiments, although of course some of them are. The terms are not labels for the occurrent and dispositional aspects of the same connotation or same denotation. "Emotions" has the wider range. Perhaps there are simple emotions, with toned experience in fusion with a simple epistemological object. There are no such simple sentiments, for there must at least be a complexity of aspects of the epistemological object, even if the quality is perfectly "blended." (And complex objects may evoke unblendable emotional qualities, in which case Broad believes that the patient rapidly alternates from one tone to another.) Again, some emotional dispositions are innate, according to our author, but all sentiments are acquired.[30]

I do not know about certain further possible differences. Conceivably Broad may intend to restrict "sentiments" to cases of conflicting disposi-

[30] Of course, factors which enter into their formation may be innate dispositions.

Probably in popular usage sentiments normally are thought of as having a dispositional status; emotions are usually thought of in the occurrent sense. But the term "moral emotion" has lately come to be so much used in either a dispositional or an occurrent sense that one feels it would be a bit pedantic to insist upon a separation of usage. Possibly there are some direct innate moral dispositions, in which case—on occasion of their pure or unhabituated excitation—a purist would speak of "moral emotions;" but probably most moral emotions are acquired, and acquired in complexes, and we should then rather speak of "moral sentiments," dispositional and occurrent.

tions toward aspects of complex objects or toward symbols thereof.[31] I see no reason to suppose that this is the case, but it is very important to recognize that a sentiment can contain both *pro* and *anti* coefficients. This is the locus of a difference with one quite popular usage.

I do not know whether Broad means that occurrent sentiments must be "motived," must contain awarenesses of the aspects of the perceived or conceived object with respect to which different emotional tones do or at least tend to arise, or whether, on the other hand, a perceptual object might directly elicit the activities of traces which produce the blend or produce an alternation between unblendable emotional tones. If there is consciousness of the "motives," surely it is sometimes pretty dim from familiarity. And one may infer that a lot of occurrent sentiments are complex second-hand conceptual emotions and a lot are something very like complex second-hand perceptual emotions (although Broad may strictly confine second-hand emotions to conceptual emotions). Of course, all the conceptual ones would be motived, in Broad's view, but the perceptual ones (if they exist) would not on the same grounds have to be motived.

Sentiments would not be produced were it not for three noteworthy conditions among other background conditions. (*a*) Were there no more or less stable objects (*b*) which are complex and (*c*) which enter into a variety of situations, there would be no sentiments. The unity of a sentiment, on Broad's meaning, is a matter of its reference to this object, and in some other important aspects it does not manifest unity. It is a nexus of emotional dispositions toward the complex object, some of which component dispositions may be much in contrast with others in tendency to tonality, tendency to action,[32] and so on. Accordingly, Broad's connotation, strictly enforced, would not permit such phrases as "sentiment of patriotism" when this means (as it often does) a selection of the disposition of pro-feeling toward one's country. Rather, a modern so-called civilized man will have a sentiment toward his country, which of course will include the dispositions to feel a certain glow on hearing

---

[31] Of course, I do not think he would attach the label of "sentiment" to a complex object occurring in a variety of contexts but toward which an agent was usually practically indifferent. Both the dispositional complex of emotional "charges" and the "complex dispositional idea" of the object seem to be essential. Although the latter and then the former may be excited by any word or symbol connected with the dispositional idea, such mode of excitation is contingent and is not definitionally essential.

[32] It is easy to see how one may learn one side of a conflicting sentiment. Suppose natively—or natively plus a minimum of learning—an animal or man has a certain propensity toward or desire of object, *O*; suppose further that he has received strong punishment sometimes on attaining it or approaching it; then the subsequent occasions of approach to *O* are likely to be ambivalent.

the national anthem and to feel a certain sort of resentment when a hostile nation lets loose a barrage of incendiary propaganda, but which will also include his proneness to feel the toned qualifications owing to some sense (or some deposit of the awareness) that his country has engaged in some bellicose acts and does (let us say) exact heavy income taxes from him.[33]

Presumably sentiments, which are acquired complexes, are materially built up from a plurality of "primary emotional dispositions." The building, however, is not just an assemblage; not only are stimuli of some component dispositions narrowed and others widened, but apparently the widening can be extended to quite new stimuli; also apparently there are emergent qualities of the resulting tonalities in experience.[34]

Blending of emotions and the establishment of sentiments obviously have some possibilities of accounting for moral emotions, including such feelings as sense of obligation, awareness of imperativeness, etc. Just for instance, what is summed up in "respect for moral rules" might be a compound made out of an urge to obey what is commanded *per se,* an urge to separate oneself from what is commanded *per se,* fear of retribution from persons in authority, desire for admiration of parents and teachers, fear of an absolute unknown moral government of the world, etc. But for psychological theoretic purposes it becomes extremely important to know what are held to be the real dispositions the simultaneous activation of which is producing the blend.

On the one hand, are there such pure dispositions? There may be, and they may be active, so to speak, in each present occurrence of the blend. On the other hand, may not the apparent mixture be both as original and as presently actual as the alleged ingredients of the mixture? Indeed, may not the "ingredients" be theoretic constructs of an illustrative schema useful for certain representational purposes and disutile

[33] Sentiments, I should believe, may be stimulated when little or none of the proper real object is there; symbols will do it. Should this be compared with the imaging of red under the stimulus of the word "red"?

Strictly, are there presumably two different—although linked—sentiments to correspond respectively to the stimulus of a physical object and to the stimulus of a word?

[34] Through learning, we greatly increase our knowledge of objects and get new sources for the stimulation of emotions. However, do we through "learning" literally make new qualities? (I think we do. Men do not think of themselves as learning to make the experience of colors; but I do think of ourselves as being conditioned or learning to make certain feelings.) Broad is suggesting that at least we make new blends. Can one make the *basis* of a new connection, not just effect the connection on antecedent bases? Are there in some radical sense "lures" to new qualities of experience? At any rate are there not somehow—how?—dimly imaged or schematically conceived possibilities which then are lures toward more full and concrete realization of qualities?

for others? Thirdly, perhaps the pure dispositions were once and for a time "there," but as the blend got activated time after time, a new disposition lapsed into desuetude and weakness. It is not implausible that, in second-hand emotions, moral words directly excite the occurrent blend.

When one would get down to a specific allegation of the origination of an important family of moral emotions it would have to be examined on its own concrete merits and demerits, as well as, of course, on the systemic status of the whole general viewpoint. No such examination can be here effected, for instance, of Broad's treatment of "Hägerström's Account of Sense of Duty and certain Allied Experiences."[35] In the end, I confess, one seems to be fortunate to have the blessed notion of "emergence" to call upon. I suspect that at a crucial spot it will be more helpful than "blending."

I close this section with a terse recapitulation of certain points with the unargued insertion of a few more.

a. As I have already said, the analogy comes off better and is in this sense more enlightening than I would have antecedently supposed. Variegation, blending, shades, etc., seem to be exemplified. So, one might add, is intensity, and possibly saturation. Perhaps there are, as Professor Hartshorne might argue, an indefinite number of similarities between the qualities of different sensations and emotions.[36] Broad touches upon this under the heading of pattern qualities. Probably different similarities, both descriptively and metaphorically expressed, would come first to mind in cases of comparison of emotions with the data of different senses.

Variegation is unexceptionably cited with respect to a total sense-field, e.g., the visual field, and it is unexceptionably cited with respect to a "total state of mind." The alleged "primary species of emotional tone" —which get blended—are presumably abstracted elements from a field, perhaps occasionally appearing in a restricted locus in practical purity. One should always keep clear the distinction between the total state of mind and an abstracted aspect, which latter may be "simple." This admonition is particularly pertinent to myself, because I use "emotion" in such a comprehensive way; perhaps Broad does too.

b. There is a texture of feeling in addition to, on the one side, mere hedonic tonality and, on the other, epistemic intensionality. I assert this on what seems to me to be fair introspection. I believe that the authority of Broad can be claimed for it. Certainly he has emotional

35 *Philosophy*, XXVI, 99–113.
36 Charles Hartshorne, *The Philosophy and Psychology of Sensation* (Chicago: University of Chicago Press, 1934).

tones which do not reduce to the pleasantness-unpleasantness continuum. However, he does not go so far as to say—as I think I would—
there are feelings "that such-and-such is the case" (and only an occasional
wayward illustration[37] could be cited for his supposing textures of this
sort, which pretty surely he would locate in the component of intentionality). In his main doctrine, what I am calling the non-hedonic
textures of concrete feelings are adverbial properties of the experienc-
ings of the person.

c. The "theory" seems particularly convenient in dealing with large
ranges of modest feeling tones. It accounts for a great multitude of
shades, if one grants it the requisite primary dispositions—I have no
idea how many—and some equally important fluid dispositional
capacity to make blends as functions of excitations of the primary dispositions. The latter wide-ranging synthetic disposition is a way of
avoiding a literally tremendous number of primary dispositions. The
apparent continua which it affords, with indefinite gradations and fine
nuances, is a strength. It contrasts favorably here with some other
theories, like that of Sartre,[38] which seem concerned only with the
strongest and most vivid emotions. Indeed, Sartre's appears to be largely
patterned on anger and terror, which it is made well to fit; correlatively
it seems to have no account of feeling tone or of petite emotions.

I find myself inclined to say that Broad is weak in the area of the strong
emotions. I will assert something akin to this in declaring that his account is deficient on the whole actional side of emotions. I hesitate to
say it about the occurrent tonality of the strong emotions. One does
not wish to be misled by the fact that Broad does not shout when he
talks about what is vivid. And one does not want to confuse the quality
of a tone with its intensity—although I should unhesitatingly say that
in these matters of aesthesis occurrent extremes of quantity are at once
part of the quality. If Broad's treatment has a defect here, it could perhaps be remedied in a paragraph about the intensities of which the
primitive emotions are capable. And, one recalls, elsewhere in treating
of motivation and decision, Broad recognizes the motivational strength
of coalitions and organized hierarchies of dispositions.

Of course the "theory" pertains to the phenomenal field of consciousness, in keeping with Broad's definition. (This is itself suggestive of
"passivity.") There is no essential reference to the organism or to intra-
somatic sensations. William James, who almost inadvertently distin-

37 "One may begin with an unmotived repulsion for a person. This may generate
the belief that he is dishonest, and we may often find in the end that he really is a
crook." *JAAC*, 207.

38 J.-P. Sartre, *The Emotions* (New York: The Philosophical Library, Inc., 1948).

guished between the "standard emotions" and other emotions, and who perhaps had several theories rather than one, was at least sometimes stating that all standard emotions are exceedingly complex composites of sensations, of various bodily sensations. Possibly he allowed a different status for the generically aesthetic emotions,[39] although this may be doubted for he basically observes that "bodily accompaniments are much more far-reaching and complicated than we ordinarily suppose."[40] Indeed, in view of the wondrous complexities of circulatory system, respiratory system, glands, skeletal muscles, smooth muscles, etc., he more than takes note of the possibility that "no shade of emotion" is "without a bodily reverberation as unique, when taken in its totality, as is the mental mood itself."[41] I realize that the last two quotations give a different doctrine than his most radical one, because of the presence of the word "accompaniments" in the first and the distinction between "mental mood" and "bodily reverberation" in the second; but in both cases there is reference to the body. Broad avoids all such confusions as these of James; still one may question whether a considerable price is not paid in the asepsis of his introspection and in his avoidance of the risks of getting muddied here by involvements in body-mind problems. Broad of course has also the advantage of still holding his cards; with the temporary adoption of a proper theory of the ego, he can allow disembodied human emotions. James radically (and therewith creating some inconsistencies) says: "A purely disembodied human emotion is a non-entity. . . . The more closely I scrutinize my states, the more persuaded I become, that whatever moods, affections, and passions I have, are in very truth constituted by and made up of, those bodily changes we ordinarily call their expression or consequence. . . ."[42] James has a sort of theory of "blending"—of blending of intro-somatic sensations— or perhaps it should more accurately be labelled a theory of "summation."

d. With respect to the number of "primary emotional dispositions," Broad says a "fairly small number," and his initial remarks illustratively use fear, anger and pubertial love-feeling (thus reminding one of Watson, who, however, found behavioral love in infants). Taking pure emotions, native or instinctive emotions, and elementary emotions to

[39] Knight Dunlap rightly observes that in the *Principles of Psychology* "James concedes much more to the esthetic and spiritual emotions in the way of independence of somatic and visceral processes than he does in the former." Knight Dunlap (ed.), *The Emotions* (Baltimore: Williams and Wilkins Co., 1922), p. 6. I do not see how James' views in the *Varieties of Religious Experience* can be reconciled with some statements in his later theory of emotions short of something approaching panpsychism or at least a wider psychism than is common.

[40] *Ibid.*, 14.   [41] *Ibid.*, 15.   [42] *Ibid.*, 18.

denote the same group, I would suppose that one would read Spinoza as having three, namely, joy, sadness, and desire (although Spinoza's definitions of quite a long list make fascinating reading in their systemic context). His distinction of active *vs.* passive in effect yields an extra dimension. Descartes is somewhat better off with six: admiration, love, hate, desire, joy, sadness. *Unless Broad is going to bank upon emergence,* he is going to need more than the three mentioned and, I believe, more than a "small number." Where, for instance, are felt imperativeness, reverence, exaltation? Except for the invocation of emergence, one must have "elements" resembling those to be explained. I do not think that recourse to the features of the intentional object meets the need.

e. In general, the "hypothesis" of blending and the doctrine of emergence in pattern qualities seem to me to be pretty independent, although each is utilized in the analogy of emotional tones with colors. I associate continuity and regularity of change with the notion of blends; I associate discontinuity with irregular appearances at antecedently unknown critical points with emergence.

f. Is the analogy an hypothesis? What predictions, if any, does it enable us to make? So far, I have not thought of any important predictions which should be tested, and I have conceived of the analogy as obtaining chiefly in the role of a descriptive device. But I should suppose that with some further articulation the notion of "blending" would suggest specific hypotheses and that these would be tested by careful introspection or inspection.

g. On the negative side of the analogy, it has already been noted that the data of vision are phenomenally objective and ostensibly externally located in a way that cannot be claimed for all or many feeling tones. Going beyond the phenomenal realm, one observes certain other presumptive differences. Color, one may presume, is relatively unmodifiable by learning. We cannot appreciably restrict or generalize the stimulus. (Outside apparatuses—telescopes, microscopes, prisms— do not count.) However, probably we do learn some pattern qualities in both cases. It is upon these that "artistic effects" depend. In the sphere of the emotions, conditioning seems to have a large role, transferring qualities and making them occur where they would not natively arise. Second-hand emotions are treated as genuine emotions, and yet are (differentially) produced by a verbal stimulus. Images may be produced by a verbal stimulus, but we would *not* say they are genuine sensations, nor even that they are ostensibly such. Nor do we get anywhere toward teaching people to see purple as orange by presenting the colors together and then dropping one stimulus out.

h. Correlated with the above, I believe, is the physiological fact of the basic involvement of one organ in the seeing of colors. I presume there are definite and indefinite linkages of many organs in the having of emotions. The functioning of the eyes has a relatively greater autonomy. There is, accordingly, a greater stability of the former. Presumably also, there is a greater intersubjectivity of visual data (and other sensory data) than of emotional quality (although taste may give one pause over the wider generalization).

i. Visual data are relatively uncharged; many of the vivid emotional tones are highly charged toward action. A complexity of the propulsive aspect may be further noted. Except in some very refined aesthetic sense, there is no feeling of conflict or contradiction whatever in noting that there is a blue patch here and a white patch there in the same field of vision. There is a feeling of conflict if there is an object in the foreground of consciousness which is at once attractive and repulsive to me, in reference to different dispositions in my being. Likewise if there are two impellingly attractive objects in the field of consciousness which lie inevitably along different courses.

Accepting desires as emotions, non-introspected properties of some emotions—or non-inspected properties of some emotions—are very important. Perhaps the deficiency is not inherent in introspection; perhaps it is not wholly incapable of noting the "force" or "tension" of desires, but in this case the habits of inspecting presentations (as momentary static objects) lead to a surface view of desires. At any rate, in practice the introspective sort of definition of emotion predisposes toward a neglect of the actional side of emotions generally and of desires in particular.

On Broad's definition of emotion, his classification of desires as emotions is correct. On the other hand, in view of the differences between desires and other emotions, it could be urged that it is inconvenient to have classed the former as a species of the latter. The major root of the inconvenience serves to raise the question whether conation might not have better been taken as fundamental; one then might have been led to look for actual functional relationships even if he were then disposed to let the questions of static classification pass as infertile taxonomy. Or, one might recommend the schema—as I have inclinations to do—of supposing that all contents theoretically have a dynamic aspect; where the tensional aspects are quite low and do not tend to manifest themselves overtly, the experiences will naturally fail to get themselves labelled as desires in ordinary usage.

One "bad thing" about the analogy of emotional tones and visual colors, we are saying, is the "passivity" suggested. This is entirely in keeping with the "spectator" orientation of Broad's definition; it illustrates it. In the case of fearing, desiring, abhorring, etc., what is most characteristic and what is usually most important is not the tonality but that there is an active tendency and presumably some marshalling of energies toward some goal or against some outcome. Discussion of desires and aversions, and of the complications over multiple candidates for "objects" and over the development of their "objects" under the processes of inquiry, is so large a subject as to require separate treatment elsewhere.

The main weight of this section has been positive. It is interesting that Broad makes an analogy across the separation of what he otherwise treats as ostensibly objective on one side and adverbial on the other. The materials of the analogy are of much theoretic interest to one who, like myself, is concerned with general theory of the modalities of consciousness and who might hanker after construction of as much as possible of a multi-dimensional spectrum of subjective contents.

6. *Some Classifications of Emotions. Placement and Appropriateness.*

In addition to emotional dispositions *vs.* occurrent emotions, and pure *vs.* mixed emotions (and therewith blended *vs.* complementary emotions), there are several further distinctions which Broad offers as important in discussing emotions: properly placed *vs.* misplaced emotions; appropriate *vs.* inappropriate emotions; motived *vs.* unmotived emotions; and first-hand *vs.* second-hand emotions.

Certain of these distinctions overlap, I believe; and one wonders if a species under one heading and a species under another heading may not exhibit redundancy. Present compass precludes an attempt at permitting all the combinations, or all the non-redundant combinations, and laying them out in a table, with examples and with queries as to whether some combinations are not vacuous where examples do not come to mind. I am rather sure that when the threefold distinction on a cognitive basis is imposed, there are some connoted combinations which mark null classes. As is his wont, however, Broad has certainly provided us with an extensive schema for making, not simply a two-dimensional table, but an *n*-dimensional volume of combinations.

Are the distinctions based on *placement* and those based on the questions of *appropriateness* alternative ways of thinking of and naming the same things? At first blush it may seem so. *E.g.*, accepting the notion that every sort of emotional tone, or at least every sort of supposed elementary emotional tone, is justified in a certain sort of context, one may think of an emotion as *misplaced* when it fails to have the appropriate sort of context. And accepting the notion that every sort of situation deserves or allows on the part of a participating mind some sort of appropriate attitude—including indifference—one may think of an emotion as inappropriate when the situation deserves another sort of attitude or at least does not deserve the reaction which is being made. Thus, one might think of the difference as a pseudo-difference, arising simply from what one took as base of mental reference—the emotion or the situation.

Is this Broad's meaning? No, I think it is not. True, both pairs of distinctions have to do with sorts of appropriateness, but they are with respect to different "objects." As Broad more restrictedly uses the terms, *"appropriateness"* and *"inappropriateness"* (as we shall momentarily see) mark a relation between the *epistemological object* and the tone of the emotion, whether or not the object be veridical. *Misplacement* has grounding in the ontological questions. Does the emotion exist with respect to a real object, *i.e.,* does its epistemological object exist as presumed in the emotion?—is the ostensible cognition in the emotion veridical? And if the main object there accepted does exist, does it have the attributes which it is assumed to possess and which are assumed relevantly to ground the emotion? (One presumes that this last distinction applies only to "motived" emotions.)

An emotion may be said to be 'misplaced' if either (i) it is felt towards an object which is believed to exist but does not really do so, or (ii) it is felt towards an object which really does exist in respect of attributes which do not really belong to it. In the first case it may be said to be *totally* misplaced, in the second *partially* misplaced.[43]

Broad observes that conceptual emotions may be "completely misplaced," indeed, that such complete misplacement occurs quite commonly among sane waking men, as the history of religion illustrates. Counting dreams, *quasi*-perceptual emotions too may be "completely hallucinatory." However, "Completely hallucinatory perceptions are very rare in sane waking, healthy persons."[44]

I should suppose that emotions which are intuitive on their cognitive side are not misplaced, and indeed, cannot be misplaced, on the assumption that the ontological questions do not arise. My supposition may be in error, but I think not. Broad does allow for errors in introspection,

---

43 *Ibid.,* 208. It appears then that, as would become clearer after a discussion of "motived emotions," a partially misplaced emotion is a motived emotion the motivating character of which lacks objective existence. (Possibly this would have to be revised for the species of emotions which are desires; perhaps their motivating characters would correlatively lack possibility of realization.) Although only "partial," surely this error is a very serious one, for it is an ontological error concerning the focal aspect of the object.

44 *Ibid.,* 209.

but the intuitions of sensibilia, images and experiences are not introspective.

Broad advises us to notice that "all emotions which are felt towards other persons in respect of their supposed mental and moral qualities must be in part conceptual on the cognitive side," since "one cannot literally *perceive* another person's mind. . . ." The remark carries its obvious implication of the danger of errors of placement in judg=ments of moral comment upon the doings of others.

In the text from which I am drawing, Broad does not discuss whether any misplacement can occur in aesthetic experience of, for example, drama and literature where the feigned cognition is recognized not to be of entities in the actual world. One may suppose, however, that there is misplacement in the admiration or the elegance of a lovely mathematical "proof" the only defect of which is its fallaciousness.

If a very extensive meaning of emotion is used—correlative with the supposition that every cognition is accompanied by some emotional tone —then every error in cognition is an error in emotion. Perhaps in part we do not usually think of it as such because we are normally concerned with the cognition and not the tone. Often the tone is not conspicuous, and may suffer little change in itself while there is much change in the epistemological objects as inquiry brings them into view. In addition, of course, only rather strong emotions get noticed and named "emotions."

With respect to *appropriateness,* we wish to raise—or at least adequately allude to—several points and issues.

First of all, it is fair to say that, although Broad gives it only three short paragraphs in the recent article upon which we have been heavily leaning, he has been much occupied with the topic. He justly observes that the "notion of a certain fittingness or unfittingness, in kind or in degree, between emotional tone and epistemological object, is plainly of the utmost importance to ethics and to aesthetics." The breadth of this statement certainly permits one to be relevantly reminded of the sort of cognitivism which G. E. Moore held in asserting intuitions of "good" in different complexes which were goods; presumably one's appropriate response to a sublimely beautiful object would be toned differently from one's response to a pleasure of dining. Broad, I believe, has done almost nothing publicly with the concept of fittingness in aesthetics, but he has repeatedly focussed upon it in ethics. His lines of inquiry which for so long caused him to be classed beside Ross among the deontologists manifest his preoccupation with objective fittingness, within the denotation of which moral "rightness" presumably named a primary species.

In 1954, Broad evaluated the work of others and of himself on the concept by making the remark that "it still awaits an adequate analysis."

It is assumed, I take it, that there is appropriateness and inappropriateness as well as right placement and wrong placement. The most radical sceptic may dissent from this, devotedly eschewing all ostensible "normative" implications. A given sceptic, however, should make clear whether he simply denies a supposed universal categorical obligation to conform to objective (trans-human) appropriateness or whether he denies criteria relative to the species or whether he denies criteria relative to a culture or whether he holds that the whole miscellany of such ostensible judgments is a result of so great a confusion of mixed "mechanisms" as to resist any ordering save that of a thankless tedious causal analysis. The "informalist" approach eludes questions of wholesale scepticism and would require an analysis of "appropriateness" anyway, because its familiar usages (or usages of kindred terms, for, whether Broad has here centered on common usage may well be questioned) have their "logic." It is doubtful, however, whether our author means to run with the ordinary language people even if he agrees with them here in considering, rather than rejecting, the phenomena.[45] He writes as if he were talking about appropriateness and inappropriateness and not about the language rules to be found by observing how the members of some culture employ the terms. And, although he is on amiable rather than hostile terms with common sense, he does not look to extracting more wisdom from linguistic usage than has been put in. We here assume that the predications under question are not an aggregate of accidental homonyms and that there are grounds is one of the focal questions in ethical theory. Whether one will or will not assert categorical obligations to try to make one's responses appropriate is not logically to be determined by the anthropological facts. If this decision has grounds as well as causes, these grounds come from wider sources than neutral noting of patterns of behavior. I parenthetically opine, however, that no cultures will be found in which it is taken to be appropriate to hate all of one's own young or to feel enmity toward all who are friendly.

Thirdly, in Broad's recognition of different "kinds of emotional quality" which are fitting respectively to different sorts of objects, he seems to be rightly far beyond any simple distinction of "pro" and "anti" feelings. The analysis is here implicitly differentiated further than it is

---

[45] Assumption of a gulf between Broad and the informalists is not incompatible with attaching a good deal of importance to a remark our author makes in his review of Stephen Toulmin's, *The Place of Reason in Ethics* (*Mind,* Jan. 1952).

at the end of his "Moral Sense" article, where he notes "pro" tendencies and "anti" tendencies in respect to different characteristics of a contemplated course of action but apparently is interested in the motivational resultant and in the misleading way in which one announces it to oneself and to others. The simile of physical vectors is a very familiar one; it is not clear that Broad is endorsing it, or saying anything about possible antecedent determination of forces, their commensurability, and whether or not the field is mono-dimensional. It is not evident that he is either affirming or denying that moral situations are distinguished by a unique quality, or that he is giving (as we shall urge later) any indication of how morally relevant factors are selected out of the situation.

The present is a not irrelevant place to ask whether Broad supposes that "moral" situations are distinguished, when appropriately felt, by some distinctive common emotional tone, and whether "aesthetic" situations are distinguished, when appropriately felt, by some common emotional tone. Or, reversely, are "moral emotions" cognitively distinguished by the presence of objective moral properties or some relational moral property, and moral emotions arise in response? Perhaps moral emotions are marked by their relationship to situations of choice or action, restricted by some further differentia, and extended to include lively consideration of past and feigned situations of choice? Or, possibly are moral emotions distinguished initially by their status as second-order emotions, relating to the "traffic flow" and "traffic control" (so to speak) of other first-level values? (It has to be admitted, I think, that sometimes they do not feel as if they are second-order emotions— they sometimes seem phenomenally to be as direct as any others.) It is empirically the case, it seems to me, that our concrete feelings which possess a component of "pro-ness" are nevertheless quite varied; even what we take to be moral pro-emotions are quite varied. Plainly there are kinds of pro-ness and anti-ness which are not felt to be "moral" but rather as morally indifferent. One's anti-feeling toward limburger cheese is different from the feeling toward genocide. Further, the noble, with its aspect of attractiveness, is different in its concrete quality from the just, which likewise has its attractiveness to a morally trained person. Similarly, concrete aversions, including moral aversions, are diverse in quality. Broad, like Sidgwick, has drawn attention to the likelihood of careless confusion of a moral sentiment with a quasi-moral sentiment. However, Sidgwick and Broad would, I am sure, say that only carelessness permits the confusion; and Sidgwick and the earlier Broad would, I think, have based the source of the distinction on the intellectual or non-emotional side of the experience and have treated the difference in emotional quality as an effect.[46]

The later Broad may well have a different view. He does not say what that view is, either with respect to the mode of distinction of the generically moral from the non-moral or of the positively moral from the immoral. We do have, as we especially note later, his confession of how he seems to himself to make first-hand deliberated moral decisions. And this is not, as he gives it, by a cognitive descrying of moral properties but rather by some sort of outcome of the play of forces of "pro" and "anti" emotions toward aspects of entertained courses of action, which aspects are somehow accepted as, or discerned to be, morally relevant aspects. For my part, I have said that it seems to be that the tones felt with respect to different aspects of the morally problematic situation—even with respect to aspects toward which the emotional components point in the same behavioral direction, either "for" or "against" —are qualitively different in their full concreteness. (I would say the same thing about tonalities with respect to different aesthetic objects, all of them praiseworthy, and perhaps about tonalities with respect to different aspects of the same aesthetic object when the fusion of the totality is broken down in a detailed examination.) This descriptive observation may most naturally point in a direction of not supposing that the generically moral is distinguished from the non-moral by the presence of some one common quality and in a direction of not supposing that the positively moral is distinguished from the non-moral by the presence of some one common quality. But there is no inconsistency, I think, in making these suppositions, provided one holds that the differentiating common quality is a quality in or of the concrete qualities.

[46] Sidgwick noted that if his pronouncement "the air is sweet" were challenged, he might content himself with simply affirming the existence of certain feelings in himself, but that the situation with the moral feelings was fundamentally different. Here, I assume, he would, in principle, have to take up the challenge to a pronouncement or let the feelings change from moral feelings into another kind. "The peculiar emotion of moral approbation is, in my experience, inseparably bound up with the conviction, implicit or explicit, that the conduct approved is 'really' right— i.e. that it cannot, without error, be disapproved by any other mind. If I give up this conviction . . . I may no doubt still retain a sentiment prompting to the conduct in question . . . but this sentiment will no longer have the special quality of 'moral sentiment' strictly so called." *Methods of Ethics* (London: Macmillan and Co., 7th ed., 1930), p. 27. I do not have the slightest doubt that Sidgwick was giving an accurate rendering of his own experience and that of many of the rest of us. This does not prove that a person reared from the cradle with an explicit Stevensonion ideology would have similar experience. Cf., *Ethics and Language,* p. 31. Broad remarks that Richard Price would have viewed the "interjectional" analysis of deontic sentences as "fantastically absurd" since such a theory "can be swallowed only after one has undergone a long and elaborate process of 'conditioning. . . .'" Sellars and Hospers, p. 365.

Although each morally problematic situation may be unique in its full quality, perhaps it is first recognized as moral because of a quality of its global quality. And possibly Broad would assent to our affirmation of the qualitative differences of the feelings toward different aspects of a morally problematic situation which are passed in review, but would assert that the tonal differences are due to blendings of what one might call the positive moral quality and the negative moral quality with other component qualities.

The first of these—that a quality of concrete qualities in certain problematic situations may first distingiush generically moral situations —I find highly credible. At the same time, I would find myself appalled by the assignment to indicate just what this common quality might be. It is most doubtful whether the presence of felt imperativeness would do for a criterion of *all* moral emotions, for it pertains directly only in the first person, present tense (and perhaps future tense), whereas we feel that we are having moral emotion when passing comment upon our own past acts or upon the present or past acts of others or even upon vivid presentations of hypothetical acts. Possibly—but it is very doubtful—emphatic processes can be taken as providing adequate "carry-over" to other cases from first-personal cases.

There is no doctrinal incompatibility in defining emotions as ostensible cognitions accompanied by tones of feeling and in asserting synthetically that certain emotions are markedly "pro" and others markedly "anti" emotions in some dynamic aspect (or, indeed, that all emotions have a conative aspect although some hover about the zero point). There are, however, one may opine, two different trains of intellectual habits connected with this definition and with treating the synthetic assertion as focal. Some persons are so taken by the behavioral-functional perspective that what "should be" material assertions and therewith should be scrutinized are somehow converted into either definitions or the rails of a methodological *a priori*. Broad may surely be exempted from this charge. He combines an introspective definition with the possibility of asserting whatever synthetic connections may be found. If there are deficiencies correlative with the respective merits of following the different trends, we should have to make the loose generalization that he centers on an internal-spectator view of emotion with, one fears, relative deficiency on the side of the actional or conational dimension. However, the latter is not missing; the present point is only that his brief discussions of it do not contain notations of the nuances of feeling, whereas a strength of his general treatment of tones of emotions and an implicit strength of his brief remarks on appropriateness is the recognition of such variety. For I should assume that appropriateness and inappropriateness are vastly more complex and qualitied than simply having the dimension of pro-ness and anti-ness. To be sure, if one is "anti" in feeling toward something to which he should be "pro," or *vice versa*, this is a gross form of inappropriateness. (How it is determined—if it can be determined—when one should be "pro" and when one should be "anti" is another crucial question, which is here assumed to have some answer. Moral innovators have attacked accepted notions of appropriateness. "Love your enemies.") Plainly unfittingness in *kind* of emotion, as Broad uses it, does not simply refer to feeling "pro-emotion," toward what should be an object of "anti-emotion," and *vice versa*. And unfittingness in *degree* presupposes fittingness in kind, with many more kinds than "pro" and "anti." One sort of "pro-emotion" is what is especially appropriate rather than any other of a long list: to feel favorably toward Beethovens *Ninth Symphony*, sensing that it is "quite cute," is inappropriate; to appreciate *The Pirates of Penzance* as "majestic, sublime" is inappropriate.

Lastly, it may be observed that Broad's restriction of "appropriateness" to a relation of the tone to the epistemological object stipulates a usage which has both an inconvenience and a convenience. (a) The chief inconvenience is due to the departure from common usage. (b) The convenience is that of being provided with a label to mark a distinction instead of using a label that covers two distinctions.

Often when A's response is deemed inappropriate, the judgment is made with respect to the real object (or to what the speaker takes to be the real object) and not with respect to A's subjective object. Further, some word other than "inappropriate" is likely to be employed if A's emotions do not fit his recognized objects; he will perhaps be called "perverse," "pathological," "abnormal," "apathetic," etc. Usually in such cases it is well recognized that a quite different mode of treatment is needed than if A's odd response is due to a mistaken view of the situation. Attempts to correct the latter will involve whatever techniques have been found useful in leading others to correct their views of objects. One will not resort to these techniques if he is sure that the problem is of the former sort, although Stevenson has well illustrated that this would be a terminal conclusion rather than an initial assumption. Radical "inappropriateness" of emotion response (in Broad's sense) may stimulate apprehensiveness in observers; often it has made the patient a target for punishment; to humane observers it may characteristically draw out recommendations of therapy and sometimes recommendations of protective custody. To be sure, inappropriateness is not always taken as important. We are likely to be practically concerned with a man who takes ecstatic delight at the sight of blood or of burning buildings; collectively we pay little heed to one who apparently does not "hear" music or "see" selected paintings. Toward the latter we may act superciliously; we may ignore him; we may pity him; we may, if he is young, give art lessons to help him to perceive aesthetic objects, assuming him to be not wholly devoid of capacity. Common sense has no settled assumption—and I doubt whether psychology as a whole has any settled theory—as to what is native here and what is or can be acquired; nor, with respect to the latter, is there knowledge of what is modifiable by communication of value-free information, of what is modifiable by value-charged symbolic means, of what is modifiable only by lessons of first personal experience, and lastly of what is modifiable only by—let us roughly say—physical and chemical interference. Certainly therapists and many other psychologists assume that men's actual emotionalities are products of learning, but the dominant practical interest here may distract attention away from that upon which presumably the modifications are worked. If there were a definitive theory of this, the discussion of those conflicts which Stevenson regards as typically ethical and the discussion of their resolution could be carried farther. Stevenson has heightened for everyone the major distinction between what may be called cognitive and non-cognitive ways of altering occurrent attitudes. If anyone combines a Stevensonian view of the nature of ethical conflicts and of their contrasting modes of resolution with, on the other hand, some view of the objective appropriateness of certain attitudes toward certain objects, then he will find—regardless of any little deviation from common usage—much convenience in Broad's narrow definition of "appropriateness" and of its difference from the issues of "placement."

7. Motived vs. Unmotived Emotions. Mediating Characteristics in Objects of Emotions.

Here is a distinction not only made but used by Broad. A further specification of it would seem to me to be very important in aesthetic and moral criticism. The distinction between motived and unmotived emotions is not equivalent to the division between, respectively, those emotions for which no sincere reasons are given and those for which sincere reasons are given, but the last is a species of ostensibly motived emotions. At first glance, the distinction appears to be a quite simple one; on examination, however, it becomes a little perplexing. But some of the complications hinge upon very interesting issues, material and methodological. Broad does not tell us how a person discerns the motivating characteristic (or characteristics) of an emotion when the person does discriminate it (or them), nor how the outside observer sometimes knows that the patient is in error in what he takes to be a motivating characteristic. The latter, at least, surely is beyond the pale of introspective method in psychology.

First of all, I should make a terminological remark which may at the same time be a significant confession of inadequacy. I have not noticed any definite difference between "motivation" and "mediation" of emotions in Broad's usage, and therefore I shall treat them as synonymous. In a way, "mediation" is a happier term, because of the heavy associations of "motivation" with action, while some of the most placid emotions may be clearly "motived."[47] Broad might suppose that they have no tendency toward action. If we assume all emotions to have a conational component, still some of these cases may register near the zero point. Of course, my treating mediation and motivation as synonymous does linguistically commit our exegesis to accepting unconscious mediation. With my assumption of degrees of explicitness and implicitness, I do not balk at this—even if it were more than a consequence of a stipulation. Broad may eschew such usage, although he explicitly asserts unconsciously motived emotions. Possibly he means "evocation" as another wider term, with "mediation" as a much narrower one; then, with respect to a motived emotion the motivating characteristic of which is operating unconsciously, one could designate the characteristic as an "evoking" characteristic but not as a "mediating" one. Possibly, too, an emotion must be dominantly a conceptual emotion before it can be "mediated."

One of Broad's introductions to the topic of motivation of emotions gives one an easy sense of familiarity. A person "may feel an emotion towards an object without consciously distinguishing any attributes of it with regard to which one could say: 'I feel this emotion towards that object in *respect of* those attributes of it.' " Some emotions just seem to be direct. Other emotions, however, are "more complex" experiences, for instance, when one dislikes a person "in respect of certain qualities, which one takes him to possess."[48] One is soon forced to notice, however, that these two groups of emotions are not the class of unmotived emotions and the class of motived emotions, respectively. Instead, they describe or illustrate *ostensibly* unmotived emotions and *ostensibly* motived emotions. The *fundamentum divisionis* apparently does not lie between them, but elsewhere. The real distinction for Broad seems to turn on whether "the emotion E really is not evoked by any knowl-

---

[47] Also, when one thinks of motives in a deliberative occasion of an agent's experience, one is usually, so to speak, thinking from an emotional-volitional state on toward overt action. In Broad's present usage, the emotional state is the effect; he seems to be inviting us to think backward from the emotion to its stimulus.

[48] *JAAC,* 206.

edge or beliefs which the person who feels it towards O has about the attributes of O" (in which case the emotion is unmotived) or whether the "person's emotion E towards O *really is* evoked by his knowledge or belief that O has a certain attribute P" (in which case the emotion is "actually motived" and P is the "actual motivating attribute").

One problem could be put in this way. Are we supposed here to have four different classes on two quite independent bases of division, or is one or the other of the latter fundamental?[49] Should one view ostensibly motived emotions as wholly distinct from really motived emotions, or is not there a reasonable presumption—as I should wish to assume— that usually what is ostensibly motived is really motived in the main in the way in which it consciously seems to be? If the latter is the case, has the distinction of "real" motivation been appended because non-introspective methods have occasionally found consciousness to be in error, or is the basic distinction intended to be one concerning causation but it happens that sometimes consciousness discloses with apparent directness the major differential stimulus of an emotion?

Related to the preceding problem is the question of whether just a differential cause-component is involved, or whether causation by specific "knowledge or beliefs" is definitionally involved. (Derivatively, in the latter case, some critics would urge the illegitimacy of the notion of unconscious knowledge; we would dissent from them.) Such phrasings as "in respect of," "calling forth the emotion," and "explicitly noticed" which are employed about the motive may suggest knowledge as the referent to which they are leading but they certainly do not themselves require it, and would be compatible with some other kind of stimulus. An essential part of this question, of course, is the scope of the tacit definition of "knowledge or belief." Broad obviously cannot mean "consciously explicit propositional knowledge or beliefs"—else he could not acknowledge a form of error which he does enumerate; and happily elsewhere he uses "cognition" and "knowledge" very widely, admitting immediate knowledge and treating the prehending of sensibilia, images, and one's "own experiences" as intuitive cognitions. Indeed, when sensibilia and images are included, the conception of knowledge is so wide that part of the problem will devolve into the question of whether there can be any unmotived emotions and why Broad is sure that animals have only unmotived emotions.

Probably some help would be afforded had Broad delivered a word

[49] This may look like a question of the history of Broad's stipulations, but I intend it to refer further to grounds for taking one or other as more fundamental. Gross unreliability of conscious or ostensible deliverances would be good reason for not taking ostensible motives as basic. On the other hand, good uses to be made of them in ethics would be one possible ground of according them primacy.

on how "motivating" characters are discerned, or had he made separate declarations on how ostensible motivating characters are discerned and on how actually motivating characters are determined. His remark that a motived emotion is a more complex experience than an unmotived one easily lends itself to the supposition that in the former there lies some added experience of introspection or added reflexive act of the mind. Two complexities, however, arise. The first is that sometimes we seem *directly* to recognize the motivating character—it is, if not indeed the delimited object itself, then some differentially significant aspect of what Broad calls the "object." Köhler urges the fact of this sort of directness against Hume's account of causation. It is conceivable, to be sure, that reflexive operations take place very rapidly here, but the experience does not seem to be dual or compound—nor inferential. (I do think that we can acknowledge, with Professor Earle, the ubiquitous character of some touch of reflexivity in various conscious processes.) The second difficulty for the suggestion that motivation is discerned by the compounding of the basic emotion with an introspective or reflexive act is that Broad holds that some actually motivating characters are not ostensible or raised to consciousness. This consideration is wholly useless for showing that no motives are discerned in the manner suggested; it is useful, however, for indicating that a consistent interpretation of Broad will require that the hypothesis be restricted in its application to ostensibly motived emotions, including, of course, those that are also really motived. And it indirectly serves to illuminate the fact, as I take it to be, that the patient's mode of cognition of the ostensibly motivating characteristics of his own emotions is quite different from the mode of cognition of real motivating characteristics in those cases in which these differ from the ostensible ones. Where the patient might compare a number of his similar occurrent emotions and employ Mill's canons to determine motivating characteristics—perhaps to correct his own ostensibly immediate deliverances—his method may be essentially the same as that of an external observer, although he happens to have access to the data in a way in which the behavioristic psychologist does not. But this method, requiring a number of similar cases and classification of the factors involved, seems to me to be quite different, on the one hand, from the patient's sense of the phenomenal givenness of motivation in some instances, and quite different, on the other hand, from the methods pursued by a depth psychologist.

I would speculatively suggest that unconscious motives of emotions are non-conscious in two significantly different statuses: there are the motives of which one is not aware because they happen not to have been raised to attention or simply lay inconspicuously covered by much else;

and there are the motives of which one is not aware because they have been repressed. I do suppose that in some cases a sense of derivation accompanies the emotional quality; if this "perception in the mode of causal efficacy" is not fundamental in the way that Whitehead contends, still it does characterize some experience. Some of it, in turn, may be causally accounted for by a very rapid funded use of Mill's method of difference: other things being taken as remaining the same, the presence of something new is taken as the source of the difference introduced into qualitative experience. I do not think that all cases are of this sort. And I repeat that the experiences do not seem to be dual and do not seem to be inferential.

Let it be supposed that we are correct in believing that knowledge of motives comes by three different avenues: (a) in a direct sense of derivation; (b) as a result of comparing a number of similar experiences and using the methods of agreement, difference and of estimated concomitant variations upon them; and (c) by the probing techniques which a depth psychologist would employ to find repressed motives. A strict operationalist would then, according to his operational definition of concepts, presumably assert three different pairs of motives vs. unmotived emotions. I feel that, although such a procedure has the merit of drawing attention to the different sources of probable discernments of motives, still it would be a mistake to leave the three matters separated. Broad has only the two distinctions; possibly he does not acknowledge our first pair; it is not clear, anyway, that the second and third mark his distinction between ostensible and real motivation, for he makes no explicit comment in the present context about psycho-analytic methods and there is no antecedent reason why mistakes in attributions of ostensible motives might not be made by non-analytic methods.

I believe that the starting point is and ought to be what the agent takes to be the "motives." I hesitate to put this in the form of saying "Ostensible motives represent the fundamental distinction and real motives are an appended class" (although with luck this might succeed in conveying my main intent), for the agent or patient takes his felt motives to be the real motives. The qualification of "ostensible" is not primitive; it is a later critical addition, owing to a recognition of the possibility of error, not owing to anyone's complacency with the suggestion that his ostensible motives are, in wholesale fashion, nonveridical. References to motives are of prime importance in art criticism and in moral discussion, and the references are made with the assumption that what is phenomenally a motive is really a motive. The chief practical rôle of appeal to "real motive" is to check hypocrisy or to help to overcome a pathological condition.

Broad takes all emotions to be caused. Either then "evoked by" is much more restricted in scope than "stimulated by" or than "caused by," or "knowledge or beliefs" must be the significant restriction among objects or aspects of stimulating objects—else there would be no un-motived emotions.

An *actually unmotived* emotion, our author says, is one for which the emotion *"really is not* evoked by any knowledge or beliefs which the person who feels it" has about the object. One reaction to this formula-tion may be: How can an emotion even be *at* an object if there be no "knowledge or beliefs" on the part of the patient with respect to the object, for how can it be an object without standing as a target of at least some tacit beliefs? Is it not impossible for one to have an object devoid of a status of figuring in his knowledge or beliefs? Then is not "unmotived emotion" coincident with objectless emotion and, accord-ing to Broad's definition, to be called unmotived *tonality* rather than emotion, since emotion requires an object whereas the supposed phe-nomenon would not have any?

There are, I suppose, ways out of this. We have already indicated doubts, textually based, that Broad is taking what otherwise would be the most plausible course. If "knowledge or beliefs" is construed rather strictly, *e.g.,* to require, for instance, propositional form or conscious acts of judging, then pretty plainly men and (one supposes) animals may have objects without knowledge or beliefs. Between sheer objectless experiences (if any) and experiences of explicit knowing and believing there is room left for what I referred to as "tacit" beliefs—*e.g.,* implicit acknowledgments, behavioral recognitions, habitual peripheral per-ceptions and perhaps even some dimmer sensitivities. When objects can be identified in some one or other of these looser ways and the mo-tivating attributes have to be identified in a stricter and more focal way, then it is possible to have an object without having "knowledge or beliefs" of its properties or of the specific properties evoking an emo-tion. Quite plainly Broad assumes that human beings have unmotived emotions and that all animal emotions belong in this class. Construed as we have done, our author's assertion of actual unmotived emotions is or would be a proposition which we want, for it shows or would show that he does recognize sensitivities to aspects of an object which aspects are not matters of explicitly conscious knowledge or belief. On a looser usage than his, one may say that these are items of implicit belief, for they are "there" although they have not attracted attention or been raised to consciousness.

On this understanding should one presume that unmotived emotions exist only toward real objects? I feel relatively sure of the negative implication of this with respect to objects constituted by connotative think-ing.[50] I am not quite so sure with respect to imaged objects; it would seem that if one of these is somewhat detailed and very vivid, an emo-tion arising from it is almost as apt to be unmotived as one arising from a perceived object. (Both have some relations to our other motivations —the one in order to be created and the other in order to be noticed; but neither need be so explicitly differentiated as to facilitate the con-necting of emotions with specific parts of them.)

A second way out of the problem set by asserting unmotived emotions and yet holding at the same time that all emotions have differential causal stimuli may be found by banking heavily upon the tacit distinc-tion of substantive object as against adjectival and relational attributes. Although by definition an emotion always has an object, one may then contend that sometimes the stimulus is the gross object whereas at other times certain aspects or relational properties of this object may be the differential stimulus and at some of these times the motivational rôle of these aspects is noticed (and on occasion incorrectly observed). De-spite his having taken a very wide view of the various objects of emo-tion, it is possible that when thinking of the topic of motived emotions Broad has habitually entertained substantial continuants as the objects of these emotions. A few of his illustrations take persons as the objects. Perhaps animals are asserted to have no motived emotions because they are presumed to make no conceptual distinction between substance and attribute.

If Broad has shifted, when thinking of the motives of emotions, to taking objects always as substantial continuants, this is, I opine, a mis-take. It is a not unnatural one, because of its not being a mistake in some of the happiest illustrations of motivation. But it is plainly in-consistent with Broad's analysis of objects in the cases of desires—which are treated by him as emotions. A situational perspective upon and analysis of emotions would serve to obviate the presumed error. The subject's own view of his situation is one in which often some fore-ground continuing object is conspicuous and hence gets called "the object." This focussed selection is all the more natural when possible blame is likely to be involved, for then one is keyed to watching him-self and other agents in the present-and-prospective situation. It is

---

[50] Or, positively put, all such objects are involved only with motived emotions. In so far as an object is constituted by connotative thinking, surely one is aware of the characteristics of the object, and pretty surely one senses his emotional tones as related to the different characteristics. To be sure, it is just possible that one be almost oblivious of the relation of his emotion to a characteristic. It is more likely that for certain reasons one might distort the relating of his emotion to one or more characters; then there is mistake with respect to the motive, not a confusion of taking an unmotived emotion to be motived.

only with such disciplined demands as a few religions charge or as serious responsibility may introduce that we are enjoined not to hate the sinner but sin, or not to blame the actor but to seek to improve his performance. For the most part, when it is persons that are involved, we do, I suppose, react to and dispose ourselves toward persons as a whole. However, under some pressure toward discrimination, as when we are asked for evaluation or when we are challenged for justification or when we find ourselves faced with the brute fact of our own internal conflict, or under some analytic mood following an aesthetic one, we distinguish different characteristics and how these different characteristics tend to make us feel or to judge. In gross practice, it is thus suggested, our Gestalten exhibit our habits of picking on dominant foreground objects which, some learning having been funded, are tacitly deemed likely to continue as factors in future situations. (It is not just the relative stability of continuants that is responsible for their being selected; indeed, when they are permanent static features they tend to be dismissed into the general background and ignored; a flash excites attention better than they do. But persons are active as well as being continuants.) Further discrimination is normally made when there is occasion to inspect our own present response, as, for example, when its propriety is challenged.

These tendencies make natural what Broad has apparently done. One might, on present assumptions, wax forensic with impetuous queries: What is the object of an emotion? Had not the whole encompassing nexus of causal conditions better be taken as the object? Or, if a narrow differential cause is to be selected, had not the actuating motive better be taken as the object? In the first case, what is usually taken as the object is really too narrow, reflecting certain economical tendencies of attention. In the latter case, what is usually taken as the object is too wide, but the intellectual slovenliness of so doing is presumably often due to certain practical deployments with respect to continuants in the future.

Rather than waxing rhetorical, however, one chooses the better procedure if he simply bears the situational perspective in mind, uses the distinctions of substantial objects and motivational characteristics when these are convenient, and employs further distinctions when such prove needful. The last task will be found to be lightened by certain highly useful formal distinctions which have already been provided by Broad in another connection. Reference is made not only to his analysis of causation but to his analysis of motives in decisions. *E.g., mutatis mutandis,* and considering degree of intensity of emotions as well as qualities, doubtless one will find convenient recourse to be made to such distinctions as total motive *vs.* motive-components, motive-component for *vs.* motive-components against, and pure *vs.* mixed motives.[51] Some distinctions may seem to fit only questions about the relative force of different vectors in a decision—e.g., sufficient *vs.* necessary and predominant *vs.* supplementary-but-superfluous motives—but possibly these have their analogies in accounts of dominant occurrent emotions and certainly their schema is relevant in those cases in which the agent is taking up an emotional attitude and is instituting it or defending it as his authorized disposition.[52] Such deliberate endorsement is akin to the adoption of a policy.

In addition to the advantage of avoiding commitment to the substance-attribute pattern of analysis and at the same time exhibiting its naturalness in many cases, a good reason for specifying "situational" perspective is to get away from the habits of thinking in terms of disconnected series of stimuli, of isolated responses (whether instinctive or in virtue of conditioned reflexes) to stimuli. Positively one wishes to be open to the organic relatedness of the emotional processes, to their *Gestalt*-aspects and to the ways in which emotions seem to be functions of teleological activity. There is abundant evidence that these possibilities are not vacuous. In "situational" analysis, I assume that one will distinguish between: first, subjective situation; second, relevant situation as disclosed and as, in principle, discoverable through inquiry; and, third, the inclusive cosmic environment. Ostensible motives lie in the first. Broad's recourse to real motives which are not noticed by the patient requires the second.

If Broad had restricted motives to ostensible motives, if by definition motives were required to be conscious, a number of complications—although they would not have been ultimately obviated—would have been transferred to another heading. Again, if Broad had not acknowledged unmotived emotions, at least certain problems of exegesis would

---

[51] Cf. "Conscience and Conscientious Action," in *EHP*, esp. 256–262. Presumably Broad is in this connection considering "motives" as conative (which is in accord with common usage) rather than in the extended way in which he employs the term in analysis and classification of emotions.

[52] To be sure, something is called for in a situation of decision which is not required in many cases in which our emotions are a sort of running commentary on the kaleidoscopic scenes of life; to wit, speaking in the first person, I have to decide to act in some way in a situation of forced decision, even though I continue to have some emotional conflict over the matter; whereas, in my rôle as spectator, there is relative absence of exigency to integrate, resolve or decide between mixed and competing strands of feeling. However, in so far as I feel myself called upon to be consistent, to prepare myself for possible action, to possess a policy in my emotional dispositions, or in so far as others hold me responsible for my emotions, I have a problem akin to that of a decision, indeed, akin to that of making a decision on principle where antecedently conflicting principles obtain.

not have been so patent, and "real motives" could have been taken as differential stimuli, whether or not noticed by the patient. But plainly Broad both asserts real motives which may not be recognized and he asserts unmotived emotions. His statement of four or five kinds of error about motives is of intrinsic as well as instrumental interest.[53]

(1) A patient may rightly recognize that a certain believed-in property is actually the motivating property, *i.e.,* the ostensible and the real motives coincide, *but* his belief in the existence of the property may be in error. There are, as has been indicated, errors of misplacement; in the present category motivating characters themselves are instances of partial misplacement. Here one might say that the error is an ontological one and not strictly an error in inspection.

(2) A patient may mistake what the actual motivating property is, although he is correct in taking his emotion as motived. Here the ostensible and actual motives are different. No doubt this error can be compounded with other errors, such as the ontological error above, but it need not be. Broad repeatedly observes tendencies which incline men to distort their motives as well as even to fabricate them. Perhaps there are sheer accidental errors of not recognizing which of one's beliefs about characteristics of the object is more particularly stimulating one's emotions; surely not infrequently persons possess tensions not to admit to themselves or to others an actually motivating character, and in the context this may tend to the substitution of some other character as the conscious relevant character.

(3) Similar to (2) are cases in which an ostensibly motivating character is in error—but not as substituting for the actual motive, since in this case there is none. Broad holds that there are unmotived emotions, and a patient may mistakenly suppose his unmotived emotion to be motived.

(4) The reverse error is possible: taking one's emotion as unmotived when it is motived. A distinguishable species of this genus of cases is demarcated by taking those in which the patient recognizes that he has beliefs about the object but is *unconscious that* one or more of these conscious beliefs is evoking the emotion.

(5) Of the same general sort of error as (4), there is another distinguishable species, namely, those in which an *unconscious belief* is operating as crucial stimulus of the emotion. Broad's explanation is to be observed: such unconscious beliefs are beliefs which for some reason the patient fails to notice or are beliefs which exist in a dispositional form.

One wonders if, in repeated occurrences of "an" emotion, the emo-

[53] *JAAC,* 206f.

tion can, if motived, become unmotived, or, if unmotived, become motived.

Can a given lengthy occurrent emotion which is unmotived become motived? On the definition of unmotived emotion as having no motive that is "explicitly noticed," could not the unmotived emotion become motived as soon as a crucial evoking character—or evoking belief about a character—is raised to explicit notice? Yes. This usage requires that the given emotion was not motived until the explicit noting took place. Availing oneself of the distinction of ostensible *vs.* real, however, one might amend the definition and say that this act of noticing made the emotion ostensibly motived but it was really already motived. Accordingly, on this revision, conscious acts of veridical noticing and acts of mistaken noticing can render an emotion ostensibly motived but not change its status as really motived or really unmotived. There is an apparent exception when an invented motive which is an instance of genuine self-delusion happens to take on an effective stimulating rôle itself. Assuming such cases to exist, the remainder is a matter of following the definitions. Broad explicitly describes a process in which an unmotived emotion[54] generates beliefs about its object, thus becoming ostensibly motived; if the beliefs then actually heighten the subsequent occurrences of the emotion, or even sustain it, the emotion has become partly or wholly actually motived. This instances, Broad supposes, "rationalization."

Can a motived emotion through familiarity or conditioning or repression become unmotived? If explicit noticing were requisite to motivation, doubtless familiarity would tend to make "repeated" emotions become habitual and unmotived. But if explicit noticing is not required, the material question becomes how genuinely one can forget. Probably we can more easily forget what has never been in the focus of consciousness than what has. And there are psycho-analytic reasons for supposing that we make ourselves forget certain sorts of things which have been focal in consciousness; but it is also a tenet of orthodox analysis that nothing is forgotten in the sub-conscious.

I take some interest in these possible cases because of their analogy with the questions concerning the "objects" themselves, toward which I thought it sensible to say that sometimes the object emerges from what has dominantly been feeling and in other cases the intentionality almost collapses into immediacy. The phenomena here also illustrate degrees of explicitness of consciousness.

54 He cannot mean a single occurrent emotion; he must mean that the emotional disposition becomes modified so that subsequent occurrent emotions related to the same-but-modified-disposition exhibit the change asserted when compared with their early predecessors.

Certain hasty material opinions, not unconnected with methodological concerns, are now offered on the assumption that we may take "motive" as some sort of differentially significant stimulus-factor and take "ostensible motive" as differentially significant stimulus-factors noticed by the agent (but not precluding error in what is thus noticed).

If Broad were contending that in any case of a motived emotion the emotion is taken up wholly "in respect of" one character or at most a very few motivating characters, I should deem it a mistake. I should think that normally in a concrete situation there are many motives—it is arguable that one does respond to the whole situation—and that in situations which are conceived with some detail there will often be quite a few motives. A merit of recourse to motives is that this gives some opportunity for discussion, for processes of criticism, for such improvement and movement toward social agreement as piecemeal consideration and comparison may yield. A danger of this recourse is that it will probably be quite incompletely carried out, but may be treated as though it were complete; moreover, there may be some tendency to lose sight of the concrete and to deal with only the "counters" which have been abstracted. I have opined that in a healthy personality attention is normally correct in what it locates as motives, but that it tends to produce distortion by its natural oversimplifications. In highly abstracted conceptual situations, set up for the express purpose of illustrating what are normally motive-components, it is, of course, appropriate to speak of *the* motivating character. Normally, however, especially in existential situations, it would be better to speak, not of what is *the* motive, but in some such manner as this: in respect to the aspect m_1, a tendency toward feeling f_1 enters the fusion; in respect to m_2, a tendency toward f_2 enters as a component in the fusion; and so on.

One's total emotional state of mind nearly always has many motives with a plurality of major strands. Theoretically one might analyze the strands down into sub-strands, where each of the latter would be "pure," *i.e.*, would be due to one motive or to one evoking characteristic plus background conditions. But I do deem this imagined procedure to be "theoretical" in the vulgar sense. The major strands of feeling, as felt with their intentionalities and various tones and overtones, are immensely complicated. Moreover, some of the dominating strands, in so far as one would think of them as having *one* motive, exist "in respect of" a *Gestalt*. The latter is at once "one" character and something grounded in the relational structures of a number of components which may themselves also—sometimes at least—be viewed as "motives." The material for motivational analysis thus gets very complex.

I have suggested that normally what is introspectively picked as "the" motivating characteristic or as "a" motivating characteristic of an emotional strand is *a* motivating characteristic. That is to say, I do not think that when one consciously notices a motive of his own that he is very likely to be in sheer error. But I do now wish to suggest that what he notices is likely to be a gross oversimplification of the operative real stimulating situation. Unless what he selects as "the" motive is a quite complex *Gestalt,* it probably represents selectivity to the point of distortion. Background stimuli figure in the total *Gestalt* but are not explicitly noticed. It is not unlikely that, when one takes himself to be having a certain emotion toward a thing "in respect of certain qualities," he is having it in causal respect of more properties than he can name. I strongly opine that, if there is strictly any denotation for "sufficient" motives, these must be very complex—more complex than either the patient or the observer is likely to bring to explicit notice. Of course, one practically uses "sufficient" with a tacit assumption of an indefinite number of background conditions. Restricting the application to conscious and unconscious stimuli, still we do not know enough to proceed far with predications of "necessary conditions." If, further, necessary negative conditions are to be listed as portions of the requisite patterns—and absences could be said to be as important as presences in *Gestalten*—it is obvious that no listing of them can possibly approach completeness.

8. *Some Uses of Noticing Motives.*

We turn now to a few remarks about the importance and use of the distinctions of motived and unmotived and of ostensibly motived and ostensibly unmotived emotions. Of course, a discovery of a stimulus or of a complex stimulus pattern anywhere is of psychological interest; and discovery of ostensible stimuli is of psychological interest to anyone who has some confidence in, or fascination with, introspective materials. The prime connection which presumably is of concern to philosophers lies in that much more restricted range—by no means narrow —where "criticism" takes place.[55] Publicly conducted criticism requires

[55] Thus, for examples, the philosopher of jurisprudence may be interested in data in the psychology of respect for, and of conscientious modification of, legal institutions; the philosopher of religion may be interested in data in the psychology of whatever seems to differentiate religious objects, in the psychology of the "perception" of the numinous, or of the convictions of the prophet and of how he supports his authority; the philosopher of art may be concerned to know what more differentially affects connoisseurs in their appreciative evaluations of a certain art object; the philosopher of morals may be interested in the felt differentia of generically moral situations, of what within them seems to the agent to be especially relevant morally, and of how accepted relevant factors are weighed and personal differences concerning them mediated.

some mediated discriminations in order to have anything to talk about; and such factors as may be felt to be peculiarly crucial are convenient handles for processes of self-criticism.

Rôles of the discrimination of motives may be noticed both in moral experience and in moral discussion, although our reference to the former may transgress for a moment our self-imposed stricture against here saying anything about the processes of decision. Recognition of motive by an agent may lead to some alteration of his motivational complex, for recognition of motive may excite into activity other and higher order dispositions. These, in turn, may fortify the vector tendencies of the given motive or may conflict with these tendencies. The latter cases will furnish the more conspicuous instances. Thus, in moral experience, speaking of conative-emotional tendencies, Broad notes: ". . . awareness of one's beliefs about a desired object may lead to recognition of conative tendencies to which it is appealing; this may excite conative dispositions of the second order which would not otherwise have been excited; and this may make a profound difference to our final action. . . ."[56] It is plausible that a parallel statement would hold for cases that are less conspicuously conative. Quite conceivably there are analogies in the revision of one's aesthetic judgment by the excitation of higher order dispositions, which occasions might be translated a bit too formally by rendering them as "adherences to higher order criteria."

If taken alone any citing of a reason is tacitly an assertion of—or appeal to—a criterion. However, in view of the need of "criticism" of such first level claims in the light of other first level claims, it is sensible to restrict "criteria" to the products of such comparative integrative criticism. Then "criteria" are rules on a level above "motives," ideally asserting the validity or relative validity (orders of priority) of them or of clusters of them. Criteria may equally well be about "bads" and "degrees of bad" in art, morals or technology, as about "goods" and "degrees of good" (or "rights" and "degrees of obligatoriness"). Of course, criteria may be put forward with more gentleness or tentativity than these statements suggest, and I would hold that it is appropriate that they be thus put forward. Not taking criteria to be revealed or self-evident (though I have no doubt of some of them), I do not see that the evidential material for them is other than material found ultimately in first-handed feeling, but of course it is such material reviewed, gone over for "consistency" (logical and aesthetic), repeated for feelings of degree and importance, checked portion against portion for practical coherence. And, naturally, there is reference to "consequences"—e.g.,

[56] *FTET,* 28.

effects in respect to health, pleasantnesses, etc.—and to "structures"—
e.g., fulfillments of promises, payment of debts, etc.—in the complexes
of relational characters which are surveyed; but were such complexes
of relational characters envisioned as completely neutral, or adverbially
viewed with complete neutrality, there would be no moral directedness
and no moral appraisal.

Generically, when there is citation of motivating characters to justify
a response, a distinction could be drawn between cases in which the
characters are cited as having been differentially influential in stimulating a response which has already taken place and cases in which one is
trying to decide what considered response to make and hence what shall
be accepted as motivating characteristics and what shall be taken as
justifying. These latter are cases of deliberated moral decision. One is
not in them primarily examining an emotion which has taken place;
a new emotion, oriented to action, is in process, and a review or new
view of objects is undertaken in which the cognitive side of the inclusive emotion undergoes change and the component tonalities or tonality-
tendencies undergo correlative change. One may scarcely feel that tendencies to component tonality are subject to voluntary control; but one
does feel—I do—that the main outcome is one for which one is responsible, that the components have to receive evaluation in this process, that they are therein accorded kinds of authorization, suppression,
sublimation, etc. We have found it necessary here to eschew the temptations to go into theory of decision; accordingly, we simply remark that
Broad has done quite a bit elsewhere with theory of the hierarchies of
sentiments; it is quite plausible that these come into play in those experiences in which "deeper" or "higher" or more inclusive interests
overcome vivid ones. One may suppose that an agent whom Hume
would describe as having a steady preference for the calm passions is
one in whom there are strong habits of self-administration and of examination of situations. A person who is responsible in the praiseworthy
sense is one who considers whether he can continue to endorse the
component values and comparative valuations which his present decision involves.

However, it would be an obvious mistake to imply that the only way
past emotions are viewed is "factually." When they are thus viewed they
are not a part of moral discussion; they belong to history, biography,
the empirical data available to psychology, and so on. But past emotions
—and imagined ones—may be treated evaluatively. They are accordingly not taken just as events or facts of behavior, but as pieces of
conduct. They are attacked and defended. A "normative" component
is involved.

When one gives ostensibly good reasons for his response, present or past, he characteristically cites to others the motivating properties or relations and conveys the tacit assumption that his sort of response is appropriate to the situation in virtue of its possession of these characters. Some contextual background is assumed; one cannot say everything; but in the presumed context these cited aspects are supposed to be crucial in material justification of their response. If their presence and relevance are granted by the challenger, attack may turn to other characters which should have been recognized and which are put forward as calling for vectors which should have overridden the responses which were dominant; argument may continue over the relative importance of competing values, absolutely or in the context—such argument constituting disagreement over criteria. When one thus engages in "justifying" an emotion, he is doing something akin to defending a policy. The emotion under question is no longer simply something that happened to one, or an instance of a kind of emotion that happens to one. It is being endorsed by the person and certain principles are implicitly being endorsed at the same time. He is claiming for it a place in a system of dispositions which are justified as an orientation of enjoying and of meeting the world.

For purposes of simple illustration we have been speaking of the cases in which an agent takes his own responses as justified and in which, if there is any challenge, it comes from the outside. However, a patient may, of course, feel at once that he has a certain motive for an emotion within his total emotionality and that this emotion is unjustified. Presumably, then, other emotional components which he accepts as justified seem incompatible with the given emotion or he has adopted criteria which rate the emotion in the non-justified category. Morally educated agents have habits of circumspection which attempt to examine all of their more conspicuous responses. "Bad conscience" and "remorse" are too familiar to need more than allusion. Obviously in human beings much "criticism" and "challenge" is internal; Freud, I suppose, thought that there is too much of it, although at least some of it is inevitably required for civilized life.

Discussions of motive naturally arise in problems of justification where the "object-side" or "stimulus-side" is being explored. Assertions that an ostensible motivating character does not exist—that its attribution is misplaced—is one way to attack an occurrent emotion. Discussions of "appropriateness" seem to arise when the "subject-side" or "response-side" is under challenge. "Appropriateness," I assume, may be predicated of a component factor in a larger emotion or of the larger emotion itself, providing, of course, that the latter has sufficient unity.[57]

Recourse to the category of motivating characters affords one way of asking about the relation of supposedly non-ethical but right-making characteristics to ethical characteristics. (Conceivably in aesthetics there are analogous questions of the relation of beauty-making characteristics to aesthetic predicates, although I am unfamiliar with their development.)[58] A slight inconvenience may lie in a predisposition toward a contingent psychological answer. In the epistemology of morals, of course, an important issue is the locus and status of distinctively moral properties. Are moral properties literally to be ascribed to the "objective correlate" in experiences which issue in ostensible moral judgments? Are there only non-moral characteristics to serve as motives, but somehow certain of these stimulate the responses which are generically moral —the moral dimension accordingly not emerging until there is emotional response?

Along the lines of the last question, if Broad has lately sketched his own emotive theory of deliberated moral decisions and ostensible (but misleading) moral "judgments," motivating characters bear an indis-

[57] At least in preliminary ways, one may look at a given complex experience in either of two manners; either as a compound of many component emotion-tendencies in which the components are correlated with different motivating characteristics, or as one big *Gestalt*-response to one very complex motivating character which is inclusive of what are treated in the former view as a plurality. I believe that sometimes there are good reasons for preferring the latter description and approach, namely, in those cases in which the experience feels highly unified and a *Gestalt* aspect is dominant. (I include emergent *Gestalten* in novel situations where much learning may be funded; I do not confine *Gestalten* to native structures in perception or instinctive complexes in response.) However, the former way—of looking at components—sometimes seems more natural, especially when the experience is conflicting and not unified; and perhaps it always enjoys the practical advantage of facilitating piecemeal discussion, where one may have hope of modifying disagreement.

I suspect that, when "elemental" feelings of component emotions are at once highly idiosyncratic but not of marked consequence to others or to the vital interests of the agent, they are passed off with the idea of "Let us not dispute tastes." Where they seem to be of social consequences or considerably injurious to the agent, they are likely to be denoted "perverse." Most disputes, I opine, are about preferences rather than absolute differences in qualitative response to component factors. When one says this he is manifestly using the notion of components and is not thinking of the comprehensive *Gestalten* as elemental.

[58] In aesthetics, references are made to motives in quasi-perceptual language; still it is assumed that what is thus discriminated are component factors of what calls for a certain kind of complex appropriate appreciative emotion. In practice or morals, references are made to characteristics (whether perceptual or derived by inference) which are taken as calling for—other factors not altering or outweighing them— certain kinds of action, it being understood that some sorts of appropriate feeling are the springs of the required action. In moral commentary much the same sort of thing goes on, only it is recognized that any present imperatives concern taking up certain attitudes; there are no imperatives to do over the past.

pensable rôle therein. The most interesting range of cases and at the same time the class of cases about which one most easily asks the crucial questions are the instances of deliberated first-hand emotions. Before delineating the rôle of motives in them we therefore turn to "handedness" of emotions.

10. *First-hand vs./and Second-hand Emotions.*

This is such a suggestive pair of labels that it is natural for a reader at once to suppose that he knows the contrasted meanings and to proceed without due caution to make his own denotations. William James and others have used similar descriptive terms in the study of religious experiences. In fact, I shall wish—more or less in exemplification of one motif of Broad's demarcation—to supplement his distinction with an extension in the area of what are primarily perceptual emotions.

Broad's distinction is not that of emotions which are innate *vs.* acquired emotions. It is not cut out on the criterion of first-personal autonomy *vs.* social authority, although there is much correlation here. Of course, it is not the antithesis of genuine *vs.* feigned emotions. Nor for Broad is the cleavage between emotions had in novel situations and habitual emotions—although this guess is, in a childhood phrase, "warm."

What are our author's meanings? It appears (1) that Broad restricts the use of the distinction to "emotions which are conceptual on the cognitive side."[59] It appears (2) that a first-hand emotion requires the logical product of the following characteristics: (a) the patient must be "really thinking at the time of the qualities and relations" which constitute a description of the object, and (b) the patient must believe in the existence of the object.[60] It appears (3) that if one is to try to say positively what second-hand emotions are he may say something like this: emotions which are stimulated by the value-charge which certain words—heard or spoken *sotto voce*—carry for the patient, without his attending to the cognitive meaning of the words.

There are some problems of the scope of the denotations of these terms and some obscurities about their inter-relations. Does the distinction between first-hand and second-hand emotions make a dichotomous division of all emotions? Does it effect a dichotomy of the genus conceptual emotions? Or do the classes simply constitute two species out of many more? Do not the actual members of each class embody the respective differentiating characteristics in important differences of de-

59 *JAAC*, 209.   60 *Ibid.*, 210.

gree, with the consequence that a given emotion is a poor or a fair or a good exemplification of its type?

The "important distinction" between first and second-hand emotions "arises," it is said, with respect to conceptual emotions. The remark would normally be taken to mean that the two classes are two species (whether the only two, or whether two out of three or more species) of conceptual emotions, and that they have residence under no other genus. However, it is possible that the remark means that the distinction arises to importance only in the area of conceptual emotions, perhaps because non-conceptual emotions are entirely peopled by members of one of these two species, or at least that the other species is a null class. A distinction has little practical use where one side of it has no members—though observing that this is the case may be very important to theory.

That the distinction applies only in the area of conceptual emotions would be true—formally—if it is stipulated for application only here, or if being a conceptual emotion is part of the connotation of each class. That the distinction applies only in the area would be a material truth if the characteristics constituting the two connotations—defined in genuine independence of reference to conceptual emotions—are found to have exemplification only in this region.

If one strictly takes first-handedness as requiring the *holding in mind* of the qualities and relations which constitute a *definition or description* of the object, then first-hand emotions are clearly conceptual. And I should say that the definition is *not* in genuine independence of the meaning of "conceptual." It is more difficult to deal with second-handedness, for in this case—in a pure instance—the patient is "not thinking of the object or its attributes at all." I am inclined to say that there is tacit reference to the idea that the patient might well be supposed by others and himself to be thinking of them—but is this enough to bring it in the domain of conceptual emotions? A little later I will urge the suggestion that pure "second-hand emotions" are not emotions by Broad's definition, which outcome would quite take the immediate issue away from us. But I shall also say that impure second-hand emotions can still be emotions and are presumably vaguely conceptual.

One particular obscurity about the relationship of the class of first-hand emotions to the class of second-hand emotions doubtless impressed the reader at the outset: are the classes contradictory within the universe of discourse of their genus? Within the encompassing proximate genus do all emotions belong either to one class or to the other and not both? It is most doubtful that this is the case. Is it not rather that, in the dichotomous division of "first-hand" and "non-first-hand," second-hand emotions are only one species among the latter? This is pretty surely the case, as evidenced by a weaker consideration and by a stronger consideration. Are not the second-hand emotions those, and only those, which are triggered into occurrence by value-charged words? May there not be other non-first-hand emotions which are stimulated in some other way, for instance, by "background music"? The easiest illustrations seem to be of non-conceptual emotions. But there may also be conceptual non-first-hand emotions which are other than second-hand on Broad's definition.[61]

The stronger reason for denying that first-hand and second-hand emotions are contradictory classes under their genus follows; and it readily suggests conceptual emotions which are neither first-hand nor second-hand. One remembers that there are two important differentiae of first-hand emotions, the second of which is that the object is believed to exist. Heretofore, we have been leaving the second characteristic untouched while thinking of some types of possible emotion compatible with denying the first differentia. First-hand emotions (in the proximate

---

[61] I am not wedded to any particular illustration, but I think that music, to which reference has just been made, affords some possible examples and introduces some interesting topics. Whatever the difficulties over assimilating the cognitive side with the stimulus may be, I think Broad would say that normal listening to music is emotional experience; it is not just mood and it is not pure perception. The stimuli of an emotion in the case of pure music are presumably the tones and patterns of tones themselves; the stimuli of the emotion in the case of program music may be in significant degree the images which are aroused by the patterns of tones. If this be correct, the experience of program music would be the more complex experience. In view of the nature of the cognitive or stimulus side in the case of pure music, it is not conceptual, at least if one is only hearing the tones as "background." Emotions in relation to program music would afford admixtures of intuitive, perceptual and conceptual elements on the cognitive side, the last of the three being what makes the music "representative" or "program" music. Conceivable cases of non-verbal stimuli which would correspond in role to the verbal stimuli of Broad's second-hand emotions can be devised. Suppose the background music is program music which is not "listened" to but it does intrude the image of moonlight into consciousness; and this image is associated with certain emotional tones which then are excited. Is not this non-verbal but comparable in function with the charged words in second-hand emotion? Or, again, I am told that considerable oriental music is—no less than stylized dancing—designative; in a wide sense of language, this consequently exists in the medium of language; it sets scenes, it tells stories, etc. Now suppose that a person who is very familiar with all this stylized meaning is not generally attending to what he is hearing but some designative passage registers and produces the associated feeling tones. Is not this parallel?

I shall not pursue here the whole question of the complications of what "the object" is. In perceptual experience, the main object is not sensa; in music one certainly cannot exclude the stimuli; in between, so to speak, is an illustration of which Homer reminds us, where the individuals, "grieving for Patroclus in seeming," were each again grieving their own private losses—yet surely they are not unmindful of the dead Patroclus. Perhaps the apparent plurality of objects can be managed by saying that there are several associated emotions which at once manifest a high degree of fusion.

genus) can be negated by denying the second portion of the connotation without denying the first. Surely the resulting class is not null; there are emotions in which the patient is thinking of qualities and relations which constitute the description of the object without believing that the object exists. Men think of unicorns, mermaids, the perfect Presidential candidate, the "dream car of 1980," etc., without believing the objects to exist, and there are tonal accompaniments in some or all of these cases.

Summing up this far, I have given some reasons for holding the following: Broad restricts the application of first-hand and second-hand emotion to conceptual emotions; the members of the two classes are thus not taken as exhausting the higher genus of emotions, nor do they exhaust the proximate genus to which they belong, namely, the class of conceptual emotions.

Next I wish to urge that exemplification of certain characteristics used respectively in defining both sorts of emotions occurs as a matter of degree. It seems to me that one may be more or less intensively and more or less focally "really thinking" of qualities and relations of an object believed to exist. And one may be more or less not attending to the cognitive meaning of words at the same time as he is manifesting a responsiveness which constitutes illustration of their emotive meaning for him. Further, in the latter region—that of second-hand emotions—it appears that a perfect or complete case is no longer an emotion; if Broad maintains it to be an emotion it would seem to commit him at least to accepting unconscious intentionality. An emotion, by his definition, has to have an object; yet a "second-hand emotion" may be devoid of any *thought of* an object.[62] Perhaps we had better treat this as a limiting case (if Broad rejects unconscious intentionality)[63] and say that where the object vanishes we are left with a verbally triggered mood.

Even if first and second-hand emotions occur in continuous gradations, this does not affect the practical worth of the labels for dealing with the more marked instances.

Broad does not, in so far as I have noticed, assert that second-hand emotions must be less intense than their first-hand ancestors in any manner comparable with memory as decaying sense, for Hobbes, or

62 Indeed, some phrasings strictly imply that it must be devoid of any thought of the object. In describing what a second-hand emotion is he says that when one feels certain tones because of hearing or using certain emotionally charged words, one "will tend to think that one is feeling a certain emotion towards a certain object in respect of certain of its attributes, when really one is not thinking of the object or of its attributes at all." *JAAC*, 210.

63 In a sense he accepts it when he asserts unconscious motives.

reminiscent of ideas as less vivid than impressions, for Hume. Nor does he develop any law of progressive weakening of second-hand emotions. He does note that second-hand emotions are significantly powerful and that they play very great rôles in moral, political and religious life. On the quite general grounds of evidences that the psychophysical organism manifests tendencies to economize its activities, I should be prepared to expect that "repetition" would be accompanied by diminution in such aspects of emotion as represent disorganization and in the intensity of conscious tonality itself. One of Broad's examples of second-hand emotion is possibly meant in part to illustrate this point, which it very satisfactorily does. Unhappily, I deem it a very poor—because very unreliable—illustration of a second-hand emotion. Reference is made to the case of a person, bereaved for a considerable time but pumping up the feelings which, as it seems to him, he ought to have. In the example, there certainly has been decrease in intensity of feeling and in personal disorganization. Doubtless in a number of such cases second-hand emotions are induced, by the individual stimulating himself with words like "death," "loss," "tragedy." But I should think that the emotion which is "pumped up" is first-hand if it springs from definite thoughts of features of the deceased person's death and character or of features of the situation which his death leaves, which features are believed to have been or to be veridical. That in some cases any pumping needs to be done may indicate conflict in addition to any weakening through time; then the situation resembles those moral situations in which part of one's self succeeds in making one review aspects of history or actuality which another part of the self is opposed to reviewing. One may entirely lack the occurent emotion which some higher order dispositions—or image of oneself—specify as appropriate. These dispositions may lead to the securing of stimuli to evoke the emotion, or lead to disciplines to provide the needed proximate dispositions. If at any time the immediate result is feigned emotion, it does not qualify as second-hand emotion. I take it that a second-hand emotion is still supposed to be a genuine, not a faked emotion. It lacks the authenticity of fresh fully conscious personal response; its ground is unexamined but it is not hypocritical. Feigned emotion is not emotion—at least not of the kind which it purports to be.

Suppose one understands the initial motive for distinguishing first and second-hand emotions is to recognize that emotions are not always "fresh," that they may be rather habitually made to stimuli which are stale enough to be less than fully noticed. There is present the idea of the "shorting-out" of the cognitive routings—due to the economizing tendencies of the organism. Roughly the motive is an appreciation of the tendencies called "habit," but there is not just habit in the tonal responding (where, as usual, it is thought of as later or dependent) but there is habit in the cognizing, too. Indeed, it is Broad's point that there is ellipsis of the cognizing.

Taking this as the principle, I do not think that the distinction—or rather now the modified form of the distinction—need be restricted to conceptual emotions. I am ready to neglect the intuitive emotions, which, when we discussed them earlier, were noted to be somewhat on the borderline of emotions and some other sort of reaction; but, if many of them qualified as cognitions in a wide sense, I should think the amended distinction applies in degree. If there were genuine attention or concentrated awareness, reactions, although native, would be first-hand; recognition and reactions conditioned by much repetition would presumably be second-hand, in the modified sense. Among perceptual emotions there can be second-hand emotions to a significant degree. All that is required, on the amended meaning, is that the perceiver recognize (or misperceive) some fragmentary part or aspect or sign of the object, and that this token perception trigger off the emotion of the sort associated with the tacitly assumed object.

Many emotions—most, I think—are not purely intuitive or purely perceptual or purely conceptual. Two or more of these types of cognition are frequently stacked up in gross experience. If when one were perceiving he could not be thinking at the time of the qualities and relations which are partially constitutive or present in the object, then plainly on the strict interpretation of Broad's demarcation of first-handed emotions, the patient could not be having them. His emotion would not be conceptual on the cognitive side. But the facts are that when one is perceiving he can also be thinking of some of the qualities and relations of the object. On many of these occasions he will not be thinking of these qualities and relations as defining the object, but he will be taking some conscious account of some of them. It is normal in perceiving to have belief in the existence of the object. Thus with lively continuing perception—which incidentally is shot through with conceptual processes—one is having emotion which is significantly first-handed.[64] This is materially true, with little fudging of Broad's definition. When a man is in a situation or continuing situations of activity,

[64] Indeed, with these facts of actual perception in mind, the initial reaction of a reader of Broad may have been, "Of course all perceptual emotions are first-hand, for the patient is confronted with the object and its properties and is unquestionably accepting their existence." And from thence it might not be an abnormal response to construe the lack of application of the distinction of handedness to perceptual emotions as practical only, owing to there being no second-hand perceptual emotions. But this, as we have seen, would be a hasty and mistaken interpretation of Broad.

he may act on a relatively few explicit cues.[65] (I entertain the hypothesis
that he is acting on a much larger body of unconscious or dimly conscious perceptions, that the situation is not one of a number of other
sorts.) When, however, his existential situation is relatively dramatic,
rather surely his emotional field—whether very diverse or largely fused
—will have components which on the cognitive side are intuitive, perceptual and conceptual. Presuming him to have an intent to know and
to deal with the real situation, a first-hand emotion presumably ensues.
Both perceptual data and conceptual factors will be important. With
respect, however, to the shape of, and his use of, what he takes to be
given, I should like to note that there is a series of possible distinctions.
Suppose that the situation is one of conflict, and that the motivating
characteristics which make it one of conflict are highly conventional.
If the agent examines and thinks of the situation (including its consequences) in terms of the conventional characteristics and criteria, his
decision above the rival moral vectors is still first-hand. Suppose that, in a
situation which he accepts as a morally problematic one, he not only
reviews it in relation to conventional morally motivational characteristics but runs over the aspects of the situation and introduces some
further motivational characteristics as relevant. Is not this first-hand in
a higher degree, or in a compound sense? And if a person was in a situation which his society regarded as non-moral but which he came to view
as moral, finding his own morally motivating characteristics, would not
this be first-hand in a pre-eminent sense?

A value which is exemplified in second-hand emotions is the value
possessed generally by habit: efficiency or economy, freeing whatever
powers are represented under the name "concentrated attention" for
other more strategic uses. One cannot imagine what life would be like
without such efficiencies; it could not be human life or higher animal
life as we know them. This observation in no way constitutes a value
judgment restraining piecemeal examination of second-hand emotions,
or attempting to prevent their alteration. For, as a human being and
as a citizen, I deplore many of the manipulative uses made of second-
hand emotions.

The characteristic dangers of these emotions are the same as those
of habit: perpetuating what is less than the best solution in the first
place, and not being sufficiently sensitive to nuances in fresh situations.

---

[65] Possibly, with the addition of another step, Broad's usage can be brought into
relation with the above observation. It may be done in this way: the agent notes a
few accepted motivating characteristics as his cues and then pronounces *sotto voce*
the supposedly proper morally charged word which is connected thus antecedently
with the moral-making characteristics and is connected subsequently with the emotion.

Whether a given habit was originally very adequate or not, there is the persistent tendency to let what is now an inadequate habit to discharge, to run its wonted part of the show.

If the cognitive side of second-hand emotions represent funded discriminations from the past (even if these be absent from conscious attention), they contribute to what I call post-discursive sensitivities. If Broad is read as saying that the discriminations are elided into nothingness, if his second-hand emotions are pure conditioned reflexes with certain verbal stimuli, then I speak of second-hand emotions in some wider sense and view his as special limiting cases beyond the range of my reference. When an agent, hastily administering his practice, ingenuously attaches a moral label, he presumably is sensitive to some features of his situation. (If these features are always really non-moral properties themselves, then one theory of the epistemology of moral judgments is true as against certain traditional ones. Into this subject we do not here go, although we may touch it again in the next section. In mentioning features of the situation which serve as cues for the labelling I assume that we are connecting with the theory of motives, although in the case described the agent is hardly conscious at the moment of the motivating characters which he implicitly acknowledges.)

As to the philosophical value of making the distinction between first-hand and second-hand emotions, it may seem that exaggeration is easy. The prime use of the distinctions would seem to lie in social psychology. In aesthetics the utility of the distinction is only indirect.[66] However, in ethics the distinction—or one something like it—is highly useful for locating different sorts of experience.

The last observation may be supplemented by a further important point. Perhaps some types of ethical theory have been framed when their authors primarily held first-hand moral emotions before their minds. Perhaps some other types of ethical theory have had their central structural features suggested by looking at second-hand emotions. And perhaps still other theories have received their focal cue from some other experience or other phenomenon—as surely Kant was impressed by the

---

66 If toward art objects one is content to have simply emotions of acknowledgment or second-hand emotions, he has missed the point of contemplating them and they are not aesthetic objects to him. Does the art object function as aesthetic object only if it is cognized and felt as a moving first-hand experience? (Some critics seem to be able to separate the cognizing from the feeling.) One may be disposed to answer in the affirmative. However, the question of whether one can have first-hand emotions, in Broad's sense, toward a drama or novel, for instance, is complicated by the defined requirement of belief in existence. Either these emotions are flatly excluded by the second differentia of first-hand emotions or else one brackets the usual meaning of "existence" and stretches the word to cover objects in the universes of successful artistic presentation. To avoid the gymnastics of the latter alternative, one may want another category akin to Broad's first-hand emotions but distinct.

awesomeness of felt categorical obligation, and as surely many anthropo-logically oriented thinkers look primarily at the various patterns of *mores* and relatively little at the structure of the feelings of individuals. Now, as a matter of fact, I would confidently guess that proponents of perceptual intuitionism or aesthetic intuitionism have had their eyes on first-hand emotions; so, too, usually have other proponents of the moral sense and of utilitarianism, the latter group thinking more speci-fically of economic deliberation. I would guess that some emotivists have well noted certain features of second-hand emotions and have taken major cues therefrom. At this distance and in the comfortable absence of specific details, it is a plausible hypothesis that Broad's doc-trine of second-hand emotions, taught during the 1920's, lies in the ancestry of moral emotivism. The emotive meaning of ethical terms is focal in both. I mean to assert no identity of doctrine; Stevenson and others have developed a large body of analyses and auxiliary comment. As compared with what Broad says about fine examples of second-hand emotions, Stevenson is more ready to allow that ethical terms in use may carry much cognitive meaning, but, of course, it is their emotive mean-ing which makes them ethical. It would be unjust to Stevenson to imply that he overlooks first-personal deliberation; he well knows that we talk to ourselves, even if his primary interests do not direct him to such phe-nomena. Broad is calling attention to first-hand moral experience.

Among those who attempt in one way or another to do normative ethics and who survey both first and second-hand emotion, much will depend upon which of these they count on to give the more reliable cognitions upon which sound morals should operate and moral theory be built. Viewing the individual as provincial and full of idiosyncrasies, some may feel that the societal wisdom is deposited in those condition-ings which second-hand emotions embody. In what there obtains, the thought may run, the rough edges of many eccentric dispositions have been knocked off, the objective needs of society have been registered and perchance a collective mind has been operative. Probably a person occu-pying such a standpoint would choose a different pair of labels than those which have been employed here; he might refer to idiosyncratic emotional responses as against the responses following from rational moral training. In contrast with all this one detects in the very choice of labels which Broad has used the suggestion that the first-hand are the source of whatever significant content (if any) may obtain in emotions of either of these classes. It is doubtful whether Broad himself is ready to endorse the idea of normative ethics, or to enunciate moral truths. But it is a good guess that if he does acknowledge them he will expect them first to manifest themselves in first-hand emotion where—whether empirical or *a priori*—they will constitute the cognitive side of an emotion or of an emotion-component in a larger emotion.

11. *Emotion in a Trans-subjective Moral Sense Theory.*

In this last section we shall look at the rôle of emotion in a dispositional moral sense theory which in the mid-1940's Broad put forward as at least a credible viewpoint—and possibly more. The assignment of such a status marked a promotion for it at the hands of our author. I assume that his earlier cognitivism in ethics is well-known, and accordingly I am not taking space to give it any documentation. Our concern in the main will still be psychological, but as the nature of the general textual reference invites trespass into moral theory, I shall not be scrupulous about observing boundaries.

A. We shall first attempt—after making one focal citation and giving a little context—to get the main points of what emotion does in first-hand moral decision according to Broad's outline of the non-sensuous trans-subjective dispositional moral sense theory. This can be done quite briefly. The simplest interpretation which is in accord with the text will be the one which ascribes maximum rôle to emotion and a minimum rôle to cognition as this is usually understood. According to our author's definition of emotion, of course, emotions contain "cognitions" (in his unconventionally wide sense) and some of these "cognitions" have important mediating functions in moral emotions.

B. Next, we shall raise several obvious questions, and will select a couple of clusterings of a few of them for further discussion.

C. One of these clusters will center around whether Broad is or could be a cognitivist if he endorses the moral sense theory for which he has provided much defense. Some development of this will move away—perhaps in a spirit of compromise—from the most parsimonious exegesis and will involve itself in rather elastic meanings of cognition.

D. A few of the questions relating to (possible) moral qualities and to whether qualities might provide the differentia of the moral will receive the briefest treatment themselves; but some oblique reference will be made to them when I rashly offer a series of opinions which are associated in my mind with my beliefs that there are a plurality of sources of what gets deemed moral and that there are phenomenally for some people a number of moral qualities of varying shadings.

A. In "Some Reflections on Moral-Sense Theories in Ethics," which appeared in the 1944–45 *Proceedings of the Aristotelian Society* (and has been reprinted in the anthology edited by Sellars and Hospers), Broad is mainly concerned with the epistemology of moral judgments, more particularly with the analysis of deontic sentences and with the-ories of ostensible deontic cognition. Dividing theories first into Inter-jectional, Objective and Subjective, he is here, of course, primarily con-cerned with the last, which might loosely be called Psychical or Experi-ence-Theories, for moral judgments are held to be about "human experiences, certain sensations or emotions or desires." Subjective The-ories first divide into Sensational and Emotional, "according to whether moral feeling is held to be analogous to sensation . . . or whether the feeling is held to be a form of emotion . . ."[67] He throws out the first-personal or "Intra-subjective" species of Subjective Theories, leaving the Trans-subjective; and, on another cross classification, he likewise dispatches all the "Occurrent" forms of the theories, saving the "Dis-positional" forms. Meantime he rejects a moral sense view which would think of the basis of singular deontic statements as highly analogous with visual or tactual sensations—on the same grounds, I think, as he has for rejecting a naively realistic view of the alleged properties as against a dispositional view. He less definitively rejects the analogy with sensations of taste or smell, partly because no one takes a naively realistic version of these data. In fact, he utilizes in exposition the similarity of "That act is right" and "That food is nice." But it is plain that he views the Sensational forms of Moral Sense Theory as less than credible.[68] Eventually he is considering the Emotional Trans-subjective Disposi-tional Moral Sense Theory as the best candidate among all Subjective Theories. It faces three formidable obstacles. In the course of answering the third objection[69] occurs the paragraph which we must quote. The paragraph either is or, I feel, will become a classic passage. It is intro-duced as a "very tentative answer" ("based on . . . imperfect intro-spection") to the question of "What is happening when a person is said to be feeling a *first-hand* moral emotion towards an act in respect of his belief that it is right or that it is wrong?"

67 *S&H*, 365.

68 His analyses are carefully done; this is not the place to review them. In another locus he calls "ridiculous" the idea that, when (if it can) the presence of goodness is directly observed, the "process of observing it is of the nature of sense-perception or introspection." The remark occurs in Broad's comment on the paper by C. H. Waddington in the "Symposium on the Relations between Science and Ethics," *Proceedings of the Aristotelian Society*, N.S. XLII (1941–42), 100D. Of course one may employ mild language about an analogy which will deserve violent language if the analogy is turned into an identity.

69 It *seems* to be the case that "moral pro-emotion is felt towards an act in respect of the characteristic of *rightness*," etc., *S&H*, 376.

It *seems* to me that in such cases I do not first recognise or think that I recognise a quality or relation of rightness or wrongness in the act, and *then* begin
to feel a moral pro-emotion or anti-emotion towards it in respect of this
knowledge or belief. What I seem to do is to consider the act and its probable
consequences under various familiar headings. "Would it do more harm than
good? Would it be deceitful? Should I be showing ingratitude to a benefactor
if I were to do it? Would I be shifting onto another person's shoulders a
burden or a responsibility which I do not care to bear for myself?" In respect
of each of these aspects of the act and its consequences I have a tendency to
feel towards the act a certain kind of moral emotion of a certain degree of
intensity. These emotional dispositions were largely built up in me by my
parents, schoolmasters, friends and colleagues; and I know that in the main
they correspond with those of other persons of my own nation and class. It
seems to me that I call the act "right" or "wrong" in accordance with my final
moral-emotional reaction to it, after viewing it under all these various aspects,
and after trying to allow for any permanent or temporary emotional peculiarities in myself which may make my emotional reaction eccentric or unbalanced.
By the time that this has happened the features which I had distinguished
and had viewed and reacted to separately have fallen into the background
and are again fused. They are the real mediating characteristics of my moral
pro-emotion or anti-emotion; but I now use the omnibus words "right" or
"wrong" to cover them all, and say that I feel that emotion towards the act in
respect of my belief that it is right or that it is wrong.[70]

Were it not for the tenor of the article as a whole and Broad's habitudes
of spreading carefully analyzed alternatives before one, I believe the
reader would—despite the introductory sentences expressing tentativity
—take this as Broad's endorsement of the type of theory described. Moreover, the passage enjoys the special dignity of being the closing paragraph of the article. As matters stand, however, I read it as an endorsement of the possible acceptability of a type of theory which our author
had earlier rejected.

Gone is the necessity of synthetic *a priori* judgments; gone is the
necessity of objective fittingness. Presumably a form of what he had
called "Public Psychological Naturalism"[71] is credible. The supposed
necessity of moral cognitivism is also gone.

Let us incidentally note the use of some of the distinctions which have
previously been made and, more importantly, record a few structural
features found in Broad's description of his introspective results.

(1) The observations are said to pertain to first-hand emotion. The
consequent problem over what the object is may be passed over for a
moment. The emotion is not, according to our usage, as first-handed as
it might be. It is not pre-eminently first-hand, for the situation is accepted as a "moral" one and certain criteria are accepted for breaking

---

[70] *S&H*, 387f.   [71] *FTET*, 259.

it down; the finding of his own motivating characteristics is not left to the agent.

(2) The analysis uses "motives." Among the important points, however, is that moral characteristics are not motives: apparently there are no such objective characteristics to serve in this rôle, unless, to be sure, some are defined into this status as dispositional powers. Instead, certain natural facts—albeit social ones—are the differential stimuli of moral emotions.

(3) The component emotional tendencies, in respect to these different relevant—right-making and wrong-making—natural characteristics presumably correspond with W. D. Ross' old *prima facie* duties. But these parti-resultant tendencies do not embody synthetic *a priori* moral truths; they represent contingent facts of the psychical structure of the agent. The trans-subjective aspect of the theory banks upon the assumption that many human beings, at least in the same culture, are similar in these contingent dispositions, whether due to native factors or to education.

(4) Again reminiscent of Ross' pattern, there is an outcome which might be called toti-resultant after the various parti-resultant factors have been contemplated and their impact felt. Even Ross did not hold that the decision issuing from this stage was either deductive or intuited as a self-evident moral certainty.[72] Instead it was a sort of result of considering the relative stringency of the different and sometimes conflicting *prima facie* duties involved. Broad's resultant is a pro-emotion or an anti-emotion toward the contemplated act, and it misleadingly delivers itself of the ostensible judgment that the act is right or wrong. I am unclear as to whether the participating sub-emotions are supposed to be fused in the concluding emotion—I should doubt this, especially where there is marked conflict—but the considerations which were motives are spoken of as falling "into the background" and being "again fused."

Now I have made, in the outline above, the most severe interpretation. This is not proof that it is the correct interpretation, although I believe that it is. And it does not preclude the possibility that something more complex is the truth, either about Broad's intent, or about the moral realities, or both. Certain compromises might be more comforting to our mental conflicts; and I must acknowledge that there are phrasings in our author's account which make it sound more "cognitivistic" than the rendition which I have given.

B. Certain questions are rather obviously to be asked.

(1) Incidentally, what is "the object" of the emotion during such a

---

[72] *The Right and the Good* (Oxford: Clarendon Press, 1930), 30f.

deliberative process? Is it the situation as a whole? Are there several objects, at least one for each distinct motivating characteristic? Or is the object the contemplated act, and the motivating characteristics attach to it? It seems that one is primarily focussing on the candidate-act. Technically, however, there is an objection. The presiding emotion is said to be first-hand. A requirement of a first-hand emotion is that the subject believe that the object exists. An act which is being considered for possible enactment does not exist as an act. Possibly the criterion of belief in existence will be stretched here, for one is thinking of what the envisaged act would do in existence. Or possibly one says that the situation is the object.

(2) What determines for the agent what he considers as morally relevant facts? How does the conscientious man pick them out? If he does it by appeal to authority, how did they get selected and become part of the authoritative? Granting that there are social pressures which nominate certain relations to be considered as morally relevant, are there not reasons to doubt that the origin of all moral discrimination has this for its matrix?

(3) What is the nature of the "final moral-emotional reaction" to the various contemplated relevant facts which are passed in review? Is the "pro-ness" (or "anti-ness") a quality? Is it a quality of the blended resultant quality? Are "pro-ness" and "anti-ness" dimensions of a continuum running through all emotions? Are "pro-ness" and "anti-ness" primarily non-qualitative features in depth—non-surface dynamic features—of emotions? Are they non-inspectible? What distinguishes the "final moral-emotional reaction" as *moral*-emotional? Is it simply in virtue of the fact that it is toward facts which have antecedently somehow been deemed morally relevant? Then how did they get thus segregated, as in (2) above? Were they not each somewhere picked out in first-hand experience? Does the pro-emotion spoken of have any qualitative distinctiveness as against a toti-resultant pro-emotion toward something which is of first-personal interest? Does the moral anti-emotion possess a distinctive quality in comparison with anti-emotions toward consolidated threats of injury? How and why do final moral emotions issue pseudo-descriptive judgments?

(4) May there not, sometimes at least, be a toti-resultant moral quality in experience? May it be so brief, oftentimes passing at once into action, that it is hardly noticed? Perhaps cases of conflict of *prima facie* duties constitute unfavorable circumstances for its emergence, since attention is upon the relevant discursive factors. Indeed, possibly complication or conflict often makes a simple quality impossible. It is easy to see a

square "simply;" it is impossible to see a hundred-sided polygon in the simple qualitative way. One may, however, see speckled hens and many-sided polygons with phenomenal directness. May there not sometimes emerge one or other out of an indefinite number of moral qualities?

(5) It is implied by the theory—is it not?—that "right" does not name an experienced property at all, unless, indeed, it name a very compli-cated relational property on the order somewhat of the - disposition - which - I - find - my - psycho - physical - organism - takes - up - toward - the - object - under - question - when - I - feel - that - my - response - is - normal - and - hence - is - in - accord - with - what - the - response - of - standard - man - would - be. "Right" is said to be an omnibus word covering all the mediating characteristics and presumably one's reaction to them. It seems to be a deceptively discursive monument erected over the outcomes of brooded problematic situations which somehow have been classed as "moral." But is one so sure that "right" never names a phenomenal *Gestalt* quality? May such quality not occur in contem-plating single or groups of right-making characteristics, although con-sciousness—too modestly when under pressure to produce evidence and already prepared to keep its adverbial qualities separate from objective qualities—reminds itself that what it has are motivating characteristics and constellations of motivating characteristics? (Similarly for wrong and wrong-making characteristics.) An affirmative answer would equip itself with a way of sorting the morally relevant from the morally irrele-vant in first-hand emotion, would it not? And it would also be prepared sometimes to distinguish generically moral situations from other situa-tions, although of course after certain characteristics have been accepted as relevant or "moral-making" their presence provides another avenue for locating moral situations, the only method available to those who do not experience moral qualities phenomenally.

(6) Is the final resultant pro-emotion or anti-emotion supposed to be cognitive?

(7) Is the final resultant pro-emotion or anti-emotion subject to appraisal as objectively appropriate or fitting, or not?

(8) Does the description and psychological analysis provide any ade-quate account of imperatives and their imperativeness? I comment a little. If one is either exploring or endorsing the trans-subjective form of the emotional moral sense theory, one is interested in what revisions this entails for an account of the "authoritativeness" of the resultant mediated moral emotion, which seems to be selected because it is moral but which really is called moral (presumably) because it is what emerges with maximum (moral?) pro-emotion in a process which encompasses

sundry mediated moral emotions. It is perhaps superfluous again to deny that the quality of felt obligingness is adequately expressed as a felt pro-ness. The pro-ness may, so to speak, be an essential property for him who recognizes obligation, for anyone with a "moral sense," yea, for any normal human being. But qualitatively the differences are great. They are even very noticeable between different sorts of imperatives. The "oomph" toward a hypothetical imperative based on transient desire is qualitatively quite different to the "force of authority" of a felt categorical imperative. Perhaps the problem will disappear as persons become re-conditioned by the new doctrine. Meantime, possibly, Broad has examined Hägerström because of the psychological light the latter can throw upon the sense of duty.

(9) Were one to go further into problems of motivation and decision, he would want to ask other questions here. Does the resultant pro-emotion have dynamic force?—is it in effect a dominant desire, or at least if it does not include such a desire is it in normally trained persons hitched up with strong conditioned desires? May these desires sometimes be weaker than other interested desires, engender conflict, and lose? If so, may not the proposed course of action under survey produce both "a final moral-emotional reaction" and a final non-moral emotional reaction, with the two not infrequently in conflict? What are the conditions of the separated deliverance of the former—why is it not overwhelmed in the latter?

C. One of the most interesting problems which runs through a few of the preceding questions is whether—on the supposition that Broad is accepting his preferred emotional moral sense theory—our author may not still be a cognitivist. This possibility also affects the legitimacy of our first list of exegetical statements, which we ourselves described as giving the simplest and most severe interpretation. Besides, there are phrasings in the cited quotation itself and elsewhere which suggest a sort of cognitivism.

What hesitations do we feel, based on the text or the pattern, to declaring that Broad's own emotivism is non-cognitive, that it, too, is an "Interjectional Theory," although the interjection disguises itself, comes at the end of a long process of mixed thinking and private emoting, is very complex and full of collapsed mediation, is evidently highly deferential toward public opinion, and, lastly, segregates its interjections which are thus deferential from those that are felt to be private, calling the former "moral"?

First, we already noted how similar the pattern is to that of the ethics of Ross and of the earlier Broad. The process looks like a perceptual intuitionism,[73] with its first-handedness, with any maxims or presumptive tools for judging relevance coming out of such experiences, and with emotions doing the intuiting (instead of reason or sensation). Moreover, some sort of cognitivism seems to be implied by the label "moral sense."

Other phrasings might be noted. We drew attention to the appearance of the ubiquitous adjective "moral," qualifying both parti-resultant ponderings and the final toti-resultant emotional reaction. How does it appear so definitively? But we failed to lead our reader to note especially the sentence which refers to one's allowing for "any permanent or temporary emotional peculiarities in myself which may make my emotional reaction eccentric or unbalanced." Moreover, elsewhere in speaking of second-hand emotions he mentions that one can learn to react "consistently and correctly" to ethical terms.[74]

But the strongest consideration of all is the one which throws all the other citations into a somewhat different light. Whether or not his description of his introspection illustrates it, is not Broad's basic intention the examination of, and the offering of a possible defense of, a certain kind of Subjective Theory with a naturalistic analysis of moral terms (dispositional and trans-subjective) and with material truths which employ these terms? His introspective account does not really illustrate the theory, but it is a strategic part of the defense. We will all grant Broad's observation that a man may have "moral anti-emotion towards an act in respect of his belief that it is wrong" without feeling it "in respect of the beliefs that it has those characteristics which

---

[73] Broad's description of his introspection is largely compatible with someone saying: "On various undramatic occasions I assume that I know what my duty is, and from these instances I am acquainted with a feeling of duty or obligation. Now there are other occasions when—from complexity and even from apparent conflict of directives which are contained in moral maxims—I am puzzled as to what to do and consequently do not as yet feel a duty toward any particular line of action. Then I review possible actions, analyzing them and thinking of them under various aspects; usually I come to feel that one of them is my duty. I call it 'right' and feel obligation to do it." We did not believe that this was what Broad was saying, because, among other things, he explicitly observes that, so far as he can notice, he does "not first recognise . . . a quality or relation of rightness or wrongness," but that he has a "moral-emotional reaction" which leads to his calling a surveyed act "right" or "wrong."

[74] *JAAC*, 210. As I construe him, he is observing that it is possible (and normal) to learn to use the emotionally charged ethical names "consistently and correctly," and that it is possible (and normal) to learn to react "consistently and correctly" to the things or situations thus emotively named. If he asserts the latter, as I take him to be doing, it would be in ethics very important to find out the analysis of "correctly" —whether it just means "correctly" according to social usage, as it surely does in respect to the naming, or whether it may mean appropriately to the realities named in such a way as might correct extant *mores*.

he holds to be the correct analysis of 'being wrong.' "[75] Surely this is possible when one is inattentive; for persons who hold a rather unusual analysis of moral terms it probably is true of all their relatively second-hand moral emotions. But as I would myself use "first-hand emotions," it would be analytically impossible for a person to fail so far in knowing what he is doing when he was having a genuinely first-hand moral emotion. Broad senses that it looks problematic for an agent having his type of first-hand moral emotion but the possibility is not definitionally foreclosed and hence the question is one of fact. The question of fact is answered; Broad's own experience is the exhibit. In our usual interpretation of our moral experience we suppose our most distinctive moral emotions to have their tonal factors in response to our discernment of rightness and wrongness; if this view is accurate, Broad thinks it is fatal to the naturalistic analysis lying at the core of the view he is examining. Far from being accurate, it is an unwitting deception. Danger to the trans-subjective emotional moral sense theory from this quarter is removed. One remembers, however, that Broad initially expressed tentativity; I would reiterate it.

I will remark that description of the phenomenon of the final moral emotional reaction seems to be counter to our author's almost inveterate habit of putting the explicit cognition first when thinking of emotions; here, true enough, component motivating characteristics are first, but the final moral emotion has no one object first, and what is supposed by many to be its distinctively proper object does not exist.[76] If I am disposed to amend Broad's account it will be not only by repeating that in one sense the whole situation is the object and that it may be "implicitly" taken account of in ways which are not explicitly noted, but it will be also by offering the hesitant suggestion that the toti-resultant emotion sometimes—perhaps when fusion takes place, as it often fails to do—produces a quality which phenomenally qualifies integrally the materials which are falling back into the background.

I shall go on in one or more ways to say that I am a bit troubled by the difficulty of getting these two things together: in one strict sense the final emotional reaction has no distinctive moral object; in some other sense it has as its implicit object a very complex proposition apparently about how normal men in normal states would feel about the appropriateness of a contemplated act.

Recognizing that Broad is *in situ* dealing with his naturalistic trans-

---

[75] *S&H*, 386.

[76] Broad thus seems to be withdrawing from his analogue of singular moral judgment "That is nasty," for I do have some positive occurrent quality of nastiness in some experiences; the recognition in many of those cases that I am making a dispositional statement is quite secondary.

subjective dispositional theory, I will desist from foolishly attempting
to expound it as some sort of non-naturalistic intuitive theory. (By
altering at least one of the two meanings of "naturalistic," I am not
averse to trying to do this for myself.) However, his treatment is not
devoid of aspects which are suggestive of a naturalistic intuitive theory.
Nor, of course, is it devoid of aspects of describing first-personal occurrent preferring, and hence some of our own list of questions may have
seemed to forget that the main theory under our author's scrutiny is
trans-subjective and dispositional. Broad's brief introspective account
of his first-hand process of decision did not impressionistically strike
me as primarily an attempted determination of reciprocal dispositions
in classes of objects and in normal men under standard conditions. Is
the thing that saves it from being intra-subjective and occurrent in status
the fact that, besides using socially established canons in selecting
motivating characters, it is prepared to make allowances for personal
peculiarities? Why does it do this?—because balanced emotions afford
better intuitive cognitions? This is a plausible reading; but in view
of the general theory under general consideration it is probably to
be rejected. Is the reason then because such emotions provide better
samples for what one is—intellectually—engaged in determining,
namely, how hypothetical normal man in a normal state views something? If the deliberative activity is about other people and their
reactions, or about the "spirit of the laws," is it not addressing itself
to fact, and had one not better resort to sociology? But Broad's
description of his introspected processes impressed me that they were
addressed to: "What shall I do?" and not to: "How would standard man
feel?"

Under usual assumptions, we may (I think) sharpen this into a sort
of dilemma: Either the processes should be empirical and inferential
about a highly complex fact, or they are legitimately emotional in
determining one's own choice, one's own reaction, to be executed in
the as yet indeterminate future. If what is being determined is the
dispositional property of certain things (e.g., an act) for normal men,
or—otherwise put—how normal men would or will react to certain
things, then a question of fact is before one, and it is such a very complex question of fact as would require a lot of inferential processes. If,
on the other hand, one is making up his response, he does it in whatever way he does it—not devoid of reference to others, for he is a social
being—but surely neither he nor we ask him to be a mirror duplicating
others, who in turn are to duplicate others in morals, and so on.

There is, of course, the following kind of reconciling possibility.
Instead of resorting to sociology—especially because there is not time

to do so when one must act—one may try to "feel out" the answer to one's very complex question of fact which, according to the view, will be the only kind of moral truth he can have or use. This kind of moral truth cannot tell him why he should be like others or abide by the developing standards of the group—if doubt has really assailed him. (Very unlike Prichard's moral truth in its content, it is very like it in this respect.) But it provides him with a guess as to what the normal reaction would be. There are available at least two epistemological versions—one quasi-scientific and one wholly unscientific—of how the agent would secure his makeshift answer to the scientific moral question. (a) He may use himself as a sample in experimentation, and then reflexively examine what happened, making whatever corrections past experience indicates that his deviant tendencies require. Broad says nothing about this method, unless his sentence referring to allowing for one's own emotional peculiarities is to be assumed to call for this context. Poor as the sampling has to be, I label this the quasi-scientific method. (b) One may "feel out" the result without any second-level of observation or use of inductive inference—much in the way, as I imagine, a novelist or dramatist works. I would not balk at calling even the latter "cognitive," but we must be clear that it does not qualify as such according to the tacit criteria of public approved procedures.

To the question whether, if Broad accepted the best emotional moral sense theory which he sketched and defended, he would be or could be a cognitivist in ethics, the answer is: he would be a cognitivist. In view of the proffered analysis of moral terms, it is more than a little surprising that moral reflection in the life of practice is so unwitting about what it is supposed to be knowing. The complexity of the facts to be determined, according to the theory, would on popular views render the task quite formidable for the relatively immediate processes of emotion. Two gross ways in which those processes either are used or perform the task themselves have been suggested. The second especially has been given no analysis. In thus wholistically regarding emotions, it may be observed, they are not even broken down into the components of cognition and tone which characterizes Broad's general treatment.

D. It has been indicated that schematically one possible way of distinguishing the generically moral, and the positively moral against the positively immoral, is by the postulate of qualitative differences in emotional content. We cannot here examine this scheme for its defects. It does seem to be a way which is highly congruent with regarding firsthand emotion as the *fons* of what is utilized (but so poorly noted) in second-hand experience. From the presence of phenomenal moral qualities—assuming them to exist—we can determine the objects which normally stimulate them. The objective correlates need not literally possess the qualities. On any doctrine like that of secondary properties, the objective correlates are specified in relation to a standard observer, and the quality is dispositionally predicated of the correlates. Motivating characteristics are, of course, macroscopic objective correlates. Feeling of qualities can vary greatly in intensity. Indeed, for guidance of behavior, they need not in some cases be present, provided there is independent sensitivity to the objective correlates, to the actual relationships (including potential ones).

In what follows, beginning far below the level of moral experience, I will hastily set down some unargued opinions which have points of incidence upon the relations of qualitative experience with the existential involvements of the living being and his natural and social environments. If the remarks lack logical order, they enjoy, I think, a certain psychological consecutiveness. All of these dicta are tentative, and some are highly so. It is brevity only which is responsible for any tone of dogmatism.

(1) There is sometimes qualitative perception of situations. Some of these are "confirmed" in indirect ways. Existent relations are found which are focally the objective correlate of a given quality and justify it.

(2) Many cases of this sort are found which concern the relation of the human organism to the physical environment. One reasonably projects analogous qualitative experience to the higher animals other than man. Also on general evolutionary grounds one may give some little "credit" to a quality where its grounds cannot be confirmed.

(3) Some of these partially "confirmable" qualitative apprehensions, which may subsequently be differentiated into an explicit recognition of certain relationships, evidently occur in the psycho-physical human being in the medium of a social environment. Confirmation of the quality—as a valuation of the situation by the organism—is again sometimes possible, by the examination of the relations which are accepted as relevant to that quality. Of course such confirmation accepts certain contexts and criteria. Where there is evidently some question or some conflict, our habitudes of verification may extend themselves by courtesy, so to speak, but in making their declarations they protect their cognitive honor by the insertion of the proper qualifications, e.g., "Assuming the survival of the organism to be the prime good . . . ," "Taking as pre-eminent the need of the person to 'belong' to the group . . . ," or even "From the standpoint of the interests of the criminal as he understands those interests . . ."

(4) Obviously the indirect means of confirmation give out wherever the accepted context and criteria fail to obtain. Thus it gives out well

below where what are felt to be typically moral questions arise. (To us in one culture there might be no hesitation in applying it to some item with which a person is morally struggling in another culture. This is because we have no hesitation in using our criteria which cover the case and whereby, for instance, we are perfectly confident that he is struggling to overcome a "superstition." Were we more sensitive to his context we might be much less confident of the application of our criterion—but then, again, we might become even more indignant than we were.) In our own culture all the "higher" more complex values, located far from the obvious requirements of the biological base, are not—even taken singly—met by any one acceptable principle of endorsement or of test, and far less are conflicts between them provided with an accepted criterion.

(5) The tendency of the psyche to make qualities—as I rashly opine—out of what are presumably non-conscious ingatherings of features of a situation—features some of which may subsequently be stated in propositional form—goes on without the slightest inhibition from the improbability or impossibility of "confirmation."

Phenomenally some persons experience some moral qualities.

(6) The regular kind of confirmation of which we have been speaking is not available in the moral area. If some criterion or criteria are accepted, and if operational meaning can be assigned to the crucial terms then, of course, procedures of test of actions (or of maxims or of whatever is grist for the mill thus set up) can follow. If we could agree, for example, that maximum psychical health of mankind was the criterion, we should then find that we are just started on the process of filling it with empirical meaning and of securing criteria for it and for the deficiencies it would illuminate, etc., but at least there would in principle be a large working area for empirical methods. But, as everyone knows, normative ethics has a variety of conflicting norms and this situation constitutes half of its problem; there is more agreement over what is right and wrong, anyway within one culture, than over the standards whereby they are to be judged right or wrong.

Broad's trans-subjective emotional dispositional moral sense theory is thus far a part of epistemological analysis. But when, if ever, its consequences in terms of actual moral judgments are spelled out, it will be evident that it constitutes an invitation to employ a certain consolidated procedure in practice. I do not expect this kind of meta-ethical study to be brought down to the arena of morals; but, if this happens, I do not think the invitation will be widely accepted.

(7) There is, of course, a different sort of "confirmation" of ascriptions of quality and of judgments of preference. (It is available *within*

such an ethical theory as Broad was scrutinizing, and that theory might be developed to give excellent criteria for the predication of dispositions.) This kind of "confirmation" is rather typically non-scientific, although possibly it is used a little bit in science in sub-areas having to do with qualities, e.g., "Does this surface really look red?" One can look again and again, perhaps with some variation in the circumstances. One can ask others if they find the quality. Similarly with the preferring.

With the decorum which fits the area, this type of confirmation is sought in aesthetic criticism.

If Broad wishes—as I would—still to make evaluative judgments of the fittingness or appropriateness of choices, attitudes and feelings, only this sort of "confirmation" is available in the superstructure of culture. Facts of similarity of response are found. Where they are found, and where not, are empirical data. These are not to be regarded as worthless, but in the social area all predications are complicated by the large unknown role of conditioning.

(8) Whether or not one "perceives" moral qualities is of no practical import if he—call him Mr. A—uses criteria which arrive at the same outcome as others do. There would then be a presumption, however, that what are motivating characters or objective correlates of qualities in the persons who experience them are properties or relations which come relevantly under A's criteria. To those who have the qualities, A is somewhat like a blind man doing good optics. But, in this analogy, there are a great many more persons blind and color-blind in morals than in physics and there seem to be somewhat different spectral bands.

(9) Some qualities form after learning. One may opine that *Gestalt* principles are not limited in application to what is native. I think one cannot otherwise account well for the degree of training which is possible in appreciation of the fine arts.

(10) But this is, if true, a source of embarrassment—as well as a boon —to a program of trying to develop any obvious type of empirical ethics. The suspicion is always open that one makes certain data by "cooking" human nature in certain ways. In attempting the predication of qualities in more than a private way, one may have recourse—following the device of Broad and many others—to specify a "normal person" in a "normal state of mind." If education can be distinguished from propaganda, perhaps circularity can be avoided.

(11) Moral qualities do not form in difficult cases. Parti-resultant qualities may form or be already formed, but then it is their conflict which makes the situation morally problematic. If the question were: "Shall I murder my best friend at this moment in order to illustrate an existential truth?" the chances are that it would not be a difficult prob-

lem. Now I do not think that a normal person finds a moral quality dominant here; the non-moral repulsiveness of the monstrous proposal overshadows the moral odiousness, but I suppose the latter is blended in the former. Possibly some difficult novel situations do get qualified phenomenally during the process of decision, but I suspect that the quality which many of them wear until the end is "dilemmatic" or "tragic."

(12) If I were seeking to develop further the interjectional emotive theory of ethics, I would make a wider empirical survey within the phenomenal field of kinds of emotive reaction. The result might well increase the literary persuasiveness of the position. The abstract compression of various rich attitudes into blanket categories of pro-attitudes and anti-attitudes is a loss of data which reacts adversely upon the felt plausibility of the scheme. If anyone is convinced that there are phenomenally no moral qualities, let him ask himself if he supposes that the meaning and use of all such words as noble, fair, honorable, heinous, odious, etc., are wholly learned by analytic definition or by denotation of neutral structures and not in the slightest by direct method in which quality precedes noting of relational properties.

Broad has raised grave doubts about whether moral predicates (or one basic moral predicate, e.g., good) name simple non-natural properties. (And in his emotional moral sense account, he doubts whether they apply to qualities at all.) Perhaps not all his strictures apply to a complex *Gestalt* property. Such a form-quality may be non-natural if this mean "dependent" and non-natural if this mean possessing or connected with certain unique feeling tones, e.g. of obligation. It is, of course, non-natural if "natural" here refers to the orthodox senses. However, it is natural if "natural" mean normally arising from human endowment in human social context; it is possibly natural if it mean probably emergent from properties in contexts which can be studied by methods of the socio-natural sciences; it is natural if this mean compatible with a non-reductive metaphysics of naturalism. But I am troubled as to whether "morally right" is often—or, with certainty, ever—such a *Gestalt* quality. Perhaps rightness is somewhat like one of W. E. Johnson's determinables. I am sure that I experience concrete oughtness.

The later Broad is, so far as I found, rather silent on the question of how generically the moral is distinguished, unless this is effected by reference to "peculiar" qualities of feeling. For purposes of discussion, of course, it is frequently distinguished by the use of certain terms. But I assume that men do have to be sensitive in one way or another to certain distinctions before they mark them with words.

Too many things preclude a recapitulation. We have seen Broad's analysis of emotion into what have been treated as two components although they may be aspects in organic fusion. The definition was made from a generically introspective standpoint; this has not seemed happy to us, but we have noticed that Broad has not confined himself to an introspective standpoint for data or for permissible entities. His discussion is tuned to objects; this is natural in view of the facts of attention, but a focussing upon the more conspicuous objects in situations tends to obscure both the vaguer donations and the sense of situations as wholes. In contrast with popular meanings, emotions are by definition intentional. The complications over "the object," however, are in some cases formidable. Broad, we thought, tended to assign the cognitive factor in emotion a status of primacy and of temporal priority. If the cognition is supposed to be explicit, we have dissented and have asserted that there are pre-discursive cases of feeling which differentiate and yield explicit cognition. The reverse process of a "collapse into immediacy" is frequently acknowledged. Our author's notations about tendencies of moods and of censorious dispositions to fabricate and to alter objects were apt. Broad made an interesting application to the formation of emotion tones of principles found in color experience. The intrinsic interest of this was heightened by virtue of its being an analogy across the adverbial *vs.* adjective boundary, and thus contained some hints for a general theory of a spectrum of consciousness. He is well set up for recognizing the varieties of qualitied response—in addition to the dimension of pro-ness and anti-ness. Various distinctions which Broad has found to be useful in discussing emotions were surveyed and the sundry pathologies under them signalized: ontological errors of misplacement, inappropriateness in kind or intensity, and the various errors about motives. Discrimination of motives seems to be requisite to provide citation in any procedure of justification of emotions. Whether or not Broad accepts an emotional moral sense theory, he assigned, in the course of defense, a larger rôle to emotions than previously. If he accepts the proffered emotional moral sense theory, it seems to commit emotions to performing some quite complicated cognitions.

ROBERT W. BROWNING

DEPARTMENT OF PHILOSOPHY
NORTHWESTERN UNIVERSITY

THE PHILOSOPHER REPLIES

C. D. Broad

A REPLY TO MY CRITICS

I PROPOSE to consider the comments and criticisms, which have been contributed to this volume, under the following nine general headings, viz., (I) *Nature, Subdivisions, and Methods of Philosophy,* (II) *Philosophy and Religion,* (III) *Formation of Empirical Concepts,* (IV) *Substance, Process, and Causation,* (V) *Induction and Laws of Nature,* (VI) *Time in general, and Precognition in particular,* (VII) *The Psychophysical Individual,* (VIII) *Sense-perception and Matter,* and (IX) *Moral Philosophy.* I think that this covers the contents of all the contributions, except the parts of Professor Patterson's paper which are devoted to details in my exposition of McTaggart's philosophy. In some cases different parts of a single essay fall under different headings.

(I) *Nature, Subdivisions, and Methods of Philosophy*

Under this heading come the whole of Professor Körner's essay and parts of the essays by Professors Nelson and Patterson.

(A) "CRITICAL" AND "SPECULATIVE" PHILOSOPHY. I find nothing to dissent from and little to comment upon in Professor Nelson's remarks on my dealings with the branches of philosophy which in some of my later writings I distinguished under the names of "Analysis," "Synopsis," and "Synthesis." The history of English and American philosophy since 1923 has shown clearly that, when I wrote *Scientific Thought,* I greatly overestimated the certainty which could be hoped for in what I called "Critical Philosophy." It is no less true that I failed to notice the extent to which a philosopher's practice of Analysis is influenced (often unwittingly) by "metaphysical" presuppositions which, if made explicit, would fall within the province of Synopsis and of Synthesis.

Since the days when I first used the expressions "critical" and "speculative" philosophy, and alleged that an essential part of the former is "analysis of concepts," much work has been done in analysing the concept of analysis, and distinctions have been drawn which I had not recognised. Professor Körner may be said to be examining through a modern telescope a nebula which I had scanned with an old-fashioned opera-glass.

Professor Körner distinguishes two kinds of analysis, which he calls

711

"exhibition" and "replacement." Both presuppose "rules which we or others have accepted for the use of signs as concepts." We are told that a sign is made "conceptual" by being used by a person in accordance with a certain rule which he accepts, and that a person may habitually *conform* to rules which he could not formulate. The business of *exhibition*-analysis is to elicit and formulate the *de facto* rules governing the use of certain words, phrases, etc., without attempting to criticise those rules, or, if they should be unsatisfactory, to substitute others for them.

It seems to me that this does include an essential part of the business of critical philosophy, but that, unless certain restrictions are put on the terms "rule," "sign," "usage," etc., it covers much that would not commonly be included in philosophy. Surely e.g., as it stands it would include the work of a grammarian, in the strict sense of that term, and of a prosodist. What is a writer of a Greek grammar doing, except to formulate the rules which ancient Greeks unwittingly followed in using words, phrases, and sentences when speaking or writing? And what is a writer on Greek prosody doing, except to formulate the rules in accordance with which words are strung together in lines, and lines in verses, in various kinds of Greek poetry?

Professor Körner says, quite rightly, that exhibition-analysis leads to *empirical* propositions about usage. In view of this it is important to note the following fact, and neither to underestimate nor to exaggerate its importance. With nearly all general names, e.g., "body," "animal," "person," etc., the situation is as follows. There are (a) innumerable cases where hardly anyone familiar with the language would *refuse* to apply the name; (b) innumerable cases where hardly any such person would *consent* to do so; and (c) a great many marginal cases where such a person would hesitate whether to apply it or to withhold it. In the group of marginal cases various possibilities exist. It may be that many such persons would unhesitatingly consent to apply the name, that many would unhesitatingly refuse to do so, and that many would hesitate. Again, it is often possible to present, not merely one, but several different series of marginal cases of the following kind. At one end of such a series most of such persons would feel little hesitation in consenting to apply the name; at the other end most of them would feel little hesitation in refusing to do so; and there would be a more or less continuous change in this respect as one presented intermediate instances in order.

This is certainly an important fact, and neglect of it may lead to tiresome and futile controversy. But it does seem to me to have gone to the heads of some contemporary philosophers, and to have produced the impression that endless dithering about series of marginal cases is all that is required of them. What is needed is, not to stand moonstruck at a very simple fact which has been well recognised since the time of Locke (to go no further), but to proceed roughly as follows. In the first place, to compare and contrast the cases where people *unhesitatingly consent* to apply the name with those where they *unhesitatingly refuse* to do so, and to note the features common and peculiar to the first group. We thus get a set of rules for the application of the name "N" to what might be called "typical" or "indubitable" N's. Next, in the light of this, to look into the various series of marginal cases which diverge in different directions from the indubitable N's, and to note (a) what features distinguish one such series from another, and (b) the characteristic ways in which the distinguishing features of each such series vary as it diverges further and further from the indubitable N's. Thus we may hope to end with a set of rules for the application of "N" to *indubitable* N's, qualified by a set of generalisations as to typical ways in which the applicability of "N" shades off in various directions from the indubitable N's to the indubitable non-N's.

The above reflexions are not meant as a criticism on Professor Körner's remarks on exhibition-analysis. Passing now to what he calls "replacement-analysis," I find myself in general agreement with him. Certainly a person would have little motive for attempting to replace rules of usage, formulated as a result of exhibition-analysis, unless he held them to be defective in one way or another. That being granted, it is plainly desirable to make explicit the standards or requirements by which one is judging them, and the precise respects in which one thinks that they fall short. Lastly, it is important to make explicit what Professor Körner calls the "analysing relation," i.e., the kind of logical relation in which the replacing rules are supposed to stand to the rules which they are intended to replace. I have no doubt that I have often failed to fulfil these desiderata (if for no other reason, because they were not explicitly before my mind), and that the clear formulation of them by Professor Körner should help future analysts to do better in these respects.

Professor Körner says that exhibition-analysis leads to contingent propositions, and replacement-analysis to necessary ones. What he has in mind is true; but it is important to understand precisely what that is, and not to confuse it with something else.

It is true that any proposition to the effect that correct users of a language L have no hesitation in applying the name "N" when and only when the conditions $c_1 c_2 \ldots \ldots c_n$ are fulfilled, is *contingent*. And it is true that any proposition to the effect that conditions $c'_1 c'_2 \ldots \ldots c'_m$ are a replacement of conditions $c_1 c_2 \ldots \ldots c_n$, given that the analysing relation is R, is *necessarily* true or *necessarily* false. But a proposition to the effect that the conditions $c_1c_2 \ldots \ldots c_n$ are fulfilled in a given case may be either contingent or necessarily true or necessarily false. That will depend on the nature of the subject-matter. If, e.g., a particular animal fulfils (or fails to fulfil) the conditions under which an animal would unhesitatingly be called a "bird," that is a *contingent* fact about it. But, if the sum of a certain infinite series in pure mathematics fulfils (or fails to fulfil) the conditions under which a number would be un-hesitatingly called "transcendental," that is a *necessary* fact about it. If the fulfilment (or the non-fulfilment), in a particular case, of the conditions formulated in an exhibition-analysis is *contingent,* then the fulfilment (or non-fulfilment) of the conditions substituted for them is also *contingent.* And the same would hold with "necessary" written for "contingent" in both places in the previous sentence.

I pass now to Professor Körner's discussion about the nature of what I have called "speculative philosophy." In order to state clearly what I take to be the points at issue, I will begin with the notion of a *sentence in the indicative mood.* When a person utters or writes such a sentence he *prima facie* intends to assert or to deny or to offer for consideration or to put on record something which can significantly be said to be *true* or *false.* And when a person hears or reads such a sentence in a language which he understands, he expects *prima facie* to have presented for his consideration something which can significantly be said to be *true* or *false.* Every such sentence, then, serves *prima facie* to state, record, or convey *factual information* (correct or incorrect). We can sum this up by saying that every sentence in the indicative is "ostensibly informative."

Now it is plausibly alleged that certain kinds of sentences in the indicative are in this respect misleading. Those who utter them are not in fact offering or recording information (correct or incorrect), though they may think that they are doing so. They are really only expressing an emotion, issuing a command, proferring advice, or so on. And those who hear or read such sentences understandingly are not thereby receiving any information (correct or incorrect), but are being emotionally stimulated, commanded, admonished, or so on. (This does not, of course, exclude the possibility that the hearer or reader may be led, either through explicit inference or through association, from hearing or reading such a sentence to forming a more or less confident opinion about the intentions, emotions, etc., of the speaker or writer.) I will describe such indicative sentences as "non-informative." Non-informative indicatives can then be classified in accordance with the positive functions which they perform, e.g., as evocative, admonitory, and so on.

Now any treatise on speculative philosophy certainly consists of sen-

tences in the indicative, and there is no doubt that most speculative philosophers have thought that most of the indicatives which they wrote or
read in such treatises conveyed *factual information.* So one set of questions to be raised is this. Is this a complete mistake? Are *all* such indicatives really non-informative? If so, what functions do they perform (a)
for those who speak or write them, and (b) for those who hear or read
them understandingly? Again, if so, why are those functions habitually
performed by the inappropriate and misleading means of sentences in
the indicative?

Suppose that this extreme position were rejected. Suppose it were
alleged that some at least of the indicatives in treatises on speculative
philosophy really do *state propositions* (which the writers accept or reject or are uncertain about), and really do present those propositions to
the consideration of those who read such treatises understandingly.
Then two kinds of question could be raised, one logical or ontological,
and the other epistemological.

The logical or ontological question is this. Is every proposition, stated
by those indicatives in treatises on speculative philosophy which are
really informative, either *necessarily* true or *necessarily* false? Or are
they all *contingent?* Or are some of one kind, and some of the other
kind?

The epistemological question is closely connected with this. But it is
a different question, and it is important to distinguish the two. We may
introduce it as follows. If a proposition is *contingent,* the only legitimate
ground on which it can be accepted or rejected is *empirical.* If, on the
other hand, a proposition is *necessarily true,* it is theoretically possible
to have purely *a priori* grounds for accepting it; and, if it is *necessarily
false,* it is theoretically possible to have purely *a priori* grounds for rejecting it. But a proposition might in fact be *necessarily* true (if true) and
necessarily false (if false), and a person might even know that this is so,
and yet he might have nothing better than *empirical* grounds for accepting or rejecting it. (That is the case, e.g., in regard to some propositions
in the Theory of Numbers, such as Fermat's "last theorem.") So the
epistemological question is this. Supposing (i) that some at least of the
indicatives of speculative philosophy are informative, and (ii) that some
at least of them state propositions which are necessarily true or necessarily false, has any speculative philosopher produced cogent *a priori*
reasons for accepting any of the former or for rejecting any of the latter?

The above questions were certainly not all of them distinctly before
my mind when I wrote about the nature of speculative philosophy and
its relations to critical philosophy. Therefore no unambiguous answers
to them will be found in my writings or can be elicited from them. What

little I can now say on this topic is perhaps best discussed in connexion with one section of Professor Patterson's essay. For, in the summary at the end of it, he raises the general objection that I have failed to make a satisfactory case against the *a priori* deductive method in metaphysics.

B) NATURE AND METHODS OF SPECULATIVE PHILOSOPHY. I should evidently be in a much stronger position, if I held that metaphysical sentences in the indicative must from the nature of the case be non-informative. But I have never been in the least impressed by the *general* argument, from the alleged nature of significant assertion, which has been put forward to prove this. It seems to me to depend on taking a very narrow and highly arbitrary definition of "significant assertion," and then ruling out by definition those indicatives as non-informative. I suppose that one may fairly say by this time that this kind of argument is characteristic of a philosophical school which (in the words of Oscar Wilde) "has a great future behind it." It seems to me plain that those who use this argument have at the back of their minds a number of ontological and epistemological premises which constitute a part of an unformulated system of speculative philosophy. It seems to presuppose *inter alia* that there can be no *a priori* concepts, that all necessarily true propositions are analytic and all necessarily false ones are self-contradictory, and that all significant synthetic propositions are such that they can be validated or invalidated by reference to sense-perception or introspection. I am not convinced of any of these presuppositions.

That would of course leave it open to me to hold that some (or even all) of the indicatives which occur in works on speculative philosophy are *in fact* non-informative. It may well be that some of them are, but it seems to me that many of them convey to the reader propositions for consideration, for reasoned acceptance or for reasoned rejection or for suspension of judgment. Take, e.g., Leibniz's doctrine that what appears to us as an inorganic material thing, e.g., a stone, is in fact a collection of a vast number of animated organisms of a very low order; that what appears to us as an animated body is in fact a collection of minds of a lower order of intelligence related in a certain specific way to a single mind of a higher order; and that what we take to be the laws of inorganic matter are statistical regularities concerning such groups of very numerous minds of very low intelligence. I can understand these statements in outline by analogy with what I know, e.g., of a swarm of gnats appearing as a cloud, of habitual and instinctive action in men and animals, of crowd-psychology, and so on. They do not seem to me to be radically different in nature from the extremely difficult statements which theoretical physicists make about the ultra-microscopic constituents of macroscopic phenomena. They may happen to uplift, depress, or admonish the reader; but, if they should do so, that seems to me to be incidental, as contrasted with the informative function which they perform.

Certainly they cannot be tested, as scientific theories can, by deducing from them consequences as to what should be perceptible by the senses under assigned experimentally producible conditions. A metaphysical theory has to be appraised by reference to such criteria as (i) its internal consistency or inconsistency, (ii) its coherence or incoherence with certain very general principles (positive or negative) which seems self-evident to the reader, and (iii) its ability (given that it fulfils the first two conditions to the reader's satisfaction) to unify in an illuminating way a number of very general and pervasive features of the inorganic, the organic, and the psychological aspects of the world. It is evident that universal or even very general agreement can hardly be expected, in view of the fact that general principles which seem self-evident to some persons will not seem so to others even of the same period and culture, and that principles which seem self-evident to most persons of a given culture at a given period may not seem so to those of other cultures or at other periods.

Suppose we take what Professor Patterson calls the "*a priori* deductive method in philosophy" to be the attempt to infer a set of far-reaching and surprising speculative conclusions from a comparatively few premises, each of which is either found to be self-evident on reflexion or states a very general and obvious empirical fact which no-one would be likely to question. Then I am certainly not in a position to assert *a priori* that "the *a priori* method in philosophy" *must* be futile.

For here too I am in certain respects much less fortunately situated than many contemporary "anti-metaphysicians." I am not convinced that every proposition which is necessarily true must be *analytic*. And, if there be propositions which are synthetic and necessary, I see no reason why some of them should not be *self-evident* on careful inspection to most intelligent persons of appropriate training and interests. Again, it is obvious that there are very general empirical facts, e.g., that there appears to be *change* in general and *motion* in particular, which no sane person is likely to question. I am therefore not prepared to deny in principle that there might be premises available for a satisfactory system of deductive metaphysics.

Granted this, it would be idle to make the general objection that no important and surprising conclusions are likely to be deducible from a few very abstract premises. For in geometry the most beautiful and surprising consequences *have been* deduced from such premises. And in theoretical physics such extremely abstract and negative principles as the Entropy Principle, the Relativity Principle, and the Uncertainty Principle *have led* to highly interesting and unexpected results.

I am therefore reduced, as Professor Patterson says, to appealing to the alleged lack of success of deductive metaphysicians in the past. That is certainly not a very strong argument, and Professor Patterson questions even the empirical basis of it. Have Descartes, Spinoza, Leibniz, and Hegel, e.g., he asks, accomplished *nothing?*

To this I would answer as follows. They have done much to illuminate the problems which they have discussed, but I do not know of anything of importance which they have *established deductively.* Spinoza is in fact the only one of them who even claimed to do this, and I think that most of his readers would feel that what is valuable in his work is independent of, and tends to be obscured and distorted by, his deductive method of expounding it.

It does seem to me that nothing comparable to the results obtained in geometry and theoretical physics by the deductive method has in fact been achieved by that method in speculative philosophy. There seems to me to be good empirical ground for thinking it very unlikely that others will succeed where so many men of such outstanding ability through so many centuries have failed. And it may well be that a careful study of the peculiarities of the subject-matter of geometry and of theoretical physics would provide a more positive and detailed ground for scepticism as to the possibility of a system of mainly deductive speculative philosophy.

(II) *Philosophy and Religion*

From Speculative Philosophy there is a natural transition to the Philosophy of Religion. So I will consider next Professor Stace's essay.

I will begin with his remark that the really important conflict between science and religion is that the general spirit of science, as expressed in what he calls "the philosophy of naturalism," conflicts with any sort of religious view. We must either abandon naturalism or abandon religion or find some way of reconciling the two.

The "philosophy of naturalism," as I understand it, holds *inter alia* that all consciousness (and *a fortiori* personality) is completely and one-sidedly dependent on the fulfilment of certain physico-chemical, physiological, and anatomical conditions. Every particular experience depends one-sidedly on a particular occurrence in a certain brain or nervous system, and each person's dispositions, character, personality, knowledge, and skills depend one-sidedly on the particular minute structure and organisation of his brain and nervous system.

Now, on the one hand, everything to which we attach value or disvalue seems to reside in or to relate to *persons,* who experience sensations, thoughts, desires, emotions, etc., and have elaborately organised cognitive, conative, and emotional dispositions. On the other hand, the physico-chemical, physiological, and anatomical conditions of consciousness in general and of organised personality in particular seem to be highly specialised, narrowly localised in time and space, extremely delicate and unstable, and altogether at the mercy of that part of nature which is organised at a lower level of complexity.

Any such view is plainly incompatible with what most people in the West and many in the East have understood by religion. For Christians, Jews, and Mohammedans, at any rate, the following propositions, taken quite literally, are essential. (1) The specifically *moral* values and disvalues, which inhere in human persons and express themselves in their volitions, emotions, thoughts, and actions, are *not* just transitory by-products of conditions to which no kind of intrinsic value or disvalue can significantly be assigned and which cannot significantly be said to have any preference for the one over the other. On the contrary, there is in every human being an essential factor which is existentially independent of his body and is destined to endure endlessly, though it may always need to be connected with an appropriate organism of some kind in order to constitute a full personality.

(2) Again, it is held that an essential part of the total environment in which human beings live falls outside the range of sense-perception and the ken of natural science. It contains non-human spiritual beings, good and evil, who are either bodiless or embodied in organisms composed of a kind of matter with which natural science has not hitherto been concerned. This non-human and non-material environment is so organised that a human being who makes morally wrong choices and entertains morally evil thoughts, desires, and emotions during the life of his present body, will inevitably suffer after his death, not only *moral* degradation, but also unhappiness, pain, and misfortune. And a similar proposition is held to be true, *mutatis mutandis,* of those who make morally right decisions and entertain morally good thoughts, desires, and emotions.

It seems to me certain that this much is held *quite literally,* in outline, by nearly all sincere Christians and by many other religious persons. Moreover, it is not held only by simple and ignorant men, though the wisest of those who hold it are the most ready to admit that we know very little of the details and can speak of them only in metaphors and analogies drawn from our present experience. The most usual and the most intelligible analogy is that of a society of spiritual beings, with one supreme spirit in complete control of their environment and standing to them in the relation of a wise, just, and loving father or king. This is certainly an essential part of what religion means for ordinary religious persons, and of what it has meant for such men as Aquinas, Leibniz, Berkeley, Kant, James, and Ward. I can see no good reason for ignoring this, and confining the connotation of the word to what it may have meant and may still mean for Hindu philosophers and mystics of one particular school and for some few Christian and Mohammedan mystics of dubious orthodoxy.

Now there is no doubt that religion, in this sense, is in head-on collision with the philosophy of naturalism, as I have described it above. It is to religion in this sense that the results of psychical research might possibly be relevant, in view of this collision. I will now explain what this possible relevance might be.

I do not need to be told that the temporary survival of bodily death, or even the endless duration of a human personality, if it could be empirically established, would not entail theism and would be compatible with a wholly non-religious view of the world. It would, e.g., be consistent with the view that each of us will persist endlessly as a sequence of embodied persons, more or less like oneself and one's neighbours as we now are, living on earth or on other planets much as we now do. Plainly that, in itself, is completely irrelevant to religion. I am sure that I have never been under the least illusion on that point.

Where psychical research might conceivably be relevant is here. It might establish facts about human cognition and about the effects of human volition which are extremely difficult or impossible to reconcile with the epiphenomenalist view of consciousness in general and of human personality in particular. That might happen as a result of experiments and observations which have no *direct* bearing on the question of human survival of bodily death, e.g., those concerned with alleged cases of clairvoyance, of telepathy, or of telekinesis. I do not suggest that this is the *only* way to attack the philosophy of naturalism. I think that it can be shown, on purely logical and epistemological grounds, to be an incoherent doctrine based on shaky foundations. But such arguments are difficult to follow, and there is little agreement among experts as to their validity. On the other hand, the philosophy of naturalism is supported psychologically by the immense prestige which the methods of natural science now enjoy, and for many persons it could be undermined only by counter-instances established by the same methods.

Now it is undoubtedly true that there have been deeply religious men who explicitly rejected the religious ideas and beliefs which I have outlined above. I do not know enough in detail about Hindu philosophy or religion to venture to speak about it. Instead, I shall take as my example Spinoza, a man brought up in a religious and philosophical tradition with which we are all more or less familiar.

I have studied Spinoza's *Ethics* carefully, and have striven to understand it in order to explain it to my pupils. What I think I understand of the first four books is enough to convince me that he was a great and a very honest thinker, of an extremely "tough-minded" sort, and the last man in the world to indulge in edifying verbal mystifications. But, when I come to the dividing line in Book V, where he says: "It is now time for me to pass to those things which concern the duration of the mind without relation to the body," I begin to be lost. I am sure that the language used in the latter part of Book V is sincerely meant, not only to *express* a deep religious conviction, but also to *justify it rationally* to others. But I am quite unable to grasp what Spinoza has in mind when he talks of "the Third Kind of Knowledge," "human immortality," and "the intellectual love of God." And when, after the account of the human mind and the human body in the previous books, he says in Book V: *Sentimus experimurque nos aeternos esse*, I am left gasping. Either he is expressing in appropriate language an experience, of which I have never had a glimmering; or he is expressing an experience, which I have had, in language so inappropriate that I cannot recognize and identify his reference. Naturally the former alternative is much the more likely.

However that may be, the following things seem certain. Spinoza must have thought it *intelligible* to talk of a person's mind existing out of relation to his present body, at any rate as that body is known to the person himself by organic sensation and to others by external sense-perception and its elaboration by natural science. He must have held that a person's mind, out of that relation, exists *timelessly* (and therefore neither for a short time nor a long one nor sempiternally). He must have regarded this as an *essential doctrine of religion*. And he asserts explicitly that the doctrine of the unending duration of the human mind is an attempt to express its *timeless* existence in temporal terms suited to the needs and intellectual limitations of the vulgar. He argues that there can be no coherent thought answering to the phrase "unending duration." But he is no less certain that there is a clear positive idea answering to the phrase "eternity" or "timeless existence," and that it can be grasped by any intelligent person, of philosophical training and aptitude, who will take enough trouble.

I do not know whether Spinoza had mystical experiences or not. If he did, he never (so far as I am aware) mentioned the fact, and he certainly never appeals to such experiences in himself or in others.

I think he would have regarded any such appeal by a philosopher in a philosophical work as a breach of the rules of the game,—an unsportsmanlike attempt to hit his readers below (or above) the intellect.

Now to this kind of religion the results of psychical research would be irrelevant. The utmost that psychical research could do would be to produce overwhelming evidence for believing that an essential element in a person *persists after* the death of his body and *continues* to have experiences, to initiate actions, and so on. It moves in the same sphere, viz., that of succession and duration, as that in which the philosophy of naturalism moves. But, when Spinoza alleges that a person's mind has an existence independent of his body, and that that existence is eternal, he is plainly intending to assert something which falls *outside* that sphere of temporality which is common to the orthodox scientist and the psychical researcher. The difficulty is to attach a meaning to what he asserts, to understand his reasons for holding it, and to see how it can be reconciled with the kind of facts with which *both* orthodox science and psychical research are concerned.

On the far side of Spinoza comes the kind of extreme monistic mysticism which Professor Stace seems to regard as the only form of religion which an intelligent and instructed person nowadays need seriously consider. It certainly enjoys all and more than all the advantages, ascribed by Oscar Wilde to the writings of contemporary liberal theologians, of "leaving the unbeliever with nothing to disbelieve in." Evidently it would be futile for me to write at length about an experience which I have never had, and of which I learn from Professor Stace that the only significant statement which can be made is that no statement about it could possibly be significant.

I will content myself therefore with a few platitudinous comments on one typical sentence, viz., that there is for a mystic "no distinction between himself and his experience on the one hand and God on the other hand, because he and his experience are simply identical with God."

Now, if we try to get down to brass tacks, I suppose that what this comes to is roughly the following. When Mr. Chatterji, who has had a mystical experience and returned to normal consciousness, tries to recollect it and to describe it to himself and to his friend Mr. Mukerji, he notes that while having it there seemed to him to be no distinction between (i) himself and his experience, (ii) his experience and God, and (iii) himself and God. He also, we will suppose, recollects that the experience seemed to him at the time to be a clear and illuminating one, and not a confused and muzzy one, such as he has had when about to faint or to go to sleep.

Now, if I were in a position to interrogate Mr. Chatterji before he "passed out" again, I should raise the following questions. (1) When you say that there seemed at the time to be no distinction between yourself, your mystical experience, and God, do you mean that you then considered the question whether there was or was not a distinction, and that you *noticed* on inspection that there was *not?* Or do you mean only that the question of identity or difference did not present itself to you at the time, and that the experience was so absorbing that you *did not notice* that there was any distinction, and probably *would not* have done so even if there had been one?

(2) Your mystical experiences, like your other experiences, begin at certain moments, last for so long, and then cease. There are innumerable other experiences, going on simultaneously or successively in yourself or in other men or animals. If you say that *this* experience of yours is identical with God, and mean that statement to be taken literally, then God is identical with *it*. If so, God must have any characteristic that belongs to it, and so must begin when it begins, end when it ends, and be one among innumerable other items simultaneous or successive. Obviously that is not what you believe.

(3) When you speak of "identity" in this context, do you mean identity in the strict sense in which it occurs, e.g., when we say that the 49th word, reading from the left and downwards on a certain page of a certain book, is identical with the 476th word, reading from the right and upwards on the same page? Or are you using the expression only to assert and to emphasize a *specially intimate relationship* between several *diverse* entities, which are commonly but mistakenly thought to be existentially independent of each other and only externally interrelated?

(4) As regards your recollection that the experience seemed at the time to be a peculiarly clear and illuminating one, I would remind you (for what, if anything, it may be worth) that this feature has often been noted by persons in the experiences which they have had when going into or coming out of the anaesthesia produced by nitrous oxide and certain other narcotics.

Let us now leave Mr. Chatterji "alone with the Alone," and turn to some other matters which are more susceptible of rational discussion.

Professor Stace asserts, on grounds which are independent of any reference to mystical experience, that all arguments for the existence of God *must* be futile. The reason alleged is this. "Existence," as predicated of God, does not mean the same as "existence" when predicated of a particular thing, e.g., the Albert Memorial, or of a class of such things, e.g., cows. In the latter sense "to exist" means to be a part of the universe; in the former application it cannot mean that. Now arguments from "certain observed facts about the world" could prove existence only in the sense of being a part of the universe. On this I would make the following comments.

(1) The point about the ambiguity of "existence," as applied to God (or to the universe) and to finite individuals or classes of such, has not escaped the notice of such men as Aquinas, Leibniz, and Spinoza. They have explicitly insisted on it. Yet, in full consciousness of it, they have not hesitated to deploy arguments for the existence of God. This suggests that the case may not be so simple as one might think on reading Professor Stace's remarks.

(2) When Professor Stace speaks of arguments starting from "certain observed facts about the world," this seems to apply primarily to the Teleological Argument. This argues *from* certain concrete characteristics, especially in living organisms and their environment, which may be described as "internal teleology and external adaptation," *to* the existence of an intelligent designer and controller of nature. (As Professor Stace rightly points out, it is an argument *to* design, not *from* design.) Then, again, it makes use of the notion of causation, in the sense in which that occurs in ordinary life and in natural science. I think it would be generally agreed that such an argument, if valid, could establish only the existence of a certain very powerful and (in some ways) very intelligent *inhabitant* of the world, and that is *not* what the higher religions understand by "God."

(3) But it is not at all obvious that this applies to such an argument as the Cosmological Argument in its various forms. What this sets out *from* is the *contingency,* not only of each particular thing and event in nature, but also of the *whole causal network,* in which the existence of each thing and the occurrence of each event is "explained" only by reference to things which existed and events which happened before it, and in which the "explanation" is only in terms of causal laws which have no trace of necessity. It argues, from this extremely general *modal* feature of the whole order of nature, that the latter cannot be self-subsistent. And it infers from this that the whole order of nature must stand in a relation of one-sided dependence (quite different from the relation of cause-and-effect, which connects finite things and events *within* nature) to something else, whose existence is *intrinsically necessary.*

I think that this line of argument is open to serious criticism, and I have stated my objections to it in my writings. But it must be criticised on its own grounds. I am quite sure that Professor Stace's *general* objection, quoted above, to all arguments for the existence of God, is irrelevant to it.

(III) *The Formation of Empirical Concepts*

Under this heading I shall deal with a part, but not the whole, of Professor Turnbull's admirably acute and thorough paper, viz., that which is concerned with the account which I have given of what is commonly called "abstraction" and of what I call "descriptive ideas." In discussing this essay I shall not attempt to use the formidable technical terminology which Professor Turnbull deploys at the beginning of it. That is not because I have failed to understand it, or because I think it unsuitable for its purpose. It is because I am sure that all that I have to say here can be stated accurately enough in a simpler and more homely way.

(A) ABSTRACTION. This is the process by which, it is alleged, a person forms a dispositional idea of such a characteristic as *red* or *round* from perceiving with his senses objects which present themselves sensibly to him as red or as round. I must confess that I took over the account which I gave of this process very uncritically from a tradition which goes back (I suppose) through Locke to the Scholastics. I tried to state it as clearly as I could, but I did not seriously question its presuppositions. When one is forced to consider them, they do seem rather shaky. It is plain that Professor Turnbull rejects the whole traditional story and would offer a very different one in its stead. But he also claims to detect inconsistencies between certain statements *within* my exposition of the traditional theory. I shall here deal mainly with these alleged internal inconsistencies.

(1) The first point which I will consider is this. In my account of the origin of the dispositional idea of a determinate colour, e.g., *red*, I assumed that what a person compares and contrasts are *physical objects*, e.g., skeins of coloured wool, coloured crayons, the tablets of pigment in a paint-box, and so on. Much later on, when I came to deal with the analysis of sense-perception I suggested that to see a physical object consists in (i) being sensibly acquainted with ("prehending") a certain particular which sensibly presents itself as having a certain determinate colour, shape, etc., and (ii) taking it uncritically and non-inferentially as part of the surface of a *body,* with certain other parts and certain other properties which are *not* at the moment being sensibly presented to one. In this connexion I threw out (without laying much weight on it) the following suggestion about such sentences as "That body *is* red," as contrasted with "That body is *now presenting itself to my sight as* red." I thought that the propositions expressed by the former might

have to be analysed in terms of those expressed by the latter, e.g., as asserting that that body *would* present itself as red to the sight of any person with normal eyesight, if he were to view it directly under normal illumination. At any rate, I was inclined to think that it was only if such sentences were understood in some such way as this, that there would be good reasons for accepting what they state as *true* in the cases where we all do in fact do so.

Now Professor Turnbull seems to think that these latter reflexions about the analysis of sense-perception, and about the interpretation of such sentences as "That body is red," somehow *conflict with* the original account of abstraction and demand a *radical revision* of it. If he does think so, I do not agree with him. The account of abstraction is and remains in terms of colours, shapes, etc., of *bodies* as *seen*. We are all perfectly familiar with such situations as we should describe as "seeing two skeins of wool of the same shape and different colours" and as "seeing a skein of wool and a postage-stamp which are visibly alike in colour and unlike in shape." According as there are various suggested analyses of "seeing a body as of such and such a shape and of such and such a colour," there will be as many different *analyses* of the process of comparing and contrasting seen bodies in respect of the colours and shapes which they present to sight. But the process is in any case just the one which I have indicated, and which I am sure that anyone can recognize from my description.

(2) I pass now to a much more radical criticism. If I understand him aright, Professor Turnbull holds that my whole account of abstracting (no matter what analysis, if any, be given of sense-perception) is *logically circular*. The reason alleged is that to see a body as, e.g., red, presupposes that the person who has that experience already has the dispositional idea of *red*. Professor Turnbull does not argue this point, he seems to find it obvious.

Now it is not in the least obvious to me. Suppose that a young child (or possibly a cat or a dog) with normal eyesight looks in daylight at a body, such as a ripe tomato, which Professor Turnbull and I (who have acquired the dispositional idea of *red* and the use of the word "red") would describe as red. Then I assume that the percipient would have a visual experience which differs in a characteristic way from the one which he would have if he were to look, in similar circumstances, at another thing, similar to it in shape and size, such as an unripe tomato, which Professor Turnbull and I (who have acquired the dispositional idea of *green* and the use of the word "green") would describe as green.

All that my account of abstraction presupposes is that there are *in fact* such characteristic unlikenesses and such characteristic likenesses between certain visual perceptual experiences of young children. Obviously a percipient could not *describe* these differences as "seeing this as red and seeing that as green," and he could not *understand* such descriptions, unless and until he had acquired the dispositional ideas of *red* and of *green* and the proper use of the words "red" and "green." But that is no reason why he should not have experiences which *in fact* differ in the ways which *we* so describe, nor is it any reason why he should not come to *recognise* that fact about his experiences.

(3) Professor Turnbull raises the question: What do I suppose to be *innate* in reference to the dispositional ideas of *red,* of *blue,* and so on? I suppose that, in order to be able to acquire the idea of *red,* the idea of *blue,* and so on, one must have the innate capacity to have visual experiences which in fact differ in all those characteristic ways which we come to describe as "seeing a thing as red," "seeing a thing as blue," and so on. Since it is logically possible (and also causally possible, as the facts of "colour-blindness" show) to have some of these capacities without the others, one must presumably postulate a number of logically (and to some extent causally) independent innate colour-sensation capacities. Given these, I should have thought that one and the same general innate capacity to notice, compare, contrast, and abstract would be involved in regard to each particular colour-likeness and colour-unlikeness experienced. However that may be, I do not think that any valid objection can be made to the traditional doctrine of abstraction, on the ground that it may need to postulate a very large number of innate capacities. Since *some* have to be postulated by everyone, the *precise number* required by a particular theory seems to be a minor matter.

(4) The questions so far considered might be called "psychological" or "epistemological." But Professor Turnbull also raises a question which might be called "ontological," viz: *What* is supposed to be abstracted from *what?*

I fear that I cannot offer much positive information on this point. What is supposed to be *abstracted* is, of course, a quality or a relational property or a relation. What it is supposed to be *abstracted from* is a particular which sensibly presents itself as qualified by that quality or relational property, or a set of particulars which sensibly present themselves as inter-related by that relation.

Obviously all expressions which suggest that a particular stands to a characteristic which characterises it as a whole stands to a part of it, and that abstraction is analogous to the physical separation of a part from a whole, are hopelessly misleading. When the idea of *red* has been abstracted from a number of red particulars, they have not thereby lost their redness, as if abstraction were a process of leaching or bleaching! What has happened is that a person has acquired the ability to *think of* a characteristic, which did (and, for all that concerns the process of abstraction, may still) characterise those particulars, without needing at the time to *perceive* those or any other particulars as characterised by it. In some sense it is certain that this phrase describes something with which we are all perfectly familiar. The difficulty is to give a satisfactory analysis of this state of affairs. I am quite willing to believe that the traditional account of abstraction fails to do this, and that it may tempt one to ask silly questions or may call up absurd associations. I find little difficulty myself in resisting the temptations and ignoring the associations.

(5) This leads on to a fundamental objection raised by Professor Turnbull. I said that, when a person has acquired the dispositional idea of, e.g., *red,* he has *ipso facto* acquired the ability to "contemplate" the characteristic *red* without needing at the time to be acquainted, either in sense-perception or in imagery, with a particular which presents itself as red to him. And I said that a person is having an occurrent idea of, e.g., *red,* whenever he is in fact "contemplating" the characteristic *red.*

Now some of Professor Turnbull's comments on this do seem to me to be mainly verbal. He shows quite conclusively that the experience described as "contemplating the characteristic *red*" is extremely unlike various other experiences which are commonly and more literally described as "contemplating so-and-so." That in itself would show only that the name "contemplating" (which, like *all* names applied to intellectual operations, is used metaphorically) is not a happy one, and is more likely to mislead than to illuminate.

But behind this verbal skirmishing there is an attack which I regard as serious, and to which I have no satisfactory defence. The point may be put as follows. I have been inclined uncritically to regard the experience of thinking of a characteristic (e.g., of *red*), when one is not being presented either sensibly or in imagery with anything that presents itself as red, as analogous to *being acquainted with a particular.* I have spoken as if the only difference were on the side of the *object,* viz., in one case a particular and in the other a universal. I have in fact been still more specific, for I have undoubtedly tended to regard the experience as analogous to that acquaintance with a particular which is an essential factor in *seeing* a body or such a physical event as a flash of lightning. Moreover, I have tended to think of the process of becoming aware of a *necessary connexion or disconnexion* between two characteristics, e.g., between equilateral and equiangular triangularity, as analogous to prehending two coloured particulars and noting, e.g., that the red one is *adjoined to* the blue one.

The use of language drawn from visual perception evidently comes naturally to speakers of Indo-European languages. (I do not know whether it extends beyond them.) We all talk of "seeing" or "failing to see" a logical connexion. If it be a bad habit, it is one that we have inherited from our prehistoric ancestors; for the Latin *video* and the English *wit* (with its kith and kin *wissen* in German, *veta* in Swedish, *witan* in Anglo-Saxon, etc.) have a common root, which means "to see." Nevertheless, when one is made aware of the habit and begins to reflect on what one has been doing, the analogy suggested by the verbal expressions is found to be faint in the extreme. I am now fully aware of the fact that the experience of thinking of a characteristic, in the absence of any perceived or imaged instance of it, is and must be utterly unlike the experience of seeing in the literal sense. I am sure that, through applying the language of visual perception to intellectual operations, I have often been led unwittingly through its associations to make unjustifiable assertions about them. The driving home of this point is for me the main positive outcome of Professor Turnbull's criticisms.

(6) As regards the relation between acquiring a dispositional idea, e.g., that of *red,* and acquiring the power to use and understand correctly the corresponding word, e.g., "red," all that I have to say is this. I take it that Professor Turnbull's view as to the correct analysis of the notion of having a dispositional idea of *red* is such that it would be *logically* impossible either (i) to acquire the dispositional idea without acquiring the corresponding verbal ability, or (ii) to acquire the latter without the former.

Now I certainly gave an account of the acquirement of the dispositional idea which made no mention of the acquirement of the corresponding verbal ability. So it may fairly be concluded that I held that the acquirement of the former is *logically* independent of the acquirement of the latter. It cannot fairly be concluded that I held it to be *causally* possible for a human being to acquire the dispositional idea without acquiring the corresponding verbal ability. Still less could it fairly be concluded that I held that there are any known instances of a human being acquiring the former without acquiring the latter. I should think it most unlikely that there have been or will be. And I am inclined to think (though without any strong conviction) that it may be causally impossible that there should be such a case.

(B) "DESCRIPTIVE IDEAS." I developed this notion in reference to a question which Hume raises in Sect. I of Part I of Book I of his *Treatise of Human Nature.* Suppose that Jones has never seen anything which presented to him any shade of red between the two shades s_1 and s_2. Suppose he has seen things which presented to him the shade s_1, and has seen things which presented to him the shade s_2, and has formed what I called an "intuitive idea" of those shades. Then I alleged that the sentence: "Jones is thinking of the *shade of red* between s_1 and s_2" means what is meant by the sentence: "Jones is thinking of the *proposition* that there is one and only one shade of red between s_1 and s_2." Professor Turnbull objects to this, on the ground that to think of a *shade of colour* cannot be the same as to think of a *proposition.*

That certainly seems very plausible at first sight, since a shade of colour and a proposition are obviously entities of two entirely different types. Nevertheless, I do not find the objection conclusive on reflexion. Remember that there may in fact be *no* shade between s_1 and s_2 (for the series of possible shades may be discontinuous, and these may be immediate successors in the series), or, on the other hand, that there may be *more than one;* and yet that the fulfilment of either of those possibilities would be quite compatible with Jones having an experience correctly describable as "thinking of *the* shade between s_1 and s_2." In view of this, is it not somewhat naive to argue, from the premiss that a shade of colour is not a proposition, to the conclusion that "Jones is thinking of the shade of colour between the shades s_1 and s_2" *cannot* mean what is meant by "Jones is thinking of such and such a proposition"?

I would make a similar rejoinder *mutatis mutandis* to Professor Turnbull's in principle similar objection to my account of such experiences as would be described by saying, e.g., "Jones is thinking of a fire-breathing serpent."

But I agree that his hypothetical example shows that a case is conceivable where an *idea* which would be simple, according to my criterion, would have as its *ideatum* a characteristic which could quite properly be called "complex." I would say that, when a person has an idea which is simple, in accordance with my criterion, he has *no positive reason to think* that its *ideatum* is complex, in the sense illustrated in Professor Turnbull's example. But a person in that position ought always to be ready to admit the possibility that the *ideatum may* be complex, in that sense.

(IV) *Substance, Process, and Causation*

I shall be concerned in this Section with parts of Professor Blanshard's and of Professor Patterson's essays and with the whole of Professor L. J. Russell's.

(A) SUBSTANCE. I propose to open the discussion by distinguishing between an "empirical substance" and "substance in the metaphysical sense."

There is no difficulty in giving clear instances and clear counter-instances of *empirical* substances. They include such existents as would commonly be described as "things" or "plants" or "animals" or "persons." A stone, an oak-tree, a pig, and a man are instances which everyone would admit. On the other hand, I suppose that everyone would decline to describe as an empirical substance either (a) a flash of lightning or a twinge of toothache, or (b) such a localised and dated occurrence of redness and hotness as exists when a poker has been held in the fire for a time and is withdrawn. The last mentioned would be described as a temporary "state of" a certain thing, viz., the poker, or as a more or less prolonged "phase in the history of" that thing. A flash of lightning seems to be very much like it in its intrinsic nature, but there is no very obvious empirical substance of which a flash of lightning or a peal of thunder could be said to be a "state." I will class together such existents as clearly fall under either (a) or (b) under the technical name of "empirical occurrents."

By comparing such existents as would unhesitatingly be described as "things" or "plants" or "animals" or "persons," and by contrasting them with such existents as flashes of lightning, twinges of toothache, etc., we could discover a set of properties which might be described as together characteristic of a *typical* empirical substance. In a similar way we could discover a set of properties which might be described as together characteristic of a *typical* empirical continuant. We must not assume, however, that every existent will fall neatly into one or other of the two classes thus demarcated. There are marginal cases, e.g., a whirlpool, which have some features of the one and some of the other, and not all the features of either. Again, there may be existents which do not answer very well to *either* description. What is one to say, e.g., of a man's *mind*, as distinct from his *body* (which is a typical living thing of the animal kind), and from the *man himself* (who is a typical person)?

Now the notion of substance in the *metaphysical* sense arises when one begins to philosophise about typical substances in the *empirical* sense. One feature of any typical empirical substance is the specially close unity between a number of dissimilar *contemporary* occurrents, so that they together constitute a single total state of that thing or plant or animal or person. Another feature is the specially close unity between certain *successive* total states, so that they together constitute the *history* of that empirical substance, with various overlapping subordinate strands (monotonous or variegated) within it. A third feature is the presence of *dispositional properties,* some invariant and others variable in accordance with dispositional properties of "higher order." (An example of the former would be mass, and of the latter magnetisation, in the case of a bit of iron.)

The notion of a substance in the *metaphysical* sense is an attempt to account for these features of substances in the *empirical* sense. It involves the notion of a peculiar existent, other than the various empirical occurrents which are counted as states of an empirical substance. This is held to be utterly different in kind from each of the latter severally, and from the complex whole composed of them all collectively in their mutual relations. Let us call such a supposed existent a "substratum."

For each empirical substance there is supposed to be *one and only one* substratum, and for each *different* empirical substance a *different* substratum. The substratum corresponding to a given empirical substance is supposed (i) to unify various contemporary empirical occurrents into a single total state of that empirical substance, (ii) to unify successive total states of it into the total history of it; and (iii) to carry its dispositional properties. In order to perform the first function a substratum is supposed to be completely *unvariegated* at any given moment, as against the many and various simultaneous empirical occurrents which it unifies. In order to perform the second function it is supposed to be completely *invariant* through lapse of time (either by enduring without variation or by existing timelessly), as against the many and various successive total states. The substratum corresponding to a given empirical substance is supposed to stand to each empirical occurrent which counts as a state of that substance in an asymmetrical dyadic relation of a unique kind. This is called by the metaphorical name "supporting." The converse of it is called by the equally metaphorical name "inhering."

Now I think that the word "substance," in the metaphysical sense, has been used in two different ways by philosophers. Sometimes it denotes a *substratum,* considered *apart from* the empirical occurrents which inhere in it and constitute the states (contemporary or successive) of an empirical substance. At other times it denotes the *complex whole,* consisting of a substratum *together with* the empirical occurrents which inhere in it, considered as organised by the relation of inherence. For anyone who accepts the theory and uses his terms in the *former* way, a substance in the metaphysical sense is *one constituent,* of a unique kind, in a substance in the empirical sense. For one who uses his terms in the *latter* way, "substance in the empirical sense" and "substance in the metaphysical sense" coincide in *extension.* Any empirical substance is so constituted as to be a substance in the metaphysical sense, i.e., a

unified whole, consisting of a substratum and the occurrents which inhere in it, organised by this relation of inherence.

Now so far as concerns the application of this metaphysical theory to
such empirical substances as stones, trees, pigs, etc., I should agree with
what I take to be Professor Blanshard's view of it. The theory is hardly
worth discussing in that connexion. And that is because there is nothing
to be said about the alleged substratum except either (i) to reiterate the
properties which constitute the definition of the term "substratum," or
(ii) to talk about the *particular* occurrents and the *particular* dispositional properties which belong either (a) to the substratum of a *particular* empirical substance (e.g., Bucephalus), or (b) to the substrata of
all members of a *species* of empirical substances (e.g., horses). As regards
(i), it is true that you can say of a substratum that it "supports" the
states, qualities, and dispositions of an empirical substance, and thus
provides them with their characteristic unity at each moment and
through successive moments. But does this really tell us anything? As
regards (ii), the reference to substrata seems to be idle. Nothing is lost
if we talk simply of particular empirical substances and species of empirical substance, and drop all mention of their alleged substrata. So
far I agree with Professor Blanshard's criticisms on what I have written.

We must note, however, that the notion of a *particular* in the empirical sense is wider than that of a substance in that sense; for it covers
both empirical substances and empirical occurrents and some existents
which we might hesitate to classify as either, e.g., a stone, a flash of
lightning, and a whirlpool. Now it might be asked whether we are not
brought back to the notion of something like a substratum when we
reflect on the nature of empirical occurrents. Certainly we have to distinguish in the case of any empirical occurrent (e.g., a flash of lightning)
the following two aspects. One of them is the completely determinate,
but none the less *universal,* characteristics, of which it is an instantiation
or manifestation, e.g., a certain absolutely determinate shade of blue-
ness, and a certain absolutely determinate shape, extension, and duration. The other is the particularity of *this* instantiation of those absolutely determinate universals, as contrasted with *other* actual or
possible instantiations of precisely the same determinate universals,
either simultaneously at other locations or successively at the same location with an interval of time between.

Now there certainly is a temptation to deal with these two essential
and correlated aspects of any empirical occurrent in somewhat the way
in which the substratum-theory treats empirical substances. An em-
perical occurrent is then thought of in one or other of the two following ways. (i) As consisting of (a) a short-lived substratum, in which cer-

tain determinate qualities inhere so long as it lasts, and which stands while it lasts in determinate spatial relations to other such substrata which are contemporary with it; and (b) the determinate but universal qualities which inhere in it. (The name "occurrent particular," in the *metaphysical* sense, might then be given either to such a short-lived substratum considered in *abstraction from* the qualities which inhere in it; or to the empirical occurrent, considered as consisting of such a substratum *together with* the qualities which it "supports" and thus unifies.) (ii) The other alternative is to take seriously the existence of Absolute Space, as a kind of single persistent substratum, and to think of any empirical occurrent as a region of Absolute Space, of determinate shape, size, and location, pervaded and thus marked out from the rest by certain determinate qualities for a certain period from a certain date.

I know that all that I have been saying about empirical occurrents must be as familiar to Professor Blanshard as it is to me; and I find the two alternatives, which I have tried to formulate, as unilluminating as he no doubt does. But I have nothing positive of my own to offer, and I must content myself with the following platitudes.

(1) It is not worth while to get rid of substrata in connexion with empirical *substances,* if they have to be re-introduced in connexion with empirical *occurrents.*

(2) The alternative which presupposes Absolute Space, as a kind of *materia prima* for all empirical occurrents, seems unfitted to deal with *mental* occurrents. Can one plausibly (or even intelligibly) allege that, e.g., an experience of anticipating with apprehension a forthcoming visit to one's dentist consists of a certain region of Absolute Space qualified for a certain period by apprehensiveness? The late Professor Alexander was capable of saying such things, but the stomachs of most of us are not strong enough to swallow and digest them.

(3) In the case of those empirical substances which are *persons,* we cannot perhaps dismiss the substratum theory so cavalierly as in the case of non-living bodies and plants and non-rational animals. To be a person involves being aware of one's own *unity,* as contrasted with one's various contemporary experiences, and being aware of one's own *identity* throughout the sequence of one's successive experiences. Now it has been argued that this is unintelligible except on the hypothesis of a Pure Ego (which would seem to be a substratum of a very special kind), and on the hypothesis that each person is acquainted with his own Pure Ego as well as with his own experiences. In that case he would presumably be intuitively aware of the relation of "supporting," in which the former stands to the latter. And, having acquired the notion of that relation in this way, he might proceed to apply it (justifiably or unjusti-

fiably) to empirical substances other than persons, e.g., to animals, plants, stones, etc. I do not say that I find these contentions convincing. But no account of the unity of a person, with which I am acquainted, seems to me very convincing. So I think that they deserve to be taken seriously, and to be met on their own ground and not just waived aside under the pretext of the *general* futility of the notion of a substratum. I do not suppose that Professor Blanshard would seriously disagree with this.

(B) THING AND PROCESS. Under this heading I shall be concerned mainly with one part of Professor Russell's paper. But before doing so I will comment very briefly on some remarks by Professor Patterson on this topic.

Professor Patterson says that the phrase "absolute process" conveys nothing intelligible to him. In so far as that is the case, it is not worth while to argue with him about it. But he proceeds to develop some consequences which he thinks would follow from certain statements of mine about processes. I strongly suspect that there is a misunderstanding here, and I will try to clear it up.

Professor Patterson ascribes to me the opinion that a process is always composed of shorter successive phases which *partially overlap*. The consequences which he develops seem to be derived from this alleged partial overlapping of successive phases.

Now, so far as I am aware, I spoke of partial overlapping *only* in reference to the doctrine of the Specious Present. I thought that the combination of discreteness and continuity, which seems to be involved in the facts (i) that what is speciously present to a person at any moment stretches back for a short period from that moment, with the degree of presentedness tailing off from the later to the earlier extremity of it, and (ii) that nevertheless his experience does not come in successive "jerks" or "pulses;" could best be represented as follows. I supposed that the short slice which is speciously present to him at any moment t, and the short slice which is speciously present to him at a later moment t', *overlap* to some extent, if and only if t' be near enough to t; and that the *nearer* t' is to t the *more* does the slice speciously present to him at t' overlap that which was speciously present to him at t. It will be evident therefore that my talk of partial overlapping occurs wholly in a psychological or epistemological context, viz., in reference to the contents *speciously present to a person* at successive instants in his experience. It has nothing to do with the successive phases of a process as such. I have always taken for granted that any process of finite duration can be regarded as composed of, or divisible into, a sequence of successive shorter phases, each adjoined to its immediate predecessor and its immediate successor without gaps and without overlaps. If a process be completely uniform (e.g., an invariant whistling noise), or if it vary continuously (e.g., a whistling noise changing continuously in pitch), there is indeed no *natural* division into such a sequence of adjoined successive phases, each of finite duration. But there is also no question here of partially overlapping successive phases. So it seems to me that the difficulties raised by Professor Patterson, on the assumption that I hold that any process must consist of a sequence of *partially overlapping* phases, do not arise for me.

I turn now to Professor Russell's essay. This seems to me to give in every instance an extremely fair and adequate summary of what I have written in my *Examination of McTaggart's Philosophy* on the present subject. I will therefore confine myself to a few reflexions which I have been led to make on re-reading those sections in the light of his comments.

(1) *The beginning-to-exist and ceasing-to-exist of a Thing.* I said that I found no particular difficulty in the notions of *beginning-to-exist* and *ceasing-to-exist*, when applied to a thing which is admittedly composed of other things, which enter at a certain time into certain characteristic intimate inter-relations, remain in them for a period, and then gradually or suddenly cease to be inter-related in that particular intimate way. A typical example is provided by an artificial thing, such as a table or a clock. The account would cover also such natural things as, e.g., a crystal of rock-salt. It would need to be considerably elaborated and modified to deal with the case of a living organism, such as an oak-tree or a cat; but I do not think that any fundamental change of principle would be required.

I said, on the other hand, that I found it difficult to make intelligible to myself the notion of a *simple* thing beginning or ceasing to exist. For that purpose I meant by a "simple thing" one that does *not* consist of other things of various kinds inter-related in a characteristic intimate way for a longer or shorter period.

It seems to me now that this needs more careful consideration. Let us confine our attention to *material* things, in a fairly wide sense. We ought, I now think, to begin by distinguishing the following two cases, viz., (i) a thing which is extended but *continuous* and *completely homogeneous,* and (ii) a thing which is supposed to be *literally punctiform,* having position but no extension. As examples of (i) we might take (a) a drop of pure water, as it would be if it were just as it appears and if we ignore all chemical theories about its composition, and (b) an old-fashioned "billiard-ball" atom. As an example of (ii) we can take an atom as it would be on Boscovich's theory.

Now anything that is extended is, in a sense, composite, even if it be completely continuous and homogeneous. It is therefore *in principle* capable of ceasing to exist through the separation of smaller extended parts (all qualitatively exactly like itself and like each other), which were formerly adjoined so that their volumes together exactly made up its volume. It is also *in principle* capable of coming into existence through the coalescence of such things of the same kind, which were formerly separated. No doubt the old-fashioned "billiard-ball" atom was held to be "indivisible." But that was a contingent physical fact about it, or simply a matter of definition.

I think that a difficulty might still be felt about the notion of a completely continuous homogeneous extended thing breaking up *spontaneously* into parts. For it would, so to speak, have no "natural joints." If it is to break up, it must do so in a certain definite way. And, if it is to break up *spontaneously*, it is difficult to see why it should do so in any one rather than in any other of the innumerable ways which are geometrically possible. But, if it were to break up as a result of *external forces*, the configuration of these would no doubt determine the particular way in which it would do so.

Moreover, it seems to me that one could also conceive of another manner in which such a thing could cease to exist or come into existence. This would be by something analogous to *evaporation* or *condensation,* as those processes appear at the level of unsophisticated common-sense, and not as a person familiar with molecular theories would regard them. What I have in mind is this. A billiard-ball atom, e.g., might gradually become smaller and smaller without limit through the literal *annihilation* of one layer after another from circumference to centre, and not through a mere *change of state* without annihilation of stuff as when water changes gradually from the liquid to the gaseous state. Similarly, one could imagine such a thing coming into existence. A billiard-ball atom, e.g., might gradually grow from nothing to its limiting size through the literal *generation* of one layer after another from centre to circumference, and not through a mere *change of state* without generation of stuff as when water changes gradually from the gaseous to the liquid state.

It might be remarked, however, that reflective persons have *not* rested content with the *prima facie* appearances in the case of evaporation and condensation or in that of chemical generation and destruction. This might suggest that there *is* some intellectual difficulty in the notions of the literal annihilation or generation of a homogeneous continuous extended thing. Against this it might be said that the sophisticated interpretation (in terms, e.g., of the physical theory of molecules and the chemical theory of atoms) synthesises a large number of very pervasive facts, which reveal themselves only at a fairly advanced stage of observation and experiment, and that it is *these facts* which originally suggested it and are the only evidence for it. Yet, on the other hand, it should be noted that atomic theories were put forward long before these facts were known or suspected. So one may be inclined to think that they were motivated by difficulties felt in the notions of the literal annihilation or generation of a homogeneous continuous extended thing.

However that may be, I conclude that I must greatly tone down my remarks about the *a priori* objection to the coming-into-existence or the ceasing-to-exist of a simple thing, when "simple" is taken to include as one possibility being extended but completely continuous and homogeneous.

I pass therefore to the case of a thing which is "simple," in the sense of being literally punctiform, e.g., a Boscovichian atom. Obviously it could not come into existence *either* by the coalescence of pre-existing smaller things of the same kind, which were formerly separated, *or* by gradual generation of fresh layers about a centre. Nor could it cease to exist by the converse of either of those processes. Now, in order to count as a "thing," such an existent would have to have *some* dispositional properties. It would be possible to distinguish, at any rate *verbally*, between the following two cases, viz., (i) beginning to exist at t, and (ii) having existed before t with nothing but unactualised dispositions, and some or all of these being actualised for the first time at t. One could also distinguish, *verbally* at any rate, between ceasing to exist at t, on the one hand, and, on the other hand, continuing to exist after t with nothing but unactualised dispositions which will never again be actualised. By taking the second alternative in each case, one could always avoid admitting in so many words the generation or annihilation of a punctiform thing. But the distinction is certainly very thin, and anyone who is inclined towards a "verificationist" account of meaning, might fairly describe it as insignificant.

I would sum up about things which are simple, in the sense of punctiform, as follows. Since such a thing could not begin or cease to exist in any of the ways which are familiar and seem intelligible to us, there is a temptation (into which I have tended to fall) to say that it is unintelligible that it should begin or cease to exist. A person who wished to maintain that proposition, and yet was presented with *prima facie* instances to the contrary, could always *verbally* save his case by adopting the expedient mentioned in the preceding paragraph. But whether anything significant corresponds to the distinction which he draws in words, might fairly be doubted.

(2) "*Absolute Process.*" Professor Russell says that I have given an account of "processes" which seems to suggest that a process could not be perceived by more than one person, and to make it doubtful whether there could be unperceived processes. If anything that I wrote gives that impression, it is to that extent misleading, for I certainly had no intention of denying the possibility *either* of a process being perceived by more than one person, *or* of there being unperceived or even imperceptible processes.

I suspect that the misunderstanding may have arisen in the following way. (i) I gave the instance of a *sound* (in the sense of something which has the *sensible* features of pitch, loudness, etc., as actually experienced) as illustrating *in certain respects* what I had in mind when I talked of an "absolute process." (ii) I then remarked that it might be, and has been, doubted whether a sound, in that sense of the word, could exist except as a factor in an auditory experience of some one particular individual on some one particular occasion. I think it is fairly plain that Professor Russell took me to be giving this example as illustrating *in all respects* what I meant by an "absolute process." For he proceeds (quite rightly) to point out that it does not answer all the requirements, in view of the facts or possibilities stated under (ii) above.

The example of a sound (in the sense in question) is useful only in so far as it illustrates the notion of a process which is not at all obviously a *state of invariance* or a *state of change* in the qualities or the relationships of any "thing." Its *prima facie* defect as an illustration (apart from the one just mentioned, which led Professor Russell astray) is that we all believe a sound to be *causally dependent* on processes in what we commonly take to be things, viz., the outer air, the auditory nerves, the brain, and so on. But I do not think that this is really a defect. It was no part of my notion of an "absolute process" that it should not be *causally dependent* on processes which are themselves states of invariance or of change in the qualities or relationships of things. (The use of the word "absolute" may have been misleading here.) The essential point was that it should not *itself be* a state of invariance or of change in the qualities or relationships of any thing. I admit, of course, that the example, even if it were certainly an instance of an absolute process, could not be used in support of the alleged possibility of *dispensing* with the notion of things and describing *all* the facts in terms of absolute processes.

I fully agree with Professor Russell that there is no hope of realising the latter possibility unless we are prepared to admit the existence of absolute processes which are not in fact perceived, and of ones which are in principle imperceptible. But I see no objection to the possibility of such absolute processes.

When physicists talk of electro-magnetic fields, of trains of electro-magnetic waves, and so on, and when they at the same time disclaim all belief in the old-fashioned substantial ether, what *can* they have in mind except what I have called "absolute processes"? If that be so, it would reinforce what Professor Russell contends as to the possibility and the necessity of ascribing *dispositional properties* to absolute processes. Obviously a wireless beam, e.g., carrying a pattern of modulations, has plenty of dispositional properties. And, if there be no substantial ether, these must be ascribed to the *beam itself,* and not to any "thing," of which the beam is a state.

(C) CAUSATION. A part of Professor Blanshard's essay is concerned with questions about causation which are mainly epistemological, and a part of Professor Russell's paper with questions about causation which are mainly analytical. I will take the two in turn.

(1) *Epistemological Questions.* What Professor Blanshard has to say on this topic occurs in his discussion of the power of "intuiting necessary connexions," which is one of the functions that has been ascribed to "Reason." I would make the following comments.

(i) I do not think that there would be any inconsistency in combining the following two views:— (a) That we have *a priori* knowledge of certain *general principles about causation,* and (b) that we have *no a priori* knowledge of any *particular causal law.*

(ii) Again, there seems to me to be no inconsistency, at any rate at the first move, in combining the following two views:—(a) That the notion of causation is (or contains as an essential ingredient) a concept which is *not empirical,* and (b) that our knowledge of any particular causal law *is* empirical.

Suppose, however, that we then raise the question:—Assuming that the notion of causation is not wholly empirical, how do we come to have it? Suppose, further, that we are not content to say that the capacity and the tendency to formulate causal judgments is *innate,* though requiring certain specific kinds of experience to activate and direct it. Then we might be forced to conclude that we must have derived the notion (or at any rate the non-empirical ingredient in it) from being acquainted, in some non-sensuous and non-introspective way, with instances of it. And that would seem to be equivalent to saying that in *some* cases we must have had *a priori* knowledge of particular instances of causal connexion.

(iii) Professor Blanshard gives examples where he thinks it plausible to hold that we do in fact see, by merely reflecting on the natures of the events in question, that any event of a certain kind has at least an *intrinsic tendency* to be accompanied or immediately followed by an event of a certain other kind in a certain relation to it. One alleged example is that an experience of expecting to suffer severe pain has an intrinsic tendency to be accompanied or immediately followed in the same conscious being by an experience of fear.

I admit the *prima facie* plausibility of such examples; but I suspect that the apparent synthetic *a priori* judgment may really be a conflation of one which is *a priori* but analytic with another which is synthetic but empirical. I think that the word "fear" connotes (a) an experience involving certain *feelings* associated with certain bodily states (e.g., a "sinking feeling" in the stomach, the feelings associated with a cold sweat, and so on), and (b) a reference to certain *kinds of situation* (e.g., dangerous, painful, or embarrassing ones). Now it is an *analytic* proposition that a person will tend to experience "fear" (in the sense of that complex of feelings, whatever it may be, which are commonly felt in dangerous or painful or embarrassing situations) when he is or expects to be in such a situation. It is a *synthetic* proposition that he will tend to experience "fear" (in the sense of a certain familiar complex experience, including a sinking feeling in the stomach, the feeling associated with a cold sweat, and so on) when he is or expects to be in a dangerous or painful or embarrassing situation. And the latter proposition seems to me to be purely contingent. But, since the word "fear" combines *both* these features in its connotation, we are liable to think that we are contemplating a *single* proposition, which is *both* synthetic and necessary. I have taken one particular example, but I have a strong suspicion that any other example adduced for the same purpose could be dealt with on the same lines.

(2) *Analytical Questions.* Professor Russell very justifiably finds much that is obscure in my remarks about causation in *Examination of McTaggart's Philosophy* Vol. I Chapter XIII. He tries to lighten the darkness by restating what I may have had in mind in terms of the notions of necessary condition and sufficient condition. I am sure that that is the right course. I have pursued it myself in later writings. I think that the simplest way for me to clear up the matter is to begin by giving some definitions and making some statements based on the contents of Pp. 15 to 18 of the first of my papers entitled, "Hr. von Wright on the Logic of Induction," in *Mind*, Vol. LIII.

(i) *P* is a *sufficient precursor* ("S.Pr.") of *Q*, if from any instant into which a *P*-event were to enter a *Q*-event would issue.

(ii) *P* is a *necessary precursor* ("N.Pr.") of *Q*, if into any instant from which a *Q*-event were to issue a *P*-event would have entered.

(iii) *P* is a *smallest sufficient precursor* ("S.S.Pr.") of *Q*, if (a) it is a sufficient precursor of *Q*, and (b) it is either (α) a simple characteristic *p*, or (β) a conjunctive characteristic $p_1 \& p_2 \& \ldots \cdot p_n$, such that, if any of the conjuncts be omitted, what remains is *not* a sufficient precursor of *Q*.

(iv) A *contributory precursive condition* ("Cy.Pr.Cn.") of *Q* is any simple characteristic, or any conjunction of such characteristics, which is a conjunct in a S.S.Pr. of *Q*.

(v) *P* is a *smallest necessary precursor* ("S.N.Pr.") of *Q*, if (a) it is a necessary precursor of *Q*, and (b) it is either (α) a simple characteristic *p*, or (β) a *disjunctive* characteristic $p_1 or\text{-}p_2 or\text{-} \ldots \cdot p_n$, such that, if any of the alternants be omitted, what remains is *not* a necessary precursor of *Q*.

(vi) A *substitutable precursive requirement* ("Sb.Pr.Rq.") of *Q* is any simple characteristic, or any disjunction of such characteristics, which is an alternant in any S.N.Pr. of *Q*.

(vii) If *Q* has *only one* S.S.Pr., every conjunct in it may be described as an *indispensable contributory precursive condition* ("I.Cy.Pr.Cn.") of *Q*. If, on the other hand, *Q* has several alternative S.S.Pr's, then any characteristic which is a *conjunct in all of them* may be so described.

So much by way of definition. It is important to be clear about the logical relationships of the two notions of *necessary precursor* and *indispensable contributory precursive condition*.

(a) It is logically possible for *P* to be an I.Cy.Pr.Cn. of *Q without being* a N.Pr. of *Q*. For, whether there be only one S.S.Pr. of *Q* or several alternative S.S.Pr's of *Q*, it remains *logically possible* that there should be cases in which a *Q*-event issues from an instant into which *no* S.S.Pr. of *Q* has entered. Now, in order for *P* to be a N.Pr. of *Q*, a *P*-event would have to enter into *every* instant from which a *Q*-event issues. So a *P*-event would have to enter *inter alia* into those instants (if any) from which a *Q*-event issues *without any* S.S.Pr. of *Q* having entered. But, in order for *P* to be an I.Cy.Pr.Cn. of *Q*, it has only to be a conjunct in *every* S.S.Pr. of *Q*. Obviously that does not guarantee the entry of a *P*-event into those instants from which a *Q*-event issues without any S.S.Pr. of *Q* having entered. Since it is logically possible that there should be such instants, it is logically possible for *P* to be an I.Cy.Pr.Cn. of *Q* without being a N.Pr. of *Q*.

(b) This possibility would be ruled out, if and only if we were to assume that in *every* case in which a Q-event issues from an instant there is *some* S.S.Pr. of Q. This might be called the *Postulate of Smallest Sufficient Precursors*. On that assumption any I.Cy.Pr.Cn. of Q must be a N.Pr. of Q.

(c) It is logically necessary that a conjunction of all the I.Cy.Pr.Cn's of Q should be a S.Pr. of Q. But it is *not* logically necessary that a conjunction of all the N.Pr's of Q should be a S.Pr. of Q. The latter proposition would, however, follow from the Postulate of Smallest Sufficient Precursors.

Now it is certain that neither the above distinctions, nor consequently the logical relations between the notions distinguished, were clearly before my mind when I wrote the chapter on Causation. In terms of them I will make the following comments on certain things which I wrote there.

(i) I think that what is generally understood by the phrase "*total cause* of such and such a change issuing from an instant *t*" is a S.S.Pr. for changes of that kind. Therefore the most obvious interpretation of the sentence: "All changes of such and such a kind are caused" would be that in every case where a change of that kind issues from an instant there is a S.S.Pr. for it. That would be quite consistent with holding that there is a *plurality* of alternative S.S.Pr's for changes of that kind; that in some cases one is present and in other cases another; and that perhaps in some cases several of them are present together. The most obvious interpretation of the sentence: "*All* changes *whatever* are caused" would be a generalisation of the above statement about all changes of *such and such a kind*. It would in fact be the Postulate of Smallest Sufficient Precursors.

(ii) Any reader might be excused for thinking that it was *this* proposition which I claimed to find self-evident when I wrote (*Examination* Vol. I P. 232) "Every change has a cause," and said that this was to me evidently true. But in fact I did *not*, and do *not*, find it self-evident that for every case in which a change of any kind issues from an instant there must be a S.S.Pr. for a change of that kind issuing from that instant.

If the reader should continue until he reaches the discussion of voluntary decision on P. 238 of the volume in question, he will find that what I there claim to be self-evident would be expressed (at any rate to a first approximation) by the following sentence:— "In every case in which a change of any kind issues from an instant there must be a change entering into that instant, such that a change of the former kind *would not have* issued *unless* one of the latter kind had entered."

Now this, as Professor Russell rightly points out, is an assertion about *necessary* precursors, and not about sufficient precursors.

The above statement needs a certain amount of elucidatory comment, in view of the fact (which I did not recognise at the time) that a N.Pr. need not be simple, and that the S.N.Pr. for a given kind of change may be a *disjunction*. (I owe the recognition of this to Professor von Wright.)

It might be that an event of the Q-kind would not issue from any instant unless an event of a certain kind P_1-or-P_2 should have entered into that instant, but that in some cases the entering event is of the kind P_1 and there is none of the kind P_2, that in others it is of the kind P_2 and there is none of the kind P_1, and that in yet others perhaps there is either a single entering event of the two kinds or two entering events one of each kind.

What I claimed to find self-evident might therefore be re-stated as follows. The issuing of an event of any given kind (say Q) from any instant must be preceded by the entry into that instant of an event which is either (a) of a certain *one* kind (the same in all such cases), or (b) of one or another of a *certain limited number* of alternative kinds (in some such cases of one, and in other such cases of another, of these alternative kinds.)

I think I may say of this proposition the following two things. (a) The contradictory of it is certainly not self-contradictory. (b) When I reflect on the contradictory of it, and try to consider "what such a state of affairs would be like," I find it almost impossible to think that it could be true.

(iii) I should not now be inclined to attach much, if any, weight to the proposition which I asserted, at the bottom of P. 233 of Vol. I of *Examination,* to be self-evident. This to the effect that a given change issuing from a given instant cannot have "more than one total cause." I should now identify "a total cause" of a particular change with any S.S.Pr. of such changes which enters into the instant from which that change issues. If there should be only one S.S.Pr. entering into the instant in question, we can talk of "*the* total cause" of the change on that occasion. But such a change may have several alternative S.S.Pr's, and it does not seem to me self-evidently impossible that more than one of them should enter into a given instant from which such a change issues. In that case, it seems to me, we must be content to say that the particular change in question has *several coexisting* total causes, and therefore that there is nothing that can be called "*the* total cause" of it. I should describe such a change as "over-determined." It would be easy to produce quite plausible *prima facie* instances of over-determination.

(V) *Induction and Laws of Nature*

It will be convenient to discuss this topic immediately after the above discussion of the notion of Causation. It forms the subject of essays by Dr. Hanson, Professor Nelson, and Professor von Wright.

(A) LAWS OF NATURE. I take it that the main point which Dr. Hanson is concerned to make is that "law-sentences" (and in particular those which are said to state the laws of motion and the law of gravitation) have a number of different, though interconnected, uses; that the same law-sentence is often used in different ways by one and the same scientist in the course of a single spell of work or a single bit of scientific writing; and that it is futile for anyone philosophising on the topic of these laws to pick out one sense, and claim that it is the only legitimate one. I certainly do not wish to dispute this, and I will content myself with the following remarks on it.

(1) The question of fact could be settled only by a careful examination of the writings, the conversations, and the behaviour on relevant occasions of representative scientists from Newton's time to the present day.

(2) I suspect that it would often be very hard to be sure of the sense in which a given scientist was using a given law-sentence on a given occasion. I should not expect to get much useful information by asking the scientist himself. If he had *not* had a philosophical training, he would probably not understand the question or see the point of asking it, and he would certainly not have the technical equipment to answer it intelligibly. If he *had* had a philosophical training, the chances are that he would not be a first-rate working scientist; and, even if he were, he would probably be committed to some particular (and often already exploded) philosophical view, which would bias his answers. In fact, those two modern oracles, "the plain man" and "the working scientist," resemble in one respect their ancient forerunners. The artless prattlings of the former and the sophisticated technicalities of the latter stand in as much need of expert interpretation as did the inspired ravings of the Pythia at Delphi or the Sybil at Cumae.

(3) If the question of fact can be settled, I agree that it is then the business of the philosopher of science to accept the situation, and not to pretend that there is one and only one legitimate sense in which a law-sentence can be used.

Dr. Hanson mentions five different uses of a law-sentence. The second, third, and fourth of these agree in that in each of them such a sentence expresses something that can significantly be lescribed as "true" or "false." In the first use such a sentence formu11ates a *definition* of the technical meaning of a term, e.g., "force," which may already have had a long-standing use in ordinary speech. In that case it can hardly be said to be true or false, but it can be judged by various criteria to be well or ill fitted for its purpose. The fifth use itself covers five very different alternatives, according to Dr. Hanson; but they all agree in making a law-sentence express something which (though not a definition) can hardly be said to be true or false.

On all these matters I will confine myself to the following comments.

(1) Dr. Hanson distinguishes, among others, the following uses of a law-sentence, viz., (i) to express a proposition which it is "psychologically impossible" to think of as false, and (ii) to express a proposition, the rejection of which would have extremely upsetting repercussions in departments of science which have for long been regarded as models of complete and detailed explanation and absolutely reliable prediction.

I should suppose that the state of affairs described under (ii) is an important factor in causing that which is described under (i). The alleged psychological impossibility of contemplating the falsity of what is expressed by a law-sentence would seldom be of much philosophical interest unless it sprang from some such cause.

(2) In his discussion of the attitudes of scientists toward the law of gravitation, Dr. Hanson makes the following remark. A most important function of such a law is that it unifies a great many empirical facts through being a *common premiss* from which they all follow. He speaks of the typical situation in modern theoretical physics as "observation-statements in search of a premiss." And he alleges that philosophers of science have failed to recognise this, and have concentrated their attention too much on empirical correlations. By these I take him to mean straightforward inductive arguments from all the observed *S*'s having been *P* to the conclusion that all past, present, and future *S*'s respectively have been, are, or will be *P*.

My comments on this are as follows. (i) I agree that the procedure in question is most important in all advanced sciences. (ii) I do not agree that it has been ignored or underrated by philosophers of science. I should have thought that it was adequately recognised, e.g., by Mill in his *Logic* (Cf. Book III, Chapters XI to XIV, both inclusive) and by Jevons in his *Principles of Science,* to mention only two of the older English writers.

(iii) As a matter of logic, it seems to me that philosophers of science nevertheless do well to lay great stress on the problem of straightforward inductive generalisation. For all the "facts," which are shown to follow from the supposed law, are themselves propositions which have been accepted as straightforward inductive generalisations. If the original inductive arguments for accepting them cannot be defended, then there is to that extent a doubt whether they *are* facts; and, unless they are, they cannot support the more general law which entails them.

Of course I am well aware that the evidence for each of these more restricted general propositions is greatly strengthened by its being entailed by a single more general law, which also entails many other such propositions, each of which was originally accepted only as an independent inductive generalisation. In this way the whole system becomes comparable to a net, as contrasted with a lot of separate threads. But the net is made of threads, and the ultimate strength or weakness of the threads depends in the last resort on the validity or invalidity of straightforward inductive generalisation.

(3) Among what I may call the "non-informative " uses of law-sentences Dr. Hanson mentions their use (a) as rules of inference, and (b) as principles for constructing instruments. It seems to me that both of these *presuppose* an "informative" use of such sentences, i.e., to state a proposition which can significantly be described as "true" or as "false," and which is in fact held to be *true*.

This is surely obvious when it is a question of constructing an instrument. A sane person constructs an instrument to perform certain functions, and he designs it in such a way as he believes will ensure its performing those functions efficiently. If he uses a law-sentence prescriptively in giving directions for constructing an instrument, or if he understands it in that sense in receiving and following such directions, it must be because he already accepts as true the propositions about nature which it states when used, not prescriptively, but informatively.

This is perhaps less obvious in reference to the use of a law-sentence as a *rule of inference*. If so, that is because it is not altogether clear what that phrase means in the present connexion. But surely this at least can be said. Such a "principle" is admittedly *not* one of pure logic or of pure mathematics, like the principle of the syllogism or the formula $(x + y)$ $(x - y) = x^2 - y^2$. If, then, the conclusions which one "deduces in accordance with it" are to have any relevance to actual or causally possible natural phenomena, the "principle of inference" must surely rest on a general proposition which is held to be *true* of the relevant department or aspect of nature.

(B) INDUCTION. The topics treated in Professor Nelson's and Professor von Wright's essays partly overlap and partly diverge, so in some of the sub-sections which follow I shall be concerned with what is common to both and in others with what is peculiar to one or the other.

(1) *The so-called "Problem of Induction."* This question is treated

by both writers. Professor von Wright quotes a dilemma, in which I summed up my position in the paper entitled "Mechanical and Teleological Causation," in Aristotelian Society's *Supplementary Volume* XIV. He suggests that, instead of pursuing the course which seems inevitably to end in that dilemma, we should begin with the question: What do we *mean* by calling an inductive belief "grounded" (as opposed to "groundless" or "ill-founded"), and what do we *mean* by "rationally believing" in reference to an inductive generalisation? He is inclined to think that, if we do this, we shall see that what we call "grounds of rational belief in induction" are *just* empirical premises *without* support of any general principles. He does not attempt to argue his case, but hopes that I may comment on it. So I will take this as the text of my sermon in this sub-section.

I would suggest that what must presumably have happened in the case of *deductive* logic may be useful as an analogy and a contrast. Here, I suppose, we could distinguish in theory three stages, though very likely they overlapped historically.

(1) There would have been a number of particular bits of deductive argument which all or most sane persons *accepted* in the law-courts, in monetary calculations, in mensuration, and so on, except when under the influence of some strong desire or emotion which was known to distort a person's judgment. There would have been a number of particular bits of deductive argument which all or most sane persons, with similar qualifications, *rejected*. Finally, there would be a number of particular bits of deductive argument which were accepted by some and rejected by other sane persons when in an emotionally calm state.

(2) It would be natural, then, to compare and contrast the generally accepted with the generally rejected arguments, in order to see whether there were other features, beside general acceptance, common and peculiar to the former. This stage might be illustrated by the discovery and formulation of the traditional rules of the syllogism. At this stage it might be agreed to be a fair test, in the case of a disputed argument, to note whether it did or did not have the characteristics which had been found to be in fact common and peculiar to arguments commonly accepted by sane men in their calmer moments.

(3) One might still, however, see *no reason why* an argument having all the characteristics in question should be valid, and *why* one which lacked any of them should be invalid. There is nothing, e.g., *obviously* wrong with a syllogism having a negative conclusion and two affirmative premises. The next stage, then, would be to try to get behind the empirical tests, and to show that they are consequences of more fundamental principles which are *self-evident*. That can be done in various alter-

native ways, which I need not describe here, for the rules of the syllogism.

Let us now compare and contrast this with the case of inductive arguments. In the case of *deductive* inference we are all, I suppose, agreed as to what we *mean* by calling an argument "valid." At any rate there is one condition which would generally be acknowledged to be necessary and sufficient for the validity of a *deductive* argument. It is this. It must be *impossible* that the premisses should be true and the conclusion false; and this impossibility must rest, not on the impossibility of the premisses (though they *may* be impossible, as in a *reductio ad absurdum* argument in pure mathematics), nor on the necessity of the conclusion (though it *may* be necessary, as it always is in the case of any valid argument from true premisses in pure mathematics), but on a certain relationship between the *logical form* of the premisses and the *logical form* of the conclusion. The task for philosophers of *deduction* is to classify arguments which answer to this admittedly necessary and sufficient condition of validity; to elicit the formal features common and peculiar to them; and then, if possible, to bring them under one or a few general principles, which all or nearly all sane and competent persons find self-evident. That programme has in the main been accomplished.

But it is not obvious what we *mean* by calling an *inductive* argument "valid"; or, if you prefer it, there is no one condition which is generally acknowledged to be necessary and sufficient for the validity of such an argument. What is quite certain is this. If we use the accepted definition or criterion of "validity" as applied to a *deductive* argument, and if we take the *complete* premiss of an *inductive* argument to be: *This, that, and the other S (which are all that have so far been observed) have been P,* and the conclusion to be: *All S's, past, present or future, respectively have been, are, or will be P,* then *all* inductive arguments are *invalid.* Now we all use inductive arguments, and we all accept the conclusions of many of them and guide important actions by reference to these. So reflective persons cannot but find this situation intellectually disturbing.

Now at this point there seem to be two alternatives open to us. One is to suppose that the definition or accepted necessary and sufficient condition of "validity," as applied to *deductive* arguments, applies also to *inductive* ones. The other is to deny this, and to set out from that point. I will now say something about each of these alternatives in turn.

(1) If we are going to use the old definition or accepted necessary and sufficient condition of "validity," and yet to admit the possibility that some inductive arguments are valid, we must try to save the situation in one or other or a combination of the following ways. We might suppose either (i) that a valid inductive argument has an additional *implicit premiss* beside the instantial propositions which are its only explicit

premisses, or (ii) that the *conclusion* of a valid inductive argument must take a *weaker form* than the unqualified *All S is P*. I think that it is now quite plain that anything on these lines needs *both* expedients in order to be at all hopeful, viz., adding some kind of universal premiss to the explicit instantial premisses, and stating the conclusion in terms of probability.

If that were done, it is evident that the *principles* (as distinct from the premisses) of inductive inference would include, beside those of non-problematic deductive inference, at least the formal principles of the calculus of probability, e.g., the axiom of addition concerning the probability of a disjunctive proposition, and the axiom of multiplication concerning that of a conjunctive one. I do not think that this in itself would be felt to raise any special difficulty.

Anyone who follows this line will have to deal with the following three questions, which might be described respectively as "logical," "ontological," and "epistemological." (i) What are the minimal universal premisses which, if added to the explicit instantial premisses, would make very highly probable the conclusions of those inductive arguments which are commonly accepted as practically certain by sane and instructed persons? (ii) What account of the structure of nature as a whole, or of certain departments of nature, would best fit in with the assumed truth of these universal premisses? (iii) How, if at all, do we know that these premisses are true or that they are highly probable? I think that this agrees almost exactly with the scheme outlined by Professor Nelson.

Before considering the other alternative, suggested by Professor von Wright, I will make the following comments on the alternative outlined above.

(a) There is no guarantee that the whole enterprise may not break down at the first stage. In that case we should have to admit that, so far as we can tell up to date, *no* inductive arguments are valid, in the sense of "validity" supposed, even when their conclusions are stated in terms of probability.

(b) Even if the logical problem can be solved satisfactorily, the epistemological problem would (as both Professor Nelson and I have emphasised) remain very troublesome. The additional premiss (and still more obviously the propositions about the "structure of nature" which have to be assumed in order that it shall be applicable) must be *general*, and it cannot be *merely analytic*. Yet our acceptance of it cannot, without circulatory, be based on *induction;* and, even if the possibility of necessary synthetic propositions were admitted (which it is not by most contemporary English and American philosophers), no additional premiss which has been plausibly alleged to fulfill the conditions has any trace of *self-evidence*.

(c) This leads me to the following two reflexions, (α) Even if the epistemological difficulties should be insoluble, that would not diminish the value of the analytic and the ontological sections of this line of thought. The justification of induction, where it is thought to be justifiable, would have to be stated *conditionally,* and not categorically. But even that would be no small gain in insight. (β) The situation would be remarkably like that which Kant (as I understand him) contemplated in regard to such allegedly synthetic *a priori* propositions as he held to be capable of "transcendental proof." People claim to *know,* or to have *good grounds for very strongly believing* certain general propositions as a result of inductive reasoning. Suppose we grant their claim. Suppose we can show that it can be valid, *if and only if* certain propositions about the structure of nature are true. Then we are entitled to accept those propositions, even though they be synthetic and though they have no trace of self-evidence. They would be "synthetic *a priori* propositions" in precisely the sense in which Kant held that, e.g., the law of universal causation and the conservation of mass are so.

(2) Let us now consider the other alternative, suggested by Professor von Wright, which is nowadays much the more popular of the two. The contention is that if an *inductive* argument can properly be described as "valid" or "invalid," those words must be understood in a special sense, appropriate to such arguments. On that supposition, it is of course quite possible that certain inductive arguments may be "valid," in the appropriate sense, *without* the addition of any implicit general premiss to their explicit instantial premisses, and perhaps without reformulating their conclusions in terms of probability. On this suggestion I would make the following comments.

(i) Plainly the first task would be to formulate a definition, or generally acceptable necessary and sufficient condition, of what I will call "inductive validity." Here we may compare and contrast this enquiry with Stage (1) of what I supposed above to have happened in the case of *deductive* arguments. We should have to consider typical *inductive* arguments, which all or most sane persons in their calmer moments accept, and compare and contrast them with typical inductive arguments which all or most of such persons under such conditions reject. But the difference would be this. In the case of *deductive* arguments there was from the outset no doubt as to what is *meant* by "valid" and "invalid" as applied to them. The object of the comparison and the contrast was not to elicit the *meaning* of "validity," but to discover, and if possible to rationalise, *tests* for its presence or absence in any deductive argument. But in the case of *inductive* arguments the primary object of this comparison and contrast would be to discover what competent persons, who use and criticise such arguments, *mean* when they call some of them "valid" and others "invalid."

Unless it turned out that inductive validity had some fairly close and important analogies to deductive validity, it would be better not to use the word "validity" or "invalidity" of inductive arguments, but to coin some other technical term. I should think that the irreducible minimum of analogy would be that the "validity" of an inductive argument should depend in some assignable way on relationships of *logical form* between its premisses and its conclusion.

(ii) However that may be, it might still be worth while, after having elicited an agreed definition of "inductive validity" in this or in some other way, to proceed thenceforth as logicians did with deductive arguments. That procedure would be as follows. (a) To try to discover features, other than those which enter into the definition of "inductive validity," which are common and peculiar to arguments which are inductively valid. (b) If that can be done, to try to show *why* the presence of all these features entails inductive validity, and the absence of any of them entails inductive invalidity. (c) To try to reduce these features as far as possible to one or a few very general headings. If all this could be accomplished, there would remain the following typically philosophical questions. What is the nature of the ultimate principles on which the tests for inductive validity rest? Are all of them analytic, or are some of them synthetic? If some of them are synthetic, how are they known or rationally believed to be true?

(iii) Now it *might* happen that, when one elicited the meaning of "inductive validity," the consequence which Professor von Wright thinks would follow, viz., that the grounds of rational belief in induction are *just* empirical premisses *without* support of any general principles, would be seen to follow. Or it might not. All that I will say in conclusion is this. We must of course distinguish between the *premisses* of a valid argument, and the *principles* which the argument exemplifies and which ensure and make evident its validity. In the valid syllogism, e.g., *All men are mortal, and all Greeks are men, therefore all Greeks are mortal* the only *premisses* are the two propositions which are stated before the word "therefore." The *principles* which the argument exemplifies, and which together make evident its validity, are such propositions as the following:—(a) If a class is empty, every sub-class of it is empty; and (b) If every member of an exhaustive set of sub-classes of a class is empty, then that class is empty. Now I should think it certain that, if there are any *principles* for the "validity" of inductive arguments (no matter what meaning be attached to "inductive validity"), they must be *general* propositions. But that would leave open the question whether a valid deductive argument does or does not have to include one or more general propositions among its *premisses*.

(2) *Professor Nelson's account of Inductive Argument.* I found this of very great interest. I will first try to state it, as I understand it, in my own words, and will then make a few comments on it. To simplify the exposition I will confine myself to inductive generalisation where the instantial premiss is that N instances of S have been observed (say $S_1, S_2, \ldots \ldots S_N$) and that all of them have been P. With that understanding I would summarise Professor Nelson's theory as follows.

(i) If the argument is to be defensible, the conclusion must not take the unqualified non-modal form *All S is P*. It must take the form *It is likely, to such and such a degree, that all S is P.*

(ii) This must be carefully distinguished from any statement of the form: "The proposition *All S is P* has such and such a degree of probability with respect to the datum q." The following points are very important to notice here. (a) "Likely," in the sense in which Professor Nelson uses it, is analogous (except in that what it stands for is capable of degree) to "true." (b) On the other hand, the statement that p has such and such a degree of probability with respect to q is comparable to the statement that p is entailed by q. Like it, it is a statement which is *necessarily* true or *necessarily* false, as the case may be. And, like it, its truth or falsity depends on certain relations between the *forms* of p and of q, and not on their individual necessity or impossibility, truth or falsity, likelihood or unlikelihood.

(iii) Nevertheless, in order to establish inductively the conclusion *It is likely to such and such a degree that all S is P*, we require such a proposition as is expressed by the sentence: "With respect to the proposition that N instances of S have been observed and all of them have been P, it is probable to such and such a degree that all S is P." I will symbolise the proposition, expressed by the sentence in inverted commas, by $\Pi_N(\sigma)$ where σ is the degree of probability in question.

(iv) The part played by $\Pi_N(\sigma)$ in establishing a conclusion *inductively* may be compared with that which is played, in establishing *deductively* that all Greeks are mortal from the premiss that all men are mortal and all Greeks are men, by the proposition which is expressed by the sentence: "*All men are mortal & All Greeks are men* entails *All Greeks are mortal.*" The following points are important to notice here:—

(a) In the deductive argument we use a principle of "Deductive Detachment." Knowing that in fact all men *are* mortal and all Greeks *are* men, we are entitled to drop those premisses and to accept as *true* the proposition that all Greeks are mortal. In the inductive argument we need a comparable principle of "Inductive Detachment." Knowing that in fact N instances of S *have* been examined and that all of them *were P*, we are entitled to drop that premiss and to accept as *likely to such and such a degree* that all S is P.

(b) According to Professor Nelson, the degree of likelihood which it is justifiable to assign to *All S is P*, under the conditions supposed, is a function of the degree of probability σ, which *All S is P* has with respect to the premisses in the complex proposition $\Pi_N(\sigma)$. As to this function he will say no more than the following. The degree of likelihood of *All S is P*, given that the premisses in $\Pi_N(\sigma)$ are known to be true and can therefore be dropped, increases with σ, the degree of probability of *All S is P* in respect to those premisses.

(v) The last point in the theory is this. Professor Nelson holds that we never have any good reason to accept such a proposition as $\Pi_N(\sigma)$ *on its own merits,* as we have, e.g., to accept the proposition expressed by the sentence: "*All Greeks are mortal* is entailed by *All men are mortal & All Greeks are men.*" The only ground for accepting such a proposition as $\Pi_N(\sigma)$ is that it is *entailed by* a certain other proposition, which he calls the "Principle of Induction," and that we *know* this to be *true*. We will denote this principle by P_I. It is important to note the following points about it. (a) Professor Nelson does not claim to be able to formulate it satisfactorily. But he thinks that progress has been made towards doing so, and that this is illustrated, e.g., by the substitution of Keynes's "Principle of Limited Variety" for Mill's "Uniformity of Nature." (b) He draws a distinction between P_I itself, and the characteristics which we must ascribe to the actual world if P_I is to be true and applicable to natural phenomena. The proposition that nature has these characteristics is ontological, whilst P_I itself is described as "formal."

Supposing this to be a fair account of Professor Nelson's very interesting theory, I will make the following comments.

(i) I wonder why he uses P_I as a premiss which entails $\Pi_N(\sigma)$, instead of modifying $\Pi_N(\sigma)$ by introducing P_I into it as an additional premiss. The modified proposition, which we will denote by $\Pi'_N(\sigma)$, would then be expressed by the sentence: "The proposition *All S is P* has probability of degree σ with respect to the conjunction of P_I with the premisses of $\Pi_N(\sigma)$." I do not see any obvious objection to this. And, unless there be some objection, I should think it would have one obvious advantage. For $\Pi'_N(\sigma)$ would hold in virtue of the *form* of its premisses and its conclusion, just as a valid syllogism does; whilst $\Pi_N(\sigma)$ would not do so (if I understand Professor Nelson aright), though I suppose that the proposition that P_I entails $\Pi_N(\sigma)$ would do so.

(ii) Professor Nelson puts the argument in terms of a definite degree of probability σ, and a definite degree of likelihood, which increases with σ. I take it that he does not suppose that these can be exactly measured in any particular case. It would be enough that in favourable cases one should know that σ was high enough to ensure that the degree of likelihood of *All S is P* is considerable.

(iii) As regards P_I itself I have two remarks to make. (a) Taking it as a "formal" principle, I feel rather uncomfortable about a premiss which it is admitted that no one has so far managed to formulate satisfactorily. In order to "detach" P_I in Professor Nelson's form of the argument, one must *know* that it is true (or at any rate "highly likely"). But unless one knows what it is, how can one know this about it? I suppose we should have to say that what one knows is that there is *some* formulable proposition (never as yet satisfactorily formulated), which has the logical properties ascribed to P_I and which is true or highly likely.

(b) I think that the distinction between the "formal" principle and its ontological ground might be rather difficult to define. Would it come to this? The *formal* principle would state in extremely abstract terms the conditions which must be fulfilled in *any possible world* in which inductive generalisation would be a valid process leading in favourable cases to highly likely conclusions. The *ontological* principle would be a much more concrete statement as to the structure of the *actual world* which ensures that these conditions are fulfilled in it.

(iv) On the notion of "likelihood" I will make the following comments:—

(a) When a person accepts a proposition (rightly or wrongly, reasonably or unreasonably) as *true,* he is prepared (so far as he is not hindered by temperamental or occasional defects, intellectual or moral) to apply it without hesitation in practice where it is relevant, to accept without question in theory any consequences which seem to him to follow from it, to use it unhesitatingly as a basis for his further reflexions and investigations, and so on. Now there is undoubtedly an attitude which we often have towards a proposition, where all this holds good with the substitution of "with very considerable confidence" for "unhesitatingly." The latter may fairly be described as accepting a proposition (justifiably or unjustifiably) as *more or less likely.*

(b) One important way in which a person comes to accept a proposition as *true* is by noting that it seems to him to be logically entailed by certain other propositions, which he accepts as true. In such cases we may say that he accepts it as "deductively established." One important way in which a person comes to accept a general proposition as *more or less likely* is by what he takes to be a valid inductive argument from premises which he accepts as true. These always include *at least* a number of favourably instantial propositions, together with a proposition to the effect that these are all the relevant instances that have been observed. In such cases we may say that he accepts it as "inductively supported."

(c) If a person accepts a proposition as *true*, because *deductively established*, he cannot hope to strengthen his case through the possible discovery of additional true propositions which entail that conclusion. These will only provide him with *alternative* lines of proof, all of which could be dispensed with, and each of which could be substituted for his original line of proof. They are like a lot of ropes, each attached to a different hook, and each amply sufficient to support a certain weight. But suppose a person accepts a general proposition as *likely to at least a certain degree*, because *inductively supported*. Then he can hope to strengthen his case (though he must also fear its complete collapse) by the examination of further relevant instances. The mere addition of further true premises of the same kind (provided that the proposition that they include all the observed instances remains true) will inductively support the conclusion *still more strongly* and will justify one in accepting it as *likely to a still higher degree*. Here the additional true premises are comparable to additional strands in a single rope, which is always liable suddenly to give way.

(v) Lastly, I would like to say how fully I agree with the following contention of Professor Nelson's. It is hopeless to consider the principles of induction in isolation from the other principles and categories which are involved in the notion of a world of persistent things with varying states, co-existing and inter-acting in a single spatio-temporal system. Whatever defects there may be in Kant's discussion of the "Principles of Pure Understanding," he had at least grasped this essential point, which his predecessors had failed to note and which most of his successors seen to have forgotten.

(3) *Assumptions about Antecedent Probability.* Professor von Wright discusses this in connexion with problems in probability concerned with drawing counters from a bag, noting their colours, and thence arguing to the probability of various propositions about the colours of the counters in the bag. I have considered such problems in "Induction and Probability" and in "The Principles of Problematic Induction".

In the former I assumed that the $n+1$ alternatives, that a bag containing n counters should contain 0 or 1 or . . . . n counters of an assigned colour (e.g., white), would be equi-probable antecedently to any of them being drawn and looked at. In the latter paper, after having read Keynes's *Treatise on Probability*, I argued that this assumption leads

to a contradiction. I there assumed instead that there are v distinguishable colours (including black and white), and that it is antecedently equi-
probable with regard to any counter in the bag that it would have any
one of these colours. Professor von Wright mentions a third possible
assumption, which I did not consider in either paper, viz., that every
possible "constitution" of the contents of the bag with respect to an
assigned colour (e.g., white) is antecedently equally probable. He
expresses regret that I did not work out the consequences of this.

Now I think that this third possible assumption can be dismissed
quite briefly. I take it to be equivalent to assuming that it is antecedently
equi-probable with regard to any counter in the bag that it would either
have or *not have* the assigned colour (e.g., white). For all purposes of
mathematical deduction that is equivalent to putting $\sqrt{} = 2$ in the
calculations in "Principles of Problematic Induction". It seems to me
obvious that the assumption as to equi-probability which I made there
is more defensible than the assumption of equi-probability of "constitutions." For the latter lumps together under the heading "other-than-
white" all the remaining colours, and then counts this *disjunction of
colours* as precisely on a level with the *single colour* white.

Professor von Wright says that he thinks there is no possibility of
proving or of disproving any of these alternative assumptions about
equi-probability. I am inclined to agree with him as to the impossibility
of *proving* any of them without making factual assumptions. I think,
e.g., that the assumption which I made in *P. of P. I.* would be reasonable
only if one had the following information, or something formally
equivalent to it, viz., that the bag had been filled by drawing n counters
from *another* bag, which contained *equal large numbers* of counters
of each of the v colours, well mixed with each other. But I should
have thought that it was possible to *refute* some assumptions by showing
that they lead to consequences which are plainly absurd. I do not see
anything wrong with the argument by which I tried to show in *P. of
P. I.* that the assumption made by me in "Induction and Probability"
leads to absurdities, if we admit that there is *more than one colour* (e.g.,
red and blue) besides the assigned one (e.g., white), which might belong
to one or more of the counters in the bag.

(4) *The notion of "Loading."* From problems concerned with drawing counters from bags the transition is natural to problems concerned
with throwing dice, spinning roulette-wheels, and so on. The notion
of "loading" has its most obvious applications in reference to the latter
problems. It is discussed both by Professor von Wright and by Professor
Nelson. I will take their remarks in turn.

In *P.P.I.* I made the following assertions. (i) "The notion of loading is the notion of a constant cause-factor which operates throughout the whole series of throws, and co-operates with other and variable cause-factors to determine the actual result of each throw." (ii) "I shall say that the counter is loaded to degree *s* in favour of red, if and only if the antecedent probability of its turning up red would be *s* for anyone who knew in detail how it was constructed." Professor von Wright finds this obscure. He says that he would understand by "load" a certain *antecedent probability*. And he asks whether I suppose the "constant cause-factor" to be this probability *itself* or some feature in the *physical world* which may be held *responsible for* the "load," in his sense.

The answer is that I meant the following. I thought of the load, *not* as a probability, but as a *physical* factor (e.g., the location of the centre of gravity at such and such a position in relation to the geometrical centre of the body in question) *determining* the antecedent probability of a face of such and such a colour coming up. It would strike me as linguistically barbarous to talk of a *probability* as a cause-factor, and I should not wittingly do so.

My statement that induction, in such cases, presupposes a reference to causation was therefore intended to mean something different from the minimum which Professor von Wright suggests that I might have meant by it. In the context it was intended to mean something like the following. The fact that the antecedent probability of a loaded die turning up a 6 on any occasion is so-and-so is determined jointly by the following facts. (i) That the position at which it comes to rest on any occasion is causally determined jointly by (a) the position of its centre of gravity in relation to its geometrical centre, (b) its geometrical, elastic, and other permanent properties, (c) the correlative properties of the surface on which it falls, and (d) the angle at which it hits the surface. (ii) That it is antecedently equally likely to hit the surface at any one of the innumerable alternative geometrically possible angles. (I suspect that this second statement would need some modification, but I think that the notion of the equi-probability of certain alternative geometrical possibilities being fulfilled would still enter.)

Passing now to Professor Nelson's "roulette-wheel," I would make the following comments:—

(i) He contrasts the case of a wheel which is "honest" and one which is not. But ought we not rather to contrast one that is *known* to the player to be honest, and one which is *not known* to him to be so or not to be so. In the latter case the possibility that it is biased is admitted from the beginning.

If the wheel is *known* to the player to be honest, then no run of a single number, however long, and no sequence of numbers, however often repeated, would give him any rational ground for betting in favour of a repetition of that number or of that sequence. That is almost, if not quite, an analytical proposition. But, if the bare possibility of bias is admitted from the first, then it might be argued that a sufficiently preponderant proportion of a certain number, or of a certain sequence of numbers, would provide a ground for a rational belief that it *is* biased *in a certain way*. That in turn would provide a reasonable ground for betting in a corresponding way on its future behaviour.

Professor Nelson does in fact consider this kind of argument in connexion with his criticism of the "Precept Theory." The essential point seems to me to be one which he himself makes. A glance at the formula for the application of the principles of inverse probability shows that all that an accumulation of uniformly favourable instances can do for a hypothesis is continually to *multiply by a new factor its initial probability*. Now, if that is to lead to a final probability whose upper limit is 1, we must have reason to believe beforehand, not merely that the initial probability is greater than 0, but that the *lower limit of its possible values* is greater than 0. Now that is not secured merely by the negative fact that it is not impossible that the wheel may be loaded in one way or another.

(ii) About artificial cases, such as roulette-wheels, the following points may be worth making:—

(a) No one in practice is in a position to *know* (even in the popular sense of that word) that a roulette-wheel is honest. At most he may have extremely good reasons to believe that it has been made by a competent and reliable firm in accordance with the accepted methods for making honest roulette-wheels, that it has not become worn or tampered with, and so on.

(b) Conversely, in certain circumstances one might have very good reasons for thinking it quite probable antecedently that a certain roulette-wheel would *not* be honest. In all artificial cases an essential part of one's ground for holding any reasonable opinion on the antecedent probability of the machine being honest or being biased is knowledge of the general laws of human motivation and of the characters and motives of certain particular individuals. Again, an essential part of one's ground for inferring, from the supposed construction of the machine and its observed performance up to date, to any conclusion about its future behaviour in any assigned respect, is one's knowledge of the general laws of physics and of the properties of specific kinds of matter.

(c) It might therefore seem that there is a risk of *circularity* in taking, as a model for the inductive inference of natural uniformities from observed regularities of co-existence or of sequence, the case of inferring

from the past results of spinning a roulette-wheel to the probable results of further spins. I mention this *appearance* of circularity only in
order to say that I do *not* think it harmful for the purpose for which the
analogy is used. That purpose is simply to exhibit the presuppositions
of an inductive argument in a case where they are very obvious, and to
suggest (α) that inductive generalisation *everywhere* presupposes the
finite antecedent probability of something *analogous to bias* in the case
of a roulette-wheel or a die, and (β) that this *always* rests on some view
about the "concealed structure and mechanism" (to use those words very
widely) of nature as a whole or of a particular department of it.

(5) *Induction by Simple Enumeration and the Hypothetical Method.*
Under this heading I will discuss a number of inter-related points raised
by Professor von Wright.

I alleged that induction by simple enumeration (so far as it is exemplified by taking counters out of a bag, noting their colours, and then drawing conclusions with more or less probability as to the original proportion of counters in the bag) is a particular case of the hypothetical
method. Professor von Wright objects to this. I think that his objection
rests partly on a mere difference in the use of words, and partly on an important matter of principle.

(i) The matter on which I think there is no real difference is this. Let
$h_0, h_1, \ldots \ldots h_n$ be a set of mutually exclusive and collectively exhaustive
alternative propositions, which it is proposed to test by specific experiment or observation. Let f be any relevant data which one may have
before undertaking the test, and let Q_N be a summary of the relevant information that has accumulated at the N-th stage of carrying out the
test. Then for any typical one of these alternatives h_r the probability
relative to the conjunction of f with Q_N is given by the equation

$$h_r/f\&Q_N = \left[(h_r/f) \times (Q_N/f\&h_r) \right] \div \left[\sum_{r=0}^{r=n} (h_r/f) \times (Q_n/f\&h_r) \right]$$

where any symbol of the form "p/q" stands for the probability of the
proposition p given the proposition q.

Now in the case of bag-problems the propositions of the form h_r are
alternative "hypotheses" to the effect that exactly so many of the n
counters in the bag are of such and such a colour. The proposition Q_N is
a summary, at any given stage of the experiment, of the accumulated information as to the whiteness or non-whiteness of the counters drawn
and inspected up to that point.

In what is commonly called "the hypothetical method" we use what
is *in principle* the same formula, but there are the following important
differences in detail. (a) Instead of considering a number of mutually ex-

clusive and collectively exhaustive alternative propositions h_0, h_1, ... h_n, we consider just a *single* proposition H and its *logical contra-dictory* $\overline{H}$. (b) H is such that at every stage $Q_N/f\&H$ is either O (in which case the hypothesis is *refuted* and the experiment comes to a natural end), or 1 (in which case there is no reason why the experiment should not be continued). (c) In the bag experiment H is analogous to the single alternative h_n, viz. that *all* the counters in the bag are white. And $Q_N/f\&H$ is either O (if Q_N includes the information that at least 1 *non-white* counter has been drawn), or 1 (if it consists of the information that *all* the counters drawn up to that stage have been *white*). The formula therefore reduces to

$$H/f\&Q_N = (H/f) \div \left[(H/f) + (\overline{H}/f) \times (Q_N/f\&\overline{H}) \right].$$

So what I was trying to say could be more accurately expressed as follows. The reasoning in induction by simple enumeration (so far as this is accurately represented by experiments in drawing counters from a bag), and the reasoning in the hypothetical method, are instances of essentially the *same general formula* in the calculus of probability. And the latter can fairly be regarded as in certain respects a *more restricted* case of that formula, since it is by definition subject to the three conditions stated above.

(ii) The important difference in principle is this. Is the kind of hypothesis which is tested in what is ordinarily called the "hypothetical method" *really* on all fours with the $(n + 1)$-th. of the alternative "hypotheses" which are tested in an artificial experiment with counters in a bag? Is *All swans are white* a proposition of the same logical kind as *All the n counters in the bag are white*? Professor von Wright objects that the former are propositions about what he calls "open classes" and that the latter are about "closed classes," and that these two are fundamentally dissimilar kinds of proposition.

I think that he is right to object, and that I was wrong to overlook this distinction, but that his objection hardly goes far enough. It seems to me now that we have to contrast at least *three* fundamentally different kinds of proposition, (a) "All S is P" might express simply the proposition that S_1 is P & S_2 is P &......S_n is P, and that these are all the S's that there are. (b) It might express a rather complicated proposition of the following form. Consider a sequence of collections of the following kind, viz., (S_1), $(S_1 \& S_2)$, ...$(S_1 \& S_2 \&......S_n)$, ... Let the percentage of the members of these collections which are P be respectively $p_1, p_2,......p_n$, ... Then "All S is P" might be taken to mean the same as "p_n tends to the limiting value 100% as n tends to infinity." This latter sentence is itself a highly condensed expression for a rather complicated proposition, but we need not unpack it further here. (c) "All S is P" might be taken to mean that in the actual world (though not in all possible worlds) *any* instance of S *would be* an instance of P. I do not know how to analyse such propositions further. But I can perhaps indicate their peculiarity by remarking that one is tempted to say of any such proposition (α) that, if it is true, it is *necessary*, but (β) that the fact that it is necessary is *contingent*. (In contrast with this, one can say of the necessity of a true *a priori* proposition that its belonging to that proposition is itself a *necessary* fact.)

We might call these respectively the "enumerative," the "limiting-frequency," and the "nomic" interpretations of such a sentence as "*All S is P.*" It is immediately obvious that (b) differs from (a). If it is not immediately obvious (as I think it should be) that (c) differs from (b), this becomes evident when one reflects that (b) is compatible with there being any finite number of S's which are *not P,* whilst (c) is not compatible with there being a single S which is not P.

Now the "limiting-frequency" interpretation certainly presupposes "open classes," in the sense of classes which contain an infinite number of members. For that is involved in the notion of a limit. For that very reason I doubt whether it has any application outside pure mathematics. The "nomic interpretation" does not presuppose "open classes" in that sense. For the proposition that *any* instance of S *would* be an instance of P in the actual world is consistent with the number of actual instances in the whole course of the world's history being finite or even zero. What it does presuppose is the notion of classes determined by *intension* as distinct from by *enumeration* of their members.

It seems to me that what we commonly try to test by the so-called "hypothetical method" is universal propositions in the *nomic* sense. If so, they *are* fundamentally different from such propositions as *All the n counters in the bag are white.* But the difference is even more fundamental than would be suggested by the contrast between "open" and "closed" classes.

(6) *The Theory of "Generators."* I have very little to object to in Professor von Wright's comments in what I said about this in *P. P. I.*

(i) He is correct in saying that the argument on P. 27 of that paper does not presuppose that the number of *generated* characteristics is finite. It presupposes only that n, the number of *generating* characteristics, is finite. The further argument, in the section entitled *Effect of the Relative Values of n and N* certainly assumes N to be finite when considering the alternatives that N is less than or equal to n, since n is assumed throughout to be finite. In discussing the alternative that N is greater than n, I certainly did assume in my own mind that N is finite; and, although the mere supposition that N is greater than n does not entail this, there are many steps in the argument which presuppose it.

(ii) He is correct also in saying that I have nowhere shown that the factor $(\mu_r \& \nu_s)/h$ in the formula on P. 27 is greater than O. This is the probability (relative to the general assumption of the theory of generators, and to the special assumption that each generated characteristic is generated by *only one* set of generators) of the proposition expressed by the sentence: "In a generalisation, whose subject is a conjunction of μ generated characters, and whose predicate is a conjunction of ν generated characters, the former require exactly r, and the latter exactly s, generating factors respectively to generate them."

(iii) He says, rightly, that all my arguments presuppose that the antecedent probability of a generalisation "can be linked with a ratio of true generalisations among a class of generalisations." But he complains that the nature and justification of this link are not made clear. I do not see exactly what the difficulty is here. If it could be shown that at least a certain proportion of possible generalisations of a certain kind *must* be true, e.g., at least $p\%$ of generalisations with a μ-fold subject and a ν-fold predicate, surely the antecedent probability of any generalisation of that kind would be at least

$$\frac{p}{100}.$$

(iv) He mentions my remarks on P. 41 of *P. of P. I.*, that the generating factors must be supposed to be *determinable* characters, and that it would follow that the generated characters must be so too. He finds the notion of "determinables" and "determinates" obscure, and asks me to try to clarify it.

I regret that it is impossible for me to go into this very large question here. The following very sketchy and therefore rather obscure remarks must suffice. (a) My account of generating factors explicitly assumes that no conjunction of such factors is either logically necessary or logically impossible. The statement about generating factors having to be determinable characters is bound up with this. (b) That is because of the following properties of determinable characters and of determinate characters. Supreme determinables are all logically independent of each other. But it is logically necessary that any thing which possesses a determinate character should possess all the determinables, of whatever order, under which this falls. And it is logically impossible that any thing should possess two determinate characters of the same order which fall under one and the same determinable.

I *think* that a more accurate statement of what I had in mind would run as follows. A complete collection of generating factors would have either (a) to contain nothing but *supreme determinables;* or (b) to contain nothing but *determinates,* each of which falls under a *different* supreme determinable; or (c) to be a *mixture* of (α) supreme determinables, and (β) determinates, none of which fall under any of these determinables, and each of which falls under a different supreme determinable.

(7) *Necessary Conditions and Sufficient Conditions.* I take some credit for seeing by 1930, when I published my two papers on "Demonstrative Induction," that these are the essential concepts involved in demonstrative induction, and for having worked out the formal logic of them in some detail and without serious mistakes, though not without one very serious omission. But all that I have written on this topic has now been superseded by Professor von Wright's more thorough and more accurate work.

I agree with him that it sounds odd to say: "The ground becoming wet is a necessary condition of rain having fallen in the neighbourhood," and I agree that both he and I are committed by our definitions to saying such things. I agree too that the verbal paradox is bound up with the conviction that a *causal* condition must be fulfilled *before* that which it conditions begins. That is why, in the present essay, I have introduced the terms "necessary *precursor*" and "sufficient *precursor*," when discussing, in Section IV, C, 2 above, Professor Russell's comments on my account of Causation in the *EMcP*.

I should be inclined to say that we must distinguish between a "condition," in the sense of a *ground for inference,* and a "condition" in the sense of a *factor in causation.* Given a knowledge of causal laws, one can often infer from knowledge of a *later* event to the conclusion that such and such an *earlier* event must have happened. (Unless one is a prophet, one cannot of course infer from knowledge of a *future* event to the occurrence of such and such an event in the *present or the past,* since one cannot be in possession of such knowledge.) But, when a person makes such an inference from a later to an earlier event, he does so because he has reason to believe that the later state of affairs (e.g., the ground being wet) would have come into being *only* if it had been preceded by a state of affairs containing such and such an event (e.g., a fall of rain in the neighbourhood) as a cause-factor.

(VI) *Time in general and Precognition in particular*

Under this heading I shall be concerned with a part of Professor Ducasse's essay and with the whole of those by Professors Flew and Mundle.

(A) TIME IN GENERAL. Professor Mundle's researches show that I have "boxed the compass" about time, and in the course of doing so, have written some things which now make me blush. It may be interesting and possibly illuminating to mention very briefly the main influences under which the three accounts of time considered by Professor Mundle were written. At the back of all of them is McTaggart's paper "The Unreality of Time," published in *Mind* in 1908. I felt from the first, and I still feel, that the difficulty which he raises is (a) embarrassing enough *prima facie* to demand the serious attention of anyone who philosophises about time; but (b) almost certainly due to some purely linguistic source (common, and perhaps peculiar, to the Indo-European verb-system), which it ought to be possible to indicate and make harmless.

At the period when I wrote the *Encyclopaedia* article (which, I must confess, I had wholly forgotten until Professor Mundle's essay reminded me of it) I was almost completely under the influence of Bertrand Russell in his extreme realist phase, and of Meinong as I understood him. By the time I wrote *Scientific Thought* I was greatly influenced by books recently published by Alexander and by Whitehead. The talk in *Scientific Thought* about "the sum-total of existence continually increasing by Becoming," and in the *Examination of McTaggart's Philosophy* about "Absolute Becoming," goes back to this source. To the influence of Whitehead was due the shocking remarks in *Scientific Thought* about a thing or a person *being* "a long event."

By the time I wrote the *Examination* I had got free from the worst of that kind of crudity, largely through the careful work which had been done in the meanwhile by Moore and others on the notion of "logical constructions." What I was putting in a terribly slovenly way in *Scientific Thought* on this topic could be stated with more polish as follows. A sentence, whose grammatical subject is the name or a description of a *thing or a person,* and whose grammatical predicate is appropriate to such a substantive word or phrase, can be replaced without loss, gain, or distortion of meaning, by a complex of sentences, in each of which there occur *only* names or descriptions of *processes,* with grammatical predicates appropriate to process-words. (This is certainly not "snappy," and it may not be true; but at any rate it is not "sick-making," like: "A thing or a person is a long event.")

In writing each later account of time I started afresh, and was not concerned with its consistency or inconsistency with earlier accounts. What I have said on this topic in the *EMcP* was meant to supersede what I had said on former occasions, wherever there was a conflict between the two. The reader may assume that I continue to hold (though with much hesitation in view of the difficulty of the subject) any opinion which I expressed in the *EMcP,* unless I explicitly question or withdraw it in what follows below. I hope that this statement will justify me in confining my attention here, as I intend to do, to the *third* account and to Professor Mundle's comments on *it.*

(1) *Qualitative Change and "Absolute Becoming."* It seems to me that there is an irreducibly characteristic feature of time, which I have called "Absolute Becoming." It must be sharply distinguished from qualitative change, though there is no doubt a connexion between the two. In the experience of a conscious being Absolute Becoming manifests itself as the continual *supersession* of what was the latest phase by a new phase, which will in turn be superseded by another new one. This seems to me to be the rock-bottom peculiarity of time, distinguishing *temporal sequence* from all other instances of one-dimensional order, such as that of points on a line, numbers in order of magnitude, and so on.

It is plain that Absolute Becoming is different from qualitative change. An example of the latter would be the gradual melting of a lump of ice in the sunshine, the sudden alteration in the pitch of the sound heard when a whistling locomotive rushes by one, and so on. The contrary opposite to qualitative change is *qualitative invariance.* An example would be the sound heard when a whistling noise of constant pitch, loudness, and tone-quality is made by a locomotive in presence of a hearer who is at rest relatively to it. Now Absolute Becoming is indifferent to whether there be qualitative variation or qualitative invariance. A superseding phase may be qualtitatively indistinguishable from that which it supersedes and from that which supersedes it. Again, in the case of a qualitative variation it is sensible to ask: At what speed is it taking place? We know that the speed of some such changes is greater than that of others, and the speed of any particular qualitative change is a matter for empirical investigation. But there is no sense in asking: At what speed does a certain phase, which was present, retreat into the past? And there is no sense in the suggestion that some might do this faster than others.

Nevertheless, there is undoubtedly a very strong temptation to talk of Absolute Becoming in terms of qualitative change, and particularly in terms of some kind of *motion.* I am quite sure that all such ways of talking are misleading for the reasons given above. Moreover, if offered as an analysis of Absolute Becoming, they involve a kind of vicious circle. For the notions both of qualitative change and of qualitative invariance plainly *presuppose* that of Absolute Becoming, in the sense of that phrase which I have indicated. This circularity is the fundamental objection to *all* such metaphors. Particular forms of the metaphor have, in addition, particular defects characteristic of each. The "policeman's bulls-eye" metaphor, e.g., if taken seriously, presupposes that what has not yet supervened and what has already been superseded in some sense "coexist" with each other and with what is now occurring. Again the metaphor of the history of the world "growing continually longer in duration by the addition of new slices," which I took seriously in *Scientific Thought,* presupposes that phases, which have already supervened and been superseded, in some sense "co-exist" with each other and with that which is now happening.

Let us, then, avoid metaphors and similies and concentrate on the following very simple example, viz., a prolonged sound, continuing for a minute without any variation in pitch, loudness, or tone-quality. Here there is the minimum temptation to imagine that the phases which have been superseded, e.g., the first 30 seconds of this sound, "*continue* somehow to exist," or that the phases which have not yet supervened, e.g., the last 30 seconds of the sound, "*already* somehow exist." And, since we have explicitly excluded all variation in quality, there is no temptation to confuse Absolute Becoming, i.e., the supersession of earlier phases by later ones, with qualitative variation.

(2) *The notion of "Successive Phases."* We seem now to be faced with a serious difficulty. I have spoken of one "phase" of a process "superseding" another, and of its being in turn "superseded by" another. But what is a single phase? Is it supposed to have duration, or is it supposed to be quite literally momentary?

(i) Suppose we ascribe *any* duration, however short, to a phase which has supervened and has not yet been superseded. Then it seems plain that it must consist of an earlier *sub-phase* adjoined to a later one, and that *either* the earlier one has already been superseded by the later one, *or* the later one has not yet supervened on the earlier one. On either alternative *only one* of the two actually exists now. Obviously the same argument applies to each sub-phase itself, and so on without end.

If that is denied, it would seem that the denier is committed to some such view as the following. He must suppose that the sequence of successive moments is *discrete* (like the sequence of integers); that there is an *intrinsically indivisible unit of duration* (viz., the interval between one moment and the next); and that each phase supervenes at one moment and is superseded at the *next,* and therefore has the intrinsically indivisible unit duration. Now I find this quite unintelligible. I can write the words "phase of finite, but intrinsically indivisible, duration," but I can attach no clear idea to what I have written. So I cannot regard this as a genuine alternative.

(ii) Suppose, then, that we say that each phase is *literally momentary* and has literally *no* duration. Then, assuming the continuity of time and therefore that the phrase "next moment" is meaningless, we shall have to say that *at one and the same moment* a phase supervenes and is superseded. To many this may sound palpably absurd, but I am not sure that it is so.

Let us, for once and for this special purpose, do what I have been warning the reader against, and compare Absolute Becoming with *motion*. Everyone must admit that a moving particle *leaves* each point which it traverses at *literally the same moment* at which it *enters* it. "Entering" refers essentially *back* to positions occupied *before,* and "leaving" refers essentially *forward* to positions occupied *after,* the moment and the point in question. Might not similar remarks apply *mutatis mutandis* to "supervening" and "being superseded?" These refer respectively backwards to phases which have been, and forward to phases which will be; but any momentary phase just *momentarily is.*

(iii) Even if this answer to the alleged difficulty in question be accepted, I think that one tends to feel dissatisfied with the notion of literally momentary phases on another count. Surely the notion of a literally momentary phase (like that of a geometrical point or line or surface) is the notion *either* of a boundary between successive adjoined phases, each of *finite* duration, *or* of a limit to an endless sequence of shorter and shorter durations, one inside another, like an endless nest of Chinese boxes? If so, it *presupposes* the existence of phases of finite duration. And surely (it might be added) the latter alone could be actual existents. The literally momentary, like the literally punctiform, bears all the marks of an abstraction, incapable of actual concrete existence, as opposed to an existent particular.

As a preliminary comment on this last objection I will ask the reader to consider for a moment the following geometrical analogue, viz., points without any spatial magnitude, lines with length but no area or volume, and surfaces with area but no thickness. We, whose spatial experiences are of the 3-dimensional kind, consider all these to be abstractions, of the nature of boundaries or limits. We regard objects extended in three dimensions as the only possible kind of extended particular existents. But a creature whose spatial experiences were of the 4-dimensional kind would presumably think of what we call a "solid" in the sort of way in which we think of a 2-dimensional surface. He would think of it as a *boundary* or *limit* with reference to objects extended in four dimensions, and he would regard the *latter* as the only possible kind of extended particular existents. Conversely, a creature whose spatial experiences were of the 2-dimensional kind would presumably think of what we call a "surface," *not* as a mere boundary or limit with reference to objects extended in three dimensions, but as the only possible kind of extended particular existent.

These reflexions seem to show that the question whether a person will regard a *spatial* entity of a given number of dimensions as a particular existent or as a mere boundary or limit, depends on the number of dimensions characteristic of his spatial experience. If the entity is of *that* number of dimensions (e.g., 3 in the case of human beings), he will regard it as a particular existent (e.g., as a cubical block, a spherical globe, and so on). If it is of *less* than that number of dimensions, he will regard it as a mere boundary or limit (e.g., as a face of a cube, the surface of a sphere, and so on). If it is of *more* than that number of dimensions (e.g., 4 or more in the case of a human being), he cannot perceive it as such. He can perceive only what a 4-dimensional being would regard as various 3-dimensional *boundaries* of it, and he will take these to be *particular existents*. This at least enables one to see that the question whether a given *spatially extended* entity is a particular existent or a mere boundary or limit, is not so simple and unambiguous as it might seem at first sight.

But I doubt if this really helps us in the present case. The question is whether we could regard *literally momentary* phases as actual existents, or whether we must regard them as limits or boundaries of phases of finite duration. Now our temporal experience is at least 1-dimensional, whilst a momentary phase would be an entity of *zero* temporal dimension. So, on the principles laid down in the preceding paragraph for *spatially* extended entities, it would seem that we could not help regarding a literally momentary phase as a mere boundary or limit, and not as a particular existent.

(3) *The theory of 2-dimensional Time.* The only solution that I can think of is to allege that Time is of at least *two* dimensions, and that a phase which has zero duration in the dimension which we commonly recognise has a finite "duration" in the other dimension.

A theory on these lines has been put forward and argued in detail by my friend and former pupil, Mr. H. A. C. Dobbs, in the *British Journal for the Philosophy of Science* for August 1951. His object was primarily to deal with (a) the facts which are summarised under the phrase "the specious present," and (b) certain notions of quantum physics. I shall here state in my own way a simplified form of the theory, as I understand it, without reference to the specious present or to the quantum theory. The reader should direct his attention to the diagram below:—

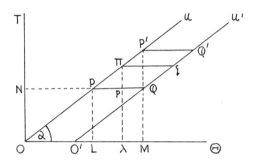

I am going to call the two temporal dimensions the "Θ-dimension" and the "T-dimension." A *completely* instantaneous "phase-particle," as I will call it, would be represented by a *point* in the diagram, whose co-ordinates are $\Theta = \theta$, and $T = t$. It might be denoted by the symbol $p(\theta,t)$. What we have been calling a "momentary phase" occurring at the instant t is represented in the diagram, *not* by a point, but by a *straight line* of finite length and no thickness parallel to the Θ-axis. It may therefore be described as "T-instantaneous," but it has a certain extension, which we will call "Θ-duration" in the Θ-dimension. Suppose that such a phase occurs at $T = t$ in the T-dimension, and that it extends from $\Theta = \theta_p$ to $\Theta = \theta_q$ in the Θ-dimension. Then we can denote it by $\phi(t, \theta_p \rightarrow \theta_q)$. In the diagram the line PQ represents such a phase. ON represents $T = t$, OL represents $\Theta = \theta_p$, and OM represents $\Theta = \theta_q$.

So much by way of notation and diagrammatic representation. We can now formulate the details of the theory as follows:—

(i) We assume that there is a certain fixed direction in the 2-dimensional time-field, represented in the diagram by a fixed straight line OU, making an angle α with the axis OΘ. (It does not matter for our present purpose what the magnitude of α may be, provided it is between O and $\frac{\pi}{2}$.)

(ii) Every T-instantaneous phase stretches in the Θ-dimension from a phase-particle represented by a point, such as P, on the line OU, to a phase-particle represented by a point, such as Q, on a line O'U' parallel to OU and at a fixed distance from it along the Θ-axis. (For the present purpose it does not matter what may be the magnitude of the Θ-duration represented by the distance OO'.)

(iii) For each *successive* T-instantaneous phase, as the value of T

continuously *increases,* the initial phase-particle is *further* along the line OU.

(iv) Between any two T-instantaneous phases, no matter how near together be the respective values of T, there is a *third* T-instantaneous phase.

It will be noted that we have secured by these suppositions a consistent combination of (a) *continuity* of transition, (b) the *finite* Θ-duration of each T-successive term, and (c) the *instantaneity* of each T-successive term. This is secured by the fact that T-instantaneous phases, though *completely* successive in the T-dimension, *partially overlap* in the Θ-dimension provided that the difference in their T-dates does not excede a certain maximum, and that the nearer their T-dates are to each other the more nearly complete is this overlap.

A glance at the diagram will show that there must be a kind of "natural unit" of T-time-lapse, correlated with the "natural unit" of Θ-duration represented in the diagram by the distance OO′. (This might be compared with the natural unit of 4 right-angles in the case of angles.) In the diagram let the straight line MQ be produced upwards until it cuts the fixed line OU at P′. Then the phase P′Q′ is the *first* successor to the phase PQ which does *not* overlap PQ *at all.* Thus the line QP′ represents a kind of natural unit of T-time-lapse. This is obviously connected with the natural unit of Θ-duration and the fixed angle α by the relation $\dfrac{P'Q}{PQ} = \dfrac{P'Q}{OO'} = \tan\alpha$. Let us denote the natural unit of T-time-lapse by τ, and the natural unit of Θ-duration by σ. Then $\tau = \sigma\tan\alpha$.

It is plaint that τ, the natural unit of T-time-lapse, can belong only to a T-sequence of *phase-particles,* all of which have *the same* value of Θ. Such a sequence *begins* with a phase-particle (such as Q) which is at the *terminal end* of a complete T-instantaneous phase (such as PQ), and it *ends* with a phase-particle (such as P′) which is at the *initial end* of a certain later complete T-instantaneous phase (such as P′Q′).

It will be of interest to consider next the T-time-lapse belonging to a sequence of *sub-phases,* all of which have the same initial value and the same terminal value of Θ. For this purpose we can consider the sub-phase represented by the segment pQ of the line PQ (which represents a complete phase). Through p draw a line parallel to OT. Let it cut the fixed line OU at Π, and the axis OΘ at λ. Then it is evident that there will be a sub-phase extending from $\Theta = O\lambda$ to $\Theta = OM$ in every successive complete phase from PQ to Πq, both inclusive, and in no others. So the T-time-lapse belonging to this sequence of sub-phases is represented by Πp. Now $\Pi p = Pp \tan_\alpha$. But $Pp = (PQ - pQ) = (\sigma - pQ)$. And we have already shown that $\tan_\alpha = \dfrac{\tau}{\sigma}$. So $\Pi p = (\sigma - pQ)\dfrac{\tau}{\sigma} = \tau(1 - \dfrac{pQ}{\sigma})$. If we put $\Pi p = t$, and $pQ = s$, we can write this in the form $t = \tau(1 - \dfrac{s}{\sigma})$. So the T-time-lapse belonging to such a sequence of sub-phases varies between the limits 0 (when $s = \sigma$, and the "sub-phase" is supposed to swell into a *complete* phase of natural unit Θ-duration) and τ (when $s = 0$, and the "sub-phase" is supposed to shrink into a mere *phase-particle*.)

(4) *The Specious Present.* This brings me to the question of the Specious Present. What I have to say about this is in principle the same as what I said in Vol. II, Part I, of the *Examination* (Pp. 281–288). But on the one hand it becomes considerably clearer when stated in terms of 2-dimensional Time, and on the other hand it provides a concrete illustration of the abstract account of the latter given above.

It is evident that the 2-dimensional diagram at the top of P. 285 in my account of the specious present in the *EMcP* would have to be replaced by a 3-dimensional diagram. For we have now to represent *two* temporal dimensions (instead of one only, as in the *EMcP*), and in addition (as there) the magnitude which I called "degree of presentedness." The modifications needed will be understood without difficulty, if the reader will refer back to the diagram given above in expounding the general theory of 2-dimensional Time.

Suppose now that the lines PQ, Πq, P′Q′, etc., in that diagram represent the Θ-durations of T-successive *specious presents*. Then we should have to represent *degree of presentedness* by distances along a *third* axis, sticking out at right-angles from the plane of the paper. We must regard each of these lines as the base of a right-angled triangle, e.g.,

turned about PQ so that QR is normal to the plane of the paper. The length QR then represents the *maximal* degree of presentedness, viz., that of the *latest* end of the content of a specious present. The degree of presentedness tails off to zero at the *earliest* end of that content. For the details of this I refer the reader to the account in the *Examination*.

It may be of interest, however, to add a diagram representing in terms of this theory the hearing of the sound of a short word, e.g.,

"RAG," which falls well within the Θ-duration of a human specious present. The diagram is in principle the same as that given above, but it now must be regarded as the *plan* in the T-Θ-plane of the complete 3-dimensional diagram.

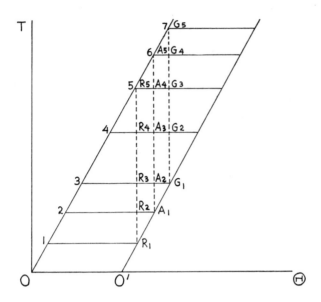

Consider the above sequence of seven lines all parallel to OΘ. They represent seven T-successive specious presents out of a continuous sequence of specious presents. In No. 1 the sound "R," and nothing more of the sound "RAG," is just being presented to the hearer, at the *latest* end of a specious present, and therefore with *maximal* degree of presentedness. In No. 2 this is true of the "A" sound. The "R" sound is still being presented, but now with less than maximal degree of presentedness. So the "RA" sound as a whole is being presented. In No. 3 the "RAG" sound as a whole is for the first time presented. The "G" sound has now the maximal degree of presentedness, the "A" sound less, and the "R" sound still less. In No. 4 (and in all the innumerable successive specious presents between those represented in the diagram by No. 3 and by No. 5) the "RAG" sound as a whole continues to be presented, but with steadily diminishing degree of presentedness. In No. 5 the "R" sound is just on the point of ceasing to be *presented* and being at most *remembered*. In No. 6 only the "AG" sound is still presented; the "RA" sound has ceased to be presented. In No. 7 nothing is any longer presented of the sound "RAG" except the ghost of the "G" sound in the act of vanishing.

(B) PRECOGNITION. This topic forms the theme of a part of Professor Ducasse's paper and of the whole of Professor Flew's. I will begin with Professor Ducasse's "Theory Theta." Although this is put forward primarily to deal with the problem of non-inferential precognition, it is a *general* theory of time, and therefore highly relevant to the topics which we have been discussing above.

(1) *Professor Ducasse's "Theory Theta."* The theory falls into three divisions, viz., (i) Inter-relations of *physical events,* (ii) Inter-relations of *experiences,* and (iii) Relations *between* experiences and physical events. I will take these points in turn.

(i) *Inter-relations of Physical Events.* (a) Purely physical events, which do not overlap each other, form a 1-dimensional *quasi-*temporal series ordered by an *irreducibly triadic relation,* which I will call "chronical betweenness." By saying that this relation is *irreducibly triadic* we mean that the statement that the physical event Y is chronically between the physical events X and Z is *not* analysable into the statement that *either* X is earlier than Y and Y earlier than $Z,$ *or* X is later than Y and Y later than $Z.$ In the sequence of purely physical events there is no asymmetrical dyadic relation, such as earlier-and-later, which would give an intrinsic direction to it.

(b) If we take any *two* terms U and U' in such a series, we can subdivide all the remaining terms in it into two mutually exclusive and collectively exhaustive sub-classes, as follows, viz., (α) those which are on *the same side* of U' as U is, and (β) those which are on *the opposite side* of U' to U (i.e., those of which it is true that U' lies between them and U.)

(c) Let us now consider a term $X,$ which is on the *same* side of U' as U is. Then there are two mutually exclusive and collectively exhaustive possibilities, viz., (α) that X is between U and U' (i.e., that X is "chronically *nearer*" to U' than U is), or (β) that U is between X and U' (i.e., that X is "chronically *further*" from U' than U is.) These are the two possibilities which Professor Ducasse would formulate respectively as: "X is *past* to U from U'" and "X is future to U from U'." So these two statements may be defined as follows:—

(α) "X is *past* to U from U'" means the same as "X is chronically on the *same* side of U' as $U,$ and is chronically nearer to U' than is $U.$" I will denote this by $\Pi\,(X,\,U;\,U').$

(β) "X is *future* to U from U'" means the same as "X is chronically on the *same* side of U' as $U,$ and is chronically *further* from U' than is $U.$" I will denote this by $\Phi\,(X,U;U').$

I think it is wiser to keep to the symbols and their definitions, and *not* to use the phrases "past to . . . from" and "future to . . . from," when talking of the *quasi*-temporal inter-relations of purely physical events. For these phrases inevitably have associations which may mislead us.

It should be noted that, although the two relationships Π $(X,U;U')$ and Φ $(X,U;U')$ are *mutually exclusive,* they are *not* collectively exhaustive. Both of them presuppose that X is on the *same* side of U' as U is. Obviously there remains the possibility that X should be on the *opposite* side of U' to U. In that case obviously X and U' would be on the *same* side of U, and X would be *further* from U than is U'. So we should have Φ $(X,U';U)$. So it would seem that for any three non-overlapping purely physical events the three mutually exclusive and collectively exhaustive possibilities would be Π $(X,U;U')$, Φ $(X,U;U')$, and Φ $(X,U';U)$.

It is also worth noting that Π $(X,U;U')$ is equivalent to Φ $(U,X;U')$. For to say that X is *nearer* to U' than is U, is obviously equivalent to saying that U is *further* from U' than is X.

I hope that the above is a complete and correct formal statement of Professor Ducasse's account of the *quasi*-temporal order of purely physical events. It may be remarked that it is precisely analogous to the *intrinsic spatial* order of points on a straight line. There is no *intrinsic* "sense" in the order of points on a line. When we ascribe one to it, we do so either by reference to our right and left hands, or by imagining something traversing it and so occupying certain points earlier and others later.

(ii) *Inter-relations of Experiences.* I am not at all sure that I fully understand Professor Ducasse's account of the temporal order of *experiences.* I think it is plainly concerned primarily with the experiences which together make up the mental history of some *one* conscious individual. Again, I think it is concerned *both* (a) with what almost everyone would call "experiences," e.g., feeling a twinge of toothache, or the popping up into consciousness of a name which one had been trying to recall, *and* (b) with what some (but not all) philosophers would refuse to call "experiences," but would prefer to describe as the "immediate objects" of certain experiences, and would call "sense-data," "mental images," and so on. I shall cover both cases here by saying that "*x* is *present to P,*" if and only if *x* is either (a) an experience, or (b) a sense-datum or a mental image or (in general) a "prehensum"; and *P* is either (a) having that experience, or (b) sensing that sensum or imaging that image or (in general) "prehending" that prehensum.

On these assumptions, I think that this part of the theory certainly includes the following propositions:—

(a) What is "present to" a person at any given moment consists of a certain set of *sub-phases.* All of these are then present to him with *some* degree or other of what Professor Ducasse calls "liveness," and each different one of them is present to him with a *different* degree of liveness. One and only one of them (which may itself be internally complex) is then present to him with the *maximal* degree of liveness. I propose to call them "degree-of-liveness sub-phases."

(b) It follows that what is present to a person at any given moment constitutes a *finite segment,* in respect of the different degrees of liveness, from maximal to minimal, with which each different sub-phase is then present to him. Let us call this a "degree-of-liveness segment."

(c) What is present to a person at any moment is not merely *in fact* a degree-of-liveness segment. It is *presented to him as* such a segment, and he can formulate these facts about it if he inspects it and reflects on his findings.

(d) That sub-phase of what is present to a person at any moment which is then present to him with *maximal* degree of liveness, is at that moment *strictly present.* All the other sub-phases in the segment are then *strictly past.* The *degree* of pastness of each is correlated *conversely* with its degree of liveness.

(e) Every degree-of-liveness sub-phase of the segment which is present to a person at any moment may be called "*speciously* present." This serves to contrast them all with sub-phases which have been present to the person, but are no longer so, and with others which have never been present to him but may be so later.

Now it will be noted that all the propositions which I have ascribed above with some confidence to Professor Ducasse have involved the phrase "at any one moment." I find it impossible to state the theory (or indeed *any* account of "specious presentness") without introducing that phrase, or some equivalent of it. But it is plain that the theory would be hopelessly inadequate unless it also referred to a *plurality of successive* specious presents, and it is at this point that I feel very uncertain as to Professor Ducasse's meaning.

It seems to me that at least the following statements would need to be added, but I am not sure which (if any) of them Professor Ducasse would accept:—

(a) If a sub-phase is present to a person with the *maximal* degree of liveness at the moment t_1, then (α) at *no* moment before t_1 was it present to him at all; (β) at each successive moment *after* t_1 (up to and including a certain moment t_2) it will be present to him with a lesser and lesser degree of liveness, and at t_2 with *minimal* degree; and (γ) after t_2 it will never be present to him again.

(b) If a sub-phase is present to a person with a degree of liveness *less than the maximal* at the moment t, then there is a moment t_1 (*earlier* than t) such that it was present to him with *maximal* degree of liveness at t_1. (My account of specious presentness in the *Examination,* and the amended account given above in terms of 2-dimensional Time, was intended to represent, by means of the series of triangles with partly overlapping bases, this irreducible feature of continuous transition.)

Now one reason why I am doubtful whether I have fully understood Professor Ducasse's theory is this. On the one hand, he appears to make such statements as the following. To call any phase "strictly present" *means* simply and solely that it is present to one with the maximal degree of liveness. To call any phase "strictly past" *means* simply and solely that it is either (a) present to one with less than the maximal degree of liveness, or (b) not present to one, but capable of being attended to only by "recalling" it in memory. Again, he says explicitly that statements about the specious present should *not* be made in *temporal* terms, as if we knew *independently* what such terms mean. And the reason given is that liveness and its degrees are the experiential basis, not only of our notion of *presentness,* but also of our notion of *earlier* and *later,* and therefore of our notion of Time. On the other hand, he does speak of events "popping into" the specious present, in the direction from maximal to minimal degree of liveness.

Now I agree that the ordered degrees of liveness with which a number of different sub-phases are present to a person at any given moment of his life may well be *one* essential factor in the experiential basis of our notions of past and present, of earlier and later, and so of Time. But surely a no less essential factor is the experience (a) of what *was just lately* present to one with maximal liveness being *now* present to one with lesser liveness, (b) of something which *just lately* was not present to one at all being *now* present to one with *maximal* liveness, and (c) of what was *just lately* present to one with minimal liveness being *now no longer* present to one at all. So far as I can see, none of these features in our experience can be described except in such temporal terms as "at a given moment," "now," "just lately," "no longer," etc. If so, it would seem impossible to admit that our notion of Time can be defined or described, completely and without circularity, simply in terms of maximal and lesser degrees of presentness to an experient. Perhaps Professor Ducasse has no intention of denying this. But my impression is that his explicit statements are (and are probably intended to be) equivalent to denying it. If so, I cannot see how the theory can be adequate to the facts of our experience.

(iii) *Relations of Experiences to Physical Events.* I doubt if I fully understand Professor Ducasse's account of the relation between the triadic *quasi*-temporal order of purely physical events and the dyadic genuinely temporal order of experiences. It is this which plays an essential part in his theory of Precognition. The following points seem to be certain:—

(a) To say of a *physical* event that it is "present" at a certain moment *means* simply and solely that it is then the object of a *perception* which is *strictly present* to some percipient. (b) It is logically possible that one and the same physical event should be *perceived* on several different occasions (either by the same person or by different persons), and therefore, by definition, that it should be *present* on as many different occasions. (c) In a genuine case of precognising non-inferentially a physical event *e,* what would happen would be this. (α) The person who is said to "precognise" *e* in fact *perceives* it, but in an *abnormal* way, viz., *not* by means of sensations (which Professor Ducasse describes as "vivid images caused at the time through the functioning of the sense-organs"). (β) *Later* he, or someone else, perceives *e* in the *normal* way, i.e., by means of sensations.

It seems to me that these three statements would at any rate need the following qualifications. (a) I think that the first of them would need to be amplified somewhat as follows. A physical event *e* is present at any moment, if e*ither* (α) it is then the object of a perception which is strictly present to a percipient, *or* (β) it is *contemporary with* another physical event *e',* of which this is true. Unfortunately Professor Ducasse has given no account of "simultaneity" between purely physical events.

(b) As Professor Ducasse recognises, it would be necessary (in view of the finite velocity of light and sound and of the transmission of nervous impulses) to modify the original statement somewhat as follows. A physical event, perceived normally by the senses, which would be called "present" in accordance with the proposed definition, would always in fact be *earlier* (and in some cases very much earlier) than the strictly present sense-perception of it. It would therefore be really *past* at the moment when, if the definition were taken as it stands, it would be called "present."

(c) Professor Ducasse admits the possibility that a physical event which is non-sensuously "perceived" by one person may *later* be perceived normally by *another* person. This presupposes some temporal correlation between the mental histories of *different* persons. Obviously there is such a correlation. But all Professor Ducasse's statements about the temporal interrelations of expriences have been confined to those which fall within the mental history of a single person.

The above are comments on matters of detail. The two following are more general. (a) What are we to understand by the kind of *non-sensuous* perception of a physical event, which Professor Ducasse postulates in contrast with ordinary sense-perception? He seems to assume that there is some generally admitted definition or description of the genus or determinable "perception," which leaves the two possibilities "sensuous" and "non-sensuous" open as specifications of it. But, if so, what is it?

(b) At an earlier stage of his essay, in dealing with the alleged "fatalistic objection" to the possibility of non-inferential precognition, Professor Ducasse asserts (quite rightly) that many of the instances of "veridical precognition" are not instances of *cognition* (i.e. knowledge) of the future event which will in course of time verify or refute the "precognition." I do not see how this fits in with the later suggestion that in cases of veridical precognition one and the same physical event is twice perceived, first non-sensuously and later sensuously, by the same person or by different persons.

(2) *Professor Flew's Comments.* I pass now to Professor Flew's essay. This is concerned with my treatment of three *prima facie* objections which I alleged that many people feel in connexion with the very notion of veridical non-inferential foreseeing. I called these the "Epistemological," the "Causal," and the "Fatalistic" objections.

(i) *The Epistemological Objection.* As Professor Flew agrees in the main with my statement of this and with my answer to it, I will comment only on the following point. I stressed an alleged analogy between ostensible *foreseeing* and ostensible *remembering* of incidents, persons, and things. In doing so, I said that a present *image* is involved in ostensible remembering, and I asserted or implied that one would be involved in ostensible foreseeing also. Professor Flew points out that in *The Mind and its Place in Nature* I had denied that a present image is necessarily involved in ostensible remembering, and he speculates on the cause of my "backsliding."

In point of fact I have never seen occasion to alter the opinion on this point which I expressed in *MPN*. The explanation of my apparent "backsliding" in "The Philosophical Implications of Precognition" is this. I was thinking exclusively of the *sporadic* cases on record at the time in the books and papers which I mentioned. The experimental work in connexion with card-guessing, which has since become the most important evidence for "precognition," was not then available. Now images (in a wide sense which includes the *quasi*-sensa of dreams and waking hallucinations) *are* involved in most of the sporadic ostensibly precognitive experiences, and images *are* involved in many experiences of ostensibly remembering events, persons, or things. In the paper in question I was concerned to stress the resemblance to memory, and to undermine the common assumption that veridical non-inferential precognition, if it occurs, *must* be of the nature of *perception*.

It is plain that the card-guessing results bear very little resemblance to experiences of ostensible remembering, and do not fit at all into the framework of my Aristotelian paper. This is of considerable importance in reference to Professor Flew's essay, for it is evident that the empirical data which he has in mind are correlations between a sequence of guess-values and a sequence of target-values, as in a card-guessing experiment.

Here the only relevant property of any guess is that it is a guess that the target-card bears such and such a one of a small number of known alternative symbols, e.g., a *cross,* where the alternatives are known to the guesser to be, e.g., a cross, a square, a circle, a wavy line, or a triangle. No-one would say here of *any particular* correct guess that it is "at least a very remarkable coincidence." One would say this only of the *proportion* of correct guesses in a long sequence of guesses. And one would say it only if that proportion were to differ (either by excess or defect) from "the proportion most probable on the hypothesis of chance-coincidence" by several times the "standard deviation" for such a sequence on that hypothesis. At a certain point, which would differ from person to person, one would be inclined to say: "This excess (or defect) is altogether too great to be reasonably regarded as a mere freak of chance."

Now the kind of case which I had in mind was different. Here a person is presented on a certain one occasion with an image or a *quasi*-sensum of a very detailed and elaborate kind, and no obvious cause can be suggested for the occurrence of that experience in him at that time. Not too long afterwards there happens an event in the external world, which could not normally have been expected by him at the time, and it corresponds in a remarkable way in its details with the experience in question. One is inclined to say of *any particular* pair of events of this kind that it constitutes "at least a very remarkable coincidence." And if the singularity and unexpectedness of the later event, and the degree of detailed correspondence between it and the earlier experience, surpass a certain point (which again would differ from person to person), one would be inclined to say: "This correspondence is altogether too peculiar and too detailed to be reasonably regarded as a mere freak of chance."

Since Professor Flew confines himself to evidence of the *first* kind, I shall do so too. I will only remark that I think it would be very difficult, in the case of some of his arguments, to adapt them to evidence of the *second* kind, which is what I had in mind in writing the paper on which he is commenting.

(ii) *The Causal Objection.* I think that Professor Flew's formulation of the alleged objection is essentially correct, but I will re-state it in my own way. A certain person P makes a sequence of guesses as to which one of a small number of known alternative symbols will be on the face of the *next* card which is about to be turned up in a certain experiment. Here a "hit" is a case where the symbol guessed is the *same* as that on the face of the card next turned up after the guess has been made. What is said to be "too great to be a mere chance coincidence" is the deviation (positive or negative) between the actual proportion of hits in the whole sequence and what is called "the most probable proportion of hits, on the hypothesis of chance coincidence, in such a sequence."

Now (a) by *definition* we are *not* to count the results as evidence for *foreseeing*, if the difference between the actual and the most probable proportion of hits *can* be dismissed as "merely a remarkable coincidence." But (b) to deny that it is a mere coincidence is to allege that there is *some causal connexion* between (a) some at least of the events described as "a guess that the next card will have such and such a symbol on its face" and (β) some of the events described as "the turning up, immediately after the making of that guess, of a card with such and such a symbol (the same or different) on its face." Let us call these respectively a "G-event" and its "A-correlate." Now (c) it is contrary to the notion of causation that the A-correlate to a G-event should be a factor in *causing* the latter. For the A-correlate does not *begin* until after the G-event in question has *ceased*. Therefore (d) the only kinds of causal connexion that are possible are the following. Either (a) a G-event is a cause factor in a *causal ancestor* of its A-correlate; or (β) a G-event and its A-correlate are effect factors respectively in an earlier and in a later *causal descendant* of some *common causal ancestor*; or (γ) the G-event was determined by the result of an *inference* as to the nature of its forthcoming A-correlate, either made somehow by the guesser himself or made by someone else and somehow imparted by him to the guesser. But (e) all these alternatives are so many ways of accounting for the difference between the actual and the most probable proportion of hits in the sequence *without* supposing that any of the guesses is an instance of veridical non-inferential precognising. (f) It would seem, therefore, that my *definition* of "foreseeing" rules out the possibility of any of the guesses counting as instances of *foreseeing* the nature of the target-card, no matter how great may be the deviation between the actual proportion of hits and the proportion which would be most probable on the hypothesis of chance-coincidence.

In the above reasoning it is the *second* step to which Professor Flew takes exception, viz., the transition from *denying* that so great a divergence can be a mere chance coincidence to *asserting* that there must be some causal connexion between some at least of the G-events and their A-correlates. Professor Flew's alternative, as I understand it, may be stated as follows:—

(a) It is a fact, with regard to certain persons P_1, P_2, ... P_n, who have been investigated, that on all or most occasions when any of them has made a long sequence of guesses under certain assigned conditions, the proportion of hits has differed significantly from the most probable proportion on the hypothesis of chance-coincidence. (b) It is reasonable to believe that the guess made by such a person on any occasion is causally determined, and it is reasonable to believe that the immediately subsequent turning up of a card with such and such a symbol on its face by the experimenter is causally determined. But in a properly designed experiment there is *no* reason to believe that there is *any causal connexion,* direct or indirect, between the former event and the latter, whether the guess be a hit or a miss.

Notwithstanding this complete lack of causal connexion, the following expectations might reasonably be entertained and the following enquiries might reasonably be undertaken, according to Professor Flew. (a) It would be reasonable to expect, with regard to any of these persons, that, if he were to make a further sequence of guesses under similar conditions, the proportion of hits would *still* diverge significantly and in the same direction from the most probable proportion on the hypothesis of chance-coincidence. (b) It would be sensible to compare these persons with each other, and to contrast them with others who (under apparently similar conditions) consistently make scores which do *not* differ significantly from what might be expected on the hypothesis of chance-coincidence, in order to discover some characteristic ψ, common and peculiar to the former. If such a characteristic were found, it would be reasonable to put forward, and to test by further experiment and observation, following wider generalisation:—Most (if not all) persons having the characteristic ψ, and few (if any) who lack it, would, if making a sequence of guesses under conditions C, score a proportion of hits significantly different from the most probable proportion on the hypothesis of chance-coincidence. (c) Even if only the narrower extrapolation, labelled (a) above, were available, the following statement would be true. Suppose that an observer O accepted this extrapolation. Suppose he knew that on a certain occasion one of these persons P_r had guessed that the next card to be turned up would be of such and such a kind. Then O would be justified in conjecturing, with *greater* conviction than would otherwise have been warranted, that such a card *would* be turned up next (if P_r's previous performance had shown a significant *positive* deviation), or that such a card would *not* be turned up next (if P_r's previous performance had shown a significant *negative* deviation).

Now, as regards the logic of the question, I find myself largely in agreement with Professor Flew here. Let us assume that the cards are properly randomised, that the experiments are properly conducted so as to eliminate all possibility of fraud, sensory leakages, and so on. Then the conclusion which can legitimately be drawn from a successful series of such experiments can be accurately stated in the following rather complex sentence: "In view of the actual results obtained with the subject S, it is *extremely unlikely* that the probability of his assigning any particular one of the alternative symbols to the next card to be turned up is the *same* no matter whether *that* symbol or any of the alternatives to it will *in fact* be on the face of that card." Now this can be expressed loosely by saying that, in view of the actual results, it is extremely unlikely that the nature of a guess is not "to some extent *influenced by*" the nature of the symbol borne by the card which will be turned up immediately afterwards. The latter expression, taken as it stands, does suggest some kind of *causal connexion* between G-events and their A-correlates. But we must remember that it is simply a shorthand translation of the longer and more complex sentence given above. Now that sentence certainly does not *explicitly* contain any reference to causation. It is couched in terms of "probability," and of variation or non-variation in "probability" according as the data are of one form or another.

That is the *prima facie* case in favour of Professor Flew's contention. I think it is strong, but not absolutely conclusive. Both "probability" and "causation" are extremely obscure and ambiguous notions, and one cannot be quite sure that sentences which explicitly mention only the former may not implicitly refer to the latter.

Without entering into that question, we can ask ourselves the following one:— Under what circumstances would one's initial impression, that the deviation of the actual proportion of hits from the proportion which would be most probable on the hypothesis of chance-coincidence is too great to be a chance-coincidence, be *strengthened?* And under what circumstances would it be *weakened?* It seems to me plain that it would be strengthened or weakened according as the answers to such questions as the following were affirmative or negative. Are the results as a whole repeatable, (a) in the sense that there are generally a few subjects who can produce them, and (b) that each such subject can go on producing them over a longish period when the known conditions are kept as constant as possible? Do they vary concomitantly with certain variations in the conditions? Is there a certain "statistical pattern," which manifests itself in each successive sequence of guesses made by the same subject with the same agent and the same experimenter under the same experimental conditions?

Before concluding this sub-section I would add the following remark.

If we consider in detail how card-guessing experiments are designed and conducted, it seems that in most of those which are said to provide evidence for "precognitive telepathy or clairvoyance" there is no *necessity* to postulate *foreknowledge* at all. The results could in fact be interpreted *causally*, and the causation would involve no *temporal* difficulties or paradoxes, though it would be in other respects extremely peculiar.

This is not the place to develop the point in detail, and the following general hint must suffice. Suppose we assume that the bodily action which the "telepathic agent" performs, on receipt of his cue from the experimenter that the subject has made a guess, is *completely determined causally*. Then a complete causal ancestor of that action must have already existed *immediately before* the subject made his guess. Now it is this action, together with the experimental set-up, which determines *what symbol* the agent will perceive on the receipt by him of his cue from the experimenter. Suppose we assume that the bodily action which the subject performs, in writing down such and such a symbol as his guess about the card which the agent is about to look at, is also *completely determined causally*. Then all that we need to assume in order to account causally for (say) a significant *predominance of hits* is this. We must suppose that that causal ancestor of the *agent's* future action of selecting and looking at such and such a card, which immediately precedes the *subject's* present action of writing down his guess as to the nature of that card, contains a factor which influences the subject to write down as his guess the symbol which it is already determined that the agent will perceive. This would be a very odd kind of causal law, but its oddity would arise from its unfamiliarity and not from its involving causal influence from future to present or later to earlier.

(iii) *The Fatalistic Objection.* I will begin by re-stating the objection. Suppose that at t_1 a person A veridically foresees an event which in due course happens at t_3; and suppose that an essential factor in causally pre-determining that event was a voluntary decision, made at a certain *intermediate* moment t_2 either by A himself or by another person B. (The following would be an example. Mr. Jones correctly foresees at t_1 that Mr. Smith will be killed in an aeroplane-crash at t_3; and a necessary precondition of this happening was that Mr. Smith decided at t_2 to travel by a certain plane and not by another plane or by boat.)

Then the argument runs as follows. (a) Since the event was correctly foreseen at t_1, it must have been completely predetermined causally by that time. (b) It must therefore have been completely predetermined causally at the later moment t_2. (c) Therefore the voluntary decision made by B at t_2, which was an essential factor in the causal ancestor at t_2

of the event in question, must have been completely pre-determined causally at least as early at t_1. (d) We must therefore draw the following conclusion in such a case. *Either* (*a*) B's voluntary decision at t_2 was *not* (as we had assumed it to be) a causally necessary precondition of the occurrence of the foreseen event. *Or* (*β*) that decision was completely predetermined causally at least as early at t_1.

Now both alternatives are highly *distasteful to the feelings* of many, though that is of course no reason for holding that neither of them could be *true*. The first alternative is in the worse position. We have as good reason for holding that Mr. Smith, in my example, would not have travelled by the plane in question, unless he had decided at an intermediate moment to do so, as we have for almost any empirical belief as to the consequences of unfulfilled conditions.

In commenting on this "objection," as I originally stated it, Professor Flew makes the following points:—

(a) He says that he rejects the assumption that freedom to decide between alternatives entails that voluntary decisions are not completely predetermined causally. If the reader will look at my re-statement above, he will see that that assumption is *not* involved. All that I allege is that many people find it distasteful to think that their voluntary decisions are completely predetermined causally long before they come to be made. I think that they would do this, even though they admitted that such decisions would still be *free* in a number of important senses, which were mentioned by Locke and have been repeated *ad nauseam* by other philosophers since his time.

(b) The premiss in this "objection" which I myself questioned was that which comes first in the above re-statement, viz., that, if an event were correctly foreseen at a certain moment, it must have been completely predetermined causally at that moment. I do not know what attitude Professor Flew would himself take towards this premiss. But he does argue that to *reject* it (as I was inclined to do) is inconsistent with certain things which I said or implied about veridical foreseeing.

The point is this. (a) My definition of "veridical foreseeing" entails that an event would *not* be said to have been "veridically foreseen" *unless* there were some kind of *causal connexion* between the experience of "foreseeing" and that event "foreseen." For, otherwise, according to what I said, the correspondence between the two would be no more than a remarkable coincidence. (b) My account of an event being "completely predetermined causally at *t*" was this. There is a set of facts about the states and dispositions at *t* of the various things and persons then existing, which, together with the laws of nature, logically entail that an event of precisely that kind would happen at the time and place at which that event did happen or will happen. (c) Now suppose that there occurs at t an experience answering to my definition of "veridical foreseeing." Then *it* must be included among "the states and dispositions at t of the various things and persons then existing." And among the "laws of nature" we must include, not only the laws of normal physics and psychology, but also those causal laws (whatever they may be), in accordance with which experiences of veridically foreseeing and the events veridically foreseen are (according to my definition) causally interconnected. (d) But, when that is done, it is not open to me (consistently with my definitions) to question that, if an event is veridically foreseen at t, it must be causally predetermined at t.

I accept this criticism of Professor Flew's on my consistency, at any rate to the following extent. I certainly did forget to include the experience of veridically foreseeing *itself* among the states and dispositions of the various things and persons existing at the time when it occurred. And I certainly failed to notice that my assertion that there must be some kind of *causal* connexion between an earlier experience and a corresponding later event, if the former is to count as a "veridical foreseeing" of the latter, implies that among the laws of nature there are laws concerning *just that kind* of causal connexion. But it does not seem to me to follow, even when these factors are taken into account, that the event foreseen at t must be *completely* predetermined causally at t. It might at that moment be causally predetermined *only within certain limits*.

This has a bearing on the last point which I will consider under this head. Consider the following modification of our previous example. Mr. Smith, hearing of the experience in which Mr. Jones ostensibly foresees his death in the crash of a certain plane (or, alternatively, having such an experience himself), cancels his booking and thus saves his life, though that plane does crash and all the passengers on it are killed. It is sometimes said that in such cases the occurrence of a *veridical* foreseeing causes voluntary action to be taken which prevents it from being fulfilled.

About all such cases it seems to me that Professor Ducasse is right. In so far as it is known that a claim has been made to foresee that a certain kind of event will happen at such and such a time and place, and in so far as that knowledge leads to action which *prevents* an event of *exactly* that kind from happening there and then, the claim *as it stands* is mistaken. But, if the claim were re-stated in a *conditional* form, or in a *less determinate* categorical form, there may be no reason against and good reasons for admitting it.

(VII) *The Psycho-Physical Individual*

Under this heading I shall consider comments on what I have written on the nature of the human mind and on the relation between the mental and the bodily aspects of a human being. These topics are the subject of the whole of Mr. Kneale's essay and of parts of the essays of Professor Ducasse and Professor Patterson.

I will begin by expressing my complete agreement with Mr. Kneale's criticisms of the views which he ascribes to a certain influential group of contemporary philosophers in England and U.S.A. I fully accept his conclusion that "all talk of minds presupposes the occurrence of experiences," in a sense in which statements about experiences are *not* reducible to statements about behaviour and tendencies to behave.

As to the persons, mentioned by Mr. Kneale, who profess to be unable to understand what is intended by familiar technical terms, like "experience," "sensation," "event," etc., unless these are used in certain special senses in which they occur in popular speech and writing, I can only say this. I have always given them the credit of not being in fact such fools as they would need to be if their professions of impotence could be taken literally. It is, after all, a very common device, in philosophic and other controversies among well-bred disputants, to use: "I don't *understand* what Mr. X means" as a polite euphemism for: "I understand quite well what Mr. X means, but I think it such obvious rubbish that I shall not waste time in refuting it." By this device two advantages are gained. One gracefully pretends to take upon oneself the blame for stupidity, whilst in fact imputing it to one's opponent. And one avoids the labour of controverting him in detail.

There is one other quite minor point in Mr. Kneale's paper which I will dispose of at once. It concerns my use of the word "know." (i) I agree, of course, that this is primarily a *dispositional* word, though it connotes *inter alia* a disposition to have certain experiences, and not only to speak, write, or otherwise behave in certain ways. (ii) But it certainly is sometimes used in a predominantly occurrent sense. Cf., e.g., the following sentences:— "When that black thunder-cloud blew up during my afternoon's walk, I *knew* that I was in for a wetting" and "All the time he was talking to me I *knew* his thoughts were elsewhere." (iii) Certainly the word "know," like many other cognition-words, such as "see," "remember," etc., is not *merely* descriptive of the experience which the subject is thought to be having at the time or of his supposed disposition. To say that a person "knows" so-and-so, evinces a belief on the part of the speaker that so-and-so is the case. And similar remarks apply *mutatis mutandis* to the statement that a person is "seeing" so-

and-so or that he is "remembering" so-and-so. None of this is precisely news to me. I have insisted on it almost *ad nauseam* in my writings, though probably more in later than in earlier ones.

Passing now to matters of detail, I will take in turn the following matters:— (A) Professor Patterson's comments on certain points in my account of McTaggart's doctrine of the Self and of Self-knowledge, (B) Mr. Kneale's discussion on Epiphenomenalism, and (C) Professor Ducasse's proposed amendments to my "Compound Theory" of the human individual.

(A) THE SELF AND SELF-KNOWLEDGE ACCORDING TO MCTAGGART. On this topic I will make the following comments.

(1) We must begin by reminding ourselves that McTaggart's doctrine of the self is very peculiar, and that it must be taken together with his doctrine of time. In judging it one has to bear in mind, and try to harmonise, the following facts. (i) For him a self, as it really is, is a *timeless* existent; and what appears to it and to others as its successive experiences are really *timeless* existents, ordered in a *non-temporal* series, by a certain asymmetrical dyadic relation of *"containing"* and *"contained in."* Thus a self and its experiences, though of course not literally extended, have a property which is in important respects formally analogous to spatial extension. (ii) On the other hand, his argument to show that every self is directly acquainted with itself is based on alleged facts about our everyday experience, as it appears to us under the partly misleading form of a *temporal* sequence of *dated* and *fleeting* mental events. (iii) For McTaggart a self, as it really is, is a non-temporal *whole,* of which its apparently successive total states are, in reality, *parts,* in a sense formally analogous to that in which, e.g., the representation of the Queen's head on an English postage-stamp is a part of the whole design on the front of the stamp. (iv) According to him there is a certain part of each such whole which stands to that whole in the *cognitive* relation of prehension to prehended object.

(2) Since neither Professor Patterson nor I can accept this account of the self, I need say no more about it. But Professor Patterson suggests, as an alternative, that a self may be "present in" the events which make up its history, "as the whole is in the part."

I find two difficulties in this. (i) In what sense is *any* whole *ever* present in any part of it? In what sense, e.g., is the whole design on the front of a penny stamp present in the representation of the Queen's head, which forms a part of it? (ii) I understand that Professor Patterson agrees with me in denying that a self's experiences are *parts* of it. In that case a self cannot stand to its experiences in *exactly* that relation (whatever it may be) which is described by saying that a whole is "present in" each part of it. At best there might be some kind of important *analogy* between the two relations. But what exactly is the analogy?

(3) I drew a distinction between "perception" and "prehension," and substituted the latter term throughout for the former as used by McTaggart. Professor Patterson objects to this.

Now there is no doubt about the following facts. (i) McTaggart intended to use "perception" for what Lord Russell called "acquaintance with particulars." (ii) He held that, whenever a person is acquainted with a particular, it *presents itself to him* as characterised in certain ways, e.g., as red, as squeaky, as having the emotional tone of anger, and so on. (iii) He regarded it as an almost intolerable paradox to suppose that a particular could *present itself,* to a person who is acquainted with it, as having any character which does *not* in fact characterise it at the time. (iv) "Perception" is commonly used as a general name for such experiences as "seeing," "touching," "hearing," etc.; and what we ostensibly see, touch, hear, etc., is either of the nature of *bodies* (e.g., tables or bells or lamps) or of the nature of *physical events* (e.g., flashes of lightning, peals of thunder, etc.).

Now, everyone admits that the experience of ostensibly seeing, e.g., a cow, *involves* as an essential factor being acquainted with a particular which sensibly presents itself as having a certain characteristic shape, size, arrangement of colours, and so on. And this holds *mutatis mutandis* of the other species of perception. So "perception," in the ordinary sense, certainly *involves* "perception" in McTaggart's sense. But it seems equally plain that it involves something *more* and something *different*. In the first place, a person would not claim to be "seeing a cow" unless he took himself to be in the presence of something which has many specific characteristics, e.g., being an animal that gives milk, which the particular which he is acquainted with at the moment is certainly *not* sensibly presenting itself to him as having. Secondly, no one finds any difficulty or paradox in a *perceived* object being *perceived as having* a characteristic which it does not in fact have at the time. There is, e.g., no paradox in the fact that a stick, which is *in fact straight,* is *seen as bent* when half in air and half in water.

For these reasons I hold to my view that McTaggart used "perception" in an unusual sense; that this usage is liable to mislead through the associations of the ordinary usage; and that it is best therefore to substitute some technical term, such as "prehension" for what he obviously had in mind.

Professor Patterson says that what I call "perception" is "an unholy amalgam of prehension and judgment." As to "unholy," hard words break no bones. As to "judgment," a rather similar point is raised by

Professor Blanshard in his essay, and I may as well deal with it here. Professor Blanshard is inclined to assert that a rudimentary kind of non-demonstrative *inference* is involved in sense-perception. The reason that he gives is that there certainly are *data,* e.g., the visual appearance of the object; that there certainly is a kind of *transition* from them; and that what is reached by that transition must be a *judgment,* since it can significantly be said to be "true" or "false."

Now I think that this question largely turns on the usage of certain words. I should not talk of "judgment" unless a person had before his mind a proposition with a subject and a predicate. I should not talk of "inference" unless that person (a) saw or thought he saw a certain *logical relation* of entailment or of probabilification between that proposition and another proposition, and (b) *in virtue of this,* and of his full or partial conviction of the truth of the former proposition, took up an attitude of full or partial belief in the latter. Professor Blanshard (and, I think, Professor Patterson too) would wish to use both "judgment" and "inference" much more widely than this. Both the wider and the narrower usages have certain advantages and certain disadvantages; but, so long as each party realises how he is using his terms and how the other party is using the same terms, there is no occasion for controversy between them.

Before leaving this topic, I wish to emphasise that the reasons stated above for distinguishing prehension from perception are quite independent of whether or not the object prehended is ever identical with, or a part of, the object perceived.

(4) In terms of this distinction it seems to me that a person's awareness of *himself* must be much more like "perception," in my sense of the word, than like "perception" in McTaggart's sense, i.e., *prehension.* For, assuming the reality of time, a self is something with a long *history,* consisting of its successive experiences, and it is something with an elaborately organised *system of dispositions.* That being so, I should suppose that self-consciousness would resemble *perception* (i) in involving non-discursive awareness of certain particulars as having certain psychological qualities and standing in certain psychological relations to each other, and (ii) in including another kind of cognition (based on the former) which so far resembles judgment as to be significantly describable as "true" or "false," "veridical" or "delusive." But I should not consider the analogy to *sense*-perception to be at all close in any other respect. One's simultaneous non-discursive awareness of one's own experiences is obviously extremely *unlike* sensation, and *reminiscence* obviously plays an all-important part in one's consciousness of one's self.

(5) Lastly, I think it is misleading to say, as Professor Patterson does, that to hold a "bundle-theory" of the self is equivalent to "denying that there is any self at all." A bundle-theory would claim to admit all the facts which we summarise by saying that certain simultaneous and successive experiences "belong to a certain self," and that certain others "belong to a certain other self." What it then professes to do is to give a satisfactory account of these facts wholly in terms of *direct inter-relations between experiences*. Ordinary language does undoubtedly suggest a quite different view, viz., that the experiences which "belong to a certain self" *derive* their characteristic inter-relations from a common relationship in which they all stand to something which is *not* an experience or a group of experiences. Let us call this a "Pure Ego." Then a bundle-theory *does* "deny that there is any self at all," in the sense of a *Pure Ego;* and in so doing it *does* go against the suggestions of ordinary language. But, if it does not ignore any relevant introspectable fact, and if it does give a satisfactory account of all the relevant introspectable facts, it cannot fairly be charged with "denying that there is a self at all." At worst it denies a certain *theory of the self*, which is so embodied in the language in which we speak of mental facts that we have a difficulty in separating it from them and in realising that it *is* a theory.

(B) EPIPHENOMENALISM. I think that Epiphenomenalism, (in the sense in which Mr. Kneale takes it, is equivalent to what T. H. Huxley called the "conscious automaton theory." It may be summed up in the following three propositions:—

(1) An experience is not a state or modification of any substance, if "substance" be understood to mean a particular existent of a peculiar kind, *other than* a set of intimately inter-related events, which *has* qualities, states, and dispositions, but *is not* a quality or a state or a disposition of anything. (2) The *complete* immediate cause of any experience is a simultaneous *bodily* event in the brain or nervous system of some one living organism. (3) No experience is a cause-factor in the total cause of any *bodily* event. (It is unnecessary to add that no experience is a cause-factor in the total cause of any *mental* event, for that follows immediately from Proposition (2) above.) So far as I can see, these three propositions are logically independent of each other.

This is not the place for me to consider at length the arguments which might be adduced for and against these propositions. As regards the second and the third of them, I will content myself with the following remarks. Both are in *prima facie* conflict with notorious facts. This is admitted by all intelligent epiphenomenalists, and there are certain well known opening moves in the game of trying to reconcile these propositions with the facts. I would summarise my impression of the whole controversy as follows. I do not think that there is any adequate empirical evidence for either of these two propositions. As to Proposition (2) the utmost that can be said is this. There is fair, but far from conclusive, empirical evidence for holding that a *necessary* condition for the occurrence of any experience is a simultaneous event in the brain or nervous system of some living organism. And there is no *strong* empirical evidence against this, though some fairly well established phenomena of trance-mediumship seem difficult to reconcile with it. Proposition (3) is in a still weaker position. There is such strong *prima facie* evidence against it that it is an extreme paradox. It could be accepted only on *a priori* grounds. And it can be defended empirically only by making liberal drafts on the unobserved and the unobservable; by drawing a distinction between *de facto* invariable accompaniment and causal conditioning; and by holding that only the *former* relation holds between a brain-event and its mental correlate, whilst the latter holds between certain bodily events.

As to Proposition (1) and its logical relationship to the other two propositions, I would make the following remarks. So far as I can see, Proposition (2) is quite consistent with there being *non-causal* relations of the most intimate and peculiar kind, which hold between all or some of the mental correlates of events in *one and the same* brain, and do not hold between any of the mental correlates of events in *different* brains.

Suppose we grant that it is intelligible to talk of a mental event which is not a modification or state of any kind of *substratum*. Then Proposition (2) is compatible with the view that the mental correlates of events in a single highly organised brain constitute a single *mental* system, highly organised in its own characteristic way. That is what a mind would be, on such a view. It might fairly be described as an "empirical substance," except for the following important defect. An essential part of the notion of an empirical substance is that *dispositional* properties of specific kinds can be ascribed to it. Now, if Proposition (2) be assumed, dispositional properties could be ascribed to a mind only by courtesy. Strictly speaking, they would all belong to the *brain*, with which that mind is correlated in the way described.

I will now consider two closely inter-connected objections which Mr. Kneale puts forward. They concern, not so much the *possibility* of a view of minds which takes the notion of an experience or mental event as primary and self-sufficient, as the *consistency* of that view with certain statements which I have made about (i) what I call "prehension" or acquaintance with particulars, and (ii) introspection. I will take these two points in turn.

(1) The first seems to come to this. I talk in many places as if the statement that X is prehending so-and-so (e.g., is aware of a squeaky noise) consists in a subject S_X (X's "ego") standing in a certain asymmetrical dyadic relation of "prehending" (in this case auditorily sensing) to a certain particular (in this case an auditory sensible of a squeaky kind). Now, it is said, Proposition (1) explicitly rules out such an entity as S_X, and therefore is incompatible with this account of prehension.

No doubt that it is true. But the following modification of the above account of prehension would remove the inconsistency. Let us say that the asymmetrical dyadic relation is not that of prehend*ing*, but that of *being-a-prehension-of*; and let us say that this relation relates, not a "subject" but a *mental event*, to a certain particular. The proposition that X is prehending so-and-so, now consists of a conjunction of the following two propositions:— (i) In that system of organised experiences which is X's mind there is a certain experience e, and (ii) e has to so-and-so the relation of prehension to prehensum.

(2) The point about introspection seems to be this. I alleged that introspection is comparable, not to *sensation* (which I regard as a species of prehension), but to *sense-perception* (which I consider to involve sensation, but to involve also something fundamentally different). But the appropriate object of sense-perception is a *body*. Now, according to epiphenomenalism, a mind differs from a body in the absolutely fundamental respect that it is *not a substance*, whilst a body *is*.

To this objection I would answer as follows. (i) The *only* analogy which I wanted to draw between introspection and sense-perception was this. In both there is *prima facie* a prehensive factor. In the former this is an immediate *non-sensuous* awareness of some contemporary experience or complex of experiences; in the latter it is an immediate awareness of some *sensibile*. In both there is certainly another factor, based upon the former, but carrying the mind beyond what is being prehended at the moment. The "something more," which is "accepted" introspectively in the one case and perceptually in the other, is of extremely different character in the two cases. But that is irrelevant for the present purpose.

(ii) The prehensive factor in introspection could be treated, consistently with a "bundle-theory" of the mind, on the lines indicated above for sensation in my answer to Mr. Kneale's first objection.

(iii) Epiphenomenalists do no doubt regard a *body* as a "substance" in the *empirical* sense; but they are not, as such, committed to holding that it involves a "substance" in the *metaphysical* sense of a substratum. Now, as I have argued above, they are not precluded from holding that a human mind is at any rate a "half-blown" substance in the *empirical* sense. (It could not be a "full-blown" empirical substance for them, because they deny it to have any dispositional properties.) So I do not think that the statement that for epiphenomalists the objects of sense-perception are substances, whilst the objects of self-awareness are *not,* will bear the weight which Mr. Kneale attaches to it.

(C) THE "COMPOUND" THEORY. I fully agree with Professor Ducasse as to the four defects which he enumerates in the theory of a "psycho-genic" factor, as put forward by me on various occasions. I welcome his attempt to substitute something on the same lines, but more definite and therefore more susceptible to experimental confirmation or invalidation. I will confine myself to the following comments on his proposals.

(1) The theory is a form of substantival dualism. As that type of theory is unfashionable at the moment, and as it has been held in forms which are almost certainly untenable and can easily be made to appear ridiculous by anyone who has a happy turn for phrase-making, I would like to say explicitly that I see no objection *in principle* to substantival dualism.

According to Professor Ducasse's form of the theory, a living human being from his conception to his death is composed of two *substances* intimately interconnected. One of these is purely *physical,* viz., a brain; the other is purely *psychical,* but it is *not* at first a *mind.* It is provided from the first with certain *aptitudes,* i.e., dispositions to acquire certain dispositions; and it is not unless and until it has acquired a number of these dispositions, and they have become organised, that it becomes a mind. Until then it can be called only a "psychical germ."

(2) If we ask what exactly is meant by calling such a germ a *"psychical"* substance, we are told that such a substance may be defined as one that has *some "psycho-psychical"* dispositions, and *no "physico-physical"* dispositions. If we consider Professor Ducasse's definitions of these terms, and of their congeners "psycho-physical" and "physico-psychical" dispositions, we are referred back finally to "psychical" and "physical" as applied to what may be called "stimulus-*events*" and "reaction-*events.*" I think that Professor Ducasse might fairly say that the meaning of "psychical" and of "physical," as applied to events, can be made quite plain (except to the hopelessly stupid or the artfully naive) by instances and counter-instances. E.g., a twinge of toothache, as actually felt, is certainly a *psychical* event (whether or not it be in some sense *also* physical). And an electrical disturbance in a certain part of the

brain is certainly a *physical* event (whether or not it be in some sense *also* psychical). A general, and perfectly well understood, name for a psychical event is an "experience," as that word is used in books by psychologists and epistemologists. And physical events may be quite satisfactorily indicated for the present purpose by saying that they are the kind of events which are discussed in books on physics and chemistry and physiology.

That being understood, we can define a "purely *psychical* substance" as follows. It would be a substance which (a) has *some* dispositions which both need an experience to stimulate them, and when thus stimulated react (if at all) by producing an experience; and (b) has *no* dispositions which both need a physical event to stimulate them, and when thus stimulated react (if at all) by producing a physical event. A "purely *physical* substance" could be defined *mutatis mutandis* in a similar way, viz., by substituting "no" for "some" in (a), and "some" for "no" in (b). It is evident from the definitions that no substance could be both "purely psychical" and "purely physical," in the senses defined. But it would be a question of fact whether there are any purely psychical or any purely physical substances. And, even if there were, it would be another question of fact whether there are or are not also substances which possess all four kinds of disposition, and might be called "psycho-physical substances."

(3) I think that there are some obscurities in Professor Ducasse's general account of dispositions, on which the above definitions depend. We are told that to say S has a disposition D is to say: "In circumstances of the kind C the occurrence of an event of the kind E causes S to respond in the manner R." One would like to be told rather more about *where* the stimulus-event is supposed to happen, and *where* the reaction-event is supposed to happen. It seems plain that the stimulus-event and the reaction-event, in the case of a psycho-physical or a physico-psychical disposition, would have to be in *different* substances (and therefore could not both be in the substance S) on Professor Ducasse's theory of the human individual. For in such a case one would be in his brain, and the other in his psychical germ (or, at a later stage, his mind).

Suppose, e.g., that there is telepathic interaction between embodied human minds, and that this is not mediated by their brains. Then it would involve *psycho-psychical* dispositions, for which the stimulus-event is in one psychical substance and the reaction-event in another. In view of all this, one is inclined to ask: What is the criterion for attributing a disposition D to a certain one substance S? Suppose that a stimulus-event E in S, under the kind of circumstances C, gives rise to a reaction-event of the kind R in a different substance S'. Are we to assign the disposition always to S (the seat of the stimulus-event), or always to S' (the seat of the reaction-event), or in some cases to one and in others to the other? Or are we to assign two complementary dispositions, D and D', one to S and the other to S'?

(4) Lastly, I am not altogether happy about Professor Ducasse's attempt to explain in terms of his theory the case of a man, hitherto of an amiable and benevolent disposition, who becomes violent and morose after an injury to his brain.

As I understand it, the explanation proposed comes to this. A man, who predominantly often responds in a *friendly* way to external stimuli which might be responded to either in a friendly or an unfriendly manner, may, when certain transitory internal conditions are fulfilled (e.g., when he is very tired or in a state of great anxiety), respond in an *unfriendly* way to similar stimuli. This shows that he has a disposition to respond in a predominantly unfriendly way, *in addition to* his disposition to respond in a predominantly friendly way, to such stimuli. The prevailing *internal condition* of a benevolent man is such that his disposition to a friendly response generally passes into action, whilst his co-existing disposition to an unfriendly response generally fails to do so. In the case of a morose man we have only to substitute "unfriendly" for "friendly" and conversely, in the last sentence.

Suppose now that a man, who has hitherto been benevolent, becomes morose after suffering a brain-injury; or that one, who has hitherto been morose, becomes benevolent after an operation on his frontal lobes. Then, according to Professor Ducasse, we must say, not that the *dispositions* of his mind have been changed, but that the *internal conditions* necessary for the functioning of a certain one disposition have been suspended, whilst those necessary for the functioning of a co-existent disposition of the opposite kind have been fulfilled.

Now my original difficulty with ordinary dualism was that the facts about changes of character and temperament, after brain-injuries or operations, made it very difficult in principle to know what dispositions to ascribe to a man's *mind*, as such. I do not find this difficulty much lightened by being told that we may and must ascribe to a man's mind all kinds of *opposite* dispositions, and ascribe the predominance of some over others in his habitual reaction to his fellows to the prevalence of this or that background condition of his body or his mind or both.

(VIII) *Sense-perception and Matter*

Beginning with *PPR* (1914) and ending (for the present) with "Berkeley's Denial of Material Substance" (*Philosophical Review,* 1954), I have treated the subject of sense-perception on nine main occasions. The various essays were written in different contexts, and each usually without reference to its predecessors. It will be obvious to anyone who may take the trouble to collate them that the definitions of such terms as "*sensibile*," "sense-datum," "sensum," etc., which are stated or implied in some of them, are not consistent with those which are stated or implied in others. This seems to me to be a matter of very little interest except to the minute historians of minor philosophers, and I shall not waste time in discussing it. I now think that the least unsatisfactory treatment is to be found in the two latest, viz., "Elementary Reflexions on Sense-perception" (*Philosophy*, 1952) and the already mentioned "Berkeley's Denial of Material Substance." I would, however, warn possible readers that the word "sensum" is used in the former, and the words "*sensibile*" and "sense-datum" are *not*, whilst the *opposite* is true of the latter article.

The contributions of Professors Price, Marc-Wogau, and Yolton are wholly concerned with certain aspects of this question, and I shall now consider them in turn.

(A) PROFESSOR PRICE'S PAPER. Professor Price is concerned mainly with the following two questions:— (1) Does the "act-object" analysis apply to *all* sensations, or do some at least of them require instead the "internal accusative" analysis? (2) Can the so-called "Sensum Theory" deal satisfactorily with certain experiences which a person would commonly express by saying that an object *O* "looks" or "sounds" so-and-so to him?

(1) *Range of Applicability of the "Act-Object" Analysis.* I begin by accepting practically all that Professor Price says in Sections I and II of his paper. All that I need say is that in writings later than *The Mind and its Place in Nature* I have recognised and tried to deal with some of the points which I had hitherto overlooked.

In "Berkeley's Denial of Material Substance," e.g., I admit that the "internal accusative" analysis is quite plausible in regard to vague, peripheral, and unusual *visual* sensations, whilst the "act-object" analysis seems obviously appropriate to the visual sensations which are an essential factor in ostensibly seeing a body of definite outline in the middle of the field of view. Again, although I nowhere deal with sensations of *smell*, I have considered rather fully (in "Normal Cognition, Clairvoyance, and Telepathy" and in later writings) the phenomenological likenesses and unlikenesses between (a) intra-somatic and extra-somatic ostensible perceptions; and (b) among the latter, between ostensible seeing, hearing, and touching. Lastly, in dealing with "touch," I have considered temperature-sensations (both of radiant heat and those associated with ostensibly touching a hot surface) and what I call "dynamic experiences."

All this, however, serves only to underline my substantial agreement with Professor Price's conclusion in Section II. The distinction between sensations to which the "act-object" analysis seems appropriate, and those to which the "internal accusative" analysis seems appropriate, has to be made *within* sensations of the same sense, and not just between the sensations of certain senses and those of others. And there are always marginal cases, where it seems arbitrary to say that the one type of analysis is more or less applicable than the other.

Professor Price's doctrine, as I understand it, comes to this. When a sensation of *any* kind is occurring, there is always a sensation of a *total sense-field* of the corresponding kind. Let us call such an experience an *"integral* sensation," of the visual kind, of the auditory kind, and so on. The "act-object" analysis applies to *integral* sensations of *every* kind. To have an integral sensation of any kind always consists in sensing a total sense-field of that kind, or (to put it otherwise) in having such a total sense-field *sensibly presented* to one.

But the total sense-field presented in an integral sensation may take three alternative forms. (a) It may not be appreciably differentiated at all. An example would be the total visual field of a person who is gazing up into a cloudless sky. (b) It may be differentiated into several sharply localised and bounded items, standing out from a relatively undifferentiated background. An example would be if the blue sky, in the former example, had a number of small fairly definite flecks of white cloud scattered about it. (c) It may be differentiated, but not in that particular way. An example might be the visual field of a person looking into an iridescent mist.

In cases (a) and (c) we should *not* be inclined to say that the integral sensation is differentiated into a number of constituent sensations, each with its own object. But in case (b) we *are* inclined to say this; and then we apply the "act-object" analysis, not only to the integral sensation, but also to each of these constituent sensations. In cases (a) and (c) we may say that there is *no sensum* at all, but only a *sense-field,* undifferentiated in the one case and differentiated in the other. Or, if we like, we can say that in each of these cases there is a *single sensum,* undifferentiated in the one case and differentiated in the other.

It must be admitted, however, that there are sensory experiences which it is natural to express in language which seems to imply the *"internal-accusative"* analysis, and which it would be extremely strained and unnatural to express in terms which imply the "act-object" analysis. The most obvious examples are certain *organic* sensory experiences, such as one naturally expresses by saying: "I feel tired," "I feel sick," and so on.

Professor Price deals with these as follows. In such cases a person is having an integral organic sensation of an organic sense-field, which is very little differentiated, and is certainly not differentiated into outstanding localised organic sensa, such as an ache here and a tickle there. He perceptually accepts this organic sense-field as a state of *his own body*. Now on many occasions a person regards his own body as part of *himself*. On other occasions he regards his body, not as a part of himself, but as one thing in the material world, to which he stands in certain uniquely intimate relations. A person tends to use phrases like "I feel tired" when (a) the integral organic sensation, by which he is perceiving his own body, is not differentiated into a number of constituent sensations with localised organic sensa as their objects; and (b) he is taking his body, so perceived, as a part of himself.

Professor Price suggests that there are occasions (rare for most of us, but not uncommon in the lives of certain poets and nature-mystics) when something analogous to condition (b) is fulfilled even in the case of *visual* sensation. The percipient takes, not only his body, as intrasomatically perceived, but also the total object of his visual perception, to be included in himself. He is most likely to do this when his visual field is not differentiated into a number of outstanding strongly localised and bounded sensa. In such cases he tends to describe his visual experience in terms suggestive of the "internal accusative" analysis. (The reader will find a good example in Byron's *Childe Harold*, Canto III, Stanza 72.)

I will now make a few comments on Professor Price's doctrine:—

(i) I wonder why Professor Price is so sure that the "act-object" analysis applies to all *integral* sensations. Is he really sure of this, or would he be content to say that it is *not obviously inapplicable* to any such sensation? For my part, I would not be prepared to go further than this. The cases where the "act-object" analysis seems most obviously applicable are those *partial* sensations which occur as essential factors in ostensible perceptions of bodies with sharp outlines, or of physical events (such as a flash of forked lightning) which are presented as definitely localised and shaped. It is difficult to believe that there is not something significant in the high positive correlation between these two features in a sensation. Yet the latter feature is conspicuously *absent* in most cases of an integral sensation of a total sense-field.

(ii) We must, no doubt, distinguish between (a) the question of what kind of analysis is applicable to a sensation, and (b) the question whether the sensibile which it presents (when the "act-object" analysis seems plainly applicable) could conceivably exist except as a sense-datum to one particular person on one particular occasion. But the two are closely inter-connected. For the "act-object" analysis leaves the latter question open, whilst the "internal-accusative" analysis entails a negative answer to it. It is therefore natural, in cases where the independent existence of the presented sensibile not only seems possible but is commonly taken for granted, to accept the "act-object" analysis. It is no less natural, in cases where the existence of the sensibile independently of the sensation seems (for whatever reason) incredible, to favour the "internal-accusative" analysis.

Now it is illuminating, in this connexion, to compare and contrast in this respect (a) the visual sense-datum involved in ostensibly seeing a near-by familiar body of sharp outline in the middle of the field of view, and (b) a vivid and detailed "visual image" (recognised by the experient to be such) of such a body. *Intrinsically* the sensation and the image-experience are very much alike. It would seem equally plausible *prima facie* to apply the "act-object" analysis in both cases, and to say that in the one a sensibile is prehended and in the other an imaginabile is prehended. But the *sense-datum* is uncritically and unhesitatingly taken to exist independently of being sensibly presented on this particular occasion to this particular person, and to have *other* sensible qualities (e.g., hardness, smoothness, coldness, etc.) which it is not sensibly presenting at the time. For the sense-datum is uncritically and unhesitatingly taken to be a part of the surface of the body which the experient is ostensibly seeing, in and through his visual sensation. In view of all this we have no hesitation, if the question is raised, in applying the "act-object" analysis here. But in the case of the *visual image* (recognised as such) all this is lacking. The person who is aware of it does not take it to be part of a body, which he is perceiving in and through imaging it; he does not take it to have any other qualities beside those which it is now presenting to him; and (perhaps because of this) most of us find it hard to conceive of a mental image existing except as imaged by some one person on some one occasion. One is therefore strongly inclined *on reflexion* to apply the *"internal-accusative"* analysis to all image-experiences, though *prima facie* many of them seem to demand the "act-object" analysis.

(iii) In view of this, might there not be something to be said for the following opinion, which I take to have been held, e.g., by Stout and by Prichard? The "internal-accusative" analysis applies alike to *all* sensations, integral or partial. The so-called "act-object analysis" is not really an *analysis*. It is a statement, not about the *internal constitution* of any sensation, but about the part which certain sensations play in certain

ostensible perceptions. No doubt there are intrinsic dissimilarities between those sensations which are, and those which are not, fitted to
play this part. But these intrinsic dissimilarities concern the "content"
or "*quale*" of the two kinds of sensation, and not the kinds of analysis
applicable to the one and to the other.

(2) "*Appearing so-and-so*" *and the* "*Sensum Theory.*" The question
which Professor Price discusses under this head may be stated as follows.
Does every proposition of the form: *That body appears ϕ to S* entail
a proposition of the form: *S is sensing a certain sensibile as characterised
by ϕ?* Here "appearing ϕ" is used as a general name to cover "looking ϕ,"
"feeling ϕ," "sounding ϕ," etc., though most of the cases discussed
by Professor Price are in fact instances of *looking* so-and-so. It is to
be clearly understood that "appearing ϕ" is used here in such a way
that to appear ϕ neither *entails* nor *excludes* being in fact ϕ.

I think that Professor Price tacitly makes the following two assumptions. (i) That any quality which a sensibile is *sensed as having* must
in fact belong to it, and the sensibile must have that quality in *the very
same determinate form* as that in which it is sensed as having it. (ii) That
in no case is the sensibile which a person senses identical with any part
of the surface of the body which he ostensibly perceives through sensing
it. Nor *a fortiori* is it identical with any part of any *other body.* I will
call the first assumption the "Assumption of Inerrancy," and the second
the "Assumption of Non-corporeality."

But I do not think that either of these assumptions is essential to
Professor Price's argument here. What he is concerned to do is to call
our attention to a series of cases of the following kind. In *all* of them
one would say: "That body appears ϕ to S." But, as one goes along the
series, one would be increasingly disinclined to admit that *S is* (or even
in some cases that he *could be*) sensing a sensibile as ϕ.

I agree with Professor Price that no serious difficulty for the general
principle under discussion arises until we come to cases where the mode
of appearing is appropriate to one sense (e.g., sight), whilst the characteristic which the perceived body is said to appear to have is appropriate
to another sense (e.g., touch). An obvious example is when a person,
looking at a block of ice or at a picture of a field covered with snow,
says: "It looks cold."

I should be inclined to treat such cases as follows. When a person,
who has often both seen and felt such things as snow and ice, merely
looks at such an object, the sensibile which he visually senses is no doubt
subtly modified in a characteristic way through the excitement of traces
left by his past associated tactual experiences. But I see no reason to
think that this modification consists in the sensibile literally having the

quality of *sensible coldness,* in addition to such qualities as hue, brightness, distribution of light and shade, etc. I should suppose that it is *these latter qualities* which are modified in a subtle and characteristic way. But we have no simple adjective available to name such characteristic modifications of hue, brightness, distribution of light and shade, etc., and none for the *visual gestalt-quality* in which they are integrated. So we express its presence by using the *verbally* paradoxical adjective "cold-looking."

The following analogy may be helpful. When a person says that something looks cream-coloured, no one supposes that the *sensibile* which he senses is made of cream. We know that he uses this phrase simply because there is no simple adjective, like "red" or "purple," available to name the hue in question. Why should we not treat such phrases as "cold-looking," "hard-looking," etc., on similar lines *mutatis mutandis?*

The next critical point in Professor Price's series is where the characteristic, which a perceived object is said to appear to have, is or involves something of such a nature that it cannot be literally present to *any* sense. Examples are: "He looks angry," "He looks ill," etc. To be angry, e.g., is to be feeling certain emotions, to be disposed to speak and act in certain ways, and so on. These are plainly not *sensible* qualities of *any* kind.

The analysis which Professor Price offers of *O appears φ to S,* in such cases, seems to come to the following. (a) The sensation, in and through which *S* is perceiving *O,* is a sensing by him of a sensibile which he senses as having a *sensible* quality *ψ,* of a certain characteristic kind. (b) In *S*'s past experience objects which have presented that kind of appearance have generally or always been found to have the *non-sensible* characteristic *φ.*

I think that this is a plausible account of the circumstances under which such experiences happen, but that it is hardly an adequate account of the experiences themselves. I would suggest that when a creature (man or animal of the higher kind), whose past experiences have been of the kind described under (b), has a sensation of the kind described under (a), he feels certain characteristic emotions (e.g., apprehension) towards *O,* and that dispositions in him to react in certain ways are stirred and certain feelings arise in connexion with this. These emotions and feelings blend with the purely cognitive factor in the experience. I suggest that the experience which a *person* might express by saying "*O* looks angry to me," and which a *dog* might have but could not express in words, is this blended state of cognition, emotion, and feeling. And I would suggest a similar account of other such experiences.

(B) PROFESSOR MARC-WOGAU'S PAPER. Professor Marc-Wogau confines his discussion to *visual* perception of *bodies,* and I shall here follow his lead. I think that the question which he is primarily concerned to discuss may be stated as follows:—

Let us grant, for the sake of argument, that whenever a person is ostensibly seeing a certain body, e.g., a cricket-ball, he is directly apprehending a certain particular existent, which sensibly presents itself to him as having certain qualities, e.g., brownness, roundness, convexity, etc. Let us also grant, for the sake of argument, that such a directly apprehended particular must *have* any characteristic which it sensibly presents itself as having, and that it must have it in *the precise determinate form* in which it presents itself as having it. It has been alleged that, even when the ostensible perception is veridical and non-hallucinatory (e.g., when there really is a cricket-ball in front of the percipient, and when his ostensible perception really is evoked by the stimulus of light coming to his eyes from it) the particular which he directly apprehends is *never* identical with the body which he sees or with any part of it, and *a fortiori* is never identical with any *other* body or any part of one. I will call this doctrine "the non-corporeality of visual sensibilia." It is this doctrine which Professor Marc-Wogau is concerned to discuss. His thesis is that, whether it be true or false, the reasons which have been alleged for it are inconclusive or positively fallacious.

I shall not waste time in discussing whether the non-corporeality of visual sensibilia becomes *analytic,* if we substitute the phrase "visual sensum" for the phrase "particular which a person directly apprehends when he ostensibly sees a body." That depends on how certain philosophers may have defined a certain technical term. But a person must *already* have persuaded himself that such particulars are never bodies or parts of bodies, *before* he would make that property a part of his definition of the technical term "visual sensum," by which he proposes to call them.

Professor Marc-Wogau is obviously right when he says that we need to be clear as to what we mean by "body" and by "part of a body" before we can appraise the doctrine in question. Suppose, e.g., you allow that the name "body" may be given to any complex of sensibilia inter-related in a certain characteristic intimate way, and that the phrase "being a part of a body" may be applied to the relationship of being a constituent of such a complex. Then some of the arguments which have been used in support of the non-corporeality of visual sensibilia cease to be relevant.

In this connexion Professor Marc-Wogau makes some highly pertinent comments on statements which I have made in various places about "the common-sense view of bodies." The essential point is that I seem to suggest that certain beliefs about the nature of a body are implicit in the language and behaviour of plain men; that these can be formulated, and constitute an essential part of the connotation of the word "body" and the phrase "part of a body," as plain men understand them; and that it can be seen on reflexion that the sensibile which a person senses when he sees a body *never* answers to the conditions required for being a "body" or a "part of a body," in the popularly accepted sense of those words. Professor Marc-Wogau says that I seem to ascribe a *philosophic theory* to plain men; and that it is very doubtful whether they have one, and whether (if they have) I have formulated it correctly. He remarks that sometimes I seem to make it an *objection* to a philosophic theory about bodies and sense-perception that it would "shock common-sense," and at other times advise common-sense to "go out and hang itself" like Judas Iscariot.

What I would now say about this is the following. (1) I still think that ordinary language and practice about bodies and parts of bodies do at least *strongly suggest* that the words "body" and "part of a body" connote certain characteristic properties, for most men at most times, in the entities to which they are applied. I would hardly describe these beliefs as constituting a "philosophic theory." But that phrase is no doubt highly elastic, and I do not wish to dispute about words.

(2) At any rate I would admit (and indeed assert) this. When a professional philosopher, who has reflected on these topics and has been led thereby to draw distinctions which are not recognised and not needed in our ordinary practical dealings with bodies, tries to formulate what he takes to be suggested by ordinary language and practice, the result of his efforts will always be open to the following objections. (i) The beliefs which he ascribes to the plain man are likely to be severally much clearer and collectively much more coherent than those which plain men hold at most times. (ii) It will be of very little use to enquire of supposedly representative plain men whether they do or do not hold the beliefs ascribed to them. The witness will not understand your questions, or see the point of your putting them to him, until you have got him to see distinctions which he would not have noticed if left to himself. At that stage he has ceased to be a "representative plain man," and his conditioning at your hands has probably biased him in favour of an affirmative or of a negative answer to your questions.

(3) In view of this, it is perhaps presumptuous for a philosopher to describe his formulation of what he takes to be connoted by "body" and by "part of a body" as "the common-sense belief." The important thing is that he should formulate it clearly, and that it should not *obviously*

conflict with common-sense notions, vague, incoherent, and half-baked as these may be. I think that the account which I have offered fulfils these modest conditions.

(4) Lastly, I do *not* think that the fact that a philosophic theory (e.g., the Leibnitzian theory that what we ostensibly perceive as a body is in fact a certain kind of collection of very low-grade minds) would "shock common-sense," is by itself any good reason for doubting it. As one who is, in his non-professional hours, the plainest of plain men, I would like to do what I can for "poor dear common-sense." But I refuse to regard that thing of rags and tatters as an oracle. And, as a professional philosopher, I should not hang my head or feel wistful, if I should find myself obliged (as a result of recognising distinctions which the plain man ignores, and of viewing synoptically facts which he views only severally, and of some of which he is entirely ignorant) to "shock common-sense" quite severely.

I will now pass from these generalities to Professor Marc-Wogau's criticism of certain specific arguments, which have been put forward in support of the non-corporeality of visual sensibilia. Before doing so I will make two explanatory remarks.

(1) The word "see" is used in ordinary speech in a looser and in a stricter sense. In the looser sense one would talk of seeing a *body* (e.g., a certain cricket-ball). In the stricter sense one would say that, from any one position at any one moment, one sees only *a certain part of the external surface* of the body which one is seeing in the looser sense. Now the only question worth discussing here is whether or not the visual *sensibile* which a person senses, when he "sees" (in the looser sense) a certain body, is or is not ever identical with that part of the external surface of that body which he is then "seeing" in the strict sense.

(2) Suppose I were looking at a body whose surface is variegated in colour, e.g., a geographical globe with the representation of the U.S.A. facing me, and with the various States represented by adjoined patches of various colours. Then what I understand by the statement that the *sensibile* which I am visually sensing is identical with the part of the surface of the globe which I am strictly seeing, is this. The total coloured particular which I am visually sensing is a part of a certain complete coloured surface of spherical shape (the *rest* of which I am *not* visually sensing), in precisely the way in which the representation of the State of Nebraska (which I *am* visually sensing) is a part of the representation of the U.S.A. (which I also *am* visually sensing). I assume that what Professor Marc-Wogau questions is the cogency of various arguments which have been adduced to show that such propositions as this are *never* true.

Of the three specific arguments which Professor Marc-Wogau considers, I need not dilate upon what he calls the "Argument from Delusive Perceptual Situations." As he says, I have discussed that argument pretty fully in *Mind,* Vol. LVI, Pp. 104–107, and have admitted it to be *inconclusive.* I have not altered my opinion. But I continue to think that the argument has *some* weight. The other two arguments are (1) an argument from *continuity,* and (2) an argument based on the *finite velocity of light.* I will now take these in turn.

(1) *Argument from Continuity.* This argument is based on the alleged continuity in the series of sensibilia visually sensed by a person when the same part of the same body (e.g., the whole of the top of a penny) is seen from a series of positions at various distances from it and at various angles to the normal through its centre. Professor Marc-Wogau complained, quite justifiably, that those who use this argument have generally ignored the fact of "phenomenal constancy," which has been established by experimental psychologists. I alleged that this merely shifts the point of application of the argument to the dividing line between the sub-class of this series of sensibilia within which phenomenal constancy holds and the sub-class for which it breaks down.

To this he answers that there is no reason why *all* the sensibilia on the one side of this line should not be identical with the top of the penny, whilst *none* of those on the other side of it are so. (It may be remarked that, strictly speaking, there would be, on the view in question, only *one* sensibile on the former side of the dividing line, though it would answer to a number of different descriptions, each of the form "the *sensibile* sensed by X from position P.") Professor Marc-Wogau suggests that the difference between the two sub-groups of sensibilia might be compared with the difference between a set of trees which could be called a "wood" and a set which could be called a "grove."

This analogy seems to me to be faulty. (i) Since one of the sub-groups would, as I have pointed out, contain *only one* member, it would be analogous to *a single tree* and neither to a wood nor a grove. (ii) When we say that a "wood" and a "grove" melt imperceptibly into each other, *all* that we mean is that there is a rather indefinite range of size and density within which either *name* is equally applicable to a collection of trees. But what is involved in the present case is not a question of the applicability of one name or another. It is the *factual* difference between (a) being identical with a certain part of the surface of a certain body, and (b) not being a part of the surface of any body. This is a difference of kind. If it occurs at all within the series of sensibilia in question, it must separate them at a certain definite point into two sub-classes of radically different kinds, one of which contains only one member, and the other an indefinite plurality of members.

What seems to me so paradoxical is to suppose that such a series of visual sensations, evoked under conditions which vary continuously, should fall into two sub-classes, having objects of such radically different ontological status.

(2) *Argument from the finite velocity of Light.* I have dealt very fully with this argument in *Scientific Thought,* and again (with special reference to Professor Marc-Wogau) in *Mind,* Vol. LVI, Pp. 120–124. All that I wish to add here is the following.

Professor Marc-Wogau says that we need not consider the argument except in cases where the body seen is so near to the percipient's body that the time-interval between the emission or reflection of light from the former and its arrival at the latter is extremely small compared with the duration of the percipient's specious present. The reason which he gives is that, in the case of a very distant body, e.g., the sun, it is obvious, from a mere comparison of the characteristics which the sensibile is sensed as having with those which the body is known to have, that the former cannot be identical with a part of the surface of the latter. The argument in question is therefore *unnecessary* in such cases.

That is no doubt true. But the fact that the argument is not *needed* in the case of very distant bodies does not affect its *validity* in such cases. Nor do I think that Professor Marc-Wogau would claim that it does. But, if that be admitted, the question of continuity comes in. The case where the body seen is near to the percipient's body cannot fairly be considered in isolation from cases where it is very remote. We see bodies which are at all sorts of distances, from close at hand to many millions of miles away. The external causal conditions of the visual perceptions are, so far as we know, precisely similar in kind in all these cases. Is it really credible that there is a certain range of distance, on one side of which the immediate objects of visual sensations are parts of the surfaces of bodies emitting light to the percipient's eye, and on the other side of which they are of a wholly different nature?

To sum up. I think that *all* the arguments for the non-corporeality of visual sensibilia rest on considerations of continuity. In view of the continuity in the external conditions of our visual sensations, I find it very hard to believe that *some* of the visual sensibilia which we sense *are* parts of the surfaces of the bodies which we see, and that others are *not* parts of the surface of *any* body, if to be a "body" and to be "a part of the surface of a body" be understood in the simple literal way which I have tried to state and illustrate. Now I also find it very hard to believe that *all* the visual sensibilia which we sense *are* parts of the surfaces of the bodies which we see, if "body" and "part of the surface of a body" are understood in that way. Therefore I am strongly inclined to think that *none* of them are. I admit that neither severally nor collectively are the arguments conclusive. What I may call Professor Marc-Wogau's "half-and-half" theory *is* logically possible; but it is the kind of theory of which I can only say: "If it should be true, I'll eat my hat!"

I will conclude, however, by adding this remark. I have been mainly concerned to work out, for good or ill, theories which presuppose the non-corporeality of visual and other sensibilia. But I have *always* recognised that there are other alternative views of sense-perception which an intelligent and instructed philosopher might take. Moreover, as I have grown older I have realised more and more that the plausibility of that presupposition rests on certain assumptions, e.g., the analysis of ostensible perception into sensation *plus* perceptual acceptance founded upon it, the "act-object" analysis of sensation, and the assumption of inerrancy. And I realise that I was formerly inclined to take all these too much for granted.

(C) PROFESSOR YOLTON'S PAPER. I shall discuss Professor Yolton's paper under the following three headings, viz., (1) the three "alternative ontologies" which he mentions, (2) the notion of "ontological construction," and (3) the alleged "phenomenalist" and "dualist" strands in my writings.

(1) *"Phenomenalism," "Phenomenalist Realism," and "Dualist Realism."* Professor Yolton defines the first two of these theories in terms of what he calls "sense-qualities." I think he must mean what I should call "sense-qualified occurrents," and I shall so interpret his statements. On that interpretation one might say, e.g., that Berkeley held a form of "Phenomenalism," and that Lord Russell has propounded in some of his works a form of "Phenomenal Realism."

I note that Professor Yolton includes among "sensible qualities" the property of being made of oak. Surely that involves having certain *causal* or *dispositional* properties, which are certainly not *sense-given,* in the way in which, e.g., redness and coldness are. However that may be, it seems to me certain that causal and dispositional properties are an essential element in the notion of a body. But "phenomenalists" and "phenomenal realists" might wish to give an account of such properties as inertia, elasticity, gravitational mass, etc., which "dualist realists" would not accept, and *vice versa.*

I take "Dualist Realism" to involve at least the following propositions. (i) That there certainly or probably are "bodies," in the sense of more or less persistent substances within closed surfaces, e.g., spheres, cubes, etc., which have (a) non-dispositional "extensible qualities" diffused over their surfaces or throughout their volumes, (b) dispositional properties, e.g., inertial mass, elasticity, etc., and (c) positions in a spatial order of at least three dimensions. (2) That when a person ostensibly sees or touches a body, he is immediately aware of certain sense-qualified occurrents, but that these are *in no case* bodies or parts of the surfaces of bodies, in the literal way in which one such sense-qualified occurrent often is a spatial part of another. They are particulars of a radically different kind. And it may be doubted whether any of them ever exists except as the objective factor in a particular sensation had by a particular individual on a particular occasion.

Now, if this be what is implied by "dualist realism," it seems plain that there is *prima facie* another alternative, which might be called "direct realism." This would accept (1) and reject (2) in the above summary. I think that the phrase "to reject (2)" covers two very different attitudes, which might be called "pre-critical" and "post-critical." At the *pre-critical* stage no clear distinction is drawn between the notion of what I have called "sense-qualified occurrents" and the notion of bodies or parts of the surfaces of bodies. Speaking in terms of a conceptual distinction which is not clearly recognised by the persons concerned, we, who have recognised that distinction, can say that the percipient simply *takes for granted* (at any rate in perceptual situations which are not regarded by him as decidedly abnormal) that the particular which he is visually or tactually sensing is literally a part of the surface of the body which he is ostensibly seeing or touching. At the *post-critical* stage we have philosophers, who *have* recognised the distinction in question, and are well aware of the arguments against identifying the particulars sensed with parts of the surfaces of bodies seen or touched, but *nevertheless* hold that the former *are* identical with the latter, at any rate in normal perceptual situations.

I suppose that Reid would be an adherent of what I should call "post-critical direct realism." I agree with Professor Yolton and Professor Marc-Wogau that it is dangerous, and perhaps almost a contradiction in terms, to ascribe any philosophical theory to plain men. Yet I am inclined to think that the language and behaviour of plain men, and of philosophers in their non-professional hours, implies or suggests what I should call "pre-critical direct realism."

When *all* the relevant facts, viz., those of physics, physiology, anatomy, and psychology, are taken into account, I think that *direct realism* is very difficult to maintain. I do not doubt that, with enough ingenuity and a good deal of special pleading, it could be saved from downright refutation. But I confess that I do not think that it is worth such intellectual acrobatics. On the other hand, I do not wish to depart further from pre-critical direct realism than I am forced to do by a fair synoptic consideration of all the relevant facts. That is not because I regard any proposition as sacrosanct, merely because it seems to me to be implied or strongly suggested by common language and everyday behaviour. At most I should say that there is a *prima facie* case for treating such propositions seriously, and seeing how far and in what sense they can be maintained in face of relevant facts which were unknown when ordinary language was formed, and which are seldom or never viewed synoptically even by those to whom they are known.

I think that a form of *dualist* realism can be stated, which fulfils these various conditions on the whole better than any alternative theory known to me. I have in the main tried to work out such a theory. I have never doubted that other types of theory, better in some ways but perhaps not so good in others, can be coherently formulated and plausibly defended. I think, however, that most of them demand more boldness and speculative originality than I have ever possessed, and that it was better for me to stick to my last.

(2) *"Ontological Construction."* Professor Yolton defines this as an attempt to derive physical objects from instantaneous punctiform event-particles. He rightly contrasts it with what he calls "linguistic construction," which he defines as an attempt to derive, from the phenomenal world, meaningful concepts to apply to the physical world.

I am sure that Professor Yolton exaggerates the significance of what I have said about ontological construction, in this sense, in relation to my account of the physical world. I suggest that this is because he ignores the very special context in which it occurs, and the very special purpose which I had in mind.

So far as I am aware, *all* that I have said on this topic will be found on Pp. 587–603 of *The Mind and its Place in Nature.* It occurs in a chapter devoted to the nature of the *unity of a mind.* The context is a discussion of the question whether it is possible to take the notion of *mental event* as primary, and to regard a *mind* as a certain kind of complex composed of appropriately inter-related mental events. In order to elucidate this I threw out for discussion the question whether it is possible to take the notion of *physical event* as primary, and to regard a *body* as a certain kind of complex composed of such events.

I did not want to devote much space to the development of what was a side-issue of a side-issue. I therefore stated the case in terms of literally punctiform instantaneous qualified event-particles, and talked as if I thought that *these* might be actually existent particulars, and as if bodies might be *literally composed of these.* But I never seriously believed this to be a possible view. Professor Yolton has taken all this too seriously and with too little reference to its peculiar context. I do not think that it would be profitable to pursue the question further here.

(3) *The "phenomenalist" and the "dualist" strands.* The above mis-understanding (as I think it) does not, however, affect the validity of what I take to be Professor Yolton's main criticism. This, if I am not mistaken, comes to the following. I make great use of the notion of logical construction, and in particular of Whitehead's Method of Extensive Abstraction. But there is a standing ambiguity as to what I supposed to be accomplished by this. Sometimes I write as if I held that statements in which physical-object words and phrases occur can be replaced, without loss or gain of meaning, by more complicated statements which are about nothing but sense-data, sensible qualities, and sensible relations. At other times I write as if I held that physical objects are particular existents of a certain kind, and sense-data (or the sensations in which they are the objective factor) are particular existents of a radically different kind; that there are intimate *causal* relations between certain of the former and certain of the latter; and that the logical constructions serve only to define, in terms of sensible qualities and relations, the concepts in terms of which we have to think of physical objects, their qualities, and their relations. We may call these respectively the "phenomenalist strand" and the "dualist strand."

I should not be much ashamed of this, if each tendency occurred only in different writings, and if those writings differed considerably in date and in main purpose. But I must admit that statements exemplifying each tendency are to be found in one and the same book, e.g., *Scientific Thought.*

I believe that my main intention at the time was to expound and defend a form of *dualism,* viz., what I call in *Scientific Thought* the "Critical Scientific Theory." This may fairly be described as an attempt to refurbish (in the light of criticisms made by later philosophers, and with the help of tools provided by later logicians) the much decried "theory of Representative Perception" or "Causal Theory of Perception," which goes back through Locke to Descartes. Much water (and still more hot air) has passed through the bridges of philosophy since I wrote. But I still think such a theory defensible, and I have not met with any alternative which seems to me less unsatisfactory in view of *all* the relevant facts. The philosophy of the physical world and of our perception of it becomes analogous in certain respects (though profoundly dissimilar in certain others) to the making and testing of a far-reaching *scientific hypothesis.* I am well aware that (to parody St. Paul) all this is "to the Phenomenalists a stumbling-block and to the Wittgersnappers foolishness." But I have always thought that Vienna contributed more notably to culture by its *Schnitzel* than by its *Kreis*, and *ich kann nicht anders.*

There is one further remark that I would make here. Professor Yolton speaks of the "Principle of Isomorphism," and says that it is essential to my way of philosophising about sense-perception and the world of bodies and physical events. I am inclined to think that what I had in mind was something less determinate and more flexible than what Professor Yolton understands by that principle.

What I would say is this. There is no reason *a priori* why the locus of those physical events which are the rather remote causal ancestors of the various groups of inter-connected sensations by which various persons ostensibly perceive a certain body, should *resemble* at all closely the *percepta* of those persons. There is also no reason *a priori* why it should *not* do so. Antecedently, then, we are free to postulate as much or as little resemblance as we choose between (a) the qualities and inter-relations of the hypothetical system of physical things and events, and (b) the qualities and relations which the objects that we ostensibly perceive present themselves to us in sense-perception as having.

The latter is certainly the only source from which we can derive the *empirical* concepts, in terms of which we think of the physical system as a whole, and of its detailed contents and their varying states and mutual relations. Undoubtedly our thought of these involves also concepts which I regard as *non-empirical,* in that they are not and could not possibly be *sense-given,* in the way in which, e.g., the concepts of colour, of shape, of position, of motion, etc., are so. Examples of such non-empirical concepts, essential to the thought of a system of physical things and events, are the notions of substance, of cause, of disposition, of potentiality and actuality, and so on. But nothing concrete can be thought of *wholly* in terms of categories; there must be a non-categorial "filling" and specification, and this can come only from what is sense-given.

If this be allowed, I am willing to leave to experts to decide (i) in what *respects* it is necessary to postulate isomorphism, if we are to form any workable and fruitful conception of the actual physical world; and (ii) to what *degree* it is necessary, and within what limits it is permissible, to postulate isomorphism in those respects.

(IX) *Moral Philosophy*

Under this heading come the papers by Professors Frankena, Hedenius, and Kuhn; Mr. Hare's paper; and one section of Professor Blanshard's.

(A) PROFESSOR FRANKENA'S QUESTIONS. In order to formulate the questions which Professor Frankena puts to me, I will begin by introducing the phrase "moral sentence in the indicative." This is to denote a sentence in the indicative mood, in which the grammatical subject is a name or a description of a person, an action, an experience, or a disposition (or of a class of such), and the grammatical predicate is some word like "ought" or "ought not," "right" or "wrong," "good" or "evil," used in its *specifically moral* sense. It would not be difficult to show by instances and counter-instances what I have in mind.

In terms of this phraseology, I think that what Professor Frankena asks me may be summarised as follows:—Have I any decided opinion, and, if so, why do I hold it, on the following interconnected questions? (1) Do moral sentences in the indicative express *judgments* or not? (2) If *not*, what does the utterance of such a sentence express? (3) If *so*, do words such as "ought" and "ought not," etc., when used in their specifically moral sense, stand for predicates of a *certain peculiar kind*, which has been described as "non-natural?" (4) If such words stand for predicates which are *"natural,"* what account should be given of the "natural" characteristics for which typical words of this kind stand?

Now a short answer, and a true one so far as it goes, to Professor Frankena's questions would be: No! I have no decided opinion on any of these points. But I could say the same about almost any philosophical question. The reasons which incline one to or against a certain opinion on any one philosophical question are always highly complex, and they are always bound up with the reasons which incline one to or against certain opinions on many other philosophical questions. Here, as elsewhere in philosophy, I have tried to clear up the questions and to indicate logical connexions between certain answers to some of them and certain answers to others. These are necessary preliminaries to any attempt to come to a reasoned decision about them. But it does not follow that it is sufficient to enable a person to do this. So far as I am concerned, I find myself now inclined to favour one kind of alternative and now another, but never to come down decisively in favour of any. At most I feel fairly confident that some proposed answers to some of the questions are *inadequate* by themselves.

I will now try to be a little more concrete. Let us give the name "predicative" to all theories which hold that moral sentences in the indicative express *judgments,* in which a *moral attribute* is ascribed to a person or action or experience or disposition. I will begin by mentioning and dismissing one general argument against all predicative theories, which has been thought by many intelligent contemporaries to be conclusive.

It is alleged that a sentence can express a synthetic judgment, if and only if one can conceive and describe some kind of possible perceptual situation or introspectable situation which, if realised, would tend to confirm it or to invalidate it. Now consider such a sentence as, e.g., "Acts of promise-breaking tend as such to be morally wrong." If this expresses a judgment at all, the judgment is certainly not analytic. But, it is said, one cannot suggest any possible perceptual or introspectable situation which, if realised, would tend to confirm or to invalidate what it expresses. So it is concluded that it cannot express a judgment. And a similar argument is applied to all moral sentences in the indicative.

This argument leaves me wholly unmoved. The account of synthetic judgments, which is its main premiss, is obviously a generalisation based *exclusively* on a review of *non-moral* indicatives, and in particular of statements about *physical* and *psychological* phenomena. Now there are admittedly whole classes of sentences in the indicative which seem *prima facie* to express synthetic judgments, and which are plainly *not* of that kind. Moral indicatives are important instances of them. If you first exclude all such sentences from your purview, in making your generalisation about the conditions under which alone a sentence can express a synthetic judgment, and then use that generalisation to show that such sentences cannot express synthetic judgments, you are simply begging the question. For the only legitimate ground for excluding these from your purview, and nevertheless holding that your generalisation covers *all* sentences which express synthetic judgments, would be a *prior* conviction that *these* sentences do not express synthetic judgments.

Dismissing this kind of argument as circular, I would next remark that there are two general principles to which I should appeal in preferring one type of theory to another. They sound rather platitudinous when stated baldly; but, in default of anything better, they are not to be despised. (1) Other things being equal, a theory is to be preferred if it does not have to postulate anything of a kind which is not already admitted as a fact and found to be readily intelligible. (2) Other things being equal, a theory is to be preferred if it does not have to suppose that all men are *fundamentally mistaken* on certain matters with which the whole race is and has always been constantly concerned. Unfortunately these two principles sometimes point in opposite directions.

On the *second* principle, taken by itself, I should be strongly inclined *prima facie* to prefer an ethical theory of the *predicative* kind to one of the non-predicative kind. The normal use of uttering a sentence in the indicative is undoubtedly to *convey information* (true or false). The fact that our moral utterances are commonly couched in the indicative mood strongly suggests that most men at most times take for granted that they are making and expressing and conveying to others *moral judgments* on such occasions. If they are in fact doing nothing of the kind, but are only e.g., evincing or evoking certain emotions, issuing certain admonitions or commands, etc., their mode of expression seems to betray a fundamental misapprehension of their situation.

On the *first* principle, taken by itself, I should be inclined *prima facie* to favour an ethical theory which holds that moral concepts are *empirical,* in the sense that they are derived from data presented in sense-perception or introspection, in the familiar ways in which, e.g., the concepts *red* or *angry* are derived, and the concepts *mermaid* or *hot-tempered* are derived. On the same principle I should be inclined *prima facie* to favour a theory which makes universal propositions of the form: *Anything that had the non-moral character N would have the moral character M* to be either (a) empirical generalisations, or (b) analytic propositions.

Now, in formulating the two principles I have prefixed to each the conditional clause "other things being equal." The basic requirement of a philosophic theory is that it shall do justice to *all* the facts characteristic of the region with which it deals (including, of course, "higher-order" facts about the inter-relations of the "lower-order" facts), and that it shall neither ignore nor distort any of them. When this fundamental condition of inclusiveness and non-distortion is taken into account, I think that the two principles point in opposite directions.

I have tried to show, in various papers quoted by Professor Frankena, that it is doubtful whether any *predicative* theory can do justice to the facts unless it admits (a) that the concepts of moral attributes are *non-empirical,* and (b) that there are universal propositions, connecting certain non-moral attributes with certain moral ones, which are *synthetic* and yet *necessary.* Now, as I have said above, the second principle would incline one to favour *predicative* theories, whilst the first principle would incline one to favour theories which do not involve either *non-empirical concepts* or *synthetic a priori judgments.*

It is plain that philosophers of two different kinds, who might agree in accepting my argument up to this point, would here diverge from each other. (1) Some are quite convinced that there *can* be no non-empirical concepts and no synthetic *a priori* judgments. They will have to accept some form of non-predicative theory, and make the best of it. (2) Others (including myself) have no such convictions. They will be in a freer position. They are not *obliged* at the next move to accept any form of non-predicative theory, but they are equally not obliged at this stage to *reject* all forms of it. They can view that type of theory sympathetically as a praiseworthy attempt to do without non-empirical concepts and synthetic *a priori* judgments in an important region of human experience. They may even offer a helping hand, as I have tried to do in certain of the writings quoted by Professor Frankena.

Those who feel obliged to accept some form of non-predicative theory will be most usefully occupied in the following tasks. (i) In trying to account plausibly, in terms of their theory, for the main outstanding facts which seem *prima facie* to demand a theory of the *predicative* type. (ii) In trying to adduce facts which seem to fit better into a *non-predicative* type of theory than into any of the predicative type. One such fact, e.g., is that the state of mind (whatever it may be) which is expressed by uttering sincerely and wittingly such a sentence as "That act would be wrong," always tends to evoke a reaction *against* doing the act in question. It might be alleged that this seems to be a *necessary* proposition, and not a mere empirical generalisation about human nature. Now it might be argued that, if what such a sentence expresses is a *judgment,* one will have to hold either (a) that the psychological proposition in question *is* merely an empirical generalisation, or (b) that it is a *necessary synthetic proposition* known *a priori.* The former alternative seems unplausible; and the latter is one to be avoided, if possible, in accordance with my first Principle. Now it might fairly be alleged that, on some forms of the non-predicative theory, the proposition in question would be *analytic.* That would certainly be a point in favour of such forms of non-predicative theory.

Whether the non-predicativists have succeeded in these tasks or not, I think that there is no doubt that, in the course of their very strenuous efforts to perform them, they have made some valuable contributions to moral philosophy. At the time when I wrote *FTET* moral philosophy in England and the U.S.A. might fairly be described as dormant and apparently moribund. Since then, partly owing to the writings of certain predicativists (like Prichard and Ross) and partly owing to those of certain non-predicativists (like Professor Stevenson and Mr. Hare), it has become one of the liveliest branches of philosophy. *Plurimi pertransibunt et multiplex erit scientia.*

There is one other topic, closely connected with those which I have discussed above, on which I will briefly comment. That is the phrase "non-natural characteristic." As a student at Cambridge I was brought up to believe that it is a fundamentally important proposition of ethics that moral attributes belong to a peculiar category called "non-natural," and that there is something called "the naturalistic fallacy," which most moralists had committed who had written before the light dawned in 1903. When I became Professor of Moral Philosophy, and had to write a course of lectures on ethics, I was unable to discover any intelligible and tenable account of the meaning of this distinction between "natural" and "non-natural" attributes. It also seemed to me that, unless "fallacy" be used in the improper and question-begging sense of "mistaken opinion," instead of in its proper sense of "invalid bit of reasoning," there was nothing which can be described as "the naturalistic fallacy."

I do not propose to traverse again now this much trodden ground, but I will state briefly and dogmatically the conclusion which it seems fair to draw. *If* words like "morally good (or evil)," "morally right (or wrong)," etc., stand for characteristics, *then* the characteristics for which they stand differ from non-moral ones in being *dependent on the latter* in a way in which no *non-moral* characteristic appears to be dependent on others. No doubt some *non-moral* characteristics are *necessarily* dependent on others, e.g., to have a shape entails having a size. But none of these cases of necessary connexion between non-moral characteristics seems to be at all like the connexion between being a breach of promise and being morally wrong, which we express by saying that being a breach of promise necessarily contributes towards making an act morally wrong.

Now a non-predicativist might accept all this, and simply use it as water for his own mill. He might proceed to argue, in accordance with my first Principle, that any ethical theory which can avoid postulating characteristics of such an odd kind as moral ones would have to be, if there were such, is to be preferred (other things being equal) to one which has to postulate them. Suppose he could then explain in detail, in terms of a certain form of non-predicative theory, how it comes about that moral adjectives *seem* to stand for characteristics of this peculiar kind. Then I think that there would be a fairly strong *prima facie* case for preferring his form of the non-predicative theory to any form of predicative theory known to me.

Now non-predicativists have attempted such detailed explanations. I am impressed, if not completely convinced, by their efforts up to date; and I am inclined to think, at the moment of writing, that it is likely that the truth lies somewhere in that direction rather than on predicative lines. I could not be more definite if Professor Frankena (that kindest of men) were to hold a pistol to my head, which I cannot imagine him doing.

(B) MORAL PHILOSOPHY AND MORAL PRACTICE. The main topic which Mr. Hare discusses is the bearing or lack of bearing of moral philosophy on moral practice. As regards the historical part of his essay I would make the following comments.

Mr. Hare rightly mentions Moore and Prichard as the two most influential English moral philosophers at the time when I was young and for many years afterwards. Each held that the moral concepts which he took as fundamental are not only unanalysable, but also of a unique and peculiar kind. Now anyone who takes such a view must, if he would be consistent, hold that any proposition, in which the subject is described in purely *non-moral* terms and the predicate is or involves one of these moral notions, must be *synthetic*. Mr. Hare thinks that this commits such a philosopher to the particular epistemological view, called by Sidgwick "aesthetic intuitionism." This view he ascribes to Moore and to Prichard, and he thinks that for those who hold it moral philosophy can give no guidance to those who seek to know what they ought to do in various types of situation.

Now I do not think that a person who holds the Moore-Prichard type of theory as to the nature of moral concepts is necessarily committed to aesthetic intuitionism. The latter view may be stated roughly as follows. The only way to discover what is morally good or morally obligatory (as the case may be) in a particular situation is to put oneself actually or imaginatively into that situation, and to note what kind of value-judgment or deontic judgment one then makes. Now I do not doubt that it would be a *necessary preliminary* to giving practical guidance to others that one should oneself often have done what the aesthetic intuitionist has in mind. It would also be a *necessary preliminary* that other men should have done the like, and should have recorded the moral judgments which they then made. But at that stage there are the following two conceivable developments.

(1) Suppose a person admits (as Sidgwick certainly did, and as I imagine both Moore and Prichard would do) the possibility of necessary *synthetic* universal propositions, which can be seen to be true *ex vi terminorum*. Then it is conceivable that one might arrive by "intuitive induction" at a number of synthetic *a priori* axioms, stating necessary connexions between certain non-moral and certain specifically moral characteristics. This alternative would no doubt be rejected unhesitatingly by Mr. Hare and by most of his English and American contemporaries. But in a *historical* account it must be remembered that it has been held by many eminent and influential moral philosophers.

(2) Even if this alternative be rejected, there remains the theoretical possibility of *inductive generalisations,* of a high order of generality and reliability, similar in content to the alleged synthetic *a priori* axioms of the rejected view.

Now such a set of moral axioms, or of well established moral inductive generalisations, *might* be capable of elaborate deductive development, and *might* be found to entail consequences which no one could have foreseen. These consequences, together with factual information about the situation in which a particular person is placed, and about the probable consequences of this, that, or the other alternative action, *might* enable a moral philosopher to provide him with valuable (though never infallible) guidance as to how he morally ought to act.

The legitimate source of scepticism here is of course the very general conviction that none of these "mights" is in fact realised. The first alternative would involve admitting that there are *synthetic* necessary propositions knowable *a priori,* and this is very commonly held to be an exploded superstition. The second of them, though it might be admitted to be theoretically possible, seems not in fact to be true. *Either* (a) there are no well established inductive generalisations in morals; *or* (b) if there are, they do not (like, e.g., the laws of motion and the law of gravitation) form a system capable of elaborate deductive development and detailed application.

Passing from the historical to the other parts of Mr. Hare's essay, I agree that many young persons take up the study of philosophy because they are morally perplexed and hope that moral philosophy will give them practical guidance. But I think that this attitude covers a number of different troubles and demands, and I propose to distinguish some of them.

(1) A person may have been brought up to accept as *unconditional* a number of general moral principles, as to how one ought or ought not to act in any instance of certain frequently recurring types of situation. It may be that each of these maxims, considered in isolation on its merits, still seems to him on reflexion to be obviously true. But he may become aware, either in his own life or in the lives of others, of situations in which several of these principles are relevant and it is impossible to act in accordance with one without acting against another.

Moral philosophy could help here, if it could carry out the following programme. (i) Indicate a certain more general principle, which seems on its merits to be at least as obviously true as any of the more special ones. (ii) Show that, in acting on each of the more concrete principles in the relevant kinds of situation, one will *generally* (though not invariably) be acting in accordance with this more general one. (iii) Show that, in the exceptional situations, where several of the more concrete principles are relevant but it is impossible to act in accordance with all of them, this more general principle provides a satisfactory answer to the question how one ought to act. (iv) Suggest the causes which may have made the more concrete maxims seem to be true in their *unconditional* form, when really they are true only in the majority of situations in which they are relevant. This is the kind of programme which, e.g., Utilitarianism claims to carry out; and it has allayed, or at any rate mitigated this kind of perplexity in many highly intelligent and conscientious persons, such as J. S. Mill and Sidgwick.

(2) A great many conscientious plain men and several very eminent moral philosophers, e.g., Plato, Butler, and Sidgwick, seem to hold the following conviction. *All* moral maxims are subject to a certain implicit condition. When this is made explicit, any acceptable moral maxim would take the form: "In situations of the kind *S* one ought always to behave in the way *W, if and only if* such behaviour would not be in the end and on the whole detrimental to one's own interests." Now the difficulty is that there are kinds of behaviour which seem to many of these very persons to be morally obligatory or to be morally forbidden even in situations where the condition just mentioned seems *prima facie not* to be fulfilled.

If such a person appealed to moral philosophy in his perplexity, its first move should be to clear up the many ambiguities in the phrase "one's own interest." Is this supposed to be confined to one's own *happiness or unhappiness;* or is it to be extended to cover the improvement or worsening of one's own character, intellect, and personality? If the latter, is it to be confined to improvement or deterioration in *non-moral* respects, or is it to be extended to cover *specifically moral* improvement or deterioration also?

So much might fairly be regarded as within the range of *moral* philosophy. But what might be demanded is an assurance that behaviour, which we all agree to be morally obligatory, but which often *seems to be to all appearances* detrimental to the agent's long-term "interest" (however that may be interpreted), can never *really* be so, and therefore is no exception to the general principle in question. Now it seems to me that any attempt to show this would fall outside the realm of specifically *moral* philosophy, since it would turn on the nature and destiny of the human individual and the organisation of the rest of the universe. Philosophy has traditionally been held to be closely concerned with such questions, but the prevalent view among professional philosophers in England and America at the present time is that that is an elementary mistake.

(3) What troubles many intelligent and conscientious persons nowadays is something still more fundamental. There is a certain view of the nature and destiny of man, which seems to have the whole weight of biology and experimental psychology behind it, viz., a "behaviourist" or "epiphenomenalist" view, which I will call for short "scientific materialism." To many people it seems that, if this view be true, the notion of moral obligation must be a mere figment, which arose somehow in the

days of men's ignorance of their nature and destiny, and now survives precariously like a vestigial organ. When they contemplate the scientific evidence they cannot help accepting the materialist account of human nature. When they are engaged in co-operating or competing with their fellow-men they cannot help thinking that they have moral obligations. When they try to bring together these two convictions into one focus it seems impossible to reconcile them. They naturally, and I think quite legitimately, appeal to professional philosophers to help them.

Now philosophers might seek, and in fact have sought, to do this in various ways. One is to try to show that, when the scientific materialist view of human nature and the notion of moral obligation are both properly understood, there is no incompatibility between accepting the former and continuing to hold that men are subject to moral obligations. This type of solution will be helpful, only if it can succeed without having to give such an account of moral obligation as seems to the intelligent and conscientious non-philosopher to distort it or eviscerate it or altogether to dissolve it. Another way would be to admit the conflict, but to deny the adequacy and the ultimate coherency of the scientific materialist account of human nature, whilst granting its plausibility and usefulness in the limited context in which it has arisen. I think that the first type of answer might fairly be said to fall within *moral* philosophy, and the second only within *philosophy* in a wider sense.

It would take me too far afield to attempt to discuss adequately the "test" for rightness or wrongness, which Mr. Hare very tentatively puts forward at the end of his essay. I will consider only the following point. Mr. Hare says that A will be inclined to judge it to be *wrong* for him to treat B in a certain way, if, on imagining himself to be in a similar situation as *patient* instead of agent, he finds that he would *dislike* to be treated in that way. What is not clear to me is what Mr. Hare takes to be the relevance of this "dislike" on A's part.

It seems to me that all that is *logically* relevant is that A should judge that it would be *wrong* for another to treat him as he is proposing to treat B. Whether he would *dislike* or *like* being treated in that way seems logically irrelevant.

Perhaps Mr. Hare wishes to assert only the *psychological* proposition that A will be inclined to judge that it would be wrong for another to treat him as he is proposing to treat B, if and only if he would *dislike* to be treated in that way. If so, I think it is a very doubtful generalisation. Perhaps, then, what Mr. Hare wishes to assert is only the following. A needs to be convinced that he would dislike to be treated in the way in question, *not* in order to judge that such action by another towards him would be wrong, *nor* in order to judge (in accordance with Mr. Hare's principle) that such action by him towards B would be wrong, but in order that the latter conviction should have *any practical effect* on his conduct towards B. If that is what Mr. Hare means, I think it is a rash generalisation about human motivation.

I am inclined to think that the only relevance of A's *disliking* the experience which he would have if he were to be treated as he is thinking of treating B is this. (i) An *important,* though neither a necessary nor a sufficient reason for thinking that it would be *wrong* to treat B in a certain way, is that B would dislike to be so treated. (ii) An *important,* and perhaps indispensable, way for A to gain a *vivid* and *practically effective* belief that B would dislike a certain experience is that A should imagine himself to be having a similar experience in similar circumstances, and should find the idea strongly distasteful. The vivid and practically effective belief thus gained is not, of course, infallible. It seems to me likely, e.g., that many soldiers do not find the experience of hand-to-hand fighting as horrible as I feel that it must be when I try to imagine myself in their situation. But, though not infallible, it is a most valuable corrective to a common tendency to perform, without any concrete realisation of the consequences, actions which will produce, in those affected by them, experiences which the latter would intensely dislike.

(C) "OUGHT" AND "CAN." The relations between the former and the latter of these notions form the main topic of Professor Hedenius's paper. I would like at the outset to make the following general remark. The treatment of the whole subject in my lecture "Determinism, Indeterminism, and Libertarianism" is extremely condensed and somewhat dogmatic. It omits much that should be included in any adequate discussion; the points raised are not sufficiently developed; and objections and counter-arguments are not considered. Such defects are inevitable when a vast and intricate subject has to be handled in the course of an hour's lecture.

Professor Hedenius draws a distinction between acts which are morally *obligatory* and acts which are morally *imputable* to the agent. He argues that a conceivable act, which it is impossible or inevitable for an agent to do, may nevertheless be morally obligatory. But he holds that, for an act to be morally imputable, it must be at any rate what I have called "conditionally substitutable." I am inclined to think that any difference between us on this matter depends mainly on different usages of certain terms, which undoubtedly are used sometimes in a wider and sometimes in a narrower sense. I will now proceed to develop this suggestion.

Consider the statement that A is under an obligation to do X at t. Does this entail (1, 1) that it is *not impossible* for him to do X at t? And does it entail (1, 2) that it is *not inevitable* for him to do X at t? Next consider the statement that A is under an obligation *not* to do Y at t. Does this entail (2, 1) that it is *not inevitable* for him to do Y at t? And does it entail (2, 2) that it is *not impossible* for him to do Y at t?

I think it is easy to show that (2, 1) can be reduced to the form of (1, 1), and (2, 2) to the form of (1, 2). In order to do this one need only note that an obligation *not* to do Y is equivalent (subject to two conditions which I will state in a moment) to an obligation to do *something-other-than-Y*. The two conditions are these. (i) It is to be understood that "to do something other than Y" includes, as one alternative, refraining from all positive relevant action, e.g., just *not* answering a question. (ii) It is also to be remembered that to be under an obligation to behave in *one-or-another* of several alternative ways does *not* entail being under an obligation to behave in *any particular one* of those ways. Subject to these explanations, I propose to confine the discussion to questions (1, 1) and (1, 2).

Professor Hedenius is undoubtedly right in saying that we often use expressions which seem to imply that the alleged entailment in (1, 1) does *not* hold. Here are some examples. "He ought to have lectured from 9 to 10 A.M. yesterday; but it was impossible, since he was then undergoing an operation." "He ought to be lecturing now; but it is impossible, since he is now stricken with aphasia." "He ought to begin to lecture at 6 P.M. in London this evening; but that will be impossible, since it is now 5 P.M. and the train in which he is travelling from Cambridge is held up by a derailment at Bishop's Stortford."

I am very doubtful, however, whether these expressions in fact show that the entailment alleged in (1, 1) does not hold. I suggest that in each of them "ought" is used in a certain *conditional* sense; that the condition is regarded as obvious and as nearly always fulfilled; and therefore is not explicitly stated. I would expand my first example as follows:— "If and only if he had been able (as he normally would have been) to lecture from 9 to 10 A.M. yesterday, he *would have been* under an obligation to do so. But (owing to the exceptional circumstances of undergoing an operation at the time) it was then impossible for him to do so, and therefore he was *not* in fact under an obligation to do so." The other two examples can be treated on similar lines.

It should be noted that the collapse of a categorical obligation, through the impossibility of performing the relevant action, very often imposes on the agent a categorical obligation to perform a certain *other* action, which *is* in his power. The lecturer in the delayed train, e.g., ought, if he can, to send a telegram to the person in charge of the arrangements for his intended lecture in London.

Let us now consider the alleged entailment (1, 2), i.e., that if A is under an obligation to do X at t, it follows that it is *not inevitable* for him to do X at t. Can we think of a relevant and obvious counter-instance?

The first point to notice is this. An action, such as answering (truly or falsely) a question, returning or withholding a borrowed article, etc., has to be considered in two aspects, viz., in reference to the person affected by it and in reference to the person doing it. In respect of the *patient* the important question is: Does the action *in fact* treat him as he has a right to be treated in the situation? In respect of the *agent* the important question is: Is the action done from the *intention (inter alia)* of treating the patient as he has a right to be treated in the situation? An action of the former kind may be called "right-*securing*," and one of the latter kind "right-*intending*."

Now I think it is certain that we often use "obligation" and "obligatory" in such a way that an action which the agent is under an obligation to do is one that is right-*securing*, whether or not it be right-intending. If we use our terms in that way, it is obvious that an action which the agent could not help doing may be obligatory upon him. (It is equally obvious that one which he could not possibly do might be obligatory on him.)

But I think it is no less certain that we often use "obligation" and "obligatory" in such a way that an action which the agent is under an obligation to do must be right-*intending*. Now it seems to be that an action, which the agent *could not help* doing, might indeed be *in accordance with* an intention on his part to treat the patient as he has a right to be treated in the situation. But one could hardly say that such an action was done *from that intention (inter alia)*. So I do not think that an action which the agent could not help doing could be called "obligatory," if that word is used (as it often is) to connote right-intending and not merely right-securing.

Professor Hedenius says, quite correctly, that we can talk of a man being *forced* to do his duty in a certain manner, e.g., forced to repay money that he owes. I doubt, however, whether this is relevant to the issue. In the first place, "duty" is here used in the first of the two senses which I have just distinguished. What we mean is that A is forced to do an act which in fact treats B as he has a right to be treated. And, secondly, to say that A was forced to do X is not generally equivalent to saying that it was *inevitable* for him to do X. What it generally means is that A would have preferred antecedently not to do X, but that he was in a situation where it was practically certain that the consequences to him of not doing it would be extremely unpleasant. It was open to him to refrain from doing X and to put up with the unpleasant consequences. So his doing of X was not inevitable.

Very likely I used "obligable" in my lecture in roughly the sense in which Professor Hedenius uses "morally imputable." Let us assume this for the sake of argument, and use the latter phrase in the rest of the discussion. I understand that Professor Hedenius is inclined to agree, up to a certain point, with my account of the conditions which must be fulfilled if it is to be morally imputable to A that he behaved in the way W in a certain situation S. He agrees with me up to the point that A's behaving in the way W would not be morally imputable unless it were, *in a certain sense,* "determined by A's ego or self." Now I offered a certain analysis of this latter condition, and said that it seemed to me self-evident that it could not be fulfilled. Professor Hedenius offers an alternative analysis, which would not be open to that objection.

If I understand him aright, the essential features in his account are as follows. We have at the back of our minds a reference to a certain large class of persons (e.g., contemporary middle-class Englishmen above the age of puberty); and we have the thought of a certain type of personality as *normal* in that class in respect to the nature and strength and organisation of a number of important conative-emotional dispositions (e.g., desire for food and drink, desire for money, sexual desire, tendency to react with hostility when thwarted, and so on). The agent is assumed to be a member of such a class of persons. We regard a bit of behaviour on the part of a member of such a class as "determined by his ego or self," when and only when the following conditions are fulfilled. (1) The stimulus must be of a kind to which (i) all members of the class are quite often subjected, and (ii) in response to which most of them on most occasions would behave in a certain way Z. (2) The individual in question A behaved, when so stimulated, in a markedly different way W.

Now I think that the distinctions which Professor Hedenius draws are important in reference to the degree of *merit or demerit* which we ascribe to a person in respect of a bit of intentional behaviour. We do not get morally excited when a person behaves rightly under circumstances which frequently occur in the lives of all of us, and in which most of us generally do act rightly. Nor do we get morally excited when a person behaves wrongly under circumstances which are highly exceptional, and in which one suspects that most such persons would act wrongly and is very doubtful whether one would have acted rightly oneself.

It seems to me that all this comes fairly easily under the sense of "ought" and "ought not" which I described in paragraph (ii) of the Section entitled, '*Various Senses of "Obligable"*' in my lecture. I said of this that "a clear-headed Determinist should hold either that this is the only sense, or that, if there is another sense, in which obligability entails *categorical* substitutability, it has no application." But I added that I am inclined to think that we often use "ought" and "ought not" in another sense, and that in this other sense they entail categorical substitutability. I think that this is most obvious when one makes judgments about *oneself*, of the form "I ought to have done so-and-so" (which I did not do), or "I ought not to have done so-and-so" (which I did). I cannot help thinking that a reference to what the average middle-class Englishman above the age of puberty would or woud not generally do, when subjected to the stimulus to which I was subjected, would serve only as a rough measure of the degree of my delinquency, and not at all as an analysis of my conviction that *I*, under the very circumstances in which I in fact failed to do my duty, *could* instead have done it.

(D) THE "EXISTENTIAL" ACCOUNT OF HUMAN PERSONALITY. I understand Professor Kuhn to be using "existence" throughout nearly the whole of his essay in a certain technical sense, viz., to denote the peculiar kind of being which he holds to be characteristic of a *person,* and to be revealed to each of us by the reflexive awareness which is an essential factor in personality. If I understand Professor Kuhn aright, what he takes such reflexive awareness to reveal to each person may be described as follows. What a person now *is* is what he has *made himself,* through the reaction of himself as active, spontaneous, and selective, upon himself as passive and malleable. Furthermore, he, as he *now is,* is actively engaged in determining and generating himself *as he will become,* by a further process of selection and action. This interest in, and self-direction towards, the *future* is particularly characteristic of a person. Moreover, each person has a unique and fundamental concern for *himself,* and this is alleged to be an essential condition of "the absolute validity of moral obligation and moral claims in a person."

I am willing to accept much of this, if I am allowed to interpret it as follows, and to put certain qualifications upon it. In the first place, it is certainly characteristic of human beings (as contrasted with other animals, and especially with certain insects) to be born with extremely few and comparatively unimportant *first-order* dispositions. They are born, instead, with what Professor Ducasse calls "aptitudes," i.e., dispositions to *acquire* dispositions and to *organise* those which they acquire. In so far as statements to the effect that a person is not "an entity fixed and bound by its own whatness" are interpreted in this way, I think that they are true and important.

On the other hand, we must not overlook the fact that what a person can make of himself, even under the most favourable conditions, *is* limited by his innate endowments. It is true that no one knows even approximately what are his own or another person's ultimate limitations. It is true too that it is generally undesirable for a person to dwell on this topic in his own case, or for his neighbours to express a confident and narrow view about it. Lastly, it is true that experience shows that a person, who seems *prima facie* to be hopelessly handicapped, physically or intellectually or morally, sometimes does (if he seriously takes himself in hand, and if others give him understanding help) achieve a development of personality which seems well nigh miraculous. But I see no reason to believe that the possibilities are in fact unlimited in any case, or that the limits in each particular case are not fixed by the innate constitution of the individual.

Allowing that there is an important sense in which it is true that each of us is continually making and re-making himself, we must not exaggerate the part played by the *deliberate action* of the individual himself in this process. In the case of most of us it is but fitfully and for short periods that one "takes oneself in hand" and sets out to make oneself a person of such and such a kind. In the main each man's personality is moulded for him in early life by the pressures of family, of school, of business, by the newspapers, the wireless, and the films. These influences are (after occasional struggles, which leave their scars in all, and mar the personalities and wreck the lives of some) generally assimilated fairly thoroughly, though of course *in modo recipientis*. Thereafter the reactions of most men of a given social group in normal situations are almost automatic. Doubtless the power to make a hard deliberate choice, which one realises will profoundly modify one's life and personality, remains latent in everyone. If faced with a crisis, some few of us might make such a choice. But I suspect that in most men that power has become so repressed and overlaid and atrophied in middle life that the chance of its being exercised, if a crisis should face one, is negligible.

"Existentialism," as presented by Professor Kuhn, seems to me to be an account of human nature derived from contemplating men of forceful and original character, making hard (and for themselves and those near and dear to them, at any rate) far-reaching decisions. It is certainly most important not to neglect this heroic side of human nature, and not to forget that it can and does show itself in what we might be tempted to regard as very ordinary men and women in very humdrum circumstances. But that should not make us ignore the dim and petty background (against which these cases shine forth by their rarity), summed up in the epitaph which might so fittingly commemorate most of us:—

Too bad for heaven, too good for hell;
So where he's gone I cannot tell.

Professor Kuhn's main criticism on what I have written about human personality is that I have treated a person and his doings and sufferings as if they were exactly like a physical thing and what happens to it, and have treated voluntary action as if it were exactly like physical causation. I must admit that there is much truth in this, as regards my published works. I can, however, assure Professor Kuhn that I am not, and have never been, a "physicalist" (as I understand that word) about human nature. I regard the differences between men and any non-human animals of whom we have knowledge, as quite fundamental, however they may have arisen in the course of evolution. And I consider that causation, as it shows itself in rational cognition, deliberation, voluntary decision, and considered action, has certain unique peculiarities as contrasted with either purely physical causation or psychological causation at the non-rational level.

The only other matter on which I will comment is this. Professor Kuhn twits me with some *obiter dicta,* which occur towards the end of *The Mind and its Place in Nature,* to the effect that the human race might possibly escape disaster by applying psychology and genetics to "deliberately altering the emotional constitution of mankind, and deliberately constructing more reasonable forms of social organisation." He asks me what I think about that now.

My answer is as follows. It seems to me even more likely now than it did then that, unless opportunities for organised scientific research should be destroyed in the near future, the *knowledge* and the *power* will be available to determine the kind of individuals who shall be born (or incubated), and to mould their nature at will after birth. Such knowledge or power *could* be used on a large scale at any moment only by that person or that group who then have control in a given society. They *would* be used only in so far as those in control knew of them and desired to use them, and the *ends* for which they would in that case be used would depend on the wishes and ideals of the controllers. Given all this, the scheme would be *effective* only in so far as those in control could apply it on a large scale by consent or through inadvertence, or impose it by fraud or by force or by propaganda on the rest of the society.

Plainly that would give an unprecedented power for good or for ill to those who are in a position to use it. Beyond that platitude there is little that I can say except to add the following supplementary platitudes.

(1) There is little likelihood that the scientists, who had the knowledge, would be any more than the tools, or at best the willing technical advisers, of those who had the power to apply it. (2) Even if, by some strange chance, the relevant scientists should also be in effective control, that would be no guarantee that a good use would be made of the power.

There is no reason to think that the ideals of psychologists and genet-icists, as such, in regard to human nature and society, would be better (as distinct from more practicable) than those of trades-unionists, business-men, lawyers, soldiers, or professional politicians. Nor is there any rea-son to think that psychologists and geneticists, as such, would be any less susceptible than other men to the corruptions of power. (3) I am inclined to believe that there is a rather strong *negative* correlation between the qualities which help a man to get and to keep power in a highly or-ganised industrial society of the modern type (whether capitalist, social-democratic, or communist), and the qualities which tend to endow a man with high ideals of human personality and human society. I should there-fore think it much more likely that the powers in question, if used at all, would be *misused* than that they would be applied to good ends. (4) On the other hand, it seems to me plainer than ever that, *unless* the emo-tional make-up of the average citizen throughout the world *be* pro-foundly modified in certain ways in the fairly near future, the chance of humanity escaping a large-scale disaster is very slender.

Existing societies are composed of persons whose emotional reactions are largely infantile or anachronistic, i.e., adapted to situations utterly different from those with which men are now faced. They are wholly dependent for their livelihood on a complex and delicate web of eco-nomic conditions, which no individual understands. They are now brought into ever closer and more irritating contact with each other, through the development of means of quick communication and the inordinate growth of population, and their emotions are continually played upon by wireless propaganda. All the conditions for an explosion are thus given. And now such persons and societies, whom a sensible parent would hesitate to trust with a popgun, are provided with atomic and hydrogen bombs, and with rockets to convey them. So there is every prospect that the explosion, when it comes, will be shatteringly de-structive.

These seem to me to be reasonably probable inferences from fairly plain empirical facts, and I do not think that their plausibility is much affected by whether one holds a "physicalist" or an "existentialist" view of the nature of human personality.

*   *   *   *   *

Philosophy is essentially a middle-aged man's game, though certain philosophers (notably Plato and Kant) have put up their best perfor-mances when they were well past middle life. Those of us who are not Platos or Kants are well advised to retire gracefully before they have too obviously lost their grip. Medical science would almost have made the world safe for senility, if physics had not made it unsafe for every-body; and there are far too many old clowns arthritically going through their hoops, to the embarrassment of the spectators:—

> From *X*'s eyes the streams of dotage flow,
> And *Y* expires a driveller and a show.

My younger colleagues would have no difficulty in substituting appropri-ate constants for the variables in these lines. Moreover, though philoso-phies are never refuted, they rapidly go out of fashion, and the kind of philosophy which I have practised has become antiquated without hav-ing yet acquired the interest of a collector's piece:—

> New forms arise, and different views engage,
> Superfluous lags the veteran on the stage.

So this veteran now definitely makes his last bow as a professional per-former, though he may occasionally make a graceful appearance "by re-quest" at a matinee for charity.

Cambridge, 14 December, 1956

BIBLIOGRAPHY OF THE WRITINGS OF

C. D. BROAD

TO THE END OF JULY 1959

Compiled by

C. LEWY

Acknowledgement

I am grateful to Professor Broad for looking through a draft of this bibliography, and drawing my attention to three items which I had out as well as to ten items which were published unsigned or under a pseudonym.

C. Lewy

Cambridge
August 1959

WRITINGS OF C. D. BROAD
To the end of July 1959

1906

The Philosophy of Omar Khayyam and its Relation to that of Schopenhauer. *The Westminster Review,* v. 166, November 1906, pp. 544–56.

1912

Review of *Proceedings of the Aristotelian Society, 1910–11* (London, 1911). *Mind,* n.s., v. 21, April 1912, pp. 260–4.
Signed D. Broad.
Review of W. R. Sorley, *The Moral Life and Moral Worth* (Cambridge, 1911). *Int. J. of Ethics,* v. 22, April 1912, pp. 352–3.
Review of J. E. Boodin, *Truth and Reality: An Introduction to the Theory of Knowledge* (New York, 1911). *Mind,* n.s., v. 21, July 1912, pp. 449–51.
Review of V. Welby, *Significs and Language: The Articulate Form of our Expressive and Interpretive Resources* (London, 1911). *Mind, n.s.,* v. 21, July 1912, pp. 455–6.
Review of James Ward, *The Realm of Ends or Pluralism and Theism* (Cambridge, 1911). *Int. J. of Ethics,* v. 23, October 1912, pp. 77–84.

1913

Critical Notice of A. Meinong, *Über Annahmen* (Leipzig, 1910). *Mind,* n.s., v. 22, January 1913, pp. 90–102.
Note on Achilles and the Tortoise. *Mind,* n.s., v. 22, April 1913, pp. 318–9.
Review of R. A. P. Rogers, *A Short History of Ethics: Greek and Modern* (London, 1911). *Int. J. of Ethics,* v. 23, April 1913, pp. 359–61.
Lord Hugh Cecil's "Conservatism." *Int. J. of Ethics,* v. 23, July 1913, pp. 396–418.
Critical Notice of A. Cournot, *Essai sur les Fondements de nos Connasissances et sur les Caractères de la Critique Philosophique* (Paris, 1912). *Mind,* n.s., v. 22, July 1913, pp. 399–402.
Review of *Proceedings of the Aristotelian Society, 1911–12* (London, 1912). *Mind,* n.s., v. 22, July 1913, pp. 408–10.
Review of W. T. Marvin, *A First Book in Metaphysics* (New York, 1912). *Mind,* n.s., v. 22, October 1913, pp. 580–2.
Review of H. Wildon Carr, *The Problem of Truth* (London and Edinburgh, 1912). *Int. J. of Ethics,* v. 24, October 1913, pp. 104–7.

1914

PERCEPTION, PHYSICS, AND REALITY; AN ENQUIRY INTO THE INFORMATION THAT PHYSICAL SCIENCE CAN SUPPLY ABOUT THE REAL. Cambridge: at the University Press, 1914, pp. xii + 388. (Abbr.: *PPR*)

1915

Critical Notice of F. Enriques, *Problems of Science* (tr. by K. Royce; Chicago and London, 1914). *Mind*, n.s., v. 24, January 1915, pp. 94–8.

Critical Notice of A. Aliotta, *The Idealistic Reaction against Science* (tr. by A. McCaskill; London, 1914). *Mind*, n.s., v. 24, January 1915, pp. 107–12.

Review of B. Russell, *On Our Knowledge of the External World* (Chicago and London, 1914). *Int. J. of Ethics*, v. 25, January 1915, pp. 259–63.

Review of H. Wildon Carr, *The Philosophy of Change* (London, 1914). *The Hibbert Journal*, v. 13, January 1915, pp. 448–51.

Extracts from the re-found Mycenean "Kronoi." *College Echoes* (*St. Andrews University Magazine*), n.s., v. 10, March 16, 1915, pp. 242–3.
Signed: Oculus-Testis. By C. D. Broad and J. H. Duncan.

Phenomenalism. *Proc. Aristotelian Soc.*, n.s., v. 15, 1914–15, pp. 227–51.
Read April 12, 1915.

Critical Notice of B. Russell, *On Our Knowledge of the External World* (Chicago and London, 1914). *Mind*, n.s., v. 24, April 1915, pp. 250–4.

Review of H. Poincaré, *Wissenschaft und Methode* (German tr. by F. and L. Lindemann; Leipzig, 1914). *Mind*, n.s., v. 24, April 1915, p. 275.
Signed C. D. B.

What do we mean by the question: Is our Space Euclidean? *Mind*, n.s., v. 24, October 1915, pp. 464–80.

Critical Notice of A. A. Robb, *A Theory of Time and Space* (Cambridge, 1914). *Mind*, n.s., v. 24, October 1915, pp. 555–61.

1916

The Prevention of War. *Int. J. of Ethics*, v. 26, January 1916, pp. 241–57.

Review of L. T. More, *The Limitations of Science* (London, 1915). *Mind*, n.s., v. 25, January 1916, pp. 113–6.

Review of E. Mach, *Science of Mechanics* (*Supplementary Volume*) (Chicago and London, 1915). *Mind*, n.s., v. 25, January 1916, pp. 118–9.

Review of G. Cantor, *Contributions to the Founding of the Theory of Transfinite Numbers* (tr. by P. E. B. Jourdain; Chicago and London, 1915). *Mind*, n.s., v. 25, January 1916, pp. 120–1.

On the Function of False Hypotheses in Ethics. *Int. J. of Ethics*, v. 26, April 1916, pp. 377–97.

Review of *Proceedings of the Aristotelian Society, 1914–15* (London, 1915). *Mind*, n.s., v. 25, April 1916, pp. 270–2.

Note on Connotation and Denotation. *Mind*, n.s., v. 25, April 1916, pp. 287–8.

Review of G. A. Johnston, *An Introduction to Ethics* (London, 1915). *Int. J. of Ethics*, v. 26, July 1916, pp. 561–4.

The Nature and Geometry of Space. *Mind*, n.s., v. 25, October 1916, pp. 522–4.

1917

Hume's Theory of the Credibility of Miracles. *Proc. Aristotelian Soc.*, n.s., v. 17, 1916–17, pp. 77–94
Read Jan. 8, 1917.

Critical Notice of G. Boole, *Collected Works, Vol. II: Laws of Thought*

(Chicago and London, 1916). *Mind,* n.s., v. 26, January 1917, pp. 81–99.

Critical Notice of A. De Morgan, *A Budget of Paradoxes* (Chicago and London, 1915). *Mind,* n.s., v. 26, April 1917, pp. 226–30.

Review of P. Richardson and E. H. Landis, *Numbers, Variables, and Mr. Russell's Philosophy* (Chicago and London, 1916). *Mind,* n.s., v. 26, April 1917, pp. 235–6.

Lord Kilsby: An Impossible Tale. *College Echoes (St. Andrews University Magazine),* n.s., v. 12, May 18, 1917, pp. 42–3.
Verse. Signed: H. B.

1918

Body and Mind. *The Monist,* v. 28, April 1918, pp. 234–58.

Critical Notice of J. Laird, *Problems of the Self* (London, 1917). *Mind,* n.s., v. 27, April 1918, pp. 234–43.

The Dukedom of Hampshire. *College Echoes (St. Andrews University Magazine),* n.s., v. 13, June 5, 1918, pp. 75–8.
Unsigned.

A General Notation for the Logic of Relations. *Mind,* n.s., v. 27, July 1918, pp. 284–303.

Critical Notice of *Proceedings of the Aristotelian Society, 1916–17* (London, 1917). *Mind,* n.s., v. 27, July 1918, pp. 366–70.

On the Relation between Induction and Probability (I.). *Mind,* n.s., v. 27, October 1918, pp. 389–404.

In What Sense is Survival Desirable? *The Hibbert Journal,* v. 17, October 1918, pp. 7–20.

Critical Notice of B. Russell, *Mysticism and Logic* (London, 1918). *Mind,* n.s., v. 27, October 1918, pp. 484–92.

Note. *Mind,* n.s., v. 27, October 1918, p. 508.
Concerning the article on "A General Notation for the Logic of Relations."

1919

Mechanical Explanation and its Alternatives. *Proc. Aristotelian Soc.,* n.s., v. 19, 1918–19, pp. 86–124.
Read Jan. 6, 1919.

Symposium: Is there "Knowledge by Acquaintance?" By G. Dawes Hicks, G. E. Moore, B. Edgell, and C. D. Broad. *Aristotelian Soc. Supp. Vol. 2,* 1919, pp. 159–220.
Broad's contribution: pp. 206–20.

The Antecedent Probability of Survival. *The Hibbert Journal,* v. 17, July 1919, pp. 561–78.

Critical Notice of E. Jones, *Papers on Psycho-Analysis* (London, 1918). *Mind,* n.s., v. 28, July 1919, pp. 340–7.

Review of C. E. Bechhofer and M. B. Reckitt, *The Meaning of National Guilds* (London, 1918). *Int. J. of Ethics,* v. 29, July 1919, pp. 504–5.

Review of P. E. B. Jourdain, *The Philosophy of Mr. B*rtr*nd R*ss*ll* (London, 1919). *Mind,* n.s., v. 28, October 1919, pp. 485–6.

The Notion of a General Will. *Mind,* n.s., v. 28, October 1919, pp. 502–4.

Reality. *Encyclopaedia of Religion and Ethics.* Edited by James Hastings *et al.* Vol. X, Edinburgh and New York, 1919, pp. 587–592.

1920

The Relation between Induction and Probability (II.). *Mind,* n.s., v. 29, January 1920, pp. 11–45.

Review of A. N. Whitehead, *An Inquiry Concerning the Principles of Natural Knowledge* (Cambridge 1919). *The Hibbert Journal,* v. 18, January 1920, pp. 397–406.

A Romance of the New Jerusalem. *College Echoes (St. Andrews Universitᵛ Magazine),* n.s., v. 15, March 10, 1920, pp. 88–90.
Unsigned.

Euclid, Newton, and Einstein. *The Hibbert Journal,* v. 18, April 1920, pp. 425–58.

Critical Notice of A. N. Whitehead, *An Inquiry Concerning the Principles of Natural Knowledge* (Cambridge, 1919). *Mind,* n.s., v. 29, April 1920, pp. 216–31.

Review of *Aristotelian Society Supp. Vol. 2* (London, 1919). *Mind,* n.s., v. 29, April 1920, pp. 232–5.

"Euclid, Newton, and Einstein." Reply to G. A. Sexton. *The Hibbert Journal,* v. 18, July 1920, p. 802.

Critical Notice of B. Bosanquet, *Implication and Linear Inference* (London. 1920). *Mind,* n.s., v. 29, July 1920, pp. 323–38.

The Philosophical Aspects of the Theory of Relativity. Symposium between A. S. Eddington, W. D. Ross, C. D. Broad, and F. A. Lindemann. *Mind,* n.s., v. 29, October 1920, pp. 414–45.
Broad's contribution: pp. 430–7.

1921

Prof. Alexander's Gifford Lectures (I.). *Mind,* n.s., v. 30, January 1921, pp. 25–39.
On S. Alexander's *Space, Time and Deity.*

Review of E. Freundlich, *The Foundations of Einstein's Theory of Gravitation* (tr. by H. L. Brose; Cambridge, 1920). *Mind,* n.s., v. 30, January 1921, pp. 101–2.

Review of A. N. Whitehead, *The Concept of Nature* (Cambridge, 1920). *The Hibbert Journal,* v. 19, January 1921, pp. 360–6.

Symposium: The Character of Cognitive Acts. By John Laird, G. E. Moore, C. D. Broad, and G. Dawes Hicks. *Proc. Aristotelian Society,* n.s., v. 21, 1920–21, pp. 123–60.
Broad's contribution: pp. 140–51.

Prof. Alexander's Gifford Lectures (II.). *Mind,* n.s., v. 30, April 1921, pp. 129–50.

Review of M. Schlick, *Space and Time in Contemporary Physics* (tr. by H. L. Brose; Oxford, 1920). *Mind,* n.s., v. 30, April 1921, p. 245.

Critical Notice of J. McT. E. McTaggart, *The Nature of Existence,* Vol. I (Cambridge, 1921). *Mind,* n.s., v. 30, July 1921, pp. 317–32.

Review of Clerk Maxwell, *Matter and Motion* (ed. by Sir J. Larmor; London, 1920). *Mind*, n.s., v. 30, July 1921, p. 372.
Signed C. D. B.

Review of F. Cajori, *A History of the Conceptions of Limits and Fluxions in Great Britain from Newton to Wodehouse* (Chicago and London, 1919). *Mind*, n.s., v. 30, July 1921, p. 372.
Signed C. D. B.

The External World. *Mind*, n.s., v. 30, October 1921, pp. 385–408.

Review of J. McT. E. McTaggart, *The Nature of Existence, Vol. I.* (Cambridge, 1921). *The Hibbert Journal*, v. 20, October 1921, pp. 172–5.

Review of E. Cunningham, *Relativity, the Electron Theory and Gravitation* (London, 1921). *Mind*, n.s., v. 30, October 1921, p. 490.
Signed C. D. B.

Review of A. A. Robb, *The Absolute Relations of Space and Time* (Cambridge, 1921). *Mind*, n.s., v. 30, October 1921, p. 490.
Signed C. D. B.

Time. *Encyclopaedia of Religion and Ethics*. Edited by James Hastings *et al.* Vol. XII, Edinburgh and New York, 1921, pp. 334–45.

1922

Critical Notice of J. M. Keynes, *A Treatise on Probability* (London, 1921). *Mind*, n.s., v. 31, January 1922, pp. 72–85.

Reply to a Note by B. Bosanquet. *Mind*, n.s., v. 31, January 1922, pp. 122–3. Title of Bosanquet's Note: "Prof. Broad on the External World."

A Neglected Method of Psychical Research. Letter to the Editor of the Journal of the S.P.R. *J. of the Society for Psychical Research*, v. 20, March 1922, pp. 251–2.

Critical Notice of W. E. Johnson, *Logic, Part II* (Cambridge, 1922). *Mind*, n.s., v. 31, October 1922, pp. 496–510.

1923

SCIENTIFIC THOUGHT. London, Kegan Paul, Trench, Trubner & Co., 1923, pp. 555. (Abbr.: *ST*)

Contents. Preface. Introduction: The Subject-matter of Philosophy, and its relations to the Special Sciences—*Part I. The Traditional Concepts of Mathematical Physics, and their gradual modification within the Region of Physical Science*—I. The Traditional Conception of Space, and the Principle of Extensive Abstraction—II. The General Problem of Time and Change—III. The Traditional Kinematics, and its gradual Modification in the Region of Physics. (1) The Absolute and the Relational Theories—IV. Modification of the Traditional Kinematics in the Region of Physics (*Continued*). (2) The Special Theory of Relativity—V. The Traditional Kinetics, and its gradual Modification in the Region of Physics. (1) Newton's *Laws of Motion and Gravitation*—VI. Modification of the Traditional Kinetics (*Continued*). (2) The General Theory of Relativity. Summary of Part I—*Part II. The Sensational and Perceptual Basis of our Scientific Concepts*—VII. Matter and its Appearances; Preliminary Definitions—VIII. The Theory of Sensa, and the Critical Scientific Theory

—IX. The Positions and Shapes of Sensa and of Physical Objects—X. The Dates and Durations of Sensa and of Physical Objects and Events—XI. Sensible and Physical Motion—XII. Sensible and Physical Space-Time—XIII. The Physiological Conditions of Sensations, and the Ontological Status of Sensa.

A Correction [to the Critical Notice of Johnson's *Logic*]. *Mind*, n.s., v. 32, January 1923, p. 139.

Various Meanings of the Term "Unconscious." *Proc. Aristotelian Soc.*, n.s., v. 23, 1922–23, pp. 173–98.

Read April 9, 1923.

Critical Notice of A. N. Whitehead, *The Principle of Relativity* (Cambridge, 1922). *Mind*, n.s., v. 32, April 1923, pp. 211–9.

Butler as a Theologian. *The Hibbert Journal*, v. 21, July 1923, pp. 637–56. Reprinted in *Religion, Philosophy and Psychical Research*, 1953.

Review of R. J. Boscovich, *Theoria Philosophiae Naturalis* (Chicago and London, 1922). *Mind*, n.s., v. 32, July 1923, p. 374.

Butler as a Moralist. *The Hibbert Journal*, v. 22, October 1923, pp. 44–63.

1924

Critical and Speculative Philosophy. *Contemporary British Philosophy: Personal Statements* (First Series). Edited by J. H. Muirhead. London, G. Allen and Unwin, 1924, pp. 77–100.

For Italian translation of this see 1939.

Two Extracts from "The Jerusalem Times." *The Trinity Magazine*, v. 5, March 1924, pp. 44–5.

Signed C. D. B.

Symposium: Critical Realism: Is the Difficulty in affirming a Nature Independent of Mind overcome by the Distinction between Essence and Existence? By J. Loewenberg, C. D. Broad, and C. J. Shebbeare. *Aristotelian Soc. Supp. Vol. 4*, 1924, pp. 86–129.

Broad's contribution: pp. 106–15.

Mr. Johnson on the Logical Foundations of Science (I.). *Mind*, n.s., v. 33, July 1924, pp. 242–61.

On W. E. Johnson's *Logic, Part III*.

Mr. Johnson on the Logical Foundations of Science (II.). *Mind*, n.s., v. 33, October 1924, pp. 369–84.

1925

THE MIND AND ITS PLACE IN NATURE. London, Kegan Paul, Trench, Trubner & Co., 1925, pp. x + 674. (Abbr.: *MPN*)

Contents. Preface—I. Introduction. General Remarks on Method. Pluralism and Monism—*Section A. Alternative Theories of Life and Mind at the level of Enlightened Common-sense*—II. Mechanism and its Alternatives—III. The Traditional Problem of Body and Mind—*Section B. The Mind's Knowledge of Existents*—IV. Sense-perception and Matter—V. Memory—VI. Introspection—VII. The Mind's Knowledge of Other Minds—*Section C. The Unconscious*—VIII. Various Meanings of the Term "Unconscious"—IX. The Alleged Evidence for Unconscious Mental Events and Processes—X. The Nature of Traces and Dispositions—

Section D. The Alleged Evidence for Human Survival of Bodily Death— XI. Ethical Arguments for Human Survival—XII. Empirical Arguments for Human Survival—*Section E. The Unity of the Mind and the Unity of Nature*—XIII. The Unity of the Mind—XIV. The Status and Prospects of Mind in Nature.

The Late Dr. McTaggart. *The Cambridge Review,* v. 46, January 30, 1925, pp. 213–4.
Unsigned.

The Late Dr. McTaggart. *The Trinity Magazine,* v. 6, March 1925, pp. 21–3.
Signed C. D. B.

[Introduction to] Guide to Trinity College. *The Trinity Magazine,* v. 6, June 1925, pp. 61–3.
Unsigned.

The Validity of Belief in a Personal God. *The Hibbert Journal,* v. 24, October 1925, pp. 32–48.
Address given by request to the Student Christian Movement in Cambridge. Reprinted in *Religion, Philosophy and Psychical Research,* 1953.

Review of E. Meyerson, *La Déduction Relativiste* (Paris, 1925). *Mind,* n.s., v. 34, October 1925, pp. 504–5.

1926

THE PHILOSOPHY OF FRANCIS BACON. Cambridge: At the University Press, 1926, pp. 67.
An Address delivered at Cambridge on the occasion of the Bacon Tercentenary, 5 October 1926. Reprinted in *Ethics and the History of Philosophy,* 1952.

Kant's First and Second Analogies of Experience. *Proc. Aristotelian Society,* n.s., v. 26, 1925–26, pp. 189–210.
Read April 19, 1926.

Symposium: The Validity of the Belief in a Personal God. By J. L. Stocks, C. D. Broad, and W. G. de Burgh. *Aristotelian Soc. Supp. Vol. 6, 1926,* pp. 69–111.
Broad's contribution: pp. 84–97.

The Necromantic Tripos. *The Trinity Magazine,* v. 8, December 1926, pp. 6–9.
Signed C. D. B.

1927

THE NATURE OF EXISTENCE, Vol. II. By John McTaggart Ellis McTaggart. Edited by C. D. Broad. Cambridge: At the University Press, 1927, pp. xlvii + 479.
Editor's Preface: pp. v–vi.

Sir Isaac Newton. *Proc. of the British Academy,* v. 13, 1927, pp. 173–202.
Annual Lecture on a Master Mind. Henriette Hertz Trust.
Read July 15, 1927. Reprinted in *Ethics and the History of Philosophy,* 1952.

John McTaggart Ellis McTaggart, 1866–1925. *Proc. of the British Academy,* v. 13, 1927, pp. 307–34.
Reprinted in *Ethics and the History of Philosophy,* 1952.

The Principles of Problematic Induction. *Proc. Aristotelian Soc.,* n.s., v. 28, 1927–28, pp. 1–46.
Presidential Address. Read November 7, 1927.
Interviews with Famous Men [C. D. Broad]. *The Trinity Magazine,* v. 8, March 1927, pp. 34–6.
Unsigned. Broad's Biography; concocted by Richard Martineau on the basis of an interview.

1928

Critical Notice of B. Russell, *The Analysis of Matter* (London, 1927). *Mind,* n.s., v. 37, January 1928, pp. 88–95.
Symposium: Time and Change. By J. Macmurray, R. B. Braithwaite, and C. D. Broad, *Aristotelian Soc. Supp. Vol. 8,* 1928, pp. 143–88.
Broad's contribution: pp. 175–88.
Analysis of Some Ethical Concepts. *J. of Philosophical Studies [Philosophy],* v. 3, July 1928, pp. 285–99.

1929

Critical Notice of F. R. Tennant, *Philosophical Theology, Vol. I* (Cambridge, 1928). *Mind,* n.s., v. 38, January 1929, pp. 94–100.
Review of *Hegel's Science of Logic* (tr. by W. H. Johnston and L. G. Struthers, London, 1929). *Mind,* n.s., v. 38, July 1929, pp. 392–3.

1930

FIVE TYPES OF ETHICAL THEORY. London, Kegan Paul, Trench, Trubner & Co., 1930, pp. xxv + 288. (Abbr.: *FTET*)
Contents. Preface—I. Introduction—II. Spinoza—III. Butler—IV. Hume —V. Kant—VI. Sidgwick—VII. Conclusion.
SOME DOGMAS OF RELIGION. By John McTaggart Ellis McTaggart. Second Edition. With an Introduction by C. D. Broad. London, Edward Arnold, 1930, pp. lii + 299.
Broad's Introduction: pp. xxv–lii.
The Principles of Demonstrative Induction (I.). *Mind,* n.s., v. 39, July 1930, pp. 302–17.
Critical Notice of A. C. Ewing, *The Morality of Punishment* (London, 1929). *Mind,* n.s., v. 39, July 1930, pp. 347–53.
The Principles of Demonstrative Induction (II.). *Mind,* n.s., v. 39, October 1930, pp. 426–39.
Critical Notice of F. R. Tennant, *Philosophical Theology, Vol. II* (Cambridge, 1930). *Mind,* n.s., v. 39, October 1930, pp. 476–84.

1931

WAR-THOUGHTS IN PEACE-TIME. London, Humphrey Milford, 1931, pp. 44. Earl Grey Memorial Lecture, No. 13. Delivered March 13, 1931. Reprinted in *Religion, Philosophy and Psychical Research,* 1953.
Critical Notice of G. F. Stout, *Studies in Philosophy and Psychology* (London, 1930). *Mind,* n.s., v. 40, April, 1931, pp. 230–4.

Review of C. J. Wright, *Miracle in History and in Modern Thought* (London, 1930). *J. of the Society for Psychical Research*, v. 27, May 1931, pp. 84–6.

Symposium: Indeterminacy and Indeterminism. By C. D. Broad, A. S. Eddington, and R. B. Braithwaite. *Aristotelian Soc. Supp. Vol. 10,* 1931, pp. 135–96.

Broad's contribution: pp. 135–60.

Critical Notice of A. E. Taylor, *Faith of a Moralist* (London, 1930). *Mind,* n.s., v. 40, July 1931, pp. 364–75.

William Ernest Johnson, 1858–1931. *Proc. of the British Academy,* v. 17, 1931, pp. 491–514.

Reprinted in *Ethics and the History of Philosophy,* 1952.

McTaggart's Principle of the Dissimilarity of the Diverse. *Proc. Aristotelian Soc.,* n.s., v. 32, 1931–32, pp. 41–52. Read Dec. 7, 1931.

1932

Critical Notice of G. F. Stout, *Mind and Matter* (Cambridge, 1931). *Mind,* n.s., v. 41, July 1932, pp. 351–70.

Review of G. Lowes Dickinson, *J. McT. E. McTaggart* (Cambridge, 1931). *Philosophy,* v. 7, July 1932, pp. 343–4.

1933

EXAMINATION OF MCTAGGART'S PHILOSOPHY. Volume I. Cambridge: at the University Press, 1933, pp. lvi + 460. (Abbr.: *EMcP*)

Contents. Preface. Directions to the Reader—*Book I. Preliminary Considerations*—I. McTaggart's Method and its Relations to other Methods—II. Reality and Existence—III. Is Existence co-extensive with Reality? (I) Characteristics and Possibilities—IV. Is Existence co-extensive with Reality? (II) Propositions—*Book II. Characteristics and Particulars*—V. Characteristics. (I) Division into Qualities and Relations—VI. Characteristics. (II) Division into Simple, Compound, and Complex—VII. Particulars. (I) The Notion of Substance—VIII. Particulars. (II) The Plurality of Particulars—IX. The Dissimilarity of the Diverse—X. The Principle of Sufficient Descriptions—*Book III. Determination*—XI. Intrinsic Determination—XII. Presupposition and Requirement—XIII. Causation—XIV. Extrinsic Determination—*Book IV. The Composition and Division of Particulars*—XV. Groups—XVI. Compound Particulars. The Universe—XVII. Manifestation and Organic Unity—XVIII. The Subdivision of the Universe—XIX. The Endless Divisibility of Particulars—XX. The Implications of Endless Divisibility—*Book V. Determining Correspondence*—XXI. The Principle of Determining Correspondence—XXII. Determining Correspondence and Unities within the Universe—XXIII. The Discrimination of Primary Parts—XXIV. Determining Correspondence and the Structure of the Universe. Retrospect.

John Locke. *The Hibbert Journal,* v. 31, January 1933, pp. 249–67.

Reprinted in *Ethics and the History of Philosophy,* 1952.

Prof. Hallett's *Aeternitas* (I.). *Mind,* n.s., v. 42, April 1933, pp. 150–69.

Prof. Hallett's *Aeternitas* (II.). *Mind,* n.s., v. 42, July 1933, pp. 299–318.

Review of T. Brailsford Robertson, *A Note Book* (Adelaide, 1932), *J. of the Society for Psychical Research,* v. 28, July 1933, pp. 112–4.

1934

DETERMINISM, INDETERMINISM, AND LIBERTARIANISM. Cambridge: At the University Press, 1934, pp. 48.
> An Inaugural Lecture. Reprinted in *Ethics and the History of Philosophy,* 1952.

Is "Goodness" a Name of a Simple Non-Natural Quality? *Proc. Aristotelian Soc.,* n.s., v. 34, 1933–34, pp. 249–68.
> Read June 11, 1934.

1935

Critical Notice of S. V. Keeling, *Descartes* (London, 1934). *Mind,* n.s., v. 44, January 1935, pp. 70–5.

Mr. Dunne's Theory of Time in "An Experiment with Time." *Philosophy,* v. 10, April 1935, pp. 168–85.
> Reprinted in *Religion, Philosophy and Psychical Research,* 1953.

Symposium: Mechanical and Teleological Causation. By C. A. Mace, G. F. Stout, A. C. Ewing, and C. D. Broad. *Aristotelian Soc. Supp. Vol. 14,* 1935, pp. 22–112.
> Broad's contribution: pp. 83–112.

Normal Cognition, Clairvoyance, and Telepathy. *Proc. of the Society for Psychical Research,* v. 43, October 1935, pp. 397–438.
> Presidential Address. Read May 1, 1935. Reprinted in *Religion, Philosophy and Psychical Research,* 1953.

Review of J. McT. E. McTaggart, *Philosophical Studies* (ed. by S. V. Keeling; London, 1934). *Mind,* n.s., v. 44, October 1935, pp. 531–2.

1936

"Ought we to fight for our country in the next war?" *The Hibbert Journal,* v. 34, April 1936, pp. 357–67.
> Reprinted in *Ethics and the History of Philosophy,* 1952.

Symposium: Are there Synthetic a priori Truths? By C. D. Broad, A. J. D. Porteous and R. Jackson. *Aristotelian Soc. Supp. vol. 15,* 1936, pp. 102–53.
> Broad's contribution: pp. 102–17.

An Ostensibly Precognitive Dream Unfulfilled. *J. of the Society for Psychical Research,* v. 30, June 1937, pp. 82–3.

Letter to the Hon. Editor, *J. of the Society for Psychical Research,* v. 30, October 1937, p. 124.

1937

The Philosophical Implications of Foreknowledge. *Aristotelian Soc. Supp. vol. 16,* 1937, pp. 177–209.

The Philosophical Implications of Precognition. Discussion between C. D. Broad and H. H. Price. *Aristotelian Soc. Supp. Vol. 16,* 1937, pp. 211–45.
> Broad's contribution: pp. 229–45. Pp. 211–45 published separately.

Critical Notice of R. von Mises, *Wahrscheinlichkeit, Statistik, und Wahrheit* (Wien, 1936). *Mind,* n.s. v. 46, October 1937, pp. 478–91.

McTaggart, John McTaggart Ellis (1866–1925). *Dictionary of National Biography, 1922–1930.* Edited by J. R. H. Weaver (London, 1937), pp. 550–1.

1938

EXAMINATION OF MCTAGGART'S PHILOSOPHY. Volume II (in 2 parts). Cambridge: at the University Press, 1938, pp. lxxiv + 796. Volume II. Part I, pp. lxxiv + 514. Volume II. Part II, pp. 515–796. (Abbr.: *EMcP*)

Contents. *Volume II. Part I*—Preface. Directions to the Reader. Introduction—*Book VI. The Psychological and Epistemological Foundations* —XXV. Classification of Ostensible Experiences: Ostensible Cogitations— —XXVI. Certain Kinds of Ostensible Cogitations. (I) Ostensible Prehension—XXVII. Certain Kinds of Ostensible Cogitations. (II) Ostensible Sense-perception—XXVIII. Ostensible Volition—XXIX. Ostensible Emotion and Ostensible Pleasure-Pain—XXX. Ostensible Selfhood and Ostensible Self-knowledge—*Book VII. The Trial of Ostensibly Exemplified Characteristics*—XXXI. Ostensible Selfhood and Ostensible Prehension —XXXII. Ostensibly Non-prehensive Cogitations—XXXIII. Ostensible Sense-qualities and Ostensible Materiality—XXXIV. McTaggart's Form of Mentalism and its Consequences—XXXV. Ostensible Temporality— *Book VIII. The Real Foundations of Temporal Appearances—Section A. Time and Error*—XXXVI. General Remarks on Error—XXXVII. Error and C-series—XXXVIII. Necessary Conditions of any Theory of Error and C-series—XXXIX. Statement of the Theory of C-series—XL. The Complete Correctness of ω—Prehensions—XLI. The Partial Incorrectness of r—Presensions—XLII. The Existence and Nature of the C-dimension —XLIII. Compliance with the Conditions—XLIV. Ostensible Sensa and Ostensible Matter—XLV. Ostensible Prehensions—XLVI. Ostensible Judgments—XLVII. Ostensible Inference—XLVIII. Other Ostensible Forms of Cogitation—XLIX. Maximal and Pre-maximal Emotion and Volition—*Volume II. Part II—Book VIII. The Real Foundations of Temporal Appearances—Section B. Time and Eternity*—L. Direction in C-series and in Ostensible B-series—LI. Apparent Temporal Position and Real C-position—LII. Ostensible Duration—*Book IX. Immortality and God*—LIII. Ostensible Immortality—LIV. Ostensible Pre-existence and Post-existence—LV. God—*Book X. Value in the Universe*—LVI. General Theory of Value—LVII. The Bearers of Value—LVIII. The Value associated with the Maximal End-term of a primary C-series—LIX. Concluding Remarks on Value. Retrospect.

Review of L. S. Stebbing, *Philosophy and the Physicists* (London, 1937). *Philosophy,* v. 13, April 1938, pp. 221–6.

Henry Sidgwick. *The Hibbert Journal,* v. 37, October 1938, pp. 25–43. Reprinted in *Ethics and the History of Philosophy,* 1952.

Science and Psychical Phenomena. *Philosophy,* v. 13, October 1938, pp. 466–75. Review of G. N. M. Tyrrell's *Science and Psychical Phenomena.*

Henry Sidgwick and Psychical Research. *Proc. of the Society for Psychical Research,* v. 45, December 1938, pp. 131–61. Reprinted in *Religion, Philosophy and Psychical Research,* 1953.

1939

Filosofia critica e speculativa. *Filosofi Inglesi Contemporanei.* A cura di J. H. Muirhead. Con una introduzione di Antonio Banfi. Traduzione della Dott. Daria Menicanti. Milano, Valentino Bompiani, 1939, pp. 253–83. Translation of "Critical and Speculative Philosophy," 1924.

Arguments for the Existence of God (I.). *J. of Theological Studies,* v. 40, January 1939, pp. 16–30.
Reprinted in *Religion, Philosophy and Psychical Research,* 1953.

Arguments for the Existence of God (II.). *J. of Theological Studies,* v. 40, April 1939, pp. 156–67.
Reprinted in *Religion, Philosophy and Psychical Research,* 1953.

The Present Relations of Science and Religion. *Philosophy,* v. 14, April 1939, pp. 131–54.
Reprinted in *Religion, Philosophy and Psychical Research,* 1953.

1940

John Albert Chadwick, 1899–1939. *Mind,* n.s., v. 49, January 1940, pp. 129–31.

Conscience and Conscientious Action. *Philosophy,* v. 15, April 1940, pp. 115–30.
Reprinted in *Ethics and the History of Philosophy,* 1952.

Critical Notice of W. D. Ross, *Foundations of Ethics* (Oxford, 1939). *Mind,* n.s., v. 49, April 1940, pp. 228–39.

Introduction to Mr. Whately Carington's and Mr. Soal's papers. *Proc. of the Society for Psychical Research,* v. 46, June 1940, pp. 25–33.
Experiments on the Paranormal Cognition of Drawings. By Whately Carington, pp. 34–150; Fresh Light on Card Guessing—Some New Effects. By S. G. Soal, pp. 152–98.

A Physical Analogy. *Proc. of the Society for Psychical Research,* v. 46, June 1940, pp. 150–1.
Appendix to Whately Carington, "Experiments on the Paranormal Cognition of Drawings."

Sir Arthur Eddington's *The Philosophy of Physical Science. Philosophy,* v. 15, July 1940, pp. 301–12.

1941

Review of S. Alexander, *Philosophical and Literary Pieces* (ed. by J. Laird; London, 1939). *Mind,* n.s., v. 50, April 1941, pp. 197–8.

Critical Notice of J. Laird, *Theism and Cosmology* (London, 1940). *Mind,* n.s., v. 50, July 1941, pp. 294–9.

Review of G. H. Hardy, *A Mathematician's Apology* (Cambridge, 1940). *Philosophy,* v. 16, July 1941, pp. 323–6.

1942

Kant's Theory of Mathematical and Philosophical Reasoning. *Proc. Aristotelian Soc.,* v. 42, 1941–42, pp. 1–24.
Read Feb. 19, 1942.

Berkeley's Argument about Material Substance. *Proc. of the British Academy,* v. 28, 1942, pp. 119–138.
Annual Philosophical Lecture. Henriette Hertz Trust.
Read March 25, 1942.

Critical Notice of J. Laird, *Mind and Deity* (London, 1941). *Mind,* n.s., v. 51, April 1942, pp. 180–8.

Symposium on the Relations between Science and Ethics. By C. H. Waddington, A. C. Ewing, and C. D. Broad. *Proc. Aristotelian Soc.,* v. 42, 1941–42, pp. 65–100 H.

Broad's contribution: pp. 100A–100H.

Certain Features in Moore's Ethical Doctrines. *The Philosophy of G. E. Moore.* Edited by P. A. Schilpp. Evanston and Chicago, Northwestern University, 1942, pp. 43–67.

Review of *The Philosophy of Alfred North Whitehead.* Edited by P. A. Schilpp. (Evanston and Chicago, 1941). *The Mathematical Gazette,* v. 26, December 1942, pp. 223–25.

1943

Obituary: Mr H. F. Saltmarsh. *Proc. of the Society for Psychical Research,* v. 47, December 1943, pp. 151–53.

1944

Hr. Von Wright on the Logic of Induction (I). *Mind,* n.s., v. 53, January 1944, pp. 1–24.

Hr. Von Wright on the Logic of Induction (II). *Mind,* n.s., v. 53, April 1944, pp. 97–119.

Hr. Von Wright on the Logic of Induction (III). *Mind,* n.s., v. 53, July 1944, pp. 193–214.

Critical Notice of J. Huxley, *Evolutionary Ethics* (Oxford, 1943). *Mind,* n.s., v. 53, October 1944, pp. 344–67.

Reprinted in H. Feigl and W. Sellars (ed.), *Readings in Philosophical Analysis* (New York, 1949).

The Experimental Establishment of Telepathic Precognition. *Philosophy,* v. 19, November 1944, pp. 261–75.

L. S. Stebbing Memorial Fund. *Mind,* n.s., v. 53, July 1944, p. 287. *Philosophy,* v. 19, July 1944, p. 191.

Signed by C. D. Broad, G. Jebb, C. A. Mace, John Macmurray, G. E. Moore, H. H. Price, and Helen M. Wodehouse.

Case: An apparently precognitive incident in a dream-sequence. Reported by C. D. Broad. *J. of the Society for Psychical Research,* v. 33, November-December 1944, pp. 88–90.

The New Philosophy: Bruno to Descartes. *The Cambridge Historical Journal,* v. 8, 1944, pp. 22–54.

A lecture delivered in Cambridge on March 4, 1944, in the series, arranged by the History of Science Committee, on *Science in the Sixteenth and Seventeenth Centuries.*

Reprinted in *Ethics and the History of Philosophy,* 1952.

1945

Some Reflections on Moral-Sense Theories in Ethics. *Proc. of the Aristotelian Society,* n.s., v. 45, 1944–45, pp. 131–66.

Reprinted in W. Sellars and J. Hospers (ed.), *Readings in Ethical Theory* (New York, 1952).

Professor G. F. Stout (1860–1944). *Mind,* n.s., v. 54, July 1945, pp. 285–88.

1946

Spinoza's Doctrine of Human Immortality. *Festskrift till Anders Karitz. Skrifter utgivna av Föreningen för filosofi och specialvetenskap* I, 1946, pp. 139–48.

Leibniz's last controversy with the Newtonians. *Theoria,* v. 12, 1946, pp. 143–68.

Reprinted in *Ethics and the History of Philosophy,* 1952.

Critical Notice of A. E. Taylor, *Does God Exist?* (London, 1945). *Mind,* n.s., v. 55, April 1946, pp. 173–78.

Discussion of Prof. Rhine's paper and the foregoing comments upon it. *Proc. of the Society for Psychical Research,* v. 48, June 1946, pp. 20–25.

On J. B. Rhine's "Telepathy and Clairvoyance Reconsidered," *ibid.,* pp. 1–7, and on the comments by W. Whately Carington, *ibid.,* pp. 8–10, J. Hettinger, *ibid.,* pp. 10–15, R. H. Thouless, *ibid.,* pp. 15–17, and G. N. M. Tyrrell, *ibid.,* pp. 17–19.

Some of the Main Problems of Ethics. *Philosophy,* v. 21, July 1946, pp. 99–117.

Lecture given to the British Institute of Philosophy on October 8, 1945. Reprinted in H. Feigl and W. Sellars (ed.), *Readings in Philosophical Analysis* (New York, 1949).

1947

Professor Marc-Wogau's *Theorie der Sinnesdata* (I). *Mind,* n.s., v. 56, January 1947, pp. 1–30.

Professor Marc-Wogau's *Theorie der Sinnesdaten* (II). *Mind,* n.s., v. 56, April 1947, pp. 97–131.

Philosophical Implications of Precognition. *The Listener,* v. 37, 8 May 1947, pp. 709–710.

Trinity College and Psychical Research. *Trinity Magazine,* June 1947, pp. 13–17.

Some Methods of Speculative Philosophy. *Aristotelian Soc. Supp. Vol. 21,* 1947, pp. 1–32.

Address. Read July 5, 1947.

Critical Notice of *The Philosophy of Bertrand Russell.* Edited by P. A. Schilpp. (Evanston and Chicago, 1944). *Mind,* n.s., v. 56, October 1947, pp. 355–64.

Review of Bertrand Russell, *A History of Western Philosophy and its Connection with Political and Social Circumstances from the Earliest Times to the Present Day* (New York, 1945). *Philosophy,* v. 22, November 1947, pp. 256–64.

1948

Symposium: A program for the next ten years of research in para-psychology: A letter from Professor C. D. Broad. *J. of Parapsychology,* v. 12, March 1948, pp. 2–6.

Alfred North Whitehead (1861–1947). *Mind,* n.s., v. 57, April 1948, pp. 139–45.

Obituary Notice. Ian Gallie. *Mind,* n.s., v. 57, October 1948, pp. 401–02.

Review of Signe Toksvig, *Emanuel Swedenborg* (New Haven, 1948). *J. of Parapsychology*, v. 12, December 1948, pp. 296–301.

1949

Review of A. W. Brown, *The Metaphysical Society, 1869–1880* (New York and London, 1947). *Mind*, n.s., v. 58, January 1949, pp. 101–04.

Leibniz's Predicate-in-Notion Principle and some of its alleged consequences. *Theoria*, v. 15, March 1949, pp. 54–70.

Letter to the Editor. *The Times*, no. 51, 487, 15 September 1949, p. 5.
> Signed by C. D. Broad, Gilbert Murray and W. H. Salter. Headed: Telepathy.

The Relevance of Psychical Research to Philosophy. *Philosophy*, v. 24, October 1949, pp. 291–309.
> Reprinted in *Religion, Philosophy and Psychical Research*, 1953.

Review of W. Whately Carington, *Matter, Mind and Meaning* (London, 1949). *Proc. of the Society for Psychical Research*, v. 49, November 1949, pp. 51–52.

Dr. J. N. Keynes. *Nature*, v. 164, December 1949, pp. 1031–32.

1950

Dr Soal's Forskning i Telepati och Framtidsförnimmelse. Stockholm, 1950, p. 22.
> Swedish translation by Maud von Steyen (assisted by Eva Hellström, J. O. Roos of Hjelmstär and Ulf Hellsten) of a lecture given on September 22, 1949 to *Sältskapet för parapsykologisk forskning* in Stockholm. Privately printed for members of the Society.

Egoism as a Theory of Human Motives. *The Hibbert Journal*, v. 48, January 1950, pp. 105–14.
> Reprinted in *Ethics and the History of Philosophy*, 1952.

Critical Notice of W. Kneale, *Probability and Induction* (Oxford, 1949). *Mind*, v. 59, January 1950, pp. 94–115.

Review of H. J. Paton, *The Moral Law or Kant's* Groundwork of the Metaphysic of Morals (London, n.d.), *Philosophy*, v. 25, January 1950, pp. 85–86.

Some Common Fallacies in Political Thinking. *Philosophy*, v. 25, April 1950, pp. 99–113.
> Reprinted in *Religion, Philosophy and Psychical Research*, 1953.

Some Trinity Philosophers: 1900–1950. *Trinity Magazine*, May Term 1950, pp. 2–6.

Dr. J. N. Keynes (1852–1949). *The Economic Journal*, v. 60, June 1950, pp. 403–07.

Immanuel Kant and Psychical Research. *Proc. of the Society for Psychical Research*, v. 49, July 1950, pp. 79–104.
> Reprinted in *Religion, Philosophy and Psychical Research*, 1953.

Review of A. N. Prior, *Logic and the Basis of Ethics* (Oxford, 1949). *Mind*, v. 59, July 1950, pp. 392–95.

Review of W. Whately Carington, *Matter, Mind and Meaning* (London, 1949). *Philosophy*, v. 25, July 1950, pp. 275–77.

Imperatives, Categorical and Hypothetical. *The Philosopher,* n.s., v. 2, September 1950, pp. 62–75.
Read before the Philosophical Society of England on May 10, 1950.
Critical Notice of H. A. Prichard, *Moral Obligation* (Oxford, 1949). *Mind,* n.s., v. 59, October 1950, pp. 555–66.

1951

Hägerström's Account of Sense of Duty and Certain Allied Experiences. *Philosophy,* v. 26, April 1951, pp. 99–113.
Locke's Doctrine of Substantial Identity and Diversity. *Theoria,* v. 17, May 1951, pp. 13–26.
A Logistic Analysis of the Two-Fold Time Theory of the Specious Present. *British J. for the Philosophy of Science,* v. 2, August 1951, pp. 137–41.
Appendix to H. A. C. Dobbs, "The Relation between the Time of Psychology and the Time of Physics, Part I," *ibid.,* pp. 122–37.
Review of "Symposium: Is Psychical Research Relevant to Philosophy?" by Mrs. M. Kneale, Mr. R. Robinson, and Mr. C. W. K. Mundle, from Aristotelian Society's Supplementary Volume XXIV, *Psychical Research, Ethics and Logic* (London, 1950). *J. of Parapsychology,* v. 15, September 1951, pp. 216–23.

1952

ETHICS AND THE HISTORY OF PHILOSOPHY. London, Routledge and Kegan Paul Ltd., 1952, pp. xiii + 274. (Abbr.: *EHP*) Contents. *Section I. Biography*— Sir Isaac Newton (1927)—John Locke (1933)—Henry Sidgwick (1938)— John McTaggart Ellis McTaggart (1927)—William Ernest Johnson (1931) —*Section II. Philosophy of Science*—The Philosophy of Francis Bacon (1926)—The New Philosophy: Bruno to Descartes (1944)—Leibniz's Last Controversy with the Newtonians (1946)—*Section III. Ethics*—Determinism, Indeterminism, and Libertarianism (1934)—Egoism as a Theory of Human Motives (1950)—Ought we to fight for our country in the next war? (1936)—Conscience and Conscientious Action (1940).
Some Elementary Reflexions on Sense-Perception. *Philosophy,* v. 27, January 1952, pp. 3–17.
Iyer Lecture delivered before the Royal Institute of Philosophy on June 8, 1951.
Critical Notice of S. E. Toulmin, *An Examination of the Place of Reason in Ethics* (Cambridge, 1950). *Mind,* v. 61, January 1952, pp. 93–101.
Review of M. M. Moncrieff, *The Clairvoyant Theory of Perception: a New Theory of Vision* (London, 1951). *Philosophy,* v. 27, July 1952, pp. 255–59.

1953

RELIGION, PHILOSOPHY AND PSYCHICAL RESEARCH. London, Routledge and Kegan Paul Limited, 1953, pp. vii + 308. (Abbr.: *RPPR*) Contents. *Section I. Psychical Research*—The Relevance of Psychical Research to Philosophy (1949)—Normal Cognition, Clairvoyance and Telepathy (1935)— Mr. Dunne's Theory of Time (1935)—Henry Sidgwick and Psychical Research (1938)—Immanuel Kant and Psychical Research (1950)—Postscript on Kant and Swedenborg—*Section II. Religion*—The Validity of Belief in a Personal God (1925)—Arguments for the Existence of God (1939)— Bishop Butler as a Theologian (1923)—The Present Relations of Science and Religion (1939)—*Section III. Politics*—War Thoughts in Peace Time (1931)—Postscript: Afterthoughts in Time of Cold War—Fallacies in Political Thinking (1950).

Axel Hägerström, *Inquiries into the Nature of Law and Morals,* edited by Karl Olivecrona, translated by C. D. Broad. Uppsala, Almqvist & Wiksells Boktryckeri Aktiebolag, 1953, pp. xii + 377.

Also published as *Skrifter Utgivna av Kungl. Humanistiska Vetenskaps-samfundet i Uppsala (Acta Societatis Litterarum Humaniorum Regiae Upsaliensis)* Band 40. Translator's preface pp. vii–ix.

Review of John Björkhem, *Det ockulta Problemet* (Uppsala, 1951). *J. of the Society for Psychical Research,* v. 37, January–February 1953, pp. 35–38.

Phantasms of the Living and of the Dead. *Proc. of the Society for Psychical Research,* v. 50, May 1953, pp. 51–66.

Berkeley's Theory of Morals. *Revue Internationale de Philosophie,* v. 7, fasc. 1–2, 1953, pp. 72–86.

1954

Letter to the Editor. *J. of the Society for Psychical Research,* v. 37, January–February 1954, pp. 254–56.

Reply to a letter by Hornell Hart entitled "Phantasms of the Living and of the Dead," *ibid.,* pp. 253–54.

Berkeley's Denial of Material Substance. *The Philosophical Review,* v. 63, April 1954, pp. 155–81.

Critical Notice of H. H. Price, *Thinking and Experience* (London, 1953). *Mind,* v. 63, July 1954, pp. 390–403.

Synopses of his papers published in *Proceedings of the Aristotelian Society* and *Aristotelian Society Supplementary Volumes* from 1915 to 1947. *A Synoptic Index to the Proceedings of the Aristotelian Society 1900–1949.* Edited by J. W. Scott. Oxford, 1954, pp. 022–035.

Synopsis of "Some Reflections on Moral-Sense Theories in Ethics" (1945) prepared editorially. "The Philosophical Implications of Precognition" (1937) not indexed.

Kant's Mathematical Antinomies. *Proc. Aristotelian Soc.,* n.s., v. 55, 1954–55, pp. 1–22.

Presidential Address. Read November 8, 1954.

Emotion and Sentiment. *The Journal of Aesthetics and Art Criticism,* v. 13, December 1954, pp. 203–14.

1955

HUMAN PERSONALITY AND THE POSSIBILITY OF ITS SURVIVAL. Berkeley and Los Angeles, University of California Press, 1955, pp. 27.

The Agnes E. and Constantine E. A. Foerster Lecture on the Immortality of the Soul. Delivered May 20, 1954.

The Phenomenology of Mrs Leonard's Mediumship. *J. of the American Society for Psychical Research,* v. 49, April 1955, pp. 47–63.
    Lecture delivered to the Society on June 18, 1954.

1956

The End of Borley Rectory? *The Cambridge Review,* v. 77, March 10, 1956, pp. 439–41.
    Review of *The Haunting of Borley Rectory: A Critical Survey of the Evidence,* by Eric J. Dingwall, Kathleen M. Goldney and Trevor H. Hall (London, 1956; and *Proc. of the Society for Psychical Research,* v. 51, January 1956).
Review of A. A. Luce, *Sense without Matter, or Direct Perception* (Edinburgh, 1954), *Philosophy,* v. 31, April 1956, pp. 169–71.
A Half-Century of Psychical Research. *J. of Parapsychology,* v. 20, Dec. 1956, pp. 209–28.

1957

Correspondence: Heaven and Hell. *The Aryan Path,* v. 28, January 1957, pp. 45–46.
    Comment on H. H. Price's "Heaven and Hell from the Point of View of Psychical Research," *The Aryan Path,* v. 27, January and February 1956.
The Local Historical Background of Contemporary Cambridge Philosophy. *British Philosophy in the Mid-Century.* Edited by C. A. Mace. London, G. Allen and Unwin, 1957, pp. 13–61.
Eräita Tuomas Akvinolaisen filosfian peruskäsitteitä. *Ajatus,* v. 19, 1956, pp. 59–79.
    Translated by K. Jaakko J. Hintikka.
Obituary Notice: Dr. F. R. Tennant.† *The Times,* no. 53, 945, September 13, 1957, p. 13.
    Unsigned.

1958

PERSONAL IDENTITY AND SURVIVAL. London, Society for Psychical Research, 1958, pp. 32.
    The Thirteenth Frederic W. H. Myers Memorial Lecture 1958.
Philosophy. *Inquiry* [Norway] v. 1, no. 2, 1958, pp. 99–129.
Critical Notice of M. Cranston, *John Locke, A Biography* (London, 1957). *Mind,* n.s., v. 67, Oct. 1958, pp. 548–54.
Obituary Notice: G. E. Moore.† *The Manchester Guardian,* no. 34, 936, October 25, 1958, p. 3.
    Unsigned.
    Reprinted (signed) with corrections and additions in G. E. Moore, *Philosophical Papers* (London, 1959), pp. 11–12.
Frederic Robert Tennant, 1866–1957. *Proc. of the British Academy,* v. 44, 1958, pp. 241–52.

1959

Dreaming, and some of its Implications. *Proc. of the Society for Psychical Research,* v. 52, February 1959, pp. 53–78.
　　Presidential Address 1958.
Review of Norman Malcolm, *Ludwig Wittgenstein: A Memoir* (London, 1958). *Universities Quarterly,* v. 13, May 1959, pp. 304–6.

INDEX

(arranged by Robert P. Sylvester)